Also by America's Test Kitchen

When Southern Women Cook

Umma

Food Gifts

America's Test Kitchen 25th Anniversary Cookbook

A Very Chinese Cookbook

Boards

Gatherings

The Skillet

Cook It in Your Dutch Oven

Cook It in Cast Iron

Ultimate Air Fryer Perfection

Kitchen Gear

Baking for Two

Everyday Bread

The Cook's Illustrated Baking Book

The Perfect Cookie

The Perfect Pie

The Perfect Cake

The Cook's Illustrated Baking Book

The Science of Good Cooking

Cook's Science

The New Cooking School Cookbook: Fundamentals

The New Cooking School Cookbook: Advanced Fundamentals

Mostly Meatless

Vegan for Everybody

Vegan Cooking for Two

Cooking with Plant-Based Meat

Vegetables Illustrated

How Can It Be Gluten Free Cookbook Collection

The Complete Plant-Based Cookbook

The Complete Beans and Grains Cookbook

The Complete Mediterranean Cookbook

The Complete Cooking for Two Cookbook

The Complete Diabetes Cookbook

The Complete Vegetarian Cookbook

The Complete One Pot

The Complete Autumn and Winter Cookbook

The Complete Summer Cookbook

The Complete Modern Pantry

The Complete Salad Cookbook

The Complete America's Test Kitchen TV Show Cookbook

For a full listing of all our books:

CooksIllustrated.com

AmericasTestKitchen.com

Praise for America's Test Kitchen Titles

"This 'very' Chinese cookbook from a father-son duo is a keeper. The book—ATK's first devoted to Chinese cooking—proves that you can teach and entertain in the same volume. . . All in all, it's one of the most charming works I've seen in years, and already want to get a second copy."
The Washington Post on *A Very Chinese Cookbook*

A Best Cookbook of 2023
New York Times on *A Very Chinese Cookbook*

"An exhaustive but approachable primer for those looking for a 'flexible' diet. Chock-full of tips, you can dive into the science of plant-based cooking or just sit back and enjoy the 500 recipes."
Minneapolis Star Tribune on *The Complete Plant-Based Cookbook*

"This comprehensive guide is packed with delicious recipes and fun menu ideas but its unique draw is the personal narrative and knowledge-sharing of each ATK chef, which will make this a hit."
Booklist on *Gatherings*

"A mood board for one's food board is served up in this excellent guide . . . This has instant classic written all over it."
Publishers Weekly (starred review) on *Boards: Stylish Spreads for Casual Gatherings*

"Reassuringly hefty and comprehensive, *The Complete Autumn and Winter Cookbook* by America's Test Kitchen has you covered with a seemingly endless array of seasonal fare . . . This overstuffed compendium is guaranteed to warm you from the inside out."
NPR on *The Complete Autumn and Winter Cookbook*

"Here are the words just about any vegan would be happy to read: 'Why This Recipe Works.' Fans of America's Test Kitchen are used to seeing the phrase, and now it applies to the growing collection of plant-based creations in *Vegan for Everybody*."
The Washington Post on *Vegan for Everybody*

"Another flawless entry in the America's Test Kitchen canon, *Bowls* guides readers of all culinary skill levels in composing one-bowl meals from a variety of cuisines."
BuzzFeed Books on *Bowls*

"The book's depth, breadth, and practicality makes it a must-have for seafood lovers."
Publishers Weekly (starred review) on *Foolproof Fish*

"*The Perfect Cookie* . . . is, in a word, perfect. This is an important and substantial cookbook . . . If you love cookies, but have been a tad shy to bake on your own, all your fears will be dissipated. This is one book you can use for years with magnificently happy results."
Huffpost on *The Perfect Cookie*

"The book offers an impressive education for curious cake makers, new and experienced alike. A summation of 25 years of cake making at ATK, there are cakes for every taste."
The Wall Street Journal on *The Perfect Cake*

"The go-to gift book for newlyweds, small families, or empty nesters."
Orlando Sentinel on *The Complete Cooking for Two Cookbook*

"If you're one of the 30 million Americans with diabetes, *The Complete Diabetes Cookbook* by America's Test Kitchen belongs on your kitchen shelf."
Parade.com on *The Complete Diabetes Cookbook*

"True to its name, this smart and endlessly enlightening cookbook is about as definitive as it's possible to get in the modern vegetarian realm."
Men's Journal on *The Complete Vegetarian Cookbook*

THE COMPLETE Cook's Country TV SHOW COOKBOOK

EVERY RECIPE AND EVERY REVIEW FROM ALL EIGHTEEN SEASONS

AMERICA'S TEST KITCHEN

Copyright © 2025 by America's Test Kitchen

All rights reserved. No part of this book may be reproduced or transmitted in any manner whatsoever without written permission from the publisher, except in the case of brief quotations embodied in critical articles or reviews.

Photo of Edna Lewis on page 123: John T. Hill

Photo of Colonel Sanders on page 135: Bettmann/Getty

Image of Count Pavel Stroganov on page 148:
Asar Studios/Alamy Stock Photo

Illustration of Michele Pezza on page 428:
Ganiew Gallery/Alamy Stock Photo

Photo of Tatin sisters on page 656: Creative Commons

America's Test Kitchen
21 Drydock Avenue
Boston, MA 02210

The Complete Cook's Country TV Show Cookbook
Every Recipe and Every Review from All Eighteen Seasons

ISBN 978-1-954210-44-8
ISSN 2330-5726

Printed in China

10 9 8 7 6 5 4 3 2 1

Distributed by Penguin Random House Publisher Services
Tel: 800-733-3000

- facebook.com/AmericasTestKitchen
- instagram.com/TestKitchen
- youtube.com/AmericasTestKitchen
- tiktok.com/@TestKitchen
- x.com/TestKitchen
- pinterest.com/TestKitchen

Editor in Chief, Cook's Country Toni Tipton-Martin
Editorial Director, Cook's Country Tucker Shaw
Executive Editor, Culinary Travel, Cook's Country Bryan Roof
Executive Editor, Cook's Country Scott Kathan
Executive Editor, Creative Content, Cook's Country Morgan Bolling
Deputy Food Editor, Cook's Country Nicole Konstantinakos
Senior Editors, Cook's Country Matthew Fairman and Jessica Rudolph
Senior Photo Test Cook, Cook's Country Lawman Johnson
Test Cooks, Cook's Country Mark Huxsoll, Amanda Luchtel, and Kelly Song
Executive Managing Editor, Magazines Todd Meier
Art Director, Cook's Country Maggie Edgar

Editorial Director, Books Adam Kowit
Executive Managing Editor, Books Debra Hudak
Assistant Editor, Books Julia Arwine
Design Director, Books Lindsey Timko Chandler
Art Director, Books Katie Barranger
Photography Director Julie Bozzo Cote
Senior Photography Producer Meredith Mulcahy
Featured Photography Steve Klise
Senior Staff Photographer Daniel J. van Ackere
Staff Photographer Kritsada Panichgul
Additional Photography Pableaux Johnson, Joseph Keller, Carl Tremblay, and Kevin White
Featured Food Stylist Elle Simone Scott
Food Stylists Joy Howard, Sheila James, Catrine Kelty, Chantal Lambeth, Kendra McKnight, Ashley Moore, Christie Morrison, Marie Piraino, Kendra Smith, and Sally Staub
Photo Shoot Support Alli Berkey, Hannah Fenton, Eric Haessler, Lawman Johnson, Gina McCreadie, Christa West, and Faye Yang
Illustrations Rose Flynn and Sophie Greenspan
Project Manager, Books Kelly Gauthier
Senior Print Production Specialist Lauren Robbins
Production and Imaging Coordinator Amanda Yong
Production and Imaging Specialist Tricia Neumyer
Production and Imaging Assistant Chloe Petraske
Historical Researcher Meg Ragland
Copyeditors Christine Campbell, April Poole, Cheryl Redmond, and Rachel Schowalter
Proofreader Vicki Rowland
Indexer Elizabeth Parson

Chief Executive Officer Dan Suratt
Chief Content Officer Dan Souza
Senior Content Adviser Jack Bishop
Executive Editorial Directors Julia Collin Davison and Bridget Lancaster
Senior Director, Book Sales Emily Logan

CooksCountry.com
AmericasTestKitchen.com

contents

VIII   WELCOME TO COOK'S COUNTRY

1   **Season Eighteen**
119   **As Good as Grandma's**
163   **Fork-in-the-Road Favorites**
273   **Steakhouse Specials**
309   **Our Sunday Best**
379   **Tex-Mex and More**
417   **Everybody Loves Italian**
457   **The State of Grilling**
545   **Rise-and-Shine Breakfast and Breads**
595   **Great American Cakes and Cookies**
651   **Old-Fashioned Fruit Desserts and Puddings**
669   **Save Room for Pie**

700   SHOPPING FOR EQUIPMENT
730   STOCKING YOUR PANTRY
754   EPISODE DIRECTORY
766   CONVERSIONS AND EQUIVALENTS
768   INDEX

welcome to cook's country

The on-set joy captured in a photo of me with Bryan Roof, our Executive Editor of Culinary Travel, beautifully expresses the sweet spot where journalism and recipe development come together. And this new edition of *The Complete Cook's Country TV Cookbook* seems like a good opportunity to share the ways that we are bringing these two worlds together more and more in the magazine and on the show.

We have aimed our sights on an approach to recipe storytelling that honors the life histories of America's cooks, discovering unknown cooking knowledge and sharing uncelebrated techniques so that you know the who, what, when, and where, not just the why and how of recipes. Bryan is talking more about the new techniques he learns when he travels to big cities and small towns across America—from the addition of fresh turmeric in a Georgia coast paella to the light touch that makes Maryland crab cakes special.

Other cast members are also telling you more about the source of their recipes, whether the idea started with a great cookbook or we learned it from a celebrated local cook. And segments in my cookbook library tell you all you ever wanted to know about the cooks behind our food, whether they created icebox cakes or they are midwestern sorghum farmers.

As we roast poblano chiles and skin and seed them, chop a fresh jalapeño and cilantro, and blend a creamy Mexican combination of milk, sour cream, and cream cheese for our Green Spaghetti recipe, we are thinking of you, our viewers, and the many options that are out there for you to watch people cook on screen. We want to make sure that what you get with *Cook's Country* is a *complete* show, one that is as delicately balanced as our sweet tea brine for fried chicken, and the rich traditions behind the dish—from the ingredients, techniques, and equipment needed to create it to the science and history that inspired its creation. It is a unique approach that we hope ignites your kitchen curiosity and makes learning fun.

Peek into a pot of the American classic gumbo, for instance, and you'll see vestiges of the many groups who have settled in New Orleans. The base, a roux, arrived with the French; smoked sausage was brought by Germans and Acadians (from northeastern Canada); the okra came from Africa (as does its name: Gombo is the West African word for okra), and ground sassafras (filé powder) was used by Native Americans. Many Louisiana natives fondly remember waking up to the smell of cooking roux, which mom would stir for hours over low heat until it was chocolate-colored. Aromatic vegetables were added, then homemade stock, and finally, the meat: Poultry, sausage, game, and seafood are all traditional, depending upon her taste preferences.

Or consider the nuances of pizza beyond the boundaries of New York and Chicago. Connie Piccinato created Detroit-style pizza by adapting a classic formula with locally produced brick cheese to satisfy a craving for the pies of her youth, while St. Louis–style pizza is made without yeast, has a wafer-thin crust, and gets a flavorful lift from another regional ingredient—Provel cheese. Here, the ingredients available to the cook are what give the dish character.

How closely do these Americanized versions resemble the original dishes brought to this country by first-generation immigrants? Not much. But adaptations of home-cooking, family histories, and immigrant tastes paint a rich and broad portrait of the American culinary landscape. From coast to coast, to the city and the country, through the suburbs, and down back roads, they tell us something hopeful about American cooking today.

It is true that fewer and fewer of us live as adults in the same town where we were born and raised. We are a mobile, peripatetic people. As each generation reaches farther afield, its tether to its roots frays a little. We pass on fewer traditions. We carry less of our history into the future. Our children know little about our own childhoods.

It is also true that all this moving from house to house and city to city encourages us to connect with new traditions. We exchange ideas with our neighbors and mix some of their way of doing things with ours. We learn to appreciate bold tastes and alluring aromas. Our family favorites grow beyond the borders of our old neighborhoods and our way of doing things.

Consider the young woman who moves from the Carolina Lowcountry to New York and longs for the taste of her grandmother's shrimp gravy. She samples recipes for shrimp and grits in restaurants, but fancy creations just don't compare to the comforting dish of tender shrimp, silky sauce, and creamy grits she remembers from childhood. She sends up a flare for the family recipe, then adapts it according to the ingredients she can source in her new hometown. She gets the taste just right and shares the recipe with new friends. Soon, one of the friends is inspired to make the dish her own, too. To honor the origin story of the dish, she places a special order for stone-ground grits from a miller of heirloom grains located near the Sea Islands of Carolina. She makes the dish her own. When asked about her recipe, the cook tells the story behind her version. It is a tribute to the original, she says.

This action captures something special about American food: Traditional dishes that are ethnically and regionally diverse are evolving, and that encourages a return to the simple pleasures of the table and inspires cooking with love. Here, at *Cook's Country*, we celebrate them all. We look at rural foods, from Lowcountry grits to high desert tacos. We look at city foods, from New Orleans gumbo to New York cheesecake. We search high, low, and in between for recipes from every community in the country, the old ones and the new, from centuries-old switchel to modern-day monkey bread. And we also share the history of these dishes, offering inspiration from the people behind the recipes, the "cooks of the country"—from Native farmers and Mexican tamale vendors to Italian fishermen, Chinese noodle makers, and Southern pitmasters.

It's been 17 years since *Cook's Country* presented its first recipe. Since then, our hard-working crew of test cooks, editors, and instructors have carried on the mission to find these recipes and work hard to perfect them. We look for ways to refine the ingredients and techniques to jibe with contemporary cooking habits, while zealously maintaining the integrity and spirit of the originals. It can take weeks of experimentation, tinkering with seasoning amounts and cooking times until we get things just right. And we don't stop there. These recipes inspire brand-new ideas for simple, straightforward, easy meals that mix time-tested knowledge with fresh discoveries.

Our goal is to produce recipes that are easy, clear, and rewarding enough that you'll want to make them too. We work to clarify concepts, streamline processes, and shorten the distance from hunger pang to dinner time. Over the past 18 seasons, we've been proud to share thousands of recipes with you. And as we work into our second decade, we've added to our cast of characters. These new faces, in our test kitchen and on our TV show and website, represent a whole new set of cooking traditions to explore.

It can take us weeks, or maybe months, to produce even a simple, two-step recipe. But it's worth it. Because by getting these dishes from our kitchens to your table, we believe we're helping to preserve, and expand, our shared American recipe book.

It's a big country, Cook's Country, and there's no better time to celebrate America's incredibly rich, incredibly broad, and incredibly deep cooking traditions. There's plenty of room in the kitchen, no matter where you're from.

Welcome home. Now, grab an apron. Let's cook.

Toni Tipton-Martin
Editor in Chief
Cook's Country magazine

This book has been tested, written, and edited by the folks at America's Test Kitchen. Located in Boston's Seaport District in the historic Innovation and Design Building, it features 15,000 square feet of kitchen space including multiple photography and video studios. It is the home of *Cook's Country* and *Cook's Illustrated* magazines and is the workday destination for more than 60 test cooks, editors, and cookware specialists. The test kitchen tests recipes over and over again until we understand how and why they work and until we arrive at the best version.

Cook's Country celebrates cooking in America. Our mission is to seek out America's best cooking ideas and create easy-to-follow recipes for bringing people together.

Bridget Lancaster and Julia Collin Davison are the hosts of the show and have the answers to the questions you might ask. It's the job of our chefs, Morgan Bolling, Lawman Johnson, Ashley Moore, and Christie Morrison, to demonstrate our recipes, and Bryan Roof travels the country to talk to the cooks behind the recipes. Editor in Chief Toni Tipton-Martin gives viewers historical and cultural context for our recipes. Jack Bishop shares helpful information about ingredients such as cucumbers, sheep's milk cheese, and tinned fish while Hannah Crowley reveals the test kitchen's recommended equipment, including panini presses, cold brew coffee makers, and leave-in temperature probes.

Although only a handful of cooks appear on the television show, dozens more worked to make the show a reality. Executive Producer Kaitlin Keleher conceived and developed each episode along with Supervising Producer Caroline Rickert with support from Director of Production Diane Knox. Additional support came from Producer Alex Curran-Cardarelli, Associate Producer Angelica Quintanilla, and Equipment and Production Coordinator Mitchell Farias. Special thanks to Director Herb Sevush and Director of Photography Dan Anderson.

The Complete Cook's Country TV Show Cookbook

Along with the on-air crew, Director of Culinary Production Erin McMurrer, Culinary Producer Alli Berkey, and Managing Culinary Producer Meri Lesogor helped plan and organize the 26 television episodes shot in September 2024 and May 2025, and ran the "back kitchen," cooking all the food that appeared on camera. They were supported by Culinary Production Coordinator Heather Tolmie and Assistant Culinary Producers Brooke Calhoun and Mel Velasco. Chase Brightwell, Valerie Sizhe Li, Sarah Sandler, and Crispin Lopez organized the ingredient and equipment segments. Additional editorial support came from Matthew Fairman, Megan Ginsberg, Mark Huxsoll, Scott Kathan, Nicole Konstantinakos, Amanda Luchtel, and Jessica Rudolph.

During filming, chefs Graciel Caces, Rob Chalmers, Leslie Garetto, Lee Tan, and Christine Tobin cooked all the food needed on set. Food stylists Ashley Moore and Kendra Smith were responsible for ensuring all the food looked beautiful. Culinary Assistant Malcolm Jackson, Kitchen Facilities and Video Equipment Associate Ethan Rogers, and Assistant Culinary Producer Wes Lane helped coordinate the kitchen with the television set by readying props, equipment, and food. Manager of Procurement and Kitchen Facilities Rachel Appelbaum, Ingredient Receiving Specialist Christopher Miller, and Kitchen Operations and Facilities Assistant Ian Watson were charged with making sure all the ingredients and kitchen equipment we needed were on hand.

We also appreciate the hard work of the television crew including Mick Bell, Ian Bishop, Mikaela Bloomberg, Fletcher Burns, Mike Duca, Eric Fisher, Rose Fortuna, Eric Goddard, Brian Henderson, Amanda Hennessey, Harlem Logan, Lee Holloway, Anthony Phelps, Justin Perro, Brad Price, Jay Maurer, Keith McManus, Laelia Mitchell, Taylor Steele, and Jennifer Tawa. Madeline Langlieb, Irene Wong, Steve Klise, Matthew Young, and Ryan Moody supported our On the Road segments.

Additional thanks to our Editors, Steven Huffaker, Hamilton Jones, Nick Perlman, Sean Sandefur, Herb Sevush, and Edit House Productions; our Senior Director of Post Production, Chen Margolis; Post Production Technician and Colorist William Rogan; and Assistant Editors Caroline Barry, Ruthie LaMay, and Ben Mushinski. Anne Howard assisted with all the historical and photography research. We also would like to thank Senior Vice President of TV, Video, and Podcast Nina Giannelli. Special thanks to Judy Barlow, Tom Davison, and Reina Roberts at American Public Television, which presents the show.

season eighteen

- 3 Grilled Hilltribe Chicken with Kua Txob
- 6 Pickle-Brined Fried Chicken Sandwiches
- 10 Chicken Cordon Bleu
- 12 Slow Roasted Ducks with Blackberry Sauce
- 15 Barbecued Chuck Roast
- 16 Frito Pie
- 19 Jitto's-Style Steak Bombs
- 20 Cajun Meatball Fricassee
- 22 Cornish Pasties
- 26 Mesquite-Grilled Tacos Rasurados
- 28 Alcapurrias
- 32 Grilled Brined Pork Chops with Garlic-Herb Oil
- 34 Porchetta Abruzzese
- 36 Indoor Barbecued Ribs
- 38 Honey-Glazed Pork Shoulder
- 40 Skillet Eggs Sardou
- 42 Rillons
- 44 American-Style Egg Rolls
- 46 Grilled Lamb Burgers
- 50 Coastal Georgia Paella
- 52 Seafood Risotto
- 54 Zephyr Wright–Inspired Shrimp Curry
- 56 Shrimp with Garlic and Jalapeño Butter
- 58 Clams Casino
- 60 Grilled Mussels
- 62 Green Spaghetti
- 64 Pesto Lasagna
- 66 One-Pot Shrimp Piccata Pasta
- 68 Shanghai Scallion Oil Noodles
- 70 Bean Bourguignon
- 72 Cutty's-Inspired Eggplant Spuckie
- 74 Tomatillo and Bibb Lettuce Salad with Tomatillo Ranch
- 76 Ultimate Caesar Salad
- 78 Tomatoes with Fontina Sauce and Cornichon Dressing
- 80 Quick-Braised Broccoli Rabe with Garlic and Anchovies
- 82 Creamy Potatoes and Leeks
- 84 Sweet Potato Fritters with Feta, Dill, and Cilantro
- 86 Air-Fryer Jalapeño Poppers
- 88 Cast Iron Potato Kugel
- 90 Gullah Lowcountry Red Rice
- 92 Double-Chocolate Banana Bread
- 95 Bolos Lêvedos (Portuguese Muffins)
- 98 Pastéis de Nata (Portuguese Egg Tarts)
- 100 Sufganiyot (Hanukkah Jelly Doughnuts)
- 102 Conchas
- 104 Chocolate-Dipped Potato Chip Cookies
- 106 Chocolate-Marshmallow Sandwich Cookies
- 108 Chocolate Brownie Cookies
- 110 Rhubarb Shortcakes with Buttermilk Whipped Cream
- 112 Aunt Jule's Pie
- 114 Peach Ripple Ice Cream
- 116 Coquito

Recipe Photos (from top to bottom): Shanghai Scallion Oil Noodles, Coastal Georgia Paella

ON THE ROAD
MINNESOTA

"Our Food Is Actually Our Story"

A HMONG MENU IN MINNEAPOLIS TELLS A FLAVORFUL TALE.

by Bryan Roof; photos by Steve Klise

It's the summer of 2023, and I'm standing with Minneapolis chef Yia Vang, talking about the menu. His restaurant, Union Hmong Kitchen (previously Mee-Ka), features a variety of Hmong-American dishes, such as a meatloaf of beef, pork, and glass noodles topped with a fried egg and oyster sauce–ketchup; smash cheeseburgers with fermented radishes and kua txob (pronounced "kuwah-tsaw") ranch dressing; and the more traditional nqaij tsaws (pronounced "ngai chah-uh"), braised pork and mustard greens with roasted vegetables and pickled onions.

Vang, who also owns a second location of Union Hmong Kitchen in Minneapolis's North Loop, says the inspiration for the menu was about "digging into these dishes that we grew up eating. So it was Hmong sausage that my dad made, or the way he grilled pork, or the way he grilled chicken. A lot of the side dishes are stuff that was inspired by Mom. Our very basic hot sauce, kua txob, which literally translates to 'pepper sauce,' is from my mom."

Today, Minnesota boasts one of the largest Hmong populations in the United States, due in large part to the Vietnam war, when many people from Southeast Asia's Hmong ethnic group aided American soldiers and took part in the covert, CIA-operated Secret War in Laos. Because of their participation, they were labeled traitors by Communist leaders throughout Southeast Asia. Fearing for their lives, many fled to the Ban Vinai refugee camp in Thailand, which is where Vang was born. "Vinai" is also the name of Vang's forthcoming restaurant, which he says will be a "love letter to my mom and dad."

Top to bottom: The exterior of Union Hmong Kitchen (formerly called Mee-Ka) in Minneapolis; Chef Yia Vang standing outside Union Hmong Kitchen; a forkful of kua txob; the crowded Minneapolis skyline.

After the war, many Hmong refugees resettled in Minnesota, and over the years family members and friends joined them stateside.

"When you have a group of people that does not have a land of their own, a home of their own, a country of their own, or an anthem of their own; when war determines where your next location's gonna be, no matter where you are in the world; if there's another Hmong person there, that's home," Vang says. "Our cultural DNA is intricately woven into the foods that we eat. If you want to know our people, then you gotta know our food, because our food is actually our story."

A typical Hmong meal consists of meat, vegetables, rice, and hot sauce, and grilling plays a primary role. "That's one thing that I really love about the way that Hmong food is done, even the way that my mom and dad does food: You can put whatever you want on the grill."

In the kitchen, Vang seasons a chicken with a mixture of salt, pepper, smoked paprika, and granulated garlic. Although the chicken is butterflied, the backbone has been left intact rather than removed. Nothing is wasted; he calls the bony, fat-laden bits of the backbone "chef snacks." He sandwiches the splayed chicken in a grill basket, and we head to the narrow back patio where he fires up a small charcoal grill and stokes the coals with a bamboo fan.

He casually grills the chicken, flipping it every so often for even cooking, fanning the coals when he wants to kick up the heat. The dish isn't on his menu, but the preparation is similar to how his father likes to cook chicken and exemplifies something he feels encapsulates Hmong cooking: straightforward preparations with powerful flavors.

When the chicken comes off the grill, the skin is perfectly char-streaked and crisp. After the chicken has rested, Vang breaks it down into 10 pieces and arranges them on a platter. He drops a handful of fermented mustard greens on one side of the platter and scatters another handful of pickled red onions over the chicken. Just before he brings it to the table, he showers the chicken with scallions and torn leaves of cilantro and mint. He serves it with a jar of kua txob—Vang's take on the cilantro, garlic, chile, lime, and fish sauce condiment inspired by his mother's version—and we douse bites of chicken with the sauce. The bold, simple dish is pure comfort.

He calls it "Grilled Hilltribe Chicken," explaining, "'Hilltribe' to us is not a description of tribes in the hills, but it's a people group who has embraced who they are."

Vang says that for the last year, he's been inspired by a Mark Twain quote: "The two most important days in your life are the day you are born and the day you find out why."

"I know why I'm here and what I was created for. The moment you realize that . . . you become unstoppable."

Grilled Hilltribe Chicken with Kua Txob

SERVES 4

WHY THIS RECIPE WORKS This recipe, inspired by chef Yia Vang, is a simple take on grilled chicken that he feels showcases Hmong cooking philosophy and technique. Following Vang's lead, we butterflied the chicken but left the backbone intact so that nothing went to waste. We seasoned the chicken with salt, pepper, smoked paprika, and granulated garlic and then cooked it bone-side down on a covered grill, where it picked up gentle smokiness from the coals. To finish, we flipped the chicken to briefly brown and crisp the skin. Finally, we served the chicken with kua txob (pronounced "kuwah-tsaw" and meaning "pepper sauce"), a potent sauce of cilantro, fish sauce, lime juice, chiles, and garlic.

Note that if you're cooking the chicken on a gas grill, there is no need to flip it to brown the skin; unlike with a charcoal grill, which loses heat over time, heat in a gas grill continues to build. When butterflying the chicken in step 1, we cut along only one side of the backbone and do not remove it. Chef Yia Vang calls the meat on the backbone "chef snacks." Haam choy is the pickled mustard green that's sold whole or halved in brine; it can be found in Asian markets. The kua txob should have a little bit of heat to it, though the lime juice balances this out. We like to leave the seeds in the red Fresno chile when chopping it, but if you prefer a milder sauce, you can remove the seeds first. A red jalapeño or one or two Thai chiles can be substituted for the Fresno.

Chicken

- 1 (3½- to 4-pound) whole chicken, giblets discarded
- 1 tablespoon kosher salt
- 1½ teaspoons granulated garlic
- 1 teaspoon pepper
- 1 teaspoon smoked paprika
- 1 cup haam choy (pickled mustard greens)
- ¼ cup pickled red onions
- ¼ cup fresh cilantro leaves
- ¼ cup fresh mint leaves, torn into large pieces
- 2 scallions, sliced thin

Kua Txob

- 1 cup cilantro leaves and stems, chopped
- 2 tablespoons plus 1 teaspoon lime juice (2 limes)
- 1 red Fresno chile, stemmed and minced
- 2 tablespoons fish sauce
- 2 garlic cloves, minced

1. For the Chicken Place chicken breast side down on cutting board. Using kitchen shears, cut along length of 1 side of backbone. Flip chicken breast side up and open chicken on board. Using palm of your hand, press firmly on center of breast to flatten chicken. Tuck wingtips under breasts.

2. Combine salt, granulated garlic, pepper, and paprika in bowl. Season chicken all over with spice mixture.

3. For the Kua Txob Combine all ingredients in bowl; set aside.

4a. For a Charcoal Grill Open bottom vent completely. Light large chimney starter filled with charcoal briquettes (6 quarts). When top coals are partially covered with ash, pour evenly over grill. Set cooking grate in place, cover, and open lid vent completely. Heat grill until hot, about 5 minutes.

4b. For a Gas Grill Turn all burners to high; cover; and heat grill until hot, about 15 minutes. Turn all burners to medium.

5a. For a Charcoal Grill Clean and oil cooking grate. Place chicken in center of grill, skin side up. Cover and cook until breasts register 150 degrees and thighs register at least 170 degrees, 40 to 45 minutes. Flip chicken skin side down and cook until skin is browned and breasts register 160 degrees and thighs register at least 175 degrees, 5 to 10 minutes.

5b. For a Gas Grill Clean and oil cooking grate. Place chicken in center of grill, skin side up. Cover and cook until breasts register 160 degrees and thighs register at least 175 degrees, 40 to 45 minutes.

6. Transfer chicken to carving board, skin side up, and let rest for 20 minutes. Carve chicken and arrange on serving platter. Place haam choy and onions on side of platter. Sprinkle chicken with cilantro leaves, mint, and scallions. Serve with kua txob.

Butterfly the Chicken

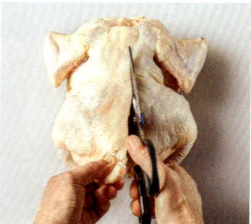 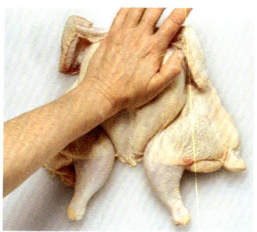

1. Cut: Use kitchen shears to cut along 1 side of backbone.

2. Flatten: Flip chicken breast side up and press down to flatten.

Vang using a fan to stoke the coals under his grilled chicken.

SEASON 18

Pickle-Brined Fried Chicken Sandwiches

SERVES 4

WHY THIS RECIPE WORKS We wanted a fried chicken sandwich where pickle juice was front and center. Adding brine in three separate stages achieved this. We started by soaking boneless thighs in pickle juice fortified with fresh dill, garlic, and dry mustard. Then we dredged the thighs in a seasoned flour dredge. We added a little pickle brine to the flour mixture for more pickle flavor and to create bits that would fry up craggy and crisp. We refrigerated the breaded thighs to help the coating stay on during frying. Just 10 minutes in the oil resulted in crispy, golden-brown chicken. To top off these sandwiches, we mixed mayonnaise, chopped pickles, finely chopped red onion, more dill and garlic, a pinch of cayenne, and a tablespoon of pickle brine for a creamy, crunchy, pickle-y slaw. In three words: crispy, tangy, delicious.

A 24-ounce jar of pickles is large enough to yield the 1¼ cups plus 1 tablespoon brine needed for this recipe.

Dill Pickle Topping
- ¼ cup mayonnaise
- ¼ cup chopped kosher dill pickles, plus 1 tablespoon brine
- ½ small red onion, chopped fine
- 2 tablespoons minced fresh dill
- 2 garlic cloves, minced
- Pinch cayenne pepper

Chicken Sandwiches
- 4 (3- to 5-ounce) boneless, skinless chicken thighs, trimmed
- 1¼ cups kosher dill pickle brine, divided
- 8 sprigs fresh dill, plus 2 tablespoons minced fresh dill, divided
- 6 garlic cloves, smashed
- 5 teaspoons dry mustard, divided
- 5 teaspoons kosher salt, divided
- 5 teaspoons pepper, divided
- 1¼ cups all-purpose flour
- ½ cup cornstarch
- 2 teaspoons granulated garlic
- 1 teaspoon baking powder
- 3 cups vegetable oil for frying
- ¼ cup mayonnaise
- 4 hamburger buns
- 2 cups shredded iceberg lettuce

1. For the Dill Pickle Topping Combine all ingredients in bowl and refrigerate until ready to serve. (Topping can be refrigerated for up to 2 days.)

2. For the Chicken Sandwiches Combine chicken, 1 cup pickle brine, dill sprigs, smashed garlic, 1 tablespoon mustard, 1 tablespoon salt, and 1 tablespoon pepper in bowl. Cover with plastic wrap and refrigerate for at least 6 hours or up to 12 hours.

3. Set wire rack in rimmed baking sheet. Whisk flour, cornstarch, granulated garlic, baking powder, minced dill, remaining 2 teaspoons mustard, remaining 2 teaspoons salt, and remaining 2 teaspoons pepper together in second bowl. Add remaining ¼ cup pickle brine to flour mixture and rub between your fingers until tiny craggy bits form throughout.

4. Working with 1 piece of chicken at a time, remove chicken from brine and transfer to flour mixture. Using your hands, toss chicken in flour mixture, pressing on coating to adhere and breaking up clumps, until coated on all sides. Transfer chicken to prepared wire rack. Refrigerate for at least 30 minutes or up to 2 hours. Discard brine.

5. Heat oil in Dutch oven over medium-high heat to 350 degrees. Carefully add chicken and fry until chicken is golden brown and registers at least 175 degrees, 8 to 12 minutes, flipping chicken halfway through frying. (Adjust heat as needed to maintain oil temperature between 325 and 350 degrees.) Transfer chicken to paper towel–lined plate.

6. Spread mayonnaise evenly on bun bottoms. Place chicken on bun bottoms, then top with dill pickle topping, lettuce, and bun tops. Serve.

Buffalo Pickle-Brined Fried Chicken Sandwiches
Omit dill pickle topping, mayonnaise for bun bottoms, and lettuce. Toss 4 thinly sliced celery ribs, ½ cup crumbled blue cheese, and ¼ cup mayonnaise together. Whisk ½ cup Frank's RedHot Original Cayenne Pepper Sauce and 4 tablespoons melted unsalted butter together in medium bowl. Toss each piece of fried chicken in hot-sauce mixture before placing chicken on bun bottoms. Top with celery topping, ¼ cup celery leaves, and bun tops before serving.

Eating Out the Old-Fashioned Way

IN WISCONSIN, TWO POPULAR RESTAURANTS OFFER A LINK TO THE PAST—
AND A GLIMPSE OF THE FUTURE.

by Bryan Roof; photos by Steve Klise

Ubiquitous throughout the state, Wisconsin's famous "supper clubs" have been part of the fabric of life for a century or more. Many were begun in converted dance halls in the early twentieth century, offering a casual, relaxed atmosphere where patrons would unwind from the stresses of the work week, often with some form of live entertainment. Today, there are over 250 supper clubs scattered throughout Wisconsin, each offering its own unique experience.

Supper clubs hit their stride in the 1950s and '60s as true dining destinations. Many were family-owned establishments located in the woods and off the beaten path and required traveling some distance to reach, which only added to their allure. According to Bob Prosser, owner and operator of Ishnala Supper Club in Lake Delton, Wisconsin, a supper club "only serves supper; a cheese spread and crackers are on the table when guests are seated; and brandy old fashioneds are pretty much a requirement."

Ishnala is a prime example of a classic midcentury supper club. The restaurant, which was built in 1953, is perched on the edge of Mirror Lake, offering views of the water from every seat in the house. Prosser says the club was constructed to incorporate 13 of the surrounding pine trees, some of which jut through the floor and out the roof, and was laid on over 76 tons of flagstone. One of their bars actually hovers above the lake. They routinely serve more than 500 guests on weeknights, well over a thousand on weekends.

Guests typically start the evening with a brandy old fashioned at the bar, ordered "sweet," "sour," or "press"—somewhere in between sweet and sour. Prosser tells me they sold 108,504 brandy old fashioneds at Ishnala in 2023; when I visited in spring 2024, the current year's count was over 35,000. Wisconsin consumes more brandy than any other state.

ON THE ROAD
WISCONSIN

After a cocktail or two, guests move to a table, where they may be greeted with a cheese spread or relish tray—an assortment of pickles, olives, crudité, and deviled eggs. And then, perhaps, a simple preparation of local lake fish, a "turf" option of prime rib or steaks, or throwback favorites like shrimp cocktail and French onion soup.

Since he took ownership in 1973, Prosser has personally welcomed hundreds of thousands of guests to Ishnala. "When we open the door, I get to greet all the customers that are standing in line. I just love that. I get to say hi to everybody, I get to shake everybody's hand, and I get to thank them," Prosser says. "One of our sayings is, 'it's not the number of people we serve, it's the number of people we please.' And to this day, we carry that through."

If Ishnala represents the classic supper club model, The Harvey House in Madison pushes the concept deep into the twenty-first century. There, husband-and-wife owners Joe and Shaina Papach honor their Midwestern roots through a wholly contemporary lens, honed after years of experience in high-end restaurants on the coasts.

"When we moved back to Madison, we both really wanted to start a restaurant that felt authentic to us, but also had a Midwestern sense of place. We really fell in love with a few different aspects of supper clubs: the sense of generosity, the sense of hospitality, and the aesthetic feel," says Shaina, who is also the creative director for the restaurant.

The Harvey House reflects these ideals. Located in a rehabbed train station, the dining room was originally the baggage handler's building. Shaina points out that you can still see marks where bags were thrown against the exterior walls. The kitchen, which Joe helms as chef, is open, polished, and tidy. The kitchen staff follows a traditional French brigade system, and each cook adheres to their specific role, a structure Joe absorbed during his tenure at The French Laundry in California. "It's like a dance," he says. "We're all working together in a way you don't get to see very often in other restaurants."

The menu pays homage to traditional supper clubs, but with the Papach's signature flair. "The direction of the menu really started out with pure continental cuisine," Joe says. "All those great American dishes like sizzling shrimp de jonghe, chicken cordon bleu, Caesar salad. Classic combinations. But at the same time we elevate it a little. We make everything from scratch in the restaurant [and] build multiple layers of flavors, but we don't take it too far beyond that. We create a really well composed dish that's real food, a good portion, and recognizable."

Joe's interpretation of chicken cordon bleu speaks to his years of training, and his knack for allowing the simplicity of a dish to speak for itself, even when the preparation is more involved. He begins by removing the thigh bone from a chicken leg quarter, while leaving the leg bone intact. A fat baton of Gruyere cheese is wrapped with both prosciutto and locally smoked Wisconsin ham, then encased in the thigh. Next, the leg quarter is cooked sous vide at 155 degrees for an hour, then chilled and refrigerated overnight. Next, the cooked-and-cooled leg quarter is dunked into a mixture of cornstarch and beaten egg whites that resembles white glue in consistency and color, and tossed in panko bread crumbs. Finally, the leg is deep-fried to golden brown and then finished in the oven.

Although The Harvey House is a new addition to the supper club roster in Wisconsin, the Papachs are fully aligned with the tradition of warm welcomes. "In the Midwest, the hospitality comes with a kindness and a generosity that I think is a little bit different than in larger markets," Shaina says. "And the guest experience is really about letting go, having an extra drink, ordering an extra appetizer, and really enjoying the people you're with."

Clockwise from left: Joe Papach assembles chicken cordon bleu in the Harvey House kitchen; the Harvey House bar in the original baggage handler's room; retro-modern decor gives the antique dining car a cozy feel; a classic supper club relish tray, complete with deviled eggs.

Chicken Cordon Bleu

SERVES 4 TO 8

WHY THIS RECIPE WORKS For our version of this supper club classic, we took inspiration from the Harvey House in Madison, Wisconsin. We began by deboning skin-on chicken thighs, which cook up moister than breast meat. We pounded and seasoned the thighs and then filled them with smoked ham, prosciutto, and Gruyère cheese. Once rolled, the skin helped keep it all contained. After chilling, we rolled the chicken in a mixture of egg whites and cornstarch before dredging in panko for the crunchiest coating. We briefly fried the chicken to ensure even color, then finished it in the oven so that it cooked through evenly. We served the chicken over a soubise—a béchamel fortified with sweet onions.

Do not trim excess skin from the chicken thighs; it is used to wrap the chicken after rolling. To form the eight batons of Gruyere cheese called for here, we call for starting with one 6-ounce block of cheese; you may have some cheese left over after cutting the batons.

Chicken

- 8 thin slices Black Forest deli ham
- 8 thin slices prosciutto
- 1 (6-ounce) block Gruyère cheese, cut into 8 (2-inch by ½-inch) batons
- 8 (5- to 7-ounce) bone-in chicken thighs
- 2 teaspoons grated lemon zest
- 2 teaspoons chopped fresh thyme
- 1 teaspoon kosher salt
- ½ teaspoon pepper
- 3 large egg whites
- ½ cup plus 1 tablespoon (2¼ ounces/255 grams) cornstarch
- 4 cups panko bread crumbs, divided
- 2 quarts peanut or vegetable oil for frying

Soubise

- 3 tablespoons unsalted butter
- ½ cup finely chopped onion
- 1 teaspoon kosher salt, divided
- 1 tablespoon all-purpose flour
- 1 cup whole milk
- ¼ cup sour cream
- ⅛ teaspoon grated nutmeg
- ¼ teaspoon pepper

1. For the Chicken Lay 1 slice of ham on cutting board with short side parallel to counter edge, then place 1 slice prosciutto on top of ham in same direction. Place 1 Gruyère baton crosswise along bottom edge of ham stack. Roll ham once around cheese, tuck in sides of ham, and continue to roll until cheese is fully encased; transfer to plate. Repeat with remaining ham, prosciutto, and Gruyère; refrigerate until needed.

2. Place thighs skin side down on cutting board. Using tip of sharp boning knife, cut slits along either side of length of bone to expose bone. Slip knife under bone, and carve out and scrape meat from bone; discard bone and cartilage. Repeat with remaining thighs.

3. Working with 1 thigh at a time, place boned-out thigh skin side down on cutting board and cover with plastic wrap. Using meat pounder, pound to even approximate ¼-inch thickness; set aside. Repeat with remaining thighs.

4. Sprinkle flesh sides of thighs evenly with lemon zest, thyme, salt, and pepper. Place 1 ham-and-cheese packet crosswise along short side of each thigh and roll thigh around it, gently stretching any excess skin over seam. Wrap each thigh tightly in plastic wrap and twist ends to create tight cylinder shape. Refrigerate for at least 4 hours or up to 24 hours.

5. Process 2 cups panko in food processor until finely ground, about 15 seconds. Transfer to 13 by 9-inch baking pan, and stir in remaining 2 cups panko. Whisk egg whites and cornstarch together in medium bowl until smooth.

6. Working with 1 packet at a time, unwrap chicken; dip into egg-white mixture, allowing excess to drip off; then coat evenly with panko. Transfer to plate. Repeat with remaining packets, and refrigerate for at least 20 minutes or up to 2 hours.

7. About 15 minutes before cooking chicken, adjust oven rack to middle position and heat oven to 350 degrees. Set wire rack in rimmed baking sheet. Add oil to large Dutch oven until it measures about 1½ inches deep and heat over medium-high heat to 350 degrees.

8. Place 4 thighs in hot oil and fry, turning often, until evenly golden brown, about 2 minutes; transfer to prepared rack. Return oil to 350 degrees and repeat with remaining chicken. Transfer chicken to oven and bake until center of chicken registers 175 degrees, about 30 minutes.

9. For the Soubise While chicken is baking, melt butter in medium saucepan over medium-low heat. Add onion and ½ teaspoon salt; cover; and cook, stirring occasionally, until onion is translucent, about 10 minutes.

Whisk in flour and cook for 1 minute. Whisk in milk, increase heat to medium-high, and bring to boil. Continue to cook, whisking constantly, until thickened, about 30 seconds longer. Remove from heat and whisk in sour cream, pepper, nutmeg, and remaining ½ teaspoon salt. Cover to keep warm.

10. Divide sauce evenly among 4 to 8 serving plates. Place 1 to 2 pieces cordon bleu over sauce on each plate. Serve.

Slow Roasted Ducks with Blackberry Sauce

SERVES 8

WHY THIS RECIPE WORKS We wanted showstopping centerpiece ducks for our holiday table (or any occasion worthy of gorgeous roast birds), and we hoped for as little hands-on work as possible. While many recipes for roast duck call for scoring or pricking the skin and often for turning the bird multiple times, we were looking for a simpler approach. Salting the ducks well in advance—48 hours was best—seasoned them thoroughly, helped to keep them juicy during long cooking, and produced the driest, crispiest skin. Ladling a mixture of hot water, soy sauce, and honey over the ducks' skin before roasting yielded birds with a breathtaking, lacquered shine while adding complex umami and depth. Roasting the ducks low and slow (300 degrees for a little over 3 hours) produced super-tender, succulent meat, and blasting them briefly at 450 degrees finished rendering the fat and crisped the skin. While the ducks roasted, we made a dead-simple sweet-and-sour blackberry duck sauce by cooking down whole berries with honey, sherry vinegar, and thyme for a perfect complement to the rich roast duck.

Pekin ducks may also be labeled as Long Island ducks and are typically sold frozen. Thaw the ducks in the refrigerator for 24 to 48 hours. This recipe was developed with Diamond Crystal kosher salt. If using Morton kosher salt, use 25 percent less. We prefer to salt the ducks for 48 hours before roasting them for crispier skin, but they will still be very good after 24 hours. Even when the duck is fully cooked, its juices will have a reddish hue.

Ducks
- 2 (5½- to 6-pound) whole Pekin ducks, neck and giblets discarded
- ¼ cup plus 2 teaspoons kosher salt, divided
- 2 navel oranges, halved
- 4 cups water
- ½ cup soy sauce
- ¼ cup honey

Blackberry Duck Sauce
- 15 ounces (3 cups) fresh or frozen blackberries
- ¾ cup honey
- ¾ cup plus ½ teaspoon sherry vinegar, divided
- 3 sprigs fresh thyme
- ¼ teaspoon pepper
- ⅛ teaspoon kosher salt

1. For the Ducks Set wire rack in rimmed baking sheet. Working with 1 duck at a time, use your hands to remove large fat deposits from bottom of cavity. Using kitchen shears, trim excess neck skin from top of breast and from cavity; remove tail and first 2 segments from each wing, leaving only drumette.

2. Rub 2 teaspoons salt into cavity of each duck. Rub 5 teaspoons salt into skin of each duck. Place ducks on prepared baking sheet. Refrigerate uncovered for 24 to 48 hours.

3. Adjust oven rack to lower-middle position and heat oven to 300 degrees. Stuff cavity of each duck with 2 orange halves. Tie legs together with kitchen twine. Set V-rack in roasting pan. Position ducks breast side up crosswise in V-rack, side by side, in opposite directions, without touching.

4. Bring water, soy sauce, and honey to boil in small saucepan over high heat; remove from heat. Ladle boiling water mixture evenly over skin of both ducks. Roast ducks until thermometer inserted into thickest part of thighs registers 190 to 195 degrees, 3¼ to 3½ hours.

5. Remove ducks from oven and increase temperature to 450 degrees. Once oven has reached 450 degrees, continue to roast ducks until skin is deeply browned all over, 10 to 25 minutes. Let ducks rest on V-rack in pan for 45 minutes.

6. For the Blackberry Sauce Meanwhile, bring all ingredients to simmer in medium saucepan over medium-high heat. Cook, stirring often and mashing berries with potato masher, until mixture is thickened and registers 218 to 220 degrees, 15 to 20 minutes. Strain mixture through fine-mesh strainer into bowl, scraping strainer and pressing on solids to extract as much sauce as possible; discard solids. Stir remaining ½ teaspoon vinegar into sauce and transfer to serving bowl. (Sauce can be refrigerated for up to 5 days; serve warm.)

7. Carve duck and serve with sauce.

Slow-Roasted Ducks with Soy-Honey Sauce

Substitute Soy-Honey Duck Sauce for the Blackberry Duck Sauce.

Soy-Honey Duck Sauce
MAKES ABOUT 1 CUP

Shaoxing wine is a staple in Chinese cooking that contributes distinctive nutty flavors to food. We use Shaoxing cooking wine, which has added salt and can be found at Chinese grocery stores and online; dry sherry can be substituted.

- ¾ cup honey
- 6 tablespoons soy sauce
- 3 tablespoons hoisin sauce
- 3 tablespoons Shaoxing wine
- 3 garlic cloves, smashed and peeled
- 1 (3-inch) piece ginger, peeled and smashed
- ½ cinnamon stick
- 1 star anise pod
- ⅛ teaspoon cayenne

Bring honey, soy sauce, hoisin, Shaoxing wine, garlic, ginger, cinnamon stick, star anise, and cayenne to boil in medium saucepan over medium-high heat. Cook, stirring often, until mixture is thickened and registers 235 degrees, 4 to 7 minutes. Strain mixture through fine-mesh strainer into bowl; discard solids. Transfer to serving bowl. Serve. (Sauce can be refrigerated for up to 5 days; serve warm.)

Deep in the Heart of Clod Country

FORKS FALL BY THE WAYSIDE AT KREUZ MARKET IN LOCKHART, TEXAS, WHERE THE FOCUS IS ON ONE THING ONLY: MEAT.

by Bryan Roof; photos by Steve Klise

ON THE ROAD
TEXAS

In 1999, the year Kreuz Market in Lockhart, Texas, celebrated its 99th anniversary, Roy Perez shoveled several pounds of smoldering coals from the restaurant's barbecue pit into a metal washtub. With a few media representatives in tow and a police escort to divert traffic, he and a coworker dragged the washtub down the road to the establishment's new location, where he carefully emptied the coals into a brand-new pit. The gesture was more than a photo op; this fire had been burning continuously for a century, and pit master Perez refused to allow it to go out on his watch. Superstition? Maybe, or maybe just efficiency: Kreuz's hungry regulars expected barbecue even on moving day, and Perez, determined to serve them, needed a hot fire.

Seventeen years later, I made the trek to Kreuz Market on a quest for shoulder clod, a regional barbecue specialty. The immensity of the place engulfed me as I passed through a cavernous concrete hallway toward the barbecue pit where the mutton-chopped Perez spends most days. The stripped plywood walls held a patchwork of antique signage, black-and-white photos, and rusted butcher's tools. A menu above the counter offered promise: ribs, brisket, smoked ham, shoulder clod. Despite its magnitude, there was a warmth to the place, and wood-fire aromas perfumed the air.

I waited in line until I was called on to place my order, which I did with a mild fear of being recognized as the outsider I was. I ordered clod along with some sliced brisket and ribs, all in ½-pound increments. The cashier turned toward the pit and called out the order in a thick, rapid-fire patois that I struggled to understand.

Perez speared the meat with a large carving fork and moved it from the pit to a chunky, round butcher block well-greased from years of slicing fatty meat. Post oak logs burned in shallow craters at the ends of the sooty brick pits, and sawdust covered the surrounding floor to sop up errant drips of fat. A young man wrapped my order neatly in paper, propped a stack of sliced white bread on top, and handed it over to me as the next customers, a pair of police officers, stepped up to the counter.

I made my way to the dining room and found a seat at one of the long, unfinished wood tables, where paper towels and bottles of spice mix were stationed every few feet.

I noticed a sign declaring "No Forks (They're at the end of your arm)." Empowered, I tore into the shoulder clod with my fingers, a little self-consciously at first but then with abandon as I surrendered to the primal pleasure of using my bare hands to eat meat—profoundly gratifying meat—that had been cooked over a century-old fire.

Barbecued Chuck Roast

SERVES 8 TO 10

WHY THIS RECIPE WORKS Beef shoulder clod, a sacred cut in some corners of Texas, delivers supremely beefy flavor underneath a coal-colored crust spiced with black pepper, cayenne, and salt. However, it often tips the scales at somewhere between 13 and 21 pounds. To make a more manageable version, we used chuck-eye roast, which is cut from the shoulder clod. Salting the roast overnight seasoned it throughout. Cooking the roast over indirect heat on a hot grill outfitted with a packet of soaked wood chips infused the beef with smoky flavor. And pulling the roast off the grill when it registered 155 degrees and slicing it paper-thin yielded ultratender meat.

The roast must be seasoned at least 18 hours before cooking.

- 1½ tablespoons kosher salt
- 1½ teaspoons pepper
- ¼ teaspoon cayenne pepper
- 1 (5-pound) boneless beef chuck-eye roast, trimmed
- 2 cups wood chip

1. Combine salt, pepper, and cayenne in bowl. Pat roast dry with paper towels. Place roast on large sheet of plastic wrap and rub all over with spice mixture. Wrap tightly in plastic and refrigerate for 18 to 24 hours.

2. Just before grilling, soak wood chips in water for 15 minutes, then drain. Using large piece of heavy-duty aluminum foil, wrap soaked chips in 8 by 4½-inch foil packet. (Make sure chips do not poke holes in sides or bottom of packet.) Cut 2 evenly spaced 2-inch slits in top of packet.

3a. For a Charcoal Grill Open bottom vent completely. Light large chimney starter filled with charcoal briquettes (6 quarts). When top coals are partially covered with ash, pour evenly over half of grill. Place wood chip packet on coals. Set cooking grate in place, cover, and open lid vent completely. Heat grill until hot and wood chips are smoking, about 5 minutes.

3b. For a Gas Grill Remove cooking grate and place wood chip packet directly on primary burner. Set cooking grate in place; turn all burners to high; cover; and heat grill until hot and wood chips are smoking, about 15 minutes. Leave primary burner on high and turn off other burner(s). (Adjust primary burner [or, if using three-burner grill, primary burner and second burner] as needed to maintain grill temperature of 350 degrees.)

4. Clean and oil cooking grate. Place roast on cooler side of grill. Cover grill (positioning lid vent directly over roast if using charcoal) and cook until meat registers 155 to 160 degrees, 2 to 2½ hours. Transfer roast to carving board, tent with foil, and let rest for 20 minutes. Slice thin and serve.

SEASON 18

Frito Pie

SERVES 6 TO 12

WHY THIS RECIPE WORKS Frito (or Fritos) pie—beef chili served over Fritos right in the bag—is one of those things that is hotly debated and personal, so for a solid starting point, we began with a chili recipe written by Kaleta Doolin, the daughter of the founder of Fritos. This chili is designed to come together fairly easily and quickly. During research, we saw a lot of different garnishes that could be added here, but we felt it was important to keep it as simple as possible and opted for cheddar cheese and raw onion. We cut the bag open along the side to give us the largest surface area so that we could cover the Fritos evenly. The wider and shallower opening also made eating easier.

If you can't find 85 percent lean ground beef, you can use 80 percent. We prefer the flavor of Pacifico or other Mexican lagers in this chili, but if they are unavailable, Budweiser or another mild lager will work just fine. Do not use bolder beers, which can make the chili too bitter. For a milder chili, use the smaller quantity of chipotle. We developed this recipe with original flavor Fritos corn chips. You can assemble and eat the Frito pie right out of the bag, or you can portion Fritos (2 to 4 ounces per serving) and chili (½ cup to 1 cup per serving) into individual serving bowls. This recipe will serve six as a meal or 12 as a snack or as part of a larger spread.

- 2 tablespoons vegetable oil
- 1½ pounds 85 percent lean ground beef
- 2 teaspoons table salt
- 2 onions, chopped fine (2 cups), divided
- 6 garlic cloves, minced
- 2 tablespoons cornmeal
- 2 tablespoons chili powder
- 2 teaspoons pepper
- 1½ teaspoons ground cumin
- 1 teaspoon dried oregano
- 1 (28-ounce) can crushed tomatoes
- 1½ cups mild lager
- 1–2 tablespoons minced canned chipotle chile in adobo sauce
- 12 (2-ounce) bags Fritos corn chips
- 12 ounces mild yellow cheddar cheese, shredded (3 cups)

1. Heat oil in Dutch oven over medium-high heat until just smoking. Add beef and salt and cook, using wooden spoon to break meat into ¼-inch pieces, until beef is browned and fond begins to form on bottom of pot, 12 to 14 minutes.

2. Reduce heat to medium. Add 1 cup onions and cook, stirring occasionally, until onions are softened and lightly browned, about 5 minutes. Stir in garlic, cornmeal, chili powder, pepper, cumin, and oregano and cook until fragrant, about 1 minute.

3. Stir in tomatoes, beer, and chipotle, scraping up any browned bits. Bring to simmer; reduce heat to low; and cook, stirring occasionally, until thickened, about 1 hour, adjusting heat as needed to maintain gentle simmer.

4. Using scissors, cut long sides of Fritos bags from end to end. Gently fold back top edge of each bag to form cuff. Scoop about ½ cup chili into each Fritos bag. Top chili with cheddar and remaining 1 cup onions. Serve.

The American Table

According to the book *Fritos Pie: Stories, Recipes, and More* (2011) by Kaleta Doolin, the daughter of Fritos founder C. E. Doolin, her father purchased the recipe for fried corn chips in 1932 (along with an extruding press for making them, plus 19 customer accounts) from a gentleman who ran a gas station in San Antonio, Texas. The grand sum was $100. According to Forbes, Frito-Lay was recently valued at $16.3 billion and was named the 39th most valuable brand in the world—not a bad return on investment. That $100 transaction was the start of the Fritos company. The company went on to merge with Lays to become Frito-Lay in 1961; in 1965 it became a subsidiary of PepsiCo.

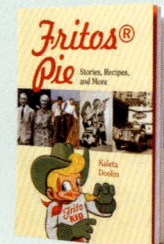

16   *The Complete Cook's Country TV Show Cookbook*

ON THE ROAD
NEW HAMPSHIRE

A Delicious Legacy

A TWIST ON TRADITION MAKES THIS SANDWICH THE BOMB.

by Bryan Roof; photos by Steve Klise

Jitto's Super Steak in Portsmouth, New Hampshire, looks more like a sprawling home than it does a proper restaurant. This feeling carries through to the inside, too, which has low ceilings and exposed wooden beams and an echo of familiar conversation between the bartender and the band of regulars seated around her. The neon glow of beer lights on the walls guides you through the dining room to a line of customers placing orders at a long take-out counter. And a glimpse into the open kitchen offers up the smells and sounds of a bustling restaurant, where the clang of metal spatulas on the flat-top griddle seems to keep time with the songs on the radio.

Jerry and Linda Nadeau opened Jitto's Super Steak in 1979. Kathy Nadeau and her late husband, Danny, took over the business from her in-laws in the mid-1980s. Kathy tells me that the name Jitto stems from the French pronunciation of "Jerry."

Over the years, Jitto's has become famous for its version of New England's beloved steak bomb, which Kathy explains "is a steak sandwich with all the fixins: mushrooms, peppers, onions, extra cheese, and salami." At Jitto's they also add a considerable smear of mayonnaise and recommend American cheese over provolone. But what really sets this steak bomb apart is the steak: hearty cubes of steak tips cooked to medium and hit with an assertive sprinkle of Lawry's Seasoned Salt.

The recipe for the steak bomb hasn't changed since 1979, and to this day it remains Jitto's biggest seller. "That's why our shirts say 'Bomb Squad.' Just don't wear [the shirt] to the airport," Kathy jokes. To keep up with demand, Jitto's goes through 350 to 450 pounds of steak each week, which Kathy cuts by hand every day.

After Danny passed away in 2015, Kathy made the choice to keep the restaurant going. To her and Danny, it was more than a business—it was where they first met, got married, and raised a family. As Kathy hands me a sandwich for the road, she leans in close and says, "I don't want to get teary, but my husband was the best. That's why I keep doing it."

Top to Bottom: Cook John Gray lays down some cheese on the flattop; there's no missing this grand entryway; owner Kathy Nadeau tops off a steak bomb; Jitto's regulars gather at the bar.

Jitto's-Style Steak Bombs
SERVES 4

WHY THIS RECIPE WORKS To make this New England classic inspired by Jitto's Super Steak in Portsmouth, New Hampshire, we started by cutting steak tips into small, bite-size pieces. We seasoned the steak tips with Lawry's Seasoned Salt and pretoasted the rolls with a spread of mayonnaise. Next, we lightly browned the onion and then added the bell pepper and mushrooms, cooking them until they were softened. We transferred the vegetables to a bowl and seared the seasoned pieces of steak tips in the same skillet, adding in the salami so that some of its fat rendered and flavored the steak. Finally, we stirred together the meats and vegetables, piled the filling into the toasted rolls, layered on some melty American cheese, and baked the sandwiches until the cheese was hot and gooey.

Sirloin steak tips are often sold as flap meat. Lawry's Seasoned Salt is usually stocked with other spice blends in the grocery store. We developed this recipe with a red bell pepper, but any color pepper can be used. Keep the sub rolls hinged when splitting them; otherwise, these extra-full sandwiches have a tendency to fall apart when fully assembled.

- 2 tablespoons plus 1 teaspoon vegetable oil, divided
- 1 onion, halved and sliced ¼ inch thick
- 1 red bell pepper, stemmed, seeded, and cut into ¼-inch-wide strips
- 4 ounces white mushrooms, trimmed, halved, and sliced ¼ inch thick
- 2 teaspoons Lawry's Seasoned Salt, divided
- 4 (8-inch) sub rolls, split but hinged
- 6 tablespoons mayonnaise
- 1 pound sirloin steak tips, trimmed and cut into ¾-inch chunks
- 1½ ounces thinly sliced deli salami, quartered
- 8 thin slices deli American cheese (4 ounces)

1. Adjust oven rack to middle position and heat oven to 400 degrees. Heat 2 tablespoons oil in 12-inch non-stick skillet over medium-high heat until just smoking. Add onion and cook, stirring frequently, until beginning to brown, about 4 minutes.

2. Add bell pepper, mushrooms, and 1 teaspoon seasoned salt and cook until vegetables are tender, about 6 minutes. Transfer to bowl; set aside skillet.

3. Arrange rolls on rimmed baking sheet. Spread mayonnaise evenly on cut sides of each roll (1½ tablespoons each). Bake rolls until crusty and warmed through, about 5 minutes.

4. Meanwhile, heat remaining 1 teaspoon oil in now-empty skillet over medium-high heat until just smoking. Add steak tips and sprinkle with remaining 1 teaspoon seasoned salt. Scatter salami over top and cook, without stirring, until steak tips are browned on bottom, about 5 minutes.

5. Off heat, stir onion mixture into steak tips. Divide steak mixture evenly among rolls. Layer 2 slices American cheese over steak mixture on each roll. Bake until cheese is melted, about 1 minute. Serve immediately.

Don't Shave That Steak

Cut the steak tips into small pieces for the filling.

Cajun Meatball Fricassee

SERVES 4 TO 6

WHY THIS RECIPE WORKS We were after tender, juicy, Cajun-spiced meatballs and a rich, boldly seasoned gravy with a balanced kick of heat. Using saltines in place of fresh bread in the meatballs got rid of some of the moisture, making the meatballs less gummy, while a hefty dose of Worcestershire sauce, Creole seasoning, and dried thyme ensured that they tasted supermeaty and exceptionally flavorful. Roasting the meatballs in the oven gave them flavorful browning and kept us from having to laboriously fry them on the stovetop. The signature flavor of a Cajun gravy comes from a deeply browned roux—a mixture of flour and fat. For ours, we sped things up by preheating the oil until it was just smoking before adding in the flour. Once the flour was the color of milk chocolate, we added chopped onion, bell pepper, and celery (the so-called "Cajun Trinity") for a backbone of aromatic sweetness and depth and to quickly stop the flour from getting any darker. Finally, simmering the browned meatballs in the gravy brought it all together, making for an exceptionally comforting stew to serve over rice for dinner.

We recommend using a #16 portion scoop to divvy up the meatball mixture. To make shaping easier, wet your hands slightly. Serve with a dash of Louisiana-style hot sauce.

Meatballs
- 22 square saltines
- 1 cup milk
- 2 tablespoons Worcestershire sauce
- 2 pounds 85 percent lean ground beef
- 2 ounces Parmesan cheese, grated (1 cup)
- 1 tablespoon Tony Chachere's Original Creole Seasoning
- 1½ teaspoons dried thyme
- 1 teaspoon pepper

Stew
- ⅓ cup vegetable oil
- ⅓ cup all-purpose flour
- 1 onion, chopped
- 1 green bell pepper, stemmed, seeded, and chopped
- 1 celery rib, chopped
- 2 slices bacon, cut into ½-inch pieces
- 6 scallions, white and green parts separated and sliced thin
- 3 garlic cloves, minced
- ½ teaspoon Tony Chachere's Original Creole Seasoning
- 4 cups chicken broth
- 1 tablespoon Worcestershire sauce
- Cooked white rice

1. For the Meatballs Adjust oven rack to upper-middle position and heat oven to 425 degrees. Set wire rack in aluminum foil–lined rimmed baking sheet and spray rack evenly with vegetable oil spray.

2. Place saltines in large zipper-lock bag, seal bag, and crush saltines fine with rolling pin. Whisk saltines, milk, and Worcestershire together in large bowl. Let sit for 5 minutes to soften saltines. Whisk saltine mixture until smooth paste forms. Add beef, Parmesan, Creole seasoning, thyme, and pepper and mix with your hands until thoroughly combined.

3. Divide mixture into about 24 scant ¼-cup portions. Roll portions between your slightly wet hands to form meatballs and evenly space on prepared wire rack. Roast meatballs until lightly browned on top, about 25 minutes.

4. For the Stew Meanwhile, heat oil in large Dutch oven over medium-high heat until just smoking. Using heat-resistant silicone spatula, stir in flour and cook, stirring constantly, until mixture is color of peanut butter, 2 to 5 minutes. Reduce heat to medium and continue to cook, stirring constantly, until roux has darkened to color of milk chocolate, 5 to 10 minutes longer.

5. Stir in onion, bell pepper, celery, and bacon and cook until vegetables are softened, 7 to 10 minutes. Stir in scallion whites, garlic, and Creole seasoning and cook until fragrant, about 1 minute. Whisk in broth and Worcestershire until thoroughly combined. Bring to boil over medium-high heat.

6. Add meatballs to stew; reduce heat to low; and cook, covered, until flavors have melded, about 20 minutes. Uncover; increase heat to medium-high; and cook until thickened to texture of heavy cream, 8 to 12 minutes. Serve over rice, sprinkled with scallion greens.

Shades of Roux

A roux is simply a mixture of flour and fat (butter or oil) cooked together. In Louisiana-style cooking, a roux is almost always made with oil; Cajun cooks often cook the roux for an hour or more to get the nutty, complex flavors a dark roux provides. Our technique takes only 15 minutes. The three important steps are preheating the oil until it's just smoking, stirring the roux constantly, and adding the vegetables to the pot right when you've reached the desired milk-chocolate color; the vegetables stop the roux from darkening further.

PEANUT-BUTTER COLOR

MILK-CHOCOLATE COLOR

SEASON EIGHTEEN 21

Cornish Pasties

SERVES 4

WHY THIS RECIPE WORKS These handheld turnovers should be rich and flaky, not tough and dry. For the best version, we toss the uncooked meat (skirt steak) and vegetables (onion, potato, and rutabaga) with a little flour before wrapping the filling tightly in our dough rounds. The flour combines with the filling's exuded juices as the pasties bake to create the gravy right inside the crust. We didn't want to stray very far from the pasties' Michigan roots, but we did add some garlic and fresh thyme to punch up the flavor of the filling. To ensure easy dough assembly, we use sour cream to make it both pliable and rip-resistant.

You can substitute turnips for rutabagas if you like. If you can't find skirt steak, you can use 1½ pounds of blade steak. The extra ¼ pound accounts for the trimming required with the blade cut. The pasties fit best on the baking sheet when placed crosswise in two rows of three. Serve the pasties with ketchup, if desired.

Crust
- ⅔ cup sour cream, chilled
- 1 large egg, lightly beaten
- 3 cups (15 ounces) all-purpose flour
- 1¾ teaspoons table salt
- 16 tablespoons unsalted butter, cut into ½-inch pieces and chilled

Filling
- 1 tablespoon unsalted butter
- 1 onion, chopped fine
- 2¼ teaspoons table salt, divided
- ¾ teaspoon pepper
- 1 tablespoon minced fresh thyme
- 2 garlic cloves, minced
- 1¼ pounds skirt steak, trimmed and cut into ½-inch pieces
- 10 ounces russet potatoes, peeled and cut into ½-inch pieces
- 10 ounces rutabaga, peeled and cut into ½-inch pieces
- ¼ cup all-purpose flour
- 1 large egg

1. For the Crust Whisk sour cream and egg together in small bowl. Process flour and salt in food processor until combined, about 3 seconds. Add butter and pulse until only pea-size pieces remain, about 10 pulses. Add half of sour cream mixture and pulse until combined, about 5 pulses. Add remaining sour cream mixture and pulse until dough begins to form, about 15 pulses.

2. Transfer mixture to lightly floured counter and knead briefly until dough comes together. Form dough into 6-inch disk, wrap tightly in plastic wrap, and refrigerate for 30 minutes. (Dough can be refrigerated for up to 24 hours; let chilled dough sit on counter for 15 minutes to soften before rolling.)

3. For the Filling Melt butter in 10-inch skillet over medium heat. Add onion and ¼ teaspoon salt and cook until softened, about 5 minutes. Add thyme and garlic and cook until fragrant, about 30 seconds. Let cool slightly, about 5 minutes. Combine cooled onion mixture, steak, potatoes, rutabaga, remaining 2 teaspoons salt, and ¾ teaspoon pepper in bowl. Add flour and toss to coat.

4. Adjust oven rack to upper-middle position and heat oven to 375 degrees. Line rimmed baking sheet with parchment paper. Remove dough from refrigerator and cut into 6 equal pieces (about 5 ounces each); cover with plastic wrap. Divide filling into 6 equal portions, about 1 heaping cup each.

5. Working with 1 piece of dough at a time, roll into 10 by 8-inch oval (about ⅛ inch thick) on lightly floured counter. Place 1 portion filling in center of dough. Moisten edges of dough with water, then fold narrow end of oval over filling to form half-moon shape. Press dough around filling to adhere.

6. Trim any ragged edges, then crimp edges with fork to seal; transfer to prepared sheet. (For more decorative edge, trim any ragged edges and, starting at one end, pinch and slightly twist dough diagonally across seam between your thumb and index finger. Continue pinching and twisting dough around seam.) Repeat with remaining dough and filling.

7. Using paring knife, cut 1-inch vent hole on top of each pasty. Whisk egg and 2 teaspoons water in bowl. Brush pasties with egg wash. Bake until crust is golden brown and filling is bubbling up through vent hole, about 45 minutes, rotating sheet halfway through baking. Transfer pasties to wire rack and let cool for 10 minutes before serving.

The American Table: Miners' Meals

Starting in 1843, the wilderness of Michigan's Upper Peninsula was the site of an epic copper boom. Miners flocked to the region from around the world; many came from Cornwall, England. By 1903 Red Jacket, the region's primary city, had a 50,000-volume library, an elaborate opera house where Caruso and Bernhardt performed, and eight separate foreign-language newspapers. Then, in 1913, a long, bloody strike started the city's slow but steady decline. Today Red Jacket, renamed Calumet, is a village of some 700 people in a region of ghost towns. Not everything has vanished, though; as is so often the case, food is the last tradition to die, and the Cornish pasty lives on to recall the glory days of King Copper. –John Willoughby

To Make Ahead Pasties can be prepared through step 6, then frozen on baking sheet. Once frozen, pasties can be stored in zipper-lock bag for up to 1 month. To cook from frozen, bake at 350 degrees for 1 hour 5 minutes to 1 hour 10 minutes.

SEASON EIGHTEEN   23

ON THE ROAD — TUCSON

Embracing the Rhythm of a Tucson Taqueria

CHARCOAL, MEAT, AND SALT MAKE MAGIC.

by Bryan Roof; photos by Steve Klise

As I arrive at the 12th Avenue location of Tacos Apson in South Tucson, Arizona, I'm immediately hit with the aromas of charred beef and mesquite smoke hanging thick in the air. After placing my order at the small takeout window, I do my best to peer through the glass wall of the kitchen, fogged over with smoke and soot from the grill directly behind it. On that grill sit thin sheets of carne asada and burly slabs of beef ribs being salted and flipped, salted and flipped.

After I grab my order of carne asada, rasurado, and tripa tacos, I make my way to the salsa bar, taking in its assortment of red and green salsas, aguamole (a puree of avocados, lime juice, and water), chopped cabbage, wedged baby limes, and a mix of diced onions and cilantro. Sitting at one of the picnic tables in the shade of the corrugated tin roof, I eat while taking in the view of Sentinel Peak against the cornflower-blue sky.

Owners Yazmin Aldecoa-Durazo and Francisco Javier Durazo opened Tacos Apson in April 2001, less than a year after they were married. Francisco had always wanted to put something of his own out into the world, to be his own boss, and opening a taco shop was a dream the couple shared. They envisioned a "home-style" taco shop with dishes based on family recipes, with a few innovations of their own.

Neither Yazmin nor Francisco was directly involved in restaurants prior to opening. "We thought the restaurant business was going to be really good, and it is very good. But it's a very big thing," says Yazmin. "A lot of people don't know that. They think that opening a restaurant is just going inside your kitchen and cooking. No. It's a passion for us—food, recipes, creating stuff—but it's also a lot of work."

Nearly 20 years later, at the height of the COVID-19 pandemic in 2020, Yazmin and Francisco opened a second location north of Tucson. It's tucked into a nondescript strip mall with surroundings bearing little

Top to bottom: Yazmin Aldecoa-Durazo, co-owner of Tacos Apson; the North Tucson location of Tacos Apson; owner Franciso Javier Durazo pulls a rack of ribs from the grill.

resemblance to the mountain views and charm of the original, but the food is still made with the same loving care and mesquite smoke flavor.

The taqueria is named in tribute to Francisco's father, also Francisco Durazo, who in 1957 started a Mexican rock-and-roll band called Los Apson with his brother. Even up to Yazmin and Francisco's wedding day, Yazmin, who had heard of the band, never knew they were related to her future husband. The name "Apson" is an acronym for Agua Prieta, Sonora, the town and state in Mexico where the band, Yazmin, and Francisco all hail from.

Most taqueria menus in Tucson have some similarities. You'll almost always find carne asada (steak tacos), burros (Tucson's version of burritos, often filled only with meat and without garnish), and the ubiquitous Sonoran hot dogs (bacon-wrapped hot dogs served in bolillo rolls and topped with beans, onions, tomatoes, salsa verde, crema, and yellow mustard). Those items are as much a part of Tucson culture as the towering saguaro cacti that fill the surrounding desert.

But what sets Tacos Apson apart is their tacos rasurados: flour tortillas filled with the rich, über-flavorful meat shaved from the bones of grilled beef ribs ("rasurado" means "shaved" in Spanish). It's a technique that Francisco says he first encountered in Mexico but really only put into practice at the restaurant when his son started wearing braces and could no longer eat ribs off the bone. The family enjoyed the tacos so much that they put them on the menu, and today the tacos are one of Tacos Apson's biggest sellers.

Francisco's mornings begin by heaving a 40-pound bag of mesquite lump charcoal into the grill. He lights the fire, busies himself around the kitchen, and keeps a watchful eye on the coals. When the coals are covered in a layer of thin, gray ash, he spreads them evenly over the grill, kicking up sparks in the process. He covers nearly the entire grill grate with vegetables for the salsa tatemada (charred salsa)—plum tomatoes, halved white onions, whole jalapeños. Their skins slowly blacken as he meticulously rotates each vegetable with the tongs that never seem to leave his left hand. The tomatoes, plump and oozing, are the last to come off; he'll combine them with the other grilled vegetables for a salsa to serve with the tacos. Customers also munch on cebollitas (bulbous spring onions) and more jalapeños, squirted with lime juice and dipped in salt, on the side, like French fries with a burger.

While the vegetables cool and the coals are still hot, Francisco lifts the hefty seven-bone racks of beef ribs onto the sturdy iron bars of the grill. They land with a thud, bone side down, and he maneuvers them like pieces of a jigsaw puzzle. He reaches into the metal receptacle to the left of the grill that's filled with coarse Mexican sea salt and grabs a fistful. He casually showers the ribs with the chunky granules. Most of it bounces against the meat and settles; some falls into the fire, where it crackles and pops. Soon after, the aromas of singed beef fat mingle with mesquite smoke and fill the kitchen. The fatty ribs occasionally flare up in quick, tall bursts, but Francisco quickly and calmly douses the flames with a squirt of water before they get out of hand.

After grilling and salting both sides, he slices the racks between the bones to break them down into their individual ribs. Working with about three at a time, Francisco stacks the ribs on their sides, each spooning the next, and returns them to the grill, cut sides down. Again, he showers them with salt. The meat on these cut sides is the payoff, and he's looking for it to brown and crisp nicely.

Francisco lands the mahogany ribs onto a carving board just as the orders start rolling in. He grabs his 10-inch chef's knife and stands the ribs upright on the board with the tongs. As he begins shaving the ribs, the knife moves in a blur, slapping in rhythm onto the cutting board as he works all sides of the ribs, removing the tender meat with surgical precision. The meat piles up on the board in long strands, and placing his hand on top of the knife to steady it, he gives it a final coarse chop. With the side of the knife, he scoops the meat into a warm flour tortilla, and in the blink of an eye the tacos are on their way to the dining room. Francisco, a man of few—but very calculated—words, turns to me and says, "Charcoal, meat, and salt. That's all you need."

Cebollitas, beef ribs, and jalapeños on the grill.

SEASON EIGHTEEN   25

Mesquite-Grilled Tacos Rasurados

SERVES 6

WHY THIS RECIPE WORKS These hearty beef tacos—loaded with the heady mesquite smoke flavor that gives Tucson-style barbecue its distinctive character—are inspired by the tacos rasurados served at Tacos Apson in South Tucson, Arizona. We grilled rich, fatty beef ribs over a hot fire, twice: First, we grilled the whole rack of ribs to cook the meat and create a flavorful browned exterior, and then we separated the rack into individual ribs and finished them on the grill with a generous sprinkle of coarse salt to create a deeply savory crust and maximize the mesquite-grilled flavor. We made a pair of fresh sauces to top the beef—aguamole (a blend of avocado, lime juice, water, garlic, and salt) and salsa tatemada (made from grilled onion, tomatoes, jalapeños, cilantro, and lime juice)—and served it with grilled spring onions and fresh flour tortillas.

You will need a charcoal grill, a squeeze bottle filled with water, and mesquite hardwood charcoal for this recipe. Mesquite adds a unique flavor to the ribs, typical of Tucson taquerias, and a squeeze bottle is important for extinguishing flare-ups, which are common when grilling fatty meats such as beef back ribs. If at any time the flare-ups get difficult to manage, pull the ribs off the grill and let the fire die down before proceeding. If you can't find spring onions, you can substitute scallions; they will cook more quickly.

Aguamole
- ⅔ cup water, divided
- ½ avocado
- 1 tablespoon lime juice, plus extra as needed
- 1 small garlic clove, minced
- ¾ teaspoon table salt

Salsa Tatemada and Garnish
- 12 spring onions
- 7 jalapeño chiles
- 3 plum tomatoes
- ½ small onion, halved through root end into 2 wedges
- ¼ cup fresh cilantro leaves and stems
- 1½ teaspoons lime juice, plus extra for seasoning, plus lime wedges for serving
- ½ teaspoon table salt
- 1 cup finely chopped cabbage

Ribs
- 1 (3½- to 4-pound) rack beef back ribs (about 7 bones)
- 3 tablespoons coarse sea salt, divided
- 12 (6-inch) flour tortillas, warmed

1. For the Aguamole Process ⅓ cup water, avocado, lime juice, garlic, and table salt in blender until smooth, about 10 seconds, adding remaining ⅓ cup water as needed to achieve pancake batter–like consistency. Season with table salt to taste; set aside for serving.

2. Open bottom vent of charcoal grill completely. Light large chimney starter filled with mesquite hardwood charcoal (6 quarts). When top coals are partially covered with ash, pour evenly over half of grill. Set cooking grate in place, cover, and open lid vent completely. Heat grill until hot, about 5 minutes. Clean and oil cooking grate.

3. For the Salsa Tatemada and Garnish Place spring onions, jalapeños, tomatoes, and onion wedges on hotter side of grill. Cook, turning occasionally, until charred all over, 10 to 15 minutes, transferring items to platter as they finish cooking; set aside. (Spring onions will likely be done first, followed by jalapeños, then onion and tomatoes.)

4. For the Ribs Adjust oven rack to middle position and heat oven to 200 degrees. Place ribs on hotter side of grill, bone side down. Sprinkle meaty side of ribs with 2¼ teaspoons coarse salt. Cook until well browned on first side, about 6 minutes, extinguishing any flare-ups with small squirts of water from squeeze bottle. Flip ribs and sprinkle bone side with 2¼ teaspoons coarse salt. Continue to cook until well-browned on second side, about 6 minutes longer.

5. Transfer ribs to carving board. Cut rack between bones to separate ribs. Nestling 2 or 3 ribs together (bones oriented same way), return ribs to hotter side of grill, cut sides down. Sprinkle ribs with 2¼ teaspoons coarse salt and cook until well browned on cut sides, about 5 minutes.

6. Flip ribs so second cut sides are down, sprinkle with remaining 2¼ teaspoons coarse salt, and cook until well browned on second side, about 5 minutes. Transfer ribs to rimmed baking sheet and keep warm in oven while finishing salsa.

7. To finish salsa, core tomatoes, remove root ends from onion wedges, and stem 1 jalapeño. Process tomatoes, onion wedges, stemmed jalapeño, cilantro, lime juice, and table salt in blender on low speed until coarsely chopped, about 7 seconds. Transfer to serving bowl; season with table salt and lime juice to taste.

8. Hold individual ribs vertically on carving board and, using chef's knife or boning knife, shave meat from ribs. Using chef's knife, chop meat into small bite-size pieces. (For crispier meat, cook chopped meat in 12-inch nonstick skillet over medium-high heat until fat is rendered and meat is crisp all over, 3 to 5 minutes.)

9. Fill tortillas with meat, cabbage, salsa, and aguamole. Serve with spring onions, remaining 6 jalapeños, and lime wedges.

Grill Cut Sides of Ribs

After searing racks, cut into individual ribs. Nestle 2 or 3 ribs together (with bones oriented same way). Grab rib bundles with tongs, return to grill, and brown on both cut sides.

Slice Meat off Bones

When fully cooked, hold individual ribs vertically on carving board and, using chef's knife or boning knife, shave meat from ribs. Using chef's knife, chop meat into small bite-size pieces.

Get Ready to Grill

CHARCOAL GRILL
Build a half-grill fire.

SQUEEZE BOTTLE
Use to quell flare-ups.

MESQUITE HARDWOOD CHARCOAL
Add smoky flavor.

Spotlight on Spring Onions

Spring onions, or cebollitas, which look like larger scallions with fatter bulb ends, are actually young onions (and, if left in the ground, will mature into full-size onions). They are available in spring and summer at farmers' markets and some grocery stores.

Alcapurrias

SERVES 6 TO 8 (MAKES 18 ALCAPURRIAS)

WHY THIS RECIPE WORKS Alcapurrias are a popular street food at the many chinchorros (fry shacks) along Puerto Rico's coastal highways. Sometimes filled with picadillo (seasoned ground beef), sometimes with a seasoned crab mixture, alcapurrias are as unique to each vendor as a fingerprint. The biggest challenges with making alcapurrias come from the composition of the masa (dough) and shaping the alcapurrias. Masa has many iterations and is usually built on one or more starchy root vegetables such as yautia, cassava, yucca, or taro, often with the addition of green banana or green plantain. Each ingredient contributes a unique taste and texture to the final alcapurrias, and impacts how easy or difficult they are to shape. With this in mind, we took a somewhat unconventional approach and used 100 percent green plantains for our masa. This not only condensed the shopping, but the starchy, comparatively dry nature of the processed plantains (versus some of the root vegetables) also made shaping the alcapurrias less difficult. It was important to grate the plantains first before processing them in the food processor to ensure a cohesive dough. We then seasoned the masa with the typical addition of annatto oil and salt. The picadillo was fortified with our homemade sofrito, a touch of earthy cumin, and briny olives, and then processed very briefly post-cooking to make it more consistently fine and easier to stuff into the masa. Alcapurrias are typically served with pique, a vinegar-based hot sauce, of which there are many variations. Ours encapsulates the general spirit of pique, but you can riff on the concept by adding more chiles, garlic, and/or herbs.

Look for plantains that have very few brown spots, as they're easier to peel when they're more consistently green. If you want to peel the plantains ahead of time (up to 6 hours), submerge the peeled plantains in cold water to prevent them from browning.

Picadillo
- 6 ounces 85 percent lean ground beef
- ½ cup chopped onion
- 3 garlic cloves, minced
- 1 teaspoon pepper
- 1 teaspoon ground cumin
- 1 teaspoon granulated garlic
- 1 teaspoon dried oregano
- ¾ teaspoon table salt
- ½ cup Sofrito (recipe follows)
- 1 tablespoon tomato paste
- 2 tablespoons water
- ½ cup pimento-stuffed green olives, chopped coarse
- ¼ cup cilantro leaves and stems, chopped

Masa
- ¼ cup vegetable oil
- 1½ teaspoons annatto seeds
- 5 pounds green plantains (about 9 medium), peeled
- 4 teaspoons table salt, divided
- 2 quarts peanut or vegetable oil for frying

Pique (recipe follows)

1. For the Picadillo Cook beef, onion, garlic, pepper, cumin, granulated garlic, oregano, and salt in 12-inch nonstick skillet over medium-high heat, breaking up meat with wooden spoon, until meat is no longer pink, 5 to 7 minutes. Stir in sofrito and cook until fragrant, about 1 minute.

2. Stir in tomato paste and cook, stirring constantly, for 1 minute. Stir in water and cook until evaporated and tomato paste coats meat mixture, about 30 seconds. Remove from heat and stir in olives and cilantro. Let picadillo cool for 15 minutes.

3. Transfer picadillo to food processor and pulse until finely chopped, about 6 pulses, scraping down sides of bowl halfway through pulsing. Transfer to bowl, cover with plastic wrap, and refrigerate for at least 1 hour or up to 2 days. Divide picadillo into 18 (1-tablespoon) portions, and place on large plate. Cover and refrigerate until needed.

recipe continues

4. For the Masa Meanwhile, heat ¼ cup oil and annatto seeds in small saucepan over low heat, swirling occasionally, until bubbles begin to form around seeds and oil takes on deep red-orange color, 5 to 7 minutes. Remove from heat and let sit for 10 minutes. Strain oil through fine-mesh stainer into liquid measuring cup and set aside; discard seeds. (Annatto oil can be stored in an airtight container for up to 1 week.)

5. Fit clean food processor with shredding disk, and shred plantains. Transfer shredded plantains to large bowl (you needn't wash processor). Fit now-empty food processor with chopping blade. Add half of shredded plantains, 2 tablespoons annatto oil, and 2 teaspoons salt to food processor. Process until cohesive dough forms and begins to clear sides of bowl, about 1 minute, scraping down bowl halfway through processing.

6. Transfer masa to clean, large bowl, and repeat process with remaining shredded plantains, 2 tablespoons annatto oil, and 2 teaspoons salt. Transfer second batch of masa to bowl with first batch, and stir to combine. (Masa can be covered with plastic wrap and refrigerated for up to 6 hours.)

7. Line rimmed baking sheet with parchment paper and spray parchment generously with vegetable oil spray. Spray ¼ cup measuring cup with vegetable oil spray, and use cup to portion 18 level ¼-cup scoops of masa (about 2½ ounces/71 grams each), respraying cup as needed; place scoops on prepared sheet. Divide any remaining masa evenly among scoops.

8. To shape alcapurrias, grease your hands well. Place one scoop of masa in your palm and pat into 4-inch patty. Place 1 portion of picadillo in center of masa patty, and gently fold masa over picadillo to create half-moon shape (like an empanada), pinching to seal. With gentle pressure, roll alcapurria between your hands to create tapered football shape, about 4 inches long. Return shaped alcapurria to greased parchment. Repeat filling and shaping with remaining masa and picadillo. (Alcapurrias can be frozen on sheet, transferred to zipper-lock bag, and frozen for up to 1 month; do not thaw before frying.)

9. Set wire rack in rimmed baking sheet and line half of rack with triple layer of paper towels. Heat 3 quarts oil in large Dutch oven over medium-high heat to 350 degrees. Add 6 alcapurrias to hot oil and fry until deep golden brown and hot throughout, about 5 minutes, gently nudging alcapurrias after 30 seconds of frying to keep from sticking to bottom of pot. (Adjust heat as needed to maintain oil temperature at 350 degrees.)

10. Transfer alcapurrias to paper towel–lined side of rack and let drain for about 30 seconds, then transfer to unlined side of rack. Return oil to 350 degrees and repeat frying twice more with remaining alcapurrias. Serve with Pique (below). (If frying from frozen, increase frying time to about 10 minutes per batch.)

Sofrito
MAKES ABOUT 2 CUPS

Recao is sometimes called culantro. Sofrito makes a great addition to all kinds of soups, stews, ground meat dishes, and sauces.

- 1 (8 ounce) onion, chopped coarse
- 1 large Cubanelle pepper (5 ounces), stemmed, seeded, and chopped coarse
- 4 ounces ajíes dulces, stemmed, seeded,
- 8 garlic cloves, smashed and peeled
- 1 ounce recao leaves and tender stems (1 cup)
- 1 ounce cilantro leaves and stems (¾ cup)

Process all ingredients in food processor until finely chopped, about 20 seconds, scraping down sides of bowl halfway through processing. (Sofrito can be refrigerated for up to 2 days or frozen in zipper-lock bags or plastic containers for up to 2 months; freeze in ¼-cup or ½-cup portions if desired.)

Pique
MAKES ABOUT 2 CUPS

- 1½ ounces fresh Thai chiles, stemmed
- 4 garlic cloves, peeled and halved lengthwise
- 5 sprigs fresh oregano (¼ ounce)
- 2 teaspoons table salt
- 2 teaspoons peppercorns
- 2 cups distilled white vinegar, plus extra as needed

Combine chiles, garlic, oregano, salt, and pepper in 16-ounce bottle with tight-fitting cap. Using funnel, pour vinegar over chiles mixture to cover, adding extra vinegar as needed. Cover bottle and let sit at room temperature for at least 12 hours. Serve. (Pique can be refrigerated for up to 1 month; flavor will continue to mature over time.)

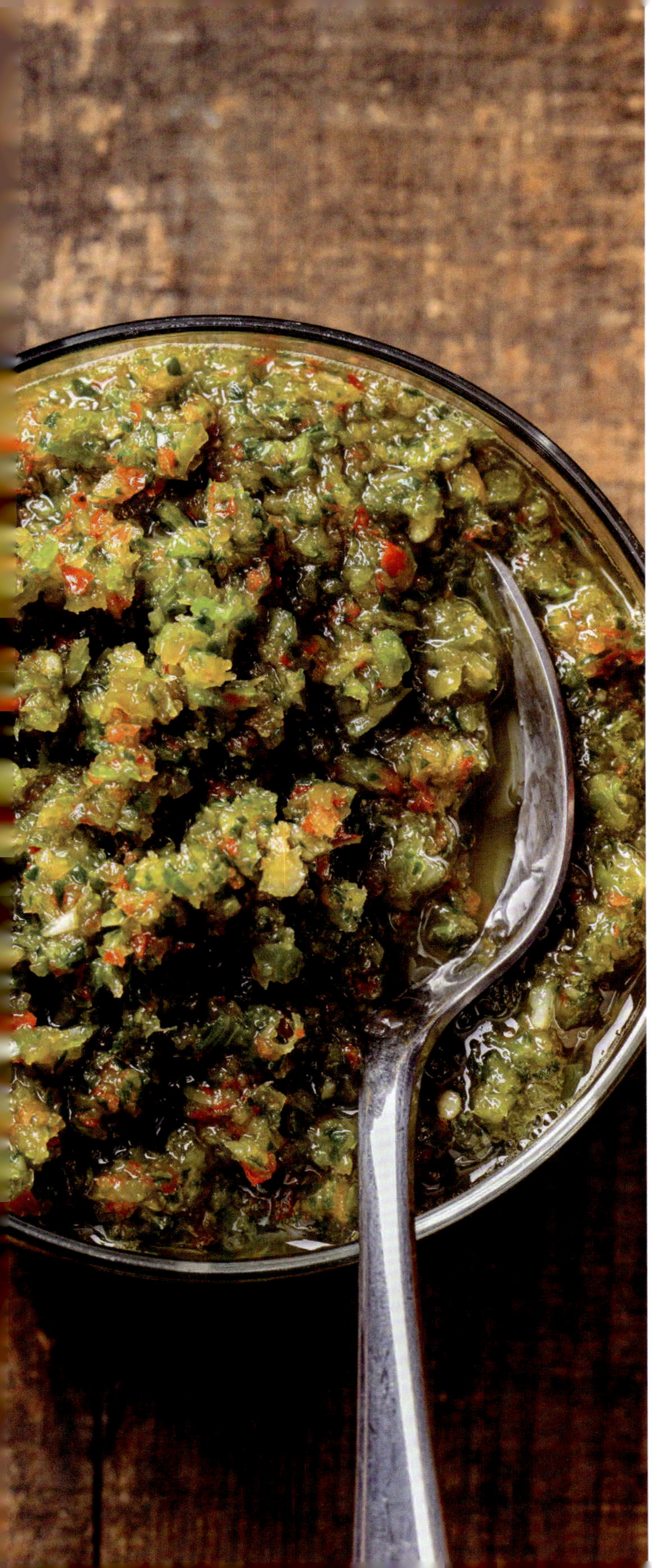

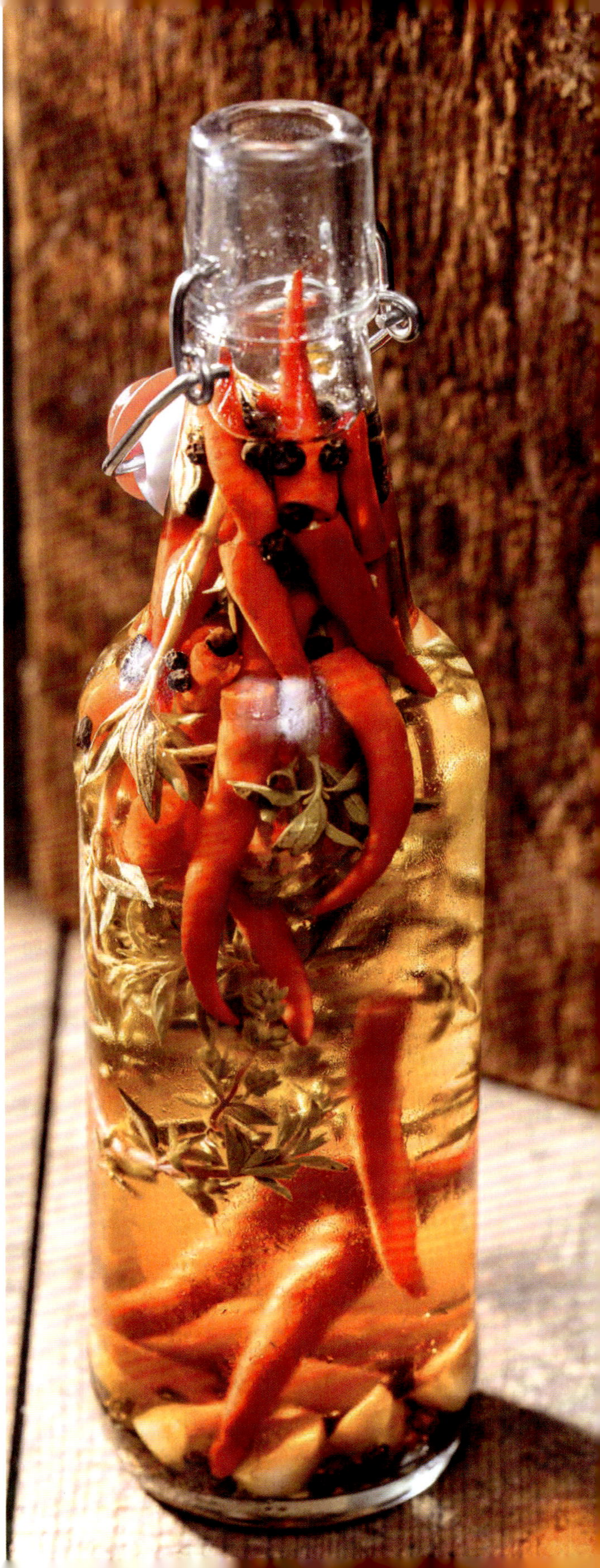

SEASON 18

Grilled Brined Pork Chops with Garlic-Herb Oil

SERVES 4

WHY THIS RECIPE WORKS Making a truly memorable grilled pork chop—one that's exceptionally juicy, tender, and flavorful—takes care. We chose 1-inch-thick bone-in rib chops (T-bone-style center-cut chops also work very well). The well-marbled meat around the bone is more flavorful than the relatively lean loin, and the bone helps safeguard against overcooking. We brined our chops in an aromatic mix of water, salt, sugar, vodka, and the seasonings that make up the classic profile of Italian sausage. The alcohol helped coax out the full spectrum of flavors from the garlic and spices, since some of their flavor compounds more readily dissolve in alcohol than in just water. Setting up our grill with hotter and cooler zones allowed us to sear the chops over the flames and then gently finish cooking them over indirect heat. To take advantage of the fat-soluble flavors, we sizzled a portion of the aromatics in olive oil to create a delectable garlic-herb oil for finishing the chops.

You can use pork chops that are slightly over or under the weight range as long as they measure about 1 inch thick. These pork chops are very flavorful after 2 hours of brining, but you can brine them for up to 24 hours; the longer they brine, the more the flavors will come through. We include vodka in the brine to extract flavors from the alcohol-soluble aromatics, but you can substitute an equal amount of water.

- ⅓ cup packed light brown sugar for brining
- ¼ cup table salt for brining
- ¼ cup vodka for brining
- 2 tablespoons fennel seeds, toasted and ground coarse, divided
- 2 tablespoons chopped fresh rosemary, divided
- 8 garlic cloves (6 smashed and peeled, 2 minced)
- 4 teaspoons pepper, divided
- 3½ teaspoons dried oregano, divided
- 3½ teaspoons red pepper flakes, divided
- 1 tablespoon grated lemon zest plus 1 tablespoon juice
- 4 (12- to 14-ounce) bone-in pork rib or center-cut chops, about 1 inch thick, trimmed
- 6 tablespoons extra-virgin olive oil
- ⅛ teaspoon table salt

1. Combine 6 cups cold water, sugar, ¼ cup salt, vodka, 4 teaspoons ground fennel, 4 teaspoons rosemary, smashed garlic, 1 tablespoon pepper, 1 tablespoon oregano, 1 tablespoon pepper flakes, and lemon zest in large bowl. Whisk to dissolve sugar and salt. Submerge pork chops in brine, cover, and refrigerate for at least 2 hours or up to 24 hours.

2. Combine oil, remaining 2 teaspoons ground fennel, remaining 2 teaspoons rosemary, remaining 2 minced garlic cloves, remaining 1 teaspoon pepper, remaining ½ teaspoon oregano, remaining ½ teaspoon pepper flakes, and salt in small saucepan. Heat oil mixture over medium heat until sizzling and fragrant, 1 to 2 minutes. Off heat, stir in lemon juice. Transfer garlic-herb oil to small bowl and refrigerate until ready to grill pork.

3. Set wire rack in rimmed baking sheet. Transfer chops to prepared rack and thoroughly pat dry, removing any whole spices with paper towels. Cut slits about 2 inches apart through fat around each chop. Refrigerate chops on rack, uncovered, for at least 30 minutes or up to 24 hours.

4a. For a Charcoal Grill Open bottom vent completely. Light large chimney starter mounded with charcoal briquettes (7 quarts). When top coals are partially covered with ash, pour evenly over half of grill. Set cooking grate in place, cover, and open lid vent completely. Heat grill until hot, about 5 minutes.

4b. For a Gas Grill Turn all burners to high; cover; and heat grill until hot, about 15 minutes. Leave primary burner on high and turn off other burner(s).

5. While grill heats, microwave garlic-herb oil until just warm, 15 to 30 seconds. Transfer 2 tablespoons garlic-herb oil to small bowl for brushing chops; reserve remaining garlic-herb oil for serving.

6. Clean and oil cooking grate. Grill chops (covered if using gas) on hotter side of grill until well browned, 2 to 4 minutes per side. Move chops to cooler side of grill. Stir garlic-herb oil for brushing to recombine, then brush onto tops of chops. Grill chops, covered, until meat registers 135 degrees, 3 to 7 minutes. Transfer chops to platter, tent with aluminum foil, and let rest for 10 minutes.

7. Serve with reserved garlic-herb oil.

SEASON 18

Porchetta Abruzzese

SERVES 8 TO 10

WHY THIS RECIPE WORKS This showstopper of a holiday roast is packed with the classic flavors associated with porchetta—garlic, fennel seeds, sage, rosemary, and red pepper flakes—plus an added burst of fresh orange. Many porchetta recipes apply these aromatics to pork shoulder roasts, but here we aimed to replicate some of the elements of a traditional South Philly–style pig roast, which involves whole, boneless pigs, roasted on spits, in the style of Abruzzo, Italy, the region from which many Italian immigrants made their way to Philadelphia. Rich and juicy pork belly; tender, succulent loin; and crackly, puffed skin come together to form a gorgeous showpiece. After pounding and seasoning the pork belly, we rolled it around a tenderloin, tied the roll with kitchen twine, and then roasted it low and slow until the meat was meltingly tender. A quick blast in a hot oven at the end of cooking gave the skin its characteristic deep golden color and shatteringly crisp texture.

If you don't have a spice grinder, you can use a mortar and pestle. Look for a pork belly that is mostly uniform in thickness. If you don't have two wire racks, carefully transfer the first rack into a clean rimmed baking sheet in step 6 (this avoids a very smoky oven). We recommend using a probe thermometer with an alarm to determine doneness precisely. If you don't have a probe thermometer, you can use an instant-read thermometer, but take care not to leave the oven open for too long. Be sure to position the pork belly with the short side parallel to the counter in step 3.

- 1 (1-pound) pork tenderloin, trimmed
- ¼ cup kosher salt, divided
- 1 orange
- 1 tablespoon coarsely chopped fresh sage
- 1 tablespoon coarsely chopped fresh rosemary
- 1 tablespoon fennel seeds, toasted
- 1 teaspoon black peppercorns
- 1 teaspoon crushed red pepper flakes
- 5 garlic cloves, minced
- 1 (6- to 7-pound) skin-on fresh pork belly, about 12 inches long by 10 inches wide and 1½ inches thick
- 1 recipe Mint Salsa Verde (recipe follows)

1. Slice tenderloin in half lengthwise, stopping ½ inch from edge so halves remain attached. Open up tenderloin and sprinkle all over with 1 teaspoon salt. Fold halves together (returning tenderloin to original shape) and place on large plate; set aside.

2. Grate 2 teaspoons zest from orange and transfer to small bowl. Cut away peel and pith from orange. Halve orange lengthwise, then slice halves crosswise ¼ inch thick; set aside. Pulse sage, rosemary, fennel seeds, peppercorns, and pepper flakes in spice grinder until finely chopped, about 8 pulses. Transfer mixture to bowl with orange zest and stir in garlic and 2 tablespoons salt; set aside.

3. Place pork belly skin side up on cutting board. Using paring knife or metal skewer, poke holes through skin at 1-inch intervals. Flip belly skin side down, with short side parallel to counter edge, and cover with plastic wrap. Using meat mallet or rolling pin, pound portions of belly that are thicker than 1½ inches to about 1½ inches. Using sharp knife, cut 1-inch crosshatch pattern, about ¼ inch deep, on flesh side.

4. Rub flesh side of belly evenly with salt mixture. Arrange orange slices in single row across center of belly. Place tenderloin on top of orange slices. (Tuck thin end of tenderloin under itself as needed to line up with edge of belly.) Tightly roll belly away from you, around tenderloin, and place seam side down on cutting board. Starting at center of belly, tie roast at 1-inch intervals with kitchen twine. Sprinkle skin evenly with remaining 5 teaspoons salt. Transfer roast to large plate or platter and refrigerate, uncovered, for at least 1 day or up to 2 days.

5. Adjust oven rack to lower-middle position and heat oven to 325 degrees. Set wire rack in rimmed baking sheet. Remove porchetta from refrigerator and place on 1 prepared rack. Insert thermometer probe about 6 inches into pork belly, horizontally from end of roast, about 1 inch underneath skin (take care to not insert probe into tenderloin). Roast until internal temperature of belly reaches 190 degrees, about 4½ hours.

6. Set wire rack in second rimmed baking sheet. Remove porchetta from oven and increase oven temperature to 450 degrees. Using tongs and large spatula, carefully transfer porchetta to second prepared rack. Once oven has reached 450 degrees, return porchetta to oven and roast until skin is blistered and deep caramel brown, 5 to 15 minutes. Remove porchetta from oven and let rest on rack for at least 30 minutes or up to 2 hours. Carefully remove twine, taking care not to tear skin. Using large serrated knife, slice porchetta ½ inch thick. Serve with salsa verde.

Mint Salsa Verde
SERVES 8 TO 10 (MAKES 1 CUP)

WHY THIS RECIPE WORKS This vibrant, Italian-style salsa verde is packed with grassy parsley, fragrant mint, extra-virgin olive oil, tangy vinegar, briny capers, and a hint of garlic. Traditionally, salsa verde is made with parsley and sometimes with additional tender herbs. We chose mint to heighten the more assertive aromatic qualities of the sauce, making it a perfect foil for the rich, meaty flavors of Porchetta Abruzzese or other roasted meats. We also love this salsa verde drizzled or spread onto almost anything that could use a bright kick, from fish and chicken to roasted vegetables or even a cold-cuts sandwich or a fresh salad.

- 3 cups fresh parsley leaves
- 1 cup fresh mint leaves
- ½ cup extra-virgin olive oil, plus extra for serving
- 3 tablespoons white wine vinegar
- 2 tablespoons capers, rinsed
- 1 garlic clove, minced
- ½ teaspoon table salt

Pulse all ingredients in food processor until finely chopped, about 10 pulses, scraping down sides of bowl as needed. Transfer mixture to bowl and adjust consistency with extra oil, if desired. (Salsa verde can be refrigerated for up to 4 days; bring to room temperature before serving.)

SEASON 18

Indoor Barbecued Ribs

SERVES 6 TO 8

WHY THIS RECIPE WORKS For oven-cooked ribs that tasted like they came off a wood-burning smoker, we brined St. Louis–style ribs in a combination of liquid smoke, salt, sugar, and water. The liquid smoke gave them a deep, smoky flavor while the sugar and salt kept them juicy during cooking. Roasting the ribs in a low 275-degree oven turned them meltingly tender. Brushing them with a tangy barbecue sauce (with an extra dose of liquid smoke) at the halfway point allowed the sauce to tighten on the ribs for deeper flavor. And applying a second dose of that sauce after baking gave them a nice, fresh, saucy shine.

If you want to get a fake smoke ring, substitute 1 tablespoon of Morton Tender Quick for 1 tablespoon of kosher salt in the pepper mixture in step 2. We developed this recipe with Diamond Crystal kosher salt. If using smaller-grained Morton Kosher Salt, use ⅔ cup in the brine and 1 tablespoon on the ribs.

Ribs
- 2 (2½- to 3-pound) racks St. Louis–style spareribs, trimmed
- ¾ cup kosher salt for brining
- ⅓ cup granulated sugar for brining
- ¼ cup liquid smoke
- 1½ tablespoons kosher salt
- 2 tablespoons pepper
- 1 tablespoon granulated garlic
- ¼ teaspoon cayenne pepper

Barbecue Sauce
- 1 tablespoon vegetable oil
- ½ cup finely chopped onion
- 1 cup ketchup
- ½ cup cider vinegar
- ¼ cup packed brown sugar
- 1½ tablespoons Worcestershire sauce
- 1 teaspoon pepper
- 1 teaspoon liquid smoke
- ½ teaspoon ground cumin

1. For the Ribs Cut each rib rack in half between 2 center bones. Combine 3 quarts cold water, ¾ cup salt, sugar, and liquid smoke in stockpot or large plastic container and whisk until sugar is dissolved. Add ribs, pressing to submerge. Cover with plastic wrap and refrigerate for at least 1 hour or up to 4 hours.

2. Adjust oven rack to middle position and heat oven to 275 degrees. Line rimmed baking sheet with aluminum foil and set wire rack in sheet. Combine salt, pepper, garlic, and cayenne in small bowl.

3. Remove ribs from brine. Pat dry with paper towels and sprinkle ribs all over with pepper mixture. Place ribs meat side up on prepared wire rack. Roast for 2½ hours.

4. For the Barbecue Sauce Meanwhile, heat oil in medium saucepan over medium heat until just shimmering. Add onion and cook until softened, about 5 minutes. Stir in ketchup, vinegar, sugar, Worcestershire, pepper, liquid smoke, and cumin. Bring to boil and cook until slightly thickened, about 4 minutes; set aside off heat.

5. Brush meat sides of ribs with ¼ cup sauce. Return to oven and continue to roast until tender and fork inserted into meat meets little resistance, 2 to 2½ hours longer.

6. Remove from oven and brush meat side of ribs with additional ¼ cup sauce. Tent with foil and let rest for 30 minutes. Cut ribs between bones and serve, passing remaining barbecue sauce separately.

Smoke in a Bottle

Liquid smoke is thought to have been invented in 1895 by Ernest H. Wright, a pharmacist in Missouri, when he observed droplets of liquid fall down a stovepipe and realized the smoke was hitting cold air above, causing it to liquefy (this eventually led to the production of Wright's Liquid Smoke, a product still commonly available today). There are brands of liquid smoke that are chemically fabricated with artificial smoke flavor, and you should avoid them (check the ingredient list). But good liquid smoke is manufactured in a relatively similar way to how Wright is first thought to have witnessed it: by pulling smoke from smoldering wood through a condenser. The condenser quickly cools the vapors and converts them into liquid.

SEASON 18

Honey-Glazed Pork Shoulder

SERVES 8 TO 10

WHY THIS RECIPE WORKS Pork and sugar play well together, so we wanted to enhance a holiday-worthy pork roast with fruity, floral honey. A Boston butt (or pork butt) was a good starting point since it is relatively inexpensive and has plenty of fat and connective tissue that—with low, slow cooking—melt out as the meat becomes tender and silky. Coating the roast in honey before roasting resulted in an overcaramelized (read: burnt) roast, no matter how low of an oven temperature we used. Instead, we stirred together a spiced honey with spicy red pepper flakes and aromatic five-spice powder. We waited to brush this onto the pork until the final half-hour of cooking, which created a juicy roast with a beautiful brown crust and a shiny honey glaze. To make it even better, we topped the finished roast with an extra layer of spiced honey and saved some to drizzle over the sliced meat. This allowed all the pork, even the interior pieces, to be saturated with that bold, sweet honey flavor.

Plan ahead: The roast must be seasoned at least 12 hours before cooking. We developed this recipe with clover honey.

- 3 tablespoons kosher salt
- 3 tablespoons packed light brown sugar
- 1 (6- to 7-pound) bone-in pork butt roast with fat cap
- ½ cup honey
- 1½ tablespoons soy sauce
- 2 teaspoons red wine vinegar
- ¾ teaspoon red pepper flakes
- ¼ teaspoon five-spice powder

1. Combine salt and sugar in bowl. Using sharp knife, cut 1-inch crosshatch pattern about ¼ inch deep in fat cap of roast, being careful not to cut into meat. Place roast on 2 large sheets of plastic wrap and rub salt mixture over entire roast and into slits. Wrap roast tightly with plastic. Place on large plate and refrigerate for 12 to 24 hours.

2. Adjust oven rack to lowest position and heat oven to 325 degrees. Line rimmed baking sheet with aluminum foil and set wire rack in prepared sheet. Unwrap roast and place on rack. Cover sheet tightly with foil. Transfer to oven and cook for 2 hours. Remove foil and continue to cook until meat registers 180 degrees in several places, 2½ to 3½ hours longer.

3. Combine honey, soy sauce, vinegar, pepper flakes, and five-spice powder in bowl. Remove roast from oven. Brush top and sides of roast with ¼ cup honey mixture (set aside remainder). Return roast to oven and continue to cook until meat registers 190 degrees and fork slips easily in and out of meat, 30 to 45 minutes longer. Transfer roast to carving board and let rest for 1 hour.

4. Brush pork with 2 tablespoons reserved honey mixture. Using boning or paring knife, cut around inverted T-shaped bone until it can be pulled free and removed from roast (use clean dish towel to grasp bone if necessary). Using serrated knife, slice roast ½ inch thick. Drizzle with remaining honey mixture and serve.

Bone Removal

1. Cut around bone
Using boning knife, carefully separate bone from meat.

2. Remove bone
Grasp bone (with clean dish towel if bone is hot) and pull.

Skillet Eggs Sardou

SERVES 4

WHY THIS RECIPE WORKS Traditionally, eggs sardou (a New Orleans brunch classic) is a Benedict-like preparation of poached eggs set atop tender artichoke bottoms and creamed spinach, all topped with luscious hollandaise and a garnish of minced ham and truffle. For an updated and streamlined version, we reimagined the dish, poaching the eggs directly in a skillet of spinach and artichoke cream sauce punched up with smoky, spicy tasso ham and Parmesan cheese. Cracking the eggs into a slotted spoon before adding them to the skillet drained off the loose, watery egg whites, creating neat poached eggs. For the lemony, creamy hollandaise, we turned to our bulletproof method, using the blender rather than constantly whisking over a double boiler. Spooned over toasted English muffins, it all made for a decadent, elegant brunch.

Use your favorite vinegary hot sauce. If you can't find tasso ham (spiced, smoked pork shoulder steaks that are a specialty of Louisiana), you can substitute andouille sausage, which has a similar flavor. You will need one 12-ounce jar of marinated artichoke hearts to yield the 1⅓ cups called for here. Use a rasp-style grater to grate the Parmesan.

8	large eggs, plus 2 large egg yolks
1	tablespoon lemon juice
2	teaspoons hot sauce, divided, plus extra for serving
1	teaspoon table salt, divided
14	tablespoons unsalted butter, divided, plus 2 tablespoons softened
1	tablespoon all-purpose flour
6	ounces tasso ham, cut into ¼-inch pieces
3	garlic cloves, minced
10	ounces (10 cups) baby spinach
1⅓	cups marinated artichoke hearts, chopped
3	ounces Parmesan cheese, grated (1½ cups)
1	cup heavy cream
¾	teaspoon pepper, divided
	Pinch ground nutmeg
4	English muffins, split and toasted
2	tablespoons minced fresh parsley

1. Process egg yolks, lemon juice, 1 teaspoon hot sauce, and ¼ teaspoon salt in blender until frothy, about 10 seconds, scraping down sides of blender jar as needed. Melt 12 tablespoons butter in small saucepan over medium heat and cook until butter registers 180 degrees, about 1 minute. Transfer butter to 1-cup liquid measuring cup. With blender running, very slowly drizzle hot butter into yolk mixture and process until mixture is emulsified, about 1 minute. Adjust consistency with hot water as needed, a teaspoon at a time, until hollandaise sauce drips slowly from spoon; set aside.

2. Using fork, mash 2 tablespoons softened butter and flour together in bowl to form smooth paste; set aside. Melt remaining 2 tablespoons butter in 12-inch nonstick skillet over medium heat. Add ham and cook until browned, about 5 minutes. Using slotted spoon, transfer about half of ham to plate; set aside.

3. Stir garlic into ham remaining in skillet and cook over medium heat until fragrant, about 30 seconds. Add spinach, 1 handful at a time, allowing each to wilt slightly before adding next; cook until uniformly wilted, about 4 minutes. Stir in artichokes, Parmesan, cream, ½ teaspoon pepper, nutmeg, ½ teaspoon salt, and remaining 1 teaspoon hot sauce until combined and bring to simmer. Stir in flour mixture until incorporated. Cook until cream mixture thickens and clings to spinach, about 1 minute.

4. Off heat, use silicone spatula to clear eight 1½-inch wells in spinach mixture (7 wells around perimeter and 1 in center; cream will run back into bottom of wells.) Rest large slotted spoon in bottom of shallow bowl. Crack 1 egg into slotted spoon, then lift and hold spoon until watery portion of egg white drains away from egg, about 10 seconds. Use spatula to hold 1 well open with free hand, then gently transfer egg from slotted spoon to well. Repeat with remaining 7 eggs. Sprinkle eggs with remaining ¼ teaspoon salt and remaining ¼ teaspoon pepper; discard watery egg whites.

5. Bring mixture to simmer over medium heat (there should be small bubbles across most of surface). Cover, reduce heat to medium-low, and cook, rotating skillet as needed to ensure even cooking, until yolks are opaque and whites are softly but uniformly set, 3 to 6 minutes. (If you prefer fully set yolks, set covered skillet aside off heat until eggs have firmed up, about 2 minutes.)

6. Spoon individual portions of egg and spinach mixture onto each English muffin half. Drizzle eggs with hollandaise sauce, and sprinkle with reserved ham and parsley. Serve with extra hot sauce.

SEASON 18

Rillons

SERVES 6 TO 8

WHY THIS RECIPE WORKS This recipe for morsels of tender, rich pork coated in a sweet-savory red-wine caramel is inspired by the rillons we tried at Toups' Meatery in New Orleans and adapted from the cookbook *Chasing the Gator: Isaac Toups and the New Cajun Cooking* (2018). Curing the pork with a precise amount of salt overnight seasoned it thoroughly and kept it juicy through long cooking. Browning the pork in batches allowed us to pour off the excess fat that would otherwise pool in the finished sauce, and cooking that sauce to exactly 225 degrees guaranteed that it was perfectly thick and glaze-like.

Medium-bodied red wines, such as Côtes du Rhône or Pinot Noir, are best for this recipe.

- 3¾ pounds skinless pork belly
- 5½ teaspoons kosher salt
- 1½ teaspoons pepper
- 2 tablespoons vegetable oil
- 3 cups red wine
- 1½ cups packed light brown sugar
- 9 sprigs fresh thyme

1. Slice pork belly into 1½-inch-thick strips, then cut strips crosswise into 1½-inch-thick pieces. Transfer pork to large bowl, sprinkle with salt and pepper, and toss until evenly coated. Cover and refrigerate for at least 12 hours or up to 24 hours.

2. Pat pork dry with paper towels. Heat oil in large Dutch oven over medium-high heat until just smoking. Add half of pork and cook, turning occasionally, until fat is rendered and pork is well browned on all sides, 12 to 15 minutes. Using slotted spoon, transfer pork to large plate. Repeat with remaining pork. Pour off fat from pot and reserve for another use.

3. Add wine and sugar to now-empty pot and stir until sugar is dissolved, about 30 seconds. Add thyme sprigs and pork and bring to simmer over medium-high heat. Cover; reduce heat to low; and simmer until pork is tender, 1½ to 2 hours, stirring once halfway through cooking.

4. Using slotted spoon, transfer pork to large plate; discard thyme sprigs. Cook wine mixture over high heat, stirring often, until sauce is thick and syrupy and registers 225 degrees, 10 to 15 minutes. Off heat, return pork to sauce and stir to coat. Let cool for 10 minutes, then stir again to coat with sauce. Serve.

Getting the Caramel Right
Cook caramel until it is thick and syrupy and registers 225 degrees.

Cutting Rillons

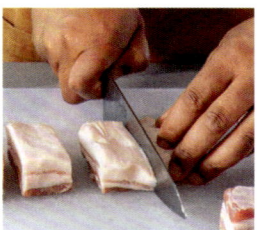 

1. Slice pork belly into 1½-inch strips.

2. Cut strips crosswise into 1½-inch-thick pieces.

American-Style Egg Rolls

MAKES 12 EGG ROLLS

WHY THIS RECIPE WORKS This recipe was inspired by the egg rolls at Chef's Special Cocktail Bar in Chicago, Illinois. The rolls' pork-shrimp filling reminded us of shu mai, which gave us a few clues for how to replicate it. First, we whipped ground pork in a stand mixer with lard until it turned snowy white, for a rich, sticky filling base. Then we chopped shrimp coarse for textural contrast and added it to the filling with shu mai–like seasonings: soy sauce, sugar, sesame oil, Shaoxing wine, rice vinegar, salt, white pepper, and five-spice powder—plus oyster sauce and chicken bouillon powder for an extra umami boost. Cooked cabbage and carrot, plus mung bean noodles, rounded out the filling. We used square egg roll wrappers and fried the rolls in peanut oil until deep golden brown.

Look for freshly ground pork sold at the butcher counter, which has more fat and a coarser texture than prepackaged pork. Adding a small amount of lard makes for even richer egg rolls. Serve with Plum Sauce (recipe follows) and/or hot mustard.

- 12 ounces ground pork
- 2 tablespoons lard, cut into 4 pieces, room temperature (optional)
- 4 ounces shrimp (any size), peeled, deveined, tails removed, and coarsely chopped
- 2 tablespoons soy sauce, divided
- 4 teaspoons sugar, divided
- 1 tablespoon oyster sauce
- 1 tablespoon chicken bouillon powder
- 1½ teaspoons toasted sesame oil
- 1½ teaspoons Shaoxing wine
- 1½ teaspoons Chinese white rice vinegar
- 1 teaspoon table salt
- ½ teaspoon white pepper
- ¼ teaspoon five-spice powder
- 1 teaspoon vegetable oil
- 2 cups chopped green cabbage
- 1 carrot, peeled and shredded
- 1½ ounces dried mung bean glass noodles
- 12 (8-inch) square egg roll wrappers
- 2 quarts peanut or vegetable oil for frying

1. Using stand mixer fitted with paddle, beat pork and lard, if using, on medium speed until well combined and mixture has lightened in color, about 2 minutes. Reduce speed to medium-low and add shrimp, 1 tablespoon soy sauce, 1 tablespoon sugar, oyster sauce, bouillon powder, sesame oil, Shaoxing wine, vinegar, salt, pepper, and five-spice powder. Mix until just combined, about 30 seconds. Cover bowl with plastic wrap and refrigerate for 30 minutes.

2. Heat empty 14-inch flat-bottomed wok over high heat until just beginning to smoke. Reduce heat to medium-high, drizzle vegetable oil around perimeter of wok, and heat until just smoking. Add cabbage, carrot, remaining 1 tablespoon soy sauce, and remaining 1 teaspoon sugar and cook, tossing slowly but constantly, until cabbage is just softened, about 2 minutes. Transfer vegetable mixture to large plate; spread into even layer; and refrigerate until cooled slightly, about 15 minutes.

3. Meanwhile, soak noodles in 4 cups hot water in bowl for 15 minutes. Drain noodles and rinse under cold running water until chilled. Drain noodles again, then transfer to cutting board and chop into rough 1-inch lengths. Return bowl with pork mixture to mixer fitted with paddle. Add vegetable mixture and noodles and mix on low speed until well combined, about 1 minute.

4. Fill small bowl with water. Working with 1 wrapper at a time, arrange on counter so 1 corner points toward edge of counter. Place rounded ¼ cup filling on lower half of wrapper and mold it with your fingers into neat 4-inch-long cylinder parallel to edge of counter. Dip your fingertip in water and moisten entire border of wrapper with thin film of water.

5. Fold bottom corner of wrapper over filling and press gently along length of filling to remove air pockets. Fold side corners over to enclose filling snugly; gently roll to form tight cylinder and press edges to seal. Transfer egg roll seam side down to parchment paper–lined plate and cover with damp paper towel while shaping remaining egg rolls. Stack egg rolls as needed, separating layers with additional parchment. (Egg rolls can be frozen until solid, then transferred to zipper-lock bag and stored in freezer for up to 1 month. Do not thaw before frying; increase frying time by 2 minutes.)

6. Set wire rack in rimmed baking sheet and line rack with triple layer of paper towels. Add peanut oil to clean, dry, 14-inch flat-bottomed wok or large Dutch oven until it measures about 1½ inches deep and heat over medium-high heat to 350 degrees. Using tongs, carefully add 6 egg rolls seam side down to hot oil and cook until deep golden brown, 4 to 8 minutes, flipping egg rolls halfway through frying. Adjust burner, if necessary, to maintain oil temperature between 325 and 350 degrees. Using tongs, transfer egg rolls to prepared rack and let drain. Return oil to 350 degrees and repeat with remaining 6 egg rolls; transfer to prepared rack and let drain. Serve.

Plum Sauce

MAKES: ABOUT 1 CUP

Sour pickled plums offset the sweetness and mellow the acidity of this sauce. If pickled plums are unavailable, they can be omitted; add an extra 1 tablespoon vinegar to the sauce mixture before simmering. Dip your crispy egg rolls here.

- 1 cup apricot preserves or jam
- ½ cup Chinese white rice vinegar
- ½ cup water
- 2 salted pickled plums, pitted and mashed (2 tablespoons)
- 1 (1-inch) piece ginger, sliced thin
- ⅛ teaspoon Sichuan chili flakes

Whisk apricot preserves, vinegar, and water together in small saucepan until combined. Stir in plums, ginger, and chili flakes. Bring to simmer over medium heat and cook, stirring occasionally, until slightly thickened and sauce coats back of spoon, about 15 minutes. Discard ginger. Let sauce cool to room temperature before serving, about 15 minutes. (Sauce can be refrigerated for up to 1 week; let come to room temperature before serving.)

SEASON EIGHTEEN

Grilled Lamb Burgers

SERVES 4

WHY THIS RECIPE WORKS We wanted a bulletproof method for getting juicy medium-rare (or medium) burgers with a gorgeous, seared-on spice crust every time. First, to ensure a consistent cook on each burger, we started with store-bought ground lamb, portioned the patties precisely (using 8 ounces per burger), and shaped them into rounds with a consistent thickness and diameter. Second, we made a dimple in the center of each patty to prevent the patties from swelling into round meatballs on the grill. Then we placed the patties on a platter and froze them for about 30 minutes, until they were firm but not frozen solid. Chilling the patties allowed for extra time on the grill, meaning that the burgers had plenty of time to get a flavorful, seared-on crust without overcooking in the middle. Finally, generously coating the ground lamb patties with a spice rub consisting of salt, pepper, earthy cumin, and a kiss of cinnamon added an uncommonly delicious complexity and warmth that accentuated the subtle differences between the lamb and the usual ground beef.

These burgers develop great char and stay perfectly medium-rare (or medium) at the center because we freeze the patties slightly before putting them on the grill. After lighting, it takes about 20 minutes for the charcoal to be ready, so plan the freezing of the patties accordingly. The amount of spice mixture may seem excessive, but it helps form the crust, so be sure to use all of it. These burgers are great topped with our Five-Spice Tomato Chutney (recipe follows), feta cheese, and sliced red onion.

- 2 pounds ground lamb
- 2 teaspoons table salt
- 1½ teaspoons ground cumin
- 1 teaspoon pepper
- ½ teaspoon ground cinnamon
- 4 brioche hamburger buns, toasted and buttered

1. Divide lamb into four 8-ounce portions and roll between your hands to form balls. Working on baking sheet, press each ball into 4½-inch-diameter patty, about ¾ inch thick. Using your thumb or fingers, make 1-inch-wide by ¼-inch-deep depression in center of each patty. (Patties can be covered with plastic wrap and refrigerated for up to 24 hours at this point.)

2. Transfer patties to platter and freeze until firm but not frozen solid, 30 to 45 minutes. Combine salt, cumin, pepper, and cinnamon in bowl; set aside.

3a. For a Charcoal Grill Light large chimney starter three-quarters filled with charcoal briquettes (4½ quarts). When top coals are partially covered with ash, pour evenly over half of grill. Set cooking grate in place, cover, and open lid vent completely. Heat grill until hot, about 5 minutes.

3b. For a Gas Grill Turn all burners to high; cover; and heat grill until hot, about 15 minutes. Turn all burners to medium.

4. Clean and oil cooking grate. Sprinkle patties on both sides with spice mixture (use all of it), using spatula to flip patties so they don't become misshapen.

5. Grill patties indentation side down (uncovered and directly over coals for charcoal; covered for gas), without moving them, until browned and they release easily from grill, about 5 minutes.

6. Flip burgers and grill (covered for gas) until browned on second side and meat registers 125 degrees (for medium-rare), about 5 minutes, or 135 degrees (for medium), about 7 minutes. Transfer burgers to wire rack set in rimmed baking sheet and let rest for 5 to 10 minutes.

7. Transfer burgers to buns. Serve.

Five-Spice Tomato Chutney

SERVES 8

If you're spice averse, consider removing the seeds from the jalapeño before mincing it. We recommend wearing gloves when working with chiles.

- 1 pound plum tomatoes, cored and cut into ½-inch pieces
- ½ cup plus 2 tablespoons packed dark brown sugar
- 6 tablespoons cider vinegar
- 2 tablespoons fish sauce
- 3 garlic cloves, minced
- 1 large jalapeño chile, stemmed and minced
- 2 teaspoons grated fresh ginger
- ¾ teaspoon five-spice powder

1. Combine all ingredients in 12-inch nonstick skillet. Bring to boil over medium-high heat. Cook, stirring often, until mixture is syrupy and slightly darkened in color, 10 to 15 minutes.

2. Off heat, mash tomato mixture with potato masher to even consistency. Return to simmer over medium heat and cook until silicone spatula leaves distinct trail when dragged across bottom of skillet, 1 to 3 minutes. (Note: Chutney will continue to thicken as it cools, so don't over-reduce.)

3. Transfer chutney to jar and let cool completely before serving, about 1 hour. (Cooled chutney can be refrigerated for up to 1 month.)

Grown in Georgia

A SIXTH-GENERATION FARMER BRINGS IT BACK TO THE LAND.

by Bryan Roof; photos by Steve Klise

I arrive at 9 a.m., just as the April sun starts to bear down over the eastern side of Gilliard Farms in Brunswick, Georgia. The owner, Matthew Raiford, waves to me as I park beneath a series of enormous moss-draped oaks, ubiquitous in coastal Georgia. We meet at the chicken coop, where Raiford is feeding the flock bright-yellow turmeric-infused rice, leftovers from a meal he made for his daughter days earlier. He talks sweetly to the chickens as he tosses the feed, just like he talks to me. He's equally kind to the plants.

I ask about a small bonfire of burning brush in front of the main house. Raiford says he often cooks large paellas over the fire for parties. We spend more than an hour walking around a small portion of the 28-acre property as he tells stories of the previous five generations in his family who lived here. He points out the house where his mother was born and a once-upon-a-time one-room schoolhouse that until 1954 was the only school for 20 miles that Black children could attend. We walk through a patch of wild huckleberry bushes and amble through the muscadine vines.

Raiford pulls bunches of carrots from soft, black dirt in raised beds and then points out the massive iron-and-log sugarcane press gifted to his great-grandparents on their wedding day in 1919. After he explains how he roasts oysters on a panel of fire-heated corrugated metal, we end our tour near the back of the property, where he introduces me to his passel of long-haired, spotted Ossabaw Island hogs, which he summons with a pitch-perfect "SOOEY!"

Throughout the morning, Raiford talks of the soil as "a living thing" that needs to be cared for and nurtured. He claims he's more chef than farmer but says he's finding his way. "I understand food and cooking, and I'm learning about farming."

As we talk, he offers wisdom about planting techniques, symbiotic relationships between different species, and various culinary and medicinal uses of plants that, to the untrained eye, look like invasive weeds. He also speaks to the appeal of cooking what you grow.

"There's a whole difference between going to the store

Matthew Raiford watering raised beds (top) and mending fences at Gilliard Farms (bottom). Next page, clockwise from top left: signage on the chicken coop; pulling carrots from the dirt; rinsing local clams to remove sand from their shells; straining shrimp stock; a pair of Ossabaw Island hogs rooting in the soil.

and buying something and having the flavor of something you raised or grew. When I go out and eat a tomato from here, that thing was not pulled off when it was green and put somewhere until it was ripe and then shipped to me. I'm eating it at the point that I'm supposed to eat it."

We make our way into the satellite kitchen attached to the main house, where Raiford does much of his culinary experimentation and prep work for events on the property. "I spend a lot of time in here. Sometimes doing nothing," he says with a smile. The space resembles a garage-turned-kitchen, with concrete floors and a wide, live-edge butcher block counter running down the center. A large bowl of freshly harvested turmeric root, still covered in dirt, sits on the counter. Wooden shelves hold glasses, plates, and cookbooks, and numerous wire racks house a variety of dry ingredients. The drawers of an antique library card catalog hold an alphabetized collection of heirloom seeds that Raiford will cultivate into this year's harvest.

Raiford and I set up at a stainless-steel prep table and begin peeling shrimp to make a version of his coastal paella. We're riffing on the concept a bit, omitting the sausage he typically includes because there's none on hand today and using earthy ground turmeric instead of more delicate saffron; the turmeric creates a beautiful golden color.

"I like the flavor of turmeric more so than I like the lightness of saffron. Turmeric is more accessible to people anyhow." He says paella was introduced by the Spanish when they occupied the area but that the concept of one-pot rice dishes has deep roots in Southern cooking.

The shrimp shells and turmeric join garlic, smoked paprika, peppercorns, red pepper flakes, sea salt, and a lemon half in a large pot that he then fills with water. The stock simmers briefly before he moves the solids to the compost bin, where they'll eventually develop into a nutrient-rich mixture he'll use to feed future plantings.

Raiford sautés peppers and onions in a small paella pan for several minutes before stirring long-grain rice into the softened vegetables. He adds the stock, and once the liquid simmers down to the level of the top of the rice, he studs the paella with fresh local clams and the peeled shrimp. He covers the pan and allows the rice to finish cooking to perfect tenderness as the seafood gently steams and the clams open.

We sit down to glasses of iced tea made with hibiscus from the farm and the stunning paella, which he scatters with lemon wedges. Before we dig in he says, "These shrimp were in the ocean two, three days ago. You can't get it any fresher than this. These clams were in the ocean less than a week ago. Being able to have something at its purest, finest point, at its peak, that's what this is about."

Then, reiterating the point with his arms opened wide, as though to embrace the entirety of Gilliard Farms, he repeats the sentiment with even more feeling, "That's what all this is about."

SEASON EIGHTEEN 49

Coastal Georgia Paella

SERVES 6

WHY THIS RECIPE WORKS This recipe, inspired by chef and farmer Matthew Raiford, is a fresh, personalized take on traditional paella. Following Raiford's lead, we started with shell-on shrimp, peeled them, and used the shells to make a quick but flavorful stock seasoned with turmeric and smoked paprika. To mirror Raiford's version, we used long-grain rice and added shrimp and clams to the paella. Finally, we finished this showstopping dish with chopped parsley and a drizzle of good olive oil and served it with lemon wedges.

This recipe is based on an interview with Matthew Raiford at his farm, Gilliard Farms, in Brunswick, Georgia. It is important to use untreated shrimp—those without added sodium or preservatives such as sodium tripolyphosphate—in this recipe; treated shrimp contain too much sodium and may have off-flavors. Most frozen E-Z peel shrimp have been treated (the ingredient list should tell you). If you don't have fine sea salt, you can use an equal measure of table salt. We developed this recipe using our winning 14-inch paella pan, the Matfer Bourgeat Black Carbon Steel Paella Pan; you can make this recipe in a slightly larger or smaller paella pan, but the texture of the finished rice may vary.

Shrimp Stock

- 6½ cups water
- 1 pound extra-large shrimp (21 to 25 per pound), peeled, deveined, and tails removed; shells reserved
- ½ onion, halved
- 1 garlic head, halved crosswise
- 1 tablespoon ground turmeric
- 2 teaspoons fine sea salt
- 2 teaspoons smoked paprika
- 1 teaspoon peppercorns
- ¼ teaspoon red pepper flakes
- ½ lemon

Paella

- 1 teaspoon fine sea salt, divided
- ½ teaspoon pepper
- ¼ cup extra-virgin olive oil, plus extra for drizzling
- 1 red bell pepper, stemmed, seeded, and sliced thin
- 1 onion, halved and sliced thin
- 3 garlic cloves, minced
- 1½ cups long-grain white rice
- 12 littleneck clams, scrubbed
- 1 tablespoon chopped fresh parsley
-   Lemon wedges

1. For the Shrimp Stock Combine water, shrimp shells, onion, garlic, turmeric, salt, paprika, peppercorns, and pepper flakes in large saucepan. Squeeze lemon into saucepan and add spent half to saucepan. Bring to boil over high heat. Reduce heat to medium-low and simmer for 10 minutes. Strain stock through fine-mesh strainer set over bowl, pressing on solids to extract as much liquid as possible; compost or discard solids. (You should have at least 6 cups shrimp stock; if not, add water to make up difference.)

2. For the Paella Press large sheet of aluminum foil over top of cold 14-inch paella pan to form lid shape; set foil aside. Sprinkle shrimp with ¾ teaspoon salt and pepper; set aside. Heat oil in paella pan over medium heat until shimmering. Add bell pepper, onion, and remaining ¼ teaspoon salt and cook, stirring occasionally, until bell pepper is beginning to soften and onion is lightly browned, about 10 minutes. Stir in garlic and cook until fragrant, about 30 seconds. Stir in rice and cook, stirring often, until rice is coated with oil and translucent at edges, about 2 minutes.

3. Stir in 6 cups shrimp stock and bring to boil over high heat. Cook, stirring occasionally, until stock has reduced to level of rice, about 8 minutes. Reduce heat to medium. Press clams hinge side down into rice mixture, arranging evenly in pan (do not stir rice from this point on). Cover with prepared foil lid and cook until clams just start to open, about 6 minutes.

4. Gently press shrimp into rice mixture around clams. Re-cover with foil and cook for 5 minutes. Remove paella from heat and let sit, covered, for 5 minutes. Sprinkle with parsley and garnish with lemon wedges. Drizzle with extra oil and serve.

Seafood Risotto

SERVES 8

WHY THIS RECIPE WORKS This risotto is all about maximizing the seafood flavors of shrimp, mussels, and squid. We began by making a rich seafood broth. Cooking the shrimp shells in butter added a robust depth to the browned shells. Steaming mussels over shrimp-infused wine flavored the mussels and added flavor to the broth. From there, we set the mussels aside and added water and fennel stalks. After a 15-minute cook, we strained the broth and kept it warm. For a flavorful background, we sweated onion, fennel, garlic, and tomato paste before stirring in the squid and the rice. We added wine and a large amount of the warm broth to jumpstart the rice. Adding the remaining broth little by little allowed us to control the finished texture of the rice. When the rice was nearly done, we stirred in the raw shrimp, cooked mussels, fresh herbs, and butter, laying the mussels on top. The residual heat was enough to just cook the shrimp through, finish the rice, and heat the mussels.

Arborio rice, which is high in starch, gives risotto its characteristic creaminess; do not substitute other types of rice. The final texture of this risotto should be slightly creamy, similar to loose oatmeal, but it will thicken as it sits. You may have leftover shellfish broth; this broth is flavorful and can be saved for use in other dishes.

- 1 (12-ounce) fennel bulb
- 12 tablespoons unsalted butter, divided
- 1 pound extra-large shrimp (21 to 25 per pound), peeled, deveined, and cut into ¾-inch pieces, shells reserved
- 2 cups dry white wine, divided
- 2 pounds mussels, scrubbed and debearded
- 7 cups water
- 1 cup finely chopped onion
- 3½ teaspoons table salt, divided
- 3 garlic cloves, minced
- 2 tablespoons tomato paste
- 8 ounces squid, bodies sliced crosswise into ¼-inch-thick rings, tentacles cut in half
- 2 cups arborio rice
- 2 tablespoons chopped fresh parsley
  Lemon wedges

1. Coarsely chop fennel stalks; core and finely chop fennel bulb (you should have about 1 cup); chop fennel fronds to yield ¼ cup; set aside.

2. Melt 4 tablespoons butter in large saucepan over medium-high heat. Add reserved shrimp shells and cook, stirring often, until shells begin to turn spotty brown, about 3 minutes. Stir in fennel stalks, 1 cup wine, and mussels and bring to simmer. Cover saucepan and cook, stirring occasionally, until mussels open, about 5 minutes. Off heat, use tongs to transfer mussels to bowl (gathering any errant mussels that fall out of shells); leave shrimp shells and wine mixture in saucepan.

3. Add water to wine-shell mixture in saucepan and bring to boil over medium-high heat. Reduce heat to low, cover, and cook for 10 minutes. Strain broth through fine mesh-strainer set over large bowl; discard solids. Return broth to saucepan, cover, and keep warm over low heat.

4. Meanwhile, shell all but 8 mussels; reserve shelled and unshelled mussels separately.

5. Melt 4 tablespoons butter in Dutch oven over medium heat. Add fennel bulb, onion, and 1 teaspoon salt and cook, covered, until vegetables are softened but not browned, 5 to 7 minutes, stirring occasionally. Stir in garlic and tomato paste and cook, uncovered, until fragrant, about 1 minute. Add squid and cook, stirring often, until squid are opaque and fond just begins to form on bottom of pot, about 3 minutes.

6. Stir in rice and cook until edges of grains are translucent, about 2 minutes. Add remaining 1 cup wine and cook, stirring often, until wine is absorbed, about 2 minutes. Stir in 5 cups warm broth and remaining 2½ teaspoons salt and bring to simmer. Reduce heat to medium-low and cook, stirring every 3 minutes, until broth is mostly absorbed and spoon leaves trail on bottom of pot that fills in slowly, 20 to 22 minutes.

7. Stir in 1 cup broth and cook, stirring constantly, until rice is al dente, about 3 minutes. Cut remaining 4 tablespoons butter into 4 pieces; stir butter, shrimp, shelled mussels, 2 tablespoons fennel fronds, and parsley into risotto. Cook, stirring constantly, until butter is incorporated, about 1 minute. Cover; remove from heat; and let stand until shrimp are fully cooked through, about 5 minutes.

8. Adjust consistency of risotto with additional broth (¾ cup to 1 cup) to achieve texture of loose oatmeal. Season with salt to taste. Gently press 8 unshelled mussels into top of risotto, hinge side down. Sprinkle with remaining 2 tablespoons fennel fronds. Serve with lemon wedges.

SEASON 18

Zephyr Wright–Inspired Shrimp Curry

SERVES 4

WHY THIS RECIPE WORKS Zephyr Wright was a Black woman who cooked for Lyndon B. Johnson and his family during a large chunk of his political career. This recipe is inspired by her recipe for shrimp curry. Making a béchamel sauce with butter, flour, curry powder, milk, and a mixture of bouillon and water gave this curry a flavorful yet creamy sauce base. Cooking the shrimp directly in the sauce for just a few minutes kept the dish easy since it used only one pan. And finishing with 2 teaspoons of lemon juice added a nice hit of acidity for a simple yet comforting and deeply satisfying meal.

If preferred, you can substitute 1 cup of chicken broth for the boiling water and chicken bouillon cube (omit step 1). Serve over white rice.

- 1 cup boiling water
- 1 (½-ounce) chicken bouillon cube
- 2 pounds extra-large shrimp (21 to 25 per pound), peeled, deveined, and tails removed
- 1 teaspoon table salt, divided
- ¼ teaspoon pepper
- 2 tablespoons unsalted butter
- 1 small onion, chopped fine
- 1 tablespoon all-purpose flour
- 1½ teaspoons curry powder
- ½ teaspoon sugar
- ½ teaspoon ground ginger
- 1 cup whole milk
- 2 teaspoons lemon juice

1. Combine boiling water and bouillon cube in liquid measuring cup and stir to dissolve bouillon; set aside.

2. Sprinkle shrimp with ½ teaspoon salt and pepper. Melt butter in 12-inch skillet over medium heat. Add onion and remaining ½ teaspoon salt and cook until onion is softened, about 5 minutes.

3. Stir in flour, curry powder, sugar, and ginger and cook for 1 minute. Add milk and reserved bouillon mixture and bring to simmer. Add shrimp and cook, stirring occasionally, until shrimp are opaque and just cooked through, 2 to 4 minutes. Off heat, stir in lemon juice and season with salt and pepper to taste. Serve.

The American Table: The Taste of Equality

According to Kate Andersen Brower in her book *The Residence* (2015), President Johnson often leaned on the experiences of Zephyr Wright and other Black members of his staff to help inform his political decisions. President Johnson told a story about how Wright influenced his civil rights efforts: Wright would accompany the Johnsons back and forth on their trips from Texas to Washington, D.C., so she could cook for them in both places. But this was the Jim Crow South. Along the ride, Wright and other Black staffers were often not allowed to stay in hotels or enter restaurants, even when the Johnsons insisted. Wright eventually put her foot down and insisted on staying in D.C. rather than going on these segregated trips. When President Johnson signed the Civil Rights Act of 1964, Wright stood by his side. After signing, Johnson handed Wright the pen and said, "You deserve this more than anyone else."

SEASON 18

Shrimp with Garlic and Jalapeño Butter

SERVES 4

WHY THIS RECIPE WORKS This recipe is patterned after the House Special Shrimp at the now-closed Royal Capital Seafood Restaurant, located in the Little Saigon district of Garden Grove, California, where flash-fried shrimp got tossed in a buttery, umami-rich garlic-jalapeño sauce. Brining the shrimp in water, salt, and baking soda ensured that they remained plump and juicy during the high-temperature frying process. A dredge in potato starch imparted a light, ultracrispy crust that held up long after being in contact with the sauce. Finally, tossing the fried shrimp in a mixture of garlic-jalapeño butter, lime juice, and fish sauce made them rich, vibrant, and irresistibly savory.

We prefer untreated shrimp—those not treated with sodium or additives such as sodium tripolyphosphate (STPP). Most frozen E-Z peel shrimp have been treated (the ingredient list should tell you). Serve with rice and sliced cucumber. If you don't have a frying thermometer, just stick a wooden chopstick into the oil—if it bubbles vigorously, then the oil is hot enough.

- ¼ cup kosher salt for brining
- 1 tablespoon baking soda for brining
- 2 pounds jumbo shrimp (16 to 20 per pound), peeled and deveined
- 1 tablespoon fish sauce
- 1 tablespoon lime juice
- 1 tablespoon sugar
- 1½ teaspoons pepper
- ⅔ cup potato starch, divided
- 1 quart peanut or vegetable oil for frying
- 3 tablespoons unsalted butter
- 4 scallions, white parts sliced thin, green parts cut into ¾-inch pieces
- 3 tablespoons minced garlic
- 2 jalapeños, stemmed, seeded, and cut into ¼-inch pieces

1. Combine 2 quarts cold water, ¼ cup salt, and baking soda in large bowl and whisk until salt is dissolved. Add shrimp and let soak for 20 minutes. Combine fish sauce, lime juice, sugar, and pepper in small bowl; set aside.

2. Transfer shrimp to colander and rinse well with cold water. Pat shrimp dry with paper towels and transfer to large mixing bowl. Sprinkle ⅓ cup potato starch over shrimp and toss to coat. Add remaining ⅓ cup potato starch and toss until shrimp are well coated. Transfer shrimp to rimmed baking sheet, shaking off any excess starch.

3. Line large mixing bowl with paper towels. Add oil to 12-inch skillet until it measures about ¾ inch deep. Heat oil over medium-high heat to 400 degrees. Add half of shrimp to skillet, spacing them so they don't touch. Fry until lightly golden and crisp, 60 to 90 seconds per side.

4. Using spider skimmer or slotted spoon, transfer fried shrimp to prepared bowl. (Exterior of shrimp should be crisp when tapped. If not, return shrimp to oil and fry for another 15 seconds on both sides.) Repeat with remaining shrimp.

5. Melt butter in small saucepan over medium heat. Add scallion whites and garlic and cook until fragrant, about 1 minute. Add jalapeños and fish sauce mixture and cook, stirring often, until sugar is melted and sauce just comes to boil, about 30 seconds.

6. Remove paper towels from bowl with shrimp. Pour sauce over shrimp and sprinkle with scallion greens. Toss until shrimp are evenly coated in sauce. Transfer to serving platter. Serve.

Spud Starch

Potato starch is made by grinding raw potatoes, then purifying and dehydrating the milky liquid that comes out. Generally, you can use potato starch similarly to cornstarch, but because it has larger granules, it is a stronger thickener; use 2 teaspoons of potato starch for every tablespoon of cornstarch. Potato starch thickens faster than cornstarch and produces a slightly different texture in the liquids it is used to thicken.

SEASON 18

Clams Casino

SERVES 6 TO 8

WHY THIS RECIPE WORKS Clams Casino, the retro appetizer from the early 1900s, takes inspiration from popular seafood recipes from that era, often adding toasted breadcrumbs for added texture. For our recipe, we opted to simply steam the clams in white wine just until they opened. We removed the clams, strained the liquid, and then reduced it with lightly cooked bacon and green bell peppers, and then mixed it with softened butter to create a compound butter. We removed one half of each shell from the cooked clams, loosened the tender clam meat from the shell, topped the clam with the deeply flavorful butter, and sprinkled with pre-toasted bread crumbs mixed with fresh herbs. A few minutes in a 450-degree oven warmed the clams through and crisped up the crunchy crumb topping.

Look for clams that measure 1½ to 2½ inches across. Eastern littleneck clams average eight to 12 clams per pound; you will need 3½ to 4½ pounds for this recipe. Discard any raw clams with unpleasant odors, with cracked or broken shells, or with open shells that won't close when tapped. Scrub the clams before cooking to remove any sand on their shells. If you don't have a coffee filter for straining the clam broth, you can use a triple layer of cheesecloth.

- 10 tablespoons butter, softened, divided
- ¾ cup panko bread crumbs
- 3 garlic cloves, minced
- 1 tablespoon minced fresh thyme
- ¼ cup minced fresh parsley
- 36 littleneck clams, scrubbed
- ½ cup dry white wine
- 6 slices bacon, chopped
- ½ green bell pepper, chopped fine (½ cup)
- 2 shallots, minced
  Lemon wedges

1. Adjust oven rack to upper-middle position and heat oven to 450 degrees. Lightly crumple 26-inch length aluminum foil into loose ball. Uncrumple foil and use to line rimmed baking sheet.

2. Melt 2 tablespoons butter in 12-inch nonstick skillet over medium heat. Add panko and cook, stirring occasionally, until panko is golden brown, 2 to 5 minutes. Add garlic and thyme and cook until fragrant, about 30 seconds. Off heat, add parsley and stir to combine; transfer to plate and set aside. Wipe skillet clean with paper towels.

3. Line fine-mesh strainer with coffee filter and set over bowl or large measuring cup. Combine clams and wine in now-empty skillet. Cover and cook over medium-high heat, shaking pan occasionally to redistribute, until clams just open, 4 to 10 minutes. Using slotted spoon, transfer clams to large bowl as they open (discard any unopened clams). Set aside until cool enough to handle, about 15 minutes. Strain clam broth through prepared strainer. Set aside ½ cup broth (if you have less than ½ cup, add enough dry white wine to equal ½ cup). Rinse and wipe skillet clean with paper towels.

4. Cook bacon in now-empty skillet over medium heat until lightly browned, 7 to 10 minutes. Add bell pepper and shallots and cook until softened, 2 to 5 minutes. Add ½ cup reserved broth. Bring to vigorous simmer and cook until almost dry, 3 to 5 minutes. Transfer to bowl and refrigerate until completely cooled, about 15 minutes.

5. Remove clam meat from shells using paring knife or your clean hands. Separate joined clamshells. Arrange half of shells on prepared sheet, pressing each shell into foil to keep shell level (discard remaining shells). Place 1 clam in each shell.

6. Add remaining 8 tablespoons butter to cooled bacon mixture and mash with fork until combined. Using 2 spoons, evenly distribute butter mixture among clamshells (scant 2 teaspoons each). Spread butter mixture evenly over each clam.

7. Evenly distribute bread crumb mixture over each buttered clam (about 1 teaspoon each), pressing lightly to adhere. Roast clams until butter has melted and crumbs are deep golden brown, about 5 minutes. Serve immediately with lemon wedges.

To Make Ahead Cooled bread crumb mixture, prepared through step 2, can be stored in airtight container overnight. Buttered clams, prepared through step 6, can be wrapped in plastic and refrigerated overnight; top with bread crumb mixture before roasting, and increase roasting time to 6 to 8 minutes.

SEASON 18

Grilled Mussels

SERVES 4 TO 6

WHY THIS RECIPE WORKS We wanted a flame-kissed take on cooking mussels to change things up from the typical indoor steaming method. To start, we melted butter on the stove and stirred in garlic, dill, lemon, pepper flakes, and salt and pepper for a dead-simple flavored butter to accompany the mussels. Grilling the mussels covered trapped steam and smoke inside the grill, helping the delicate mussels cook through evenly and giving them a subtle smoky flavor. Cooking the 4 pounds of mussels (enough to serve a decent gathering as a snack or appetizer) in two batches kept the number of pieces on the grill manageable. Once they were cooked—which took mere minutes—we transferred the mussels to a large bowl and drizzled and tossed them with that irresistible butter.

Discard any raw mussels with unpleasant odors, cracked or broken shells, or with shells that won't close when tapped. If you don't have a bowl large enough to accommodate 4 pounds of mussels, divide the mussels into two bowls in step 3 and drizzle each with half the garlic butter in step 4. A colander makes it quick and easy to spread the mussels over the grill without excess liquid.

- 8 tablespoons unsalted butter
- 4 garlic cloves, minced
- 2 tablespoons chopped fresh dill
- 1 tablespoon lemon juice
- 1 teaspoon table salt
- ½ teaspoon pepper
- ½ teaspoon red pepper flakes
- 4 pounds mussels, scrubbed and debearded, divided

1. Melt butter in small saucepan over medium heat. Off heat, add garlic, dill, lemon juice, salt, pepper, and pepper flakes; cover to keep warm and set aside off heat.

2a. For a Charcoal Grill Open bottom vent completely. Light large chimney starter filled with charcoal briquettes (6 quarts). When top coals are partially covered with ash, pour evenly over grill. Set cooking grate in place, cover, and open lid vent completely. Heat grill until hot, about 5 minutes.

2b. For a Gas Grill Turn all burners to high; cover; and heat grill until hot, about 15 minutes. Turn all burners to medium-high. (Adjust burners as needed to maintain grill temperature between 350 and 400 degrees.)

3. Clean and oil cooking grate. Place half of mussels in large colander to drain off any accumulated liquid, then pour mussels from colander onto grill, spreading them evenly over cooking grate. Cook, covered, until mussels begin to open, 3 to 5 minutes. Using tongs, remove each mussel as it opens and transfer to large bowl. Repeat with remaining mussels.

4. Drizzle ¼ cup reserved garlic butter over mussels and toss to coat. Serve immediately with remaining garlic butter.

Flex Your Mussels

1. After scrubbing the mussels, use a paring knife to remove and discard the bristly beards.

2. Cook the mussels just until they open and then transfer them to a large bowl.

SEASON 18

Green Spaghetti

SERVES 6

WHY THIS RECIPE WORKS We asked chef Chuck Charnichart, a pitmaster at Barbs-B-Q in Lockhart, Texas, to help us develop our version of this creamy, green pepper spaghetti. Green spaghetti, or "espagueti verde" in Spanish, is a dish of noodles coated in poblano-pepper sauce that has roots in both Mexican and Tex-Mex cuisine. To make the sauce, we roasted poblano peppers until blackened and then removed the skins and seeds to prevent bitterness. We blended the peppers with raw jalapeño for a slight kick, along with chopped cilantro for freshness and a vivid green hue. For a tangy, creamy balance, we incorporated a typical Mexican combination of milk, sour cream, and cream cheese, along with chicken bouillon powder (a Mexican and Mexican American pantry staple) for ultrasavory depth. We briefly cooked the blended sauce in butter to warm the dairy and mellow any raw flavors before tossing it with cooked spaghetti and thinning it to a desired consistency with reserved pasta cooking water. We love it alongside barbecued brisket (a Texan trend) or stuffed chicken (a common Mexican combination) or simply on its own.

Knorr brand chicken bouillon is traditional; if you can't find the loose powder, you can crush three bouillon cubes and then measure 2 tablespoons. You can also replace all the bouillon with 2 teaspoons table salt, though the dish will taste less savory. The jalapeño can be seeded or omitted if you desire a milder dish. The sauce will thicken quite a bit as it sits; serve the pasta immediately from the hot pot for the best texture.

2–3 poblano chiles (8½ ounces), stemmed, halved, and seeded
2 teaspoons vegetable oil
2 cups roughly chopped fresh cilantro leaves and stems
8 ounces cream cheese, cut into 8 pieces
1 cup milk
¼ cup sour cream
2 tablespoons chicken bouillon powder
1 jalapeño chile, stemmed and chopped (optional)
1 pound spaghetti
 Table salt for cooking pasta
2 tablespoons unsalted butter

1. Adjust oven rack 6 inches from broiler element and heat broiler. Line rimmed baking sheet with aluminum foil. Brush poblanos all over with oil and arrange skin side up on baking sheet. Broil until skins are spotty brown and beginning to blacken, 4 to 6 minutes. Using tongs, flip poblanos and broil until other side is starting to brown and peppers are softened, 4 to 6 minutes. Let peppers cool slightly, then remove and discard skins.

2. Process skinned poblanos; cilantro; cream cheese; milk; sour cream; chicken bouillon powder; and jalapeño, if using, in blender until smooth, about 1 minute. Set aside.

3. Bring 4 quarts water to boil in large pot. Add pasta and 1 tablespoon salt and cook, stirring often, until al dente. Reserve 1 cup cooking water and drain pasta.

4. Melt butter in now-empty pot over medium heat. Add sauce and bring to simmer, stirring occasionally, until bubbling and slightly thickened, 3 to 5 minutes. Add pasta and cook, tossing constantly with tongs, until pasta is evenly coated with sauce. Adjust consistency with reserved cooking water as needed. Serve immediately.

SEASON 18

Pesto Lasagna

SERVES 8 TO 10

WHY THIS RECIPE WORKS This recipe combines what we love about fresh basil pesto and rich, comforting lasagna. For a lasagna with substantial chew and layers that didn't just melt together, we chose boiled dried lasagna noodles over no-boil noodles. For a creamy base, we made a rich béchamel sauce, and then we made a fresh, fragrant pesto with lots of blanched basil. Blanching resulted in basil that tasted cleaner and had a more vibrant green color. (We saved steps and extra pots by cooking the noodles in the same water we blanched the basil in.) We added the basil to a blender along with olive oil, pine nuts, garlic, and salt. Using a blender gave us a finer pesto compared with pesto in a food processor. We stirred the basil into the béchamel and then added Parmesan and lemon zest to finish our sauce. Then we simply layered our pesto-béchamel sauce between the lasagna noodles. This was easier than layering the sauces separately and gave us the rich, creamy texture we were looking for. A final sprinkle of Parmesan and toasted pine nuts on top made our lasagna dinner-party ready and reinforced the flavors within.

Use a good-quality, relatively mild extra-virgin olive oil for the best results. Toast the pine nuts in a dry skillet over medium heat, stirring often, until they are lightly browned and fragrant. A 1-pound box of lasagna noodles should yield enough for this recipe, but sometimes it's best to buy two boxes in case some of the noodles are broken. Depending on the exact sizes of your lasagna noodles (which can vary slightly by brand) and baking dish, you may not need to use the half noodles called for in steps 4 and 5. You can also make this recipe in a 13 by 9-inch metal baking pan.

Béchamel
- 7 tablespoons unsalted butter
- 7 tablespoons all-purpose four
- 5½ cups whole milk
- 1 teaspoon pepper
- ⅛ teaspoon grated nutmeg

Pesto
- 4 ounces fresh basil leaves
- 1 tablespoon table salt, plus salt for blanching basil
- ½ cup extra-virgin olive oil
- ¼ cup pine nuts, toasted
- 2 garlic cloves, peeled
- 2 ounces grated Parmesan cheese (1 cup)
- 2 teaspoons grated lemon zest

Lasagna
- 17 curly-edged lasagna noodles
- Vegetable oil spray
- 1 ounce grated Parmesan cheese (½ cup), plus extra for serving
- ¼ cup pine nuts, toasted

1. For the Béchamel Melt butter in medium saucepan over medium heat. Whisk in flour and cook, whisking constantly, until mixture is evenly combined but still very pale in color, about 1 minute. Slowly whisk in milk, increase heat to medium-high, and bring to boil. Add pepper and nutmeg and continue to cook, whisking constantly, until mixture is thickened and smooth, about 1 minute longer. Transfer béchamel to large bowl and let cool while making pesto, about 20 minutes.

2. For the Pesto Bring 4 quarts water to boil in large pot. Add basil leaves and 1 tablespoon salt and cook until basil is just wilted but still bright green, 5 to 10 seconds. Using spider skimmer or slotted spoon, transfer basil directly to salad spinner and spin to remove excess water; do not discard water in pot. (If you don't have a salad spinner, pat basil dry with clean dish towel and squeeze thoroughly to remove excess water.)

3. Transfer basil to blender. Add oil, pine nuts, garlic, and salt and process until smooth, about 1 minute, scraping down sides of blender jar as needed. Transfer pesto to bowl with béchamel. Stir in Parmesan and lemon zest until combined; set aside.

4. For the Lasagna Adjust oven rack to middle position and heat oven to 375 degrees. Return water in pot to boil. Add noodles and cook, stirring occasionally, until fully tender. Drain noodles and transfer to rimmed baking sheet. Spray noodles lightly with oil spray and toss gently to coat. Cut 2 noodles in half crosswise.

5. Spread 1 heaping cup béchamel mixture evenly over bottom of 13 by 9-inch baking dish. Arrange 3 noodles in even layer over sauce, with short ends of noodles flush with 1 short side of dish, leaving gap at 1 end. Arrange 1 half noodle crosswise to fill gap. Spread 1 cup béchamel mixture evenly over noodles. Repeat layering of noodles and béchamel mixture 3 more times, switching position of half noodle in each layer.

6. Arrange remaining 3 noodles over top (there is no half noodle for top layer). Spread remaining 1 cup béchamel mixture over noodles, then sprinkle evenly with Parmesan and pine nuts. Bake until top of lasagna is spotty brown and edges are bubbling, 40 to 50 minutes. Let lasagna cool for 45 minutes. Slice and serve with extra Parmesan.

To Make Ahead After sprinkling top of lasagna with Parmesan and pine nuts in step 6, cover dish with greased aluminum foil and refrigerate for up to 24 hours. Bake lasagna, covered, on middle rack of 375-degree oven for 20 minutes. Remove foil and continue to bake, uncovered, until top is spotty brown and edges are bubbling, 40 to 50 minutes longer.

SEASON 18

One-Pot Shrimp Piccata Pasta

SERVES 4

WHY THIS RECIPE WORKS This one-pot shrimp pasta dish is a cross between a garlicky scampi and a zippy, lemony piccata, with a creamy (almost Alfredo-like) sauce tossed in for good measure. We wanted tender, succulent shrimp and lots of rich, silky sauce balanced with just enough vibrant lemon and briny capers. The sauce needed to be fully flavored with garlic and white wine, but it also needed to support (not upstage) the star of the show: the shrimp. So we began by shopping for good-quality shrimp. For the best flavor, we looked for individually quick frozen (IQF) shell-on shrimp that were wild caught in U.S. waters and that were untreated with salt or any additives. To get the most out of those shrimp, we began by browning the shrimp shells in oil and then adding wine and water and simmering them for just 5 minutes, building a flavorful base for the pasta sauce. Cooking the pasta right in the garlicky shrimp stock (after we removed the shells) meant that we needed only one pot, and we never had to pull out a colander. More important, cooking the pasta in just enough flavorful stock meant that the starches from the pasta thickened the cooking liquid, yielding a luscious, creamy sauce. Adding fresh, citrusy parsley; a squeeze of lemon juice and grated lemon zest; and a sprinkling of capers provided just enough of an acidic counterpoint to balance the richness of the creamy sauce, and grated Parmesan added a salty, savory finishing touch.

You can substitute 12 ounces (4½ cups) of medium pasta shells for the orecchiette, if desired. We prefer untreated shrimp (those not treated with salt or additives such as sodium tripolyphosphate). Most frozen E-Z peel shrimp have been treated (the ingredient list should tell you). If you're using treated shrimp, do not salt the shrimp in step 1. You can use medium or large shrimp, but you may need to reduce the cooking time in step 5. The pasta will not absorb all the cooking liquid in step 4; stirring vigorously in step 5 helps thicken the sauce so that it coats the pasta.

- 1 pound extra-large shrimp (21 to 25 per pound), peeled, deveined, and tails removed, shells reserved
- 2½ teaspoons table salt, divided
- ¼ cup extra-virgin olive oil
- 7 garlic cloves, peeled (6 smashed, 1 minced)
- 2 anchovy fillets, rinsed (optional)
- ½ cup dry white wine
- 3½ cups water
- 12 ounces (3⅓ cups) orecchiette
- ⅓ cup chopped fresh parsley
- 2 tablespoons capers, rinsed
- ½ teaspoon grated lemon zest plus 1 tablespoon juice
- ½ teaspoon red pepper flakes
- Grated Parmesan cheese

1. Cut shrimp crosswise into thirds. Sprinkle shrimp with ½ teaspoon salt; set aside. Combine reserved shrimp shells; oil; smashed garlic; and anchovies, if using, in large Dutch oven and cook over medium heat until shells are spotty brown, 5 to 7 minutes.

2. Stir in wine and cook until liquid is nearly evaporated, about 2 minutes. Add water and remaining 2 teaspoons salt, increase heat to high, and bring to boil. Reduce heat to medium-low, cover, and simmer for 5 minutes.

3. Using spider skimmer or slotted spoon, remove shells from shrimp stock and transfer to bowl. (Some garlic cloves may be inadvertently removed at this point; this is OK.) Pour any stock that has accumulated in bottom of bowl back into pot. Discard shells.

4. Stir pasta into stock and bring to simmer. Cover; reduce heat to medium-low; and simmer, stirring occasionally, until pasta is al dente, 10 to 14 minutes (some liquid will remain in bottom of pot when pasta is al dente).

5. Stir in shrimp and cook, uncovered, until opaque, about 2 minutes, stirring often. Off heat, stir in parsley, capers, lemon zest and juice, pepper flakes, and minced garlic. Stir vigorously until sauce is thickened, about 1 minute. Serve with Parmesan.

SEASON 18

Shanghai Scallion Oil Noodles

SERVES 4 TO 6

WHY THIS RECIPE WORKS Scallion oil noodles, a popular Shanghainese dish, are springy wheat noodles dressed with scallion-infused oil, savory soy sauce, and sugar for balance. We slowly simmered scallion whites and thinly sliced shallot in peanut oil to draw out their aromatic flavors, with thin strips of ginger added for freshness. Dark soy sauce, light soy sauce, and sugar added to the scallion mixture helped form a glossy, savory-sweet sauce. Fresh wheat noodles, which have a tender, chewy texture, were tossed to coat in the sauce. The dish can be served plain or enhanced with a range of toppings, including blanched bok choy, stir-fried ground pork, or crispy fried eggs. We opted for the traditional route of garnishing with crispy scallion greens, which are shallow-fried until nearly blackened and shatteringly crisp.

Look for fresh, raw wheat noodles (without egg), preferably a Chinese brand, that are about the thickness of cooked spaghetti; thinner noodles (the thickness of cooked thin spaghetti or thinner) will not work here. Fresh Korean or Japanese wheat noodles of the same thickness can also be used. Other traditional toppings include crispy fried eggs or blanched baby bok choy.

- ¼ cup light soy sauce
- 2 tablespoons dark soy sauce
- 5 teaspoons sugar
- 15–18 scallions (6 ounces), white and green parts separated
- 1 (1-inch) piece ginger, peeled
- 1 pound fresh Chinese wheat noodles
- ⅔ cup peanut or vegetable oil
- ⅛ teaspoon table salt
- 1 shallot, halved and sliced thin

1. Combine light soy sauce, dark soy sauce, and sugar in small bowl; set aside. Halve scallion whites lengthwise, then slice into 1½-inch segments. Slice green parts into 1½-inch segments; reserve white and green parts separately. Slice ginger crosswise into thin rounds. Stack rounds and slice into thin matchsticks.

2. Bring 4 quarts water to boil in large pot. Add noodles and cook, stirring often, until just tender. Drain noodles, rinse well, and drain again; set aside.

3. Meanwhile, heat oil and scallion greens in 14-inch wok or 12-inch nonstick skillet over medium-high heat and cook, stirring constantly, until most scallions are browned and crispy, 8 to 10 minutes. Off heat, use slotted spoon to transfer scallion greens to small bowl; sprinkle with salt and set aside.

4. Add shallot, scallion whites, and ginger to oil remaining in wok and cook over medium-low heat, stirring often, until scallion whites and shallot are golden and wilted, 11 to 13 minutes.

5. Stir soy sauce mixture to recombine and add to scallion mixture in wok. Cook, stirring often, until sugar is dissolved and sauce is rapidly bubbling, 1 to 2 minutes. Add noodles and toss until evenly coated in sauce and heated through, 2 to 3 minutes. Transfer noodles to serving bowls and top with scallion greens. Serve.

Ingredient Spotlight

Chinese Wheat Noodles We developed this recipe using Twin Marquis Thin Shanghai Style Plain Noodles, but any fresh, eggless noodles of a similar size (about the thickness of cooked spaghetti when raw) will work here.

Light Soy Sauce Dark Soy Sauce Light soy sauce is thin and very salty. Dark soy sauce (lao chou) has a thicker texture, darker color, and sweeter flavor.

SEASON 18

Bean Bourguignon

SERVES 4 TO 6

WHY THIS RECIPE WORKS Creamy, chestnut-like Christmas lima beans meet tender, earthy portobello mushrooms in a rich, velvety sauce for a vegan version of the French classic, as luxurious and satisfying as the original. The ability of mushrooms to create fond, plus umami-boosting miso, soy sauce, and tomato paste, create a supremely savory sauce. Simmering beans in this acidic sauce slows down their cook time, leading to uneven results, so we cook them separately and add them to the sauce for the last 15 minutes to infuse them with the stew's flavors. You can substitute dried shiitake mushrooms for the porcini and yellow or red miso for white. Leave the mushroom gills intact; they enhance the stew's color and flavor. Serve over polenta.

Substitution: You can use dried large lima beans in place of the Christmas lima beans.

- 1½ tablespoons table salt for brining
- 8 ounces (1⅓ cups) dried Christmas lima beans, picked over and rinsed
- ½ teaspoon table salt, plus salt for cooking beans
- ¼ cup extra-virgin olive oil, divided
- 1½ pounds portobello mushroom caps, cut into 1-inch pieces
- ¼ teaspoon pepper
- 2 carrots, peeled, and chopped fine
- 1 large shallot, minced
- ½ ounce dried porcini mushrooms, rinsed and minced
- 4 garlic cloves, minced
- 2 teaspoons minced fresh thyme or ¾ teaspoon dried
- 3 tablespoons all-purpose flour
- 1 cup plus 2 tablespoons dry red wine, divided
- 2 tablespoons white miso
- 2 tablespoons soy sauce
- 1 tablespoon tomato paste
- 2 bay leaves
- 1 cup frozen pearl onions, thawed
- ¼ cup minced fresh parsley

1. Dissolve 1½ tablespoons table salt in 2 quarts cold water in large container. Add beans and soak at room temperature for at least 8 hours or up to 24 hours. Drain and rinse well. (If you're pressed for time, see page 530 for information on quick soaking your beans.)

2. Bring soaked beans and 7 cups water to simmer in large saucepan. Simmer, partially covered, over medium-low heat until beans are tender, 20 to 30 minutes. Remove from heat, stir in 1½ teaspoons salt, cover, and let sit for 15 minutes. Drain beans and set aside.

3. While beans cook, add ¼ cup water and 2 tablespoons oil to Dutch oven and bring to simmer over medium-high heat. Add portobello mushrooms, salt, and pepper. Cover and cook for 5 minutes, stirring occasionally (mushrooms will release liquid).

4. Uncover and continue to cook, stirring occasionally, until pot is dry and dark fond forms, 6 to 8 minutes longer. Add carrots, shallot, and remaining 2 tablespoons oil to pot and cook, stirring frequently, until vegetables start to brown, 3 to 4 minutes. Add porcini mushrooms, garlic, and thyme and cook until fragrant, about 30 seconds. Stir in flour and cook for 30 seconds. Whisk in 1 cup wine, scraping up any browned bits.

5. Whisk in miso, soy sauce, and tomato paste, then stir in 5 cups water and bay leaves. Bring to boil over high heat. Reduce heat to maintain vigorous simmer and cook, stirring occasionally and scraping bottom of pot to loosen any browned bits, until sauce is reduced and has consistency of heavy cream, 20 to 25 minutes.

6. Stir in cooked beans, pearl onions, and remaining 2 tablespoons wine. Cover and cook over low heat, stirring occasionally, until pearl onions are tender, about 15 minutes. Discard bay leaves and stir in parsley. Serve.

SEASON 18

Cutty's-Inspired Eggplant Spuckie

SERVES 4

WHY THIS RECIPE WORKS A spuckie is what some old school Bostonians call a sub sandwich. This particular spuckie, inspired by one at the Boston-area sandwich shop Cutty's, is a test kitchen favorite. The star of the show is the eggplant, which we broiled until it turned silky soft and browned. We paired it with thick slices of mozzarella for a satisfying sandwich filling. The briny carrot-olive spread came together quickly in the food processor and added flavor and crunch while gluing the sandwich together. Piling it all on chewy, airy ciabatta rolls rounded out every bite.

It's OK to use the tender, thin stems at the base of the parsley leaves.

- 1½ pounds eggplant, sliced into ½-inch-thick rounds
- ½ cup extra-virgin olive oil, divided
- 1 teaspoon table salt, divided
- ¾ cup pitted kalamata olives
- ½ cup fresh parsley leaves
- ½ cup jarred roasted red peppers, coarsely chopped
- 1 teaspoon red wine vinegar
- 1 small garlic clove, minced
- ¼ teaspoon red pepper flakes
- 1 cup shredded carrots
- 4 ciabatta sandwich rolls, halved lengthwise
- 8 ounces fresh mozzarella cheese, sliced into ¼-inch-thick rounds

1. Adjust oven rack 6 inches from broiler element and heat broiler. Line rimmed baking sheet with foil and spray with vegetable oil spray. Brush eggplant slices with 2 tablespoons oil, sprinkle with ¾ teaspoon salt, and arrange on prepared sheet. Broil eggplant until softened and beginning to brown, 10 to 14 minutes, flipping halfway through cooking. Transfer eggplant to plate and set aside.

2. Pulse olives, parsley, red peppers, vinegar, garlic, pepper flakes, and remaining ¼ teaspoon salt in food processor until chopped, 8 to 10 pulses. Transfer to bowl and stir in carrots and 2 tablespoons oil.

3. Arrange rolls on now-empty sheet and brush cut sides with remaining ¼ cup oil. Broil rolls, cut sides up, until golden brown, 2 to 5 minutes. Spread carrot-olive mixture evenly on cut sides of each roll. Distribute mozzarella and eggplant evenly among roll bottoms, then cap with roll tops. Serve.

SEASON 18

Tomatillo and Bibb Lettuce Salad with Tomatillo Ranch

SERVES 4

WHY THIS RECIPE WORKS Tomatillos, a husked nightshade fruit, have a distinctly firm texture and tart, floral flavor. While tomatillos are usually cooked before serving, our tomatillo salad showcases the unique flavors of the raw fruit. To prepare the tomatillos, we removed the husks and rinsed the skins to wash off any sticky residue. We sliced the fruits thin, which broke up their skins, exposed more pulp, and revealed a visually stunning cross section. We macerated the slices in salt and sugar, which softened the skins, drew out their juices, and seasoned them. Then we tossed the tomatillos with Bibb lettuce, which added crunch without excessive moisture. To create a creamy ranch-style dressing inspired by the dressing served at Cafe Rio (a Mexican grill chain based in Salt Lake City), we blended tomatillos with mayonnaise, jalapeño, cilantro, chives, dill, and spices (the tomatillos added natural acidity in lieu of buttermilk or vinegar). We drizzled the zippy, spicy dressing atop the salad and garnished it with pepitas for extra crunch.

Use fresh tomatillos (purchased or harvested with their husks intact) here.

Coat Check
Tomatillos are enclosed in papery husks. To remove the husks, peel them away from the fruit. Then, run the tomatillos under cold water and rub away any remaining husk and sticky residue using your fingers.

Dressing
- 3 ounces tomatillos, husks and stems removed, rinsed well, dried, and quartered
- ⅔ cup coarsely chopped fresh cilantro leaves and stems
- ⅓ cup mayonnaise
- 1 jalapeño chile, stemmed and chopped
- 2 tablespoons minced fresh chives
- 1 tablespoon chopped fresh dill
- 1 teaspoon granulated garlic
- ½ teaspoon table salt
- ¼ teaspoon pepper

Salad
- 1 pound tomatillos, husks and stems removed, rinsed well, dried, and sliced thin
- 1 teaspoon sugar
- ½ teaspoon table salt
- 8 ounces Bibb lettuce leaves
- 2 tablespoons roasted, salted pepitas

1. For the Dressing Process all ingredients in blender until smooth, about 90 seconds. (Dressing can be refrigerated for up to 4 days. If separated, stir to recombine before serving.)

2. For the Salad Toss tomatillos, sugar, and salt together in large bowl and let sit until tomatillos are shiny and slightly juicy, about 10 minutes. Drain tomatillos in colander and return to now-empty bowl (do not rinse).

3. Add lettuce to tomatillos and toss until lettuce is lightly coated with tomatillo juices. Arrange salad in even layer on large serving platter. Drizzle with ½ cup dressing and sprinkle with pepitas. Serve, passing remaining dressing separately.

Ultimate Caesar Salad

SERVES 4

WHY THIS RECIPE WORKS There are precious few salads as popular as the classic Caesar, and when you have a good one, it's easy to see why. To create a recipe for a Caesar salad that could truly live up to the hype, we threw it back to the classic method, slowly whisking extra-virgin olive oil into a pungent mix of egg yolk, lemon juice, Dijon mustard, minced anchovies, and Worcestershire sauce to create a luscious, creamy dressing. For the perfect buttery, crisp garlic-flavored croutons, we cut ciabatta bread into ½-inch cubes and tossed them in garlic oil before baking them until crisp and golden. To infuse the entire salad with savory Parmesan cheese, we stirred finely grated Parmesan into the dressing and tossed coarsely shredded Parmesan into the salad. When it all came together with the crunchy, lightly sweet romaine lettuce, we remembered why everyone knows the name Caesar.

Use a rasp-style grater or the fine holes of a box grater to grate the Parmesan. To shred it, use the large holes of a box grater. The size of the lettuce is important here. To cut the lettuce into 1-inch pieces, first cut off the core and then cut each romaine heart in half lengthwise. Cut the halves in half lengthwise. Finally, cut crosswise into 1-inch pieces.

- ¾ cup extra-virgin olive oil
- 2 garlic cloves, minced
- ½ teaspoon table salt, divided
- ½ teaspoon pepper, divided
- 4 ounces ciabatta, cut into ½-inch cubes (4 cups)
- 1 large egg yolk
- 1 tablespoon lemon juice
- 2 teaspoons Worcestershire sauce
- 2 teaspoons Dijon mustard
- 2 anchovy fillets, rinsed and minced, plus extra fillets for serving (optional)
- ¼ cup grated Parmesan cheese, plus 1½ ounces shredded (½ cup)
- 2 romaine lettuce hearts (12 ounces), cut into 1-inch pieces

1. Adjust oven rack to middle position and heat oven to 350 degrees. Stir ¼ cup oil, half of garlic, ¼ teaspoon salt, and ¼ teaspoon pepper together in large bowl. Add bread and toss to combine. Transfer bread to rimmed baking sheet and bake until light golden, about 18 minutes, stirring halfway through baking. Let cool completely. Wipe bowl clean with paper towels.

2. Form damp dish towel into ring shape on counter. Set now-empty bowl on towel to stabilize. Whisk egg yolk, lemon juice, Worcestershire, mustard, anchovies, remaining ¼ teaspoon salt, remaining ¼ teaspoon pepper, and remaining garlic together in bowl. Whisking constantly, slowly drizzle in remaining ½ cup oil until emulsified. Whisk in grated Parmesan.

3. Add lettuce, croutons, and shredded Parmesan to bowl with dressing and toss to combine. Season with salt and pepper to taste. Serve, garnished with extra anchovies, if using.

SEASON 18

Tomatoes with Fontina Sauce and Cornichon Dressing

SERVES 4 TO 6

WHY THIS RECIPE WORKS Fonduta is a rich cheese sauce from Northern Italy. It is often served during the cooler months, but we wanted to make a dish with it that would be perfect for a summer evening. We started the cheesy fonduta sauce by reducing heavy cream and incorporating funky fontina with nutty, savory Parmesan cheese. For a surprising contrast, we paired it with bright, ripe tomatoes drizzled with a simple dressing of cornichons, cornichon brine, olive oil, and shallot. The combination of bold cheeses and fresh tomatoes, both balanced by the acidity of the dressing, created a delectable appetizer. Fresh thyme rounded out the dish, which we suggest serving with toasted or grilled bread.

We prefer smaller tomatoes, such as Campari or Kumato (sometimes labeled "cocktail tomatoes"); other tomato varieties, cut into rough 1- to 2-inch pieces, will also work. Shred the fontina on the large holes of a box grater and grate the Parmesan cheese on a rasp-style grater. Do not use pregrated Parmesan here; it may contain additives that can affect the sauce's texture. Serve with crusty bread, toasted or grilled.

Tomato Salad
- ¼ cup cornichons, sliced thin on bias, plus 1 tablespoon brine
- 3 tablespoons extra-virgin olive oil
- 1 small shallot, minced
- ¾ teaspoon table salt, divided
- 1 pound small tomatoes, cored and cut into 1-inch-thick wedges
- ½ teaspoon pepper
- 2 teaspoons fresh thyme leaves
- ¼ teaspoon flake sea salt

Cheese Sauce
- 2 cups heavy cream
- 2 ounces fontina cheese, shredded (½ cup)
- 1½ ounces Parmesan cheese, grated (¾ cup)
- ¼ teaspoon table salt

1. For the Tomato Salad Toss cornichons and brine, oil, shallot, and ¼ teaspoon table salt together in bowl; set aside. Toss tomatoes gently with pepper and remaining ½ teaspoon table salt.

2. For the Cheese Sauce Bring cream to boil in large saucepan over medium-high heat. Reduce heat to medium-low and simmer, whisking occasionally, until cream is reduced to 1½ cups, 15 to 18 minutes. (If mixture begins to boil over, briefly remove saucepan from heat; adjust heat as needed to maintain consistent simmer.) Off heat, add fontina, Parmesan, and salt and whisk until cheeses are fully melted and sauce is smooth, about 30 seconds.

3. Immediately transfer cheese sauce to large platter and spread into even layer (sauce may appear thin at first; it will thicken quickly as it cools). Arrange tomatoes in even layer over cheese sauce. Drizzle cornichon dressing over tomatoes. Sprinkle with thyme and flake sea salt. Serve.

Getting the Fonduta Just Right

1. To achieve the proper texture, it is important to simmer the cream until reduced to 1½ cups and then return it to the saucepan.

2. Whisk in the fontina and Parmesan off the heat to ensure even melting.

SEASON 18

Quick-Braised Broccoli Rabe with Garlic and Anchovies

SERVES 6 TO 8

WHY THIS RECIPE WORKS Rather than cooking broccoli rabe in two distinct stages (starting with blanching, a commonly used method to purge it of its bitterness, before sautéing or roasting), we shortened the path to tender, well-balanced rabe by turning the typical blanch-sauté process on its head. We started by blooming a few key aromatics in olive oil before sautéing the rabe briefly over high heat. Then we lowered the heat, stirred in savory chicken broth, covered the pot, and briefly braised the rabe in the broth. To serve, we removed the rabe from the pot with a slotted spoon, leaving behind the braising liquid, which had extracted just the right amount of bitterness from our greens while also rendering them tender and flavorful. Extra olive oil and fresh lemons added their own point and counterpoint of fruitiness and pepperiness to finish the dish.

Look for broccoli rabe (also known as rapini) with dark green leaves, stems, and florets (without any yellowing) and a firm texture.

- ½ cup extra-virgin olive oil, plus extra for drizzling
- 6 garlic cloves, sliced thin
- 6 anchovy fillets, minced
- ½ teaspoon red pepper flakes
- 2 pounds broccoli rabe, trimmed and cut into 2-inch pieces
- ¾ teaspoon table salt
- ½ cup chicken broth
- Lemon wedges

1. Cook oil, garlic, anchovies, and pepper flakes in Dutch oven over medium-low heat until garlic is golden, about 3 minutes.

2. Add broccoli rabe and salt; increase heat to medium-high; and cook, stirring often, until rabe is bright green, about 2 minutes. Stir in broth, scraping up any browned bits, and bring to simmer. Cover pot; decrease heat to medium-low; and cook until broccoli rabe is tender but still bright green, 6 to 8 minutes.

3. Using slotted spoon, transfer broccoli rabe to platter, leaving behind braising liquid. Drizzle broccoli rabe generously with extra oil. Serve with lemon wedges.

Creamy Potatoes and Leeks

SERVES 6

WHY THIS RECIPE WORKS Potatoes and leeks are a classic pairing. This rustic yet elegant side dish uses one skillet to make creamy and rich potatoes with melted leeks and a crispy panko topping. We started this side dish by toasting panko bread crumbs in butter for a crispy topping. Then, we softened leeks in more butter before adding chunks of potatoes. We cooked the potatoes in chicken broth and wine, instead of water, which gave the dish depth and brightness. To enrich the final dish, we added some heavy cream and allowed the potatoes to cook past al dente to create an even creamier consistency. Just as the cream reduced, we stirred in a handful of nutty Gruyère cheese and topped the potatoes and leeks with the buttery toasted bread crumbs and earthy fresh thyme leaves.

We prefer to use leeks measuring about 1 inch in diameter for this recipe because they're more tender than larger leeks. Larger leeks will work, but discard their more fibrous outer layers.

- 4 tablespoons unsalted butter, cut into 4 pieces, divided
- ½ cup panko bread crumbs
- 1¼ teaspoons table salt, divided
- 2 pounds leeks, white and light-green parts only, halved lengthwise, sliced ½ inch thick, and washed thoroughly
- 1½ pounds Yukon Gold potatoes, unpeeled, cut into ¾-inch pieces
- 1½ cups chicken broth
- ¼ cup dry white wine
- ¾ cup heavy cream
- ½ teaspoon pepper
- 2 ounces Gruyère cheese, shredded (⅔ cup)
- 2 teaspoons chopped fresh thyme or oregano

1. Melt 2 tablespoons butter in 12-inch nonstick skillet over medium heat. Add panko and ½ teaspoon salt and cook, stirring often, until golden brown, 3 to 6 minutes. Transfer to bowl; set aside. Wipe skillet clean with paper towels.

2. Melt remaining 2 tablespoons butter in now-empty skillet over medium heat. Add leeks and ¼ teaspoon salt and cook, covered, until softened, about 6 minutes, stirring halfway through cooking.

3. Stir in potatoes, broth, wine, and remaining ½ teaspoon salt and spread into even layer. Cover and bring to vigorous simmer over medium-high heat. Reduce heat to medium-low and simmer, covered, until potatoes are fork-tender, 20 to 25 minutes.

4. Stir in cream and pepper and return to simmer. Continue to cook, uncovered, until spatula leaves trail when dragged through mixture, 4 to 6 minutes longer. Off heat, stir in Gruyère. Sprinkle evenly with panko mixture and thyme. Serve.

When is It Done?
The cream has reduced enough once a spatula leaves a trail when dragged through the mixture. Then, it's time to add the cheese.

Leek Prep
Leeks grow concentrically, and each ring can trap dirt, so it's important to chop them before washing them. A salad spinner works for washing cut leeks.

Keys to This Dish

Melted Leeks
Cover the sliced leeks to steam and "melt" them down with butter to ensure that they are softened before adding the potatoes.

Flavorful Potatoes
For maximum flavor in one skillet, simmer the potatoes in a mixture of chicken broth (for depth) and white wine (for brightness and acidity). As the potatoes cook, the liquids reduce into a base for the sauce.

Cream and Cheese
Add cream to the partially cooked potatoes, allowing their starches to slightly thicken the liquid as it reduces. Then, stir in shredded Gruyère for richness and a hint of nuttiness.

Crunchy Topping
Toast panko bread crumbs in melted butter for a quick, crispy topping without heating the oven. Sprinkle the cooked potatoes with these crispy bits and some fresh thyme just before serving.

SEASON 18

Sweet Potato Fritters with Feta, Dill, and Cilantro

SERVES 4 TO 6

WHY THIS RECIPE WORKS We were after lightly crisp sweet potato fritters with savory exteriors and creamy, sweet insides. We started by following a tried-and-true method for making mashed sweet potatoes that calls for steaming the spuds in a small amount of water (rather than boiling them in an abundance of water, which dilutes their flavor). After cooking the potatoes, we mashed them, purposefully leaving a few small chunks for contrasting texture. Adding eggs and flour to the mash made the fritters fluffier, with extra-crunchy edges. Shallow frying was easier to manage—and clean up—than deep frying. Sliced scallions, chopped fresh cilantro and dill, and some briny feta cheese made each bite of these fritters exciting.

Using two spatulas to flip the fritters helps prevent splattering.

- 1½ pounds sweet potatoes, peeled and sliced ¼ inch thick
- ¼ cup water
- 1½ teaspoons table salt
- 3 ounces feta cheese, crumbled (¾ cup)
- ½ cup all-purpose flour
- 2 large eggs
- 4 scallions, sliced thin
- ¼ cup chopped fresh cilantro
- ¼ cup chopped fresh dill
- 1 teaspoon ground cumin
- ½ teaspoon pepper
- ½ cup peanut or vegetable oil for frying
  Sour cream
  Lemon or lime wedges

1. Combine potatoes, water, and salt in large saucepan. Cover and cook over medium-low heat, stirring occasionally, until paring knife inserted into potatoes meets no resistance, about 20 minutes.

2. Remove from heat. Using potato masher, mash potatoes until mostly smooth with some small chunks remaining. Let cool until no longer hot to touch, about 30 minutes. (Mashed sweet potatoes can be transferred to bowl, covered with plastic wrap, and refrigerated for up to 2 days.)

3. Set wire rack in rimmed baking sheet and line half of rack with triple layer of paper towels. Stir feta, flour, eggs, scallions, cilantro, dill, cumin, and pepper into potato mixture until fully combined.

4. Heat oil in 12-inch nonstick skillet over medium heat to 350 degrees (to take temperature, tilt skillet so oil pools on 1 side). Using greased ¼-cup dry measuring cup, place 6 portions of potato mixture in skillet. Press portions into approximate 3-inch disks with back of spoon.

5. Cook fritters until deep brown, 2 to 3 minutes per side, using 2 spatulas to carefully flip. Transfer fritters to paper towel–lined side of prepared rack to drain for 15 seconds on each side, then move to unlined side of rack. Return oil to 350 degrees and repeat with remaining potato mixture. Serve with sour cream and lemon wedges.

Sweet Potato Fritters with Cheddar and Chipotle

Substitute shredded sharp cheddar for feta and 2 tablespoons minced canned chipotle chile in adobo sauce for dill.

SEASON 18

Air-Fryer Jalapeño Poppers

SERVES 4 (MAKES 12 POPPERS)

WHY THIS RECIPE WORKS We adapted a recipe for bacon-wrapped jalapeño poppers to fit the convenience and efficiency of an air fryer. We stemmed and halved the jalapeños and then seeded them to tame their intense heat. Next, we stuffed them with cream cheese and cheddar cheese, which soften into a melty filling; a little cornstarch prevented the filling from separating and leaking out of the peppers. We added scallion for fresh flavor, lime zest for brightness, and pickled jalapeños for acidity and to reinforce the chile flavor. We made sure that when we wrapped the poppers with bacon the seams were down so that they remained neat little bites when cooking.

Look for large jalapeños that are about 4 inches long and 1¼ inches thick at the stem end. If your jalapeños are smaller, do not overfill them; the filling should be level with the cut sides. This recipe can easily be doubled. If doubling, cook the poppers in two batches. This recipe was developed using a basket-style air fryer, but you can cook the poppers in an oven-style air fryer. Some air-fryer models have preheating functions; the cook-time range in this recipe is intended to work with either a cold or preheated air fryer.

6 jalapeño chiles, halved lengthwise with stems left intact, seeds and ribs removed
¼ teaspoon table salt
4 ounces sharp cheddar cheese, shredded (1 cup)
4 ounces cream cheese, softened
1 scallion, sliced thin
1 tablespoon chopped pickled jalapeño chiles
1 tablespoon minced fresh cilantro
2 teaspoons cornstarch
1 teaspoon grated lime zest
6 slices bacon, halved crosswise

1. Arrange jalapeño halves cut side up on cutting board and sprinkle evenly with salt. Stir cheddar, cream cheese, scallion, pickled jalapeños, cilantro, cornstarch, and lime zest in bowl until well combined.

2. Divide cheese mixture evenly among jalapeño halves (about 1 tablespoon per half), gently pressing filling into cavities so it is flush with cut edges. Wrap each popper with bacon, overlapping ends of bacon pieces underneath jalapeño halves. (Bacon-wrapped poppers can be refrigerated for up to 24 hours; arrange on large plate and cover with plastic wrap until ready to cook.)

3. Arrange poppers in even layer in air-fryer basket. Place basket in air fryer and set temperature to 400 degrees. Cook until jalapeños are tender and bacon is golden and crispy, 10 to 14 minutes. Serve.

SEASON 18

Cast Iron Potato Kugel

SERVES 8

WHY THIS RECIPE WORKS We were after an easy yet supersavory potato dish that was crisp on the outside but had a tender, fluffy interior. We used shredded russet potatoes for their starchiness and treated them with a saltwater solution to keep them from oxidizing to an unappetizing gray tinge. We flavored the spuds with sautéed onions and a generous amount of rendered chicken fat (schmaltz) and added eggs to bind it all together. Using a preheated cast-iron skillet gave us an extra-crispy edge.

You can find rendered chicken fat (schmaltz) in the frozen foods section of larger supermarkets. If you can't find it, you can substitute extra-virgin olive oil. We prefer using the shredding disk of a food processor to shred the potatoes, but you can also use the large holes of a box grater. Making this kugel in a well-seasoned cast-iron skillet ensures that it will have a crisp crust, but if you don't have one, you can use a 10-inch ovensafe nonstick skillet. Serve with sour cream, if desired.

- 6 tablespoons rendered chicken fat (schmaltz), divided
- 2 cups finely chopped onions
- ¾ teaspoon table salt, plus salt for tossing potatoes
- 3 pounds russet potatoes, unpeeled
- 4 large eggs
- 1¼ teaspoons pepper
- 1 tablespoon minced fresh chives

1. Adjust oven rack to upper-middle position and heat oven to 425 degrees. Heat 2 tablespoons chicken fat in 10-inch cast-iron skillet over medium-high heat until shimmering. Add onions and cook, stirring occasionally, until softened, about 3 minutes. Transfer to bowl and set aside.

2. Whisk 2 cups water and 2 tablespoons salt in large bowl until salt is dissolved. Fit food processor with shredding disk. Peel potatoes and halve or quarter lengthwise as needed to fit through processor feed tube. Shred potatoes. Transfer potatoes to salt water and toss briefly to coat.

3. Drain potatoes in colander. Place one-quarter of shredded potatoes in center of clean dish towel. Gather ends of towel and twist tightly to wring out excess moisture from potatoes. Transfer dried potatoes to now-empty bowl. Repeat 3 more times with remaining potatoes. Stir eggs, pepper, onions, and remaining ¾ teaspoon salt into potatoes until thoroughly combined.

4. Heat remaining ¼ cup chicken fat in now-empty skillet over medium-high heat until just smoking. Add potato mixture to skillet and distribute into even layer but do not press down or smooth top. Cook for 1 minute to set bottom.

5. Transfer to oven and bake until kugel is lightly browned on top, about 45 minutes. Let cool for 5 minutes. Cut into wedges in skillet. Sprinkle with chives and serve.

> **Color Saver**
> Shredding potatoes releases an enzyme that can cause them to turn a blue-gray color. A simple toss with salted water neutralizes this reaction and keeps the spuds white.
>
>
>
> **LIGHT AND LOVELY**
> The salt water preserves the spuds' color.
>
>
>
> **GRAY AND GHOULISH**
> The shreds turn gray without the salt water.

SEASON 18

Gullah Lowcountry Red Rice

SERVES 4 TO 6

WHY THIS RECIPE WORKS Gullah Lowcountry red rice, a tomato and pork pilaf (or "purloo" in the Lowcountry) that is similar to West African jollof rice, should be fluffy, with a flavor that's at once rich and bright. Chef Kardea Brown, Charleston-born and of Gullah Geechee descent, says the rice has intense tomato flavor but avoids tasting too acidic thanks to the addition of a dash of sugar. This version starts with a rich base created by rendering the fat from salt pork and browning smoked sausage in that fat. Rinsing the red rice thoroughly removes excess starch that could otherwise turn the finished dish gummy; baking the rice cooks it gently and evenly to ensure that it is uniformly fluffy. Pureed fresh tomatoes lend brightness, while tomato paste offers depth and savory complexity. This recipe uses Carolina Gold rice, traditionally cultivated by the Gullah Geechee in the Lowcountry and coveted for its fluffiness and intensely nutty aroma and flavor. We used Rollen's Raw Grains Carolina Gold rice, which you can purchase online at rollensrawgrains.com. Carolina Gold is standard in this dish, but another long-grain white rice can also be used. Look for a fatty piece when purchasing the salt pork so that it renders enough fat for sautéing. Note that not all salt pork is sold with its rind on.

- 1½ cups Carolina Gold rice
- 2 tomatoes (12 ounces), cored and quartered
- 4 ounces salt pork, rind removed, rinsed, patted dry, and cut into ½-inch pieces
- 8 ounces smoked sausage, cut in half lengthwise and sliced ¼ inch thick
- 1 cup chopped onion
- 1 cup chopped green bell pepper
- ¼ cup tomato paste
- 1¼ cups chicken broth
- 1 teaspoon sugar (optional)
- 1 teaspoon pepper
- 1 teaspoon granulated garlic
- ½ teaspoon table salt
- ½ teaspoon onion powder
- ¼ teaspoon cayenne pepper

1. Adjust oven rack to middle position and heat oven to 350 degrees. Place rice in fine-mesh strainer and rinse under cold running water for 1½ minutes. Shake strainer vigorously to remove all excess water; set aside.

2. Process tomatoes in food processor until smooth, about 30 seconds, scraping down sides of bowl as needed. Transfer tomatoes to liquid measuring cup; you should have 1½ cups (if necessary, spoon off excess or top off with water so that volume equals 1½ cups).

3. Cook salt pork in Dutch oven over medium heat, stirring often, until pork is browned and fat has rendered, 10 to 12 minutes. Increase heat to medium-high, add sausage, and cook until browned, about 3 minutes. Add onion and bell pepper and cook until nearly softened, about 3 minutes. Stir in rice until grains are evenly coated with fat and cook, stirring often, until edges of rice are translucent and vegetables are softened, about 4 minutes. Stir in tomato paste and cook until darkened, about 1 minute.

4. Stir in broth; pureed tomatoes; sugar, if using; pepper; granulated garlic; salt; onion powder; and cayenne and bring to boil, scraping up any browned bits. Cover pot with sheet of aluminum foil, then cover with lid. Transfer to oven; bake for 35 minutes.

5. Remove rice from oven and let stand, covered, for 10 minutes. Fluff rice gently with fork and let stand, uncovered, for an additional 5 minutes. Serve.

SEASON 18

Double-Chocolate Banana Bread

MAKES 1 LOAF

WHY THIS RECIPE WORKS We wanted a dead-simple banana bread recipe that packed a big banana-chocolate punch and wasn't really "bready" at all. We were after a chocolaty slice that was tender, moist, buttery, just the right amount of sweet, and (most important) heavy with the aroma and flavor of bananas. To get there, we started by adding more bananas than we thought was possible, and then we added even more. After extensive testing, we arrived at a recipe that called for more than a pound of sweet, very ripe bananas and two types of chocolate (cocoa powder and chopped bittersweet chocolate). Plus, it was as easy as mixing the wet and dry ingredients together in a bowl. This version packs in a bit more butter and loads more bananas than the average recipe. What's more, we think it tastes a lot better, and we think you will too.

Be sure to use very ripe, heavily speckled (or even black) bananas in this recipe. Use a potato masher to thoroughly mash the bananas. The test kitchen's preferred loaf pan measures 8½ by 4½ inches; if you use a 9 by 5-inch loaf pan, start checking for doneness 5 minutes earlier than advised in the recipe. We place the loaf pan on a rimmed baking sheet in case the batter overflows in the oven.

- 1¼ cups (6¼ ounces) all-purpose flour
- ¼ cup (¾ ounce) Dutch-processed cocoa powder
- 1¼ teaspoons baking soda
- ¾ teaspoon table salt
- 2 cups mashed very ripe bananas (about 4 bananas)
- 1 cup packed (7 ounces) dark brown sugar
- 10 tablespoons unsalted butter, melted and cooled slightly
- 2 large eggs
- 4 ounces bittersweet chocolate, chopped
- 2 tablespoons granulated sugar

1. Adjust oven rack to middle position and heat oven to 350 degrees. Spray 8½ by 4½-inch loaf pan with vegetable oil spray.

2. Whisk flour, cocoa, baking soda, and salt together in bowl. Whisk bananas, brown sugar, melted butter, and eggs in large bowl until thoroughly combined, making sure to break up any clumps of brown sugar with whisk. Add flour mixture to banana mixture and whisk gently until just combined (batter will be lumpy). Fold in chocolate.

3. Place prepared pan on rimmed baking sheet. Transfer batter to prepared pan and sprinkle granulated sugar over top. Bake until toothpick inserted in center comes out clean, about 1 hour 10 minutes.

4. Let bread cool in pan on wire rack for 30 minutes. Tilt pan and gently remove bread. Let bread continue to cool on wire rack at least 30 minutes longer. Serve warm or at room temperature. (Cooled bread can be wrapped tightly in plastic wrap and stored at room temperature for up to 5 days.)

The Perfect Overripe Banana
Heavily speckled—or even black—bananas are best in this recipe. Why? As bananas age, their starch turns to sugar. If you have darkening bananas on the counter and wish to freeze them for making banana bread later, we recommend peeling them before freezing them.

DIY Overripe Bananas
No overripe bananas? Make your own by baking just-ripe, unpeeled yellow bananas in a 325-degree oven for 20 minutes, until they're entirely black. Be sure to let them cool completely before using them in this recipe.

The Complete Cook's Country TV Show Cookbook

ON THE ROAD — RHODE ISLAND

A Mighty Muffin

PORTUGUESE PERFECTION AT A FAMILY BAKERY

by Bryan Roof; photos by Steve Klise

Central Bakery in Tiverton, Rhode Island, makes only one thing: bolos lêvedos. But brothers Paul and David Lopes believe this laser focus is the key to their 30-plus years of success.

"My mom and dad came to the United States and realized no one was making the muffins. In 1974, they started making them in their garage, then opened up their first bakery," Paul says. The muffins were based on the recipe Lopes's grandmother used back on São Miguel, an island in the Azores.

Business took off, thanks to word of mouth. "One of my dad's first big hits was on Cape Cod [in the late 1970s]," Paul says. Vacationing New Yorkers brought word of the muffins back to the city, starting a sales boom.

Paul credits the company's evolution to his customers. "In Portugal, the only thing they used the muffins for was breakfast. But the American public got really creative," Paul says. "Now, the number one use for this product is a hamburger bun." Central Bakery, an exclusively wholesale operation today, supplies Madison Square Garden and Yankee Stadium, among others.

The Lopes brothers (above), second-generation operators of Central Bakery, based their recipe for bolos lêvedos (also called Portuguese muffins) on a family recipe brought from the Azores. Their mother, Leonor (left), and father, Tiberio, started the business in 1974.

Sticking to a single product confounds some customers. "I'll talk to a retailer and he'll say, 'What else do you have?' and I'll say, 'This is it,' and he'll say, 'You make just one product since 1974?' But it's keeping our doors open."

That extreme focus extends to the recipe and process, too. The brothers keep the specifics top secret. "We've tried to adapt, but it's not the same."

Bolos Lêvedos (Portuguese Muffins)

MAKES 8 MUFFINS

WHY THIS RECIPE WORKS Though they look a lot like English muffins, these Portuguese "cakes" ("bolos" means "cakes" and "lêvedos" means "leavened"), originally from the Azores, are denser and richer, with a fair amount of sweetness and a rich crumb thanks to whole milk, eggs, and butter. Inspired by a visit to Central Bakery, a Portuguese bakery in Tiverton, Rhode Island, that turns out dozens of bolos lêvedos a day, we set out to create a small-scale recipe for the home kitchen. First, to ensure that the dough would be hydrated enough to create a tender finished product, we followed a method called tangzhong, which involves quickly heating a small portion of flour and liquid to form a paste before mixing it in with the rest of the ingredients. This helped hydrate the dough quickly and created a more workable dough (it also helped the cooked bolos stay fresh longer). To further ensure full hydration and tender bolos, we included an autolyse step: mixing everything together (except for the sugar and salt) and allowing it to rest for 15 minutes to fully hydrate and get a head start on gluten development. After a traditional two-stage rise, we browned our muffins in a skillet and finished cooking them in the oven, which yielded slightly sweet, moist cakes fit for breakfast, lunch, and dinner.

If you don't own a microwave, the flour paste can also be made in a small saucepan over medium heat. Just be sure to whisk it constantly so that the ingredients don't scorch. Split the muffins with a knife. Serve them with butter or use them as sandwich bread or burger buns.

Flour Paste
- ⅔ cup water
- ¼ cup (1¼ ounces) all-purpose flour

Dough
- 6 tablespoons whole milk
- 4 tablespoons unsalted butter, cut into 4 pieces and softened
- 2 large eggs
- 3 cups (15 ounces) all-purpose flour, plus extra for shaping
- 1 teaspoon instant or rapid-rise yeast
- ½ cup (3½ ounces) sugar
- 1 teaspoon table salt
- 1 teaspoon vegetable oil

SEASON EIGHTEEN   95

1. For the Flour Paste Whisk water and flour in medium bowl until no lumps remain. Microwave, whisking every 20 seconds, until mixture thickens to stiff, smooth, pudding-like consistency, 40 to 80 seconds. Transfer paste to bowl of stand mixer.

2. For the Dough Whisk milk into flour paste in bowl of stand mixer until combined. Whisk in butter until fully incorporated. Whisk in eggs until fully incorporated.

3. Add flour and yeast to paste mixture. Fit mixer with dough hook and mix on low speed until dough comes together and no dry flour remains, about 2 minutes. Turn off mixer, cover bowl with dish towel or plastic wrap, and let dough stand for 15 minutes.

4. Add sugar and salt to dough and mix on low speed until incorporated, about 1 minute. Increase speed to medium and mix until dough is elastic and pulls away from sides of bowl but still sticks to bottom (dough will be sticky), about 8 minutes. Transfer dough to greased large bowl; cover tightly with plastic wrap; and let rise until doubled in size, about 1½ hours.

5. Line rimmed baking sheet with parchment paper. Turn out dough onto clean counter and divide into 8 equal pieces, about 4 ounces each. Working with 1 piece of dough at a time, cup dough with your palm and roll against counter in circular motion into smooth, tight ball. (Dough will be sticky; very lightly flour dough and hands as needed, but avoid excess flour in order to maintain tackiness necessary to roll dough into tight ball.)

6. Sprinkle ¼ cup flour on counter. Working with 1 dough ball at a time, turn dough ball in flour and press with your hand to flatten into 3½- to 4-inch disk. Transfer dough disks to prepared sheet. Lay second sheet of parchment over dough disks, then place second rimmed baking sheet on top to keep disks flat during second rise. Let rise for 30 minutes. Adjust oven rack to middle position and heat oven to 350 degrees.

7. Heat oil in 12-inch nonstick skillet over medium-low heat until shimmering. Using paper towels, carefully wipe out oil from skillet.

8. Transfer 4 dough disks to skillet and cook until deeply browned on both sides, 2 to 4 minutes per side. Return toasted disks to sheet. Repeat with remaining 4 dough disks.

9. Bake until muffins register 190 degrees in center, 11 to 14 minutes. Transfer muffins to wire rack and let cool for 30 minutes. Serve. (Muffins can be stored in airtight container for up to 3 days or frozen for up to 1 month.)

Bolos Lêvedos (Portuguese Muffins) with Lemon and Cinnamon

Add 1½ teaspoons grated lemon zest and ¼ teaspoon ground cinnamon with flour in step 3.

Easy Techniques

In this recipe we use a technique called tangzhong, which involves heating a mixture of water and flour (we use the microwave) until it forms a paste and then mixing it into the dough. This method helps the flour absorb the liquid it is cooked with, resulting in a moister final product. We also employ a technique called autolyse, giving the dough a short, 15-minute rest before we add the salt and sugar. This rest allows the flour to fully absorb the liquid and develop just the right amount of gluten for a satisfyingly chewy bolo.

Building the Bolos
Here's how we shape the muffins.

1. Portion After first rise, divide dough into 8 equal pieces.

2. Round Cup each piece and roll in circles to create taut dough balls.

3. Flatten Use your hand to flatten each ball into disk.

4. Weight Top with baking sheet so disks don't puff too much before browning.

SEASON 18

Pastéis de Nata (Portuguese Egg Tarts)

MAKES 12 EGG TARTS

WHY THIS RECIPE WORKS This recipe is inspired by the pastéis de nata handmade by owner and baker Tony Rodrigues at Barcelo's, his Portuguese bakery in Fall River, Massachusetts. For our take on these sweet, creamy egg tarts, we baked the pastéis in a muffin tin instead of the traditional pastel cups, and at a home-oven-friendly 450 degrees rather than the 600+ degrees they use at the bakery. Layering softened butter between thin layers of dough resulted in the memorable crisp crust iconic to these tarts. To get the classic swirled pastry layers, we rolled the laminated dough into a log, sliced it into rounds, and pressed it into the muffin tin cups to ensure that the dough was even and thin. For the custard, we found that just flour was needed to thicken the mixture and withstand the high temperature needed to achieve the traditional spotty-brown surface. Serve these tarts warm or at room temperature sprinkled with cinnamon and powdered sugar.

The softened butter called for here should be easily spreadable (about 72 degrees) but not warm or melted. A baking steel can be used in place of the baking stone, but lower the cooking range to 25 to 27 minutes. You can use traditional 3-ounce pastel cups measuring approximately 1 inch tall, 1¾ inches in diameter along the bottom, and about 3 inches across the top. (These cups are available in Portuguese grocery stores or online.) If using pastel cups, cut the 12-inch dough log into 16 (¾-inch) pieces, place the cups on a rimmed baking sheet, and decrease the baking time in step 10 to 21 to 25 minutes. To rewarm the tarts and refresh the pastry, bake them on a rimmed baking sheet on the middle rack of a 350-degree oven for 5 to 7 minutes; let cool for about 5 minutes before serving.

Dough
- 1¼ cup (6¼ ounces/177 grams) all-purpose flour, plus extra for work surface
- ½ teaspoon table salt
- ½ cup water
- 15 tablespoons unsalted butter, cut into ½ inch pieces and softened, divided

Custard
- 1¼ cups whole milk, divided
- 3 tablespoons all-purpose flour
- ¾ teaspoon table salt
- 6 large egg yolks, lightly beaten
- 1½ teaspoons vanilla extract (optional)
- 1¼ cup (8¾ ounces/248 grams) granulated sugar
- ½ cup water
- Confectioners' sugar
- Cinnamon

1. For the Dough Whisk flour and salt together in bowl of stand mixer. Fit mixer with dough hook; add water; and mix on low speed until cohesive dough forms, 2 to 3 minutes, scraping down bowl as needed. Transfer dough to liberally floured counter. Pat dough into 4-inch square. Lightly flour top of dough, cover with plastic wrap, and let rest at room temperature for 15 minutes.

2. Roll dough into 15 by 13-inch rectangle with short side parallel to counter's edge, using bench scraper to release dough and re-flouring counter as needed. Brush excess flour from top of dough. Scatter one-third butter pieces crosswise over center third of dough. Using small offset spatula, spread butter evenly into 5 by 12-inch rectangle, leaving ½-inch border on each side.

3. Fold top third of dough over butter layer, then brush away excess flour from folded portion. Fold bottom third of dough over top third to create 5 by 13-inch rectangle (like business letter), and brush away excess flour.

4. Rotate dough 90 degrees. Re-flour counter, and repeat rolling dough, spreading butter, folding, and rotating dough twice more with remaining butter.

5. Line rimmed baking sheet with parchment paper. Roll dough into 15 by 13-inch rectangle with short side parallel to counter edge, and brush excess flour from dough. Using moistened finger, brush top edge of dough lightly with water. Starting at short side, roll dough away from you into tight log and pinch seam to seal. Transfer log to prepared sheet, seam side down; cover loosely with

The Complete Cook's Country TV Show Cookbook

plastic wrap, and refrigerate until firm, at least 1 hour or up to 12 hours.

6. Spray 12-cup muffin tin with vegetable oil spray. Using sharp knife, trim ends of dough log to create 12-inch log. Cut log into 12 equal pieces, and place 1 piece into each muffin cup, cut side up.

7. Using moistened fingers, press dough pieces evenly into bottoms and up sides of muffin cups until dough just reaches tops of cups, taking care to press dough evenly into corners and avoid tearing. (If dough is very cold, allow pieces to sit in cups at room temperature for 5 to 10 minutes until dough can be pressed without cracking around edges.) Cover tin with plastic and refrigerate until dough is well chilled, at least 1 hour or up to 12 hours.

8. For the Custard Whisk ¼ cup milk, flour, and salt together in bowl until smooth. Whisk egg yolks and vanilla, if using, together in second bowl. Set fine-mesh strainer over 4-cup liquid measuring cup.

9. Combine sugar, water, and remaining 1 cup milk in medium saucepan and bring to simmer over medium-high heat. Cook, stirring occasionally, until sugar is dissolved, about 2 minutes. Off heat, slowly whisk hot milk mixture into flour mixture until smooth. Gently whisk warm flour mixture into egg yolks until evenly combined. Strain mixture through prepared strainer into measuring cup; discard solids. (Custard will be thin.)

Let custard sit at room temperature for up to 1 hour, or refrigerate for up to 12 hours. (If custard was refrigerated, let it sit at room temperature while the oven is preheating for an hour in step 10.)

10. One hour before baking, adjust oven rack to upper-middle position, place baking stone on rack, and heat oven to 450 degrees. Just before baking, whisk custard to recombine. Divide custard evenly among dough cups in muffin tin, filling to just below rim and being careful not to overfill. (You may have extra custard; this is OK.) Bake until custard is puffed and spotty brown on most tarts and dough is deep golden brown and crisp around edges, 27 to 30 minutes.

11. Let tarts cool in muffin tin on wire rack for 5 minutes. Using small offset spatula, transfer tarts to wire rack and let cool for at least 30 minutes. Dust tops of tarts with confectioners' sugar and cinnamon, if desired. Serve warm or at room temperature.

Pastéis de Nata with Lemon and Cinnamon

Omit vanilla. Add 2 (3-inch) strips lemon zest and 1 cinnamon stick when heating milk mixture in step 7. Let zest and cinnamon stick steep in custard for at least 1 hour before straining.

SEASON 18

Sufganiyot (Hanukkah Jelly Doughnuts)

MAKES 12 DOUGHNUTS

WHY THIS RECIPE WORKS To make fluffy, tender, and perfectly puffy jelly doughnuts, we started with an enriched dough. We mixed together flour, yeast, and a scant amount of warm spices (just enough to round out the flavor) with milk and eggs and then let it rest, which fully hydrated the flour and built a strong gluten network. Then we mixed in ample sugar and salt, kneaded the dough well, and slowly incorporated softened butter for richness. We allowed for a long rise to combat the heaviness from the added fat and then used plenty of flour when rolling out the soft, sticky dough and cutting it into rounds. After a second rise, we fried the doughnuts at a low temperature so that they didn't get too brown. Then we filled them with jelly from the top, which allowed for greater precision.

Heating the oil slowly makes it easier to control the temperature when frying. Use a large Dutch oven that holds 6 quarts or more. You can substitute any flavor jam you like (if it's too chunky to pipe, blitz it in the food processor until smooth) or use lemon curd, Nutella, or dulce de leche. If you prefer, you can coat the doughnuts in granulated sugar instead of confectioners' sugar. To do so, roll the doughnuts in sugar before filling them in step 6.

- 3½ cups (17½ ounces) all-purpose flour
- 2¼ teaspoons instant or rapid-rise yeast
- ⅛ teaspoon ground cinnamon
  Pinch ground nutmeg
- 1 cup milk
- 2 large eggs
- ⅓ cup (2⅓ ounces) granulated sugar
- 1¼ teaspoons table salt
- 6 tablespoons unsalted butter, cut into ½-inch pieces and softened
- 2 quarts vegetable oil for frying
- 1 cup strawberry jam
  Confectioners' sugar

1. Stir flour, yeast, cinnamon, and nutmeg together in bowl of stand mixer fitted with dough hook. Add milk and eggs. Mix on low speed until dough comes together and no dry flour remains, about 2 minutes, scraping down bowl and dough hook as needed. Turn off mixer, cover bowl with dish towel or plastic wrap, and let stand for 20 minutes.

2. Add granulated sugar and salt and mix on low speed until dough is smooth and elastic and clears sides of bowl, 5 to 7 minutes. With mixer running, add butter, a few pieces at a time. Increase speed to medium-low and continue to mix until butter is fully incorporated and dough is smooth and elastic, 8 to 12 minutes longer, scraping down bowl halfway through mixing.

3. Transfer dough to lightly greased large bowl. Gather edges up and fold inward to form loose ball shape, then flip dough seam side down. Cover bowl tightly with plastic and let dough rise at room temperature until doubled in size, 1½ to 2 hours. (Unrisen dough can be refrigerated for at least 8 hours or up to 24 hours; let sit at room temperature for 2 hours before rolling.)

4. Line rimmed baking sheet with parchment paper and lightly grease parchment. Transfer dough to floured counter and sprinkle with flour. Gently press dough to expel air, then press and roll dough to ½-inch thickness (approximately 10 by 13 inches). Using 3-inch round cutter dipped in flour, cut 12 rounds. (Reserve dough scraps for doughnut holes or discard.) Carefully transfer dough rounds to prepared sheet using thin metal spatula (flour spatula as needed). Cover sheet with plastic and let dough rise at room temperature until puffy, about 1 hour.

5. About 20 minutes before end of rising time, add oil to large Dutch oven until it measures about 1½ inches deep and heat over medium-low heat to 335 degrees. Set wire rack in second rimmed baking sheet and line with triple layer of paper towels. Using both your hands, gently drop 4 dough rounds into hot oil and fry until golden brown, about 2 minutes per side. Adjust heat as needed to maintain oil temperature between 330 and 340 degrees. Transfer doughnuts to prepared rack. Return oil to 335 degrees and repeat with remaining doughnuts. Let cool almost completely, about 10 minutes.

6. Discard paper towels, leaving doughnuts on rack. Spoon jam into pastry bag or zipper-lock bag fitted with ¼-inch round pastry tip. Working with 1 doughnut at a time, use chopstick or skewer to poke hole through top of each doughnut, about halfway through, rotating to widen opening to about ½ inch. Insert pastry tip into opening and squeeze gently until jam just starts to appear around opening, about 1 tablespoon jam per doughnut. Dust doughnuts with confectioners' sugar. Serve warm or at room temperature.

Sufganiyot's (Yeasted) Rise To Fame

According to historian Gil Marks in his *Encyclopedia of Jewish Food* (2010), the history of jelly doughnuts can be traced back to a German cookbook from 1485, which featured a recipe for two round pieces of bread stuffed with jam and then fried in lard. Fried jelly pastries took on various identities across Europe: krapfen in Austria, Berliners in Germany, and pączki in Poland (ponchiks when fried in kosher fat). European migrants, fleeing increasing antisemitism, brought these traditions to what is now Israel in the early 20th century. Histradut, Israel's national trade union center, is to thank for sufganiyot achieving its iconic Hanukkah status. In the late 1920s, they pushed for sufganiyot to replace latkes as the go-to Hanukkah food item. Since latkes are easily made at home but doughnuts are more often left to the pastry professionals, this created more job opportunities in Jewish quarters.

Handling the Raw Doughnuts

1. Using thin metal spatula, carefully transfer dough rounds to prepared baking sheet to rise.

2. Using 2 hands, gently drop 4 dough rounds into hot oil and fry until golden brown.

Fill 'er Up

1. Poke hole in top of each doughnut with chopstick. Angle and turn chopstick to widen hole.

2. Carefully insert pastry tip into hole and squeeze to fill doughnut just until jam emerges from hole.

SEASON 18

Conchas

MAKES 12 CONCHAS

WHY THIS RECIPE WORKS Buttery, light, and tender and Mexico's best-known pan dulce (sweet bread), conchas are a lightly sweet, enriched bread topped with a sweet, melt-in-your-mouth crust that's scored to look like a shell. We used a brioche method to create the breads' base. We made the topping from equal parts confectioners' sugar, flour, and vegetable shortening and pressed it into thin rounds to cover each shaped bun. (The higher melting point of the shortening helps preserve the iconic seashell scoring during baking.) A butter knife made quick work of the design without the need for a traditional concha cutter.

Conchas are best eaten the day they are made.

Dough
- 3⅔ cups (20⅛ ounces) bread flour
- 1 tablespoon instant or rapid-rise yeast
- 1¼ cups (10 ounces) water, room temperature
- 2 large eggs, room temperature
- ¼ cup (1¾ ounces) granulated sugar
- 2 teaspoons table salt
- 13 tablespoons unsalted butter, cut into 13 pieces and softened

Vanilla Crust
- 1 cup (4 ounces) confectioners' sugar
- ¾ cup (4⅛ ounces) bread flour, plus extra for rolling
- 10 tablespoons (4 ounces) vegetable shortening
- 2 teaspoons vanilla extract
- ⅛ teaspoon table salt

1. Make Dough Whisk flour and yeast together in bowl of stand mixer. Whisk water and eggs in 4-cup liquid measuring cup until combined. Using dough hook on low speed, add water mixture to flour mixture and mix until cohesive dough starts to form and no dry flour remains, about 2 minutes, scraping down bowl as needed. Let rest for 15 minutes.

2. Add sugar and salt to dough and knead on medium-low speed until incorporated, about 30 seconds. Increase speed to medium and, with mixer running, add butter 1 piece at a time, allowing each piece to incorporate before adding next, 4 to 6 minutes total, scraping down bowl and dough hook as needed. Continue to knead until dough is elastic and pulls away cleanly from sides of bowl, about 10 minutes longer.

3. First Rise Transfer dough to greased large bowl or container; cover with greased plastic wrap; and let dough rise at room temperature until doubled in volume, about 1 hour.

4. Make Vanilla Crust While dough rises, combine all ingredients in clean, dry mixer bowl. Fit mixer with paddle attachment and mix on low speed, scraping down bowl as needed, until mixture is homogeneous and has texture of Play-Doh, about 2 minutes. Transfer mixture to counter and divide into 12 equal pieces. Roll into balls, place on large plate, and cover with plastic; refrigerate for 30 minutes. Draw or trace 4-inch circle in center of 1 side of zipper-lock bag. Cut open seams along both sides of bag, leaving bottom seam intact so bag opens completely; set aside.

5. Shape Dough Line 2 rimmed baking sheets with parchment paper. Transfer concha dough to clean counter and divide into 12 equal pieces. Cover loosely with greased plastic. Form 1 piece of dough into rough ball by bringing edges of dough together and pinching edges to seal so top is smooth. Place ball seam side down on clean counter and, using your cupped hand, drag in small circles until dough feels taut and round. Repeat with remaining dough pieces, scraping counter clean with bench scraper as needed (keep remaining pieces covered). Evenly space 6 dough balls on each prepared sheet. Poke any air bubbles in dough balls with tip of paring knife.

6. Second Rise Cover rolls loosely with greased plastic and let rise at room temperature until doubled in size, 1 to 1½ hours.

7. While rolls rise, place reserved cut bag marked side down on counter. Place ⅓ cup flour in small bowl; working with 1 ball of crust at a time, toss gently in flour to generously coat, then open bag and place ball in center of circle. Fold other side of bag over ball and, using glass pie plate or baking dish, gently press crust to 4-inch diameter, using circle drawn on bag as guide. Carefully peel bag away from crust to remove, then place crust on top of 1 ball of concha dough, pressing gently to mold crust to dough. Repeat with remaining balls of crust and remaining concha dough balls, wiping bag clean as needed. (Don't wait until after dough rises to top dough balls with crust.)

8. Using butter knife and pressing gently, score crust of each roll with series of concentric curved lines emanating from single point to create seashell pattern, being careful not to cut through topping completely.

9. Bake Adjust oven racks to upper-middle and lower-middle positions and heat oven to 350 degrees. Bake until buns are golden brown and register at least 205 degrees, 20 to 25 minutes, switching and rotating sheets halfway through baking. Transfer sheets to wire racks and let cool for 15 minutes. Serve.

Chocolate Conchas
Reduce bread flour in Vanilla Crust to ⅔ cup (3⅔ ounces) and add 3 tablespoons unsweetened cocoa powder.

Assembling Conchas

1. Toss ball of crust in flour.

2. Press crust into circle.

3. Place crust on top of concha.

4. Score pattern.

Chocolate-Dipped Potato Chip Cookies

MAKES 24 COOKIES

WHY THIS RECIPE WORKS They were conceived by potato chip companies decades ago in an effort to boost sales, and the salty-sweet morsels have stood the test of time. Surprisingly, we found that these buttery cookies are best when made with low-fat potato chips, and a rolling pin makes quick work of crushing them. For texture, we use both granulated and confectioners sugar in equal parts to get the best balance of shortness and chew.

Cape Cod 40% Reduced Fat Potato Chips is the test kitchen favorite among reduced-fat chips. In this recipe, they make for extremely crunchy cookies. To prevent sticking, dip the drinking glass in flour before flattening each cookie. Toast the pecans in a small, dry skillet over medium heat, shaking the skillet often, until they begin to darken, 3 to 5 minutes.

- ¾ cup (3¾ ounces/106 grams) all-purpose flour
- 1½ ounces (43 grams) reduced-fat potato chips, crushed fine (½ cup)
- ¼ cup pecans, toasted and chopped fine
- ¼ teaspoon table salt
- 8 tablespoons unsalted butter, cut into 8 pieces, softened but still cool
- ¼ cup (1¾ ounces/50 grams) granulated sugar
- ¼ cup (1 ounce/28 grams) confectioners' sugar
- 1 large egg yolk
- ½ teaspoon vanilla extract
- 8 ounces (227 grams) bittersweet chocolate (6 ounces/170 grams chopped fine, 2 ounces/57 grams grated)
- 1–2 teaspoons flake sea salt, such as Maldon

1. Adjust oven rack to middle position and heat oven to 350 degrees. Line 2 rimmed baking sheets with parchment paper. Combine flour, potato chips, pecans, and salt in bowl.

2. Using stand mixer fitted with paddle, beat butter, granulated sugar, and confectioners' sugar on medium-high speed until pale and fluffy, about 3 minutes. Add egg yolk and vanilla and beat until combined. Reduce speed to low and slowly add flour mixture in 3 additions. Roll dough into 1-inch balls and space 3 inches apart on baking sheets. Refrigerate dough until just firm, about 10 minutes. Flatten dough balls into 2-inch rounds (about ¼ inch thick) with bottom of floured drinking glass.

3. Bake, 1 sheet at a time, until cookies are just set and lightly browned on bottom, 10 to 13 minutes, rotating sheet halfway through baking. Let cookies cool completely on sheets, about 15 minutes.

4. Microwave chopped chocolate in bowl at 50 percent power, stirring often, until about two-thirds melted, 1 to 2 minutes. Remove bowl from microwave, add grated chocolate, and stir until fully melted, returning to microwave for no more than 5 seconds at a time to complete melting as needed. Carefully dip half of each cooled cookie in chocolate, scraping off excess with offset spatula, and place on parchment paper–lined baking sheet. Sprinkle flake salt over warm chocolate and refrigerate until chocolate sets, about 15 minutes. Serve. (Cookies can be stored in airtight container for up to 2 days.)

Use Reduced-Fat Chips

It's a tough job, but somebody has to do it: We fearlessly ate many batches of cookies baked with potato chips of every sort. In the end, we preferred reduced-fat chips in this recipe. Because of the extra oil, the edges of cookies made with ordinary fried chips get too dark before the cookie is fully baked. Also, some testers detected a disagreeable fried taste in cookies that were made with fried potato chips.

The American Table: Crazy for Chips

Today we've got sliders, kale chips, and cupcakes, to name a few, but food trends are nothing new. America's love affair with potato chips, for one, began more than 150 years ago when an enterprising chef at Moon's Lake House in Saratoga Springs, New York, sent thin slices of potato on a historic salty plunge into the deep-fryer and unwittingly changed the snack food business forever.

Saratoga Springs was (and is) a small, upstate town. But plenty of well-heeled New Yorkers relaxed there during the summer in the 1850s, which may account for the spotlight shone on the early chip.

"You begin to eat fried potatoes so soon as you arrive at the Lake; you continually eat them till you depart; and I have heard of ladies who have taken French cambric pocket-handkerchiefs full of fried potatoes home with them, and kept them under their pillows," British journalist George Augustus Sala wrote in *The Daily Telegraph*. (He was reporting on American manners and customs during the Civil War.)

"I have seen them eaten by ladies with lavender kid gloves on," he continued, "and they are so crisp and croquant and so clean-looking, that you generally dispense with a plate while eating them at dinner, and keep a pile of fried potatoes on the table-cloth by your side. They are eaten with fish, they are eaten with game, they are eaten with sherry-coblers, and they are eaten with ice-creams."

Reports appeared in *The New York Times* and *The Philadelphia Inquirer*, and the news traveled fast. In 1874, Chicago's *Pomeroy's Democrat* ran an article on eating-house slang in which the reporter learned that "Saratoga" had become kitchen code for orders of deep-fried potatoes.

Over the decades, that usage has been lost, but the snack it describes has gone on to global fame. You can munch on potato chips in China, India, the Middle East, Africa, and just about anywhere else, enjoying flavors as varied as lychee or hot chili–squid (no lavender kid gloves required). Nineteenth-century visitors to Saratoga Springs would be amazed.

SEASON 18

Chocolate-Marshmallow Sandwich Cookies

MAKES 12 SANDWICH COOKIES

WHY THIS RECIPE WORKS Our homemade MoonPies are a delicious construction of marshmallow layered between two graham cookies fully coated in a thin layer of chocolate. We made the cookies first, using an even mix of all-purpose and graham flours to give the cookies a slightly coarse texture and toasty flavor. Once the cookies cooled, we sandwiched homemade marshmallow between them, working quickly while the marshmallow was still warm and malleable. To ensure even distribution, we applied gentle pressure and a light twisting motion. Finally, we carefully melted our chocolate along with a tablespoon of coconut oil to help it maintain a spreadable and fluid consistency throughout the dipping process. We dipped the sandwich cookies and used an offset spatula to help smooth out the chocolate layer on the pies to achieve a consistently thin layer of chocolate all around. After 20 minutes in the refrigerator to let the chocolate set, this treat is ready to be devoured.

Graham flour, also known as stone-ground whole-wheat flour, is coarser and less processed than conventional whole-wheat flour. The marshmallow filling quickly starts to set after whipping, so have everything ready to assemble the cookies in step 7 before you begin.

Cookies

- 1¼ cups (6¼ ounces) all-purpose flour
- 1 cup plus 2 tablespoons (6¼ ounces) graham flour
- ¾ cup (5¼ ounces) sugar
- 1 teaspoon baking powder
- 1 teaspoon baking soda
- ¾ teaspoon table salt
- ¼ teaspoon ground cinnamon
- 12 tablespoons unsalted butter, melted and cooled
- 5 tablespoons water
- 2 tablespoons molasses
- 1 teaspoon vanilla extract

Filling

- 6 tablespoons water, divided
- 2 teaspoons unflavored gelatin
- ¼ cup light corn syrup
- ⅔ cup (4⅔ ounces) sugar
- ⅛ teaspoon table salt
- 1 teaspoon vanilla extract
- 12 ounces bittersweet chocolate (9 ounces chopped fine, 3 ounces grated)
- 1 tablespoon coconut oil

1. For the Cookies Adjust oven rack to middle position and heat oven to 350 degrees. Line 2 rimmed baking sheets with parchment paper. Whisk all-purpose flour, graham flour, sugar, baking powder, baking soda, salt, and cinnamon together in bowl of stand mixer. Add melted butter, water, molasses, and vanilla. Using paddle attachment, mix until dough comes together, about 20 seconds.

2. Transfer dough to counter and divide into 2 equal pieces. Working with 1 piece of dough at a time (keep remaining piece covered with plastic wrap), roll into 12-inch circle, ⅛ inch thick, between 2 large sheets of parchment. Remove top piece of parchment. Using 3-inch round cookie cutter, cut dough into 8 rounds; carefully transfer rounds to prepared sheets, spacing ½ inch apart. Gently reroll scraps into 8-inch circle, ⅛ inch thick, then cut into 4 rounds and transfer to sheets.

3. Bake cookies, 1 sheet at a time, until edges are set, about 10 minutes, rotating sheet halfway through baking. Transfer sheet to wire rack and let cookies cool completely. (Cookies can be stored in airtight container for up to 1 day.)

4. For the Filling Whisk 3 tablespoons water and gelatin together in clean, dry bowl of stand mixer fitted with whisk attachment. Let sit until very firm, about 5 minutes.

5. Meanwhile, combine corn syrup and remaining 3 tablespoons water in small saucepan. Pour sugar and salt into center of saucepan (do not let sugar hit saucepan

The Complete Cook's Country TV Show Cookbook

sides). Bring to boil over medium-high heat and cook, gently swirling saucepan, until sugar has dissolved completely and mixture registers 240 degrees, 4 to 6 minutes.

6. Turn mixer speed to low and carefully pour hot syrup into gelatin mixture, avoiding whisk and sides of bowl. Gradually increase speed to high and whip until mixture is very thick and stiff and coats whisk, about 7 minutes, scraping down bowl as needed. Add vanilla and mix until incorporated, about 15 seconds.

7. To assemble, place 12 cookies upside down on counter. Working with 1 cookie at a time, place 2 tablespoons marshmallow filling in center of cookie and spread evenly with back of spoon. Place second cookie on top of filling, right side up, and gently press and twist until filling is even with edges of cookies. Let sit for 15 minutes until filling is set.

8. Line baking sheet with clean sheet of parchment. Microwave chopped chocolate in medium bowl at 50 percent power, stirring often, until about two-thirds melted, 2 to 4 minutes. (Melted chocolate should not be much warmer than body temperature; check by holding bowl in palm of your hand.) Add grated chocolate and coconut oil and stir until smooth, returning to microwave for no more than 5 seconds at a time to finish melting if necessary.

9. Rotate filling-exposed side of 1 sandwich cookie in chocolate until filling and cookie edges are fully covered. Place sandwich cookie in chocolate and, using 2 forks, gently flip to fully coat all sides. Lift cookie out of chocolate with fork. Using offset spatula, spread chocolate on top of cookie into thin, even layer, allowing excess to run off sides. Tap fork against edge of bowl, then wipe underside of fork on edge of bowl to remove excess chocolate from bottom of cookie. Use second fork to slide sandwich cookie onto prepared sheet. Repeat with remaining sandwich cookies, returning chocolate to microwave for no more than 5 seconds at a time if it becomes too firm.

10. Refrigerate sandwich cookies until chocolate is set, about 20 minutes, before serving. (Sandwich cookies can be stored at room temperature for up to 2 days.)

Chocolate Brownie Cookies

MAKES 20 COOKIES

WHY THIS RECIPE WORKS We wanted cookies with all the best qualities of brownies—rich and chewy, with a deep chocolate flavor and a crackly, shiny top. To maximize the chocolate complexity, we used both melted bittersweet chocolate and cocoa powder, plus a good dose of salt. The key to chewiness was the right mix of butter and vegetable oil; and whipping the eggs and sugar together in a stand mixer delivered the shiny, crackly top, giving these cookies showstopping appeal.

We developed this recipe using Ghirardelli 60% Cacao Bittersweet Chocolate Premium Baking Bar and Droste Cacao Dutch-processed cocoa powder.

- 1 cup (5 ounces) all-purpose flour
- ¼ cup (¾ ounce) Dutch-processed cocoa powder
- 1 teaspoon baking powder
- ¼ teaspoon baking soda
- ¾ teaspoon table salt
- 10 ounces bittersweet chocolate, chopped, divided
- 3 tablespoons vegetable oil
- 1 tablespoon unsalted butter
- 2 tablespoons whole milk
- 1 cup (7 ounces) sugar
- 2 large eggs

1. Adjust oven racks to upper-middle and lower-middle positions and heat oven to 300 degrees. Line 2 rimmed baking sheets with parchment paper. Whisk flour, cocoa, baking powder, baking soda, and salt together in bowl; set aside.

2. Microwave 6 ounces chocolate, oil, and butter in medium bowl at 50 percent power, stirring halfway through microwaving, until melted, about 3 minutes. Whisk milk into chocolate mixture until combined.

3. Using stand mixer fitted with whisk attachment, whip sugar and eggs on medium-high speed until very thick and pale, about 4 minutes. Remove bowl from mixer. Add melted chocolate mixture and whisk by hand until uniform. Fold in flour mixture with silicone spatula until thoroughly combined and no dry pockets remain. Fold in remaining 4 ounces chocolate.

4. Using 1-tablespoon measure or #30 scoop, scoop 10 heaping-tablespoon portions of batter onto each prepared sheet (you should have 20 cookies total). (Use soupspoon to help scrape batter from tablespoon, if necessary.) Bake until cookies are puffed and covered with large cracks (cookies will look raw between cracks and seem underdone), about 16 minutes, switching and rotating sheets halfway through baking.

5. Let cookies cool completely on sheets, about 30 minutes. Slide thin spatula under cookies to remove from sheets. Serve. (Cookies can be stored in airtight container at room temperature for up to 3 days.)

> **Easy Melting**
> Microwave method: Chop chocolate and nuke on 50 percent power, stirring often, until no chunks remain.
>
> **Cooling Time**
> These cookies will look underbaked when you remove them from the oven. They'll firm up as they cool on the sheet for 30 minutes.
>
> **Sticky Batter?**
> Grease your portioning measure (a 1-tablespoon measure or #30 scoop) so the batter doesn't stick.
>
> **Two Fats**
> Vegetable oil and butter combine for the right mix of saturated and unsaturated fats to create the perfect chew.

SEASON 18

Rhubarb Shortcakes with Buttermilk Whipped Cream

SERVES 8

WHY THIS RECIPE WORKS Our rhubarb shortcake is a unique and delicious take on the classic strawberry shortcake. Rhubarb breaks down quickly when cooked, so we slowly baked it to keep its texture and shape. To balance rhubarb's distinct bitter taste, we added a carefully calibrated amount of sugar; we also added some lemon juice to brighten the flavor. For the rustic shortcakes, we used generous amounts of butter and buttermilk to give them a buttery, tangy flavor. We cut them into squares to minimize waste and squared off the edges to ensure that they puffed up and stayed square. Adding buttermilk to the whipped cream accentuated the tartness of the rhubarb, and omitting vanilla extract allowed the buttermilk's flavor to shine.

To highlight the red hue of the cooked rhubarb, we suggest looking for raw rhubarb that is mostly red. This recipe works best with rhubarb stalks that are ½ to ¾ inch thick. If stalks are thicker than 1 inch, cut them in half lengthwise before cutting them into ¾-inch pieces.

Rhubarb
- 2¼ pounds rhubarb, trimmed and cut into ¾-inch pieces
- 1¼ cups (8¾ ounces) sugar
- 2 teaspoons lemon juice
- ¼ teaspoon table salt

Shortcakes
- 2 cups (10 ounces) all-purpose flour
- ⅓ cup (2⅓ ounces) sugar, plus 2 teaspoons for sprinkling
- 1 tablespoon baking powder
- 1 teaspoon table salt
- 12 tablespoons cold butter, cut into ½-inch pieces, plus 2 tablespoons melted for brushing
- ½ cup plus 2 tablespoons buttermilk, chilled

Whipped Cream
- 1 cup heavy cream, chilled
- ½ cup buttermilk, chilled
- ⅓ cup (2⅓ ounces) sugar
- Pinch table salt

1. For the Rhubarb Adjust oven rack to upper-middle position and heat oven to 325 degrees. Toss all ingredients in large bowl until evenly combined. Arrange rhubarb mixture in even layer in 13 by 9-inch baking dish. Cover dish tightly with aluminum foil and bake for 20 minutes. Remove dish from oven and carefully remove foil. Stir rhubarb mixture and redistribute into even layer. Continue to bake, uncovered, until paring knife inserted into rhubarb meets little resistance, 30 to 35 minutes longer. Let rhubarb mixture cool completely in dish, about 1 hour. (Rhubarb can be refrigerated for up to 1 day and used chilled.)

2. For the Shortcakes While rhubarb cools, increase oven temperature to 425 degrees. Line rimmed baking sheet with parchment paper. Process flour, sugar, baking powder, and salt in food processor until combined, about 5 seconds. Scatter cold butter over top and pulse until mixture resembles coarse crumbs and butter pieces are no larger than peas, about 10 pulses. Add buttermilk and pulse until dough forms clumps and no dry flour remains, about 12 pulses, scraping down sides of bowl as needed.

3. Turn dough onto lightly floured counter and knead briefly until dough just comes together, about 3 turns. Using your lightly floured hands and bench scraper, shape dough into 8 by 4-inch rectangle, about 1¼ inches thick. Using sharp, floured bench scraper or chef's knife, trim no more than ⅛ inch dough from each side of rectangle to create even shape; discard dough scraps. Cut dough in half crosswise into two 4-inch squares, then cut each square into four 2-inch squares, flouring bench scraper or knife as needed.

4. Arrange dough squares at least 2 inches apart on prepared sheet. (Dough squares can be refrigerated, covered with plastic wrap, for up to 12 hours.)

5. Brush tops of dough squares with melted butter and sprinkle evenly with remaining 2 teaspoons sugar (¼ teaspoon each). Bake until tops of shortcakes are light golden brown, 10 to 14 minutes, rotating sheet halfway through baking. Transfer shortcakes to wire rack and let cool completely before filling, about 10 minutes. (Fully cooled shortcakes can be wrapped tightly in plastic wrap and stored at room temperature for up to 1 day.)

6. For the Whipped Cream Using stand mixer fitted with whisk attachment, whip cream, buttermilk, sugar, and salt on medium-low speed until foamy, about 1 minute. Increase speed to high and whip until stiff peaks form, 1 to 3 minutes.

7. Using serrated knife, split shortcakes in half horizontally, then place bottoms on serving plates. Divide rhubarb mixture evenly over bottoms, dollop with whipped cream, and top with shortcake tops. Serve immediately.

Strawberry-Elderflower Rhubarb Shortcakes with Buttermilk Whipped Cream

Reduce sugar in rhubarb mixture to ½ cup and increase lemon juice to 1 tablespoon. Add ½ cup strawberry jam and 3 tablespoons elderflower liqueur to rhubarb mixture when tossing ingredients in large bowl in step 1.

Cutting Square Shortcakes

1. Using your lightly floured hands and bench scraper, shape dough into 8 by 4-inch rectangle, about 1¼ inches thick.

2. Using sharp, floured bench scraper or chef's knife, trim no more than ⅛ inch dough from each side of rectangle to create even shape; discard dough scraps.

3. Cut dough in half crosswise into two 4-inch squares, then cut each square into four 2-inch squares, flouring bench scraper or knife as needed.

SEASON 18

Aunt Jule's Pie

SERVES 8

WHY THIS RECIPE WORKS In the *Cook's Country* archives, we used to have a recipe for Jefferson Davis Pie. We learned that this pie, named after the Confederate general, was most likely invented by, and should have been attributed to, an enslaved woman, Aunt Jule. So we asked baker and activist Arley Bell to redevelop our old pie recipe. And we've named it after the woman who deserves the credit. Per a suggestion from Arley Bell's husband, we love serving this pie with Bourbon Whipped Cream (page 686) made with Uncle Nearest Bourbon.

- 1 recipe Single-Crust Pie Dough (page 670)
- 8 tablespoons unsalted butter
- ½ cup golden raisins
- ½ cup pitted dates
- ½ cup pecans, toasted and roughly chopped
- ¾ teaspoon table salt, divided
- 1 cup packed (7 ounces) light brown sugar
- 3 tablespoons all-purpose flour
- ½ teaspoon ground nutmeg
- ¼ teaspoon ground allspice
- 5 large egg yolks
- 1¼ cups heavy cream
- 1 teaspoon cider vinegar

1. Roll dough into 12-inch circle on floured counter. Loosely roll dough around rolling pin and gently unroll it onto 9-inch pie plate, letting excess dough hang over edge. Ease dough into plate by gently lifting edge of dough with your hand while pressing into plate bottom with your other hand.

2. Trim overhang to ½ inch beyond lip of plate. Tuck overhang under itself; folded edge should be flush with edge of plate. Crimp dough evenly around edge of plate. Wrap dough-lined plate loosely in plastic wrap and refrigerate until firm, about 30 minutes. Adjust oven rack to bottom position and heat oven to 325 degrees.

3. Melt butter in 8-inch skillet over medium heat. Cook, swirling skillet constantly, until solids turn color of milk chocolate and have toasty aroma, 3 to 5 minutes. Immediately remove skillet from heat and scrape browned butter into small heatproof bowl; set aside to cool.

4. Combine raisins, dates, pecans, and ¼ teaspoon salt in food processor and process until finely ground, about 30 seconds.

5. Combine brown sugar, flour, nutmeg, allspice, and remaining ½ teaspoon salt in large bowl. Add browned butter and whisk until fully combined. Whisk in egg yolks until fully combined. Whisk in cream and vinegar.

6. Press nut and fruit mixture into bottom of chilled pie crust. Pour custard over top. Transfer to oven and bake until center of pie registers 185 to 190 degrees and is set (filling will jiggle slightly when pie is shaken), about 1 hour. Let pie cool on wire rack until set, at least 4 hours. Serve.

SEASON 18

Peach Ripple Ice Cream

SERVES 8 (MAKES ABOUT 1 QUART)

WHY THIS RECIPE WORKS For a peach ice cream that screams peach, a no-custard base was essential to let the delicate fruit flavor come through. A combination of fresh and cooked peaches yielded juicy peach aroma and flavor that permeated each spoonful. Using half-and-half gave the base a creamy consistency while tangy sour cream complemented the natural piquancy of peaches. To keep the ice cream base largely free from ice crystals, light corn syrup did just the trick. Jammy ribbons of peach ripple layered through the ice cream were the perfect accent to highlight the zingy peach flavor without disrupting the smooth texture of the ice cream.

We recommend using ripe, in-season peaches for this recipe, but you can substitute 3 cups of frozen sliced peaches. The vodka helps reduce iciness in the ice cream. You can omit it if you like, but note that the ice cream will be icier and not as soft. An instant-read thermometer is critical for the best results. Using a prechilled metal loaf pan and working quickly in step 5 will help prevent melting and refreezing of the ice cream and will speed the hardening process. If using a canister-style ice cream maker, be sure to freeze the empty canister at least 24 hours and preferably 48 hours before churning. For self-refrigerating ice cream makers, prechill the canister by running the machine for 5 to 10 minutes before pouring in the custard.

- 1½ pounds ripe peaches, peeled, halved, pitted, and cut into ½-inch pieces (about 3 cups)
- 1⅔ cups (11⅔ ounces) sugar, divided
- ½ teaspoon plus 2 tablespoons lemon juice, divided
- Pinch table salt
- 1½ cups half-and-half
- ¾ cup sour cream
- ⅓ cup light corn syrup
- 2 tablespoons vodka

1. Place 8½ by 4½-inch loaf pan in freezer. Combine peaches, ½ cup sugar, ½ teaspoon lemon juice, and salt in bowl; let sit until about ½ cup liquid accumulates in bowl and peaches soften slightly, 1 to 1½ hours. Drain peaches in fine-mesh strainer set over second bowl. Reserve ½ cup liquid; discard remaining liquid.

2. Process drained peaches in blender until smooth, about 1 minute. Transfer ½ cup peach puree to small saucepan; reserve remaining puree. Add ½ cup sugar and remaining 2 tablespoons lemon juice to saucepan and bring mixture to boil over medium heat. Cook, stirring and scraping bottom of saucepan constantly with rubber spatula, until mixture turns deep orange color, becomes translucent, and registers 218 to 220 degrees, 6 to 8 minutes. Transfer cooked peach mixture to bowl; let cool slightly, cover, and refrigerate until needed.

3. Bring reserved drained peach liquid to simmer in now-empty saucepan over medium heat and cook, stirring often, until liquid is thick and syrupy and registers 218 to 220 degrees, 6 to 8 minutes. Transfer syrup to large bowl. Add half-and-half, sour cream, corn syrup, vodka, remaining ⅔ cup sugar, and remaining reserved uncooked peach puree and whisk until smooth, about 30 seconds. Cover and refrigerate ice cream base until temperature registers 40 degrees, about 4 hours. (Chilled mixture can be refrigerated for up to 24 hours.)

4. Transfer ice cream base to ice cream maker and churn until mixture resembles thick soft-serve ice cream, 25 to 30 minutes.

5. Spread one-third of ice cream in even layer in prepared loaf pan. Drizzle one-third of reserved cooked peach mixture evenly over ice cream. Repeat 2 more times with remaining ice cream and peach mixture. Drag skewer through ice cream (in rough zigzag and circular patterns all the way to bottom of pan) to create swirls. Freeze ice cream until firm, at least 2 hours. Serve.

How to Ripple

1. Spread one-third of ice cream in even layer in pan.

2. Drizzle one-third of cooked peach mixture over ice cream.

3. Repeat spreading ice cream and drizzling with peach mixture 2 more times.

4. Drag skewer through ice cream, touching bottom of pan, to create swirls.

SEASON 18

Coquito

SERVES 8 TO 10

WHY THIS RECIPE WORKS "Coquito" means "little coconut" in Spanish, and many families with Latin American heritage make their own treasured version of this celebratory holiday recipe. This one is based on a Puerto Rican cocktail, served over ice—but some folks swear by drinking it chilled, without ice. It's your call! It packs plenty of creamy coconut richness with both a can of coconut milk and a can of cream of coconut. A modest amount of golden rum adds spirited punch, and vanilla, cinnamon, and nutmeg provide warm spiciness. Blending the drink right before serving time ensures that everything is fully combined; plus, it gives the cocktail a delightful slight frothiness.

We tested this recipe using Coco López brand cream of coconut, which is often found in the soda and drink-mix aisle of the grocery store.

- 1 (15-ounce) can cream of coconut
- 1 (14-ounce) can coconut milk
- 1 (12-ounce) can evaporated milk
- 1¼ cups gold rum
- 1 teaspoon vanilla extract
- ½ teaspoon ground cinnamon
- ¼ teaspoon ground nutmeg, plus extra for serving

1. Whisk all ingredients together in large pitcher until combined. Refrigerate for at least 1 hour or up to 3 days.

2. Just before serving, working in batches, transfer cream of coconut mixture to blender and process until slightly frothy, about 1 minute per batch. Serve over ice, garnished with extra nutmeg.

> **Cream of Coconut**
> Not to be confused with coconut cream—the heavy, rich layer of cream that rises to the top of coconut milk after it sits for a while—cream of coconut is a heavily sweetened, emulsified product used in desserts and cocktail mixes. You still need to whisk it up or vigorously shake it to reincorporate. Cream of coconut provides enough sweetness for this drink that no additional sugar is needed.

116 *The Complete Cook's Country TV Show Cookbook*

as good as grandma's

120 Old-Fashioned Chicken Noodle Soup	**140** Chicken Florentine
120 Slow-Cooker Chicken Stock	**141** One-Pot Chicken Jardinière
122 Chicken and Pastry	**142** Double-Crust Chicken Pot Pie
123 Classic Tomato Soup	**143** Glazed Meatloaf
124 Best Potluck Macaroni and Cheese	**145** Frosted Meatloaf
124 Pimento Mac and Cheese	**145** Meatloaf with Mushroom Gravy
126 Macaroni and Cheese with Tomatoes	**146** Bacon-Wrapped Meatloaf
127 Cheeseburger Mac	**148** Ground Beef Stroganoff
128 Creamy Cheese Grits	**148** Salisbury Steak
129 Extra-Cheesy Grits	**149** Tater Tot Hotdish
129 Strawberry Pretzel Salad	**150** Swiss Steak with Tomato Gravy
130 Roasted Green Beans with Goat Cheese and Hazelnuts	**151** Jamaican Oxtail
132 Classic Tuna Salad	**152** Jamaican Rice and Peas
132 Green Goddess Dressing	**153** Olympia Provisions–Style Choucroute Garnie
133 Green Goddess Roast Chicken	**155** Milk-Can Supper
134 Cast Iron Baked Chicken	**156** Pan-Fried Pork Chops
135 One-Batch Fried Chicken	**157** Pan-Fried Pork Chops with Milk Gravy
136 Southern-Style Smothered Chicken	**157** Smothered Pork Chops
137 Chicken Paprikash and Buttered Spaetzle	**158** Cider-Braised Pork Chops
138 Hot-Honey Chicken	**159** Crispy Fried Shrimp
139 Chicken Divan	**160** Crispy Fish Sticks with Tartar Sauce
	161 Lemonade with Honey

Recipe Photos (from left to right): Crispy Fried Shrimp; Classic Tuna Salad

Old-Fashioned Chicken Noodle Soup

SERVES 4 TO 6

WHY THIS RECIPE WORKS There's nothing more comforting when you're feeling under the weather than a warm bowl of chicken noodle soup. This easy recipe is deeply flavorful and starts by browning bone-in chicken parts then simmering them in store-bought chicken broth, which created an intensely savory base. A standard mix of onion, celery, and carrot simmered with the chicken enhanced the broth's richness. Though egg noodles are common in homemade chicken noodle soup, we preferred spaghetti broken into bite-size pieces that cooked right in the soup. The final product gave a nostalgic nod to canned versions but had loads more flavor.

If you prefer, 4 ounces (2 cups) of egg noodles can be substituted for the spaghetti. Fresh dill can be substituted for the parsley.

- 1½ pounds bone-in chicken breasts and/or thighs, trimmed
- ½ teaspoon table salt, divided
- ¼ teaspoon pepper
- 1 tablespoon vegetable oil
- 8 cups chicken broth
- 1 onion, chopped
- 1 carrot, peeled and cut into ½-inch pieces
- 1 celery rib, cut into ½-inch pieces
- 2 sprigs fresh thyme
- 1 bay leaf
- 5 ounces spaghetti, broken into 1-inch pieces (1½ cups)
- 1 tablespoon minced fresh parsley

1. Pat chicken dry with paper towels and sprinkle with ¼ teaspoon salt and pepper. Heat oil in Dutch oven over medium-high heat until shimmering. Cook chicken until well browned all over, 8 to 10 minutes.

2. Add broth, onion, carrot, celery, thyme sprigs, bay leaf, and remaining ¼ teaspoon salt, scraping up any browned bits. Bring to boil, cover, and reduce heat to low. Simmer until breasts register 160 degrees and/or thighs register at least 175 degrees, 14 to 17 minutes.

3. Remove pot from heat; discard thyme sprigs and bay leaf. Transfer chicken to plate and let cool slightly. Using 2 forks, shred chicken into bite-size pieces; discard skin and bones.

4. Return soup to boil over medium-high heat and add pasta. Cook, uncovered, until pasta is tender, 9 to 11 minutes, stirring often. Add chicken and parsley and cook until chicken is warmed through, about 2 minutes. Season with salt and pepper to taste. Serve.

The American Table: Campbell's Noodle with Chicken Soup

Time was, radio advertisements weren't prerecorded interruptions; rather, a host would simply take a moment out of the show to read some copy prepared by the sponsor. Sometimes, this would lead to misreadings. So it went in 1938, when a radio host misread his script touting "Campbell's Noodle with Chicken Soup," instead calling it "Chicken Noodle Soup." Campbell's wasn't happy, but consumers loved the catchy name: Thousands thought this was a new product and soon started asking for it at local grocers. What could have been a disaster quickly became a boon—rather than fight the tide, Campbell's changed the product name and the packaging, and sales took off. Today, Campbell's sells nearly 200 million cans of the stuff each year, and its iconic label remains one of the most recognizable in American supermarkets. And while the name may have changed, the company's slogan has remained the same since the product was introduced in 1934: "M'm! M'm! Good!"

Slow-Cooker Chicken Stock

MAKES ABOUT 3 QUARTS

WHY THIS RECIPE WORKS Homemade stock tastes a lot better than even the best store-bought broths. This rich, savory stock is remarkably easy in the slow cooker. We piled vegetables and leftover cooked chicken bones in cold water, added seasonings, and set it on high. The slow cooker prevented evaporation, so the bones remained submerged. Refrigerating the strained stock allowed the fat to rise to the top and solidify, making it easy to discard.

This stock is great to use in any of our recipes calling for chicken broth. You can freeze chicken carcasses one at a time until you have the 2½ pounds needed for this recipe; three to four rotisserie chicken carcasses or one 6-pound roaster carcass will weigh about 2½ pounds. This recipe was developed using bones from cooked chicken. Buy fresh carrots with greens attached for the best flavor. Buy loose celery heads, not bagged celery heads or hearts.

- 3 quarts water
- 2½ pounds roasted chicken bones
- 1 onion, chopped
- 2 carrots, peeled and cut into 1-inch chunks
- 2 celery ribs, chopped
- 1 teaspoon black peppercorns
- 1 teaspoon table salt
- 1 bay leaf

1. Place all ingredients in slow cooker. Cover and cook on high for 8 to 10 hours.

2. Let stock cool slightly, then strain through fine-mesh strainer set over large bowl. Use immediately or let cool completely, then refrigerate until cold. (When cold, surface fat will solidify and can be easily removed with spoon. Stock will keep, refrigerated, for up to 5 days, or frozen for up to 2 months.)

Stock Storage

Frozen homemade chicken stock lasts for up to two months. Freeze small and medium amounts in ice cube trays or muffin tins; once frozen, pop out the stock blocks and keep them in zipper-lock bags for easy access when making pan sauces or gravy. Freeze larger amounts in plastic quart containers or zipper-lock bags, which are easy to stack in crowded freezers.

SMALL AMOUNTS | MEDIUM AMOUNTS | LARGE AMOUNTS

Old-Fashioned Chicken Noodle Soup

Slow-Cooker Chicken Stock

Chicken and Pastry

Classic Tomato Soup

Chicken and Pastry
SERVES 4 TO 6

WHY THIS RECIPE WORKS We first ate "Chicken and Pastry" at Red's Little Schoolhouse in Grady, Alabama. It features tender shreds of chicken and chewy bites of pastry in an ultrasavory stock. To prepare a flavorful base, we browned chicken thighs before pouring in broth and water. For the trademark pastry dumplings, we took a cue from Edna Lewis and cut the dough into diamond shapes to give this homey dish a touch of style. Once stirred in and simmered, the pastry became tender and its starch thickened the soup, making it rich and velvety.

Keep the root ends of the onion halves intact so the petals don't separate during cooking and the onion is easy to remove from the pot.

- 1½ cups (7½ ounces) all-purpose flour
- 2 teaspoons baking powder
- ½ teaspoon table salt
- 1 teaspoon pepper, divided
- ½ cup milk
- 2 tablespoons unsalted butter, melted, plus 1 tablespoon unsalted butter
- 2 pounds bone-in chicken thighs, trimmed
- 4 cups chicken broth
- 1 cup water
- 1 onion, peeled and halved through root end
- 1 celery rib, halved crosswise

1. Combine flour, baking powder, salt, and ½ teaspoon pepper in large bowl. Combine milk and melted butter in second bowl (butter may form clumps). Using rubber spatula, stir milk mixture into flour mixture until just incorporated. Turn dough out onto lightly floured counter and knead until no flour streaks remain, about 1 minute. Return dough to large bowl, cover with plastic wrap, and set aside.

2. Pat chicken dry with paper towels and sprinkle with remaining ½ teaspoon pepper. Melt remaining 1 tablespoon butter in Dutch oven over medium-high heat. Add chicken, skin side down, and cook until golden brown, 3 to 5 minutes. Flip chicken and continue to cook until golden brown on second side, 3 to 5 minutes longer.

3. Add broth and water, scraping up any browned bits. Nestle onion and celery into pot and bring to boil. Reduce heat to low, cover, and simmer for 25 minutes.

4. Meanwhile, roll dough into 12-inch square, about ⅛ inch thick. Using pizza cutter or knife, cut dough lengthwise into 1-inch-wide strips, then cut diagonally into 1-inch-wide strips to form diamonds (pieces around edges will not be diamonds; this is OK).

5. Remove pot from heat. Transfer chicken to plate and let cool slightly. Discard onion and celery. Return broth to boil over medium-high heat and add pastry. Reduce heat to low, cover, and simmer, stirring occasionally, until pastry is tender and puffed, about 15 minutes. While pastry cooks, shred chicken into bite-size pieces, discarding skin and bones.

6. Stir chicken into stew and cook, uncovered, until warmed through and stew has thickened slightly, 2 to 4 minutes. Season with salt and pepper to taste. Serve.

The American Table: Southern Cooking with Style

A descendant of formerly enslaved people, Edna Lewis grew up on a subsistence farm in rural Virginia and had made a life as a farmer, a seamstress, and a celebrated New York City chef before legendary cookbook editor Judith Jones convinced her to compile her recipes and share her wisdom. That book, *The Taste of Country Cooking* (1976), became a cornerstone of the American cookbook shelf; Julia Child, Alice Waters, and Craig Claiborne praised its pure recipes and intimate tone.

At Café Nicholson in New York, where she cooked in the 1950s, Lewis was known for comforting meals (roast chicken was a specialty) presented with a chic flourish (cheese soufflé on the side). It was this sense of style that inspired her to cut her dumplings into diamond shapes, as we do in our Chicken and Pastry; it's a bit of elegance in a dish whose mission is to deliver deep homespun flavor.

Edna Lewis died in 2006, having emphatically accomplished the goal she articulated to the *New York Times* in 1989: "As a child in Virginia, I thought all food tasted delicious. After growing up, I didn't think food tasted the same, so it has been my lifelong effort to try and recapture those good flavors of the past."

Classic Tomato Soup

SERVES 6 TO 8

WHY THIS RECIPE WORKS We were shocked that the key to a satiny, well-balanced classic tomato soup turned out to be just ½ teaspoon of baking soda, which also helped neutralize the metallic taste and acidity of the canned tomatoes. To enhance the tomatoes' complexity, we browned most of them in a Dutch oven to concentrate their flavor—and saved some to add at the end of cooking to keep the soup fresh. We were tempted to add a variety of classic seasonings—but found that they made the soup taste like marinara sauce. Tasters were most satisfied with a single bay leaf, chicken broth, and the richness of heavy cream.

Use unseasoned canned tomatoes.

- 2 (28-ounce) cans diced tomatoes
- ¾ cup low-sodium chicken broth
- 3 tablespoons unsalted butter
- 1 onion, chopped
- 1 bay leaf
- 1 teaspoon brown sugar
- 2 tablespoons tomato paste
- 2 tablespoons all-purpose flour
- ½ teaspoon baking soda
- ½ teaspoon table salt
- ½ cup heavy cream

1. Drain tomatoes in colander set over large bowl, pressing lightly to release juices. Transfer tomato juice and chicken broth to large measuring cup (mixture should measure about 4 cups); reserve.

2. Melt butter in Dutch oven over medium heat. Add onion and cook until softened, about 5 minutes. Add two-thirds of drained tomatoes, bay leaf, and brown sugar and cook, stirring occasionally, until tomatoes begin to brown, about 15 minutes.

3. Add tomato paste and flour to pot and cook, stirring frequently, until paste begins to darken, 1 to 2 minutes. Slowly stir in reserved tomato juice–broth mixture, remaining tomatoes, baking soda, and salt and bring to boil. Reduce heat to medium-low and simmer until slightly thickened, about 5 minutes. Remove from heat.

4. Discard bay leaf. Puree soup in batches. Return pureed soup to pot and stir in cream. Season with salt and pepper to taste. Serve. (Soup can be refrigerated for 3 days.)

Best Potluck Macaroni and Cheese

SERVES 8 TO 10

WHY THIS RECIPE WORKS We can thank James Hemings, the enslaved French-trained chef of Thomas Jefferson, for helping to make macaroni and cheese so popular today. Early recipes consisted of pasta, cheese, and butter, but Hemings' version included cream, turning it into a rich baked casserole that was served at the White House. Our recipe follows the creamy tradition, incorporating evaporated milk and American cheese; the stabilizers in these ingredients kept the sauce from breaking, so it emerged from the oven satiny smooth.

Block American cheese from the deli counter is best here, as prewrapped singles result in a drier macaroni and cheese.

- 4 slices hearty white sandwich bread, torn into quarters
- 4 tablespoons unsalted butter, melted, plus 4 tablespoons unsalted butter
- ¼ cup grated Parmesan cheese
- 1 pound elbow macaroni
- 2 teaspoons table salt, plus salt for cooking pasta
- 5 tablespoons all-purpose flour
- 3 (12-ounce) cans evaporated milk
- 2 teaspoons hot sauce
- 1 teaspoon dry mustard
- ⅛ teaspoon ground nutmeg
- 8 ounces extra-sharp cheddar cheese, shredded (2 cups)
- 5 ounces American cheese, shredded (1¼ cups)
- 3 ounces Monterey Jack cheese, shredded (¾ cup)

1. Adjust oven rack to middle position and heat oven to 350 degrees. Pulse bread, melted butter, and Parmesan in food processor until ground to coarse crumbs, about 8 pulses. Transfer to bowl.

2. Bring 4 quarts water to boil in large pot. Add macaroni and 1 tablespoon salt and cook, stirring often, until just al dente, about 6 minutes. Reserve ½ cup macaroni cooking water, then drain and rinse macaroni in colander under cold running water. Set aside.

3. Melt remaining 4 tablespoons butter in now-empty pot over medium-high heat. Stir in flour and cook, stirring constantly, until mixture turns light brown, about 1 minute. Slowly whisk in evaporated milk, hot sauce, mustard, nutmeg, and 2 teaspoons salt and cook until mixture begins to simmer and is slightly thickened, about 4 minutes. Off heat, whisk in cheeses and reserved cooking water until cheese melts. Stir in macaroni until completely coated.

4. Transfer mixture to 13 by 9-inch baking dish and top evenly with bread-crumb mixture. Bake until cheese is bubbling around edges and top is golden brown, 20 to 25 minutes. Let sit for 5 to 10 minutes before serving.

To Make Ahead The macaroni and cheese can be made in advance through step 3. Increase amount of reserved macaroni cooking water to 1 cup. Scrape mixture into 13 by 9-inch baking dish, cool, lay plastic wrap directly on surface of pasta, and refrigerate for up to 1 day. Breadcrumb mixture may be refrigerated for up to 2 days. When ready to bake, remove plastic, cover with aluminum foil, and bake for 30 minutes. Uncover, sprinkle bread crumbs over top, and bake until topping is golden brown, about 20 minutes longer. Let sit before serving.

Pimento Mac and Cheese

SERVES 8 TO 10

WHY THIS RECIPE WORKS Pimento cheese is an American favorite, especially in the South, but it's often relegated to sandwiches or crackers. To expand its range, we aimed to add it to macaroni and cheese. Folding store-bought pimento cheese into our macaroni and cheese recipe resulted in a broken sauce. Instead, we made a flavored béchamel, a thickened milk sauce, to help us control the amount of fat in the sauce and prevent breaking. Adding the cheese to the sauce before adding the macaroni also reduced the risk of it breaking. For a flavor punch, we turned to pungent dry mustard, savory Worcestershire sauce, black pepper, and hot sauce. For color, we relied on a cup of minced ruby-red pimentos.

We developed this recipe with Frank's RedHot Original Cayenne Pepper Sauce. Creamette makes our favorite elbow macaroni.

- 1 pound elbow macaroni
- ½ teaspoon table salt, plus salt for cooking pasta
- ¾ teaspoon pepper
- 3 tablespoons unsalted butter
- 2 tablespoons all-purpose flour
- 1 tablespoon dry mustard

- 2 cups whole milk
- 2 cups heavy cream
- 1 pound extra-sharp cheddar cheese, shredded (4 cups)
- 2 ounces cream cheese
- 2 tablespoons hot sauce
- 1 tablespoon Worcestershire sauce
- 3 (4-ounce) jars pimentos, drained, patted dry, and minced

1. Adjust oven rack to upper-middle position and heat oven to 375 degrees. Bring 4 quarts water to boil in Dutch oven. Add macaroni and 1 tablespoon salt and cook for 5 minutes. Drain macaroni; set aside.

2. Add butter to now-empty pot and melt over medium-high heat. Stir in flour, mustard, pepper, and salt and cook until mixture is fragrant and bubbling, about 30 seconds. Slowly whisk in milk and cream and bring to boil. Reduce heat to medium-low and simmer until sauce is thick enough to coat back of spoon, about 2 minutes, whisking frequently.

3. Remove pot from heat. Add 3 cups cheddar, cream cheese, hot sauce, and Worcestershire to sauce and whisk until cheese is melted. Add pimentos and macaroni and stir until macaroni is thoroughly coated in sauce. Transfer to 13 by 9-inch baking dish and sprinkle with remaining 1 cup cheddar. Bake until edges are lightly browned and filling is bubbling, 18 to 20 minutes. Let rest for 20 minutes. Serve.

To Make Ahead Fully assembled casserole can be wrapped tightly in plastic wrap and refrigerated for up to 24 hours. When ready to serve, remove plastic and bake until heated through, 40 to 45 minutes.

The Trouble with Aged Cheese

Aged cheeses such as cheddar are notoriously difficult to melt smoothly. That's because the aging process causes the cheese to lose a lot of water, which allows its protein clusters to move closer together and form stronger bonds. Cheddar also contains a lot of fat. This fat can melt long before the protein begins to flow, resulting in a separation of the fat and protein—a greasy, messy problem known as "breaking." Our recipe minimizes breaking by stabilizing the cheddar with flour. The starch in the flour coats the protein clusters, preventing them from coming apart and releasing droplets of fat as they melt.

Best Potluck Macaroni and Cheese

Pimento Mac and Cheese

Macaroni and Cheese with Tomatoes

Macaroni and Cheese with Tomatoes

SERVES 8 TO 10

WHY THIS RECIPE WORKS To pack our mac with bright tomato flavor, we discovered that undercooking the pasta and adding petite canned diced tomatoes with their juices to the drained macaroni allowed the pasta to soak up more of the tomato flavor. Finally, to avoid a curdled sauce, we added fat in the form of half-and-half (cut with some chicken broth) and a mix of sharp and mild cheddar cheeses.

Let the finished dish rest for 10 to 15 minutes before you serve it; otherwise, it will be soupy.

- 1 pound elbow macaroni
- 1 teaspoon table salt, plus salt for cooking pasta
- 1 (28-ounce) can petite diced tomatoes
- 6 tablespoons unsalted butter
- 1/2 cup all-purpose flour
- 1/4 teaspoon cayenne pepper
- 4 cups half-and-half
- 1 cup chicken broth
- 1 pound mild cheddar cheese, shredded (4 cups)
- 8 ounces sharp cheddar cheese, shredded (2 cups)
- 1 teaspoon pepper

1. Adjust oven rack to middle position and heat oven to 400 degrees. Bring 4 quarts water to boil in large Dutch oven. Add macaroni and 1 tablespoon salt and cook, stirring often, until just al dente, about 6 minutes. Drain pasta and return to pot. Pour diced tomatoes with their juices over pasta and stir to coat. Cook over medium-high heat, stirring occasionally, until most of liquid is absorbed, about 5 minutes. Set aside.

2. Meanwhile, melt butter in medium saucepan over medium heat. Stir in flour and cayenne and cook until golden, about 1 minute. Slowly whisk in half-and-half and broth until smooth. Bring to boil, reduce heat to medium, and simmer, stirring occasionally, until mixture is slightly thickened, about 15 minutes. Off heat, whisk in cheeses, 1 teaspoon salt, and pepper until cheeses melt. Pour sauce over macaroni and stir to combine.

3. Scrape mixture into 13 by 9-inch baking dish set in rimmed baking sheet and bake until top begins to brown, 15 to 20 minutes. Let sit for 10 to 15 minutes before serving.

An Automat Classic

Home cooks have long put their stamp on plain macaroni and cheese, but one appealing, old-fashioned variation is practically endangered: baked macaroni and cheese with tomatoes. In this version, the bright acid of the tomato cuts the richness of the cheese. Today, people of a certain age remember tomato mac and cheese from Horn and Hardart's automats.

Automats started in Germany in 1896 as a way to quickly feed hundreds of thousands of workers during their lunch hour. Rather than ordering their meals through a server, patrons would drop coins into a slot to open a glass door in front of a compartment holding a menu item. Frank Hardart brought back the automat idea after a visit to Germany. Hardart, along with his partner, Joseph B. Horn, hired an engineer to simplify the German system so they could turn their traditional lunch counter into an automat in 1902. Automats may be a thing of the past, but a good recipe for macaroni and cheese shouldn't be.

To Make Ahead The macaroni and cheese can be made in advance through step 2. Scrape mixture into 13 by 9-inch baking dish, cool, lay plastic wrap directly on surface of pasta, and refrigerate for up to 2 days. When ready to bake, remove plastic, cover with aluminum foil, and bake for 30 minutes. Uncover and bake until top is golden brown, about 15 minutes. Let sit for 10 to 15 minutes before serving.

Cheeseburger Mac
SERVES 4 TO 6

WHY THIS RECIPE WORKS One bite of this cheeseburger mac and you'll never buy the boxed stuff again. We soaked the ground beef briefly in a baking soda solution to keep it tender while we cooked it on the stovetop, making sure to sear it for deep, burger-like flavor. For the macaroni, we cooked the pasta right in the skillet with just enough milk and water to cook it to al dente. The best part of a cheeseburger is the toppings, which we didn't skimp on here. Stirring American and cheddar cheese, ketchup, mustard, pickles, and chopped raw onion into the pasta gave it all the familiar burger flavors, while a splash of Worcestershire sauce boosted the meatiness. A short stint under the broiler browned and bubbled the cheese, making this mac look as irresistible as it tastes.

Tossing the beef with the baking soda solution in step 1 helps keep it tender.

- 1½ tablespoons plus 1½ cups water, divided
- 1 teaspoon table salt, divided
- 1 teaspoon pepper
- ½ teaspoon baking soda
- 1 pound 85 percent lean ground beef
- 1 tablespoon vegetable oil
- 8 ounces (2 cups) elbow macaroni
- 1 cup whole milk
- 8 ounces American cheese, chopped (2 cups), divided
- 8 ounces sharp cheddar cheese, shredded (2 cups), divided
- ½ cup finely chopped onion, plus extra for serving
- ¼ cup finely chopped dill pickles, plus extra for serving
- 2 tablespoons ketchup
- 2 tablespoons yellow mustard
- 1 tablespoon Worcestershire sauce

Cheeseburger Mac

1. Stir 1½ tablespoons water, ½ teaspoon salt, pepper, and baking soda in medium bowl until baking soda and salt are dissolved. Add beef and mix until thoroughly combined. Let sit for 15 minutes.

2. Heat oil in 12-inch broiler-safe skillet over medium-high heat until just smoking. Add beef and cook, breaking up meat with wooden spoon, until well browned, 6 to 8 minutes.

3. Add macaroni, milk, and remaining 1½ cups water and bring to simmer. Cover; reduce heat to medium-low; and cook until macaroni is al dente, about 5 minutes, stirring halfway through cooking.

4. Adjust oven rack 6 inches from broiler element and heat broiler. Stir 1½ cups American cheese, 1½ cups cheddar, onion, pickles, ketchup, mustard, Worcestershire, and remaining ½ teaspoon salt into macaroni until fully combined and cheese is melted, about 2 minutes.

5. Off heat, sprinkle remaining ½ cup American cheese and remaining ½ cup cheddar over top of macaroni. Broil until spotty brown, about 2 minutes. Let cool for 5 minutes. Sprinkle with extra onion and pickles. Serve.

Creamy Cheese Grits

Extra-Cheesy Grits

Creamy Cheese Grits
SERVES 4 TO 6

WHY THIS RECIPE WORKS Grits are a Southern staple, but their appeal can be lost in bland, gluey incarnations. We set out to take this down-home dish from dull to delicious. Replacing some of the cooking water with milk gave a creamy sweetness to the unadorned grits. We found that a combination of Monterey Jack and sharp cheddar lent both smoothness and pronounced cheesy flavor. To give the dish more depth, we sautéed scallion whites and added real pureed corn for an extra boost of flavor.

The grits are ready when they are mostly creamy but still retain a little bite. If the grits get too thick, whisk in a little water. If you are using frozen corn, thaw it first.

- ½ cup fresh or frozen corn kernels
- 3½ cups water, divided
- 4 tablespoons unsalted butter, divided
- 4 scallions, white parts minced, green parts sliced thin
- 1 cup milk
- ½ teaspoon hot sauce
- ½ teaspoon table salt
- ½ teaspoon pepper
- 1 cup old-fashioned grits
- 4 ounces Monterey Jack cheese, shredded (1 cup)
- 4 ounces sharp cheddar cheese, shredded (1 cup)

1. Puree corn and ¼ cup water in blender until smooth, about 1 minute; set aside. Melt 2 tablespoons butter in medium saucepan over medium heat. Add scallion whites and cook until softened, about 2 minutes. Stir in remaining 3¼ cups water, milk, hot sauce, ½ teaspoon salt, and ½ teaspoon pepper and bring to boil.

2. Slowly whisk grits into saucepan until no lumps remain. Reduce heat to low and cook, stirring frequently, until thick and creamy, about 15 minutes.

3. Off heat, stir in Monterey Jack, cheddar, pureed corn, and remaining 2 tablespoons butter until incorporated. Season with salt and pepper to taste. Serve sprinkled with scallion greens.

Know Your Corn

Cornmeal Cornmeal is corn kernels that are dried and ground to a powder.

Grits Grits are cornmeal, but the name also refers to the cooked porridge popular in the South.

Hominy Grits Hominy grits are corn kernels with the hull and bran removed before grinding.

Polenta Polenta is cornmeal, but the name also refers to the cooked Italian porridge, which is traditionally enriched with butter and Parmesan.

Extra-Cheesy Grits

SERVES 4 TO 6

WHY THIS RECIPE WORKS In recent history, grits have transformed from a simple mixture of water and ground corn to a creamy, savory—and often cheesy—culinary staple. These extra-cheesy grits benefited from flavor-boosting ingredients inspired by macaroni and cheese. Worcestershire sauce, Dijon mustard, and hot sauce added complexity and savoriness, while cooking the grits in a mixture of milk and water provided both creaminess and thorough hydration. Less flavorful cheeses, such as American and mild cheddar, tasted too bland and milky when mixed into the grits; using extra-sharp cheddar and a hint of Parmesan allowed the cheesy flavors to shine through. These ultrasavory grits are as flavorful as they are versatile; pair them with bacon and runny eggs for breakfast, spoon them next to a pile of garlicky greens, or simply enjoy them by the bowlful with extra hot sauce.

We developed this recipe with widely available Quaker Old Fashioned Grits. If you use our winning grits (Anson Mills Pencil Cob Grits), or other more coarsely ground grits, you will need to increase the simmering time in step 1 to about 50 minutes.

- 2¼ cups whole milk
- 2 cups water, plus extra for thinning
- ½ teaspoon table salt
- ½ teaspoon pepper
- 1 cup grits
- 6 ounces extra-sharp cheddar cheese, shredded (1½ cups)
- 2 ounces Parmesan cheese, grated (1 cup)
- 2 tablespoons unsalted butter
- 2 teaspoons Dijon mustard
- 2 teaspoons hot sauce, plus extra for seasoning
- 2 teaspoons Worcestershire sauce

1. Bring milk, water, salt, and pepper to boil in medium saucepan over medium-high heat. Slowly whisk in grits. Reduce heat to low, cover, and simmer, whisking often, until grits are thick and creamy, about 25 minutes. (Add extra water, 2 tablespoons at a time, if grits become too stiff while cooking.)

2. Whisk cheddar, Parmesan, butter, mustard, hot sauce, and Worcestershire into grits until cheese is melted, about 1 minute. Off heat, season with salt, pepper, and hot sauce to taste. Serve.

Strawberry Pretzel Salad

SERVES 10 TO 12

WHY THIS RECIPE WORKS This tri-layer Midwestern specialty doesn't much resemble salad, but the sweet-salty, creamy-crunchy combination grabbed our attention. We knew we could make this slightly offbeat potluck favorite shine with some homemade elements. We replaced the "whipped topping" with real cream, which we whipped into softened cream cheese with some sugar for a tangy, not-too-sweet middle layer. The top layer, traditionally made from boxed Jell-O, got an upgrade to plain gelatin flavored with real pureed strawberry juice and sliced frozen berries. The time it took to make these elements from scratch was well worth the extra effort.

For a sturdier crust, use (thinner) pretzel sticks, not (fatter) rods. Thaw the strawberries in the refrigerator the night before you begin the recipe. You'll puree 2 pounds of the strawberries and slice the remaining 1 pound.

6½ ounces pretzel sticks
2¼ cups (15¾ ounces) sugar, divided
12 tablespoons unsalted butter, melted and cooled
8 ounces cream cheese
1 cup heavy cream
3 pounds (10½ cups) frozen strawberries, thawed
¼ teaspoon table salt
4½ teaspoons unflavored gelatin
½ cup cold water

1. Adjust oven rack to middle position and heat oven to 400 degrees. Spray 13 by 9-inch baking pan with vegetable oil spray. Pulse pretzels and ¼ cup sugar in food processor until coarsely ground, about 15 pulses. Add melted butter and pulse until combined, about 10 pulses. Transfer pretzel mixture to prepared pan. Using bottom of measuring cup, press crumbs into bottom of pan. Bake until crust is fragrant and beginning to brown, about 10 minutes, rotating pan halfway through baking. Set aside crust, letting it cool slightly, about 20 minutes.

2. Using stand mixer fitted with whisk, whip cream cheese and ½ cup sugar on medium speed until light and fluffy, about 2 minutes. Increase speed to medium-high and, with mixer still running, slowly add cream in steady stream. Continue to whip until soft peaks form, scraping down bowl as needed, about 1 minute longer. Spread whipped cream cheese mixture evenly over cooled crust. Refrigerate until set, about 30 minutes.

3. Meanwhile, process 2 pounds strawberries in now-empty food processor until pureed, about 30 seconds. Strain mixture through fine-mesh strainer set over medium saucepan, using underside of small ladle to push puree through strainer. Add remaining 1½ cups sugar and salt to strawberry puree in saucepan and cook over medium-high heat, whisking occasionally, until bubbles begin to appear around sides of pan and sugar is dissolved, about 5 minutes; remove from heat.

4. Sprinkle gelatin over water in large bowl and let sit until gelatin softens, about 5 minutes. Whisk strawberry puree into gelatin. Slice remaining strawberries and stir into strawberry-gelatin mixture. Refrigerate until gelatin thickens slightly and starts to cling to sides of bowl, about 30 minutes. Carefully pour gelatin mixture evenly over whipped cream cheese layer. Refrigerate salad until gelatin is fully set, at least 4 hours or up to 24 hours. Serve.

The American Table: Salad Days

Baked beans, marshmallows, fruit cocktail, flavored gelatin, grated American cheese, ginger ale, sauerkraut . . . Do the words "salad fixings" spring to mind? Probably not, but then you aren't a well-bred, middle-class lady living in the first half of the 20th century. Had you been reared on the tenets of the domestic science movement that dominated American cooking at that time, such a list would indeed have suggested salad. As a "progressive housekeeper," you would have cringed at the very idea of what we call salad today. As culinary historian Laura Shapiro has detailed in *Perfection Salad: Women and Cooking at the Turn of the Century*, vegetables had to be tamed, and the very best way to render untidy raw vegetables harmless was to encase them in gelatin. After molding and chilling her salad, she could gild the lily with a few stuffed prunes, rococo swirls of thinned mayonnaise, and a carved tomato tulip. Pretzel salad is a direct descendant of such "Festive for Special Occasions Salads," as Betty Crocker's *New Picture Cook Book* grouped similar concoctions as late as 1961. Even today, despite the Cool Whip and the strawberry Jell-O, pretzel salad is not dessert—it's a salad.

Roasted Green Beans with Goat Cheese and Hazelnuts

SERVES 4 TO 6

WHY THIS RECIPE WORKS For tender green beans with a hint of flavorful browning, we developed a hybrid method—first steaming the beans under a foil cover and then removing the foil and allowing them to roast. Adding a bit of sugar to the beans promoted the browning and blistering we wanted in the oven's high heat. Tossing the beans with a light citrus dressing and goat cheese brightened their flavor, while toasted hazelnuts provided a welcome crunch.

To trim green beans quickly, line up a handful so the stem ends are even and then cut off the stems with one swipe of the knife.

1½	pounds green beans, trimmed
5½	tablespoons extra-virgin olive oil, divided
¾	teaspoon sugar
1	teaspoon kosher salt, divided
¾	teaspoon pepper, divided
2	garlic cloves, minced
1	teaspoon grated orange zest plus 2 teaspoons juice
2	teaspoons lemon juice
1	teaspoon Dijon mustard
2	tablespoons minced fresh chives
2	ounces goat cheese, crumbled (½ cup)
¼	cup hazelnuts, toasted, skinned, and chopped

1. Adjust oven rack to lowest position and heat oven to 475 degrees. Combine green beans, 1½ tablespoons oil, sugar, ¾ teaspoon salt, and ½ teaspoon pepper in bowl. Evenly distribute green beans on rimmed baking sheet.

2. Cover sheet tightly with aluminum foil and roast for 10 minutes. Remove foil and continue to roast until green beans are spotty brown, about 10 minutes longer, stirring halfway through roasting.

3. Meanwhile, combine garlic, orange zest, and remaining ¼ cup oil in medium bowl and microwave until bubbling, about 1 minute; let steep for 1 minute. Whisk orange juice, lemon juice, mustard, remaining ¼ teaspoon salt, and remaining ¼ teaspoon pepper into garlic mixture.

4. Transfer green beans to bowl with dressing, add chives, and toss to combine. Transfer to serving platter and sprinkle with goat cheese and hazelnuts. Serve.

Roasted Green Beans with Almonds and Mint

Omit orange zest and juice, substitute with 1 teaspoon grated lime zest and 4 teaspoons lime juice; ¼ cup torn fresh mint leaves for chives; and ¼ cup whole blanched almonds, toasted and chopped, for hazelnuts. Omit goat cheese.

Roasted Green Beans with Pecorino and Pine Nuts

Omit orange zest and juice, substitute with 1 teaspoon grated lemon zest and 4 teaspoons lemon juice; 2 tablespoons chopped fresh basil for chives; 1½ ounces Pecorino Romano cheese, shredded, for goat cheese; and ¼ cup pine nuts, toasted, for hazelnuts.

Strawberry Pretzel Salad

Roasted Green Beans with Goat Cheese and Hazelnuts

Classic Tuna Salad

MAKES 2 CUPS; ENOUGH FOR 4 SANDWICHES

WHY THIS RECIPE WORKS A classic lunch box staple, tuna salad too often turns out watery, chalky, and/or bland. It may sound odd, but the key to great tuna salad is to first thoroughly drain chunked tuna and dry it with paper towels. Mashing the dried tuna with a fork made for a nice, uniform consistency. To moisten the salad, we quickly infused olive oil with chopped onion in the microwave and added it to the tuna, along with a bit of sugar, lemon juice, and mayo to round out the flavor. We tasted every variety of canned tuna and the runaway winner was solid white tuna packed in water.

For slightly milder salads, use an equal amount of shallot instead of onion.

- 1/4 cup finely chopped onion
- 2 tablespoons extra-virgin olive oil
- 3 (5-ounce) cans solid white tuna in water
- 1/2 cup plus 2 tablespoons mayonnaise
- 1 celery rib, minced
- 2 teaspoons lemon juice
- 1/2 teaspoon sugar

1. Combine onion and oil in small bowl and microwave until onion begins to soften, about 2 minutes. Let onion mixture cool for 5 minutes. Place tuna in fine-mesh strainer and press dry with paper towels. Transfer tuna to medium bowl and mash with fork until finely flaked.

2. Stir mayonnaise, celery, lemon juice, sugar, 1/2 teaspoon salt, 1/2 teaspoon pepper, and onion mixture into tuna until well combined. Season with salt and pepper to taste. Serve. (Salad can be refrigerated for up to 24 hours.)

Tuna Salad with Hard-Cooked Eggs, Radishes, and Capers

Substitute 6 tablespoons extra-virgin olive oil for mayonnaise. Add 2 thinly sliced hard-cooked eggs; 2 trimmed, halved, and thinly sliced radishes; and 1/4 cup capers, minced, to salad.

Tuna Salad with Apple, Walnuts, and Tarragon

Add 1 apple, cored and cut into 1/2-inch pieces; 1/2 cup walnuts, toasted and chopped coarse; and 1 tablespoon minced fresh tarragon to salad.

Tuna Salad with Cornichons and Whole-Grain Mustard

Add 1/4 cup finely chopped cornichons, 1 tablespoon minced fresh chives, and 1 tablespoon whole-grain mustard to salad.

Tuna Salad with Curry and Grapes

Add 1 teaspoon curry powder to bowl with onion and oil before microwaving. Add 1 cup green grapes, halved, to salad.

Green Goddess Dressing

MAKES 1 1/4 CUPS; ENOUGH FOR 6 WEDGES OF LETTUCE

WHY THIS RECIPE WORKS Too often a bright, crisp romaine salad is weighed down by an overly heavy dressing, so we set out to make a light and flavorful green goddess dressing. We achieved this by using three kinds of herbs: tarragon, parsley, and chives. To discreetly add depth, we used a single anchovy fillet, and for the creamiest texture, we used mayo and sour cream and prepared the dressing in a blender. While modern versions of green goddess dressing often contain avocado, the original version, credited to chef Philip Roemer of the Palace Hotel in San Francisco in the 1920s, does not, so we skipped it.

To appreciate the full flavor of this rich dressing, drizzle it over chilled wedges of mild iceberg lettuce or romaine lettuce leaves. A blender yields a brighter, slightly more flavorful dressing, but a food processor will work, too.

- 2 teaspoons dried tarragon
- 1 tablespoon lemon juice
- 1 tablespoon water
- 3/4 cup mayonnaise
- 1/4 cup sour cream
- 1/4 cup coarsely chopped fresh parsley
- 1 garlic clove, chopped
- 1 anchovy fillet, rinsed and dried
- 1/4 cup chopped chives

1. Combine tarragon, lemon juice, and water in small bowl and let sit for 15 minutes.

2. Blend tarragon mixture, mayonnaise, sour cream, parsley, garlic, and anchovy in blender until smooth, scraping down sides as necessary. Transfer to medium bowl, stir in chives, and season with salt and pepper to taste. Chill until flavors meld, about 1 hour. (Dressing can be covered and refrigerated for up to 1 day.)

Green Goddess Roast Chicken

SERVES 4 TO 6

WHY THIS RECIPE WORKS Made with fresh herbs and rich mayonnaise, green goddess dressing is usually a creamy complement to salads and crudités. We thought it might make a flavorful marinade for chicken with one key change. We used buttermilk in the marinade instead of mayo to provide deeper seasoning and tangy flavor. Before marinating the chicken, we reserved some of the mixture to use as a sauce for the roasted chicken. To give our herby sauce more creamy richness, we reintroduced some mayo and a splash more buttermilk. Roasting the chicken at high heat for just 25 minutes yielded nicely browned skin and juicy meat.

Don't spend a lot of time chopping the herbs and garlic. Chop them just enough to measure them, and then let the blender do the bulk of the work.

- ½ cup chopped fresh chives
- ½ cup chopped fresh parsley
- ¼ cup plus 1 tablespoon buttermilk, divided
- 2 tablespoons lemon juice
- 4 teaspoons chopped fresh tarragon
- 2 garlic cloves, chopped
- 2 anchovy fillets, rinsed
- ¼ cup mayonnaise
- 1½ teaspoons table salt
- 3 pounds bone-in chicken pieces (2 split breasts cut in half crosswise, 2 drumsticks, and 2 thighs), trimmed

Green Goddess Dressing

Green Goddess Roast Chicken

1. Process chives, parsley, ¼ cup buttermilk, lemon juice, tarragon, garlic, and anchovies in blender until smooth, about 30 seconds, scraping down sides of blender jar as needed.

2. Transfer 2 tablespoons herb mixture to bowl; add mayonnaise and remaining 1 tablespoon buttermilk and stir to combine. Cover and set aside until ready to serve.

3. Combine salt and remaining herb mixture in 1-gallon zipper-lock bag. Add chicken to bag, press out air, seal bag, and turn to coat chicken in marinade. Refrigerate for at least 2 hours or up to 24 hours.

4. Adjust oven rack to middle position and heat oven to 475 degrees. Line rimmed baking sheet with aluminum foil. Place chicken, skin side up, on prepared sheet (do not brush off marinade that sticks to chicken). Make sure skin is not bunched up on chicken. Roast until breasts register 160 degrees and drumsticks/thighs register 175 degrees, 25 to 30 minutes.

5. Transfer chicken to platter, tent with foil, and let rest for 10 minutes. Serve chicken with sauce.

Cast Iron Baked Chicken

SERVES 4

Cast Iron Baked Chicken

WHY THIS RECIPE WORKS For baked chicken with the crispiest possible skin, we turned to kitchen workhorse and heat-retainer extraordinaire: a cast-iron skillet. We carefully placed colorful paprika-seasoned chicken pieces skin side down into the preheated skillet to get an instant sizzle, achieving that trademark rendered skin. After a quick flip halfway through, our chicken emerged from the oven with an evenly browned exterior that crunched faintly against the juicy meat. Sprigs of thyme and some butter mingled together with the pan juices to create a silky sauce that we spooned over the top for an herby finish.

Note that the cast-iron skillet should be preheated along with the oven; this is key to getting crispy, well-browned skin. You will not achieve the same type of browning with a conventional skillet. A 4-pound whole chicken will yield the 3 pounds of parts called for in the recipe.

- 2 teaspoons paprika
- 2 teaspoons table salt
- 1 teaspoon pepper
- ½ teaspoon onion powder
- ½ teaspoon granulated garlic
- 3 pounds bone-in chicken pieces (2 split breasts, 2 drumsticks, 2 thighs, and 2 wings with wingtips discarded), trimmed
- 2 tablespoons unsalted butter
- 6 sprigs fresh thyme

1. Adjust oven rack to middle position, place 12-inch cast-iron skillet on rack, and heat oven to 450 degrees. Combine paprika, salt, pepper, onion powder, and granulated garlic in bowl. Pat chicken dry with paper towels and sprinkle all over with spice mixture.

2. When oven is heated, carefully remove hot skillet. Add butter, let it melt, and add thyme sprigs. Place chicken in skillet skin side down, pushing thyme sprigs aside as needed. Transfer skillet to oven and bake for 15 minutes.

3. Remove skillet from oven and flip chicken. Return skillet to oven and bake until breasts register 160 degrees and drumsticks/thighs register at least 175 degrees, about 15 minutes longer.

4. Let chicken rest in skillet for 10 minutes. Transfer chicken to platter and spoon pan juices over top. Serve.

One-Batch Fried Chicken

SERVES 4

WHY THIS RECIPE WORKS Inspired by the covered pressure-frying machine in which Colonel Sanders created his famous fried chicken, we set out to find a faster way to fry that would get a full cut-up chicken on the table in one batch. To fit all the chicken into a Dutch oven, we had to decrease the amount of oil. Covering the pot for the first half of cooking allowed the oil, which dropped in temperature when we added the chicken, to quickly heat up again. We let the pieces fry undisturbed, so the coating set almost entirely around each piece before flipping and frying the chicken uncovered to allow excess moisture to escape.

Use a Dutch oven that holds 6 quarts or more. To take the temperature of the chicken pieces, take them out of the oil and place them on a plate; this is the safest way and provides the most accurate reading.

Brine and Chicken
- 2 cups buttermilk
- 1 tablespoon table salt
- 3 pounds bone-in chicken pieces (2 split breasts cut in half crosswise, 2 drumsticks, and 2 thighs), trimmed
- 1½ quarts peanut or vegetable oil for frying

Coating
- 3 cups all-purpose flour
- 3 tablespoons white pepper
- 1 tablespoon pepper
- 1 tablespoon celery salt
- 1 tablespoon granulated garlic
- 1 tablespoon ground ginger
- 1 tablespoon Italian seasoning
- 1 tablespoon baking powder
- ½ teaspoon table salt
- 6 tablespoons buttermilk

1. For the Brine and Chicken Whisk buttermilk and salt in large bowl until salt is dissolved. Submerge chicken in buttermilk mixture. Cover with plastic wrap and refrigerate for at least 1 hour or up to 24 hours.

2. For the Coating Whisk flour, white pepper, pepper, celery salt, granulated garlic, ginger, Italian seasoning, baking powder, and salt together in large bowl. Add buttermilk and, using your fingers, rub flour mixture and buttermilk together until craggy bits form throughout.

The American Table: The Colonel

His iconic white suit is part of what makes Harland Sanders's image an indelible one in the American food landscape, but according to Josh Ozersky's biography *Colonel Sanders and the American Dream* (2012), the Colonel's original suit was black. "It came with a string tie and was distinctive enough in its way, but something about it lacked oomph, panache."

Eventually, in a bid to portray the image of a "paternal-looking Southern gentleman," Sanders bleached his beard and changed up the suit; as Ozersky tells it, "television producers told him the white suit made him stand out, giving him a visual signature."

One-Batch Fried Chicken

> ### How to Split and Trim Breasts
>
>
>
> **1.** With whole breast skin side down on cutting board, center knife on breastbone, then apply pressure to cut through and separate breast into two halves.
>
>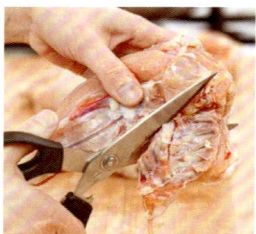
>
> **2.** Using kitchen shears, trim off rib section from each breast, following vertical line of fat from tapered end of breast up to socket.
>
>
>
> **3.** Using chef's knife or kitchen shears, trim excess fat and skin from breasts.

3. Set wire rack in rimmed baking sheet. Working with 2 pieces of chicken at a time, remove from buttermilk mixture, allowing excess to drip off, then drop into flour mixture, turning to thoroughly coat and pressing to adhere. Transfer to prepared rack, skin side up. Refrigerate, uncovered, for at least 1 hour or up to 2 hours.

4. Set second wire rack in second rimmed baking sheet and line with triple layer of paper towels. Add oil to large Dutch oven until it measures about 1 inch deep and heat over medium-high heat to 350 degrees. Add all chicken to oil, skin side down in single layer (some slight overlap is OK) so that pieces are mostly submerged. Cover and fry for 10 minutes, rotating pot after 5 minutes. Adjust burner, if necessary, to maintain oil temperature around 300 degrees.

5. Uncover pot (chicken will be golden on sides and bottom but unset and gray on top) and carefully flip chicken. Continue to fry, uncovered, until chicken is golden brown and breasts register 160 degrees and drumsticks/thighs register 175 degrees, 7 to 9 minutes longer. Transfer chicken to paper towel–lined rack and let cool for 10 minutes. Serve.

Southern-Style Smothered Chicken

SERVES 4

WHY THIS RECIPE WORKS For perfectly tender, evenly cooked Southern-style smothered chicken, we started with chicken parts rather than a whole bird. We browned the pieces and then shallow-braised them in a gravy built from pantry ingredients: chicken broth, flour, sautéed onions, celery, garlic, and dried sage. We found that we needed just 2 tablespoons of flour to thicken the gravy to a rich consistency. A splash of cider vinegar brightened the sauce and helped the chicken's flavor shine.

Serve with rice or potatoes. You can substitute ¼ teaspoon ground sage for the dried sage leaves, if desired.

- 3 pounds bone-in chicken pieces (split breasts cut in half crosswise, drumsticks, and/or thighs), trimmed
- 1½ teaspoons table salt, divided
- 1 teaspoon pepper, divided
- ½ cup plus 2 tablespoons all-purpose flour
- ¼ cup vegetable oil
- 2 onions, chopped fine
- 2 celery ribs, chopped fine
- 3 garlic cloves, minced
- 1 teaspoon dried sage leaves
- 2 cups chicken broth
- 1 tablespoon cider vinegar
- 2 tablespoons minced fresh parsley

1. Pat chicken dry with paper towels and sprinkle with ½ teaspoon salt and ½ teaspoon pepper. Spread ½ cup flour in shallow dish. Working with 1 piece at a time, dredge chicken in flour, shaking off excess, and transfer to plate.

2. Heat oil in Dutch oven over medium-high heat. Add half of chicken to pot, skin side down, and cook until deep golden brown, 4 to 6 minutes per side; transfer to plate. Repeat with remaining chicken, adjusting heat if flour begins to burn.

3. Pour off all but 2 tablespoons fat and return pot to medium heat. Add onions, celery, remaining 1 teaspoon salt, and remaining ½ teaspoon pepper, and cook until softened, 6 to 8 minutes. Stir in garlic, sage, and remaining 2 tablespoons flour and cook until vegetables are well coated with flour and garlic is fragrant, about 1 minute. Whisk in broth, scraping up any browned bits.

Southern-Style Smothered Chicken

4. Nestle chicken into sauce, add any accumulated juices from plate, and bring to boil. Reduce heat to low, cover, and simmer until breasts register 160 degrees and drumsticks/thighs register 175 degrees, 30 to 40 minutes.

5. Transfer chicken to serving dish. Stir vinegar into sauce and season with salt and pepper to taste. Pour sauce over chicken, sprinkle with parsley, and serve.

Chicken Paprikash and Buttered Spaetzle

SERVES 4 TO 6

WHY THIS RECIPE WORKS We learned a lot about paprika from visiting Balaton in Cleveland, Ohio. Chicken paprikash is a Hungarian stew that sings of the toasty flavor of paprika, but paprika is sensitive to heat. To prevent it from burning and tasting bitter, we added it to the pot with chicken broth rather than blooming it in oil. Cayenne provided balanced warmth, and red bell pepper and onion lent sweetness. Bone-in chicken thighs turned tender in the stew—removing their skin prevented greasiness. We like to serve paprikash with spaetzle, a homey cross between egg noodles and dumplings, which we made using a makeshift spaetzle press.

We call for removing the skin from bone-in chicken thighs here. Rather than discarding the skin, try crisping it in a skillet in a little oil set over medium-high heat and setting it aside for a snack. Be sure to use sweet Hungarian paprika here, not hot or smoked, and make sure it's fresh (once opened, paprika loses its flavor quickly). Serve with Buttered Spaetzle (recipe follows) or buttered egg noodles.

- ¼ cup extra-virgin olive oil
- 1 large onion, halved and sliced thin
- 1 red bell pepper, stemmed, seeded, and sliced thin
- 1 (14.5-ounce) can diced tomatoes, drained
- 5 garlic cloves, chopped fine
- 2 teaspoons table salt, divided
- 8 (5- to 7-ounce) bone-in chicken thighs, skin removed, trimmed
- ¾ teaspoon pepper
- 2½ cups chicken broth
- 2 tablespoons paprika, plus extra for serving
- ¼ teaspoon cayenne pepper
- ⅓ cup sour cream, plus extra for serving
- 3 tablespoons all-purpose flour
- 2 tablespoons chopped fresh parsley

1. Heat oil in Dutch oven over medium-high heat until shimmering. Add onion, bell pepper, tomatoes, garlic, and 1 teaspoon salt and cook, stirring often, until vegetables are softened and fond begins to develop on bottom of pot, about 10 minutes.

2. Sprinkle chicken with pepper and remaining 1 teaspoon salt. Stir broth, paprika, and cayenne into pot, scraping up any browned bits. Submerge chicken in broth mixture and bring to simmer. Reduce heat to medium-low, cover, and simmer until chicken is very tender and registers at least 195 degrees, about 30 minutes, stirring and flipping chicken halfway through simmering.

3. Whisk sour cream and flour together in bowl. Slowly whisk ½ cup cooking liquid into sour cream mixture. Stir sour cream mixture into pot until fully incorporated. Continue to simmer, uncovered, until thickened, about 5 minutes longer. Off heat, season with salt and pepper to taste. Let stand for 5 minutes. Sprinkle with parsley and serve with extra paprika and extra sour cream.

AS GOOD AS GRANDMA'S

Chicken Paprikash and Buttered Spaetzle

3. Add 1 tablespoon salt to boiling water and set prepared disposable pan on top of Dutch oven. Transfer half of batter to disposable pan. Use spatula to scrape batter across holes, letting batter fall into water. Boil until spaetzle float, about 1 minute. Using spider skimmer or slotted spoon, transfer spaetzle to colander set in large bowl to drain. Repeat with remaining batter.

4. Discard any accumulated water in bowl beneath colander. Pour spaetzle into now-empty bowl. Add melted butter and toss to combine. Serve.

Hot-Honey Chicken
SERVES 4

WHY THIS RECIPE WORKS Honey and hot sauce make an enticing combination of flavors in this one-pan chicken recipe. We seasoned and seared the chicken pieces to get the best browning, then poured the sauce—a mixture of equal parts honey and Frank's RedHot, plus a couple cloves of garlic—over the chicken before roasting it to glossy doneness in the oven. Whipping up a pan sauce from the accumulated juices was just a matter of briefly reducing the liquid back on the stovetop, then adding butter for richness and lime juice for a bit of brightness. A sprinkling of scallions brought it all together into an appealing blend of sweet, spicy, and savory.

If you're using table salt instead of kosher salt, cut the amount in half.

- ¼ cup honey
- ¼ cup Frank's RedHot Original Cayenne Pepper Sauce
- 2 garlic cloves, minced
- 2 teaspoons kosher salt
- 1 teaspoon ground cumin
- 3 pounds bone-in chicken pieces (2 split breasts cut in half crosswise, 2 drumsticks, and 2 thighs), trimmed
- 1 tablespoon vegetable oil
- 2 tablespoons unsalted butter, cut into 2 pieces
- 2 teaspoons lime juice
- 2 scallions, sliced thin

1. Adjust oven rack to middle position and heat oven to 425 degrees. Combine honey, hot sauce, and garlic in bowl; set aside. Combine salt and cumin in separate bowl. Pat chicken dry with paper towels and sprinkle all over with salt mixture.

Buttered Spaetzle
SERVES 6 TO 8

The 13 by 9-inch disposable aluminum pan serves as a makeshift sieve for portioning the batter.

- 2 cups all-purpose flour
- ¾ teaspoon table salt, plus salt for cooking spaetzle
- ½ teaspoon pepper
- ¼ teaspoon ground nutmeg
- ¾ cup whole milk
- 3 large eggs
- 1 (13 by 9-inch) disposable aluminum pan
- 2 tablespoons unsalted butter, melted

1. Whisk flour, salt, pepper, and nutmeg together in large bowl. Whisk milk and eggs together in second bowl. Slowly whisk milk mixture into flour mixture until smooth. Cover and let rest for 15 to 30 minutes.

2. While batter rests, use scissors to poke about forty ¼-inch holes in bottom of disposable pan. Bring 4 quarts water to boil in Dutch oven.

138 *The Complete Cook's Country TV Show Cookbook*

Hot-Honey Chicken

Chicken Divan

SERVES 4

WHY THIS RECIPE WORKS Once-trendy chicken Divan's original recipe calls for many different components and even more cooking steps. We wanted to stay true to the original flavor of the dish but streamline the cooking process. To do this, we batch-cooked the broccoli first, then the chicken. While the broccoli and chicken rested, we used the same pan to prepare our sauce. And instead of making a separate hollandaise sauce, like the traditional chicken Divan recipes demand, we whisked egg yolks and lemon juice together, tempered the mixture with the hot pan sauce, and whisked in butter at the end.

Use one small onion instead of the shallots, if desired.

- 3 tablespoons vegetable oil, divided
- 1 pound broccoli florets, cut into 1-inch pieces
- 2½ cups chicken broth, divided
- ¼ cup all-purpose flour
- 4 (6-ounce) boneless, skinless chicken breasts, trimmed
- ½ teaspoon table salt
- ½ teaspoon pepper
- 2 shallots, minced
- 1 cup heavy cream
- ½ cup dry sherry
- 2 teaspoons Worcestershire sauce
- 3 ounces Parmesan cheese, grated (1½ cups), divided
- 3 large egg yolks
- 1 tablespoon lemon juice
- 3 tablespoons unsalted butter

1. Adjust oven rack to lower-middle position and heat broiler. Heat 1 tablespoon oil in large skillet over medium-high heat until just smoking. Add broccoli and cook until spotty brown, about 1 minute. Add ½ cup broth, cover, and steam until just tender, about 1½ minutes. Remove lid and cook until liquid has evaporated, about 1 minute. Transfer broccoli to plate lined with paper towels; rinse and wipe out skillet.

2. Heat remaining 2 tablespoons oil in now-empty skillet over medium-high heat until smoking. Meanwhile, place flour in shallow dish. Sprinkle chicken with salt and pepper and dredge in flour to coat. Cook chicken until golden brown on both sides, 4 to 6 minutes. Transfer chicken to plate.

2. Heat oil in 12-inch ovensafe skillet over medium-high heat until just smoking. Add chicken and cook until golden brown on both sides, about 4 minutes per side. Transfer chicken to plate, skin side up.

3. Pour off fat from skillet. Return chicken to now-empty skillet, skin side up; pour honey mixture evenly over chicken. Transfer skillet to oven and roast until breasts register 160 degrees and drumsticks/thighs register at least 175 degrees, 17 to 22 minutes. Let chicken rest in skillet for 10 minutes.

4. Transfer chicken to shallow platter. Bring juices in skillet to boil over medium-high heat (skillet handle will be hot). Cook until slightly thickened, 1 to 2 minutes. Reduce heat to low and whisk butter and lime juice into juices in skillet until butter is melted. Spoon sauce over chicken. Sprinkle with scallions and serve.

AS GOOD AS GRANDMA'S

Chicken Divan

3. Add shallots to skillet and cook until just softened, about 1 minute. Add remaining 2 cups broth and cream and scrape browned bits from bottom of pan. Return chicken to skillet and simmer over medium-high heat until cooked through, about 10 minutes. Transfer chicken to clean plate and continue to simmer sauce until reduced to 1 cup, about 10 minutes. Add sherry and Worcestershire and simmer until reduced again to 1 cup, about 3 minutes. Stir in 1 cup Parmesan.

4. Whisk egg yolks and lemon juice in small bowl, then whisk in about ¼ cup sauce. Off heat, whisk egg yolk mixture into sauce in skillet, then whisk in butter.

5. Cut chicken into ½-inch-thick slices and arrange on broiler-safe platter. Scatter broccoli over chicken and pour sauce over broccoli. Sprinkle with remaining ½ cup Parmesan and broil until golden brown, 3 to 5 minutes. Serve.

Chicken Florentine
SERVES 4 TO 6

Chicken Florentine

WHY THIS RECIPE WORKS To restore chicken Florentine to its elegant roots, we started with fresh spinach. To prevent the water from the spinach from washing out the other flavors in the dish, we drained excess liquid from the cooked spinach by pressing the leaves with the back of a spoon in a colander. For flavor, we seared the chicken breasts first and then poached them in the sauce before broiling. We used cream to make the sauce silky and built volume with equal amounts of chicken broth and water. We also added a squeeze of lemon juice and a hit of zest, along with Parmesan cheese for its nutty, savory punch.

Draining Spinach
As it cooks, spinach releases a lot of moisture, which can make dishes like our Chicken Florentine watery. To prevent that, we transferred the spinach to a colander and pressed the leaves with a spoon to force the liquid out. We drained nearly ¼ cup of liquid from the 12 ounces of spinach used in this recipe.

We like tender, quick-cooking bagged baby spinach here; if using curly-leaf spinach, chop it before cooking.

- 2 tablespoons vegetable oil, divided
- 12 ounces (12 cups) baby spinach
- 4 (6-ounce) boneless, skinless chicken breasts, trimmed
- ½ teaspoon table salt
- ½ teaspoon pepper
- 1 shallot, minced
- 2 garlic cloves, minced
- 1¼ cups chicken broth
- 1¼ cups water
- 1 cup heavy cream
- 6 tablespoons grated Parmesan cheese, divided
- 1 teaspoon grated lemon zest plus 1 teaspoon juice

1. Adjust oven rack to upper-middle position and heat broiler. Heat 1 tablespoon oil in 12-inch skillet over medium-high heat until shimmering. Add spinach and cook, stirring occasionally until wilted, 1 to 2 minutes. Transfer spinach to colander set over bowl and press with spoon to release excess liquid. Discard liquid.

2. Pat chicken dry with paper towels and sprinkle with salt and pepper. Wipe out pan and heat remaining 1 tablespoon oil over medium-high heat until just smoking. Cook chicken on both sides until golden, 4 to 6 minutes. Add shallot and garlic to skillet and cook until fragrant, about 30 seconds. Stir in broth, water, and cream and bring to boil.

3. Reduce heat to medium-low and simmer until chicken is cooked through, about 10 minutes; transfer chicken to plate and tent with aluminum foil. Continue to simmer sauce until reduced to 1 cup, about 10 minutes. Off heat, stir in 4 tablespoons Parmesan and lemon zest and juice.

4. Cut chicken crosswise into ½-inch-thick slices and arrange on broiler-safe platter. Scatter spinach over chicken and pour sauce over spinach. Sprinkle with remaining Parmesan and broil until golden brown, 3 to 5 minutes. Serve.

One-Pot Chicken Jardinière

SERVES 4 TO 6

WHY THIS RECIPE WORKS "Gardener's Stew" doesn't cut it in English, but borrow a French word and you've got Chicken Jardinière, an elegant braise of bone-in chicken parts and vegetables flavored with garlic, herbs, and wine. This streamlined version can be prepared in just one pot. We started by browning the chicken to build a rich base for the sauce. Sautéing the carrots and mushrooms proved unnecessary, so we stirred them directly into the sauce. Simmering the dark meat in the sauce before adding the white meat ensured that all the chicken was done at the same time. Frozen peas and fresh tarragon finished our stew with color and brightness.

Buy a 4-ounce hunk of pancetta from the deli counter. Try to buy potatoes with a 1-inch diameter. If you can find only slightly larger potatoes, up to 2 inches in diameter, cut them in half. Do not substitute russet potatoes for Yukon Gold potatoes. Note that the dark and white meat are added to the pot at different times in step 3.

One-Pot Chicken Jardinière

Double-Crust Chicken Pot Pie

SERVES 6 TO 8

WHY THIS RECIPE WORKS With a flaky crust topping savory chicken and vegetables suspended in a velvety cream gravy, it's hard to imagine anything more comforting than a traditional pot pie, but we upped the ante by adding a second buttery crust underneath. Incorporating sour cream and egg into the dough made it easy to handle after an hour-long rest in the fridge, and using rotisserie chicken streamlined the process (and cut down on dirty dishes). Letting the pie cool on a wire rack for 45 minutes gave the filling time to firm up, producing a pie that was satisfyingly sliceable.

The pie may seem loose when it comes out of the oven; it will set up as it cools. You can substitute 3 cups of turkey meat for the chicken, if desired.

Crust
- ½ cup sour cream, chilled
- 1 large egg, lightly beaten
- 2½ cups (12½ ounces) all-purpose flour
- 1½ teaspoons table salt
- 12 tablespoons unsalted butter, cut into ½-inch pieces and chilled

Filling
- 4 tablespoons unsalted butter
- 1 onion, chopped fine
- 2 carrots, peeled and cut into ¼-inch pieces (⅔ cup)
- 2 celery ribs, cut into ¼-inch pieces (½ cup)
- ½ teaspoon table salt
- ½ teaspoon pepper
- 6 tablespoons all-purpose flour
- 2¼ cups chicken broth
- ½ cup half-and-half
- 1 small russet potato (6 ounces), peeled and cut into ¼-inch pieces (1 cup)
- 1 teaspoon minced fresh thyme
- 1 (2½-pound) rotisserie chicken, skin and bones discarded, meat shredded into bite-size pieces (3 cups)
- ¾ cup frozen peas
- 1 large egg, lightly beaten

- 3 pounds bone-in chicken pieces (split breasts cut in half, drumsticks, and/or thighs), trimmed
- ¾ teaspoon table salt, divided
- ¾ teaspoon pepper, divided
- 1 teaspoon vegetable oil
- 4 ounces pancetta, cut into ½-inch pieces
- 1 onion, chopped fine
- 3 garlic cloves, minced
- 2 teaspoons minced fresh thyme
- 3 tablespoons all-purpose flour
- 2 cups chicken broth
- ¾ cup dry white wine
- 12 ounces small Yukon Gold potatoes, unpeeled
- 8 ounces small white mushrooms, trimmed and halved
- 4 carrots, cut into 1-inch chunks
- ½ cup frozen peas
- 1 tablespoon chopped fresh tarragon or parsley
- Lemon wedges

1. Pat chicken dry with paper towels and sprinkle with ¼ teaspoon salt and ¼ teaspoon pepper. Heat oil in Dutch oven over medium-high heat until shimmering. Add chicken, skin side down, and cook until well browned on both sides, about 3 minutes per side. Transfer chicken to plate.

2. Reduce heat to medium. Add pancetta, onion, garlic, thyme, and remaining ½ teaspoon salt to now-empty pot and cook until onion just begins to soften, about 4 minutes. Stir in flour and cook for 1 minute. Slowly whisk in broth and wine. Stir in potatoes, mushrooms, carrots, chicken drumsticks and thighs, and remaining ½ teaspoon pepper and bring to simmer. Cover and simmer for 25 minutes.

3. Uncover and stir. Add chicken breasts and any accumulated juices to pot; return to simmer. Cover and continue to cook until breasts register 160 degrees and drumsticks/thighs register at least 175 degrees, about 20 minutes longer. Off heat, stir in peas and let sit uncovered for 5 minutes. Stir in tarragon and season with salt and pepper to taste. Serve with lemon wedges.

Double-Crust Chicken Pot Pie

1. For the Crust Combine sour cream and egg in bowl. Process flour and salt in food processor until combined, about 3 seconds. Add butter and pulse until only pea-size pieces remain, about 10 pulses. Add half of sour cream mixture and pulse until combined, 5 pulses. Add remaining sour cream mixture and pulse until dough begins to form, about 10 pulses.

2. Transfer mixture to lightly floured counter and knead briefly until dough comes together. Divide dough in half and form each half into 4-inch disk. Wrap disks tightly in plastic wrap and refrigerate for 1 hour. (Wrapped dough can be refrigerated for up to 2 days or frozen for up to 2 months. If frozen, let dough thaw completely on counter before rolling.)

3. Let chilled dough sit on counter to soften slightly, about 10 minutes, before rolling. Roll 1 disk of dough into 12-inch circle on lightly floured counter. Loosely roll dough around rolling pin and gently unroll it onto 9-inch pie plate, letting excess dough hang over edge. Ease dough into plate by gently lifting edge of dough with your hand while pressing into plate bottom with your other hand.

4. Roll other disk of dough into 12-inch circle on lightly floured counter, then transfer to parchment paper–lined baking sheet; cover with plastic. Refrigerate both doughs for 30 minutes.

5. For the Filling Meanwhile, adjust oven rack to lowest position and heat oven to 450 degrees. Melt butter in large saucepan over medium heat. Add onion, carrots, celery, salt, and pepper and cook until vegetables begin to soften, about 6 minutes. Add flour and cook, stirring constantly, until golden, 1 to 2 minutes. Slowly stir in broth and half-and-half and bring to boil over medium-high heat.

6. Stir in potato and thyme. Reduce heat to medium and simmer until sauce is thickened and potato is tender, about 8 minutes. Off heat, stir in chicken and peas.

7. Transfer filling to dough-lined pie plate. Loosely roll remaining dough round around rolling pin and gently unroll it onto filling. Trim overhang to ½ inch beyond lip of plate. Pinch edges of top and bottom crusts firmly together. Tuck overhang under itself; folded edge should be flush with edge of plate. Crimp dough evenly around edge of plate using your fingers. Cut four 2-inch slits in top of dough.

8. Brush top of pie with egg. Place pie on rimmed baking sheet. Bake until top is light golden brown, 18 to 20 minutes. Reduce oven temperature to 375 degrees, rotate sheet, and continue to bake until crust is deep golden brown, 12 to 15 minutes longer. Let pie cool on wire rack for at least 45 minutes. Serve.

Glazed Meatloaf

SERVES 6 TO 8

WHY THIS RECIPE WORKS For our old-fashioned meatloaf, we cut ground beef with an equal portion of sweet ground pork for better flavor. For seasoning, we stuck with tradition: salt, pepper, Dijon mustard, Worcestershire sauce, thyme, parsley, sautéed onion, and garlic. We combined the meat with a panade (paste) of milk and saltines for a cohesive, tender structure. To evaporate the surface moisture that was inhibiting the formation of a crust, we broiled the loaf prior to baking and glazing.

Both ground sirloin and ground chuck work well here, but avoid ground round—it is gristly and bland.

AS GOOD AS GRANDMA'S   143

Glazed Meatloaf

Frosted Meatloaf

Glaze
- 1 cup ketchup
- ¼ cup packed brown sugar
- 2½ tablespoons cider vinegar
- ½ teaspoon hot sauce

Meatloaf
- 2 teaspoons vegetable oil
- 1 onion, chopped fine
- 2 garlic cloves, minced
- 17 square or 19 round saltines
- ⅓ cup whole milk
- 1 pound 90 percent lean ground beef
- 1 pound ground pork
- 2 large eggs plus 1 large yolk
- ⅓ cup finely chopped fresh parsley
- 2 teaspoons Dijon mustard
- 2 teaspoons Worcestershire sauce
- ½ teaspoon dried thyme
- 1 teaspoon table salt
- ¾ teaspoon pepper

1. For the Glaze Whisk all ingredients in saucepan until sugar dissolves. Reserve ¼ cup glaze mixture, then simmer remaining glaze over medium heat until slightly thickened, about 5 minutes. Cover and keep warm.

2. For the Meatloaf Line rimmed baking sheet with aluminum foil and coat lightly with vegetable oil spray. Heat oil in nonstick skillet over medium heat until shimmering. Cook onion until golden, about 8 minutes. Add garlic and cook until fragrant, about 30 seconds. Transfer to large bowl.

3. Process saltines and milk in food processor until smooth, about 30 seconds. Add beef and pork and pulse until well combined, about 10 pulses. Transfer meat mixture to bowl with cooled onion mixture. Add eggs and yolk, parsley, mustard, Worcestershire, thyme, salt, and pepper to bowl and mix with hands until combined.

4. Adjust 1 oven rack to middle position and second rack 4 inches from broiler element; heat broiler. Transfer meat mixture to prepared baking sheet and shape into 9 by 5-inch loaf. Broil on upper rack until well browned, about 5 minutes. Brush 2 tablespoons unreduced glaze over top and sides of loaf and then return to oven and broil until glaze begins to brown, about 2 minutes.

5. Transfer meatloaf to lower rack and brush with remaining unreduced glaze. Reduce oven temperature to 350 degrees and bake until meatloaf registers 160 degrees, 40 to 45 minutes. Transfer to cutting board, tent with foil, and let rest for 20 minutes. Slice and serve, passing remaining reduced glaze at table.

Frosted Meatloaf

SERVES 6 TO 8

WHY THIS RECIPE WORKS Meatloaf and potatoes are an unbeatable combination, so frosted meatloaf—meatloaf coated in a layer of mashed potatoes—was an idea we could get behind. To perfect this nearly forgotten 1950s classic, we found that we had to broil the meatloaf in stages to keep the potatoes from slipping off: First, it was broiled to create a crust and then coated with a tangy, ketchup-based glaze for flavor and broiled again. After cooking through, the meatloaf was frosted with creamy mashed potatoes and broiled for a final stint to turn the fluffy crown of potatoes beautifully brown.

If you don't have a ricer or a food mill, just mash the potatoes thoroughly.

- 1/4 cup ketchup
- 1 tablespoon packed light brown sugar
- 1 tablespoon cider vinegar
- 1/2 teaspoon hot sauce
- 8 tablespoons unsalted butter, divided
- 1 onion, chopped fine
- 3 garlic cloves, minced
- 17 square or 19 round saltines, crushed (2/3 cup)
- 1 cup whole milk, divided
- 1 pound ground pork
- 2 large eggs plus 1 large yolk
- 1/3 cup minced fresh parsley
- 2 teaspoons Dijon mustard
- 2 teaspoons Worcestershire sauce
- 2 teaspoons table salt, divided
- 3/4 teaspoon pepper
- 1/2 teaspoon dried thyme
- 1 pound 90 percent lean ground beef
- 2 pounds russet potatoes, peeled and cut into 1-inch pieces

1. Adjust oven racks to upper-middle and lower-middle positions and heat broiler. Line rimmed baking sheet with aluminum foil, set wire rack in sheet, and place 14 by 6-inch piece of foil in center of rack. Whisk ketchup, sugar, vinegar, and hot sauce together in bowl; set aside glaze.

2. Melt 2 tablespoons butter in 10-inch skillet over medium heat. Add onion and cook until just softened, 3 to 5 minutes. Add garlic and cook until fragrant, about 30 seconds. Set aside off heat.

3. Combine saltines and 1/3 cup milk in large bowl and mash with fork until chunky paste forms. Add pork, eggs and yolk, parsley, mustard, Worcestershire, 1 teaspoon salt, pepper, thyme, and onion mixture and knead with your hands until mostly combined. Add beef and knead until combined.

4. Transfer meat mixture to foil rectangle on wire rack and form into 9 by 6-inch loaf. Broil on upper-middle oven rack until well browned, 5 to 7 minutes. Brush glaze over top and sides of meatloaf, return to upper-middle rack, and broil until glaze begins to brown, 3 to 5 minutes. Move meatloaf to lower-middle oven rack, adjust oven temperature to 350 degrees, and bake until meatloaf registers 160 degrees, 40 to 45 minutes. Remove from oven.

5. Meanwhile, bring potatoes and 2 quarts water to boil in Dutch oven over high heat. Reduce heat to medium-low and simmer until potatoes are tender, 20 to 25 minutes; drain potatoes thoroughly in colander. Set ricer or food mill over now-empty pot and press or mill potatoes into pot. Stir remaining 1 teaspoon salt, remaining 6 tablespoons butter, and remaining 2/3 cup milk into potatoes until combined.

6. Using offset spatula, spread mashed potatoes evenly over top and sides of meatloaf. Heat broiler and return meatloaf to lower-middle oven rack. Broil until potatoes are browned, about 15 minutes. Using foil as sling, transfer meatloaf to carving board and let rest for 15 minutes. Slice and serve.

Meatloaf with Mushroom Gravy

SERVES 8

WHY THIS RECIPE WORKS We wanted to make a rustic meatloaf with a deep-brown crust and hearty mushroom gravy. Sliced button mushrooms plus minced porcini gave the gravy an earthy richness. To further boost the flavor of the meatloaf, we added the porcini soaking liquid and more button mushrooms, which we ground in a food processor and sautéed. To keep things simple, we baked the meatloaf in the same skillet. Then, while the loaf was resting, we used the skillet and the meat drippings to build our gravy.

If you're short the 2 tablespoons of meatloaf drippings needed to make the gravy, supplement the drippings with melted butter or vegetable oil.

AS GOOD AS GRANDMA'S

1	cup water
¼	ounce dried porcini mushrooms, rinsed
16	square or 18 round saltines
10	ounces white mushrooms, trimmed, divided
1	tablespoon vegetable oil
1	onion, chopped fine
1½	teaspoons table salt, divided
4	garlic cloves, minced
1	pound ground pork
2	large eggs
1	tablespoon plus ¾ teaspoon Worcestershire sauce
¾	teaspoon pepper
1	pound 85 percent lean ground beef
¾	teaspoon minced fresh thyme
¼	cup all-purpose flour
2½	cups chicken broth

1. Adjust oven rack to middle position and heat oven to 375 degrees. Microwave water and porcini in covered bowl until steaming, about 1 minute. Let sit until softened, about 5 minutes. Strain porcini through fine-mesh strainer lined with coffee filter, reserving liquid. Mince and reserve porcini.

2. Process saltines in food processor until finely ground, about 30 seconds; transfer to large bowl and reserve. Pulse 5 ounces of white mushrooms in processor until finely ground, 8 to 10 pulses.

3. Heat oil in 12-inch nonstick oven-safe skillet over medium-high heat until shimmering. Add onion and cook until browned, 6 to 8 minutes. Stir in processed mushrooms and ¼ teaspoon salt and cook until liquid evaporates and mushrooms begin to brown, about 5 minutes. Add garlic and cook until fragrant, about 30 seconds. Transfer to bowl with saltines and let cool to room temperature, about 15 minutes. Wipe out skillet with paper towels.

4. Add pork, ¼ cup reserved porcini liquid, eggs, 1 tablespoon Worcestershire, 1 teaspoon salt, and pepper to cooled mushroom-saltine mixture and knead gently until nearly combined. Add beef and knead until well combined. Transfer meat mixture to now-empty skillet and shape into 10 by 6-inch loaf. Bake until meatloaf registers 160 degrees, 45 to 55 minutes. Transfer meatloaf to carving board and tent loosely with aluminum foil.

5. Slice remaining 5 ounces white mushrooms. Discard any solids in skillet and pour off all but 2 tablespoons fat. Heat fat over medium-high heat until shimmering. Add sliced mushrooms and reserved porcini and cook, stirring occasionally, until deep golden brown, 6 to 8 minutes. Stir in thyme and remaining ¼ teaspoon salt and cook until fragrant, about 30 seconds. Add flour and cook, stirring frequently, until golden, about 2 minutes. Slowly whisk in broth, ½ cup reserved porcini liquid, and remaining ¾ teaspoon Worcestershire, scraping up any browned bits, and bring to boil. Reduce heat to medium and simmer, whisking occasionally, until thickened, 10 to 15 minutes. Season with salt and pepper to taste. Slice meatloaf and serve with gravy.

Bacon-Wrapped Meatloaf
SERVES 6 TO 8

WHY THIS RECIPE WORKS What's even better than a bacon-wrapped meatloaf? A bacon-wrapped meatloaf that also has chopped bacon added to the ground beef inside. To make shaping easy, we lined a loaf pan with plastic wrap and then shingled slices of bacon in the pan. After pressing the meatloaf mixture into the pan, we turned it out onto a piece of foil set on a wire rack inside a rimmed baking sheet. This allowed the fat from the meat to drain away from the loaf as it cooked. A pass under the broiler ensured that the bacon was crispy and that the spicy-sweet glaze caramelized to perfection.

Bull's-Eye Original is our favorite barbecue sauce. Do not use thick-cut bacon for this recipe, as the package will yield fewer strips for wrapping the meatloaf.

¼	cup barbecue sauce, plus extra for serving
1	tablespoon cider vinegar
1	tablespoon Worcestershire sauce
1	tablespoon spicy brown mustard
17	square or 19 round saltines, crushed (⅔ cup)
4	slices coarsely chopped bacon, plus 8 whole slices
1	onion, chopped coarse
3	garlic cloves, minced
⅓	cup whole milk
2	large eggs plus 1 large yolk
⅓	cup minced fresh parsley
¾	teaspoon table salt
½	teaspoon pepper
1½	pounds 90 percent lean ground beef

1. Adjust oven rack to upper-middle position and heat oven to 375 degrees. Line rimmed baking sheet with aluminum foil and set wire rack in sheet. Whisk barbecue sauce, vinegar, Worcestershire, and mustard together in bowl; set glaze aside.

2. Process saltines in food processor until finely ground, about 30 seconds; transfer to large bowl. Pulse chopped bacon and onion in now-empty processor until coarsely ground, about 10 pulses. Transfer bacon mixture to 10-inch nonstick skillet and cook over medium heat until onion is soft and translucent, about 5 minutes. Add garlic and cook until fragrant, about 30 seconds. Set aside off heat.

3. Add milk, eggs and yolk, parsley, salt, pepper, and 2 tablespoons glaze to saltines and mash with fork until chunky paste forms. Stir in bacon mixture until combined. Add the beef and knead with your hands until combined.

4. Lightly spray 8½ by 4½-inch loaf pan with vegetable oil spray. Line pan with large sheet of plastic wrap, with extra plastic hanging over edges of pan. Push plastic into corners and up sides of pan. Line pan crosswise with remaining 8 bacon slices, overlapping them slightly and letting excess hang over edges of pan (you should have at least ½ inch of overhanging bacon). Brush bacon with 3 tablespoons glaze. Transfer meatloaf mixture to bacon-lined pan and press mixture firmly into pan. Fold bacon slices over mixture.

5. Using metal skewer or tip of paring knife, poke 15 holes in one 14 by 3-inch piece of foil. Center foil rectangle on top of meatloaf. Carefully flip meatloaf onto wire rack so foil is on bottom and bacon is on top. Gripping plastic, gently lift and remove pan from meatloaf. Discard plastic. Gently press meatloaf into 9 by 5-inch rectangle.

6. Bake until bacon is browned and meatloaf registers 150 degrees, about 1 hour. Remove from oven and heat broiler. Brush top and sides of meatloaf with remaining 2 tablespoons glaze. Broil meatloaf until glaze begins to char and meatloaf registers 160 degrees, 3 to 5 minutes. Using foil as sling, transfer meatloaf to carving board and let rest for 15 minutes. Slice and serve, passing extra barbecue sauce.

That's a Wrap

Invert the foil-topped loaf, bacon and all, onto a wire rack set in a baking sheet, remove the loaf pan and plastic, press the meatloaf into shape, and bake.

Meatloaf with Mushroom Gravy

Bacon-Wrapped Meatloaf

Ground Beef Stroganoff

SERVES 4

WHY THIS RECIPE WORKS Many upscale versions of beef Stroganoff call for pricey beef tenderloin, while the weeknight version of this recipe features ground beef with canned cream of mushroom soup. We set out to create an easy and comforting Stroganoff that kicked the can to the curb while remaining quick and inexpensive. For the sauce, we used a combination of chicken broth and white wine. Increasing the amounts of each allowed us to cook the egg noodles right in the sauce. Sautéed fresh mushrooms boosted the dish's meatiness, and sour cream added tang and richness. To finish, we sprinkled the dish with bright-green chives for oniony bite.

Pennsylvania Dutch Wide Egg Noodles are our favorite.

- 2 tablespoons vegetable oil, divided
- 8 ounces white mushrooms, trimmed and sliced thin
- 1 teaspoon table salt, divided
- ¾ teaspoon pepper, divided
- 1 onion, chopped fine
- 2 garlic cloves, minced
- 1 pound 85 percent lean ground beef
- 3 tablespoons all-purpose flour
- 4 cups chicken broth
- ¼ cup dry white wine
- 8 ounces (4 cups) egg noodles
- ½ cup sour cream, plus extra for serving
- 2 tablespoons minced fresh chives

1. Heat 1 tablespoon oil in Dutch oven over medium-high heat until shimmering. Add mushrooms and ¼ teaspoon salt and cook until liquid has evaporated and mushrooms begin to brown, 5 to 7 minutes; transfer to bowl.

2. Add remaining 1 tablespoon oil to now-empty pot and return to medium-high heat until shimmering. Add onion, garlic, ½ teaspoon salt, and ½ teaspoon pepper and cook, stirring occasionally, until onion begins to soften, about 5 minutes. Add beef, remaining ¼ teaspoon salt, and remaining ¼ teaspoon pepper and cook, breaking up meat with spoon, until no longer pink, 5 to 7 minutes.

3. Add flour and stir until beef is well coated; cook for 1 minute. Stir in broth and wine and bring to simmer, scraping up any browned bits. Cook until mixture is slightly thickened, about 3 minutes. Stir in noodles; reduce heat to medium; and cook, uncovered, until noodles are tender, 10 to 12 minutes, stirring occasionally.

4. Off heat, stir in sour cream and mushrooms until fully combined. Season with salt and pepper to taste. Transfer to shallow platter and sprinkle with chives. Serve, passing extra sour cream separately.

The Namesake of a Favorite Noodle Dish

Picture him with his knee-high riding boots, tousled hair, and piercing eyes: Count Pavel Stroganov cut a striking figure in 18th-century Russia. At that time, members of the Russian court were Francophiles, speaking French and turning to Paris for cultural inspiration. Beef Stroganoff was likely created by a French chef in honor of the Count. As was often the case when cooking for a patron, the dish was named for him, and the name stuck even as it reached American shores a century after his death. In the 1950s, the dish enjoyed a minor vogue in fancy stateside restaurants; after a few decades in obscurity, it's seen a revival in recent years.

Salisbury Steak

SERVES 4

WHY THIS RECIPE WORKS We wanted to rescue this American classic from the frozen foods aisle for a great weeknight option. We started by mixing a panade into ground beef to help bind the meat and preserve moisture, but this made the dish taste too much like meatloaf. We added mashed potatoes instead and were impressed with the silky texture and great flavor of the patties. To make the dish easier, we swapped in instant potato flakes. We browned the patties on both sides and let them finish cooking in the rich sauce, which kept the beef tender.

When shaping the patties in step 1, be sure to wet your hands to prevent sticking. Tawny port or dry sherry can be substituted for the ruby port. Do not use potato granules, which add an off-flavor.

½	cup milk
7	tablespoons instant potato flakes
1	pound 90 percent lean ground beef
1	teaspoon table salt, divided
½	teaspoon pepper
4	tablespoons unsalted butter, divided
1	onion, halved and sliced thin
1	pound white mushrooms, trimmed and sliced thin
1	tablespoon tomato paste
2	tablespoons all-purpose flour
1¾	cups beef broth
¼	cup ruby port

1. Whisk milk and potato flakes in large bowl. Add beef, ½ teaspoon salt, and pepper and knead until combined. Shape into four ½-inch-thick oval patties and transfer to parchment paper–lined plate. Refrigerate for at least 30 minutes or up to 4 hours.

2. Melt 1 tablespoon butter in 12-inch nonstick skillet over medium-high heat. Cook patties until well browned on each side, about 10 minutes. Transfer to plate.

3. Add onion and remaining 3 tablespoons butter to now-empty skillet and cook until onion is softened, about 5 minutes. Add mushrooms and remaining ½ teaspoon salt and cook until liquid has evaporated, 5 to 7 minutes. Stir in tomato paste and flour and cook until browned, about 2 minutes. Slowly stir in broth and port and bring to simmer. Return patties to skillet, cover, and simmer over medium-low heat until cooked through, 12 to 15 minutes. Season sauce with salt and pepper to taste. Serve.

Tater Tot Hotdish

SERVES 6 TO 8

WHY THIS RECIPE WORKS Hotdish is to Minnesotans what a casserole is to the rest of the country. For a fresh take on the classic, we skipped the typical cream of mushroom soup (to bind everything together) and made our own sauce by sprinkling flour over the meat and vegetables, adding chicken broth and milk, and stirring in Parmesan cheese. Using a shallow baking dish kept the tots from sinking into the filling, and placing the dish on the upper-middle oven rack browned the tots nicely.

Be sure to buy cylinder-shaped frozen Tater Tots (not crispy crowns or coins). Do not thaw the tots or the vegetables; they go into the hotdish frozen. Serve with ketchup.

Ground Beef Stroganoff

Salisbury Steak

Tater Tot Hotdish

1½ pounds 85 percent lean ground beef
1 pound white mushrooms, trimmed and sliced thin
1 onion, chopped
4 garlic cloves, minced
1 tablespoon minced fresh thyme
1½ teaspoons table salt
1½ teaspoons pepper
3 tablespoons all-purpose flour
1½ cups whole milk
1½ cups chicken broth
3 ounces Parmesan cheese, grated (1½ cups)
1 cup frozen peas
1 cup frozen corn
1 (2-pound) bag frozen Tater Tots

1. Adjust oven rack to upper-middle position and heat oven to 450 degrees. Combine beef, mushrooms, onion, garlic, thyme, salt, and pepper in Dutch oven. Cook over medium-high heat until nearly all liquid has evaporated, 25 to 28 minutes, stirring occasionally and breaking up meat with spoon.

2. Stir in flour until fully incorporated and cook for 1 minute. Stir in milk and broth and bring to simmer, scraping up any browned bits. Cook until mixture is slightly thickened, about 3 minutes. Off heat, stir in Parmesan. Transfer mixture to 13 by 9-inch baking dish.

3. Sprinkle peas and corn evenly over beef mixture. Lightly arrange Tater Tots in even layer over top, but do not press into mixture (you may have extra Tater Tots). Bake until Tater Tots are deep golden brown and filling is bubbling, 35 to 38 minutes, rotating dish halfway through baking. Let cool for 15 minutes before serving.

To Make Ahead At end of step 2, let beef mixture cool completely, then cover with aluminum foil and refrigerate for up to 24 hours. To serve, bake beef mixture, covered, until hot in center, 15 to 20 minutes. Remove foil, stir beef mixture, sprinkle with peas and corn, arrange Tater Tots on top, and bake as directed in step 3.

Swiss Steak with Tomato Gravy

SERVES 6 TO 8

WHY THIS RECIPE WORKS The point of Swiss steak is to transform a tough, inexpensive cut of meat into a delicate meal so tender you can almost eat it with a spoon. Many recipes called for tenderizing the meat by pounding it before cooking, but we know from experience that pounding meat does nothing to tenderize it. Instead we relied on a slow braise to create the ideal texture. To flavor the Swiss steak gravy, we found that a combination of sautéed onion, diced tomatoes, and sun-dried tomatoes was ideal.

Top blade roast may also be labeled chuck roast first cut, top chuck roast, flat iron roast, or simply blade roast.

1 (3½- to 4-pound) boneless top blade roast, trimmed
1 teaspoon table salt
1 teaspoon pepper
2 tablespoons vegetable oil, divided
1 onion, halved and sliced thin
2 tablespoons tomato paste
1 tablespoon all-purpose flour
3 garlic cloves, minced
½ teaspoon dried thyme
1 (14.5-ounce) can diced tomatoes
1½ cups chicken broth

1 tablespoon sun-dried tomatoes packed in oil, rinsed, patted dry, and minced
1 tablespoon minced fresh parsley

1. Adjust oven rack to middle position and heat oven to 300 degrees. Cut roast crosswise into quarters. Working with one piece at a time, turn meat on its side to expose line of gristle that runs through center. Remove center line of gristle by slicing through meat on either side of gristle to yield 2 "steaks."

2. Pat steaks dry with paper towels and season lightly with salt and pepper. Heat 1 tablespoon oil in Dutch oven over medium-high heat just until smoking. Brown 4 steaks on both sides, about 6 minutes. Transfer to plate and repeat with remaining oil and steaks.

3. Add onion to empty pot and cook until softened, about 5 minutes. Add tomato paste, flour, garlic, and thyme and cook until fragrant, about 1 minute. Stir in diced tomatoes and broth and bring to boil.

4. Return steaks and any accumulated juices to pan. Cover, transfer to oven and cook until steaks are fork-tender, about 2 hours. Transfer steaks to platter, tent with aluminum foil, and let rest for 5 minutes. Skim fat from sauce. Stir in sun-dried tomatoes and parsley. Season with salt and pepper to taste. Pour sauce over steaks. Serve.

Swiss Steak with Tomato Gravy

Jamaican Oxtail

SERVES 6 TO 8

WHY THIS RECIPE WORKS Jillian Atkinson, a food writer living in Brooklyn, New York, learned this dish from her grandma. A staple of Jamaican cuisine, oxtails feature a round bone surrounded by a bit of tough meat. A long braise tenderizes the meat and extracts gelatin from the bone. While some cook their oxtail in caramelized sugar before braising it (a step called browning). Jillian's grandmother would occasionally omit browning entirely and replace it with thick, dark soy sauce. This recipe uses both techniques, striking a balance between salty and sweet.

Plan ahead: The oxtails need to marinate for at least 4 hours before cooking. Note that the oxtail marinade is reserved and added to the pot in step 9. We call for using dark soy sauce here, which is thicker and slightly sweeter than regular soy sauce. Search for it online or at an Asian grocery store. Butter beans are also called baby lima beans. If you can't find them canned, you can substitute 1½ cups (about 8 ounces) of

Jamaican Oxtail

frozen beans. You can substitute a habanero chile for the Scotch bonnet chile, if desired. It's important to have the hot water called for in step 6 ready to add as soon as the sugar has properly browned. The wide time range for the reduction in step 10 accounts for the varying heating capabilities of different stovetops. Be sure to reduce the liquid until it is thickened and just below the top of the oxtails. Jamaican Rice and Peas (recipe follows) is a traditional side dish.

Oxtail

- 5 pounds oxtails, 2 to 2½ inches thick, trimmed
- 2 onions, halved and sliced thin
- 10 sprigs fresh thyme
- 2 scallions, crushed with side of knife, then chopped
- 2 tablespoons distilled white vinegar
- 1 tablespoon table salt
- 1 tablespoon pepper
- 1 tablespoon Worcestershire sauce
- 1 tablespoon dark soy sauce
- 3 garlic cloves, chopped
- 1 teaspoon onion powder
- 1 teaspoon garlic powder
- 8 whole allspice berries
- 6 cups hot water
- 1 Scotch bonnet chile
- 1 (15.5-ounce) can butter beans, rinsed
- ¼ cup ketchup

Browning

- ¼ cup sugar
- ¼ cup hot water

1. For the Oxtail Place oxtails in large bowl and fill with cold water. Agitate to remove any loose bone and fat fragments. Drain and repeat, then drain again.

2. Add onions, thyme sprigs, scallions, vinegar, salt, pepper, Worcestershire, soy sauce, garlic, onion powder, garlic powder, and allspice berries to bowl with oxtails and toss to thoroughly combine. Cover and refrigerate for at least 4 hours or up to 24 hours.

3. Brush marinade off oxtails and transfer oxtails to plate; reserve marinade to use in step 9.

4. For the Browning Add sugar to center of large Dutch oven. Place pot over medium-low heat and cook, without stirring, until edges of sugar begin to liquefy and turn golden, about 4 minutes. Using long-handled wooden spoon or heat-resistant rubber spatula, pull edges of melted sugar inward to help melt remaining sugar.

5. Continue to cook until sugar turns dark chocolate brown, 4 to 6 minutes longer, stirring often for even cooking. (Browning will smoke; we recommend turning on your hood vent.)

6. Carefully add ¼ cup hot water to browning (mixture will sputter and let off steam) and stir to incorporate. Simmer until reduced by half and large bubbles break surface, 1½ to 2 minutes.

7. Add oxtails to browning and increase heat to medium-high (pot will be crowded). Cook, turning oxtails frequently, until oxtails have picked up significant color from sugar-based browning, some fond has begun to form on bottom of pot, and most moisture has cooked off to point where sizzling can be heard, 10 to 12 minutes.

8. Add 6 cups hot water to pot and bring to boil. Cover; reduce heat to medium-low; and cook at strong simmer for 2½ hours, stirring and turning oxtails occasionally.

9. Stir reserved marinade into pot. Poke small hole in Scotch bonnet with tip of paring knife and add to pot. Cover and continue to simmer until largest oxtails are fork-tender and meat begins to fall easily off bone, about 1 hour longer, stirring occasionally and being mindful not to burst Scotch bonnet as you stir.

10. Stir in butter beans and continue to simmer, covered, until meat falls easily off bone, about 30 minutes longer. Stir in ketchup and cook, uncovered, until liquid has thickened and reduced to just below surface of oxtails, 5 to 15 minutes. Serve.

Jamaican Rice and Peas

SERVES 6

WHY THIS RECIPE WORKS Rice and peas is so foundational in Jamaican cooking that it has been called the nation's "coat of arms." For our version, we remained faithful to traditional recipes, soaking dried red kidney beans (Jamaicans call them peas) before simmering them in a mixture of chicken broth and coconut milk. To ensure that our recipe resulted in the right amount of leftover liquid to cook the rice, we strained the beans over a measuring cup, settling on a precise 3½ cups (and adding water as necessary). Placing a sheet of aluminum foil under the saucepan lid created a tight seal against excess evaporation that might have left us with too little liquid.

If you can't find a Scotch bonnet chile, you can substitute a habanero. Rinse the rice in a fine-mesh strainer until the water runs clear. Once the saucepan is covered in step 4, do not uncover it until after the 10-minute rest.

Jamaican Rice and Peas

3. Drain bean mixture in fine-mesh strainer set over 8-cup liquid measuring cup or large bowl. Discard thyme sprigs and Scotch bonnet. Return bean mixture to saucepan along with 3½ cups bean cooking liquid (add water to compensate if necessary; reserve any excess for another use or discard).

4. Stir rice and butter into bean mixture. Bring to boil over high heat. Once boiling, stir and place large sheet of aluminum foil over saucepan and cover tightly with lid. Reduce heat to low and cook for 20 minutes. Remove from heat and let rest, covered, for 10 minutes. Transfer rice and bean mixture to shallow serving bowl. Fluff rice with fork and serve.

Olympia Provisions–Style Choucroute Garnie

SERVES 8

WHY THIS RECIPE WORKS At its simplest, choucroute garnie is a rustic, rib-sticking, country-style dish that puts the focus on the meat. The dish has roots in the Alsace region of France: "Choucroute" means "sauerkraut" in French. And while there's plenty of sauerkraut in this dish, it's garnished with lots of pork. Our recipe is inspired by Elias Cairo, co-owner and lead salumist of Olympia Provisions in Portland, Oregon. He explained to us that each butcher and chef has their own version that they serve for friends or as a family meal at their restaurant. The trick is to create a dish that's rich and meaty but also tempered with just enough acidity and contrasting texture to keep things in balance. Scoring three kinds of sausages before pan-frying them allowed them to get crispier in the pan. Seared ham and rendered bacon drove home the porky richness, and if you count lard, brought the pork count to six. Cooking potatoes in sauerkraut brine infused them with tons of flavor. Combining the potatoes, kraut, meats, and some slightly acidic Riesling and letting everything simmer together melded the flavors.

Note that we call for fully cooked bratwurst here. Two pounds of sauerkraut typically yields 1 to 1½ cups of brine, depending on the brand. The variability is OK; just add enough water to the potato-brine mixture to cover the potatoes by 1 inch. This recipe was developed with Olympia Provisions meats and sauerkraut, but other brands can be used.

- 1 cup dried red kidney beans, picked over and rinsed
- 3 cups chicken broth
- 1 (14-ounce) can coconut milk
- 10 sprigs fresh thyme
- 2 scallions, sliced thin
- 4 garlic cloves, chopped coarse
- 1 Scotch bonnet chile
- 2 teaspoons table salt
- ½ teaspoon pepper
- ¼ teaspoon whole allspice berries
- 2 cups long-grain white rice, rinsed
- 2 tablespoons unsalted butter

1. Combine 1 quart cold water and beans in bowl and soak at room temperature for at least 8 hours or up to 24 hours.

2. Drain beans and transfer to large saucepan. Add broth, coconut milk, thyme sprigs, scallions, garlic, Scotch bonnet, salt, pepper, and allspice berries. Bring to boil over high heat. Cover; reduce heat to medium-low; and simmer until beans are tender, 45 minutes to 1 hour.

AS GOOD AS GRANDMA'S   153

Olympia Provisions–Style Choucroute Garnie

Milk-Can Supper

2	pounds sauerkraut, drained with brine reserved
1¼	pounds Yukon gold potatoes, unpeeled and cut into 1¼- to 1½-inch pieces
2	teaspoons table salt
12	ounces kielbasa sausage, cut crosswise into 4 pieces
12	ounces Frankfurters, halved crosswise
12	ounces cooked bratwurst
1	tablespoon lard, or vegetable oil
8	ounces ham steak, ½ inch thick, patted dry and quartered
6	ounces skinless slab bacon, cut into ¾-inch pieces
1	cup off-dry Riesling
1	cup whole-grain mustard

1. Combine sauerkraut brine, potatoes, salt, and enough water to cover potatoes by 1 inch (4 to 5 cups) in large saucepan. Bring to boil over high heat, reduce heat to medium-low, and simmer until paring knife inserted into potatoes meets no resistance, about 10 minutes. Off heat, let potatoes sit in cooking liquid while preparing sausages. (Once cooled, potatoes can be refrigerated overnight in liquid.)

2. Meanwhile, score kielbasa, Frankfurters, and bratwurst on 2 opposing sides, ⅛ inch deep, about every ½ inch. Heat lard in 12-inch nonstick skillet over medium-high heat until just smoking. Add about two-thirds of sausages to pan and cook until browned on each scored side, 2 to 3 minutes per side; transfer to plate. Repeat with remaining sausages and ham (ham will only brown slightly), then transfer to plate.

3. Cook bacon in large Dutch oven over medium-low heat until fat is rendered and bacon is nearly crispy, 10 to 12 minutes. Increase heat to medium and stir in drained sauerkraut and wine. Drain potatoes and stir into sauerkraut mixture. Bring to simmer over medium heat, cover, and cook for 5 minutes.

4. Nestle sausages and ham into sauerkraut mixture (some sausages will need to sit on top; this is OK). Cover and continue to cook 5 minutes longer. Transfer sausages and ham to plate. Transfer sauerkraut mixture to large, shallow platter, then top with sausages and ham. Serve with mustard.

On the Road: A Dish Meant to be Customized

"Choucroute is a local dish that everybody kind of puts their own spin on," says Eric Joppie, culinary director at Olympia Provisions in Portland, Oregon. "I've seen big pieces of salt pork, big pieces of smoked bacon, everything from different types of sausages to also having whole pieces of hocks and shanks. I've even seen some recipes that contain duck confit or goose fat." In other words, according to Eric, choucroute garnie is a flexible, elastic, and ultimately personal dish.

"Apples would be good in this, I think. Other root vegetables would be good. Sauerkraut made with kohlrabi." Eric continues to brainstorm, the ideas flowing like water. "It's a nice dish."

Milk-Can Supper

SERVES 6 TO 8

WHY THIS RECIPE WORKS Traditionally, cowboys layered vegetables and meat (usually sausage) into a giant milk can, then cooked it over an open fire to feed large groups of cowhands. To bring this all-in-one dish into the home kitchen, we opted to use a Dutch oven but keep the basic technique of layering ingredients according to cooking time. Browning the Bratwurst first created flavorful fond. We lined the bottom of the pot with sturdy red potatoes to protect the other vegetables from burning, and we added the quick-cooking green bell peppers halfway through cooking. Traditional lager as a cooking liquid gave our meat-and-potatoes meal toasty depth.

If your Dutch oven is slightly smaller than 8 quarts, the lid may not close all the way when you start cooking. But as the contents of the pot cook, they will decrease in volume, so you'll soon be able to clamp on the lid. Use small red potatoes, measuring 1 to 2 inches in diameter. Light-bodied American lagers, such as Budweiser, work best in this recipe.

- 1 tablespoon vegetable oil
- 2½ pounds bratwurst (10 sausages)
- 2 pounds small red potatoes, unpeeled
- 1 head green cabbage (2 pounds), cored and cut into 8 wedges
- 3 ears corn, husks and silk removed, ears cut into 3 pieces
- 6 carrots, peeled and cut into 2-inch pieces
- 1 onion, halved and cut through root end into 8 wedges
- 4 garlic cloves, peeled and smashed
- 10 sprigs fresh thyme
- 2 bay leaves
- 1 teaspoon table salt
- ½ teaspoon pepper
- 1½ cups beer
- 2 green bell peppers, stemmed, seeded, and cut into 1-inch-wide strips

1. Heat oil in 8-quart Dutch oven over medium heat until shimmering. Add bratwurst and cook until browned all over, 6 to 8 minutes. Remove pot from heat. Transfer bratwurst to cutting board and halve crosswise.

2. Place potatoes in single layer in now-empty Dutch oven. Arrange cabbage wedges in single layer on top of potatoes. Layer corn, carrots, onion, garlic, thyme, bay leaves, salt, and pepper over cabbage. Pour beer over vegetables and arrange browned bratwursts on top.

3. Bring to boil over medium-high heat (wisps of steam will be visible). Cover, reduce heat to medium, and simmer for 15 minutes. Add bell peppers and continue to simmer, covered, until potatoes are tender, about 15 minutes. (Use long skewer to test potatoes for doneness.)

4. Transfer bratwurst and vegetables to large serving platter (or roasting pan, if your platter isn't large enough); discard thyme sprigs and bay leaves. Pour 1 cup cooking liquid over platter. Season with salt and pepper to taste. Serve, passing remaining cooking liquid separately.

Pan-Fried Pork Chops

Pan-Fried Pork Chops
SERVES 4

WHY THIS RECIPE WORKS Not all pork chops are created alike—for pan-frying, we found that center-cut or bone-in pork chops worked best. The bone added valuable flavor to the meat and prevented it from drying out. Simply dredging the pork chops in flour, as most recipes instructed, produced a spotty, insubstantial crust that wouldn't stay put. We have had success letting floured chicken rest before re-dredging and frying, and we wondered if the same treatment would work for pork. Sure enough, our double-dipped chops emerged from the pan with a hefty, crisp, golden-brown crust.

Chops between ¾ and 1 inch thick will work in this recipe.

- 1 teaspoon garlic powder
- ½ teaspoon paprika
- ½ teaspoon table salt
- ½ teaspoon pepper
- ¼ teaspoon cayenne pepper
- 1 cup all-purpose flour
- 4 (8- to 10-ounce) bone-in pork rib or center-cut chops, about ¾ inch thick, trimmed
- 3 slices bacon, chopped
- ½ cup vegetable oil

1. Combine garlic powder, paprika, salt, pepper, and cayenne in bowl. Place flour in shallow dish. Pat chops dry with paper towels. Cut 2 slits about 2 inches apart through fat and connective tissue on edge of each chop. Season both sides of chops with spice mixture, then dredge chops lightly in flour (do not discard flour). Transfer to plate and let rest for 10 minutes.

2. Meanwhile, cook bacon in 12-inch nonstick skillet over medium heat until fat renders and bacon is crisp, 5 to 7 minutes. Using slotted spoon, transfer bacon to paper towel–lined plate and reserve for another use. Do not wipe out pan.

3. Add oil to fat in pan and heat over medium-high heat until just smoking. Return chops to flour dish and turn to coat chops again. Cook chops until well browned on each side, 6 to 8 minutes. Serve.

Pan-Fried Pork Chops with Milk Gravy

BBQ Pan-Fried Pork Chops

Replace first 5 ingredients with 3 tablespoons light brown sugar, 1 teaspoon chili powder, 1 teaspoon paprika, ½ teaspoon salt, ½ teaspoon dry mustard, ¼ teaspoon ground cumin, and ¼ teaspoon cayenne pepper.

Herbed Pan-Fried Pork Chops

Replace first 5 ingredients with ½ teaspoon dried marjoram, ½ teaspoon dried thyme, ¼ teaspoon dried basil, ¼ teaspoon dried rosemary (crumbled), ¼ teaspoon dried sage, pinch ground fennel, and ½ teaspoon salt.

Pan-Fried Pork Chops with Milk Gravy

SERVES 4

WHY THIS RECIPE WORKS To produce pan-fried pork chops with a supercrunchy coating, we added a small amount of milk to seasoned flour to create a shaggy dough that readily stuck to the chops. Refrigerating the coated chops briefly before frying them helped keep their coatings in place. We tried loin, blade, and rib chops and settled on rib chops for their moist meat. Shallow-frying the chops in two batches allowed us to use less oil. The gravy came together easily. To the fat left in the skillet, we whisked in a bit more flour, added some milk, and let the mixture simmer and thicken for just a few minutes. Just one teaspoon of pepper provided the perfect smattering of flecks and pushed this gravy over the finish line.

Use pork chops no more than ½ inch thick to ensure that the meat cooks through before the breading begins to burn. If you can find only chops that are slightly thicker than ½ inch, thin them with a meat pounder.

- 1 cup plus 2 tablespoons all-purpose flour, divided
- 2 teaspoons garlic powder
- 2½ teaspoons table salt, divided
- 2½ teaspoons pepper, divided
- ½ teaspoon cayenne pepper
- 2 tablespoons plus 1½ cups whole milk, divided
- 2 large eggs
- 4 (5- to 7-ounce) bone-in pork rib chops, ½ inch thick, trimmed
- 1 cup vegetable oil

1. Whisk 1 cup flour, garlic powder, 1½ teaspoons salt, 1 teaspoon pepper, and cayenne together in shallow dish. Add 2 tablespoons milk to flour mixture; using your fingers, rub flour and milk together until milk is fully incorporated and shaggy pieces of dough form. Whisk eggs together in second shallow dish.

2. Set wire rack in rimmed baking sheet. Pat chops dry with paper towels and sprinkle with ½ teaspoon salt and ½ teaspoon pepper. Working with 1 chop at a time, dredge chops in flour mixture, shaking off any excess; dip into eggs to thoroughly coat, letting excess drip back into dish; and dredge again in flour mixture, pressing gently to adhere. Transfer to prepared wire rack. Refrigerate coated chops for at least 15 minutes or up to 2 hours.

3. Line large plate with triple layer of paper towels. Heat oil in 12-inch nonstick skillet over medium-high heat to 375 degrees. Add 2 chops and cook until golden brown and meat registers 140 degrees, 2 to 3 minutes per side. Transfer to prepared plate. Repeat with remaining 2 chops.

4. Carefully pour off all but 2 tablespoons fat from skillet and place skillet over medium heat. Whisk in remaining 2 tablespoons flour, remaining 1 teaspoon pepper, and remaining ½ teaspoon salt and cook until bubbly and fragrant, about 30 seconds. Whisk in remaining 1½ cups milk, bring to boil, and cook until slightly thickened, about 2 minutes. Serve gravy with chops.

Smothered Pork Chops

SERVES 4

WHY THIS RECIPE WORKS Bone-in chops were a must for smothered pork chops, because the bone kept the meat moist and added flavor to the sauce. Caramelizing the onions made the sauce too sweet and took almost an hour. We had better luck cooking them in butter until they were lightly browned. We swapped out chicken broth in favor of meatier beef broth, which greatly improved the flavor of our sauce. Adding dried thyme, a bay leaf, and cider vinegar bumped up the flavor even more. To thicken our broth, we made a cornstarch-and-broth slurry. The results? A silky sauce that clung to our chops.

Chops thicker than ½ inch won't be fully tender in the allotted cooking time.

AS GOOD AS GRANDMA'S

- 1 teaspoon onion powder
- ½ teaspoon paprika
- ½ teaspoon table salt
- ½ teaspoon pepper
- ¼ teaspoon cayenne pepper
- 4 (8- to 10-ounce) bone-in blade-cut pork chops, about ½ inch thick, trimmed
- 1½ tablespoons vegetable oil
- 1 tablespoon unsalted butter
- 2 onions, halved and sliced ¼ inch thick
- 2 garlic cloves, minced
- ¼ teaspoon dried thyme
- ¾ cup plus 1 tablespoon beef broth
- 1 bay leaf
- 1 teaspoon cornstarch
- 1 teaspoon cider vinegar

1. Adjust oven rack to middle position and heat oven to 300 degrees. Combine onion powder, paprika, salt, pepper, and cayenne in small bowl. Pat chops dry with paper towels. Cut 2 slits about 2 inches apart through fat and connective tissue on edge of each chop. Rub chops with spice mixture.

2. Heat oil in large skillet over medium-high heat until just smoking. Brown chops on both sides, 6 to 8 minutes, and transfer to plate. Melt butter in now-empty skillet over medium heat. Cook onions until browned, 8 to 10 minutes. Add garlic and thyme and cook until fragrant, about 30 seconds. Stir in ¾ cup broth and bay leaf, scraping up any browned bits, and bring to boil. Return chops and any accumulated juices to pan, cover, and transfer to oven. Cook until chops are completely tender, about 1½ hours.

3. Transfer chops to platter and tent with aluminum foil. Discard bay leaf. Strain contents of skillet through fine-mesh strainer into large liquid measuring cup; reserve onions. Let liquid settle, then skim fat. Return 1½ cups defatted pan juices to now-empty skillet and bring to boil. Reduce heat to medium and simmer until sauce is reduced to 1 cup, about 5 minutes.

4. Whisk remaining 1 tablespoon broth and cornstarch in bowl until no lumps remain. Whisk cornstarch mixture into sauce and simmer until thickened, 1 to 2 minutes. Stir in reserved onions and vinegar. Season with salt and pepper to taste. Serve.

Cider-Braised Pork Chops
SERVES 6

WHY THIS RECIPE WORKS The apple flavor in cider-braised pork chops can be fleeting. We wanted tender, juicy chops infused with deep, rich cider flavor. Tasters preferred 1-inch blade chops for their heft, silky meat, and rich taste. Patting the chops dry before adding them to the heated Dutch oven helped them develop a flavorful crust. Apple cider lent both sweetness and tartness to the braising mixture and sauce, while a bit of fresh thyme provided a heady herbal component. Jarred apple butter added further apple flavor, and its natural pectin gave the sauce a thick, glossy consistency. A splash of cider vinegar provided brightness.

Do not use chops thinner than 1 inch. In step 3, a fat separator makes quick work of defatting the sauce.

- 6 (8- to 10-ounce) bone-in blade-cut pork chops, about 1 inch thick, trimmed
- ½ teaspoon table salt
- ½ teaspoon pepper
- 2 tablespoons vegetable oil

Smothered Pork Chops

browned bits with wooden spoon, and bring to boil. Add browned chops and any accumulated juices to pot, cover, and transfer to oven. Braise until chops are completely tender, about 1½ hours.

3. Transfer chops to serving platter. Strain sauce, then skim off fat. Whisk in vinegar, parsley, and remaining 2 tablespoons apple butter. Season with salt and pepper to taste. Serve, passing sauce at table. (Pork chops and sauce can be refrigerated separately for up to 2 days. To serve, reheat sauce and chops together over medium heat until chops are warmed through.)

Crispy Fried Shrimp
SERVES 4 TO 6

WHY THIS RECIPE WORKS Our goal for these fried shrimp was impeccably seasoned, crispy, tender morsels with an irresistible dipping sauce. We used extra-large shrimp because they could withstand enough time in the hot oil to get good browning. For a breading that would adhere well and get golden and crispy quickly, we dipped the seasoned shrimp in a light batter of seasoned flour, egg, and water and then into ultracrispy panko bread crumbs. Combining ketchup and horseradish with mayo, Worcestershire, lemon juice, cayenne, and Old Bay seasoning created a delectable spicy-creamy hybrid of cocktail and tartar sauce.

For this recipe, we like using extra-large shrimp (21 to 25 per pound), but jumbo shrimp (16 to 20 per pound) also work. We prefer untreated shrimp—those not treated with sodium or additives such as sodium tripolyphosphate (STPP). Most frozen E-Z peel shrimp have been treated (the ingredient list should tell you). If you're using treated shrimp, reduce the salt sprinkled on the shrimp in step 3 to ¼ teaspoon. Use a Dutch oven that holds 6 quarts or more. Serve with lemon wedges.

Sauce
- ½ cup ketchup
- ½ cup mayonnaise
- ¼ cup prepared horseradish
- 2 teaspoons Worcestershire sauce
- 1 teaspoon lemon juice
- ½ teaspoon Old Bay seasoning
- ½ teaspoon cayenne pepper

Cider-Braised Pork Chops

- 1 onion, chopped
- ¼ cup apple butter, divided
- 2 tablespoons all-purpose flour
- 3 garlic cloves, minced
- 1 cup apple cider
- 1 sprig fresh thyme
- 1 teaspoon cider vinegar
- 1 tablespoon finely chopped fresh parsley

1. Adjust oven rack to lower-middle position and heat oven to 300 degrees. Pat chops dry with paper towels. Cut 2 slits about 2 inches apart through fat and connective tissue on edge of each chop. Sprinkle chops with salt and pepper. Heat oil in Dutch oven over medium-high heat until just smoking. Brown 3 chops on each side, about 8 minutes; transfer to plate, and then repeat with remaining 3 chops.

2. Pour off all but 1 tablespoon fat from pot and cook onion over medium heat until softened, about 5 minutes. Stir in 2 tablespoons apple butter, flour, and garlic and cook until onion is coated and mixture is fragrant, about 1 minute. Stir in cider and thyme, scraping up any

AS GOOD AS GRANDMA'S   159

Shrimp

- ½ cup all-purpose flour
- ½ cup water
- 2 large eggs
- 1¼ teaspoons table salt, divided
- ½ teaspoon pepper, divided
- 2 cups panko bread crumbs
- 1 teaspoon garlic powder
- ¼ teaspoon cayenne pepper
- 1½ pounds extra-large shrimp (21 to 25 per pound), peeled, deveined, and tails left on
- 1½ quarts vegetable oil for frying

1. For the Sauce Whisk all ingredients in bowl until combined; set aside.

2. For the Shrimp Whisk flour, water, eggs, ½ teaspoon salt, and ¼ teaspoon pepper in bowl until no lumps remain. Spread panko in shallow dish.

3. Combine garlic powder, cayenne, remaining ¾ teaspoon salt, and remaining ¼ teaspoon pepper in small bowl. Pat shrimp dry with paper towels and sprinkle with spice mixture.

4. Working with 1 shrimp at a time, hold shrimp by tail and dip into batter, letting excess drip back into bowl, then coat with panko, pressing gently to adhere. Arrange breaded shrimp on rimmed baking sheet. Refrigerate while heating oil (breaded shrimp can be refrigerated for up to 2 hours).

5. Line platter with triple layer of paper towels. Add oil to large Dutch oven until it measures about 1 inch deep and heat over medium-high heat to 350 degrees. Add one-third of shrimp, one at a time, to hot oil. Fry, stirring gently to prevent shrimp from sticking together, until shrimp are golden brown, 1 to 2 minutes after adding last shrimp.

6. Transfer shrimp to prepared platter. Return oil to 350 degrees and repeat with remaining shrimp in 2 more batches. Serve immediately with sauce.

To Make Ahead At end of step 4, freeze breaded shrimp on sheet until firm, then transfer to zipper-lock bag and freeze for up to 1 month. Do not thaw before cooking; increase cooking time by 1 to 2 minutes.

Crispy Fish Sticks with Tartar Sauce

SERVES 4

WHY THIS RECIPE WORKS Forget the boxed varieties in the frozen foods aisle—our homemade fish sticks are fresh and crisp, and fry up in just minutes. Our recipe calls for cod, but halibut, haddock, and catfish are all worthy substitutes. Eggs beaten with mayonnaise helped our coating of crisp saltines and fresh bread crumbs adhere to the fish. We pan-fried the fish in two batches to ensure they cooked up even and crisp.

Be sure to rinse the capers, otherwise the tartar sauce will be too salty. Halibut, haddock, or catfish can be substituted for the cod.

- 4 slices hearty white sandwich bread, torn into quarters
- 16 square or 18 round saltines
- ½ cup all-purpose flour
- 2 large eggs
- 1 cup mayonnaise, divided
- 2 pounds skinless cod, cut into 1-inch-thick strips
- ½ teaspoon table salt
- ½ teaspoon pepper
- ¼ cup finely chopped dill pickles, plus 1 tablespoon pickle juice
- 1 tablespoon capers, rinsed and minced
- 1 cup vegetable oil, divided

1. Adjust oven rack to middle position and heat oven to 200 degrees. Pulse bread and saltines in food processor to fine crumbs, about 15 pulses; transfer to shallow dish. Place flour in second shallow dish. Beat eggs with ¼ cup mayonnaise in third shallow dish.

2. Pat fish dry with paper towels and season with salt and pepper. One at a time, coat fish strips lightly with flour, dip in egg mixture, and then dredge in crumbs, pressing on both sides to adhere. Transfer breaded fish to plate. Combine remaining ¾ cup mayonnaise, pickles, pickle juice, and capers in small bowl and set aside.

3. Heat ½ cup oil in large 12-inch nonstick skillet over medium heat until just smoking. Fry half of fish strips until deep golden and crisp on both sides, about 4 minutes. Drain on paper towel–lined plate and transfer to oven to keep warm. Discard oil, wipe out skillet, and repeat with remaining ½ cup oil and remaining fish. Serve with tartar sauce.

Lemonade with Honey

SERVES 6 TO 8

WHY THIS RECIPE WORKS This sweet, tart, refreshing lemonade is based on a recipe by Mikaila Ulmer, owner of Me & The Bees Lemonade. We muddled lemon slices with granulated sugar to extract the oils in the peels for deep flavor in addition to the bright, freshly squeezed lemon juice. Following Mikaila's wisdom, we added a little honey for a lightly floral flavor. After combining all the ingredients, we strained the lemonade to catch any stray lemon seeds and chilled it for at least one hour. Served over ice, it's a lovely twist on a summertime classic.

When purchasing lemons, choose large ones that give to gentle pressure; hard lemons have thicker skin and yield less juice. Lemons are commonly waxed to prevent moisture loss, increase shelf life, and protect from bruising during shipping. Scrub them with a vegetable brush under running water to remove wax, or buy organic lemons. Don't worry about the seeds in the extracted juice; the entire juice mixture is strained at the end of the recipe.

- ¾ cup sugar
- 13 lemons (2 sliced thin, 11 juiced to yield 2 cups)
- 56 ounces cold water
- ½ cup honey

1. Using potato masher, mash sugar and half of lemon slices in large bowl until sugar is completely wet, about 1 minute.

2. Add water and lemon juice and whisk until sugar is completely dissolved, about 1 minute. Strain mixture through fine-mesh strainer set over serving pitcher, pressing on solids to extract as much juice as possible; discard solids.

3. Discard any ends from remaining lemon slices. Stir in honey and remaining lemon slices and refrigerate until chilled, at least 1 hour or up to 3 days. Stir to recombine before serving over ice.

Ginger Lemonade
Mash ½ cup peeled, thinly sliced ginger with sugar and half of lemon slices.

Mint Lemonade
Mash 1 cup fresh mint leaves with sugar and half of lemon slices. Add ½ cup fresh mint leaves to strained lemonade.

Crispy Fish Sticks with Tartar Sauce

Lemonade with Honey

fork-in-the-road favorites

- 164 Batter-Fried Chicken
- 165 Creole Fried Chicken
- 166 Extra-Crunchy Fried Chicken
- 167 Lard-Fried Chicken
- 168 Nashville Hot Fried Chicken
- 170 Honey Fried Chicken
- 171 Garlic Fried Chicken
- 172 North Carolina Dipped Fried Chicken
- 173 Mimosa Fried Chicken
- 175 Hawaiian-Style Fried Chicken
- 175 Ranch Fried Chicken
- 177 Sweet Tea–Brined Fried Chicken Thighs
- 178 Chicken Nuggets
- 179 Popcorn Chicken
- 180 Greek Chicken
- 180 Chicken Sauce Piquant
- 182 Lemon Pepper Chicken Wings
- 183 Cajun Stuffed Turkey Wings
- 184 Fish and Chips
- 185 Fried Catfish
- 186 Miso Black Cod
- 187 Eastern North Carolina Fish Stew
- 188 Monterey Bay Cioppino
- 189 Woodman's-Style Clam Chowder
- 191 Okra and Shrimp Stew
- 192 Gumbo
- 194 Shrimp Mozambique
- 194 Charleston Shrimp Perloo
- 195 Shrimp and Grits
- 196 New Orleans Barbecue Shrimp
- 197 Pickled Shrimp
- 198 Shrimp Po' Boys
- 199 South Carolina Shrimp Burgers
- 201 Hot Buttered Lobster Rolls
- 202 Tuna Poke
- 203 Salmon Teriyaki Poke
- 203 Guanimes con Bacalao (Cornmeal Dumplings with Salt Cod)
- 205 Neorm Sach Moan (Cambodian Chicken Salad)
- 206 Chinese Chicken Salad
- 207 Chicken Chow Mein
- 208 Bourbon Chicken
- 209 Almond Boneless Chicken
- 210 Soy Sauce Chicken Wings
- 210 Khao Man Gai (Thai-Style Chicken and Rice)
- 212 Kombdi, Jira Ghalun (Cumin-Scented Chicken)
- 213 Pad Gra Prow (Holy Basil Stir-Fry)
- 214 Slow-Cooker Chinese Barbecued Pork
- 215 St. Paul Sandwich
- 216 New Orleans Muffulettas
- 217 Croque Monsieur
- 218 Boogaloo Wonderland Sandwiches
- 220 Patty Melts
- 221 Diner-Style Patty Melts
- 222 Sliders
- 223 Oklahoma Fried Onion Burgers
- 224 Wisconsin Butter Burgers
- 225 Atlanta Brisket
- 226 Slow-Cooker BBQ Beef Brisket
- 227 Tennessee Whiskey Pork Chops
- 228 Memphis-Style Wet Ribs for a Crowd
- 229 Slow-Cooker Memphis-Style Wet Ribs
- 230 Okinawan Taco Rice
- 231 Sinigang (Filipino Pork and Vegetable Stew)
- 232 Sisig
- 234 Iowa Skinny
- 235 Baltimore Pit Beef
- 236 Philadelphia Pork Sandwiches
- 237 Cuban Sandwiches
- 238 Cuban Roast Pork with Mojo
- 239 Cuban Bread
- 240 South Carolina Barbecue Hash
- 241 Cincinnati Chili
- 242 Colorado Green Chili
- 243 Beef Yakamein (New Orleans Spicy Beef Noodle Soup)
- 244 Natchitoches Meat Pies
- 245 Delta Hot Tamales
- 247 Cajun Rice Dressing
- 248 Hoppin' John
- 249 St. Louis–Style Pizza
- 250 Chicago Thin-Crust Pizza
- 251 Easy Sweet Italian Sausage
- 252 New England Bar Pizza
- 253 Detroit-Style Pizza
- 255 Philly Tomato Pie
- 256 Pepperoni French Bread Pizza
- 257 Potato-Cheddar Pierogi
- 258 North Carolina Cheese Biscuits
- 259 Crunchy Potato Wedges
- 260 Crispy Potato Tots
- 262 Gobi Manchurian
- 263 Texas Potato Pancakes
- 263 Crispy Vegetable Fritters
- 264 Ultimate Extra-Crunchy Onion Rings
- 265 Beer-Battered Onion Rings
- 266 Fried Cheese Curds with Ranch Dressing
- 268 Charred Cherry Tomatoes with Roasted Red Bell Peppers and Fresh Mozzarella
- 268 Hawaiian Macaroni Salad
- 269 Ballpark Pretzels
- 270 Baba Ghanoush
- 271 Piña Coladas

Recipe Photos (clockwise from top left): Ballpark Pretzels, Texas Potato Pancakes, Charleston Shrimp Perloo

Batter-Fried Chicken

SERVES 4 TO 6

WHY THIS RECIPE WORKS The old-fashioned method of batter-fried chicken calls for dipping chicken parts in a batter not unlike pancake batter before frying. For juicy meat, we brined our chicken. To ensure a crisp crust, we replaced the milk in our initial batters with plain old water. With milk, the sugars in the milk solids browned too fast and produced a soft crust. Using equal parts cornstarch and flour in the batter also helped ensure a crisp crust on the chicken. And baking powder added lift and lightness without doughiness.

Use a Dutch oven that holds 6 quarts or more for this recipe.

Brine and Chicken
- ¼ cup table salt
- ¼ cup sugar
- 4 pounds bone-in chicken pieces (breasts halved crosswise and leg quarters separated into drumsticks and thighs), trimmed

Batter
- 1 cup all-purpose flour
- 1 cup cornstarch
- 5 teaspoons pepper
- 2 teaspoons baking powder
- 1 teaspoon table salt
- 1 teaspoon paprika
- ½ teaspoon cayenne pepper
- 1¾ cups cold water
- 3 quarts peanut or vegetable oil for frying

1. For the Brine and Chicken Dissolve salt and sugar in 1 quart cold water in large container. Submerge chicken in brine, cover, and refrigerate for 30 minutes or up to 1 hour.

2. For the Batter Meanwhile, combine flour, cornstarch, pepper, baking powder, salt, paprika, and cayenne in large bowl, add water, and whisk until smooth. Refrigerate batter while chicken is brining.

3. Set wire rack in rimmed baking sheet. Add oil to large Dutch oven until it measures about 2 inches deep and heat over medium-high heat to 350 degrees. Using tongs, remove chicken from brine and pat dry with paper towels. Rewhisk batter. Transfer half of chicken to batter and turn to coat. Remove chicken from batter, 1 piece at a time, allowing excess to drip back into bowl, and transfer to oil. Fry chicken, adjusting burner as necessary to maintain oil temperature between 300 and 325 degrees, until deep golden brown and breasts register 160 degrees and thighs and drumsticks register 175 degrees, 12 to 15 minutes. Drain chicken on prepared baking sheet. Return oil to 350 degrees and repeat with remaining chicken. Serve.

Keys to Best Batter-Fried Chicken

1. Whisk together flour, cornstarch, baking powder, spices, and water to make thin batter for crisp crust.

2. After dipping chicken in batter, let excess drip off (back into bowl) to avoid doughy coating.

3. To prevent chicken pieces from sticking together in oil, don't crowd the pot. Fry chicken in 2 batches.

Creole Fried Chicken

SERVES 4 TO 6

WHY THIS RECIPE WORKS This crispy fried chicken is seasoned with the bold flavors of Creole cooking of New Orleans. We built our own Creole seasoning based on its three traditional ground peppers: three parts black, two parts cayenne, and one part white. One of the hallmarks of Creole cooking is its layering of flavors, so we took a three-step approach: After brining the chicken, we sprinkled the raw pieces with our homemade seasoning for added flavor. We also added seasoning to the chicken's flour coating to lend a potent punch. And for a peppery finish, we sprinkled the hot chicken with more seasoning when it came out of the oil.

In step 1, do not soak the chicken longer than 8 hours, or it will be too salty. Use a Dutch oven that holds 6 quarts or more for this recipe.

Seasoned Brine and Chicken

- ¼ cup sugar
- 3 tablespoons Worcestershire sauce
- 3 tablespoons hot sauce
- 2 tablespoons table salt
- 1 tablespoon garlic powder
- 4 pounds bone-in chicken pieces (breasts halved crosswise and leg quarters separated into drumsticks and thighs), trimmed

Creole Seasoning

- 1 tablespoon pepper
- 1 tablespoon dried oregano
- 1 tablespoon garlic powder
- 2 teaspoons onion powder
- 2 teaspoons cayenne pepper
- 1 teaspoon white pepper
- 1 teaspoon celery salt
- 2 cups all-purpose flour
- 3 quarts peanut or vegetable oil for frying

1. For the Seasoned Brine and Chicken Dissolve sugar, Worcestershire, hot sauce, salt, and garlic powder in 1 quart cold water in large container. Submerge chicken in brine, cover, and refrigerate for 1 hour or up to 8 hours.

Batter-Fried Chicken

Creole Fried Chicken

2. For the Creole Seasoning Combine pepper, oregano, garlic powder, onion powder, cayenne, white pepper, and celery salt in large bowl; reserve ¼ cup spice mixture. Add flour to bowl with remaining spice mixture and stir to combine. Set wire rack in rimmed baking sheet.

3. Remove chicken from brine and pat dry with paper towels. Sprinkle chicken with 3 tablespoons reserved spice mixture and toss to coat. Dredge chicken pieces in flour mixture. Shake excess flour from chicken and transfer to wire rack. (Do not discard flour mixture.)

4. Adjust oven rack to middle position and heat oven to 200 degrees. Set second wire rack in second rimmed baking sheet. Add oil to large Dutch oven until it measures about 2 inches deep and heat over medium-high heat to 375 degrees. Return chicken pieces to flour mixture and turn to coat. Fry half of chicken, adjusting burner as necessary to maintain oil temperature between 300 and 325 degrees, until deep golden brown and breasts register 160 degrees and thighs and drumsticks register 175 degrees, 10 to 12 minutes. Transfer chicken to prepared baking sheet and place in oven. Return oil to 375 degrees and repeat with remaining chicken. Sprinkle crisp chicken with remaining 1 tablespoon spice mixture. Serve.

Extra-Crunchy Fried Chicken

SERVES 4

WHY THIS RECIPE WORKS For well-seasoned, extra-crunchy fried chicken we started by brining the chicken in heavily salted buttermilk. For the crunchy coating, we combined flour with a little baking powder, then added buttermilk to make a thick slurry, which clung tightly to the meat. Frying the chicken with the lid on the pot for half the cooking time contained the spatter-prone oil and kept it hot.

Keeping the oil at the correct temperature is essential to producing crunchy fried chicken that is neither too brown nor too greasy. Use a Dutch oven that holds 6 quarts or more for this recipe. If you want to produce a slightly lighter version of this recipe, remove the skin from the chicken before soaking it in the buttermilk. The chicken will be slightly less crunchy.

- 2 tablespoons table salt
- 2 cups plus 6 tablespoons buttermilk
- 1 (3½-pound) whole chicken, cut into 8 pieces and trimmed (4 breast pieces, 2 drumsticks, 2 thighs), wings discarded
- 3 cups all-purpose flour
- 2 teaspoons baking powder
- ¾ teaspoon dried thyme
- ½ teaspoon pepper
- ¼ teaspoon garlic powder
- 1 quart peanut or vegetable oil for frying

1. Dissolve salt in 2 cups buttermilk in large container. Submerge chicken in brine, cover, and refrigerate for 1 hour.

2. Whisk flour, baking powder, thyme, pepper, and garlic powder together in large bowl. Add remaining 6 tablespoons buttermilk; with your fingers rub flour and buttermilk together until buttermilk is evenly incorporated into flour and mixture resembles coarse, wet sand. Set wire rack inside rimmed baking sheet.

3. Dredge chicken pieces in flour mixture and turn to coat thoroughly, gently pressing flour mixture onto chicken. Shake excess flour from each piece of chicken and transfer to prepared baking sheet.

Extra-Crunchy Fried Chicken

4. Line platter with triple layer of paper towels. Add oil to large Dutch oven until it measures about ¾ inch deep and heat over medium-high heat to 375 degrees. Place chicken pieces skin side down in oil, cover, and fry until deep golden brown, 8 to 10 minutes. Remove lid after 4 minutes and lift chicken pieces to check for even browning; rearrange if some pieces are browning faster than others. Adjust burner, if necessary, to maintain oil temperature between 300 and 315 degrees. Turn chicken pieces over and continue to fry, uncovered, until chicken pieces are deep golden brown on second side and breasts register 160 degrees and thighs and drumsticks register 175 degrees, 6 to 8 minutes. Using tongs, transfer chicken to prepared platter; let stand for 5 minutes. Serve.

Extra-Spicy, Extra-Crunchy Fried Chicken

Add ¼ cup hot sauce to buttermilk-salt mixture in step 1. Replace dried thyme and garlic powder with 2 tablespoons cayenne pepper and 2 teaspoons chili powder in step 2.

Lard-Fried Chicken

SERVES 4

WHY THIS RECIPE WORKS In 1836, Mary Rudolph's cookbook, *The Virginia Housewife*, called for frying chicken in a "good quantity of boiling lard." Our modern-day inspiration comes from Indiana, where chicken pieces are seasoned with salt and black pepper, dunked in a light coating of flour, and then fried in lard (aka rendered pork fat). The result is fried chicken with a crisp exterior, a juicy interior, and supersavory flavor. For our version, we dipped the chicken in flour, then water, then back in flour. For fast frying, we cooked the chicken all in one batch. Keeping the lard at a low temperature ensured that the coating became golden brown all over without developing any off-flavors.

Use a Dutch oven that holds 6 quarts or more for this recipe. We developed this recipe using John Morrell Snow Cap Lard, but you can substitute 1 quart of peanut or vegetable oil, if desired, although the taste will be different. If you're breaking

Breaking Down a Chicken

1. Orient bird on board breast side up with wings away from you. Gather chef's knife, boning knife, and shears.

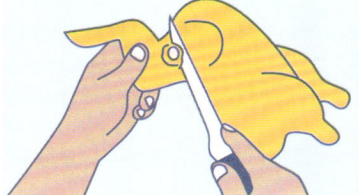

2. Use boning knife to slice between wing joint and breast to free wing. Repeat on other side. Reserve wings for another use.

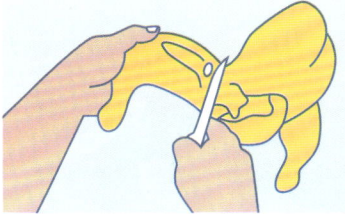

3. Bend leg quarters down to "pop" and expose joint. Maneuver tip of boning knife around base of joint and cut leg free. Repeat on other side

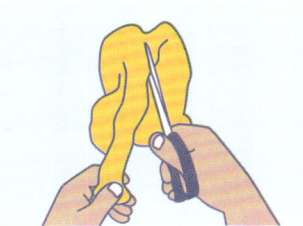

4. Flip chicken breast side down with cavity facing you. Using shears, cut on both sides of backbone to remove it. Reserve backbone for stock.

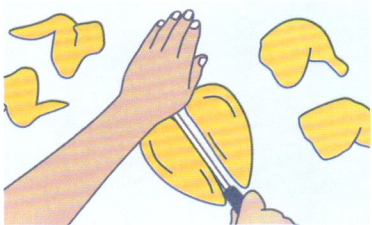

5. Flip chicken breast side up. With both your hands on chef's knife, cut through breastbone to split breasts in two.

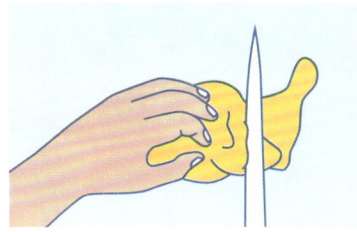

6. Use chef's knife to cut at seam that naturally separates drumstick from thigh. Repeat with other leg.

down a whole chicken for this dish, a 4½-pound chicken would yield the necessary pieces. If you're using table salt, reduce the amount by half. To take the temperature of the chicken pieces, take them out of the oil and place them on a plate; this is the safest way and provides the most accurate reading.

- 3 pounds bone-in chicken pieces (2 split breasts cut in half crosswise, 2 drumsticks, and 2 thighs), trimmed
- 5 teaspoons kosher salt, divided
- 1 tablespoon pepper
- 1½ cups all-purpose flour
- 1½ teaspoons baking powder
- 4 cups water
- 2 pounds lard

1. Sprinkle chicken all over with 2 teaspoons salt and pepper. Whisk flour, baking powder, and remaining 1 tablespoon salt in large bowl until combined. Place water in medium bowl.

2. Working with 1 piece of chicken at a time, dredge chicken in flour mixture, shaking off excess; dunk in water, letting excess drip off; then dredge again in flour mixture, pressing to adhere. Transfer to large plate and refrigerate for at least 30 minutes or up to 2 hours.

3. Set wire rack in rimmed baking sheet and line half of rack with triple layer of paper towels. Melt lard in large Dutch oven and heat over medium-high heat to 350 degrees.

4. Add all chicken to lard, skin side down, in single layer (some slight overlap is OK) so pieces are mostly submerged. Fry for 10 minutes, rotating pot 180 degrees after 5 minutes. Adjust burner, if necessary, to maintain oil temperature between 300 and 325 degrees.

5. Carefully flip chicken and continue to fry until golden brown and breasts register 160 degrees and drumsticks/thighs register 175 degrees, 5 to 9 minutes longer. Transfer chicken to paper towel–lined side of prepared rack and drain for about 10 seconds per side, then move to unlined side of rack. Let cool for 10 minutes. Serve.

Nashville Hot Fried Chicken

SERVES 4 TO 6

WHY THIS RECIPE WORKS Mimicking the heat of the hot fried chicken we sweated through at Prince's Hot Chicken Shack in Nashville was harder than we anticipated. We created a spicy exterior to the chicken by blooming the spices (cooking them in oil for a short period) to create a complex yet still lip-burning spicy flavor. We also added a healthy amount of hot sauce to our brine to inject into the chicken, making the flavor more than skin deep.

Chicken quarters take longer to cook than smaller pieces. To ensure that the exterior doesn't burn before the inside cooks through, keep the oil temperature between 300 and 325 degrees while the chicken is frying. Use a Dutch oven that holds 6 quarts or more for this recipe. Serve the chicken as they do in Nashville, on white bread with pickles.

Brine and Chicken
- ½ cup hot sauce
- ½ cup table salt
- ½ cup sugar
- 1 (3½- to 4-pound) whole chicken, quartered

Lard-Fried Chicken

Coating

- 3 quarts peanut or vegetable oil for frying
- 1 tablespoon cayenne pepper
- ½ teaspoon paprika
- ½ teaspoon sugar
- ¼ teaspoon garlic powder
- Salt and pepper
- 2 cups all-purpose flour

1. For the Brine and Chicken Dissolve hot sauce, salt, and sugar in 2 quarts cold water in large container. Submerge chicken in brine, cover, and refrigerate for 30 minutes or up to 1 hour.

2. For the Coating Heat 3 tablespoons oil in small saucepan over medium heat until shimmering. Add cayenne, paprika, sugar, garlic powder, and ½ teaspoon salt and cook until fragrant, about 30 seconds. Transfer to small bowl.

3. Set wire rack in rimmed baking sheet. Remove chicken from brine and pat with paper towels. Combine flour, ½ teaspoon salt, and ½ teaspoon pepper in large bowl. Dredge chicken pieces two at a time in flour mixture. Shake excess flour from chicken and transfer to prepared baking sheet. (Do not discard seasoned flour.)

4. Adjust oven rack to middle position and heat oven to 200 degrees. Set second wire rack in second rimmed baking sheet. Add remaining oil to large Dutch oven until it measures about 2 inches deep and heat over medium-high heat to 350 degrees. Return chicken pieces to flour mixture and turn to coat. Fry half of chicken, adjusting burner as necessary to maintain oil temperature between 300 and 325 degrees, until deep golden brown and breast meat registers 160 degrees and legs register 175 degrees, 20 to 25 minutes. Drain chicken on prepared baking sheet and place in oven. Return oil to 350 degrees and repeat with remaining chicken. Stir spicy oil mixture to recombine and brush over both sides of chicken. Serve.

Nashville Extra-Hot Fried Chicken

For spiced oil in step 2, increase oil to ¼ cup, cayenne to 3½ tablespoons, and sugar to ¾ teaspoon and add 1 teaspoon dry mustard. Continue with recipe as directed.

Nashville Hot Fried Chicken

The American Table: The Prince of Shacks

Prince's Hot Chicken Shack, the granddaddy of all hot chicken shacks, sits in a nondescript strip mall in east Nashville. The business got its start in 1945, when, according to legend, Thornton Prince's "lady friend" doused his chicken dinner in hot sauce to teach him a lesson—she'd caught him fooling around. But, her plan backfired: He liked the chicken, and the seed of Prince's Hot Chicken Shack was born. Word spread. The turquoise walls of the "shack" are papered with tacked-up Styrofoam plates that bear autographs from the many Grand Ole Opry stars who have made Prince's famous. Country singers drop in after their shows for late-night snacks of the blazingly hot chicken, says the current proprietor—and Thornton's grand-niece—André Prince Jeffries. These days, Prince's attracts club-goers in the wee hours as well as young couples, old couples, and families. Everybody in Nashville, it seems, has a taste for hot chicken.

Honey Fried Chicken

Honey Fried Chicken

SERVES 4

WHY THIS RECIPE WORKS Really good honey fried chicken is juicy and tender on the inside with a crispy, sticky, honey-flavored coating. To keep the meat moist, we brined the chicken first. For the coating, we dusted the chicken in cornstarch and dipped it in a thin cornstarch-and-water batter. The hardest part was glazing the fried chicken in honey without making the crust soggy. We found that the key was to double-fry the chicken: We partially fried the chicken, let it rest to allow moisture from the skin to evaporate, then fried it again for an incredibly crunchy crust that stayed crispy when dunked in a glaze of warm honey and hot sauce.

If using kosher chicken, do not brine. Use a Dutch oven that holds 6 quarts or more for this recipe.

Brine and Chicken
- ½ cup table salt
- ½ cup sugar
- 3 pounds bone-in chicken pieces (breasts halved crosswise and leg quarters separated into drumsticks and thighs), trimmed

Batter
- 1½ cups cornstarch
- ¾ cup cold water
- 2 teaspoons pepper
- 1 teaspoon table salt
- 3 quarts peanut or vegetable oil for frying

Honey Glaze
- ¾ cup honey
- 2 tablespoons hot sauce

1. For the Brine and Chicken Dissolve salt and sugar in 2 quarts cold water in large container. Submerge chicken in brine, cover, and refrigerate for 30 minutes to 1 hour.

2. For the Batter While chicken is brining, whisk 1 cup cornstarch, water, pepper, and salt together in large bowl until smooth. Refrigerate batter.

3. Set wire rack inside rimmed baking sheet. Sift remaining ½ cup cornstarch into shallow bowl. Remove chicken from brine and dry thoroughly with paper towels. Working with 1 piece at a time, coat chicken thoroughly with cornstarch, shaking to remove excess; transfer to platter.

4. Add oil to large Dutch oven until it measures about 2 inches deep and heat over medium-high heat to 350 degrees. Whisk batter to recombine. Using tongs, transfer half of chicken to batter and turn to coat. Remove chicken from batter, 1 piece at a time, allowing excess to drip back into bowl, and transfer to hot oil. Fry chicken, stirring to prevent pieces from sticking together, until slightly golden and just beginning to crisp, 5 to 7 minutes. Adjust burner, if necessary, to maintain oil temperature between 325 and 350 degrees. (Chicken will not be cooked through at this point.) Transfer parcooked chicken to platter. Return oil to 350 degrees and repeat with remaining raw chicken and batter. Let each batch of chicken rest for 5 to 7 minutes.

5. Return oil to 350 degrees. Return first batch of chicken to oil and fry until breasts register 160 degrees and thighs/drumsticks register 175 degrees, 5 to 7 minutes. Transfer to prepared baking sheet. Return oil to 350 degrees and repeat with remaining chicken.

6. For the Honey Glaze Combine honey and hot sauce in large bowl and microwave until hot, about 1½ minutes. Add chicken pieces to honey mixture, one at a time, and turn to coat. Return to baking sheet, skin side up, to drain. Serve.

Garlic Fried Chicken
SERVES 4

WHY THIS RECIPE WORKS For fried chicken loaded with garlic flavor, we started by tossing a mix of chicken pieces in a marinade chock-full of both fresh and granulated garlic. We further reinforced our key flavor by dipping the parts in beaten egg whites and dredging them in flour boosted with more granulated garlic. After frying the chicken in peanut oil, we created a potent garlic-parsley butter that took the chicken's flavor right over the top.

Use a Dutch oven that holds 6 quarts or more for this recipe. Mince the garlic with a knife rather than with a garlic press.

Chicken
- 3 tablespoons extra-virgin olive oil
- 2 tablespoons garlic powder
- 5 garlic cloves, minced
- Kosher salt and pepper
- 3 pounds bone-in chicken pieces (split breasts cut in half crosswise, drumsticks, thighs, and/or wings), trimmed
- 2 cups all-purpose flour
- 4 large egg whites
- 3 quarts peanut or vegetable oil for frying

Garlic Butter
- 8 tablespoons unsalted butter, softened
- 2 tablespoons minced fresh parsley
- ¼ teaspoon kosher salt
- ¼ teaspoon pepper
- 8 garlic cloves, minced
- 1 tablespoon water

Garlic Fried Chicken

On the Road: Basque Cooking in California

Though it might seem out of place, Basque food is as comfortable in California as any other cuisine. Immigrants from the Basque lands—primarily the Pyrenees Mountains separating Spain and France—flooded California during the Gold Rush in the mid-19th century; when gold proved elusive, they turned to agriculture and shepherding in and around Bakersfield, California, which boasts one of the largest Basque populations in the United States.

During our visit to this region, we were struck by how the vibrant fare at the Pyrenees Cafe stands firmly against the city's ever-present heat. There we feasted on plates of garlic fried chicken, Basque-style green beans, cabbage and bean soup dotted with spicy salsa, thin slices of pickled veal tongue, and a few glasses of chilled house wine, before enjoying the customary Basque dessert: vanilla ice cream doused with red wine.

1. For the Chicken Combine olive oil, 1 tablespoon granulated garlic, minced garlic, 2 teaspoons salt, and 2 teaspoons pepper in large bowl. Add chicken and toss to thoroughly coat with garlic mixture. Cover with plastic wrap and refrigerate for at least 1 hour or up to 24 hours.

2. Set wire rack in rimmed baking sheet. Whisk flour, remaining 1 tablespoon garlic powder, 2 teaspoons salt, and 2 teaspoons pepper together in separate bowl. Lightly beat egg whites together in shallow dish.

3. Remove chicken from marinade and brush away any solidified clumps of oil with paper towels. Working with 1 piece at a time, dip chicken into egg whites to thoroughly coat, letting excess drip back into dish; then dredge in flour mixture, pressing firmly to adhere. Transfer chicken to prepared wire rack and refrigerate, uncovered, for at least 30 minutes or up to 2 hours.

4. Set second wire rack in second rimmed baking sheet and line with triple layer of paper towels. Add peanut oil to large Dutch oven until it measures about 2 inches deep and heat over medium-high heat to 325 degrees. Add half of chicken to hot oil and fry until breasts register 160 degrees and drumsticks/thighs register 175 degrees, 13 to 16 minutes. Adjust burner, if necessary, to maintain oil temperature between 300 and 325 degrees. Transfer to paper towel–lined rack, return oil to 325 degrees, and repeat with remaining chicken.

5. For the Garlic Butter While chicken rests, combine 7 tablespoons butter, parsley, salt, and pepper in bowl; set aside. Melt remaining 1 tablespoon butter in 8-inch nonstick skillet over medium heat. Add garlic and water and cook, stirring frequently, until garlic is softened and fragrant, 1 to 2 minutes. Add hot garlic mixture to butter-parsley mixture and whisk until well combined.

6. Transfer chicken to platter and spoon garlic butter over top. Serve.

North Carolina Dipped Fried Chicken

SERVES 4

WHY THIS RECIPE WORKS For this unusual "dipped" fried chicken, we started with a brine to keep the meat moist and tender. We then coated the pieces in a seasoned mixture of flour, cornstarch, and baking powder. A quick stint in the refrigerator ensured that the coating stuck. We based our sauce on Texas Pete Original Hot Sauce, a North Carolina specialty. We spooned the sauce over the chicken, which was less messy than dipping. The coating absorbed the lip-tingling sauce and still retained crisp texture.

Plan ahead: The chicken needs to brine for at least 1 hour before being coated in step 3. Do not brine the chicken longer than 4 hours or it will be too salty. Use a Dutch oven that holds 6 quarts or more. You'll need one 12-ounce bottle of Texas Pete Original Hot Sauce for this recipe.

Chicken

- Table salt and pepper
- ¼ cup sugar
- 3 pounds bone-in chicken pieces (split breasts cut in half, drumsticks, thighs, and/or wings), trimmed
- 1¼ cups all-purpose flour
- ¾ cup cornstarch
- 1 teaspoon granulated garlic
- 1 teaspoon baking powder
- 3 quarts peanut or vegetable oil for frying

Sauce

- 1¼ cups Texas Pete Original Hot Sauce
- 5 tablespoons Worcestershire sauce
- 5 tablespoons peanut or vegetable oil
- 2 tablespoons molasses
- 1 tablespoon cider vinegar

1. For the Chicken Dissolve ½ cup salt and sugar in 2 quarts cold water in large container. Submerge chicken in brine, cover, and refrigerate for at least 1 hour or up to 4 hours.

2. Whisk flour, cornstarch, granulated garlic, baking powder, 2 teaspoons pepper, and 1 teaspoon salt together in large bowl. Add 2 tablespoons water to flour mixture; using your fingers, rub flour mixture and water together until water is evenly incorporated and shaggy pieces of dough form.

3. Set wire rack in rimmed baking sheet. Working with 1 piece at a time, remove chicken from brine, letting excess drip off; dredge chicken in flour mixture, pressing to adhere. Transfer to prepared rack. Refrigerate chicken, uncovered, for at least 30 minutes or up to 2 hours.

4. Set second wire rack in second rimmed baking sheet and line half of rack with triple layer of paper towels. Add oil to large Dutch oven until it measures 2 inches deep and heat over medium-high heat to 350 degrees.

North Carolina Dipped Fried Chicken

The American Table: The Rise of Texas Pete

Thad W. Garner's initial plan was to take the money he'd put aside for college and, rather than pursue his studies, buy and run a barbecue restaurant near his family's home in North Carolina. And he did just that. But it was 1929, and within months the Great Depression killed the business. Garner was left with nothing—nothing, that is, except a recipe for a bracing, peppery hot sauce his customers loved.

Determined, Garner spent the next decade selling the sauce door to door. He called it "Texas Pete" to capitalize on the country's Hollywood-driven nostalgia for cowboy movies; even in a troubled economy, enough households could afford it for Garner to eke out a living.

By the mid-1940s, the economy was booming again, and the newly incorporated T. W. Garner Food Company was booming, too, selling hot sauce, jams, jellies, and more. But Texas Pete was—and remains—its most popular product.

Add half of chicken to pot and fry until breasts register 160 degrees and drumsticks/thighs/wings register 175 degrees, 13 to 16 minutes. Adjust burner, if necessary, to maintain oil temperature between 325 and 350 degrees.

5. Transfer chicken to paper towel–lined side of prepared rack. Let chicken drain on each side for 30 seconds, then move to unlined side of rack. Return oil to 350 degrees and repeat with remaining chicken. Let chicken cool for 10 minutes.

6. For the Sauce Meanwhile, whisk all ingredients together in bowl. Microwave, covered, until hot, about 2 minutes, stirring halfway through microwaving.

7. Transfer chicken to shallow platter. Spoon sauce over chicken. Serve.

Mimosa Fried Chicken

SERVES 4 TO 6

WHY THIS RECIPE WORKS After sampling the juicy, crunchy boneless chicken thighs layered with bright orange notes at Biscuit Head in Asheville, North Carolina, we wanted to create our own version. Marinating our chicken in orange juice and zest, white wine, salt, garlic, coriander, and pepper flakes infused it with the flavors of its namesake drink. Mixing a little water into our breading mixture (equal parts flour and cornstarch with a bit of baking powder) created hunks of breading that fried up extra-crunchy. Finally, adding coriander to the marinade and the breading mixture and using it as a finishing touch for the fried chicken layered bright, citrusy flavor throughout, reinforcing the flavor of sweet, vibrant orange.

Use a Dutch oven that holds 6 quarts or more here. If you like, you can use our Butter and Lard Biscuits (page 561) to create sandwiches. Other dry white wines can be substituted for the sparkling wine, if desired.

FORK-IN-THE-ROAD FAVORITES

Mimosa Fried Chicken

Hawaiian-Style Fried Chicken

Marinade and Chicken
- ½ cup dry sparkling white wine, such as prosecco or cava
- 2 tablespoons grated orange zest plus ½ cup juice (2 oranges)
- 5 garlic cloves, smashed and peeled
- 1 tablespoon table salt
- 2 teaspoons ground coriander
- ¼ teaspoon red pepper flakes
- 2 pounds boneless, skinless chicken thighs, trimmed
- 2 quarts peanut or vegetable oil for frying

Coating
- 1½ cups all-purpose flour
- 1¼ cups cornstarch
- 4 teaspoons ground coriander, divided
- 2 teaspoons garlic powder
- 2 teaspoons baking powder
- 2 teaspoons table salt
- 2 teaspoons pepper
- ½ teaspoon cayenne pepper
- 3 tablespoons water

1. For the Marinade and Chicken Combine wine, orange zest and juice, garlic, salt, coriander, and pepper flakes in large bowl. Add chicken to marinade and toss to coat. Cover and refrigerate for at least 1 hour or up to 24 hours.

2. For the Coating Whisk flour, cornstarch, 1 tablespoon coriander, garlic powder, baking powder, salt, pepper, and cayenne together in second large bowl. Add water and, using your fingers, rub flour mixture and water together until craggy bits form throughout.

3. Working with 1 piece of chicken at a time, remove from marinade, allowing excess to drip off, then drop into flour mixture, turning to thoroughly coat and pressing to adhere. Transfer to rimmed baking sheet. Refrigerate, uncovered, for at least 30 minutes or up to 2 hours.

4. Set wire rack in second rimmed baking sheet and line half of rack with triple layer of paper towels. Add oil to large Dutch oven and heat over medium-high heat to 350 degrees. Add half of chicken to oil and fry until golden brown and registering at least 175 degrees, about 7 minutes. Adjust burner, if necessary, to maintain oil temperature between 325 and 350 degrees.

5. Transfer chicken to paper towel–lined side of rack and let drain on each side for 30 seconds, then move to unlined side of rack. Return oil to 350 degrees and repeat with remaining chicken. Transfer chicken to platter and sprinkle with remaining 1 teaspoon coriander. Serve.

Hawaiian-Style Fried Chicken

SERVES 4 TO 6

WHY THIS RECIPE WORKS In Hawaii, fried chicken comes in many varieties. Our favorite is karaage, which is marinated in soy sauce, brown sugar, sake, ginger, and garlic, before being coated in potato flour, fried until shatteringly crisp, and then served with a tangy dipping sauce. Potato flour offered maximum crunch, but we couldn't get it to stick on its own, so we added baking powder and sesame seeds, firmly pressed the coating into the marinated chicken thighs, and then refrigerated them until the coating became fully saturated with the marinade. Rice vinegar, soy sauce, and lemon juice made a sweet and sour sauce that was ripe for dunking.

Use a Dutch oven that holds 6 quarts or more for this recipe. Plan ahead: The chicken marinates for at least an hour before breading. Pressing the chicken after dredging it in the starch ensures a more uniform coating.

Chicken

- 1 (3-ounce) piece ginger, unpeeled, cut into ½-inch pieces
- 4 garlic cloves, peeled
- 1 cup water
- ½ cup soy sauce
- 3 tablespoons packed light brown sugar
- 1 tablespoon toasted sesame oil
- 2 pounds boneless, skinless chicken thighs, trimmed and halved crosswise
- 2¼ cups potato starch
- 2 tablespoons sesame seeds
- 1½ teaspoons baking powder
- Salt and pepper
- 3 quarts peanut or vegetable oil for frying

Dipping Sauce

- ½ cup seasoned rice vinegar
- ¼ cup soy sauce
- ¼ cup lemon juice (2 lemons)
- Pepper

1. For the Chicken Process ginger and garlic in food processor until finely chopped, about 15 seconds; transfer to large bowl. Add water, soy sauce, sugar, and sesame oil and whisk to combine. Add chicken and press to submerge. Cover bowl with plastic wrap and refrigerate for at least 1 hour or up to 3 hours.

2. For the Dipping Sauce Whisk vinegar, soy sauce, and lemon juice together in bowl. Season with pepper to taste.

3. Line rimmed baking sheet with parchment paper. Set wire rack in second rimmed baking sheet. Whisk potato starch, sesame seeds, baking powder, 1 teaspoon salt, and 1 teaspoon pepper together in large bowl.

4. Working with 1 piece of chicken at a time, remove from marinade, allowing excess to drip back into bowl. Dredge chicken in potato starch mixture, pressing to adhere. Gently shake off excess and transfer chicken to parchment-lined sheet. Coating will look mottled; using your hand, press on chicken to smooth out coating. Cover sheet tightly with plastic wrap and refrigerate for at least 30 minutes or up to 1 hour.

5. Add peanut oil to large Dutch oven until it measures about 2 inches deep; heat oil over medium-high heat to 375 degrees. Carefully add one-third of chicken to pot and fry until deep golden brown and cooked through, about 5 minutes, stirring gently as needed to prevent pieces from sticking together. Adjust burner, if necessary, to maintain oil temperature between 350 and 375 degrees.

6. Transfer chicken to prepared rack. Return oil to 375 degrees and repeat in 2 more batches with remaining chicken. Serve chicken with sauce.

Ranch Fried Chicken

SERVES 4 TO 6

WHY THIS RECIPE WORKS Hot oil is the key to crunchy fried chicken, but it can be deadly to fresh herbs. To get the flavors to last throughout the frying process, the key was to fry for as little time as possible. Thin boneless chicken thighs took half as long to fry as bone-in chicken parts, which allowed the fresh herb flavors to flourish. Also, thighs are less expensive. After a few tests, we settled on a three-part technique for the chives, dill, and cilantro; we added them to the tangy buttermilk dip, the flour coating, and the dipping sauce. This triple punch provided the classic aroma and flavor we know and love as "ranch."

Use a Dutch oven that holds 6 quarts or more for this recipe.

Ranch Fried Chicken

Sweet Tea–Brined Fried Chicken Thighs

Chicken
- 8 (5- to 7-ounce) boneless, skinless chicken thighs, trimmed
- Salt and pepper
- 2 quarts peanut or vegetable oil for frying

Buttermilk Mixture
- 1 cup buttermilk
- 2 tablespoons minced fresh chives
- 2 tablespoons minced fresh cilantro
- 2 teaspoons minced fresh dill
- 2 teaspoons distilled white vinegar
- 1 garlic clove, minced
- ½ teaspoon table salt
- Pinch cayenne pepper

Coating
- 1¼ cups all-purpose flour
- ½ cup cornstarch
- 3 tablespoons minced fresh chives
- 3 tablespoons minced fresh cilantro
- 1 tablespoon minced fresh dill
- 1½ teaspoons garlic powder
- 1½ teaspoons table salt
- ¾ teaspoon pepper

Ranch Sauce
- ½ cup mayonnaise
- Salt and pepper

1. For the Chicken Pat chicken dry with paper towels and season with salt and pepper.

2. For the Buttermilk Mixture Whisk all ingredients together in bowl. Set aside ¼ cup buttermilk mixture for ranch sauce.

3. For the Coating Whisk all ingredients together in large bowl.

4. Set wire rack in rimmed baking sheet. Set second wire rack in second rimmed baking sheet and line half of rack with triple layer of paper towels.

5. Working with 1 piece at a time, dip chicken in remaining buttermilk mixture to coat, letting excess drip back into bowl; then dredge in coating, pressing to adhere. Transfer chicken to first wire rack (without paper towels). (At this point, coated chicken may be refrigerated, uncovered, for up to 2 hours.)

6. Heat oil in large Dutch oven over medium-high heat until it reaches 350 degrees. Add half of chicken to hot oil and fry until golden brown and registers 175 degrees,

7 to 9 minutes. Adjust burner, if necessary, to maintain oil temperature between 325 and 350 degrees.

7. Transfer chicken to paper towel–lined side of second wire rack to drain on each side for 30 seconds, then move to unlined side of rack. Return oil to 350 degrees and repeat with remaining chicken.

8. For the Ranch Sauce Whisk mayonnaise into reserved buttermilk mixture. Season with salt and pepper to taste.

9. Transfer chicken to platter and serve with ranch sauce.

Sweet Tea–Brined Fried Chicken Thighs

SERVES 4

WHY THIS RECIPE WORKS Inspired by Chef John Fleer's recipe in *The Blackberry Farm Cookbook: Four Seasons of Great Food and the Good Life* (2009), this dish combines two of the South's best-known culinary icons. Fleer favors dark meat for fried chicken, so we turned to bone-in chicken thighs, which we brined in a mixture of strong black tea, sugar, salt, and lemon. This ensured that the tea's subtle aromatic flavor came through when the chicken was cooked. A quick dip in buttermilk before dredging in a seasoned mix of flour and cornstarch helped create a substantial coating that fried up crunchy and crispy. Because the increased sugar content of the brine caused the chicken to brown quickly, we heated our frying oil to a relatively low 325 degrees and pulled the pieces out when they were perfectly golden brown, then finished cooking them in a low oven. It's a flavor match made in heaven—or rather, in Tennessee.

Use a Dutch oven that holds 6 quarts or more for this recipe. We developed this recipe using Lipton tea bags. This fried chicken is very flavorful after 12 hours of brining, but if you have the time, you can brine it for up to 48 hours. The longer it brines, the more the tea flavor will come through.

- 6 family-size or 24 single-cup black tea bags
- ½ cup sugar for brining
- ¼ cup table salt for brining
- 1 tablespoon grated lemon zest plus 3 tablespoons juice, plus lemon wedges for serving
- 8 (5- to 7-ounce) bone-in chicken thighs, trimmed
- 1½ cups all-purpose flour
- 1¼ cups cornstarch
- 1 tablespoon paprika
- 1 tablespoon granulated garlic
- 1 tablespoon pepper
- 2 teaspoons table salt
- 2 teaspoons baking powder
- ¾ teaspoon cayenne pepper
- 1 cup buttermilk
- 3 quarts peanut or vegetable oil for frying

1. Bring 1 quart water to boil in medium saucepan over high heat. Off heat, add tea bags and steep for 5 minutes. Strain hot tea into large bowl, pressing gently on tea bags with back of spoon. Whisk in sugar, ¼ cup salt, and lemon zest and juice until salt and sugar are dissolved. Stir 1 quart ice water into tea until ice is melted and mixture is cold. Submerge chicken in brine, cover, and refrigerate for at least 12 hours or up to 48 hours.

2. Drain chicken in colander. Whisk flour, cornstarch, paprika, garlic, pepper, salt, baking powder, and cayenne together in large bowl. Add 3 tablespoons water to flour mixture; using your fingers, rub flour mixture and water together until water is evenly incorporated and shaggy pieces of dough form. Add buttermilk to medium bowl.

3. Set wire rack in rimmed baking sheet. Working with 1 piece at a time, add chicken to buttermilk and turn to coat; remove chicken from buttermilk, letting excess drip off; dredge chicken in flour mixture, pressing to adhere; and transfer to prepared rack, skin side up. Refrigerate chicken, uncovered, for at least 30 minutes or up to 2 hours.

4. Adjust oven rack to middle position and heat oven to 300 degrees. Set second wire rack in second rimmed baking sheet and line with triple layer of paper towels. Add oil to large Dutch oven until it measures 2 inches deep and heat over medium-high heat to 325 degrees. Add half of chicken to pot and fry until dark golden brown and crisp, about 10 minutes, flipping once halfway through frying. (Adjust burner, if necessary, to maintain oil temperature between 300 and 325 degrees.) Transfer chicken to paper towel–lined rack. Return oil to 325 degrees and repeat with remaining chicken.

5. Discard paper towels and bake chicken until it registers at least 175 degrees, 10 to 14 minutes. Transfer to paper towel–lined serving platter. Let chicken cool for at least 10 minutes. Serve with lemon wedges.

Chicken Nuggets

SERVES 4 TO 6

WHY THIS RECIPE WORKS We opted for boneless, skinless chicken breasts for our nuggets. Brining the chicken prevented it from drying out, and seasoning the breast meat combated its bland flavor. Ground-up panko bread crumbs, flour, and baking soda made a crispy coating. Using whole eggs to adhere the coating made the nuggets too eggy. Egg whites alone didn't have enough binding power, but resting the nuggets before frying solved the problem.

Do not brine the chicken longer than 30 minutes or it will be too salty. To crush the bread crumbs, place them inside a zipper-lock bag and lightly beat it with a rolling pin. Use a Dutch oven that holds 6 quarts or more for this recipe. This recipe doubles easily and freezes well.

- 4   (6-ounce) boneless, skinless chicken breasts, trimmed
- 2   cups water
- 2   tablespoons Worcestershire sauce
- 1   teaspoon salt, plus salt for brining
- ¾   teaspoon pepper
- 1   cup all-purpose flour
- 1   cup panko bread crumbs, crushed
- 2   teaspoons onion powder
- ½   teaspoon garlic powder
- ½   teaspoon baking soda
- 3   large egg whites
- 1   quart peanut or vegetable oil for frying
- 1   recipe dipping sauce (recipes follow)

1. Cut each chicken breast diagonally into thirds, then cut each third diagonally into ½-inch-thick pieces. Whisk water, Worcestershire, and 1 tablespoon salt in large bowl until salt dissolves. Add chicken pieces, cover, and refrigerate for 30 minutes.

2. Remove chicken from brine and pat dry with paper towels. Combine flour, panko, onion powder, salt, pepper, garlic powder, and baking soda in shallow dish. Whisk egg whites in second shallow dish until foamy. Coat half of chicken with egg whites and dredge in flour mixture, pressing gently to adhere. Transfer to plate and repeat with remaining chicken (don't discard flour mixture). Let sit for 10 minutes.

3. Adjust oven rack to middle position and heat oven to 200 degrees. Set wire rack in rimmed baking sheet. Add oil to large Dutch oven until it measures about ¾ inch deep and heat over medium-high heat to 350 degrees. Return chicken pieces to flour mixture and turn to coat, pressing flour mixture gently to adhere. Fry half of chicken until deep golden brown, about 3 minutes, turning halfway through cooking. Transfer chicken to prepared baking sheet and place in oven. Return oil to 350 degrees and repeat with remaining chicken. Serve with dipping sauce.

To Make Ahead Let fried nuggets cool, transfer to zipper-lock bag, and freeze for up to 1 month. To serve, adjust oven rack to middle position and heat oven to 350 degrees. Place nuggets on rimmed baking sheet and bake, flipping once, until heated through, about 15 minutes.

Honey-Mustard Sauce
MAKES ¾ CUP

- ½   cup yellow mustard
- ⅓   cup honey

Whisk mustard and honey in medium bowl until smooth. Season with salt and pepper to taste.

Sweet and Sour Sauce
MAKES ¾ CUP

- ¾ cup apple, apricot, or hot pepper jelly
- 1 tablespoon white vinegar
- ½ teaspoon soy sauce
- ⅛ teaspoon garlic powder
- Pinch ground ginger
- Pinch cayenne pepper

Whisk jelly, vinegar, soy sauce, garlic powder, ginger, and cayenne in medium bowl until smooth. Season with salt and pepper to taste.

Popcorn Chicken
SERVES 6 TO 8

WHY THIS RECIPE WORKS Popcorn chicken can require a lot of work for all those little pieces. Some versions are easier to make but have just a thin layer of fried flour that flakes off. Tossing our chicken pieces in beaten egg helped the dredge stick, and working water into a mixture of flour and cornstarch created craggy bits that fried up extra-crunchy. A small amount of sugar added to the dredge helped it brown more quickly while imparting a faint, pleasing sweetness. We brought the frying oil to a higher temperature so that the chicken could brown and cook through quickly without drying out. A simple honey–hot sauce dip completed this fun snack.

Use a Dutch oven that holds 6 quarts or more. We prefer Frank's RedHot Original Cayenne Pepper Sauce here, but you can substitute your favorite hot sauce, if desired. Freezing the chicken breasts makes them easier to cut.

- 1½ pounds boneless, skinless chicken breasts, trimmed
- 2¾ cups all-purpose flour, divided
- ½ cup cornstarch
- 1½ tablespoons granulated garlic
- 1½ tablespoons sugar
- 1 tablespoon baking powder
- 5 teaspoons plus pinch kosher salt, divided
- 1 teaspoon pepper
- 2 teaspoons onion powder
- 1 teaspoon cayenne pepper
- ½ cup water
- 2 large eggs, lightly beaten
- 1½ quarts peanut or vegetable oil for frying
- 6 tablespoons honey
- 2 tablespoons Frank's RedHot Original Cayenne Pepper Sauce

1. Place chicken on large plate and freeze until firm but still malleable, about 40 minutes.

2. Whisk 2½ cups flour, cornstarch, granulated garlic, sugar, baking powder, 1 tablespoon salt, onion powder, cayenne, and pepper together in large bowl. Add water and rub flour mixture between your hands until tiny craggy bits form throughout and mixture holds together like damp sand when squeezed.

3. Cut chicken into ½-inch pieces. Toss chicken, eggs, and 2 teaspoons salt together in second bowl. Transfer half of chicken to flour mixture and toss with your hands, pressing on coating to adhere and breaking up clumps, until chicken is coated on all sides. Pick chicken out of flour mixture and spread in even layer on rimmed baking sheet. Whisk remaining ¼ cup flour into flour mixture until combined, then repeat coating process with remaining chicken.

4. Line second rimmed baking sheet with triple layer of paper towels. Add oil to large Dutch oven until it measures about 1 inch deep and heat over medium-high heat to 400 degrees.

Popcorn Chicken

5. Using spider skimmer or slotted spoon, carefully add half of chicken to hot oil in several spoonfuls. Immediately stir to break up clumps. Fry until chicken is evenly golden brown and cooked through, 2 to 3 minutes, stirring occasionally. Using clean spider skimmer or slotted spoon, transfer chicken to paper towel–lined sheet. Return oil to 400 degrees and repeat with remaining chicken. Let cool for 5 minutes.

6. Whisk honey, hot sauce, and remaining pinch salt together in small bowl. Serve chicken with honey sauce.

Greek Chicken

SERVES 4

WHY THIS RECIPE WORKS We found inspiration for this tasty Greek baked chicken at Johnny's Restaurant in Homewood, Alabama. Their chicken is juicy, marinated and roasted to perfection, and flavored with tons of herbs and lemon. To be sure the marinade penetrated the chicken, we cut ½-inch-deep slashes in each piece and tossed the chicken with the herb mixture. A 12-inch skillet kept the pieces tightly packed to minimize evaporation of the marinade and the chicken juices, transforming that liquid into a deeply flavorful pan sauce. To achieve a lovely brown color, we finished the chicken with a blast under the broiler.

Use a vegetable peeler to remove six strips of zest from the lemon. If you have a rasp-style grater and prefer to use it to zest the lemon, you will need about 1 tablespoon of zest. Make sure to use kosher salt here; we developed this recipe using Diamond Crystal Kosher Salt.

- ¼ cup extra-virgin olive oil
- 2 tablespoons chopped fresh rosemary
- 2 tablespoons chopped fresh thyme
- 5 garlic cloves, chopped
- 6 (3-inch) strips lemon zest, chopped, plus 1 tablespoon juice
- 1 tablespoon kosher salt
- 1½ teaspoons dried oregano
- 1 teaspoon ground coriander
- ½ teaspoon red pepper flakes
- ½ teaspoon pepper
- 3 pounds bone-in chicken pieces (2 split breasts, 2 drumsticks, 2 thighs, and 2 wings, wingtips discarded)

1. Combine oil, rosemary, thyme, garlic, lemon zest, salt, oregano, coriander, pepper flakes, and pepper in large bowl. Cut three ½-inch-deep slits in skin side of each chicken breast, two ½-inch-deep slits in skin side of each thigh, and two ½-inch-deep slits in each drumstick; leave wings whole. Transfer chicken to bowl with marinade and turn to thoroughly coat, making sure marinade gets into slits. Cover and refrigerate for at least 30 minutes or up to 2 hours.

2. Adjust oven rack 6 inches from broiler element and heat oven to 425 degrees. Place chicken, skin side up, in 12-inch ovensafe skillet. Using rubber spatula, scrape any remaining marinade from bowl over chicken. Roast until breasts register 160 degrees and drumsticks/thighs register 175 degrees, 30 to 35 minutes.

3. Remove skillet from oven and spoon pan juices over top of chicken to wet skin. Heat broiler. Broil chicken until skin is lightly browned, about 3 minutes, rotating skillet as necessary for even browning. Let chicken rest in skillet for 10 minutes. Transfer chicken to shallow platter. Stir lemon juice into pan juices, then spoon over chicken. Serve.

Chicken Sauce Piquant

SERVES 6 TO 8

WHY THIS RECIPE WORKS A lively mix of Creole and Cajun flavors, spicy Sauce Piquant features chicken (though locals sometimes use wild game or alligator tail) braised in a cayenne-spiked, roux-thickened tomato sauce. We found we could skip the roux and mimic its consistency and flavor by dredging boneless chicken thighs in flour and shallow-frying them, and then cooking vegetables with flour before adding crushed tomatoes and chicken broth. We stirred in a few glugs of Worcestershire and Tabasco for depth and heat and some bacon for a meaty, smoky edge and popped it into the oven to thicken and finish cooking.

Louisiana seasoning is typically a mix of paprika, garlic powder, thyme, cayenne, celery salt, oregano, salt, and black pepper. If you don't want to make your own, the test kitchen's taste test winner is Tony Chachere's Original Creole Seasoning.

- ½ cup all-purpose flour
- 2 pounds boneless, skinless chicken thighs, trimmed and quartered
- 3½ teaspoons Louisiana seasoning, divided

- 5 tablespoons vegetable oil, divided
- 1 onion, chopped
- 1 green bell pepper, stemmed, seeded, and chopped
- 1 celery rib, chopped
- 2 garlic cloves, minced
- 1 (28-ounce) can crushed tomatoes
- 3 cups chicken broth
- 2 slices bacon
- 2 tablespoons Worcestershire sauce
- 1 bay leaf
- 1 teaspoon Tabasco sauce, plus extra for serving
  Table salt and pepper
- 4 cups cooked rice
- 4 scallions, sliced thin

1. Adjust oven rack to lower-middle position and heat oven to 350 degrees. Place flour in large bowl. Season chicken with 1 tablespoon Louisiana seasoning. Transfer chicken to bowl with flour and toss to coat.

2. Heat ¼ cup oil in Dutch oven over medium-high heat until shimmering. Shaking off excess flour, add half of chicken to pot and cook until golden brown, 3 to 5 minutes per side; transfer to plate. Repeat with remaining chicken. Reserve remaining flour.

3. Add onion, bell pepper, celery, garlic, remaining ½ teaspoon Louisiana seasoning, remaining 1 tablespoon oil, and reserved flour to now-empty pot. Cook, stirring often, until vegetables are just softened, about 5 minutes.

4. Stir in tomatoes, broth, bacon, Worcestershire, and bay leaf, scraping up any browned bits. Nestle chicken into pot and add any accumulated juices. Bring to simmer, cover, and transfer to oven. Cook until chicken is tender, about 45 minutes.

5. Remove pot from oven. Discard bacon and bay leaf, stir in Tabasco, and season with salt and pepper to taste. Serve over rice, sprinkled with scallions, passing extra Tabasco separately.

Louisiana Seasoning
MAKES ABOUT ¾ CUP

- 5 tablespoons paprika
- 2 tablespoons garlic powder
- 1 tablespoon dried thyme
- 1 tablespoon cayenne pepper
- 1 tablespoon celery salt
- 1 tablespoon table salt
- 1 tablespoon pepper

Combine all ingredients in a bowl.

Greek Chicken

Chicken Sauce Piquant

Lemon Pepper Chicken Wings

SERVES 4 TO 6

WHY THIS RECIPE WORKS Lemon pepper chicken wings are an Atlanta favorite. Our version is based on the popular "lemon pepper wet" style, which douses the wings in a special sauce after frying. For our homemade lemon pepper seasoning, we dehydrated lemon zest in the microwave and stirred in plenty of coarsely ground black pepper. We tossed the uncooked wings in lemon juice to reinforce the lemon flavor and dredged them in cornstarch and flour for a crispy coating. A mixture of melted butter and hot sauce made a rich, bright sauce to finish the wings.

Citric acid gives our homemade lemon pepper seasoning the signature punchy tartness present in most commercial lemon pepper blends. When possible, buy whole wings and butcher them yourself because they tend to be larger than wings that come split. If you can find only split wings, look for larger ones. Twelve whole wings should ideally equal 3 pounds and will yield 24 pieces (12 drumettes and 12 flats, with the tips discarded). Serve the wings with blue cheese dressing.

Lemon Pepper Seasoning
- 3 tablespoons grated lemon zest (3 lemons)
- 1 tablespoon coarsely ground pepper
- 1 teaspoon kosher salt
- 1 teaspoon granulated garlic
- 1 teaspoon onion powder
- 1 teaspoon ground coriander
- ½ teaspoon sugar
- ½ teaspoon citric acid (optional)
- ½ teaspoon ground turmeric
- ¼ teaspoon cayenne pepper

Wings
- ¾ cup cornstarch
- ¼ cup all-purpose flour
- 2 teaspoons baking powder
- 3 pounds chicken wings, cut at joints, wingtips discarded
- 3 tablespoons lemon juice
- 1 tablespoon kosher salt
- 1 teaspoon pepper
- 2 quarts peanut or vegetable oil for frying

Sauce
- 8 tablespoons unsalted butter, melted
- 1½ tablespoons Frank's RedHot Original Cayenne Pepper Sauce
- 1½ tablespoons lemon juice
- 1 tablespoon mayonnaise
- 1 tablespoon honey

1. For the Lemon Pepper Seasoning Spread lemon zest evenly on plate and microwave until dry and lemon zest separates easily when crumbled between your fingers, about 2 minutes, stirring halfway through microwaving.

2. Combine pepper; salt; granulated garlic; onion powder; coriander; sugar; citric acid, if using; turmeric; cayenne; and lemon zest in bowl. Set aside. (Seasoning can be stored in airtight container at room temperature for up to 1 month.)

3. For the Wings Adjust oven rack to middle position and heat oven to 200 degrees. Line rimmed baking sheet with triple layer of paper towels. Whisk cornstarch, flour, and baking powder together in bowl. Toss wings with lemon juice, salt, and pepper in large bowl until wings are evenly coated. Add cornstarch mixture and use your hands to toss and thoroughly coat wings in cornstarch mixture, pressing and rubbing cornstarch mixture into wings to adhere; set aside while heating oil.

4. Heat oil in large Dutch oven over medium-high heat to 375 degrees. Using tongs, add half of wings to oil and fry until golden and crispy, about 10 minutes. Using slotted

Lemon Pepper Chicken Wings

spoon or spider skimmer, transfer fried wings to prepared sheet. Transfer sheet to oven to keep warm. Return oil to 375 degrees and repeat with remaining wings.

5. For the Sauce Meanwhile, whisk all ingredients in second large bowl until uniform.

6. Add wings and 2 tablespoons lemon pepper seasoning to bowl with sauce and toss until wings are uniformly coated. Serve, sprinkled with extra lemon pepper seasoning as desired.

Cajun Stuffed Turkey Wings

SERVES 4

WHY THIS RECIPE WORKS At Laura's II in Lafayette, Louisiana, meaty turkey wings are slit open, stuffed with garlic cloves and a powerful mix of spices, and braised to tenderness. To re-create that secret spice mix, we tinkered our way to a mixture heavy on paprika and granulated garlic. Browning the wings gave them beautiful color and created flavorful fond in the pot, to which we added flour to make a caramel-colored roux. After a slow braise in the oven, the wings were fall-off-the-bone tender and draped in a complex and delicious gravy.

Serve with rice.

Spice Mix
- 1¾ teaspoons paprika
- 1 teaspoon granulated garlic
- ¾ teaspoon table salt
- ¾ teaspoon pepper
- ½ teaspoon onion powder
- ½ teaspoon celery salt
- ¼ teaspoon cayenne pepper

Turkey
- 4 (12- to 16-ounce) whole turkey wings, cut at joints into flats and drumettes, wingtips discarded
- 12 garlic cloves, peeled (8 halved lengthwise, 4 smashed)
- ¼ cup vegetable oil
- ¼ cup all-purpose flour
- 1 cup finely chopped green bell pepper
- 1 cup finely chopped onion
- ¼ cup finely chopped celery
- 1 tablespoon chopped fresh thyme
- 3 cups chicken broth

1. For the Spice Mix Combine all ingredients in bowl. Measure out 1½ teaspoons spice mix and set aside.

2. For the Turkey Adjust oven rack to middle position and heat oven to 300 degrees. Make one 1-inch-long incision, about ½ inch deep, on either side of each drumette bone and one 2-inch-long incision, about ½ inch deep, between bones on underside of each flat. Sprinkle wings inside and out with remaining 4 teaspoons spice mix. Stuff 1 piece halved garlic into each pocket of each drumette and 2 pieces into pocket of each flat.

3. Heat oil in Dutch oven over medium-high heat until shimmering. Add wings and cook until browned on both sides, about 10 minutes. Transfer wings to plate. Reduce heat to medium and add flour to fat left in pot. Cook, stirring often, until roux is caramel-colored, about 3 minutes.

4. Add bell pepper, onion, celery, thyme, smashed garlic, and reserved spice mix and cook, stirring occasionally and scraping up any browned bits, until vegetables are just beginning to soften, about 5 minutes.

5. Stir in broth and bring to simmer. Nestle wings into broth mixture. Cover, transfer pot to oven, and cook for 1 hour. Remove pot from oven and flip wings. Cover, return pot to oven, and continue to cook until tender, about 45 minutes longer.

Cajun Stuffed Turkey Wings

6. Transfer wings to clean plate. Bring gravy to boil over high heat and cook until slightly thickened, about 7 minutes. Off heat, season with salt and pepper to taste. Return wings to pot and gently turn to coat with gravy. Serve.

On the Road: Laura's II, Lafayette, Louisiana

The turkey wings at Laura's II in Lafayette, Louisiana, are an impressive sight: probably close to 2 pounds each, well browned, and braised in their own juices. The area along the drumstick of each wing is "stuffed" with a mixture of garlic and spices, of which cayenne is surely one, while the others remain secret.

Owner Madonna Broussard learned from her grandmother, Laura Broussard, who ran a restaurant out of the back of her house in the 1960s. It was one of Lafayette's first soul food "plate lunch" spots, where working-class residents could find a reasonably priced square meal.

The restaurant and home were destroyed by a fire in the 1970s, and Laura's relocated to a residential neighborhood. In 2000, the restaurant moved again, to a busy commercial strip on West University Avenue, reopening as Laura's II—a name chosen to acknowledge that the location had changed while reassuring longtime customers that the food had not.

As Madonna says, "When people eat here they are gonna feel like this is a home. And it's a good home."

Fish and Chips

SERVES 4

WHY THIS RECIPE WORKS The best fish and chips are usually found at a proper English pub, but we wanted to create a worthy version at home. To make the crispiest coating, we needed just four ingredients: beer, flour, cornstarch, and baking powder. The beer helped to create a coating that stuck well to the tender pieces of cod and also added a malty sweetness to each bite. For the chips, we fry the potatoes first, then the fish, then quickly finish the fries by frying again until deep golden brown. Yukon Gold potatoes worked best; they were less starchy and more crisp once fried than other potato varieties.

Try to find large Yukon Gold potatoes, 10 to 12 ounces each, that are similar in size. We prefer peanut or vegetable oil for frying and do not recommend using canola oil since it can impart off-flavors. Use a Dutch oven that holds 6 quarts or more. A light-bodied American lager, such as Budweiser, works best here. If you prefer to cook without alcohol, substitute seltzer for the beer. We prefer to use cod for this recipe, but haddock and halibut will also work well. Serve with Tartar Sauce (recipe follows), if desired.

- 1 cup (5 ounces) all-purpose flour
- 1 cup (4 ounces) cornstarch
- Salt and pepper
- 1 teaspoon baking powder
- 1½ cups beer
- 1 (2-pound) skinless cod fillet, about 1 inch thick
- 2½ pounds large Yukon Gold potatoes, unpeeled
- 8 cups peanut or vegetable oil
- Lemon wedges

1. Whisk flour, cornstarch, 1½ teaspoons salt, and baking powder together in large bowl. Add beer and whisk until smooth. Cover with plastic wrap and refrigerate for at least 20 minutes.

2. Cut cod crosswise into 8 equal fillets (about 4 ounces each). Pat cod dry with paper towels and season with salt and pepper; refrigerate until ready to use.

3. Square off each potato by cutting ¼-inch-thick slice from each of its 4 long sides. Cut potatoes lengthwise into ¼-inch-thick planks. Stack 3 to 4 planks and cut into ¼-inch fries. Repeat with remaining planks. (Do not place potatoes in water.)

4. Line rimmed baking sheet with triple layer of paper towels. Combine potatoes and oil in large Dutch oven. Cook over high heat until oil has reached rolling boil, about 7 minutes. Continue to cook, without stirring, until potatoes are limp but exteriors are beginning to firm, about 15 minutes longer. Using tongs, stir potatoes, gently scraping up any that stick, and continue to cook, stirring occasionally, until just lightly golden brown, about 4 minutes longer (fries will not be fully cooked at this point). Using spider skimmer or slotted spoon, transfer fries to prepared sheet. Skim off any browned bits left in pot.

5. Set wire rack in second rimmed baking sheet. Transfer fish to batter and toss to evenly coat. Heat oil over medium-high heat to 375 degrees. Using fork, remove 4 pieces of

184   *The Complete Cook's Country TV Show Cookbook*

fish from batter, allowing excess batter to drip back into bowl, and add to hot oil, briefly dragging fish along surface of oil to prevent sticking. Adjust burner, if necessary, to maintain oil temperature between 350 and 375 degrees.

6. Cook fish, stirring gently to prevent pieces from sticking together, until deep golden brown and crispy, about 4 minutes per side. Using spider skimmer or slotted spoon, transfer fish to prepared rack and skim off any browned bits left in pot. Return oil to 375 degrees and repeat with remaining 4 pieces of fish.

7. Return oil to 375 degrees. Add fries to oil and cook until deep golden brown and crispy, about 1 minute. Using spider skimmer or slotted spoon, transfer fries back to prepared sheet and season with salt. Transfer fish and chips to platter. Serve with lemon wedges.

Tartar Sauce
MAKES ABOUT 1 CUP

The test kitchen's favorite mayo is Blue Plate Real Mayonnaise, which is not available in all areas of the United States. Hellmann's Real Mayonnaise, which is available nationwide, was a close second and is a great option.

- ¾ cup mayonnaise
- ¼ cup dill pickle relish
- 1½ teaspoons distilled white vinegar
- ½ teaspoon Worcestershire sauce
- ½ teaspoon pepper
- ⅛ teaspoon table salt

Combine all ingredients in small bowl. Cover with plastic wrap and refrigerate until flavors meld, about 15 minutes.

Fried Catfish
SERVES 4 TO 6

WHY THIS RECIPE WORKS This fried catfish is made in the style of the Mississippi Delta, with a cornmeal-based coating, bold seasoning, and spicy comeback sauce. For the best crunchy texture of the breading, we processed half the cornmeal into a superfine powder before mixing it with the unground cornmeal and spices. Buttermilk and hot sauce whisked together made a flavorful dredge that helped the cornmeal mixture stick to the fish. Before coating and frying the catfish, we cut the fillets in half lengthwise along their natural seams. This made it easier to manage the smaller

Fish and Chips

Fried Catfish

pieces when frying; the strips cooked faster and more evenly; and we got a better ratio of crunchy crust to flesh on every piece. The tangy, spicy Comeback Sauce came together quickly and easily in a blender.

Use a Dutch oven that holds 6 quarts or more. If your spice grinder is small, grind the cornmeal in batches or process it in a blender for 60 to 90 seconds.

- 2 cups buttermilk
- 1 teaspoon hot sauce
- 2 cups cornmeal
- 4 teaspoons table salt
- 2 teaspoons pepper
- 2 teaspoons granulated garlic
- 1 teaspoon cayenne pepper
- 4 (6- to 8-ounce) catfish fillets, halved lengthwise along natural seam
- 2 quarts peanut or vegetable oil for frying
- Lemon wedges

1. Set wire rack in rimmed baking sheet and line half of rack with triple layer of paper towels. Whisk buttermilk and hot sauce together in shallow dish. Process 1 cup cornmeal in spice grinder to fine powder, 30 to 45 seconds. Whisk salt, pepper, granulated garlic, cayenne, remaining 1 cup cornmeal, and ground cornmeal together in second shallow dish.

2. Pat fish dry with paper towels. Working with 1 piece of fish at a time, dip fish in buttermilk mixture, letting excess drip back into dish. Dredge fish in cornmeal mixture, shaking off excess, and transfer to large plate.

3. Add oil to large Dutch oven until it measures about 1½ inches deep and heat over medium-high heat to 350 degrees. Working with 4 pieces of fish at a time, add fish to hot oil. Adjust burner, if necessary, to maintain oil temperature between 325 and 350 degrees. Fry fish until golden brown and crispy, about 5 minutes. Transfer fish to paper towel–lined side of prepared rack and let drain for 1 minute, then move to unlined side of rack. Return oil to 350 degrees and repeat with remaining fish. Serve with lemon wedges.

Comeback Sauce
SERVES 4 TO 6 (MAKES ABOUT 1 CUP)

Chili sauce, a condiment similar to ketchup, has a sweet flavor and subtle spicy kick; do not substitute Asian chili sauce.

- ½ cup mayonnaise
- ⅓ cup chopped onion
- 2 tablespoons vegetable oil
- 2 tablespoons chili sauce
- 1 tablespoon ketchup
- 2½ teaspoons Worcestershire sauce
- 2½ teaspoons hot sauce
- 1 teaspoon yellow mustard
- 1 teaspoon lemon juice
- 1 garlic clove, minced
- ¾ teaspoon pepper
- ⅛ teaspoon paprika

Process all ingredients in blender until smooth, about 30 seconds. Sauce can be refrigerated for up to 5 days.

Miso Black Cod
SERVES 4

WHY THIS RECIPE WORKS Chef Nobuyuki "Nobu" Matsuhisa made his name nearly synonymous with the technique of marinating black cod in sweet white miso when he began serving it at a Los Angeles sushi bar in the 1980s. The dish was a hit and was part of what propelled him to open his own restaurant, Matsuhisa (now one of many worldwide). The technique, known in Japanese as saikyo-zuke, results in firm, succulent fish that browns gorgeously under the broiler. Black cod has a higher fat content than Atlantic cod, which keeps it from drying out during cooking. We marinated the cod with miso, sugar, mirin, sake, soy sauce, and sesame oil. Then all it took was a stint under the broiler to achieve restaurant quality at home.

Black cod often contains a row of small pin bones running down the center line of the fillet; they are difficult to remove from the raw fillets but slide out easily after cooking. It's also easy to cut on either side of the center line of the cooked fillets to avoid them. Salmon (farmed or wild), Chilean sea bass, or arctic char can be substituted for the black cod. If using wild salmon or arctic char, cook the fillets to 120 degrees (for medium-rare), and start checking for doneness early. Red miso can be substituted for the white miso. Garnish with scallions, if desired.

- 1 cup white miso
- ⅔ cup sugar
- ⅓ cup mirin

Miso Black Cod

Eastern North Carolina Fish Stew

SERVES 8

WHY THIS RECIPE WORKS Locals in the Tar Heel State have loved this hearty tomatoey, bacon-infused Sunday stew for decades. After crisping bacon, we cooked onion and red pepper flakes in the rendered fat before adding a whole can of tomato paste for intense tomato flavor. With the spicy broth in place, we turned to the rest of the stew. We gave potato slices a head start before nestling chunks of whitefish into the pot. A surprising addition to this dish is poached eggs, which we layered atop the stew and cooked gently in the covered pot until just set.

Fishing for Stew in Deep Run

"Throwing a fish stew" is what they say in Deep Run, North Carolina, and it's as good an excuse as any for a low-key gathering. They usually happen in the fall, during vest season.

Walking behind the main house, Greg Smith and his father, Emmett, are gathering supplies outside their party shack (formerly a tobacco packhouse). To one side sits a large, black iron kettle. Emmett found this cauldron years ago in a "manure field," as he describes it, and this gets a rise out of the guests, all longtime friends who grew up together in the small town. He clarifies: It was technically a cow pasture, but you can see the connection. The pot was nearly completely buried when he unearthed it, but with determination, he scrubbed it back to life. Emmett estimates that his pot has held more than 500 stews.

Emmett and Greg fire up the propane burner under the pot and then drop in a pound and a half of chopped bacon to cook until its fat has rendered. Guests emerge from the kitchen in a procession, each bearing an offering for the stew: 10 pounds of sliced potatoes, 5 pounds of sliced onions, and 7 pounds of local rockfish. Emmett layers it all into the pot. One guest spoons in a couple of cans of tomato paste—his only job, but he performs it with authority.

Emmett throws in a heavy handful of red pepper flakes and stands guard as the stew simmers away. He eventually adds the final, and most surprising, ingredient: four dozen eggs, cracked and dropped one by one into the stew—just enough for 20 people.

¼ cup sake
3 tablespoons soy sauce
1 tablespoon toasted sesame oil
4 (6- to 8-ounce) skin-on black cod fillets
    Pickled sliced ginger

1. Whisk miso, sugar, mirin, sake, soy sauce, and oil together in medium bowl. Pat cod dry with paper towels and place in 1-gallon zipper-lock bag. Pour miso mixture over cod. Press out air, seal bag, and turn to coat cod in marinade. Refrigerate for at least 8 hours or up to 24 hours, turning occasionally.

2. Adjust oven rack 8 inches from broiler and heat broiler. Set wire rack in rimmed baking sheet and line with aluminum foil. Lightly spray foil with vegetable oil spray. Wipe excess marinade from cod with your fingers, leaving thin layer on cod, and transfer to prepared wire rack, skin side down.

3. Broil until cod is deeply browned and registers 125 degrees, 8 to 12 minutes, rotating sheet halfway through broiling and shielding fillets with foil if they begin to get too dark. Serve with pickled ginger.

Any mild, firm-fleshed whitefish, such as bass, rockfish, cod, hake, haddock, or halibut, will work well in this stew. Our favorite supermarket bacon is Oscar Mayer Naturally Hardwood Smoked Bacon. Serve this rustic stew with soft white sandwich bread or saltines.

- 6 slices thick-cut bacon, cut into ½-inch-wide strips
- 2 onions, halved and sliced thin
- 1½ teaspoons table salt
- ½ teaspoon red pepper flakes
- 6 cups water
- 1 (6-ounce) can tomato paste
- 1 pound red potatoes, unpeeled, sliced ¼ inch thick
- 1 bay leaf
- 1 teaspoon Tabasco sauce, plus extra for serving
- 2 pounds skinless whitefish fillets, 1 to 1½ inches thick, cut into 2-inch chunks
- 8 large eggs

1. Cook bacon in Dutch oven over medium heat until crispy, 9 to 11 minutes, stirring occasionally. Add onions, salt, and pepper flakes and cook until onions begin to soften, about 5 minutes.

2. Stir in water and tomato paste, scraping up any browned bits. Add potatoes and bay leaf. Increase heat to medium-high and bring to boil. Reduce heat to medium and cook at vigorous simmer for 10 minutes.

3. Reduce heat to medium-low and stir in Tabasco. Nestle fish into stew but do not stir. Crack eggs into stew, spacing them evenly. Cover and cook until eggs are just set, 17 to 22 minutes. Season with salt to taste. Serve, passing extra Tabasco separately.

Monterey Bay Cioppino

SERVES 6 TO 8

WHY THIS RECIPE WORKS To create a home recipe inspired by the rich, complex cioppino served at Phil's Fish Market & Eatery in Moss Landing, California, we added pesto's key ingredients (olive oil, basil, and garlic) to the mix, instead of making a traditional basil pesto to flavor the stew like Phil does. Phil's version uses a wide range of seafood, including clams and calamari, but we opted instead for easy-to-find shrimp, scallops, sea bass, and mussels. Adding our seafood to the pot in stages and finishing the cooking off-heat ensured that no item was overcooked.

We recommend buying "dry" scallops, which don't have chemical additives and taste better than "wet" scallops. Dry scallops will look ivory or pinkish; wet scallops are bright white. If you can't find fresh dry scallops, you can substitute thawed frozen scallops. If you can't find sea bass, you can substitute cod, haddock, or halibut fillets.

Marinara

- 3 tablespoons extra-virgin olive oil
- 1 large onion, halved and sliced thin
- 3 garlic cloves, sliced thin
- ¾ teaspoon table salt
- 1 (15-ounce) can tomato sauce
- 1 cup canned tomato puree
- ½ cup chopped fresh basil
- 1 tablespoon packed light brown sugar
- 1½ teaspoons Worcestershire sauce
- ¼ teaspoon ground cinnamon

Cioppino

- 1½ pounds skinless sea bass fillets, 1 to 1½ inches thick, cut into 1½-inch pieces
- 12 ounces extra-large shrimp (21 to 25 per pound), peeled, deveined, and tails removed
- 12 ounces large scallops, tendons removed, cut in half horizontally
- Salt and pepper
- 3 tablespoons extra-virgin olive oil
- 1 pound mussels, scrubbed and debearded
- ½ cup chopped fresh basil
- ¼ cup dry sherry
- 3 garlic cloves, minced
- 1 teaspoon Worcestershire sauce
- ½ teaspoon saffron threads, crumbled
- 2 (8-ounce) bottles clam juice
- 1 (12-inch) baguette, sliced and toasted
- Lemon wedges

1. For the Marinara Heat oil in large saucepan over medium heat until shimmering. Add onion, garlic, and salt and cook until onion is softened and just beginning to brown, about 8 minutes. Add tomato sauce, tomato puree, basil, sugar, Worcestershire, and cinnamon and bring to boil. Reduce heat to medium-low and simmer until marinara is slightly thickened, 10 to 12 minutes. Remove from heat, cover, and set aside.

2. For the Cioppino Season sea bass, shrimp, and scallops with salt and pepper; set aside. Heat oil in Dutch oven over medium-high heat until shimmering. Add mussels, basil, sherry, garlic, Worcestershire, saffron, and ½ teaspoon salt. Cover and cook until mussels start to open, about 2 minutes.

3. Stir in clam juice and marinara until combined. Nestle sea bass and scallops into pot and bring to boil. Reduce heat to medium, cover, and simmer until seafood is just turning opaque, about 2 minutes. Nestle shrimp into pot and return to simmer. Cover and cook until all seafood is opaque, about 3 minutes. Remove from heat and let sit, covered, for 5 minutes. Serve with baguette slices and lemon wedges.

Seafood Substitutions

Our version of Phil's cioppino uses a carefully considered collection of seafood, but that doesn't mean you can't make it if you can't find everything on the ingredient list. For instance, sea bass is our first choice, but you can also use cod, haddock, or halibut fillets of a similar size. Here are a few more options:

- Double the amount of shrimp or scallops if you can't find one or the other.

- Use small clams in place of the mussels, or use half clams and half mussels.

- Garnish the stew with cooked crabmeat—or, for the full Phil's effect, cooked crab legs—before serving.

Woodman's-Style Clam Chowder

SERVES 6 TO 8

WHY THIS RECIPE WORKS Woodman's of Essex in Massachusetts uses fresh clams in their chowder, but our version relies on convenient and affordable canned clams (both chopped and whole baby clams), which deliver a satisfying flavor and texture. We parcooked diced potatoes, mixed them with the chopped clams and their juice, and let the mixture marinate in the fridge to meld the flavors. To prevent rubbery clams, we kept the chowder below a simmer and added the whole baby clams toward the end. Light cream and a knob of butter enriched the chowder.

Eastern North Carolina Fish Stew

Monterey Bay Cioppino

Woodman's-Style Clam Chowder

Okra and Shrimp Stew

To make this recipe more accessible, we call for two kinds of canned clams: chopped clams and whole baby clams. Purchase the best-quality canned clams you can find. The Woodman's clam chowder is relatively thin compared with other New England clam chowders. We use instant mashed potato flakes to thicken ours slightly; if you prefer a thinner chowder, omit them. If you can't find light cream, substitute 1½ cups of heavy cream mixed with ½ cup of whole milk.

- 1¾ pounds russet potatoes, peeled and cut into ½-inch dice
- 2 (6.5-ounce) cans chopped clams
- 2 cups finely chopped onion
- 2½ teaspoons table salt, divided
- 2 teaspoons pepper
- 2 (10-ounce) cans whole baby clams
- 2 cups light cream
- 2 tablespoons unsalted butter
- 2 tablespoons instant mashed potato flakes (optional)
- Oyster crackers

1. Place potatoes in large saucepan and cover with water by 1 inch. Bring to boil over high heat. Reduce heat to medium-low and simmer until potatoes are al dente and paring knife inserted into them still meets some resistance, about 3 minutes. Drain potatoes in colander and transfer to medium bowl. Let potatoes cool completely, about 30 minutes.

2. Add chopped clams and their juice, onion, 1 teaspoon salt, and pepper to potatoes and stir to combine. Transfer mixture to 1-gallon zipper-lock bag, seal bag, and refrigerate for at least 1 hour or up to 24 hours.

3. When ready to finish cooking chowder, drain whole clams in fine-mesh strainer set over bowl; reserve juice (you should have about 1 cup; add water if necessary to make up difference).

4. Combine potato mixture, reserved clam juice, and remaining 1½ teaspoons salt in large saucepan. Bring to bare simmer over medium heat (bubbles should just begin to form along edge of saucepan), stirring often (it will take about 10 minutes to reach bare simmer). Reduce heat to medium-low and cook, stirring often and adjusting heat to keep chowder just below simmer, until potatoes are mostly tender, about 5 minutes.

5. Stir in whole clams and cream. Increase heat to medium and cook, stirring often to keep chowder just below simmer, until potatoes are fully tender and chowder is hot throughout, about 5 minutes. Off heat, stir in butter and potato flakes, if using, until combined. Season with salt and pepper to taste. Serve with oyster crackers.

On the Road: Woodman's of Essex

Woodman's of Essex is famous for fried seafood; steamed lobsters; and all things clam, from cakes to chowder. Situated on a piece of inland marsh on the North Shore of Massachusetts, the area offers up all the elements of an ideal coastal setting: rocky shorelines, tangerine sunsets, and sweet salt air. On any given weekend at Woodman's, a line of customers waiting to place their orders—most of them still sandy from the beach—stretches 50 people long out the door, and the hunger in the air is as palpable as the fog of fried seafood that hangs over the place. Inside, a view into the open kitchen reveals a crew of at least 20 seemingly high school–aged kids frantically working 10 deep-fryers and ladling out cupfuls of clam chowder for hungry customers. It's hard to believe that it all started with a desire to sell fresh clams.

Steve and Doug Woodman now co-own the business that their grandfather, Lawrence Woodman, started in 1914 as a simple roadside stand.

"My grandfather's nickname was Chubby," Steve says. "He was a short man with a big barrel chest. He was a trolley engineer at the time and was digging clams to make some extra money." When the stand opened up, it carried a few grocery items to draw customers in, but ultimately "Chubby was really trying to sell his clams."

Chubby eventually began selling homemade potato chips. Then, on July 3, 1916, at the suggestion of a customer, he breaded and fried clams and sold them during Essex's Fourth of July parade. Steve says, "They put a sign up: 'Fried Essex Clams.' And people came in and bought them. My grandfather took in $35 that day, which was the most money he'd ever taken in on any day he was open. So, he wasn't a stupid man, he kept them on the menu."

Soon the menu expanded to include clam cakes; clam rolls; and their famous, award-winning family recipe for clam chowder, a true New England classic.

Okra and Shrimp Stew

SERVES 8 TO 10

WHY THIS RECIPE WORKS Okra and shrimp stew is popular in the Carolina Lowcountry, which is home to the Gullah, or Gullah Geechee, people. Known by different names, including okra stew and okra gumbo, this long-simmered, complexly flavored mix of vegetables and seafood is a gumbo-style dish, but it uses okra as a thickener instead of a roux or filé powder. We started our stew with a homemade ham stock and then added in vegetables, spices, andouille sausage, and the meat from the ham hocks. Once the stew was thickened and reduced by half, we quickly poached the shrimp in the stew.

If you can find medium shrimp (41 to 50 per pound), use those and leave them whole. Look for meaty ham hocks. If you buy the test kitchen's preferred brand of andouille sausage, Jacob's World Famous Andouille, which tends to be thicker than other products, halve it lengthwise before slicing it crosswise.

- 4 quarts water
- 1–1¼ pounds smoked ham hocks
- 1 onion, quartered
- 1 bay leaf
- 1 tablespoon vegetable oil
- 12 ounces andouille sausage, sliced ¼ inch thick
- 1 pound frozen or fresh okra (stemmed and cut crosswise ½ inch thick for fresh)
- 1 (14.5-ounce) can diced tomatoes
- 1½ cups frozen baby lima (aka butter) beans
- 4 garlic cloves, minced
- 2 teaspoons table salt
- 1 teaspoon pepper
- 1 teaspoon granulated garlic
- 1 teaspoon onion powder
- ½ teaspoon paprika
- 1 pound large shrimp (26 to 30 per pound), peeled, deveined, and tails removed, cut into thirds
  Cooked white rice

Gumbo

SERVES 6 TO 8

WHY THIS RECIPE WORKS This hearty Louisiana specialty combines culinary traditions from many different cultures (gombo means okra in many parts of West Africa). Our challenge was to find an easier way to prepare the dark-brown roux, the fat and flour paste that thickens the stew and adds flavor. We created a relatively hands-off roux by toasting the flour on the stovetop, adding the oil, and finishing the roux in the oven. For the soup base, instead of making our own shrimp stock, we switched to store-bought chicken broth fortified with fish sauce. Tasters preferred the flavor of meaty chicken thighs over breasts.

A heavy cast-iron Dutch oven yields the fastest oven roux. If a lightweight pot is all you've got, increase the oven time by 10 minutes. The chicken broth must be at room temperature to prevent lumps from forming. Fish sauce lends an essential savory quality. Since the salt content of fish sauce varies among brands, taste the finished gumbo before seasoning with salt.

1. Combine water, ham hocks, onion, and bay leaf in large Dutch oven and bring to boil over high heat. Reduce heat to medium-low; cover, with lid slightly ajar; and simmer until ham hocks are fork-tender, 2½ to 3 hours.

2. Remove pot from heat and transfer ham hocks to cutting board. Let ham hocks rest until cool enough to handle; discard onion and bay leaf from broth. Transfer broth to large bowl; measure out 8 cups broth (add enough water to equal 8 cups if necessary; reserve any excess for another use). Remove ham from bones, discard bones, and cut ham into bite-size pieces. (Broth and chopped ham can be refrigerated separately for up to 2 days. If fat solidifies on top of broth after chilling, you can discard fat before proceeding, if preferred.)

3. Heat oil in now-empty pot over medium-high heat until shimmering. Add sausage and cook until lightly browned on both sides, about 5 minutes. Add okra, tomatoes and their juice, beans, minced garlic, salt, pepper, granulated garlic, onion powder, paprika, 8 cups broth, and ham to pot. Bring to boil over high heat.

4. Reduce heat to medium and cook at strong simmer, uncovered, until reduced by about half and thickened to stew-like consistency, 55 minutes to 1 hour 5 minutes, stirring occasionally. Reduce heat to low; stir in shrimp; and cook until shrimp are just cooked through, about 3 minutes. Remove from heat and season with salt and pepper to taste. Serve over rice.

On the Road: The Gullah Influence on Lowcountry Cuisine

The marshy, coastal area of South Carolina known as the Lowcountry is home to the Gullah, or Gullah Geechee, people. Descendants of West Africans who were sought after for their rice-farming skills and enslaved on coastal plantations on the mainland and throughout the Sea Islands, the Gullah applied African cooking techniques to ingredients that were accessible to them, namely fresh seafood; wild game; and African foods imported during the slave trade, including rice, okra, peanuts, and benne (sesame) seeds. Many Gullah dishes, such as Frogmore stew, hoppin' John, and shrimp and grits, are now known outside the Lowcountry and eaten throughout the South and beyond. Chefs such as Alexander Smalls and BJ Dennis, who grew up on Gullah cuisine, have been educating diners and bringing recognition to this style of cooking. Smalls featured Gullah dishes at his first restaurant, Café Beulah, in New York, while Dennis became an ambassador of Gullah culture, hosting pop-ups in the Lowcountry showcasing regional foods and dishes. A testament to the tight-knit Gullah community, the Lowcountry remains defined by Gullah cuisine and traditions, which are celebrated annually at the Original Gullah Festival in Beaufort, South Carolina.

¾	cup plus 1 tablespoon all-purpose flour
½	cup vegetable oil
1	onion, chopped fine
1	green bell pepper, stemmed, seeded, and chopped
1	celery rib, chopped fine
5	garlic cloves, minced
1	teaspoon minced fresh thyme
¼	teaspoon cayenne pepper
1	(14.5-ounce) can diced tomatoes, drained
3¾	cups chicken broth, room temperature
¼	cup fish sauce
2	pounds bone-in chicken thighs, skin removed, trimmed
	Table salt and pepper
8	ounces andouille sausage, halved lengthwise and sliced thin
2	cups frozen okra, thawed (optional)
2	pounds extra-large shrimp (21 to 25 per pound), peeled and deveined

1. Adjust oven rack to lowest position and heat oven to 350 degrees. Toast ¾ cup flour in Dutch oven over medium heat, stirring constantly, until just beginning to brown, about 5 minutes. Off heat, whisk in oil until smooth. Cover, transfer pot to oven, and cook until mixture is deep brown and fragrant, about 45 minutes. (Roux can be refrigerated for 1 week. To use, heat in Dutch oven over medium-high heat, whisking constantly, until just smoking, and continue with step 2.)

2. Transfer Dutch oven to stovetop and whisk cooked roux to combine. Add onion, bell pepper, and celery and cook over medium heat, stirring frequently, until vegetables are softened, about 10 minutes. Stir in remaining 1 tablespoon flour, garlic, thyme, and cayenne and cook until fragrant, about 1 minute. Add tomatoes and cook until dry, about 1 minute. Slowly whisk in broth and fish sauce until smooth. Season chicken with pepper. Add chicken to vegetable mixture and bring to boil.

3. Reduce heat to medium-low and simmer, covered, until chicken is tender, about 30 minutes. Skim fat and transfer chicken to plate. When chicken is cool enough to handle, cut into bite-size pieces and return to pot; discard bones.

4. Stir in sausage and okra, if using, and simmer until heated through, about 5 minutes. Add shrimp and simmer until cooked through, about 5 minutes. Season with salt and pepper to taste. Serve. (Gumbo can be refrigerated for 1 day.)

Gumbo

Newcomer to the Bayou

Asian fish sauce in a gumbo recipe? Admittedly, it's an unconventional idea. And here's the cool part: New Orleans has a well-established Vietnamese community that began after the Vietnam War. As far as we know, we're the first to put fish sauce in gumbo, but there's no question that these immigrants to New Orleans are having an impact on the city's storied food traditions: They've tossed lemongrass into crawfish boils, organized a farmers' market with such items as ngo gai (an herb), banana buds, and longan fruit, and put banh mi on the city's must-eat food list, right there next to the city's signature po' boys.

To Make Ahead Gumbo can be made through step 3 and refrigerated for 3 days. To serve, bring gumbo to simmer, covered, in Dutch oven. Remove lid and proceed with recipe as directed.

FORK-IN-THE-ROAD FAVORITES 193

Shrimp Mozambique

SERVES 4

WHY THIS RECIPE WORKS This buttery, garlicky, peppery shrimp dish has roots in southeast Africa, where Portuguese colonists cultivated the piri-piri pepper that traditionally gives this dish its heat. While looking for a stand-in for the piri-piri pepper, we realized Frank's RedHot Original Cayenne Pepper Sauce was, like many piri-piri sauces, a puree of peppers, vinegar, and oil. To give it body and balance, we blended Frank's with olive oil, garlic, parsley, paprika, and torn bread. Cooking the shrimp until just opaque in the sauce with a splash of white wine and finishing it off with butter brought together this spicy and velvety seafood dish.

We prefer untreated shrimp—those without added sodium or preservatives such as sodium tripolyphosphate. Most frozen E-Z peel shrimp have been treated (the ingredient list should tell you). If you're using treated shrimp, do not sprinkle the shrimp with salt in step 2. We developed this recipe with Frank's RedHot Original Cayenne Pepper Sauce, which is similar to the piri-piri sauce called for in the traditional recipe. Serve with crusty bread or over white rice.

Sauce
- 2 tablespoons Frank's RedHot Original Cayenne Pepper Sauce
- 2 tablespoons extra-virgin olive oil
- 2 tablespoons water
- ¼ slice hearty white sandwich bread, torn into small pieces
- 1 tablespoon chopped fresh parsley
- 2 garlic cloves, chopped
- 2 teaspoons paprika
- ½ teaspoon pepper

Shrimp
- 2 pounds extra-large shrimp (21 to 25 per pound), peeled, deveined, and tails removed
- Table salt and pepper
- 1 tablespoon extra-virgin olive oil
- ½ cup finely chopped onion
- 3 garlic cloves, sliced thin
- 1 cup dry white wine
- 2 tablespoons unsalted butter, cut into 2 pieces
- 2 tablespoons chopped fresh parsley

1. For the Sauce Process all ingredients in blender until smooth, about 2 minutes, scraping down sides of blender jar as needed.

2. For the Shrimp Sprinkle shrimp with ½ teaspoon salt and ¼ teaspoon pepper; set aside. Heat oil in 12-inch nonstick skillet over medium heat until shimmering. Add onion and ½ teaspoon salt and cook until softened, about 5 minutes. Add garlic and cook until fragrant, about 1 minute. Add wine and bring to boil. Cook until reduced by half, about 4 minutes.

3. Add shrimp and cook, stirring occasionally, until opaque and just cooked through, about 4 minutes. Stir in butter and sauce and cook until butter is melted and sauce is heated through, about 1 minute. Season with salt and pepper to taste. Sprinkle with parsley and serve.

Charleston Shrimp Perloo

SERVES 4 TO 6

WHY THIS RECIPE WORKS Perloo (pronounced "PUHR-low"), a staple in South Carolina's Low Country, is a tomatoey rice dish simmered in broth. To start, we went the classic route and used reserved shrimp shells to create and flavor shrimp stock, which is surprisingly easy and practical to make from scratch. For the rice, we stuck to the traditional flavor base of onions, celery, and bell pepper. Sautéing the rice with the vegetables firmed up the grains' exterior and prevented mushiness. Just before removing the rice from the heat, we folded in the shrimp and let them rest, covered, for perfectly cooked shrimp and tender rice in a delicious one-pot meal.

After adding the shrimp to the pot, fold it in gently; stirring the rice too vigorously will make it mushy. Any extra stock can be refrigerated for 3 days or frozen for up to 1 month. Serve with hot sauce.

- 5 tablespoons unsalted butter
- 1½ pounds extra-large shrimp (21 to 25 per pound), peeled and deveined, shells reserved
- 2 onions, chopped
- 4 celery ribs, chopped
- Table salt
- 4 cups water
- 1 tablespoon peppercorns
- 5 sprigs fresh parsley
- 2 bay leaves

1 green bell pepper, stemmed, seeded, and chopped
2 cups long-grain white rice
2 garlic cloves, minced
1 teaspoon minced fresh thyme
¼ teaspoon cayenne pepper
1 (14.5-ounce) can diced tomatoes

1. Melt 1 tablespoon butter in large saucepan over medium heat. Add shrimp shells, 1 cup onion, ½ cup celery, and 1 teaspoon salt and cook, stirring occasionally, until shells are spotty brown, about 10 minutes. Add water, peppercorns, parsley, and bay leaves. Increase heat to high and bring to boil. Reduce heat to low, cover, and simmer for 30 minutes. Strain shrimp stock through fine-mesh strainer set over large bowl, pressing on solids to extract as much liquid as possible; discard solids.

2. Melt remaining 4 tablespoons butter in Dutch oven over medium heat. Add bell pepper, remaining onion and celery, and ½ teaspoon salt and cook until vegetables are beginning to soften, 5 to 7 minutes. Add rice, garlic, thyme, and cayenne and cook until fragrant and rice is translucent, about 2 minutes. Stir in tomatoes and their juice and 3 cups shrimp stock (reserve remainder for another use) and bring to boil. Reduce heat to low, cover, and cook for 20 minutes.

3. Gently fold shrimp into rice until evenly distributed, cover, and continue to cook 5 minutes longer. Remove pot from heat and let sit, covered, until shrimp are cooked through and all liquid is absorbed, about 10 minutes. Serve.

Shrimp and Grits

SERVES 4

WHY THIS RECIPE WORKS Known locally in the Carolinas for generations as "breakfast shrimp," there are many versions of shrimp and grits. We kept it simple: tender flavorful shrimp, silky sauce, and creamy grits. We used the shrimp shells to make a stock for the sauce base. To avoid overcooking the shrimp, we lightly sautéed them in bacon fat, set them aside while creating the sauce in the same skillet, then finished them in the sauce. Toasting the grits in butter coaxed more corn flavor out of them before we added liquid. Sliced scallions added a fresh finish.

We prefer untreated shrimp—those without added sodium or preservatives like sodium tripolyphosphate. Most frozen

Shrimp Mozambique

Shrimp and Grits

E-Z peel shrimp have been treated (the ingredient list should tell you). If you're using treated shrimp, do not add the salt in step 4. If you use our winning grits (Anson Mills Pencil Cob Grits) or other fresh-milled grits, you will need to increase the simmering time by 25 minutes.

Grits
- 3 tablespoons unsalted butter
- 1 cup grits
- 2¼ cups whole milk
- 2 cups water
- Table salt and pepper

Shrimp
- 3 tablespoons unsalted butter
- 1½ pounds extra-large shrimp (21 to 25 per pound), peeled and deveined, shells reserved
- 1 tablespoon tomato paste
- 2¼ cups water
- 3 slices bacon, cut into ½-inch pieces
- 1 garlic clove, minced
- Table salt and pepper
- 2 tablespoons all-purpose flour
- 1 tablespoon lemon juice
- ½ teaspoon Tabasco sauce, plus extra for serving
- 4 scallions, sliced thin

1. For the Grits Melt 1 tablespoon butter in medium saucepan over medium heat. Add grits and cook, stirring often, until fragrant, about 3 minutes. Add milk, water, and ¾ teaspoon salt. Increase heat to medium-high and bring to boil. Reduce heat to low, cover, and simmer, whisking often, until thick and creamy, about 25 minutes. Remove from heat, stir in remaining 2 tablespoons butter, and season with salt and pepper to taste. Cover and keep warm.

2. For the Shrimp Meanwhile, melt 1 tablespoon butter in 12-inch nonstick skillet over medium heat. Add shrimp shells and cook, stirring occasionally, until shells are spotty brown, about 7 minutes. Stir in tomato paste and cook for 30 seconds. Add water and bring to boil. Reduce heat to low, cover, and simmer for 5 minutes.

3. Strain shrimp stock through fine-mesh strainer set over bowl, pressing on solids to extract as much liquid as possible; discard solids. You should have about 1½ cups stock (add more water if necessary to equal 1½ cups). Wipe out skillet with paper towels.

4. Cook bacon in now-empty skillet over medium-low heat until crisp, 7 to 9 minutes. Increase heat to medium-high and stir in shrimp, garlic, ½ teaspoon salt, and ½ teaspoon pepper. Cook until edges of shrimp are just beginning to turn pink, but shrimp are not cooked through, about 2 minutes. Transfer shrimp mixture to bowl.

5. Melt 1 tablespoon butter in now-empty skillet over medium-high heat. Whisk in flour and cook for 1 minute. Slowly whisk in shrimp stock until incorporated. Bring to boil, reduce heat to medium-low, and simmer until thickened slightly, about 5 minutes.

6. Stir in shrimp mixture, cover, and cook until shrimp are cooked through, about 3 minutes. Off heat, stir in lemon juice, Tabasco, and remaining 1 tablespoon butter. Season with salt and pepper to taste. Serve over grits, sprinkled with scallions, and passing extra Tabasco.

> **Shrimp Jumps the Shark**
>
> For decades, the savory Southern dish known as "shrimp and grits" was little known outside a small swath of the southeastern U.S. coast. There, the entrenched combination was an inevitable outcome of abundance—the Carolina shores teemed with shrimp, and grits were plentiful and cheap. Its profile grew through places like Crook's Corner restaurant in Chapel Hill, North Carolina, where Chef Bill Neal's Brunswick stew, hoppin' John, and shrimp and grits preserved the regional dishes of the area.

New Orleans Barbecue Shrimp
SERVES 4

WHY THIS RECIPE WORKS Named for the "barbecue" color rather than the cooking method, this New Orleans skillet shrimp dish relies on a velvety, butter-based sauce to flavor shell-on shrimp. To cook the shrimp perfectly, we seared them to partially cook them and then later returned the shrimp to the finished sauce to gently cook through. By using a roux to thicken the sauce and sautéing the aromatics with tomato paste, we were able to create a silky, flavorful sauce that clung well to the shrimp. We replaced time-consuming seafood stock with bottled clam juice.

Although traditional barbecue shrimp is always made with shell-on shrimp, peeled and deveined shrimp may be used. Light- or medium-bodied beers work best here. Serve with Tabasco sauce and French bread, if desired.

2. Melt 1 tablespoon butter in empty skillet over medium heat. Add flour, tomato paste, rosemary, thyme, oregano, and garlic and cook until fragrant, about 30 seconds. Stir in clam juice, beer, and Worcestershire, scraping up any browned bits, and bring to boil. Return shrimp and any accumulated juices to skillet. Reduce heat to medium-low and simmer, covered, until shrimp are cooked through, about 2 minutes. Off heat, stir in remaining butter until incorporated. Serve.

Pickled Shrimp

SERVES 6 TO 8

WHY THIS RECIPE WORKS This recipe for pickled shrimp is inspired by one given to us by Sheila Williams from Escondido, California. We gently cooked the shrimp in salted water to help season them, taking them off the heat once they turned pink to let them firm up without overcooking. For a flavorful pickling liquid to pour over the shrimp, we quickly dissolved sugar in vinegar in the microwave and then added oil, capers, slices of red onion, lemon wedges, and other seasonings. Placing a small plate over the shrimp fully submerged them in the pickling liquid, ensuring that they soaked up flavor.

The shrimp need to be refrigerated for at least 3 hours before serving.

New Orleans Barbecue Shrimp

- 2 pounds extra-large (21 to 25 per pound) shrimp
- ½ teaspoon table salt
- ½ teaspoon cayenne pepper
- 2 tablespoons vegetable oil
- 6 tablespoons unsalted butter, cut into 6 pieces
- 2 teaspoons all-purpose flour
- 1 teaspoon tomato paste
- 1 teaspoon minced fresh rosemary
- 1 teaspoon minced fresh thyme
- ½ teaspoon dried oregano
- 3 garlic cloves, minced
- ¾ cup bottled clam juice
- ½ cup beer
- 1 tablespoon Worcestershire sauce

1. Pat shrimp dry with paper towels and sprinkle with salt and cayenne. Heat 1 tablespoon oil in large skillet over medium-high heat until just smoking. Cook half of shrimp, without moving, until spotty brown on one side, about 1 minute; transfer to large plate. Repeat with remaining oil and shrimp.

- 2 pounds extra-large shrimp (21 to 25 per pound), peeled and deveined
- 1 teaspoon table salt, plus salt for cooking shrimp
- 8 cups ice
- 1 cup cider vinegar
- ¼ cup sugar
- 2 garlic cloves, smashed and peeled
- 3 bay leaves
- 1 teaspoon allspice berries
- 1 teaspoon coriander seeds
- ½ teaspoon red pepper flakes
- 1 cup extra-virgin olive oil
- ¼ cup capers, minced
- 2 tablespoons Dijon mustard
- 2 tablespoons minced fresh dill
- 1 tablespoon hot sauce
- 1 tablespoon Worcestershire sauce
- 1 cup thinly sliced red onion
- 1 lemon, cut into 6 wedges

FORK-IN-THE-ROAD FAVORITES 197

Pickled Shrimp

1. Combine 4 cups cold water, shrimp, and 2 teaspoons salt in Dutch oven. Set pot over medium-high heat and cook, stirring occasionally, until water registers 170 degrees and shrimp are just beginning to turn pink, 5 to 7 minutes. Remove from heat, cover, and let sit until shrimp are completely pink and firm, 5 to 7 minutes. Stir ice into pot and let shrimp cool completely, about 5 minutes. Drain shrimp in colander. Transfer shrimp to paper towel–lined baking sheet and pat dry.

2. Combine vinegar, sugar, garlic, bay leaves, allspice, coriander seeds, and pepper flakes in large bowl and microwave until hot, about 2 minutes. Stir to dissolve sugar. Let cool completely. Whisk in oil, capers, mustard, dill, hot sauce, Worcestershire, and 1 teaspoon salt until combined.

3. Stir onion, lemon wedges, and shrimp into vinegar mixture until thoroughly combined. Push to submerge shrimp in marinade, then place small plate on top to keep submerged. Cover and refrigerate, stirring occasionally, for at least 3 hours or up to 48 hours. To serve, remove shrimp from marinade using slotted spoon.

Shrimp Po' Boys
SERVES 4

Shrimp Po' Boys

WHY THIS RECIPE WORKS For our version of the New Orleans poor boy sandwich served on pillowy bread slathered with a pungent rémoulade and piled with fried shrimp, we packed flavor into every element. We started by tossing the shrimp in a flour, cornmeal, and Creole seasoning mixture. Next, to ensure that the batter stayed put when fried, we first dipped the shrimp in a paste-like batter of beaten eggs bolstered with a bit of the Creole-seasoned dry mixture, and dredged them again in the flour mixture before letting them rest in the refrigerator. Our superflavorful rémoulade dressing added another jazzed-up layer of flavor.

Use refrigerated prepared horseradish, not the shelf-stable kind, which contains preservatives and additives. Frank's RedHot Original Cayenne Pepper Sauce is best here. Use a Dutch oven that holds 6 quarts or more. Do not refrigerate the breaded shrimp for longer than 30 minutes, or the coating will be too wet. It may seem like you're spreading a lot of rémoulade on the rolls, but it will be absorbed by the other ingredients.

Rémoulade

- 2/3 cup mayonnaise
- 2 tablespoons prepared horseradish
- 1 tablespoon Worcestershire sauce
- 1 tablespoon hot sauce
- 1/4 teaspoon pepper

Shrimp

- 2 cups all-purpose flour
- 1/4 cup cornmeal
- 2 tablespoons Creole seasoning
- 4 large eggs
- 1 pound medium-large shrimp (31 to 40 per pound), peeled, deveined, and tails removed
- 2 quarts peanut or vegetable oil for frying
- 4 (8-inch) sub rolls, toasted
- 2 cups shredded iceberg lettuce
- 2 large tomatoes, cored and sliced thin
- 1 cup dill pickle chips

1. For the Rémoulade Whisk all ingredients together in bowl. Set aside.

2. For the Shrimp Set wire rack in rimmed baking sheet. Whisk flour, cornmeal, and Creole seasoning together in shallow dish. Whisk eggs and 1/2 cup flour mixture together in second shallow dish.

3. Place half of shrimp in flour mixture and toss to thoroughly coat. Shake off excess flour mixture, dip shrimp into egg mixture, then return to flour mixture, pressing gently to adhere. Transfer shrimp to prepared wire rack. Repeat with remaining half of shrimp. Refrigerate shrimp for at least 15 minutes or up to 30 minutes.

4. Line large plate with triple layer of paper towels. Add oil to large Dutch oven until it measures about 1 1/2 inches deep and heat over medium-high heat to 375 degrees. Carefully add half of shrimp to oil. Cook, stirring occasionally, until golden brown, about 4 minutes. Using slotted spoon or spider skimmer, transfer shrimp to prepared plate. Return oil to 375 degrees and repeat with remaining shrimp.

5. Spread rémoulade evenly on both cut sides of each roll. Divide lettuce, tomatoes, pickle chips, and shrimp evenly among rolls. Serve.

The American Table: The Birth of a Sandwich

Nineteen twenty-nine was a bumpy year for New Orleans—and not just because of the famous October stock market crash. Several months earlier, streetcar workers went on strike. They took to the streets on July 1, stomachs growling. Bennie Martin and his brother Clovis, former streetcar workers who'd since opened their Martin Brothers' Coffee Stand and Restaurant, came along to feed the picketers with their "poor boy" sandwiches, distributed free of charge. The sometimes-violent strike lasted in varying degrees for several years, and the sandwiches, originally filled with beef, became a signature New Orleans lunch. Eventually variations on po' boys—shrimp, for one—caught on and spread to other Gulf Coast towns.

South Carolina Shrimp Burgers

SERVES 4

WHY THIS RECIPE WORKS South Carolina is the undisputed home of the shrimp burger. The best ones—like at the Shrimp Shack in Beaufort, South Carolina—are almost pure shrimp, with no bready fillers. To achieve the perfect consistency, we finely chopped a third of our raw, peeled shrimp in a food processor, then coarsely chopped the remaining shrimp. This made the shrimp slightly sticky for easy binding, aided further by some cayenne-seasoned mayo. Chopped scallions gave our burgers extra fresh flavor. Before pan-frying our patties, we dredged them in finely ground panko bread crumbs. We like to serve our shrimp burgers with a smear of homemade tartar sauce.

We prefer untreated shrimp—those without added sodium or preservatives like sodium tripolyphosphate (STPP). Most frozen shrimp have been treated (the ingredient list should tell you). If you're using untreated shrimp, increase the amount of salt to 1/2 teaspoon. If you're purchasing shell-on shrimp, you should buy about 1 1/2 pounds.

South Carolina Shrimp Burgers

Tartar Sauce
- ¾ cup mayonnaise
- 3 tablespoons finely chopped dill pickles plus 1 teaspoon brine
- 1 small shallot, minced
- 1 tablespoon capers, rinsed and chopped fine
- ¼ teaspoon pepper

Burgers
- 1 cup panko bread crumbs
- 1¼ pounds peeled and deveined large shrimp (26 to 30 per pound), tails removed
- 2 tablespoons mayonnaise
- ¼ teaspoon pepper
- ⅛ teaspoon table salt
- ⅛ teaspoon cayenne pepper
- 3 scallions, chopped fine
- 3 tablespoons vegetable oil
- 4 hamburger buns
- 4 leaves Bibb lettuce

1. For the Tartar Sauce Combine all ingredients in bowl and refrigerate until needed.

2. For the Burgers Pulse panko in food processor until finely ground, about 15 pulses; transfer to shallow dish. Place one-third of shrimp (1 cup), mayonnaise, pepper, salt, and cayenne in now-empty processor and pulse until shrimp are finely chopped, about 8 pulses. Add remaining two-thirds of shrimp (2 cups) to shrimp mixture in processor and pulse until coarsely chopped, about 4 pulses, scraping down sides of bowl as needed. Transfer shrimp mixture to bowl and stir in scallions.

3. Divide shrimp mixture into four ¾-inch-thick patties (about ½ cup each). Working with 1 patty at a time, dredge both sides of patties in panko, pressing lightly to adhere, and transfer to plate.

4. Heat oil in 12-inch nonstick skillet over medium heat until shimmering. Place patties in skillet and cook until golden brown on first side, 3 to 5 minutes. Carefully flip and continue to cook until shrimp registers 140 to 145 degrees and second side is golden brown, 3 to 5 minutes longer. Transfer burgers to paper towel–lined plate and let drain, about 30 seconds per side. Place lettuce on bun bottoms, then place burgers on top. Spread tartar sauce on burgers and cover with bun tops. Serve.

A Family Affair
Plenty of restaurants in Beaufort, South Carolina, offer shrimp burgers, but only the Shrimp Shack, an institution since 1978, uses "Captain Bob" Upton's special recipe, which relies on local shrimp—and not much else. Upton, a local fisherman, and his wife, Hilda Upton, opened the Shack in his front yard that year, after a particularly poor fishing season. Daughters Hilda "Sis" Godley and Julie Madlinger run the place now, using local shrimp and Captain Bob's recipe.

The Complete Cook's Country TV Show Cookbook

Hot Buttered Lobster Rolls

SERVES 4

WHY THIS RECIPE WORKS For the perfect hot buttered lobster rolls, we started by simmering the lobsters whole in heavily seasoned water until they were tender but still slightly undercooked. Once we removed the lobster meat and cut it into bite-size pieces, we finished cooking it in a skillet with butter and minced shallot, then spooned the buttered lobster into toasted buns. A sprinkle of chives and a squeeze of lemon brightened up the summery rolls.

For the best results, use live lobsters. If you cannot find live lobsters, eight 4- to 5-ounce frozen lobster tails can be substituted; reduce the cooking time in step 1 to 4 minutes, or cook until the meat registers 135 degrees. If New England–style hot dog buns, also known as "split-top" buns, are unavailable, you can substitute regular hot dog buns or, in a pinch, hamburger buns.

- 3 (1½-pound) live lobsters
- ¼ teaspoon table salt, plus salt for cooking lobsters
- 2 tablespoons unsalted butter, softened, plus 6 tablespoons cut into 6 pieces
- 4 New England–style hot dog buns
- 1 small shallot, minced (optional)
- 2 teaspoons minced fresh chives
- Lemon wedges

1. Bring 6 quarts water to boil in large stockpot over high heat. Add lobsters and 3 tablespoons salt, making sure lobsters are completely submerged. Reduce heat to medium-low, cover, and cook for 10 minutes. Transfer lobsters to rimmed baking sheet and let cool for 10 minutes.

2. Remove lobster meat from claws and tails. Cut meat into rough ¾-inch pieces; set aside. Spread softened butter evenly on outer cut sides of buns. Toast outside of buns in 12-inch skillet over medium heat. Transfer buns to serving platter.

3. Melt remaining 6 tablespoons butter in now-empty skillet over medium-low heat. Stir in shallot, if using; lobster; and salt and cook until lobster is heated through, about 2 minutes.

4. Using slotted spoon, divide lobster mixture among buns. Sprinkle lobster rolls with chives and drizzle with any remaining butter from skillet, if desired. Serve with lemon wedges.

Removing Cooked Lobster Meat

This is wet, messy work: Hold the lobster using clean dish towels to ensure a secure grip and protect yourself from cuts since the shells are sharp. Lobster crackers and forks are nice if you have them, but you can get by with kitchen shears, a chef's knife, and a butter knife for digging out the meat.

CLAWS
1. Twist to remove.
2. Separate claw pieces and knuckles.
3. Crack shells and dig out meat.

BODY
There are tasty morsels within the lobster's body, but they take a bit of work to get to. The small side legs are great for snacking on—some say their fine shreds of meat are the sweetest.

TAIL
1. Twist to separate from body.
2. Pull off small flippers.
3. Use shears to cut through underside of shell, or use your fingers to push meat out through larger (body side) opening.

Hot Buttered Lobster Rolls

Tuna Poke

Salmon Teriyaki Poke

Tuna Poke

SERVES 4

WHY THIS RECIPE WORKS For inspiration, we looked to simple, classic recipes from Hawaii. This tuna poke is a version of ahi shoyu poke—one of Hawaii's most popular recipes—and it rests on a foundation of fresh, dense, clean-tasting yellowfin tuna. We dressed our poke with a simple, savory mix of soy sauce and sesame oil. Sweet onion, scallions, pepper flakes, ginger, and garlic added pungency, spice, and texture. A garnish of furikake (a multitextured Japanese seasoning blend commonly containing dried seaweed, bonito flakes, and sesame seeds) layered on various textures and gave us an all-in-one ingredient for boosting the umami in our tuna poke.

Vidalia, Maui, or Walla Walla sweet onions will all work here. If you can't find sweet onions, you can substitute a yellow onion by soaking the thinly sliced onion in ice water for 20 minutes and then draining and patting it dry. Serve this poke as a snack or an appetizer, or make it a meal by serving it over warm rice.

- 1 pound skinless yellowfin tuna, cut into ¾-inch cubes
- ¼ cup thinly sliced sweet onion (halved and sliced through root end)
- ⅓ cup finely chopped salted dry-roasted macadamia nuts
- 3 scallions, white and green parts separated and sliced thin on bias
- 3 tablespoons soy sauce
- 2 tablespoons vegetable oil
- 2 teaspoons toasted sesame oil
- 2 teaspoons grated fresh ginger
- 1 garlic clove, minced
- ¾ teaspoon red pepper flakes
   Furikake (optional)

Gently combine tuna, onion, macadamia nuts, scallion whites, soy sauce, vegetable oil, sesame oil, ginger, garlic, and pepper flakes in large bowl using rubber spatula. Season with salt to taste. Serve, sprinkled with furikake, if using, and scallion greens. (Poke can be refrigerated for up to 24 hours.)

Salmon Teriyaki Poke

SERVES 4

WHY THIS RECIPE WORKS Poke ("poh-KAY") translates from Hawaiian as "to cut or slice into pieces" and refers to a raw fish salad that's become popular across the rest of the United States. Our recipe was inspired by one in Martha Cheng's *The Poke Cookbook: The Freshest Way to Eat Fish* (2017). The success of this recipe rests on a foundation of fresh, rich, clean-tasting salmon. We dressed the salmon with a savory-sweet teriyaki sauce. Toasted sesame oil added roasty depth, while scallions, diced cucumber, and Fresno chile added pungency, texture, and spice. A final garnish of furikake (a Japanese seasoning blend) boosted the umami.

You can serve this poke as a snack or an appetizer, or you can make it a meal by serving it over warm rice.

- 3 tablespoons soy sauce
- 1 tablespoon mirin
- 2 teaspoons sugar
- 2 teaspoons grated fresh ginger
- 1 garlic clove, minced
- 1 pound skinless farm-raised salmon, cut into ¾-inch cubes
- 1 small avocado, halved, pitted, and cut into ½-inch pieces
- ¼ English cucumber, cut into ½-inch pieces (½ cup)
- 3 scallions, white and green parts separated and sliced thin on bias
- 1 Fresno chile, stemmed, halved, seeded, and sliced thin
- 2 teaspoons toasted sesame oil
- 1 teaspoon kosher salt
  Furikake (optional)

1. Microwave soy sauce, mirin, sugar, ginger, and garlic in bowl until steaming, 30 to 60 seconds. Stir to dissolve sugar. Refrigerate until no longer warm, about 15 minutes.

2. Gently combine salmon, avocado, cucumber, scallion whites, Fresno chile, oil, salt, and soy sauce mixture in large bowl using rubber spatula. Serve, sprinkled with furikake, if using, and scallion greens. (Poke can be refrigerated for up to 24 hours.)

Poke Fish Primer

Freshness is key when serving fish raw. The raw tuna and salmon flesh should appear moist and shiny; feel firm (the flesh should spring right back when pressed); and smell clean, not fishy. Ask your fishmonger to slice tuna steaks to order, ideally those that have little to no connective tissue, which can be too chewy raw. Similarly, ask to have salmon cut to order from a center-cut fillet that has little to none of the thin belly attached, as it can be tough and fatty when eaten raw.

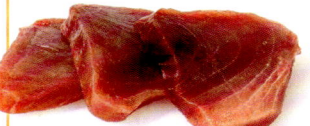

TUNA   SALMON

Guanimes con Bacalao (Cornmeal Dumplings with Salt Cod)

SERVES 4

WHY THIS RECIPE WORKS Guanimes con bacalao, a stew widely eaten in Puerto Rico, combines the brininess of salt cod with the fruitiness of peppers in a lusciously rich sauce. For our version, which was inspired by the one served at Casa Vieja in Ciales, Puerto Rico, we soaked the salt cod in water for 24 hours before boiling it to soften it and remove much of its salinity. We softened onions, garlic, Cubanelle pepper, and ajíes dulces (sweet chiles) in annatto oil before adding the salt cod and finishing with sliced olives and chopped cilantro (traditional recipes call for culantro). Just before serving, we topped our cornmeal dumplings with the boldly flavored stew.

If possible, use pieces of salt cod that vary in thickness. The thicker pieces will remain saltier after soaking and boiling, and the thinner pieces will be less salty. This variety is ideal. If you can find only thinner tail pieces (about ½ inch or less), then soak it for only 18 hours (still changing the water once). The guanimes can be shaped ahead of time, but boil them only just before serving and once the cod mixture is finished cooking. Guanimes are best when eaten

**Guanimes con Bacalao
(Cornmeal Dumplings with Salt Cod)**

Neorm Sach Moan (Cambodian Chicken Salad)

immediately after boiling (their texture will become dense and dry the longer they sit). We strongly recommend weighing the cornmeal here. If you can't find ajíes dulces, you can substitute ½ cup of chopped red bell pepper; the flavor of the dish will be slightly different, though still very good.

Bacalao

- 1 pound salt cod
- ½ cup vegetable oil
- 1½ teaspoons annatto seeds
- 2¼ cups chopped onion
- 1 large Cubanelle pepper (5 ounces), stemmed, seeded, halved crosswise, and cut into thin strips (1 cup)
- 4 ounces ajíes dulces, stemmed, seeded, and chopped (about ½ cup)
- 5 garlic cloves, minced
- ¾ teaspoon table salt
- ½ teaspoon dried oregano
- 2 tablespoons tomato paste
- ⅓ cup coarsely chopped fresh cilantro leaves and stems
- ¼ cup thinly sliced pimento-stuffed Manzanilla olives

Guanimes

- ¾ teaspoon table salt
- 1¼ cups (6¼ ounces) cornmeal

1. For the Bacalao Rinse salt cod of excess surface salt. Place cod in medium bowl and cover with about 2 quarts water. Transfer to refrigerator and let cod soak for 24 hours, changing water halfway through soaking.

2. Heat oil and annatto seeds in small saucepan over low heat, swirling occasionally, until bubbles begin to form around seeds and oil takes on deep orange color, about 5 minutes. Remove from heat and let sit for 10 minutes. Strain oil through fine-mesh stainer into liquid measuring cup and set aside; discard seeds. (Annatto oil can be stored in airtight container for up to 1 week.)

3. Drain cod. Place cod in large saucepan, cover with 2 quarts water, and bring to boil over high heat. Reduce heat to medium and simmer for 10 minutes. Reserve 1 cup cooking water. Drain cod; transfer to bowl; and let sit until cool enough to handle, 5 to 10 minutes. Using your fingers or potato masher, flake or mash cod until finely shredded. (Shredded cod can be refrigerated for up to 2 days.)

4. Heat ¼ cup annatto oil in 12-inch nonstick skillet over medium heat until shimmering. Add onion, Cubanelle, ajíes dulces, garlic, salt, and oregano and cook, stirring occasionally, until vegetables are softened, about 7 minutes.

5. Stir in tomato paste and cook for 1 minute. Stir in cod and reserved cooking water and bring to simmer. Reduce heat to low; cover; and cook, stirring occasionally, until mixture deepens in color and flavors meld, about 15 minutes. Off heat, stir in cilantro and olives. Season with salt to taste and cover to keep warm.

6. For the Guanimes Bring 1½ cups water and salt to boil in medium saucepan over high heat. Once boiling, immediately remove from heat. Using wooden spoon, quickly stir in cornmeal until mixture thickens and no lumps remain. Let mixture cool for 3 to 5 minutes. Divide guanimes mixture into 20 equal portions, about 1 tablespoon each. Roll guanimes between your lightly moistened hands to form smooth balls and transfer to plate. (Shaped guanimes can be refrigerated in zipper-lock bag for up to 24 hours.)

7. Bring 3 quarts water to boil in large saucepan over high heat. (Simultaneously begin reheating bacalao mixture, if necessary.) Drop guanimes into boiling water and cook until beginning to float, about 5 minutes. Using spider skimmer or slotted spoon, transfer 5 guanimes to each of 4 serving bowls. Top with bacalao mixture and drizzle with remaining annatto oil to taste. Serve.

Neorm Sach Moan (Cambodian Chicken Salad)

SERVES 4

WHY THIS RECIPE WORKS For a lively and refreshing herb-packed chicken salad, we turned to a chef who has made it her mission to bring Cambodian food to America. This recipe is adapted from Nite Yun, owner and chef of Nyum Bai in Oakland, California. Her neorm sach moan is a cabbage salad with shreds of chicken and a bold dressing made with rice vinegar and fish sauce. The salad is layered and nuanced with heat from a Thai chile, umami from the fish sauce, and herbal notes from handfuls of fresh mint, cilantro, and Thai basil. After tossing together the dressing, shredded vegetables, and gently poached chicken, all there is to do is put the salad on a platter and enjoy.
You can substitute Italian basil for Thai basil. If you can't find a Persian cucumber, use 1 cup of thinly sliced English cucumber. A mandoline makes quick work of evenly shredding the cabbage and slicing the radishes and cucumber.

- 1 (6- to 8-ounce) boneless, skinless chicken breast, trimmed
- ¼ teaspoon table salt, plus salt for poaching chicken
- 6 tablespoons fish sauce
- ¼ cup sugar
- ¼ cup unseasoned rice vinegar
- 1 Thai chile, minced
- 1 garlic clove, minced
- 4 cups shredded green cabbage
- 2 ounces (2 cups) baby mizuna or baby arugula, chopped coarse
- 1 cup shredded red cabbage
- 1 red bell pepper, stemmed, seeded, and sliced thin
- 1 Persian cucumber, halved crosswise and sliced thin lengthwise
- 4 radishes, trimmed and sliced thin
- ¼ cup chopped fresh cilantro, plus 2 tablespoons leaves
- ¼ cup chopped fresh Thai basil
- ¼ cup chopped fresh mint
- ¼ cup salted dry-roasted peanuts, chopped

1. Combine chicken, 4 cups water, and 2 teaspoons salt in large saucepan. Cook over medium heat until water just begins to simmer, about 10 minutes. Cover pot, reduce heat to low, and simmer gently until chicken registers 160 degrees, 12 to 17 minutes.

2. Transfer chicken to plate or cutting board and let cool for 15 minutes. Shred into thin, bite-size strips.

3. Whisk fish sauce, sugar, vinegar, Thai chile, garlic, and salt together in large bowl until sugar is dissolved. Add green cabbage, mizuna, red cabbage, bell pepper, cucumber, radishes, chopped cilantro, Thai basil, mint, and shredded chicken and toss thoroughly to combine. Top with remaining cilantro leaves and peanuts. Serve.

Bitter Is Better

Mizuna is a Japanese mustard green you can likely find at Asian markets, specialty produce stores, or farmers' markets. It has the pepperiness of arugula and a little bitterness like frisée. It adds a really nice complexity here. But if you can't find it, 2 cups of arugula works well.

Chinese Chicken Salad

SERVES 6

Chinese Chicken Salad

WHY THIS RECIPE WORKS Despite its name, Chinese chicken salad is an American dish, invented in the 1908s by chef Wolfgang Puck for his Chinois on Main restaurant in Los Angeles. From there, it trickled down to family-friendly chains and turned up on mall menus across the country. Although it is a beloved salad, we wanted to give it a fresh makeover. The typical salad-bar pile ons, from chow mein noodles to water chestnuts, got the ax. We started with romaine lettuce, napa cabbage, bell peppers, cilantro, and scallions. To keep the chicken from tasting like an afterthought, we poached chicken breasts in soy sauce, orange juice, rice vinegar, and ginger, setting some aside to whisk with sesame and vegetable oils for a bold dressing. We finished the dish with oranges and roasted peanuts.

You can substitute 1 minced clove of garlic and ¼ teaspoon of cayenne pepper for the chili-garlic sauce.

- 2 oranges
- ¼ cup rice vinegar
- ¼ cup soy sauce
- 3 tablespoons grated fresh ginger
- 3 tablespoons sugar
- 1 tablespoon chili-garlic sauce
- 3 tablespoons vegetable oil
- 2 tablespoons toasted sesame oil
- 4 (6- to 8-ounce) boneless, skinless chicken breasts, trimmed
- 2 romaine lettuce hearts (12 ounces), sliced thin
- ½ small head napa cabbage, cored and sliced thin (6 cups)
- 2 red bell peppers, stemmed, seeded, and cut into 2-inch-long matchsticks
- 1 cup fresh cilantro leaves
- 1 cup salted, dry-roasted peanuts, chopped
- 6 scallions, sliced thin

1. Cut thin slice from top and bottom of each orange, exposing fruit. Slice off rind and pith, cutting from top to bottom. Working over bowl, cut orange segments from thin membrane and transfer segments to second bowl; set aside. Squeeze juice from membrane into first bowl (juice should measure ¼ cup).

2. Combine orange juice, vinegar, soy sauce, ginger, sugar, and chili-garlic sauce in bowl. Transfer ½ cup of orange juice mixture to 12-inch skillet. Slowly whisk vegetable oil and sesame oil into remaining orange juice mixture to make vinaigrette; set aside.

3. Bring orange juice mixture in skillet to boil. Add chicken, reduce heat to medium-low, cover, and simmer until meat registers 160 degrees, 10 to 15 minutes, flipping halfway through cooking. Transfer chicken to plate and let rest for 5 to 10 minutes.

4. Meanwhile, boil pan juices until reduced to ¼ cup, 1 to 3 minutes, and set aside. Using 2 forks, shred chicken into bite-size pieces. Off heat, add chicken, any accumulated juices, and 2 tablespoons vinaigrette to skillet. Toss to coat and let sit for 10 minutes.

5. Toss lettuce, cabbage, bell peppers, cilantro, peanuts, and scallions with remaining vinaigrette in large bowl. Transfer to serving platter and top with chicken and oranges. Serve.

Chicken Chow Mein

SERVES 4

Chicken Chow Mein

WHY THIS RECIPE WORKS Like many dishes you'll find in America's Chinese restaurants, chow mein has deep roots in China, where chao mian ("fried noodles") has been around for centuries. To help the chicken in this takeout standard retain moisture, we soaked sliced chicken in water and baking soda followed by a quick soak in Shaoxing wine and cornstarch. For the chow mein's sauce, oyster sauce added meaty notes, and more rice wine added sweet brightness. To avoid a gloppy sauce, we used just a bit of cornstarch as thickener then added plenty of bean sprouts for fresh crunch.

Purchase thin, round fresh Chinese egg noodles, not flat and/or dried noodles, or substitute 6 ounces of dried chow mein, ramen, or wheat vermicelli.

- 1 (9-ounce) package fresh Chinese noodles
- 1 tablespoon toasted sesame oil
- 1 teaspoon baking soda
- 2 (6-ounce) boneless, skinless chicken breasts, trimmed and cut crosswise into ¼-inch-thick slices
- 3 tablespoons Shaoxing wine or dry sherry
- 1 tablespoon cornstarch
- ½ cup chicken broth
- 3 tablespoons soy sauce
- 3 tablespoons oyster sauce
- ¼ teaspoon white pepper
- 2 tablespoons vegetable oil
- 6 ounces shiitake mushrooms, stemmed and sliced thin
- 1 carrot, peeled and cut into 2-inch matchsticks
- 2 celery ribs, cut on bias into ¼-inch-thick slices
- 4 scallions, white and green parts separated and sliced thin
- 3 garlic cloves, minced
- 1 tablespoon grated fresh ginger
- 4 ounces (2 cups) mung bean sprouts

1. Bring 4 quarts water to boil in large pot. Add noodles to boiling water and cook until tender, 2 to 4 minutes. Drain noodles, rinse thoroughly with cold water, then drain again. Toss noodles with sesame oil in bowl; set aside.

2. Meanwhile, dissolve baking soda in ½ cup cold water in bowl. Add chicken and let sit at room temperature for 15 minutes. Drain chicken, rinse under cold water, then drain again. Pat chicken dry with paper towels. Combine 1 tablespoon rice wine, 2 teaspoons cornstarch, and chicken in bowl; set aside.

3. Whisk broth, soy sauce, oyster sauce, pepper, remaining 2 tablespoons rice wine, and remaining 1 teaspoon cornstarch together in bowl; set aside.

4. Heat oil in 12-inch nonstick skillet over high heat until just smoking. Add chicken and cook, stirring frequently, until opaque, about 2 minutes. Add mushrooms and carrot and cook, stirring frequently, until tender, about 2 minutes. Add celery and cook until crisp-tender, about 1 minute. Add scallion whites, garlic, and ginger and cook until fragrant, about 30 seconds.

5. Whisk broth mixture to recombine, then add to skillet and cook until thickened and chicken is cooked through, about 2 minutes. Add bean sprouts and noodles and toss until sauce evenly coats noodles, about 1 minute. Transfer to platter and sprinkle with scallion greens. Serve.

Bourbon Chicken

SERVES 4

Bourbon Chicken

WHY THIS RECIPE WORKS Our recipe for Bourbon Chicken—dark meat chicken pieces in a sticky, sweet-savory sauce—was inspired by the one we sampled at Today's Cajun Seafood in New Orleans. Brown sugar added complex sweetness to our sauce and balanced the soy sauce's umami. Toasted sesame oil added roasty depth, while minced garlic and grated ginger provided pungent bite. A shot of bourbon imparted aromatic notes of vanilla and caramel. We employed a velveting technique (tossing the bite-size chicken thigh pieces in a combination of cornstarch and some of the sauce mixture) to ensure tender and juicy chicken and a thick-yet-glossy sauce. Cider vinegar stirred in at the end added brightness.

Use a good-quality soy sauce—such as Kikkoman Soy Sauce—for this recipe. Serve with rice.

- ½ cup soy sauce
- ½ cup packed brown sugar
- ¼ cup water
- 2 tablespoons bourbon
- 1 teaspoon toasted sesame oil
- ½ teaspoon pepper
- 2 pounds boneless, skinless chicken thighs, trimmed and cut into 1-inch pieces
- 2 tablespoons cornstarch
- 2 tablespoons vegetable oil
- 2 garlic cloves, minced
- 1 teaspoon grated fresh ginger
- 2 teaspoons cider vinegar

1. Combine soy sauce, sugar, water, bourbon, sesame oil, and pepper in 2-cup liquid measuring cup. Microwave until hot, about 2 minutes. Whisk to dissolve sugar. Toss chicken, cornstarch, and 2 tablespoons soy sauce mixture in bowl until thoroughly combined.

2. Heat vegetable oil in 12-inch nonstick skillet over medium-high heat until shimmering. Add chicken (skillet will be full) and cook, stirring occasionally, until browned and cooked through, about 10 minutes.

3. Stir in garlic, ginger, and remaining soy sauce mixture. Bring to boil and cook until sauce is syrupy and rubber spatula dragged through it leaves wide trail before filling back in, 6 to 8 minutes. Off heat, stir in vinegar. Serve.

On the Road: A Crescent City Gem

The menu at Today's Cajun Seafood reads like a beautiful mash-up of cultures: shrimp and sausage gumbo, smothered pork chops, boiled crawfish, General Tso's chicken, baked spaghetti, bourbon chicken. New Orleans is known for its modernized takes on blended cuisines—its culinary influences range from the home cooking of the descendants of French settlers in rural Louisiana to the foods of enslaved West Africans, Spanish and Chinese immigrants, Native Americans, and Vietnamese refugees—the latter of which includes the owners of Today's Cajun Seafood, Huong Vu Nguyen (Rose) and her husband Hao (Howie).

They opened the restaurant in the years following Hurricane Katrina and, by welcoming every guest as if into their own home and overfilling plates with every kind of comfort food, strived to make life a little easier for their community. When asked why his restaurant sells bourbon chicken, Howie answered pragmatically, "It's Bourbon Street. People like it."

Almond Boneless Chicken

SERVES 4 TO 6

Almond Boneless Chicken

WHY THIS RECIPE WORKS Also known as ABC, this Chinese American staple is on menus in the Detroit region. When we were testing batter recipes, one puffed up like a doughnut, while a thinner batter produced a coating that wasn't crisp enough. So we turned to an ingredient often used in coatings: beer. It added a welcome flavor, and its carbonation lightened the batter. Almond boneless chicken is traditionally sprinkled with chopped almonds, but we wanted to include the nuts more deeply. Adding toasted almonds to the batter made the almond flavor much more pronounced and our tasters, even the Michigan purists, called it an improvement.

Use a Dutch oven that holds 6 quarts or more. Choose a mild lager or pilsner for this recipe. In addition to iceberg lettuce, this dish is usually served with rice.

Sauce
- 1 tablespoon cornstarch
- 1 tablespoon cold water
- 1 cup chicken broth
- 2 teaspoons dry sherry
- 2 teaspoons hoisin sauce
- 2 teaspoons soy sauce
- ⅛ teaspoon table salt

Chicken
- 4 (6- to 8-ounce) boneless, skinless chicken breasts, trimmed
- Table salt and pepper
- ½ cup sliced almonds, toasted, divided
- 2 cups all-purpose flour
- 1 cup cornstarch
- 1 teaspoon garlic powder
- 1 teaspoon baking powder
- ½ teaspoon baking soda
- 1¼ cups lager or pilsner beer
- 1 large egg, lightly beaten
- 2 quarts peanut or vegetable oil for frying
- ½ head iceberg lettuce (4½ ounces), cored and sliced thin crosswise
- 3 scallions, sliced thin on bias

1. For the Sauce Dissolve cornstarch in water in small bowl and set aside. Combine broth, sherry, hoisin, soy sauce, and salt in small saucepan and bring to boil over medium-high heat. Whisk in reserved cornstarch mixture, return to boil, and cook until thickened, about 30 seconds. Remove from heat, cover, and keep warm, stirring occasionally.

2. For the Chicken Line rimmed baking sheet with parchment paper. Set wire rack in second rimmed baking sheet and line rack with triple layer of paper towels. Halve chicken breasts horizontally to form 8 cutlets. Pat cutlets dry with paper towels and season with salt and pepper.

3. Finely chop ¼ cup almonds. Whisk chopped almonds, 1 cup flour, cornstarch, garlic powder, baking powder, baking soda, 1 teaspoon salt, and ¾ teaspoon pepper together in large bowl. Whisk in beer and egg. Combine remaining 1 cup flour and 1 teaspoon salt in shallow dish.

4. Working with 1 at a time, dip cutlets into batter to thoroughly coat, letting excess drip back into bowl. Dredge battered cutlets in flour to coat, shaking off excess, and place on parchment-lined sheet. Let cutlets sit while oil heats.

5. Add oil to large Dutch oven until it measures about 1½ inches deep and heat over medium-high heat to 350 degrees. Working in batches, add half of cutlets to hot oil. Adjust burner as necessary to maintain oil temperature between 325 and 350 degrees. Fry, stirring gently to prevent pieces from sticking together, until cutlets are golden and register 160 degrees, about 4 minutes, flipping halfway through frying. Transfer to prepared wire rack to cool while frying remaining cutlets.

6. Place lettuce on platter. Cut each cutlet crosswise into ½-inch-thick slices. Arrange slices over lettuce and drizzle with sauce. Sprinkle with scallions and remaining ¼ cup almonds. Serve.

Soy Sauce Chicken Wings

SERVES 4 TO 6

WHY THIS RECIPE WORKS We found that whole wings were cumbersome to eat and stayed a bit flabby at the joint. Splitting the wings into flats and drumettes allowed more fat to render and made the pieces easier to handle. To give our split wings savory flavor with a touch of sweetness and heat, we marinated them in a combination of soy sauce, vegetable oil, brown sugar, garlic, and cayenne pepper. We opted for fresh garlic rather than garlic powder in the marinade, as the powder burned in the oven and turned bitter. We arranged the wings on a baking sheet before baking them for about an hour in a moderate 350 degree oven; this gave us meltingly tender meat; any less time and the fat didn't fully render, leaving the skin unpleasantly chewy.

We prefer to buy whole chicken wings and butcher them ourselves because they tend to be larger than wings that come presplit. If you can find only presplit wings, opt for larger ones, if possible. Three pounds of chicken wings is about 12 whole chicken wings, which will yield about 24 pieces of chicken (12 drumettes and 12 flats) once broken down.

- ¾ cup soy sauce
- ¼ cup vegetable oil
- ¼ cup packed brown sugar
- 12 garlic cloves, smashed and peeled
- ½ teaspoon cayenne pepper
- 3 pounds chicken wings, cut at joints, wingtips discarded
- 2 scallions, sliced thin on bias

1. Combine soy sauce, oil, sugar, garlic, and cayenne in 1-gallon zipper-lock bag. Add wings to marinade, press out air, seal bag, and turn to distribute marinade. Refrigerate for at least 2 hours or up to 6 hours.

2. Adjust oven rack to middle position and heat oven to 350 degrees. Line rimmed baking sheet with aluminum foil and spray with vegetable oil spray. Remove wings from marinade and arrange in single layer, fatty side up, on prepared sheet; discard marinade. Bake until evenly well browned, about 1 hour 5 minutes. Transfer wings to platter, sprinkle with scallions, and serve.

Soy Sauce, Savannah-Style

During the 17th and 18th centuries, when Asian ingredients were first being imported to Europe and North America on a big scale, the terms "soy sauce" and "catchup" were often used to refer to the same (or variations on the same) product: a fermented cooking sauce used to add savory depth. By 1766, Samuel Bowen was producing a product, Bowen's Patent Soy, near Savannah, Georgia, to sell in American ports and in England. It wasn't until later that "ketchup" was used to refer to a tomato-based product.

Khao Man Gai (Thai-Style Chicken and Rice)

SERVES 4 TO 6

WHY THIS RECIPE WORKS After feasting on the famous chicken and rice at Nong's Khao Man Gai in Portland, Oregon, we came back to the test kitchen excited to create a recipe for home cooks. Following the lead of the cooks at Nong's, we began by poaching the chicken whole with garlic and ginger, resulting in perfectly juicy meat and flavorful chicken broth. The jasmine rice cooked in the poaching liquid while the bird rested, resulting in a rich, poultry-infused rice. To re-create Nong's sauce, we whisked together white vinegar, soy sauce, Thai soybean paste, garlic, ginger, and Thai chiles into a bright, savory, spicy sauce.

You can substitute 1 tablespoon of chili-garlic sauce for the Thai chiles, if desired. Use a Dutch oven with at least a 7-quart capacity to comfortably fit the chicken. Thai soybean paste is sometimes labeled as yellow bean sauce or soybean sauce; you can substitute Japanese red miso in a pinch.

Chicken and Broth
- 12 cups water
- 1 (2-inch) piece ginger, peeled and sliced into ¼-inch-thick rounds
- 2 tablespoons table salt
- 6 garlic cloves, smashed and peeled
- 1 (3½- to 4-pound) whole chicken, giblets discarded

Rice
- 1 tablespoon vegetable oil
- 1 shallot, chopped fine
- 1 (2-inch) piece ginger, peeled and cut in half lengthwise
- 2 garlic cloves, minced
- ¼ teaspoon table salt
- 2 cups jasmine rice, rinsed
- 1 cup fresh cilantro leaves and stems
- ½ English cucumber, sliced into thin rounds

Sauce
- ¼ cup Thai soybean paste
- ¼ cup soy sauce
- ¼ cup distilled white vinegar
- 2 tablespoons sugar
- 3 garlic cloves, minced
- 2 Thai chiles, stemmed and minced
- 1 teaspoon grated fresh ginger
- 2 scallions, sliced thin

1. For the Chicken and Broth Combine water, ginger, salt, and garlic in large Dutch oven. Add chicken to pot, breast side up, and bring to simmer over high heat. Place large sheet of foil over pot, then cover with lid. Reduce heat to low and simmer until breast registers 160 degrees and thighs register at least 175 degrees, 25 to 35 minutes.

2. Transfer chicken to bowl, tent with foil, and let rest while making rice. Using slotted spoon, skim foamy residue from surface of chicken broth. Set aside 3 cups broth for cooking rice. Cover remaining broth.

3. For the Rice Heat oil in large saucepan over medium heat until shimmering. Add shallot, ginger, garlic, and salt and cook until shallot is softened, about 2 minutes. Add rice and cook, stirring frequently, until edges begin to turn translucent, about 2 minutes.

4. Stir in reserved 3 cups broth and bring to boil over medium-high heat. Stir once more, then cover and reduce heat to low. Cook for 20 minutes. Without removing lid, remove saucepan from heat and let sit, covered, for 10 minutes.

Soy Sauce Chicken Wings

Khao Man Gai (Thai-Style Chicken and Rice)

5. For the Sauce Whisk all ingredients in bowl until sugar is dissolved, about 1 minute. (Sauce can be refrigerated for up to 2 days.)

6. Rewarm remaining broth over medium heat. Using boning knife, remove breast meat from chicken carcass; discard skin. Remove chicken leg quarters by dislocating thigh joint from carcass. Using 2 forks, shred leg quarter meat into bite-size pieces; discard skin and bones. Slice breasts crosswise ½ inch thick.

7. Transfer rice to large serving platter. Arrange shredded chicken on top of rice. Arrange sliced breast meat on top of shredded chicken. Place cilantro in pile in 1 corner of platter and shingle cucumber along side of platter.

8. Portion four to six 1-cup servings of remaining hot broth into individual soup bowls and sprinkle with scallions (you will have more than 6 cups broth; reserve extra broth for another use). Serve chicken and rice with sauce and portions of broth.

Kombdi, Jira Ghalun (Cumin-Scented Chicken)

SERVES 4 TO 6

WHY THIS RECIPE WORKS This simple, aromatic recipe was adapted by us from Kaumudi Marathé's *The Essential Marathi Cookbook* (2009) and shared with Kaumudi by her friend Anuradha Samant. This dish proves the rule that braising meats produces deeply nuanced flavors. We first marinated the chicken in yogurt, garlic, and ginger and then braised it in a tomato-onion sauce until it was tender and cooked through. Unlike north Indian recipes, which often rely on warm spices such as cinnamon, cardamom, and cloves to add aromatic flavor, this dish calls only for freshly ground cumin, which we stirred in just before serving so that it added smoky top notes to both the chicken and the sauce. It all came together into a quick, fragrant, oh-so-satisfying dinner, served with rice or naan and extra yogurt or Onion Raita (recipe follows).

You can substitute 2 tablespoons of Indian red chile powder for the paprika and cayenne, if desired. We strongly recommend toasting and grinding your own whole cumin seeds for this recipe, but you can substitute 7 teaspoons ground cumin, if desired. If using ground cumin, toast it in an 8-inch skillet over medium heat until fragrant, about 1½ minutes. This recipe can also be made with 2¾ pounds of boneless, skinless chicken breasts instead of the drumsticks. If using breasts, cook until the meat registers 160 degrees in step 6, 18 to 25 minutes. For a milder version of this dish, reduce the amount of cayenne to ½ teaspoon.

3⅓	cups water, divided
¼	cup plain whole-milk yogurt, plus extra for serving
8	garlic cloves, smashed and peeled
1	(2-inch) piece ginger, peeled and chopped coarse
1½	tablespoons paprika
1	tablespoon table salt, divided
1½	teaspoons cayenne pepper
2	tomatoes, cored and chopped coarse
2¾	pounds chicken drumsticks (about 8 large drumsticks)
3	tablespoons cumin seeds
¼	cup vegetable oil
1	large onion, chopped fine
½	cup fresh cilantro leaves

1. Process ⅓ cup water, yogurt, garlic, ginger, paprika, 2 teaspoons salt, and cayenne in blender until smooth, about 2 minutes, scraping down sides of blender jar as needed. Transfer yogurt marinade to bowl.

2. Process tomatoes in now-empty blender until coarsely pureed, about 5 seconds. Transfer to second bowl.

3. Add chicken to bowl with yogurt marinade and toss to coat, rubbing marinade into chicken. Cover and refrigerate for at least 1 hour or up to 24 hours (if marinating longer than 1 hour, cover and refrigerate tomatoes as well).

4. Heat cumin seeds in 8-inch skillet over medium heat, stirring frequently, until fragrant, about 3 minutes. Transfer to spice grinder or mortar and pestle and grind to powder; set aside.

5. Heat oil in large Dutch oven over medium-high heat until just smoking. Add onion and remaining 1 teaspoon salt and cook until onion is softened, 5 to 7 minutes. Add tomatoes; increase heat to high; and cook until mixture darkens slightly and begins to stick to bottom of pot, 5 to 7 minutes.

6. Add chicken, along with any marinade left in bowl, and remaining 3 cups water and bring to boil. Cover; reduce heat to medium-low; and simmer, stirring occasionally, until chicken registers at least 175 degrees, 25 to 30 minutes.

7. Using tongs, transfer chicken to large plate. Increase heat to high and cook, uncovered and stirring occasionally, until sauce is thickened and reduced to about 2¾ cups, 12 to 15 minutes. Stir cumin into sauce. Add chicken back to pot and stir to coat with sauce. Serve, sprinkled with cilantro and passing extra yogurt separately.

Onion Raita

SERVES 4 TO 6 (MAKES ABOUT 1¼ CUPS)

This recipe is best with plain whole-milk yogurt. Do not use low-fat, nonfat, or Greek yogurt in this raita.

- 1 cup plain whole-milk yogurt
- ¾ teaspoon ground cumin
- ½ teaspoon sugar
- ½ teaspoon table salt
- ⅓ cup finely chopped onion
- 1 tablespoon chopped fresh cilantro

Whisk yogurt, cumin, sugar, and salt in bowl until thoroughly combined. Stir in onion and cilantro. Season with salt to taste. Serve.

Pad Gra Prow (Holy Basil Stir-Fry)

SERVES 4

WHY THIS RECIPE WORKS A spicy stir-fry featuring vibrant holy basil, pad gra pow is a popular street food in Thailand. We made sure to use plenty of holy basil here; its peppery flavor and notes of clove set it apart from other basil varieties. We started by browning a paste of garlic, shallots, and Thai chiles in a wok. Ground pork came next, followed by a savory-sweet mixture of Thai fish sauce, thin soy sauce, sweet soy sauce, and oyster sauce and handfuls of holy basil. A crispy Thai-style fried egg on top brought richness, and a chile sauce awakened all the flavors.

If you can't find holy basil (also called tulsi or gra prow), you can substitute Italian or Thai basil. Look for lean ground pork (85 percent or leaner). Ground chicken, lean ground beef, or crumbled extra firm-tofu can be substituted for the pork. It's typical for recipes to call for more than eight chilies for this amount of meat; start with two chiles for an extra-mild version of this dish; four chiles for medium-mild, etc. If you can't find Thai chiles, one serrano chile can be substituted for every two Thai chiles. We recommend turning on your hood vent while stir-frying to help reduce the risk of breathing in aerosolized chiles. Serve with Kai Dao (Thai-Style Fried Eggs [recipe follows]), nam prik nam pla (chile fish sauce), and jasmine rice.

Kombdi, Jira Ghalun (Cumin-Scented Chicken)

Pad Gra Prow (Holy Basil Stir-Fry)

2	shallots, chopped coarse
8	garlic cloves, smashed and peeled
2–8	Thai chiles, stemmed
2	tablespoons Thai fish sauce
2	tablespoons Thai thin soy sauce
2	tablespoons Thai sweet soy sauce
2	tablespoons Thai oyster sauce
¾	teaspoon ground white pepper
2	tablespoons vegetable oil
1½	pounds 85 percent lean ground pork
3	cups fresh holy basil leaves

1. Add shallots, garlic, and chiles to food processor and pulse until finely chopped, 10 to 12 pulses, scraping down sides of bowl as needed. Transfer shallot mixture to bowl. Combine fish sauce, thin soy sauce, sweet soy sauce, oyster sauce, and white pepper in second bowl.

2a. For a Wok Heat oil in 14-inch wok over medium-high heat until just smoking. Add shallot mixture and cook, stirring frequently, until just beginning to brown, about 2 minutes. Increase heat to high. Add pork and cook, stirring frequently and breaking up meat with wooden spoon, until pork is nearly cooked through, 3 to 5 minutes.

2b. For a Nonstick Skillet Heat oil in 12-inch nonstick skillet over medium-high heat until just smoking. Add shallot mixture and cook, stirring frequently, until just beginning to brown, about 3 minutes. Add pork and cook, breaking up meat with wooden spoon, until pork is nearly cooked through, 3 to 5 minutes.

3. Stir in fish sauce mixture and cook, stirring frequently, until liquid is nearly entirely evaporated and pork is darkened and sizzling, 3 to 5 minutes for wok, 5 to 7 minutes for skillet. Stir in basil, one handful at a time, allowing each handful to wilt slightly before adding next. Cook until basil is just wilted, about 1 minute. Serve.

Kai Dao (Thai-Style Fried Eggs)
SERVES 4 (MAKES 4 FRIED EGGS)

To take the temperature of the oil, we suggest tilting the wok or skillet slightly so the oil pools on 1 side.

½	cup vegetable oil for frying
4	large eggs

1. Line large plate with paper towels. Crack 1 egg into small bowl.

2a. For a Wok Add oil to 14-inch wok and heat over medium-high heat to 350 degrees. Add egg to oil and cook, gently swirling oil in wok and spooning some oil over egg white to cook it through, until egg is browned around edges and egg white is opaque, 30 to 60 seconds.

2b. For a Nonstick Skillet Add oil to 8-inch nonstick skillet and heat over medium-high heat to 350 degrees. Add egg to oil, cover, and cook until egg is browned around edges and egg white is opaque, 30 to 60 seconds.

3. Using thin spatula, transfer egg to prepared plate (tilting egg to drain off excess grease). Repeat with remaining eggs, adjusting burner, if necessary, to maintain oil temperature between 325 and 350 degrees. Serve.

Slow-Cooker Chinese Barbecued Pork

SERVES 8

WHY THIS RECIPE WORKS Unlike what we typically think of as barbecue, Chinese barbecued pork is made neither on a grill nor in a smoker: It's usually cooked (and then glazed) in an oven. We made this dish even more convenient by adapting it to the slow cooker. Boneless pork butt renders lots of flavorful fat and pork juices as it cooks. This fat diluted any sauce we tried, so we instead used a dry rub and then cooked the pork with a glazy sauce under the broiler. The finished pork was tender with a shiny, slightly charred exterior that tasted even better than it looked.

Pork butt roast is often labeled Boston butt in the supermarket. Look for five-spice powder and hoisin sauce near the Asian ingredients at your supermarket.

1½	teaspoons table salt
1½	teaspoons five-spice powder, divided
½	teaspoon pepper
1	(5- to 6-pound) boneless pork butt roast, trimmed and sliced crosswise into 1-inch-thick steaks
⅓	cup hoisin sauce
⅓	cup honey
¼	cup sugar
¼	cup soy sauce
¼	cup ketchup
2	tablespoons dry sherry
1	tablespoon toasted sesame oil
1	tablespoon grated fresh ginger
2	garlic cloves, minced

Slow-Cooker Chinese Barbecued Pork

St. Paul Sandwich

SERVES 4

WHY THIS RECIPE WORKS The traditional version of this regionally famous sandwich is made by deep-frying a large omelet filled with bean sprouts, onions, and meat; to make handling and cleanup easier, we chose to shallow-fry smaller patties in a skillet. Transferring the egg foo yong patties to a paper towel–lined plate after frying kept them from being greasy. We arranged the patties on white bread with mayonnaise, shredded iceberg lettuce, tomato slices, and dill pickle chips. The final sandwich features salty and tangy flavors with soft yet crispy textures in every bite.

Be sure to pat the ham steak dry with paper towels before adding it to the skillet in step 1; this will keep it from splattering as it cooks.

- 4 large eggs
- ½ teaspoon table salt
- ½ teaspoon white pepper
- ½ teaspoon granulated garlic
- 2 ounces (1 cup) mung bean sprouts, coarsely chopped
- 1 cup chopped onion
- 5 ounces ham steak, patted dry and cut into ½-inch pieces
- ½ cup vegetable oil for frying
- 4 tablespoons mayonnaise
- 8 slices hearty white sandwich bread
- 2 cups shredded iceberg lettuce
- 8 thin tomato slices
- 16 dill pickle chips

1. Combine salt, ¾ teaspoon five-spice powder, and pepper in bowl. Rub spice mixture all over pork and transfer to slow cooker. Cover and cook on low until pork is just tender, 5 to 6 hours.

2. When pork is nearly done, combine hoisin, honey, sugar, soy sauce, ketchup, sherry, oil, ginger, garlic, and remaining ¾ teaspoon five-spice powder in bowl. Set wire rack inside aluminum foil–lined rimmed baking sheet. Pour 1 cup water into sheet. Adjust oven rack 4 inches from broiler element and heat broiler.

3. Using tongs, transfer pork from slow cooker to prepared wire rack in single layer. Brush pork with one-third of hoisin mixture and broil until lightly caramelized, 5 to 7 minutes. Flip pork, brush with half of remaining hoisin mixture, and broil until lightly caramelized on second side, 5 to 7 minutes. Brush pork with remaining hoisin mixture and broil until deep mahogany and crispy around edges, about 3 minutes. Transfer to carving board and let rest for 10 minutes. Slice crosswise into thin strips. Serve.

1. Beat eggs, salt, white pepper, and granulated garlic together in medium bowl. Stir in bean sprouts, onion, and ham until thoroughly combined.

2. Heat oil in 12-inch nonstick skillet over medium heat until just smoking. Using ½-cup dry measuring cup, portion 4 evenly spaced scoops of egg mixture in skillet. (Eggs may run together; this is OK.) Cover and cook, without stirring, until bottoms of egg foo yong patties are browned and tops are set, about 5 minutes.

3. Using spatula, cut and separate egg foo yong patties in skillet. Flip each patty and continue to cook, covered, until browned on second side, about 3 minutes longer. Transfer egg foo yong patties to paper towel–lined plate and let drain for 1 minute.

FORK-IN-THE-ROAD FAVORITES

4. Spread mayonnaise on 1 side of each piece of bread. Top each of 4 slices of bread with ½ cup lettuce, 1 egg foo yong patty, 2 tomato slices, 4 pickles, and 1 slice of bread. Serve.

> ### On the Road: A Misleading Name
> Rudy Lieu first ate egg foo yong (a deep-fried omelet filled with bean sprouts, onions, and meat smothered in a savory brown gravy) at the age of 15 on a visit to his uncle's Chinese restaurant in St. Louis. On the same trip, Rudy tried St. Louis's famous St. Paul sandwich: an egg foo yong patty nestled between two slices of white bread with iceberg lettuce, tomatoes, pickles, and mayonnaise. "When you have it for the first time, it's like, Whoa! This is interesting." In the early 1980s, Rudy's uncle, Anthony Lieu, worked for a man named Stephen Yuen at his restaurant Park Chop Suey. Rudy refers to Yuen as a "pioneer" of the Chinese restaurant scene at that time. Yuen had moved to St. Louis from St. Paul, Minnesota, a city he loved, so he invented the St. Paul sandwich as an homage. "It started selling like hotcakes," says Rudy. He smiles and says, "In St. Louis, nobody doesn't know what a St. Paul sandwich is." Luckily for us, this crispy egg foo yong sandwich tastes great in any city.

St. Paul Sandwich

New Orleans Muffulettas

New Orleans Muffulettas
SERVES 8

WHY THIS RECIPE WORKS This Italian sandwich is a New Orleans classic, and we wanted to do it justice. We started by emulating Central Grocery's famous olive salad. Combining olives, capers, giardiniera, garlic, herbs, and spices gave us the salty, tangy mixture we wanted. We baked store-bought pizza dough into perfect puffy rounds, which we sprinkled with sesame seeds. Alternating layers of meats and cheese gave our sandwich stability, making it easier to eat. Lastly, we pressed the assembled sandwiches for an hour to allow the olive salad to properly soak into the bread.

You will need one 16-ounce jar of giardiniera to yield 2 cups drained; our favorite brand is Pastene. If you like a spicier sandwich, increase the amount of pepper flakes to ½ teaspoon.

2	(1-pound) balls pizza dough
2	cups drained jarred giardiniera
1	cup pimento-stuffed green olives
½	cup pitted kalamata olives
2	tablespoons capers, rinsed
1	tablespoon red wine vinegar
1	garlic clove, minced
½	teaspoon dried oregano
¼	teaspoon red pepper flakes
¼	teaspoon dried thyme
½	cup extra-virgin olive oil
¼	cup chopped fresh parsley
1	large egg, lightly beaten
5	teaspoons sesame seeds
4	ounces thinly sliced Genoa salami
6	ounces thinly sliced aged provolone cheese
6	ounces thinly sliced mortadella
4	ounces thinly sliced hot capicola

1. Form dough balls into 2 tight round balls on oiled baking sheet, cover loosely with greased plastic wrap, and let sit at room temperature for 1 hour.

2. Meanwhile, pulse giardiniera, green olives, kalamata olives, capers, vinegar, garlic, oregano, pepper flakes, and thyme in food processor until coarsely chopped, about 6 pulses, scraping down sides of bowl as needed. Transfer to bowl and stir in oil and parsley. Let sit at room temperature for 30 minutes. (Olive salad can be refrigerated for up to 1 week.)

3. Adjust oven rack to middle position and heat oven to 425 degrees. Keeping dough balls on sheet, flatten each into 7-inch disk. Brush tops of disks with egg and sprinkle with sesame seeds. Bake until golden brown and loaves sound hollow when tapped, 18 to 20 minutes, rotating sheet halfway through baking. Transfer loaves to wire rack and let cool completely, about 1 hour. (Loaves can be wrapped in plastic and stored at room temperature for up to 24 hours.)

4. Slice loaves in half horizontally. Spread one-fourth of olive salad on cut side of each loaf top and bottom, pressing firmly with rubber spatula to compact. Layer 2 ounces salami, 1½ ounces provolone, 3 ounces mortadella, 1½ ounces provolone, and 2 ounces capicola in order on each loaf bottom. Cap with loaf tops and individually wrap sandwiches tightly in plastic.

5. Place baking sheet on top of sandwiches and weigh down with heavy Dutch oven or two 5-pound bags of flour or sugar for 1 hour, flipping sandwiches halfway through pressing. Unwrap and slice each sandwich into quarters and serve. (Pressed, wrapped sandwiches can be refrigerated for up to 24 hours. Bring to room temperature before serving.)

A Weighty Solution

If you don't have a heavy Dutch oven, use two 5-pound bags of flour or sugar to weigh down the wrapped muffulettas.

Pressing the assembled sandwiches for an hour helps the olive salad properly soak into the bread.

Croque Monsieur
SERVES 4

WHY THIS RECIPE WORKS Croque monsieurs are the perfect mix of crisp, buttery toast; salty-sweet ham; a creamy white sauce; and plenty of nutty Gruyère cheese. For a truly impressive version of this French bistro favorite we chose to amp up the béchamel sauce by adding both Gruyère and Parmesan cheeses. To ensure that the sandwiches were ready to eat at the same time, we assembled all four of them on a baking sheet, layering in the cheese sauce and slices of Black Forest ham before topping them with more sauce and cheese. A trip under the broiler was all that was needed to meld the sandwich together and create a bubbly-browned top.

For the best results, be sure to use a good-quality Gruyère here.

FORK-IN-THE-ROAD FAVORITES

Sandwiches

- 8 slices hearty white sandwich bread
- 4 tablespoons unsalted butter, melted
- 12 ounces thinly sliced Black Forest deli ham
- ¼ cup grated Parmesan cheese
- 4 ounces Gruyère cheese, shredded (1 cup)

Mornay Sauce

- 2 tablespoons unsalted butter
- 2 tablespoons all-purpose flour
- 1 cup whole milk
- 4 ounces Gruyère cheese, shredded (1 cup)
- ¼ cup grated Parmesan cheese
- ½ teaspoon table salt
- ¼ teaspoon pepper
- Pinch ground nutmeg

1. For the Sandwiches Adjust oven rack 6 inches from broiler element and heat oven to 375 degrees. Line rimmed baking sheet with aluminum foil and spray with vegetable oil spray.

2. Brush bread on both sides with melted butter and place on prepared sheet. Bake until light golden brown on top, about 10 minutes. Remove sheet from oven and flip slices. Return to oven and bake until golden brown on second side, about 3 minutes. Reserve 4 slices for sandwich tops; evenly space remaining 4 slices on sheet.

3. For the Mornay Sauce Melt butter in small saucepan over medium heat. Whisk in flour and cook for 1 minute. Slowly whisk in milk and bring to boil. Once boiling, remove from heat and quickly whisk in Gruyère, Parmesan, salt, pepper, and nutmeg until smooth.

4. Spread 1 tablespoon Mornay on each slice of toast on sheet. Then, folding ham slices over themselves multiple times so they bunch up, divide ham evenly among slices of toast. Spread 2 tablespoons Mornay on 1 side of each reserved slice of toast and place slices Mornay side down on top of ham.

5. Spread 2 tablespoons Mornay evenly over top of each sandwich, making sure to completely cover toast, including edges (exposed edges can burn under broiler). Sprinkle sandwiches with Parmesan, followed by Gruyère.

6. Bake until cheese on top of sandwiches is melted, about 5 minutes. Turn on broiler and broil until cheese bubbles across tops of sandwiches and edges are spotty brown, about 5 minutes. Serve.

Croque Madame

Top each sandwich with a fried egg.

Boogaloo Wonderland Sandwiches

SERVES 4

WHY THIS RECIPE WORKS This sandwich bears a passing resemblance to the classic sloppy joe, but it's bigger and bolder, spicier and tangier. The Detroit staple was reinvented at Chef Greg's Soul "N" the Wall and features spicy, saucy ground beef that's topped with American cheese and sautéed onions and piled onto soft sub rolls. The original recipe for the sauce is top secret, so we puzzled out our own version, adding chili powder and dry mustard for heat and spice. Toasting the sandwiches in the oven created crunchy edges on the bread and melted the cheese. We reserved some sauce to spoon over the toasted sandwiches for a zesty finish.

Croque Monsieur

Heinz Organic Tomato Ketchup and Heinz Filtered Apple Cider Vinegar are our favorites. Both light and dark brown sugar will work in this recipe. Don't be tempted to substitute another kind of cheese for the American; nothing melts like it. Serve with your favorite hot sauce, if desired.

Sauce
- 1 cup ketchup
- 3 tablespoons cider vinegar
- 2 tablespoons packed brown sugar
- 2 tablespoons Worcestershire sauce
- ¾ teaspoon dried thyme
- ¾ teaspoon dry mustard
- ¾ teaspoon granulated garlic
- ¾ teaspoon chili powder
- ¼ teaspoon pepper

Sandwiches
- 1 tablespoon vegetable oil
- 1¼ pounds 85 percent lean ground beef
- 1 onion, sliced thin
- 1 teaspoon pepper
- ¾ teaspoon table salt
- 4 (6-inch) Italian sub rolls, sliced lengthwise with 1 side intact
- 8 slices American cheese

1. For the Sauce Combine all ingredients in small saucepan and bring to boil over medium-high heat. Cook, whisking constantly, until slightly thickened, about 3 minutes.

2. For the Sandwiches Adjust oven rack to middle position and heat oven to 350 degrees. Heat oil in 12-inch nonstick skillet over medium-high heat until just smoking. Add beef, onion, pepper, and salt and cook, breaking meat into small pieces with spoon, until liquid has evaporated and meat begins to sizzle, about 10 minutes. Add 1 cup sauce and bring to boil. Reduce heat to medium and simmer until slightly thickened, about 1 minute.

3. Place rolls on rimmed baking sheet. Divide meat mixture evenly among roll bottoms. Top each sandwich with 2 slices American cheese. Bake until cheese is melted and rolls are warmed through, about 5 minutes. Divide remaining sauce equally among sandwiches. Fold roll tops over meat and serve.

Boogaloo Wonderland Sandwiches

On the Road: New Life for an Old Sandwich

Chef Gregory Emilis Beard opened Chef Greg's Soul "N" the Wall in Detroit in 2006 where he serves his own style of food that he calls "urban flavor with a twist." The spot was formerly occupied by Brother's Bar-B-Que, one of whose specialties was the so-called Boogaloo sandwich, a barbecue-flavored Sloppy Joe–style hero smothered with cheese and sauce and served on a sub roll. Beard had never heard of, much less tasted, a Boogaloo but customers kept asking for it. Through trial and error and with plenty of feedback from fans, he finessed a recipe and brought the sandwich back to life. He named this new version the Boogaloo Wonderland sandwich in honor of his friend, Grammy award–winning songwriter and Detroit native Allee Willis, who wrote the song "Boogie Wonderland" for Earth, Wind & Fire in 1979.

As Beard sees it, he "found something old, borrowed the concept, and turned it into something new."

Patty Melts

Diner-Style Patty Melts

Patty Melts
SERVES 4

WHY THIS RECIPE WORKS Because the ground beef patty for patty melts is traditionally cooked twice—browned once in butter and a second time while the sandwich is griddled—many recipes produce something resembling dried-out hockey pucks. To solve the problem, we incorporated a panade (a paste of bread and milk) into the meat. To bump up the flavor of our burgers, we used rye bread and onion powder in the panade. Covering the cooking onions with the patties trapped some of the steam and helped the onions to soften quicker. This also allowed the flavors of the meat to seep into the onions and vice versa.

To make sure that the melts hold together, use rye bread that's sliced about ½ inch thick.

- 10 slices hearty rye sandwich bread
- 2 tablespoons whole milk
- ¾ teaspoon onion powder
- 1¼ teaspoon table salt, divided
- ½ teaspoon pepper
- 1½ pounds 85 percent lean ground beef
- 3 tablespoons unsalted butter, divided
- 2 onions, halved and sliced thin
- 8 ounces Swiss cheese, shredded (2 cups)

1. Adjust oven rack to middle position and heat oven to 200 degrees. Tear 2 pieces of bread into ½-inch pieces. Using potato masher, mash torn bread, milk, onion powder, ¾ teaspoon salt, and pepper in large bowl until smooth. Add beef and gently knead until well combined. Divide meat into 4 equal portions. Shape each portion into 6 by 4-inch oval.

2. Melt 1 tablespoon butter in 12-inch nonstick skillet over medium-high heat. Cook 2 patties until well browned on first side, about 5 minutes. Transfer to large plate, browned side up, and repeat with remaining 2 patties.

3. Pour off all but 1 teaspoon fat from pan. Add onions and remaining ½ teaspoon salt and cook, stirring occasionally, until golden brown, 5 to 7 minutes. Arrange patties, browned side up, on top of onions, pouring any accumulated juices into pan. Reduce heat to medium and cook, shaking pan occasionally, until onions are tender and burgers are cooked through, about 5 minutes.

4. Divide 1 cup cheese among 4 slices bread. Top with patties, onions, remaining cheese, and remaining bread. Wipe out skillet with paper towels. Melt 1 tablespoon butter in now-empty skillet over medium heat. Cook 2 sandwiches until golden brown and cheese is melted, 3 to 4 minutes per side. Transfer to rimmed baking sheet and keep warm in oven. Repeat with remaining 1 tablespoon butter and remaining 2 sandwiches. Serve.

> ### The American Table: Heyday of the Sandwich
>
> When it comes to inventive sandwiches, you can't top 1920s America. Just a decade earlier, New Yorkers were said to eat only six types of sandwich: sardine, tongue, roast beef, Swiss cheese, liverwurst, and egg, according to William Grimes's book *Appetite City: A Culinary History of New York*. But three factors—Prohibition, the newfound popularity of automobiles, and women's increasing independence—had created a tearoom craze across the country, making sandwiches so popular that one New Yorker counted nearly 1,000 different types. In these newly minted salons of sandwiches, customers chose among dubious combinations like cheese-ketchup, lemon-prune, and baked bean–celery. Cookbooks reflected the trend, offering other odd partnerships, such as peanut butter and chili sauce, not to mention shredded coconut, cucumber, and mayonnaise. Makes Elvis's prized fried sandwich of peanut butter, banana, and bacon sound almost tame.

Diner-Style Patty Melts

MAKES 4 SANDWICHES

WHY THIS RECIPE WORKS These patty melts boast juicy beef, jammy onions, perfectly melted cheese, and buttery griddled rye bread that's exquisitely crisp. To get here, we started by lightly toasting the bread to make it sturdier. Pressing out thin beef patties a bit larger than our slices of toast made for quick-cooking burgers with loads of flavorful crust. Placing the seared patties directly on the cheese (American for creamy melting, Swiss for nutty flavor) jump-started the melting process. Further, it kept the beef juices from making the toast soggy. Finally, making a quick onion jam with ketchup, brown sugar, cider vinegar, and Worcestershire sauce in the same skillet we used to cook the patties took these melts to the next level.

We developed this recipe using Pepperidge Farm Jewish Rye Bread. For the best flavor, buy American cheese from the deli counter, not cellophane-wrapped cheese slices. It's helpful to weigh the cheese to account for differences in thickness of deli slices. This recipe can be halved (note that you'll need to decrease the cooking times for the onions).

- 2 teaspoons kosher salt, divided
- 1½ teaspoons pepper, divided
- ½ cup water
- 2 tablespoons ketchup
- 2 tablespoons cider vinegar
- 2 teaspoons packed brown sugar
- 2 teaspoons Worcestershire sauce
- 8 slices seeded rye bread, lightly toasted, divided
- 8 slices deli Swiss cheese (6 ounces), divided
- 4 slices deli American cheese (3 ounces)
- 1 pound 80 percent lean ground beef
- 6 tablespoons unsalted butter, cut into six 1-tablespoon pieces, divided
- 2 onions, sliced thin (3 cups)

1. Adjust oven rack to middle position and heat oven to 200 degrees. Set wire rack in rimmed baking sheet; place in oven. Combine 1½ teaspoons salt and 1 teaspoon pepper in small bowl; set aside. Combine ½ cup water, ketchup, vinegar, sugar, and Worcestershire sauce in second small bowl; set aside.

2. Lay 4 slices rye toast in single layer on clean counter. Shingle 1 slice Swiss cheese and 1 slice American cheese on toast (breaking up cheese slices as necessary to keep from hanging over edges of toast). Divide beef into 4 equal portions and, working on flat surface, use your hands to press each portion into very thin oval patty (no more than ¼ inch thick) about ¼ inch larger than slices of rye toast.

3. Heat 12-inch cast-iron skillet over medium-high heat for 5 minutes. Sprinkle tops of patties with half of salt mixture. Swirl 1 tablespoon butter into hot skillet until melted. Using 2 hands, carefully pick up 2 patties and add to skillet seasoned side down. Sprinkle tops with half of remaining salt mixture. Cook until well browned on both sides, 60 to 90 seconds per side. Transfer patties to 2 cheese-topped slices of toast. Melt 1 tablespoon butter in now-empty skillet. Add remaining 2 patties, seasoned side down, and repeat cooking process, sprinkling with remaining salt mixture.

4. Add onions, 1 cup water, remaining ½ teaspoon salt, and remaining ½ teaspoon pepper to now-empty skillet and stir to scrape up any browned bits. Cover and cook over medium-high heat until water has evaporated and onions are sizzling, 8 to 10 minutes.

5. Uncover and continue to cook, stirring often, until onions are softened, 5 to 7 minutes. Stir in ketchup mixture and cook until liquid has evaporated and onions are uniformly browned, 5 to 7 minutes. Off heat, divide onions evenly over patties and immediately top with remaining 4 slices Swiss cheese and remaining 4 slices toast. Rinse out skillet, scraping up any stuck-on bits, and wipe clean with paper towels.

6. Melt 1 tablespoon butter in now-empty skillet over medium heat, swirling to coat skillet. Transfer 2 patty melts to skillet. Cover and cook until bottoms are golden brown and crisp, 3 to 5 minutes, moving sandwiches occasionally to ensure even browning.

7. Using spatula, carefully flip sandwiches. Add 1 tablespoon butter to center of skillet between sandwiches and tilt to distribute butter as it melts. Cover and cook until golden brown and crisp, about 3 minutes, reducing heat to medium-low if toast begins to turn deep brown or browns unevenly. Transfer to wire rack in oven.

8. Repeat with remaining 2 tablespoons butter and remaining 2 patty melts. Slice sandwiches in half and serve.

The Creation of a Classic

The patty melt was popularized (and perhaps created) by the six-foot-four, 300-pound William Wallace "Tiny" Naylor at his iconic 1950s Los Angeles drive-in. Open 24 hours and operating from 1949 to 1980, Tiny Naylor's was a popular destination for movie stars (who could dine in anonymity in their cars) and high school students alike. The iconic restaurant, with its bright lights and soaring concrete wing, stood on the corner of La Brea Avenue and Sunset Boulevard as a textbook example of futurist Googie architecture. These days, you can find "Tiny's Classic Patty Melt" on the menu at another L.A. institution, Du-par's, which was owned from 2004 to 2018 by Tiny's son "Biff."

Sliders

MAKES 12 SLIDERS

WHY THIS RECIPE WORKS Miniature burgers known as sliders (popularized by the White Castle chain) satisfy a lot of cravings: tender burger, soft roll, gooey cheese, and sweet onions. Since the burgers are small, it's important they're all the same size to prevent overcooking. To portion the patties, we weighed the beef and pressed it with a clear pie plate. The way to achieve classic slider flavor is to sprinkle finely chopped onion on the patties when they first hit the skillet and then press the onion into the meat. Adding water and covering the skillet softened the buns, finished cooking the onion, and melted the cheese.

This recipe moves quickly, so be sure to have everything ready before you begin cooking.

Sauce
- ¼ cup mayonnaise
- 2 tablespoons ketchup
- 1 teaspoon sweet pickle relish
- 1 teaspoon sugar
- 1 teaspoon distilled white vinegar
- 1 teaspoon pepper

Sliders
- 1½ pounds 85 percent lean ground beef
- 12 (2½-inch) slider buns or soft dinner rolls, halved horizontally
- 6 slices deli American cheese (6 ounces)
- 1½ teaspoons kosher salt
- 1 teaspoon pepper
- 2 teaspoons vegetable oil, divided
- ½ cup finely chopped onion
- ¼ cup water

1. For the Sauce Whisk all ingredients together in bowl; refrigerate until ready to use.

2. For the Sliders Cut sides of 1-quart zipper-lock bag, leaving bottom seam intact. Divide beef into twelve 2-ounce portions, then roll into balls. Working with 1 ball at a time, enclose in split bag. Using clear pie plate (so you can see size of patty), press ball into even 4-inch-diameter patty. Remove patty from bag and place on baking sheet. Cover sheet with plastic wrap and refrigerate until ready to cook. (Patties can be shaped up to 24 hours in advance.)

3. Divide sauce evenly among bun bottoms. Arrange bun bottoms, sauce side up, on platter; set aside. Stack American cheese and cut into quarters (you will have 24 pieces). Combine salt and pepper in bowl.

4. Sprinkle both sides of patties with salt-pepper mixture. Heat 1 teaspoon oil in 12-inch nonstick skillet over medium heat until just smoking. Using spatula, transfer 6 patties to skillet. Sprinkle ¼ cup onion evenly over tops of patties and press firmly into patties with back of spatula.

5. Cook patties, uncovered and without moving them, for 2 minutes. Flip patties and top each with 2 pieces American cheese; add bun tops. Add 2 tablespoons water to skillet (do not wet buns), cover, and continue to cook until cheese is melted, about 90 seconds longer.

6. Transfer sliders to prepared bun bottoms and tent with aluminum foil. Wipe skillet clean with paper towels. Repeat with remaining 1 teaspoon oil, 6 patties, ¼ cup onion, American cheese, bun tops, and 2 tablespoons water. Serve immediately.

Sliders

Oklahoma Fried Onion Burgers

SERVES 4

Oklahoma Fried Onion Burgers

WHY THIS RECIPE WORKS These Oklahoma specialties feature a thin beef patty topped with a crispy crust of caramelized griddled onions served on a grilled bun with mustard, pickles, and American cheese. To make them at home, we salted the onions and squeezed out their excess moisture so they'd brown quickly and stick to the burgers. We mashed the onions into the burgers then browned them on a buttered skillet, onion side down. To sear and finish them, we flipped the patties and turned up the heat.

A mandoline makes quick work of slicing the onion thinly. Squeeze the salted onion slices until they're as dry as possible, or they won't adhere to the patties. These burgers are traditionally served with yellow mustard and dill pickles.

- 1 large onion, halved and sliced ⅛ inch thick
  Table salt and pepper
- 12 ounces 85 percent lean ground beef
- 1 tablespoon unsalted butter
- 1 teaspoon vegetable oil
- 4 slices American cheese (4 ounces)
- 4 hamburger buns, buttered and toasted

1. Combine onion and 1 teaspoon salt in bowl and toss to combine. Transfer to colander and let sit for 30 minutes, tossing occasionally. Using tongs, transfer onion to clean dish towel, gather edges, and squeeze onion dry. Sprinkle with ½ teaspoon pepper.

2. Divide onion mixture into 4 separate mounds on rimmed baking sheet. Form beef into 4 lightly packed balls and season with salt and pepper. Place beef balls on top of onion mounds and flatten beef firmly so onion adheres and patties measure 4 inches in diameter.

3. Melt butter with oil in 12-inch nonstick skillet over medium heat. Using spatula, transfer patties to skillet, onion side down, and cook until onion is deep golden brown and beginning to crisp around edges, 6 to 8 minutes. Flip burgers, increase heat to high, and cook until well browned on second side, about 2 minutes. Place 1 slice cheese on each bottom bun. Place burgers on buns, add desired toppings, and serve.

Wisconsin Butter Burgers

SERVES 4

Wisconsin Butter Burgers

WHY THIS RECIPE WORKS The butter burgers at Solly's Grille in Milwaukee feature thin, crispy-edged patties topped with American cheese, stewed onion, and a generously buttered bun. For our version, we cooked the patties in a hot skillet, without moving them, until they developed that signature crisp crust. We flipped them, topped them with cheese, and then spooned over the stewed onion (cooked simply with water, butter, and salt until it was softened and just beginning to brown). A bun slathered in salted butter topped off each burger.

Our favorite domestic salted butter is Kate's Homemade.

- 9 tablespoons salted butter, softened, divided
- 1 onion, chopped
- 1 tablespoon water
-   Table salt and pepper
- 1 pound 90 percent lean ground beef
- 4 hamburger buns, toasted
- ½ teaspoon vegetable oil
- 4 slices American cheese

1. Melt 1 tablespoon butter in medium saucepan over medium heat. Add onion, water, and ¼ teaspoon salt and cook, covered, until tender, about 5 minutes. Remove lid and continue to cook until translucent and just beginning to brown, about 3 minutes. Cover and keep warm.

2. Transfer beef to rimmed baking sheet and separate into 4 equal mounds. Gently shape each mound into 4½-inch-wide by ½-inch-thick patty. Combine ¾ teaspoon salt and ¾ teaspoon pepper in bowl and sprinkle both sides of patties with mixture. Refrigerate until ready to cook, up to 30 minutes.

3. Spread 2 tablespoons butter onto each bun top; set aside. Heat oil in 12-inch skillet over high heat until just smoking. Using spatula, transfer patties to skillet and cook without moving them for 3 minutes. Flip patties and cook for 1 minute. Top each burger with 1 slice of American cheese and continue to cook until cheese is melted, about 30 seconds longer.

4. Transfer burgers to bun bottoms. Divide onion mixture among burgers and cover with buttered bun tops. Serve immediately.

Atlanta Brisket

SERVES 6

WHY THIS RECIPE WORKS Atlanta brisket is a Southern braise featuring onion soup mix, ketchup, and Atlanta's own Coca-Cola. We wanted to keep the regional charm but update the convenience-product flavor. To season the brisket, we pierced it with a fork, salted it, and let it sit overnight. For a great crust, we seared the brisket weighed down with a heavy pot. Finally, for the characteristic braising liquid, we mixed cola and ketchup and replaced the artificial-tasting soup mix with our own blend of sautéed onions, onion and garlic powders, brown sugar, and dried thyme. The mixture both flavored the meat and became a sweet, tangy sauce for serving.

Parchment paper provides a nonreactive barrier between the cola-based braising liquid and the aluminum foil. A whole brisket is comprised of two smaller roasts: the flat cut and the point cut. For this recipe, we prefer the flat cut, which is rectangular in shape and leaner than the knobby, well-marbled point cut. The flat cut is topped with a thick fat cap; make sure that the fat cap isn't overtrimmed.

- 1 (3½-pound) beef brisket, flat cut, fat trimmed to ¼ inch thick
- Table salt and pepper
- 4 teaspoons vegetable oil, divided
- 1 pound onions, halved and sliced ½ inch thick
- 2 cups cola
- 1½ cups ketchup
- 4 teaspoons onion powder
- 2 teaspoons packed dark brown sugar
- 1 teaspoon garlic powder
- 1 teaspoon dried thyme

1. Using fork, poke holes all over brisket. Rub entire surface of brisket with 1 tablespoon salt. Wrap brisket in plastic wrap and refrigerate for at least 6 or up to 24 hours.

2. Adjust oven rack to lower-middle position and heat oven to 325 degrees. Pat brisket dry with paper towels and season with pepper. Heat 2 teaspoons oil in 12-inch nonstick skillet over medium-high heat until just smoking. Place brisket fat side down in skillet; weigh down brisket with heavy Dutch oven or cast-iron skillet and cook until well browned on bottom, about 4 minutes. Remove pot, flip brisket, and replace pot on top of brisket. Cook on second side until well browned, about 4 minutes longer. Transfer brisket to plate.

3. Heat remaining 2 teaspoons oil in now-empty skillet over medium heat until shimmering. Add onions and cook, stirring occasionally, until soft and golden brown, 10 to 12 minutes. Transfer onions to 13 by 9-inch baking dish and spread out in even layer.

4. Combine cola, ketchup, onion powder, sugar, garlic powder, thyme, 1 teaspoon salt, and 1 teaspoon pepper in bowl. Place brisket fat side up on top of onions and pour cola mixture over brisket. Place parchment paper over brisket and cover dish tightly with aluminum foil. Bake until tender and fork slips easily in and out of meat, 3½ to 4 hours. Let brisket rest in liquid, uncovered, for 30 minutes.

5. Transfer brisket to carving board. Skim any fat from top of sauce with large spoon. Slice brisket against grain into ¼-inch-thick slices and return to baking dish. Serve brisket with sauce.

To Make Ahead Follow recipe through step 4. Allow brisket to cool in sauce, cover, and refrigerate overnight or up to 24 hours. To serve, slice brisket, return to sauce, and cover with parchment paper. Cover baking dish with aluminum foil and cook in 350-degree oven until heated through, about 1 hour.

Atlanta Brisket

Slow-Cooker BBQ Beef Brisket

SERVES 8 TO 10

Slow-Cooker BBQ Beef Brisket

WHY THIS RECIPE WORKS Barbecued brisket in the slow cooker? You bet. To minimize the moisture absorbed by the brisket (which traditionally isn't cooked directly in liquid), we came up with an unorthodox solution: elevating the meat off the bottom of the slow cooker with an inverted loaf pan. The liquid exuded from the meat during cooking was drawn under the loaf pan by a vacuum effect, which meant that the slow cooker more closely mimicked the dry heat of real barbecue. To bump up the flavor of this liquid, we added sautéed onion, garlic, tomato paste, and chipotle chiles.

Scoring the fat on the brisket at ½-inch intervals will allow the rub to penetrate the meat. Two disposable aluminum loaf pans stacked inside one another can be substituted for the metal loaf pan.

Spice Rub and Brisket
- ½ cup packed dark brown sugar
- 2 tablespoons minced canned chipotle chile in adobo sauce
- 1 tablespoon ground cumin
- 1 tablespoon paprika
- 2 teaspoons pepper
- 1 teaspoon table salt
- 1 (4- to 5-pound) brisket roast, fat trimmed to ¼ inch thick and scored lightly

Aromatics and Sauce
- 3 tablespoons vegetable oil
- 1 onion, chopped fine
- 2 tablespoons tomato paste
- 1 tablespoon chili powder
- 1 tablespoon minced canned chipotle chile in adobo sauce
- 2 garlic cloves, minced
- ½ cup water, plus extra as needed
- ¼ cup ketchup
- 1 tablespoon cider vinegar
- ¼ teaspoon liquid smoke
- Table salt and pepper

1. For the Spice Rub and Brisket Combine sugar, chipotle, cumin, paprika, pepper, and salt in bowl. Rub sugar mixture all over brisket. Cover with plastic wrap and let sit at room temperature for 1 hour or refrigerate for up to 24 hours.

2. For the Aromatics and Sauce Heat oil in 12-inch skillet over medium-high heat until shimmering. Cook onion until softened, about 5 minutes. Add tomato paste and cook until beginning to brown, about 1 minute. Stir in chili powder, chipotle, and garlic and cook until fragrant, about 30 seconds. Mound onion mixture in center of slow cooker, arrange inverted metal loaf pan over onion mixture, and place brisket fat side up on top of loaf pan. Add water to slow cooker, cover, and cook on high until fork inserted in brisket can be removed with no resistance, 7 to 8 hours (or cook on low for 10 to 12 hours).

3. Transfer brisket to 13 by 9-inch baking dish, cover with aluminum foil, and let rest for 30 minutes. Carefully remove loaf pan from slow cooker. Pour onion mixture and accumulated juices into large bowl and skim fat. (You should have about 2 cups defatted juices; if you have less, supplement with water.)

4. Transfer brisket to carving board, slice thin against grain, and return to baking dish. Pour 1 cup reserved defatted juices over sliced brisket. Whisk ketchup, vinegar, and liquid smoke into remaining juices. Season with salt and pepper to taste. Serve, passing sauce at table.

To Make Ahead In step 3, wrap brisket tightly in foil and refrigerate for up to 3 days. (Refrigerate juices separately.) To serve, transfer foil-wrapped brisket to baking dish and heat in 350-degree oven until brisket is heated through, about 1 hour. Reheat juices in microwave or saucepan set over medium heat. Continue with recipe as directed.

Preventing Waterlogged Brisket

To minimize the moisture absorbed by the brisket, we place the meat on top of a loaf pan. The juices exuded by the meat are drawn under the pan by a vacuum effect, creating less moisture directly below the meat.

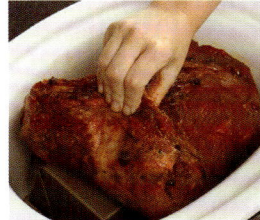

1. Pile onion mixture under inverted loaf pan and place brisket on top.

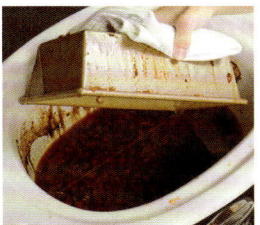

2. After cooking, release juices from loaf pan and reserve for use in barbecue sauce.

Tennessee Whiskey Pork Chops

SERVES 4

WHY THIS RECIPE WORKS We wanted a foolproof recipe for this Southern specialty. We started by making a whiskey-flavored marinade, then steeped the chops in it for at least 1 hour prior to cooking. We cooked the chops in a hot skillet and then used the same pan to prepare the glaze—browned bits left behind by the chops in the pan added deep, meaty flavor. Allowing the cooked chops to sit in the pan in the glaze for a few minutes before serving helped ensure that it clung to the meat.

Bourbon tastes fine, but we think it's worth purchasing the real deal—Jack Daniel's Tennessee Whiskey—for this recipe. Watch the glaze closely during the last few minutes of cooking—the bubbles become very small as it approaches the right consistency.

- ½ cup Jack Daniel's Tennessee Whiskey or bourbon
- ½ cup apple cider
- 2 tablespoons packed light brown sugar
- 4 teaspoons cider vinegar, divided
- 1 tablespoon Dijon mustard
- ½ teaspoon vanilla extract
- ⅛ teaspoon cayenne pepper
- 4 (8- to 10-ounce) bone-in, center-cut pork chops, about 1 inch thick, trimmed
- 2 teaspoons vegetable oil
  Table salt and pepper
- 1 tablespoon unsalted butter

1. Whisk whiskey, cider, sugar, 2 teaspoons vinegar, mustard, vanilla, and cayenne together in bowl. Transfer ¼ cup whiskey mixture to 1-gallon zipper-lock bag, add pork chops, press air out of bag, and seal. Turn bag to coat chops with marinade and refrigerate 1 to 2 hours. Reserve remaining whiskey mixture separately.

Tennessee Whiskey Pork Chops

2. Remove chops from bag, pat dry with paper towels, and discard marinade. Heat oil in 12-inch skillet over medium-high heat until just beginning to smoke. Season chops with salt and pepper and cook until well browned on both sides and a peek into thickest part of a chop using paring knife yields still-pink meat ¼ inch from surface, 6 to 8 minutes, flipping chops halfway through cooking. Transfer chops to plate and cover tightly with aluminum foil.

3. Add reserved whiskey mixture to skillet and bring to boil, scraping up any browned bits with wooden spoon. Cook until reduced to thick glaze, 3 to 5 minutes. Reduce heat to medium-low and, holding on to chops, tip plate to add any accumulated juices back to skillet. Add remaining 2 teaspoons vinegar, whisk in butter, and simmer glaze until thick and sticky, 2 to 3 minutes. Remove pan from heat.

4. Return chops to skillet and let rest in pan, turning chops occasionally to coat both sides, until sauce clings to chops and meat registers 145 degrees, about 5 minutes. Transfer chops to platter and spoon sauce over. Serve.

Memphis-Style Wet Ribs for a Crowd

SERVES 8 TO 12

WHY THIS RECIPE WORKS For these saucy Memphis wet ribs, a potent spice rub performs double duty, seasoning the meat and creating the backbone for our barbecue sauce. Tying two racks together allowed us to double our yield and cook four hefty racks of ribs at once. To keep the ribs moist, we grilled them over indirect heat and basted them with a traditional "mop" of juice and vinegar. After a few hours of smoking on the grill, we brushed the ribs with our flavorful barbecue sauce and transferred them to the steady, even heat of the oven to finish tenderizing.

Spice Rub
- ¼ cup paprika
- 2 tablespoons packed brown sugar
- 2 tablespoons table salt
- 2 teaspoons pepper
- 2 teaspoons onion powder
- 2 teaspoons granulated garlic

Barbecue Sauce and Mop
- 1½ cups ketchup
- 1¼ cups apple juice
- ¼ cup molasses
- ½ cup cider vinegar
- ¼ cup Worcestershire sauce
- 3 tablespoons yellow mustard
- 2 teaspoons pepper

Ribs
- 4 (2½- to 3-pound) racks St. Louis–style spareribs, trimmed, membrane removed
- 2 cups wood chips, soaked in water for 15 minutes and drained
- 1 (13 by 9-inch) disposable aluminum roasting pan (if using charcoal) or 1 (8½ by 6-inch) disposable aluminum pan (if using gas)

1. For the Spice Rub Combine all ingredients in bowl.

2. For the Barbecue Sauce and Mop Combine ketchup, ¾ cup apple juice, molasses, ¼ cup vinegar, Worcestershire, 2 tablespoons mustard, and 2 tablespoons spice rub in medium saucepan and bring to boil over medium heat. Reduce heat to medium-low and simmer until thickened and reduced to 2 cups, about 20 minutes. Off heat, stir in pepper; set barbecue sauce aside. For the mop, whisk ½ cup apple juice, ¼ cup vinegar, 1 tablespoon mustard, and ¼ cup barbecue sauce together in bowl.

3. For the Ribs Pat ribs dry with paper towels and season with remaining spice rub. Place 1 rack of ribs, meaty side down, on cutting board. Place second rack of ribs, meaty side up, directly on top of first rack, arranging thick end over tapered end. Tie racks together at 2-inch intervals with kitchen twine. Repeat with remaining 2 racks of ribs for two bundles. Using large piece of heavy-duty aluminum foil, wrap soaked chips in foil packet and cut several vent holes in top.

4a. For a Charcoal Grill Open bottom vent halfway and place disposable roasting pan on 1 side of grill. Fill pan with 2 quarts water. Arrange 3 quarts unlit charcoal briquettes on other side of grill. Light large chimney starter half filled with charcoal briquettes (3 quarts). When top coals are partially covered with ash, pour evenly over unlit coals. Place wood chip packet on coals. Set cooking grate in place, cover, and open lid vent halfway. Heat grill until hot and wood chips are smoking, about 5 minutes.

4b. For a Gas Grill Place wood chip packet and disposable pan over primary burner and fill pan with 2 cups water. Turn primary burner to high (leave other burners off), cover, and heat grill until hot and wood chips are smoking, about 15 minutes. (Adjust primary burner as needed to maintain grill temperature of 275 to 300 degrees.)

5. Clean and oil cooking grate. Place ribs on cooler side of grill and baste with one-third of mop. Cover (positioning lid vent over ribs for charcoal) and cook for 2 hours, flipping and switching positions of ribs and basting again with half of remaining mop halfway through cooking.

6. Adjust oven racks to upper-middle and lower-middle positions and heat oven to 300 degrees. Line 2 rimmed baking sheets with foil. Cut kitchen twine from racks. Transfer 2 racks, meaty side up, to each sheet. Baste with remaining mop and bake for 2 hours, switching and rotating sheets halfway through baking.

7. Remove ribs from oven and brush evenly with ½ cup barbecue sauce. Return to oven and continue to bake until tender, basting with ½ cup barbecue sauce and switching and rotating sheets twice during baking, about 45 minutes. (Ribs do not need to be flipped and should remain meaty side up during baking.) Transfer ribs to carving board. Brush evenly with remaining ½ cup barbecue sauce, tent loosely with foil, and let rest for 20 minutes. Cut ribs in between bones to separate. Serve.

Slow-Cooker Memphis-Style Wet Ribs

SERVES 4 TO 6

WHY THIS RECIPE WORKS To serve up saucy Memphis wet ribs without ever leaving the kitchen, we turned to our slow cooker. After applying a zesty spice rub, we arranged two racks of St. Louis–style ribs in the slow cooker. The ribs cooked low and slow in their own flavorful juices, no other liquid required. Hours later, the ribs were tender and perfectly cooked. We made a thick glazy sauce and brushed it over our ribs before sliding them under the broiler to create truly "wet" barbecue ribs indoors.

Try to find ribs of equal shape to ensure even cooking. These ribs should be tender but not falling off the bone.

Memphis-Style Wet Ribs for a Crowd

Slow-Cooker Memphis-Style Wet Ribs

Ribs

- 2 tablespoons paprika
- 1 tablespoon packed brown sugar
- 1 tablespoon kosher salt
- 2 teaspoons pepper
- 2 teaspoons onion powder
- 2 teaspoons granulated garlic
- 2 (2½- to 3-pound) racks St. Louis–style spareribs, trimmed and each rack cut in half

Barbecue Sauce

- ¾ cup ketchup
- 6 tablespoons apple juice
- 2 tablespoons molasses
- 2 tablespoons cider vinegar
- 2 tablespoons Worcestershire sauce
- 1 tablespoon yellow mustard
- 1 teaspoon pepper
- ¼ teaspoon liquid smoke

1. For the Ribs Combine paprika, sugar, salt, pepper, onion powder, and granulated garlic in bowl. Reserve 1 tablespoon spice rub for sauce. Pat ribs dry with paper towels and coat all over with remaining 5 tablespoons rub.

2. Arrange ribs vertically with thick ends pointing down and meaty side against interior wall of slow cooker (ribs will overlap). Cover and cook until ribs are just tender, 5 to 6 hours on high or 6 to 7 hours on low.

3. For the Barbecue Sauce Meanwhile, whisk ketchup, apple juice, molasses, vinegar, Worcestershire, mustard, pepper, liquid smoke, and reserved 1 tablespoon spice rub together in medium saucepan. Bring to boil over medium heat, then reduce heat to medium-low and simmer, stirring occasionally, until thickened and reduced to 1 cup, about 10 minutes. (Sauce can be refrigerated for up to 3 days.)

4. Line rimmed baking sheet with aluminum foil and set wire rack in sheet. Using tongs, transfer ribs, meaty side up, to prepared rack. Let ribs sit for 10 minutes to allow surface to dry out.

5. Adjust oven rack 3 inches from broiler element and heat broiler. Liberally brush ribs with ½ cup sauce and broil until sauce is bubbling and beginning to char, about 4 minutes. Remove ribs from oven, brush with remaining ½ cup sauce, tent with foil, and let rest for 20 minutes. Cut ribs in between bones to separate. Serve.

Okinawan Taco Rice

SERVES 4

WHY THIS RECIPE WORKS Matsuzo Gibo created taco rice in 1984 to cater to U.S. Marines stationed in Okinawa, Japan, and the delicious, satisfying, and affordable dish has since flourished within Okinawan cuisine. The key to our weeknight-friendly recipe was the seasoning for the ground beef. We enhanced the typical taco seasoning with umami-rich instant dashi, sweet and complex mirin, and savory soy sauce. Steamed short-grain rice provided the perfect foil for the flavorful beef, while Monterey Jack cheese, shredded iceberg lettuce, diced avocado, and tangy salsa took our taco rice to irresistible heights.

We developed this recipe with Hondashi instant dashi and McCormick taco seasoning; you can use other brands, but be aware that salt levels and flavors may vary slightly. Look for instant dashi in well-stocked supermarkets, in Asian markets, or online. You can substitute a batch (¼ cup) of our Homemade Taco Seasoning (recipe follows) for the store-bought packet of seasoning, if you prefer.

- 2 cups sushi rice
- 3½ cups water, divided
- 2 tablespoons vegetable oil
- 1 onion, chopped fine
- 1 pound 90 percent lean ground beef
- 1 (1-ounce) packet taco seasoning
- 2 tablespoons ketchup
- 2 tablespoons mirin
- 2 tablespoons soy sauce
- 1 teaspoon Hondashi instant dashi
- 4 ounces Monterey Jack cheese, shredded (1 cup)
- 2 cups shredded iceberg lettuce
- 1 avocado, halved, pitted, and cut into ½-inch pieces (optional)
- ½ cup jarred tomato salsa
- Lime wedges

1. Place rice in fine-mesh strainer and rinse under running water until water running through rice is clear, about 1½ minutes, swishing rice occasionally with your hand. Drain rice well.

2. Combine rice and 2½ cups water in large saucepan and bring to boil over high heat. Cover, reduce heat to low, and simmer for 20 minutes. Remove rice from heat and let stand, covered, for 10 minutes.

3. Heat oil in 12-inch nonstick skillet over medium-high heat until shimmering. Add onion and cook until softened, 3 to 5 minutes. Add beef and cook, using wooden spoon to break meat into pieces, until beef is no longer pink, 3 to 5 minutes. Stir in taco seasoning and cook until fragrant, about 30 seconds.

4. Stir in ketchup, mirin, soy sauce, instant dashi, and remaining 1 cup water; bring to boil; and cook until liquid is slightly thickened, 3 to 5 minutes. Gently fluff rice with fork. Top individual portions of rice with beef; Monterey Jack; lettuce; avocado, if using; and salsa (in that order), and serve with lime wedges.

Homemade Taco Seasoning
SERVES 4 (MAKES ¼ CUP)

- 2 tablespoons chili powder
- 2 teaspoons cumin
- 2 teaspoons cornstarch
- 1 teaspoon paprika
- 1 teaspoon table salt
- ½ teaspoon granulated garlic
- ½ teaspoon onion powder
- ½ teaspoon dried oregano

Place all ingredients in airtight container and shake to thoroughly combine. (Taco seasoning can be stored at room temperature for up to 1 month.)

Sinigang (Filipino Pork and Vegetable Stew)

SERVES 4 TO 6

WHY THIS RECIPE WORKS Our version of this tangy stew is based on a dish by Janice Dulce, chef and owner of FOB Kitchen in Oakland, California. Following her lead, we used a rack of St. Louis–style spareribs, cut in half crosswise through the bones. This exposes lots of marrow and gelatin within the bones, which lends the soup body and richness during cooking. The soup gets its signature flavor from tamarind paste, fish sauce, and lemon juice. For the vegetables, we decided to include daikon radishes, Japanese eggplant, and green beans, which cook directly in the soup. This savory-sour dish is served with rice and a mixture of fish sauce and Thai chiles.

Okinawan Taco Rice

Sinigang (Filipino Pork and Vegetable Stew)

Cutting the ribs crosswise through the bones will have to be done with a bandsaw, so ask your butcher to do this for you. This recipe will still work if you aren't able to get the ribs cut crosswise, but you should separate them into single bone portions if that's the case. One average-size Japanese eggplant is about 6 ounces. Note that we call for a coarse-mesh strainer for straining the tamarind paste.

- 5 ounces tamarind paste
- 1 (3-pound) rack St. Louis–style spareribs, cut in half crosswise through bones
- 2 teaspoons kosher salt
- 1 tablespoon vegetable oil
- 1½ cups thinly sliced onion
- 1 (2-inch) piece ginger, peeled and julienned
- 6 ounces vine-ripe tomatoes, chopped (1 cup)
- 3 Thai chiles, minced, divided
- 8 ounces daikon radish, peeled, halved lengthwise, and sliced thin crosswise ¼ inch thick
- ½ cup fish sauce, divided
- ¼ cup lemon juice (2 lemons)
- 6 ounces green beans, trimmed and halved crosswise
- 6 ounces Japanese eggplant, sliced crosswise on slight bias ½ inch thick
- Cooked white rice

1. Combine tamarind paste and 1 cup boiling water in bowl, and let sit for 15 minutes. Using your hands, squish tamarind paste until diluted into water. Strain mixture though coarse-mesh strainer set over bowl, pressing on solids with ladle to extract as much tamarind mixture as possible. Scrape bottom of strainer with rubber spatula. Discard remaining pulp; set tamarind mixture aside.

2. Separate ribs into 2-bone sections by cutting in between bones. Pat ribs dry with paper towels. Season ribs all over with salt. Heat oil in large Dutch oven over medium-high heat. Add half of ribs, starting meaty side down, and cook until browned on both sides, 3 to 5 minutes per side. Transfer to baking sheet and repeat with remaining ribs; transfer to sheet with first batch of ribs.

3. Add onion and ginger to now-empty pot and cook until softened, about 2 minutes. Add tomatoes and 2 chiles and cook until tomatoes have broken down, 3 to 5 minutes. Add 4 cups water, daikon, ¼ cup fish sauce, lemon juice, and tamarind mixture to pot and stir to combine, scraping up any browned bits from bottom of pot.

4. Add daikon and ribs and press below surface of liquid. Bring to boil. Reduce heat to medium-low, cover, and cook at strong simmer until ribs are fork tender, 1½ hours to 1¾ hours, stirring occasionally.

5. Meanwhile, combine remaining ¼ cup fish sauce with remaining 1 chile in bowl. Divide evenly among 4 to 6 small ramekins; set aside.

6. Stir green beans and eggplant into stew and increase heat to medium. Cook, uncovered, until vegetables are tender, about 15 minutes, stirring occasionally to make sure vegetables are submerged in liquid. Remove stew from heat and season with salt to taste.

7. To serve, portion stew among 4 to 6 shallow bowls; portion rice onto 4 to 6 plates; give each guest 1 ramekin of fish sauce mixture. Transfer portions of stew to plate with rice and spoon small amounts of fish sauce mixture over food, as desired, before each bite. Hold spoon in your right hand and fork in your left, and "bulldoze" food onto your spoon with fork.

Sisig

SERVES 4

WHY THIS RECIPE WORKS Defined by sharp flavors and contrasting textures, sisig is a traditional Filipino dish of chopped pork, onions, and chiles made sour with vinegar or calamansi juice. We were inspired by a dish created by Bobby Punla and Jan Dela Paz and served at their pop-up restaurants in Oakland, California. Marinating the pork in cane vinegar and soy sauce brightened up the rich meat, and grilling it added smoky char. We chopped the pork, combined it with mayonnaise, chiles, and onions, then crisped the meat to perfection in a superhot skillet.

We used Datu Puti cane vinegar, but you can use distilled or cider vinegar, if desired. Maggi liquid seasoning can be used in place of the Knorr. When grilling the pork, be prepared for flareups to occur. Adding the pork to the preheated cast-iron skillet will create smoke, so turn on your exhaust fan or crack open a window prior to cooking. This dish is traditionally made with calamansi juice and served with calamansi halves as a garnish. If you're not able to find them, use lemon juice and lemon wedges. Serve with Garlic Fried Rice (recipe follows).

- ½ cup cane vinegar
- ⅓ cup soy sauce
- 1½ tablespoons Knorr liquid seasoning, divided
- 4 teaspoons garlic powder
- 4 teaspoons onion powder
- 2 teaspoons gochugaru
- 2 teaspoons kosher salt

- 1¼ pounds skinless pork belly, sliced ¼ to ½ inch thick
- 1 pound boneless pork butt roast, sliced ¼ to ½ inch thick
- ½ cup diced red onion, divided
- 6 tablespoons mayonnaise
- 1 serrano chile, stemmed and sliced into thin rings, divided
- 1½ tablespoons calamansi juice or lemon juice, plus calamansi halves or lemon wedges for serving
- 3 garlic cloves, minced
- 3 large eggs
- 3 scallions, sliced thin
- ½ cup coarsely broken chicharrones (½- to ¾-inch pieces)

1. Whisk vinegar, soy sauce, 1 tablespoon liquid seasoning, garlic powder, onion powder, gochugaru, and salt together in large bowl. Add pork belly and butt and toss to thoroughly combine. Transfer pork and any excess marinade to large zipper-lock bag; seal bag; and refrigerate for at least 12 hours or up to 2 days, turning occasionally.

2a. For a Charcoal Grill Open bottom vent completely. Light large chimney starter filled with charcoal briquettes (6 quarts). When top coals are partially covered with ash, pour evenly over half of grill. Set cooking grate in place, cover, and open lid vent completely. Heat grill until hot, about 5 minutes.

2b. For a Gas Grill Turn all burners to high; cover; and heat grill until hot, about 15 minutes. Turn primary burner to medium-high and turn off other burner(s).

3. Working with half of pork, cook over hotter side of grill until browned, lightly charred, and just cooked through, about 4 minutes per side if using charcoal or 6 minutes per side if using gas, moving pork to cooler side of grill as flare-ups occur. Transfer pork to rimmed baking sheet. Repeat with remaining pork.

4. Once pork is cool enough to handle, cut into approximate ¼- to ½-inch pieces. Combine pork, ¼ cup onion, mayonnaise, half of serrano, calamansi or lemon juice, garlic, and remaining 1½ teaspoons liquid seasoning in bowl. Crack eggs into 3 separate ramekins or small bowls. Heat 12-inch cast-iron skillet over high heat until very hot, about 10 minutes.

5. Working quickly, add pork mixture to hot skillet, spread into even layer, and make 3 shallow wells for eggs. Sprinkle scallions and remaining ¼ cup onion evenly over pork mixture. Add 1 egg to each well. Sprinkle chicharrones and remaining serrano over top. Garnish with calamansi halves or lemon wedges. Bring to table while sizzling. Just before serving, stir to incorporate eggs.

Garlic Fried Rice
SERVES 4

One-and-a-half cups of raw jasmine rice cooked with 2¼ cups of water will yield 4½ cups of cooked rice. Ensure that the rice is cold before frying, or it may turn gummy. We run the cooled rice under water to break up the clumps. Let the excess water drain off the rice for at least 5 minutes before transferring it to the skillet. Serve this with the Sisig.

- 4½ cups cooked jasmine rice, cold
- 3 tablespoons vegetable oil
- 8 garlic cloves, chopped fine
- 1 teaspoon kosher salt
- 1 scallion, sliced thin

1. Transfer rice to fine-mesh strainer. Place rice under cold running water and break up clumps with your hands. Let drain for 5 minutes.

2. Combine oil and garlic in 12-inch nonstick skillet. Cook over medium heat until garlic turns golden brown, 3 to 5 minutes. Add rice and salt and cook, stirring frequently, until garlic is evenly distributed throughout rice, about 2 minutes. Off heat, season with salt to taste. Transfer to dish, sprinkle with scallion, and serve.

Sisig

Iowa Skinny

SERVES 4

WHY THIS RECIPE WORKS In the Midwest, pork is king. Iowa stands out for the "skinny"—a sandwich that showcases tender pork pounded thin, battered, and pan-fried to a crunchy golden brown, then served on a hamburger bun. A saltine mixture created a crunchy, golden-brown coating: mayonnaise on the bun added richness and tang that enhanced the pork flavor without weighing down the crust. Lettuce and tomato rounded it all out.

- 1 (1-pound) pork tenderloin, trimmed
- ¼ teaspoon table salt
- ¼ teaspoon pepper
- 3 slices hearty white sandwich bread, torn into quarters
- ½ cup all-purpose flour
- 2 large eggs
- ¼ cup mayonnaise, plus extra for serving
- 16 square or 18 round saltines
- 1 cup vegetable oil
- 4 hamburger buns
- 2 cups shredded iceberg lettuce
- 1 tomato, cored and sliced thin

1. Adjust oven rack to middle position and heat oven to 200 degrees. Set wire rack in rimmed baking sheet. Cut tenderloin in half. Cut each half in half again, cutting tapered tail piece slightly thicker than middle medallions. Cover pork pieces, cut side up, with plastic wrap and pound to ¼-inch thickness with meat pounder. Pat cutlets dry with paper towels and sprinkle with salt and pepper.

2. Pulse bread and saltines in food processor to fine crumbs, about 12 pulses; transfer to shallow dish. Spread flour in second shallow dish. Whisk eggs and mayonnaise together in third shallow dish.

3. Working with 1 cutlet at a time, dredge cutlets in flour, dip in egg mixture, then coat with crumbs, pressing gently to adhere. Transfer cutlets to prepared wire rack and let dry for 5 minutes or refrigerate for up to 1 hour.

4. Heat ½ cup oil in 12-inch nonstick skillet over medium heat until shimmering. Working with 2 cutlets at a time, fry cutlets until deep golden brown and crisp, 2 to 3 minutes per side. Transfer to paper towel–lined plate and keep warm in oven. Discard oil, wipe out skillet, and repeat with remaining ½ cup oil and remaining 2 cutlets. Serve on hamburger buns with lettuce, tomato, and extra mayonnaise.

Baltimore Pit Beef

Baltimore Pit Beef

SERVES 10

WHY THIS RECIPE WORKS Baltimore is known for its pit beef, replete with a well-seasoned, charred crust and a rosy pink interior. The meat is shaved paper thin, piled onto a kaiser roll, topped with a horseradish-y mayo known as tiger sauce, and finally covered with sliced onions. We started by cutting a beefy top sirloin roast in half and slow-cooked the meat on the cool side of the grill—a foil shield provided maximum protection so the meat didn't dry out. Then for maximum char, we generously seared both pieces all over.

When shopping for the prepared horseradish, buy the brined (not creamy) variety and, if necessary, drain it.

Tiger Sauce
- ½ cup mayonnaise
- ½ cup hot prepared horseradish
- 1 teaspoon lemon juice
- 1 garlic clove, minced
- Table salt and pepper

Pit Beef
- 4 teaspoons kosher salt
- 1 tablespoon paprika
- 1 tablespoon pepper
- 1 teaspoon garlic powder
- 1 teaspoon dried oregano
- ¼ teaspoon cayenne pepper
- 1 (4- to 5-pound) boneless top sirloin roast, trimmed and halved crosswise
- 10 kaiser rolls
- 1 onion, sliced thin

1. For the Tiger Sauce Whisk mayonnaise, horseradish, lemon juice, and garlic together in bowl. Season with salt and pepper to taste. (Sauce can be refrigerated for up to 2 days.)

2. For the Pit Beef Combine salt, paprika, pepper, garlic powder, oregano, and cayenne in bowl. Pat roasts dry with paper towels and rub with 2 tablespoons seasoning mixture. Wrap meat tightly with plastic wrap and refrigerate for 6 to 24 hours.

3a. For a Charcoal Grill Open bottom vent halfway. Light large chimney starter filled with charcoal briquettes (6 quarts). When top coals are partially covered with ash, pour evenly over half of grill. Set cooking grate in place, cover, and open lid vent halfway. Heat grill until hot, about 5 minutes.

3b. For a Gas Grill Turn all burners to high, cover, and heat grill until hot, about 15 minutes. Leave primary burner on high and turn other burner(s) off.

4. Clean and oil cooking grate. Unwrap roasts and place end to end on long side of 18 by 12-inch sheet of aluminum foil. Loosely fold opposite long side of foil around top of roasts. Place meat on cool part of grill with foil-covered side closest to heat source. Cover (positioning lid vent over meat if using charcoal) and cook until meat registers 100 degrees, 45 minutes to 1 hour.

5. Transfer roasts to plate and discard foil. Turn all burners to high if using gas. If using charcoal, carefully remove cooking grate and light large chimney starter three-quarters filled with charcoal briquettes (4½ quarts). When top coals are partially covered with ash, pour evenly over spent coals. Set cooking grate in place and cover. Heat grill until hot, about 5 minutes.

6. Pat roasts dry with paper towels and rub with remaining spice mixture. Place meat on hot part of grill. Cook (covered if using gas), turning occasionally, until charred on all sides and meat registers 120 to 125 degrees (for medium-rare), 10 to 20 minutes. Transfer meat to carving board, tent loosely with foil, and let rest for 15 minutes. Slice meat thin against grain. Transfer sliced beef to rolls, top with onion slices, and drizzle with sauce. Serve.

Preventing Pit Beef from Drying Out
Even with indirect heat, the sides of the roasts closest to the fire can overcook. A simple foil shield protects them.

Philadelphia Pork Sandwiches

SERVES 8

WHY THIS RECIPE WORKS A Philadelphia roast pork sandwich is a glorious beast: thinly sliced seasoned pork; bitter, garlicky greens; a rich, herby jus; and a fluffy sub roll topped with sharp provolone cheese (and optional hot peppers). A long braise was essential for the pork butt to reach the point of fall-apart tenderness, followed by chilling to make the meat easy to slice thin. The pork juices combined with the braising broth to create a flavorful base for the jus, which we used to warm the pork back up. Garlicky broccoli rabe took just a few minutes to make. We piled the meat and greens on rolls, topped them off with provolone, and baked the sandwiches to melty perfection.

Plan ahead: You need to let the pork cool for 1 hour and then refrigerate it for at least 1 hour to make slicing easier. Sharp provolone is often labeled "provolone picante," but you can use standard deli provolone too. If you're using table salt, cut the amounts in half.

Philadelphia Pork Sandwiches

Pork and Jus
- 1 tablespoon kosher salt
- 2 teaspoons minced fresh rosemary
- 2 teaspoons dried thyme
- 2 teaspoons dried oregano
- 2 teaspoons fennel seeds
- 1 teaspoon red pepper flakes
- 1 (4-pound) boneless pork butt roast, trimmed
- 2 cups chicken broth, plus extra as needed
- 8 garlic cloves, peeled and smashed

Broccoli Rabe
- 2 tablespoons extra-virgin olive oil
- 3 garlic cloves, sliced thin
- 1 pound broccoli rabe, trimmed and cut into ½-inch pieces
- 2 teaspoons kosher salt
- Pinch red pepper flakes

Sandwiches
- 8 (8-inch) Italian sub rolls, split lengthwise
- 12 ounces sliced sharp provolone cheese

1. For the Pork and Jus Adjust oven rack to lower-middle position and heat oven to 300 degrees. Combine salt, rosemary, thyme, oregano, fennel seeds, and pepper flakes in bowl. Tie pork with kitchen twine at 1-inch intervals. Transfer pork to large Dutch oven and season all over with salt mixture. Pour broth around pork and add garlic to pot. Cover, transfer to oven, and cook until meat registers 190 degrees, 2½ to 3 hours.

2. Transfer pork to large plate. Transfer braising liquid to 4-cup liquid measuring cup; add extra broth, if necessary, to equal 3 cups. Let pork and liquid cool completely, about 1 hour. Cover and refrigerate both for at least 1 hour or up to 2 days.

3. For the Broccoli Rabe Heat oil and garlic in Dutch oven over medium heat until garlic is golden brown, 3 to 5 minutes. Add broccoli rabe, salt, and pepper flakes and cook, stirring occasionally, until tender, 4 to 6 minutes. Transfer to bowl.

4. About 20 minutes before serving, adjust oven rack to middle position and heat oven to 450 degrees. Remove twine and cut cooled pork in half lengthwise to make 2 even-size roasts. Position roasts cut side down and slice each crosswise as thin as possible.

5. Spoon solidified fat off cooled jus and discard. Transfer jus to Dutch oven and bring to boil over high heat. Reduce heat to low, add pork, cover, and cook until pork is heated through, about 3 minutes, tossing occasionally. Cover and keep warm.

6. For the Sandwiches Arrange rolls on 2 rimmed baking sheets (4 rolls per sheet). Divide provolone evenly among rolls. Bake, 1 sheet at a time, until cheese is melted and rolls are warmed, about 3 minutes. Using tongs, divide pork and broccoli rabe evenly among rolls (about 1 cup pork and ⅓ cup broccoli rabe per roll). Serve.

On the Road: Philly's Other Sandwich

If you're ordering the house special hot roast pork sandwich at John's Roast Pork in South Philadelphia, you don't have to wait in line; that deeply satisfying sandwich of roasted pork, braised spinach, and a noticeable kick of black and red peppers can be made in short order, and you're allowed to weave through the lunch-rush crowd and up to the counter. You can be out the door while the other guy is still getting yelled at for ordering his cheesesteak all wrong. ("American wit' extra" is the way to go.) At midday, John's is a noisy place, thanks to the yelling between all the staff jammed into a tiny shoebox of a building.

By contrast, the cavernous Reading Terminal Market across town delivers a much bigger, nearly overwhelming sensory experience. That's where you'll find Tommy DiNic's, a Reading Terminal Market standby since 1980. DiNic's draws a huge and reliable lunchtime crowd, weekdays and weekends alike. Cooks pile garlicky broccoli rabe atop the thin slices of seasoned pork, along with sharp provolone cheese. Fresh bread, crunchy on the outside and soft inside, soaks up the juices and keeps everything in place. Most of the time, anyway.

Slicing Thin for the Win

We found that the braised pork shoulder we use in this recipe is most tender when sliced very thin.

To make thin slicing easy, we chill the cooked roast for between 1 hour and 2 days and then cut it into two long, skinny halves. We then cut the halves crosswise into very thin slices that make easy-to-eat sandwiches.

Cuban Sandwiches

SERVES 4

WHY THIS RECIPE WORKS To make Tampa-style Cuban sandwiches that rival the prizewinners at the International Cuban Sandwich Festival, we prepared the Cuban bread and roast pork ourselves. For the filling, we built the sandwich in the traditional order: deli ham, roast pork, Genoa salami (a signature Tampa-only addition), Swiss cheese, and pickles. We swiped the mojo sauce from our roast pork onto the bottom slice of bread for extra complexity and brightness. A heavy Dutch oven weighed down the sandwiches and yielded a crispy edge.

We strongly prefer to use our Cuban Bread (page 239) for this recipe. But if you don't have the time to make it, you can use four 7- to 8-inch soft white Italian-style sub rolls or two 15-inch loaves of soft supermarket Italian or French bread. Do not use a thick-crusted rustic or artisan-style loaf or a baguette. To make slicing the Cuban Roast Pork (page 238) easier, be sure to chill it thoroughly beforehand. Mojo and mayonnaise aren't typical ingredients in Tampa-style Cuban sandwiches, but they make nice additions.

- 1 recipe Cuban Bread (page 239)
- ¼ cup mojo from Cuban Roast Pork with Mojo (optional) (page 238)
- ¼ cup mayonnaise (optional)
- 12 ounces thinly sliced deli ham
- 10 ounces thinly sliced Cuban roast pork from Cuban Roast Pork with Mojo (2 cups) (page 238)
- 3 ounces thinly sliced deli Genoa salami with peppercorns
- 6 ounces thinly sliced deli Swiss cheese
- 16 dill pickle chips
- ¼ cup yellow mustard
- 4 tablespoons unsalted butter, cut into 4 pieces, divided

1. Adjust oven rack to middle position and heat oven to 200 degrees. Set wire rack in rimmed baking sheet. Cut bread in half crosswise, then cut each piece in half horizontally.

2. Brush bread bottoms with mojo, if using, and spread with mayonnaise, if using. Layer on ham, followed by pork, salami, cheese, and pickles, overlapping and/or folding meats as needed to keep them from overhanging sides of bread. Spread mustard on bread tops. Cap sandwiches with bread tops.

FORK-IN-THE-ROAD FAVORITES   237

On the Road: Tampa

The annual Cuban Sandwich Festival, created by Victor Padilla and Jolie Gonzalez-Padilla, has become a massive two-day event that transforms Centennial Park in Tampa's Ybor City neighborhood with music, performances, and, in 2019, a winning attempt at a world record for the longest Cuban sandwich—183 feet.

Ybor City, most historians and other experts agree, is the birthplace of the Cuban sandwich, which reflects the Cuban, Italian, German, and Spanish influences present in Tampa.

The marquee event is a contest to crown the best Cuban sandwich maker in the world. Contestants like Iliana Cordero (below) often present twists on the theme to a strict panel of judges; for example, cooks from Miami may present sandwiches "Miami-style," in which the salami, essential in Tampa-style versions, is left off.

3. Melt 1 tablespoon butter in 12-inch nonstick skillet over medium-low heat. Place 2 sandwiches in skillet, right side up, in alternating directions, and spread far apart. Place heavy Dutch oven on top and cook until bottoms of sandwiches are uniformly golden brown and feel firm when tapped, 5 to 7 minutes, rotating sandwiches in skillet as needed. (You will need to flip sandwiches to tap them.)

4. Transfer sandwiches to cutting board. Melt 1 tablespoon butter in now-empty skillet. Return sandwiches to skillet toasted side up. Place Dutch oven on top and continue to cook until second side is uniformly golden brown and feels firm when tapped, 3 to 5 minutes longer.

5. Transfer toasted sandwiches to prepared wire rack and place in oven to keep warm. Wipe skillet clean with paper towels. Repeat with remaining 2 tablespoons butter and remaining 2 sandwiches. Cut sandwiches in half on steep diagonal and serve.

Cuban Roast Pork with Mojo
SERVES 6 TO 8

Avoid buying a boneless pork butt wrapped in netting; it will contain smaller, separate lobes of meat rather than one whole roast. The pork will take longer to cook in a stainless-steel pot than in an enameled cast-iron Dutch oven. If you're using a stainless-steel pot, place a sheet of aluminum foil over the pot before affixing the lid. If you plan to make Cuban sandwiches with the leftovers, it is best to slice only what you want to serve and then slice the chilled, leftover pork for the sandwiches. If using table salt, cut the amounts of salt in half.

Pork
- ⅓ cup kosher salt
- ⅓ cup packed light brown sugar
- 1 tablespoon lime zest (2 limes)
- 1 tablespoon orange zest
- 3 garlic cloves, minced
- 2 teaspoons ground cumin
- 2 teaspoons dried oregano
- ½ teaspoon red pepper flakes
- 1 (5-pound) boneless pork butt with fat cap

Mojo
- ⅓ cup extra-virgin olive oil
- 6 garlic cloves, minced
- ⅓ cup pineapple juice
- ⅓ cup orange juice
- ⅓ cup lime juice (3 limes)

Cuban Sandwiches

1 tablespoon yellow mustard
1¼ teaspoons ground cumin
1 teaspoon kosher salt
¾ teaspoon pepper
¾ teaspoon dried oregano
¼ teaspoon red pepper flakes
 Thinly sliced onion rounds

1. For the Pork Combine salt, sugar, lime zest, orange zest, garlic, cumin, oregano, and pepper flakes in bowl. Using sharp knife, trim fat cap on pork to ¼ inch. Cut 1-inch crosshatch pattern in fat cap.

2. Place pork on large double layer of plastic wrap. Sprinkle pork all over with salt mixture. Wrap pork tightly in plastic, place on plate, and refrigerate for at least 12 hours or up to 24 hours.

3. Adjust oven rack to middle position and heat oven to 325 degrees. Unwrap pork; transfer to Dutch oven, fat side up; and pour 2 cups water around pork. Cover, transfer to oven, and cook until meat registers 175 degrees in center, 2½ to 3 hours.

4. Uncover pork and continue to cook until meat registers 195 degrees in center and fork slips easily in and out of meat, 45 minutes to 1¾ hours longer. Transfer pork to carving board, tent with aluminum foil, and let rest for 45 minutes.

5. For the Mojo While pork is resting, heat oil and garlic in small saucepan over low heat, stirring often, until tiny bubbles appear and garlic is fragrant and straw-colored, 3 to 5 minutes. Let cool for at least 5 minutes. Whisk pineapple juice, orange juice, lime juice, mustard, cumin, salt, pepper, oregano, and pepper flakes into cooled garlic oil.

6. Slice pork as thin as possible (some meat may shred; this is OK) and transfer to serving platter. Serve with onion and mojo.

Cuban Bread
MAKES TWO 15-INCH LOAVES

Covering the bread with the disposable pan during baking traps steam to create a crispier crust. You can substitute shortening for the lard, if desired. We prefer the flavor that the overnight fermentation provides, but you can ferment the sponge for at least 1 hour or up to 4 hours at room temperature instead. Be gentle when slashing the shaped loaves or they will bake up wide and squat. As a table bread, these loaves are best eaten warm, but for Cuban sandwiches, we found that two-day-old bread is still acceptable.

Cuban Roast Pork: Keys to Success

We nailed down three keys to a flavorful, moist, sliceable roast pork.

1. For juicier pork, we use an overnight dry rub instead of a wet marinade to season it.

2. For tender meat with a burnished look, we first braise the pork in water, covered, to break down its tough connective tissue and collagen. We then roast it uncovered to caramelize its exterior.

3. A garnish of crisp raw onion helps cut through all the porky richness.

On the Road: La Segunda Bakery
La Segunda Bakery in Ybor City sold its first loaf in 1915. Today, they produce 20,000 loaves of Cuban bread daily. The massive operation lacks climate control, a challenge in Florida. "The bread takes on the personality of the weather—humidity and heat," says co-owner Copeland More. Bakers adjust the process based on the weather that day—the dough might move in and out of the refrigerator or spend extra time in the steam-fed proof box to account for the temperature.

Sponge
- ¼ cup water
- ¼ cup (1¼ ounces) all-purpose flour
- ½ teaspoon instant or rapid-rise yeast

Dough
- 3 cups (15 ounces) all-purpose flour
- 2 teaspoons instant or rapid-rise yeast
- 1½ teaspoons table salt
- 1 cup warm water (110 degrees)
- ¼ cup lard
- 1 (16 by 12-inch) rectangular disposable aluminum roasting pan

1. For the Sponge Whisk all ingredients with fork in liquid measuring cup until consistency of thin pancake batter. Cover with plastic wrap and refrigerate overnight (sponge will rise and collapse).

2. For the Dough Whisk flour, yeast, and salt together in bowl of stand mixer. Add warm water, lard, and sponge. Fit mixer with dough hook and mix on low speed until no dry flour remains, about 2 minutes, scraping down bowl as needed. Increase speed to medium and knead for 8 minutes. (Dough will be sticky and clear sides of bowl but still stick to bottom.)

3. Turn out dough onto lightly floured counter, sprinkle top with flour, and knead briefly to form smooth ball, about 30 seconds. Transfer dough to greased large bowl and turn to coat. Cover with plastic and let dough rise at room temperature until doubled in size, about 45 minutes.

4. Line rimless baking sheet with parchment paper. Turn out dough onto floured counter and cut into 2 equal pieces, about 14 ounces each.

5. Working with 1 piece of dough at a time, flatten into 10 by 6-inch rectangle with long side parallel to counter's edge. Fold top edge of rectangle down to midline, pressing to seal. Fold bottom edge of rectangle up to midline, pressing to seal. Fold dough in half so top and bottom edges meet; pinch seam and ends to seal. Flip dough seam side down and gently roll into 15-inch loaf with tapered ends.

6. Transfer loaf, seam side down, to 1 side of prepared sheet. Repeat shaping with second piece of dough and place about 3 inches from first loaf on other side of sheet. Cover loosely with plastic and let rise at room temperature until puffy, about 30 minutes. Adjust oven rack to middle position and heat oven to 450 degrees.

7. Using sharp paring knife in swift, fluid motion, make ⅛-inch-deep lengthwise slash along top of each loaf, starting and stopping about 1½ inches from ends. Cover loaves with inverted disposable pan. Bake for 20 minutes. Using tongs, remove disposable pan and continue to bake until loaves are light golden brown and centers register 210 degrees, 10 to 12 minutes longer.

8. Transfer loaves to wire rack and let cool for 30 minutes. Serve warm.

To Make Ahead Fully cooled loaves can be wrapped in aluminum foil and stored at room temperature for up to 2 days. Cooled bread can also be wrapped in plastic wrap, then in foil, and frozen for up to 1 month. Unwrap and warm before serving.

South Carolina Barbecue Hash

SERVES 8 TO 10

WHY THIS RECIPE WORKS Hard to find outside South Carolina, this regional favorite features ultratender shreds of pork stewed in a tangy barbecue sauce. The result is a comforting concoction somewhere on the spectrum between a stew and a gravy. For our version, we braised pork butt with chicken broth and chicken livers to give the dish a complex, savory boost. Yellow mustard, Worcestershire sauce, and hot sauce cut through the richness of the pork, contributing to a dish that's hard to beat served over white rice.

Instead of chopping the chicken livers by hand, you can use a food processor; it will take about six pulses to get them finely chopped.

- 3 pounds boneless pork butt roast, trimmed and cut into 1½-inch chunks
- 4 cups chicken broth
- 8 ounces chicken livers, trimmed and chopped fine
- 1 large onion, chopped coarse
- 6 scallions, cut into 1-inch pieces
- 3 garlic cloves, peeled
- 1 tablespoon pepper
- 2 teaspoons table salt
- ½ teaspoon cayenne pepper, plus extra for seasoning
- 1¼ cup yellow mustard
- ⅓ cup cider vinegar
- 3 tablespoons packed brown sugar
- 1 teaspoon hot sauce
- 1 teaspoon Worcestershire sauce
- Cooked white rice

1. Adjust oven rack to lower-middle position and heat oven to 300 degrees. Combine pork, broth, livers, onion, scallions, garlic, pepper, salt, and cayenne in Dutch oven. Bring to boil over high heat. Transfer to oven and cook, uncovered, until fork inserted into pork meets little resistance, 2 to 2½ hours.

2. Transfer pot to stovetop. Using potato masher, mash pork until finely shredded. Stir in mustard, vinegar, sugar, hot sauce, and Worcestershire. Bring to boil over medium-high heat. Reduce heat to medium-low and simmer until slightly thickened, about 10 minutes. Season with salt, pepper, and extra cayenne to taste. Serve over rice.

Cincinnati Chili

SERVES 6 TO 8

WHY THIS RECIPE WORKS Warm spices and unexpected garnishes lend Cincinnati chili recipes their unique flavors—but can sometimes muddle the dish. To re-create this Midwestern recipe in our own kitchen, we narrowed our ingredient list to four spices. Tomato paste added richness to our chili, while dark brown sugar gave it a sweet tang. Boiling the beef in water kept it tender during cooking—we cooked ours directly in our spices and liquid to infuse the meat with their intense flavor. Serving our chili over spaghetti, plus cheese, onions, red beans, and oyster crackers, gave us the true Cincinnati chili experience.

Use canned tomato sauce for this recipe—do not use jarred spaghetti sauce.

- 1 tablespoon vegetable oil
- 2 onions, chopped fine
- 2 tablespoons tomato paste
- 2 tablespoons chili powder
- 1 tablespoon dried oregano
- 1½ teaspoons ground cinnamon
- 1 garlic clove, minced
- Table salt and pepper
- ¼ teaspoon ground allspice
- 2 cups chicken broth
- 2 cups canned tomato sauce
- 2 tablespoons cider vinegar
- 2 teaspoons packed dark brown sugar
- 1½ pounds 85 percent lean ground beef

South Carolina Barbecue Hash

Cincinnati Chili

Five Ways to Cincinnati

Those in the know can order their chili without a second thought, but for the uninitiated, here's a quick guide to the five ways of Cincinnati chili. The chili is almost never served on its own (one-way). Just don't forget the oyster crackers!

TWO-WAY CHILI
Served over spaghetti

THREE-WAY CHILI
Served over spaghetti and topped with cheese

FOUR-WAY CHILI
Served over spaghetti and topped with onions and cheese

FIVE-WAY CHILI
Served over spaghetti and topped with onions, red beans, and cheese

---

1. Heat oil in Dutch oven over medium-high heat until shimmering. Cook onions until soft and browned around edges, about 8 minutes. Add tomato paste, chili powder, oregano, cinnamon, garlic, 1 teaspoon salt, ¾ teaspoon pepper, and allspice and cook until fragrant, about 1 minute. Stir in chicken broth, tomato sauce, vinegar, and sugar.

2. Add beef and stir to break up meat. Bring to boil, reduce heat to medium-low, and simmer until chili is deep brown and slightly thickened, 15 to 20 minutes. Season with salt to taste, and serve. (Chili can be refrigerated for up to 3 days or frozen for up to 2 months.)

Colorado Green Chili

SERVES 6

WHY THIS RECIPE WORKS This popular Southwestern dish boasts rich bites of pork in a sauce dominated by green chiles. For our version, we used a combination of Anaheim and jalapeño peppers. To achieve the cohesive flavor and mild vegetal taste that we liked, we used canned, diced tomatoes and more than 2 pounds of chiles, along with 3 pounds of boneless pork butt—our preferred cut for its rich meatiness. To reduce the hands-on time, we started the pork with water in a covered pan to render the fat, then let the even heat of the oven cook the chili. Adding the jalapeños just before serving gave a fresh hit of heat.

The chiles can be roasted and refrigerated up to 24 hours in advance.

- 3 pounds boneless pork butt roast, trimmed and cut into 1-inch pieces
  Table salt
- 2 pounds (10 to 12) Anaheim chiles, stemmed, halved lengthwise, and seeded
- 3 jalapeño chiles
- 1 (14.5-ounce) can diced tomatoes
- 1 tablespoon vegetable oil
- 2 onions, chopped fine
- 8 garlic cloves, minced
- 1 tablespoon ground cumin
- ¼ cup all-purpose flour
- 4 cups chicken broth
  Cayenne pepper
  Lime wedges

1. Combine pork, ½ cup water, and ½ teaspoon salt in Dutch oven over medium heat. Cover and cook for 20 minutes, stirring occasionally. Uncover, increase heat to medium-high, and continue to cook, stirring frequently, until liquid evaporates and pork browns in its own fat, 15 to 20 minutes. Transfer pork to bowl and set aside.

2. Meanwhile, adjust 1 oven rack to lowest position and second rack 6 inches from broiler element. Heat broiler. Line rimmed baking sheet with aluminum foil and spray with vegetable oil spray. Arrange Anaheims, skin side up, and jalapeños in single layer on prepared sheet. Place sheet on upper rack and broil until chiles are mostly blackened and soft, 15 to 20 minutes, rotating sheet and flipping only jalapeños halfway through broiling. Place Anaheims in large bowl and cover with plastic wrap; let cool for 5 minutes. Set aside jalapeños. Heat oven to 325 degrees.

Colorado Green Chili

Beef Yakamein (New Orleans Spicy Beef Noodle Soup)

SERVES 6

WHY THIS RECIPE WORKS Yakamein (loosely translated from Chinese as "an order of noodles") originated in Chinese American restaurants all across the United States. Thanks mainly to the efforts of chef Linda Green (aka the "Yakamein Lady"), a uniquely New Orleans version has become popular. For our version, we browned beef chuck-eye roast and aromatics (the "holy trinity" of onion, bell pepper, and celery) to create a flavorful fond. We then added broth and simmered the beef until it was meltingly tender. We ladled this Creole-seasoned broth over bowls of spaghetti, the chopped beef, hard-cooked eggs, and sliced scallions, finishing the soup with soy sauce and hot sauce.

Smaller chuck-eye roasts are sometimes sold prepackaged as chuck steak. If you can find only chuck roasts larger than 2 pounds, ask the butcher to cut a smaller roast for you or cut your own roast and freeze the remaining meat. Sriracha or Tabasco can be substituted for the Crystal Hot Sauce. We developed this recipe with Kikkoman Soy Sauce and Better Than Bouillon Roasted Beef Base. Monosodium glutamate is sold under the brand name Ac'cent. Look for it in the spice aisle next to the seasoning salts.

- 1 (2-pound) boneless beef chuck-eye roast, trimmed
- 2 teaspoons kosher salt
- 2 teaspoons pepper
- 2 tablespoons vegetable oil
- 1 onion, chopped
- 1 green bell pepper, stemmed, seeded, and chopped
- 1 celery rib, chopped
- 4 garlic cloves, minced
- 1 tablespoon Tony Chachere's Original Creole Seasoning
- 1 tablespoon sugar
- 1 teaspoon onion powder
- 1/2 teaspoon Ac'cent (optional)
- 8 cups beef broth
- 1/4 cup soy sauce, plus extra for serving
- 12 ounces spaghetti
- 3 hard-cooked large eggs, halved
- 6 scallions, sliced 1/4 inch thick
  Crystal Hot Sauce

---

3. Remove skins from Anaheims. Chop half of Anaheims into 1/2-inch pieces and transfer to bowl. Process remaining Anaheims in food processor until smooth, about 10 seconds; transfer to bowl with chopped Anaheims. Pulse tomatoes and their juice in now-empty food processor until coarsely ground, about 4 pulses.

4. Heat oil in now-empty Dutch oven over medium heat until shimmering. Add onions and cook until lightly browned, 5 to 7 minutes. Stir in garlic and cumin and cook until fragrant, about 30 seconds. Stir in flour and cook for 1 minute. Stir in broth, Anaheims, tomatoes, and pork with any accumulated juices and bring to simmer, scraping up any browned bits. Cover pot, transfer to lower oven rack, and cook until pork is tender, 1 to 1 1/4 hours.

5. Without peeling, stem and seed jalapeños and reserve seeds. Finely chop jalapeños and stir into chili. Season chili with salt, cayenne, and reserved jalapeño seeds to taste. Serve with lime wedges.

1. Pat beef dry with paper towels and sprinkle with salt and pepper. Heat oil in large Dutch oven over medium-high heat until shimmering. Add beef and cook until well browned on all sides, 8 to 12 minutes. Transfer beef to plate.

2. Add onion, bell pepper, and celery to fat left in pot and cook until softened, 5 to 7 minutes. Add garlic; Creole seasoning; sugar; onion powder; and Ac'cent, if using, and cook until fragrant, about 1 minute. Stir in broth and soy sauce, scraping up any browned bits. Return beef to pot and bring to boil over high heat. Cover; reduce heat to low; and simmer until beef is tender, 1½ to 2 hours.

3. Transfer beef to cutting board and let cool until easy to handle, at least 20 minutes. Use wide spoon to skim excess fat from broth. Set colander over large bowl. Strain broth through colander, pressing on solids to extract all liquid. Discard solids in colander. Return broth to pot; cover and keep warm over low heat.

4. Meanwhile, bring 3 quarts water to boil in large saucepan. Add pasta and cook until fully tender. Drain pasta and return it to saucepan. Cover and set aside.

5. Using chef's knife, chop beef into approximate ¾-inch pieces. Divide pasta evenly among 6 serving bowls. Divide beef, eggs, and scallions evenly among serving bowls on top of pasta. Ladle hot broth into serving bowls to cover pasta (about 1½ cups each). Serve, passing hot sauce and extra soy sauce separately.

Beef Yakamein (New Orleans Spicy Beef Noodle Soup)

Natchitoches Meat Pies

Natchitoches Meat Pies

MAKES 16 PIES

WHY THIS RECIPE WORKS The Natchitoches meat pie is one of the official state foods of Louisiana. It originated in the Louisiana city of Natchitoches, which was named after the indigenous Natchitoches people. Similar to Latin American empanadas, these deep-fried hand pies are filled with savory ground meat and spices. For the filling, we used equal parts ground beef and pork along with the classic Creole combination of onions, green bell peppers, and a pinch of cayenne for heat. Chicken broth and flour made the filling cohesive, and scallions added freshness. Using chicken broth rather than milk in the dough gave the crust a subtle savory flavor. After a few minutes in hot oil, they emerged with a crisp, flaky crust and piping-hot filling.

You can make the dough and the filling up to 24 hours ahead and refrigerate them separately. You can also shape and fill the pies, refrigerating them for up to 24 hours before frying. Use a Dutch oven that holds 6 quarts or more for this recipe.

Filling

- 5 teaspoons vegetable oil, divided
- ¾ pound 85 percent lean ground beef
- ¾ pound ground pork
- Table salt and pepper
- 1 onion, chopped fine
- 1 green bell pepper, stemmed, seeded, and minced
- 6 scallions, white parts minced, green parts sliced thin
- 3 garlic cloves, minced
- ¼ teaspoon cayenne pepper
- 2 tablespoons all-purpose flour
- 1 cup chicken broth

Dough

- 4 cups (20 ounces) all-purpose flour
- 2 teaspoons table salt
- 1 teaspoon baking powder
- 8 tablespoons vegetable shortening, cut into ½-inch pieces
- 1 cup chicken broth
- 2 large eggs, lightly beaten
- 1 quart vegetable oil for frying

1. For the Filling Heat 2 teaspoons oil in 12-inch skillet over medium-high heat until just smoking. Add beef, pork, 1 teaspoon salt, and ½ teaspoon pepper and cook, breaking up pieces with spoon, until no longer pink, 8 to 10 minutes. Transfer meat to bowl.

2. Add remaining 1 tablespoon oil to now-empty skillet and heat over medium-high heat until shimmering. Add onion, bell pepper, scallion whites, ½ teaspoon salt, and ½ teaspoon pepper and cook until vegetables are just starting to brown, 3 to 5 minutes. Stir in garlic and cayenne and cook until fragrant, about 30 seconds.

3. Return meat and any accumulated juices to skillet with vegetables. Sprinkle flour over meat and cook, stirring constantly, until evenly coated, about 1 minute. Add broth, bring to boil, and cook until slightly thickened, about 3 minutes. Transfer filling to bowl and stir in scallion greens. Refrigerate until completely cool, about 1 hour. (Filling can be refrigerated for up to 24 hours.)

4. For the Dough Process flour, salt, and baking powder in food processor until combined, about 3 seconds. Add shortening and pulse until mixture resembles coarse cornmeal, 6 to 8 pulses. Add broth and eggs and pulse until dough just comes together, about 5 pulses. Transfer dough to lightly floured counter and knead until dough forms smooth ball, about 20 seconds. Divide dough into 16 equal pieces. (Dough can be covered and refrigerated for up to 24 hours.)

5. Line rimmed baking sheet with parchment paper. Working with 1 piece of dough at a time, roll into 6-inch circle on lightly floured counter. Place ¼ cup filling in center of dough round. Brush edges of dough with water and fold dough over filling. Press to seal, trim any ragged edges, and crimp edges with tines of fork. Transfer to prepared sheet. (Filled pies can be covered and refrigerated for up to 24 hours.)

6. Adjust oven rack to middle position and heat oven to 200 degrees. Set wire rack in second rimmed baking sheet. Add oil to large Dutch oven until it measures about ¾ inch deep and heat over medium-high heat to 350 degrees. Place 4 pies in oil and fry until golden brown, 3 to 5 minutes per side, using slotted spatula or spider to flip. Adjust burner, if necessary, to maintain oil temperature between 325 and 350 degrees. Transfer pies to prepared wire rack and place in oven to keep warm. Return oil to 350 degrees and repeat with remaining pies. Serve.

Delta Hot Tamales

SERVES 6 TO 8

WHY THIS RECIPE WORKS Hot tamales—rich, spicy meat wrapped in flavorful corn dough—are a favorite in the Mississippi Delta. A bit of this cornmeal mixture stirred into the uncooked ground beef kept the filling moist, and baking soda was the trick for a more tender bite. We used butter instead of the traditional lard with coarsely ground cornmeal for a more balanced taste. We cooked the tamales in groups

Cooking with Corn Husks

Cooking the tamales in corn husks—which are available in most supermarkets near the dried chiles—adds a subtle depth of flavor. Working with the husks is actually quite easy, as they become pliable when soaked in hot water.

FORK-IN-THE-ROAD FAVORITES 245

of six for more stability in the pot and made a spicy, glazy sauce with the seasoned stewing liquid and a cornstarch slurry. This was as close as we could come to being in the Delta without a plane ticket.

Use a saucepan that holds 4 quarts or more, with at least 5-inch sides. Corn husks can be found in the international aisle of most grocery stores.

24	corn husks
1½	tablespoons chili powder
1	tablespoon paprika
1	tablespoon table salt
2	teaspoons ground cumin
2	teaspoons sugar
¾	teaspoon pepper
¾	teaspoon cayenne pepper
2½	cups (12½ ounces) yellow cornmeal
1	tablespoon baking powder
12	tablespoons unsalted butter, cut into 12 pieces
½	teaspoon baking soda
1	pound 85 percent lean ground beef
2	garlic cloves, minced
2	tablespoons cornstarch combined with 2 tablespoons cold water

Delta Hot Tamales

1. Place husks in large bowl and cover with hot water; soak until pliable, about 30 minutes. Combine chili powder, paprika, salt, cumin, sugar, pepper, and cayenne in bowl.

2. Pulse cornmeal and baking powder in food processor until combined, about 3 pulses. Add butter and 1½ tablespoons spice mixture and pulse to chop butter into small pieces, about 8 pulses. Add 1¼ cups water and process until dough forms, about 30 seconds. Reserve ½ cup cornmeal mixture. Divide remaining cornmeal mixture into 24 equal portions, about 1½ tablespoons each, and place on plate.

3. Dissolve baking soda in 2 tablespoons water in large bowl. Add beef, garlic, reserved ½ cup cornmeal mixture, and 1½ tablespoons spice mixture and knead with your hands until thoroughly combined. Divide meat mixture into 24 equal portions, about 1½ tablespoons each, and place on plate.

4. Remove husks from water and pat dry with dish towel. Working with 1 husk at a time, lay husk on counter, smooth side up, with long side parallel to counter edge and wide end oriented toward right. Using small offset spatula, spread 1 portion of cornmeal mixture in 3½-inch square over lower right corner of husk, flush to bottom edge but leaving ¼-inch border on right edge.

5. Place 1 portion of meat mixture in log across center of cornmeal (end to end), parallel to long side of husk. Roll husk away from you and over meat mixture so cornmeal mixture surrounds meat and forms cylinder; continue rolling to complete tamale. Fold tapered end (left side) of tamale up leaving top open. Using scissors, trim tapered end of tamale to align with filled end (if tapered end hangs over). Set tamales aside seam side down.

6. Stack tamales on their sides in groups of 6 and tie into bundles with kitchen twine. Add remaining 2 tablespoons spice mixture to large saucepan. Stand tamales, open ends up, in pot (walls of pot should clear tops of tamales). Add about 5½ cups water to pot to come within 1 inch of tops of tamales, being careful not to pour water into tamales.

7. Bring tamales to boil. Cover, reduce heat to low to maintain gentle simmer, and cook until tamales are firm and beginning to pull away from husks, about 30 minutes. Using tongs and slotted spoon, carefully transfer tamales to serving platter and remove twine.

8. Return liquid to simmer over medium heat. Whisk in cornstarch slurry and cook until slightly thickened, about 1 minute. Serve sauce with tamales.

Cajun Rice Dressing

SERVES 8 TO 10

WHY THIS RECIPE WORKS We first encountered cajun rice dressing—an intensely flavorful side dish of rice and ground meat—at the Cochon de Lait Festival in Mansura, Louisiana. We began our dressing by sautéing the holy trinity of Cajun and Creole cooking (onions, celery, and green peppers). A 2:1 ratio of ground pork to chopped chicken livers provided a restrained savory boost. We browned the meat to develop a flavorful fond and then deglazed it with chicken broth, ensuring that the rice would soak it up.

Two cups of uncooked long-grain white rice will yield about 6 cups once cooked. You can find chicken livers in the refrigerated meat section of your supermarket or at your local butcher shop. If you prefer, you can use a food processor to chop the chicken livers; it will take about six pulses to finely chop them. For a spicier dish, use the larger amount of cayenne pepper.

- 6 tablespoons unsalted butter, divided
- 3 slices bacon, chopped
- 2 green bell peppers, stemmed, seeded, and chopped fine
- 2 onions, chopped fine
- 1 celery rib, chopped fine
- 12 scallions, cut into 1/2-inch pieces, divided
- 4 garlic cloves, minced
- 1 tablespoon chopped fresh thyme
- 2 teaspoons table salt, divided
- 1 3/4 teaspoons pepper, divided
- 1 pound ground pork
- 8 ounces chicken livers, trimmed and chopped fine
- 1 tablespoon paprika
- 1 1/2 teaspoons granulated garlic
- 1/2 teaspoon celery salt
- 1/4–1/2 teaspoon cayenne pepper
- 3 cups chicken broth
- 6 cups cooked long-grain white rice
- Hot sauce

1. Melt 4 tablespoons butter in Dutch oven over medium-high heat. Add bacon and cook until almost crispy, about 3 minutes.

Cajun Rice Dressing

On the Road: Bayou Bash

On the second day of the Cochon de Lait Festival in Mansura, Louisiana, among the sea of Cajun cooks is a group of men wielding stainless-steel canoe paddles over a gigantic iron kettle. Jimmy Armand is focused on tending to a mixture of ground meat, vegetables, and rice that is heavily perfumed with bacon grease and pungent with pork liver—the foundation for Cajun rice dressing. He seems to be in charge of the operation and explains, "All them ingredients are having a marriage right now."

Armand says that the mixture, which he calls "yum-yum sauce," needs to be in perfect balance before the rice is stirred in. He offers us what he calls a "pocket sandwich," spooning some of the "yum-yum" onto a slice of white bread and folding it in half. He looks us over and we nod in approval. Armand smiles. "Yum-yum?" It certainly is.

Hoppin' John

2. Add bell peppers, onions, celery, half of scallions, garlic, thyme, ¾ teaspoon salt, and 1 teaspoon pepper and cook until vegetables have softened, about 7 minutes, stirring occasionally.

3. Add pork, chicken livers, paprika, granulated garlic, celery salt, cayenne, ¾ teaspoon salt, ½ teaspoon pepper, and remaining 2 tablespoons butter and cook, breaking up meat with spoon, until mixture begins to fry in its own fat and fond develops on bottom of pot, 12 to 15 minutes, stirring occasionally.

4. Stir in broth, scraping up any browned bits. Stir in remaining scallions and bring to boil. Reduce heat to medium-low and simmer until slightly reduced, about 15 minutes.

5. Off heat, add rice, remaining ½ teaspoon salt, and remaining ¼ teaspoon pepper and stir until thoroughly combined. Season with salt and pepper to taste. Serve with hot sauce.

Hoppin' John

SERVES 4 TO 6

WHY THIS RECIPE WORKS We visited Ms. Emily Meggett at her Edisto Island, South Carolina, home and cooked through a recipe based on the hoppin' John recipe in her cookbook, *Gullah Geechee Home Cooking: Recipes from the Matriarch of Edisto Island* (2022). This recipe is inspired by that experience. We opted to use Sea Island red peas here, as they are considered the traditional choice for hoppin' John. We simmered the peas with water and a split ham hock, then drained the peas and reserved their cooking liquid and the pieces of ham hock to use in the finished dish. We browned salt pork and combined it with long-grain rice to season the rice and infuse it with meaty flavor. We then added granulated garlic, onion powder, the peas, reserved cooking liquid, and the ham hocks to the pot so that everything could cook together. .

We split the ham hock in half so that it cooks through at about the same rate as the peas. We enjoy adding the optional smoky pieces of ham hock to our Hoppin' John. If you prefer your rice and peas with less meat, feel free to leave it out. Note that not all salt pork is sold with its skin on.

Peas

- 1 cup Sea Island red peas
- 1 smoked ham hock, split in half vertically along bone
- 1 tablespoon table salt

St. Louis–Style Pizza

Hoppin' John

- 6 ounces salt pork, skin removed, rinsed, patted dry, and cut into ¾-inch pieces
- ¼ cup vegetable oil or lard
- 1 cup chopped onion
- 3 scallions, sliced ½ inch thick
- 1½ cups long-grain or Carolina Gold rice, unrinsed
- 1 teaspoon table salt
- ¾ teaspoon pepper
- ¾ teaspoon granulated garlic
- ½ teaspoon onion powder

1. For the Peas Place peas in medium bowl and cover with water. Slosh peas around with your hand to knock off loose dirt. Let peas settle, then pour off excess water along with any floating peas; repeat rinsing and pouring off excess water until no peas float.

2. Combine rinsed peas, 4 quarts water, ham hock, and salt in Dutch oven. Bring to boil over high heat. Reduce to medium-low; cover; and simmer until peas are tender, 50 minutes to 1 hour.

3. Reserve 2¼ cups pea cooking liquid and transfer ham hock pieces to plate to cool. Drain peas in colander in sink. (Cooked peas and liquid can be refrigerated separately for up to 24 hours or frozen for up to 1 month. Defrost before proceeding with recipe.) When cool enough to handle, chop ham hock into ½-inch pieces and reserve ¾ cup for hoppin' John, if desired (reserve remaining ham for another use or discard).

4. For the Hoppin' John Combine salt pork and oil in large saucepan. Cover and cook over medium heat until pork is evenly browned, 10 to 12 minutes, stirring occasionally and being mindful of splatter. (Pork will initially stick to bottom of pot but will eventually release as it browns.)

5. Add onion and scallions to salt pork and cook until softened, about 3 minutes. Stir in rice until grains are evenly coated with oil and cook, stirring often, until edges of rice are translucent, about 2 minutes. Stir in salt; pepper; granulated garlic; onion powder; cooked peas; reserved pea cooking liquid; and chopped ham hock, if using, and bring to simmer. Once simmering, cover pot with sheet of aluminum foil, then cover with lid. Reduce heat to low and cook for 20 minutes without removing lid.

6. Off heat, let hoppin' John sit, covered, for 10 minutes. Fluff rice with carving fork. Transfer to shallow serving dish. Serve.

On the Road: Edisto Island

At 90 years old, Ms. Emily was the undisputed queen of Edisto Island, South Carolina, a place she called home all her life. She often drove around the island handing out meals to friends and those suffering from illness or financial hardship. At Christmas she dropped off lima beans to islanders she called her "little people." When she brought her car to the mechanic, the trunk was filled with hot meals, and in return she was charged nothing for the repairs. She insisted that there is something special about Edisto Island. "Across the [McKinley] bridge is a little bit of heaven. Everybody here loves everybody."

The hoppin' John she made was the best any of us had ever tasted—rich pork, sweet onion, and earthy peas nestled among fluffy rice grains. It was hearty enough on its own, but Ms. Emily served it to us alongside cabbage and braised chicken, as well as a batch of fried chicken she made amid all the other cooking. She seemed unstoppable. When she was done feeding us, Ms. Emily headed outside to plant okra seeds in her garden.

Ms. Emily Meggett passed away in April 2023 at the age of 90.

St. Louis–Style Pizza

MAKES TWO 12-INCH PIZZAS

WHY THIS RECIPE WORKS St. Louis–style pizza is uniquely its own category with barely-there thin crust, sweet sauce, and melty Provel cheese. Adding cornstarch to the dough absorbed moisture and allowed the crust to crisp in a conventional oven. We doctored a simple pizza sauce by adding sugar, tomato paste, dried oregano, and fresh basil. The fresh herb wasn't typical, but it gave the pizza a flavorful lift. Smoky, melty Provel cheese was difficult to find outside the St. Louis area, so we crafted a respectable substitute with American cheese, Monterey Jack, and liquid smoke.

If you can find Provel cheese, use 10 ounces in place of the American cheese, Monterey Jack cheese, and liquid smoke.

Sauce and Cheeses
- 1 (8-ounce) can tomato sauce
- 3 tablespoons tomato paste
- 2 tablespoons chopped fresh basil
- 1 tablespoon sugar
- 2 teaspoons dried oregano
- 8 ounces white American cheese, shredded (2 cups)
- 2 ounces Monterey Jack cheese, shredded (½ cup)
- 3 drops liquid smoke

Dough
- 2 cups (10 ounces) all-purpose flour
- 2 tablespoons cornstarch
- 2 teaspoons sugar
- 1 teaspoon baking powder
- 1 teaspoon table salt
- ½ cup plus 2 tablespoons water
- 2 tablespoons extra-virgin olive oil

1. For the Sauce and Cheeses Whisk together tomato sauce, tomato paste, basil, sugar, and oregano in small bowl; set aside. Toss cheeses with liquid smoke in medium bowl; set aside.

2. For the Dough Combine flour, cornstarch, sugar, baking powder, and salt in large bowl. Combine water and olive oil in liquid measuring cup. Stir water mixture into flour mixture until dough starts to come together. Turn dough onto lightly floured surface and knead 3 or 4 times, until cohesive.

3. Adjust oven rack to lower-middle position, place baking stone (or inverted baking sheet) on rack, and heat oven to 475 degrees. Divide dough into 2 equal pieces. Working with 1 piece of dough at a time, press into small circle and transfer to parchment paper dusted lightly with flour. Using rolling pin, roll and stretch dough to form 12-inch circle, rotating parchment as needed. Lift parchment and pizza off work surface onto inverted baking sheet.

4. Top each piece of dough with half of sauce and half of cheese. Carefully pull parchment paper and pizza off baking sheet onto hot baking stone. Bake until underside is golden brown and cheese is completely melted, 9 to 12 minutes. Remove pizza and parchment from oven. Transfer pizza to wire rack and let cool briefly. Assemble and bake second pizza. Cut into 2-inch squares. Serve.

To Make Ahead The dough can be made in advance. At end of step 2, tightly wrap ball of dough in plastic wrap and refrigerate for up to 2 days.

Chicago Thin-Crust Pizza
MAKES TWO 12-INCH PIZZAS

WHY THIS RECIPE WORKS Chicago thin-crust—sometimes called "tavern"—pizza is the slimmer, crunchier sibling of the city's famous deep-dish version, with a lightly sweet sauce and spotty-brown cheese reaching all the way to its charred edges. Since this pizza's success rests on its snappy crust (similar to St. Louis–style) we used a food processor to ensure the dough came together quickly, minimizing gluten development. After a 2- to 2½-hour rise, we rolled out the dough and slathered it with a no-cook tomato sauce, homemade Italian sausage, and shredded mozzarella, slid it onto a preheated baking stone, and baked it until the edges were crisp.

Using cold water keeps the dough from overheating in the food processor. A baking peel is the best tool for moving the pizza in and out of the oven, but you can also use a rimless baking sheet. You can swap the sweet Italian sausage for 12 ounces of homemade Easy Sweet Italian Sausage (pages 251–252), crumbled.

Pizza
- 2½ cups (12½ ounces) all-purpose flour
- 2 teaspoons sugar
- 1½ teaspoons instant or rapid-rise yeast
- 1 teaspoon table salt
- ¾ cup plus 2 tablespoons cold water
- 2 tablespoons extra-virgin olive oil
- Cornmeal
- 12 ounces sweet Italian sausage, casings removed
- 12 ounces whole-milk mozzarella cheese, shredded (3 cups)
- ½ teaspoon dried oregano

Sauce
- 1 (8-ounce) can tomato sauce
- 1 tablespoon tomato paste
- 2 teaspoons sugar
- ½ teaspoon Italian seasoning
- ½ teaspoon fennel seeds

1. For the Pizza Process flour, sugar, yeast, and salt in food processor until combined, about 3 seconds. With processor running, slowly add cold water and oil and process until dough forms sticky ball that clears sides of bowl, 30 to 60 seconds.

2. Transfer dough to lightly oiled counter and knead until smooth, about 1 minute. Shape dough into tight ball and place in greased bowl. Cover bowl with plastic wrap and let dough rise at room temperature until almost doubled in size, 2 to 2½ hours. One hour before baking, adjust oven rack to lowest position, set baking stone on rack, and heat oven to 500 degrees.

3. For the Sauce Whisk all ingredients together in bowl. (Sauce can be refrigerated for up to 2 days.)

4. Transfer dough to lightly floured counter, divide in half, and gently shape each half into ball. Return 1 dough ball to bowl and cover with plastic. Coat remaining dough ball lightly with flour and gently flatten into 8-inch disk using your fingertips. Using rolling pin, roll dough into 12-inch circle, dusting dough lightly with flour as needed. (If dough springs back during rolling, let rest for 10 minutes before rolling again.)

5. Sprinkle pizza peel with cornmeal. Transfer dough to prepared pizza peel and carefully stretch to return to 12-inch circle. Using back of spoon or ladle, spread scant ½ cup sauce in thin layer over surface of dough, leaving ⅛-inch border around edge. Pinch 6 ounces sausage into approximate dime-size pieces and evenly distribute over sauce. Sprinkle 1½ cups mozzarella evenly over sausage to edge of pie. Sprinkle ¼ teaspoon oregano over top.

6. Carefully slide pizza onto baking stone and bake until cheese is well browned and edges of pizza are crisp and dark, 10 to 14 minutes. Slide pizza peel underneath pizza and remove pizza from oven. Slide pizza onto cutting board and let cool for 5 minutes. Repeat with remaining dough, sauce, sausage, mozzarella, and oregano. Cut pizzas into 2- to 3-inch squares and serve.

Chicago Thin-Crust Pizza

Easy Sweet Italian Sausage

MAKES ABOUT 1½ POUNDS

WHY THIS RECIPE WORKS For an easy, all-purpose Italian sausage—the perfect topping for our Chicago Thin-Crust Pizza—we started with coarsely ground pork. We toasted fennel seeds to enhance their flavor, crushed them to break them down slightly, and added them to the pork with sugar for sweetness, black and red peppers for spice, and garlic for pungency. Using a stand mixer to combine it all helped extract more sticky proteins to bind the sausage, and letting it chill helped balance and round out the flavors.

Easy Sweet Italian Sausage

Let the toasted fennel seeds cool completely before cracking them in step 1. A rasp-style grater makes quick work of turning the garlic into a paste. If you can't find coarsely ground pork (you may have to ask your butcher), you can substitute finer, more commonly available regular-grind pork, but the texture of the sausage will be denser. If desired, you can grill the patties over a medium-hot fire until they're lightly charred and register 160 degrees, about 4 minutes per side.

- 1 tablespoon fennel seeds, toasted
- 1½ pounds coarsely ground pork
- 1½ teaspoons sugar
- 1½ teaspoons salt
- 1 large garlic clove, minced to paste
- ¾ teaspoon pepper
- ¼ teaspoon dried oregano
- ¼ teaspoon red pepper flakes
- 2 teaspoons vegetable oil, divided

1. Place fennel seeds in small zipper-lock bag and seal bag. Using rolling pin, roll over seeds 2 or 3 times to coarsely crack.

2. Combine pork, sugar, salt, garlic, pepper, oregano, pepper flakes, and fennel seeds in bowl of stand mixer. Fit mixer with paddle and mix on low speed until mixture is thoroughly combined and looks sticky, 60 to 90 seconds, scraping down bowl as needed. Cover and refrigerate mixture for at least 1 hour to allow flavors to meld before using. (Sausage mixture can be refrigerated for up to 2 days.)

3. Using your wet hands and working with ½ cup sausage at a time, form six 4-inch-diameter patties, about ½ inch thick. Heat 1 teaspoon oil in 12-inch nonstick skillet over medium heat until shimmering. Add 3 patties to skillet and cook until browned on both sides and meat registers 160 degrees, about 4 minutes per side. Transfer patties to serving platter and tent with aluminum foil. Repeat with remaining 1 teaspoon oil and remaining 3 patties. Transfer to platter and serve.

New England Bar Pizza

SERVES 4

WHY THIS RECIPE WORKS Popular on Massachusetts's South Shore, bar pizza is baked in well-seasoned rimmed pans, with the dough forming a thin lip up the sides. The crust is tender yet crispy. To replicate this style of pizza, we used all-purpose flour rather than the usual bread flour for the dough. We created the distinctive edges by rolling the dough thin and baking the pies in cake pans, pressing the dough up the sides of the pan. Brushing the edges with tomato sauce and cheese gave us the "laced" edges that bar pizzas are known for. A mixture of cheddar and mozzarella best imitated the classic version's distinct tangy flavors.

Clean the food processor in between making the dough and the pizza sauce. You will have some sauce left over; reserve it for another use. Use sharp cheddar cheese, not extra-sharp (which makes the pizzas too greasy).

Dough

- 1⅔ cups (8⅓ ounces) all-purpose flour
- 1 tablespoon sugar
- 1 teaspoon instant or rapid-rise yeast
- ⅔ cup water
- 1½ teaspoons extra-virgin olive oil
- ¾ teaspoon table salt

Sauce

- 1 (14.5-ounce) can diced tomatoes
- 1 teaspoon extra-virgin olive oil
- ½ teaspoon dried oregano
- ½ teaspoon sugar
- ¼ teaspoon table salt
- ⅛ teaspoon pepper
- ⅛ teaspoon red pepper flakes

> **Mix It Up**
>
> Using a stand mixer to incorporate the seasonings into the pork increases the contact between the salt and the meat and aids in extracting more of the sticky proteins in the meat that help bind the sausage.
>
>
>
> **COARSELY GROUND PORK**
> Makes the best-textured sausage
>
> **REGULAR-GRIND PORK**
> Makes acceptable but slightly dense sausage

Topping

- 4 ounces sharp cheddar cheese, shredded (1 cup)
- 4 ounces whole-milk mozzarella, shredded (1 cup)
- 1 tablespoon extra-virgin olive oil

1. For the Dough Process flour, sugar, and yeast in food processor until combined, about 3 seconds. With processor running, slowly add water; process dough until just combined and no dry flour remains, about 10 seconds. Let dough stand for 10 minutes. Add oil and salt to dough and process until dough forms satiny, sticky ball that clears sides of workbowl, 30 to 60 seconds.

2. Transfer dough to lightly oiled counter and knead until smooth, about 1 minute. Shape dough into tight ball and place in greased bowl. Cover with plastic wrap and let rise at room temperature until almost doubled in size, 2 to 2½ hours.

3. For the Sauce Process all ingredients in clean, dry food processor until smooth, about 30 seconds; set sauce aside. (Sauce can be refrigerated for up to 2 days or frozen for up to 1 month.)

4. For the Topping One hour before baking, adjust oven rack to lowest position, set baking stone or steel on rack, and heat oven to 450 degrees. Combine cheddar and mozzarella in bowl. Using pastry brush, grease bottom and sides of 2 dark-colored 9-inch round cake pans with 1½ teaspoons oil each.

5. Transfer dough to lightly floured counter, divide in half, and shape into balls. Gently flatten 1 dough ball into 6-inch disk using your fingertips. Using rolling pin, roll disk into 10-inch round. Transfer dough to prepared pan and press into corners, forcing ¼-inch lip of dough up sides of pan. Repeat with remaining dough ball.

6. Spread ⅓ cup sauce in thin layer over entire surface of 1 dough. Using pastry brush, brush sauce over lip of dough. Sprinkle 1 cup cheese mixture evenly over pizza, including lip. Repeat with remaining dough, ⅓ cup sauce, and remaining 1 cup cheese mixture.

7. Bake until crust is browned and cheese is bubbly and beginning to brown, about 12 to 14 minutes, switching and rotating pans halfway through baking. To remove pizzas from pans, run offset spatula along top edge of pizza crust. Once loosened, slide spatula underneath pizza and slide pizza onto wire rack. Let cool for 5 minutes. Slice and serve.

New England Bar Pizza

Detroit-Style Pizza

SERVES 4

WHY THIS RECIPE WORKS Our challenge in creating a recipe for Detroit pizza—a crispy, buttery pizza from the Motor City—was figuring out how to mimic the tender crumb, melty brick cheese (which can be found only in Michigan), and vibrant sauce. The rich, hydrated dough required a 15-minute rest and a 2-hour rise to produce the tender, buttery crust we were after. We topped the dough with handfuls of shredded Monterey Jack cheese, the only acceptable substitute we found for the brick cheese typically used. Dried herbs, sugar, and canned tomatoes gave our sauce deep flavor and thick texture.

When kneading the dough on medium speed, the mixer can wobble and move on the counter. Place a towel or shelf liner under the mixer to keep it in place, and watch it closely. To add more toppings, such as pepperoni or sausage, to your pizza, press them into the dough before adding the cheese.

Detroit Style Pizza

Philly Tomato Pie

Pizza
- 1 tablespoon extra-virgin olive oil
- 2¼ cups (11¼ ounces) all-purpose flour
- 1½ teaspoons instant or rapid-rise yeast
- 1½ teaspoons sugar
- 1 cup water, room temperature
- ¾ teaspoon table salt
- 10 ounces Monterey Jack cheese, shredded (2½ cups)

Sauce
- 1 cup canned crushed tomatoes
- 1 tablespoon extra-virgin olive oil
- 1 tablespoon chopped fresh basil
- 1 garlic clove, minced
- 1 teaspoon dried oregano
- 1 teaspoon dried basil
- ½ teaspoon sugar
- ½ teaspoon pepper
- ¼ teaspoon table salt

1. For the Pizza Spray 13 by 9-inch nonstick baking pan with vegetable oil spray, then brush bottom and sides of pan with oil. Using stand mixer fitted with dough hook, mix flour, yeast, and sugar on low speed until combined, about 10 seconds. With mixer running, slowly add room-temperature water and mix until dough forms and no dry flour remains, about 2 minutes, scraping down bowl as needed. Cover with plastic wrap and let stand for 10 minutes.

2. Add salt to bowl and knead on medium speed until dough forms satiny, sticky ball that clears sides of bowl, 6 to 8 minutes. Turn dough onto lightly floured counter and knead until smooth, about 1 minute.

3. Transfer dough to prepared pan, cover with plastic, and let rest for 15 minutes. Using your well-oiled hands, press dough into corners of pan. (If dough resists stretching, let it rest for another 10 minutes before trying again to stretch.) Cover with plastic and let dough rise at room temperature until nearly tripled in volume and large bubbles form, 2 to 3 hours. Adjust oven rack to lowest position and heat oven to 500 degrees.

4. For the Sauce Combine all ingredients in bowl. (Sauce can be refrigerated for up to 24 hours.)

5. Sprinkle Monterey Jack evenly over dough to edges of pan. Spoon three 1-inch-wide strips of sauce, using ⅓ cup sauce for each, over cheese evenly down length of pan.

6. Bake until cheese is bubbly and browned, about 15 minutes. Let pizza cool in pan on wire rack for 5 minutes. Run knife around edge of pan to loosen pizza. Using spatula, slide pizza onto cutting board. Cut into 8 pieces and serve.

> **On the Road: It Couldn't Have Happened Anywhere But in Detroit**
>
> As a child in Sicily, Connie Piccinato grew up eating squared-off wedges of focaccia studded with leftover meats. As an adult in 1946, while working as a waitress at Buddy's in Detroit, she found herself craving the pies of her youth. But she faced a dilemma. Food-grade rectangular pizza pans simply didn't exist at the time, so "square pizza" wasn't known in the States. But Piccinato found inspiration in a discarded rectangular "blue steel" pan used for collecting errant nuts and bolts in the string of automobile-related factories along Six Mile Road. She and Buddy's owner, August "Gus" Guerra, pressed a batch of dough into one of the pans, nudging it into the sharp corners; topped it with cheese and sauce; and baked it off. The square pizza was a hit, and it gave Buddy's, originally a "blind pig" speakeasy selling contraband booze during Prohibition, a new lease on life.

Philly Tomato Pie

SERVES 4

WHY THIS RECIPE WORKS This South Philadelphia specialty boasts a tender yet chewy crust topped with a bright, savory tomato sauce. We achieved the signature chewy-soft crust by using less water by weight in proportion to the weight of the flour. This yielded fine holes and a pleasantly spongy chew. Letting the dough rise twice—pressing it into the pan in between—gave it maximum yeasty flavor. For the invigorating, sweet-tart, herby sauce, we started with a savory base of onion and garlic and then added a hefty amount of dried oregano along with red pepper flakes for kick. One can of tomato sauce provided just the right tomato flavor and texture, and a tablespoon of sugar contributed the sauce's signature sweetness.

When kneading the dough on medium speed, the mixer may wobble and shimmy. To keep it in place, position a dish towel or shelf liner beneath the mixer and keep a close watch on it. You will need a nonstick metal baking pan for this recipe.

Dough
- 2½ cups (12½ ounces) all-purpose flour
- ¾ teaspoon instant or rapid-rise yeast
- 1 cup water, room temperature
- 1½ tablespoons extra-virgin olive oil
- 1½ teaspoons table salt

Sauce
- 2 tablespoons extra-virgin olive oil
- ¼ cup finely chopped onion
- 2 garlic cloves, minced
- 2 teaspoons dried oregano
- ¼ teaspoon red pepper flakes
- 1 (15-ounce) can tomato sauce
- 1 tablespoon sugar

1. For the Dough Spray 13 by 9-inch nonstick baking pan with vegetable oil spray. Using stand mixer fitted with dough hook, mix flour and yeast on medium speed until combined, about 10 seconds. With mixer running, slowly add room-temperature water and oil and mix until dough forms and no dry flour remains, about 30 seconds, scraping down bowl as needed. Turn off mixer, cover bowl with plastic wrap, and let dough stand for 10 minutes.

2. Add salt to dough and knead on medium speed until dough is satiny and sticky and clears sides of bowl but still sticks to bottom, 6 to 8 minutes. Transfer dough to prepared pan, cover pan tightly with plastic, and let dough rise at room temperature until doubled in size, about 1½ hours.

3. For the Sauce While dough rises, heat oil in small saucepan over medium heat until shimmering. Add onion and cook, stirring occasionally, until softened and lightly browned, 3 to 5 minutes. Add garlic, oregano, and pepper flakes and cook until fragrant, about 30 seconds. Add tomato sauce and sugar and bring to boil. Reduce heat to medium-low and simmer until sauce is slightly thickened and measures about 1¼ cups, about 10 minutes. Let sauce cool completely.

4. Using your well-oiled hands, press dough into corners of pan. (If dough resists stretching, let it rest for 10 minutes before trying to stretch again.) Cover pan tightly with plastic and let dough rise at room temperature until doubled in size, about 1½ hours. Adjust oven rack to upper-middle position and heat oven to 450 degrees.

5. Spread sauce evenly over dough, leaving ½- to ¼-inch border. Bake until edges are light golden brown and sauce has reduced in spots, about 20 minutes. Let tomato pie cool in pan on wire rack for 5 minutes. Run knife around edge of pan to loosen pie. Using spatula, slide pie onto cutting board. Cut into 8 pieces and serve.

> ### Wait on the Salt
> To produce a chewy pizza crust, we use a technique called autolyse; this simply entails mixing the flour, yeast, and liquid but withholding the salt for a short period (10 minutes in this case). Salt slows flour's absorption of water, so delaying the addition of salt allows the flour to soak up liquid and become more thoroughly hydrated. More hydration means more gluten formation, which leads to a chewier finished crust—exactly what we were after here.

Pepperoni French Bread Pizza

SERVES 4

WHY THIS RECIPE WORKS Soft supermarket French bread stands in as a hearty, crusty alternative for pizza dough in this speedy pizza recipe. We upped the flavor ante by giving the loaf a garlic-bread treatment before topping it, brushing the cut side with a spicy garlic butter and the crusty side with olive oil and then baking it until toasty brown and crispy. A stir-together mix of crushed tomatoes, olive oil, Italian seasoning, and sugar made a bold and bright pizza sauce. Using both mozzarella and Parmesan gave us the perfect balance of melty creaminess and nutty depth. We topped these pizzas simply with a classic smattering of sliced pepperoni.

A 24 by 4-inch loaf of supermarket French bread, which has a soft, thin crust and fine crumb, works best here. If you can't find soft French bread, you can substitute one and a half 18-inch baguettes, though the crust will be slightly tougher. Cut the baguettes into six equal pieces, and distribute the toppings evenly.

Pizza
- 1 (24 by 4-inch) loaf soft French bread
- 1 tablespoon extra-virgin olive oil
- 8 tablespoons unsalted butter, melted
- 2 teaspoons granulated garlic
- ½ teaspoon table salt
- ¼ teaspoon red pepper flakes
- 12 ounces mozzarella cheese, shredded (3 cups)
- 1 ounce Parmesan cheese, grated (½ cup)
- 2 ounces thinly sliced pepperoni

Sauce
- 1½ cups canned crushed tomatoes
- 1 tablespoon extra-virgin olive oil
- 1½ teaspoons Italian seasoning
- ½ teaspoon sugar
- ½ teaspoon table salt
- ½ teaspoon pepper

1. For the Pizza Adjust oven rack to upper-middle position and heat oven to 450 degrees. Line rimmed baking sheet with aluminum foil. Cut bread in half crosswise, then halve each piece horizontally to create 4 equal pieces. Arrange pieces cut side down on prepared sheet. Brush crust with oil.

2. Combine melted butter, granulated garlic, salt, and pepper flakes in bowl. Flip bread cut side up and brush cut side evenly with melted butter mixture. Bake, cut side up, until browned around edges, about 5 minutes.

3. For the Sauce Meanwhile, combine all ingredients in bowl. (Sauce can be refrigerated for up to 24 hours.)

4. Spread sauce evenly over toasted bread, then top with mozzarella, followed by Parmesan and pepperoni (in that order). Bake until cheese is melted and spotty brown, about 15 minutes. Let pizza cool for 5 minutes. Serve.

Supreme French Bread Pizza
Decrease pepperoni to 1½ ounces. Add 2½ ounces sweet Italian sausage, casings removed, meat pinched into ½-inch pieces; ½ cup thinly sliced red onion; ½ cup thinly sliced green bell pepper, cut into 2-inch lengths; and ½ cup sliced black olives with pepperoni.

Pineapple and Bacon French Bread Pizza
Substitute ¾ cup crumbled cooked bacon and ¾ cup canned pineapple tidbits, drained and patted dry, for pepperoni.

Potato-Cheddar Pierogi

MAKES ABOUT 30 PIEROGI

WHY THIS RECIPE WORKS Our take on the Polish dumplings known as pierogi combined potatoes and cheese tucked into a tender dough. We began by thoroughly combining boiled russet potatoes, shredded cheddar cheese, and butter in a stand mixer. The heat from the potatoes melted the butter and cheese for an even consistency. We created a pliable, rollable dough using higher-protein bread flour, sour cream, and egg. We stamped out rounds with a biscuit cutter and sealed in the filling by pinching the edges together before boiling the pierogi. A caramelized onion topping mixed with the dumplings made for a traditional sweet-savory finish.

When rolling the dough in step 4, be sure not to dust the top surface with too much flour, as that will prevent the edges from forming a tight seal when pinched.

Filling
- 1 pound russet potatoes, peeled and sliced ½ inch thick
- Table salt and pepper
- 4 ounces sharp cheddar cheese, shredded (1 cup)
- 2 tablespoons unsalted butter

Dough
- 2½ cups (13¾ ounces) bread flour
- 1 teaspoon baking powder
- Table salt
- 1 cup sour cream
- 1 large egg plus 1 large yolk

Topping
- 4 tablespoons unsalted butter
- 1 large onion, chopped fine
- ½ teaspoon table salt

1. For the Filling Combine potatoes and 1 tablespoon salt in large saucepan and cover with water by 1 inch. Bring to boil over medium-high heat; reduce heat to medium and cook at vigorous simmer until potatoes are very tender, about 15 minutes.

Pepperoni French Bread Pizza

Potato-Cheddar Pierogi

2. Drain potatoes in colander. While still hot, combine potatoes, cheddar, butter, ½ teaspoon salt, and ½ teaspoon pepper in bowl of stand mixer. Fit mixer with paddle and mix on medium speed until potatoes are smooth and all ingredients are fully combined, about 1 minute. Transfer filling to 8-inch square baking dish and refrigerate until fully chilled, about 30 minutes, or cover with plastic wrap and refrigerate for up to 24 hours.

3. For the Dough Whisk flour, baking powder, and ½ teaspoon salt together in clean bowl of stand mixer. Add sour cream and egg and yolk. Fit mixer with dough hook and knead on medium-high speed for 8 minutes (dough will be smooth and elastic). Transfer dough to floured bowl, cover with plastic, and refrigerate until ready to assemble.

4. Line rimmed baking sheet with parchment paper and dust with flour. Roll dough on lightly floured counter into 18-inch circle, about ⅛ inch thick. Using 3-inch biscuit cutter, cut 20 to 24 circles from dough. Place 1 tablespoon chilled filling in center of each dough round. Fold dough over filling to create half-moon shape and pinch edges firmly to seal. Transfer to prepared sheet.

5. Gather dough scraps and reroll to ⅛-inch thickness. Cut 6 to 10 more circles from dough and repeat with remaining filling. (It may be necessary to reroll dough once more to yield 30 pierogi.) Cover pierogi with plastic and refrigerate until ready to cook, up to 3 hours.

6. For the Topping Melt butter in 12-inch skillet over medium-low heat. Add onion and salt and cook until onion is caramelized, 15 to 20 minutes. Remove skillet from heat and set aside.

7. Bring 4 quarts water to boil in Dutch oven. Add 1 tablespoon salt and half of pierogi to boiling water and cook until tender, about 5 minutes. Using spider or slotted spoon, remove pierogi from water and transfer to skillet with caramelized onion. Return water to boil, cook remaining pierogi, and transfer to skillet with first batch.

8. Add 2 tablespoons cooking water to pierogi in skillet. Cook over medium-low heat, stirring gently, until onion mixture is warmed through and adhered to pierogi. Transfer to platter and serve.

To Make Ahead Uncooked pierogi can be frozen for several weeks. After sealing pierogi in step 4, freeze them on baking sheet, about 3 hours. Transfer frozen pierogi to zipper-lock freezer bag. When ready to cook, extend boiling time in step 7 to about 7 minutes.

North Carolina Cheese Biscuits

North Carolina Cheese Biscuits

MAKES 6 BISCUITS

WHY THIS RECIPE WORKS These buttermilk biscuits found around Rocky Mount, North Carolina, are big, golden, and stuffed with gooey cheese. Regional recipes call for hoop cheese, a yellow cheese common in North Carolina but hard to find elsewhere. We settled on yellow sharp cheddar cheese for its tangy flavor and meltability. We found, while trying to stuff a loose handful of shredded cheese into a wad of wet dough, that pressing the cheese into firmly packed balls made assembly easier and didn't sacrifice meltability. Baking the wet dough in a cake pan produced a higher rise and a more tender, fluffy texture due to the increase in trapped steam.

The biscuit dough will be wet and soft. Keep your hands well floured and don't be afraid to sprinkle extra flour on the biscuits to keep them from sticking. To prevent overbrowning, use a light-colored cake pan.

- 8 ounces yellow sharp cheddar cheese, shredded (2 cups)
- 3½ cups (17½ ounces) all-purpose flour, divided
- 1 tablespoon sugar
- 1 tablespoon baking powder
- ½ teaspoon baking soda
- 1 teaspoon table salt
- 4 tablespoons unsalted butter, cut into ¼-inch pieces and chilled, plus 2 tablespoons melted
- 1½ cups buttermilk

1. Adjust oven rack to middle position and heat oven to 500 degrees. Grease light-colored 9-inch round cake pan. Working with ⅓ cup cheese, use your hands to squeeze cheese tightly into firm ball. Repeat with remaining cheese to form 5 more balls; set cheese balls aside.

2. Pulse 2½ cups flour, sugar, baking powder, baking soda, and salt in food processor until combined, about 6 pulses. Add chilled butter and pulse until mixture resembles pebbly, coarse cornmeal, 8 to 10 pulses. Transfer mixture to large bowl. Stir in buttermilk until just combined. (Dough will be very wet and slightly lumpy.)

3. Spread remaining 1 cup flour in rimmed baking sheet. Using greased ½-cup dry measuring cup, transfer 6 portions of dough to prepared sheet. Dust top of each portion with flour from sheet.

4. Using your well-floured hands, gently flatten 1 portion of dough into 3½-inch circle and coat with flour. Pick up dough and place 1 cheese ball in center. Gently pull edges of dough over cheese to enclose and pinch together to seal. Shake off excess flour and transfer to prepared pan. Repeat with remaining dough and cheese, placing 5 biscuits around edge of pan and one in center. (Biscuits will be soft and will spread slightly as they sit.)

5. Brush biscuit tops with melted butter. Bake for 5 minutes, then reduce oven temperature to 450 degrees. Continue to bake until biscuits are deep golden brown, 15 to 20 minutes longer. Let biscuits cool in pan for 2 minutes, then invert onto plate. Break biscuits apart and turn right side up. Let cool for 5 minutes; serve warm.

Filling the Biscuits with Cheese

1. Using your hands, squeeze ⅓ cup shredded cheese into firm ball. Repeat to form 5 more balls.

2. Using greased ½-cup dry measuring cup, transfer 6 portions of dough to prepared sheet. Dust top of each with flour.

3. Flatten each dough ball into 3½-inch circle and coat with flour. Enclose cheese ball in center of dough and pinch to seal.

Crunchy Potato Wedges

SERVES 6

WHY THIS RECIPE WORKS We wanted a recipe for fast food–style crunchy potato wedges that we could prepare at home. Microwaving the potatoes in a tightly covered bowl precooked them perfectly. For the coating, adding baking soda to buttermilk and replacing some of the flour with cornstarch resulted in crunchy, deep-golden-brown wedges. Finally, seasoning our crunchy potato wedges with a spice blend as they precooked in the microwave, then tossing the wedges in the seasonings when they came out of the oil, produced potatoes that were flavored from the inside out.

If you don't have buttermilk, substitute 1 cup milk mixed with 1 tablespoon lemon juice. Let the mixture sit 15 minutes before using. Use a Dutch oven that holds 6 quarts or more.

FORK-IN-THE-ROAD FAVORITES 259

4	teaspoons kosher salt
2	teaspoons onion powder
1	teaspoon garlic powder
1	teaspoon dried oregano
¾	teaspoon cayenne pepper
½	teaspoon pepper
3	large russet potatoes (about 1¾ pounds), cut into ¼-inch wedges
¼	cup peanut or vegetable oil, plus 3 quarts for frying
1½	cups all-purpose flour
½	cup cornstarch
1	cup buttermilk
½	teaspoon baking soda

1. Combine salt, onion powder, garlic powder, oregano, cayenne, and pepper in small bowl.

2. Toss potato wedges with 4 teaspoons spice mixture and ¼ cup oil in large bowl; cover. Microwave until potatoes are tender but not falling apart, 7 to 9 minutes, shaking bowl to redistribute potatoes halfway through cooking. Uncover and drain potatoes. Arrange potatoes on rimmed baking sheet and let cool until potatoes firm up, about 10 minutes. (Potatoes can be held at room temperature for up to 2 hours.)

3. Set wire rack in rimmed baking sheet and line second baking sheet with triple layer of paper towels. Add remaining 3 quarts oil to large Dutch oven until it measures about 2 inches deep and heat over medium-high heat to 340 degrees. Meanwhile, combine flour and cornstarch in medium bowl and whisk buttermilk and baking soda together in large bowl. Working in 2 batches, dredge potato wedges in flour mixture, shaking off excess. Dip in buttermilk mixture, allowing excess to drip back into bowl, then coat again in flour mixture. Shake off excess and place on wire rack. (Potatoes can be coated up to 30 minutes in advance.)

4. When oil is ready, add half of coated wedges and fry until deep golden brown, 4 to 6 minutes. Transfer wedges to large bowl and toss with 1 teaspoon spice mixture. Drain wedges on paper towel–lined baking sheet. Return oil to 340 degrees and repeat with second batch of wedges. Serve with extra spice mixture.

To Make Ahead Our Crunchy Potato Wedges freeze very well. Follow steps 1 through 4, frying each batch of wedges until they are light golden brown, 2 to 3 minutes. Do not toss with seasoning, and drain and cool potatoes completely on baking sheet lined with paper towels. Freeze wedges on baking sheet until completely frozen, about 2 hours, then transfer potatoes to zipper-lock bag for up to 2 months. When ready to eat, heat 3 quarts oil to 340 degrees and cook in 2 batches until deep golden brown, about 3 minutes. Toss with seasonings, drain, and serve.

Creamy BBQ Sauce
MAKES 1¼ CUPS

Combine ¾ cup mayonnaise, ¼ cup barbecue sauce, 3 tablespoons cider vinegar, 1 minced garlic clove, ¼ teaspoon pepper, and ⅛ teaspoon salt in small bowl.

Buffalo Blue Cheese Sauce
MAKES 1½ CUPS

Combine ¾ cup mayonnaise, ¼ cup blue cheese salad dressing, 3 tablespoons hot sauce, 1 minced garlic clove, ¼ teaspoon pepper, and ⅛ teaspoon celery salt in small bowl.

Curried Chutney Sauce
MAKES 1¼ CUPS

Combine ¾ cup mayonnaise, ¼ cup yogurt, ¼ cup minced fresh cilantro, 3 tablespoons mango chutney, 2 teaspoons curry powder, ¼ teaspoon pepper, and ⅛ teaspoon salt in small bowl.

Crispy Potato Tots
MAKES 48 POTATO TOTS

WHY THIS RECIPE WORKS Let's face it, frozen potato tots don't live up to our childhood memories. And many recipes simply mix coarsely ground potato with flour and egg, which fry up into raw, dense nuggets. We found that parcooking the chopped potato in the microwave was a step in the right direction, but the tots were still too heavy. Reducing the flour and omitting the egg helped, but they were still not light and fluffy. To minimize the gluey texture of potato starch, we tried processing the potatoes with water. Perfection. This step rinsed off the excess starch, and a small amount of salt in the mixture kept the interior downy white.

If any large pieces of potato remain after processing, chop them coarsely by hand. To make handling the uncooked tots easier, use a wet knife blade and wet hands. Once the tots are added to the hot oil, they may stick together; resist the temptation to stir and break them apart until after they have browned and set. You will need at least a 6-quart Dutch oven for this recipe.

- 2¼ teaspoons table salt
- 2½ pounds russet potatoes, peeled and cut into 1½-inch pieces
- 1½ tablespoons all-purpose flour
- ½ teaspoon pepper
- 1 quart peanut or vegetable oil for frying

1. Whisk 1 cup water and salt together in bowl until salt dissolves. Pulse potatoes and salt water in food processor until coarsely ground, 10 to 12 pulses, stirring occasionally. Drain mixture in fine-mesh strainer, pressing potatoes with rubber spatula until dry (liquid should measure about 1½ cups); discard liquid. Transfer potatoes to bowl and microwave, uncovered, until dry and sticky, 8 to 10 minutes, stirring halfway through cooking.

2. Stir flour and pepper into potatoes. Spread potato mixture into thin layer over large sheet of aluminum foil and let cool for 10 minutes. Push potatoes to center of foil and place foil and potatoes in 8-inch square baking pan. Push foil into corners and up sides of pan, smoothing it flush to pan. Press potato mixture tightly and evenly into pan. Freeze, uncovered, until firm, about 30 minutes.

3. Meanwhile, adjust oven rack to middle position and heat oven to 200 degrees. Set wire rack in rimmed baking sheet. Add oil to large Dutch oven until it measures about ¾ inch deep and heat over high heat until 375 degrees. Using foil overhang, lift potatoes from pan and cut into 48 pieces (5 cuts in 1 direction and 7 in other). Fry half of potato tots until golden brown and crisp, 5 to 7 minutes, stirring only after they are browned and set. Transfer to prepared baking sheet and place in oven. Return oil to 375 degrees and repeat with remaining potato tots. Serve.

To Make Ahead Let fried potato tots cool, transfer to zipper-lock bag, and freeze for up to 1 month. To serve, adjust oven rack to middle position and heat oven to 400 degrees. Place potato tots on rimmed baking sheet and bake until heated through, 12 to 15 minutes.

Crispy Potato Tots for a Crowd
Double all ingredients for Crispy Potato Tots. Process and drain potato mixture in 2 batches. Microwave entire potato mixture for 12 to 14 minutes, stirring halfway through cooking. Spread potato mixture over large sheet of foil to cool and press into 13 by 9-inch baking pan. After freezing, cut potato rectangle in half crosswise before cutting into potato tots per recipe. Fry in 4 batches.

Crunchy Potato Wedges

Crispy Potato Tots

Bacon-Ranch Potato Tots

Stir 1 tablespoon cider vinegar into potatoes after microwaving. Add 4 slices finely chopped cooked bacon, 1 teaspoon onion powder, ½ teaspoon garlic powder, and ½ teaspoon dried dill to potatoes with flour in step 2.

Parmesan-Rosemary Potato Tots

Stir 2 minced garlic cloves into drained potatoes before microwaving. Add 1 cup grated Parmesan cheese and 2 tablespoons minced fresh rosemary to potatoes with flour in step 2.

Southwestern Potato Tots

Add ½ cup shredded smoked gouda cheese, 3 tablespoons minced fresh cilantro, and 2 tablespoons minced jarred jalapeños to potatoes with flour in step 2.

Gobi Manchurian

SERVES 4

Gobi Manchurian

WHY THIS RECIPE WORKS Gobi Manchurian, a multinational dish with roots in the Chinese immigrant communities of Kolkata, India, features cauliflower florets that are battered and fried until crisp and then served with or tossed in a spicy, umami-rich sauce. For our "wet-style" version, we coated cauliflower florets in a light batter (made of water, cornstarch, flour, baking powder, and salt) that was wonderfully crisp when fried and could hold up to being dressed in a thick and flavorful sauce.

A whole 2½-pound head of cauliflower should yield 1 pound of florets. You can also buy precut florets if available. Use a Dutch oven that holds 6 quarts or more.

Sauce
- ¼ cup ketchup
- 3 tablespoons water
- 2 tablespoons soy sauce
- 1 tablespoon chili-garlic sauce
- 2 teaspoons lime juice, plus lime wedges for serving
- ¾ teaspoon pepper
- ½ teaspoon ground cumin
- 2 tablespoons vegetable oil
- 3 scallions, white and green parts separated and sliced thin
- 1 tablespoon grated fresh ginger
- 3 garlic cloves, minced

Cauliflower
- 1 cup water
- ⅔ cup cornstarch
- ⅔ cup all-purpose flour
- 1 teaspoon table salt
- 1 teaspoon baking powder
- 1 pound (1½-inch) cauliflower florets (4 cups)
- 2 quarts peanut or vegetable oil for frying

1. For the Sauce Combine ketchup, water, soy sauce, chili-garlic sauce, lime juice, pepper, and cumin in bowl. Heat oil in small saucepan over medium-high heat until shimmering. Add scallion whites, ginger, and garlic and cook, stirring frequently, until fragrant, about 1½ minutes. Stir in ketchup mixture and bring to simmer, scraping up any bits of ginger mixture from bottom of saucepan. Transfer sauce to clean large bowl.

2. For the Cauliflower Whisk water, cornstarch, flour, salt, and baking powder in large bowl until smooth. Add cauliflower florets to batter and toss with rubber spatula to evenly coat; set aside.

3. Line baking sheet with triple layer of paper towels. Add oil to large Dutch oven until it measures about 1½ inches deep and heat over medium-high heat to 375 degrees.

4. Using tongs, add florets to hot oil 1 piece at a time. Cook, stirring occasionally to prevent florets from sticking, until coating is firm and very lightly golden, about 5 minutes. (Adjust burner, if necessary, to maintain oil temperature between 300 and 325 degrees.) Using spider skimmer, transfer florets to prepared sheet. Let sit for 5 minutes.

5. Add cauliflower and scallion greens to bowl with sauce and toss to combine. Transfer to platter and serve with lime wedges.

Texas Potato Pancakes

SERVES 4 TO 6

WHY THIS RECIPE WORKS The Texas version of Kartoffelpuffer (German potato pancakes) boasts fluffy interiors with crunchy exteriors. When developing our recipe, we found that the potatoes' water content inhibited crispiness. Wringing out the shredded potatoes in a dish towel helped, but not enough. Using russet potatoes and some flour turned our pancakes from squishy to crisp. In Texas, the pancakes can be 10 inches across, but we found that smaller cakes were easier to flip and less likely to fall apart. Traditionally served with sour cream or applesauce, these crunchy cakes are just as good on their own.

Shred the potatoes and onion on the large holes of a box grater or with the shredding disk of a food processor. The potato shreds may take on a red hue if left to sit out for a few minutes before cooking. This does not affect their flavor.

- 2   pounds russet potatoes, peeled and shredded
- ½   cup all-purpose flour
- 2   large eggs, lightly beaten
- ⅓   cup shredded onion
-     Table salt and pepper
- 1¼ cups vegetable oil, plus extra as needed
-     Sour cream
-     Applesauce

1. Adjust oven rack to middle position and heat oven to 200 degrees. Set wire rack in rimmed baking sheet and place in oven. Line large plate with triple layer of paper towels.

2. Place half of potatoes in center of clean dish towel. Gather ends together and twist tightly to squeeze out as much liquid as possible. Transfer to large bowl and repeat with remaining potatoes.

3. Stir flour, eggs, onion, and 1¼ teaspoons salt into potatoes until combined. Heat oil in 12-inch skillet over medium heat to 325 degrees. Using ⅓-cup dry measuring cup, place 3 portions of potato mixture in skillet and press into 4-inch disks with back of spoon.

4. Cook until deep golden brown, 3 to 4 minutes per side, carefully flipping pancakes with 2 spatulas. Transfer pancakes to paper towel–lined plate to drain, about 15 seconds per side, then transfer to prepared wire rack in oven.

5. Repeat with remaining potato mixture in 3 batches, stirring mixture, if necessary, to recombine and adding extra oil to skillet as needed to maintain ¼-inch depth. Season pancakes with salt and pepper to taste. Serve immediately, passing sour cream and applesauce separately.

Crispy Vegetable Fritters

MAKES 12 FRITTERS; SERVES 4 TO 6

WHY THIS RECIPE WORKS Making vegetable fritters can transform imperfect produce into something that's crisp, delicious, and fun to eat. For a smooth batter that was light enough to not overpower the vegetables, we swapped tap water for seltzer, whisking it into equal parts cornstarch and flour (the perfect ratio for tender, not chewy, fritters), and added baking powder for leavening. Shallow-frying the fritters yielded crispy morsels bursting with flavor, and a quick dipping sauce added a final finish.

You can use tap water instead of seltzer, but the fritters won't be as light. Shred the zucchini and carrot on the large shredding disk of a food processor or the large holes of a box grater. Do not add corn; it pops in the hot oil. We season the batter just before frying because the salt causes the vegetables to shed water that thins the batter. Hold cooked fritters on a wire rack in a 200-degree oven.

Sauce
- ⅓   cup mayonnaise
- 1   tablespoon prepared horseradish, drained
- 1   tablespoon lemon juice
-     Table salt and pepper

Fritters

- ½ cup (2½ ounces) plus 1 tablespoon all-purpose flour
- ½ cup (2 ounces) plus 1 tablespoon cornstarch
- ½ teaspoon baking powder
- ¾ cup seltzer
- 1 cup thinly sliced red bell pepper
- 1 cup shredded zucchini
- ½ cup shredded carrot
- ½ cup thinly sliced onion
- ½ cup fresh cilantro leaves
- 2 scallions, cut into ½-inch pieces
- 1 garlic clove, minced
- 1½ cups vegetable oil
- Table salt and pepper

1. For the Sauce Whisk mayonnaise, horseradish, and lemon juice together in bowl and season with salt and pepper to taste; set aside.

2. For the Fritters Set wire rack in rimmed baking sheet and line half of rack with triple layer of paper towels. Whisk flour, cornstarch, and baking powder together in large bowl. Add seltzer and whisk until smooth, thick batter forms. Add bell pepper, zucchini, carrot, onion, cilantro, scallions, and garlic to batter and stir until vegetables are evenly coated.

3. Add oil to 12-inch nonstick skillet until it measures about ¼ inch deep and heat over medium-high heat to 350 degrees. Stir ½ teaspoon salt and ½ teaspoon pepper into vegetable batter.

4. Using ¼-cup dry measuring cup, place 1 portion of vegetable batter in skillet; immediately spread to 4-inch diameter with spoon so top sits slightly below surface of oil. Repeat 3 times, so you have 4 fritters in skillet. Make sure vegetables do not mound in centers of fritters. Adjust burner, if necessary, to maintain oil temperature between 300 and 325 degrees.

5. Cook on first side until deep golden brown on bottom, 2 to 4 minutes. Using 2 spatulas, flip and continue to cook until golden brown on second side, 2 to 4 minutes longer, moving fritters around skillet as needed for even browning.

6. When second side of fritters is golden brown, turn off burner so oil doesn't overheat. Transfer fritters to paper towel–lined side of prepared rack to drain for about 15 seconds per side, then move to unlined side of rack and season with salt.

7. Return oil to 350 degrees and repeat with remaining vegetable batter in 2 batches, stirring to recombine batter as needed. Serve with sauce.

Ultimate Extra-Crunchy Onion Rings

SERVES 6 TO 8

WHY THIS RECIPE WORKS For onion rings with the crunchiest, craggiest crusts and fully cooked onions, we double-breaded thick rings in a mixture of buttermilk, seasoned flour, and cornstarch. To streamline the process, we tossed all the buttermilk-soaked onions with the flour mixture in a large paper bag. A double-bag setup ensured no blowouts or leaking. We used plenty of oil and stirred gently during frying for even cooking. With the generous breading, the rings could stay in the hot oil longer, ensuring that the onions became fully tender. These crunchy rings paired perfectly with a stir-together horseradish sauce.

Look for large onions (about 1 pound each) for this recipe. Be sure to use a double-bagged large paper shopping bag in step 2. Note that the onions are double-breaded, so don't discard the flour bag after the first shake. Buy refrigerated prepared horseradish, not the shelf-stable kind, which contains preservatives and additives.

Sauce

- ½ cup mayonnaise
- 2 tablespoons prepared horseradish
- 2 tablespoons Dijon mustard
- ¼ teaspoon cayenne pepper
- ¼ teaspoon pepper

Onion Rings

- 4 cups buttermilk
- 4 cups all-purpose flour
- ½ cup cornstarch
- 2 tablespoons Lawry's Seasoned Table salt
- 2 tablespoons baking powder
- 2 teaspoons pepper
- ½ teaspoon table salt
- 2 large onions (1 pound each), peeled
- 3 quarts peanut or vegetable oil for frying

1. For the Sauce Whisk all ingredients together in bowl; set aside.

2. For the Onion Rings Adjust oven rack to middle position and heat oven to 200 degrees. Add buttermilk to large bowl. Combine flour, cornstarch, seasoned salt, baking powder, pepper, and salt in second large bowl. Transfer flour mixture to double-bagged large paper shopping bag. Slice onions crosswise into ½-inch-thick rounds. Reserve onion slices smaller than 2 inches in diameter for another use.

3. Separate remaining onion rounds into rings. Toss one-third of onion rings in buttermilk to thoroughly coat. Shake off excess buttermilk and transfer onion rings to flour mixture in bag. Repeat with remaining onion rings in 2 batches. Roll top of bag to seal and shake vigorously to coat onion rings in flour mixture. Remove onion rings from bag, shaking off excess flour mixture, and transfer to rimmed baking sheet.

4. Transfer one-third of onion rings back to buttermilk and toss to thoroughly coat. Shake off excess buttermilk and transfer onion rings back to flour mixture in bag. Repeat with remaining onion rings in 2 batches. Roll top of bag to seal and shake vigorously to coat onion rings in flour mixture. Pour contents of bag onto sheet. Separate any onion rings that stick together.

5. Line second rimmed baking sheet with triple layer of paper towels. Add oil to large Dutch oven until it measures about 2 inches deep and heat over medium-high heat to 375 degrees.

6. Add one-third of onion rings to hot oil and fry, without stirring, until breading is just set, 30 to 60 seconds. Stir gently with tongs or spider skimmer and continue to fry until dark golden brown, 3 to 5 minutes longer, flipping onion rings occasionally and separating any that stick together. Adjust burner, if necessary, to maintain oil temperature between 325 and 375 degrees. Transfer fried onion rings to paper towel-lined sheet and place in oven to keep warm.

7. Return oil to 375 degrees and repeat with remaining onion rings in 2 batches. Serve onion rings with sauce.

Beer-Battered Onion Rings

SERVES 4 TO 6

WHY THIS RECIPE WORKS We wanted sweet, tender onions for our beer-battered onion rings. After testing many different batters, we settled on a beer, flour, salt, pepper, baking powder, and cornstarch batter. The beer gave the coating flavor, and the carbonation provided lift to the batter. Baking powder yielded a coating that was substantial yet light, while cornstarch added crunch. Before frying our onion rings, we soaked the onions in a mixture of beer, malt vinegar, and salt to soften them and build flavor.

Crispy Vegetable Fritters

Ultimate Extra-Crunchy Onion Rings

In step 1, do not soak the onion rounds longer than 2 hours or they will turn soft and become too saturated to crisp properly. Ordinary yellow onions will produce acceptable rings here. We like full-bodied beers like Sam Adams in this recipe. Cider vinegar can be used in place of malt vinegar. Use a Dutch oven that holds 6 quarts or more for this recipe.

- 2 sweet onions, peeled and sliced into ½-inch thick rounds
- 3 cups ale or lager, divided
- 2 teaspoons malt vinegar
- Table salt and pepper
- 2 quarts peanut or vegetable oil for frying
- ¾ cup all-purpose flour
- ¾ cup cornstarch
- 1 teaspoon baking powder

1. Place onion rounds, 2 cups beer, vinegar, ½ teaspoon salt, and ½ teaspoon pepper in 1-gallon zipper-lock bag; refrigerate for 30 minutes or up to 2 hours.

2. Line rimmed baking sheet with triple layer of paper towels. Add oil to large Dutch oven until it measures about 1½ inches deep and heat over medium-high heat to 350 degrees. While oil is heating, combine flour, cornstarch, baking powder, ½ teaspoon salt, and ¼ teaspoon pepper in large bowl. Slowly whisk in ¾ cup beer until just combined (some lumps will remain). Whisk in remaining beer as needed, 1 tablespoon at a time, until batter falls from whisk in steady stream and leaves faint trail across surface of batter.

3. Adjust oven rack to middle position and heat oven to 200 degrees. Remove onions from refrigerator and pour off liquid. Pat onion rounds dry with paper towels and separate into rings. Transfer one-third of rings to batter. One at a time, carefully transfer battered rings to oil. Fry until rings are golden brown and crisp, about 5 minutes, flipping halfway through frying. Drain rings on prepared baking sheet, season with salt and pepper to taste, and transfer to oven. Return oil to 350 degrees and repeat 2 more times with remaining onion rings and batter. Serve.

Fried Cheese Curds with Ranch Dressing

SERVES 2 TO 4

WHY THIS RECIPE WORKS These golden nuggets of deep-fried goodness were inspired by the wildly popular fried cheese curds served by chefs Kurt Fogle and Joe McCormick at their Milwaukee restaurant, Dairyland Old-Fashioned Frozen Custard & Hamburgers. To keep the curds from melting too quickly during frying, we froze them. We made a light yet sturdy batter using all-purpose flour and cornstarch for body and crispness, plus baking powder for puff and crunch. Using a light beer added malty, mildly bitter flavors to balance the milkiness of the cheese.

Break any cheese curds that are larger than 1 inch into smaller pieces. Note that the cheese curds need to be frozen for 2 hours before frying. We recommend weighing the flour and cornstarch for the best results. Use a Dutch oven that holds 6 quarts or more. When dropping the curds into the oil, hold the bowl close to the oil to minimize splatter.

Dressing
- ⅓ cup buttermilk
- ⅓ cup mayonnaise
- 3 tablespoons sour cream
- 2 tablespoons chopped fresh cilantro
- 2 tablespoons minced fresh chives
- 1 tablespoon chopped fresh dill

Beer-Battered Onion Rings

1 garlic clove, minced
1 teaspoon white wine vinegar
½ teaspoon granulated garlic
¼ teaspoon table salt
¼ teaspoon pepper
   Pinch cayenne

Curds

1 pound cheddar cheese curds
½ cup (2½ ounces) all-purpose flour
½ cup (2 ounces) cornstarch
1½ teaspoons paprika
1 teaspoon baking powder
¾ teaspoon table salt
⅔ cup lager or other light beer
2 quarts vegetable oil for frying

1. For the Dressing Whisk all ingredients together in bowl. Refrigerate for at least 30 minutes to allow flavors to blend. Season with salt to taste. (Dressing can be refrigerated for up to 3 days.)

2. For the Curds Place cheese curds in zipper-lock bag, seal bag, and lay bag flat in freezer. Freeze until solid, about 2 hours. (Curds can be frozen for up to 1 month.)

3. When ready to fry, whisk flour, cornstarch, paprika, baking powder, and salt together in bowl. Whisk in beer until no lumps remain (texture should resemble pancake batter). Let batter sit for 5 minutes to thicken fully.

4. Divide frozen curds evenly among 3 medium bowls. Add ¼ cup batter to each bowl of curds and stir to combine (curds should be just coated with batter). Set bowls aside and discard any remaining batter. Set wire rack in rimmed baking sheet. Add oil to Dutch oven until it measures about 1½ inches deep and heat over medium-high heat to 350 degrees.

5. Working with 1 bowl at a time, position bowl close to oil and, using dinner spoon, slide curds into oil, one at a time, moving bowl as you dispense curds. Fry, without stirring, until golden brown, 1 to 1½ minutes. (Pockets of melted cheese should barely begin to show through crust. Don't worry if some curds clump together; they can be separated once removed from oil.) Using spider skimmer or slotted spoon, transfer curds to prepared rack.

6. Return oil to 350 degrees and repeat with remaining curds, stirring to recoat with batter before frying. Serve immediately with dressing.

On the Road: Milwaukee's Cheese Curd Kings

Standing in front of Dairyland Old-Fashioned Frozen Custard & Hamburgers in Milwaukee, chef and co-owner Kurt Fogle says with a calm, matter-of-fact confidence, "Milwaukee is the center of the universe for quality cheeseburgers." His Midwest politeness then kicks in and he adds, "No offense to anyone else."

He's talking about cheeseburgers, but he could easily be talking about cheese curds, a signature side dish at the restaurant he co-owns with fellow chef Joe McCormick. "Kurt and I are cosmically aligned kindred spirits," McCormick says.

Fried cheese curds are a customer favorite, more popular today, according to Fogle, than when he was growing up. While most restaurants buy frozen pre-battered curds from big food-service distributors, at Dairyland they purchase fresh curds from the nearby Clock Shadow Creamery and then batter and fry them to order in their own house-made beer batter. The goal, as McCormick says, is clear: "It's gotta be a little salty, it's gotta be crispy, it's gotta be gooey, it's gotta make you want to have another beer."

Fried Cheese Curds with Ranch Dressing

Charred Cherry Tomatoes with Roasted Red Bell Peppers and Fresh Mozzarella
SERVES 4

WHY THIS RECIPE WORKS Spooned over warm bread, these savory tomatoes and bell peppers make a satisfying appetizer. We cooked cherry tomatoes in a preheated cast-iron skillet, stirring them only once to ensure that they charred and blistered. After browning the bell peppers in the same skillet, we tossed the vegetables with a garlicky vinaigrette. Anchovies and smoked paprika boosted the flavors further. We let the mixture sit to allow the flavors to meld before stirring in fresh mozzarella and basil.

One pint of cherry tomatoes weighs about 12 ounces. Serve with warmed or grilled crusty bread.

- 1 garlic clove, peeled
- 1¾ teaspoons kosher salt, divided
- 3 tablespoons plus 1 teaspoon extra-virgin olive oil
- 1 tablespoon plus 2 teaspoons red wine vinegar
- 3 anchovies, minced
- 2 teaspoons minced fresh thyme
- 2 teaspoons lemon juice
- ½ teaspoon red pepper flakes
- ½ teaspoon smoked paprika
- 1 pound cherry tomatoes
- 1 red bell pepper, stemmed, seeded, and cut lengthwise into thin strips
- 8 ounces fresh mozzarella cheese, torn into bite-size pieces
- ½ cup fresh basil leaves, torn into 1-inch pieces

1. Mince garlic with ¼ teaspoon salt to form smooth paste. Transfer to large bowl. Add 2 tablespoons oil, vinegar, anchovies, thyme, lemon juice, pepper flakes, smoked paprika, and ½ teaspoon salt. Whisk to combine.

2. Heat 12-inch cast-iron skillet over medium heat for 10 minutes. Toss tomatoes with 2 teaspoons oil and ½ teaspoon salt in medium bowl. Add tomatoes to skillet and cook until lightly charred and blistered on two sides, 8 to 10 minutes, stirring once halfway through cooking. (Some tomatoes will start to burst.)

3. Meanwhile, toss bell pepper with remaining 2 teaspoons oil and remaining ½ teaspoon salt.

4. Transfer tomatoes to vinegar mixture. Add bell peppers to now-empty skillet set over medium heat. Cook until spotty brown on one side, about 4 minutes. Stir and continue to cook for 2 minutes longer. Transfer bell peppers to tomato mixture; toss gently to combine. Let mixture sit to cool to room temperature and to allow flavors to meld, at least 30 minutes or up to 2 hours.

5. Gently toss mozzarella and basil with tomato mixture until combined. Season with salt and pepper flakes to taste. Transfer to serving platter. Serve.

Hawaiian Macaroni Salad
SERVES 8 TO 10

WHY THIS RECIPE WORKS No al dente noodles here—the Hawaiian tradition of overcooking the pasta for their creamy macaroni salad until it's "fat," enables the noodles to absorb more dressing. To achieve maximum flavor absorption, we added 2 cups each of mayonnaise and milk to make sure that the dressing was thin enough to soak into the macaroni. For an extra boost of flavor, we added cider vinegar only to discover that it curdled the milk, so we poured the vinegar directly over the hot macaroni and let it cool slightly before stirring in the dressing and vegetables.

Low-fat milk or mayonnaise will make the dressing too thin.

- 2 cups whole milk
- 2 cups mayonnaise
- 1 tablespoon brown sugar
- 2 teaspoons pepper
- ½ teaspoon table salt, plus salt for cooking pasta
- 1 pound elbow macaroni
- ½ cup cider vinegar
- 4 scallions, sliced thin
- 1 large carrot, peeled and grated
- 1 celery rib, chopped fine

1. Whisk milk, mayonnaise, sugar, pepper, and ½ teaspoon salt together in bowl. Reserve and refrigerate 1 cup dressing for finishing salad. Set both aside.

2. Bring 4 quarts water to boil in large pot. Add 1 tablespoon salt and pasta and cook until very soft, about 15 minutes. Drain pasta in colander and shake to remove excess water. Transfer pasta to large bowl, add vinegar, and toss until vinegar is absorbed. Let pasta cool for 10 minutes.

3. Stir remaining dressing (larger portion) into pasta mixture until combined. Stir in scallions, carrot, and celery until combined. Cover and refrigerate until fully chilled, about 1 hour. Stir in reserved 1 cup dressing. Season with salt and pepper to taste. Serve.

Ballpark Pretzels
MAKES 12 PRETZELS

WHY THIS RECIPE WORKS Soft pretzels are hard to come by unless you're at a ballpark. We wanted to make them worth staying at home. We created a soft, sweet interior using bread flour—its higher gluten content produced great chew—and brown sugar, which added malty flavor. We made our own alkali solution with water and baking soda. Boiling the pretzels in this solution ensured proper browning and set the crust to protect the dough inside. We then sprinkled the pretzels with kosher salt and baked them until they turned mahogany-brown.

We use kosher salt on the exterior of our pretzels, but coarse pretzel salt may be substituted. However, be sure to still use kosher salt in the dough. Keep in mind that the dough needs to rise for 60 minutes, and then the shaped pretzels require a 20-minute rise before boiling and baking. These pretzels are best served warm, with mustard.

- 1½ cups warm water (110 degrees)
- 3 tablespoons vegetable oil, divided
- 2 tablespoons packed dark brown sugar
- 2 teaspoons instant or rapid-rise yeast
- 3¾ cups (20⅔ ounces) bread flour
  Kosher salt
- ¼ cup baking soda

1. Lightly grease large bowl. In bowl of stand mixer, combine warm water, 2 tablespoons oil, sugar, and yeast and let sit until foamy, about 3 minutes. Combine flour and 4 teaspoons salt in separate bowl. Add flour mixture to yeast mixture. Fit stand mixer with dough hook and knead on low speed until dough comes together and clears sides of bowl, 4 to 6 minutes.

2. Turn out dough onto lightly floured counter and knead by hand until smooth, about 1 minute. Transfer dough to greased bowl and cover with plastic wrap. Let dough rise at room temperature until almost doubled in size, about 60 minutes.

Charred Cherry Tomatoes with Roasted Red Bell Peppers and Fresh Mozzarella

Hawaiian Macaroni Salad

3. Gently press center of dough to deflate. Transfer dough to lightly greased counter, divide into 12 equal pieces, and cover with plastic.

4. Lightly flour 2 rimmed baking sheets. Working with 1 piece of dough at a time, roll into 22-inch-long rope. Shape rope into U with 2-inch-wide bottom curve and ends facing away from you. Crisscross ropes in middle of U, then cross again. Fold ends toward bottom of U and firmly press ends into bottom curve of U 1 inch apart to form pretzel shape. Transfer pretzels to prepared sheets, knot side up, 6 pretzels per sheet. Cover pretzels loosely with plastic and let rise at room temperature until slightly puffy, about 20 minutes.

5. Adjust oven racks to upper-middle and lower-middle positions and heat oven to 425 degrees. Dissolve baking soda in 4 cups water in Dutch oven and bring to boil over medium-high heat. Using slotted spatula, transfer 4 pretzels, knot side down, to boiling water and cook for 30 seconds, flipping halfway through cooking. Transfer pretzels to wire rack, knot side up, and repeat with remaining 8 pretzels in 2 additional batches. Let pretzels rest for 5 minutes.

6. Wipe flour from sheets and grease with remaining 1 tablespoon oil. Sprinkle each sheet with ½ teaspoon salt. Transfer pretzels to prepared sheets, knot side up, 6 pretzels per sheet. Sprinkle 1 teaspoon salt evenly over pretzels.

7. Bake pretzels until mahogany brown and any yellowish color around seams has faded, 15 to 20 minutes, switching and rotating sheets halfway through baking. Transfer pretzels to wire rack and let cool for 10 minutes. Serve.

Baba Ghanoush

SERVES 4

WHY THIS RECIPE WORKS The bedrock technique for making baba ghanoush, a deeply flavorful eggplant dip, is cooking the eggplant over an open flame until the skin is charred and the interior is tender. We pierced the eggplant to encourage moisture to evaporate and to prevent bursting. Then, we placed them either under the broiler or on the grill. To temper the raw garlic, we combined it with lemon juice and salt and let it sit while the eggplants cooled. Generous amounts of tahini and olive oil ensured creaminess. To account for the eggplants' variable size and water content, we added more lemon and salt before serving.

If the only eggplants you can find weigh more than 12 ounces, you may need to go a little heavier on the salt and lemon juice when seasoning to taste in step 6. The finished product should be assertive but not overpowering.

2	(12-ounce) eggplants
1	tablespoon lemon juice, plus extra for seasoning
1	garlic clove, minced to paste
1	teaspoon table salt
¼	cup tahini
¼	cup extra-virgin olive oil, divided
1	tablespoon chopped fresh parsley

1. Poke each eggplant about 6 times with paring knife.

2a. For the Oven Adjust oven rack 8 inches from broiler element and heat broiler. Line rimmed baking sheet with aluminum foil.

2b. For a Charcoal Grill Open bottom vent completely. Light large chimney starter filled with charcoal briquettes (6 quarts). When top coals are partially covered with ash, pour evenly over grill. Set cooking grate in place, cover, and open lid vent completely. Heat grill until hot, about 5 minutes.

2c. For a Gas Grill Turn all burners to high; cover; and heat grill until hot, about 15 minutes. Turn all burners to medium-high.

3. Place eggplants on prepared sheet (or directly on cooking grate) and broil (or grill, covered) for 20 minutes. Remove sheet from oven and flip eggplants (or flip eggplants on grill). Return sheet to oven and broil (or grill, covered) for 10 minutes. (Skin should be charred and have aroma of burning leaves.) Transfer eggplants to plate and let cool completely, about 30 minutes.

4. Meanwhile, combine lemon juice, garlic, and salt in medium bowl and let sit while eggplants cool.

5. Working with 1 eggplant at a time, split lengthwise on 1 side through skin and peel back skin to expose flesh. Using spoon, scoop out eggplant flesh; discard eggplant skin. Chop eggplant flesh fine with chef's knife and transfer to bowl with lemon juice mixture.

6. Add tahini and 2 tablespoons oil to eggplant mixture and whisk to combine. Let baba ghanoush sit for 20 minutes to allow flavors to blend, stirring occasionally. Season with extra lemon juice and salt to taste. Spread baba ghanoush in shallow bowl and drizzle with remaining 2 tablespoons oil. Sprinkle with parsley and serve.

Eggplant Dip with Scallions and Cilantro

Omit parsley. Stir 2 thinly sliced scallions, 2 tablespoons chopped fresh cilantro, and ½ teaspoon ground cumin into eggplant mixture with tahini in step 6.

Piña Coladas
MAKES 4 COCKTAILS

WHY THIS RECIPE WORKS This official drink of Puerto Rico is a magical combination of pineapple, coconut, and rum. For a frozen version bursting with tropical flavor, we found that frozen pineapple (frozen at its peak of ripeness) provided the flavor of fresh while reducing the amount of ice needed for texture. For the coconut, we chose coconut cream for its great mouthfeel and rich, natural flavor. Choosing the rum was no easy task, but white rum provided just the right flavor. For a dramatic presentation, try floating some aged rum on top.

Do not substitute cream of coconut for the coconut cream. Add a rum float by arranging bar spoon concave side down near surface of cocktail. Gently pour ½ ounce aged rum onto back of spoon and into cocktail.

- 1 (15-ounce) can coconut cream
- 6 ounces white rum
- 2 ounces Simple Syrup (recipe follows)
- 12 ounces (3 cups) frozen pineapple chunks
- 8 ounces (2 cups) ice cubes
  Fresh pineapple slices

Add coconut cream, rum, simple syrup, pineapple, and ice to blender (in that order) and process until smooth, about 1 minute, scraping down sides of blender jar as needed. Pour into chilled old-fashioned glasses or hurricane glasses. Garnish with pineapple and serve.

Simple Syrup
MAKES ABOUT 8 OUNCES

- ¾ cup sugar
- 5 ounces warm tap water

Whisk sugar and warm water together in bowl until sugar has dissolved. Let cool completely, about 10 minutes, before transferring to airtight container.

Baba Ghanoush

Piña Coladas

steakhouse specials

- **274** French Onion Soup
- **275** Slow-Cooker French Onion Soup
- **276** Grilled Steakhouse Steak Tips
- **276** Grilled Sugar Steak
- **277** Broiled Steaks
- **279** Char-Grilled Steaks
- **280** Spice-Crusted Steaks
- **281** Easy Steak Frites
- **282** Grilled Cowboy-Cut Rib Eyes
- **283** Slow-Roasted Medium-Rare Beef Short Ribs
- **284** Japanese Steakhouse Steak and Vegetables
- **285** Simple Hibachi-Style Fried Rice
- **286** Grilled Steak Burgers
- **287** Pork Grillades
- **288** Baked Stuffed Shrimp
- **289** Failproof Chicken Cordon Bleu
- **290** Garlic Mashed Potatoes
- **291** Mashed Potato Cakes
- **292** Lyonnaise Potatoes
- **293** Delmonico Potato Casserole
- **294** Lighthouse Inn Potatoes
- **295** Olive Oil Potato Gratin
- **296** Crushed Red Potatoes with Garlic and Herbs
- **297** Roasted Salt-and-Vinegar Potatoes
- **298** Torn and Fried Potatoes
- **299** Crispy Parmesan Potatoes
- **300** Crispy Baked Potato Fans
- **301** Super-Stuffed Baked Potatoes
- **302** Twice-Baked Potatoes with Bacon and Cheddar Cheese
- **303** Roasted Garlic–Parmesan Bread
- **304** Creamed Spinach
- **304** Grill-Roasted Peppers
- **305** Caesar Green Bean Salad
- **306** BLT Salad
- **307** Stuffed Tomatoes

Recipe Photos (clockwise from top right): Twice-Baked Potatoes with Bacon and Cheddar Cheese; Stuffed Tomatoes; Slow-Cooker French Onion Soup

French Onion Soup

SERVES 6

WHY THIS RECIPE WORKS The cornerstone of this bistro favorite is perfectly caramelized onions. First, we cooked sliced onions covered to steam and soften them, and then we removed the lid to allow the liquid to evaporate and cook the onions until they were soft and browned. Deglazing the pot with red wine ensured that all the tasty fond ended up in the soup, while stirring in beef broth and herbal aromatics completed the overall flavor. After ladling the soup into individual crocks, we sprinkled on a layer of Gruyère, followed by croutons and more cheese. The Gruyère under the croutons protected the bread from getting too soggy. C'est magnifique!

Be patient when caramelizing the onions; the entire process takes 55 to 70 minutes. If you don't have ovensafe soup crocks, form six individual piles of croutons on a baking sheet, cover them with the cheese, and broil them on the middle oven rack until the cheese is melted, 1 to 3 minutes. Then use a spatula to transfer the crouton portions to the individual filled soup bowls.

French Onion Soup

- 4 tablespoons unsalted butter
- 4 pounds onions, halved and sliced thin
- 1¾ teaspoons table salt, divided
- 1 teaspoon sugar
- 1 cup dry red wine
- 8 cups beef broth
- 4 sprigs fresh thyme
- 2 bay leaves
- ¾ teaspoon pepper, divided
- 6 ounces baguette, cut into 1-inch cubes
- 3 tablespoons extra-virgin olive oil
- 8 ounces Gruyère cheese, shredded (2 cups)
- 1½ ounces Parmesan cheese, shredded (½ cup)

1. Melt butter in Dutch oven over medium-high heat. Stir in onions, 1 teaspoon salt, and sugar. Cover and cook, stirring occasionally, until onions release their liquid and are uniformly translucent, about 20 minutes.

2. Uncover and cook until liquid has evaporated and browned bits start to form on bottom of pot, 5 to 10 minutes. Reduce heat to medium and continue to cook, uncovered, until onions are caramel-colored, 30 to 40 minutes longer, stirring and scraping with wooden spoon as browned bits form on bottom of pot and spreading onions into even layer after stirring. (If onions or browned bits begin to scorch, reduce heat to medium-low.)

3. Stir in wine, scraping up any browned bits, and cook until nearly evaporated, about 1 minute. Stir in broth, thyme sprigs, bay leaves, ½ teaspoon pepper, and ½ teaspoon salt. Increase heat to high and bring to boil. Reduce heat to medium-low and simmer, uncovered, for 30 minutes.

4. While onions simmer, adjust oven rack to middle position and heat oven to 350 degrees. Toss baguette, oil, remaining ¼ teaspoon salt, and remaining ¼ teaspoon pepper together in bowl. Transfer to rimmed baking sheet and bake until golden and crisp, 15 to 18 minutes. Remove sheet from oven and set aside. Increase oven temperature to 500 degrees.

5. Set six 12-ounce ovensafe crocks on second rimmed baking sheet. Discard thyme sprigs and bay leaves and season soup with salt and pepper to taste. Divide soup evenly among crocks (about 1½ cups each). Divide 1 cup

The Complete Cook's Country TV Show Cookbook

Gruyère evenly among crocks, top with croutons, and sprinkle with remaining Gruyère, then Parmesan. Bake until cheeses are melted and soup is bubbly around edges, 5 to 7 minutes. Let cool for 5 minutes before serving.

Slow-Cooker French Onion Soup

SERVES 6 TO 8

WHY THIS RECIPE WORKS It can be a hassle to stand over a pot of caramelized onions when a craving for this French classic strikes. We looked to the slow cooker for simplification. Replicating the meaty flavor of the soup was more of a challenge, as the slow, long cooking can result in washed-out flavor. We found that soy sauce, sherry, and thyme added early on helped boost flavor and the addition of beef bones to store-bought chicken and beef broths reproduced the rich meatiness of the classic. Apple butter highlighted the flavor of the onions without drawing attention to itself and also helped make for a rich, silky broth.

After halving the onions, slice them through the root end for hearty slices that will hold up to long cooking. Beef bones are stocked in the frozen foods aisle of most supermarkets.

Soup
- 2 pounds beef bones
- 4 tablespoons unsalted butter
- 4 pounds yellow onions, halved and sliced through root end into ¼-inch-thick slices
- Table salt and pepper
- 1 tablespoon packed brown sugar
- 1 teaspoon minced fresh thyme
- ¾ cup apple butter
- ¾ cup dry sherry
- 5 tablespoons all-purpose flour
- ¼ cup soy sauce
- 2 cups chicken broth
- 2 cups beef broth

Cheese Croutons
- 1 small baguette, cut into ½-inch slices
- 10 ounces Gruyère cheese, shredded (2½ cups)

1. For the Soup Arrange beef bones on paper towel–lined plate. Microwave until well browned, 8 to 10 minutes. Meanwhile, set slow cooker to high. Add butter, cover, and cook until melted. Add onions, 2 teaspoons salt, 1 teaspoon pepper, brown sugar, and thyme. Stir apple butter, sherry, flour, and soy sauce together in small bowl until smooth. Pour over onions and toss to coat. Tuck bones under onions around edge of slow cooker. Cover and cook on high heat until onions are softened and deep golden brown, 10 to 12 hours (start checking onions after 8 hours). (Cooked onions can be refrigerated for 1 day.)

2. Remove bones from slow cooker. Heat broths in microwave until beginning to boil. Stir into slow cooker. Season with salt and pepper to taste.

3. For the Cheese Croutons Adjust oven rack to upper-middle position (about 6 inches from broiler element) and heat oven to 400 degrees. Arrange bread slices in single layer on baking sheet and bake until bread is golden at edges, about 10 minutes. Heat broiler. Divide cheese evenly among croutons and broil until melted and bubbly, 3 to 5 minutes.

4. Ladle soup into bowls, top each with 2 croutons, and serve.

Slicing Onions for French Onion Soup

For this soup, we found that cutting onions with the grain (rather than across it) yielded slices that retained their shape through 10 to 12 hours in the slow cooker.

1. Using chef's knife, trim off both ends of onion. Turn onion onto cut end to steady it and slice in half, through root end.

2. Peel each half, place flat side down, and cut onion, lengthwise, into slices.

Grilled Steakhouse Steak Tips

SERVES 4 TO 6

WHY THIS RECIPE WORKS The sizzling arrival of cast-iron plates of marinated steakhouse steak tips is often the most exciting part about them, because in reality, the first bite reveals chewy meat in an overly sweet marinade. For tender tips with great beefy flavor, we relied on sirloin steak tips. As for the marinade, we replaced the usual culprits—ketchup, barbecue sauce, and cola—with a mixture of soy sauce, oil, dark brown sugar, and tomato paste for enhanced meaty flavor and maximum char.

Sirloin steak tips are often labeled "flap meat" and are sold as whole steaks, strips, and pieces. For even pieces, buy a whole steak of uniform size and cut it up yourself.

- ⅓ cup soy sauce
- ⅓ cup vegetable oil
- 3 tablespoons packed dark brown sugar
- 5 garlic cloves, minced
- 1 tablespoon tomato paste
- 1 tablespoon paprika
- ½ teaspoon pepper
- ¼ teaspoon cayenne pepper
- 2½ pounds sirloin steak tips, trimmed

1. Whisk soy sauce, oil, sugar, garlic, tomato paste, paprika, pepper, and cayenne together in bowl until sugar dissolves; transfer to zipper-lock bag. Pat beef dry with paper towels. Prick beef all over with fork and cut into 2½-inch pieces. Add meat to bag with soy sauce mixture and refrigerate for at least 2 or up to 24 hours, turning occasionally.

2a. For a Charcoal Grill Open bottom vent completely. Light large chimney starter filled with charcoal briquettes (6 quarts). When top coals are partially covered with ash, pour evenly over grill. Set cooking grate in place, cover, and open lid vent completely. Heat grill until hot, about 5 minutes. Leave burners on high.

2b. For a Gas Grill Turn all burners to high, cover, and heat grill until hot, about 15 minutes.

3. Clean and oil cooking grate. Grill beef (covered if using gas) until charred and registers 130 to 135 degrees (for medium), 8 to 10 minutes. Transfer meat to platter, tent loosely with aluminum foil, and let rest for 5 to 10 minutes. Serve.

Grilled Steakhouse Steak Tips

Grilled Sugar Steak

SERVES 4 TO 6

WHY THIS RECIPE WORKS Adding sugar to steak may at first seem strange, but trust us, the sugar provides a hint of sweetness and helps create the ultimate charred crust. To keep the sugar-salt mixture from sliding off the steaks or melting away on the grill, we sprinkled the mixture onto the steaks, let them rest for at least an hour, and then seasoned the moist steaks again just before hitting the heat. Though we typically discourage fussing with meat once it's on the grill, in this case, moving the steaks around as they cooked minimized the hot spots and evened out the heavy browning caused by the sugar.

These steaks need to sit for at least 1 hour after seasoning. You will have about 1 teaspoon of sugar mixture left over after the final seasoning of the steaks in step 3. If your steaks are more than 1 inch thick, pound them to 1 inch.

¼ cup sugar
3 tablespoons kosher salt
4 (9- to 11-ounce) boneless strip steaks, 1 inch thick, trimmed
¼ teaspoon pepper

1. Mix sugar and salt together in bowl. Pat steaks dry with paper towels and place in 13 by 9-inch baking dish. Evenly sprinkle 1½ teaspoons sugar mixture on top of each steak. Flip steaks and sprinkle second side of each steak with 1½ teaspoons sugar mixture. Cover with plastic wrap and let sit at room temperature for 1 hour or refrigerate for up to 24 hours.

2a. For a Charcoal Grill Open bottom vent completely. Light large chimney starter mounded with charcoal briquettes (7 quarts). When top coals are partially covered with ash, pour evenly over half of grill. Set cooking grate in place, cover, and open lid vent completely. Heat grill until hot, about 5 minutes.

2b. For a Gas Grill Turn all burners to high, cover, and heat grill until hot, about 15 minutes. Turn all burners to medium-high.

3. Clean and oil cooking grate. Transfer steaks to plate. (Steaks will be wet; do not pat dry.) Sprinkle steaks with 1 teaspoon sugar mixture on each side, then sprinkle with pepper.

4. Place steaks on hotter side of grill (if using charcoal) and cook (covered if using gas) until evenly charred on first side, 3 to 5 minutes, rotating and switching positions for even cooking. Flip steaks and continue to cook until meat registers 120 to 125 degrees (for medium-rare), 3 to 5 minutes, rotating and switching positions for even cooking.

5. Transfer steaks to wire rack set in rimmed baking sheet and let rest for 5 minutes. Slice and serve.

On the Road: A Denver Gem

Shaped like a circus tent, Bastien's Restaurant is a historic family-owned restaurant in Denver, Colorado, where grilled sugar steak has been the signature dish for decades. The restaurant sits on Colfax Avenue, a 50-odd-mile street that bisects Denver. It's a street of notorious contrasts (gentrification mixes with grit along its entire stretch), but as Denver's defining throughway, it was granted Heritage Corridor status in the late 1990s to help protect and preserve Bastien's and many other mid-century architectural gems.

Grilled Sugar Steak

Broiled Steaks

SERVES 4

WHY THIS RECIPE WORKS We usually rely on a red-hot skillet or the grill for our recipes that include putting a crusty sear on steaks, but we wondered if our oven's broiler could do the job just as well. Starting the steaks at a moderate temperature took the chill off, and letting them rest before putting them under the broiler produced evenly cooked meat. Covering the bottom of the pan with salt helped absorb the grease from the meat and greatly minimized smoking. To ensure a good sear on our steaks, we placed a wire rack over a 3-inch disposable pan, to bring the meat closer to the heating element.

To minimize smoking, be sure to trim as much exterior fat and gristle as possible from the steaks before cooking. Try to purchase steaks of a similar size and shape for this recipe. Note that you will need 2 cups of salt to line the roasting pan; the salt will absorb drippings from the steak and minimize smoking.

STEAKHOUSE SPECIALS

Broiled Steaks

- 4 tablespoons unsalted butter, softened
- 1 teaspoon minced fresh thyme
- 1 teaspoon Dijon mustard
- Table salt and pepper
- 1 (13 by 9-inch) disposable aluminum roasting pan, 3 inches deep
- 4 strip, rib-eye, or tenderloin steaks, 1 to 2 inches thick, trimmed

1. Adjust oven racks to upper-middle and lower-middle positions and heat oven to 375 degrees. Beat butter, thyme, mustard, ¼ teaspoon salt, and ¼ teaspoon pepper in bowl and refrigerate.

2. Spread 2 cups salt over bottom of aluminum pan. Pat steaks dry with paper towels, season with salt and pepper, and transfer to wire rack. Set rack over aluminum pan and transfer to lower oven rack. Cook 6 to 10 minutes, then remove pan from oven. Flip steaks, pat dry with paper towels, and let rest for 10 minutes.

Perfectly Broiled Steaks

The first step to perfectly broiled steaks is knowing exactly how thick your steaks are. Using a ruler, measure each steak and then follow the guidelines below.

STEAK THICKNESS	PRECOOK	BROIL
1 inch	6 minutes	Turn steaks every 2 minutes
1½ inches	8 minutes	Turn steaks every 3 minutes
2 inches	10 minutes	Turn steaks every 4 minutes

Broiler Prep

Since oven-rack positioning varies greatly from model to model, we suggest you ensure correct positioning with a dry run before turning on your oven.

Before preheating your oven and with your oven racks adjusted to the upper-middle and lower-middle positions, place a wire rack on top of a 3-inch-deep disposable aluminum pan and place it on the upper-middle rack. Place the steaks on top of the rack and use a ruler to measure the distance between the top of the steaks and the heating element of the broiler. For optimal searing, there should be ½ inch to 1 inch of space.

If there is more than 1 inch of space, here's how to close the gap: Elevate the aluminum pan by placing it on an inverted rimmed baking sheet; use a deeper-sided disposable aluminum pan; or stack multiple aluminum pans inside one another. If there's less than ½ inch of space, adjust the oven rack or use a shallower pan.

3. Heat broiler. Transfer pan to upper oven rack and broil steaks, flipping every 2 to 4 minutes, until meat registers 120 to 125 degrees (for medium-rare), 6 to 16 minutes, depending on thickness of steaks (see chart). Transfer steaks to platter, top with reserved butter mixture, and tent with aluminum foil. Let rest for 5 minutes. Serve.

Char-Grilled Steaks

SERVES 4

WHY THIS RECIPE WORKS In order to achieve a respectable crust on our restaurant-style grilled steak, the exterior of the meat must be dry. After trying numerous drying-out methods, including salting and aging, we considered the freezer. The freezer's intensely dry environment sufficiently dehydrated the steaks' exteriors, and since we were freezing them for only a short time, the interiors remained tender and juicy. We rubbed the steaks with a mixture of salt and cornstarch before freezing. The salt ensured that they were well seasoned, and cornstarch, a champ at absorbing moisture, allowed us to cut the freezing time in half.

Serve with one of the sauces that follow, if desired.

- 1 teaspoon table salt
- 1 teaspoon cornstarch
- 4 strip, rib-eye, or tenderloin steaks, about 1½ inches thick, trimmed
- ¼ teaspoon pepper
- 1 recipe steak sauce (recipes follow)

1. Combine salt and cornstarch. Pat steaks dry with paper towels and rub with salt mixture. Arrange on wire rack set in rimmed baking sheet and freeze until steaks are firm and dry to touch, at least 30 minutes or up to 1 hour.

2a. For a Charcoal Grill Open bottom vent completely. Light large chimney starter filled with charcoal briquettes (6 quarts). When top coals are partially covered with ash, pour evenly over grill. Set cooking grate in place, cover, and open lid vent completely. Heat grill until hot, about 5 minutes.

2b. For a Gas Grill Turn all burners to high, cover, and heat grill until hot, about 15 minutes. Leave burners on high.

3. Clean and oil cooking grate. Season steaks with pepper. Grill (covered if using gas) until meat registers 120 to 125 degrees (for medium-rare), 8 to 16 minutes, flipping steaks halfway through cooking. Transfer to plate, tent with aluminum foil, and let rest for 5 minutes. Serve.

Char-Grilled Steaks

Classic Steak Sauce
MAKES 1¼ CUPS

Raisins add depth and sweetness to this sauce.

- ½ cup boiling water
- ⅓ cup raisins
- ¼ cup ketchup
- 3 tablespoons Worcestershire sauce
- 2 tablespoons Dijon mustard
- 2 tablespoons distilled white vinegar
  Table salt and pepper

Combine water and raisins in bowl and let sit, covered, until raisins are plump, about 5 minutes. Puree raisin mixture, ketchup, Worcestershire, mustard, and vinegar in blender until smooth, 30 seconds to 1 minute. Season with salt and pepper to taste. (Sauce can be refrigerated for 1 week.)

STEAKHOUSE SPECIALS

Spicy Red Pepper Steak Sauce
MAKES 1¼ CUPS

This peppery sauce is a simplified version of the Spanish classic, romesco.

- 1 slice hearty white sandwich bread, toasted until golden and torn into pieces
- 2 tablespoons slivered almonds, toasted
- 1 cup jarred roasted red peppers, drained
- 1 plum tomato, seeded and chopped
- 2 teaspoons red wine vinegar
- 1 garlic clove, minced
- ⅛ teaspoon cayenne pepper
- 1 tablespoon extra-virgin olive oil
  Table salt

Process bread and almonds in food processor until finely ground, about 10 seconds. Add red peppers, tomato, vinegar, garlic, and cayenne and process until smooth, about 1 minute. Season with salt to taste. (Sauce can be refrigerated for 1 week.)

Garlic-Parsley Steak Sauce
MAKES 1¼ CUPS

A little of this aromatic vinaigrette goes a long way.

- ½ cup finely chopped fresh parsley
- ¼ cup minced red onion
- ¼ cup red wine vinegar
- 2 garlic cloves, minced
- ⅛ teaspoon red pepper flakes
- ¼ cup extra virgin olive oil
  Table salt and pepper

Combine parsley, onion, vinegar, garlic, and pepper flakes in bowl. Slowly whisk in oil. Season with salt and pepper to taste. (Sauce can be refrigerated for 1 week.)

Spice-Crusted Steaks

Spice-Crusted Steaks
SERVES 4

WHY THIS RECIPE WORKS Too often, spice-crusted steaks are overpoweringly potent and leave scorched spices stuck to the pan, not the meat. We started with rib-eye steaks, our choice for their rich and beefy flavor, that could stand up to a bold spice crust and were thick enough to provide the perfect ratio of interior meat to exterior spice. We covered them in ground coriander and dry mustard with some coarsely crushed black peppercorns and carefully cooked the steaks in a nonstick skillet (our trusty cast iron left too much crust behind). Flipping them gently with a fork every two minutes kept the crusts intact with nary a burned peppercorn in sight.

A rasp-style grater is the best tool for zesting lemons. Turning the steaks every 2 minutes helps prevent the spices from burning.

- 1 tablespoon black peppercorns
- 2 tablespoons chopped fresh rosemary
- 1 tablespoon kosher salt
- 2 teaspoons ground coriander
- 2 teaspoons grated lemon zest
- 1½ teaspoons dry mustard
- 1 teaspoon red pepper flakes
- 2 (1-pound) boneless rib-eye steaks, 1½ inches thick, trimmed
- 1 tablespoon vegetable oil

1. Place peppercorns in zipper-lock bag and seal bag. Using rolling pin, crush peppercorns coarse. Combine peppercorns, rosemary, salt, coriander, lemon zest, mustard, and pepper flakes in bowl. Season steaks all over, including sides, with spice mixture, pressing to adhere. (Use all of spice mixture.)

2. Set wire rack in rimmed baking sheet. Heat oil in 12-inch nonstick skillet over medium heat until just smoking. Add steaks and cook, flipping steaks with fork every 2 minutes, until well browned and meat registers 125 degrees (for medium-rare), 10 to 13 minutes. Transfer steaks to prepared rack, tent with aluminum foil, and let rest for 5 minutes. Slice and serve.

Easy Steak Frites

SERVES 4

Easy Steak Frites

WHY THIS RECIPE WORKS Steak frites is a favorite bistro dinner of juicy steak and crispy french fries that we wanted to make at home. For fries that did not require double frying, we added the potatoes and oil to a cold Dutch oven before cranking the heat to high. Lower-starch Yukon Golds yielded fries with crunchy exteriors and creamy interiors. For the steaks, we found that thick-cut boneless strip steaks gave us more time to get a crust on the outside without overcooking the center. To ensure that the fries and steaks were ready at the same time, we prepared all ingredients and equipment before cooking and started the fries 30 minutes before serving time.

For the best french fries, we recommend using large Yukon Gold potatoes (10 to 12 ounces each) that are similar in size. We prefer peanut oil for frying for its high smoke point and the clean taste it imparts to fried foods, but you can use vegetable oil, if desired. Use a Dutch oven that holds 6 quarts or more for this recipe.

- 4 tablespoons unsalted butter, softened
- 1 shallot, minced
- 1 tablespoon minced fresh parsley
- 1 garlic clove, minced
  Kosher salt and pepper
- 2½ pounds large Yukon Gold potatoes, unpeeled
- 6 cups plus 1 tablespoon peanut or vegetable oil
- 2 (1-pound) boneless strip steaks, 1¼ to 1½ inches thick, trimmed and halved crosswise

1. Mash butter, shallot, parsley, garlic, ½ teaspoon salt, and ¼ teaspoon pepper together in bowl; set compound butter aside.

2. Square off potatoes by cutting ¼-inch-thick slice from each of their 4 long sides; discard slices. Cut potatoes lengthwise into ¼-inch-thick planks. Stack 3 or 4 planks and cut into ¼-inch-thick fries. Repeat with remaining planks. (Do not place sliced potatoes in water.)

3. Line rimmed baking sheet with triple layer of paper towels. Combine potatoes and 6 cups oil in large Dutch oven. Cook over high heat until oil is vigorously bubbling, about 5 minutes. Continue to cook, without stirring, until

STEAKHOUSE SPECIALS 281

potatoes are limp but exteriors are beginning to firm, about 15 minutes. Using tongs, stir potatoes, gently scraping up any that stick, and continue to cook, stirring occasionally, until golden and crispy, 7 to 10 minutes longer.

4. Meanwhile, pat steaks dry with paper towels and season with salt and pepper. Heat remaining 1 tablespoon oil in 12-inch skillet over medium-high heat until just smoking. Add steaks and cook until well browned and meat registers 125 degrees (for medium-rare), 4 to 7 minutes per side. Transfer steaks to platter, top each with compound butter, tent with aluminum foil, and let rest for 10 minutes.

5. Using spider or slotted spoon, transfer fries to prepared sheet and season with salt. Serve fries with steaks.

The American Table: Our First Restaurant? French.

Roadside taverns in New England served food to travelers throughout the colonial period, but it wasn't until 1793 that America got its first restaurant—complete with menus and separate prices for each item. The place, Julien's Restorator, was decidedly French. Proprietor Jean Baptiste Gilbert Payplat, called Julien by his friends and acquaintances, cooked for the archbishop of Bordeaux before emigrating to the United States. He settled in Massachusetts and set up shop, specializing in "excellent wines and cordials, good soups and broths, pastry in all its delicious variety, . . . beef, bacon, poultry, and generally, all other refreshing viands." After Payplat's death in 1805, his customers demanded that the business remain open, so his wife Hannah took over. She went on to manage Julien's Restorator for another decade.

Grilled Cowboy-Cut Rib Eyes

SERVES 4 TO 6

WHY THIS RECIPE WORKS Oversized cowboy-cut rib eyes offer big, beefy flavor, but cooking the huge steaks all the way through while achieving a flavorful seared crust is challenging. We used a bare minimum of seasonings—salt, pepper, and oil—to highlight the flavor of the steaks. To cook them, we opted for a low and slow approach to start. To keep the fire burning long enough, we layered unlit coals under lit ones. We let the steaks come to room temperature before grilling to cut down on cooking time, and then we slow-roasted the steaks on the cooler side of the grill until they were almost done. A quick sear over hot coals gave them a flavorful dark crust.

Don't start grilling until the steaks' internal temperatures have reached 55 degrees. Otherwise, the times and temperatures in this recipe will be inaccurate.

- 2 (1¼- to 1½-pound) double-cut bone-in rib-eye steaks, 1¾ to 2 inches thick, trimmed
- 4 teaspoons kosher salt
- 2 teaspoons vegetable oil
- 2 teaspoons pepper

1. Set wire rack inside rimmed baking sheet. Pat steaks dry with paper towels and sprinkle all over with salt. Place steaks on prepared rack and let stand at room temperature until meat registers 55 degrees, about 1 hour. Rub steaks with oil and sprinkle with pepper.

2a. For a Charcoal Grill Open bottom vent halfway. Arrange 4 quarts unlit charcoal briquettes in even layer over half of grill. Light large chimney starter one-third filled with charcoal briquettes (2 quarts). When top coals are partially covered with ash, pour evenly over unlit coals. Set cooking grate in place, cover, and open lid vent halfway. Heat grill until hot, about 5 minutes.

2b. For a Gas Grill Turn all burners to high, cover, and heat grill until hot, about 15 minutes. Turn primary burner to medium-low and turn off other burner(s). Adjust primary burner as needed to maintain grill temperature of 300 degrees.

3. Clean and oil cooking grate. Place steaks on cooler side of grill with bones facing fire. Cover and cook until steaks register 75 degrees, 10 to 20 minutes. Flip steaks, keeping bones facing fire. Cover and continue to cook until steaks register 95 degrees, 10 to 20 minutes.

4. If using charcoal, slide steaks to hotter part of grill. If using gas, remove steaks from grill, turn primary burner to high, and heat until hot, about 5 minutes; place steaks over primary burner. Cover and cook until well browned and steaks register 120 degrees (for medium-rare), about 4 minutes per side. Transfer steaks to clean wire rack set in rimmed baking sheet, tent loosely with foil, and let rest for 15 minutes. Transfer steaks to carving board, cut meat from bone, and slice into ½-inch-thick slices. Serve.

Slow-Roasted Medium-Rare Beef Short Ribs

SERVES 4

WHY THIS RECIPE WORKS For a different take on a tougher cut of beef, we applied a tried-and-true technique for cooking steaks: reverse searing. We first cooked the ribs until they were medium-rare—about an hour in a 275-degree oven. Next, we quickly browned them over high heat on the stovetop to create a flavorful crust. Salting the short ribs and letting them sit for at least 2 hours or up to 24 hours before cooking seasoned them all the way through and aided in tenderizing the meat and retaining juices. The slow cook also helped break down the muscle fibers to ensure tenderness. For a luxurious sauce, we dressed up browned butter with shallot, garlic, Worcestershire sauce, and Dijon mustard.

Plan ahead: The salted short ribs need to sit for at least 2 hours before cooking. You should have about 1½ pounds of meat after trimming.

Short Ribs
- 1 tablespoon kosher salt
- 1 tablespoon pepper
- 2 pounds boneless beef short ribs, 1½ to 2 inches thick, 2 inches wide, and 4 to 5 inches long, trimmed
- 1 tablespoon vegetable oil

Browned Butter Steak Sauce
- 8 tablespoons unsalted butter
- 2 tablespoons minced shallot
- 1 garlic clove, minced
- ¼ cup Worcestershire sauce
- 2 tablespoons red wine vinegar
- 1 tablespoon Dijon mustard
- 1 tablespoon packed brown sugar
- 1 tablespoon soy sauce
- 2 teaspoons pepper

1. For the Short Ribs Combine salt and pepper in small bowl. Pat short ribs dry and sprinkle all over with salt mixture. Transfer to large plate, cover, and refrigerate at least 2 hours or up to 24 hours.

2. Adjust oven rack to middle position and heat oven to 275 degrees. Set wire rack in rimmed baking sheet. Evenly space short ribs on prepared rack. Roast until meat registers between 135 and 140 degrees, 50 minutes to 1 hour. Remove from oven and let rest for 10 minutes.

Grilled Cowboy-Cut Rib Eyes

Slow-Roasted Medium-Rare Beef Short Ribs

3. For the Browned Butter Steak Sauce Meanwhile, melt butter in medium saucepan over medium heat. Cook, whisking frequently, until milk solids in butter are color of milk chocolate and have nutty aroma, 3 to 5 minutes. Add shallot and garlic and cook for 30 seconds. Remove from heat and immediately whisk in Worcestershire, vinegar, mustard, sugar, soy sauce, and pepper; set aside.

4. Heat oil in 12-inch nonstick skillet over medium-high heat until just smoking. Sear short ribs until well browned on top and bottom, 1 to 2 minutes per side. Transfer to carving board and let rest for 5 minutes.

5. Reheat sauce over medium heat, whisking frequently, until hot, 1 to 2 minutes. Slice short ribs against grain as thin as possible. Serve, passing sauce separately.

Spice-Crusted Slow-Roasted Medium-Rare Beef Short Ribs

Add 1 tablespoon packed brown sugar, 1 teaspoon smoked paprika, 1 teaspoon ground coriander, and ½ teaspoon ground allspice with salt in step 1.

Japanese Steakhouse Steak and Vegetables

SERVES 4

WHY THIS RECIPE WORKS We wanted to deliver all the savory-sweet appeal of a hibachi steakhouse dinner at home. A large cast-iron skillet mimicked the powerful heat of the flattop; we avoided overcrowding by cooking the steak and vegetables separately. To give the vegetables a superflavorful start, we added them to the steak drippings in the still-hot skillet. We finished the sliced steaks and perfectly browned shiitakes, onion, and zucchini with a rich, savory soy-garlic butter.

Strip steaks can be substituted for the rib eyes. We like to serve the steak and vegetables with Simple Hibachi-Style Fried Rice, Spicy Mayonnaise (Yum-Yum Sauce), White Mustard Sauce, and Sweet Ginger Sauce (recipes follow on pages 274–275). If using a nonstick skillet, heat the oil in the skillet over medium-high heat until just smoking before adding the steaks in step 2.

- 3 tablespoons unsalted butter, melted
- 2 tablespoons soy sauce
- 2 garlic cloves, minced
- 2 (1-pound) boneless rib-eye steaks, 1½ to 1¾ inches thick, trimmed
- 1¼ teaspoons white pepper, divided
- 1 teaspoon table salt, divided
- 1 tablespoon vegetable oil
- 2 zucchini (8 ounces each), halved lengthwise and sliced ¾ inch thick
- 2 onions, cut into ¾-inch pieces
- 6 ounces shiitake mushrooms, stemmed and halved if small or quartered if large
- 2 tablespoons mirin

1. Combine melted butter, soy sauce, and garlic in bowl; set aside. Pat steaks dry with paper towels and sprinkle with 1 teaspoon white pepper and ¾ teaspoon salt.

2. Heat 12-inch cast-iron skillet over medium-high heat for 5 minutes. Add oil to skillet and swirl to coat. Add steaks and cook, flipping steaks every 2 minutes, until well browned and meat registers 120 to 125 degrees (for medium-rare), 10 to 13 minutes. Transfer steaks to carving board, tent with aluminum foil, and let rest.

3. While steaks rest, add zucchini, onions, mushrooms, remaining ¼ teaspoon white pepper, and remaining ¼ teaspoon salt to fat left in skillet and stir to combine. Pat vegetables into even layer and cook over medium-high heat, without stirring, until beginning to brown,

The American Table: Benihana

Hiroaki "Rocky" Aoki, a Tokyo native, came to the United States in the early 1960s on a wrestling scholarship, earned a restaurant management degree, and began to pursue his dream of opening a Japanese restaurant in New York. Aoki's father agreed to help bankroll the project under one condition: It needed to provide entertainment. When his first Benihana opened in 1964, customers loved the showy "performance" cooking that included sleight-of-hand egg-cracking tricks and onion volcanoes. By 1972, there were six Benihana locations across the country, and Aoki's success continued to grow. He encountered extreme highs and lows along the way, living lavishly but also coming under scrutiny for insider trading and nearly dying in a powerboat race under the Golden Gate Bridge. Aoki died in 2008, leaving behind dozens of restaurants.

about 3 minutes. Stir and continue to cook 2 minutes longer. Add mirin and 2 tablespoons soy-garlic butter to skillet and continue to cook until liquid has evaporated and vegetables are well browned, about 2 minutes longer.

4. Transfer vegetables to serving platter. Slice steaks ¼ inch thick and transfer to platter with vegetables. Drizzle steaks with remaining soy-garlic butter. Serve.

Simple Hibachi-Style Fried Rice

SERVES 4

WHY THIS RECIPE WORKS For a simple, comforting fried rice to accompany our Japanese Steakhouse Steak and Vegetables (page 284), we started by boiling the rice in plenty of water. This eliminated the need for leftover rice by effectively cutting the cooking time in half and rinsing away excess starch that can result in stickiness. To create a classic hibachi flavor profile, we fried the rice with scallions and scrambled egg and stirred in a mixture of soy sauce and mirin, a Japanese sweetened rice wine. A spoonful of garlic butter added richness and shine.

Mirin can be found in your supermarket's Asian foods section. Black pepper can be substituted for the white pepper, if desired.

- 1½ cups long-grain white rice
- 3 large eggs
- 1 teaspoon toasted sesame oil
- ¼ teaspoon table salt
- ¼ teaspoon white pepper
- 1 tablespoon unsalted butter, softened
- 1 garlic clove, minced
- 1 tablespoon vegetable oil
- 4 scallions, sliced ¼ inch thick
- 1½ tablespoons soy sauce
- 1½ tablespoons mirin

1. Bring 3 quarts water to boil in large saucepan over high heat. Add rice and cook, stirring occasionally, until just cooked through, about 12 minutes. Drain rice in fine-mesh strainer or colander. Whisk eggs, sesame oil, salt, and white pepper together in bowl; set aside. Combine butter and garlic in second bowl; set aside.

Japanese Steakhouse Steak and Vegetables

Simple Hibachi-Style Fried Rice

2. Heat vegetable oil in 12-inch nonstick skillet over medium-high heat until shimmering. Add egg mixture and stir with rubber spatula until set but still wet, about 15 seconds.

3. Add scallions and rice and cook until sizzling and popping loudly, about 3 minutes. Add soy sauce and mirin and cook, stirring constantly, until thoroughly combined, about 2 minutes. Stir in garlic butter until incorporated. Serve.

Spicy Mayonnaise (Yum-Yum Sauce)
SERVES 4 TO 6 (MAKES ABOUT ¾ CUP)

White miso can be substituted for the red miso, if desired.

- ½ cup mayonnaise
- 2 tablespoons water
- 1 tablespoon unsalted butter, melted
- 1 tablespoon red miso
- 1 teaspoon tomato paste
- ¼ teaspoon cayenne pepper
- ¼ teaspoon paprika
- ¼ teaspoon table salt

Whisk all ingredients together in bowl.

White Mustard Sauce
SERVES 4 TO 6 (MAKES ABOUT ⅔ CUP)

Be sure to use toasted sesame oil here. If you prefer a spicier sauce, add more dry mustard.

- ½ cup heavy cream
- 2 tablespoons soy sauce
- 1½ teaspoons dry mustard
- 1½ teaspoons toasted sesame oil
- 1 teaspoon sugar

Vigorously whisk all ingredients in bowl until combined and slightly thickened.

Sweet Ginger Sauce
SERVES 4 TO 6 (MAKES ABOUT ¾ CUP)

Be sure to use unseasoned rice vinegar here.

- ½ cup chopped onion
- 3 tablespoons sugar
- 3 tablespoons rice vinegar
- 3 tablespoons soy sauce
- 1 (¾-inch) piece ginger, peeled and chopped

Process all ingredients in blender until smooth, about 15 seconds, scraping down sides of blender jar as needed.

Grilled Steak Burgers
SERVES 4

WHY THIS RECIPE WORKS We wanted a burger with the big beefy flavor and crusty char of a grilled steak. Ground sirloin, the most flavorful ground beef, was a natural choice, but unfortunately it's also quite lean. A seasoned butter added richness to the sirloin, but something was missing. Steak sauce! In about five minutes, we simmered up our own intensely flavored sauce, perfect for serving with the burger, smearing on the bun, and even mixing into the beef before cooking.

Use kaiser rolls or other hearty buns for these substantial burgers.

Burgers
- 8 tablespoons unsalted butter
- 2 garlic cloves, minced
- 2 teaspoons onion powder
- 1 teaspoon pepper
- ½ teaspoon table salt
- 2 teaspoons soy sauce
- 1½ pounds 90 percent lean ground sirloin
- 4 hamburger buns

Steak Sauce
- 2 tablespoons tomato paste
- ⅔ cup beef broth
- ⅓ cup raisins
- 2 tablespoons soy sauce
- 2 tablespoons Dijon mustard
- 2 tablespoons balsamic vinegar
- 1 tablespoon Worcestershire sauce

1. For the Burgers Melt butter in 8-inch skillet over medium-low heat. Add garlic, onion powder, pepper, and salt and cook until fragrant, about 1 minute. Pour all but 1 tablespoon butter mixture into bowl and let cool for about 5 minutes.

2. For the Steak Sauce Meanwhile, add tomato paste to skillet and cook over medium heat until paste begins to darken, 1 to 2 minutes. Stir in broth, raisins, soy sauce, mustard, vinegar, and Worcestershire and simmer until raisins plump, about 5 minutes. Process sauce in blender until smooth, about 30 seconds; transfer to bowl.

3. Add 5 tablespoons cooled butter mixture and soy sauce to ground beef and gently knead until well combined. Shape into four ¾-inch-thick patties and press shallow divot in center of each. Brush each patty all over with 1 tablespoon steak sauce. Combine remaining 2 tablespoons cooled butter mixture with 2 tablespoons steak sauce; set aside.

4a. For a Charcoal Grill Open bottom vent completely. Light large chimney starter filled with charcoal briquettes (6 quarts). When top coals are partially covered with ash, pour evenly over grill. Set cooking grate in place, cover, and open lid vent completely. Heat grill until hot, about 5 minutes.

4b. For a Gas Grill Turn all burners to high, cover, and heat grill until hot, about 15 minutes. Leave burners on high.

5. Clean and oil cooking grate. Grill burgers (covered if using gas) until meat registers 120 to 125 degrees (for medium-rare), 3 to 4 minutes per side, or 130 to 135 degrees (for medium), 4 to 5 minutes per side. Transfer burgers to plate, tent loosely with aluminum foil, and let rest for 5 to 10 minutes. Brush cut side of buns with butter–steak sauce mixture. Grill buns, cut side down, until golden, 2 to 3 minutes. Place burgers on buns. Serve with remaining steak sauce.

Grilled Steak Burgers

Pork Grillades

SERVES 6 TO 8

WHY THIS RECIPE WORKS Despite their name, grillades are not grilled; rather, they are thinly sliced cuts of meat browned and stewed in a supersavory tomato-based gravy. For consistency and ease we opted for pork blade chops (with the bones cut off) which cooked evenly and held up to stewing. When it came time to make a roux for

Pork Grillades

the base of our gravy, dry-toasting the flour in a skillet in advance helped cut down on the cooking time. Adding our own Cajun seasoning spice blend, a traditional mix of vegetables, and a dash of Tabasco provided heat and complexity to this iconic Louisiana dish.

We prefer pork blade chops because they hold up to stewing better than loin chops. Blade chops aren't typically available boneless; ask your butcher to bone them for you. Use our recipe for Louisiana Seasoning (page 181) or the test kitchen's taste test winner, Tony Chachere's Original Creole Seasoning.

- 1 cup all-purpose flour, divided
- 8 (6- to 8-ounce) bone-in pork-blade-cut chops, ½ inch thick, bones discarded, and trimmed
- 2 tablespoons Louisiana Seasoning, divided
  Table salt and pepper
- ½ cup vegetable oil
- 1 onion, chopped
- 1 green bell pepper, stemmed, seeded, and chopped
- 1 celery rib, chopped
- 2 garlic cloves, minced
- 2 cups chicken broth
- 1 (14.5-ounce) can whole peeled tomatoes, crushed by hand
- 2 slices bacon
- 1 tablespoon Worcestershire sauce
- 1 bay leaf
- 1 teaspoon Tabasco sauce, plus extra for serving
- 4 cups cooked white rice
- 2 scallions, sliced thin

1. Adjust oven rack to lower-middle position and heat oven to 350 degrees. Toast ¼ cup flour in small skillet over medium heat, stirring constantly, until just beginning to brown, about 3 minutes; set aside.

2. Season chops with 1½ teaspoons Louisiana Seasoning, salt, and pepper. Whisk remaining ¾ cup flour and remaining 1½ tablespoons Louisiana Seasoning together in shallow dish. Working with 1 chop at a time, dredge in seasoned flour, shaking off excess; transfer chops to plate.

3. Heat oil in Dutch oven over medium heat until shimmering. Add 4 chops and cook until browned, 3 to 5 minutes per side; transfer to plate. Repeat with remaining 4 chops.

4. Remove all but ¼ cup oil from Dutch oven and return to medium heat. Add toasted flour to pot and cook, whisking constantly, until deep brown, about 2 minutes. Add onion, bell pepper, celery, and 1 teaspoon salt and cook, stirring often, until vegetables are just softened, about 3 minutes. Add garlic and cook until fragrant, about 30 seconds.

5. Stir in broth, tomatoes and their juice, bacon, Worcestershire, and bay leaf, scraping up any browned bits. Nestle chops into liquid and add any accumulated pork juices from plate. Bring to simmer, cover, and transfer to oven. Cook until fork slips easily in and out of pork, about 1 hour.

6. Remove grillades from oven. Discard bacon and bay leaf; stir in Tabasco. Season with salt and pepper to taste. Serve over rice, sprinkled with scallions and passing extra Tabasco.

Baked Stuffed Shrimp

SERVES 4 TO 6

WHY THIS RECIPE WORKS There are often two problems with baked stuffed shrimp: mushy, bland stuffing and rubbery shrimp. For our stuffing, we preferred the sweet flavor of fresh bread crumbs, toasted to ensure crispness. Butterflying the shrimp allowed us to press the stuffing into the shrimp—as the shrimp contracted in the oven, the stuffing was sealed into place. To prevent overcooked shrimp yet still achieve crisp stuffing, we cooked the shrimp for a longer time at a lower temperature.

In a pinch, chicken broth can be substituted for the clam juice. A sturdy rimmed baking sheet can be used in place of the broiler pan bottom. Shrimp that are labeled U12 contain 12 or fewer shrimp per pound.

- 4 slices hearty white sandwich bread, torn into quarters
- ½ cup mayonnaise
- ¼ cup bottled clam juice
- ¼ cup finely chopped fresh parsley
- 4 scallions, chopped fine
- 1 tablespoon Dijon mustard
- 2 garlic cloves, minced
- 2 teaspoons grated lemon zest plus 1 tablespoon juice
- ⅛ teaspoon cayenne pepper
  Table salt
- 1¼ pounds colossal shrimp (U12), peeled and deveined

1. Adjust oven rack to upper-middle position and heat oven to 375 degrees. Pulse bread in food processor to coarse crumbs, about 10 pulses. Transfer crumbs to broiler pan bottom and bake until golden and dry, 8 to 10 minutes, stirring halfway through cooking time. Remove crumbs from oven and reduce temperature to 275 degrees.

2. Combine toasted bread crumbs, mayonnaise, clam juice, parsley, scallions, mustard, garlic, lemon zest and juice, cayenne, and ¼ teaspoon salt in bowl.

3. Pat shrimp dry with paper towels and season with salt. Grease empty broiler pan bottom. To butterfly shrimp, use sharp paring knife to cut along (but not through) vein line, then open up shrimp like a book. Using tip of paring knife, cut 1-inch opening through center of shrimp. Arrange shrimp cut side down on prepared pan. Divide bread-crumb mixture among shrimp, pressing to adhere. Bake until shrimp are opaque, 20 to 25 minutes.

4. Remove shrimp from oven and heat broiler. Broil shrimp until crumbs are deep golden brown and crispy, 1 to 3 minutes. Serve.

Creole Baked Stuffed Shrimp with Sausage

The smoky, meaty flavor of kielbasa is a nice foil to the sweet shrimp in this variation.

Omit cayenne and add 1 teaspoon Creole seasoning in step 2. Fold 4 ounces kielbasa sausage, chopped fine, into filling and proceed as directed.

Failproof Chicken Cordon Bleu

SERVES 4 TO 6

WHY THIS RECIPE WORKS Making chicken cordon bleu can be fussy; we wanted an easier way. We found cutting a pocket into the breast to be much more efficient than the traditional method of pounding and rolling. To get the same swirl effect achieved by rolling the chicken around the ham and cheese, we simply rolled the ham slices into cylinders around shredded cheese and tucked the cylinders into each chicken breast. Adding a healthy dose of Dijon mustard to the egg wash boosted the flavor of our chicken, as did supplementing homemade bread crumbs with buttery Ritz cracker crumbs.

To keep the filling from leaking, thoroughly chill the stuffed breasts before breading. We like Black Forest ham here.

Baked Stuffed Shrimp

Failproof Chicken Cordon Bleu

25 Ritz crackers (about ¾ sleeve)
4 slices hearty white sandwich bread, torn into quarters
6 tablespoons unsalted butter, melted
8 thin slices deli ham (8 ounces)
8 ounces Swiss cheese, shredded (2 cups)
4 (8-ounce) boneless, skinless chicken breasts, trimmed
  Table salt and pepper
3 large eggs
2 tablespoons Dijon mustard
1 cup all-purpose flour

1. Adjust oven racks to lowest and middle positions and heat oven to 450 degrees. Pulse crackers and bread in food processor until coarsely ground, about 15 pulses. Drizzle in butter; pulse a few times to incorporate. Bake crumbs on rimmed baking sheet on middle rack, stirring occasionally, until light brown, 3 to 5 minutes. Transfer to shallow dish. Do not turn oven off.

2. Top each ham slice with ¼ cup cheese and roll tightly; set aside. Pat chicken dry with paper towels. Using paring knife, cut into thickest part of each chicken breast to create deep pocket with opening of 3 to 4 inches. Stuff each breast with 2 ham-and-cheese rolls and press closed. Season both sides of chicken with salt and pepper. Transfer chicken to plate, cover with plastic wrap, and refrigerate for at least 20 minutes.

3. Beat eggs and mustard in second shallow dish. Place flour in third shallow dish. One at a time, coat stuffed chicken lightly with flour, dip into egg mixture, and dredge in crumbs, pressing to adhere. (Breaded chicken can be refrigerated, covered, for 1 day.) Transfer chicken to clean rimmed baking sheet. Bake on lowest rack until bottom of chicken is golden brown, about 10 minutes, and then move baking sheet to middle rack and reduce oven temperature to 400 degrees. Bake until golden brown and chicken registers 160 degrees, 20 to 25 minutes. Transfer to platter, tent with aluminum foil, and let rest for 5 minutes. Serve.

Garlic Mashed Potatoes

SERVES 8 TO 10

WHY THIS RECIPE WORKS Making mashed potatoes isn't typically a quick endeavor—add roasted garlic to the mix and you've really got a project on your hands. We wanted a streamlined recipe. We cut the potatoes into small pieces to promote even, quicker cooking. The small pieces also meant the potatoes could better soak up garlicky flavor. To mimic the flavor of roasted garlic, we sprinkled in a little sugar while sautéing the garlic. Finally, we simmered the potatoes in half-and-half, butter, and the sautéed garlic to avoid the "washing away" of flavor that can come from boiling in just water.

Cutting the potatoes into ½-inch pieces ensures that the maximum surface area is exposed to soak up garlicky flavor.

4 pounds russet potatoes, peeled, quartered, and cut into ½-inch pieces
12 tablespoons unsalted butter, cut into pieces
12 garlic cloves, minced
1 teaspoon sugar
1½ cups half-and-half, divided
½ cup water
  Table salt and pepper

1. Place cut potatoes in colander. Rinse under cold running water until water runs clear. Drain thoroughly.

2. Melt 4 tablespoons butter in Dutch oven over medium heat. Cook garlic and sugar, stirring often, until sticky and straw colored, 3 to 4 minutes. Add rinsed potatoes, 1¼ cups half-and-half, water, and 1 teaspoon salt to pot and stir to combine. Bring to boil, then reduce

Stuffing, Streamlined

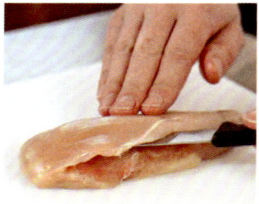
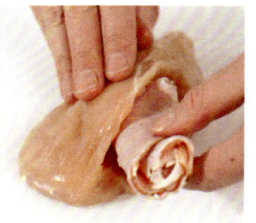
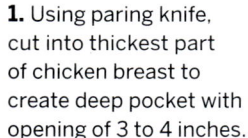

1. Using paring knife, cut into thickest part of chicken breast to create deep pocket with opening of 3 to 4 inches.

2. Stuff each pocket with 2 ham-and-cheese rolls and seal. Refrigerate chicken for at least 20 minutes before breading.

heat to low and simmer, covered and stirring occasionally, until potatoes are tender and most of liquid is absorbed, 25 to 30 minutes.

3. Off heat, add remaining 8 tablespoons butter to pot and mash with potato masher until smooth. Using rubber spatula, fold in remaining ¼ cup half-and-half until liquid is absorbed and potatoes are creamy. Season with salt and pepper to taste. Serve.

Mashed Potato Cakes
SERVES 4 TO 6

Garlic Mashed Potatoes

WHY THIS RECIPE WORKS Mashed potato cakes are equally welcome at suppertime next to a piece of meat or at breakfast under a poached egg. Leftover mashed potatoes made mushy cakes, so we started from scratch, mashing russet potatoes with Parmesan, chives, and an egg yolk for richness. Chilling the mashed potatoes made shaping the cakes easier. For a crisp crust, we dipped the disks in beaten egg to help the coating adhere. Serving the cakes with a dollop of sour cream offered a cool, tangy finish.

Using two spatulas to flip the cakes helps prevent splattering. We like to change the oil after frying the first batch of cakes because any dark panko remnants left behind will freckle the second batch. You can strain the oil through a fine-mesh strainer if you prefer to reuse it, but be careful because it is very hot. Plan ahead: The cooked mashed potatoes need to chill in the refrigerator for 1 hour.

- 2½ pounds russet potatoes, peeled, halved lengthwise, and sliced ¼ inch thick
- Table salt and pepper
- 1 ounce Parmesan cheese, grated (½ cup)
- ¼ cup chopped fresh chives
- 1 large egg yolk plus 2 large eggs
- 2 cups panko bread crumbs
- 1 cup vegetable oil, divided
- Sour cream

1. Place potatoes in medium saucepan and add water to cover by 1 inch, then stir in 1 tablespoon salt. Bring to boil over high heat. Reduce heat to medium-low and simmer until tip of paring knife inserted into potatoes meets no resistance, 8 to 10 minutes. Drain potatoes and return to saucepan; let cool for 5 minutes.

Mashed Potato Cakes

2. Add Parmesan, chives, egg yolk, ¾ teaspoon salt, and ¼ teaspoon pepper to cooled potatoes. Using potato masher, mash until smooth and well combined. Transfer potato mixture to bowl and refrigerate until completely cool, about 1 hour.

3. Beat remaining 2 eggs together in shallow dish. Place panko in second shallow dish. Divide potato mixture into 8 equal portions (about ½ cup each) and shape into 3-inch-diameter cakes, about ¾ inch thick. Working with 1 cake at a time, carefully dip cakes in egg mixture, turning to coat both sides and allowing excess to drip off; then coat with panko, pressing gently to adhere. Transfer to plate and let sit for 5 minutes.

4. Line large plate with paper towels. Heat ½ cup oil in 12-inch nonstick skillet over medium-high heat until shimmering. Place 4 cakes in skillet and cook until deep golden brown on first side, about 3 minutes. Using 2 spatulas, carefully flip cakes and continue to cook until deep golden brown on second side, about 2 minutes longer, gently pressing on cakes with spatula for even browning.

5. Transfer cakes to prepared plate. Discard oil and wipe out skillet with paper towels. Repeat with remaining ½ cup oil and remaining 4 cakes. Serve with sour cream.

Blue Cheese and Bacon Mashed Potato Cakes

Substitute ¾ cup crumbled blue cheese for Parmesan. Stir 6 slices cooked chopped bacon into potato mixture after mashing in step 2.

Cheddar and Scallion Mashed Potato Cakes

Substitute 1 cup shredded sharp cheddar cheese for Parmesan and sliced scallions for chives.

Lyonnaise Potatoes

SERVES 4

WHY THIS RECIPE WORKS Lyonnaise potatoes originated as a way to use up boiled potatoes from dinner the night before; they're sliced and pan-fried with copious amounts of butter and thin slices of onion. To avoid waiting for leftovers, we started with raw Yukon Golds (chosen for their deep flavor and tender texture). Slicing them into thick rounds prevented overcrowding the pan, and giving them a head start before lowering the heat and adding the onions ensured that everything emerged tender and browned.

Lyonnaise Potatoes

Use potatoes of similar size.

- 4 tablespoons unsalted butter
- 2 pounds Yukon Gold potatoes, peeled and sliced ½ inch thick
- Table salt and pepper
- 1 onion, halved and sliced thin
- 1 tablespoon minced fresh parsley

1. Melt butter in 12-inch nonstick skillet over medium heat. Add potatoes and ¾ teaspoon salt and cook, covered, until just tender and golden brown, about 15 minutes, flipping potatoes occasionally to ensure even browning.

2. Reduce heat to medium-low. Add onion, ½ teaspoon salt, and ½ teaspoon pepper; cover and continue to cook until onion is tender and golden brown, about 10 minutes longer, stirring occasionally. Season with salt and pepper to taste. Transfer to serving platter and sprinkle with parsley. Serve.

Delmonico Potato Casserole

SERVES 8 TO 10

WHY THIS RECIPE WORKS To revive this classic dish, we first focused on how to prep the potatoes. Boiled cubed potatoes won out over shredded because they held their texture better in the casserole. We sautéed onion and garlic, added cream and chicken broth (to cut the richness of the cream), and cooked the cubed potatoes in this mixture. Lemon juice and zest added welcome brightness. For the crusty topping, we turned to an unexpected ingredient: frozen shredded hash browns. We sautéed the thawed hash browns in butter, cream, and chicken broth to enhance their flavor before topping the casserole.

We prefer the buttery flavor of Yukon Gold potatoes here, but all-purpose and red potatoes also work. Do not use russets—their high starch content will make the casserole gluey. For the topping, we had good results with Ore-Ida Country Style Hash Browns, available in the frozen foods aisle of most supermarkets.

- 3 tablespoons unsalted butter, divided
- 1 onion, chopped fine
- 2 garlic cloves, minced
- 2½ cups heavy cream, divided
- 1½ cups chicken broth, divided
- 2½ pounds Yukon Gold potatoes, peeled and cut into ½-inch cubes
- ⅛ teaspoon ground nutmeg
- Table salt and pepper
- 1 teaspoon grated lemon zest plus 2 teaspoons juice
- 5 cups frozen shredded hash brown potatoes, thawed and patted dry with paper towels
- 1½ ounces Parmesan cheese, grated (¾ cup), divided
- ¼ cup finely chopped fresh chives

1. Adjust oven rack to upper-middle position and heat oven to 450 degrees. Melt 1 tablespoon butter in Dutch oven over medium-high heat. Cook onion until softened, about 3 minutes. Stir in garlic and cook until fragrant, about 30 seconds. Stir in 2 cups cream, 1 cup broth, Yukon Golds, nutmeg, 2 teaspoons salt, and 1 teaspoon pepper. Bring to boil, then reduce heat to medium and simmer until potatoes are translucent at edges and mixture is slightly thickened, about 10 minutes. Off heat, stir in lemon zest and juice.

Delmonico Potato Casserole

The American Table: Potatoes with Panache

In 1837, Delmonico's opened in lower Manhattan and a restaurant star was born. Owned by two Swiss men, the restaurant served French-style cuisine and became the model for many other fashionable restaurants of the era. Its lavish dining room served such luxurious fare as lobster Newburg, baked Alaska, and their signature potato side dish, Delmonico potatoes. The potatoes were boiled, finely shredded, and cooked with milk and heavy cream. When an order came in, a serving of potatoes was sprinkled with Parmesan cheese and "gratinéed" under the broiler. The result was a potato gratin with a creamy interior and a crusty, cheesy topping. But look up a modern recipe for this dish and you'll most likely find a casserole made of overboiled chunks of potatoes baked in a creamy cheddar sauce and topped with more cheese. We wanted to bring back the simplicity and elegance of the original dish but make it more practical to feed a crowd.

2. Transfer potato mixture to 13 by 9-inch baking dish and bake until bubbling around edges and surface is just golden, about 20 minutes. Meanwhile, melt remaining 2 tablespoons butter in 12-inch nonstick skillet over medium-high heat. Cook shredded potatoes until beginning to brown, about 2 minutes. Add remaining ½ cup cream, remaining ½ cup broth, and ½ teaspoon pepper to skillet and cook, stirring occasionally, until liquid has evaporated, about 3 minutes. Off heat, stir in ½ cup Parmesan and 2 tablespoons chives.

3. Remove baking dish from oven and top with shredded potato mixture. Sprinkle with remaining ¼ cup Parmesan and continue to bake until top is golden brown, about 20 minutes. Let cool for 15 minutes. Sprinkle with remaining 2 tablespoons chives. Serve.

To Make Ahead Prepare through step 1, let cool completely, transfer to baking dish, and refrigerate, covered with plastic wrap, for 1 day. To serve, proceed as directed in step 2, increasing baking time to 25 to 30 minutes.

Lighthouse Inn Potatoes
SERVES 8 TO 10

Lighthouse Inn Potatoes

WHY THIS RECIPE WORKS The Lighthouse Inn, an iconic Connecticut restaurant and hotel, was known for its rich potato side dish. To re-create its creamy sauce, we cooked russet potatoes in cream and butter; the starch released by the potatoes into the cream left the sauce rich and velvety. A little baking soda prevented curdling. Topping the mixture with cheesy bread crumbs and baking them until crunchy and golden took our recipe over the top.

We prefer the texture of light cream for this recipe, but heavy cream will also work. Do not use half-and-half; it has a tendency to break. Grate the Parmesan on a rasp-style grater. Our favorite panko bread crumbs are from Kikkoman.

- 2 ounces Parmesan cheese, grated (1 cup)
- 1 cup panko bread crumbs
- 4 tablespoons unsalted butter, melted, plus 6 tablespoons cut into 6 pieces
  Table salt and pepper
- 2½ pounds russet potatoes, peeled and cut into 1-inch chunks
- 3 cups light cream, divided
- ⅛ teaspoon baking soda

1. Adjust oven rack to middle position and heat oven to 375 degrees. Combine Parmesan, panko, melted butter, and ¼ teaspoon salt in bowl; set aside.

2. Bring potatoes, 2½ cups cream, baking soda, 2 teaspoons salt, and 1 teaspoon pepper to boil in large saucepan over medium-high heat. Reduce heat to low and cook at bare simmer, stirring often, until paring knife slides easily into potatoes without them crumbling, 20 to 25 minutes.

3. Off heat, stir remaining ½ cup cream and remaining 6 tablespoons butter into potato mixture until butter has melted, about 1 minute. Transfer potato mixture to 13 by 9-inch baking dish. Sprinkle Parmesan-panko mixture over top. Bake, uncovered, until bubbling around edges and surface is golden brown, 15 to 20 minutes. Let cool for at least 15 minutes. Serve.

To Make Ahead After potato mixture has been transferred to baking dish, let cool completely, cover with aluminum foil, and refrigerate for up to 24 hours. Before applying topping, bake, covered, until heated through, about 35 minutes. Apply topping and continue to bake, uncovered, 15 to 20 minutes longer.

The Lighthouse Inn

Locals claim that the Lighthouse Inn, originally a country house for wealthy businessmen before being turned into a resort, is haunted.

Olive Oil Potato Gratin

SERVES 6 TO 8

WHY THIS RECIPE WORKS Potato gratin is a notoriously heavy side dish, laden with cream and gooey cheese. We wanted to shift the focus of this classic side dish to the potatoes. We chose Yukon Gold potatoes for their rich flavor and moderate starch content, which helped them hold their shape when cooked. Tossing the potatoes with fruity, flavorful extra-virgin olive oil heightened the flavor of the potatoes but didn't overpower them. For a crisp, cheesy topping, we mixed more olive oil with panko bread crumbs and sprinkled the dish with sharp, salty Pecorino Romano. For added depth, we added sautéed onions, fresh thyme, and garlic.

The test kitchen's favorite supermarket extra-virgin olive oils are Carapelli Original Extra Virgin Olive Oil and California Olive Ranch 100% California Extra Virgin Olive Oil. We prefer to use a mandoline to create thin, even slices of potato.

- 2 ounces Pecorino Romano cheese, grated (1 cup)
- ½ cup extra-virgin olive oil, divided
- ¼ cup panko bread crumbs
  Table salt and pepper
- 2 onions, halved and sliced thin
- 2 garlic cloves, minced
- 1 teaspoon minced fresh thyme, divided
- 1 cup chicken broth, divided
- 3 pounds Yukon Gold potatoes, peeled and sliced ⅛ inch thick

1. Adjust oven rack to upper-middle position and heat oven to 400 degrees. Grease 13 by 9-inch baking dish. Combine Pecorino, 3 tablespoons oil, panko, and ½ teaspoon pepper in bowl; set aside.

2. Heat 2 tablespoons oil in 12-inch skillet over medium heat until shimmering. Add onions, ½ teaspoon salt, and ¼ teaspoon pepper and cook, stirring frequently, until browned, about 15 minutes. Add garlic and ½ teaspoon thyme and cook until fragrant, about 30 seconds. Add ¼ cup broth and cook until nearly evaporated, scraping up any browned bits, about 2 minutes. Remove from heat; set aside.

3. Toss potatoes, remaining 3 tablespoons oil, 1 teaspoon salt, ½ teaspoon pepper, and remaining ½ teaspoon thyme together in bowl. Arrange half of potatoes in prepared dish, spread onion mixture in even layer over potatoes, and distribute remaining potatoes over onions. Pour remaining ¾ cup broth over potatoes. Cover dish tightly with aluminum foil and bake for 1 hour.

Olive Oil Potato Gratin

4. Remove foil, top gratin with reserved Pecorino mixture, and continue to bake until top is golden brown and potatoes are completely tender, 15 to 20 minutes. Let cool for 15 minutes. Serve.

Crushed Red Potatoes with Garlic and Herbs

SERVES 4 TO 6

WHY THIS RECIPE WORKS Boiled and buttered potatoes are a reliable side dish, but they can be a bit boring; all the flavor remains on the outsides of the potatoes, leaving the interiors bland. To fix that, we simmered red potatoes until they were tender, drained them, and then melted butter in the empty pot before adding minced garlic, fresh chives, fresh parsley, salt, and pepper. We then added the hot potatoes, lightly pressed each with the back of a spoon until it broke apart, and gently stirred them with the buttery, herby goodness so that it worked its way into all the nooks and crannies. Goodbye, underseasoned spuds.

Be sure to use small red potatoes measuring 1 to 2 inches in diameter, and use a gentle hand when crushing them.

- 2 pounds small red potatoes, unpeeled
  Table salt and pepper
- 6 tablespoons unsalted butter
- 1 garlic clove, minced
- 2 tablespoons minced fresh chives
- 2 tablespoons minced fresh parsley

1. Place potatoes and 2 tablespoons salt in Dutch oven and cover with water by 1 inch. Bring to boil over high heat. Reduce heat to medium-high and simmer until paring knife slips easily in and out of potatoes, about 20 minutes. (Potatoes should be very tender.) Drain potatoes in colander.

2. In now-empty pot, melt butter over medium heat. Add garlic and cook until fragrant, about 30 seconds. Off heat, stir in chives, parsley, ½ teaspoon salt, and ¼ teaspoon pepper.

3. Add potatoes to pot. Press each potato with back of spoon or spatula to lightly crush (do not mash; potatoes should still have texture). Stir to coat potatoes with butter mixture (potatoes will break up slightly; this is OK). Transfer to platter. Serve.

Crushed Red Potatoes with Garlic and Herbs

Getting the Texture Just Right

1. Press on the cooked potatoes with a wooden spoon until they crack open and are lightly crushed.

2. Stir gently to further break down the crushed potatoes and distribute the seasoned butter mixture.

Crushed Red Potatoes with Garlic and Smoked Paprika

Substitute extra-virgin olive oil for butter and heat until shimmering. Sprinkle 1 teaspoon smoked paprika over crushed potatoes on platter before serving.

Crushed Red Potatoes with Oregano and Capers

Substitute 1 tablespoon chopped fresh oregano, 1 tablespoon rinsed capers, and 1 tablespoon lemon juice for chives and parsley. Decrease salt in step 2 to ¼ teaspoon.

Roasted Salt-and-Vinegar Potatoes

SERVES 4

WHY THIS RECIPE WORKS Cooking red potatoes in a super-saturated salt solution gave them incredibly creamy, well-seasoned interiors. After the potatoes were parcooked, we smashed them to expose some of the potato flesh, brushed them with malt vinegar, and roasted them on a well-oiled baking sheet until the exposed surface was golden and crispy. A final brush with more vinegar when the potatoes came out of the oven reinforced the irresistible salty-sour flavor of these spuds.

Use small red potatoes, measuring 1 to 2 inches in diameter. If you prefer to use kosher salt, you will need 1½ cups of Morton's or 2½ cups of Diamond Crystal. Cider vinegar is a good substitute for the malt vinegar.

- 6 tablespoons extra-virgin olive oil
- 2 pounds small red potatoes, scrubbed
- 1¼ cups table salt
- 3 tablespoons malt vinegar, divided
   Pepper

1. Adjust oven rack to upper-middle position and heat oven to 500 degrees. Set wire rack inside rimmed baking sheet. Brush second rimmed baking sheet evenly with oil. Bring 2 quarts water to boil in Dutch oven over medium-high heat. Stir in potatoes and salt and cook until just tender and paring knife slips easily in and out of potatoes, 20 to 30 minutes. Drain potatoes and transfer to wire rack; let dry for 10 minutes.

2. Transfer potatoes to oiled baking sheet. Flatten each potato with underside of measuring cup until ½ inch thick. Brush potatoes with half of vinegar and season with pepper. Roast until potatoes are well browned, 25 to 30 minutes. Brush with remaining vinegar. Transfer potatoes to platter, smashed side up. Serve.

Roasted Salt-and-Vinegar Potatoes

Malt Vinegar Substitutes

For our salt-and-vinegar potatoes, we raided the English larder for a beloved condiment: malt vinegar. Brits commonly douse fish and chips with it, so we knew it would be a perfect match for roasted potatoes. The vinegar, which is made from sprouted barley grains, gives the potatoes a pleasantly malty, tangy taste. But if you don't have it, cider or white wine vinegars are good substitutes. Avoid balsamic and rice vinegars, which tasters found too sweet, and red wine and distilled white vinegars, which were too harsh.

Torn and Fried Potatoes

Torn and Fried Potatoes

SERVES 4

WHY THIS RECIPE WORKS We figured fried potatoes with a compelling mix of textures—soft, fluffy interiors and craggy, crispy-crunchy exteriors—would be irresistible. Starchy russets offered the best interior texture and the most delicious crispy skins. We fully baked the potatoes and allowed them to cool completely before tearing them into chunks and frying them. Starting the oil quite hot and turning up the heat after adding the cold potatoes ensured crispy potatoes that cooked quickly enough to not dry out. Every bit as satisfying as the best french fries, these potatoes won't last long at your table.

Since you eat the potato skins in this recipe, make sure to scrub them well before cooking. In addition to the salt, these potatoes can be seasoned with any variety of seasoning or herb blend; they're also great dipped in ketchup or aioli.

2½ pounds russet potatoes, unpeeled, scrubbed
 1 quart vegetable oil for frying
 1 teaspoon kosher salt

1. Adjust oven rack to middle position and heat oven to 400 degrees. Prick each potato 6 times with fork. Place potatoes on rack and bake until tip of paring knife can be easily inserted into potatoes, about 1 hour 20 minutes. Let potatoes cool completely and then refrigerate until cold throughout, at least 3 hours. (Potatoes can be refrigerated for up to 2 days.)

2. Keeping skins on potatoes, use your hands to break potatoes into approximate 1½-inch pieces; transfer to bowl. Line rimmed baking sheet with triple layer of paper towels.

3. Add oil to Dutch oven and heat over medium-high heat to 375 degrees. Carefully add potatoes to hot oil and increase heat to high to compensate for oil cooling. Cook, stirring occasionally with metal spoon and taking care to scrape bottom of pot to prevent sticking, until potatoes are consistently browned and crispy, 13 to 15 minutes. Using spider skimmer or slotted spoon, transfer potatoes to prepared sheet. Sprinkle with salt. Serve.

Crispy Parmesan Potatoes

Crispy Parmesan Potatoes

SERVES 6 TO 8

WHY THIS RECIPE WORKS These crispy, cheesy Parmesan potatoes promised to be a habit-forming snack, but first we had to figure out how best to cook the potatoes and how to get the cheese to stick to them. Using thinly sliced, creamy Yukon Gold potatoes meant they wouldn't dry out during roasting. We tossed the potato slices with seasoned cornstarch to promote crisping. Parmesan, rosemary, and a little more cornstarch made for a savory coating that clung evenly to the slices. Baked in a very hot oven until golden brown and served with a cool chive sour cream, these were just the potatoes we craved.

Try to find potatoes that are 2½ to 3 inches long. Spray the baking sheet with an aerosol (not pump) vegetable oil spray. Use a good-quality Parmesan cheese here. Serve with Chive Sour Cream (recipe follows), if desired.

- 2 pounds medium Yukon gold potatoes, unpeeled
- 4 teaspoons cornstarch, divided
-   Table salt and pepper
- 1 tablespoon extra-virgin olive oil
- 6 ounces Parmesan cheese, cut into 1-inch chunks
- 2 teaspoons minced fresh rosemary

1. Adjust oven rack to lower-middle position and heat oven to 500 degrees. Spray rimmed baking sheet liberally with vegetable oil spray. Cut thin slice from 2 opposing long sides of each potato; discard slices. Cut potatoes crosswise into ½-inch-thick slices and transfer to large bowl.

2. Combine 2 teaspoons cornstarch, 1 teaspoon salt, and 1 teaspoon pepper in small bowl. Sprinkle cornstarch mixture over potatoes and toss until potatoes are thoroughly coated and cornstarch is no longer visible. Add oil and toss to coat.

3. Arrange potatoes in single layer on prepared sheet and bake until golden brown on top, about 20 minutes.

4. Meanwhile, process Parmesan, rosemary, ½ teaspoon pepper, and remaining 2 teaspoons cornstarch in food processor until cheese is finely ground, about 1 minute.

5. Remove potatoes from oven. Sprinkle Parmesan mixture evenly over and between potatoes (cheese should cover surface of baking sheet), pressing on potatoes with back of spoon to adhere. Using two forks, flip slices over into same spot on sheet.

6. Bake until cheese between potatoes turns light golden brown, 5 to 7 minutes. Transfer sheet to wire rack and let potatoes cool for 15 minutes. Using large metal spatula, transfer potatoes, cheese side up, and accompanying cheese to platter and serve.

Chive Sour Cream
MAKES ABOUT 1 CUP

This enhanced condiment makes an excellent topping for potatoes of all kinds.

- 1 cup sour cream
- ¼ cup minced fresh chives
- ½ teaspoon minced fresh rosemary
- ½ teaspoon table salt
- ½ teaspoon pepper
- ½ teaspoon garlic powder
- ¼ teaspoon onion powder

Combine all ingredients in bowl. Cover and refrigerate at least 30 minutes to allow flavors to blend.

Flipping for Frico
Using 2 forks, turn each potato slice over and return it to the same spot on the sheet. As the Parmesan bakes, it will transform into crispy cheesy bits called frico.

Crispy Baked Potato Fans

SERVES 4

WHY THIS RECIPE WORKS For this showstopper side, we found that using russet potatoes was the best choice because of their starch and fluffy texture. Rinsing the potatoes of surface starch after slicing kept them from sticking together, while trimming off the ends gave the slices room to fan out. We precooked the spuds in the microwave before baking to prevent overcooking. A cheesy, buttery bread crumb topping was the crowning touch.

To ensure that the potatoes fan out evenly, look for uniformly shaped potatoes.

Bread Crumb Topping
- 1 slice hearty white sandwich bread, torn into quarters
- 4 tablespoons unsalted butter, melted
- 2 ounces Monterey Jack cheese, shredded (½ cup)
- ¼ cup grated Parmesan cheese
- 1 teaspoon paprika
- ½ teaspoon garlic powder
- Table salt and pepper

Potato Fans
- 4 russet potatoes
- 2 tablespoons extra-virgin olive oil
- Table salt and pepper

1. For the Bread Crumb Topping Adjust oven rack to middle position and heat oven to 200 degrees. Pulse bread in food processor until coarsely ground, about 5 pulses. Bake bread crumbs on rimmed baking sheet until dry, about 20 minutes. Let cool for 5 minutes, then combine crumbs, butter, Monterey Jack, Parmesan, paprika, garlic powder, ¼ teaspoon salt, and ¼ teaspoon pepper in large bowl. (Bread crumb mixture can be refrigerated in zipper-lock bag for 2 days.)

2. For the Potato Fans Heat oven to 450 degrees. Cut ¼ inch from bottom and ends of potatoes, then slice potatoes crosswise at ¼-inch intervals, leaving ¼ inch of potato intact. Gently rinse potatoes under running water, let drain, and transfer, sliced side down, to plate. Microwave until slightly soft to touch, 6 to 12 minutes, flipping potatoes halfway through cooking.

3. Line rimmed baking sheet with aluminum foil. Arrange potatoes, sliced side up, on prepared baking sheet. Brush potatoes all over with oil and season with salt and pepper. Bake until skin is crisp and potatoes are beginning to brown, 25 to 30 minutes. Remove potatoes from oven and heat broiler.

4. Top potatoes with bread crumb mixture, pressing gently to adhere. Broil until bread crumbs are deep golden brown, about 3 minutes. Serve.

Blue Cheese and Bacon Baked Potato Fans

In step 1, substitute ⅓ cup crumbled blue cheese for Monterey Jack. In step 4, sprinkle 4 slices bacon, cooked until crispy and then crumbled, over potatoes just prior to serving.

Prepping Baked Potato Fans
These potatoes may look difficult to make, but we found a few simple tricks to ensure perfect potato fans every time.

1. Trim ¼-inch slices from bottom and ends of each potato to allow them to sit flat and to give slices extra room to fan out during baking.

2. Chopsticks provide a failproof guide for slicing potato petals without cutting all the way through.

3. Gently flex open fans while rinsing under cold running water; this rids potatoes of excess starch that can impede fanning.

Super-Stuffed Baked Potatoes

SERVES 6

WHY THIS RECIPE WORKS Our Super-Stuffed Baked Potatoes feature fluffy potato, garlic, herbs, and creamy cheese in crispy potato-skin shells. Precooking the potatoes in the microwave shaved an hour off the cooking time. And while most stuffed baked potato recipes call for cutting the potato in half, we preferred to lop off just the top quarter of the potato. Prepared this way, the potato shells held more filling. But after hollowing out the potatoes, there wasn't enough stuffing to fill each one and mound the filling on top. To make the filling go further, we cooked an extra potato and used its flesh to top off the other stuffed baked potatoes.

This recipe calls for seven potatoes but makes six servings; the remaining potato is used for its flesh.

- 7 large russet potatoes
- 3 tablespoons unsalted butter, melted, plus 3 tablespoons unsalted butter
  Table salt and pepper
- 1 (5.2-ounce) package Boursin cheese, crumbled, divided
- ½ cup half-and-half
- 2 garlic cloves, minced
- ¼ cup chopped fresh chives, divided

1. Adjust oven rack to middle position and heat oven to 475 degrees. Set wire rack in rimmed baking sheet. Prick potatoes all over with fork, place on paper towel, and microwave until tender, 20 to 25 minutes, turning potatoes over after 10 minutes.

2. Slice and remove top quarter of each potato, let cool for 5 minutes, then scoop out flesh, leaving ¼-inch layer of potato on inside. Discard 1 potato shell. Brush remaining shells inside and out with 3 tablespoons melted butter and sprinkle interiors with ¼ teaspoon salt. Transfer potatoes, scooped side up, to prepared baking sheet and bake until skins begin to crisp, about 15 minutes.

3. Meanwhile, mix half of Boursin with half-and-half in bowl until blended. Cook remaining 3 tablespoons butter and garlic in saucepan over medium-low heat until garlic is straw-colored, 3 to 5 minutes. Stir in Boursin mixture until combined.

Crispy Baked Potato Fans

Super-Stuffed Baked Potatoes

4. Set ricer or food mill over medium bowl and press or mill potatoes into bowl. Gently fold in warm Boursin mixture, 3 tablespoons chives, 1 teaspoon pepper, and ½ teaspoon salt until well incorporated. Remove potato shells from oven and fill with potato-cheese mixture. Top with remaining crumbled Boursin and bake until tops of potatoes are golden brown, about 15 minutes. Sprinkle with remaining 1 tablespoon chives. Serve.

Twice-Baked Potatoes with Bacon and Cheddar Cheese
SERVES 4

WHY THIS RECIPE WORKS These twice-baked potatoes taste as good as they look—no leathery skins or bland fillings here. Before the first bake, we pricked the potatoes all over with a fork and tossed them in a saltwater solution. Pricking the potatoes prevented steam from building up inside them, and the salty bath seasoned the skins and encouraged them to dry and crisp in the oven. For the filling, we mixed the potato interiors with butter for richness (rather than half-and-half), and incorporated sour cream, cheddar, bacon, and scallions into the mix—rather than just using them as toppings—so we got the best flavor in every bite.

Try to find potatoes of equal size and weight to ensure even cooking. Larger potatoes will work, but the baking time in step 1 will be longer. This recipe can easily be doubled.

- 4 (8- to 10-ounce) russet potatoes, unpeeled
- ¼ teaspoon table salt, plus salt for moistening potatoes
- 4 slices bacon, cut into ½-inch pieces
- 5 tablespoons unsalted butter, melted, divided
- ¼ cup sour cream
- ¼ teaspoon pepper
- 3 ounces sharp cheddar cheese, shredded (¾ cup)
- 4 scallions, sliced thin

1. Adjust oven rack to middle position and heat oven to 450 degrees. Prick each potato lightly with fork in 6 places. Dissolve 1 tablespoon salt in ½ cup water in large bowl. Add potatoes and toss so exteriors are evenly moistened. Place potatoes on wire rack set in rimmed baking sheet. Bake until centers register 205 degrees, 50 minutes to 1 hour. Let potatoes cool for 15 minutes. Reduce oven temperature to 400 degrees.

2. While potatoes bake, cook bacon in 12-inch ovensafe nonstick skillet over medium heat until crispy, 5 to 7 minutes. Using slotted spoon, transfer bacon to paper towel–lined plate; set aside. Discard fat in skillet or reserve for another use. Wipe skillet clean with paper towels.

3. With potatoes sitting on flat sides, cut off top ¼ inch and discard. Using fork, carefully remove potato flesh from remaining portion of potato by poking and twisting at insides to loosen, leaving ¼-inch wall all around inside of potato. Transfer potato flesh to medium bowl. Set aside potato shells.

4. Using potato masher, mash potato flesh until smooth. Stir in 3 tablespoons melted butter, sour cream, pepper, and salt until incorporated. Stir in cheddar, scallions, and bacon until combined. Season with salt and pepper to taste.

5. Divide filling evenly among potato shells (scant ¾ cup each), mounding filling over tops of potatoes. Fluff up top of filling with tines of fork. Brush 1 tablespoon melted butter in now-empty skillet and place potatoes in skillet. Brush remaining 1 tablespoon melted butter over tops of potatoes.

6. Bake until potatoes are warmed through and beginning to brown on top, 20 to 23 minutes. Let cool for 10 minutes before serving.

To Make Ahead At the end of step 4, let potatoes cool completely. Cover with plastic wrap and refrigerate for up to 24 hours. To serve, continue with step 5, increasing baking time by 10 minutes.

Twice-Baked Potatoes with Chorizo and Chipotle
Substitute 4 ounces Mexican-style chorizo sausage, casings removed, for bacon. Cook chorizo in 12-inch skillet over medium heat, breaking up meat with spoon, until well browned and cooked through, 5 to 7 minutes. Substitute Monterey Jack cheese for cheddar and 1 tablespoon minced canned chipotle chile in adobo sauce for pepper.

Twice-Baked Potatoes with Pancetta and Mozzarella
Substitute 4 ounces pancetta, cut into ¼-inch pieces, for bacon; 3 ounces shredded whole-milk mozzarella cheese and ¼ cup grated Parmesan cheese for cheddar; and 1 minced shallot and 1 teaspoon chopped fresh thyme for scallions.

Roasted Garlic–Parmesan Bread

SERVES 6 TO 8

Roasted Garlic–Parmesan Bread

WHY THIS RECIPE WORKS For balanced, sweet roasted garlic that was at once mellow and intense, we lopped off the top third of six heads of garlic to expose the flesh, drizzled the heads with olive oil, and sprinkled them with salt. We wrapped the heads tightly in an aluminum foil packet (to allow them to steam) and then roasted them at 400 degrees until the cloves were buttery soft and deep golden brown. Once the garlic was cool enough to handle, we easily squeezed the browned, nearly translucent paste out of the skins (squeezing from the root end up) and combined it with butter, Parmesan, chopped parsley, freshly ground pepper, and salt to use as spread for garlic bread.

A supermarket loaf of Italian bread, which has a soft, thin crust and fine crumb, works best here. Do not use a rustic or crusty artisan-style loaf.

- 8 tablespoons unsalted butter, softened
- 1 ounce Parmesan cheese, grated (½ cup)
- 1 head Roasted Garlic, squeezed to extrude garlic (recipe follows)
- 2 tablespoons chopped fresh parsley
- ½ teaspoon pepper
- ¼ teaspoon table salt
- 1 (12 by 5-inch) loaf Italian bread, halved horizontally

1. Adjust oven rack to middle position and heat oven to 400 degrees. Using fork, combine butter, Parmesan, garlic, parsley, pepper, and salt in bowl.

2. Spread butter mixture evenly on cut side of bread. Place bread on rimmed baking sheet, cut side up. Bake until golden brown, 15 to 20 minutes. Transfer bread to cutting board. Cut each half crosswise into 8 pieces. Serve warm.

Roasted Garlic
MAKES 6 HEADS

Look for larger heads of garlic when shopping. Roasted garlic freezes beautifully (see "To Make Ahead").

- 6 garlic heads
- 2 tablespoons extra-virgin olive oil
- ¼ teaspoon table salt

1. Adjust oven rack to middle position and heat oven to 400 degrees. Remove any loose outer papery skin from garlic heads by rubbing with your hands. Cut off and discard top one-third (pointed tip) of heads.

2. Set wire rack in rimmed baking sheet. Place 24 by 12-inch sheet of aluminum foil on rack. Place garlic heads on foil, cut side up. Drizzle garlic with oil and sprinkle with salt. While keeping garlic heads in single layer, pull sides of foil up around garlic and crimp tightly to seal.

3. Transfer sheet to oven and roast until garlic is soft, about 1½ hours.

4. Remove sheet from oven and let garlic cool in foil on rack for 30 minutes. To use, squeeze head from root end to extrude garlic; discard skins.

To Make Ahead Place whole heads of roasted garlic in airtight container and refrigerate for up to 1 week. Let garlic come to room temperature before squeezing out of skins. To freeze, squeeze cloves from skins into airtight container; freeze for up to 1 month. A scant ¼ cup of defrosted garlic is equal to 1 head.

Creamed Spinach

SERVES 4 TO 6

WHY THIS RECIPE WORKS Some recipes for this earthy, rich steakhouse side dish call for very complex sauces, but since we wanted the spinach flavor to shine, we called for only a handful of ingredients: cream; pungent garlic; subtly sweet shallot; and Parmesan cheese, which would add its unmistakable umami depth. We began by wilting the spinach and ridding it of excess water, which ensured a creamy rather than soupy texture. We added the cream and cooked the mixture until the cream had reduced, but by then the spinach had overcooked. To remedy this, we introduced a simple thickening trick: a paste of butter and flour, called beurre manié, which helped to thicken the sauce.

Baby spinach comes in a wide range of package sizes; this recipe works with anywhere from 15 to 18 ounces of baby spinach. You can substitute half-and-half for the heavy cream, if desired, but the resulting dish will be less rich and slightly more soupy. Preheat your serving dish in a 200-degree oven for 10 minutes so that the spinach stays warm on the table.

- 2 tablespoons unsalted butter, softened, plus 2 tablespoons unsalted butter
- 1 tablespoon all-purpose flour
- 1 shallot, minced
- 1 garlic clove, minced
- 1 pound (16 cups) baby spinach
- ½ teaspoon table salt
- ½ cup heavy cream
- 2 ounces Parmesan cheese, grated (1 cup)
- ½ teaspoon pepper
- Pinch ground nutmeg

1. Using fork, mash 2 tablespoons softened butter and flour together in bowl to form smooth paste; set aside. Melt remaining 2 tablespoons butter in Dutch oven over medium heat. Add shallot and garlic and cook until shallot is translucent, 1 to 2 minutes. Add spinach and salt and turn with tongs to coat with butter, shallot, and garlic. Cook until just wilted, about 4 minutes.

2. Add cream and bring to simmer. Stir in flour mixture until incorporated. Cook until cream thickens and clings to spinach, about 3 minutes. Off heat, stir in Parmesan, pepper, and nutmeg. Season with salt and pepper to taste. Transfer to warm shallow dish and serve.

Grill-Roasted Peppers

SERVES 4

WHY THIS RECIPE WORKS Roasting red peppers on the grill transforms their juicy crunch. We tossed stemmed and cored peppers in garlic-infused olive oil, allowing the oil to soak into the interiors' exposed flesh. To prevent flare-ups, we grilled the peppers in a foil-covered disposable pan then drained them and placed them directly on the hot grates to char. After scraping the charred skins from the peppers, we tossed them in a vinaigrette made from the leftover oil and pepper liquid. The finished peppers were tender, smoky, and infused with heady garlic flavor that complemented the sweetness.

These peppers can be refrigerated for up to 5 days.

- ¼ cup extra-virgin olive oil
- 3 garlic cloves, peeled and smashed
- Table salt and pepper
- 1 (13 by 9-inch) disposable aluminum pan
- 6 red bell peppers
- 1 tablespoon sherry vinegar

1. Combine oil, garlic, ½ teaspoon salt, and ¼ teaspoon pepper in disposable pan. Using paring knife, cut around stems of peppers and remove cores and seeds. Place peppers in pan and turn to coat with oil. Cover pan tightly with aluminum foil.

2a. For a Charcoal Grill Open bottom vent completely. Light large chimney starter filled with charcoal briquettes (6 quarts). When top coals are partially covered with ash, pour evenly over half of grill. Set cooking grate in place, cover, and open lid vent completely. Heat grill until hot, about 5 minutes.

2b. For a Gas Grill Turn all burners to high, cover, and heat grill until hot, about 15 minutes. Turn all burners to medium-high.

3. Clean and oil cooking grate. Place pan on grill (over hotter side for charcoal) and cook, covered, until peppers are just tender and skins begin to blister, 10 to 15 minutes, rotating and shaking pan halfway through cooking.

4. Remove pan from heat and carefully remove foil (reserve foil to use later). Using tongs, remove peppers from pan, allowing juices to drip back into pan, and place on grill (over hotter side for charcoal). Grill peppers, covered, turning every few minutes until skins are blackened, 10 to 15 minutes.

5. Transfer juices and garlic in pan to medium bowl and whisk in vinegar. Remove peppers from grill, return to now-empty pan, and cover tightly with foil. Let peppers steam for 5 minutes. Using spoon, scrape blackened skin off each pepper. Quarter peppers lengthwise, add to vinaigrette in bowl, and toss to combine. Season with salt and pepper to taste, and serve.

Caesar Green Bean Salad

SERVES 4 TO 6

WHY THIS RECIPE WORKS It's hard to beat a classic Caesar salad, so we wanted to translate the familiar flavor we love into a fuss-free green bean side dish. To keep the flavors bold and prevent the green beans from being waterlogged, we blanched the beans and then transferred them to a towel-lined baking sheet to cool. Dijon mustard provided great flavor and helped emulsify the dressing so it would cling well to the beans. We didn't want to skip the croutons, so we browned small baguette cubes in a skillet until they were perfectly crispy and would add just the right crunch to our beans.

For maximum crunch, use a good-quality baguette for the croutons. The dressing can be made up to 1 day in advance.

Dressing and Green Beans

- 1½ tablespoons lemon juice
- 1 tablespoon Worcestershire sauce
- 1 tablespoon Dijon mustard
- 3 garlic cloves, minced
- 3 anchovy fillets, minced to paste
  Table salt and pepper
- 3 tablespoons extra-virgin olive oil
- 1½ pounds green beans, trimmed
- 2 ounces Parmesan cheese, shaved with vegetable peeler

Croutons

- 3 ounces baguette, cut into ½-inch pieces
- 2 tablespoons extra-virgin olive oil
- ¼ teaspoon pepper

1. For the Dressing and Green Beans Whisk lemon juice, Worcestershire, mustard, garlic, anchovies, ½ teaspoon pepper, and ¼ teaspoon salt in bowl until combined. Slowly whisk in oil until emulsified; set aside.

Creamed Spinach

Grill-Roasted Peppers

Caesar Green Bean Salad

2. Line baking sheet with clean dish towel. Bring 4 quarts water to boil in large Dutch oven. Add green beans and 1½ teaspoons salt, return to boil, and cook until tender, 5 to 7 minutes. Drain green beans in colander and spread in even layer on prepared sheet. Let green beans cool completely.

3. For the Croutons Meanwhile, toss baguette, oil, and pepper in large bowl until baguette pieces are coated with oil. Transfer to 12-inch nonstick skillet (reserve bowl). Cook over medium-high heat, stirring occasionally, until golden brown and crispy, 5 to 7 minutes. Return croutons to reserved bowl.

4. Transfer dressing, green beans, and half of Parmesan to bowl with croutons and toss to combine. Season with salt and pepper to taste. Transfer to serving dish. Sprinkle with remaining Parmesan. Serve.

BLT Salad

SERVES 4

BLT Salad

WHY THIS RECIPE WORKS Our aim was to transform a classic summer sandwich into a perfectly balanced yet still satisfying main-course salad. To avoid wateriness, we cut ripe tomatoes into chunks, tossed them with salt and pepper in a bowl, and then set them aside while preparing the other ingredients. To double down on the bacon, we cooked torn pieces of ciabatta in the bacon drippings to make crunchy, supersavory croutons. For the dressing, we mixed puckery red wine vinegar and mayonnaise with a little olive oil (to tamp down the sweetness of the mayo) and stirred in spicy Dijon mustard to give it some dimension and punch. Torn fresh basil leaves contributed a fragrant freshness.

A baguette or boule can be substituted for the ciabatta, if desired. This salad is best with in-season, ripe tomatoes and is perfect for lunch or a light supper.

- 12 ounces ripe tomatoes, cored and cut into 1-inch pieces
- 1 teaspoon table salt, divided
- ½ teaspoon pepper, divided
- 8 slices bacon, cut crosswise into 1-inch pieces
- 4 ounces ciabatta bread, torn into ½-inch pieces (3 cups)
- 3 tablespoons extra-virgin olive oil
- 2 tablespoons mayonnaise
- 1 tablespoon red wine vinegar

- 2 teaspoons Dijon mustard
- 1 garlic clove, minced
- 2 romaine lettuce hearts (12 ounces), cut into 1-inch pieces
- ½ cup fresh basil leaves, torn

1. Toss tomatoes, ½ teaspoon salt, and ¼ teaspoon pepper together in bowl; set aside.

2. Line large plate with paper towels. Cook bacon in 12-inch nonstick skillet over medium heat until well browned and crispy, about 12 minutes. Using slotted spoon, transfer bacon to 1 side of paper towel–lined plate.

3. Return skillet with bacon fat to medium heat and add bread. Cook, stirring frequently, until golden brown, 3 to 6 minutes. Transfer croutons to empty side of paper towel–lined plate and let cool completely, about 5 minutes.

4. Whisk oil, mayonnaise, vinegar, mustard, garlic, remaining ½ teaspoon salt, and remaining ¼ teaspoon pepper in large bowl until combined. Add lettuce, basil, bacon, and croutons and toss to combine.

5. Using slotted spoon, transfer tomatoes to salad (leaving liquid behind) and toss gently to combine; discard tomato liquid. Serve immediately.

Stuffed Tomatoes

SERVES 6

WHY THIS RECIPE WORKS Stuffed tomatoes always sound delicious, but too often yield tasteless tomatoes and lackluster stuffing that falls out in a clump. To concentrate flavor and get rid of excess moisture, we seasoned hollowed-out tomato shells with salt and sugar and let them drain. Couscous proved the best base for the filling, and we rehydrated it with the reserved tomato juice for extra flavor. A topping of panko bread crumbs mixed with cheese added crunch and richness, and a drizzle of the cooking liquid mixed with red wine vinegar provided a piquant final touch.

Look for large tomatoes, about 3 inches in diameter.

- 6 large vine-ripened tomatoes (8 to 10 ounces each)
- 1 tablespoon sugar
- Kosher salt and pepper
- 4½ tablespoons extra-virgin olive oil, divided
- ¼ cup panko bread crumbs
- 3 ounces Gruyère cheese, shredded (¾ cup), divided
- 1 onion, halved and sliced thin
- 2 garlic cloves, minced
- ⅛ teaspoon red pepper flakes
- 8 ounces (8 cups) baby spinach, chopped coarse
- 1 cup couscous
- ½ teaspoon grated lemon zest
- 1 tablespoon red wine vinegar

1. Adjust oven rack to middle position and heat oven to 375 degrees. Cut top ½ inch off stem end of tomatoes and set aside. Using melon baller, scoop out tomato pulp and transfer to fine-mesh strainer set over bowl. Press on pulp with wooden spoon to extract juice; set aside juice and discard pulp. (You should have about ⅔ cup tomato juice; if not, add water as needed to equal ⅔ cup.)

2. Combine sugar and 1 tablespoon salt in bowl. Sprinkle each tomato cavity with 1 teaspoon sugar mixture, then turn tomatoes upside down on plate to drain for 30 minutes.

3. Combine 1½ teaspoons oil and panko in 10-inch skillet and toast over medium-high heat, stirring frequently, until golden brown, about 3 minutes. Transfer to bowl and let cool for 10 minutes. Stir in ¼ cup Gruyère.

4. Heat 2 tablespoons oil in now-empty skillet over medium heat until shimmering. Add onion and ½ teaspoon salt and cook until softened, 5 to 7 minutes. Stir in garlic and pepper flakes and cook until fragrant, about 30 seconds. Add spinach, 1 handful at a time, and cook until wilted, about 3 minutes. Stir in couscous, lemon zest, and reserved tomato juice. Cover, remove from heat, and let sit until couscous has absorbed liquid, about 7 minutes. Transfer couscous mixture to bowl and stir in remaining ½ cup Gruyère. Season with salt and pepper to taste.

5. Coat bottom of 13 by 9-inch baking dish with remaining 2 tablespoons oil. Blot tomato cavities dry with paper towels and season with salt and pepper. Pack each tomato with couscous mixture, about ½ cup per tomato, mounding excess. Top stuffed tomatoes with 1 heaping tablespoon panko mixture. Place tomatoes in prepared dish. Season reserved tops with salt and pepper and place in empty spaces in dish.

6. Bake, uncovered, until tomatoes have softened but still hold their shape, about 20 minutes. Using slotted spoon, transfer to serving platter. Whisk vinegar into oil remaining in dish, then drizzle over tomatoes. Place tops on tomatoes and serve.

our sunday best

- 310 Old-Fashioned Roast Turkey with Gravy
- 311 Cider-Braised Turkey
- 312 One-Pan Turkey Breast and Stuffing with Pomegranate-Parsley Sauce
- 313 Cornbread and Sausage Stuffing
- 315 Duck Breasts with Port Wine–Fig Sauce
- 315 Herb Roast Chicken
- 316 Roast Lemon Chicken
- 317 Apple Cider Chicken
- 318 One-Pan Roast Chicken with Root Vegetables
- 319 Cast Iron Chicken and Vegetables
- 321 Skillet-Roasted Chicken and Potatoes
- 322 Skillet-Roasted Chicken with Stuffing
- 323 Chicken Baked in Foil with Sweet Potato and Radish
- 324 Chicken and Slicks
- 325 Moravian Chicken Pie
- 326 Brunswick Stew
- 327 Transylvanian Goulash
- 328 Guinness Beef Stew
- 329 Sunday-Best Garlic Roast Beef
- 331 Classic Roast Beef and Gravy
- 331 Herbed Roast Beef
- 332 Herb-Crusted Beef Tenderloin
- 334 Classic Roast Beef Tenderloin
- 335 Holiday Strip Roast
- 336 Bottom Round Roast Beef with Zip-Style Sauce
- 337 Roasted Beef Chuck Roast with Horseradish-Parsley Sauce
- 338 Deviled Beef Short Ribs
- 339 Boneless Rib Roast with Yorkshire Pudding and Jus
- 340 One-Pan Prime Rib and Roasted Vegetables
- 341 Prime Rib with Potatoes and Red Wine–Orange Sauce
- 342 Chuck Roast in Foil
- 343 Roast Pork Loin with 40 Cloves of Garlic
- 344 Crown Roast of Pork
- 345 Slow-Cooker Pork Pot Roast
- 347 Old-Fashioned Roast Pork
- 348 Pork Pernil
- 349 Cider-Braised Pork Roast
- 350 Bacon-Wrapped Pork Roast with Peach Sauce
- 351 Pork Chops with Bourbon-Cherry Sauce and Sweet Potatoes
- 352 Slow-Roasted Fresh Ham
- 353 Cider-Baked Ham
- 354 Crumb-Crusted Rack of Lamb
- 355 Trout Amandine
- 356 Slow-Roasted Salmon with Chives and Lemon
- 357 One-Pan Roasted Salmon with Broccoli and Red Potatoes
- 358 Baked Shrimp with Fennel, Potatoes, and Olives
- 359 Gambas al Ajillo (Spanish-Style Sizzling Garlic Shrimp)
- 360 Clams with Chorizo
- 361 Parmesan-Crusted Asparagus
- 362 Brussels Sprout Gratin
- 364 Brussels Sprout Salad
- 364 Asparagus Salad with Radishes, Pecorino Romano, and Croutons
- 365 Shredded Swiss Chard Salad with Prosciutto, Basil, and Blue Cheese
- 366 Endive Salad with Oranges and Blue Cheese
- 367 Torn Potato Salad with Toasted Garlic and Herb Dressing
- 368 Whipped Potatoes
- 369 Duchess Potatoes
- 370 Mashed Potato Casserole
- 370 Syracuse Salt Potatoes
- 371 Creamy Mashed Sweet Potatoes
- 372 Roasted Butternut Squash and Apple
- 373 Roasted Beets with Lemon-Tahini Dressing
- 374 Fresh Tomato Galette
- 375 Lentilles du Puy with Spinach and Crème Fraîche
- 376 Sweet Corn Spoonbread
- 376 Spinach-Artichoke Dip

Recipe Photos (clockwise from top left): Clams with Chorizo; Pork Chops with Bourbon-Cherry Sauce and Sweet Potatoes

Old-Fashioned Roast Turkey with Gravy

Cider-Braised Turkey

Old-Fashioned Roast Turkey with Gravy

SERVES 10 TO 12

WHY THIS RECIPE WORKS For a roast turkey with moist, flavorful meat, we tried a number of options until we discovered a technique used for ages: barding. Similar to larding, it is a process of wrapping strips of lard (or other animal fat) around the meat so that it slowly releases flavor and moisture throughout roasting. After piercing the skin of the turkey breast and legs with a fork, we covered it with thin slices of salt pork before layering on cheesecloth that had been soaked in water and then aluminum foil. This insulated the meat and allowed the salt pork to slowly melt in the oven, basting the turkey with rich fat.

You will need one 2-yard package of cheesecloth for this recipe. Because we layer the bird with salt pork, we prefer to use a natural turkey here; a self-basting turkey (such as a frozen Butterball) may become too salty. If using a self-basting turkey, omit the chicken broth in the gravy and increase the amount of water to 7 cups. Make sure to start the gravy as soon as the turkey goes into the oven.

Turkey
- 1 (2-yard) package cheesecloth
- 4 cups water
- 1 (12- to 14-pound) turkey, neck, giblets, and tailpiece removed and reserved for gravy
- 1 pound salt pork, cut into ¼-inch-thick slices

Gravy
- 1 tablespoon vegetable oil
- 1 onion, chopped
- 5 cups water
- 2 cups chicken broth
- 4 sprigs fresh thyme
- 1 bay leaf
- 6 tablespoons all-purpose flour
- Salt and pepper

1. For the Turkey Adjust oven rack to lowest position and heat oven to 350 degrees. Fold cheesecloth into 18-inch square, place in large bowl, and cover with water. Tuck wings behind turkey and arrange, breast side up, on V-rack set in roasting pan. Prick skin of breast and legs of turkey all over with fork, cover breast and legs with salt pork, top with soaked cheesecloth (pouring any remaining water into roasting pan), and cover cheesecloth completely with heavy-duty aluminum foil.

2. Roast turkey until breast registers 140 degrees, 2½ to 3 hours. Remove foil, cheesecloth, and salt pork and discard. Increase oven temperature to 425 degrees. Continue to roast until breast registers 160 degrees and thighs register 175 degrees, 40 minutes to 1 hour longer. Transfer turkey to carving board and let rest 30 minutes.

3. For the Gravy Meanwhile, heat oil in large saucepan over medium-high heat until shimmering. Cook turkey neck and giblets until browned, about 5 minutes. Add onion and cook until softened, about 3 minutes. Stir in water, broth, thyme, and bay leaf and bring to boil. Reduce heat to low and simmer until reduced by half, about 3 hours. Strain mixture through fine-mesh strainer into 4-cup liquid measuring cup (you should have about 3½ cups), reserving giblets, if desired.

4. Carefully strain contents of roasting pan into fat separator. Let liquid settle, then skim, reserving ¼ cup fat. Pour defatted pan juices into measuring cup with giblet broth to yield 4 cups liquid.

5. Heat reserved fat in empty saucepan over medium heat until shimmering. Stir in flour and cook until golden and fragrant, about 4 minutes. Slowly whisk in giblet broth and bring to boil. Reduce heat to medium-low and simmer until slightly thickened, about 5 minutes. Chop giblets and add to gravy, if desired, and season with salt and pepper to taste. Carve turkey and serve with gravy.

Cider-Braised Turkey

SERVES 8 TO 12

WHY THIS RECIPE WORKS We were inspired by Chef Sean Sherman's recipe for cider-braised turkey in *The Sioux Chef's Indigenous Kitchen* (2017) to braise rather than roast our turkey. But we used a different method and flavor profile. We sought to transform tough turkey legs so that the meat practically fell off the bone. We started by salting the turkey legs overnight to season the meat all the way through and tenderize it. After braising, we blended the solids (onion, ginger, and porcini mushrooms) from the braise into a mixture that thickened the final sauce. To achieve picture-perfect turkey skin, we browned the turkey legs in the finished braising liquid in a 400-degree oven before serving.

You can use any combination of bone-in turkey thighs and drumsticks you like; look for pieces with an average weight of about 1 pound each. You can substitute vegetable oil for the sunflower oil and table salt for the fine sea salt if desired. We developed this recipe using our winning roasting pan, but it can also be made in a heavy-duty disposable aluminum pan; be sure to place the disposable pan on a baking sheet for extra support. Note that the turkey needs to be salted for at least 12 hours before cooking.

8	pounds bone-in turkey thighs and/or drumsticks, trimmed
1½	tablespoons fine sea salt, divided
2	tablespoons sunflower oil
1	onion, chopped
1	(3-inch) piece ginger, sliced into ¼-inch-thick rounds
3	cups apple cider
1	ounce dried porcini mushrooms, rinsed
6	sprigs fresh sage
2	tablespoons whole-grain mustard
2	tablespoons cider vinegar, plus extra for seasoning

1. Pat turkey dry with paper towels and sprinkle all over with 1 tablespoon salt. Transfer to large platter, cover with plastic wrap, and refrigerate for 12 to 24 hours.

2. Adjust oven rack to middle position and heat oven to 300 degrees. Heat oil in large saucepan over medium-high heat until shimmering. Add onion, ginger, and remaining 1½ teaspoons salt and cook, stirring occasionally, until vegetables are softened and lightly browned, 3 to 5 minutes. Add cider, mushrooms, and sage and bring to boil. Transfer cider mixture to roasting pan. Arrange turkey pieces in even layer in pan. Cover pan tightly with aluminum foil, transfer to oven, and cook for 1½ hours.

3. Remove pan from oven, flip turkey pieces, and re-cover pan tightly with foil. Return pan to oven and continue to cook until meat offers no resistance when pierced with fork and is beginning to fall off bones, about 1½ hours longer.

4. Remove pan from oven and increase oven temperature to 400 degrees. Transfer turkey skin side up to large platter. Strain braising liquid through fine-mesh strainer set over 8-cup liquid measuring cup or large bowl. Discard sage sprigs.

5. Transfer strained solids and 2 cups braising liquid to blender. Return remaining braising liquid to now-empty roasting pan. Process solids in blender until smooth, about 1 minute. Add blended mixture, mustard, and vinegar to braising liquid in pan and whisk to combine. Nestle turkey pieces skin side up into sauce.

Braising Arrangement

We call for braising the turkey parts in a roasting pan. The parts should be halfway submerged in the liquid (they get flipped once). An aluminum foil lid traps steam for more efficient cooking.

BRAISING LIQUID COVERS MEAT HALFWAY

On the Road: The Sioux Chef

Owamni by The Sioux Chef, the modern Indigenous restaurant in downtown Minneapolis, sits along the Mississippi River atop the ruins of an old flour mill. The chef and owner is Sean Sherman, who is Oglala Lakota from Pine Ridge Reservation in South Dakota, and whose Lakota name is Waŋblí Wathákpe, meaning Charging Eagle. He opened Owamni in July 2021 to promote the foodways of the Ojibwe and Dakota tribes with a menu of precolonial ingredients indigenous to North America.

When it comes to understanding and cooking with indigenous foods, Sherman says, "You have to know that you're not going to find some of these flavors in the grocery store. But if you look outside and learn the plants, you're going to start to see it. Go outside and learn the names of things and create a relationship. You're going to start seeing nothing but food and medicine everywhere you look."

About 70 percent of Sherman's employees identify as Indigenous, and Sherman says there are more and more Indigenous chefs cropping up throughout the country. "As Indigenous people, so many of us can reconnect with our ancestry, even if it's broken, and start to rebuild. What is a sense moving forward for us is just reclaiming our true North American foods. The true story of North America."

---

6. Return pan to oven and roast turkey, uncovered, until skin is well browned, 20 to 25 minutes. Transfer turkey to serving platter. Season sauce with salt and extra vinegar to taste and transfer to gravy boat. Serve turkey with sauce.

To Make Ahead Turn off oven after removing pan in step 4. Follow recipe through step 5, letting turkey and sauce cool completely in pan. Cover and refrigerate for up to 24 hours. To serve, cover pan with aluminum foil and heat in 400-degree oven for 15 minutes. Remove foil and continue to roast until skin is well browned and turkey registers at least 165 degrees, 30 to 45 minutes.

One-Pan Turkey Breast and Stuffing with Pomegranate-Parsley Sauce

SERVES 8 TO 10

WHY THIS RECIPE WORKS For a lower-maintenance, holiday-worthy turkey and stuffing made in one pan, we started with bone-in turkey breast instead of a whole bird. This made for easier carving and eliminated the challenge of differing cook times for white and dark meat. For the stuffing, we used ciabatta with a combo of herbs, onion, wine, and chicken broth (plus some hot Italian sausage). We roasted the turkey breast on top of the stuffing and then removed it before returning the stuffing to the oven to crisp up. A vibrant sauce of pomegranate seeds and parsley added a final holiday flourish.

The salted turkey needs to be refrigerated for at least 2 hours before cooking. If you can't find a loaf of ciabatta, you can substitute 2 pounds of another rustic, mild-tasting white bread. Do not use sourdough here; its flavor is too assertive.

Turkey
- 1½ tablespoons kosher salt
- 1 tablespoon pepper
- 1 tablespoon minced fresh thyme
- 1 (5- to 7-pound) bone-in turkey breast, trimmed

Stuffing
- ½ cup extra-virgin olive oil
- 3 cups chopped onion
- 1¾ teaspoons kosher salt, divided

- 6 garlic cloves, minced
- 3 cups chicken broth
- ⅓ cup dry white wine
- 2 tablespoons minced fresh sage
- 1 tablespoon minced fresh thyme
- ¼ teaspoon red pepper flakes
- 2 pounds ciabatta, cut into 1-inch cubes (about 20 cups)
- 1 pound hot Italian sausage, casings removed
- 1½ cups coarsely chopped fresh parsley

Sauce

- ¾ cup chopped fresh parsley
- ¾ cup pomegranate seeds
- ½ cup extra-virgin olive oil
- 1 shallot, minced
- 2 tablespoons lemon juice
- 2 garlic cloves, minced
- ¾ teaspoon kosher salt

1. For the Turkey Combine salt, pepper, and thyme in bowl. Place turkey on large plate and pat dry with paper towels. Sprinkle all over with salt mixture. Refrigerate, uncovered, for at least 2 hours or up to 24 hours.

2. For the Stuffing Adjust oven rack to lower-middle position and heat oven to 325 degrees. Spray large heavy-duty roasting pan with vegetable oil spray, then add oil to pan. Heat oil in roasting pan over medium heat until shimmering. Add onion and ¼ teaspoon salt and cook until onion is golden brown, about 10 minutes. Add garlic and cook until fragrant, about 30 seconds.

3. Off heat, stir in broth, wine, sage, thyme, pepper flakes, and remaining 1½ teaspoons salt, scraping up any browned bits. Add bread and, using tongs or your hands, toss until bread is evenly coated. Break sausage into ¾-inch chunks and toss with bread mixture to combine.

4. Nestle turkey, skin side up, into stuffing in center of roasting pan. Roast until thickest part of turkey registers 160 degrees, 2¼ to 2¾ hours.

5. For the Sauce Meanwhile, combine all ingredients in bowl; set aside.

6. Transfer turkey to carving board, skin side up, and let rest, uncovered, for at least 30 minutes or up to 1 hour.

7. Meanwhile, stir stuffing in roasting pan. Return pan to oven and cook until top of bread looks golden brown and is evenly dry, 10 to 15 minutes.

8. Remove breast meat from bone and slice thin crosswise. Toss parsley with stuffing in roasting pan. Arrange turkey over stuffing in pan. Drizzle with sauce. Serve, passing remaining sauce separately.

One-Pan Turkey Breast and Stuffing with Pomegranate-Parsley Sauce

Cornbread and Sausage Stuffing

SERVES 10 TO 12

WHY THIS RECIPE WORKS We wanted a stuffing that could stand on its own without gravy. We found our answer in cornbread, which gives the stuffing more flavor than plain white bread. We wanted plenty of stuffing, so we chose to cook it in a Dutch oven large enough to accommodate 10 to 12 portions. To compensate for the loss in richness brought by gravy, we added spicy andouille sausage. Adding chicken broth to the stuffing boosted the meaty flavor and helped keep it from drying out.

We prefer spicy andouille sausage in this recipe, but chorizo or kielbasa work well too. For the cornbread, use your favorite recipe, store-bought cornbread, or Betty Crocker Golden Corn Muffin and Bread Mix or Jiffy Corn Muffin Mix, both of which will work fine in stuffing.

Cornbread and Sausage Stuffing

Duck Breasts with Port Wine–Fig Sauce

12 cups prepared cornbread cut into ¾-inch cubes
1½ pounds andouille sausage, halved lengthwise and sliced into ¼-inch-thick half-moons
2 tablespoons unsalted butter
2 small onions, chopped fine
3 celery ribs, chopped fine
2 tablespoons minced fresh sage
3 garlic cloves, minced
1 teaspoon table salt
1 teaspoon pepper
4 cups chicken broth

1. Adjust oven racks to upper-middle and lower-middle positions and heat oven to 400 degrees. Spread cornbread evenly over 2 rimmed baking sheets. Bake until slightly crisp, 15 to 20 minutes; let cool. Carefully remove upper-middle rack from oven.

2. Cook sausage in Dutch oven over medium-high heat until lightly browned, 5 to 7 minutes. Transfer to paper towel–lined plate and pour off fat left behind in pot. Melt butter over medium-high heat, add onions and celery, and cook until softened, about 5 minutes. Stir in sage, garlic, salt, and pepper and cook until fragrant, about 1 minute. Add broth and sausage, scraping up browned bits with wooden spoon. Add cornbread and gently stir until liquid is absorbed. Cover and set aside for 10 minutes. (Stuffing can be refrigerated for 1 day; let sit at room temperature for 30 minutes before baking.)

3. Remove lid and bake until top of stuffing is golden brown and crisp, about 30 minutes. Serve.

Cornbread and Bacon Stuffing

Substitute 1 pound bacon, chopped, for sausage, 3 cups fresh or frozen corn kernels for celery, and 3 thinly sliced scallions for sage.

Drying Cornbread

Although cornbread gives stuffing great flavor, it also adds a lot of moisture, making a soggy baked mess. If you have the time, cube the cornbread, spread it out on baking sheets, and let it sit overnight on the counter. If you're in a hurry (and who isn't around the holidays?), pop the baking sheets holding the cornbread into a 400-degree oven and bake until slightly crisp, 15 to 20 minutes.

Duck Breasts with Port Wine–Fig Sauce

SERVES 4

WHY THIS RECIPE WORKS Duck is a great choice for a special meal. To help the subcutaneous fat render and the skin crisp, we scored the skin in a crosshatch pattern. We then sprinkled the breasts with salt and pepper and refrigerated them, wrapped in plastic, for at least 6 hours to help them retain moisture and to season them deeply. We started the breasts skin side down in a cold skillet and then cooked them gently over medium heat to render the fat and crisp the skin. After flipping the breasts and lowering the heat, we finished cooking them on the stovetop. A simple sauce made of port wine, dried figs, vinegar, and sugar cut perfectly through the fat and made a great pairing.

This recipe was developed with duck breasts weighing 7 to 8 ounces each. However, if you can find only larger duck breasts that weigh 10 to 12 ounces each, they will also work. They tend to come with more excess fat; once it's trimmed away, the breasts will weigh closer to 8 or 9 ounces. You may need to cook larger duck breasts about 1 minute longer on the second side to reach the desired temperature. We prefer duck cooked to medium-rare or medium. Note that the duck breasts need to be salted for at least six hours before cooking.

Duck
- 4 (7- to 8-ounce) boneless duck breasts
- 2 teaspoons kosher salt
- 1½ teaspoons pepper

Sauce
- ½ cup ruby port
- ¼ cup dried Black Mission figs, halved through stem
- ¼ cup red wine vinegar
- 3 tablespoons sugar

1. For the Duck Pat duck breasts dry with paper towels. Place breasts skin side down on cutting board. Using sharp knife, trim away excess fat around edges of breasts, then remove any visible silverskin attached to meat.

2. Flip breasts and cut ½-inch crosshatch pattern in skin and fat, being careful not to cut into meat. Sprinkle all over with salt and pepper. Place duck on large plate skin side up, cover tightly with plastic wrap, and refrigerate for at least 6 hours or up to 24 hours.

3. For the Sauce Meanwhile, combine all ingredients in small saucepan. Bring to boil over medium heat. Cook until reduced to about ½ cup, about 15 minutes; set aside off heat. Sauce will thicken to syrupy consistency as it cools. (Cooled sauce can be stored in airtight container for up to 3 days or refrigerated for up to 2 weeks.)

4. Place breasts skin side down in cold 12-inch nonstick skillet. Cook over medium heat until copious amount of fat has rendered and skin is well browned and crispy, 17 to 20 minutes.

5. Flip breasts skin side up and reduce heat to medium-low. Cook until centers of breasts register 125 to 130 degrees (for medium-rare), 1 to 2 minutes; 130 to 135 degrees (for medium), 3 to 4 minutes; 135 to 140 degrees (for medium-well), 4 to 5 minutes; or 145 to 150 degrees (for well-done), 7 to 8 minutes.

6. Transfer breasts to wire rack set in rimmed baking sheet. Tent with aluminum foil and let rest for 10 minutes.

7. Transfer duck to carving board and slice ¼ inch thick. Serve with sauce.

Crosshatch with Caution

When crosshatching the skin, be sure not to cut all the way through it to the meat.

Herb Roast Chicken

SERVES 6 TO 8

WHY THIS RECIPE WORKS Developing a recipe for a classic herb roast chicken proved surprisingly tricky. Stuffing the chicken with fresh herbs delivered zero flavor, herb butter melted off the chicken, and infused oil failed to really penetrate the meat. Our solution was to slather the chicken with a thick paste of fresh herbs and garlic, processed until smooth, then let it rest to develop a pronounced herbal flavor. So that there was plenty of meat to go around, we used two whole chickens instead of one. For a simple pan sauce, we whisked the drippings with chicken broth, white wine, cornstarch, butter, and additional herb paste while the chicken rested.

For even cooking, arrange the chickens side by side a few inches apart on the V-rack, with the legs pointing in opposite directions.

- 1 cup chopped fresh parsley
- 2 tablespoons chopped fresh thyme
- 1 tablespoon chopped fresh rosemary
- 2 garlic cloves, minced
-   Salt and pepper
- 2 tablespoons extra-virgin olive oil
- 2 (3½- to 4-pound) whole chickens, giblets discarded
- 1 cup plus 2 tablespoons water
- 2 teaspoons cornstarch
- 1¼ cups chicken broth
- ¼ cup dry white wine
- 2 tablespoons unsalted butter, chilled

1. Process parsley, thyme, rosemary, garlic, 2 teaspoons salt, and 1 teaspoon pepper in food processor until paste forms, about 30 seconds. Reserve 1 teaspoon herb paste for sauce. Combine 2 tablespoons herb paste with oil in bowl. Set aside herb-oil paste and remaining herb paste.

2. Adjust oven rack to middle position and heat oven to 450 degrees. Pat chickens dry with paper towels. Using your fingers, gently loosen skin covering breast and thighs. Rub remaining herb paste under skin of each chicken, making sure to coat breast, thigh, and leg meat. Rub herb-oil paste over outside of each chicken. Tuck wings behind back and tie legs together with kitchen twine. Transfer chickens to platter. Cover and refrigerate 1 hour.

3. Arrange chickens 2 inches apart, breast side down, on V-rack set inside large roasting pan. Roast until thigh meat registers 135 to 140 degrees, 35 to 40 minutes. Remove chickens from oven and, using 2 bunches of paper towels, flip breast side up (meat that was facing in should now be facing out). Pour 1 cup water into roasting pan. Return chickens to oven and roast until breast registers 160 degrees and thighs register 175 degrees, 25 to 30 minutes. Transfer to carving board and let rest for 20 minutes.

4. Whisk cornstarch with remaining 2 tablespoons water in bowl until no lumps remain. Pour pan juices and any accumulated chicken juices into liquid measuring cup; skim fat. Transfer ½ cup defatted pan juices to medium saucepan. Add broth and wine and bring to boil. Reduce heat to medium-low and simmer until sauce is slightly thickened and reduced to 1¼ cups, 8 to 10 minutes. Whisk in cornstarch mixture and simmer until thickened, 3 to 5 minutes. Off heat, whisk in butter and reserved 1 teaspoon herb paste. Season with salt and pepper to taste. Carve chickens and serve, passing sauce at table.

Roast Lemon Chicken

SERVES 3 TO 4

WHY THIS RECIPE WORKS The citrus flavor in roasted lemon chicken can be harsh or, on the flip side, totally absent. To infuse the meat with bright flavor, we combined lemon zest, sugar, and salt and rubbed it into the chicken under the skin. For even more lemon flavor, we roasted the chicken in a sauce of lemon juice mixed with water, more zest, and chicken broth. Roasting the bird at a high temperature ensured that the exposed skin became crisp. Before serving, we reduced the sauce to concentrate its flavor and thickened it with butter and cornstarch for sheen, body, and richness.

Avoid using nonstick or aluminum roasting pans in this recipe. The former can cause the chicken to brown too quickly, while the latter may react with the lemon juice, producing off-flavors.

- 1 (3½- to 4-pound) whole chicken, giblets discarded
- 3 tablespoons grated lemon zest plus ⅓ cup juice (3 lemons)
- 1 teaspoon sugar
-   Salt and pepper
- 2 cups chicken broth
-   Water
- 1 teaspoon cornstarch
- 3 tablespoons unsalted butter
- 1 tablespoon finely chopped fresh parsley

1. Adjust oven rack to middle position and heat oven to 475 degrees. Pat chicken dry with paper towels. Using kitchen shears, cut along both sides of backbone to remove it. Flatten breastbone and tuck wings behind back. Using your fingers, gently loosen skin covering breast and thighs. Combine lemon zest, sugar, and 1 teaspoon salt in small bowl. Rub 2 tablespoons zest mixture under skin of chicken. Season chicken with salt and pepper and transfer to roasting pan. (Seasoned chicken can be refrigerated for 2 hours.)

2. Whisk broth, 1 cup water, lemon juice, and remaining zest mixture in 4-cup liquid measuring cup, then pour into roasting pan. (Liquid should just reach skin of thighs. If it does not, add enough water to reach skin of thighs.) Roast until skin is golden brown and breast registers 160 degrees and thighs register 175 degrees, 40 to 45 minutes. Transfer to carving board and let rest for 20 minutes.

3. Carefully pour liquid from pan, along with any accumulated chicken juices, into saucepan (you should have about 1½ cups). Skim fat, then cook over medium-high heat until reduced to 1 cup, about 5 minutes. Whisk cornstarch with 1 tablespoon water in small bowl until no lumps remain, then whisk into saucepan. Simmer until sauce is slightly thickened, about 2 minutes. Off heat, whisk in butter and parsley and season with salt and pepper. Carve chicken and serve, passing sauce at table.

Apple Cider Chicken
SERVES 3 TO 4

WHY THIS RECIPE WORKS We had a tall order with our Apple Cider Chicken: It had to taste like apples, and it had to have supercrisp skin. Cooking the chicken skin side down in a skillet and then moving it to a hot oven kept the skin exceptionally crisp. When it came to flavor, apple cider alone didn't do the trick. We also needed fresh apples, apple brandy, and cider vinegar to flavor the chicken with apple goodness. For the sauce, Granny Smith apples were too sour, while other varieties turned to mush when cooked. In the end, we preferred Golden Delicious, Cortland, or Jonagold apples, which held their shape and offered sweet flavor.

Plain brandy, cognac, or Calvados (a French apple brandy) can be used in place of the apple brandy.

- 3 pounds bone-in chicken pieces, (split breasts halved crosswise, legs separated into thighs and drumsticks), trimmed
  Salt and pepper
- 2 teaspoons vegetable oil
- 1 onion, chopped fine
- 2 garlic cloves, minced
- 2 teaspoons minced fresh thyme
- 2 teaspoons all-purpose flour
- 1 large Golden Delicious, Cortland, or Jonagold apple (8 ounces), peeled, cored, and cut into ¾-inch pieces
- 1 cup apple cider
- ¼ cup apple brandy, divided
- 1 teaspoon cider vinegar

Herb Roast Chicken

Roast Lemon Chicken

Apple Cider Chicken

1. Adjust oven rack to middle position and heat oven to 450 degrees. Pat chicken dry with paper towels and season with salt and pepper. Heat oil in 12-inch oven-proof skillet over medium-high heat until just smoking. Cook chicken skin side down until well browned, about 10 minutes. Flip and brown on second side, about 5 minutes. Transfer to plate.

2. Pour off all but 1 tablespoon fat from skillet. Add onion and cook until softened, about 5 minutes. Stir in garlic, thyme, and flour and cook, stirring frequently, until fragrant and flour is absorbed, about 1 minute. Add apple, apple cider, and 3 tablespoons apple brandy and bring to boil.

3. Nestle chicken skin side up into sauce and roast in oven until breasts register 160 degrees and thighs/drumsticks register 175 degrees, about 10 minutes. Transfer chicken to platter. Stir vinegar and remaining 1 tablespoon brandy into sauce and season with salt and pepper to taste. Serve, passing sauce at table.

One-Pan Roast Chicken with Root Vegetables

SERVES 4

WHY THIS RECIPE WORKS Cooking vegetables and chicken together in the same pan often leads to unevenly cooked chicken and greasy, soggy vegetables. To get the chicken and vegetables to cook at the same rate, we used chicken parts, which contain less overall fat than a whole chicken and don't smother the vegetables underneath, which would cause them to steam. To ensure that the delicate white meat stayed moist while the darker meat cooked through, we placed the chicken breasts in the center of the pan and the thighs and drumsticks around the perimeter.

We halve the chicken breasts crosswise for even cooking. Use brussels sprouts no bigger than golf balls, as larger ones are often tough and woody.

- 12 ounces brussels sprouts, trimmed and halved
- 12 ounces red potatoes, cut into 1-inch pieces
- 8 ounces shallots, peeled and halved
- 4 carrots, peeled and cut into 2-inch pieces, thick ends halved lengthwise
- 6 garlic cloves, peeled

Preventing Flabby Skin

We avoid flabby skin with a hybrid technique that combines braising and pan roasting.

1. Brown chicken skin side down in skillet for 10 minutes until deep brown. Brown second side for 5 more minutes.

2. Finish chicken, skin side up and uncovered, in hot oven. Be sure liquid does not submerge chicken pieces.

318 *The Complete Cook's Country TV Show Cookbook*

One-Pan Roast Chicken with Root Vegetables

3. Brush chicken with herb butter and roast until breasts register 160 degrees and thighs/drumsticks register 175 degrees, 35 to 40 minutes, rotating pan halfway through cooking. Transfer chicken to serving platter, tent loosely with aluminum foil, and let rest for 5 to 10 minutes. Toss vegetables in pan juices and transfer to platter with chicken. Serve.

One-Pan Roast Chicken with Fennel and Parsnips

Replace brussels sprouts and carrots with 1 fennel bulb, stalks discarded, bulb halved, cored, and sliced into ½-inch wedges, and 8 ounces (4 medium) parsnips, peeled and cut into 2-inch pieces.

Cast Iron Chicken and Vegetables

SERVES 4

WHY THIS RECIPE WORKS We wanted a full dinner of golden, juicy roast chicken and hearty vegetables, and we wanted to cook it all in one pan to limit the cleanup. We began by butterflying a whole chicken and then rubbing the skin generously with olive oil (to help our spice mixture stick and the skin crisp). Seasoning the bird with a mixture of salt, fresh thyme, granulated garlic, and smoked paprika produced an instant hit of complex flavor with a subtle smokiness. For the side dish, we sprinkled our favorite vegetables for roasting—potatoes, fennel, onion, and carrots—with the same spice mixture that went on the chicken. We then added them to a hot cast-iron skillet with a bit more olive oil and placed the chicken on top. Starting in a preheated cast-iron skillet yielded browned rather than braised vegetables (because the juices from the bird cooked off faster), while butterflying the chicken meant that the white and dark meat cooked through at the same time. Laying the chicken out flat also meant that all the skin was exposed to the hot air in the oven. In just an hour, the chicken was cooked perfectly, and all the skin was golden and crispy. For a final touch, a bright parsley, lemon, and garlic sauce was easy enough to stir together while the chicken roasted, and it proved to be just the thing to make this comforting dinner truly memorable.

You can make this recipe in a traditional stainless-steel or ovensafe nonstick skillet, but it will take the potatoes longer to brown in step 7. Be sure to buy potatoes measuring

4	teaspoons minced fresh thyme, divided
1	tablespoon vegetable oil
2	teaspoons minced fresh rosemary, divided
1	teaspoon sugar
	Salt and pepper
2	tablespoons unsalted butter, melted
3½	pounds bone-in chicken pieces (2 split breasts halved crosswise, 2 drumsticks, and 2 thighs), trimmed

1. Adjust oven rack to upper-middle position and heat oven to 475 degrees. Toss brussels sprouts, potatoes, shallots, carrots, garlic, 2 teaspoons thyme, oil, 1 teaspoon rosemary, sugar, ¾ teaspoon salt, and ¼ teaspoon pepper together in bowl. Combine butter, remaining 2 teaspoons thyme, remaining 1 teaspoon rosemary, ¼ teaspoon salt, and ⅛ teaspoon pepper in second bowl; set aside.

2. Pat chicken dry with paper towels and season with salt and pepper. Place vegetables in single layer on rimmed baking sheet, arranging brussels sprouts in center. Place chicken, skin side up, on top of vegetables, arranging breast pieces in center and leg and thigh pieces around perimeter of sheet.

1 to 2 inches in diameter. If you use table salt instead of kosher salt, cut the amounts in half and distribute the spice mixture accordingly. If you can't find a 1-pound bulb of fennel, buy several smaller ones. The weight of the trimmed fennel going into the skillet should be about 8 ounces.

Spice Mixture
- 4 teaspoons kosher salt
- 1 tablespoon chopped fresh thyme
- 1 teaspoon granulated garlic
- 1 teaspoon pepper
- ½ teaspoon smoked paprika

Chicken and Vegetables
- 1 (3½- to 4-pound) whole chicken, giblets discarded
- 2 tablespoons extra-virgin olive oil, divided
- 1 pound small Yukon Gold potatoes, unpeeled, halved
- 1 (1-pound) fennel bulb, stalks discarded, bulb halved through root end and cut into 1-inch wedges
- 1 red onion, cut through root end into 1-inch wedges
- 2 carrots, peeled, halved lengthwise, then halved crosswise

Sauce
- 3 tablespoons extra-virgin olive oil
- 2 tablespoons chopped fresh parsley
- 1½ tablespoons lemon juice
- 1 garlic clove, minced
- 1 teaspoon chopped fresh thyme
- 1 teaspoon kosher salt
- ¼ teaspoon pepper
- ¼ teaspoon smoked paprika

1. For the Spice Mixture Combine all ingredients in bowl and set aside.

2. For the Chicken and Vegetables Adjust oven rack to middle position and heat oven to 425 degrees. With chicken breast side down on cutting board, use kitchen shears to cut through bones on either side of backbone; discard backbone or reserve for another use. Flip chicken and press on breastbone to flatten. Tuck wingtips underneath breast. Pat chicken dry with paper towels. Cut ½-inch-deep slit into drumstick-thigh joint on each side of chicken.

3. Sprinkle underside of chicken with 1 tablespoon spice mixture. Flip chicken and rub skin with 1 tablespoon oil. Sprinkle chicken skin with 5 teaspoons spice mixture.

4. Heat 12-inch cast-iron skillet over medium heat for 5 minutes. Add remaining 1 tablespoon oil to skillet and heat until just smoking. Add potatoes to skillet, cut side down. Add fennel, onion, and carrots to skillet, allowing them to come into contact with bottom of skillet as much as space permits; some vegetables will have to sit on top of potatoes. Sprinkle vegetables with remaining spice mixture.

5. Place chicken on top of vegetables, skin side up. Transfer skillet to oven and roast until breast registers 160 degrees and drumsticks/thighs register at least 175 degrees, about 1 hour.

6. For the Sauce Meanwhile, whisk all ingredients together in bowl; set aside.

7. Transfer chicken to carving board. Return skillet with vegetables to oven and roast until potatoes are browned on bottom, about 15 minutes.

8. Carve chicken, spoon sauce over top, and serve with vegetables.

Chicken Prep: Butterfly and Slash

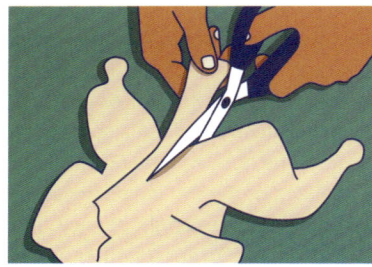

1. With chicken breast side down on cutting board, use kitchen shears to cut through bones on either side of backbone; remove backbone and save for stock.

2. Flip chicken, then use your palm to forcibly press down on breastbone to flatten.

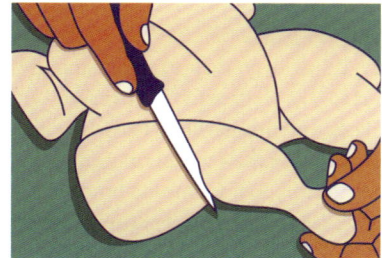

3. Tuck wingtips underneath breast, pat chicken dry, and cut ½-inch-deep slit into joint between thigh and drumstick on each side.

Skillet-Roasted Chicken and Potatoes

SERVES 4

WHY THIS RECIPE WORKS For this one-pan meal, we wanted to deliver tender potatoes and moist chicken at the same time. First, we quickly browned one side of the potatoes (2 pounds of potatoes fit into a 12-inch skillet when sliced into thick rounds). We placed the bird on top and moved it all to the oven, where flavorful juices basted the spuds. The chicken emerged golden and juicy and the potatoes had caramelized on the bottom. While the chicken rested, we returned the potatoes to the oven to finish them.

Use uniform, medium potatoes.

- 3 tablespoons extra-virgin olive oil, divided
- 2 teaspoons minced fresh thyme
- 1½ teaspoons smoked paprika
- 1½ teaspoons grated lemon zest, plus lemon wedges for serving
-   Salt and pepper
- 1 (4-pound) whole chicken, giblets discarded
- 2 pounds Yukon Gold potatoes, peeled, ends squared off, and sliced into 1-inch-thick rounds

1. Adjust oven rack to lower middle position and heat oven to 400 degrees. Combine 2 tablespoons oil, thyme, paprika, lemon zest, 1 teaspoon salt, and ½ teaspoon pepper in bowl. Pat chicken dry with paper towels and use your fingers or handle of wooden spoon to carefully separate skin from breast. Rub oil mixture all over chicken and underneath skin of breast. Tie legs together with kitchen twine and tuck wingtips behind back.

2. Toss potatoes with remaining 1 tablespoon oil, 1½ teaspoons salt, and ½ teaspoon pepper. Arrange potatoes, flat sides down, in single layer in 12-inch oven-safe nonstick skillet. Place skillet over medium heat and cook potatoes, without moving them, until brown on bottom, 7 to 9 minutes (do not flip).

3. Place chicken, breast side up, on top of potatoes and transfer skillet to oven. Roast until breast registers 160 degrees and thighs register 175 degrees, 1 to 1¼ hours. Transfer chicken to carving board, tent loosely with aluminum foil, and let rest for 20 minutes.

4. Meanwhile, cover skillet, return potatoes to oven, and roast until tender, about 20 minutes. Carve chicken and serve with potatoes and lemon wedges.

Cast Iron Chicken and Vegetables

Skillet-Roasted Chicken and Potatoes

Skillet-Roasted Chicken with Stuffing

SERVES 4

WHY THIS RECIPE WORKS To simplify Sunday-style stuffed chicken into a one-pan meal, we sped things up by taking the stuffing out of the chicken and making the entire dish in just one skillet. First we sautéed the aromatics for the stuffing, then we placed the chicken—brushed with a flavorful herb butter—right on top. We scattered the bread cubes around the bird and moved the skillet to the oven to simultaneously roast the chicken and toast the bread. As the chicken cooked, the bread soaked up its flavorful juices. Finally, while the chicken rested, a quick stir and a splash of broth mixed up the aromatics and moistened the stuffing.

You can find Italian bread in the bakery section of your grocery store. Take care when stirring the contents of the skillet in steps 4 and 5, as the skillet handle will be very hot.

- 1 (4-pound) whole chicken, giblets discarded
- 6 tablespoons unsalted butter, divided
- 2 tablespoons minced fresh sage, divided
- 2 tablespoons minced fresh thyme, divided
  Salt and pepper
- 2 onions, chopped fine
- 2 celery ribs, minced
- 7 ounces Italian bread, cut into ½-inch cubes (6 cups)
- ⅓ cup chicken broth

1. Adjust oven rack to lower-middle position and heat oven to 375 degrees. Pat chicken dry with paper towels. Melt 4 tablespoons butter in small bowl in microwave, about 45 seconds. Stir in 1 tablespoon sage, 1 tablespoon thyme, 1 teaspoon salt, and ½ teaspoon pepper. Brush chicken with herb butter.

2. Melt remaining 2 tablespoons butter in 12-inch ovensafe skillet over medium heat. Add onions, celery, ½ teaspoon salt, and ½ teaspoon pepper and cook until softened, about 5 minutes. Add remaining 1 tablespoon sage and remaining 1 tablespoon thyme and cook until fragrant, about 1 minute. Off heat, place chicken, breast side up, on top of vegetables. Arrange bread cubes around chicken in bottom of skillet.

3. Transfer skillet to oven and roast until breasts register 160 degrees and thighs register 175 degrees, about 1 hour, rotating skillet halfway through roasting.

Skillet-Roasted Chicken with Stuffing

Chicken Baked in Foil with Sweet Potato and Radish

4. Carefully transfer chicken to plate and tent loosely with aluminum foil. Holding skillet handle with potholder (handle will be hot), stir bread and vegetables to combine, cover, and let stand for 10 minutes.

5. Add broth and any accumulated chicken juice from plate and cavity to skillet and stir to combine. Warm stuffing, uncovered, over low heat until heated through, about 3 minutes. Remove from heat, cover, and let sit while carving chicken. Transfer chicken to carving board, carve, and serve with stuffing.

Chicken Baked in Foil with Sweet Potato and Radish

SERVES 4

WHY THIS RECIPE WORKS A quick meal of chicken and vegetables baked in foil sounded great to us, but our first attempts were not much better than an old-style TV dinner. Seasoning the chicken with salt on both sides and refrigerating it for at least an hour proved ideal, as did using sturdy vegetables, which held up during cooking. Placing the potato slices under the chicken insulated the meat from the oven's direct heat, and we found that leaving plenty of headroom above the chicken within the pouch gave the steam room to circulate, ensuring even cooking. An added bonus? No pots or pans to clean.

To ensure even cooking, cut the vegetables as directed and buy chicken breasts of the same size. Refrigerate the pouches for at least 1 hour before cooking.

- 5 tablespoons extra-virgin olive oil
- 6 garlic cloves, sliced thin
- 1 tablespoon grated fresh ginger
- ¼ teaspoon red pepper flakes
- 12 ounces sweet potatoes, peeled and sliced ¼ inch thick
- 4 radishes, trimmed and quartered
- 2 celery ribs, quartered lengthwise and cut into 2-inch lengths
- ½ large red onion, sliced ½ inch thick, layers separated
  Kosher salt and pepper
- 4 (6-ounce) boneless, skinless chicken breasts, trimmed
- 2 tablespoons rice vinegar
- 2 tablespoons minced fresh cilantro

1. Spray centers of four 20 by 12-inch sheets of heavy-duty aluminum foil with vegetable oil spray. Microwave oil, garlic, ginger, and pepper flakes in small bowl until garlic begins to brown, 1 to 1½ minutes. Combine potato slices, radishes, celery, onion, 1 teaspoon salt, and garlic oil in large bowl.

2. Pat chicken dry with paper towels. Sprinkle ⅛ teaspoon salt evenly over each side of each chicken breast, then season with pepper. Position 1 piece of prepared foil with long side parallel to counter edge. In center of foil, arrange one-quarter of potato slices in 2 rows perpendicular to counter edge. Lay 1 chicken breast on top of potato slices. Place one-quarter of vegetables around chicken. Repeat with remaining foil, potato slices, chicken, and vegetables. Drizzle any remaining oil mixture from bowl over chicken.

3. Bring short sides of foil together and crimp to seal tightly. Crimp remaining open ends of packets, leaving as much headroom as possible inside packets. Refrigerate for at least 1 hour or up to 24 hours.

4. Adjust oven rack to lowest position and heat oven to 475 degrees. Arrange packets on rimmed baking sheet. Bake until chicken registers 160 degrees, 18 to 23 minutes. (To check temperature, poke thermometer through foil and into chicken.) Let chicken rest in packets for 3 minutes.

5. Transfer chicken packets to individual dinner plates, carefully open (steam will escape), and slide contents onto plates. Drizzle vinegar over chicken and vegetables and sprinkle with cilantro. Serve.

Chicken Baked in Foil with Potatoes and Carrots

Substitute 12 ounces Yukon Gold potatoes (unpeeled, sliced ¼ inch thick) and 2 carrots (peeled, quartered lengthwise and cut into 2-inch lengths), for sweet potatoes, radishes, and celery; lemon juice for rice vinegar. Substitute 1 teaspoon minced fresh thyme for ginger and 2 tablespoons minced fresh chives for cilantro.

Chicken Baked in Foil with Fennel and Sun-Dried Tomatoes

Substitute 1 fennel bulb, stalks discarded, bulb halved, cored, and cut into ½-inch-thick wedges, layers separated, for celery; balsamic vinegar for rice vinegar; and minced fresh basil for cilantro. Add ¼ cup oil-packed sun-dried tomatoes, rinsed, patted dry, and chopped fine and ¼ cup pitted kalamata olives, chopped fine, to vegetables in step 1.

Chicken and Slicks

SERVES 4 TO 6

Chicken and Slicks

WHY THIS RECIPE WORKS A distant cousin to chicken and dumplings, chicken and slicks offers tender chicken in a rich, flavorful broth but swaps the traditional biscuit-style dumpling for a chewy, noodlelike version. We browned bone-in chicken pieces for the best flavor before simmering them in the broth. We replaced the traditional lard in the slicks with more readily available vegetable oil, plus some of the rendered chicken fat. Cooking the slicks in thickened broth caused them to break apart, so we cooked them in the broth before adding toasted flour to thicken it.

If you're short on chicken fat at the end of step 1, supplement it with vegetable oil.

- 1½ pounds bone-in chicken thighs, trimmed
- 2 (12-ounce) bone-in split chicken breasts, halved crosswise and trimmed
- Salt and pepper
- 6 tablespoons plus 2 cups all-purpose flour
- 3 tablespoons vegetable oil, divided
- 1 onion, chopped
- 2 teaspoons minced fresh thyme
- 7½ cups chicken broth, divided
- 2 bay leaves
- ¼ cup chopped fresh parsley

1. Pat chicken dry with paper towels and season with salt and pepper. Toast 6 tablespoons flour in Dutch oven over medium heat, stirring constantly, until just beginning to brown, about 5 minutes. Transfer flour to medium bowl and wipe out pot. Heat 1 tablespoon oil in now-empty Dutch oven over medium-high heat until just smoking. Cook chicken until browned all over, about 10 minutes; transfer to plate. When chicken is cool enough to handle, remove and discard skin. Pour fat (you should have about 2 tablespoons) into small bowl; reserve.

2. Add onion and 1 tablespoon oil to now-empty pot and cook over medium heat until softened, about 5 minutes. Stir in thyme and cook until fragrant, about 30 seconds. Add 7 cups broth, chicken, and bay leaves and bring to boil. Reduce heat to low and simmer, covered, until breasts register 160 degrees and thighs register 175 degrees, 20 to 25 minutes. Remove from heat and transfer chicken to clean plate. When chicken is cool enough to handle, shred into bite-size pieces, discarding bones.

3. Meanwhile, combine remaining ½ cup chicken broth, reserved fat, and remaining 1 tablespoon oil in liquid measuring cup. Process remaining 2 cups flour and ½ teaspoon salt in food processor until combined. With processor running, slowly pour in broth mixture and process until mixture resembles coarse meal. Turn dough onto lightly floured surface and knead until smooth. Divide in half.

4. Roll each dough half into 10-inch square about ⅛ inch thick. Cut each square into twenty 5 by 1-inch rectangles. Place handful of noodles in single layer on parchment paper–lined plate, cover with another sheet of parchment, and repeat stacking with remaining noodles and additional parchment, ending with parchment. Freeze until firm, at least 10 minutes or up to 30 minutes.

5. Return broth to simmer and add noodles. Cook until noodles are nearly tender, 12 to 15 minutes, stirring occasionally to separate. Remove 1 cup broth from pot and whisk into reserved toasted flour. Stir broth-flour mixture into pot, being careful not to break up noodles, and simmer until slightly thickened, 3 to 5 minutes. Add shredded chicken and parsley and cook until heated through, about 1 minute. Season with salt and pepper to taste. Serve.

Making Slicks

1. Roll each dough half into 10-inch square of ⅛-inch thickness. Then, using sharp knife, cut dough into twenty 5 by 1-inch rectangles.

2. Stack slicks between layers of parchment and freeze briefly before simmering.

Moravian Chicken Pie
SERVES 8

WHY THIS RECIPE WORKS Immigrants from the Czech province Moravia settled in Pennsylvania, and later North Carolina, and brought with them such homey dishes as Moravian cake, cookies, and a satisfying double-crusted chicken pie served with a rich gravy. Searing the chicken rendered its fat, which we used in a roux to thicken the gravy. For moist chicken, we poached it in chicken broth and used that broth to give our gravy flavor. Sour cream helped make for a rich, flaky pie crust that was easy to roll out.

The pie may seem loose when it comes out of the oven; it will set up as it cools.

Crust
- ½ cup sour cream, chilled
- 1 large egg, lightly beaten
- 2½ cups (12½ ounces) all-purpose flour
- 1½ teaspoons table salt
- 12 tablespoons unsalted butter, cut into ½-inch pieces and chilled

Filling
- 2 (10- to 12-ounce) bone-in split chicken breasts, halved crosswise and trimmed
- 3 (5- to 7-ounce) bone-in chicken thighs, trimmed
  Salt and pepper

Moravian Chicken Pie

- 1 tablespoon vegetable oil
- 3 cups chicken broth
- 1 bay leaf
- 2 tablespoons unsalted butter
- ¼ cup all-purpose flour
- ¼ cup half-and-half
- 1 large egg, lightly beaten

1. For the Crust Combine sour cream and egg in bowl. Process flour and salt in food processor until combined, about 3 seconds. Add butter and pulse until only pea-size pieces remain, about 10 pulses. Add half of sour cream mixture and pulse until combined, 5 pulses. Add remaining sour cream mixture and pulse until dough begins to form, about 10 pulses.

2. Transfer mixture to lightly floured counter and knead briefly until dough comes together. Divide dough in half and form each half into 4-inch disk. Wrap each disk in plastic wrap and refrigerate for at least 1 hour or up to 2 days.

3. Line rimmed baking sheet with parchment paper. Remove 1 dough disk from refrigerator and let sit for 10 minutes. Working on lightly floured counter, roll into 12-inch round and transfer to 9-inch pie plate, leaving ½-inch overhang all around. Repeat with second dough disk and transfer to prepared baking sheet. Cover both dough rounds with plastic wrap and refrigerate for 30 minutes.

4. For the Filling Pat chicken dry with paper towels and season with salt and pepper. Heat oil in large Dutch oven over medium-high heat until just smoking. Cook chicken until browned, about 10 minutes; transfer to plate. Pour fat (you should have 2 tablespoons; supplement with butter if necessary) into bowl; reserve. When chicken is cool enough to handle, remove and discard skin. Add broth, chicken, and bay leaf to now-empty pot and bring to boil. Reduce heat to low and simmer, covered, until breasts register 160 degrees and thighs register 175 degrees, 14 to 18 minutes. Transfer chicken to bowl. When chicken is cool enough to handle, shred into bite-size pieces, discarding bones. Pour broth through fine-mesh strainer into second bowl and reserve (you should have about 2¾ cups); discard bay leaf.

5. Adjust oven rack to lowest position and heat oven to 450 degrees. Heat butter and reserved fat in now-empty pot over medium heat until shimmering. Add flour and cook, whisking constantly, until golden, 1 to 2 minutes. Slowly whisk in 2 cups reserved broth and half-and-half and bring to boil. Reduce heat to medium-low and simmer gravy until thickened and reduced to 1¾ cups, 6 to 8 minutes. Season with salt and pepper to taste. Combine 1 cup gravy with shredded chicken; reserve remaining gravy for serving.

6. Transfer chicken mixture to dough-lined pie plate and spread into even layer. Top with second dough round, leaving at least ½-inch overhang all around. Fold dough under so that edge of fold is flush with rim of pie plate. Flute edges using thumb and forefinger or press with tines of fork to seal. Cut four 1-inch slits in top. Brush pie with egg and bake until top is light golden brown, 18 to 20 minutes. Reduce oven temperature to 375 degrees and continue to bake until crust is deep golden brown, 10 to 15 minutes. Let pie cool on wire rack for at least 45 minutes.

7. When ready to serve, bring remaining ¾ cup reserved gravy and remaining ¾ cup reserved broth to boil in medium saucepan. Simmer over medium-low heat until slightly thickened, 5 to 7 minutes. Season with salt and pepper to taste. Serve pie with gravy.

Brunswick Stew

SERVES 4 TO 6

WHY THIS RECIPE WORKS Brunswick stew is a fixture at many Southern barbecues, but because there is no definitive recipe for the stew, many cooks use it as a kitchen sink dump-all, resulting in variations that simply aren't appealing. After testing various versions, we settled on an eastern North Carolina style made with barbecue sauce for complex flavor and potatoes for thickness. We kept the meats simple, opting for tender chicken thighs and flavorful kielbasa. Because barbecue sauce flavors vary across brands, we created our own. Browning the ketchup before adding other ingredients helped to soften its raw edge and created a rich tomato base.

Our favorite kielbasa is Wellshire Farms Smoked Polska Kielbasa.

- 1 tablespoon vegetable oil
- 1 onion, chopped fine
- ¾ cup ketchup
- 4 cups water, divided
- 2 pounds boneless, skinless chicken thighs, trimmed
- 1 pound russet potatoes, peeled and cut into ½-inch chunks
- 8 ounces kielbasa sausage, sliced ¼ inch thick
- 6–8 tablespoons cider vinegar
- 2 tablespoons Worcestershire sauce, divided
- 1 tablespoon yellow mustard
- 1 teaspoon garlic powder
- Salt and pepper
- ¼ teaspoon red pepper flakes
- 1 cup canned crushed tomatoes
- ½ cup frozen lima beans
- ½ cup frozen corn

1. Heat oil in Dutch oven over medium-high heat until shimmering. Add onion and cook until softened, 3 to 5 minutes. Add ketchup and ¼ cup water and cook, stirring frequently, until fond begins to form on bottom of pot and mixture has thickened, about 6 minutes.

2. Add chicken, potatoes, kielbasa, 6 tablespoons vinegar, 1½ tablespoons Worcestershire, mustard, garlic powder, 1 teaspoon salt, 1 teaspoon pepper, pepper flakes, and remaining 3¾ cups water and bring to boil. Reduce heat to low, cover, and simmer until potatoes are tender, 30 to 35 minutes, stirring frequently.

3. Transfer chicken to plate and let cool for 5 minutes, then shred into bite-size pieces with 2 forks. While chicken cools, stir tomatoes, lima beans, and corn into stew and continue to simmer, uncovered, for 15 minutes. Stir in shredded chicken and remaining 1½ teaspoons Worcestershire and cook until warmed through, about 2 minutes. Season with salt, pepper, and remaining vinegar (up to 2 tablespoons) to taste. Serve.

Transylvanian Goulash
SERVES 6 TO 8

WHY THIS RECIPE WORKS A close cousin to Hungarian goulash, this hearty stew served at Józsa Corner in Pittsburgh features rich, marbled pork shoulder rather than beef. Browning the pork in batches developed flavorful fond that was enhanced by aromatic vegetables. Following the style of Józsa Corner, we used water instead of chicken broth to let the variety of flavors to shine. We introduced sauerkraut toward the end of cooking to balance the rich pork; rinsing the sauerkraut helped tame the tang. Sweet paprika provided its trademark color and intensity.

Pork butt roast is often labeled Boston butt in the supermarket. Since sweet paprika is vital to the success of this recipe, it is best to use a fresh bottle. Do not substitute hot or smoked Spanish paprika. Eden Organic jarred sauerkraut is our favorite. Rinsing the sauerkraut reduces its sharp flavor and bite; if you prefer sharper sauerkraut flavor, omit this step. Serve with white rice, if desired.

- 1 (3½-pound) boneless pork butt roast, trimmed and cut into 1½-inch pieces
- 1½ teaspoons table salt, divided
- ½ teaspoon pepper
- 1 tablespoon vegetable oil
- 1 onion, chopped fine
- 1 green bell pepper, stemmed, seeded, and chopped fine
- 2 celery ribs, chopped fine
- 1 plum tomato, chopped
- 3 tablespoons sweet paprika
- 1 tablespoon caraway seeds
- 2 garlic cloves, minced
- 3 cups water
- 2 cups sauerkraut, rinsed and drained
  Sour cream
  Minced fresh dill

Brunswick Stew

Transylvanian Goulash

On the Road: A Big, Strong Pittsburgh Belly

The unassuming Hungarian restaurant Józsa Corner occupied a distressed whitewashed building along the railroad tracks in Hazelwood, a neighborhood a few minutes from downtown Pittsburgh. The owner, Alexander Józsa Bodnar, a veteran of the Hungarian Revolution of 1956, ruled the kitchen.

One Friday a month, Bodnar hosted "Hungarian Night." You stepped through the main entrance directly into the kitchen, where Bodnar was feverishly preparing the coming meal. He welcomed everyone warmly. You then passed from the kitchen to the dining room through a sledgehammered opening in a weathered brick wall. Guests cozied up, elbow to elbow, at long tables in a converted living room where an old piano rested quietly unused.

Bodnar entered the dining room through the hole in the wall with a plate of yeasted fry bread called lángos and a bowl of mushroom paprikash to be spooned over the top, chanting "Egyetek, vegyetek, hadd nőjön a begyetek," a saying that promotes the virtues of eating for a "big, strong belly." What followed was a simple meal with a big personality: peasant soup (so called for the many bones it contains), haluska, chicken paprikash, and goulash. Although you were dining with strangers, the mood was sure to transform into one of a familiar dinner with close friends.

Alexander Józsa Bodnar passed away in February of 2022 and Józsa Corner has since closed.

1. Adjust oven rack to lower-middle position and heat oven to 325 degrees. Pat pork dry with paper towels and sprinkle with 1 teaspoon salt and pepper.

2. Heat oil in Dutch oven over medium-high heat until just smoking. Add half of pork and cook, stirring occasionally, until brown on all sides, about 8 minutes; transfer to bowl. (Reduce heat if bottom of pot begins to scorch.) Repeat with remaining pork.

3. Reduce heat to medium. Add onion, bell pepper, celery, tomato, and remaining ½ teaspoon salt to now-empty pot and cook until vegetables are softened and liquid has evaporated, 8 to 10 minutes, scraping up any browned bits.

4. Add paprika, caraway seeds, and garlic and cook until fragrant, about 1 minute. Stir in water and pork and any accumulated juices and bring to simmer, scraping up any browned bits. Cover, transfer to oven, and cook for 1 hour. Stir in sauerkraut, cover, return pot to oven, and continue to cook until pork is fully tender, about 30 minutes longer.

5. Using wide spoon, skim off any surface fat. Season with salt and pepper to taste. Serve, garnished with sour cream and dill.

Guinness Beef Stew

SERVES 6 TO 8

WHY THIS RECIPE WORKS Guinness beef stew often captures only the bitterness and none of the deep, caramelized flavors of the beer. We found the trick to rich, malty flavor was to add some of the beer at the end of cooking so that the heat didn't dull the complex flavors. We also added a little brown sugar to balance some of the bitterness. We loved the idea of just dumping the meat into the pot without searing, but the flavor was lacking. To compensate, we first browned the onions and tomato paste, then cooked the stew uncovered so that the meat could brown in the oven.

Use Guinness Draught, not Guinness Extra Stout, which is too bitter.

- 1 (3½- to 4-pound) boneless beef chuck-eye roast, pulled apart at seams, trimmed, and cut into 1½-inch pieces
  Salt and pepper
- 3 tablespoons vegetable oil
- 2 onions, chopped fine

1	tablespoon tomato paste
2	garlic cloves, minced
¼	cup all-purpose flour
3	cups chicken broth
1¼	cups Guinness Draught, divided
1½	tablespoons packed dark brown sugar
1	teaspoon minced fresh thyme
1½	pounds Yukon Gold potatoes, unpeeled, cut into 1-inch pieces
1	pound carrots, peeled and cut into 1-inch pieces
2	tablespoons minced fresh parsley

1. Adjust oven rack to lower-middle position and heat oven to 325 degrees. Season beef with salt and pepper. Heat oil in Dutch oven over medium-high heat until shimmering. Add onions and ¼ teaspoon salt and cook, stirring occasionally, until well browned, 8 to 10 minutes.

2. Add tomato paste and garlic and cook until rust-colored and fragrant, about 2 minutes. Stir in flour and cook for 1 minute. Whisk in broth, ¾ cup Guinness, sugar, and thyme, scraping up any browned bits. Bring to simmer and cook until slightly thickened, about 3 minutes. Stir in beef and return to simmer. Transfer to oven and cook, uncovered, for 90 minutes, stirring halfway through cooking.

3. Stir in potatoes and carrots and continue cooking until beef and vegetables are tender, about 1 hour, stirring halfway through cooking. Stir in remaining ½ cup Guinness and parsley. Season with salt and pepper to taste, and serve.

Preparing a Chuck Roast

1. Pull apart roast at major seams (marked by lines of fat and silverskin). Use knife as necessary.

2. With sharp chef's knife or boning knife, trim off thick layers of fat and silverskin. Cut meat into 1½-inch pieces.

Guinness Beef Stew

Sunday-Best Garlic Roast Beef

SERVES 6 TO 8

WHY THIS RECIPE WORKS Top sirloin is a more affordable roast beef alternative to prime rib—one that is faster to cook and full of flavor. We browned the roast in the oven at a high temperature and then reduced the oven temperature to cook the roast through without losing too much moisture. To give our roast an extra layer of savory flavor, we studded the roast beef with toasted garlic, rubbed it with garlic salt, and coated it while it cooked with a garlic paste.

Look for a top sirloin roast that has a thick, substantial fat cap still attached. The rendered fat will help to keep the roast moist. When making the jus, taste the reduced broth before adding any of the accumulated meat juices from the roast. The meat juices are well seasoned and may make the jus too salty. If you don't have a heavy-duty nonstick roasting pan, a broiler pan bottom works well too.

OUR SUNDAY BEST   329

Sunday-Best Garlic Roast Beef

Classic Roast Beef and Gravy

Beef
- 8 large garlic cloves, unpeeled
- 1 (4-pound) top sirloin roast, fat trimmed to ¼ inch

Garlic-Salt Rub
- 3 large garlic cloves, minced
- 1 teaspoon dried thyme
- ½ teaspoon table salt

Garlic Paste
- ½ cup extra-virgin olive oil
- 12 large garlic cloves, cut in half lengthwise
- 2 sprigs fresh thyme
- 2 bay leaves
- ½ teaspoon table salt
- Pepper

Jus
- 1½ cups beef broth
- 1½ cups chicken broth

1. For the Beef Toast garlic in 8-inch skillet over medium-high heat, tossing frequently, until spotty brown, about 8 minutes. Set aside. When cool enough to handle, peel and cut into ¼-inch slivers. Using paring knife, make 1-inch-deep slits all over roast and insert toasted garlic into slits.

2. For the Garlic-Salt Rub Combine garlic, thyme, and salt in small bowl and rub all over roast. Place roast on large plate and refrigerate, uncovered, for at least 4 hours or preferably overnight.

3. For the Garlic Paste Heat oil, garlic, thyme, bay leaves, and salt in small saucepan over medium-high heat until bubbles start to rise to surface. Reduce heat to low and cook until garlic is soft, about 30 minutes. Let cool completely, then strain, reserving oil. Discard herbs and transfer garlic to small bowl. Mash garlic with 1 tablespoon garlic oil until paste forms. Cover and refrigerate paste until ready to use. Cover and reserve garlic oil.

4. Adjust oven rack to middle position, place nonstick roasting pan on rack, and heat oven to 450 degrees. Using paper towels, wipe garlic-salt rub off beef. Rub beef with 2 tablespoons reserved garlic oil and season with pepper. Transfer meat, fat side down, to preheated pan and roast, turning as needed until browned on all sides, 10 to 15 minutes.

5. Reduce oven temperature to 300 degrees. Remove pan from oven, turn roast fat side up, and, using spatula, coat top with garlic paste. Return meat to oven and roast until it registers 120 to 125 degrees (for medium-rare), 50 minutes to 1 hour, 10 minutes. Transfer to carving board, cover loosely with aluminum foil, and let rest for 20 minutes.

6. For the Jus Pour off fat from roasting pan and place pan over high heat. Add beef broth and chicken broth and bring to boil, scraping up browned bits with wooden spoon. Simmer, stirring occasionally, until reduced to 2 cups, about 5 minutes. Add accumulated juices from roast and cook for 1 minute, then pour through fine-mesh strainer. Slice roast crosswise into ¼-inch-thick slices. Serve with jus.

Classic Roast Beef and Gravy

SERVES 6 TO 8

WHY THIS RECIPE WORKS For tender, juicy roast beef, we chose top sirloin roast with a thick fat cap, which rendered as the beef roasted and kept it moist. Searing each side before roasting helped to develop a flavorful crust. Though the right roasting temperature produced juicy meat (our roast having expelled very little liquid), it left precious few drippings in the roasting pan from which to make gravy. A good amount of beef broth, plus the rendered fat and fond left behind from searing the meat, provided volume and richness, while mushrooms, red wine, and Worcestershire sauce amped up the flavor.

For the best flavor and texture, refrigerate the roast overnight after salting. If you don't have a V-rack, cook the roast on a wire rack set inside a rimmed baking sheet.

- 1 (4-pound) top sirloin roast, fat trimmed to ¼ inch
- Salt and pepper
- 1 tablespoon vegetable oil
- 8 ounces white mushrooms, trimmed and chopped
- 2 onions, chopped fine
- 1 carrot, peeled and chopped
- 1 celery rib, minced
- 1 tablespoon tomato paste
- 4 garlic cloves, minced
- ¼ cup all-purpose flour
- 1 cup red wine
- 4 cups beef broth
- 1 teaspoon Worcestershire sauce

1. Pat roast dry with paper towels. Rub 2 teaspoons salt evenly over meat. Cover with plastic wrap and refrigerate for at least 1 hour or up to 24 hours.

2. Adjust oven rack to lower-middle position and heat oven to 275 degrees. Pat roast dry with paper towels and rub with 1 teaspoon pepper. Heat oil in Dutch oven over medium-high heat until just smoking. Brown roast all over, 8 to 12 minutes, then transfer to V-rack set inside roasting pan (do not wipe out Dutch oven). Transfer to oven and cook until meat registers 120 to 125 degrees (for medium-rare), 1½ to 2 hours.

3. Meanwhile, add mushrooms to fat left in Dutch oven and cook until golden, about 5 minutes. Stir in onions, carrot, and celery and cook until browned, 5 to 7 minutes. Stir in tomato paste, garlic, and flour and cook until fragrant, about 2 minutes. Stir in wine and broth, scraping up any browned bits with wooden spoon. Bring to boil, then reduce heat to medium and simmer until thickened, about 10 minutes. Strain gravy, then stir in Worcestershire and season with salt and pepper; cover and keep warm.

4. Transfer roast to carving board, tent with aluminum foil, and let rest for 20 minutes. Slice roast crosswise into ½-inch-thick slices. Serve with gravy.

Herbed Roast Beef

SERVES 6 TO 8

WHY THIS RECIPE WORKS For an easy roast beef dressed to impress, we created a swirl of herbs and mustard by butterflying the roast and spreading the mixture of fresh herbs and mustard over the interior of the meat before folding it back together and securing it with twine. A simple herb butter, spread over the resting roast, mingled with the juices of the meat to create a flavorful sauce.

For even deeper seasoning, refrigerate the roast overnight after filling it with the herb mixture in step 2.

- ⅓ cup minced fresh parsley
- 1 shallot, minced
- 2 tablespoons minced fresh thyme
- 2 tablespoons extra-virgin olive oil, divided
- 1 tablespoon Dijon mustard
- 4 tablespoons unsalted butter, softened
- 1 (4-pound) top sirloin roast, fat trimmed to ¼ inch
- 1 tablespoon table salt
- 1 tablespoon pepper

1. Combine parsley, shallot, and thyme in bowl. Transfer 2 tablespoons herb mixture to second bowl and stir in 1 tablespoon oil and mustard until combined; set aside. Add butter to remaining herb mixture and mash with fork until combined.

2. Butterfly roast by slicing horizontally through middle of meat, leaving about ½ inch of meat intact, and rub roast inside and out with salt and pepper. Spread herb-mustard mixture over interior of meat, fold roast back together, and tie securely with kitchen twine at 1-inch intervals. Refrigerate for at least 1 hour or up to 24 hours.

3. Adjust oven rack to middle position and heat oven to 275 degrees. Pat roast dry with paper towels. Heat remaining 1 tablespoon oil in 12-inch skillet over medium-high heat until just smoking. Brown roast all over, 8 to 12 minutes, then arrange on V-rack set inside roasting pan. Transfer to oven and roast until meat registers 120 to 125 degrees (for medium-rare), 1½ to 2 hours.

4. Transfer roast to carving board, spread with herb-butter mixture, tent with aluminum foil, and let rest for 20 minutes. Remove twine and slice roast crosswise into ¼-inch-thick slices. Serve.

Herbs Galore

Fresh parsley and thyme flavor both the interior and exterior of our roast.

1. Butterfly roast by slicing horizontally through middle of the meat. Leave about ½ inch of meat intact, then open it like a book.

2. After seasoning meat, spread herb-mustard mixture over interior of meat.

3. Fold meat back to its original position, then tie securely at 1-inch intervals with kitchen twine.

4. For second hit of herb flavor after roast is cooked, spread it with herb butter.

Herb-Crusted Beef Tenderloin

SERVES 12 TO 16

WHY THIS RECIPE WORKS Though beef tenderloin offers incomparable tenderness, its flavor could often use some embellishment. To give the meat a flavor boost, we turned to a thick herbed crust. But herbs can burn easily, lose their flavor in a hot oven, or just fall off the meat. Cooking the roast in the oven at a high temperature for part of the time gave us a perfectly caramelized exterior that made applying an herb paste easy. Adding grated Parmesan cheese to the paste gave it nutty flavor and helped the paste adhere to the meat. Fresh parsley and thyme provided a flavorful coating, and for a crisp texture, we relied on bread crumbs.

Make sure to begin this recipe 2 hours before you plan to put the roast in the oven. The tenderloin can be trimmed, tied, rubbed with the salt mixture, and refrigerated up to 24 hours in advance; make sure to bring the roast back to room temperature before putting it into the oven.

- 1 (6-pound) whole beef tenderloin, trimmed, tail end tucked, and tied at 1½-inch intervals
  Kosher salt and cracked peppercorns
- 2 teaspoons sugar
- 2 slices hearty white sandwich bread, torn into pieces
- 2½ ounces Parmesan cheese, grated (1¼ cups), divided
- ½ cup chopped fresh parsley, divided
- 6 tablespoons extra-virgin olive oil, divided
- 2 teaspoons plus 2 tablespoons chopped fresh thyme
- 4 garlic cloves, minced
- 1 recipe Horseradish Cream Sauce (recipe follows)

1. Set wire rack in rimmed baking sheet. Pat tenderloin dry with paper towels. Combine 1 tablespoon salt, 1 tablespoon pepper, and sugar in small bowl and rub all over tenderloin. Transfer to prepared baking sheet and let sit at room temperature for 2 hours.

2. Meanwhile, pulse bread in food processor to fine crumbs, about 15 pulses. Transfer bread crumbs to medium bowl and toss with ½ cup Parmesan, 2 tablespoons parsley, 2 tablespoons oil, and 2 teaspoons thyme until evenly combined. Wipe out food processor with paper towels and process remaining ¾ cup Parmesan, 6 tablespoons parsley, ¼ cup oil, 2 tablespoons thyme, and garlic until smooth paste forms. Transfer herb paste to small bowl.

3. Adjust oven rack to upper-middle position and heat oven to 400 degrees. Roast tenderloin for 20 minutes and remove from oven. Using scissors, carefully cut kitchen twine and remove it. Coat tenderloin with herb paste, then bread-crumb topping. Roast until meat registers 120 to 125 degrees (for medium-rare) and topping is golden brown, 20 to 25 minutes. (If topping browns before meat reaches preferred internal temperature, lightly cover with aluminum foil for remainder of roasting time and remove while roast rests.) Let roast rest, uncovered, for 30 minutes on wire rack. Transfer to carving board and carve. Serve with Horseradish Cream Sauce.

Herbed Roast Beef

Preparing Herb-Crusted Beef Tenderloin

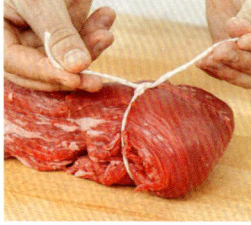 

1. To ensure even cooking, fold thin, tapered end under roast, then tie entire roast with kitchen twine every 1½ inches. Roast for 20 minutes.

2. Remove roast from oven, snip twine with scissors, and remove before adding herb paste and bread-crumb mixture. Return to oven to finish cooking.

Herb-Crusted Beef Tenderloin

Horseradish Cream Sauce
MAKES ABOUT 1 CUP

- ½ cup sour cream
- ½ cup heavy cream
- ¼ cup prepared horseradish, drained
- 2 teaspoons Dijon mustard
- 1 garlic clove, minced
- ¼ teaspoon sugar
  Salt and pepper

Mix all ingredients in bowl; add salt and pepper to taste. Cover and let stand at room temperature for 1 to 1½ hours to thicken. (Sauce can be refrigerated for up to 2 days.)

Classic Roast Beef Tenderloin

SERVES 12 TO 16

WHY THIS RECIPE WORKS A 5-pound trimmed whole beef tenderloin is a showstopper, but it can be too large to fit in a skillet to sear (our favorite method for developing a nice crust). So we started by cutting it in half, yielding two smaller roasts that were easier to manage. We salted them overnight and then roasted both pieces gently in a low oven before searing them in a piping-hot skillet just before serving, ensuring a nicely browned exterior that added flavor and visual appeal without compromising the rosy interior. A rich, glossy red wine sauce took the roast over the top.

Plan ahead: The roast must be salted and refrigerated for at least 12 hours before cooking. If you're buying an untrimmed tenderloin, be sure it weighs 6 to 7 pounds. Serve with Red Wine Sauce (recipe follows), if desired.

- 1 (5-pound) trimmed whole beef tenderloin
  Kosher salt and pepper
- 2 tablespoons vegetable oil

1. Cut tenderloin crosswise at base of head to make 2 roasts. Using kitchen twine, tie head at 1-inch intervals. Tuck tail end of second roast underneath by 3 to 5 inches to create more even shape. Tie tucked portion with kitchen twine at 1-inch intervals to secure.

2. Place 1 roast on large sheet of plastic wrap and sprinkle all over with 1 tablespoon salt. Wrap tightly in double layer of plastic. Repeat with remaining roast and 1 tablespoon salt. Refrigerate roasts for at least 12 hours or up to 24 hours.

3. Adjust oven rack to middle position and heat oven to 250 degrees. Set wire rack in rimmed baking sheet. Season roasts with pepper and place on prepared wire rack. Roast until meat registers 125 degrees (for medium-rare) or 130 degrees (for medium), 1 hour, 20 minutes to 1 hour, 40 minutes for tail-end roast and 1 hour, 40 minutes to 2 hours for head-end roast. Transfer roasts to carving board, tent with aluminum foil, and let rest for 20 minutes.

4. Pat roasts dry with paper towels. Heat oil in 12-inch nonstick skillet over medium-high heat until just smoking. Add both roasts and sear on all sides until well browned, 5 to 7 minutes. Transfer roasts to carving board, remove twine, and slice ½ inch thick. Serve.

Red Wine Sauce
MAKES ABOUT 2 CUPS

Medium-bodied red wines, such as Côtes du Rhône or Pinot Noir, are best for this recipe. You can substitute chain meat trimmed from a beef tenderloin for the stew meat.

- 5 tablespoons unsalted butter, cut into 5 pieces and chilled, divided
- 12 ounces beef stew meat, cut into 1-inch pieces
- 2 tablespoons tomato paste
- 2 cups red wine
- 2 cups beef broth
- 1 shallot, sliced thin
- 2 tablespoons soy sauce
- 1½ tablespoons sugar
- 6 sprigs fresh thyme
- 2½ teaspoons cornstarch
- 1 tablespoon cold water
  Salt and pepper

1. Melt 1 tablespoon butter in large saucepan over medium-high heat. Add beef and cook, stirring occasionally, until well browned and fond forms on bottom of saucepan, 10 to 12 minutes.

2. Add tomato paste and cook until darkened in color and fragrant, about 1 minute. Stir in wine, broth, shallot, soy sauce, sugar, and thyme sprigs and bring to boil, scraping up any browned bits. Cook until reduced to 4 cups, 12 to 15 minutes.

3. Strain sauce through fine-mesh strainer set over bowl; discard solids. Return sauce to saucepan and bring to boil over medium-high heat. Dissolve cornstarch in cold water. Whisk cornstarch mixture into sauce and boil until slightly thickened, about 30 seconds. Reduce heat to low and whisk in remaining 4 tablespoons butter, 1 piece at a time. Season with salt and pepper to taste. Remove from heat and cover to keep warm.

Holiday Strip Roast
SERVES 8 TO 10

WHY THIS RECIPE WORKS For an occasion-worthy, beefy top-loin roast, we wanted a seared crust and a perfect medium-rare throughout. Gently roasting until the meat was almost done and then setting it under the broiler for a few minutes achieved both results without the hassle of pan-searing. Scoring the fat cap before cooking helped the fat to render and the surface to crisp. We let the meat sit overnight with a spice and herb rub (and plenty of salt) to ensure a perfectly seasoned, flavorful roast.

Serve with Salsa Verde (recipe follows).

- 1 (5- to 6-pound) boneless top loin roast, fat trimmed to ¼ inch
- 2 tablespoons peppercorns
- 1 tablespoon coriander seeds
- 1 tablespoon yellow mustard seeds
- 3 tablespoons extra-virgin olive oil
- 2 tablespoons kosher salt
- 2 tablespoons chopped fresh rosemary
- 1 teaspoon red pepper flakes

1. Pat roast dry with paper towels. Using sharp knife, cut ½-inch crosshatch pattern through fat cap, ¼ inch deep. Tie kitchen twine around roast at 2-inch intervals. Grind peppercorns, coriander seeds, and mustard seeds to texture of coarse sand in spice grinder. Combine spice mixture, oil, salt, rosemary, and pepper flakes in bowl until thick paste forms. Rub paste all over roast and into crosshatch. Wrap roast with plastic wrap and refrigerate for 6 to 24 hours.

2. Set wire rack inside rimmed baking sheet. One hour before cooking, unwrap meat and place on prepared rack, fat side up. Adjust oven rack to middle position and heat oven to 275 degrees. Transfer roast to oven and cook until meat registers 115 degrees, about 90 minutes, rotating sheet halfway through cooking. Remove roast from oven and heat broiler.

Classic Roast Beef Tenderloin

Holiday Strip Roast

3. Return roast to oven and broil on middle oven rack until fat cap is deep brown and interior of roast registers 125 degrees, 3 to 5 minutes. Transfer to carving board, tent loosely with aluminum foil, and let rest for 20 minutes. Remove twine and carve into thin slices. Serve.

Salsa Verde
MAKES ABOUT 1½ CUPS

Mince the garlic before processing it, or it won't break down enough. This sauce can be prepared up to two days in advance and refrigerated. Before serving, bring it to room temperature and stir to recombine.

- 2 slices hearty white sandwich bread, torn into 1-inch pieces
- 1 cup extra-virgin olive oil
- ¼ cup lemon juice (2 lemons)
- 4 cups fresh parsley leaves
- ¼ cup capers, rinsed
- 4 anchovy fillets, rinsed
- 2 garlic cloves, minced
- ½ teaspoon kosher salt

Process bread, oil, and lemon juice in food processor until smooth, about 10 seconds. Add parsley, capers, anchovies, garlic, and salt and pulse until mixture is finely chopped, about 5 pulses, scraping down bowl as needed.

Bottom Round Roast Beef with Zip-Style Sauce

SERVES 8

WHY THIS RECIPE WORKS Over the years, many cooks have decried the poor bottom round roast as unfit to serve as a centerpiece—too tough, too liver-y, nothing at all like a tender, melty rib roast or eye round. We wanted to find a way to serve this less-expensive cut as the main event—and not to have to apologize for it. By cooking the roast in a low oven for a few hours, then turning off the heat and letting the roast finish cooking, we were able to bring the roast to a perfect, tender medium. After letting it rest, we had a beautiful, herb-covered roast that was easy to slice paper-thin and looked much more elegant than any of us had expected.

We recommend cooking this roast to medium for ease of slicing. Open the oven door as little as possible, and remove the roast from the oven when taking its temperature to prevent dropping the oven temperature too drastically. Because the sauce contains butter, it will solidify as it cools, so it's best kept warm for serving.

Beef
- 1 (4-pound) boneless beef bottom round roast, trimmed Kosher salt and pepper
- 1 tablespoon minced fresh rosemary
- 1 tablespoon minced fresh thyme
- 2 tablespoons vegetable oil

Zip-Style Sauce
- 8 tablespoons unsalted butter
- ½ cup Worcestershire sauce
- 2 garlic cloves, minced
- 2 teaspoons minced fresh rosemary
- 1 teaspoon minced fresh thyme
- ½ teaspoon kosher salt
- ½ teaspoon pepper

1. For the Beef Pat roast dry with paper towels and sprinkle with 2 teaspoons salt. Wrap in plastic wrap and refrigerate for at least 1 hour or up to 24 hours.

2. Adjust oven rack to middle position and heat oven to 250 degrees. Set wire rack in rimmed baking sheet. Combine rosemary, thyme, 2 teaspoons pepper, and 1 teaspoon salt in bowl.

3. Pat roast dry with paper towels. Brush roast all over with oil and sprinkle with herb mixture; place on prepared wire rack. Transfer to oven and cook until meat registers 120 degrees, 1¾ hours to 2¼ hours. Turn off oven and leave roast in oven, without opening door, until meat registers 135 degrees (for medium), 20 to 30 minutes longer. Transfer roast to carving board, tent with aluminum foil, and let rest for 30 minutes.

4. For the Zip-Style Sauce Meanwhile, bring butter, Worcestershire, garlic, rosemary, thyme, salt, and pepper to bare simmer in small saucepan over medium heat, whisking constantly. Remove from heat, cover, and keep warm.

5. Slice roast thin against grain and serve with sauce.

Roasted Beef Chuck Roast with Horseradish-Parsley Sauce

SERVES 8 TO 10

WHY THIS RECIPE WORKS For a celebration-worthy but affordable beef roast, we chose chuck eye because it has a big, beefy flavor and is easy to find. We pulled the roast apart at its natural line of fat and then cut away the fat to avoid any chewy, unrendered bites in the final dish. Tying the two pieces back together made for an evenly shaped, impressive-looking roast. Letting the cooked roast rest ensured moist meat. For a bright accompaniment, we stirred together a spicy horseradish-parsley sauce.

Plan ahead: The roast must be seasoned at least 18 hours before cooking. If using table salt, cut the amount in half. Buy refrigerated prepared horseradish, not the shelf-stable kind. The horseradish-parsley sauce can be refrigerated up to two days; let come to room temperature before serving.

Beef
- 1 (5-pound) boneless beef chuck-eye roast, trimmed
- 2 tablespoons kosher salt
- 2 teaspoons pepper
- 2 tablespoons extra-virgin olive oil

Sauce
- 1 cup fresh parsley leaves
- ¼ cup prepared horseradish
- 1 shallot, chopped
- 2 tablespoons capers, rinsed
- 1 tablespoon lemon juice
- 1 garlic clove, minced
- ½ teaspoon kosher salt
- ¾ cup extra-virgin olive oil

1. For the Beef Pull roast into 2 pieces at major seam delineated by line of white fat, cutting with boning knife as needed. Using knife, remove large knobs of fat from each piece.

2. Sprinkle roast pieces all over with salt and pepper. Place pieces back together along major seam. Tie together with kitchen twine at 1-inch intervals to create 1 evenly shaped roast. Wrap tightly in plastic wrap and refrigerate for 18 to 24 hours.

Bottom Round Roast Beef with Zip-Style Sauce

Roasted Beef Chuck Roast with Horseradish-Parsley Sauce

Deviled Beef Short Ribs

Boneless Rib Roast with Yorkshire Pudding and Jus

3. Adjust oven rack to lower-middle position and heat oven to 275 degrees. Set wire rack in rimmed baking sheet. Unwrap roast and rub all over with oil. Place roast on prepared wire rack. Transfer sheet to oven and roast until meat registers 145 to 150 degrees, 3¼ to 3¾ hours. Transfer roast to carving board, tent with aluminum foil, and let rest for 45 minutes.

4. For the Sauce Meanwhile, pulse parsley, horseradish, shallot, capers, lemon juice, garlic, and salt in food processor until parsley is finely chopped, 6 to 8 pulses, scraping down sides of bowl as needed. Transfer to bowl and stir in oil until combined. Season with salt to taste; set aside.

5. Slice roast thin, removing twine as you go so roast stays intact. Serve, passing sauce separately.

Chuck Eye Prep

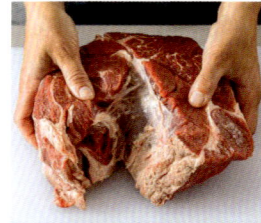

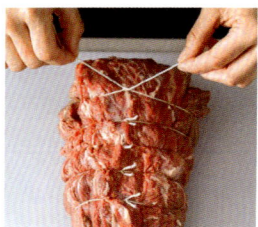

1. Bisect the roast along its natural seam (using a knife if necessary) and then trim and discard any excess fat and connective tissue.

2. Use kitchen twine to tie the two trimmed pieces together into one big roast.

Deviled Beef Short Ribs

SERVES 4 TO 6

WHY THIS RECIPE WORKS "Deviling" food usually involves flavoring it with mustard, black pepper, and other seasonings, but for our deviled short ribs we really wanted to feel the heat. We first roasted the seasoned ribs meat side down in a covered baking dish, allowing the meat to cook in its own rendered fat and juices. After cranking the heat and pouring off the juices, we brushed the ribs with a spicy glaze of dry and prepared mustards, citrus, brown sugar, and pureed jalapeños. A few rounds of brushing and roasting created a browned crust, and for a crunchy finish we coated the ribs with buttery, toasted panko bread crumbs.

English-style short ribs contain a single rib bone. For a milder sauce, use only one jalapeño and discard the seeds.

- 2/3 cup yellow mustard
- 1/3 cup orange juice
- 1/3 cup packed light brown sugar
- 1–2 jalapeño chiles, stemmed, seeds reserved, and roughly chopped
- 4 teaspoons dry mustard
- 1 tablespoon lemon juice plus 1 teaspoon grated lemon zest
- Salt and pepper
- 1/2 teaspoon cayenne pepper
- 5 pounds bone-in English-style short ribs, bones 4 to 5 inches long, 1 to 1 1/2 inches of meat on top of bone, trimmed
- 2 tablespoons unsalted butter
- 1 1/2 cups panko bread crumbs
- 1 tablespoon chopped fresh parsley

1. Adjust oven rack to middle position and heat oven to 325 degrees. Combine yellow mustard, orange juice, sugar, jalapeños and reserved seeds, dry mustard, lemon juice, and 2 teaspoons pepper in food processor and process until smooth, about 30 seconds; set aside. (Mustard mixture can be refrigerated for up to 1 week.)

2. Combine 1 tablespoon salt, 1 tablespoon pepper, and cayenne in bowl. Sprinkle ribs all over with spice mixture. Arrange ribs, meat side down, in 13 by 9-inch baking dish. Cover dish tightly with aluminum foil and roast until meat is nearly tender, about 3 hours.

3. Meanwhile, melt butter in 12-inch skillet over medium-high heat. Add panko and cook, stirring often, until golden brown, about 3 minutes. Off heat, stir in parsley and lemon zest and transfer to shallow dish.

4. Remove baking dish from oven and increase oven temperature to 425 degrees; transfer ribs to plate. Discard rendered fat and juices from dish. Brush meat (not bone) all over with one-fourth of mustard sauce and return ribs to dish, meat side up. Roast, uncovered, until beginning to brown, about 10 minutes. Brush meat again with one-third of remaining mustard sauce and continue to roast until well browned and completely tender, 10 to 15 minutes longer. Transfer ribs to serving platter, tent loosely with foil, and let rest for 15 minutes.

5. Brush meat once more with half of remaining mustard sauce and roll in panko mixture, taking care to entirely coat meat. Serve, passing remaining mustard sauce separately.

Boneless Rib Roast with Yorkshire Pudding and Jus

SERVES 8 TO 10

WHY THIS RECIPE WORKS We focused on two parts of the classic British Sunday roast dinner—beef rib roast and Yorkshire pudding—to create a failproof recipe that would have both ready simultaneously. The key was using one pan. We started with a nicely marbled, easy-to-carve boneless beef rib roast, our cut of choice, and used rendered fat from the roast and trimmings to make a Yorkshire pudding infused with meaty flavor. A quick, savory jus and horseradish sauce provided the perfect complements.

At the butcher counter, ask for a roast with an untrimmed fat cap, ideally 1/2 inch thick, in order to get enough trimmings to cook the pudding. Plan ahead: The roast must be salted and refrigerated for at least 24 hours before cooking. If you're using a dark, nonstick roasting pan, reduce the cooking time for the Yorkshire pudding by 5 minutes.

Horseradish Sauce
- 1/2 cup sour cream
- 1/2 cup prepared horseradish
- 1 1/2 teaspoons kosher salt
- 1/8 teaspoon pepper

Roast and Pudding
- 1 (5- to 5 1/2-pound) first-cut boneless beef rib roast with 1/2-inch fat cap
- Kosher salt and pepper
- 2 1/2 cups (12 1/2 ounces) all-purpose flour
- 4 cups milk
- 4 large eggs
- 1 tablespoon vegetable oil, plus extra as needed

Jus
- 1 onion, chopped fine
- 1 teaspoon cornstarch
- 2 1/2 cups beef broth
- 1 sprig fresh thyme

1. For the Horseradish Sauce Combine all ingredients in bowl. Cover and refrigerate until ready to serve. (Sauce can be refrigerated for up to 2 days.)

2. For the Roast and Pudding Using sharp knife, trim roast's fat cap to even ¼-inch thickness and refrigerate trimmings for later use. Cut 1-inch crosshatch pattern in fat cap, being careful not to cut into meat. Rub 2 tablespoons salt over entire roast and into crosshatch. Transfer to large plate and refrigerate, uncovered, for at least 24 hours or up to 4 days.

3. Adjust oven rack to lower-middle position and heat oven to 250 degrees. Spray roasting pan with vegetable oil spray. Cut reserved trimmings into ½-inch pieces. Place 3 ounces (about ¾ cup) trimmings in bottom of prepared pan. Set V-rack over trimmings in pan.

4. Season roast with pepper and place fat side up on V-rack. Roast until meat registers 115 degrees for rare, 120 degrees for medium-rare, or 125 degrees for medium, 2½ to 3 hours.

5. Meanwhile, combine flour and 1 tablespoon salt in large bowl. Whisk milk and eggs in second bowl until fully combined. Slowly whisk milk mixture into flour mixture until smooth. Cover with plastic wrap and let rest for 1 hour. (Batter can be covered and refrigerated for up to 24 hours. Let come to room temperature before proceeding.)

6. Transfer V-rack with roast to carving board, tent with aluminum foil, and let rest for 1 hour. Using fork, remove solids in pan, leaving liquid fat behind (there should be about 6 tablespoons; if not, supplement with extra vegetable oil). Increase oven temperature to 425 degrees.

7. When oven reaches 425 degrees, return pan to oven and heat until fat is just smoking, 3 to 5 minutes. Rewhisk batter and pour into center of pan. Bake until pudding is dark golden brown and edges are crisp, 40 to 45 minutes.

8. Meanwhile, pat roast dry with paper towels. Heat 1 tablespoon oil in 12-inch skillet over medium-high heat until just smoking. Sear roast on all sides until evenly browned, 5 to 7 minutes. Transfer roast to carving board.

9. For the Jus Return skillet to medium-high heat, add onion, and cook until softened, about 3 minutes, scraping up any browned bits. Whisk cornstarch into broth. Add broth mixture and thyme sprig to skillet and bring to boil. Reduce heat to medium-low and simmer until reduced by half and slightly thickened, about 7 minutes. Strain jus through fine-mesh strainer set over small saucepan; discard solids. Cover and keep warm.

10. Slice roast ¾ inch thick. Cut pudding into squares in roasting pan. Serve beef with Yorkshire pudding, jus, and horseradish sauce.

One-Pan Prime Rib and Roasted Vegetables

SERVES 8 TO 10

WHY THIS RECIPE WORKS Our goal was to produce a recipe for holiday prime rib with roasted vegetables that was simple and foolproof. We scored and salted a first-cut standing rib roast and refrigerated it for 24 hours for tender beef. A low-and-slow cooking method yielded evenly red and juicy meat, and an additional stint under the broiler turned the outside crispy and golden. Instead of forcing the vegetables to work in concert with the beef, we roasted them solo in the flavorful beef fat while the prime rib was resting. It was definitely a feast fit for a holiday—with only one pan to wash.

The roast must be salted and then refrigerated for at least 24 hours before cooking; salting and refrigerating for the full 4 days results in the most tender, flavorful meat.

- 1 (7-pound) first-cut beef standing rib roast (3 bones), fat trimmed to ¼ inch
- Kosher salt and pepper
- Vegetable oil
- 2 pounds carrots, peeled, cut into 2-inch lengths, halved or quartered lengthwise to create ½-inch-diameter pieces
- 1 pound parsnips, peeled and sliced ½ inch thick on bias
- 1 pound Brussels sprouts, trimmed and halved
- 1 red onion, halved and sliced through root end into ½-inch wedges
- 2 teaspoons minced fresh thyme

1. Using sharp knife, cut through roast's fat cap in 1-inch crosshatch pattern, being careful not to cut into meat. Rub 2 tablespoons salt over entire roast and into crosshatch. Transfer to large plate and refrigerate, uncovered, for at least 24 hours or up to 4 days.

2. Adjust oven rack to lower-middle position and heat oven to 250 degrees. Season roast with pepper and arrange, fat side up, on V-rack set in large roasting pan. Roast until meat registers 115 degrees for rare, 120 degrees for medium-rare, or 125 degrees for medium, 3 to 3½ hours. Transfer V-rack with roast to carving board, tent loosely with aluminum foil, and let rest for about 1 hour.

One-Pan Prime Rib and Roasted Vegetables

Prime Rib with Potatoes and Red Wine–Orange Sauce

SERVES 8 TO 10

WHY THIS RECIPE WORKS To ensure a juicy roast, we trimmed the excess fat, made shallow crosshatch cuts in the remaining fat cap, and rubbed the roast with salt 24 hours before cooking. We saved the trimmed fat and placed it under the roast as it cooked, creating intensely flavored drippings. We precooked the potatoes in the microwave before tossing them with the rendered fat and roasting them until crisp. Searing the cooked roast in a hot skillet added some last-minute browning to the roast's exterior. An easy red wine–orange sauce proved a bright contrast to the beef.

The roast must be salted and refrigerated for at least 24 hours before cooking. Wait until the roast is done cooking before peeling and cutting the potatoes so they don't discolor. It is crucial to use a sturdy rimmed baking sheet for this recipe. Serve with Red Wine–Orange Sauce (recipe follows).

- 1 (7-pound) first-cut beef standing rib roast (3 bones), with untrimmed fat cap
  Kosher salt and pepper
- 4 pounds Yukon gold potatoes, peeled and cut into 1½-inch pieces
- 1 tablespoon minced fresh rosemary
- 1 tablespoon vegetable oil

1. Using sharp knife, trim roast's fat cap to even ¼-inch-thickness; reserve and refrigerate trimmings. Cut 1-inch crosshatch pattern in fat cap, being careful not to cut into meat. Rub 2 tablespoons salt over roast and into crosshatch. Transfer to large plate and refrigerate, uncovered, for at least 24 hours or up to 4 days.

2. Adjust oven rack to lower-middle position and heat oven to 250 degrees. Cut reserved trimmings into ½-inch pieces. Place 1 cup of trimmings in rimmed baking sheet, then set wire rack in sheet. Season roast with pepper and place, fat side up, on wire rack.

3. Roast until meat registers 115 degrees for rare, 120 degrees for medium-rare, or 125 degrees for medium, 3 to 3½ hours. Transfer roast to carving board, tent with aluminum foil, and let rest for 1 hour. Carefully remove wire rack and reserve beef fat in baking sheet (there should be about ½ cup; if not, add vegetable oil).

3. Meanwhile, increase oven temperature to 425 degrees. Pour off all but 2 tablespoons fat from pan. (If there isn't enough fat in pan, add vegetable oil to equal 2 tablespoons.) Toss carrots, parsnips, brussels sprouts, onion, thyme, 1 teaspoon salt, and ½ teaspoon pepper with fat in pan. Roast vegetables, stirring halfway through roasting, until tender and browned, 45 to 50 minutes.

4. Remove pan from oven and heat broiler. Carefully nestle V-rack with roast among vegetables in pan. Broil roast until fat cap is evenly browned, about 5 minutes, rotating pan as necessary. Transfer roast to carving board, carve meat from bones, and cut into ¾-inch-thick slices. Season vegetables with salt and pepper to taste. Serve roast with vegetables.

4. Increase oven temperature to 450 degrees. Microwave potatoes, covered, in large bowl until they begin to release moisture and surfaces look wet, about 7 minutes. Pat potatoes dry with paper towels. Toss potatoes with rosemary, 2 teaspoons salt, and ½ teaspoon pepper. Transfer potatoes to baking sheet and carefully toss with reserved fat (fat may be hot). Roast until tender and browned, 35 to 40 minutes, redistributing halfway through cooking. Season potatoes with salt and pepper to taste.

5. Pat roast dry with paper towels. Heat oil in 12-inch skillet over medium-high heat until just smoking. Sear all sides until browned, 6 to 8 minutes total. Transfer roast to carving board. Carve meat from bones and cut into ¾-inch-thick slices. Serve with potatoes.

Red Wine–Orange Sauce
MAKES ABOUT 1½ CUPS

Medium-bodied red wines are best for this sauce.

- 6 tablespoons unsalted butter, cut into 6 pieces and chilled, divided
- 3 shallots, minced
- 1½ tablespoons tomato paste
- 1 tablespoon sugar
- 4 garlic cloves, minced
- 1 tablespoon all-purpose flour
- 3 cups beef broth
- 1½ cups red wine
- ⅓ cup orange juice
- 1½ tablespoons Worcestershire sauce
- 1 sprig fresh thyme
- Salt and pepper

1. Melt 2 tablespoons butter in medium saucepan over medium-high heat. Add shallots, tomato paste, and sugar and cook, stirring frequently, until deep brown, 4 to 5 minutes. Stir in garlic and flour and cook until garlic is fragrant and vegetables are well coated with flour, about 30 seconds.

2. Stir in broth, wine, orange juice, Worcestershire, and thyme, scraping up any browned bits. Bring to boil, reduce heat to medium, and cook at low boil until reduced to 2 cups, about 40 minutes.

3. Strain sauce through fine-mesh strainer set over bowl; discard solids. Return sauce to pot and place over low heat. Whisk in remaining 4 tablespoons butter, 1 piece at a time. Season with salt and pepper to taste.

Chuck Roast in Foil
SERVES 4 TO 6

WHY THIS RECIPE WORKS We ditched the onion soup mix traditionally used in this lazy cook's pot roast, preferring onion powder and salt. Drizzling the vegetables with soy sauce before roasting enhanced the flavor of the pan juices. Brown sugar added depth, while a little espresso powder provided toasty complexity. Halving the roast let us apply more of the spice rub to its exterior.

You will need an 18-inch-wide roll of heavy-duty aluminum foil for wrapping the roast. We prefer to use small red potatoes, measuring 1 to 2 inches in diameter, in this recipe.

Rub
- 3 tablespoons cornstarch
- 4 teaspoons onion powder
- 2 teaspoons packed light brown sugar
- 2 teaspoons table salt
- 1 teaspoon pepper
- 1 teaspoon garlic powder
- 1 teaspoon instant espresso powder
- 1 teaspoon dried thyme
- ½ teaspoon celery seeds

Chuck Roast
- 1 (4-pound) boneless beef chuck-eye roast, pulled apart at seams, fat trimmed to ¼ inch, and tied at 1-inch intervals
- 2 onions, peeled and quartered
- 1 pound small red potatoes, quartered
- 4 carrots, peeled and cut into 1½-inch pieces
- 2 bay leaves
- 2 tablespoons soy sauce

1. For the Rub Adjust oven rack to lower-middle position and heat oven to 300 degrees. Combine all ingredients in small bowl.

2. For the Chuck Roast Pat roast dry with paper towels. Place two 30 by 18-inch sheets of heavy-duty aluminum foil perpendicular to each other inside large roasting pan. Place onions, potatoes, carrots, and bay leaves in center of foil and drizzle with soy sauce. Set roasts on top of vegetables. Rub roasts all over with rub. Fold opposite corners of foil toward each other and crimp edges tightly to seal. Transfer pan to oven and cook until meat is completely tender, about 4½ hours.

3. Remove roasts from foil pouch and place on carving board. Tent meat with foil and let rest for 20 minutes. Remove onions and bay leaves. Using slotted spoon, place carrots and potatoes on serving platter. Strain contents of roasting pan through fine-mesh strainer into fat separator. Let liquid settle, then pour defatted pan juices into serving bowl.

4. Remove kitchen twine from roasts. Slice roasts thin against grain and transfer to platter with vegetables. Pour ½ cup pan juices over meat. Serve with remaining pan juices.

The American Table: Back in Fashion

Family Circle magazine once asked Peg Bracken, author of the mega-bestselling *I Hate to Cook Book*, to select her greatest-hits list for the hate-to-cook set. Her list included such gems as Stayabed Stew ("For those days when you're en negligee, en bed, with a murder story and a box of bonbons") and the Basic I-Hate-to-Cook Muffin (made by combining beer and muffin mix). But one classic super-easy dish of the day was notably absent: chuck roast with instant onion soup. "Done to death," Bracken explained, adding, "I remember years ago when every working wife in the land was sprinkling a package of dried onion soup mix onto a chunk of chuck steak . . . the thing was bigger than a Hula-Hoop, and it died, of course, of over-exposure." But guess what? The hula hoop is back, and in its new incarnation, chuck roast in foil is poised for a comeback too.

Roast Pork Loin with 40 Cloves of Garlic

SERVES 4 TO 6

WHY THIS RECIPE WORKS For a twist on the classic chicken dish, we paired 40 cloves of garlic with pork loin; the toasted garlic flavor complemented the pork's subtle sweetness. The pork needed a low oven temperature to cook evenly but couldn't pick up flavorful browning, so we first seared it in a skillet on the stovetop. Since the garlic required a higher temperature to transform from sharp to mellow, we let the peeled cloves cook with the pork in the oven and then returned them to the stovetop while the pork

Prime Rib with Potatoes and Red Wine–Orange Sauce

Chuck Roast in Foil

rested. Broth, white wine, and cream added to the skillet reduced into a glossy sauce that tied everything together.

You can use a blade-end or center-cut pork loin here. Three to four heads of garlic will yield 40 cloves. Note that the pork needs to be salted and refrigerated for at least an hour before cooking.

- 4 teaspoons minced fresh thyme, divided
- 1 tablespoon minced fresh rosemary
- 1 tablespoon kosher salt
- 2 teaspoons ground fennel
- 1 teaspoon pepper
- ¼ teaspoon red pepper flakes
- 1 (3-pound) boneless pork loin roast, trimmed
- 2 tablespoons vegetable oil
- 40 garlic cloves, peeled
- 1¼ cups chicken broth
- ⅓ cup dry white wine
- ⅓ cup heavy cream

1. Combine 2 teaspoons thyme, rosemary, salt, fennel, pepper, and pepper flakes in bowl. Sprinkle pork with thyme mixture. Wrap pork in plastic wrap and refrigerate for at least 1 hour or up to 24 hours.

2. Adjust oven rack to middle position and heat oven to 300 degrees. Heat oil in 12-inch ovensafe nonstick skillet over medium-high heat until just smoking. Unwrap pork and place in skillet. Cook until browned on all sides, about 7 minutes.

3. Scatter garlic around pork and transfer skillet to oven. Roast until pork registers 130 degrees, 40 to 50 minutes. Transfer pork to carving board, tent with aluminum foil, and let rest for 20 minutes.

4. While pork rests, place skillet with garlic over medium-high heat (skillet handle will be hot) and cook, stirring occasionally, until garlic is sizzling and light golden brown all over, about 3 minutes. Add broth, wine, cream, and remaining 2 teaspoons thyme and bring to boil. Cook until sauce has reduced to slightly more than 1 cup and is thick enough to coat back of spoon, about 10 minutes. Remove from heat and cover to keep warm.

5. Slice pork thin. Serve with sauce.

Crown Roast of Pork

SERVES 10 TO 12

WHY THIS RECIPE WORKS A crown roast—two bone-in pork loin roasts tied together in a round—can feed a holiday crowd and offers a dramatic presentation, but its shape presents serious challenges to even cooking. Simply roasting it yielded meat overcooked on the outside and undercooked around the inner circle. The solution? We turned the roast upside down to allow more air to circulate and to better expose the thickest part of the roast to the heat. For a side, we opted for potatoes, shallots, and apples roasted in the pan alongside the meat. Pureeing the apples into a rich pan sauce gave us both fruity flavor and a nice, thick consistency.

A crown roast is two bone-in pork loin roasts tied into a crown shape, with the rib bones frenched and chine bones removed. This can be difficult to do, so ask your butcher to make this roast for you. We wrap extra kitchen twine around the widest part of the roast to provide more support when flipping. Use potatoes that measure 1 to 2 inches in diameter.

- Kosher salt and pepper
- 3 tablespoons minced fresh thyme
- 2 tablespoons minced fresh rosemary
- 5 garlic cloves, minced
- 1 (8- to 10-pound) pork crown roast

Roast Pork Loin with 40 Cloves of Garlic

- 2 pounds small red potatoes
- 10 ounces shallots, peeled and halved
- 2 Golden Delicious apples, peeled, cored, and halved
- 8 tablespoons unsalted butter, melted, divided
- ½ cup apple cider
- 1 cup chicken broth

1. Combine 3 tablespoons salt, 1 tablespoon pepper, thyme, rosemary, and garlic in bowl; reserve 2 teaspoons for vegetables. Pat pork dry with paper towels and rub with remaining herb salt. Wrap kitchen twine twice around widest part of roast and tie tightly. Refrigerate roast, covered, for 6 to 24 hours.

2. Adjust oven rack to lower-middle position and heat oven to 475 degrees. Place V-rack inside large roasting pan. Toss potatoes, shallots, apples, 4 tablespoons butter, and reserved herb salt in large bowl and transfer to pan. Arrange roast bone side down in V-rack and brush with remaining 4 tablespoons butter. Roast until meat is well browned and registers 110 degrees, about 1 hour.

3. Remove roast from oven and reduce oven temperature to 300 degrees. Using 2 bunches of paper towels, flip roast bone side up. Add apple cider to pan and return to oven, rotating direction of pan. Roast until meat registers 140 degrees, 30 to 50 minutes. Place meat on carving board, tent loosely with aluminum foil, and let rest for 15 to 20 minutes.

4. Transfer apple halves to blender and potatoes and shallots to bowl. Pour pan juices into fat separator, let liquid settle for 5 minutes, then pour into blender. Add chicken broth to blender with apples and pan juices and process until smooth, about 1 minute. Transfer sauce to medium saucepan and bring to simmer over medium heat. Season with salt and pepper to taste. Cover and keep warm. Remove twine from roast and slice meat between bones. Serve with vegetables and sauce.

Crown Roast of Pork

Cooking Crown Roast of Pork Evenly

1. Using kitchen twine, make 2 loops around widest part of roast and tie securely to help crown hold its shape when flipped.

2. Place pork bone side down on V-rack and adjust bones to steady roast. Roast about 1 hour, until meat registers 110 degrees.

3. Using paper towels to protect your hands, flip hot roast bone side up and set it back on V-rack to finish cooking in gentle oven.

Slow-Cooker Pork Pot Roast

SERVES 8

WHY THIS RECIPE WORKS Pork shoulder's fat content and marbling mean it requires low and slow cooking to become tender—making it a natural for the slow cooker. For a full-flavored sauce, we browned the pork, then sautéed onions and garlic with tomato paste in the browned bits left behind before adding them to the slow cooker. A little instant tapioca produced just the right texture in the braising liquid. White wine added brightness and a splash of white wine vinegar, stirred in at the end of cooking, refreshed the wine flavor. Hearty root vegetables and diced tomatoes, which cooked along with the roast, balanced the flavors.

This roast is sometimes sold in elastic netting that must be removed before cooking. If you cannot find 2½- to 3-pound pork picnic shoulder roasts, you can substitute one 6-pound pork picnic shoulder roast; cut it into two pieces and prepare as directed.

- 2 (2½- to 3-pound) boneless pork picnic shoulder roasts, trimmed
- Salt and pepper
- 2 tablespoons vegetable oil, divided
- 2 onions, chopped
- 6 garlic cloves, minced
- 1 tablespoon tomato paste
- ½ cup white wine
- 1 (28-ounce) can diced tomatoes, drained
- 3 tablespoons instant tapioca
- 2 teaspoons minced fresh thyme
- 1 pound carrots, peeled, halved lengthwise, and cut into 2-inch pieces
- 1 pound parsnips, peeled, halved lengthwise, and cut into 2-inch pieces
- 2 teaspoons white wine vinegar

1. Open each roast and trim any excess fat, then tie each roast with kitchen twine at 1½-inch intervals and once around length of roasts. Pat roasts dry with paper towels and season with salt and pepper. Heat 2 teaspoons oil in 12-inch skillet over medium-high heat until just smoking. Brown roasts all over, about 10 minutes. Transfer to slow cooker.

2. Add onions and 2 teaspoons oil to now-empty skillet and cook until browned, about 5 minutes. Add garlic and tomato paste and cook until fragrant, about 1 minute. Stir in wine and simmer, scraping up browned bits with wooden spoon, until thickened, about 2 minutes. Stir in tomatoes, tapioca, and thyme; transfer to slow cooker.

3. Toss carrots, parsnips, ¼ teaspoon salt, ¼ teaspoon pepper, and remaining 2 teaspoons oil in bowl until vegetables are well coated. Scatter vegetable mixture over pork. Cover and cook on low until meat is tender, 9 to 10 hours (or cook on high 4 to 5 hours).

4. Transfer roasts to carving board, tent with aluminum foil, and let rest for 10 minutes. Remove twine from roasts and cut meat into ½-inch-thick slices; transfer to serving platter. Using slotted spoon, transfer carrots and parsnips to platter with pork. Stir vinegar into sauce and season with salt and pepper to taste. Serve, passing sauce separately.

Two Roasts Are Better than One

We like to use two smaller roasts for this recipe, because the meat cooks more quickly and the small roasts are easier to manage in the slow cooker—and to find in the supermarket. Most boneless pork shoulder roasts come bound in string netting, which is difficult to remove after cooking. We prefer to cut the netting off before cooking, trim the roasts, and then tie each one with kitchen twine.

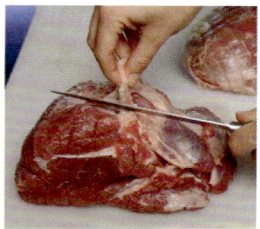

1. Remove netting from pork roasts. Open each roast and trim any excess fat.

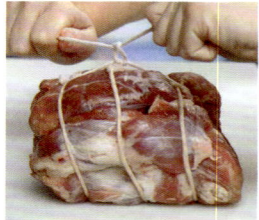

2. Tie roasts separately. To ensure even cooking, fold smaller lobes under, then tie each roast with kitchen twine every 1½ inches around circumference and once around length.

Old-Fashioned Roast Pork

SERVES 8

WHY THIS RECIPE WORKS For this Sunday dinner–worthy pork roast, we skipped lean loins and opted for a meaty and inexpensive pork butt roast, which we flavored with a spice rub of cracked peppercorns, rosemary, sage, fennel seeds, and garlic. Cooking the roast in a low oven for seven hours rendered its fat and softened its tough connective tissue. For easy slicing, we refrigerated the cooked roast overnight until firm, then reheated it in the oven while we made a simple sauce from apple cider, apple jelly, and cider vinegar.

A heavy roasting pan with 3-inch sides is the best choice for this recipe, but a shallow broiler pan also works well. Boneless pork butt roast is often labeled Boston butt in the supermarket.

- 6 pounds boneless pork butt roast, fat trimmed to 1/8 inch, tied lengthwise and crosswise
- 3 garlic cloves, minced
- 2 teaspoons peppercorns, cracked
- 1½ teaspoons table salt
- 1 tablespoon chopped fresh rosemary
- 1 tablespoon chopped fresh sage
- 1 tablespoon fennel seeds, chopped
- 2 large red onions, cut into 1-inch wedges
- 1 cup apple cider
- ¼ cup apple jelly
- 2 tablespoons cider vinegar

1. Adjust oven rack to lower-middle position and heat oven to 300 degrees. Pat pork dry with paper towels. Combine garlic, peppercorns, salt, rosemary, sage, and fennel seeds in small bowl. Rub roast with herb mixture.

2. Transfer to roasting pan and cook for 3 hours. Scatter onion wedges around roast, tossing onions in pan drippings to coat. (If roast has not produced any juices, toss onions with 1 tablespoon vegetable oil before adding to pan.) Continue roasting until meat is extremely tender and skewer inserted in center meets no resistance, 3½ to 4 hours. (Check pan juices every hour to make sure they have not evaporated. If necessary, add 2 cups water to pan and scrape up browned bits.)

Slow-Cooker Pork Pot Roast

Old-Fashioned Roast Pork

3. Transfer roast to large baking dish, place onions in medium bowl, and pour pan drippings into 2-cup liquid measuring cup, adding enough water to measure 1½ cups. Let roast, onions, and drippings cool for 30 minutes, cover each with plastic wrap, and refrigerate overnight.

4. One hour before serving, adjust oven rack to middle position and heat oven to 300 degrees. Cut meat into ¼-inch slices and overlap in large baking dish. Skim off fat from pan drippings and transfer drippings and reserved onions to medium saucepan. Add cider, jelly, and vinegar and bring to boil over medium-high heat, then reduce to simmer. Spoon ½ cup sauce over pork slices and cover baking dish with aluminum foil. Place in oven and heat until very hot, 30 to 40 minutes.

5. Just before serving, reduce sauce until dark and thickened, 10 to 15 minutes. Serve pork, spooning onion mixture over meat or passing separately.

Pork Pernil

SERVES 8 TO 10

Pork Pernil

WHY THIS RECIPE WORKS This Puerto Rican dish of long-cooked, heavily seasoned pork roast results in flavorful meat with a trademark crispy exterior. We rubbed a picnic shoulder with a salty sofrito the day before roasting, which kept the meat moist and packed a flavor punch. We then roasted the pork skin side down, covered, which helped transform tough collagen into gelatin. Next, we removed the foil cover and turned the roast skin side up on a V-rack to prepare it for the last step—a quick roast at very high heat.

You may need two bunches of cilantro, depending on their size. Crimp the foil tightly over the edges of the roasting pan in step 2 to minimize evaporation. Make sure to spray the V-rack in step 3. Serve over white rice.

1½	cups chopped fresh cilantro leaves and stems
1	onion, chopped coarse
¼	cup kosher salt
¼	cup extra-virgin olive oil
10	garlic cloves, peeled
2	tablespoons pepper
1	tablespoon dried oregano
1	tablespoon ground cumin
1	(7-pound) bone-in pork picnic shoulder
1	tablespoon grated lime zest plus ⅓ cup juice (3 limes)

1. Pulse 1 cup cilantro, onion, salt, oil, garlic, pepper, oregano, and cumin in food processor until finely ground, about 15 pulses, scraping down sides of bowl as needed. Pat pork dry with paper towels and rub sofrito all over. Wrap pork in plastic wrap and refrigerate for at least 12 hours or up to 24 hours.

2. Adjust oven rack to lower-middle position and heat oven to 450 degrees. Pour 8 cups water in large roasting pan. Unwrap pork and place skin side down in pan. Cover pan tightly with aluminum foil and roast for 90 minutes. Remove foil, reduce oven temperature to 375 degrees, and continue to roast for 2½ hours.

3. Remove pan from oven. Spray V-rack with vegetable oil spray. Gently slide metal spatula under pork to release skin from pan. Using folded dish towels, grasp ends of pork and transfer to V-rack, skin side up. Wipe skin dry with paper towels. Place V-rack with pork in roasting pan. If pan looks dry, add 1 cup water. Return to oven and roast until pork registers 195 degrees, about 1 hour. (Add water as needed to keep bottom of pan from drying out.)

4. Line rimmed baking sheet with foil. Remove pan from oven. Transfer V-rack and pork to prepared sheet and return to oven. Immediately increase oven temperature to 500 degrees. Cook until pork skin is well browned and crispy (when tapped lightly with tongs, skin will sound hollow), 15 to 30 minutes, rotating sheet halfway through cooking. Transfer pork to carving board and let rest for 30 minutes.

5. Meanwhile, pour juices from pan into fat separator. Let liquid settle for 5 minutes, then pour off 1 cup defatted juices into large bowl. (If juices measure less than 1 cup, make up difference with water.) Whisk remaining ½ cup cilantro and lime zest and juice into bowl.

6. Remove crispy skin from pork in 1 large piece. Coarsely chop skin into bite-size pieces and set aside. Trim and discard excess fat from pork. Remove pork from bone and chop coarse. Transfer pork to bowl with cilantro-lime sauce and toss to combine. Serve pork, with crispy skin on side.

Cider-Braised Pork Roast

SERVES 8

Cider-Braised Pork Roast

WHY THIS RECIPE WORKS Pork and apples are a classic combination, so we paired flavorful bone-in pork butt roast with apple cider. Rubbing the meat with a brown sugar–salt mixture and refrigerating it overnight seasoned the pork and helped keep it juicy. Onions, garlic, bay leaf, cinnamon, and thyme were welcome additions that kept the clean, sweet-tart taste of cider in focus. Apple butter and cider vinegar added more apple-y punch, and a slurry of cornstarch and reserved cider thickened the braising liquid into a beautiful sauce. Apple wedges seared in flavorful pork fat united the elements of this hearty roast.

Pork butt roast is often labeled Boston butt in the supermarket. Plan ahead: This roast needs to cure for 18 to 24 hours before cooking. If you can't find Braeburn apples, substitute Jonagold. If you don't have a fat separator, strain the liquid through a fine-mesh strainer into a medium bowl in step 4 and wait for it to settle.

- 1 (5- to 6-pound) bone-in pork butt roast
- ¼ cup packed brown sugar
- Kosher salt and pepper
- 3 tablespoons vegetable oil
- 1 onion, halved and sliced thin
- 6 garlic cloves, smashed and peeled
- 2 cups apple cider, divided
- 6 sprigs fresh thyme
- 2 bay leaves
- 1 cinnamon stick
- 2 Braeburn apples, cored and cut into 8 wedges each
- ¼ cup apple butter
- 1 tablespoon cornstarch
- 1 tablespoon cider vinegar

1. Using sharp knife, trim fat cap on roast to ¼ inch. Cut 1-inch crosshatch pattern, 1/16 inch deep, in fat cap. Place roast on large sheet of plastic wrap. Combine sugar and ¼ cup salt in bowl and rub mixture over entire roast and into slits. Wrap roast tightly in double layer of plastic, place on plate, and refrigerate for 18 to 24 hours.

2. Adjust oven rack to middle position and heat oven to 275 degrees. Unwrap roast and pat dry with paper towels, brushing away any excess salt mixture from surface. Season roast with pepper.

OUR SUNDAY BEST 349

3. Heat oil in Dutch oven over medium-high heat until just smoking. Sear roast until well browned on all sides, about 3 minutes per side. Turn roast fat side up. Scatter onion and garlic around roast and cook until fragrant and beginning to brown, about 2 minutes. Add 1¾ cups cider, thyme sprigs, bay leaves, and cinnamon stick and bring to simmer. Cover, transfer to oven, and braise until fork slips easily in and out of meat and meat registers 190 degrees, 2 hours 15 minutes to 2 hours 45 minutes.

4. Transfer roast to carving board, tent with aluminum foil, and let rest for 30 minutes. Strain braising liquid through fine-mesh strainer into fat separator; discard solids and let liquid settle for at least 5 minutes.

5. About 10 minutes before roast is done resting, wipe out pot with paper towels. Spoon 1½ tablespoons of clear, separated fat from top of fat separator into now-empty pot and heat over medium-high heat until shimmering. Season apples with salt and pepper. Space apples evenly in pot, cut side down, and cook until well browned on both cut sides, about 3 minutes per side. Transfer to platter and tent with foil.

6. Wipe out pot with paper towels. Return 2 cups defatted braising liquid to now-empty pot and bring to boil over high heat. Whisk in apple butter until incorporated. Whisk cornstarch and remaining ¼ cup cider together in bowl and add to pot. Return to boil and cook until thickened, about 1 minute. Off heat, add vinegar and season with salt and pepper to taste. Cover sauce and keep warm.

7. To carve roast, cut around inverted T-shaped bone until it can be pulled free from roast (use clean dish towel to grasp bone if necessary). Slice pork and transfer to serving platter with apples. Pour 1 cup sauce over pork and apples. Serve, passing remaining sauce at table.

Removing the Bone

Holding on to tip of T-shaped bone, use long knife to cut meat away from all sides of bone until bone is loose enough to pull out of roast.

Bacon-Wrapped Pork Roast with Peach Sauce
SERVES 8

WHY THIS RECIPE WORKS Wrapping a pork loin roast in bacon not only adds big, smoky flavor to the mild meat but also encases the roast in a layer of protective fat that bastes the pork as it renders. Achieving a rosy, moist roast with a beautifully browned bacon crust required a two-pronged cooking approach: We roasted the pork in a low 250-degree oven until it reached 90 degrees, and then we cranked the oven to 475 degrees to brown the bacon and finish cooking the pork. Brushing the bacon with a sweet-savory, quick-cooking peach sauce gave it a rich, lacquered appearance and rounded out the dish.

Buy a pork loin roast that measures about 9 inches long and is between 4 and 5 inches in diameter. Oscar Mayer Naturally Hardwood Smoked Bacon is our winning thin-sliced bacon. Do not use thick-cut bacon here. The peaches needn't be thawed before you make the sauce. The pork needs to cure for at least an hour before cooking.

Pork
- Kosher salt and pepper
- 1 tablespoon sugar
- 1 (3½-pound) boneless center-cut pork loin roast
- 2 teaspoons herbes de Provence
- 10 slices bacon

Sauce
- 20 ounces frozen peaches, cut into ½-inch pieces (3 cups)
- 1 cup dry white wine
- ½ cup sugar
- ⅓ cup cider vinegar
- 4 sprigs fresh thyme
- ½ teaspoon kosher salt
- 2 tablespoons whole-grain mustard

1. For the Pork Combine 4 teaspoons salt and sugar in bowl. Remove fat cap and silverskin from roast. Rub roast with salt-sugar mixture, wrap in plastic wrap, and refrigerate for at least 1 hour or up to 24 hours.

2. For the Sauce Bring peaches, wine, sugar, vinegar, thyme sprigs, and salt to simmer in medium saucepan over medium-high heat. Reduce heat to medium and

Bacon-Wrapped Pork Roast with Peach Sauce

6. Brush top and sides of roast with reserved 2 tablespoons sauce. Once oven reaches temperature, return pork to oven and roast until bacon is well browned and meat registers 130 degrees, 15 to 20 minutes longer. Transfer roast to wire rack and let rest for 15 minutes.

7. Stir mustard into sauce and rewarm over low heat. Transfer roast to carving board and cut into ½-inch-thick slices. Serve with peach sauce.

Pork Chops with Bourbon-Cherry Sauce and Sweet Potatoes

SERVES 4

WHY THIS RECIPE WORKS This whole meal came together in an hour; combined with its comforting flavors, that made it an ideal choice for dinner on a cold weeknight. We used pumpkin pie spice to add wintry warmth to bone-in pork chops, which we seared in a pan with butter to achieve great browning fast. Using an immersion blender to whip sweet potatoes made an ultracreamy mash. And a quick sweet and savory pan sauce inspired by the flavors of an old-fashioned (we used flavor-forward bourbon, sweet cherries, and orange marmalade) tied the dish together in an unexpected and elevated way.

You can substitute ground cinnamon for the pumpkin pie spice. Garnish this dish with chopped fresh chives.

- 2 pounds sweet potatoes, peeled and sliced ¼ inch thick
- 1 cup chicken broth, divided
- 7 tablespoons unsalted butter, divided
- 2 teaspoons table salt, divided
- 1¾ teaspoons pepper, divided
- 4 (8- to 10-ounce) bone-in pork rib chops, ¾ to 1 inch thick, trimmed
- ¼ teaspoon pumpkin pie spice
- 1 teaspoon cornstarch
- 8 ounces frozen sweet cherries, quartered
- ¼ cup bourbon
- 1 tablespoon orange marmalade

cook at strong simmer, stirring occasionally, until reduced to about 2 cups and spatula leaves trail when dragged through sauce, about 30 minutes. Remove from heat and discard thyme sprigs. Reserve 2 tablespoons of liquid portion of sauce (without peach segments) in small bowl for glazing. Cover and set aside remaining sauce.

3. Meanwhile, adjust oven rack to upper-middle position and heat oven to 250 degrees. Line rimmed baking sheet with aluminum foil and spray with vegetable oil spray. Unwrap roast and pat dry with paper towels. Sprinkle with herbes de Provence and 1 teaspoon pepper.

4. Arrange bacon slices on cutting board parallel to counter's edge, overlapping them slightly to match length of roast. Place roast in center of bacon, perpendicular to slices. Bring ends of bacon up and around sides of roast, overlapping ends of slices as needed.

5. Place bacon-wrapped roast, seam side down, in center of prepared sheet. Roast until center of pork registers 90 degrees, 30 to 40 minutes. Remove roast from oven and increase oven temperature to 475 degrees.

OUR SUNDAY BEST   351

1. Combine potatoes, ½ cup chicken broth, 4 tablespoons butter, ¾ teaspoon salt, and ½ teaspoon pepper in large saucepan. Cover and cook over medium heat, stirring occasionally, until potatoes are tender, about 20 minutes. Process with immersion blender until smooth.

2. Meanwhile, pat pork dry with paper towels and sprinkle with pie spice, 1 teaspoon salt, and 1 teaspoon pepper. Melt 1 tablespoon butter in 12-inch nonstick skillet over medium-high heat. Add pork and cook until well browned and registers 140 degrees, about 6 minutes per side. Transfer pork to platter and tent with foil.

3. Whisk cornstarch and remaining ½ cup chicken broth together in bowl. Combine cherries, bourbon, orange marmalade, chicken broth mixture, remaining ¼ teaspoon salt, and remaining ¼ teaspoon pepper in now-empty skillet. Bring to simmer over medium-high heat and cook, stirring, until mixture turns thick and translucent, about 3 minutes. Off heat, stir in remaining 2 tablespoons butter. Serve pork chops and sweet potatoes with sauce.

Slow-Roasted Fresh Ham

SERVES 12 TO 14

Slow-Roasted Fresh Ham

WHY THIS RECIPE WORKS Unlike the hams that most people are familiar with, fresh ham isn't cured, smoked, or aged. This big cut is basically an oddly shaped bone-in, skin-on pork roast, and slow roasting turned it tender and flavorful. Roasting the ham in an oven bag created a moist environment that conducted heat more effectively than a dry oven did, so the ham stayed moist and reached the ideal cooking temperature faster and remained there longer. A simple tangy glaze brushed on toward the end of roasting made for a flavorful finish. This rich ham may be just the thing to serve as a simple yet elegant centerpiece for your next big gathering.

Use a turkey-size oven bag for this recipe.

- 1 (8- to 10-pound) bone-in, shank-end fresh ham
- ⅓ cup packed brown sugar
- ⅓ cup kosher salt
- 3 tablespoons minced fresh rosemary
- 1 tablespoon minced fresh thyme
- 1 large oven bag
- 2 tablespoons maple syrup
- 2 tablespoons molasses
- 1 tablespoon soy sauce
- 1 tablespoon Dijon mustard
- 1 teaspoon pepper

1. Place ham flat side down on cutting board. Using sharp knife, remove skin, leaving ½- to ¼-inch layer of fat intact. Cut 1-inch diagonal crosshatch pattern in fat, being careful not to cut into meat. Place ham on its side. Cut one 4-inch horizontal pocket about 2 inches deep in center of flat side of ham, being careful not to poke through opposite side.

2. Combine sugar, salt, rosemary, and thyme in bowl. Rub half of sugar mixture in ham pocket. Tie 1 piece of kitchen twine tightly around base of ham. Rub exterior of ham with remaining sugar mixture. Wrap ham tightly in plastic wrap and refrigerate for at least 12 hours or up to 24 hours.

3. Adjust oven rack to lowest position and heat oven to 325 degrees. Set V-rack in large roasting pan. Unwrap ham and place in oven bag flat side down. Tie top of oven bag closed with kitchen twine. Place ham, flat side down, on V-rack and cut ½-inch slit in top of oven bag.

352   The Complete Cook's Country TV Show Cookbook

Roast until thermometer inserted in center of ham, close to but not touching bone, registers 160 degrees, 3½ to 5 hours. Remove ham from oven and let rest in oven bag on V-rack for 1 hour. Heat oven to 450 degrees.

4. Whisk maple syrup, molasses, soy sauce, mustard, and pepper together in bowl. Cut off top of oven bag and push down with tongs, allowing accumulated juices to spill into roasting pan; discard oven bag. Leave ham sitting flat side down on V-rack.

5. Brush ham with half of glaze and roast for 10 minutes. Brush ham with remaining glaze, rotate pan, and roast until deep amber color, about 10 minutes longer. Move ham to carving board, flat side down, and let rest for 20 minutes. Pour pan juices into fat separator. Carve ham into ¼-inch-thick slices, arrange on platter, and moisten lightly with defatted pan juices. Serve, passing remaining pan juices separately.

How to Season Deeply and Cook Evenly

We found two tricks for deep seasoning and even cooking of a fresh ham.

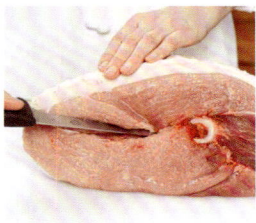

1. Cut a pocket in the meaty end and season the ham inside the pocket.

2. Tie twine around the base to create a more even shape, then season the exterior.

Cider-Baked Ham

Cider-Baked Ham

SERVES 16 TO 20

WHY THIS RECIPE WORKS Ham glazed with sweet apple cider certainly sounds great, but most recipes lack serious apple flavor—and call for frequent basting. For a relatively hands-off ham that was infused with lots of apple flavor, we marinated the ham in spiced apple cider. Baking the ham in an oven bag guarded against dried-out meat. And to create a crusty, spicy-sweet exterior, we rolled back the bag once the ham was heated through, slathered on reduced apple cider and a mixture of brown sugar and black pepper, and returned it to the oven to caramelize.

We prefer a bone-in, uncut, cured ham for this recipe, because the exterior layer of fat can be scored and helps create a nice crust. A spiral-sliced ham can be used instead, but there won't be much exterior fat, so skip the trimming and scoring in step 2. This recipe requires nearly a gallon of cider and a large oven bag. In step 4, be sure to stir the reduced cider mixture frequently to prevent scorching.

  1 cinnamon stick, broken into rough pieces
  ¼ teaspoon whole cloves
3¼ quarts apple cider, divided
  8 cups ice cubes
  1 (7- to 10-pound) cured bone-in half ham, preferably shank end
  2 tablespoons Dijon mustard
  1 cup packed dark brown sugar
  1 teaspoon pepper
     Large oven bag

OUR SUNDAY BEST

1. Toast cinnamon and cloves in large saucepan over medium heat until fragrant, about 3 minutes. Add 4 cups cider and bring to boil. Pour spiced cider into large stockpot or clean bucket, add 4 cups cider and ice, and stir until melted.

2. Meanwhile, remove skin from exterior of ham and trim fat to ¼-inch thickness. Score remaining fat at 1-inch intervals in crosshatch pattern. Transfer ham to container with chilled cider mixture (liquid should nearly cover ham) and refrigerate for at least 4 hours or up to 12 hours.

3. Discard cider mixture and transfer ham to large oven bag. Add 1 cup fresh cider to bag, tie securely, and cut 4 slits in top of bag. Transfer to large roasting pan and let stand at room temperature for 1½ hours.

4. Adjust oven rack to lowest position and heat oven to 300 degrees. Bake until ham registers 100 degrees, 1½ to 2½ hours. Meanwhile, bring remaining 4 cups cider and mustard to boil in saucepan. Reduce heat to medium-low and simmer, stirring often, until mixture is very thick and reduced to ⅓ cup, about 1 hour.

5. Combine sugar and pepper in bowl. Remove ham from oven and let rest for 5 minutes. Increase oven temperature to 400 degrees. Roll back oven bag and brush ham with reduced cider mixture. Using your fingers, carefully press sugar mixture onto exterior of ham. Return to oven and bake until dark brown and caramelized, about 20 minutes. Transfer ham to carving board, tent loosely with aluminum foil, and let rest for 15 minutes. Carve and serve.

Crumb-Crusted Rack of Lamb

Crumb-Crusted Rack of Lamb

SERVES 6 TO 8

WHY THIS RECIPE WORKS A rack of lamb with a nicely burnished exterior is the perfect festive centerpiece, but trying to get a brown crust in the oven left us with overcooked meat. So instead we employed a two-step process, first searing the racks on the stovetop and then roasting them in a relatively low oven until they emerged tender, juicy, and rosy-pink throughout. Panko crumbs seasoned with thyme, garlic, lemon zest, and anchovies added crunch and assertive flavor, and sharp, tangy Dijon mustard acted as a flavorful glue to adhere the mixture to the lamb. A lemony mint sauce added a bright and zippy finish.

We prefer the milder taste and bigger size of domestic lamb, but you may substitute lamb imported from New Zealand or Australia. Since imported lamb is generally smaller, if you can find only racks that are 1½ to 1¾ pounds, decrease the salt for each rack to ¾ teaspoon in step 2 and reduce the cooking time by about 5 minutes in step 3. Serve with Fresh Mint Sauce (recipe follows), if desired.

- 1 cup panko bread crumbs
- 2 tablespoons plus 1 teaspoon extra-virgin olive oil
- 2 tablespoons minced fresh thyme
- 6 garlic cloves, minced
- 4 anchovy fillets, rinsed, patted dry, and minced (optional)
- Kosher salt and pepper
- 2 tablespoons minced fresh parsley
- 1 tablespoon grated lemon zest
- 2 (1¾- to 2-pound) racks of lamb, fat trimmed to ⅛ inch
- ¼ cup Dijon mustard

1. Adjust oven rack to middle position and heat oven to 300 degrees. Combine panko; 2 tablespoons oil; thyme; garlic; anchovies, if using; 2 teaspoons salt; and 1 teaspoon pepper in 12-inch nonstick skillet. Cook over medium heat, stirring frequently and breaking up any clumps, until golden brown, about 5 minutes. Transfer to shallow dish. Stir in parsley and lemon zest.

2. Wipe skillet clean with paper towels. Set wire rack in rimmed baking sheet. Pat lamb dry with paper towels, sprinkle each rack with 1 teaspoon salt, and season with pepper. Heat remaining 1 teaspoon oil in now-empty skillet over medium-high heat until just smoking. Place 1 rack in skillet and cook until well browned, 2 to 4 minutes per side, using tongs as necessary to stand up rack to brown loin portion. Transfer to prepared wire rack. Pour off all but 1 teaspoon fat from skillet and repeat cooking with remaining rack of lamb. Let lamb cool for 5 minutes.

3. Brush lamb all over with mustard. Working with 1 rack at a time, transfer lamb to panko mixture, turning to coat all sides and pressing gently to adhere. Return lamb to wire rack, fat side up. Roast until lamb registers 135 degrees for medium, 40 to 50 minutes. Transfer to carving board and let rest for 15 minutes. Cut between bones to separate chops. Serve.

> ### The Details Matter
>
>
>
> **1. Trim Fat** Much of lamb's stronger flavor resides in its fat; we trim the fat on the racks' exteriors to 1/8 inch to control it.
>
> **2. Stand Up to Brown** To ensure even cooking, brown the racks on all sides, including the "bottom" of the loin.

Fresh Mint Sauce
MAKES ABOUT 1/2 CUP

Use a good-quality extra-virgin olive oil here for the best results.

- 1/2 cup chopped fresh mint
- 6 tablespoons extra-virgin olive oil
- 1/4 cup chopped fresh parsley
- 2 tablespoons lemon juice
- 1 garlic clove, minced
- 1/2 teaspoon kosher salt
- 1/4 teaspoon pepper

Combine all ingredients in bowl.

Trout Amandine
SERVES 4

WHY THIS RECIPE WORKS Trout fillets are quite thin, and their thinness means they can quickly overcook. To avoid this, we employed a simple technique: dredging the fillets in flour. The flour coating browns more quickly than an uncoated fish fillet would (so you can get good browning without overcooking the trout). The flour also protects the fillets from overcooking. For the sauce, we browned butter in the then-empty skillet and then toasted sliced almonds in the butter before adding fresh lemon juice and zest. Then we poured the butter and almond mixture over the trout and garnished it with chopped fresh parsley for a beautiful presentation.

Use raw sliced almonds here—toasted ones can burn. We developed this recipe using farm-raised rainbow trout fillets. If you can't tell the color of the butter in the nonstick skillet in step 5, quickly spoon some onto a white plate to check.

- 4 (4- to 6-ounce) skin-on trout fillets
- 1 1/4 teaspoons table salt, divided
- 1/2 teaspoon pepper
- 1/4 cup all-purpose flour
- 2 tablespoons vegetable oil, divided
- 8 tablespoons unsalted butter, cut into 8 pieces
- 1/2 cup sliced almonds
- 2 teaspoons grated lemon zest plus 4 teaspoons juice
- 2 tablespoons chopped fresh parsley

1. Pat trout fillets dry with paper towels. Sprinkle all over with 1 teaspoon salt and pepper.

2. Place flour in shallow dish. Working with 1 fillet at a time, dredge both sides in flour, pressing gently to adhere. Shake off excess and transfer to large plate.

3. Heat 1 tablespoon oil in 12-inch nonstick skillet over medium heat until just smoking. Carefully place 2 fillets skin side down in skillet and cook until browned and crispy, 2 to 4 minutes. Using fish spatula, flip fillets flesh side down and cook until flesh is opaque and begins to turn golden, about 1 minute.

4. Transfer cooked fillets to large serving platter flesh side up. Repeat cooking and transferring with remaining 1 tablespoon oil and remaining 2 fillets.

5. Add butter to now-empty skillet. Cook, stirring frequently, until butter is golden brown with toasted aroma, 1 to 2 minutes. Stir in almonds and cook, swirling skillet occasionally, until almonds are deep golden brown, about 2 minutes.

6. Immediately remove skillet from heat and quickly but carefully stir in lemon zest and juice and remaining ¼ teaspoon salt, scraping up any browned bits. Pour sauce over fillets, sprinkle with parsley, and serve.

Trout Amandine

Slow-Roasted Salmon with Chives and Lemon

SERVES 6

WHY THIS RECIPE WORKS Though slow roasting is an uncommon method for cooking fish, here it results in ultratender, buttery salmon. To feed six people, we opted to work with a single 2½-pound fillet, which would be less likely to overcook than separate, smaller pieces. We sprinkled the fish with a mixture of brown sugar and salt to evoke the flavors of cured salmon and slid it into the oven. A very low, 250-degree oven kept the fish from overcooking and minimized any residual cooking once it was out of the oven. A light, bright vinaigrette of extra-virgin olive oil, lemon zest and juice, and fresh chives perfectly complemented our succulent fish.

You can substitute granulated sugar for the brown sugar, if desired. If a 2½-pound salmon fillet is unavailable, you can use six 6- to 8-ounce skinless salmon fillets instead. In step 1, sprinkle both sides of the fillets evenly with the sugar mixture and arrange them side by side in the baking dish so that they are touching. The cooking time remains the same. We prefer farm-raised salmon here; if using wild salmon, reduce the cooking time to 45 to 50 minutes, or until the salmon registers 120 degrees. If you're using table salt, use ¾ teaspoon (½ teaspoon in step 1 and ¼ teaspoon in step 3).

- 1 tablespoon packed brown sugar
- 1½ teaspoons kosher salt, divided
- ½ teaspoon pepper
- 1 (2½-pound) skinless center-cut salmon fillet, about 1½ inches thick
- ¼ cup extra-virgin olive oil
- 2 tablespoons sliced fresh chives
- 2 teaspoons grated lemon zest plus 1½ tablespoons juice

1. Adjust oven rack to middle position and heat oven to 250 degrees. Combine sugar, 1 teaspoon salt, and pepper in small bowl. Sprinkle salmon all over with sugar mixture.

2. Place salmon, flesh side up, in 13 by 9-inch baking dish. Roast until center is still translucent when checked with tip of paring knife and registers 125 degrees (for medium-rare), 55 to 60 minutes.

Slow-Roasted Salmon with Chives and Lemon

Pull Out the Pin Bones

To remove the pin bones from a salmon fillet, drape the fillet skin side down on an overturned bowl and remove the protruding bones with tweezers or needle-nose pliers.

One-Pan Roasted Salmon with Broccoli and Red Potatoes

SERVES 4

WHY THIS RECIPE WORKS We embraced the challenge of a one-pan dinner with salmon, broccoli, and red potatoes even though all require different cooking times. We started the potatoes and broccoli together, roasting them at 500 degrees—enough time for the broccoli to brown and the spuds to soften. Then we removed the broccoli, keeping it warm under foil, and arranged the salmon fillets in its place. Reducing the oven temperature let the salmon roast gently while the potatoes finished cooking. A sharp stir-together sauce of chives, mustard, and lemon gave this simple meal some pizzazz and added a fresh note.

Use small red potatoes measuring 1 to 2 inches in diameter for this recipe.

- 4 (6- to 8-ounce) center-cut skinless salmon fillets, 1 to 1½ inches thick
- 2 teaspoons plus 5 tablespoons extra-virgin olive oil
  Salt and pepper
- 1 pound small red potatoes, unpeeled, halved
- 1 pound broccoli florets, cut into 2-inch pieces
- ¼ cup minced fresh chives
- 2 tablespoons whole-grain mustard
- 2 teaspoons lemon juice
- 1 teaspoon honey
  Lemon wedges

3. Meanwhile, combine oil, chives, lemon zest and juice, and remaining ½ teaspoon salt in bowl.

4. Remove dish from oven and immediately pour oil mixture evenly over salmon. Let rest for 5 minutes. Using spatula and spoon, portion salmon and sauce onto serving platter. Stir together any juices left in dish and spoon over salmon. Serve.

Slow-Roasted Salmon with Dill and Garlic

Substitute 1 teaspoon dry mustard for pepper. Add 1 teaspoon granulated garlic to sugar mixture. Substitute chopped fresh dill for chives.

Slow-Roasted Salmon with Parsley and Cayenne

Substitute cayenne pepper for pepper and chopped fresh parsley for chives.

OUR SUNDAY BEST

> **Broccoli-Salmon Switcheroo**
> To ensure that all three components emerge from the oven well browned and cooked just right, we roast the potatoes the entire time on the baking sheet (they take the longest) but remove the broccoli before placing the salmon fillets on the sheet.

1. Adjust oven rack to lowest position and heat oven to 500 degrees. Pat salmon dry with paper towels, then rub all over with 2 teaspoons oil and season with salt and pepper. Refrigerate until needed.

2. Brush rimmed baking sheet with 1 tablespoon oil. Toss potatoes, 1 tablespoon oil, ½ teaspoon salt, and ½ teaspoon pepper together in bowl. Arrange potatoes cut side down on half of sheet. Toss broccoli, 1 tablespoon oil, ¼ teaspoon salt, and ¼ teaspoon pepper together in now-empty bowl. Arrange broccoli on other half of sheet.

3. Roast until potatoes are light golden brown and broccoli is dark brown on bottom, 22 to 24 minutes, rotating sheet halfway through baking.

4. Meanwhile, combine chives, mustard, lemon juice, honey, remaining 2 tablespoons oil, pinch salt, and pinch pepper in bowl; set chive sauce aside.

5. Remove sheet from oven and transfer broccoli to platter, browned side up; cover with foil to keep warm. Using spatula, remove any bits of broccoli remaining on sheet. (Leave potatoes on sheet.)

6. Place salmon skinned side down on now-empty side of sheet, spaced evenly. Place sheet in oven and immediately reduce oven temperature to 275 degrees. Bake until centers of fillets register 125 degrees (for medium-rare), 11 to 15 minutes, rotating sheet halfway through baking. Transfer potatoes and salmon to platter with broccoli. Serve with lemon wedges and chive sauce.

Baked Shrimp with Fennel, Potatoes, and Olives

SERVES 4 TO 6

WHY THIS RECIPE WORKS Unlike other proteins that look anemic if not seared over direct heat, naturally vibrant pink shrimp are a great candidate for the oven. But since shrimp cook so quickly, we needed to give the rest of our one-pan meal a head start. Potatoes browned nicely in the oven, and licorice-y fennel stayed intact when sliced into wedges though the stem end. To achieve a bright flavor profile, we tossed the shrimp with oregano and lemon zest before adding them to the baking sheet with the vegetables. Salty feta cheese and kalamata olives gave our simple dish a savory finish, and a squeeze of lemon brought it all to life.

We prefer all-natural shrimp that aren't treated with sodium or preservatives. If buying frozen shrimp, the ingredient label should list only "shrimp."

- 1½ pounds Yukon Gold potatoes, peeled and sliced ½ inch thick
- 2 fennel bulbs, stalks discarded, bulbs halved lengthwise and cut into 1-inch-thick wedges through stem end
- 3 tablespoons extra-virgin olive oil, plus extra for drizzling
  Salt and pepper
- 2 pounds jumbo shrimp (16 to 20 per pound), peeled, deveined, and tails removed
- 2 teaspoons dried oregano
- 1 teaspoon grated lemon zest, plus lemon wedges for serving
- 4 ounces feta cheese, crumbled (1 cup)
- ½ cup pitted kalamata olives, halved
- 2 tablespoons chopped fresh parsley

1. Adjust oven rack to lower-middle position and heat oven to 450 degrees. Toss potatoes, fennel, 2 tablespoons oil, 1 teaspoon salt, and ¼ teaspoon pepper together in bowl. Spread vegetables in single layer on rimmed baking sheet and roast until just tender, about 25 minutes.

2. Pat shrimp dry with paper towels. Toss shrimp, oregano, lemon zest, remaining 1 tablespoon oil, ½ teaspoon salt, and ¼ teaspoon pepper together in bowl.

3. Using spatula, flip potatoes and fennel so browned sides are facing up. Scatter shrimp and feta over top. Return to oven and roast until shrimp are cooked through, 6 to 8 minutes. Sprinkle olives and parsley over top and drizzle with extra oil. Serve with lemon wedges.

> **Roast Veggies First**
> Roast the longer-cooking potatoes and fennel until they are just tender. Then, flip the vegetables so that their browned sides are facing up and scatter the oregano-and-lemon-scented shrimp and the feta on top to cook the shrimp. Sprinkle with parsley and kalamata olives before serving.
>
>

One-Pan Roasted Salmon with Broccoli and Red Potatoes

Gambas al Ajillo (Spanish-Style Sizzling Garlic Shrimp)

SERVES 4

WHY THIS RECIPE WORKS To make this dish inspired by the Spanish tapas bar classic, we reached for high-quality frozen shrimp that we thawed and peeled ourselves. We gently cooked fresh minced garlic in a generous amount of extra-virgin olive oil with red pepper flakes until golden brown. Then we added the shrimp, which we seasoned ahead of time, to the infused oil to gently cook for a few minutes per side. Using a cast-iron skillet set over medium-low heat helped keep the heat even and gentle, and it held the cooked shrimp in its leftover warmth when served directly from the skillet. Crusty bread was the perfect vehicle to soak up and enjoy the remaining oil once the shrimp had all been eaten.

Baked Shrimp with Fennel, Potatoes, and Olives

3. Add shrimp and cook until bottoms are light pink, about 2 minutes. Working quickly, flip shrimp and cook until just cooked through and pink all over, about 2 minutes longer. Off heat, stir in parsley. Serve immediately, directly from skillet, with crusty bread.

Clams with Chorizo
SERVES 2

WHY THIS RECIPE WORKS Based on a dish on offer at Ansots restaurant in Boise, Idaho, these clams will bring a taste of Basque country into your home kitchen. We started by toasting garlic and chorizo in olive oil, which both flavored the oil and turned it an appealing red color. The clams were steamed in equal parts clam juice and white wine until they popped open and added their own juice to the broth. A cornstarch slurry thickened up the broth, which was tossed with pimentos and parsley before pouring it back over the clams. Served with crusty bread, it's a simple but flavorful meal.

Scrub the clams before cooking to remove any sand on their shells. Eastern littleneck clams average eight to 10 clams per pound. You can substitute other small, hard-shelled clams, such as Manila clams, cockles, or Pacific littlenecks, but their sizes (and the number of clams per serving) and cooking times will vary. Do not use larger clams, such as cherrystones or quahogs, or soft-shelled clams. This recipe can easily be doubled in a Dutch oven; increase the cooking time for the clams to about 12 minutes.

Gambas al Ajillo (Spanish-Style Sizzling Garlic Shrimp)

It is important to use untreated shrimp—those without added sodium or preservatives such as sodium tripolyphosphate—in this recipe; treated shrimp contain too much sodium and may have off-flavors. Most frozen E-Z peel shrimp have been treated (the ingredient list should tell you). We like the heat of a full teaspoon of pepper flakes; for a milder dish, use the lesser amount.

- 1½ pounds extra-large shrimp (21 to 25 per pound), peeled, deveined, and tails removed
- 1½ teaspoons kosher salt
- ¾ cup extra-virgin olive oil
- 6 garlic cloves, minced
- ½–1 teaspoon red pepper flakes
- ½ cup chopped fresh parsley
  Crusty bread

1. Toss shrimp and salt together in large bowl. Cover and refrigerate for 15 minutes.

2. Heat oil, garlic, and pepper flakes in 12-inch cast-iron skillet over medium-low heat until garlic is light golden brown, 8 to 10 minutes.

- 1 teaspoon cornstarch
- ¾ cup dry white wine
- 2 ounces Spanish chorizo, sliced into thin rounds (scant ½ cup)
- 3 tablespoons extra-virgin olive oil
- 4 garlic cloves, sliced thin
- 2–2¼ pounds littleneck clams, scrubbed
- 2 tablespoons chopped pimentos (optional)
- 1 tablespoon chopped fresh parsley
  Crusty bread

1. Whisk cornstarch into wine in liquid measuring cup until dissolved; set aside. Combine chorizo, oil, and garlic in 12-inch skillet. Cook over medium-high heat until garlic begins to brown around edges and chorizo begins to render its fat, 3 to 4 minutes.

2. Whisk wine mixture to recombine. Add clams; pimentos, if using; and wine mixture to skillet and bring to boil. Cover and cook until clams open, 8 to 10 minutes. Remove from heat and use tongs or slotted spoon to transfer clams to deep platter. Stir parsley into sauce and pour sauce and chorizo over clams. Serve with bread.

On the Road: Tradition and Chorizo in the Heart of Basque Idaho

Ansots is a small Basque restaurant around the corner from Boise's famous Basque Block, the historic heart of Idaho's thriving Basque community, where locals gather to celebrate Basque music, dance, and food. The restaurant specializes in Basque-inspired small plates; Basque and Spanish wines; and various incarnations of house-made chorizos, which are prominently displayed in the natural wood dining room. "Almost everything in the restaurant is based on these chorizos," says chef, owner, and head charcutier Dan Ansotegui.

The curing case holds slabs of pork belly that will eventually become bacon; traditional chorizos, expertly balanced with the fruitiness of choriceros and garlic; chistorras, lightly smoked chorizos that register about five out of 10 for heat; marinated solomo that Ansotegui's daughter and the restaurant's pastry chef, Ellie, refers to as "meat candy"; and motzak, a shorter, chubbier chorizo flavored with roasted garlic and rosemary that Ansotegui says "goes with everything."

Parmesan-Crusted Asparagus

Parmesan-Crusted Asparagus

SERVES 4 TO 6

WHY THIS RECIPE WORKS Simply roasting asparagus and topping it with shaved Parmesan gives you limp spears and rubbery cheese. To get perfectly crisp-tender asparagus, we first salted it to rid it of excess moisture. For a cheesy coating that would stay put on the slender spears, we whipped a combination of honey and egg whites to soft peaks, dipped the asparagus in the mixture, then coated them with a mixture of bread crumbs and Parmesan. Finally, to reinforce the Parmesan flavor, we sprinkled the spears with more cheese at the end of roasting.

Avoid pencil-thin asparagus for this recipe. Work quickly when tossing the asparagus with the egg whites, as the salt on the asparagus will rapidly begin to deflate the whites.

OUR SUNDAY BEST   361

2 pounds (½-inch-thick) asparagus, trimmed
Salt and pepper
3 ounces Parmesan cheese, grated (1½ cups), divided
¾ cup panko bread crumbs
1 tablespoon unsalted butter, melted and cooled
Pinch cayenne
2 large egg whites
1 teaspoon honey

1. Adjust oven rack to middle position and heat oven to 450 degrees. Line rimmed baking sheet with aluminum foil and spray with vegetable oil spray. Using fork, poke holes up and down stalks of asparagus. Toss asparagus with ½ teaspoon salt and let stand for 30 minutes on a paper towel–lined baking sheet.

2. Meanwhile, combine 1 cup Parmesan, panko, butter, ¼ teaspoon salt, ⅛ teaspoon pepper, and cayenne in bowl. Transfer half of panko mixture to shallow dish and reserve remaining mixture. Using stand mixer fitted with whisk, whip egg whites and honey on medium-low speed until foamy, about 1 minute. Increase speed to medium-high and whip until soft peaks form, 2 to 3 minutes. Scrape into 13 by 9-inch baking dish and toss asparagus in mixture. Working with 1 spear at a time, dredge half of asparagus in panko and transfer to aluminum foil–lined baking sheet. Refill shallow dish with reserved panko mixture and repeat with remaining half of asparagus.

3. Bake asparagus until just beginning to brown, 6 to 8 minutes. Sprinkle with remaining ½ cup Parmesan and continue to bake until cheese is melted and panko is golden brown, 6 to 8 minutes. Transfer to platter. Serve.

Brussels Sprout Gratin

SERVES 6 TO 8

WHY THIS RECIPE WORKS It's easy to mask the taste of an unpopular vegetable with cheese, but we think the flavors of properly cooked brussels sprouts are worth showing off. We roasted them to bring out their nutty and slightly sweet notes, and meanwhile whipped up a Mornay sauce—a creamy cheese sauce (using Gruyère and Parmesan) spiked with nutmeg, cayenne, and sweet-sharp aromatics. We poured the sauce over the roasted sprouts, and then for the crunchiest possible topping for our gratin, we jump-started some panko by sautéing it in butter, sprinkled it over the top with cheese, and popped the whole dish back in the oven to crisp up.

Look for smaller brussels sprouts, no bigger than a golf ball, as they're likely to be sweeter and more tender than large sprouts. If you can find only large sprouts, quarter them. A broiler-safe dish is important because the sprouts cook at such a high temperature.

2½ pounds brussels sprouts, trimmed and halved through stem
1 tablespoon vegetable oil
Salt and pepper
3 tablespoons unsalted butter, divided
¼ cup panko bread crumbs
1 shallot, minced
1 garlic clove, minced
1 tablespoon all-purpose flour
1¼ cups heavy cream
¾ cup chicken broth
2 ounces Gruyère cheese, shredded (½ cup), divided
1 ounce Parmesan cheese, grated (½ cup)
Pinch ground nutmeg
Pinch cayenne pepper

1. Adjust oven rack to middle position and heat oven to 450 degrees. Grease 13 by 9-inch broiler-safe baking dish. Toss brussels sprouts, oil, ½ teaspoon salt, and ¼ teaspoon pepper together in prepared baking dish. Bake until sprouts are well browned and tender, 30 to 35 minutes. Transfer to wire rack and set aside to cool for at least 5 minutes or up to 30 minutes.

2. Meanwhile, melt 1 tablespoon butter in medium saucepan over medium heat. Add panko and cook, stirring frequently, until golden brown, about 3 minutes. Transfer to bowl and stir in ¼ teaspoon salt and ¼ teaspoon pepper; set aside. Wipe saucepan clean with paper towels.

3. Melt remaining 2 tablespoons butter in now-empty saucepan over medium heat. Add shallot and garlic and cook until just softened, about 1 minute. Stir in flour and cook for 1 minute. Whisk in cream and broth and bring to boil over medium-high heat. Once boiling, remove from heat and whisk in ¼ cup Gruyère, Parmesan, nutmeg, cayenne, ¼ teaspoon pepper, and ⅛ teaspoon salt until smooth.

4. Pour cream mixture over brussels sprouts in baking dish and stir to combine. Sprinkle evenly with panko mixture and remaining ¼ cup Gruyère. Bake until bubbling around edges and golden brown on top, 5 to 7 minutes. Transfer dish to wire rack and let cool for 10 minutes. Serve.

Brussels Sprout Salad

SERVES 8

WHY THIS RECIPE WORKS Raw brussels sprout salad isn't as weird as it sounds: brussels sprouts are very much like miniature cabbages in both texture and taste. To make this slaw-like salad, we thinly sliced the sprouts and tossed them with a bright, lemony vinaigrette with a touch of Dijon. We briefly marinated the salad in the vinaigrette to soften and season the sprouts. We topped the sprouts with toasted pine nuts and salty Pecorino Romano for a salad that's so delicious it can turn brussels sprout loathers into brussels sprout lovers.

Slice the sprouts as thin as possible. Shred the Pecorino Romano on the large holes of a box grater.

- 3 tablespoons lemon juice
- 2 tablespoons Dijon mustard
- 1 small shallot, minced
- 1 garlic clove, minced
  Salt and pepper
- 6 tablespoons extra-virgin olive oil
- 2 pounds brussels sprouts, trimmed, halved, and sliced very thin
- 3 ounces Pecorino Romano cheese, shredded (1 cup)
- ½ cup pine nuts, toasted

1. Whisk lemon juice, mustard, shallot, garlic, and ½ teaspoon salt together in large bowl. Slowly whisk in oil until incorporated. Toss brussels sprouts with vinaigrette and let sit for at least 30 minutes or up to 2 hours.

2. Fold in Pecorino and pine nuts. Season with salt and pepper to taste. Serve.

Brussels Sprout Salad with Cheddar, Hazelnuts, and Apple

Substitute 1 cup shredded sharp cheddar for Pecorino and ½ cup hazelnuts, toasted, skinned, and chopped, for pine nuts. Add 1 Granny Smith apple, cored and cut into ½-inch pieces.

Brussels Sprout Salad with Smoked Gouda, Pecans, and Dried Cherries

Substitute 1 cup shredded smoked gouda for Pecorino and ½ cup pecans, toasted and chopped, for pine nuts. Add ½ cup chopped dried cherries.

Brussels Sprout Gratin

Brussels Sprout Salad

Asparagus Salad with Radishes, Pecorino Romano, and Croutons

SERVES 4 TO 6

Asparagus Salad with Radishes, Pecorino Romano, and Croutons

WHY THIS RECIPE WORKS Eating raw asparagus may sound strange, but it makes a memorable salad. Slicing the spears thin was key to keeping the asparagus crunchy, not woody. An herb-based pesto dressing complemented the freshness of the asparagus by bringing in flavors of basil, mint, salty Pecorino Romano, zesty lemon, and zingy garlic. Spicy radishes, shaved pieces of Pecorino, and crunchy homemade croutons provided the finishing touches to this vibrant salad.

Parmesan can be substituted for the Pecorino Romano. Grate the cheese for the pesto with a rasp-style grater or use the small holes of a box grater; shave the cheese for the salad with a vegetable peeler. For easier slicing, select large asparagus spears, about ½ inch thick.

Croutons
- 2 tablespoons unsalted butter
- 1 tablespoon extra-virgin olive oil
- 2 slices hearty white sandwich bread, crusts removed, cut into ½-inch cubes (1⅓ cups)

Pesto
- 2 cups fresh mint leaves
- ¼ cup fresh basil leaves
- ¼ cup grated Pecorino Romano cheese
- 1 teaspoon grated lemon zest plus 2 teaspoons juice
- 1 garlic clove, minced
- ½ cup extra-virgin olive oil

Salad
- 2 pounds asparagus, trimmed
- 5 radishes, trimmed and sliced thin
- 2 ounces Pecorino Romano cheese, shaved (¾ cup)

1. For the Croutons Heat butter and oil in 12-inch nonstick skillet over medium heat until butter is melted. Add bread cubes and ⅛ teaspoon salt and cook, stirring frequently, until golden brown, 7 to 10 minutes. Transfer croutons to paper towel–lined plate. Season with salt and pepper to taste.

2. For the Pesto Process mint, basil, Pecorino, lemon zest and juice, garlic, and ¾ teaspoon salt in food processor until finely chopped, about 20 seconds, scraping down bowl as needed. Transfer to large bowl. Stir in oil until combined and season with salt and pepper to taste.

3. For the Salad Cut asparagus tips from stalks into ¾-inch-long pieces. Slice asparagus stalks ⅛ inch thick on bias into approximate 2-inch lengths. Add asparagus tips and stalks, radishes, and Pecorino to pesto and toss to combine. Season with salt and pepper to taste. Transfer salad to platter and top with croutons. Serve.

Asparagus Salad with Grapes, Goat Cheese, and Almonds

Pesto
- 2 cups fresh mint leaves
- ¼ cup fresh basil leaves
- ¼ cup grated Pecorino Romano cheese
- 1 teaspoon grated lemon zest plus 2 teaspoons juice
- 1 garlic clove, minced
- ½ cup extra-virgin olive oil

364 *The Complete Cook's Country TV Show Cookbook*

Salad

- 2 pounds asparagus, trimmed
- 6 ounces grapes, thinly sliced (1 cup)
- 4 ounces goat cheese, crumbled (1 cup)
- ¾ cup almonds, toasted and chopped

1. For the Pesto Process mint, basil, Pecorino, lemon zest and juice, garlic, and ¾ teaspoon salt in food processor until finely chopped, about 20 seconds, scraping down bowl as needed. Transfer to large bowl. Stir in oil until combined and season with salt and pepper to taste.

2. For the Salad Cut asparagus tips from stalks into ¾-inch-long pieces. Slice asparagus stalks ⅛ inch thick on bias into approximate 2-inch lengths. Add asparagus tips and stalks, grapes, goat cheese, and almonds to pesto and toss to combine. Season with salt and pepper to taste. Serve.

Asparagus Salad with Oranges, Feta, and Hazelnuts

Pesto

- 2 cups fresh mint leaves
- ¼ cup fresh basil leaves
- ¼ cup grated Pecorino Romano cheese
- 1 teaspoon grated lemon zest plus 2 teaspoons juice
- 1 garlic clove, minced
- ½ cup extra-virgin olive oil

Salad

- 2 pounds asparagus, trimmed
- 2 large oranges
- 4 ounces feta cheese, crumbled (1 cup)
- ¾ cup blanched hazelnuts, toasted and chopped

1. For the Pesto Process mint, basil, Pecorino, lemon zest and juice, garlic, and ¾ teaspoon salt in food processor until finely chopped, about 20 seconds, scraping down bowl as needed. Transfer to large bowl. Stir in oil until combined and season with salt and pepper to taste.

2. For the Salad Cut asparagus tips from stalks into ¾-inch-long pieces. Slice asparagus stalks ⅛ inch thick on bias into approximate 2-inch lengths. Cut away peel and pith from oranges. Holding fruit over bowl, use paring knife to slice between membranes to release segments. Add asparagus tips and stalks, orange segments, feta, and hazelnuts to pesto and toss to combine. Season with salt and pepper to taste. Serve.

Shredded Swiss Chard Salad with Prosciutto, Basil, and Blue Cheese

Shredded Swiss Chard Salad with Prosciutto, Basil, and Blue Cheese

SERVES 4 TO 6

WHY THIS RECIPE WORKS If it isn't already, chard could become your new favorite salad green. In addition to being rich in vitamins, minerals, and fiber, it's also delicious when simply stemmed, sliced, and tossed in dressing. Chard is tender enough to be eaten raw. It's lighter, fresher, and slightly less earthy-tasting than cooked chard. A bright, sweet vinaigrette of fig preserves, whole-grain mustard, red wine vinegar, and minced shallot complemented not only the chard but also some peppery, pungent blue cheese and salty, rich prosciutto. Shredded fresh basil added complexity, while toasted walnuts provided nuttiness and crunch.

You can use any color Swiss chard in this recipe.

12 ounces Swiss chard
3 tablespoons extra-virgin olive oil
3 tablespoons red wine vinegar
2 tablespoons fig preserves
1 small shallot, minced
2 teaspoons whole-grain mustard
½ teaspoon table salt
½ teaspoon pepper
½ cup shredded fresh basil
3 ounces thinly sliced prosciutto, torn into bite-size pieces, divided
½ cup walnuts, toasted and chopped coarse, divided
2 ounces blue cheese, crumbled (½ cup), divided

1. Stem Swiss chard, cutting out any stems thicker than ¼ inch from middle of chard leaves. Halve leaves lengthwise, then stack them on cutting board and slice crosswise ¼ inch thick.

2. Whisk oil, vinegar, fig preserves, shallot, mustard, salt, and pepper together in large bowl. Add chard, basil, half of prosciutto, half of walnuts, and half of blue cheese and toss to combine. Transfer salad to platter or individual serving plates and top with remaining prosciutto, walnuts, and blue cheese. Serve.

Stemming Swiss Chard

Lay leaves flat on cutting board and cut along sides of stems to remove any stems thicker than ¼ inch.

Endive Salad with Oranges and Blue Cheese

Endive Salad with Oranges and Blue Cheese

SERVES 4

WHY THIS RECIPE WORKS An endive salad calls for ingredients such as fruit, cheese, and nuts to complement and mellow the leaves' slight bitterness. For our recipe, we chose oranges, blue cheese, and walnuts. We segmented the oranges to eliminate the bitter pith. Marinating the orange segments and thinly sliced red onion in red wine vinegar and olive oil blended their flavors and mellowed the sharp onion. We tossed the blue cheese crumbles and walnuts in a mixture of honey and orange juice and zest. The tangy-sweet punch of the citrus nicely balanced the blue cheese's funk. A simple dressing of orange juice and honey ensured sweet citrus flavor throughout.

Toast the walnuts on a rimmed baking sheet in a 350-degree oven until they're fragrant, 5 to 7 minutes.

2 oranges, divided
½ red onion, sliced thin
3 tablespoons extra-virgin olive oil, divided
2 tablespoons red wine vinegar
½ teaspoon table salt, divided
1 tablespoon honey
2 ounces blue cheese, crumbled (½ cup)
½ cup walnuts, toasted and chopped coarse
4 heads Belgian endive (4 ounces each), root end trimmed and leaves separated
¼ teaspoon pepper

366   *The Complete Cook's Country TV Show Cookbook*

1. Using rasp-style grater, grate 1½ teaspoons zest from 1 orange; transfer zest to medium bowl. Cut away peel and pith from both oranges. Holding fruit over large bowl, use paring knife to slice between membranes to release segments. Squeeze 1 tablespoon juice from orange membranes and add to bowl with zest; set aside.

2. Add onion, 2 tablespoons oil, vinegar, and ¼ teaspoon salt to large bowl with orange segments and toss to combine. Let stand for 30 minutes to allow flavors to meld.

3. Meanwhile, whisk honey and remaining 1 tablespoon oil into orange zest mixture. Add blue cheese and walnuts and toss gently to combine.

4. Add endive, pepper, and remaining ¼ teaspoon salt to orange segment mixture; toss gently to coat. Season with salt and pepper to taste. Transfer to serving platter. Spoon walnut mixture evenly over salad. Serve.

How to Prepare Belgian Endive

1. Trim ½ inch from bottom end and separate leaves from bulb (removing only leaves that come off easily).

2. Trim ½ inch from bottom again and separate more leaves, repeating process until you reach core.

How to Supreme an Orange

1. Cut away peel and pith from orange.

2. Holding orange over bowl, use paring knife to carefully slice between membranes to release segments.

Torn Potato Salad with Toasted Garlic and Herb Dressing

SERVES 4 TO 6

WHY THIS RECIPE WORKS The unique appeal of this potato salad is the texture of the potatoes, which we boiled whole and then tore into chunks (rather than cutting them before boiling or boiling and then slicing them). Boiling baby Yukon Gold potatoes whole in extra-salty water until they were very tender (rather than just tender, as some potato salads call for), created a delightful contrast in textures between the tight, slightly firm exteriors (that "pop" a bit when you bite into them) and the creamy, well-seasoned interiors. Plus, tearing the flavorful spuds into craggy, irregular pieces created a porous and convoluted surface for the dressing not only to coat but also to be absorbed.

Look for potatoes that are similar in size, about 2 inches in diameter. You can substitute Red Bliss potatoes for the baby Yukon Gold potatoes and red or white wine vinegar for the sherry vinegar.

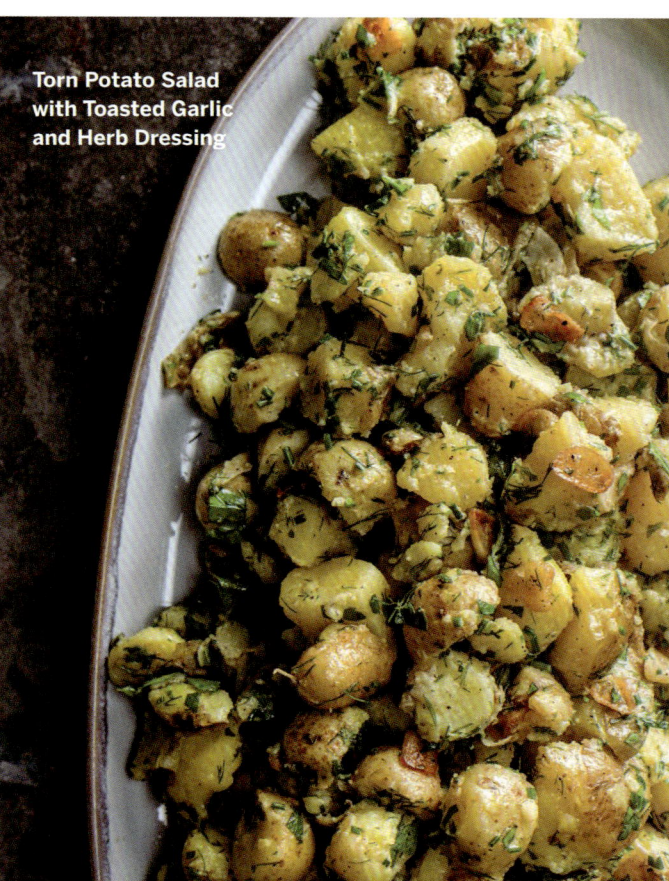

Torn Potato Salad with Toasted Garlic and Herb Dressing

- 2 pounds baby Yukon Gold potatoes, unpeeled
- 1 teaspoon table salt, plus salt for cooking potatoes
- ¼ cup extra-virgin olive oil
- 6 garlic cloves, sliced thin
- 2 tablespoons mayonnaise
- 1 tablespoon sherry vinegar, plus extra for seasoning
- ½ teaspoon pepper
- ½ cup chopped fresh chives, parsley, cilantro, and/or dill

1. Bring 3 quarts water to boil in large saucepan over high heat. Add potatoes and 3 tablespoons salt; return to boil and cook until potatoes are very tender and easily crushed but not breaking down, 20 to 25 minutes. Drain potatoes in colander and let sit until cool enough to handle but still warm, about 10 minutes.

2. Wipe saucepan clean with damp paper towels. Heat oil and garlic in now-empty saucepan over medium heat, swirling oil constantly once garlic begins to sizzle. Cook until garlic is light golden brown, 3 to 5 minutes. Immediately pour oil and garlic into large bowl. Add mayonnaise, vinegar, pepper, and salt and whisk until smooth.

3. Using your fingertips, gently tear each potato into rough 1-inch pieces and add to bowl with dressing. Add herbs and toss until evenly combined. Season with salt, pepper, and extra vinegar to taste. Serve warm, at room temperature, or chilled. (Potato salad can be refrigerated for up to 3 days; season with salt, pepper, and vinegar to taste before serving.)

Whipped Potatoes

SERVES 8 TO 10

WHY THIS RECIPE WORKS Conventional wisdom holds that anything but the gentlest treatment turns mashed potatoes into wallpaper paste, but we think our mixer-whipped spuds prove otherwise. For the lightest, fluffiest potatoes, we found high-starch russets worked best. Boiling the potatoes added extra water, resulting in a flat, not fluffy, finished dish. The best technique was to rinse excess starch from the raw potatoes, steam them, and then dry them in a pot on the stovetop over low heat. This process made them fluffier and better able to absorb the warm butter-and-milk mixture during whipping.

Whipped Potatoes

If your steamer basket has short legs (under 1¾ inches), the potatoes will sit in water as they cook and get wet. To prevent this, use balls of aluminum foil as steamer basket stilts. A stand mixer fitted with a whisk yields the smoothest potatoes, but a handheld mixer may be used as well.

- 4 pounds russet potatoes, peeled and cut into 1-inch pieces
- 1½ cups whole milk
- 8 tablespoons unsalted butter, cut into 8 pieces
- 2 teaspoons table salt
- ½ teaspoon pepper

1. Place cut potatoes in colander. Rinse under cold water until water runs clear, about 1 minute. Drain potatoes. Fill Dutch oven with 1 inch water and bring to boil. Place steamer basket in Dutch oven and fill with potatoes. Reduce heat to medium and cook, covered, until potatoes are tender, 20 to 25 minutes.

2. Heat milk, butter, salt, and pepper in small saucepan over medium-low heat, whisking until smooth, about 3 minutes; cover and keep warm.

3. Pour contents of Dutch oven into colander and return potatoes to dry pot. Stir over low heat until potatoes are thoroughly dried, about 1 minute. Using stand mixer fitted with whisk, break potatoes into small pieces on low speed, about 30 seconds. Add milk mixture in steady stream until incorporated. Increase speed to high and whip until potatoes are light and fluffy and no lumps remain, about 2 minutes. Serve.

Duchess Potatoes

SERVES 8

Duchess Potatoes

WHY THIS RECIPE WORKS Duchess potatoes take mashed potatoes to the next level, enriching them with egg and piping them into decorative rosettes before baking. To cook our spuds, we tried boiling, but this made them waterlogged; baking dried them out. Parcooking them in the microwave and finishing the rosettes in a hot oven proved best. For a potato mixture that was the right texture for piping, we stirred in butter, eggs, and cream while the potatoes were still hot, then added more butter once the potatoes had cooled. Baking powder ensured our picture-perfect Duchess Potatoes had the perfect airy, light texture to match.

For the smoothest, most uniform texture, use a food mill or ricer to mash the potatoes. Choose potatoes of the same size so that they cook evenly.

3	pounds russet potatoes
1	cup heavy cream
6	tablespoons unsalted butter, cut into ¼-inch pieces and softened, divided
1	large egg plus 1 large yolk, lightly beaten
1¼	teaspoons table salt
½	teaspoon pepper
½	teaspoon baking powder
	Pinch nutmeg
	Vegetable oil spray

1. Adjust oven rack to upper-middle position and heat oven to 475 degrees. Meanwhile, prick potatoes all over with fork, place on plate, and microwave until tender, 18 to 25 minutes, turning potatoes over after 10 minutes.

2. Cut potatoes in half. When cool enough to handle, scoop flesh into large bowl and mash until no lumps remain. Add cream, 3 tablespoons butter, egg and yolk, salt, pepper, baking powder, and nutmeg and continue to mash until potatoes are smooth. Let cool to room temperature, about 10 minutes. Gently fold in remaining butter until pieces are evenly distributed.

3. Transfer potato mixture to piping bag fitted with ½-inch star tip. Pipe eight 4-inch-wide mounds of potato onto rimmed baking sheet. Spray lightly with vegetable oil spray and bake until golden brown, 15 to 20 minutes. Serve.

To Make Ahead Once piped onto baking sheet, potatoes can be covered loosely with plastic wrap and refrigerated for 24 hours. They can also be frozen 2 hours until they're solid and then transferred to an airtight container (or left on the baking sheet). When you are ready to bake, arrange them on a rimmed baking sheet (or simply remove the plastic) and spray lightly with vegetable oil spray. They can go straight from the freezer to the oven, and they won't need any extra time.

Mashed Potato Casserole

SERVES 8

WHY THIS RECIPE WORKS Most recipes for mashed potato casserole simply dump mashed potatoes in a baking dish and pop it in the oven, but these dishes always end up bland, gluey, and dense. We wanted a casserole that delivered fluffy, buttery, creamy potatoes nestled under a savory golden crust. Using half-and-half instead of the traditional heavy cream lightened the recipe, and cutting it with chicken broth kept the potatoes moist. Beating eggs into the potato mixture helped it achieve a fluffy, airy texture. For bold flavor, we added Dijon mustard and fresh chives.

The casserole may also be baked in a 13 by 9-inch pan.

- 4 pounds russet potatoes, peeled and cut into 1-inch chunks
- 12 tablespoons unsalted butter, cut into 12 pieces
- ½ cup half-and-half
- ½ cup chicken broth
- 2 teaspoons Dijon mustard
- 1 garlic clove, minced
- 2 teaspoons table salt
- 4 large eggs
- ¼ cup finely chopped fresh chives

1. Adjust oven rack to upper-middle position and heat oven to 375 degrees. Bring potatoes and water to cover by 1 inch to boil in large pot over high heat. Reduce heat to medium and simmer until potatoes are tender, about 20 minutes.

2. Heat butter, half-and-half, broth, mustard, garlic, and salt in saucepan over medium-low heat until smooth, about 5 minutes. Keep warm.

3. Drain potatoes and transfer to large bowl. Using stand mixer fitted with paddle, beat potatoes on medium-low speed, slowly adding half-and-half mixture, until smooth and creamy, about 1 minute. Scrape down bowl; beat in eggs, 1 at a time, until incorporated, about 1 minute. Fold in chives.

4. Transfer potato mixture to greased 3-quart baking dish. Smooth surface of potatoes, then use fork to make peaked design on top of casserole. Bake until potatoes rise and begin to brown, about 35 minutes. Let cool for 10 minutes. Serve.

Mashed Potato Casserole

To Make Ahead The baking dish with the potatoes can be covered with plastic and refrigerated for up to 24 hours. When ready to bake, let the casserole sit at room temperature for 1 hour. Increase baking time by 10 minutes.

Syracuse Salt Potatoes

SERVES 6 TO 8

WHY THIS RECIPE WORKS For Syracuse salt potatoes with a well-seasoned crust and ultra-creamy interior, we cut back on the usual 3 cups of salt, which resulted in overly salty potatoes. We found that white or red potatoes proved best, but they needed to be boiled in the salted water whole—if they were cut or peeled, they absorbed too much salt. Though these potatoes are usually served with plain melted butter for dipping, we found that adding chives and black pepper to the butter brought this dish to new heights.

370 *The Complete Cook's Country TV Show Cookbook*

You will need 1¼ cups of noniodized table salt, 1½ cups of Morton kosher salt, or 2½ cups of Diamond Crystal kosher salt to equal 14 ounces. We prefer to use small potatoes, measuring 1 to 2 inches in diameter, in this recipe.

- 8 cups water
- 14 ounces salt
- 3 pounds small white or red potatoes
- 8 tablespoons unsalted butter, cut into 8 pieces
- 2 tablespoons minced fresh chives
- 1 teaspoon pepper

1. Set wire rack in rimmed baking sheet. Bring water to boil in Dutch oven over medium-high heat. Stir in salt and potatoes and cook until potatoes are just tender, 20 to 30 minutes. Drain potatoes and transfer to prepared baking sheet. Let dry until salty crust forms, about 1 minute.

2. Meanwhile, microwave butter, chives, and pepper in medium bowl until butter is melted, about 1 minute. Transfer potatoes to serving bowl and serve, passing butter separately.

Syracuse Salt Potatoes

Creamy Mashed Sweet Potatoes

SERVES 4 TO 6

WHY THIS RECIPE WORKS Deeply flavored, earthy, and subtly sweet, mashed sweet potatoes hardly need a layer of marshmallows to make them into a tempting side. For a silky and full-flavored mash, we found the secret was to thinly slice the potatoes and cook them covered, on the stovetop, over low heat in a small amount of butter and cream. Once the sweet potatoes were fall-apart tender, they could be mashed right in the pot—no draining, no straining, no fuss. Adding another spoonful of cream when we mashed the potatoes enriched them even more.

This recipe can be doubled and prepared in a Dutch oven, but the cooking time will need to be doubled as well.

- 2 pounds sweet potatoes, peeled, quartered, and sliced ¼ inch thick
- 4 tablespoons unsalted butter, cut into 4 pieces
- 3 tablespoons heavy cream, divided
- 1 teaspoon sugar
  Salt and pepper

Creamy Mashed Sweet Potatoes

1. Combine sweet potatoes, butter, 2 tablespoons cream, sugar, ½ teaspoon salt, and ¼ teaspoon pepper in large saucepan. Cook, covered, over low heat until potatoes are fall-apart tender, 35 to 40 minutes.

2. Off heat, add remaining 1 tablespoon cream and mash sweet potatoes with potato masher. Serve.

Herbed Mashed Sweet Potatoes with Caramelized Onion

If you prefer, substitute ¼ teaspoon of dried thyme for the thyme sprig.

Add 1 sprig fresh thyme to saucepan in step 1. While sweet potatoes are cooking, melt 1 tablespoon butter in 8-inch nonstick skillet and add 1 small onion, chopped, ¼ teaspoon sugar, and ¼ teaspoon salt. Cook over low heat until onion is caramelized, about 15 minutes. Remove thyme and mash potatoes as directed. Stir in onion and 1 tablespoon sour cream.

Smokehouse Mashed Sweet Potatoes

Add ⅛ teaspoon cayenne pepper to saucepan in step 1. Mash sweet potatoes with ½ cup shredded smoked Gouda cheese and cover with lid until cheese melts, about 1 minute. Sprinkle with 6 slices chopped cooked bacon and 1 thinly sliced scallion.

Roasted Butternut Squash and Apple

SERVES 4 TO 6

WHY THIS RECIPE WORKS Butternut squash is one of our favorite fall vegetables, but it can be a chore to prepare. To streamline the process, we began by peeling the tough exterior of the squash. Instead of meticulously dicing the squash into cubes, we cut the squash in half lengthwise and then crosswise into 1-inch-thick pieces. The larger pieces of squash caramelized beautifully while their interiors remained ultracreamy. For a mix of sweet and tart flavors, we added an apple partway through cooking. After removing the squash and apple from the oven, we drizzled them with a zippy vinaigrette of minced shallot, red wine vinegar, and parsley.

When peeling the squash, be sure to also remove the fibrous yellow flesh just beneath the skin.

Roasted Butternut Squash and Apple

Roasted Beets with Lemon-Tahini Dressing

Vinaigrette

- 3 tablespoons red wine vinegar
- 1 tablespoon sugar
- 1/8 teaspoon table salt
- 3 tablespoons minced shallot
- 2 tablespoons chopped fresh parsley
- 2 tablespoons extra-virgin olive oil
- 1/4 teaspoon red pepper flakes

Squash and Apple

- 1 (2¼- to 2¾-pound) butternut squash
- 3 tablespoons extra-virgin olive oil, divided
- 1 teaspoon table salt
- 1 Gala, Fuji, or Braeburn apple, unpeeled, cored, halved, and cut into ½-inch-thick wedges

1. For the Vinaigrette Stir vinegar, sugar, and salt in small bowl until sugar is dissolved. Stir in shallot, parsley, oil, and pepper flakes; set aside.

2. For the Squash And Apple Adjust oven rack to lowest position and heat oven to 450 degrees. Trim ends from squash and peel squash. Halve squash lengthwise and scrape out seeds. Place squash cut side down on cutting board and slice crosswise 1-inch thick.

3. Toss squash, 2 tablespoons oil, and salt together in bowl. Spread squash in even layer on rimmed baking sheet, cut side down. Roast until squash is tender and bottoms are beginning to brown, 14 to 16 minutes.

4. Toss apple and remaining 1 tablespoon oil together in now-empty bowl. Remove sheet from oven. Place apple between squash on sheet, cut side down. (Do not flip squash.) Return sheet to oven and continue to roast until apple is tender and squash is fully browned on bottoms (tops of squash will not be browned), about 8 minutes longer.

5. Using spatula, transfer squash and apple to shallow platter and spread into even layer. Drizzle vinaigrette over top. Serve warm or at room temperature.

Roasted Butternut Squash with Pear and Pancetta

Reduce salt for squash to ½ teaspoon. Substitute 1 teaspoon minced fresh thyme for parsley and 1 Bosc pear for apple. Add 3 ounces pancetta, cut into ½-inch pieces, to sheet with pears in step 4.

Roasted Beets with Lemon-Tahini Dressing

SERVES 4 TO 6

WHY THIS RECIPE WORKS Peeling and cutting beets before cooking them is less messy than trying to peel and cut warm beets. Plus, peeled and cut beets have more surface area to absorb flavors (we tossed ours with olive oil, smashed garlic, thyme sprigs, bay leaves, salt, and pepper before cooking) and are seasoned all the way through. Roasting the beets in a foil-covered baking pan with water created steam, which helped cook them evenly. Removing the foil once the beets were tender and continuing to roast them a little longer added savory browning to all those cut surfaces. A stir-together sauce of tahini, lemon juice, fresh thyme, and raw garlic was a perfect counterpoint to the sweet, earthy, roasted beets.

To ensure even cooking, we recommend using beets of similar size—roughly 2 to 3 inches in diameter. If your beets are larger, cut the wedges in half crosswise. Toast the sesame seeds in a dry skillet over medium heat until fragrant (about 3 minutes); immediately remove the skillet from the heat to prevent scorching.

Dressing

- 2 tablespoons tahini
- 2 tablespoons lemon juice
- 1 tablespoon extra-virgin olive oil
- 1 tablespoon water
- 1 teaspoon minced fresh thyme
- 1 garlic clove, minced
- ¼ teaspoon table salt

Beets

- 2 pounds beets, trimmed, peeled, and cut into ½-inch-thick wedges
- 3 tablespoons extra-virgin olive oil
- 4 garlic cloves, smashed and peeled
- 12 fresh thyme sprigs
- 2 bay leaves
- 1 teaspoon table salt
- ½ teaspoon pepper
- ¾ cup water
- 2 teaspoons sesame seeds, toasted
- 2 teaspoons minced fresh chives

1. For the Dressing Whisk all ingredients in medium bowl until smooth; set aside. (Dressing can be refrigerated for up to 2 days; stir to recombine and thin with water or lemon juice as needed before serving.)

2. For the Beets Adjust oven rack to middle position and heat oven to 450 degrees. Toss beets with oil, garlic, thyme sprigs, bay leaves, salt, and pepper in large bowl until evenly coated. Transfer beets to 13 by 9-inch baking pan. Pour water into pan; cover tightly with aluminum foil; and roast until beets can be easily pierced with paring knife, 1 to 1¼ hours.

3. Remove pan from oven. Carefully remove foil, letting steam escape away from you, and return pan to oven. Roast until edges of beets are beginning to caramelize, 15 to 20 minutes. Discard garlic, thyme sprigs, and bay leaves. Let beets cool for 20 minutes.

4. Spread dressing evenly over serving platter. Arrange beets on top of dressing, then sprinkle with sesame seeds and chives. Serve warm or at room temperature.

Fresh Tomato Galette

SERVES 4 TO 6

WHY THIS RECIPE WORKS "Galette" is the French term for a freeform, round crusty cake, generally with a savory filling. The idea of a rustic tomato galette is simple: slice tomatoes, season them, pile them onto flaky dough, fold the edges up, and bake until the crust is golden and crisp. To draw out the tomatoes' excess juice, we salted the slices and let them sit in a colander for just 30 minutes. We spread mustard and sprinkled Gruyère right onto the dough to water proof it before layering the tomato slices on top and finished with a sprinkle of Parmesan.

Sharp cheddar can be used in place of the Gruyère.

- 1½ cups (7½ ounces) all-purpose flour
- 2 teaspoons table salt, divided
- 10 tablespoons unsalted butter, cut into ½-inch pieces and chilled
- 6–7 tablespoons ice water
- 1½ pounds mixed tomatoes, cored and sliced ¼ inch thick
- 1 shallot, sliced thin
- 2 tablespoons extra-virgin olive oil
- 1 teaspoon minced fresh thyme
- 1 garlic clove, minced
- ¼ teaspoon pepper
- 2 teaspoons Dijon mustard
- 3 ounces Gruyère cheese, shredded (¾ cup)
- 2 tablespoons grated Parmesan cheese
- 1 large egg, lightly beaten
- 1 tablespoon chopped fresh basil

1. Process flour and ½ teaspoon salt in food processor until combined, about 3 seconds. Scatter butter over top and pulse until mixture resembles coarse crumbs, about 10 pulses. Transfer to large bowl. Sprinkle 6 tablespoons ice water over flour mixture. Using rubber spatula, stir and press dough until it sticks together, adding up to 1 tablespoon more ice water if dough doesn't come together.

2. Turn out dough onto lightly floured counter, form into 4-inch disk, wrap tightly in plastic wrap, and refrigerate for 1 hour. (Wrapped dough can be refrigerated for up to 2 days or frozen for up to 1 month.)

3. Toss tomatoes and 1 teaspoon salt together in second large bowl. Transfer tomatoes to colander and set in sink. Let tomatoes drain for 30 minutes.

4. Adjust oven rack to lower-middle position and heat oven to 375 degrees. Line rimmed baking sheet with parchment paper. Let chilled dough sit on counter to soften slightly, about 10 minutes, before rolling. Roll dough into 12-inch circle on lightly floured counter, then transfer to prepared sheet (dough may run up lip of sheet slightly; this is OK).

5. Shake colander well to rid tomatoes of excess juice. Combine tomatoes, shallot, oil, thyme, garlic, pepper, and remaining ½ teaspoon salt in now-empty bowl. Spread mustard over dough, leaving 1½-inch border. Sprinkle Gruyère in even layer over mustard. Shingle tomatoes and shallot on top of Gruyère in concentric circles, keeping within 1½-inch border. Sprinkle Parmesan over tomato mixture.

6. Carefully grasp 1 edge of dough and fold up about 1 inch over filling. Repeat around circumference of tart, overlapping dough every 2 inches, gently pinching pleated dough to secure. Brush folded dough with egg (you won't need it all).

7. Bake until crust is golden brown and tomatoes are bubbling, 45 to 50 minutes. Transfer sheet to wire rack and let galette cool for 10 minutes. Using metal spatula, loosen galette from parchment and carefully slide onto wire rack; let cool until just warm, about 20 minutes. Sprinkle with basil. Cut into wedges and serve.

Lentilles du Puy with Spinach and Crème Fraîche

SERVES 4 TO 6

WHY THIS RECIPE WORKS We were after a recipe simple enough to allow the lentilles du Puy, which are often referred to as the "caviar of lentils," to shine. To start, we gently cooked mirepoix in olive oil until the vegetables were just softened. We then added the lentils and simmered them in chicken broth until almost all the broth was absorbed and the softened lentils still held their shape. Finally, we folded in some spinach and a few spoonfuls of Dijon mustard, plus a luxurious dollop of crème fraîche.

You can substitute other French green lentils for the lentilles du Puy, but do not substitute other types of green lentils or black, brown, or red lentils—the cooking times of the other lentil varieties can vary greatly. For a vegetarian version, substitute vegetable broth for the chicken broth. If you can't find crème fraîche, sour cream works well.

- 1 tablespoon extra-virgin olive oil
- ½ cup finely chopped onion
- ¼ cup finely chopped carrot
- ¼ cup finely chopped celery
- ½ teaspoon table salt
- 2 cups chicken broth
- 1 cup dried lentilles du Puy, picked over and rinsed
  Hot water
- 2 ounces (2 cups) baby spinach
- 2 tablespoons Dijon mustard
- ¼ cup crème fraîche

1. Heat oil in large saucepan over medium heat until shimmering. Add onion, carrot, celery, and salt; cook until vegetables are tender, about 5 minutes.

2. Add broth and lentils and bring to simmer. Reduce heat to medium-low; cover; and cook, stirring occasionally, until lentils are tender but still hold their shape, about 30 minutes. (Add hot water, ¼ cup at a time, if saucepan becomes dry before lentils are cooked through.)

3. Gently fold in spinach and mustard. Let sit off heat for 5 minutes. Transfer to serving bowl and dollop with crème fraîche. Serve.

Fresh Tomato Galette

Lentilles du Puy with Spinach and Crème Fraîche

Sweet Corn Spoonbread
SERVES 6

WHY THIS RECIPE WORKS For a fluffy, soufflé-style sweet corn spoonbread with deep corn flavor, we focused on flavor, then texture. Sautéing the corn in butter, before steeping it in milk and pureeing it, ensured that the sweet corn flavor permeated our spoonbread. To make sure that the cornmeal didn't impart a gritty texture, we soaked it in the milk beforehand. And to guarantee a stable foam and an impressive rise, we beat the egg whites with a bit of cream of tartar.

You will need three ears of corn to yield 2 cups. Frozen corn, thawed and drained well, can also be used.

- 1 cup cornmeal
- 2¾ cups whole milk, divided
- 4 tablespoons unsalted butter
- 2 cups fresh corn
- 1 teaspoon sugar
- 1 teaspoon table salt
- ⅛ teaspoon cayenne pepper
- 3 large eggs, separated
- ¼ teaspoon cream of tartar

1. Adjust oven rack to middle position and heat oven to 400 degrees. Grease 1½-quart soufflé dish or 8-inch baking dish. Whisk cornmeal and ¾ cup milk in bowl until combined; set aside.

2. Melt butter in Dutch oven over medium-high heat. Cook corn until beginning to brown, about 3 minutes. Stir in remaining 2 cups milk, sugar, salt, and cayenne and bring to boil. Off heat, cover mixture and let steep for 15 minutes.

3. Transfer warm corn mixture to blender or food processor and puree until smooth. Return to pot and bring to boil. Reduce heat to low and add cornmeal mixture, whisking constantly, until thickened, 2 to 3 minutes; transfer to large bowl and let cool to room temperature, about 20 minutes. Once mixture is cool, whisk in egg yolks until combined.

4. Using stand mixer fitted with whisk, beat egg whites and cream of tartar on medium-low speed until foamy, about 1 minute. Increase speed to medium-high and whip until stiff peaks form, 3 to 4 minutes. Whisk one-third of whites into corn mixture, then gently fold in remaining whites until combined. Scrape mixture into prepared dish and transfer to oven. Reduce oven temperature to 350 degrees and bake until spoonbread is golden brown and has risen above rim of dish, about 45 minutes. Serve immediately.

Individual Sweet Corn Spoonbreads
To make individual spoonbreads, divide batter among 6 greased 7-ounce ramekins. Arrange ramekins on rimmed baking sheet and bake as directed, reducing cooking time to 30 to 35 minutes.

Egg Whites 101
Egg whites are most easily whipped in a very clean metal bowl with a pinch of cream of tartar, which promotes stabilization.

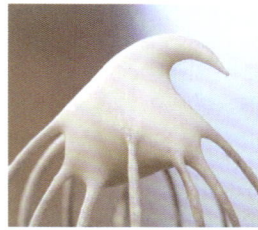

Soft Peaks
Soft peaks will droop slightly downward from tip of whisk or beater.

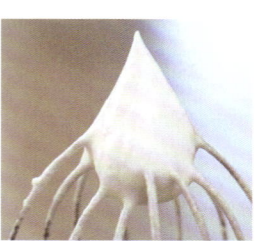

Stiff Peaks
Stiff peaks will stand up tall on their own.

Overwhipped
Overwhipped egg whites will look curdled and separated; if you reach this point, start over with new whites and clean bowl.

Spinach-Artichoke Dip
SERVES 10 TO 12

WHY THIS RECIPE WORKS To amplify the spinach and artichoke flavors in this dip, we swapped dull, fibrous frozen spinach for fresh, coarsely chopped baby spinach that we'd sautéed and tinny canned artichokes or frozen artichokes for bright, tender, marinated artichokes from a jar. Gouda's sweet and nutty flavor perfectly accentuated the subtle nuttiness of the artichokes, and it gave our dip a creamy, melty texture without causing it to congeal and turn stringy after cooling. Our streamlined preparation method calls for stirring all the ingredients together in one skillet before transferring the dip to a baking dish. After about 20 minutes in the oven, the top was golden brown and the edges were bubbling.

You will need one 12-ounce jar of marinated artichoke hearts to yield the 1⅓ cups called for here. You can substitute canned artichoke hearts if you can't find marinated. If you can find only 5-ounce packages of baby spinach, there's no need to buy a third package to make up the extra ounce; just make the dip with 10 ounces. Use the large holes of a box grater to shred the gouda and a rasp-style grater to grate the Parmesan. Serve with tortilla chips, crusty bread, pita chips, or vegetables.

- 1 tablespoon extra-virgin olive oil
- 3 garlic cloves, minced
- 11 ounces (11 cups) baby spinach, chopped coarse
- 8 ounces cream cheese, softened
- 6 ounces gouda cheese, shredded (1½ cups)
- 3 ounces Parmesan cheese, grated (1½ cups)
- 1⅓ cups marinated artichoke hearts, chopped
- 1 cup mayonnaise
- ¼ teaspoon pepper
- ⅛ teaspoon cayenne pepper

1. Adjust oven rack to middle position and heat oven to 400 degrees. Heat oil in 12-inch skillet over medium-high heat until shimmering. Add garlic and cook until fragrant, about 30 seconds. Add spinach, 1 handful at a time, allowing each to wilt slightly before adding next; cook until wilted and liquid has evaporated, about 4 minutes.

2. Off heat, add cream cheese and stir until melted and combined, about 1 minute. Stir in gouda, Parmesan, artichokes, mayonnaise, pepper, and cayenne until combined. Transfer to 2-quart baking dish and smooth top with rubber spatula.

3. Bake until spotty golden brown and bubbling around edges, about 22 minutes. Let cool for 10 minutes. Serve.

To Make Ahead At end of step 2, let dip cool completely, wrap in plastic wrap, and refrigerate for up to 2 days. When ready to serve, continue with step 3, increasing baking time by 10 minutes

Sweet Corn Spoonbread

Spinach-Artichoke Dip

tex-mex and more

- **380** Ultimate Spicy Beef Nachos
- **381** Ultimate Seven-Layer Dip
- **382** Chunky Guacamole
- **383** Huevos Rancheros
- **384** Sopa Seca
- **384** Arroz con Pollo
- **386** Garlic-Lime Fried Chicken
- **387** California-Style Fish Tacos
- **388** San Diego Fish Tacos
- **389** Ahi-Chile Tostadas
- **390** Shrimp Tacos
- **391** Easy Chicken Tacos
- **392** Carne Guisada
- **393** Puffy Tacos
- **394** Quesabirria Tacos
- **396** Gorditas
- **398** Citrus-Braised Pork Tacos
- **399** Pork Carnitas
- **400** Easier Chicken Chimichangas
- **401** Smoky Salsa Verde
- **402** New Mexican Bean-and-Cheese Turnovers with Green Chile
- **403** Tex-Mex Cheese Enchiladas
- **405** Easy Green Chile Chicken Enchiladas
- **406** Beef Enchiladas
- **406** Flank Steak in Adobo
- **408** Chicken Chilaquiles
- **409** Easy Chili con Carne
- **410** Five-Alarm Chili
- **411** Vegetarian Chili
- **412** Texas-Style Pinto Beans
- **413** Southwestern Tomato and Corn Salad
- **414** Skillet Corn with Mexican Chorizo
- **414** So-Cal Churros

Recipe Photos (clockwise from top left): Sopa Seca, Skillet Corn with Mexican Chorizo

Ultimate Spicy Beef Nachos

SERVES 8

WHY THIS RECIPE WORKS Some nacho recipes produce soggy chips loaded down with bland, greasy beef, dry beans, and cold strings of cheese. Instead, we wanted hearty nachos that are crisp, flavorful, and fresh. Boldly seasoning our beef with a mixture of spices and other flavorings caused the flavor to pop. While many nacho recipes call for cheddar cheese, we found it didn't melt nearly as well as pepper Jack, which melted smoothly and added a kick too.

Garnish the nachos with sour cream, chopped cilantro, and diced avocado.

Refried Beans
- ½ cup canned refried beans
- 3 tablespoons shredded pepper Jack cheese
- 1 tablespoon chopped canned jalapeños

Spicy Beef
- 2 teaspoons vegetable oil
- 1 small onion, chopped fine
- 3 garlic cloves, minced
- 1 tablespoon chili powder
- 1 teaspoon ground cumin
- ½ teaspoon dried oregano
- 1 teaspoon table salt
- 1 pound 90 percent lean ground beef
- 2 tablespoons tomato paste
- 1 teaspoon packed brown sugar
- 1½ teaspoons minced canned chipotle chile in adobo sauce, plus 1 teaspoon adobo sauce
- ½ cup water
- 2 teaspoons lime juice

- 1 (9.5-ounce) bag tortilla chips
- 1 pound pepper Jack cheese, shredded (4 cups)
- 2 jalapeño chiles, sliced into thin rings
- 1 recipe One-Minute Salsa (recipe follows)

1. Adjust oven rack to middle position and heat oven to 400 degrees.

2. For the Refried Beans Pulse ingredients in food processor until smooth, about 10 pulses. Transfer to bowl and cover with plastic wrap.

3. For the Spicy Beef Heat oil in large skillet over medium heat until shimmering. Cook onion until softened, about 4 minutes. Add garlic, chili powder, cumin, oregano, and salt and cook until fragrant, about 1 minute. Add beef and cook, breaking meat into small bits with wooden spoon and scraping pan bottom to prevent scorching, until no longer pink, about 5 minutes. Add tomato paste, sugar, chipotle, and adobo sauce and cook until paste begins to darken, about 1 minute. Add water, bring to simmer, and cook over medium-low until mixture is nearly dry, 5 to 7 minutes. Stir in lime juice and transfer mixture to plate lined with several layers of paper towels. Use more paper towels to blot up excess grease.

4. Spread half of chips on large ovensafe serving platter or in 13 by 9-inch baking dish. Dollop half of bean mixture over chips, then spread evenly. Scatter half of beef mixture over beans, top with 2 cups cheese and half of jalapeños. Repeat with remaining chips, beans, beef, cheese, and jalapeños. Bake until cheese is melted and just beginning to brown, 12 to 14 minutes. Serve with salsa.

One-Minute Salsa
MAKES ABOUT 1 CUP

Make sure to drain both the tomatoes and the jalapeños before processing. The salsa will keep for two days in the refrigerator. Season to taste before serving.

- ½ small red onion
- ¼ cup fresh cilantro leaves
- 2 tablespoons jarred jalapeños, drained
- 1 tablespoon lime juice
- 1 garlic clove, peeled
- ¼ teaspoon table salt
- 1 (14.5-ounce) can diced tomatoes, drained

Pulse onion, cilantro, jalapeños, lime juice, garlic, and salt in food processor until roughly chopped, about 5 pulses. Add tomatoes and pulse until chopped, about 2 pulses. Transfer mixture to fine-mesh strainer and drain briefly. Serve.

Ultimate Seven-Layer Dip

SERVES 8 TO 10

WHY THIS RECIPE WORKS With bold Southwestern flavors and an appealing ingredient list, seven-layer dip recipes sound like a hit. But most versions of this party classic assume that guests won't notice the messy layers and muted flavors. In our version, canned black beans stood in for refried beans, while garlic, chili powder, and lime juice added flavor. We found that sour cream on its own quickly watered down our dip, but combining it with cheese gave this layer more structure.

This recipe is usually served in a clear dish so you can see the layers. For a crowd, double the recipe and serve in a 13 by 9-inch glass baking dish. If you don't have time to make fresh guacamole as called for, simply mash three avocados with 3 tablespoons lime juice and ½ teaspoon salt.

- 4 large tomatoes, cored, seeded, and chopped fine
- 2 jalapeño chiles, stemmed, seeded, and minced
- 3 tablespoons chopped fresh cilantro
- 6 scallions (2 minced, 4 with green parts sliced thin and white parts discarded)
- 2 tablespoons plus 2 teaspoons lime juice (2 limes)
- ¼ teaspoon table salt, divided
- 1 (15-ounce) can black beans, drained but not rinsed
- 2 garlic cloves, minced
- ¾ teaspoon chili powder
- 1½ cups sour cream
- 1 pound pepper Jack cheese, shredded (4 cups)
- 1 recipe Chunky Guacamole (page 382)
- Tortilla chips

1. Combine tomatoes, jalapeños, cilantro, minced scallions, and 2 tablespoons lime juice in medium bowl. Stir in ⅛ teaspoon salt and let stand until tomatoes begin to soften, about 30 minutes. Strain mixture into bowl and discard liquid.

2. Pulse black beans, garlic, remaining 2 teaspoons lime juice, chili powder, and remaining ⅛ teaspoon salt in food processor until mixture resembles chunky paste, about 15 pulses. Transfer to bowl and wipe out food processor. Pulse sour cream and 2½ cups pepper Jack until smooth, about 15 pulses. Transfer to separate bowl.

Ultimate Spicy Beef Nachos

Ultimate Seven-Layer Dip

3. Spread bean mixture evenly over bottom of 8-inch square baking dish or 1-quart glass bowl. Spread sour cream mixture evenly over bean layer and sprinkle evenly with remaining 1½ cups cheese. Spread guacamole over cheese and top with tomato mixture. Sprinkle with sliced scallion greens and serve with tortilla chips. (Dip can be refrigerated for up to 24 hours. Let dip stand at room temperature for 1 hour before serving.)

Ultimate Smoky Seven-Layer Dip
Cook 4 slices bacon in 10-inch skillet over medium-high heat until crispy, about 8 minutes. Drain on paper towel–lined plate and crumble. Pulse 1 to 3 teaspoons minced canned chipotle chile in adobo sauce with black beans in step 2. Garnish dip with crumbled bacon along with scallions.

Seeding Jalapeños

Halve pepper lengthwise. Starting at end opposite stem, use melon baller to scoop down inside of each half.

Chunky Guacamole

Chunky Guacamole
MAKES ABOUT 3 CUPS

WHY THIS RECIPE WORKS The best guacamole starts with ripe avocados, but other ingredients often overwhelm their delicate flavor. Tasters liked the flavor of minced garlic in guacamole but thought raw onions were just too harsh. Instead, scallions contributed a mellower onion flavor. Steeping them in lime juice for a few minutes before combining them with the avocados mellowed their flavor even more. To provide some textural contrast to our guacamole, we chopped the avocados and then mashed just two-thirds of the chunks.

Preparing the guacamole ahead of time helps the flavors marry, but it should not be prepared more than 24 hours in advance. To prevent the dip from turning brown, press a sheet of plastic wrap directly onto the surface and refrigerate until ready to use. We prefer pebbly Hass avocados to the smoother Fuerte variety.

- 2 scallions, green and white parts separated and sliced thin
- 1 jalapeño chile, stemmed, seeded, and minced
- 1 small garlic clove, minced
- ¼ teaspoon finely grated lime zest plus 2 tablespoons juice
- 3 avocados, halved, pitted, and cubed
- 3 tablespoons chopped fresh cilantro
- Table salt

1. Combine scallion whites, jalapeño, garlic, and lime juice in large bowl. Let sit for 30 minutes.

2. Add two-thirds of avocado pieces to bowl with jalapeño mixture and mash with potato masher until smooth. Gently fold remaining avocado pieces into mashed avocado mixture. Gently stir in lime zest, scallion greens, and cilantro. Season with salt to taste. Serve.

Huevos Rancheros

SERVES 4

WHY THIS RECIPE WORKS Huevos rancheros has made its way northward from Mexico, becoming common on breakfast menus around the United States. To make this crowd-pleasing but involved dish of fried eggs, cheese, and tomato-chile sauce manageable for a group, we roasted the sauce components to brown the vegetables and replicate the char from a cast-iron skillet. We then transferred everything to a casserole dish and nestled the eggs into the sauce so that we could cook eight eggs at once. Moving this spicy dish of eggs and charred chiles to the oven gave us a perfectly timed meal that's not just for breakfast.

Use a heavyweight rimmed baking sheet; flimsy sheets will warp. Our winning sheet is the Nordic Ware Baker's Half Sheet. Serve with refried beans and hot sauce.

- 2 (28-ounce) cans diced tomatoes
- 1 tablespoon packed brown sugar
- 1 tablespoon lime juice
- 1 onion, chopped
- ½ cup chopped canned green chiles
- ¼ cup extra-virgin olive oil
- 3 tablespoons chili powder
- 4 garlic cloves, sliced thin
  Table salt and pepper
- 4 ounces pepper Jack cheese, shredded (1 cup)
- 8 large eggs
- 1 avocado, halved, pitted, and diced
- 3 scallions, sliced thin
- ⅓ cup minced fresh cilantro
- 8 (6-inch) corn tortillas, warmed

1. Adjust oven rack to middle position and heat oven to 500 degrees. Line rimmed baking sheet with parchment paper. Drain tomatoes in fine-mesh strainer set over bowl, pressing with rubber spatula to extract as much juice as possible. Reserve 1¾ cups tomato juice and discard remainder. Whisk sugar and lime juice into reserved tomato juice and set aside.

2. In separate bowl, combine onion, chiles, oil, chili powder, garlic, ½ teaspoon salt, and drained tomatoes. Transfer tomato mixture to prepared baking sheet and spread in even layer to edges of sheet. Roast until charred in spots, 35 to 40 minutes, stirring and redistributing into even layer halfway through baking. Reduce oven temperature to 400 degrees.

3. Transfer roasted tomato mixture to 13 by 9-inch baking dish and stir in tomato juice mixture. Season with salt and pepper to taste, then spread into even layer. Sprinkle pepper Jack over tomato mixture. Using spoon, hollow out 8 holes in tomato mixture in 2 rows. Crack 1 egg into each hole. Season eggs with salt and pepper.

4. Bake until whites are just beginning to set but still have some movement when dish is shaken, 13 to 16 minutes. Transfer dish to wire rack, tent loosely with aluminum foil, and let sit for 5 minutes. Spoon avocado over top, then sprinkle with scallions and cilantro. Serve with warm tortillas.

To Make Ahead The sauce can be made 24 hours in advance. Microwave until hot, about 2 minutes (stirring halfway), before transferring to baking dish and proceeding with recipe.

Huevos Rancheros

Sopa Seca

SERVES 4

WHY THIS RECIPE WORKS Sopa seca is a popular comfort food dish in many Mexican and Mexican American homes. It's built upon a base of fideos, which are short, thin, golden noodles similar to angel hair pasta. We simmered these fideos in a smoky, spicy, tomato-based sauce flavored with chipotle, chicken bouillon powder, and other spices. (Knorr brand bouillon is sometimes called the "secret ingredient" in sopa seca, providing the distinct salty, round flavor found in home-cooked versions.) To finish, we topped it off with classic fixings such as crema, avocado, queso fresco, and chicharrones.

Look for short, "broken" fideos pasta, about 1 inch in length, and not coiled noodles, which are also known as fideos. We developed this recipe using an 8-ounce package of fideos, but if all you can find is a 7-ounce package, there's no need to make up the extra ounce. If you can't find short fideos, substitute 8 ounces thin spaghetti or angel hair, broken into 1- to 2-inch lengths; loosely wrap pasta in dish towel and then press the bundle against the corner of the counter to break into short pieces. Knorr brand chicken bouillon is traditional; if you can't find the loose powder, you can crush two to three bouillon cubes and then measure 2 tablespoons. For a spicier dish, use the greater amount of chipotle chile.

- 8 ounces fideos (2 cups)
- 1/4 cup vegetable oil, divided
- 1 pound plum tomatoes, cored and quartered (4 to 6 tomatoes)
- 1 onion, chopped
- 2 garlic cloves, smashed and peeled
- 2 cups water, plus extra as needed
- 2 tablespoons chicken bouillon powder
- 1/2–1 tablespoon minced canned chipotle chile in adobo sauce
- 1 teaspoon dried oregano
- 1/2 teaspoon table salt
- 1/2 teaspoon pepper
- 1 avocado, halved, pitted, and sliced thin
- 1 1/2 ounces queso fresco, crumbled (1/3 cup)
- 1/2 cup Mexican crema
- 1/4 cup chopped fresh cilantro
- 1/2 cup crushed chicharrones (optional)

1. Heat fideos and 3 tablespoons oil in 12-inch nonstick skillet over medium-high heat, stirring constantly, until fideos are deep golden brown but not burnt, 4 to 5 minutes. Transfer fideos to large bowl; set aside. Wipe skillet clean with paper towels.

2. Heat remaining 1 tablespoon oil in now-empty skillet over medium heat until shimmering. Add tomatoes, onion, and garlic and cook until tomatoes are very soft and have released some of their juices, 8 to 10 minutes.

3. Process tomato mixture, water, bouillon powder, chipotle, oregano, salt, and pepper in blender until smooth, about 1 minute, scraping down sides of blender as needed. Transfer mixture to 8-cup liquid measuring cup; add extra water as needed to reach 5 cups.

4. Transfer tomato mixture to again-empty skillet. Using rubber spatula or wooden spoon, gently stir in fideos until fully submerged in tomato mixture. Spread fideos into even layer, and bring to simmer over medium-high heat. Reduce heat to low, cover, and simmer, stirring every 5 minutes, until fideos are tender and sauce is fully absorbed, 20 to 25 minutes, adjusting heat as needed to maintain very gentle simmer. Season with salt and pepper to taste.

5. Transfer sopa seca to serving bowls. Divide avocado, queso fresco, crema, and cilantro evenly over fideos. Sprinkle with chicharrones, if using. Serve.

Arroz con Pollo

SERVES 6

WHY THIS RECIPE WORKS Arroz con pollo is a classic Latin take on chicken and rice. For our version, we first created the dish's flavor backbone: a sofrito of onions, peppers, garlic, and spices. Next, after browning meaty skin-on chicken thighs, we used the rendered fat to soften chopped onion, toast the rice, and bloom the starring spice blend, sazón. We removed the skin from the thighs and finished cooking them nestled into the rice, studded with halved green olives, capers, and our zesty sofrito. We served our arroz con pollo with a drizzle of herby lemon sauce for a final punch of freshness.

Sazón is a spice blend common in Latin American cooking. We developed this recipe with Goya Sazón with Coriander and Annatto (or con Culantro y Achiote). It can be found in the Latin American aisle of most supermarkets; however, other brands will work. (One tablespoon of Goya Sazón equals about two packets.) If you can't find sazón, use our homemade version (recipe follows). You can substitute ¾ cup of chopped green bell pepper for the Cubanelle pepper. Allow the rice to rest for the full 15 minutes before lifting the lid to check it. Long-grain rice may be substituted for medium-grain, but the rice will be slightly less creamy.

- 1 cup fresh cilantro leaves and stems, chopped
- 1 onion, chopped (1 cup), divided
- 1 Cubanelle pepper, stemmed, seeded, and chopped (¾ cup)
- 5 garlic cloves, chopped coarse
- 1 teaspoon ground cumin
- ½ cup mayonnaise
- 3½ tablespoons lemon juice (2 lemons), divided plus lemon wedges for serving
- Table salt and pepper
- 6 (5- to 7-ounce) bone-in chicken thighs, trimmed
- 1 tablespoon vegetable oil
- 2 cups medium-grain rice, rinsed
- 1 tablespoon Goya Sazón with Coriander and Annatto
- 2½ cups chicken broth
- ¼ cup pimento-stuffed green olives, halved
- 2 tablespoons capers, rinsed
- 2 bay leaves
- ½ cup frozen peas, thawed (optional)

1. Adjust oven rack to middle position and heat oven to 350 degrees. Process cilantro, ½ cup onion, Cubanelle, garlic, and cumin in food processor until finely chopped, about 20 seconds, scraping down bowl as needed. Transfer sofrito to bowl.

2. Process mayonnaise, 1½ tablespoons lemon juice, ⅛ teaspoon salt, and 2 tablespoons sofrito in now-empty processor until almost smooth, about 30 seconds. Transfer mayonnaise-herb sauce to small bowl, cover, and refrigerate until ready to serve.

3. Pat chicken dry with paper towels and sprinkle with 1 teaspoon salt and ¼ teaspoon pepper. Heat oil in Dutch oven over medium heat until shimmering. Add chicken to pot skin side down and cook without moving it until skin is crispy and golden, 7 to 9 minutes. Flip chicken and continue to cook until golden on second side, 7 to 9 minutes longer. Transfer chicken to plate; discard skin.

4. Pour off all but 2 tablespoons fat from pot and heat over medium heat until shimmering. Add remaining ½ cup onion and cook until softened, 3 to 5 minutes. Stir in rice and Sazón and cook until edges of rice begin to turn translucent, about 2 minutes.

5. Stir in broth, olives, capers, bay leaves, remaining sofrito, remaining 2 tablespoons lemon juice, 1 teaspoon salt, and ½ teaspoon pepper, scraping up any browned bits. Nestle chicken into pot along with any accumulated juices and bring to vigorous simmer. Cover, transfer to oven, and bake for 20 minutes.

6. Transfer pot to wire rack and let stand, covered, for 15 minutes. Fluff rice with fork and stir in peas, if using. Discard bay leaves. Serve with mayonnaise-herb sauce and lemon wedges.

Homemade Sazón
MAKES 1 TABLESPOON

We add paprika in place of annatto for color. In addition to flavoring our Arroz con Pollo, this blend makes a great seasoning for eggs, beans, and fish.

- 1 teaspoon garlic powder
- ¾ teaspoon table salt
- ½ teaspoon paprika
- ½ teaspoon ground coriander
- ¼ teaspoon ground cumin

Combine all ingredients in bowl.

Arroz con Pollo

Garlic-Lime Fried Chicken

SERVES 4

WHY THIS RECIPE WORKS Fried chicken is a classic comfort food across Latin America. Each country has its own variation, but most feature a citrus and garlic marinade and a crunchy spiced coating. For our version, we used a combination of flour cut with cornstarch for a nice, light coating, and a little baking powder made it extra-crisp. Refrigerating the marinated dredged chicken before frying ensured that the coating set up nicely and thus stayed put on the chicken. Dipping the chicken in egg whites before coating it enhanced the lightness, and after frying, it was crunchy, juicy, and golden brown.

Don't let the chicken marinate any longer than 2 hours or it will toughen from the lime juice. Use a Dutch oven that holds 6 quarts or more for this recipe.

Marinade and Chicken

- 2 tablespoons kosher salt
- 6 garlic cloves, chopped coarse
- 1 tablespoon pepper
- 1 tablespoon ground cumin
- 2 teaspoons smoked paprika
- 2 teaspoons dried oregano
- 2 teaspoons grated lime zest plus ¼ cup juice (2 limes)
- 3 pounds bone-in chicken pieces (split breasts cut in half crosswise, drumsticks, thighs, and/or wings), trimmed

Coating

- 1¼ cups all-purpose flour
- ¾ cup cornstarch
- 1 tablespoon pepper
- 1 tablespoon granulated garlic
- 1 teaspoon baking powder
- 1 teaspoon white pepper
- 1 teaspoon kosher salt
- 1 teaspoon ground cumin
- ¼ teaspoon cayenne pepper
- 3 large egg whites, lightly beaten

- 3 quarts peanut or vegetable oil for frying

Garlic-Lime Fried Chicken

1. For the Marinade and Chicken Combine salt, garlic, pepper, cumin, paprika, oregano, and lime zest and juice in bowl. Add chicken and turn to coat thoroughly. Cover with plastic wrap and refrigerate for at least 1 hour or up to 2 hours.

2. For the Coating Whisk flour, cornstarch, pepper, granulated garlic, baking powder, white pepper, salt, cumin, and cayenne together in bowl. Place egg whites in shallow dish.

3. Set wire rack in rimmed baking sheet. Remove chicken from marinade and scrape off solids. Pat chicken dry with paper towels. Working with 1 piece at a time, dip chicken into egg whites to thoroughly coat, letting excess drip back into dish. Dredge chicken in flour mixture, pressing to adhere. Transfer chicken to prepared wire rack and refrigerate for at least 30 minutes or up to 2 hours.

4. Add oil to large Dutch oven until it measures about 2 inches deep and heat over medium-high heat to 325 degrees. Add half of chicken to hot oil and fry until breasts register 160 degrees and drumsticks/thighs register 175 degrees, 13 to 16 minutes. Adjust burner, if necessary, to maintain oil temperature between 300 and 325 degrees. Transfer chicken to second wire rack set in second rimmed baking sheet. Return oil to 325 degrees and repeat with remaining chicken. Serve.

California-Style Fish Tacos

SERVES 6

WHY THIS RECIPE WORKS We wanted our California-style fish tacos to be light, fresh, and simple, with a perfect balance of flavors and textures. An ultrathin beer batter using a combination of flour, cornstarch, and baking powder proved to be ideal for getting a light, crispy coating on the delicate white fish. Quick-pickled onions and jalapeños added tart spiciness, and tossing shredded cabbage with the pickling liquid just before serving added flavor without overcomplicating the dish. Lime juice and sour cream added tang to the traditional creamy white sauce.

Light-bodied American lagers, such as Budweiser, work best here. Cod, haddock, or halibut are good choices for the fish. Cut the fish on a slight bias if your fillets aren't quite 4 inches wide. You should end up with about 24 pieces of fish. Serve with green salsa, if desired.

Pickled Onions
- 1 small red onion, halved and sliced thin
- 2 jalapeño chiles, stemmed and sliced into thin rings
- 1 cup white wine vinegar
- 2 tablespoons lime juice
- 1 tablespoon sugar
- 1 teaspoon table salt

Cabbage
- 3 cups shredded green cabbage
- ¼ cup pickling liquid from pickled onions
- ½ teaspoon table salt
- ½ teaspoon pepper

White Sauce
- ½ cup mayonnaise
- ½ cup sour cream
- 2 tablespoons lime juice
- 2 tablespoons milk

California-Style Fish Tacos

Fish
- 2 pounds skinless white-flesh fish fillets, cut crosswise into 4 by 1-inch strips
  Table salt and pepper
- ¾ cup all-purpose flour
- ¼ cup cornstarch
- 1 teaspoon baking powder
- 1 cup beer
- 1 quart peanut or vegetable oil for frying

- 24 (6-inch) corn tortillas, warmed
- 1 cup fresh cilantro leaves

1. For the Pickled Onions Combine onion and jalapeños in medium bowl. Bring vinegar, lime juice, sugar, and salt to boil in small saucepan. Pour vinegar mixture over onion mixture and let sit for at least 30 minutes. (Pickled onions can be made and refrigerated up to 2 days in advance.)

2. For the Cabbage Toss all ingredients together in bowl.

3. For the White Sauce Whisk all ingredients together in bowl. (Sauce can be made and refrigerated up to 2 days in advance.)

4. For the Fish Adjust oven rack to middle position and heat oven to 200 degrees. Set wire rack inside rimmed baking sheet. Pat fish dry with paper towels and season with salt and pepper. Whisk flour, cornstarch, baking powder, and 1 teaspoon salt together in large bowl. Add beer and whisk until smooth. Transfer fish to batter and toss until evenly coated.

5. Add oil to large Dutch oven until it measures about ¾ inch deep and heat over medium-high heat to 350 degrees. Working with 5 to 6 pieces at a time, remove fish from batter, allowing excess to drip back into bowl, and add to hot oil, briefly dragging fish along surface of oil to prevent sticking. Adjust burner, if necessary, to maintain oil temperature between 325 and 350 degrees. Fry fish, stirring gently to prevent pieces from sticking together, until golden brown and crispy, about 2 minutes per side. Transfer fish to prepared wire rack and place in oven to keep warm. Return oil to 350 degrees and repeat with remaining fish.

6. Divide fish evenly among tortillas. Top with pickled onions, cabbage, white sauce, and cilantro. Serve.

San Diego Fish Tacos

SERVES 4 TO 6

WHY THIS RECIPE WORKS Our version of San Diego–style fish tacos is inspired by tacos served at Karina's Cantina in downtown San Diego. We chose cod for our tacos because it's flavorful, sturdy, and goes well with zarandeado sauce—an assertive mixture of mayonnaise, sour cream, mustard, a variety of chiles, and other ingredients. We sautéed the cod in strips with the zarandeado sauce; as the sauce reduced, it imparted its color and complex heat to the fish. Shredded cabbage, chopped tomato, cilantro, more zarandeado sauce, pickled red onion, and thinly sliced avocado finished off the tacos with style.

Make sure to prepare all your taco fixings before cooking the fish. Use a mandoline to slice the cabbage as thin as possible. The combination of red and green cabbage is for aesthetic reasons; if preferred, you can use a single variety of cabbage. Other fish, such as snapper, bass, haddock, or halibut, can be substituted for the cod. Other varieties of Mexican hot sauces can be substituted for the Tapatío.

Zarandeado Sauce
- ⅔ cup mayonnaise
- ⅓ cup sour cream
- 1 chipotle chile in adobo sauce
- 1 arbol chile, seeded
- 1 tablespoon Tapatío hot sauce
- 1 tablespoon beer
- 1 tablespoon yellow mustard
- 1 garlic clove, chopped
- ¾ teaspoon soy sauce
- ¾ teaspoon Worcestershire sauce
- ½ teaspoon Mexican oregano
- ¼ teaspoon pepper
- ¼ teaspoon kosher salt

Fish
- 4 (6- to 8-ounce) cod fillets, each cut lengthwise into 3 pieces
- 1½ teaspoons kosher salt
- ½ teaspoon pepper
- ¼ cup all-purpose flour
- 2 tablespoons vegetable oil, divided
- 2 tablespoons unsalted butter, divided

Tacos
- 1½ cups finely shredded red cabbage
- 1½ cups finely shredded green cabbage
- 12 corn tortillas, warmed
- 1 large tomato, chopped fine
- ¼ cup coarsely chopped cilantro leaves and stems
- 1 recipe Pickled Red Onion (recipe follows)
- 1 avocado, sliced thin

1. For the Zarandeado Sauce Process all ingredients in blender until smooth, about 20 seconds. Reserve 6 tablespoons sauce for cooking cod. Sauce can be prepared and refrigerated up to 2 days in advance.

2. For the Fish Adjust oven rack to middle position and heat oven to 200 degrees. Set wire rack in rimmed baking sheet. Sprinkle cod with salt and pepper. Place flour in shallow dish. Dredge cod in flour, shaking to remove excess, and transfer to large plate.

3. Heat 1 tablespoon oil in 12-inch nonstick skillet over medium-high heat until just smoking. Add 1 tablespoon butter and cook until foaming subsides. Add 6 pieces cod to skillet and cook, without moving them, for 2 minutes.

4. Drizzle cod with 3 tablespoons reserved sauce and then, using fish spatula, gently flip pieces. Shake skillet gently to distribute sauce and let cod continue to cook until just cooked through, 1 to 2 minutes longer. Remove skillet from heat and, using spatula, transfer cod to prepared wire rack.

5. Transfer cod to oven to keep warm. Wipe out skillet with paper towels and repeat with remaining 1 tablespoon oil, 1 tablespoon butter, 6 pieces cod, and 3 tablespoons reserved sauce.

6. For the Tacos Combine red and green cabbage in bowl. Build tacos by placing 1 piece of cod in center of each tortilla, followed by cabbage, tomato, cilantro, sauce, pickled onion, and avocado. Serve immediately.

Pickled Red Onion
SERVES 6 TO 8 (MAKES ABOUT 1½ CUPS)

Use a baseball-size onion for this recipe. Cider vinegar or red wine vinegar can be substituted for the distilled white vinegar.

- 1   red onion, halved and sliced thin
- 1   cup distilled white vinegar
- ⅓   cup sugar
- 1   teaspoon kosher salt

Place onion in medium bowl. Bring vinegar, sugar, and salt to simmer in small saucepan over medium-high heat, stirring occasionally, until sugar dissolves. Pour vinegar mixture over onion, pressing onion below surface of liquid. Let onion cool completely, about 30 minutes, stirring occasionally. (Pickled onion can be refrigerated for up to 1 week.)

Ahi-Chile Tostadas
SERVES 4

WHY THIS RECIPE WORKS These tostadas are a favorite from the Mariscos German Beyer food truck in San Diego, owned by Jorge Fuentes. A fresh spin on aguachile (which means "chile water" in Spanish)—a preparation that originated in Sinaloa, Mexico, in which fish (often shrimp) is quickly marinated in lime juice, chiles, and sometimes additional aromatics—these tostadas feature tender morsels of sashimi-grade tuna and sweet-tart pineapple. We tossed the fish and fruit (along with cucumber, onion, and serrano chile) in a punchy marinade containing Jugo seasoning, which is concentrated and has a subtle sweetness that makes it taste a bit like dark soy sauce. We topped the tostadas with sliced avocado.

San Diego Fish Tacos

Ahi-Chile Tostadas

You will need 1 full pound of trimmed tuna for this recipe. If the fish you're purchasing has any sinewy belly or bloodline attached, consider buying a little extra to account for trimming away and discarding those parts. The coarse flake sea salt in the ahi-chile is intended to add texture in addition to salinity. If substituting Diamond Crystal Kosher Salt, lower the amount to 2 teaspoons; if substituting Morton Kosher Salt, reduce the amount to 1½ teaspoons; if using table salt, reduce the amount to 1 teaspoon. Do not add the lime juice to the tuna until just before serving, because it will immediately begin cooking the fish.

Tostadas

- 2 cups vegetable oil for frying
- 4 (6-inch) corn tortillas
- ½ teaspoon kosher salt, divided

Ahi-Chile

- 1 pound trimmed sushi-grade ahi or bluefin tuna, cut into ¾-inch pieces
- ¾ cup ½-inch fresh pineapple pieces
- 3 ounces English cucumber, peeled, halved lengthwise, and sliced thin (½ cup)
- ½ cup thinly sliced red onion
- ¼ cup extra-virgin olive oil
- ½–1 serrano chile, seeded, sliced into thin rounds
- 1 tablespoon flake sea salt
- 1 teaspoon pepper
- ½ teaspoon Jugo Seasoning Sauce
- 3 tablespoons plus 2 teaspoons lime juice (2 limes)
- 8 thin slices avocado

1. For the Tostadas Line baking sheet with triple layer of paper towels. Heat oil in medium saucepan over medium-high heat to 350 degrees.

2. Place 1 tortilla in hot oil and press flat with potato masher or tongs for 60 seconds. Flip tortilla and fry, without pressing, until stiff and very lightly browned, about 30 seconds. Transfer tostada to prepared sheet and sprinkle with ⅛ teaspoon kosher salt. Repeat with remaining tortillas and kosher salt. Let tostadas cool completely, about 10 minutes. (Tostadas can be stored in zipper-lock bag for up to 2 days.)

3. For the Ahi-Chile Combine tuna, pineapple, cucumber, onion, oil, serrano, sea salt, pepper, and Jugo in medium bowl.

4. To serve, place 1 tostada on each of 4 individual serving plates. Stir lime juice into tuna mixture until fully incorporated. Divide ahi-chile evenly among tostadas, then top each with 2 avocado slices. Serve immediately.

On the Road: Mariscos Magic

Twenty minutes from downtown San Diego, Mariscos German Beyer food truck trades in savory fish tacos, lime-soused aguachiles, and colorful ceviches. Owner Jorge Fuentes has been in the mariscos (seafood) business since 1997. He ran a successful restaurant in Tijuana, Mexico, for four years but decided to close it when he got married. In 2005, Fuentes and a partner (the "German" in Mariscos German Beyer) turned to the food-truck business. While food trucks were already big in San Diego, Fuentes says theirs was one of the first trucks to focus entirely on mariscos (other mariscos places were sit-down restaurants.) "It kicked off right away. We had a line of people all the time," Fuentes says.

Shrimp Tacos

SERVES 4 TO 6

WHY THIS RECIPE WORKS Our goal was to combine the best parts of a taco and a quesadilla—crisped corn tortillas, gooey cheese, and a fiesta of shrimp. To do this without time-consuming stovetop batch cooking, we placed corn tortillas on baking sheets and topped them with cheese and a quick-cooked shrimp filling, baking them until the tortillas crisped and the cheese melted. To give our shrimp filling a secret boost, we stirred in some ketchup. This gave the sauce extra body, subtle sweetness, and a vinegary punch. Topping with fresh ingredients just before serving gave us the vibrancy of a taco with the warmth and comfort of a quesadilla.

We developed this recipe using Mission White Corn Tortillas, Restaurant Style, but any 100 percent corn tortillas will work here. Mexican hot sauces, such as Valentina Salsa Picante and Tapatío Salsa Picante, pair best with these tacos. For a spicier taco filling, reserve the jalapeño seeds and add them to the tomato mixture in step 1.

Shrimp Tacos

- 2 tomatoes, cored and chopped
- 1 small onion, chopped fine
- 1 jalapeño chile, stemmed, seeded, and minced
- 2 tablespoons ketchup
- 1 tablespoon lime juice, plus lime wedges for serving
- 2 garlic cloves, minced
- Table salt and pepper
- 1 pound large shrimp (26 to 30 per pound), peeled, deveined, and tails removed
- 5 tablespoons vegetable oil, divided
- 12 (6-inch) corn tortillas
- 8 ounces Monterey Jack cheese, shredded (2 cups)
- Shredded iceberg lettuce
- Diced avocado
- Chopped fresh cilantro
- Hot sauce

1. Adjust oven rack to lowest position and heat oven to 450 degrees. Combine tomatoes, onion, jalapeño, ketchup, lime juice, garlic, 1 teaspoon salt, and ¼ teaspoon pepper in large bowl; set aside. Cut shrimp into ½-inch pieces.

2. Heat 1 tablespoon oil in 12-inch skillet over medium-high heat until shimmering. Add tomato mixture and cook until liquid is slightly thickened and tomatoes begin to break down, 5 to 7 minutes. Reduce heat to medium, stir in shrimp, and cook until shrimp are just opaque, about 2 minutes.

3. Brush 2 rimmed baking sheets with 2 tablespoons oil (1 tablespoon per sheet). Arrange tortillas in single layer on prepared sheets (6 tortillas per sheet). Brush tops of tortillas with remaining 2 tablespoons oil. Divide Monterey Jack evenly among tortillas, then top with shrimp mixture. Bake, 1 sheet at a time, until cheese melts and edges of tortillas just begin to brown and crisp, 7 to 9 minutes.

4. Garnish with lettuce, avocado, cilantro, and hot sauce, then fold tacos in half. Transfer tacos to platter. Serve, passing lime wedges separately.

Easy Chicken Tacos

SERVES 6

WHY THIS RECIPE WORKS We like the convenience of boneless, skinless chicken breasts in tacos, but they can be dry. After trying a variety of cooking methods, we found that poaching produced meat that was tender and moist. Chipotle chiles gave our poaching liquid a smoky, full-bodied flavor and orange juice offered a touch of sweetness that tempered its vivid acidity. For more robust flavor, we called on two kitchen staples: Worcestershire mimicked the complex flavor of dark meat, and mustard added sharpness that balanced the sweet orange juice and smoky chipotle.

To warm the tortillas, wrap them in foil and heat them in a 350-degree oven for 15 minutes. Top the tacos with shredded lettuce, grated cheese, diced avocado, chopped tomato, and sour cream.

- 3 tablespoons unsalted butter
- 4 garlic cloves, minced
- 2 teaspoons minced canned chipotle chile in adobo sauce
- ¾ cup chopped fresh cilantro, divided
- ½ cup orange juice
- 1 tablespoon Worcestershire sauce
- 4 (6-ounce) boneless, skinless chicken breasts, trimmed
- 1 teaspoon yellow mustard
- Table salt and pepper
- 12 (6-inch) flour tortillas

TEX-MEX AND MORE   391

1. Melt butter in large skillet over medium-high heat. Add garlic and chipotle and cook until fragrant, about 30 seconds. Stir in ½ cup cilantro, orange juice, and Worcestershire and bring to boil. Add chicken and simmer, covered, over medium-low heat until meat registers 160 degrees, 10 to 15 minutes, flipping chicken halfway through cooking. Transfer to plate and tent with aluminum foil.

2. Increase heat to medium-high and cook until liquid is reduced to ¼ cup, about 5 minutes. Off heat, whisk in mustard. Using 2 forks, shred chicken into bite-size pieces and return to skillet. Add remaining ¼ cup cilantro to skillet and toss until well combined. Season with salt and pepper to taste. Serve with tortillas.

Shredding Chicken

Hold 1 fork in each hand, with tines facing down. Insert tines into chicken and gently pull forks away from each other, breaking meat apart and into long thin shreds.

Easy Chicken Tacos

Carne Guisada

SERVES 8 TO 10

WHY THIS RECIPE WORKS Carne guisada is a bold and satisfying beef, tomato, and potato stew eaten in many Latin American countries. To re-create the Mexican-style version of this comfort food enjoyed in Texas, we used a delicious mix of chili powder, oregano, cumin, and coriander in place of fresh and dried chiles. Using chicken broth for the braising liquid really let the tender beef chuck shine, and adding the potatoes and bell peppers partway through cooking guaranteed tender and intact vegetables. Using less liquid and adding some flour gave us the perfect texture, making it equally delicious as a taco filling or served with beans and rice.

Note that you are browning only half the beef in step 1. If your Dutch oven holds less than 6 quarts, you may need to brown the beef in batches to avoid overcrowding the pot. This recipe yields enough filling for about 24 tacos.

- 3 pounds boneless beef chuck-eye roast, trimmed and cut into 1-inch pieces
  Table salt and pepper
- 2 tablespoons vegetable oil
- 2 onions, chopped
- 2 tablespoons tomato paste
- 4 garlic cloves, minced
- 1 tablespoon chili powder
- 1 tablespoon dried oregano
- 2 teaspoons ground coriander
- 1½ teaspoons ground cumin
- 1 tablespoon all-purpose flour
- 1 (14.5-ounce) can diced tomatoes, drained
- 1 cup chicken broth
- 1 pound Yukon Gold potatoes, peeled and cut into ½-inch pieces
- 2 green bell peppers, stemmed, seeded, and cut into ¼-inch strips
- 24 flour tortillas, warmed
  Fresh cilantro leaves
  Lime wedges

1. Adjust oven rack to lower-middle position and heat oven to 325 degrees. Pat beef dry with paper towels and season with salt and pepper. Heat oil in Dutch oven

Carne Guisada

Puffy Tacos
SERVES 6 TO 8

WHY THIS RECIPE WORKS Puffy taco fans in San Antonio, Texas, cite Diana Barrios-Treviño's restaurant, Los Barrios, as having the best in the city. Determined to recreate a similar version, instead of using the traditional masa de maíz (finely ground hominy) we used the more widely available masa harina (dried masa flour) for our tortilla dough. Pressing the dough with a clear pie plate allowed us to gauge the diameter and to get a consistent thickness. Using a large saucepan containing just 2 quarts of oil made our taco shell prep much easier. For a flavorful filling, picadillo made with ground beef, green bell pepper, onion, garlic, and cumin fit the bill.

We used Maseca Instant Masa Corn Flour for our taco shells. The dough should not be sticky and should have the texture of Play-Doh. If the dough cracks or falls apart when pressing the tortillas, just reroll and press again.

Picadillo
- 12 ounces 85 percent lean ground beef
- ½ russet potato (4 ounces), peeled and cut into ¼-inch pieces
- Table salt and pepper
- 1 onion, chopped fine
- 1 small green bell pepper, stemmed, seeded, and chopped fine
- 3 garlic cloves, minced
- 1½ teaspoons ground cumin
- 2 teaspoons all-purpose flour
- ¾ cup water

Taco Shells
- 2½ cups (10 ounces) masa harina
- 1 teaspoon table salt
- 1⅔ cups warm water
- 2 quarts vegetable oil

Shredded iceberg lettuce
Chopped tomato
Shredded sharp cheddar cheese
Hot sauce

over medium-high heat until just smoking. Add half of beef and cook until browned on all sides, 7 to 10 minutes; transfer to plate.

2. Reduce heat to medium-low, add onions and 1 teaspoon salt to pot, and cook until softened, about 5 minutes. Stir in tomato paste, garlic, chili powder, oregano, coriander, and cumin and cook until fragrant, about 30 seconds. Stir in flour and cook for 1 minute. Stir in tomatoes and broth and bring to simmer, scraping up any browned bits. Stir in all of beef and any accumulated juices. Cover, transfer pot to oven, and cook for 1½ hours.

3. Remove pot from oven and stir in potatoes and bell peppers. Cover, return pot to oven, and continue to cook until beef and potatoes are tender, about 45 minutes longer.

4. Season with salt and pepper to taste. Spoon small amount of stew into center of each tortilla, top with cilantro, and serve with lime wedges.

TEX-MEX AND MORE

Puffy Tacos

5. Set wire rack in rimmed baking sheet and line rack with triple layer of paper towels. Add oil to large saucepan until it measures 2½ inches deep and heat over medium-high heat to 375 degrees.

6. When oil comes to temperature, enclose 1 dough ball at a time in split bag. Using clear pie plate (so you can see size of tortilla), press dough flat into 6-inch circle (about ⅛ inch thick).

7. Carefully remove tortilla from plastic and drop into hot oil. Fry tortilla until it puffs up, 15 to 20 seconds. Using 2 metal spatulas, carefully flip tortilla. Immediately press down in center of tortilla with 1 spatula to form taco shape, submerging tortilla into oil while doing so. Using second spatula, spread top of tortilla open about 1½ inches. Fry until golden brown, about 60 seconds. Adjust burner, if necessary, to maintain oil temperature between 350 and 375 degrees.

8. Transfer taco shell to prepared rack and place upside down to drain. Return oil to 375 degrees and repeat with remaining dough balls.

9. Divide picadillo evenly among taco shells, about ¼ cup each. Serve immediately, passing lettuce, tomato, cheddar, and hot sauce separately.

Quesabirria Tacos

SERVES 4 TO 6

WHY THIS RECIPE WORKS These crispy, cheesy, meaty tacos were inspired by those served at Rollies Mexican Patio in Tucson, Arizona. Flavoring shredded beef with garlic, spices, and guajillo chiles brought spice to the meat and the broth. Melty mozzarella complemented the beef, while cilantro and red onion balanced the richness—all wrapped up in tortillas cooked until crisp in chile-infused fat. Dunking these tacos into the broth before each bite ensured none of the hard-earned flavor was wasted.

We prefer not to trim the meat because we skim the chile-infused fat from the top of the broth after braising and use it to crisp the tacos. However, while shredding the meat, it is easy to remove any unwanted strands of fat. About 6 dried guajillo chiles should give you the 1½ ounces needed for this recipe. You should have enough meat for 12 or more tacos and for our Birria Ramen (recipe follows). If you can't serve these tacos immediately, keep them warm in a 200-degree oven. These tacos can also be cooked on a preheated griddle over medium heat.

1. For the Picadillo Combine beef, potato, 1 teaspoon pepper, and ¾ teaspoon salt in 12-inch nonstick skillet. Cook over medium-high heat until meat and potatoes begin to brown, 6 to 8 minutes, breaking up meat with spoon. Add onion and bell pepper and cook until softened, 4 to 6 minutes. Add garlic and cumin and cook until fragrant, about 30 seconds.

2. Stir in flour and cook for 1 minute. Stir in water and bring to boil. Reduce heat to medium-low and simmer until thickened slightly, about 1 minute. Season with salt and pepper to taste. Remove from heat, cover, and keep warm.

3. For the Taco Shells Mix masa harina and salt together in medium bowl. Stir in warm water with rubber spatula. Using your hands, knead mixture in bowl until it comes together fully (dough should be soft and tacky, not sticky), about 30 seconds. Cover dough with damp dish towel and let rest for 5 minutes.

4. Divide dough into 12 equal portions, about ¼ cup each, then roll each into smooth ball between your hands. Transfer to plate and keep covered with damp dish towel. Cut sides of 1-gallon zipper-lock bag, leaving bottom seam intact.

394   The Complete Cook's Country TV Show Cookbook

Birria

- 3½ pounds boneless beef chuck roast or short ribs, untrimmed, cut into 2- to 3-inch pieces
- 2 quarts water
- 1½ ounces dried guajillo chiles, stemmed and seeded
- 1 onion, quartered
- ¼ cup vegetable oil
- 8 garlic cloves, smashed and peeled
- 2 tablespoons paprika
- 4 teaspoons onion powder
- 4 teaspoons granulated garlic
- 4 teaspoons table salt
- 1 tablespoon Mexican oregano
- 1 tablespoon ground coriander
- 2 teaspoons pepper
- ½ teaspoon ground cinnamon
- 4 bay leaves

Tacos

- 12 (6-inch) yellow corn tortillas
- 12 ounces block mozzarella cheese, shredded (3 cups)
- 1 cup chopped red onion
- 1 cup coarsely chopped fresh cilantro, plus extra for serving

1. For the Birria Combine all ingredients in Dutch oven and bring to boil over high heat. Cover; reduce heat to medium-low; and simmer until meat is tender, about 2½ hours. Off heat, let meat rest in broth for 30 minutes. Using ladle, skim fat from surface of birria broth and transfer it to shallow dish or wide-mouthed bowl; set aside.

2. Using tongs or slotted spoon, transfer meat to large bowl. Using tongs or potato masher, smash meat until finely shredded; set aside.

3. Using immersion blender, process birria broth mixture until smooth, about 3 minutes. (If using jar blender, fill only halfway for each batch, especially if broth is hot. Process until smooth, about 20 seconds per batch.) Strain processed broth through fine-mesh strainer set over large saucepan; discard solids.

4. Stir 2 cups birria broth into shredded birria meat. Season with salt and pepper to taste and cover with aluminum foil to keep warm. Season remaining broth with salt and pepper to taste and place over low heat to keep warm.

5. For the Tacos Drag 1 side of 3 tortillas through reserved birria fat and place tortillas in 12-inch nonstick skillet, fat side down (tortillas will overlap slightly). Top each tortilla evenly with ¼ cup mozzarella. Spread scant ¼ cup birria meat over half of each tortilla. Cook over medium heat until most of cheese has melted, 2 to 3 minutes.

Quesabirria Tacos

6. Sprinkle red onion and cilantro to taste over each taco, then fold nonmeat half of tortilla over meat using spatula and tongs. Cook tacos until crisp on both sides, 1 to 2 minutes per side. Transfer tacos to serving dishes. Wipe skillet clean with paper towels. Repeat with remaining tortillas, fat, mozzarella, meat, red onion, and cilantro. (Extra meat can be refrigerated for up to 4 days.)

7. Portion ½ cup warm birria broth into each of 4 to 6 small crocks (1 for each person) and sprinkle with cilantro to taste. (Extra broth can be refrigerated for up to 4 days.) Serve tacos with broth; dunk tacos in broth before each bite.

Birria Ramen
SERVES 2

WHY THIS RECIPE WORKS This deeply comforting soup is a surprising combination of elements of traditional Mexican beef birria tacos and Japanese ramen noodle soup. Inspired by the birria ramen served by Chef-Owner Mateo Otero at Rollies Mexican Patio in Tucson, Arizona, the broth is the chile-and-spice-infused braising liquid used

TEX-MEX AND MORE 395

Birria Ramen

2. Meanwhile, cook ramen noodles according to package instructions (without seasoning packets). Drain noodles and divide between 2 deep serving bowls. Top with broth, meat, cabbage, cilantro, scallions, and jalapeño. Serve.

Gorditas

SERVES 6

WHY THIS RECIPE WORKS Inspired by the gorditas we had at Saenz Gorditas in Las Cruces, New Mexico, we combined 5 cups of corn flour (masa harina) with just the right amount of water to form a soft, putty-like dough and kneaded in a handful of shredded Colby Jack cheese for extra savoriness. This helped us avoid dry and crumbly or wet and pasty corn cakes. A version of picadillo—a mixture of ground beef, cubed potato, and plenty of seasoning—was the perfect fit as a filling. We like to further stuff the gorditas (gordita means "little fat one" in Spanish) with shredded iceberg lettuce and diced tomatoes for freshness and then top it all off with hot sauce and more tangy shredded Colby Jack cheese to make them even tastier.

We developed this recipe using Maseca Instant Corn Masa Flour. Monterey Jack or cheddar cheese can be substituted for the Colby Jack. Add hot sauce, shredded iceberg lettuce, diced tomatoes, and shredded cheese to your filled gorditas, if desired.

Filling

- 1 pound 85 percent lean ground beef
- 1 russet potato, peeled and cut into ¼-inch pieces
- 1 teaspoon table salt
- 1 teaspoon pepper
- 1 onion, chopped fine
- 1 tomato, cored and chopped fine
- 3 garlic cloves, minced
- 1½ teaspoons ground cumin
- 2 teaspoons all-purpose flour
- ¾ cup water

Dough

- 5 cups (20 ounces) masa harina
- 2 teaspoons table salt
- 3⅔ cups water, room temperature
- 3 ounces Colby Jack cheese, shredded (¾ cup)
- 6 cups vegetable oil

to slow-cook beef chuck for another Rollies specialty, quesabirria tacos. Tender ramen noodles were added to the broth and then topped with shredded beef, chopped cabbage, cilantro, scallions, and jalapeño.

You can modify the toppings to suit your taste. This recipe can easily be doubled.

- 3 cups birria broth from Quesabirria Tacos (page 394)
- ½ cup birria meat from Quesabirria Tacos (page 394)
- 2 (3-ounce) packages instant ramen noodles, seasoning packets reserved for another use
- ½ cup chopped cabbage, cut into ¼-inch pieces
- ½ cup coarsely chopped fresh cilantro
- 2 scallions, sliced thin
- 1 jalapeño chile, sliced into thin rings

1. Heat birria broth in medium saucepan over medium-high heat until just simmering. Cover and keep warm over low heat. Heat birria meat in skillet or microwave, stirring occasionally, until hot, about 5 minutes.

396   *The Complete Cook's Country TV Show Cookbook*

1. For the Filling Combine beef, potato, salt, and pepper in 12-inch nonstick skillet. Cook over medium-high heat until beef and potato begin to brown, 6 to 8 minutes, breaking up meat with wooden spoon. Add onion and tomato and cook until softened, 4 to 6 minutes. Add garlic and cumin and cook until fragrant, about 30 seconds.

2. Stir in flour and cook for 1 minute. Stir in water and bring to boil. Cook until slightly thickened, about 1 minute. Off heat, season with salt and pepper to taste. Cover and set aside.

3. For the Dough Line baking sheet with parchment paper. Whisk masa harina and salt together in large bowl. Add room-temperature water and Colby Jack and knead with your hands until mixture is fully combined. (Mixture should have texture of Play-Doh and easily hold fingerprint.)

4. Divide dough into 12 level ½-cup portions and place on large plate; divide any remaining dough evenly among portions. Working with 1 portion at a time (keep remaining dough covered with damp dish towel), roll dough into smooth ball between your wet hands, then return it to plate. Cut sides of 1-quart zipper-lock bag, leaving bottom seam intact.

5. Enclose 1 dough ball in split bag. Using clear plate or dish (so you can see size of dough round), press dough into 4-inch round, about ½ inch thick. Smooth any cracks around edges of round; transfer to prepared sheet. Repeat with remaining dough balls, placing second sheet of parchment on top once sheet is filled so you can stack dough rounds as needed. Cover with damp dish towel. (Dough rounds can be covered tightly with plastic wrap, without dish towel, and refrigerated for up to 2 hours.)

6. Set wire rack in rimmed baking sheet and line with triple layer of paper towels. Add oil to Dutch oven until it measures about ¾ inch deep and heat over medium-high heat to 375 degrees.

7. Fry 4 dough rounds until golden brown on both sides, 5 minutes per side. Adjust burner, if necessary, to maintain oil temperature between 350 and 375 degrees. Transfer fried rounds to prepared rack to drain. Return oil to 375 degrees and repeat with remaining dough rounds in 2 batches. Let fried rounds cool for 10 minutes. While rounds are cooling, reheat filling.

8. Insert paring knife into side of fried dough rounds and split 180 degrees to create pocket. Stuff each pocket with ⅓ cup filling and serve.

Gorditas

A Pressing Issue

To press the gordita dough, cut the sides of a zipper-lock bag. Then put one dough round in the bag and press it to a ½-inch thickness with a clear plate or dish (we like to use a clear pie plate).

TEX-MEX AND MORE

Citrus-Braised Pork Tacos

SERVES 6

WHY THIS RECIPE WORKS These tacos contain a rich filling inspired by cochinita pibil, a popular Mexican dish from the Yucatán Peninsula that features incredibly tender slow-roasted pork. Traditionally, to make cochinita pibil, a whole suckling pig is swaddled in bitter orange juice and banana leaves before being nestled under a pile of hot coals to roast. To make this recipe on a smaller scale, we substituted pork butt for the whole pig. Instead of using the traditional banana leaves and annatto, we added bay leaves for herbal flavor and Worcestershire for meaty tanginess. Tomato paste gave the meat its vibrant color. A quick habanero sauce and pickled red onions balanced out the rich meat.

Pork butt roast is often labeled Boston butt in the supermarket. For a spicier sauce, add an extra habanero or two; if you are spice-averse, substitute jalapeños for the habaneros. Pickled onions and habanero sauce can each be refrigerated for up to 1 week.

Pork

- 2 tablespoons vegetable oil
- 1 onion, chopped fine
- 3 garlic cloves, minced
- 1 teaspoon ground cumin
- 1 teaspoon dried oregano
- ½ teaspoon ground allspice
- ½ teaspoon ground cinnamon
- ⅓ cup tomato paste
- 1½ cups water
- ¼ cup frozen orange juice concentrate, thawed
- 3 tablespoons distilled white vinegar
- 1½ tablespoons Worcestershire sauce
- 5 bay leaves
  Table salt and pepper
- 1 (2½- to 3-pound) boneless pork butt roast, trimmed and cut into 1-inch chunks

Pickled Red Onions

- 1 red onion, halved and sliced thin
- 1 cup distilled white vinegar
- ⅓ cup sugar
- ¼ teaspoon table salt

Habanero Sauce

- 1 cup water
- 1 carrot, peeled and chopped
- 1 vine-ripened tomato, cored and chopped
- ¼ cup chopped onion
- ½ habanero chile, stemmed
- 1 garlic clove, smashed and peeled
  Table salt and pepper
- 1 tablespoon distilled white vinegar
- 1½ teaspoons lime juice, plus lime wedges for serving

- 18 (6-inch) corn tortillas, warmed

1. For the Pork Adjust oven rack to lower-middle position and heat oven to 300 degrees. Heat oil in Dutch oven over medium heat until shimmering. Add onion and cook until lightly browned, 4 to 6 minutes.

2. Add garlic, cumin, oregano, allspice, and cinnamon and cook until fragrant, about 30 seconds. Stir in tomato paste and cook, stirring constantly, until paste begins to darken, about 45 seconds. Stir in water, orange juice concentrate, 2 tablespoons vinegar, Worcestershire, bay leaves, 2 teaspoons salt, and 1 teaspoon pepper, scraping up any browned bits.

3. Add pork and bring to boil. Transfer to oven, uncovered, and cook until pork is tender, about 2 hours, stirring once halfway through cooking.

4. For the Pickled Red Onions Meanwhile, place onion in medium bowl. Bring vinegar, sugar, and salt to simmer in small saucepan over medium-high heat, stirring occasionally, until sugar dissolves. Pour over onions and cover loosely. Let onions cool completely, about 30 minutes.

5. For the Habanero Sauce Combine water, carrot, tomato, onion, habanero, garlic, and ½ teaspoon salt in now-empty saucepan. Bring to boil over medium heat and cook until carrot is tender, about 10 minutes. Remove from heat and let carrot mixture cool slightly, about 5 minutes. Transfer carrot mixture to blender, add vinegar and lime juice, and process until sauce is smooth, 1 to 2 minutes. Season with salt and pepper to taste; set aside.

6. Transfer pot to stovetop; discard bay leaves. Using potato masher, mash pork until finely shredded. Bring to simmer over medium-high heat, then reduce heat to medium-low and cook until most of liquid has evaporated, 3 to 5 minutes.

7. Off heat, stir in remaining 1 tablespoon vinegar and season with salt and pepper to taste. Serve on tortillas with pickled red onions, habanero sauce, and lime wedges.

Pork Carnitas

SERVES 8 TO 10

WHY THIS RECIPE WORKS We used 86 pounds of meat and 26 pounds of lard to develop this recipe inspired by the carnitas on offer at Carnitas Uruapan in Chicago, Illinois. While testing, we noticed that a tiny difference in our stovetop heat dial could produce surprisingly varied results, so we decided to move the carnitas operation to the more controlled heat of the oven. At 300 degrees, the pork cooked evenly and was tender, except for the corners that poked above the surface of the lard, which browned into crisp edges. Since we didn't add any seasonings or spices, the result was soft pork with unparalleled flavor. These carnitas are best chopped into bite-size pieces served in a warm tortilla with a tangy tomatillo salsa.

We developed this recipe using Morrell Snow Cap Lard, but you can substitute 4 cups of peanut or vegetable oil. Pork butt roast is often labeled Boston butt in the supermarket. The pork doesn't need to be cut into perfect 2-inch pieces; a little variation in size is fine. Serve with Quick Tomatillo Salsa (recipe follows), if desired.

- 4 pounds boneless pork butt roast, cut into 2-inch pieces
- 1½ tablespoons kosher salt
- 2 pounds lard, cut into 8 pieces
- 24 (6-inch) corn tortillas, toasted
  Finely chopped onion
  Coarsely chopped fresh cilantro
  Lime wedges

> ### The American Table: Advocating for Lard
> Many home cooks think that lard—which is simply rendered and clarified pork fat—is an antiquated, unhealthy cooking medium. We'll leave the health debate up to the professionals (many of whom claim that lard has more health benefits than butter, by the way), but we can confidently declare that lard produces great results in the kitchen. While you can cook our Pork Carnitas in vegetable oil and they'll taste great, the meat is more deeply savory when cooked in lard. Like frying oil, lard can be strained, refrigerated, and reused once or twice before being discarded.

Citrus-Braised Pork Tacos

Pork Carnitas

1. Adjust oven rack to lower-middle position and heat oven to 300 degrees. Sprinkle pork with salt. Melt lard in large Dutch oven over medium-low heat. Add pork, increase heat to medium-high, and cook until bubbling vigorously all over, about 5 minutes. Transfer to oven and cook, uncovered, until pork is tender, about 2½ hours.

2. Remove pot from oven and let stand for 30 minutes. Using spider skimmer or tongs, transfer pork to carving board; chop into bite-size pieces. Transfer pork to bowl and season with salt to taste. Divide pork among warm tortillas and garnish with onion and cilantro. Serve with lime wedges.

Quick Tomatillo Salsa
MAKES ABOUT 2 CUPS

We developed this recipe using a 28-ounce can of tomatillos, but they are also available in 26-ounce cans. If you can find only a 26-ounce can, there's no need to buy a second can to make up the extra 2 ounces. For more heat, reserve and add the jalapeño seeds.

- 1 (28-ounce) can whole tomatillos, drained, divided
- 1 tablespoon extra-virgin olive oil, divided
- 1 small onion, chopped
- ½ cup fresh cilantro leaves
- 1 jalapeño chile, stemmed, seeded, and chopped
- 3 tablespoons lime juice (2 limes)
- 1 garlic clove, minced
- ¾ teaspoon table salt
- ½ teaspoon sugar

1. Adjust oven rack 6 inches from broiler element and heat broiler. Line rimmed baking sheet with aluminum foil. Toss half of tomatillos with 1 teaspoon oil and transfer to prepared sheet. Broil until tomatillos are spotty brown and skins begin to burst, 7 to 10 minutes. Transfer tomatillos to food processor and let cool completely.

2. Add onion, cilantro, jalapeño, lime juice, garlic, salt, sugar, remaining tomatillos, and remaining 2 teaspoons oil to processor. Pulse until slightly chunky, 16 to 18 pulses. Season with salt to taste. Serve. (Salsa can be refrigerated for up to 2 days.)

Easier Chicken Chimichangas
SERVES 4

WHY THIS RECIPE WORKS Forget about tasteless fillings. We simmer the chicken and rice for our chimichangas in a chipotle broth, infusing them with a smoky bite through and through. As for construction, we noticed that the standard burrito-style wrapping method left us with doughy tortilla ends and filling that fell out. We created an easy new folding technique that kept the filling put without any floury bites.

If using a cast-iron Dutch oven, increase the broth to 1¾ cups, adding 1¼ cups in step 2. Serve with Smoky Salsa Verde (page 401).

- 1¼ cups chicken broth
- 1 tablespoon minced canned chipotle chile in adobo sauce
- ½ cup long-grain white rice
  Table salt and pepper
- 2 (6-ounce) boneless, skinless chicken breasts, trimmed
- 1 tablespoon peanut or vegetable oil, plus 3 cups for frying
- 1 onion, chopped fine
- 2 garlic cloves, minced
- 1 teaspoon chili powder
- ½ teaspoon ground cumin
- 1 (15-ounce) can pinto beans, rinsed
- 4 ounces sharp cheddar cheese, shredded (1 cup)
- ⅓ cup chopped fresh cilantro
- 1 tablespoon all-purpose flour
- 1 tablespoon water
- 4 (10-inch) flour tortillas

1. Whisk broth and chipotle together in 2-cup liquid measuring cup. Combine ½ cup chipotle broth, rice, and ¼ teaspoon salt in bowl. Cover bowl and microwave until liquid is completely absorbed, about 5 minutes. Meanwhile, pat chicken dry with paper towels and season with salt and pepper.

2. Heat 1 tablespoon oil in Dutch oven over medium-high heat until just smoking. Add onion and cook until softened, about 5 minutes. Stir in garlic, chili powder, and cumin and cook until fragrant, about 30 seconds. Add remaining ¾ cup chipotle broth, parcooked rice, and beans and bring to boil.

400   *The Complete Cook's Country TV Show Cookbook*

Easier Chicken Chimichangas

Glue and Fold

The usual burrito-style wrapping method left us between the devil and the deep blue sea: Either the filling leaked out in the pot of oil or the ends of the tortilla never crisped. Our new chimichanga folding technique solves both problems.

1. Place filling in middle of tortilla. Brush tortilla's circumference with flour-and-water paste.

2. After folding opposing sides toward center and pressing to seal, brush open flaps with more paste. Fold flaps in and press firmly to seal chimichanga shut.

3. Reduce heat to medium-low, add chicken, and cook, covered, until chicken registers 160 degrees and rice is tender, about 15 minutes, flipping chicken halfway through cooking. Transfer chicken to cutting board and let rest for 5 to 10 minutes. Cut chicken into ½-inch pieces and combine with rice and bean mixture, cheddar, and cilantro in large bowl. Wash now-empty pot.

4. Whisk flour and water together in small bowl. Stack tortillas on plate and microwave, covered, until pliable, about 1 minute. Working with one at a time, place one-quarter of chicken mixture in center of warm tortilla. Brush edges of tortilla with flour paste. Wrap top and bottom of tortilla tightly over filling. Brush ends of tortilla with paste and fold into center, pressing firmly to seal.

5. Set wire rack in rimmed baking sheet. Heat remaining 3 cups oil in clean pot over medium-high heat until 325 degrees. Place 2 chimichangas, seam side down, in oil. Fry, adjusting burner as necessary to maintain oil temperature between 300 and 325 degrees, until chimichangas are deep golden brown, about 4 minutes, turning them halfway through frying. Drain on prepared wire rack. Bring oil back to 325 degrees and repeat with remaining chimichangas. Serve.

Smoky Salsa Verde

MAKES 1¼ CUPS

WHY THIS RECIPE WORKS Our recipe for salsa verde includes the typical ingredients: tomatillos, onions, garlic, jalapeño, and lots of cilantro. To temper their sharply acidic flavor, we broiled the tomatillos just until tender. We also broiled the other vegetables to provide subtle smokiness. Our recipe calls for a large amount of cilantro to ensure that its flavor stands out from the other ingredients.

This salsa is especially good served with our Easier Chicken Chimichangas, or try it with anything you'd serve salsa with, such as tortilla chips, grilled steak, or scrambled eggs.

- 1 pound tomatillos, husks and stems removed, rinsed well, and dried
- 1 small onion, quartered
- 1 jalapeño chile, stemmed, halved, and seeded
- 1 garlic clove, peeled
- 1 teaspoon olive oil
- ½ cup fresh cilantro leaves
- 1 tablespoon lime juice
  Table salt

Smoky Salsa Verde

New Mexican Bean-and-Cheese Turnovers with Green Chile

1. Adjust oven rack 5 inches from broiler element and heat broiler. Toss tomatillos, onion, jalapeño, and garlic with oil and place on aluminum foil–lined rimmed baking sheet. Broil, shaking pan occasionally, until vegetables are lightly charred, 10 to 12 minutes. Cool slightly, about 5 minutes.

2. Add vegetables, cilantro, lime juice, and ¼ teaspoon salt to food processor and pulse until coarsely ground, 5 to 7 pulses. Season with salt to taste. Serve. (Salsa can be refrigerated for up to 3 days.)

New Mexican Bean-and-Cheese Turnovers with Green Chile
SERVES 8

WHY THIS RECIPE WORKS The golden, stuffed turnovers we ate at Mary & Tito's Cafe in Albuquerque, New Mexico, were smothered in a lightly spicy green chile sauce that coated every bite. For our version, we added baking powder to our flour tortilla dough to help it puff in the oil and some lard to tenderize it and add flavor. We enhanced our quick refried beans recipe with lard and onion. Wetting the edges of the dough circles and twisting the sealed edges kept the filling contained. We approximated the flavor of New Mexican chiles with Anaheim chiles and a jalapeño. Broiling the chiles added smokiness while intensifying their sweetness for a punchy chile sauce.

Use a Dutch oven that holds 6 quarts or more for this recipe. We developed this recipe using John Morrell Snow Cap Lard. You can substitute vegetable shortening for the lard, if desired.

Dough
- 2¾ cups (13¾ ounces) all-purpose flour
- 1½ teaspoons table salt
- ½ teaspoon baking powder
- 6 tablespoons lard, cut into ½-inch pieces

Refried Beans
- 4 tablespoons lard
- 1 cup finely chopped onion
- 2 (15-ounce) cans pinto beans, rinsed
- 1 cup chicken broth
- 1 teaspoon table salt

Green Chile

- 2 pounds Anaheim chiles
- 1 jalapeño chile
- 2 tablespoons lard
- 1 cup finely chopped onion
- 3 garlic cloves, minced
- 1 tablespoon all-purpose flour
- 1 cup chicken broth
- 1 teaspoon table salt

- 8 ounces mild cheddar cheese, shredded (2 cups)
- 2 quarts peanut or vegetable oil for frying

1. For the Dough Whisk flour, salt, and baking powder together in large bowl. Rub lard into flour mixture with your fingers until mixture resembles coarse meal. Stir in ¾ cup plus 2 tablespoons water until combined. Turn out dough onto clean counter and knead briefly to form cohesive ball, 6 to 8 turns. Divide dough into 8 equal portions, about 2¾ ounces each (scant ⅓ cup), then roll into balls. Transfer dough balls to plate, cover with plastic wrap, and refrigerate until firm, at least 30 minutes or up to 2 days.

2. For the Refried Beans Heat lard in 12-inch skillet over medium heat until shimmering. Add onion and cook until softened, about 4 minutes. Stir in beans, broth, and salt. Cook, mashing beans with potato masher, until finely mashed and mixture is thickened, about 8 minutes. Season with salt to taste. Set aside and let cool completely.

3. For the Green Chile Adjust oven rack 6 inches from broiler element and heat broiler. Line rimmed baking sheet with aluminum foil. Arrange Anaheims and jalapeño in single layer on prepared sheet. Broil until chiles are soft and mostly blackened, about 5 minutes per side, rotating sheet halfway through broiling. Transfer chiles to bowl and cover with plastic; let cool for 10 minutes.

4. Remove skins from chiles with spoon. Stem and seed Anaheims, then chop into ¼-inch pieces. Stem (but do not seed) jalapeño; chop into ¼-inch pieces.

5. Heat lard in large saucepan over medium heat until shimmering. Add onion and cook until softened, about 3 minutes. Stir in garlic and cook until fragrant, about 30 seconds. Stir in flour and cook for 1 minute. Stir in broth, salt, Anaheims, and jalapeño and bring to simmer. Simmer until slightly thickened, about 6 minutes. Season with salt to taste; cover and set aside.

6. Keeping other dough balls covered with damp dish towel, roll 1 dough ball into 7-inch circle on lightly floured counter. Lightly squeeze ¼ cup cheese in your palm to form ball. Place cheese in center of dough round, followed by ¼ cup refried beans. Moisten edges of dough round with water. Fold dough round in half, creating half-moon shape to enclose filling, and press to seal.

7. Moisten top of sealed edge with water. Starting at 1 end, fold, slightly twist, and pinch dough diagonally across sealed edge between your thumb and index finger. Continue pinching and twisting dough around seam to create decorative rope edge. Transfer to parchment paper–lined baking sheet. Repeat with remaining dough balls, cheese, and refried beans (reserve any remaining beans for another use). Using paring knife, poke ½-inch hole in center of each turnover. (Filled turnovers can be covered and refrigerated for up to 24 hours.)

8. Line baking sheet with triple layer of paper towels. Add oil to large Dutch oven until it measures about 1½ inches deep and heat over medium-high heat to 375 degrees. Add 4 turnovers to oil and fry until golden brown, about 3 minutes per side. Adjust burner as needed to maintain oil temperature between 350 and 375 degrees. Transfer fried turnovers to prepared sheet. Return oil to 375 degrees and repeat with remaining 4 turnovers.

9. Reheat green chile sauce over medium-high heat until hot. Serve turnovers topped with chile sauce.

Tex-Mex Cheese Enchiladas

SERVES 6

WHY THIS RECIPE WORKS Tex-Mex cheese enchiladas are a wildly popular dish in the Lone Star State, beloved for their relative simplicity and their chile gravy, a red sauce that's a cross between beef gravy and Mexican enchilada sauce. We found that two toasted ancho chiles ground with a combination of spices gave the sauce smoky flavors that we brightened with a little white vinegar. We skipped frying the corn tortillas, instead brushing them with oil and microwaving, resulting in soft, easy-to-roll tortillas without excess grease. For the cheesy filling, we combined sharp cheddar and Monterey Jack and used the oven to ensure melty, gooey cheese.

Dried chiles vary in size and weight. You'll get a more accurate measure if you seed and tear them first; you need about ½ cup of prepped chiles. You'll lose some flavor, but you can substitute 2 tablespoons ancho chile powder and 1 tablespoon ground cumin for the whole ancho chiles and cumin seeds, decreasing the toasting time to 1 minute.

Gravy

- 2 dried ancho chiles, stemmed, seeded, and torn into ½-inch pieces (½ cup)
- 1 tablespoon cumin seeds
- 1 tablespoon garlic powder
- 2 teaspoons dried oregano
- 3 tablespoons vegetable oil
- 3 tablespoons all-purpose flour
  Table salt and pepper
- 2 cups chicken broth
- 2 teaspoons distilled white vinegar

Enchiladas

- 12 (6-inch) corn tortillas
- 1½ tablespoons vegetable oil
- 8 ounces Monterey Jack cheese, shredded (2 cups)
- 6 ounces sharp cheddar cheese, shredded (1½ cups)
- 1 onion, chopped fine

1. For the Gravy Toast chiles and cumin in 12-inch skillet over medium-low heat, stirring frequently, until fragrant, about 2 minutes. Transfer to spice grinder and let cool for 5 minutes. Add garlic powder and oregano and grind to fine powder.

2. Heat oil in now-empty skillet over medium-high heat until shimmering. Whisk in flour, ½ teaspoon salt, ½ teaspoon pepper, and spice mixture and cook until fragrant and slightly deepened in color, about 1 minute. Slowly whisk in broth and bring to simmer. Reduce heat to medium-low and cook, whisking frequently, until gravy has thickened and reduced to 1½ cups, about 5 minutes. Whisk in vinegar and season with salt and pepper to taste. Remove from heat, cover, and keep warm.

3. For the Enchiladas Adjust oven rack to middle position and heat oven to 450 degrees. Brush both sides of tortillas with oil. Stack tortillas, then wrap in damp dish towel. Place tortillas on plate and microwave until warm and pliable, about 1 minute.

4. Spread ½ cup gravy in bottom of 13 by 9-inch baking dish. Combine cheeses in bowl; set aside ½ cup cheese mixture for topping enchiladas. Sprinkle ¼ cup cheese mixture and 1 tablespoon onion across center of each tortilla. Tightly roll tortillas around filling and lay them seam side down in dish (2 columns of 6 tortillas will fit neatly across width of dish). Pour remaining 1 cup gravy over enchiladas, then sprinkle with reserved cheese mixture.

5. Cover dish with aluminum foil and bake until sauce is bubbling and cheese is melted, about 15 minutes. Let enchiladas cool for 10 minutes, then sprinkle with remaining onion. Serve.

To Make Ahead The sauce can be made up to 24 hours in advance. To reheat, add 2 tablespoons water and microwave until loose, 1 to 2 minutes, stirring halfway through microwaving.

Tex-Mex Cheese Enchiladas

Enchilada Orientation

After spreading ½ cup chile gravy in 13 by 9-inch baking dish, fit 12 enchiladas by creating 2 snug columns of 6.

Easy Green Chile Chicken Enchiladas

SERVES 4 TO 6

Easy Green Chile Chicken Enchiladas

WHY THIS RECIPE WORKS To cut down on the prep work required for enchiladas, we started with shredded rotisserie chicken. Store-bought enchilada sauces tasted too acidic, but homemade ones required sometimes out-of-season fresh tomatillos, so we turned to canned tomatillos and bolstered them with fresh chiles. Broiling before blending with cilantro and spices added complexity, while a little water kept the sauce fluid so that the filled and rolled enchiladas did not dry out in the oven.

For more heat, reserve the jalapeño seeds and add them to the blender in step 3. Don't spend a lot of time chopping the cilantro stems and leaves for the sauce; chop them just enough to measure them, and then let the blender do the bulk of the work. Serve with hot sauce, if desired.

Sauce
- 1 (28-ounce) can whole tomatillos, drained
- 3 poblano chiles, stemmed, halved, and seeded
- 1 onion, cut into 8 wedges through root end
- 1 jalapeño chile, stemmed, halved, and seeded
- 5 garlic cloves, peeled
- 1 tablespoon vegetable oil
- ¼ cup water
- ¼ cup coarsely chopped fresh cilantro leaves and stems
- 1 teaspoon ground cumin
- 1 teaspoon dried oregano
- 1 teaspoon sugar
- 1 teaspoon table salt
- 1 teaspoon pepper

Enchiladas
- 1 (2½-pound) rotisserie chicken, skin and bones discarded, meat shredded into bite-size pieces (3 cups)
- 12 ounces sharp cheddar cheese, shredded (3 cups), divided
- 12 (6-inch) corn tortillas
- 1 tablespoon chopped fresh cilantro
- Sour cream
- Lime wedges
- Avocado
- Finely chopped onion

1. For the Sauce Adjust oven rack 6 inches from broiler element and heat broiler. Line rimmed baking sheet with aluminum foil.

2. Place tomatillos, poblanos, onion, jalapeño, and garlic on prepared sheet. Drizzle with oil and toss gently to coat. Arrange poblanos and jalapeño skin side up. Broil until poblanos, jalapeño, and tomatillos are blistered and blackened and onion wedges are dark at edges, about 15 minutes, rotating sheet halfway through broiling. (Vegetables may appear to be burning, but they are not.) Let vegetables cool on sheet for 15 minutes.

3. Turn off broiler and heat oven to 400 degrees. Transfer broiled vegetables and any accumulated juices to blender. Add water, cilantro, cumin, oregano, sugar, salt, and pepper and process until smooth, about 30 seconds, scraping down sides of blender jar as needed (you should have about 3½ cups sauce).

4. For the Enchiladas Spread ½ cup sauce in bottom of 13 by 9-inch baking dish. Combine chicken, 1½ cups cheddar, and 1 cup sauce in bowl. Stack tortillas and wrap in damp dish towel. Microwave until hot and pliable, about 1½ minutes.

5. Arrange tortillas on counter and place ¼ cup filling in center of each. Distribute any remaining filling evenly among tortillas. Roll tortillas tightly around filling and place seam side down in prepared dish.

6. Pour remaining 2 cups sauce over enchiladas and spread evenly with back of spoon. Sprinkle with remaining 1½ cups cheddar and cover dish with foil. Bake until enchiladas are heated through and cheese is melted, about 30 minutes.

7. Uncover and let cool for 15 minutes. Sprinkle with cilantro and serve with sour cream, lime wedges, avocado, and onion.

Beef Enchiladas

SERVES 4 TO 6

WHY THIS RECIPE WORKS Traditional beef enchilada recipes require simmering steak for hours. Convenience recipes call for hamburger and canned sauce. We wanted to find a middle ground. For a deeply flavored sauce, we relied on chili powder and tomato sauce, along with onions, garlic, and spices. Slicing beefy, inexpensive blade steaks into small pieces cut our cooking time considerably. Traditional recipes fry the corn tortillas and then dip them in sauce to soften and season them. Instead, we softened the tortillas in the microwave. Once filled, topped with sauce and cheese, and baked, our enchiladas tasted like the real deal.

Cut back on the jalapeños if you like your enchiladas on the mild side.

- 3 tablespoons chili powder
- 3 garlic cloves, minced
- 2 teaspoons ground coriander
- 2 teaspoons ground cumin
- 1 teaspoon sugar
- Table salt
- 1¼ pounds top blade steaks, trimmed
- 1 tablespoon vegetable oil
- 2 onions, chopped
- 1 (15-ounce) can tomato sauce
- ½ cup water
- 8 ounces Monterey Jack or mild cheddar cheese, shredded (2 cups), divided
- ⅓ cup chopped fresh cilantro
- ¼ cup chopped canned jalapeños
- 12 (6-inch) corn tortillas

1. Combine chili powder, garlic, coriander, cumin, sugar, and 1 teaspoon salt in small bowl. Pat meat dry with paper towels and sprinkle with salt. Heat oil in Dutch oven over medium-high heat until shimmering. Cook meat until browned on both sides, about 6 minutes. Transfer meat to plate. Add onions to pot and cook over medium heat until golden, about 5 minutes. Stir in garlic mixture and cook until fragrant, about 1 minute. Add tomato sauce and water and bring to boil. Return meat and juices to pot, cover, reduce heat to low, and simmer gently until meat is tender and can be broken apart with wooden spoon, about 1½ hours.

2. Adjust oven rack to middle position and heat oven to 350 degrees. Strain beef mixture over medium bowl, breaking meat into small pieces; reserve sauce. Transfer meat to bowl and mix with 1 cup cheese, cilantro, and jalapeños.

3. Spread ¾ cup sauce in bottom of 13 by 9-inch baking dish. Place 6 tortillas on plate and microwave until soft, about 1 minute. Spread ⅓ cup beef mixture down center of each tortilla, roll tortillas tightly, and set in baking dish seam side down. Repeat with remaining tortillas and beef mixture (you may have to fit 2 or more enchiladas down the sides of the baking dish). Pour remaining sauce over enchiladas and spread to coat evenly. Sprinkle remaining 1 cup cheese evenly over enchiladas, wrap with aluminum foil, and bake until heated through, 20 to 25 minutes. Remove foil and continue baking until cheese browns slightly, 5 to 10 minutes. Serve.

Flank Steak in Adobo

SERVES 4 TO 6

WHY THIS RECIPE WORKS Arrachera en adobo, a chili-like dish of steak slowly stewed in a pungent adobo sauce, is a gem of Mexican American cuisine. For a simple but rich adobo sauce, we used two kinds of dried chiles—anchos for their fruitiness and pasillas for their bitter earthiness. Seeding them tamed their heat, while toasting them gave them more complex flavor. Flank steak proved to be the ideal cut of meat. Since it is leaner, it did not add greasiness to the sauce.

Salsa verde is a green salsa made from tomatillos and green chiles. You can substitute skirt steak for flank steak here, if desired. If queso fresco is unavailable, you can substitute farmer's cheese or a mild feta. This dish is also great served over rice.

Adobo

- 1½ ounces dried ancho chiles, stemmed and seeded
- 1 ounce dried pasilla chiles, stemmed and seeded
- ¾ cup salsa verde
- ¾ cup chicken broth
- ½ cup orange juice
- ⅓ cup packed brown sugar
- ¼ cup lime juice (2 limes)
- 1½ teaspoons dried oregano
- 1 teaspoon table salt
- ½ teaspoon pepper

Flank Steak

- 2½–3 pounds flank steak, trimmed and cut into 1½-inch cubes
- Table salt and pepper
- 2 tablespoons vegetable oil, divided
- 1 onion, chopped fine
- 8 garlic cloves, minced
- 1 tablespoon ground cumin
- 12 (8-inch) flour tortillas, warmed
- 4 ounces queso fresco, crumbled (1 cup)
- ½ cup coarsely chopped fresh cilantro

1. For the Adobo Adjust oven rack to lower-middle position and heat oven to 350 degrees. Arrange anchos and pasillas on rimmed baking sheet and bake until fragrant, about 5 minutes. Immediately transfer chiles to bowl and cover with hot tap water. Let stand until chiles are softened and pliable, about 5 minutes. Drain.

2. Process salsa verde, broth, orange juice, sugar, lime juice, oregano, salt, pepper, and drained chiles in blender until smooth, 1 to 2 minutes. Set aside.

3. For the Flank Steak Reduce oven temperature to 300 degrees. Pat beef dry with paper towels and sprinkle with ½ teaspoon salt and ½ teaspoon pepper. Heat 1 tablespoon oil in Dutch oven over medium-high heat until just smoking. Add half of beef and cook, stirring occasionally, until well browned on all sides, 6 to 9 minutes. (Adjust heat, if necessary, to keep bottom of pot from scorching.) Using slotted spoon, transfer beef to large bowl. Repeat with remaining 1 tablespoon oil and remaining beef.

4. Add onion and ½ teaspoon salt to now-empty pot. Reduce heat to medium and cook, stirring occasionally, until golden brown, 3 to 5 minutes, scraping up any browned bits. Add garlic and cumin and cook until fragrant, about 30 seconds. Stir in adobo, beef, and any accumulated juices until well incorporated and bring mixture to simmer.

Beef Enchiladas

Flank Steak in Adobo

5. Cover pot and transfer to oven. Cook until beef is tender and sauce has thickened, about 1½ hours. Season with salt and pepper to taste. Serve with flour tortillas, sprinkled with queso fresco and cilantro.

Chicken Chilaquiles

SERVES 6

WHY THIS RECIPE WORKS Chilaquiles are often made from leftover meats and are considered a side dish, but we started from scratch for the best flavor and turned the dish into a meal. We began by baking our own tortilla chips. For the tomato-based red sauce, we toasted dried guajillo chiles to intensify their flavor before pureeing them with fresh poblanos, jalapeños, and other aromatic ingredients. To make the chilaquiles a complete meal, we poached boneless, skinless chicken breasts in the red sauce before shredding and mixing the tender meat back in with the chips. Finishing the dish with sour cream and queso fresco balanced the heat.

New Mexican or Anaheim chiles can be substituted for the guajillo chiles. If queso fresco is unavailable, you can substitute farmer's cheese or a mild feta. When baking the tortillas, stir them well to promote even browning.

- 16 (6-inch) corn tortillas, each cut into 8 wedges
- ¼ cup extra virgin olive oil
- Table salt
- 5 dried guajillo chiles, stemmed and seeded
- 1 (28-ounce) can whole peeled tomatoes
- 1 cup finely chopped onion, divided
- 1 poblano chile, stemmed, seeded, and chopped
- 1 jalapeño chile, stemmed, seeded, and chopped
- 8 sprigs fresh cilantro, plus 2 tablespoons chopped
- 3 garlic cloves, chopped
- 1½ cups chicken broth
- 1½ pounds boneless, skinless chicken breasts, trimmed
- 4 ounces queso fresco, crumbled (1 cup)
- 1 avocado, halved, pitted, and cut into ½-inch chunks
- 2 radishes, trimmed and sliced thin
- Sour cream
- Lime wedges

1. Adjust oven racks to upper-middle and lower-middle positions and heat oven to 425 degrees. Divide tortillas evenly between 2 rimmed baking sheets and drizzle with oil and ½ teaspoon salt. Toss until tortillas are evenly coated with oil. Bake until golden brown and crisp, 15 to 20 minutes, stirring chips and switching and rotating sheets halfway through baking.

2. Toast guajillos in Dutch oven over medium heat until fragrant and slightly darkened, about 5 minutes. Transfer to blender and process until finely ground, 60 to 90 seconds, scraping down sides of blender jar as needed.

3. Add tomatoes and their juice, ¾ cup onion, poblano, jalapeño, cilantro sprigs, garlic, and ¾ teaspoon salt to guajillos and process until very smooth, 60 to 90 seconds. Transfer sauce to now-empty Dutch oven and stir in broth. Bring sauce to boil over medium-high heat. Add chicken breasts; reduce heat to low and simmer, uncovered, until chicken registers 160 degrees, 15 to 20 minutes, flipping halfway through cooking.

4. Using tongs, transfer chicken to large plate. Increase heat to medium and continue to simmer sauce until thickened and reduced to about 4½ cups, about 5 minutes longer. While sauce simmers, shred chicken into bite-size pieces using 2 forks. Return chicken to sauce and cook until warmed through, about 2 minutes.

Entrée-Worthy Chilaquiles

1. Use 3 types of chiles.

2. Make easy homemade chips.

3. Cook chicken in sauce.

4. Finish with fresh garnishes.

5. Add chips to pot and toss to coat. Remove from heat and season with salt to taste. Cover and let stand for 2 to 5 minutes, depending on how soft you like your chips.

6. Transfer chilaquiles to serving dish and top with queso fresco, avocado, radishes, remaining ¼ cup onion, and chopped cilantro. Serve with sour cream and lime wedges.

Easy Chili con Carne
SERVES 6 TO 8

WHY THIS RECIPE WORKS Many chili con carne recipes call for toasting and grinding whole chiles. We wanted to create a simpler, but still satisfying version. For the meat, we settled on beef chuck, our favorite cut for stews because its substantial marbling provides rich flavor and tender texture after prolonged cooking. To add a smoky meatiness to our chili, we browned the beef in bacon fat instead of oil. We added a jalapeño for brightness and heat and minced chipotle for smoky, spicy depth. A few tablespoons of corn muffin mix, in place of masa harina (corn flour), helped thicken our chili and gave it a silky texture.

If the bacon does not render a full 3 tablespoons of fat in step 1, supplement it with vegetable oil. If desired, serve chili with chopped onion, avocado, shredded cheese, lime wedges, and/or hot sauce.

- 1 (14.5-ounce) can diced tomatoes
- 2 teaspoons minced canned chipotle chile in adobo sauce
- 4 slices bacon, chopped fine
- 1 (3½- to 4-pound) boneless beef chuck-eye roast, pulled apart at seams, trimmed, and cut into 1-inch pieces
     Table salt and pepper
- 1 onion, chopped fine
- 1 jalapeño chile, stemmed, seeded, and chopped fine
- 3 tablespoons chili powder
- 4 garlic cloves, minced
- 1½ teaspoons ground cumin
- ½ teaspoon dried oregano
- 4 cups water
- 1 tablespoon packed brown sugar
- 2 tablespoons yellow corn muffin mix

Chicken Chilaquiles

Easy Chili con Carne

Five-Alarm Chili

SERVES 8 TO 10

WHY THIS RECIPE WORKS As the name implies, five-alarm chili should be spicy enough to make you break a sweat—but it has to have rich, complex chile flavor as well. We used a combination of dried anchos, smoky chipotle chiles in adobo sauce, fresh jalapeños, and chili powder to create layers of spicy flavor. Ground beef added meaty bulk, and pureeing the chiles along with canned tomatoes and corn chips added extra body and another layer of flavor. Mellowed with a bit of sugar and enriched with creamy pinto beans, our chili was well balanced and spicy without being harsh.

Look for ancho chiles in the Latin American aisle at the supermarket. Light-bodied American lagers, such as Budweiser, work best here. Serve chili with lime, sour cream, diced tomato, diced avocado, scallions, and cornbread.

- 2 ounces (4 to 6) dried ancho chiles, stemmed, seeded, and cut into 1-inch pieces
- 3½ cups water, divided
- 1 (28-ounce) can whole peeled tomatoes
- ¾ cup crushed corn tortilla chips
- ¼ cup canned chipotle chile in adobo sauce plus 2 teaspoons adobo sauce
- 2 tablespoons vegetable oil, divided
- 2 pounds 85 percent lean ground beef
  Table salt and pepper
- 2 pounds onions, chopped fine
- 2 jalapeño chiles, stemmed, seeds reserved, and minced
- 6 garlic cloves, minced
- 2 tablespoons ground cumin
- 2 tablespoons chili powder
- 1 tablespoon dried oregano
- 2 teaspoons ground coriander
- 2 teaspoons sugar
- 1 teaspoon cayenne pepper
- 1½ cups beer
- 3 (15-ounce) cans pinto beans, rinsed

1. Combine anchos and 1½ cups water in bowl and microwave until softened, about 3 minutes. Drain and discard liquid. Process anchos, tomatoes and their juice, remaining 2 cups water, tortilla chips, chipotle, and adobo sauce in blender until smooth, about 1 minute; set aside.

1. Process tomatoes and chipotle in food processor until smooth. Cook bacon in Dutch oven over medium heat until crispy, about 8 minutes. Transfer bacon to paper towel–lined plate and reserve 3 tablespoons bacon fat.

2. Pat beef dry with paper towels and season with salt and pepper. Heat 1 tablespoon reserved bacon fat in now-empty Dutch oven over medium-high heat until just smoking. Brown half of beef, about 8 minutes. Transfer to bowl and repeat with 1 tablespoon bacon fat and remaining beef.

3. Add remaining 1 tablespoon bacon fat, onion, and jalapeño to again-empty Dutch oven and cook until softened, about 5 minutes. Stir in chili powder, garlic, cumin, and oregano and cook until fragrant, about 30 seconds. Stir in water, pureed tomato mixture, bacon, browned beef, and sugar and bring to boil. Reduce heat to low and simmer, covered, for 1 hour. Skim fat and continue to simmer uncovered until meat is tender, 30 to 45 minutes.

4. Ladle 1 cup chili liquid into medium bowl and stir in muffin mix; cover with plastic wrap. Microwave until mixture is thickened, about 1 minute. Slowly whisk mixture into chili and simmer until chili is slightly thickened, 5 to 10 minutes. Season with salt and pepper to taste. Serve. (Chili can be refrigerated for up to 3 days.)

Five-Alarm Chili

2. Heat 2 teaspoons oil in Dutch oven over medium-high heat until just smoking. Add beef, 1 teaspoon salt, and ½ teaspoon pepper and cook, breaking up pieces with spoon, until all liquid has evaporated and meat begins to sizzle, 10 to 15 minutes. Drain in colander and set aside.

3. Heat remaining 4 teaspoons oil in now-empty Dutch oven over medium-high heat until simmering. Add onions and jalapeños and seeds and cook until onions are lightly browned, about 5 minutes. Stir in garlic, cumin, chili powder, oregano, coriander, sugar, and cayenne and cook until fragrant, about 30 seconds. Pour in beer and bring to simmer. Stir in beans, reserved chile-tomato mixture, and reserved cooked beef and return to simmer. Cover, reduce heat to low, and cook, stirring occasionally, until thickened, 50 to 60 minutes. Season with salt to taste. Serve.

Vegetarian Chili

SERVES 6

Vegetarian Chili

WHY THIS RECIPE WORKS A meatless chili worthy of a cook-off crown is possible by using umami-packed porcini mushrooms, soy sauce, and tomato paste to build satisfying, savory flavor. For complex heat, smokiness, and sweetness, we used four different types of chiles: poblano, ancho, guajillo, and canned chipotles in adobo. In place of meat, we turned to a colorful medley of kidney, pinto, and black beans. Pearl barley provided a pleasant, chewy bite.

One ounce of ancho chiles is two to three chiles; ½ ounce of guajillo chiles is three to four chiles. Use more or fewer chipotle chiles depending on your desired level of spiciness. We like using a mix of beans, but you can use all of one type or any combination of the three. Do not substitute hulled, hull-less, quick-cooking, or presteamed barley (read the ingredient list on the package to determine this). Serve the chili with lime wedges, sour cream, diced avocado, chopped red onion, and shredded Monterey Jack or cheddar cheese.

- 1 ounce dried ancho chiles, stemmed, seeded, and torn into 1-inch pieces
- ½ ounce dried guajillo chiles, stemmed, seeded, and torn into 1-inch pieces
- 1 (28-ounce) can whole peeled tomatoes
- 1–3 canned chipotle chiles in adobo sauce
- 3 tablespoons soy sauce
- 2¼ teaspoons table salt, divided
- ¼ cup extra-virgin olive oil
- 1 onion, chopped
- 1 poblano chile, stemmed, seeded, and chopped
- 3 tablespoons tomato paste
- 6 garlic cloves, minced
- 2 tablespoons ground cumin
- 1 tablespoon dried oregano
- 1 (15-ounce) can pinto beans, rinsed
- 1 (15-ounce) can black beans, rinsed
- 1 (15-ounce) can red kidney beans, rinsed
- ¾ cup pearl barley
- ½ ounce dried porcini mushrooms, rinsed and chopped fine
- ½ cup chopped fresh cilantro

1. Place anchos and guajillos in Dutch oven and cook over medium heat, stirring often, until fragrant and darkened slightly but not smoking, 3 to 5 minutes. Immediately transfer anchos and guajillos to bowl and cover with hot water. Let sit until chiles are soft and pliable, about 5 minutes.

TEX-MEX AND MORE 411

2. Drain anchos and guajillos and combine with tomatoes and their juice, 1 cup water, chipotle(s), soy sauce, and 1½ teaspoons salt in blender. Process until smooth, 1 to 2 minutes; set aside.

3. Heat oil in now-empty Dutch oven over medium-high heat until shimmering. Add onion, poblano, and remaining ¾ teaspoon salt. Cook, stirring occasionally, until onion begins to brown, 3 to 5 minutes. Stir in tomato paste, garlic, cumin, and oregano and cook until tomato paste darkens, 1 to 2 minutes.

4. Stir in pinto, black, and kidney beans; barley; mushrooms; chile puree; and 2½ cups water. Bring to boil. Reduce heat to medium-low and simmer, stirring occasionally, until barley is tender, 35 to 45 minutes. Let sit off heat for 10 minutes (chili will continue to thicken as it sits). Season with salt to taste. Stir in cilantro and serve.

Chiles 101

Poblano Poblano chiles vary in color from very dark green (most common in American markets) to dark red or brown when ripe. Spicier than bell peppers but not as spicy as jalapeño or serrano chiles, they add subtle heat and grassy pepper notes to recipes.

Ancho Ancho chiles are almost-ripe poblanos that are dried. These chiles are dark, mahogany red and wrinkly skinned, and they have a deep, sweet, raisiny flavor with elements of coffee and chocolate.

Guajillo Guajillos are dried mirasol chiles. They are a little sweet, with a mild to medium heat. These chiles have a fruity, tangy, smoky flavor profile with notes of berries and green tea.

Canned Chipotle In Adobo Chipotles are ripe jalapeño peppers that are smoke-dried. They are sold both dried and rehydrated and packed in cans with thick, tangy adobo sauce. They are spicy, smoky, and complex.

Texas-Style Pinto Beans

SERVES 8

WHY THIS RECIPE WORKS Different from mashed or refried beans, Texas-style pinto beans are tender whole beans long-simmered with pork and served in the savory broth they are cooked in. For supremely creamy beans, we soaked dried pinto beans overnight in salted water to gradually rehydrate them so that they cooked evenly and more quickly than unsoaked beans. Plus, the salt in the soaking liquid seasoned them nicely. To cook them, we drained them, covered them with fresh water, and added a bit more salt to ensure that the bean skins were fully tender and a smoked ham hock to provide rich pork flavor. We then simmered them uncovered for 1½ hours to reduce and concentrate the cooking liquid.

If you can't find a ham hock, you can substitute 4 ounces of salt pork, omit the salt in step 2, and season to taste once finished. Monitor the water level as the beans cook: Don't let it fall below the level of the beans before they're done. If it does, add more water. Good garnishes include finely chopped onion, dill pickles, jalapeño chiles, and/or tomatoes. Use the meat from the ham hock within a few days to flavor another dish. Plan ahead: The beans need to be brined for at least 8 hours before cooking.

    Table salt
1 pound (2½ cups) dried pinto beans, picked over and rinsed
1 (10-ounce) smoked ham hock

1. Dissolve 1½ tablespoons salt in 2 quarts cold water in large container. Add beans and soak at room temperature for at least 8 hours or up to 24 hours. Drain and rinse well. (Soaked beans can be stored in zipper-lock bag and frozen for up to 1 month.)

2. Combine 12 cups water, ham hock, beans, and 1 teaspoon salt in Dutch oven. Bring to boil over high heat. Reduce heat to medium-low and simmer, uncovered, stirring occasionally, until beans are tender, about 1½ hours, skimming any foam from surface with spoon. Remove from heat and let stand for 15 minutes. Reserve ham hock for another use. Season with salt to taste. Serve.

Southwestern Tomato and Corn Salad

SERVES 4

WHY THIS RECIPE WORKS The key to this salad is choosing the best tomatoes and corn you can find. We tried adding the corn to the salad three ways: blanched, sautéed, and raw. Tasters preferred the version with the raw kernels to the two others because the kernels added bursts of sweetness that countered the acidic tomatoes. A vinaigrette (6 parts extra-virgin olive oil to 1 part lime juice) tied the salad together without obscuring the flavors of the star ingredients. For a robust Southwestern profile, we finished the salad with a sprinkling of queso fresco and some vibrant, fresh cilantro leaves.

If queso fresco is unavailable, you can substitute farmer's cheese or a mild feta.

1½	pounds ripe mixed tomatoes, cored
1	ear corn, kernels cut from cob
¼	cup extra-virgin olive oil
1	tablespoon minced shallot
1	tablespoon minced jalapeño chile
2	teaspoons lime juice
½	teaspoon table salt
¼	teaspoon pepper
2	ounces queso fresco, crumbled (½ cup)
2	tablespoons fresh cilantro leaves

1. Cut tomatoes into ½-inch-thick wedges, then cut wedges in half crosswise. Arrange tomatoes on large, shallow platter, alternating colors. Season with salt and pepper to taste. Sprinkle corn over top.

2. Whisk oil, shallot, jalapeño, lime juice, salt, and pepper together in medium bowl. Spoon dressing evenly over tomatoes. Sprinkle with queso fresco and cilantro. Serve.

Texas-Style Pinto Beans

Southwestern Tomato and Corn Salad

Skillet Corn with Mexican Chorizo

SERVES 4 TO 6

WHY THIS RECIPE WORKS We wanted a fork-friendly version of street corn with a little more oomph that didn't lose sight of what's so appealing about its muse. First, we sautéed chorizo to make the dish more substantial and add deeply savory notes. Adding fresh kernels of corn to the skillet developed a nice color to emulate grilling. Cooking it with the chorizo allowed the corn to pick up a porky flavor, and scallion whites, garlic, and oregano pumped up the flavor even more. Scallion greens, chopped cilantro, and lime juice stirred in off the heat gave the dish a pop of fresh brightness. Some quick pickled shallots added at the end punched up the flavor further while lending a sweet-sour balance to the salty, crumbly cotija cheese and tangy Mexican crema.

It's important to use fresh corn here. If you can't find fresh oregano, you can substitute 1½ teaspoons dried oregano. If you can't find Mexican crema, you can substitute a mixture of ¼ cup sour cream, 2 teaspoons lime juice, and ⅛ teaspoon table salt.

- ¼ cup red wine vinegar
- 1 tablespoon sugar
- 1 shallot, sliced into thin rings
- 8 ounces Mexican-style chorizo sausage, casings removed
- 4 scallions, white parts minced, green parts sliced thin on bias
- 2 garlic cloves, minced
- 5 ears corn, kernels cut from cobs (3¾ cups)
- 1 tablespoon minced fresh oregano
- ¾ teaspoon table salt
- ½ cup coarsely chopped fresh cilantro leaves and stems
- 1 tablespoon lime juice
- ¼ cup Mexican crema
- 2 ounces cotija cheese, crumbled

1. Combine vinegar and sugar in small bowl. Microwave until sugar is dissolved and vinegar is steaming, about 45 seconds. Add shallot and stir to combine. Cover with plastic wrap; set aside.

2. Cook chorizo in 12-inch nonstick skillet over medium-high heat, breaking up pieces with wooden spoon, until well browned, 4 to 6 minutes. Add scallion whites and garlic and cook until fragrant, about 30 seconds.

3. Add corn, oregano, and salt and cook until corn is spotty brown, about 6 minutes, stirring occasionally. Remove skillet from heat.

4. Drain shallot and discard liquid. Stir shallot, cilantro, lime juice, and scallion greens into corn mixture. Transfer to shallow bowl, drizzle with crema, and sprinkle with cotija. Serve.

Mexican Crema

Mexican crema is a rich, pourable cultured cream that is a saltier, thinner version of sour cream. You can find it the in the refrigerated section of your supermarket.

So-Cal Churros

MAKES ABOUT 18 CHURROS

WHY THIS RECIPE WORKS Churros should be crisp on the outside and soft on the inside, but piping thick pâte à choux dough into hot oil is no easy feat. We began by preparing a simple dough, precooking water, butter, sugar, vanilla, and salt before adding flour and eggs. The dough proved easier to work with when still warm, so we transferred it to a pastry bag right away. Piping the dough onto a baking sheet and frying in batches made it easier to monitor when the churros were done. A roll in cinnamon sugar and a dip in chocolate sauce made for a sweet finish.

We used a closed star #8 pastry tip, ⅝ inch in diameter, to create deeply grooved ridges in the churros. However, you can use any large, closed star tip of similar diameter, though your yield may vary slightly. It's important to mix the dough for 1 minute in step 2 before adding the eggs to keep them from scrambling.

Dough

- 2 cups water
- 2 tablespoons unsalted butter
- 2 tablespoons sugar
- 1 teaspoon vanilla extract
- ½ teaspoon table salt
- 2 cups (10 ounces) all-purpose flour
- 2 large eggs
- 2 quarts vegetable oil

Chocolate Sauce

- ¾ cup heavy cream
- 4 ounces semisweet chocolate chips
- Pinch table salt
- ¼ teaspoon vanilla extract

Coating

- ½ cup (3½ ounces) sugar
- ¾ teaspoon ground cinnamon

So-Cal Churros

1. For the Dough Line 1 rimmed baking sheet with parchment paper and spray with vegetable oil spray. Combine water, butter, sugar, vanilla, and salt in large saucepan and bring to boil over medium-high heat. Remove from heat; add flour all at once and stir with rubber spatula until well combined, with no streaks of flour remaining.

2. Transfer dough to bowl of stand mixer. Fit mixer with paddle and mix on low speed until cooled slightly, about 1 minute. Add eggs, increase speed to medium, and beat until fully incorporated, about 1 minute.

3. Transfer warm dough to piping bag fitted with ⅝-inch closed star pastry tip. Pipe 18 (6-inch) lengths of dough onto prepared sheet, using scissors to snip dough at tip. Refrigerate, uncovered, for 15 minutes to 1 hour.

4. Adjust oven rack to middle position and heat oven to 200 degrees. Set wire rack in second rimmed baking sheet and place in oven. Line large plate with triple layer of paper towels. Add oil to Dutch oven until it measures about 1½ inches deep and heat over medium-high heat to 375 degrees.

5. Gently drop 6 churros into hot oil and fry until dark golden brown on all sides, about 6 minutes, turning frequently for even cooking. Adjust burner, if necessary, to maintain oil temperature between 350 and 375 degrees. Transfer churros to paper towel–lined plate for 30 seconds to drain off excess oil, then transfer to wire rack in oven. Return oil to 375 degrees and repeat with remaining dough in 2 more batches.

6. For the Chocolate Sauce Microwave cream, chocolate chips, and salt in bowl at 50 percent power, stirring occasionally, until melted, about 2 minutes. Stir in vanilla until smooth.

7. For the Coating Combine sugar and cinnamon in shallow dish. Roll churros in cinnamon sugar, tapping gently to remove excess. Transfer churros to platter and serve warm with chocolate sauce.

Churning Out Churros

Pipe eighteen 6-inch lengths of warm dough, snipping at tip. Refrigerate 15 minutes to 1 hour to firm up before frying.

everybody loves italian

- **418** Pasta e Fagioli
- **419** Slow-Cooker Minestrone
- **420** Slow-Cooker Italian Sunday Gravy
- **421** Pork Ragu
- **422** Pasta with Sausage Ragu
- **422** Fettuccine with Butter and Cheese
- **424** Aglio e Olio (Spaghetti with Garlic and Olive Oil)
- **425** Spaghetti Carbonara
- **425** Pasta with Roasted Garlic Sauce, Arugula, and Walnuts
- **426** Pasta with Mushroom Sauce
- **427** Seafood Fra Diavolo
- **428** Instant Mashed Potato Gnocchi
- **430** Fluffy Baked Polenta with Red Sauce
- **431** Drop Meatballs
- **432** Meatballs and Marinara
- **433** Slow-Cooker Meatballs and Marinara
- **434** Slow-Cooker Baked Ziti
- **435** Italian Meatloaf
- **436** Skillet Lasagna
- **437** Hearty Beef Lasagna
- **438** Sausage Lasagna
- **439** Spinach and Tomato Lasagna
- **440** Eggplant Pecorino
- **441** Baked Manicotti with Meat Sauce
- **442** Cheesy Stuffed Shells
- **444** Grandma Pizza
- **445** Cast-Iron Skillet Pizza
- **446** Skillet Chicken Parmesan
- **447** Chicken Scampi
- **448** Chicken Scarpariello
- **448** Italian Pot Roast
- **450** Pork Chops with Vinegar Peppers
- **451** Salmon Piccata
- **451** Beans and Greens
- **452** Fried Artichokes
- **453** Prosciutto Bread
- **454** Zeppoles

Recipe Photos (from left to right): Italian Meatloaf, Sausage Lasagna

Pasta e Fagioli

SERVES 4 TO 6

WHY THIS RECIPE WORKS Every cook has a different take on "pasta fazool"—the hearty Italian American soup studded with creamy beans and little pieces of pasta. For our slightly sweet, full-bodied version, we started with chicken broth and added pancetta for meaty richness, tomato paste for savory punch, and plenty of garlic. To build body, we pureed half of the cannellini beans and added them to the broth with the remaining whole beans. Finally, for simplicity, we cooked ditalini pasta directly in the simmering soup before serving—their small size prevents them from bloating and sucking up too much of the brothy goodness.

You can use any small pasta shape, such as tubettini, elbow macaroni, or small shells, in place of the ditalini. To make this soup vegetarian, omit the pancetta and substitute vegetable broth for the chicken broth. If you do not have a food processor, you can use a blender to process the beans and water in step 1.

- 2 (15-ounce) cans cannellini beans, rinsed, divided
- 1 cup water
- 2 tablespoons extra-virgin olive oil, plus extra for drizzling
- 2 onions, chopped fine
- 2 carrots, peeled and chopped fine
- 1 celery rib, chopped fine
- 2 ounces pancetta, chopped fine
- ¾ teaspoon table salt
- ½ teaspoon pepper
- 2 tablespoons tomato paste
- 4 garlic cloves, minced
- ¼ teaspoon red pepper flakes (optional)
- 4 cups chicken broth
- 4 ounces (1 cup) ditalini
- 2 ounces Parmesan cheese, grated (1 cup), plus extra for serving
- ½ cup finely chopped fresh basil

1. Process 1 can of beans and water in food processor until smooth, about 30 seconds. Set aside.

2. Heat oil in large saucepan over medium heat until shimmering. Add onions, carrots, celery, pancetta, salt, and pepper and cook until vegetables are softened, about 10 minutes.

Pasta e Fagioli

3. Add tomato paste, garlic, and pepper flakes, if using, and cook until fragrant, about 2 minutes. Stir in broth, remaining can of beans, and pureed bean mixture. Bring to boil, reduce heat to medium-low, and simmer, stirring occasionally, until flavors have melded, about 10 minutes.

4. Increase heat to medium and bring to boil. Add pasta and cook, stirring occasionally, until pasta is al dente, about 12 minutes. Off heat, stir in Parmesan and basil. Serve, drizzled with extra oil and passing extra Parmesan separately.

To Make Ahead At end of step 3, let soup cool completely. Refrigerate soup for up to 2 days or freeze for up to 1 month. Let frozen soup thaw completely in refrigerator before reheating. To serve, bring soup to boil and continue with step 4.

> **Tiny Tubes**
> Ditalini are just the right size to add heft while still being easy to eat.
>
>

418 *The Complete Cook's Country TV Show Cookbook*

Slow-Cooker Minestrone

SERVES 6 TO 8

WHY THIS RECIPE WORKS To translate a classic minestrone to the slow cooker, we needed to find a combination of vegetables that would cook through in the same amount of time. Green beans took too long to become tender. We scrapped cauliflower because its flavor overwhelmed the soup. Zucchini squash and Swiss chard won out for texture and their similar cooking times. Canned beans disintegrated in the soup, so we used dried white beans. We started cooking the beans in the soup along with some softened carrots and onions, then added the squash, chard, and pasta toward the end of cooking so they would be perfectly tender.

We recommend using great Northern or cannellini beans here. Serve the minestrone with grated Parmesan cheese.

- 1 cup dried medium-size white beans, rinsed and picked over
- 6 tablespoons extra-virgin olive oil, divided
- 2 onions, chopped fine
- 4 carrots, peeled and cut into 1/2-inch pieces
- 8 garlic cloves, minced
- 1 (28-ounce) can whole peeled tomatoes, coarsely crushed by hand
- 8 cups chicken broth
- 3 cups water
- 2 cups fresh basil leaves, chopped, divided
- 1 teaspoon dried oregano
- 1/4 teaspoon red pepper flakes
- 2 medium zucchini, quartered lengthwise, seeded, and sliced 1/4 inch thick
- 8 ounces Swiss chard, stemmed and chopped
- 1/2 cup small dried pasta, such as ditalini, orzo, or small elbows
- Table salt and pepper

1. Bring beans and enough water to cover by 1 inch to boil in medium saucepan over high heat. Reduce heat to low and simmer, covered, until beans are just beginning to soften, about 20 minutes. Drain beans and transfer to slow cooker.

Slow-Cooker Minestrone

2. Heat 3 tablespoons oil in Dutch oven over medium heat until shimmering. Add onions and carrots and cook until softened, about 5 minutes. Stir in garlic and cook until fragrant, about 30 seconds. Add tomatoes and their juice and cook until pan is nearly dry, 8 to 12 minutes. Stir in broth, water, 1/2 cup basil, oregano, and pepper flakes and bring to boil; transfer to slow cooker. Cover and cook until beans are tender, 6 to 7 hours on low or 5 to 6 hours on high.

3. Stir zucchini, Swiss chard, and pasta into slow cooker and cook on high, covered, until pasta is tender, 20 to 30 minutes. Stir in remaining 1 1/2 cups basil and remaining 3 tablespoons oil. Season with salt and pepper to taste, and serve.

To Make Ahead Recipe can be made through step 2 and refrigerated for up to 2 days. To finish, bring to boil in Dutch oven. Stir in zucchini, chard, and pasta; reduce heat to low; and simmer until pasta is tender, about 10 minutes.

Slow-Cooker Italian Sunday Gravy

Pork Ragu

Slow-Cooker Italian Sunday Gravy

SERVES 8 TO 10

WHY THIS RECIPE WORKS We love the flavor and heartiness of Sunday gravy, but traditional recipes feature a long ingredient list and involve hours of monitoring the stovetop. For a streamlined recipe, we turned to our slow cooker and narrowed the meat selection down to three: flank steak, for meaty flavor; country-style spareribs, for tender, fall-off-the-bone meat; and sausage, for its spicy, sweet kick. Using the flavorful drippings left behind from browning the sausage to sauté our aromatics infused the whole dish with flavor. And a combination of drained diced tomatoes, canned tomato sauce, and tomato paste ensured a rich, thick sauce.

Most sausage has enough seasoning to make extra salt unnecessary. This recipe makes enough to sauce 2 pounds of pasta. We like rigatoni, ziti, or penne with this sauce.

- 1 tablespoon vegetable oil
- 1 pound sweet Italian sausage
- 1 pound hot Italian sausage
- 2 onions, chopped
- 12 garlic cloves, minced
- 2 teaspoons dried oregano
- 1 (6-ounce) can tomato paste
- ½ cup dry red wine
- 1 (28-ounce) can diced tomatoes, drained
- 1 (28-ounce) can tomato sauce
- 2 pounds bone-in country-style pork spareribs, trimmed
- 1 (1½-pound) flank steak, trimmed
- 3 tablespoons chopped fresh basil
  Pepper

1. Heat oil in Dutch oven over medium-high heat until just smoking. Add sweet sausage and cook until well browned and fat begins to render, about 8 minutes. Using slotted spoon, transfer sausage to paper towel–lined plate to drain, then place in slow cooker. Repeat with hot sausage; transfer to slow cooker.

2. Cook onions in rendered fat over medium heat until well browned, about 6 minutes. Stir in garlic and oregano and cook until fragrant, about 1 minute. Add tomato paste and cook until it begins to brown, about 5 minutes.

Stir in wine and simmer, scraping up browned bits, until wine is slightly reduced, about 3 minutes. Transfer to slow cooker. Stir in diced tomatoes and tomato sauce.

3. Submerge spareribs and steak in sauce in slow cooker. Cover and cook until meat is tender, 8 to 10 hours on low or 4 to 5 hours on high.

4. About 30 minutes before serving, remove ribs, steak, and sausages and set aside until cool enough to handle. Shred ribs and steak into small pieces, discarding excess fat and bones; slice sausages in half crosswise. Skim fat from surface of sauce, then stir sausages and shredded meat back into sauce. Stir in basil and season with pepper to taste. Serve. (Gravy can be refrigerated for up to 3 days.)

To Make Ahead Recipe can be made in advance through step 2. After stirring in diced tomatoes and tomato sauce, add browned sausages and simmer over medium-low heat until cooked through, about 12 minutes. Refrigerate sausage and sauce for up to 2 days. To cook gravy, warm sauce and sausages together over medium heat until heated through; transfer to slow cooker. Proceed with step 3.

Pork Ragu

MAKES ABOUT 8 CUPS

WHY THIS RECIPE WORKS Earthy and intense, pork ragu takes pasta to a new level. Most recipes call for pork shoulder and a hard-to-find, bony cut like neck, shank, or feet. We tried using all baby back ribs and found the resulting ragu rich and meaty. For a classic Italian flavor profile, fennel took the place of celery in the ragu's base and ground fennel rubbed into the ribs echoed the anise flavor. Simmering the garlic head whole right in the sauce yielded sweeter softened cloves that we squeezed back into the sauce when tender. With fresh herbs and red wine, our ragu tasted balanced and far more complex than its simple preparation would suggest.

This recipe makes enough sauce to coat 2 pounds of pasta. Leftover sauce may be refrigerated for up to 3 days or frozen for up to 1 month.

- 2 (2¼- to 2½-pound) racks baby back ribs, trimmed and each rack cut into fourths
- 2 teaspoons ground fennel
  Kosher salt and pepper
- 3 tablespoons extra-virgin olive oil
- 1 large onion, chopped fine
- 1 large fennel bulb, stalks discarded, bulb halved, cored, and chopped fine
- 2 large carrots, peeled and chopped fine
- ¼ cup minced fresh sage, divided
- 1½ teaspoons minced fresh rosemary
- 1 cup plus 2 tablespoons dry red wine
- 1 (28-ounce) can whole peeled tomatoes, drained and chopped coarse
- 3 cups chicken broth
- 1 garlic head, outer papery skins removed and top fourth of head cut off and discarded
- 1 pound pappardelle or tagliatelle
  Grated Parmesan cheese

1. Adjust oven rack to middle position and heat oven to 300 degrees. Sprinkle ribs with ground fennel and generously season with salt and pepper, pressing spices to adhere. Heat oil in Dutch oven over medium-high heat until just smoking. Add half of ribs, meat side down, and cook, without moving them, until meat is well browned, 6 to 8 minutes; transfer to plate. Repeat with remaining ribs; set aside.

2. Reduce heat to medium and add onion, fennel, carrots, 2 tablespoons sage, rosemary, and ½ teaspoon salt to now-empty pot. Cook, stirring occasionally and scraping up any browned bits, until vegetables are well browned and beginning to stick to pot bottom, 12 to 15 minutes.

3. Add 1 cup wine and cook until evaporated, about 5 minutes. Stir in tomatoes and broth and bring to simmer. Submerge garlic and ribs, meat side down, in liquid; add any accumulated juices from plate. Cover and transfer to oven. Cook until ribs are fork-tender, about 2 hours.

4. Remove pot from oven and transfer ribs and garlic to rimmed baking sheet. Using large spoon, skim any fat from surface of sauce. Once cool enough to handle, shred meat from bones; discard bones and gristle. Return meat to pot. Squeeze garlic from its skin into pot. Stir in remaining 2 tablespoons sage and remaining 2 tablespoons wine. Season with salt and pepper to taste.

5. Meanwhile, bring 4 quarts water to boil in large pot. Add pasta and 2 tablespoons salt and cook, stirring often, until al dente. Reserve ½ cup cooking water, then drain pasta and return it to pot. Add half of sauce and toss to combine, adjusting consistency with reserved cooking water as needed. Serve, passing Parmesan separately.

Pasta with Sausage Ragu

SERVES 4 TO 6

WHY THIS RECIPE WORKS For the long-cooked flavor of pork ragu in under 90 minutes, we looked to our food processor. Whirring fennel, onion, and fennel seeds together created a savory flavor base. Pulsing canned whole tomatoes created a silky tomato sauce, and processing sweet Italian sausage delivered bites of well-seasoned meat in every forkful. We cooked the components in stages, browning the sausage before softening the soffritto in the rendered fat. Minced garlic and dried oregano, bloomed in tomato paste, further defined the Italian flavors, and red wine offered brightness. A 45-minute simmer produced a rich ragu with the perfect consistency.

For a spicier sauce, substitute hot Italian sausage for sweet. You will have 3 cups of extra sauce, which can be used to sauce 1 pound of pasta.

- ½ fennel bulb, stalks discarded, bulb cored and chopped coarse
- ½ onion, chopped coarse
- 1 tablespoon fennel seeds
- 1 (28-ounce) can whole peeled tomatoes
- 2 pounds sweet Italian sausage, casings removed
- 1 tablespoon extra-virgin olive oil, plus extra for drizzling
- Table salt and pepper
- 2 tablespoons tomato paste
- 4 garlic cloves, minced
- 1½ teaspoons dried oregano
- ¾ cup red wine
- 1 pound pappardelle or tagliatelle
- Grated Parmesan cheese

1. Pulse fennel, onion, and fennel seeds in food processor until finely chopped, about 10 pulses, scraping down sides of bowl as needed; transfer to separate bowl. Process tomatoes in now-empty processor until smooth, about 10 seconds; transfer to second bowl. Pulse sausage in now-empty processor until finely chopped, about 10 pulses, scraping down sides of bowl as needed.

2. Heat oil in Dutch oven over medium-high heat until shimmering. Add sausage and cook, breaking up meat with spoon, until all liquid has evaporated and meat begins to sizzle, 10 to 15 minutes.

3. Add fennel mixture and ½ teaspoon salt and cook stirring occasionally, until softened, about 5 minutes. (Fond on bottom of pot will be deeply browned.) Add tomato paste, garlic, and oregano and cook, stirring constantly, until fragrant, about 30 seconds.

4. Stir in wine, scraping up any browned bits, and cook until nearly evaporated, about 1 minute. Add 1 cup water and pureed tomatoes and bring to simmer. Reduce heat to low and simmer gently, uncovered, until thickened, about 45 minutes. (Wooden spoon should leave trail when dragged through sauce.) Season with salt and pepper to taste; cover and keep warm.

5. Bring 4 quarts water to boil in large pot. Add pasta and 1 tablespoon salt and cook, stirring often, until al dente. Reserve 1 cup cooking water, then drain pasta and return it to pot. Add 3 cups sauce and ½ cup reserved cooking water to pasta and toss to combine. Adjust consistency with remaining reserved cooking water as needed. Transfer to serving dish. Drizzle with extra oil, sprinkle with Parmesan, and serve. (Remaining 3 cups sauce can be refrigerated for up to 3 days or frozen for up to 1 month.)

Fettuccine with Butter and Cheese

SERVES 4 TO 6

WHY THIS RECIPE WORKS Fettuccine with butter and cheese, aka fettuccine Alfredo, has simple roots and a rich sauce of only a few ingredients: Parmigiano-Reggiano, butter, and salt. The secret to getting a silky sauce that coats each strand? Using the pasta's cooking water. After cooking a pound of fettuccine in exactly 3 quarts of water, we reserved 1 cup of the starchy liquid and added it back to the drained pasta along with the sauce's ingredients. After a rest and some vigorous stirring, the butter, cheese, and pasta water formed a creamy, emulsified sauce. Serving the pasta in warm bowls kept the pasta hot and the sauce velvety right to the last bite.

Be sure to use imported Parmigiano-Reggiano cheese here and not the bland domestic cheese labeled "Parmesan." For the best results, grate the cheese on a rasp-style grater. Do not adjust the amount of water for cooking the pasta.

Stir the pasta frequently while cooking so that it doesn't stick together. It's important to move quickly after draining the pasta, as the residual heat from the reserved cooking water and pasta will help the cheese and butter melt. For best results, heat ovensafe dinner bowls in a 200-degree oven for 10 minutes prior to serving and serve the pasta hot. If you are using fresh pasta, increase the amount to 1¼ pounds.

- 1 pound fettuccine
- Table salt
- 4 ounces Parmigiano-Reggiano, grated (2 cups), plus extra for serving
- 5 tablespoons unsalted butter, cut into 5 pieces

1. Bring 3 quarts water to boil in large Dutch oven. Add pasta and 1 tablespoon salt and cook, stirring frequently, until al dente. Reserve 1 cup cooking water, then drain pasta and return it to pot.

2. Add Parmigiano-Reggiano, butter, reserved cooking water, and ½ teaspoon salt to pot. Set pot over low heat and, using tongs, toss and stir vigorously to thoroughly combine, about 1 minute. Remove pot from heat, cover, and let pasta sit for 1 minute.

3. Toss pasta vigorously once more so sauce thoroughly coats pasta and any cheese clumps are emulsified into sauce, about 30 seconds. (Mixture may look wet at this point, but pasta will absorb excess moisture as it cools slightly.) Season with salt to taste.

4. Transfer pasta to individual bowls. (Use rubber spatula as needed to remove any clumps of cheese stuck to tongs and bottom of pot.) Serve immediately, passing extra Parmigiano-Reggiano separately.

Keep On Stirring

When the grated Parmigiano-Reggiano cheese, butter pieces, and reserved pasta cooking water are stirred into the still-hot fettuccine, the dish will appear very watery. But don't fret: After a covered 1-minute rest and a vigorous stir, the sauce will come together, forming a creamy emulsion.

Pasta with Sausage Ragu

Fettuccine with Butter and Cheese

Aglio e Olio (Spaghetti with Garlic and Olive Oil)

Spaghetti Carbonara

Aglio e Olio (Spaghetti with Garlic and Olive Oil)

SERVES 4 TO 6

WHY THIS RECIPE WORKS We wanted to create a creamy pasta according to the traditional method—without the addition of heavy cream or cheese—letting the pasta's starch do the work of thickening the sauce for us. To start, we lightly simmered equal parts garlic and olive oil in a small saucepan to soften the harshness of the garlic and to infuse the oil. We then reserved some of the starchy pasta cooking water to use as the foundation for our sauce. We simply set the garlic oil; pasta water; and parcooked, drained pasta back over heat in the pasta cooking pot and stirred to create a full-bodied sauce while the pasta finished cooking through. As a final touch, we added chopped parsley for color and vibrancy.

Be sure to use the 3 quarts of water specified in the recipe for cooking the pasta. The starch that the pasta releases into the water is essential to achieving the proper consistency in the sauce.

- ⅓ cup extra-virgin olive oil
- 8 garlic cloves, sliced thin
- ½ teaspoon red pepper flakes
- 1 pound spaghetti
- ½ teaspoon table salt, plus salt for cooking pasta
- 3 tablespoons chopped fresh parsley

1. Heat oil and garlic in small saucepan over medium-low heat until pale golden and fragrant, about 5 minutes. Off heat, stir in pepper flakes. Set aside.

2. Meanwhile, bring 3 quarts water to boil in large Dutch oven. Add pasta and 1 tablespoon salt and cook, stirring often, until strands are flexible but still very firm in center, about 5 minutes. Reserve 3 cups cooking water, then drain pasta.

3. Combine pasta, oil mixture, ½ teaspoon salt, and 2 cups reserved cooking water in now-empty pot and bring to boil over medium-high heat. Cook, stirring often with tongs and folding pasta over itself, until water is mostly absorbed but still pools slightly in bottom of pot, about 5 minutes.

4. Let pasta sit off heat for 2 minutes. Stir in parsley and additional reserved cooking water as needed (approximately ¼ cup) to adjust consistency (noodles should be slightly wet, not oily). Serve.

Spaghetti Carbonara

SERVES 4

WHY THIS RECIPE WORKS We wanted a bulletproof version of this much-beloved Roman dish. We began by rendering guanciale (cured pork jowl) until it was slightly crisp but still chewy. For the sauce base, we whisked egg yolks and whole eggs with a hefty amount of freshly ground black pepper and the traditional Pecorino Romano cheese. Once the spaghetti was cooked to al dente, we used some of the cooking water to temper the egg mixture. Tossing the hot pasta with the guanciale, its rendered fat, and the egg mixture emulsified it all into a silky sauce.

It is important to immediately add the egg mixture to the hot pasta in step 5. The hot pasta cooks the eggs, which thickens them and creates a sauce. We call for Pecorino Romano here, but Parmesan can be used, if preferred. If guanciale is difficult to find, you can substitute pancetta; just be sure to buy a 4-ounce chunk and not presliced pancetta. It's best to use freshly ground black pepper here.

- 3 large eggs plus 2 large yolks
- 2½ ounces Pecorino Romano cheese, grated (1¼ cups), plus extra for serving
- 1 teaspoon pepper, plus extra for serving
- ¼ teaspoon table salt, plus salt for cooking pasta
- 4 ounces guanciale, cut into ½-inch chunks
- 2 tablespoons extra-virgin olive oil
- 1 pound spaghetti

1. Bring 4 quarts water to boil in large Dutch oven.

2. Meanwhile, beat eggs and yolks, Pecorino, pepper, and salt together in bowl; set aside. Combine guanciale and oil in 12-inch nonstick skillet and cook over medium heat, stirring frequently, until guanciale begins to brown and is just shy of crisp, about 6 minutes. Remove skillet from heat.

3. Add pasta and 1 tablespoon salt to boiling water and cook, stirring often, until al dente.

4. Reserve ½ cup cooking water, then drain pasta and immediately return it to pot. Add guanciale and rendered fat from skillet and toss with tongs to coat pasta.

5. Working quickly, whisk ¼ cup reserved cooking water into egg mixture, then add egg mixture to pasta in pot. Toss pasta until sauce begins to thicken and looks creamy, 1 to 2 minutes. Adjust consistency with remaining reserved cooking water as needed. Serve immediately, passing extra Pecorino and pepper separately.

Pasta with Roasted Garlic Sauce, Arugula, and Walnuts

Pasta with Roasted Garlic Sauce, Arugula, and Walnuts

SERVES 4

WHY THIS RECIPE WORKS Toasting mellows, softens, and sweetens a head of garlic. But rather than waiting the hour or more it can take to roast garlic in the oven, we set out to develop a quick pasta dish that could harness the same great flavor in short order. We browned a whopping 50 whole cloves on the stovetop and then poached the garlic in chicken broth seasoned with sweet, tangy balsamic vinegar. After a spin in the food processor, the final result was a complex and silky sauce that we combined with walnuts and spicy arugula. The best part? The whole thing took just 15 minutes—more than enough time to cook the pasta.

It takes about four heads of garlic to yield 50 cloves, but you can use prepeeled.

EVERYBODY LOVES ITALIAN   425

- 50 garlic cloves, peeled (1 cup)
- 3 tablespoons extra-virgin olive oil, plus extra for drizzling
- 1 cup chicken broth
- 2 teaspoons balsamic vinegar
  Table salt and pepper
- 1 pound spaghetti, linguine, or fettuccine
- 8 ounces (8 cups) baby arugula
- 1 cup walnuts, toasted and chopped
  Grated Pecorino Romano cheese

1. Combine garlic and oil in medium saucepan over medium-low heat. Cover and cook, stirring occasionally, until garlic is browned all over, 6 to 8 minutes. Add broth, vinegar, ¾ teaspoon salt, and ½ teaspoon pepper and bring to boil. Reduce heat to low and simmer, uncovered, until garlic is fork-tender, 5 to 7 minutes. Pour garlic mixture into food processor and process until smooth, about 1 minute.

2. Meanwhile, bring 4 quarts water to boil in large pot. Add pasta and 1 tablespoon salt and cook, stirring often, until al dente. Reserve ½ cup cooking water, then drain pasta and return it to pot. Add garlic sauce, arugula, and walnuts to pasta and toss to combine. Adjust consistency with reserved cooking water as needed. Season with salt and pepper to taste. Serve, drizzling individual servings with extra oil and passing Pecorino separately.

Pasta with Mushroom Sauce

SERVES 4

Pasta with Mushroom Sauce

WHY THIS RECIPE WORKS In order to coax as much earthy, meaty flavor as possible from supermarket mushrooms, we used fresh shiitake and white mushrooms, plus dried porcini. We coarsely chopped half of them to increase surface area for browning and quartered the rest for visual appeal and meaty texture. After deglazing the pan with wine, we added the pasta directly to the pot so it could absorb the flavorful liquid. One minute of vigorous stirring drew out the pasta's starch, adding structure to the sauce and helping it cling to the pasta.

If you can't find shiitake mushrooms, cremini mushrooms can be substituted or white mushrooms can be used exclusively, but don't omit the dried porcini. Parmesan cheese can be substituted for the Pecorino Romano.

- 12 ounces shiitake mushrooms, stemmed
- 12 ounces white mushrooms, trimmed
- 4 tablespoons unsalted butter, divided
  Table salt and pepper
- 2 shallots, minced
- 2 tablespoons minced fresh sage
- 4 garlic cloves, minced
- ¼ ounce dried porcini mushrooms, rinsed and chopped fine
- ½ cup dry white wine
- 4 cups water plus ¼ cup hot water
- 12 ounces (3¾ cups) campanelle, penne, or fusilli
- 2 ounces Pecorino Romano cheese, grated (1 cup), plus extra for serving
- 1 tablespoon lemon juice
- 2 tablespoons minced fresh chives

1. Coarsely chop half of shiitake mushrooms and white mushrooms; then quarter remaining shiitake mushrooms and white mushrooms. Melt 2 tablespoons butter in Dutch oven over medium-high heat. Add all shiitake mushrooms and white mushrooms (both chopped and quartered) and ¾ teaspoon salt. Cover and cook until mushrooms release their liquid, about 5 minutes. Uncover and continue to cook, stirring occasionally, until all liquid has evaporated and mushrooms begin to brown, about 10 minutes.

2. Add shallots, sage, garlic, and porcini mushrooms and cook until fragrant, about 1 minute. Add wine and cook until evaporated, about 2 minutes. Stir in 4 cups water, pasta, and 1¼ teaspoons salt and bring to boil. Reduce heat to medium, cover, and cook, stirring occasionally, until pasta is tender, 12 to 15 minutes.

3. Off heat, stir in Pecorino, ¼ cup hot water, lemon juice, remaining 2 tablespoons butter, and ½ teaspoon pepper. Stir vigorously for 1 minute, until sauce is thickened. Season with salt and pepper to taste. Transfer to serving dish and sprinkle with chives. Serve, passing extra Pecorino separately.

Seafood Fra Diavolo

SERVES 4 TO 6

Seafood Fra Diavolo

WHY THIS RECIPE WORKS To make this restaurant classic at home, we cooked all the ingredients in one pot. This simplified cleanup and ensured that every element of the dish was infused with fresh seafood flavor. We started by steaming our mussels, removing them from the pot, and adding whole peeled tomatoes and briny clam juice to the flavorful liquid they left behind. We then added our linguine to cook through and soak up the sauce. Once the pasta was nearly cooked through, we tossed in the shrimp and scallops. We returned the mussels to the pot and finished the dish with chopped pickled cherry peppers and fresh parsley.

We prefer shrimp not treated with salt or additives such as sodium tripolyphosphate (STPP). Most frozen E-Z peel shrimp have been treated (the ingredient list should tell you). We recommend buying "dry" scallops, which don't have chemical additives and taste better than "wet." Dry scallops will look ivory or pinkish; wet scallops are bright white. If you can't find fresh "dry" scallops, you can substitute thawed frozen scallops. If you're spice averse, use a lesser amount of pepper flakes and cherry peppers. Different brands of linguine will cook at different rates and absorb different amounts of liquid; you may not need to add any hot water in step 5, but having some on hand provides insurance against the pasta being too dry.

- 12 ounces extra-large shrimp (21 to 25 per pound), peeled, deveined, and tails removed
- 12 ounces large sea scallops, tendons removed, cut in half horizontally
- 6 tablespoons extra-virgin olive oil, divided, plus extra for drizzling
- 7 garlic cloves, minced, divided
- ¾ teaspoon table salt, divided
- 3 anchovy fillets, rinsed
- 3 tablespoons tomato paste
- 2 teaspoons dried oregano
- 1–1½ teaspoons red pepper flakes, plus extra for sprinkling
- 1 pound mussels, scrubbed and debearded
- 1 cup dry white wine
- 1 (28-ounce) can whole peeled tomatoes
- 1 (8-ounce) bottle clam juice
- 12 ounces linguine
- Hot water
- ½ cup chopped fresh parsley
- 1–2 tablespoons chopped jarred hot cherry peppers, plus 1 tablespoon brine

EVERYBODY LOVES ITALIAN

1. Toss shrimp and scallops with 2 tablespoons oil, 1 tablespoon garlic, and ½ teaspoon salt in bowl. Refrigerate until ready to use.

2. Combine anchovies, remaining ¼ cup oil, and remaining garlic in large Dutch oven and cook over medium heat until garlic is just beginning to brown, 3 to 5 minutes, breaking up anchovies with wooden spoon.

3. Add tomato paste, oregano, and pepper flakes and cook, stirring constantly, until tomato paste begins to darken, about 2 minutes. Increase heat to medium-high. Add mussels and wine and bring to boil. Cover and cook, shaking pot occasionally, until mussels have opened, 3 to 4 minutes (discard any unopened mussels). Using tongs, transfer mussels to bowl and cover to keep warm.

4. Add tomatoes and their juice, clam juice, and remaining ¼ teaspoon salt to pot. Using potato masher, mash tomatoes in pot until coarsely pureed.

5. Bring tomato mixture to boil over medium-high heat. Add pasta (it needn't be fully submerged) and cook, stirring often, until strands are flexible but still slightly firm in center, 6 to 10 minutes. (If sauce begins to dry up before pasta is done, add hot water, ½ cup at a time, and continue cooking pasta. Begin checking pasta 2 minutes shy of package instructions; it should be nearly cooked to your liking before adding seafood.)

6. Stir in shrimp and scallops and cook, stirring frequently, until pasta is al dente and seafood is opaque, about 3 minutes.

7. Off heat, add parsley, cherry peppers and brine, and mussels (along with any accumulated juices) and toss to combine. (Pasta sauce will continue to thicken. Adjust consistency with additional hot water as needed.) Season with salt to taste. Serve, sprinkled with extra pepper flakes and drizzled with extra oil.

What's in a Name?

Fra diavolo is an angry sauce named after an angry guy. Its name translates as "brother devil" and is a reference to Michele Pezza, an infamous hothead and ferocious Italian bandit who carried that nickname. Pezza was pardoned and hired to lead Italian guerilla forces fighting against the invading French in Naples at the turn of the 19th century.

Instant Mashed Potato Gnocchi

Instant Mashed Potato Gnocchi

SERVES 4 (MAKES 1½ POUNDS)

WHY THIS RECIPE WORKS These gnocchi are easy to make with a little help from a convenience product. Instead of cooking, peeling, and mashing potatoes, we simply used instant mashed potato flakes. After a quick knead and rest, the dough was easy to divide into pieces and shape into dumplings. We cooked the gnocchi in boiling water and then tossed them with a simple sauce.

We used Idahoan Original Mashed Potatoes when developing this recipe. Do not use flavored instant mashed potato flakes. It is important to knead the dough to the texture of Play-Doh in step 2, or it will be too tender and difficult to roll into ropes. In step 3, be sure to very lightly dust the counter with flour before rolling the dough into ropes to keep them from sticking. In step 5, make whichever sauce you prefer. See "Shape It Your Way" for other shaping ideas.

> ### Shape It Your Way
> Here are some popular methods for shaping gnocchi. Note that the shape you choose won't affect the cooking time.
>
>
> **Squares** Just cut the rope with your bench scraper, and you're done.
>
>
> **Spheres** Roll the cut gnocchi between your fingers to form little balls.
>
>
> **Indented** Give each gnocchi a poke, about ¼ inch deep, in its center to create a divot.
>
>
> **Ridged** Roll the cut gnocchi downward on the tines of a fork to create grooves.

- 2 cups (4 ounces) plain instant mashed potato flakes
- 1 cup (5 ounces) all-purpose flour
- 2 teaspoons table salt, plus salt for cooking gnocchi
- 1½ cups water
- 1 large egg
  Grated Parmesan cheese

1. Whisk potato flakes, flour, and salt together in large bowl. Whisk water and egg together in separate bowl. Add water mixture to potato flake mixture and stir with wooden spoon until fully combined and mixture forms dough ball. Let sit for 3 minutes for potato flakes and flour to hydrate.

2. Turn out dough onto lightly floured counter and knead until dough has texture of Play-Doh and springs back halfway when poked with your finger, about 3 minutes. Lightly dust dough with flour and let rest on counter for 5 minutes.

3. Divide dough into 6 equal pieces. On very lightly floured counter, roll 1 piece into ¾-inch-thick rope. Lightly dust rope with flour. Using floured bench scraper, cut rope crosswise into ¾-inch pieces; transfer gnocchi to lightly floured rimmed baking sheet. Repeat with remaining dough pieces.

4. Press gnocchi, cut side down, on tines of fork, then roll downward to create grooves. If dough sticks, dust your thumb and fork with flour. Return gnocchi to sheet.

5. Prepare 1 recipe sauce according to directions that follow.

6. Bring 4 quarts water to boil in large pot over high heat. Add 1 tablespoon salt to boiling water. Add half of gnocchi, then stir gently to keep from sticking. Simmer until just cooked through and gnocchi float to top, about 1½ minutes. Using spider skimmer or slotted spoon, transfer gnocchi to skillet with sauce. Return water to boil and repeat with remaining gnocchi.

7. Place skillet over medium-high heat. Cook, stirring gently, until hot throughout and gnocchi are well coated with sauce, about 2 minutes. Season with salt to taste. Sprinkle with Parmesan and serve.

Tomato-Basil Sauce
MAKES ENOUGH FOR 1½ POUNDS GNOCCHI
A good-quality jarred marinara, such as Rao's, can be substituted for the canned tomato sauce.

- 2 tablespoons extra-virgin olive oil
- 2 garlic cloves, minced
- 1 (15-ounce) can tomato sauce
- 1 teaspoon sugar
- ¼ teaspoon pepper
- ¼ teaspoon dried oregano
- ½ cup fresh basil leaves, torn into ½-inch pieces

Combine oil and garlic in 12-inch skillet. Cook over medium heat until garlic is fragrant and just beginning to turn golden, about 2 minutes. Carefully stir in tomato sauce, sugar, pepper, and oregano. Bring to simmer, then remove from heat. Stir in basil. Cover to keep warm.

Fontina Cheese Sauce
MAKES ENOUGH FOR 1½ POUNDS GNOCCHI
Fontal cheese, which is in the fontina family, can be substituted for the fontina.

EVERYBODY LOVES ITALIAN

- 2 tablespoons unsalted butter
- 1 garlic clove, minced
- 2 tablespoons all-purpose flour
- 1¼ cups whole milk
- 4 ounces fontina cheese, shredded (1 cup)
- ½ teaspoon table salt
- ¼ teaspoon pepper

Melt butter in 12-inch skillet over medium heat. Add garlic and cook until fragrant, about 30 seconds. Whisk in flour and cook for 1 minute. Slowly whisk in milk. Bring to simmer, then remove from heat. Whisk in fontina, salt, and pepper. Cover to keep warm.

Browned Butter–Caper Sauce
MAKES ENOUGH FOR 1½ POUNDS GNOCCHI
If using salt-packed capers, rinse them before mincing.

- 6 tablespoons unsalted butter
- 2 tablespoons minced shallot
- 2 tablespoons capers, minced
- 1 tablespoon lemon juice

Melt butter in 12-inch skillet over medium heat. Cook, swirling skillet often, until butter is color of milk chocolate and has toasty aroma, 3 to 5 minutes. Add shallot and cook until fragrant, about 30 seconds. Off heat, stir in capers and lemon juice. Cover to keep warm.

Fluffy Baked Polenta with Red Sauce

SERVES 6

WHY THIS RECIPE WORKS We visited Mike's Kitchen in Cranston, Rhode Island, and were inspired by Mike Lepizzera's creamy, light polenta. Cooking the cornmeal in water instead of dairy gave us clean, sweet corn flavor and an airy texture. Garlic oil boosted the savory flavor, while half-and-half and Pecorino contributed richness. While the polenta chilled, we processed canned tomatoes into a puree for a sweet-and-savory red sauce. We then sliced blocks of polenta and browned them in the oven.

We developed this recipe using Quaker Yellow Corn Meal for its desirable texture and relatively short cooking time. The timing may be different for other types of cornmeal, so be sure to cook the polenta until it is thickened and tender. Whole milk can be substituted for the half-and-half. Plan ahead: The polenta needs to cool for at least 3 hours before being cut, baked, and served.

Polenta
- 4 tablespoons unsalted butter
- 2 tablespoons extra-virgin olive oil
- 2 garlic cloves, smashed and peeled
- 7 cups water
- 1½ teaspoons table salt
- ½ teaspoon pepper
- 1½ cups cornmeal
- 3 ounces Pecorino Romano cheese, grated (1½ cups)
- ¼ cup half-and-half

Red Sauce
- 1 (14.5-ounce) can whole peeled tomatoes
- ¼ cup extra-virgin olive oil, divided
- 1 onion, peeled and halved through root end
- 1 (15-ounce) can tomato sauce
- 1 ounce Pecorino Romano cheese, grated (½ cup)
- 1½ tablespoons sugar
- ¾ teaspoon table salt
- ½ teaspoon garlic powder

1. For the Polenta Lightly grease 8-inch square baking pan. Heat butter and oil in Dutch oven over medium heat until butter is melted. Add garlic and cook until lightly golden, about 4 minutes. Discard garlic.

2. Add water, salt, and pepper to butter mixture. Increase heat to medium-high and bring to boil. Add cornmeal in slow, steady stream, whisking constantly. Reduce heat to medium-low and continue to cook, whisking frequently and scraping sides and bottom of pot, until mixture is thick and cornmeal is tender, about 20 minutes.

3. Off heat, whisk in Pecorino and half-and-half. Transfer to prepared pan and let cool completely on wire rack. Once cooled, cover with plastic wrap and refrigerate until completely chilled, at least 3 hours.

4. For the Red Sauce Process tomatoes and their juice in blender until smooth, about 30 seconds. Heat 1 tablespoon oil in large saucepan over medium heat until shimmering. Add onion, cut side down, and cook without moving until lightly browned, about 4 minutes. Add pureed tomatoes, tomato sauce, Pecorino, sugar, salt, garlic powder, and remaining 3 tablespoons oil. Bring mixture to boil, reduce heat to medium-low, and simmer until sauce is slightly thickened, about 15 minutes. Remove from heat, discard onion, cover, and keep warm.

5. Adjust oven rack to middle position and heat oven to 375 degrees. Line rimmed baking sheet with parchment paper, then grease parchment. Cut chilled polenta into 6 equal pieces (about 4 by 2⅔ inches each). Place on prepared sheet and bake until heated through and beginning to brown on bottom, about 30 minutes. Serve each portion covered with about ½ cup red sauce.

Drop Meatballs
SERVES 6 TO 8

WHY THIS RECIPE WORKS For a simpler meatball recipe, we skipped our usual browning step (good for developing a nice crust, but a lot of work) and went straight to simmering them in a sauce. But we discovered that the crust adds more than just flavor; it also keeps the meatballs intact. A crushed saltine panade (higher-moisture bread crumbs caused crumbling) saved the day, as did finishing everything in the oven so the meatballs could cook evenly without stirring. We liked the brighter, less meaty sauce, and added a hefty dose of smashed garlic and red pepper flakes for a savory edge and a slight kick.

You can use a #16 portion scoop to form the meatballs. To make shaping easier, wet your hands slightly. The recipe yields enough sauce for 2 pounds of pasta. To serve, toss the pasta with some sauce and top it with the meatballs.

Meatballs
- 22 square saltines
- 1 cup milk
- 2 pounds 85 percent lean ground beef
- 2 ounces Parmesan cheese, grated (1 cup)
- 1 teaspoon garlic powder
- 1 teaspoon dried oregano
- 1 teaspoon table salt
- ½ teaspoon pepper

Sauce
- ¼ cup extra-virgin olive oil
- 10 garlic cloves, peeled and smashed
- ½ teaspoon red pepper flakes
- 2 (28-ounce) cans crushed tomatoes
  Table salt and pepper
- 3 tablespoons chopped fresh basil

Fluffy Baked Polenta with Red Sauce

Drop Meatballs

1. **For the Meatballs** Adjust oven rack to lower-middle position and heat oven to 400 degrees. Place saltines in large zipper-lock bag, seal bag, and crush saltines fine with rolling pin (you should have 1 cup). Combine saltines and milk in large bowl and let sit for 5 minutes for saltines to soften. Mash with fork until smooth paste forms.

2. Add beef, Parmesan, garlic powder, oregano, salt, and pepper to saltine mixture and mix with your hands until thoroughly combined. Divide meat mixture into 24 scant ¼-cup portions. Roll portions between your wet hands to form balls. Transfer to plate, cover with plastic wrap, and refrigerate until ready to use. (Meatballs can be refrigerated for up to 24 hours.)

3. **For the Sauce** Combine oil and garlic in large Dutch oven. Cook over low heat until garlic is soft and golden on all sides, 10 to 12 minutes, stirring occasionally. Add pepper flakes and cook until fragrant, about 30 seconds. Stir in tomatoes and 1 teaspoon salt. Nestle meatballs into sauce. Bring to simmer over medium-high heat.

4. Cover and bake until meatballs are cooked through and tender, about 40 minutes. Let cool, uncovered, for 20 minutes. Gently stir in basil and season with salt and pepper to taste. Serve.

All in the Family

Basil DeLuca, pictured here with his daughter Carmella Garofoli, hand-rolls nearly 150 meatballs every day at Philadelphia's Villa di Roma restaurant. To keep the meatballs tender, they're careful not to pack them too tightly. The restaurant is a touchstone in Philadelphia's Italian American community, one of the oldest and most dynamic in the United States.

Meatballs and Marinara

SERVES 8

WHY THIS RECIPE WORKS Frying meatballs can be messy and take a good chunk of time when working in batches. For an easier method, we turned to the oven and roasted our meatballs at a high temperature, which ensured they developed a nice, browned crust. To keep our meatballs moist and tender, we added a panade (a paste of milk and bread). In addition to ground beef, using Italian sausage for the pork gave the meatballs a flavor boost, as did simmering them in the sauce after baking.

To keep the recipe easy and streamlined, the meatballs and sauce start with the same onion mixture. This recipe makes enough to sauce 2 pounds of pasta.

Onion Mixture
- ¼ cup extra-virgin olive oil
- 3 onions, chopped fine
- 8 garlic cloves, minced
- 1 tablespoon dried oregano
- ¾ teaspoon red pepper flakes

Marinara
- 1 (6-ounce) can tomato paste
- 1 cup dry red wine
- 1 cup water
- 4 (28-ounce) cans crushed tomatoes
- 1 ounce Parmesan cheese, grated (½ cup)
- ¼ cup chopped fresh basil
- Table salt
- 1–2 teaspoons sugar

Meatballs
- 4 slices hearty white sandwich bread, torn into pieces
- ¾ cup milk
- 8 ounces sweet Italian sausage, casings removed
- 2 ounces Parmesan cheese, grated (1 cup)
- ½ cup chopped fresh parsley
- 2 large eggs
- 2 garlic cloves, minced
- 1½ teaspoons table salt
- 2½ pounds 80 percent lean ground chuck

1. **For the Onion Mixture** Heat oil in Dutch oven over medium-high heat until shimmering. Cook onions until golden, 10 to 15 minutes. Add garlic, oregano, and pepper

432   *The Complete Cook's Country TV Show Cookbook*

Meatballs and Marinara

Slow-Cooker Meatballs and Marinara
SERVES 6

WHY THIS RECIPE WORKS To infuse our Slow-Cooker Meatballs and Marinara with depth of flavor, we used lots of onion, garlic, and tomato paste and sautéed them before adding them to the slow cooker. Microwaving the meatballs before adding them to the slow cooker rendered just enough fat (which we discarded) to ensure the sauce wouldn't be greasy. To bind and moisten the meatballs, we traded in the usual panade (a paste of milk and bread), which caused them to break apart in the slow cooker, for cream and shredded mozzarella cheese.

Microwave the meatballs on a large plate or in a casserole dish to contain the rendering fat. This recipe makes enough to sauce 1½ pounds of pasta.

Onion Mixture
- 2 tablespoons extra-virgin olive oil
- 2 onions, chopped fine
- 1 (6-ounce) can tomato paste
- 6 garlic cloves, minced
- 1 tablespoon dried oregano
- ½ teaspoon red pepper flakes
- ¼ teaspoon table salt

Marinara
- ½ cup red wine
- 2 (28-ounce) cans crushed tomatoes

Meatballs
- 4 ounces Italian sausage, casings removed
- 2 ounces mozzarella cheese, shredded (½ cup)
- 1 ounce Parmesan cheese, grated (½ cup)
- 2 large eggs
- 2 garlic cloves, minced
- ¾ teaspoon table salt
- 1¼ pounds 85 percent lean ground beef
- 3 tablespoons heavy cream

- 1 ounce Parmesan cheese, grated (½ cup)
- 2 tablespoons finely chopped fresh basil
  Table salt

flakes and cook until fragrant, about 30 seconds. Transfer half of onion mixture to large bowl and set aside.

2. For the Marinara Add tomato paste to remaining onion mixture in pot and cook until fragrant, about 1 minute. Add wine and cook until slightly thickened, about 2 minutes. Stir in water and tomatoes and simmer over low heat until sauce is no longer watery, 45 minutes to 1 hour. Stir in Parmesan and basil and season with salt and sugar to taste.

3. For the Meatballs Meanwhile, adjust oven rack to upper-middle position and heat oven to 475 degrees. Add bread and milk to bowl with reserved onion mixture and mash together until smooth. Add sausage, Parmesan, parsley, eggs, garlic, and salt to bowl and mash to combine. Add beef and knead with hands until well combined. Lightly shape mixture into 2½-inch round meatballs (about 16 meatballs total), place on rimmed baking sheet, and bake until well browned, about 20 minutes.

4. Transfer meatballs to pot with sauce and simmer for 15 minutes. Serve. (Meatballs and marinara can be frozen for up to 1 month.)

EVERYBODY LOVES ITALIAN

1. **For the Onion Mixture** Heat oil in Dutch oven over medium-high heat until shimmering. Add onions, tomato paste, garlic, oregano, pepper flakes, and salt and cook until softened and lightly browned, about 8 to 10 minutes. Transfer half of onion mixture to large bowl and set aside.

2. **For the Marinara** Add wine to remaining onion mixture in pot and cook until slightly thickened, about 2 minutes. Stir in tomatoes, then transfer to slow cooker.

3. **For the Meatballs** Add sausage, mozzarella, Parmesan, eggs, garlic, and salt to bowl with reserved onion mixture. Mash with potato masher until smooth. Add beef and cream to bowl and knead with hands until well combined. Lightly shape mixture into 2-inch round meatballs (about 12 total). Microwave meatballs on large plate until fat renders and meatballs are firm, 4 to 7 minutes. Nestle meatballs into slow cooker, discarding rendered fat. Cover and cook until meatballs are tender and sauce is slightly thickened, 4 to 5 hours on low.

4. Let meatballs and sauce settle for 5 minutes, then skim fat from surface and stir in Parmesan and basil. Season with salt to taste. Serve.

To Make Ahead Recipe can be made in advance through shaping meatballs in step 3. Uncooked meatballs and sauce can be refrigerated in separate containers for up to 24 hours. When ready to cook, add sauce to slow cooker and proceed with microwaving meatballs in step 3.

Slow-Cooker Meatballs and Marinara

Slow-Cooker Baked Ziti

Slow-Cooker Baked Ziti
SERVES 6

WHY THIS RECIPE WORKS Pasta in a slow cooker? You bet. But achieving well-cooked pasta and melty cheese in the slow cooker takes some strategy. Borrowing a technique from risotto was the key to perfect pasta—we stirred the raw pasta into the browned sausage and onion mixture, coating the starch in fat and preventing the pasta from bloating in the slow cooker. To get cheese that was evenly melted, we added it after cooking and let it sit in the residual warmth of the turned-off slow-cooker.

Our favorite crushed tomatoes are San Merican Crushed Tomatoes.

    2   tablespoons extra-virgin olive oil
    1   pound hot or sweet Italian sausage, casings removed
    1   onion, chopped

- 3 garlic cloves, minced
- ½ teaspoon dried oregano
- ½ teaspoon table salt
- ½ teaspoon pepper
- 8 ounces (2½ cups) ziti
- 1 (28-ounce) can crushed tomatoes
- 1 (15-ounce) can tomato sauce
- 8 ounces (1 cup) whole-milk ricotta cheese
- 4 ounces mozzarella cheese, shredded (1 cup)
- 2 tablespoons thinly sliced fresh basil

1. Make aluminum foil collar for slow cooker by folding 2 (18-inch-long) pieces of foil to make 2 (18 by 4-inch) strips. Line perimeter of slow cooker with foil strips and spray with vegetable oil spray.

2. Heat oil in Dutch oven over medium-high heat until just smoking. Cook sausage, breaking up pieces with spoon, until well browned, 6 to 8 minutes. Add onion and cook until lightly browned, about 5 minutes. Stir in garlic, oregano, salt, and pepper and cook until fragrant, about 1 minute.

3. Reduce heat to medium-low. Add ziti and cook, stirring constantly, until edges of pasta become translucent, about 4 minutes. Off heat, stir in crushed tomatoes and tomato sauce, scraping up any browned bits. Transfer mixture to prepared slow cooker. Cover and cook on low until pasta is tender, about 3 hours.

4. Using tongs, remove foil collar from slow cooker. Dollop ricotta over ziti and sprinkle with mozzarella. Cover and let sit for 20 minutes to let cheeses melt. Garnish with basil and serve.

Italian Meatloaf

SERVES 6 TO 8

WHY THIS RECIPE WORKS This Italian meatloaf is essentially an excellent, no-fuss meatballs and marinara recipe. We started with a flavorful meat mixture of ground beef, Italian sausage, Parmesan cheese, garlic, and oregano. Instead of rolling dozens of meatballs, we made one big loaf-shaped one. Mixing in a paste of crushed saltines, eggs, and milk helped the meatloaf hold its shape and stay moist. We whipped up a garlicky 5-minute tomato sauce, poured it on top, and baked the two together, elevating both meatloaf and sauce in the process. For a finishing touch, we topped the meatloaf with melty fontina and a sprinkling of fresh basil.

Grate the Parmesan using a rasp-style grater; shred the fontina on the large holes of a box grater.

Sauce

- 1 tablespoon extra-virgin olive oil
- 5 garlic cloves, sliced thin
- 1 (28-ounce) can crushed tomatoes
- 1 (15-ounce) can tomato sauce
- ¼ teaspoon red pepper flakes
- ¼ teaspoon table salt

Meatloaf

- 35 square saltines
- ¾ cup whole milk
- 2 large eggs
- 1 pound 85 percent lean ground beef
- 1 pound sweet Italian sausage, casings removed
- 2 ounces Parmesan cheese, grated (1 cup)
- 1 teaspoon granulated garlic
- 1 teaspoon dried oregano
- ½ teaspoon table salt
- ½ teaspoon pepper
- ¼ teaspoon red pepper flakes
- 4 ounces fontina cheese, shredded (1 cup)
- 3 tablespoons chopped fresh basil

1. For the Sauce Adjust oven rack to middle position and heat oven to 400 degrees. Heat oil in large saucepan over medium heat until shimmering. Add garlic and cook until lightly browned, about 1 minute. Stir in tomatoes, tomato sauce, pepper flakes, and salt. Bring to simmer and cook until flavors have melded, about 5 minutes. Remove from heat; cover to keep warm.

2. For the Meatloaf Spray broiler-safe 13 by 9-inch baking dish with vegetable oil spray. Place saltines in large zipper-lock bag, seal bag, and crush saltines to fine crumbs with rolling pin. Whisk saltines, milk, and eggs together in large bowl. Let sit until saltines are softened, about 5 minutes. Whisk saltine mixture until smooth paste forms. Add beef, sausage, Parmesan, granulated garlic, oregano, salt, pepper, and pepper flakes and mix with your hands until thoroughly combined.

3. Transfer beef mixture to prepared dish. Using your wet hands, shape into 9 by 5-inch rectangle; top should be flat and meatloaf should be 1½ inches thick. Pour sauce over meatloaf. Cover dish with aluminum foil and place on rimmed baking sheet. Bake until meatloaf registers 160 degrees, 1 hour 5 minutes to 1¼ hours.

4. Remove sheet from oven, uncover dish, and sprinkle meatloaf evenly with fontina. Heat broiler. Broil meatloaf until cheese is melted, about 2 minutes. Let rest for 15 minutes.

5. Using 2 spatulas, transfer meatloaf to cutting board. Spoon off any excess grease from tomato sauce. Slice meatloaf 1 inch thick. Transfer slices back to sauce in dish, sprinkle with basil, and serve.

Skillet Lasagna
SERVES 4 TO 6

Skillet Lasagna

WHY THIS RECIPE WORKS To get our lasagna fix without spending hours in the kitchen, we made the entire dish, from start to finish, in a 12-inch skillet. After sautéing aromatics, we browned our meat in the pan, then added the noodles and sauce. Meatloaf mix (a blend of ground beef, pork, and veal) contributed deep, meaty flavor. Canned diced tomatoes and tomato sauce, thinned with water, provided ample liquid to cook our noodles and thickened to just the right consistency after a brief simmer. For a rich, creamy topping, we dropped big dollops of ricotta cheese over the noodles and covered the pan so they'd melt.

A 12-inch nonstick skillet with a tight-fitting lid works best for this recipe.

- 1 (28-ounce) can diced tomatoes
  Water
- 1 tablespoon extra-virgin olive oil
- 1 onion, chopped fine
  Table salt and pepper
- 3 garlic cloves, minced
- 1/8 teaspoon red pepper flakes
- 1 pound meatloaf mix
- 10 curly-edged lasagna noodles, broken into 2-inch lengths
- 1 (8-ounce) can tomato sauce
- 1 ounce Parmesan cheese, grated (1/2 cup), plus 2 tablespoons, grated, divided
- 8 ounces (1 cup) whole-milk or part-skim ricotta cheese
- 3 tablespoons chopped fresh basil

1. Place tomatoes in 4-cup liquid measuring cup. Add water until mixture measures 4 cups.

2. Heat oil in 12-inch nonstick skillet over medium heat until shimmering. Add onion and 1/2 teaspoon salt and cook until onion begins to brown, about 5 minutes. Stir in garlic and pepper flakes and cook until fragrant, about 30 seconds. Add meat and cook, breaking up meat into small pieces with wooden spoon, until it is no longer pink, about 4 minutes.

3. Scatter pasta over meat but do not stir. Pour tomato mixture and tomato sauce over pasta, cover, and bring to simmer. Reduce heat to medium-low and simmer, stirring occasionally, until pasta is tender, about 20 minutes.

4. Off heat, stir in 1/2 cup Parmesan and season with salt and pepper to taste. Dollop heaping tablespoons of ricotta over top, cover, and let sit for 5 minutes. Sprinkle with basil and remaining 2 tablespoons Parmesan. Serve.

Skillet Lasagna with Sausage and Red Pepper
Substitute 1 pound Italian sausage, casings removed, for meatloaf mix. Add 1 chopped red bell pepper to skillet with onion.

436 *The Complete Cook's Country TV Show Cookbook*

Hearty Beef Lasagna

SERVES 10 TO 12

Hearty Beef Lasagna

WHY THIS RECIPE WORKS We wanted to streamline the lasagna-making process and also amp up the meatiness. We chose 90 percent lean ground beef for its rich flavor and added a panade (a mixture of bread and milk), which produced an easy-to-layer meat sauce. Instead of a traditional béchamel sauce or layer of ricotta, we created a no-cook sauce made with cottage cheese, heavy cream, Pecorino Romano, and cornstarch to bind and thicken it. Since the meat sauce continued to cook in the oven as the lasagna baked, we could skip the long simmer on the stovetop.

We developed this recipe using dried curly-edged lasagna noodles; do not use no-boil noodles. There are about 20 individual noodles in a 1-pound box of lasagna noodles, enough for this recipe.

Lasagna

- Vegetable oil spray
- 17 curly-edged lasagna noodles
- 1 tablespoon table salt
- 12 ounces mozzarella cheese, shredded (3 cups), divided
- ¼ cup grated Pecorino Romano cheese

Meat Sauce

- 2 slices hearty white sandwich bread, torn into small pieces
- ¼ cup milk
- 1½ pounds 90 percent lean ground beef
- ¾ teaspoon table salt
- ½ teaspoon pepper
- 1 tablespoon extra-virgin olive oil
- 1 onion, chopped fine
- 6 garlic cloves, minced
- 1 teaspoon dried oregano
- ¼ teaspoon red pepper flakes
- 1 (28-ounce) can crushed tomatoes

Cream Sauce

- 8 ounces (1 cup) cottage cheese
- 4 ounces Pecorino Romano cheese, grated (2 cups)
- 1 cup heavy cream
- 2 garlic cloves, minced
- 1 teaspoon cornstarch
- ¼ teaspoon table salt
- ¼ teaspoon pepper

1. For the Lasagna Adjust oven rack to middle position and heat oven to 375 degrees. Spray rimmed baking sheet and 13 by 9-inch baking dish with oil spray. Bring 4 quarts water to boil in large Dutch oven. Add noodles and salt and cook, stirring often, until al dente. Drain noodles and transfer them to prepared sheet. Using tongs, gently turn noodles to coat lightly with oil spray. Cut 2 noodles in half crosswise.

2. For the Meat Sauce Mash bread and milk in bowl until smooth. Add beef, salt, and pepper and knead with your hands until well combined; set aside. Heat oil in now-empty Dutch oven over medium heat until shimmering. Add onion and cook until softened, about 5 minutes. Stir in garlic, oregano, and pepper flakes and cook until fragrant, about 1 minute.

3. Add beef mixture, breaking meat into small pieces with wooden spoon, and cook until no longer pink, about 4 minutes. Stir in tomatoes and bring to simmer, scraping up any browned bits. Reduce heat to medium-low and simmer until flavors have melded, about 5 minutes.

4. For the Cream Sauce Whisk all ingredients in bowl until combined.

5. Lay 3 noodles lengthwise in prepared dish with ends touching 1 short side of dish, leaving gap at far end. Lay 1 half noodle crosswise to fill gap (if needed).

6. Spread 1½ cups meat sauce over noodles, followed by ½ cup cream sauce and finally ½ cup mozzarella. Repeat layering of noodles, meat sauce, cream sauce, and mozzarella 3 more times, switching position of half noodle to opposite end of dish each time.

7. Lay remaining 3 noodles over top (there is no half noodle for top layer). Spread remaining cream sauce over noodles, followed by remaining 1 cup mozzarella. Sprinkle Pecorino over top.

8. Spray sheet of aluminum foil with oil spray and cover lasagna. Set lasagna on rimmed baking sheet. Bake for 30 minutes. Discard foil and continue to bake until top layer of lasagna is spotty brown, 25 to 30 minutes longer. Let lasagna cool for 30 minutes. Slice and serve.

To Make Ahead At end of step 7, cover dish with greased aluminum foil and refrigerate for up to 24 hours. When ready to eat, bake lasagna as directed in step 8, increasing covered baking time to 55 minutes.

Sausage Lasagna

SERVES 8 TO 10

WHY THIS RECIPE WORKS Fennel, onion, sage, garlic, fennel seeds, and pepper flakes pulsed together in a food processor gave the sauce a flavor boost. Slightly undercooking the noodles meant that they stayed firm when baked. To ensure full coverage in the bottom of the pan (and structural integrity), we cut two of the noodles in half. For the cheese, we relied on a combo of creamy mozzarella, flavorful provolone, and supersavory Pecorino Romano. Because ricotta cheese can turn gritty when baked, we opted for cottage cheese, which contains more moisture and so is more apt to stay pillowy-soft and creamy.

A 1-pound box of dry lasagna noodles should yield enough for this lasagna. Note that we call for grinding the Pecorino Romano in a food processor; you can use preground Pecorino Romano, if desired. To make quick work of shredding the mozzarella and provolone, use your processor's shredding disk or the large holes of a box grater.

Sauce
- 1 (1-pound) fennel bulb, stalks discarded, bulb halved, cored, and chopped coarse
- 1 onion, chopped coarse
- 3 tablespoons chopped fresh sage
- 4 garlic cloves, peeled
- 1 tablespoon fennel seeds
- ½ teaspoon red pepper flakes
- 1 tablespoon extra-virgin olive oil
- 2 pounds hot or sweet Italian sausage, casings removed
- 1 (28-ounce) can crushed tomatoes
- 1 (15-ounce) can tomato sauce

Lasagna
- 17 curly-edged lasagna noodles
- Table salt for cooking pasta
- Vegetable oil spray
- 1 pound whole-milk mozzarella cheese, shredded (4 cups)
- 8 ounces provolone cheese, shredded (2 cups)
- 4 ounces Pecorino Romano cheese, ground fine in food processor (¾ cup)
- 1½ teaspoons dried oregano
- 1 pound (2 cups) whole-milk cottage cheese

1. For the Sauce Combine fennel, onion, sage, garlic, fennel seeds, and pepper flakes in food processor and pulse until finely chopped, about 10 pulses; set aside. Heat oil in Dutch oven over medium-high heat until just smoking. Add sausage and cook, breaking up meat with potato masher, until sausage begins to sizzle in its own fat, about 15 minutes.

2. Reduce heat to medium and add fennel mixture. Cook until vegetables are softened and fragrant, about 4 minutes. Add crushed tomatoes and tomato sauce and bring to simmer. Reduce heat to medium-low and cook for 5 minutes to allow flavors to blend. Set aside off heat. Reserve 2 cups sauce for topping.

3. For the Lasagna Bring 4 quarts water to boil in large pot. Add noodles and 1 tablespoon salt and cook until just shy of al dente, about 7 minutes. Drain noodles and transfer to rimmed baking sheet. Spray noodles lightly with oil spray; toss gently to coat (to prevent them from sticking to each other). Cut 2 noodles in half crosswise.

4. Adjust oven rack to middle position and heat oven to 375 degrees. Spray 13 by 9-inch baking dish with oil spray. Combine mozzarella, provolone, Pecorino, and oregano in bowl. Reserve 2 cups mozzarella mixture for topping.

5. Lay 3 noodles lengthwise in prepared dish with ends touching short side of dish, leaving gap at far end. Lay 1 half noodle crosswise to fill gap. Spread 1½ cups meat sauce over noodles; dollop ½ cup cottage cheese over sauce. Use back of spoon to spread cottage cheese evenly over sauce. Sprinkle with 1 cup mozzarella mixture.

6. Repeat layering of noodles, meat sauce, cottage cheese, and mozzarella mixture 3 more times, switching position of half noodle to opposite end of dish each time.

7. Lay remaining 3 noodles over top (there is no half noodle for top layer). Spread reserved 2 cups sauce over noodles, then sprinkle with reserved 2 cups mozzarella mixture.

8. Spray sheet of aluminum foil with oil spray and cover lasagna. Set lasagna on foil-lined rimmed baking sheet. Bake for 30 minutes. Discard foil covering lasagna and continue to bake until top layer of lasagna is spotty brown and lasagna is hot throughout, about 30 minutes longer. Let lasagna cool for 45 minutes. Slice and serve.

To Make Ahead At end of step 7, cover dish with greased aluminum foil and refrigerate for up to 24 hours. To serve, bake lasagna as directed in step 8, increasing covered baking time to 55 minutes.

30	ounces frozen chopped spinach
2	tablespoons extra-virgin olive oil
1	onion, chopped fine
5	garlic cloves, minced
⅛	teaspoon red pepper flakes
2	(28-ounce) cans crushed tomatoes
	Table salt and pepper
6	tablespoons chopped fresh basil, divided
1½	pounds (3 cups) whole-milk or part-skim ricotta cheese
3	ounces Parmesan cheese, grated (1½ cups)
2	large eggs
12	no-boil lasagna noodles
12	ounces whole-milk mozzarella cheese, shredded (3 cups), divided

1. Adjust oven rack to middle position and heat oven to 375 degrees. Microwave spinach in covered large bowl until completely thawed, about 15 minutes, stirring halfway through cooking. Squeeze spinach dry, reserving ⅓ cup liquid. Pulse spinach in food processor until ground, 8 to 10 pulses, scraping down bowl every few pulses. Wipe out large bowl with paper towels. Transfer spinach to now-empty bowl; set aside.

Spinach and Tomato Lasagna

SERVES 8 TO 10

WHY THIS RECIPE WORKS To make a spinach lasagna worthy of its name, we increased the amount of spinach. Frozen spinach tasted just as good as fresh and cut down on kitchen time. For the most even texture, we used the food processor to chop the spinach. For extra spinach flavor we included some of the drained spinach liquid (we combined it with the ricotta in the food processor) but not enough to make the lasagna watery. To keep the spinach flavor front and center, we nixed the traditional creamy béchamel in favor of a fresh, herb-flecked tomato sauce but still layered in plenty of mozzarella and Parmesan for richness.

Our favorite brand of no-boil lasagna noodles is Barilla. You can thaw the spinach overnight in the refrigerator instead of microwaving it, but be sure to warm the spinach liquid to help smooth the ricotta.

Spinach and Tomato Lasagna

2. Heat oil in large saucepan over medium heat until shimmering. Add onion and cook until softened, about 5 minutes. Stir in garlic and pepper flakes and cook until fragrant, about 30 seconds. Add tomatoes, ½ cup processed spinach, 1 teaspoon salt, and ½ teaspoon pepper and cook until slightly thickened, about 10 minutes. Off heat, stir in 3 tablespoons basil; set aside.

3. Process ricotta and reserved spinach liquid in food processor until smooth, about 30 seconds. Add Parmesan, remaining 3 tablespoons basil, eggs, 1½ teaspoons salt, and ½ teaspoon pepper and process until combined. Stir ricotta mixture into remaining processed spinach.

4. Cover bottom of 13 by 9-inch baking dish with 1¼ cups sauce. Top with 3 noodles and spread one-third of ricotta mixture evenly over noodles. Sprinkle with ⅔ cup mozzarella and cover with 1¼ cups sauce. Repeat twice, beginning with noodles and ending with sauce. Top with remaining 3 noodles, remaining sauce, and remaining 1 cup mozzarella.

5. Cover pan tightly with aluminum foil sprayed with vegetable oil spray and bake until bubbling around edges, about 40 minutes. Discard foil and continue to bake until cheese is melted, about 10 minutes. Let cool on wire rack for 30 minutes. Serve.

Eggplant Peccorino

Eggplant Pecorino

SERVES 6

WHY THIS RECIPE WORKS For a more refined take on eggplant Parmesan that showcases the eggplant paired with a rich, bright sauce, we took inspiration from La Campagna, in Westlake, Ohio. For our version, we skipped bread crumbs and instead fried the eggplant in a thin flour and egg coating, which created a light, fluffy shell around each thin eggplant slice rather than a thick, bready coating. We replaced the traditional Parmesan with Pecorino Romano, which added a nutty, tangy flavor, elevating the mild eggplant. Topping our eggplant stacks with creamy shredded fontina and finishing them under the broiler gave them an irresistible melted browned top.

Do not use eggplants weighing more than 1 pound each or the slices won't fit in the baking dish. Use a rasp-style grater to grate the Pecorino Romano; shred the fontina on the large holes of a box grater. Depending on the size of your eggplants, you may not need to use all three to get the 20 slices needed to assemble the casserole.

Sauce

- 2 tablespoons unsalted butter
- ¼ cup finely chopped onion
- 3 garlic cloves, minced
- 2 anchovy fillets, rinsed and minced
- ¾ teaspoon table salt
- ¼ teaspoon red pepper flakes
- ¼ teaspoon dried oregano
- 1 (28-ounce) can crushed tomatoes
- 1 (14.5-ounce) can diced tomatoes
- ½ teaspoon sugar
- ¼ cup chopped fresh basil
- 1 tablespoon extra-virgin olive oil

Eggplant

- 3 (10- to 16-ounce) eggplants
- ½ cup all-purpose flour
- 4 large eggs
- 1 cup extra-virgin olive oil for frying
- 4 ounces Pecorino Romano cheese, grated (2 cups)
- 4 ounces fontina cheese, shredded (1 cup)

1. For the Sauce Melt butter in medium saucepan over medium-low heat. Add onion, garlic, anchovies, salt, pepper flakes, and oregano and cook until onion is softened, about 3 minutes. Stir in crushed tomatoes, diced tomatoes and their juice, and sugar; increase heat to medium-high; and bring to simmer. Reduce heat to medium-low and simmer until slightly thickened, about 10 minutes. Off heat, stir in basil and oil. Season with salt and pepper to taste. Set aside. (Sauce can be refrigerated for up to 48 hours.)

2. For the Eggplant Cut stem end off eggplants and discard. Cut ¼-inch-thick slice from 1 long side of each eggplant and discard. Using mandoline or slicing knife and starting on cut side, slice eggplants lengthwise ¼ inch thick until you have 20 slices total (you may not need all 3 eggplants).

3. Place flour in shallow dish. Beat eggs in second shallow dish. Line baking sheet with triple layer of paper towels. Heat oil in 12-inch skillet over medium heat to 350 degrees (to take temperature, tilt skillet so oil pools on 1 side). Working with 3 or 4 slices at a time (depending on size of eggplant), dredge eggplant in flour, shaking off excess; dip in egg, allowing excess to drip off; then place in hot oil. Fry until lightly browned on both sides, about 1½ minutes per side. Transfer to prepared sheet. (As eggplant slices cool, you can stack them to make room on sheet.)

4. Adjust oven rack 6 inches from broiler element and heat oven to 375 degrees. Spread 1 cup sauce in bottom of broiler-safe 13 by 9-inch baking dish. Starting with largest slices of eggplant, place 4 eggplant slices side by side over sauce in dish. Spread ½ cup sauce over eggplant, then sprinkle ½ cup Pecorino over top. Repeat layering 3 times to make 4 stacks of 4 slices. Place remaining eggplant slices on top. Spread remaining sauce over top layer of eggplant, then sprinkle with fontina.

5. Bake until bubbling around edges and center of casserole is hot, about 30 minutes. Broil until fontina is lightly browned, 1 to 3 minutes. Let cool for 20 minutes. Serve.

Baked Manicotti with Meat Sauce

Baked Manicotti with Meat Sauce

SERVES 6 TO 8

WHY THIS RECIPE WORKS For fuss-free but flavorful manicotti, we started by substituting no-boil lasagna noodles for the manicotti tubes. Briefly soaking them in hot water made them pliable and easy to roll up. Using the food processor to break down the ground beef allowed its flavor to permeate the sauce quickly so it needed just a short simmer. For even more meaty flavor, we added a popular pizza topping—pepperoni—which gave the sauce a spicy backbone. To liven up the filling, we included assertive provolone, plus a portion of the processed ground beef and pepperoni; a single egg helped to bind it all together.

You will need 16 no-boil lasagna noodles for this recipe. The test kitchen's preferred brand, Barilla, comes 16 noodles to a box, but other brands contain only 12. It is important to let the dish cool for 15 minutes after baking.

EVERYBODY LOVES ITALIAN   441

Meat Sauce

- 1 onion, chopped
- 6 ounces thinly sliced deli pepperoni
- 1 pound 85 percent lean ground beef
- 5 garlic cloves, minced
- 1 tablespoon tomato paste
- ¼ teaspoon red pepper flakes
- 2 (28-ounce) cans crushed tomatoes
- Table salt and pepper

Manicotti

- 1½ pounds (3 cups) ricotta cheese
- 10 ounces mozzarella cheese, shredded (2½ cups), divided
- 6 ounces provolone cheese, shredded (1½ cups), divided
- 1 large egg, lightly beaten
- ¼ cup finely chopped fresh basil
- ½ teaspoon table salt
- ½ teaspoon pepper
- 16 no-boil lasagna noodles

1. For the Meat Sauce Adjust oven rack to upper-middle position and heat oven to 375 degrees. Pulse onion and pepperoni in food processor until coarsely ground, about 10 pulses. Add beef and pulse until thoroughly combined, 5 to 8 pulses.

2. Transfer mixture to large saucepan and cook over medium heat, breaking up mixture with wooden spoon, until no longer pink, about 5 minutes. Using slotted spoon, transfer 1 cup meat mixture to paper towel–lined plate and reserve. Add garlic, tomato paste, and pepper flakes to pot and cook until fragrant, about 1 minute. Stir in tomatoes and simmer until sauce is slightly thickened, about 20 minutes. Season with salt and pepper to taste. (Meat sauce can be refrigerated for up to 3 days.)

3. For the Manicotti Combine ricotta, 2 cups mozzarella, 1 cup provolone, egg, basil, salt, pepper, and reserved meat mixture in large bowl. Pour 1 inch boiling water into 13 by 9-inch baking dish and slip noodles into water, one at a time. Let noodles soak until pliable, about 5 minutes, separating noodles with tip of knife to prevent sticking. Remove noodles from water and place in single layer on clean dish towels; discard water and dry off baking dish.

4. Spread half of meat sauce over bottom of baking dish. Spread ¼ cup ricotta mixture evenly over bottom of each noodle. Roll noodles up around filling and lay them seam side down in baking dish. Spread remaining sauce over top to cover pasta completely. Cover dish tightly with aluminum foil and bake until bubbling around edges, about 40 minutes. Remove foil and sprinkle with remaining ½ cup mozzarella and ½ cup provolone. Bake until cheese is melted, about 5 minutes. Let cool for 15 minutes. Serve.

Manicotti Made Easy

Manicotti shells are hard to fill without tearing. For easy-to-fill manicotti, we found a better solution in no-boil lasagna noodles.

1. After soaking no-boil lasagna noodles briefly in hot water, spread filling across bottom of each and roll into tube.

2. Arrange rolled manicotti seam side down over sauce in baking dish.

Cheesy Stuffed Shells

SERVES 6 TO 8

WHY THIS RECIPE WORKS Stuffed shell recipes can be frustrating. For a quicker version of stuffed shells with better results, we chose raw jumbo shells with wide openings and piped in the filling. For a supercheesy filling, we mixed creamy ricotta, shredded fontina, and grated Pecorino Romano cheeses with savory minced garlic, fragrant chopped fresh basil, and dried oregano. Adding cornstarch to the ricotta kept it from becoming grainy when baked. Smothering the shells in a thin tomato sauce meant the raw pasta cooked during baking, absorbing the liquid while still leaving behind a full-bodied sauce.

Shred the fontina on the large holes of a box grater. Be sure to use only open, unbroken shells. We developed this recipe using Barilla Jumbo Shells and were able to find at least 25 open shells in each 1-pound box we used. Pipe each shell only about three-quarters full on your first pass, and then divide the remaining filling evenly among the shells.

442 *The Complete Cook's Country TV Show Cookbook*

Sauce

- 2 tablespoons extra-virgin olive oil
- 1 onion, chopped
- ½ teaspoon table salt
- ½ teaspoon pepper
- 6 garlic cloves, minced
- ¼ teaspoon red pepper flakes
- 1 (28-ounce) can tomato puree
- 2 cups water
- 1 teaspoon sugar

Filling

- 10 ounces (1¼ cups) whole-milk ricotta cheese
- 4 ounces fontina cheese, shredded (1 cup)
- 2 ounces Pecorino Romano cheese, grated (1 cup)
- 2 large eggs
- 3 tablespoons chopped fresh basil
- 1½ tablespoons cornstarch
- 2 garlic cloves, minced
- 1 teaspoon dried oregano
- ½ teaspoon table salt

Shells

- 25 jumbo pasta shells
- 8 ounces fontina cheese, shredded (2 cups)
- 1 tablespoon chopped fresh basil

Cheesy Stuffed Shells

1. For the Sauce Heat oil in large saucepan over medium heat until shimmering. Add onion, salt, and pepper and cook, stirring occasionally, until softened and lightly browned, about 10 minutes.

2. Stir in garlic and pepper flakes and cook until fragrant, about 30 seconds. Stir in tomato puree, water, and sugar and bring to simmer. Reduce heat to medium-low and cook until flavors have melded, about 5 minutes. (Cooled sauce can be refrigerated for up to 3 days.)

3. For the Filling Stir all ingredients in bowl until thoroughly combined. Transfer filling to pastry bag or large zipper-lock bag (if using zipper-lock bag, cut 1 inch off 1 corner of bag).

4. For the Shells Adjust oven rack to middle position and heat oven to 400 degrees. Place shells open side up on counter. Pipe filling into shells until each is about three-quarters full. Divide remaining filling evenly among shells.

5. Spread 1 cup sauce over bottom of 13 by 9-inch baking dish. Transfer shells, open side up, to prepared dish. Pour remaining sauce evenly over shells to completely cover.

6. Cover dish tightly with aluminum foil and set on rimmed baking sheet. Bake until shells are tender and sauce is boiling rapidly, about 45 minutes. Remove dish from oven and discard foil; sprinkle fontina over top. Bake, uncovered, until fontina is lightly browned, about 15 minutes. Let shells cool for 25 minutes. Sprinkle with basil. Serve.

To Make Ahead At end of step 2, let sauce cool completely. At end of step 5, cover dish tightly with aluminum foil and refrigerate for up to 24 hours. When ready to eat, bake shells as directed in step 6.

Grandma Pizza

Cast-Iron Skillet Pizza

Grandma Pizza

SERVES 4

WHY THIS RECIPE WORKS Grandma pizza is a thin-crust pan pizza topped with a modest amount of cheese and chunks of tomatoes. To re-create this Long Island specialty, bread flour and lengthy kneading gave us the chewy crust we wanted, but the dough was difficult to stretch thin. Proofing the dough on the same sheet pan that we used to bake the pizza let it stretch on its own as it proofed. For a fresh, easy tomato topping that wouldn't make our crust soggy, we tossed drained diced tomatoes with salt, olive oil, garlic, and oregano. Baking the pizza on the lowest rack then cooling it on a wire rack perfectly crisped the bottom crust.

If the dough snaps back when pressed to the corners of the baking sheet, cover it, let rest for 10 minutes, and try again.

Dough
- 3 tablespoons extra-virgin olive oil, divided
- ¾ cup water
- 1½ cups (8¼ ounces) bread flour
- 2¼ teaspoons instant or rapid-rise yeast
- 1 teaspoon sugar
- ¾ teaspoon table salt

Topping
- 1 (28-ounce) can diced tomatoes
- 1 tablespoon extra-virgin olive oil
- 2 garlic cloves, minced
- 1 teaspoon dried oregano
- ¼ teaspoon table salt
- 8 ounces mozzarella cheese, shredded (2 cups)
- ¼ cup grated Parmesan cheese
- 2 tablespoons chopped fresh basil

1. For the Dough Coat rimmed baking sheet with 2 tablespoons oil. Combine water and remaining 1 tablespoon oil in 1-cup liquid measuring cup. Using stand mixer fitted with dough hook, mix flour, yeast, sugar, and salt on low speed until combined. With mixer running, slowly add water mixture and mix until dough comes together, about 1 minute. Increase speed to medium-low and mix until dough is smooth and comes away from sides of bowl, about 10 minutes.

2. Transfer dough to greased baking sheet and turn to coat. Stretch dough to 10 by 6-inch rectangle. Cover loosely with plastic wrap and let rise in warm place until doubled in size, 1 to 1½ hours. Stretch dough to corners of pan, cover loosely with plastic, and let rise in warm place until slightly puffed, about 45 minutes. Meanwhile, adjust oven rack to lowest position and heat oven to 500 degrees.

3. For the Topping Place tomatoes in colander and drain well. Combine drained tomatoes, oil, garlic, oregano, and salt in bowl. Combine mozzarella and Parmesan in second bowl. Sprinkle cheese mixture over dough, leaving ½-inch border around edges. Top with tomato mixture and bake until well browned and bubbling, about 15 minutes. Slide pizza onto wire rack, sprinkle with basil, and let cool for 5 minutes. Serve.

> **The American Table:**
> **Where Was Grandma Pizza Born?**
>
> In a 2003 piece in the Long Island newspaper *Newsday*, writer Erica Marcus traced grandma pizza's origins to Umberto's Pizzeria in New Hyde Park. According to Marcus, in the early 1970s proprietor Umberto Corteo would ask his pizza man to create a simple pizza like the one his mother used to make in Italy. The Corteos opened a second pizzeria, King Umberto's, in nearby Elmont. It was later bought by two former Umberto's pizza makers, who built a best-selling item out of their former boss's favorite lunch, naming it grandma pizza sometime in the late 1980s. Within 10 years, other Long Island pizzerias were offering the pie, and a phenomenon was born.

Cast-Iron Skillet Pizza

SERVES 4

WHY THIS RECIPE WORKS Getting crisp pizza crust from your oven can be a challenge, but with just a few tweaks and the right tools, you'll have homemade pizza that's miles better than offerings from the freezer or the delivery guy. We started by rolling pizza dough out thin and then gently pressing it into our cast-iron skillet. Heating the pizza dough in the skillet on the stove gave our crust a jump start before going into the oven. Once in the oven, the skillet functioned like a pizza stone and crisped up our crust in just minutes. Our simple, classic toppings—pizza sauce, mozzarella, and basil—allowed our crust to shine.

We like to use our Classic Pizza Dough and No-Cook Pizza Sauce (recipes follow); however, you can use ready-made pizza dough and sauce from the local pizzeria or supermarket.

- ¼ cup extra-virgin olive oil, divided
- 1 pound pizza dough, room temperature
- 1 cup pizza sauce
- 12 ounces fresh mozzarella cheese, sliced ¼ inch thick
- 2 tablespoons chopped fresh basil

1. Adjust oven rack to upper-middle position and heat oven to 500 degrees. Grease 12-inch cast-iron skillet with 2 tablespoons oil.

2. Place dough on lightly floured counter, divide in half, and cover with greased plastic wrap. Press and roll 1 piece of dough (keeping remaining dough covered) into 11-inch round. Transfer dough to prepared skillet and gently push it to corners of pan. Spread ½ cup sauce over surface of dough, leaving ½-inch border around edge. Top with half of mozzarella.

3. Set skillet over medium-high heat and cook until outside edge of dough is set, pizza is lightly puffed, and bottom crust is spotty brown when gently lifted with spatula, 2 to 4 minutes. Transfer skillet to oven and bake until edge of pizza is golden brown and cheese is melted, 7 to 10 minutes.

4. Using potholders, remove skillet from oven and slide pizza onto wire rack using spatula; let cool slightly. Sprinkle with 1 tablespoon basil, cut into wedges, and serve. Being careful of hot skillet, repeat with remaining 2 tablespoons oil, dough, sauce, mozzarella, and 1 tablespoon basil. Cut into wedges and serve.

Classic Pizza Dough
MAKES 1 POUND

- 2 cups (11 ounces) plus 2 tablespoons bread flour
- 1⅛ teaspoons instant or rapid-rise yeast
- ¾ teaspoon table salt
- 1 tablespoon extra-virgin olive oil
- ¾ cup warm water (110 degrees)

1. Pulse flour, yeast, and salt together in food processor to combine, about 5 pulses. With processor running, add oil, then water, and process until rough ball forms, 30 to 40 seconds. Let dough rest for 2 minutes, then process for 30 seconds longer. (If after 30 seconds dough is very sticky and clings to blade, add extra flour as needed.)

EVERYBODY LOVES ITALIAN 445

2. Transfer dough to lightly floured counter and knead by hand to form smooth, round ball, about 1 minute. Place dough in large, lightly greased bowl, cover tightly with greased plastic wrap, and let rise until doubled in size, 1 to 1½ hours. (Alternatively, dough can be refrigerated for at least 8 hours or up to 16 hours.)

No-Cook Pizza Sauce
MAKES 2 CUPS

While it is convenient to use ready-made pizza sauce, we think making your own yields tastier results.

- 1 (28-ounce) can whole peeled tomatoes, drained with juice reserved
- 1 tablespoon extra-virgin olive oil
- 1 teaspoon red wine vinegar
- 2 garlic cloves, minced
- 1 teaspoon dried oregano
- Table salt and pepper

Process tomatoes with oil, vinegar, garlic, and oregano in food processor until smooth, about 30 seconds. Transfer mixture to 2-cup liquid measuring cup and add tomato juice until sauce measures 2 cups. Season with salt and pepper to taste. (Sauce can be refrigerated for up to 1 week or frozen for up to 1 month.)

Skillet Chicken Parmesan
SERVES 4

WHY THIS RECIPE WORKS To streamline chicken Parmesan and still keep its flavors and textures intact, we browned boneless, skinless chicken breasts, which we had sliced into cutlets, in a nonstick pan, then made a simple tomato sauce and simmered the chicken right in the sauce so it could absorb the flavors. For the cheesy layer, we supplemented the traditional mozzarella with provolone (preferably the sharp variety) for a much richer flavor. And rather than breading the chicken, we sprinkled the bread crumbs, which we toasted and seasoned with Parmesan and basil, over the finished dish so they stayed ultra-crisp.

We like the assertive flavor of sharp provolone here, but mild provolone works well, too.

- 2 slices hearty white sandwich bread, torn into large pieces
- 3 tablespoons extra-virgin olive oil, divided
- 2½ ounces Parmesan cheese, grated (1¼ cups), divided
- ¼ cup chopped fresh basil, divided
- 1 (28-ounce) can crushed tomatoes
- 2 garlic cloves, minced
- Table salt and pepper
- 4 (6-ounce) boneless, skinless chicken breasts, trimmed
- ½ cup all-purpose flour
- 3 tablespoons vegetable oil, divided
- 3 ounces mozzarella cheese, shredded (¾ cup)
- 3 ounces provolone cheese, shredded (¾ cup)

1. Pulse bread in food processor to coarse crumbs, about 10 pulses. Toast bread crumbs in 12-inch nonstick skillet over medium-high heat until browned, about 5 minutes, and transfer to bowl. Toss with 1 tablespoon olive oil, ¼ cup Parmesan, and half of basil. In separate bowl, combine remaining 2 tablespoons olive oil, ¼ cup Parmesan, remaining basil, tomatoes, garlic, and salt and pepper to taste.

2. Using sharp knife, and holding chicken securely, slice each breast horizontally into 2 cutlets of even thickness. Place flour in shallow dish. Season chicken with salt and pepper and dredge in flour. Heat 2 tablespoons vegetable oil in now-empty skillet over medium-high heat until shimmering. Add 4 cutlets and cook until golden brown on both sides, about 5 minutes. Transfer to plate and repeat with remaining cutlets and remaining 1 tablespoon vegetable oil.

3. Reduce heat to medium-low and add tomato mixture to now-empty skillet. Return cutlets to pan in even layer, pressing down to cover with sauce. Sprinkle mozzarella, provolone, and remaining ¾ cup Parmesan over chicken. Cover and cook until cheese is melted, about 5 minutes. Sprinkle with bread crumb mixture and serve.

Making Cutlets from Breasts

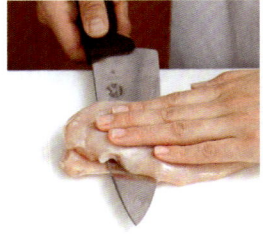

Use your hand to hold breast in place, keeping your fingers straight and parallel to breast. Starting at thickest end of breast, slice in half horizontally, producing 2 even cutlets.

Chicken Scampi

SERVES 4 TO 6

WHY THIS RECIPE WORKS Chicken scampi is a popular restaurant dish, and we wanted to find out why. The dish consists of fried chicken tenders served in the style of shrimp scampi, with a classic lemony, garlicky sauce. To achieve a golden, crisp coating, we dredged chicken tenderloins in egg and flour, shallow-fried them in just 2 tablespoons of oil, and paired them with a garlicky sauce studded with strips of tender red bell pepper. We finished the sauce with lemon for brightness and butter for richness and the proper consistency—perfect for swiping up with crusty bread or pouring over pasta.

If you can't find chicken tenderloins, slice boneless, skinless chicken breasts lengthwise into ¾-inch-thick strips. You can use torn basil in place of the parsley, if desired. Serve with crusty bread and lemon wedges.

- 2 large eggs
- Table salt and pepper
- ¾ cup plus 1 tablespoon all-purpose flour
- 2 pounds chicken tenderloins, trimmed
- 6 tablespoons extra-virgin olive oil, divided
- 1 red bell pepper, stemmed, seeded, and sliced thin
- 8 garlic cloves, sliced thin
- 1¼ cups chicken broth
- ¾ cup dry white wine
- 4 tablespoons unsalted butter, cut into 4 pieces
- 2 tablespoons chopped fresh parsley

1. Lightly beat eggs and ½ teaspoon salt together in shallow dish. Place ¾ cup flour in second shallow dish. Pat chicken dry with paper towels and season with salt and pepper. Working with 1 piece of chicken at a time, dip in eggs, allowing excess to drip off, then dredge in flour, shaking off any excess. Transfer to large plate.

2. Heat 2 tablespoons oil in 12-inch nonstick skillet over medium-high heat until just smoking. Add half of chicken and cook until golden brown and registering 160 degrees, about 3 minutes per side. Transfer chicken to clean plate and tent with aluminum foil. Wipe skillet clean with paper towels and repeat with 2 tablespoons oil and remaining chicken.

Skillet Chicken Parmesan

Chicken Scampi

3. Wipe skillet clean with paper towels. Heat remaining 2 tablespoons oil in now-empty skillet over medium-high heat until just smoking. Add bell pepper and ½ teaspoon salt and cook until softened and well browned, 5 to 7 minutes. Add garlic and cook until fragrant and golden brown, about 1 minute. Stir in remaining 1 tablespoon flour and cook for 1 minute.

4. Stir in broth and wine and bring to boil, scraping up any browned bits. Cook until mixture is reduced to about 1½ cups, 5 to 7 minutes. Reduce heat to low and stir in butter until melted. Return chicken to skillet and cook, turning to coat with sauce, until heated through, about 2 minutes. Season with salt and pepper to taste. Transfer to shallow serving platter and sprinkle with parsley. Serve.

Chicken Scarpariello

SERVES 4 TO 6

WHY THIS RECIPE WORKS We wanted our version of this Italian American dish to be bright and flavorful, but not too briny or too spicy. Removing the cherry peppers' seeds tempered their heat, and using some of their vinegary brine added extra flavor. After browning the chicken and sausage, we sautéed the vegetables, then nestled in the chicken and sausage to finish cooking in the oven, which kept the chicken skin crispy. Flour and chicken broth created a sauce that coated the meat perfectly.

We used sweet Italian sausage to balance the spiciness of the cherry peppers. Feel free to substitute hot Italian sausage if you prefer a spicier dish.

- 3 pounds bone-in chicken pieces (2 split breasts cut in half crosswise, 2 drumsticks, and 2 thighs), trimmed
- Table salt and pepper
- 1 tablespoon vegetable oil
- 8 ounces sweet Italian sausage, casings removed
- 1 onion, halved and sliced thin
- 1 red bell pepper, stemmed, seeded, and sliced thin
- 5 jarred hot cherry peppers, seeded, rinsed, and sliced thin (½ cup), plus 2 tablespoons brine
- 5 garlic cloves, minced
- 1 teaspoon dried oregano
- 1 tablespoon all-purpose flour
- ¾ cup chicken broth
- 2 tablespoons chopped fresh parsley

1. Adjust oven rack to middle position and heat oven to 350 degrees. Pat chicken dry with paper towels and season with salt and pepper. Heat oil in 12-inch skillet over medium-high heat until just smoking. Add chicken to skillet, skin side down, and cook without moving until well browned, about 5 minutes. Flip chicken and continue to cook until browned on second side, about 3 minutes. Transfer chicken to plate.

2. Add sausage to fat left in skillet and cook, breaking up with spoon, until browned, about 3 minutes. Transfer sausage to paper towel–lined plate.

3. Pour off all but 1 tablespoon fat from skillet and return to medium-high heat. Add onion and bell pepper and cook until vegetables are softened and lightly browned, about 5 minutes. Add cherry peppers, garlic, and oregano and cook until fragrant, about 1 minute. Stir in flour and cook for 30 seconds. Add broth and cherry pepper brine and bring to simmer, scraping up any browned bits.

4. Remove skillet from heat and stir in sausage. Arrange chicken pieces, skin side up, in single layer in skillet and add any accumulated juices. Transfer skillet to oven and cook until breasts register 160 degrees and drumsticks/thighs register 175 degrees, 20 to 25 minutes.

5. Carefully remove skillet from oven (handle will be very hot). Transfer chicken to serving platter. Season onion mixture with salt and pepper to taste, then spoon over chicken. Sprinkle with parsley. Serve.

Italian Pot Roast

SERVES 4 TO 6

WHY THIS RECIPE WORKS The bolder cousin of American-style pot roast, Italian Pot Roast trades the potatoes, carrots, and gravy for mushrooms, onion, and a thick sauce based on tomatoes, red wine, garlic, and herbs. For our version, we started with a chuck-eye roast for its beefy flavor and ample fat. Canned diced tomatoes, tomato sauce, and tomato paste gave us a thick, rich sauce; a double dose of red wine added depth and brightness. Simmering a whole head of garlic with our roast ensured the meat and sauce were infused with mellow garlic flavor.

Start checking the roast for doneness after 2 hours; if there is a little resistance when prodded with a fork, it's done. Light, sweeter red wines, such as a Merlot or Beaujolais, work especially well with this recipe.

- 1 (3½- to 4-pound) boneless beef chuck-eye roast, trimmed, tied at 1-inch intervals
- Table salt and pepper
- 2 tablespoons vegetable oil
- 1 onion, chopped
- 1 celery rib, minced
- 1 pound cremini or white mushrooms, trimmed and quartered
- 2 tablespoons tomato paste
- 1 (14.5-ounce) can diced tomatoes
- ½ cup canned tomato sauce
- ½ cup water
- 1 cup red wine, divided
- 2 teaspoons sugar
- 1 large garlic head, outer papery skins removed, halved
- 1 sprig fresh thyme
- 1 sprig fresh rosemary

1. Adjust oven rack to middle position and heat oven to 300 degrees. Pat roast dry with paper towels and season with salt and pepper.

2. Heat oil in Dutch oven over medium-high heat until just smoking. Brown roast on all sides, 8 to 12 minutes. Transfer roast to large plate. Reduce heat to medium, add onion, celery, mushrooms, and tomato paste and cook until vegetables begin to soften, about 8 minutes. Add diced tomatoes, tomato sauce, water, ½ cup wine, sugar, garlic, and thyme. Add roast, with accumulated juices, to pot and bring to simmer over medium-high heat. Place piece of aluminum foil over pot, cover with lid, and transfer pot to oven.

3. Cook until roast is just fork-tender, 2½ to 3½ hours, turning roast after 1 hour. Remove lid and foil and let roast rest for 30 minutes, skimming fat from surface of liquid after 20 minutes. Transfer roast to carving board and tent with foil.

4. Remove and reserve garlic head and skim remaining fat. Add remaining ½ cup wine to pot, bring to boil over medium-high heat, and cook until sauce begins to thicken, about 12 minutes. Meanwhile, carefully squeeze garlic cloves from their skins and mash into paste. Add rosemary to pot and simmer until fragrant, about 2 minutes. Remove rosemary and thyme sprigs, stir in mashed garlic, and season with salt and pepper to taste.

5. Remove twine from roast and slice meat against grain into ½-inch-thick slices or pull apart into large pieces. Transfer meat to serving platter and pour ¾ cup sauce over meat. Serve, passing remaining sauce separately.

Chicken Scarpariello

Italian Pot Roast

Pork Chops with Vinegar Peppers

Pork Chops with Vinegar Peppers
SERVES 4

WHY THIS RECIPE WORKS Choosing the right pork chop and the right kind of peppers was essential to getting this dish right. We decided on thick-cut, bone-in rib chops, which we brined briefly to ensure seasoned and moist meat. Jarred sweet vinegar peppers held up≈to braising and had a mild tang that we liked. To give long-cooked flavor to our quick-cooked braising sauce, we added a secret ingredient—anchovy fillets—which contributed savory depth but did not impart any fishy flavor. We thickened the sauce in two ways: by flouring the chops (which also aided browning) and by reducing the sauce slightly after the pork was done.

Our favorite chicken broth is Swanson Chicken Stock.

- 3 tablespoons sugar
- Table salt and pepper
- 4 (8- to 10-ounce) bone-in pork rib chops, 1 inch thick, trimmed
- 1/3 cup all-purpose flour
- 2 tablespoons extra-virgin olive oil, divided
- 1 onion, halved and sliced thin
- 8 garlic cloves, lightly crushed and peeled
- 2 anchovy fillets, rinsed, patted dry, and minced
- 2 cups thinly sliced sweet green vinegar peppers
- 1 sprig fresh rosemary
- 1 cup chicken broth
- 1/2 cup red wine vinegar
- 1 tablespoon unsalted butter

1. Dissolve sugar and 3 tablespoons salt in 1½ quarts cold water in large container. Add chops, cover, and refrigerate for 30 minutes or up to 1 hour.

2. Place flour in shallow dish. Remove chops from brine. Pat chops dry with paper towels and season with pepper. Working with 1 chop at a time, dredge both sides in flour, shaking off excess. Heat 1 tablespoon oil in 12-inch skillet over medium-high heat until just smoking. Add chops and cook until well browned on first side, 5 to 7 minutes. Flip chops and cook on second side for 1 minute; transfer to plate, browned side up.

3. Reduce heat to medium and add remaining 1 tablespoon oil, onion, garlic, and anchovies to now-empty skillet. Cook, stirring frequently, until

Salmon Piccata

onion is softened and golden brown, 6 to 8 minutes. Add peppers and rosemary and cook until peppers begin to caramelize, about 5 minutes. Add broth and vinegar and bring to boil.

4. Arrange chops, browned side up, in skillet and add any accumulated juices from plate. Reduce heat to low, cover, and simmer until chops register 145 degrees, 6 to 10 minutes. Transfer chops to serving platter and tent loosely with aluminum foil.

5. Increase heat to high and boil sauce until slightly thickened, about 3 minutes. Off heat, stir in butter and season with salt and pepper to taste. Stir any accumulated juices from platter into sauce. Discard rosemary and spoon sauce over chops. Serve.

Salmon Piccata

SERVES 4

WHY THIS RECIPE WORKS Tangy, bold piccata sauce is a great pairing for salmon's rich, full flavor. To keep the salmon fillets from breaking apart, we covered the pan and steamed the fish without flipping it. We built the sauce in the same pan, using garlic, white wine, capers, and lemon zest and juice for punchy flavor. We whisked in butter off the heat to ensure silkiness and then finished with fresh dill.

To ensure uniform pieces of fish, we prefer to purchase a whole center-cut salmon fillet and cut it into four equal pieces. For skinless salmon, we refer to the side opposite where the skin used to be, which is typically more pink in color and more rounded than the flesh side.

- 1 (2-pound) center-cut skinless salmon fillet, about 1½ inches thick
- 1 teaspoon table salt, divided
- 1 teaspoon pepper, divided
- 1 tablespoon extra-virgin olive oil
- 3 garlic cloves, sliced thin
- 2 teaspoons all-purpose flour
- ½ cup dry white wine
- ¼ cup water
- 2 tablespoons capers, rinsed
- 1 teaspoon grated lemon zest plus 1 tablespoon juice
- 4 tablespoons unsalted butter, cut into 4 pieces
- 3 tablespoons chopped fresh dill

1. Cut salmon crosswise into 4 equal fillets. Pat salmon dry with paper towels and sprinkle all over with ½ teaspoon salt and ½ teaspoon pepper.

2. Heat oil in 12-inch nonstick skillet over medium-high heat until just smoking. Add salmon flesh side down. Cover and cook until browned on bottom and registering 125 degrees (for medium-rare), about 5 minutes, or 135 degrees (for medium), about 7 minutes. Remove skillet from heat and transfer salmon, browned side up, to platter or individual plates.

3. Return skillet to medium heat. Add garlic and cook until fragrant, about 30 seconds. Stir in flour and cook for 15 seconds. Whisk in wine, water, capers, lemon zest and juice, remaining ½ teaspoon salt, and remaining ½ teaspoon pepper. Bring to boil and cook for 30 seconds.

4. Off heat, whisk in butter, 1 piece at a time, until combined. Stir in dill. Spoon sauce over salmon. Serve.

Beans and Greens

SERVES 4

WHY THIS RECIPE WORKS A staple restaurant menu item in Pennsylvania's Western Valley, beans and greens features hearty greens cooked down in a flavorful broth and tossed with tender white beans. We kept things simple, sautéing some aromatics before adding one head of escarole, which we cut into pieces. Once the greens were wilted, we stirred in drained canned cannellini beans, cooked them for a few minutes, and finished the dish by sprinkling some nutty Parmesan cheese and extra olive oil over the top.

Don't be alarmed by what may seem like the large amount of greens we call for. Once added to the pot, they wilt down significantly within minutes.

- 2 tablespoons extra-virgin olive oil, plus extra for drizzling
- 1 onion, chopped fine
- ½ teaspoon table salt
- ½ teaspoon pepper
- 3 garlic cloves, minced
- 1 teaspoon chopped fresh rosemary
- ½ teaspoon red pepper flakes
- ½ cup chicken broth
- 1 head escarole (1 pound), trimmed and cut into 2-inch pieces
- 1 (15-ounce) can cannellini beans, rinsed
- 1 ounce Parmesan cheese, grated (½ cup), divided

1. Heat oil in Dutch oven over medium-high heat until shimmering. Add onion, salt, and pepper and cook until softened and beginning to brown, 5 to 7 minutes. Add garlic, rosemary, and pepper flakes and cook until fragrant, about 30 seconds.

2. Reduce heat to medium-low. Stir in broth, scraping up any browned bits. Stir in escarole; cover and cook, stirring occasionally, until wilted, 6 to 8 minutes.

3. Add beans and cook, uncovered and stirring occasionally, until escarole is tender, about 5 minutes. Off heat, stir in ¼ cup Parmesan. Season with salt and pepper to taste. Transfer greens to serving dish. Sprinkle with remaining ¼ cup Parmesan and drizzle with extra oil. Serve.

Beans and Greens

Fried Artichokes
SERVES 4 TO 6

WHY THIS RECIPE WORKS We set out to make fried artichokes using frozen hearts for convenience. We quickly found that thawed-then-battered frozen artichoke hearts were too wet to fry to crispiness. Using a dry coating of flour, cornstarch (to absorb excess moisture and help with crispiness), baking powder (to lighten the coating), and seasonings gave these artichokes a shatteringly crispy fried exterior. Best of all, the thawed-and-patted-dry artichoke hearts were moist enough to hold on to the coating without any additional breading steps. A quick, easy marinara sauce made from canned crushed tomatoes, garlic, extra-virgin olive oil, and Parmesan cheese was the perfect accompaniment.

These artichokes also go well with our Lemon Aioli (recipe follows).

Marinara Sauce
- 2 tablespoons extra-virgin olive oil
- 2 garlic cloves, minced
- 1 (14.5-ounce) can crushed tomatoes
- ¼ teaspoon table salt
- ¼ cup grated Parmesan cheese
- ⅛ teaspoon sugar

Artichokes
- 1¼ cups all-purpose flour
- ¼ cup cornstarch
- 1 tablespoon garlic powder
- 2 teaspoons table salt

Fried Artichokes

- 1 teaspoon baking powder
- ½ teaspoon pepper
- 1½ pounds frozen quartered artichoke hearts, thawed and patted dry
- 1 quart vegetable or peanut oil for frying

1. For the Marinara Sauce Heat oil and garlic in small saucepan over medium heat, stirring frequently, until fragrant but not browned, about 2 minutes. Stir in tomatoes and salt and simmer until slightly thickened, about 5 minutes. Stir in Parmesan and sugar. Remove from heat; cover to keep warm.

2. For the Artichokes Whisk flour, cornstarch, garlic powder, salt, baking powder, and pepper together in large bowl. Add artichokes to flour mixture and toss with your hands to coat evenly.

3. Set wire rack in rimmed baking sheet and line with triple layer of paper towels. Heat oil in Dutch oven over medium-high heat to 375 degrees.

4. Gently shake off excess flour mixture from half of artichokes and carefully add to hot oil. Immediately stir with spider skimmer or slotted spoon to break up clumps. Fry until artichokes are golden brown, 5 to 7 minutes. (Adjust burner, if necessary, to maintain oil temperature around 350 degrees.)

5. Transfer fried artichokes to prepared rack. Return oil to 375 degrees and repeat with remaining artichokes. Transfer fried artichokes to platter and serve immediately with sauce.

Lemon Aioli
SERVES 24 (MAKES ABOUT 1½ CUPS)

Do not substitute olive oil for the vegetable oil; the aioli will turn out bitter.

- 1 large egg
- 3 tablespoons lemon juice
- 1½ teaspoons Dijon mustard
- 1 garlic clove, minced
- ¾ teaspoon table salt
- ¼ teaspoon sugar
- Pinch cayenne pepper
- 1½ cups vegetable oil
- 2 tablespoons extra-virgin olive oil

Process egg, lemon juice, mustard, garlic, salt, sugar, and cayenne in food processor until combined, about 5 seconds. With processor running, slowly drizzle in vegetable oil until emulsified and mixture is thick, about 2 minutes. Scrape down sides of bowl with rubber spatula and continue to process 5 seconds longer. Transfer to jar and stir in olive oil. Affix jar lid and refrigerate until ready to use. (Aioli can be refrigerated for up to 1 week.)

Prosciutto Bread
MAKES 2 LOAVES

WHY THIS RECIPE WORKS Prosciutto bread is a specialty at G. Esposito and Sons Jersey Pork Store in Brooklyn: a rustic loaf studded with tiny chunks of cured meats and flavored with black pepper. For a dough with a strong gluten structure that wouldn't collapse under the weight of the meat, we opted for high-protein bread flour. Adding beer boosted the bread's yeasty flavor while cutting down on rising time. Standard thin slices of deli meat got wadded up, but thick slabs cut into ½-inch pieces incorporated nicely. Prosciutto, capicola, and pepperoni gave the bread a balance of peppery sweetness, and provolone underscored the savoriness.

We love the combination of prosciutto, pepperoni, and capicola in this bread, but you can use 9 ounces of any combination of your favorite cured meats; just be sure to have each sliced ¼ inch thick at the deli counter. Do not use thinly sliced deli meats, as they will adversely affect the bread's texture. Use a mild lager, such as Budweiser; strongly flavored beers will make this bread taste bitter.

- 3 cups (16½ ounces) bread flour
- 1½ teaspoons instant or rapid-rise yeast
- 1 teaspoon table salt
- 1 cup mild lager, room temperature
- 6 tablespoons water, room temperature
- 3 tablespoons extra-virgin olive oil
- 5 ounces (¼-inch-thick) sliced provolone cheese, cut into ½-inch pieces (optional)
- 3 ounces (¼-inch-thick) sliced prosciutto, cut into ½-inch pieces
- 3 ounces (¼-inch-thick) sliced pepperoni, cut into ½-inch pieces
- 3 ounces (¼-inch-thick) sliced capicola, cut into ½-inch pieces
- 1½ teaspoons coarsely ground pepper
- Cornmeal

1. Whisk flour, yeast, and salt together in bowl of stand mixer. Whisk beer, room-temperature water, and oil together in 2-cup liquid measuring cup.

2. Fit mixer with dough hook. Mix flour mixture on low speed while slowly adding beer mixture until cohesive dough starts to form and no dry flour remains, about 2 minutes, scraping down bowl as needed. Increase speed to medium and knead until dough is smooth and elastic and clears sides of bowl, about 8 minutes.

3. Reduce speed to low and add provolone, if using, prosciutto, pepperoni, capicola, and pepper. Continue to knead until combined, about 2 minutes longer (some meats may not be fully incorporated into dough at this point; this is OK). Transfer dough and any errant pieces of meats to lightly floured counter and knead by hand to evenly incorporate meats into dough, about 1 minute.

4. Form dough into smooth, round ball and place seam side down in lightly greased large bowl. Cover tightly with plastic wrap and let dough rise at room temperature until doubled in size, about 1½ hours.

5. Line baking sheet with parchment paper and lightly dust with cornmeal. Turn out dough onto counter and gently press down to deflate any large air pockets. Cut dough into 2 even pieces. Press each piece of dough into 8 by 5-inch rectangle with long side parallel to counter's edge.

6. Working with 1 piece of dough at a time, fold top edge of rectangle down to midline, pressing to seal. Fold bottom edge of rectangle up to midline and pinch to seal. Flip dough seam side down and gently roll into 12-inch loaf with tapered ends. Transfer loaf to 1 side of prepared sheet. Repeat shaping with second piece of dough and place loaf about 3 inches from first loaf on sheet. Cover with greased plastic and let rise at room temperature until puffy and dough springs back slowly when pressed lightly with your finger, about 45 minutes.

7. Adjust oven rack to middle position and heat oven to 450 degrees. Using sharp paring knife in swift, fluid motion, make ½-inch-deep lengthwise slash along top of each loaf, starting and stopping about 1½ inches from ends. Bake until loaves register 205 to 210 degrees, 22 to 25 minutes. Transfer loaves to wire rack and let cool completely, about 3 hours. Serve.

To Make Ahead Make dough through step 3, form into ball, and place seam side down in lightly greased large bowl. Cover tightly with plastic wrap and refrigerate for at least 16 hours or up to 24 hours. Let dough come to room temperature, about 3 hours, before proceeding with step 5.

Shaping the Loaf

After patting half the dough into a rectangle, fold the top down and the bottom up, pressing to seal as you go. Flip it seam down and roll it into a 12-inch loaf.

Zeppoles

MAKES 15 TO 18 ZEPPOLES

WHY THIS RECIPE WORKS To make zeppoles, a cross between doughnuts and fried dough, we discovered that two leaveners were better than one. Although typically used independently, in the case of these Italian fritters, a combination of baking powder and yeast created the perfect fluffy confection. We fried the wet, sticky dough at 350 degrees, which yielded a crispy exterior that didn't overcook by the time the interior had finished cooking. These light, tender zeppoles are best served warm with a dusting of powdery confectioners' sugar.

This dough is very wet and sticky. If you own a 4-cup liquid measuring cup, you can combine the batter in it to make it easier to tell when it has doubled in volume in step 1. Zeppoles are best served warm.

- 1⅓ cups (6⅔ ounces) all-purpose flour
- 1 tablespoon granulated sugar
- 2 teaspoons instant or rapid-rise yeast
- 1 teaspoon baking powder
- ½ teaspoon table salt
- 1 cup warm water (110 degrees)
- ½ teaspoon vanilla extract
- 2 quarts peanut or vegetable oil
  Confectioners' sugar

1. Combine flour, granulated sugar, yeast, baking powder, and salt in large bowl. Whisk water and vanilla into flour mixture until fully combined. Cover tightly with plastic wrap and let rise at room temperature until doubled in size, 15 to 25 minutes.

2. Set wire rack in rimmed baking sheet and line rack with triple layer of paper towels. Adjust oven rack to middle position and heat oven to 200 degrees. Add oil to large Dutch oven until it measures about 1½ inches deep and heat over medium-high heat to 350 degrees.

3. Using greased tablespoon measure, add 6 heaping tablespoonfuls of batter to oil. (Use dinner spoon to help scrape batter from tablespoon if necessary.) Fry until golden brown and toothpick inserted in center of zeppole comes out clean, 2 to 3 minutes, flipping once halfway through frying. Adjust burner, if necessary, to maintain oil temperature between 325 and 350 degrees.

4. Using slotted spoon, transfer zeppoles to prepared wire rack; roll briefly so paper towels absorb grease. Transfer sheet to oven to keep warm. Return oil to 350 degrees and repeat twice more with remaining batter. Dust zeppoles with confectioners' sugar and serve.

Instant Yeast

Instant, or rapid-rise, yeast is much like active dry yeast, but it has undergone a gentler drying process that has not destroyed the outer cells. Instant yeast does not require proofing and can be added directly to the dry ingredients when making bread—hence the name "instant." Our recipes call for instant yeast because it's easier to use. In breads that contain butter, sugar, and other flavorings, we find virtually no difference in flavor between instant and active dry yeasts. If you have a recipe that calls for active dry yeast, you can use instant as long as you reduce the amount of yeast by 25 percent. For example, if the recipe calls for 1 packet, or 2¼ teaspoons, of active dry yeast, use 1¾ teaspoons of instant yeast.

Prosciutto Bread

Zeppoles

the state of grilling

458 Huli Huli Chicken	494 Texas-Style Smoked Beef Ribs	519 Grilled Bone-In Leg of Lamb with Charred-Scallion Sauce
459 Cornell Barbecued Chicken	495 Smoked Prime Rib	520 Pomegranate-Glazed Grilled Lamb Chops
460 Alabama Barbecued Chicken	495 Smoked Prime Rib Sandwiches with Green Chile Queso	521 Wood-Grilled Salmon
461 Classic Barbecued Chicken		522 Cedar-Planked Salmon with Cucumber-Yogurt Sauce
462 Grilled Jerk Chicken	497 Kalbi (Korean Grilled Flanken-Style Short Ribs)	523 Grilled Salmon Steaks with Lemon-Caper Sauce
464 Chicken Teriyaki	498 South Carolina Smoked Fresh Ham	524 Smoked Fish Tacos
465 Smoked Citrus Chicken	499 North Carolina Barbecue Pork	525 Grilled Jalapeño and Lime Shrimp Skewers
466 Smoked Bourbon Chicken	501 Lexington-Style Pulled Pork	526 Husk-Grilled Corn
467 Grilled Butterflied Lemon Chicken	502 South Carolina Pulled Pork	527 Grilled Corn on the Cob
468 Grilled Chicken Wings	503 Tennessee Pulled Pork Sandwiches	528 Backyard Barbecue Beans
469 Grill-Fried Chicken Wings	504 Hoecakes	529 California Barbecued Beans
471 Smoked Chicken Wings	506 Grilled Pork Burgers	530 Grilled Potato Packs
472 Grilled Chicken Leg Quarters	507 Grilled Sausages with Bell Peppers and Onions	531 Grilled Sweet Potatoes with Maple Chile Crisp
473 BBQ Chicken Thighs	508 Texas Thick-Cut Smoked Pork Chops	532 Grilled Broccoli with Lemon and Parmesan
474 Grilled Chicken Diavolo	509 Smoked Double-Thick Pork Chops	533 Grilled Caesar Salad
475 Barbecued Pulled Chicken	510 Grilled Thin-Cut Pork Chops	534 Tangy Apple Cabbage Slaw
476 Tennessee Pulled Turkey Sandwiches	511 Monroe County–Style Pork Chops	535 Memphis Chopped Coleslaw
478 Barbecued Burnt Ends	512 St. Louis BBQ Pork Steaks	536 Shredded Carrot and Serrano Chile Salad
479 Shashlik-Style Beef Kebabs	514 Chinese-Style Glazed Pork Tenderloin	536 All-American Potato Salad
480 Grilled Bourbon Steaks	514 Chinese-Style Barbecued Spareribs	537 Smoky Potato Salad
481 Grilled Thick-Cut Porterhouse Steaks	516 Barbecued Country-Style Ribs	538 Amish Potato Salad
482 Grilled Steak Fajitas	516 South Dakota Corncob-Smoked Ribs	539 Ranch Potato Salad
483 Grilled Flank Steak with Basil Dressing	518 Grilled Mustard-Glazed Pork Loin	540 Dill Potato Salad
484 California Barbecued Tri-Tip		540 Texas Potato Salad
486 Shredded Barbecued Beef		541 Smashed Potato Salad
487 Texas Barbecue Brisket		542 Lemon and Herb Red Potato Salad
488 Jucy Lucy Burgers		543 Potato, Green Bean, and Tomato Salad
489 Grilled Bacon Burgers with Caramelized Onion		
490 Green Chile Cheeseburgers		
491 Chicago-Style Barbecued Ribs		
492 Texas Barbecued Beef Ribs		

Recipe Photos (clockwise from top left): Chicken Teriyaki; Grilled Salmon Steaks; Smoked Prime Rib; and Potato, Green Bean, and Tomato Salad

Huli Huli Chicken

SERVES 4 TO 6

Huli Huli Chicken

WHY THIS RECIPE WORKS Traditional Hawaiian huli huli chicken is typically something home cooks buy instead of make. The birds are continually basted with a sticky-sweet glaze and "huli"-ed, which means "turned" in Hawaiian. For the teriyaki-like glaze, we developed a version with soy sauce, rice vinegar, ginger, garlic, chili sauce, ketchup, brown sugar, and lots and lots of pineapple juice. We boiled the sauce down until it was thick, glossy, and sweet. To mimic a Hawaiian rotisserie, we spread the coals in a single layer. The direct heat rendered the fat and crisped the skin, but the chicken was far enough from the coals to avoid burning.

Mesquite wood chips give this recipe the best flavor, but you can substitute another variety.

Chicken
- 2 (3½- to 4-pound) whole chickens
- 2 quarts water
- 2 cups soy sauce
- 1 tablespoon vegetable oil
- 6 garlic cloves, minced
- 1 tablespoon grated fresh ginger

Glaze
- 3 (6-ounce) cans pineapple juice
- ¼ cup packed light brown sugar
- ¼ cup soy sauce
- ¼ cup ketchup
- ¼ cup rice vinegar
- 4 garlic cloves, minced
- 2 tablespoons grated fresh ginger
- 2 teaspoons chili-garlic sauce
- 2 cups wood chips, soaked in water for 15 minutes and drained

1. For the Chicken Using kitchen shears, cut along both sides of backbone to remove it. Trim any excess fat or skin at neck. Flip chicken over and, using chef's knife, cut through breastbone to separate chicken into halves. Repeat with other chicken. Combine water and soy sauce in large bowl. Heat oil in large saucepan over medium-high heat until shimmering. Add garlic and ginger and cook until fragrant, about 30 seconds. Stir into soy sauce mixture. Add chicken and refrigerate, covered, for at least 1 hour or up to 8 hours.

2. For the Glaze Combine pineapple juice, sugar, soy sauce, ketchup, vinegar, garlic, ginger, and chili-garlic sauce in empty saucepan and bring to boil. Reduce heat to medium and simmer until thick and syrupy (you should have about 1 cup), 20 to 25 minutes. Using large piece of heavy-duty aluminum foil, wrap soaked chips in foil packet and cut several vent holes in top.

3a. For a Charcoal Grill Open bottom vent halfway. Light large chimney starter three-quarters filled with charcoal briquettes (4½ quarts). When top coals are partially covered with ash, pour evenly over grill. Place foil packet on coals. Set cooking grate in place, cover, and open lid vent halfway. Heat grill until hot and wood chips are smoking, about 5 minutes.

3b. For a Gas Grill Place wood chip packet directly on primary burner. Turn all burners to high, cover, and heat grill until hot and wood chips are smoking, about 15 minutes. Turn all burners to medium-low. (Adjust burners as needed to maintain grill temperature of 350 degrees.)

4. Clean and oil cooking grate. Remove chicken from brine and pat dry with paper towels. Place chicken skin side up on grill (do not place chicken directly above foil packet). Cover and cook chicken until well browned on bottom and thighs register 120 degrees, 25 to 30 minutes. Flip chicken skin side down and continue to cook, covered, until skin is well browned and crisp and thighs register 175 degrees, 20 to 25 minutes longer. Transfer chicken to platter, brush with half of glaze, and let rest for 5 minutes. Serve, passing remaining glaze at table.

To Make Ahead Both brine and glaze can be made ahead and refrigerated for up to 3 days. Do not brine chicken for longer than 8 hours or it will become too salty.

> ### Huli History Lesson
> In 1955, Hawaiian chicken farmer Ernie Morgado served local farmers barbecued chickens he'd made with his mom's homemade teriyaki-style sauce. They liked it so much that he launched a catering business using specially designed barbecue troughs that held chicken halves between two grates. When the chickens were ready to turn, the workers would yell "Huli!" ("turn," in Hawaiian), and all the chickens would be rotated in one go. Morgado named his sauce Huli Huli.

Cornell Barbecued Chicken

SERVES 4 TO 6

WHY THIS RECIPE WORKS Invented in the 1940s by Robert Baker, a Cornell University professor, this tangy, crisp-skinned grilled chicken recipe has been a star attraction at the New York State Fair ever since. Grilling two split chickens over gentle direct heat worked best here. To crisp the skin without burning it, we started the chicken skin side up to render the fat slowly, then flipped the chicken skin side down to brown until crisp. The traditional poultry seasoning worked great as a rub but tasted dusty in the sauce, so we replaced it with fresh rosemary and sage. Dijon mustard contributed even more flavor to the sauce and thickened it perfectly.

Do not brine the chicken longer than 2 hours or the vinegar will turn the meat mushy. Poultry seasoning is a mix of herbs and spices that can be found in the spice aisle of most supermarkets.

Chicken
- 2 (3½- to 4-pound) whole chickens
- ¼ cup table salt
- 3½ cups cider vinegar

Seasoning and Sauce
- 1 tablespoon ground poultry seasoning
- Table salt and pepper
- ½ cup cider vinegar
- 3 tablespoons Dijon mustard
- 1 tablespoon chopped fresh sage leaves
- 1 tablespoon chopped fresh rosemary
- ½ cup olive oil

1. For the Chicken Using kitchen shears, cut along both sides of backbone to remove it. Trim any excess fat or skin at neck. Flip chicken over and, using chef's knife, cut through breastbone to separate chicken into halves. Repeat with other chicken. In large container, dissolve salt in vinegar and 2 quarts water. Submerge chickens in brine, cover, and refrigerate for 1 to 2 hours.

2. For the Seasoning and Sauce Combine poultry seasoning, 2 teaspoons salt, and 2 teaspoons pepper in small bowl; set aside. Process vinegar, mustard, sage, rosemary, ½ teaspoon salt, and ½ teaspoon pepper in blender until smooth, about 1 minute. With blender running, slowly add oil until incorporated. Transfer vinegar sauce to small bowl and reserve for basting chicken in steps 5 and 6.

3. Remove chickens from brine, pat dry with paper towels, and rub evenly with poultry seasoning mixture. Measure out ¾ cup vinegar sauce and set aside for cooking; reserve remaining sauce for serving.

4a. For a Charcoal Grill Open bottom vent completely. Light large chimney starter three-quarters filled with charcoal briquettes (4½ quarts). When top coals are partially covered with ash, pour evenly over grill. Set cooking grate in place, cover, and open lid vent halfway. Heat grill until hot, about 5 minutes.

4b. For a Gas Grill Turn all burners to high, cover, and heat grill until hot, about 15 minutes. Turn all burners to medium-low. (Adjust burners as needed to maintain grill temperature around 350 degrees.)

THE STATE OF GRILLING 459

Cornell Barbecued Chicken

5. Clean and oil cooking grate. Place chicken skin side up on grill and brush with 6 tablespoons vinegar sauce for cooking. Cover and cook chicken until well browned on bottom and thighs register 120 degrees, 25 to 30 minutes, brushing with more sauce for cooking halfway through grilling.

6. Flip chicken skin side down and brush with remaining sauce for cooking. Cover and continue to cook chicken until skin is golden brown and crisp and breasts register 160 degrees and thighs register 175 degrees, 20 to 25 minutes longer.

7. Transfer chicken to carving board and let rest for 10 minutes. Carve chicken and serve with reserved sauce.

> **The Chicken Man of Cornell University**
>
> Robert Baker (1921–2006) developed the recipe for Cornell chicken while employed at Pennsylvania State University, but his recipe didn't take off until he had moved on to the Animal Sciences Department at Cornell University (his alma mater) and published it in a school journal. This vinegary chicken wasn't Dr. Baker's only contribution to the culinary world: He also had a hand in developing the vacuum packaging still used by much of the poultry industry and was the inventor of chicken nuggets, turkey ham, and chicken hot dogs.

Alabama Barbecued Chicken

Alabama Barbecued Chicken

SERVES 4 TO 6

WHY THIS RECIPE WORKS For Alabama-inspired barbecued chicken, we ditched the tomato and slathered a mayonnaise-based sauce on hickory-smoked chicken. Smoking generally takes hours, but our recipe expedites the process by cutting the chickens in half and cooking them in the middle of the grill, sandwiched between piles of smoking coals topped with hickory chips. We coated our chickens with the traditional Alabama mixture of seasoned mayonnaise and vinegar two times during cooking so the hot chicken absorbed the sauce and was flavored through and through.

Hickory wood chips are traditional here; however, any type of wood chips will work fine. Two medium wood chunks, soaked in water for 1 hour, can be substituted for the wood chips on a charcoal grill.

Sauce
- ¾ cup mayonnaise
- 2 tablespoons cider vinegar
- 2 teaspoons sugar
- ½ teaspoon prepared horseradish
- ½ teaspoon table salt
- ½ teaspoon black pepper
- ¼ teaspoon cayenne pepper

Chicken
- 1 teaspoon table salt
- 1 teaspoon black pepper
- ½ teaspoon cayenne pepper
- 2 (3½- to 4-pound) whole chickens
- 2 cups wood chips, soaked in water for 15 minutes and drained
- 1 (13 by 9-inch) disposable aluminum roasting pan (if using charcoal)

1. For the Sauce Process ingredients in blender until smooth, about 1 minute. Refrigerate for at least 1 hour or up to 2 days.

2. For the Chicken Combine salt, pepper, and cayenne in small bowl. Using kitchen shears, cut along both sides of backbone to remove it. Trim any excess fat or skin at neck. Flip chicken over and, using chef's knife, cut through breastbone to separate chicken into halves. Repeat with other chicken. Pat chickens dry with paper towels and rub them evenly with spice mixture. Using large piece of heavy-duty aluminum foil, wrap soaked chips in foil packet and cut several vent holes in top.

3a. For a Charcoal Grill Open bottom vent halfway and place disposable pan in center of grill. Light large chimney starter filled with charcoal briquettes (6 quarts). When top coals are partially covered with ash, pour into 2 even piles on either side of pan. Place wood chip packet on 1 pile of coals. Set cooking grate in place, cover, and open lid vent halfway. Heat grill until hot and wood chips are smoking, about 5 minutes.

3b. For a Gas Grill Place wood chip packet directly on primary burner. Turn all burners to high, cover, and heat grill until hot and wood chips are smoking, about 15 minutes. Turn all burners to medium-low. (Adjust burners as needed to maintain grill temperature around 350 degrees.)

4. Clean and oil cooking grate. Place chicken skin side down on grill (in center of grill if using charcoal). Cover (positioning lid vent over chicken if using charcoal) and cook chicken until well browned on bottom and thighs register 120 degrees, 35 to 45 minutes.

5. Flip chicken skin side up. Cover and continue to cook chicken until skin is golden brown and crisp and breasts register 160 degrees and thighs register 175 degrees, 15 to 20 minutes longer.

6. Transfer chicken to carving board and brush with 2 tablespoons sauce. Tent chicken with foil and let rest for 10 minutes. Brush chicken with remaining sauce, carve, and serve.

Keeping BBQ in the Family
Famous for its white mayonnaise-based sauce, Big Bob Gibson's has been serving hickory-smoked barbecue in Decatur, Alabama, since 1925. Now run by Big Bob's grandchildren and great-grandchildren, the restaurant has expanded several times. The current pit smoker can cook 175 chickens, 110 slabs of ribs, and 60 whole turkeys at the same time. Although Big Bob used the sauce mostly on chicken, his grandson Don McLemore says nowadays people put it on everything from pork to potato chips.

Classic Barbecued Chicken

SERVES 4 TO 6

WHY THIS RECIPE WORKS Despite its popularity, barbecued chicken recipes cause grillers plenty of headaches. Most recipes call for searing chicken quickly over high heat, but we found that starting the chicken over low heat slowly rendered the fat without the danger of flare-ups. Using a method called "grill roasting" ensured that we had almost completely cooked chicken before we were ready to add our sauce. We created a thick, complex layer of barbecue flavor for our grilled chicken by applying the sauce in coats and turning the chicken frequently as it cooked over moderate heat and then finishing it over higher heat.

Don't try to grill more than 10 pieces of chicken at a time; you won't be able to line them up on the grill as directed in step 5.

Quick Barbecue Sauce

- 3 cups store-bought barbecue sauce
- ½ cup molasses
- ½ cup ketchup
- ¼ cup cider vinegar
- 3 tablespoons brown mustard
- 2 teaspoons onion powder
- 1 teaspoon garlic powder

Chicken

- 1 teaspoon table salt
- 1 teaspoon pepper
- ¼ teaspoon cayenne pepper
- 3 pounds bone-in chicken pieces, breasts halved crosswise and leg quarters separated into thighs and drumsticks, trimmed
- 1 (13 by 9-inch) disposable aluminum roasting pan (if using charcoal)

1. For the Quick Barbecue Sauce Whisk all ingredients in medium saucepan and bring to boil over medium-high heat. Reduce heat to medium and cook until sauce is thick and reduced to 3 cups, about 20 minutes. (Sauce can be refrigerated for up to 1 week.)

2. For the Chicken Combine salt, pepper, and cayenne in small bowl. Pat chicken dry with paper towels and rub evenly with spice mixture.

3a. For a Charcoal Grill Open bottom vent completely. Place disposable pan on 1 side of grill. Light large chimney starter filled with charcoal briquettes (6 quarts). When top coals are partially covered with ash, pour evenly over half of grill, opposite pan. Set cooking grate in place, cover, and open lid vent completely. Heat grill until hot, about 5 minutes.

3b. For a Gas Grill Turn all burners to high, cover, and heat grill until hot, about 15 minutes. Leave primary burner on high and turn other burner(s) off. (Adjust primary burner as needed to maintain grill temperature around 350 degrees.)

4. Clean and oil cooking grate. Place chicken, skin side down, on cool side of grill. Cover (positioning lid vent over chicken if using charcoal) and cook until chicken begins to brown, 30 to 35 minutes. Reserve 2 cups barbecue sauce for cooking; set aside remaining 1 cup sauce for serving.

5. Slide chicken into single line between hot and cool sides of grill and continue to cook, uncovered, flipping chicken and brushing with half of sauce for cooking every 5 minutes, until sticky, about 20 minutes.

6. Slide chicken to hot side of grill and continue to cook, flipping and brushing chicken with remaining sauce for cooking, until well glazed and breasts register 160 degrees and thighs/drumsticks register 175 degrees, about 5 minutes.

7. Transfer chicken to platter, tent loosely with aluminum foil, and let rest for 10 minutes. Serve with reserved sauce.

Grilled Jerk Chicken

SERVES 4

WHY THIS RECIPE WORKS Our bold but nuanced grilled jerk chicken starts with the paste. A blend of habaneros, scallions, garlic, and thyme sprigs made a big herby punch. Soy sauce added savory depth, cider vinegar brightness, and warm spices characteristic jerk flavor. After marinating the chicken, we cooked it on the cooler side of the grill, covered, which helped the marinade stick. Once the chicken was cooked through, we brushed it with a little marinade for a fresh burst of jerk flavor and seared it on the hotter side of the grill. Tasters preferred the chicken charred, not smoked per tradition, because the jerk flavor came through more clearly.

Plan ahead: The chicken needs to marinate for at least 1 hour before cooking. Use more or fewer habaneros depending on your desired level of spiciness. You can also remove the seeds and ribs from the habaneros or substitute jalapeños for less heat. We recommend wearing rubber gloves or plastic bags on your hands when handling the chiles. Use thyme sprigs with a generous amount of leaves; there's no need to separate the leaves from the stems. Keep a close eye on the chicken in step 5 since it can char quickly.

- 4 scallions
- ¼ cup vegetable oil
- ¼ cup soy sauce
- 2 tablespoons cider vinegar
- 2 tablespoons packed brown sugar
- 1–2 habanero chiles, stemmed

	10	sprigs fresh thyme
	5	garlic cloves, peeled
2½		teaspoons ground allspice
1½		teaspoons table salt
½		teaspoon ground cinnamon
½		teaspoon ground ginger
	3	pounds bone-in chicken pieces (split breasts cut in half crosswise, drumsticks, and/or thighs), trimmed
		Lime wedges

1. Process scallions, oil, soy sauce, vinegar, sugar, habanero(s), thyme sprigs, garlic, allspice, salt, cinnamon, and ginger in blender until smooth, about 30 seconds, scraping down sides of blender jar as needed. Measure out ¼ cup marinade and refrigerate until ready to use.

2. Place chicken and remaining marinade in 1-gallon zipper-lock bag. Press out air, seal bag, and turn to coat chicken in marinade. Refrigerate for at least 1 hour or up to 24 hours, turning occasionally.

3a. For a Charcoal Grill Open bottom vent completely. Light large chimney starter mounded with charcoal briquettes (7 quarts). When top coals are partially covered with ash, pour evenly over half of grill. Set cooking grate in place, cover, and open lid vent completely. Heat grill until hot, about 5 minutes.

3b. For a Gas Grill Turn all burners to high, cover, and heat grill until hot, about 15 minutes. Leave primary burner on high and turn off other burner(s). (Adjust primary burner [or, if using 3-burner grill, primary burner and second burner] as needed to maintain grill temperature between 450 and 500 degrees.)

4. Clean and oil cooking grate. Place chicken skin side up on cooler side of grill, with breast pieces farthest away from heat. Cover and cook until breasts register 160 degrees and drumsticks/thighs register 175 degrees, 22 to 30 minutes, transferring pieces to plate, skin side up, as they come to temperature. (Re-cover grill after checking pieces for doneness.)

5. Brush skin side of chicken with half of reserved marinade. Place chicken skin side down on hotter side of grill. (Turn all burners to high if using gas.) Brush with remaining reserved marinade and cook until lightly charred, 1 to 3 minutes per side. Check browning often and move pieces as needed to avoid flare-ups.

6. Transfer chicken to platter, tent with aluminum foil, and let rest for 5 to 10 minutes. Serve with lime wedges.

Classic Barbecued Chicken

Grilled Jerk Chicken

Chicken Teriyaki

SERVES 6 TO 8

WHY THIS RECIPE WORKS Inspired by the signature menu item at Toshi's Teriyaki Grill just outside Seattle, Washington, this recipe for chicken teriyaki features juicy, flavorful chicken with a shiny, caramelized crust. A handful of powerhouse ingredients worked together in a potent marinade: soy sauce, sugar, mirin, ginger, and garlic. Letting boneless, skinless chicken thighs soak up all that flavor for anywhere from one to 24 hours was all it took to get them ready for grilling. A short stint at medium-high heat on a charcoal grill gave the chicken its characteristic color and char. Sliced into thin strips and served with reserved teriyaki sauce and Japanese-style short-grain rice, it's a meal that's as simple as it is delicious.

Mirin is a sweet rice wine that is a common ingredient in Japanese cooking. It can be found in the international section of most supermarkets. Serve with white rice.

- 1 cup soy sauce
- ½ cup sugar
- 2 tablespoons mirin
- 1 (2-inch) piece ginger, peeled and sliced thin
- 5 garlic cloves, peeled
- 3 pounds boneless, skinless chicken thighs, trimmed

1. Bring soy sauce, sugar, and mirin to boil in small saucepan over medium-high heat, stirring to dissolve sugar. Remove from heat and let teriyaki sauce cool completely.

2. Combine ¾ cup teriyaki sauce, ginger, and garlic in blender and process until smooth, about 20 seconds. Set aside remaining teriyaki sauce for serving (you should have about ½ cup).

3. Place chicken in 1-gallon zipper-lock bag and add teriyaki sauce–ginger mixture. Press out air, seal bag, and turn to coat chicken with marinade. Refrigerate for at least 1 hour or up to 24 hours.

4a. For a Charcoal Grill Open bottom vent completely. Light large chimney starter filled with charcoal briquettes (6 quarts). When top coals are partially covered with ash, pour evenly over grill. Set cooking grate in place, cover, and open lid vent completely. Heat grill until hot, about 5 minutes.

4b. For a Gas Grill Turn all burners to high, cover, and heat grill until hot, about 15 minutes. Turn all burners to medium-high.

5. Clean and oil cooking grate. Place chicken on grill and cook (covered if using gas) until chicken is lightly charred and registers at least 175 degrees, 6 to 8 minutes per side, rearranging as needed to ensure even browning. Transfer to cutting board, tent with aluminum foil, and let rest for 5 minutes. Slice crosswise ½ inch thick and serve with reserved teriyaki sauce.

On The Road: Toshi's Teriyaki Grill

When Seattle cooking legend Toshi Kasahara invited me for a teriyaki lunch at his restaurant in Mill Creek, Washington, about 30 minutes outside of the city, I hadn't pictured a strip-mall storefront with just three tables and a view of Staples and Rite Aid out front. But that's where I find him, tucked away in the tiny kitchen of Toshi's Teriyaki Grill, a space filled with the iconic aromas of ginger, garlic, and grilled meats.

Toshi smiles as he cooks, sharing his story in a soft voice that is nearly drowned out by the dull hum of the range hood. He arrived in Seattle in 1976 with a business degree and a plan: to change the city's understanding of what teriyaki should be. Toshi's teriyaki sauce is simple, tasting only of

soy sauce, sugar, and a mildly boozy splash of mirin. The sauce doubles as a marinade when he adds ginger and garlic. It's a balanced combination that resembles nothing of the cloying, overly sweet versions of teriyaki that pass at many restaurants.

Customers responded favorably, and Toshi's business grew. He franchised the concept, and at one time, more than 30 restaurants bore his name. Many still do, but Toshi is no longer involved with them. His focus is here at his shop in Mill Creek, where his attention is on the food. Its pristine execution is what fulfills him.

Today, regulars line up for Styrofoam containers of chicken and beef teriyaki served with rice and slaw. Toshi moves with focus and intensity to fill the orders. He knows what he's doing.

Smoked Citrus Chicken

SERVES 4 TO 6

WHY THIS RECIPE WORKS This recipe was inspired by the citrus-and-spice infused char-grilled chicken served at El Pollo Loco, the restaurant chain founded by Juan Francisco "Pancho" Ochoa. Bone-in chicken pieces were easier to grill than the halves served at the restaurant. Cutting slits into the pieces gave the bold marinade of citrus zest, cumin, garlic, cinnamon, and cayenne more surface area to cling to. We set up a half-grill fire—all the briquettes arranged on one side of the grill—to provide two heat zones. Cooking the chicken on the cooler side over a packet of wood chips infused the meat with a smoky flavor, while charring it on the hotter side of the grill for the last few minutes gave it a deeper color.

If you prefer, you can use two wood chunks in place of the wood chip packet if you're using a charcoal grill. We tested this recipe with applewood, cherrywood, and hickory wood chips, but feel free to use any type of wood chips you like.

- ¼ cup extra-virgin olive oil
- 4 garlic cloves, minced
- 1 tablespoon kosher salt
- 1½ teaspoons grated orange zest, plus orange wedges for serving
- 1½ teaspoons ground cumin
- 1 teaspoon grated lemon zest, plus lemon wedges for serving
- ¾ teaspoon ground cinnamon
- ½ teaspoon pepper
- ⅛ teaspoon cayenne pepper
- 3 pounds bone-in chicken pieces (split breasts cut in half crosswise, drumsticks, and/or thighs), trimmed
- 1 cup wood chips

1. Whisk oil, garlic, salt, orange zest, cumin, lemon zest, cinnamon, pepper, and cayenne together in large bowl. Cut two ½-inch-deep slits in skin side of each chicken breast half, two ½-inch-deep slits in skin side of each thigh, and two ½-inch-deep slits in each drumstick. Transfer chicken to bowl with marinade and turn to thoroughly coat. Cover and refrigerate for at least 1 hour or up to 24 hours.

2. Using large piece of heavy-duty aluminum foil, wrap wood chips in 8 by 4-inch foil packet. (Make sure chips do not poke holes in sides or bottom of packet.) Cut 2 evenly spaced 2-inch slits in top of packet.

3a. For a Charcoal Grill Open bottom vent completely. Light large chimney starter mounded with charcoal briquettes (7 quarts). When top coals are partially covered with ash, pour evenly over half of grill. Place wood chip packet on coals. Set cooking grate in place, cover, and open lid vent completely. Heat grill until hot, about 5 minutes.

3b. For a Gas Grill Remove cooking grate and place wood chip packet directly on primary burner. Set grate in place; turn all burners to high; cover; and heat grill until hot, about 15 minutes. Leave primary burner on high and turn off other burner(s). (Adjust primary burner [or, if using 3-burner grill, primary burner and second burner] as needed to maintain grill temperature between 350 and 400 degrees.)

4. Clean and oil cooking grate. Place chicken skin side up on cooler side of grill, with breast pieces farthest away from heat. Cover and cook until breasts register 160 degrees and drumsticks/thighs register 175 degrees, 22 to 28 minutes, transferring pieces to plate, skin side up, as they come to temperature. (Re-cover grill after checking pieces for doneness.)

5. Transfer chicken, skin side down, to hotter side of grill. Cook until skin is well browned, 2 to 5 minutes, moving pieces as needed for even browning. Transfer chicken to platter, tent with foil, and let rest for 10 minutes. Serve with orange and lemon wedges.

> ### Smoky, but Not Too Smoky
> When we make wood chip packets in the test kitchen, we often use a large amount of chips and soak them (so that they burn and smoke longer). But here we wanted lighter smoke flavor to make sure that the bright citrus and spice flavors came through. So we used a relatively small amount of chips (1 cup) and didn't soak them. The resulting chicken had just the right amount of smoke to balance—but not overwhelm—the other flavors.

Smoked Bourbon Chicken

SERVES 4

Smoked Bourbon Chicken

WHY THIS RECIPE WORKS The combination of bourbon and smoke flavors sounded perfect, but first we had get the savory taste we wanted while keeping the chicken from drying out. The key was a mopping sauce: a sauce that is applied during long-grilling recipes to help keep the meat moist. And since smoke is attracted to moisture, keeping the chicken skin damp enhanced the smoky flavor. For even tastier chicken, we split them in half and cut slashes into the meat to create more surface area to soak up the flavor. By basting the chicken every 15 minutes, we ended up with moist, browned chicken with smokin' good bourbon taste.

Use a bourbon you'd be happy drinking. Use all the basting liquid in step 5.

- 1¼ cups bourbon
- 1¼ cups soy sauce
- ½ cup packed brown sugar
- 1 shallot, minced
- 4 garlic cloves, minced
- 2 teaspoons pepper
- 2 (3½- to 4-pound) whole chickens, giblets discarded
- 1 cup wood chips
- 4 (12-inch) wooden skewers

1. Bring bourbon, soy sauce, sugar, shallot, garlic, and pepper to boil in medium saucepan over medium-high heat and cook for 1 minute. Remove from heat and let cool completely. Set aside ¾ cup bourbon mixture for basting chicken. (Bourbon mixture can be refrigerated for up to 3 days.)

2. With chickens breast side down, using kitchen shears, cut through bones on both sides of backbones; discard backbones. Flip chickens and, using chef's knife, split chickens in half lengthwise through centers of breastbones. Cut ½-inch-deep slits across breasts, thighs, and legs, about ½ inch apart. Tuck wingtips behind backs. Divide chicken halves between two 1-gallon zipper-lock bags and divide remaining bourbon mixture between bags. Seal bags, turn to distribute marinade, and refrigerate for at least 1 hour or up to 24 hours, flipping occasionally.

3. Just before grilling, soak wood chips in water for 15 minutes, then drain. Using large piece of heavy-duty aluminum foil, wrap soaked chips in foil packet and cut several vent holes in top. Remove chicken halves from marinade and pat dry with paper towels; discard marinade. Insert 1 skewer lengthwise through thickest part of breast down through thigh of each chicken half.

4a. For a Charcoal Grill Open bottom vent halfway. Light large chimney starter filled with charcoal briquettes (6 quarts). When top coals are partially covered with ash, pour into steeply banked pile against side of grill. Place wood chip packet on coals. Set cooking grate in place, cover, and open lid vent halfway. Heat grill until hot and wood chips are smoking, about 5 minutes.

4b. For a Gas Grill Remove cooking grate and place wood chip packet directly on primary burner. Set grate in place, turn all burners to high, cover, and heat grill until hot and wood chips are smoking, about 15 minutes. Leave primary burner on high and turn off other burners. (Adjust primary burner as needed to maintain grill temperature between 350 to 375 degrees.)

5. Clean and oil cooking grate. Place chicken halves skin side up on cooler side of grill with legs pointing toward fire. Cover and cook, basting every 15 minutes with reserved bourbon mixture, until breasts register 160 degrees and thighs register 175 degrees, 75 to 90 minutes, switching placement of chicken halves after 45 minutes. (All of bourbon mixture should be used.) Transfer chicken to carving board, tent loosely with foil, and let rest for 20 minutes. Carve and serve.

How to Cut a Chicken in Half

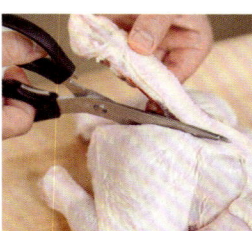 

1. Remove backbone Using poultry shears, cut through bones on both sides of backbone; discard backbone.

2. Cut through breast Flip chicken and use chef's knife to halve chicken through center of breastbone.

Grilled Butterflied Lemon Chicken

SERVES 8

WHY THIS RECIPE WORKS For perfectly grilled butterflied lemon chicken, we banked all the coals on one side of the grill, placing the chicken opposite the coals and setting the lid on the grill. This allowed the fat under the chicken's skin to render slowly; the relatively gentle heat resulted in a moister bird. Placing the chicken on the grill skin side down reduced cooking time and allowed the most fat to render. A final sear directly over the coals at the end of cooking crisped and browned the skin nicely. To finish with intense lemon flavor, we caramelized lemon halves over the grill and made a sauce from their juice.

Chicken and Rub
- 2 (3½- to 4-pound) whole chickens
- 2 teaspoons grated lemon zest (reserve lemon for vinaigrette)
- 2 teaspoons table salt
- 1 teaspoon pepper
- 1 (13 by 9-inch) disposable aluminum roasting pan (if using charcoal)

Vinaigrette
- 4 lemons, halved; plus zested, halved lemon from rub
- 2 tablespoons minced fresh parsley
- 2 teaspoons Dijon mustard
- 1 garlic clove, minced
- 1 teaspoon sugar
- ½ teaspoon table salt
- ½ teaspoon pepper
- ⅔ cup extra-virgin olive oil

1. For the Chicken and Rub Set wire rack in rimmed baking sheet. With 1 chicken breast side down, using kitchen shears, cut along both sides of backbone to remove it. Flip chicken and flatten breastbone. Use your hands to loosen skin over breast and thighs and remove any excess fat. Repeat with other chicken. Combine lemon zest, salt, and pepper in bowl. Rub zest mixture under chicken skin and tuck wings behind back. Transfer chickens to prepared baking sheet and refrigerate, uncovered, for 30 minutes. (Chickens may be prepared up to this point 24 hours in advance; allow chickens to sit at room temperature for 30 minutes before grilling.)

THE STATE OF GRILLING   467

Grilled Butterflied Lemon Chicken

5. Slide chicken to hot side of grill and continue to cook (covered if using gas) until deeply browned and breasts register 160 degrees and thighs register 175 degrees, about 5 minutes longer. Transfer chicken to carving board, tent loosely with aluminum foil, and let rest for 10 minutes.

6. For the Vinaigrette While chicken cooks, squeeze ⅓ cup juice from grilled lemons into bowl. Stir in parsley, mustard, garlic, sugar, salt, and pepper, then slowly whisk in oil until emulsified.

7. Carve chicken and transfer to serving platter. Pour ⅓ cup vinaigrette over chicken and serve, passing remaining vinaigrette separately.

Butterflying a Whole Chicken

1. Cut through bones on either side of backbone and trim any excess fat or skin at neck.

2. Flip chicken and use heel of your hand to flatten breastbone.

2a. For a Charcoal Grill Open bottom vent completely and place disposable pan on 1 side of grill. Light large chimney starter filled with charcoal briquettes (6 quarts). When top coals are partially covered in ash, pour into steeply banked pile against side of grill (opposite disposable pan). Evenly scatter 20 unlit coals on top of hot coals. Set cooking grate in place, cover, and open lid vent completely. Heat grill until hot, about 5 minutes.

2b. For a Gas Grill Turn all burners to high, cover, and heat grill until hot, about 15 minutes. Leave primary burner on high and turn off other burner(s). (Adjust primary burner as needed to maintain grill temperature around 350 degrees.)

3. Clean and oil cooking grate. Place lemon halves, cut side down, on hot side of grill and cook until deep brown and caramelized, 5 to 8 minutes. Transfer to bowl.

4. Place chicken skin side down on cool side of grill, with legs closer to hot side. Cover (positioning lid vent over chicken if using charcoal) and cook until skin is well browned, 45 to 55 minutes.

Grilled Chicken Wings
MAKES 24 WINGS

WHY THIS RECIPE WORKS To get crisp, well-rendered chicken wings, we tossed the wings in cornstarch and pepper and grilled them over a gentle medium-low heat. We began grilling with the thicker skin side facing up so that the fat could slowly render, and then we flipped the wings at the end of cooking to crisp the skin. Also, though we normally cook white chicken meat to 160 degrees, wings are chock-full of collagen, which begins to break down upwards of 170 degrees. Cooking the wings to 180 degrees produced meltingly tender wings.

If you buy whole wings, cut them into two pieces before brining. Don't brine the wings for more than 30 minutes or they'll be too salty.

4. Clean and oil cooking grate. Grill wings (covered if using gas), thicker skin side up, until browned on bottom, 12 to 15 minutes. Flip chicken and grill until skin is crisp and lightly charred and meat registers 180 degrees, about 10 minutes. Transfer chicken to platter, tent loosely with aluminum foil, and let rest for 5 to 10 minutes. Serve.

BBQ Grilled Chicken Wings

Reduce pepper to ½ teaspoon. Add 1 teaspoon chili powder, 1 teaspoon paprika, ½ teaspoon garlic powder, ½ teaspoon dried oregano, and ½ teaspoon sugar to cornstarch mixture in step 2.

Creole Grilled Chicken Wings

Add ¾ teaspoon dried oregano, ½ teaspoon garlic powder, ½ teaspoon onion powder, ½ teaspoon white pepper, and ¼ teaspoon cayenne pepper to cornstarch mixture in step 2.

Tandoori Grilled Chicken Wings

Reduce pepper to ½ teaspoon. Add 1 teaspoon garam masala, ½ teaspoon ground cumin, ¼ teaspoon garlic powder, ¼ teaspoon ground ginger, and ⅛ teaspoon cayenne pepper to cornstarch mixture in step 2.

Grilled Chicken Wings

Grill-Fried Chicken Wings

SERVES 4 TO 6

WHY THIS RECIPE WORKS It's possible to make great fried chicken without deep frying. We found a way to get deeply seasoned meat and a crunchy coating on the grill. We separated whole chicken wings into drumettes and flats and brined them to ensure they stayed moist. Then we coated the chicken with heavily seasoned flour and built a hot fire with the coals banked on one side of the grill. We put the chicken on the cooler side of the grill to cook until the coating was dry and set. Then, to get the fried texture we were looking for, we brushed the wings with vegetable oil halfway through cooking, which helped the coating turn golden brown.

½ cup table salt
2 pounds chicken wings, wingtips discarded, trimmed
1½ teaspoons cornstarch
1 teaspoon pepper

1. Dissolve salt in 2 quarts cold water in large container. Prick chicken wings all over with fork. Submerge chicken in brine, cover, and refrigerate for 30 minutes.

2. Combine cornstarch and pepper in bowl. Remove chicken from brine and pat dry with paper towels. Transfer wings to large bowl and sprinkle with cornstarch mixture, tossing until evenly coated.

3a. For a Charcoal Grill Open bottom vent completely. Light large chimney starter half filled with charcoal briquettes (3 quarts). When top coals are partially covered with ash, pour evenly over grill. Set cooking grate in place, cover, and open lid vent completely. Heat grill until hot, about 5 minutes.

3b. For a Gas Grill Turn all burners to high, cover, and heat grill until hot, about 15 minutes. Turn all burners to medium-low.

THE STATE OF GRILLING 469

We prefer to buy whole chicken wings and butcher them ourselves because they tend to be larger than wings that come presplit. If you can find only presplit wings, opt for larger ones, if possible. Ideally, 12 whole wings should equal 3 pounds, which will yield 24 pieces of chicken (12 drumettes and 12 flats, tips discarded) once broken down. Do not brine the chicken for longer than 3 hours in step 1 or it will become too salty. Charcoal grills tend to produce more-intense heat than gas grills do, hence the difference in cooking times.

Table salt and pepper
¼ cup sugar
3 pounds chicken wings, cut at joints, wingtips discarded
2 cups all-purpose flour
1 tablespoon granulated garlic
2 teaspoons paprika
½ teaspoon cayenne pepper
3 tablespoons vegetable oil

1. Dissolve ¼ cup salt and sugar in 2 quarts cold water in large container. Add chicken and refrigerate, covered, for at least 1 hour or up to 3 hours.

2. Set wire rack in rimmed baking sheet. Whisk flour, granulated garlic, paprika, cayenne, 1 tablespoon pepper, and 1 teaspoon salt together in large bowl. Remove chicken from brine. Working in batches of four, dredge chicken pieces in flour mixture, pressing to adhere. Place chicken on prepared rack. Refrigerate chicken, uncovered, for at least 30 minutes or up to 2 hours.

3a. For a Charcoal Grill Open bottom vent completely. Light large chimney starter mounded with charcoal briquettes (7 quarts). When top coals are partially covered with ash, pour into steeply banked pile against side of grill. Set cooking grate in place, cover, and open lid vent completely. Heat grill until hot, about 5 minutes.

3b. For a Gas Grill Turn all burners to high, cover, and heat grill until hot, about 15 minutes. Turn primary burner to high and turn off other burner(s). (Adjust primary burner [or, if using three-burner grill, primary burner and second burner] as needed to maintain grill temperature of 425 degrees.)

4. Clean and oil cooking grate. Place chicken, fatty side up, on cooler side of grill, arranging drumettes closest to coals. Cook chicken, covered, until lightly browned and coating is set, about 30 minutes for charcoal or about 45 minutes for gas.

Grill-Fried Chicken Wings

5. Brush chicken with oil until no traces of flour remain (use all oil). Cover and continue to cook until coating is golden brown and chicken registers between 180 and 200 degrees, about 30 minutes longer for charcoal or about 45 minutes longer for gas. Transfer chicken to clean wire rack and let cool for 10 minutes. Serve.

Buffalo-Style Grill-Fried Chicken Wings

Add ½ cup Frank's RedHot Original Cayenne Pepper Sauce to brine in step 1. While chicken is cooling, microwave ½ cup Frank's RedHot Original Cayenne Pepper Sauce and 4 tablespoons unsalted butter in covered large bowl until butter is melted, about 1 minute. Whisk to fully combine. Add chicken and toss to coat before serving.

Smoked Chicken Wings

SERVES 4 TO 6

WHY THIS RECIPE WORKS We wanted smoked wings with tender, juicy meat; a balanced, pronounced smokiness; and crisp, fully rendered skin. Our wings got a quick brine before they hit the grill to keep the meat from drying out. A spice rub including paprika, chili powder, oregano, garlic powder, and cayenne gave the wings heat and aromatic complexity. To let the wings cook through with plenty of smoke, we built a two-level fire in the grill, starting them over indirect heat and then moving them over the coals to sear and crisp the skin. To make the wings shine, we mixed melted butter with cider vinegar and ketchup to create a savory sauce.

We prefer to buy whole wings and butcher them ourselves because they tend to be larger than wings that come split. If you can find only split wings, look for larger ones. Twelve whole wings should ideally equal 3 pounds and will yield 24 pieces (12 drumettes and 12 flats, tips discarded). Do not brine the chicken for longer than 3 hours in step 1 or it will become too salty.

Wings
- ¼ cup table salt, for brining
- ¼ cup sugar, for brining
- 3 pounds chicken wings, cut at joints, wingtips discarded
- 2 teaspoons paprika
- 2 teaspoons chili powder
- 1¼ teaspoons dried oregano
- 1¼ teaspoons pepper
- 1¼ teaspoons garlic powder
- 1 teaspoon sugar
- ¼ teaspoon cayenne pepper
- 2 cups wood chips

Sauce
- 4 tablespoons unsalted butter
- 2 tablespoons cider vinegar
- 2 tablespoons ketchup
- ¼ teaspoon table salt

1. For the Wings Dissolve salt and ¼ cup sugar in 2 quarts cold water in large container. Submerge wings in brine, cover, and refrigerate for at least 1 hour or up to 3 hours. Combine paprika, chili powder, oregano, pepper, garlic powder, 1 teaspoon sugar, and cayenne in bowl. Measure out 1 tablespoon spice mixture and set aside.

2. For the Sauce Melt butter in small saucepan over medium-low heat. Add reserved 1 tablespoon spice mixture and cook until fragrant, about 30 seconds. Carefully add vinegar (mixture will bubble up). Bring to quick simmer, then remove from heat. Whisk in ketchup and salt. Cover and set aside.

3. Remove wings from brine and pat dry with paper towels. Sprinkle wings all over with remaining spice mixture.

4. Just before grilling, soak wood chips in water for 15 minutes, then drain. Using large piece of heavy-duty aluminum foil, wrap soaked chips in 8 by 4½-inch foil packet. (Make sure chips do not poke holes in sides or bottom of packet.) Cut 2 evenly spaced 2-inch slits in top of packet.

5a. For a Charcoal Grill Open bottom vent completely. Light large chimney starter mounded with charcoal briquettes (7 quarts). When top coals are partially covered with ash, place wood chip packet on 1 side of grill and pour coals evenly over half of grill, covering wood chip packet. Set cooking grate in place, cover, and open lid vent completely. Heat grill until hot and wood chips are smoking, about 5 minutes.

Smoked Chicken Wings

5b. For a Gas Grill Remove cooking grate and place wood chip packet directly on primary burner. Turn all burners to high, cover, and heat grill until hot and wood chips are smoking, about 15 minutes. Leave primary burner on high and turn off other burner(s). (Adjust primary burner [or, if using 3-burner grill, primary burner and second burner] as needed to maintain grill temperature of 400 degrees.)

6. Clean and oil cooking grate. Place wings, fatty side up, on cooler side of grill, arranging drumettes closest to coals. Cover and cook until wings are darkened in color and meat registers at least 180 degrees, about 40 minutes, flipping wings halfway through cooking.

7a. For a Charcoal Grill Slide half of wings to hotter side of grill and cook, uncovered, until charred in spots, 1 to 3 minutes per side. Transfer wings to platter and tent with foil. Repeat with remaining wings.

7b. For a Gas Grill Turn all burners to high and cook, uncovered, until wings are charred in spots, 5 to 7 minutes per side. Transfer wings to platter and tent with foil.

8. Reheat sauce over medium heat, about 2 minutes. Toss wings and sauce together in bowl. Serve.

Grilled Chicken Leg Quarters

SERVES 4

WHY THIS RECIPE WORKS Chicken leg quarters seem like a perfect candidate for the grill—the rich leg and thigh meat has plenty of skin to crisp up. But the thick joint takes longer to cook than the rest of the leg, so grilling often results in overcooking. To remedy this, we took a two-pronged approach. To prepare the chicken, we made slashes down to the bone, a technique often used for large cuts of meat. This helped the chicken cook evenly, and also ensured deep seasoning. We then used our two-level grilling technique, starting the chicken over a low flame, then searing it over a hot fire. A citrus-y dressing provided a welcome hit of brightness.

A garlic press makes quick work of mincing the 6 cloves called for here. You can use 1 teaspoon of dried oregano in place of the fresh called for in the dressing. Do not use dried cilantro.

6 garlic cloves, minced
4 teaspoons kosher salt
1 tablespoon sugar
2 teaspoons grated lime zest plus 2 tablespoons juice
2 teaspoons plus ¼ cup extra-virgin olive oil
1½ teaspoons ground cumin
1 teaspoon pepper
½ teaspoon cayenne pepper
4 (10-ounce) chicken leg quarters, trimmed
2 tablespoons chopped fresh cilantro
2 teaspoons chopped fresh oregano

1. Combine garlic, salt, sugar, lime zest, 2 teaspoons oil, cumin, pepper, and cayenne in bowl and mix to form paste. Reserve 2 teaspoons garlic paste for dressing.

2. Position chicken skin side up on cutting board and pat dry with paper towels. Leaving drumsticks and thighs attached, make 4 parallel diagonal slashes in chicken: 1 across drumsticks, 1 across leg joints; and 2 across thighs (each slash should reach bone). Flip chicken over and make 1 more diagonal slash across back of drumsticks. Rub remaining garlic paste all over chicken and into slashes. Refrigerate chicken for at least 1 hour or up to 24 hours.

3a. For a Charcoal Grill Open bottom vent completely. Light large chimney starter filled with charcoal briquettes (6 quarts). When top coals are partially covered with ash, pour two-thirds evenly over half of grill, then pour remaining coals over other half of grill. Set cooking grate in place, cover, and open lid vent completely. Heat grill until hot, about 5 minutes.

3b. For a Gas Grill Turn all burners to high, cover, and heat grill until hot, about 15 minutes. Turn primary burner to medium and turn other burner(s) to low. (Adjust primary burner as needed to maintain grill temperature of 400 to 425 degrees.)

4. Clean and oil cooking grate. Place chicken on cooler side of grill, skin side up. Cover and cook until underside of chicken is lightly browned, 9 to 12 minutes. Flip chicken, cover, and cook until leg joint registers 165 degrees, 7 to 10 minutes.

5. Transfer chicken to hotter side of grill, skin side down, and cook (covered if using gas) until skin is well browned, 3 to 5 minutes. Flip chicken and continue to cook until leg joint registers 175 degrees, about 3 minutes longer. Transfer to platter, tent loosely with aluminum foil, and let rest for 5 to 10 minutes.

6. Meanwhile, whisk lime juice, remaining ¼ cup oil, cilantro, oregano, and reserved garlic paste together in bowl. Spoon half of dressing over chicken and serve, passing remaining dressing separately.

Grilled Chicken Leg Quarters

Making Flavorful, Well-Cooked Chicken Leg Quarters

1. Slash Make bone-deep slashes in each quarter so the seasonings can penetrate and the meat cooks more readily.

2. Rub Massage the garlicky seasoning paste into the slashes and all over the chicken and refrigerate for up to 24 hours.

BBQ Chicken Thighs

SERVES 4 TO 6

WHY THIS RECIPE WORKS For juicy grilled chicken thighs slick with a shiny barbecue glaze, we started by applying a sweet-meets-spicy rub. We braised spice-rubbed chicken thighs in a pan of flavorful bottled barbecue sauce and chicken broth. After 30 minutes, we poured off the cooking liquid, applied a sticky glaze and more spice rub, and arranged the thighs directly on the grill to render the skin. With a final layer of glaze and a brief rest, we had the ultimate finger-licking chicken.

The seasoned chicken thighs need to sit for 1 hour before grilling. We prefer Frank's RedHot Original Cayenne Pepper Sauce for this recipe. If you use Tabasco, reduce the amount to 2 teaspoons in the broth mixture and 1 teaspoon in the glaze.

- 2 tablespoons packed brown sugar, divided
- 1 tablespoon kosher salt
- 1 tablespoon paprika
- 1 teaspoon pepper
- 1 teaspoon white pepper
- ¾ teaspoon granulated garlic
- 4 pounds bone-in chicken thighs, trimmed
- 1 (13 by 9-inch) disposable aluminum roasting pan
- ½ cup plus 2 tablespoons bottled barbecue sauce
- ½ cup chicken broth
- 7 garlic cloves (6 sliced thin, 1 minced)
- 3 tablespoons Worcestershire sauce
- 3 tablespoons hot sauce, divided
- 2 tablespoons apple jelly
- 1½ cups wood chips

1. Combine 1 tablespoon sugar, salt, paprika, pepper, white pepper, and granulated garlic in bowl. Set aside 4 teaspoons spice mixture. Place chicken in disposable pan and season all over with remaining spice mixture. Flip chicken skin side down and let sit at room temperature for 1 hour.

2. Meanwhile, whisk ½ cup barbecue sauce, broth, sliced garlic, Worcestershire sauce, and 2 tablespoons hot sauce together in bowl; set aside. In separate bowl, microwave jelly until melted, about 30 seconds. Stir minced garlic, remaining 2 tablespoons barbecue sauce, remaining 1 tablespoon sugar, and remaining 1 tablespoon hot sauce into jelly; set glaze aside.

THE STATE OF GRILLING   473

5. Pour broth mixture over chicken in pan. Place pan on cooler side of grill, cover (positioning lid vent over chicken for charcoal), and cook for 30 minutes (chicken will be about 140 degrees).

6. Remove pan from grill. Using tongs, transfer chicken skin side up to cooler side of grill. (Discard cooking liquid.) Brush chicken skin with half of glaze, then sprinkle with reserved spice rub. Cover and cook for 15 minutes.

7. Brush chicken skin with remaining glaze. Cover and cook until glaze has set and chicken registers 175 degrees, 25 to 30 minutes longer. Transfer chicken to platter, tent loosely with foil, and let rest for 15 minutes. Serve.

Grilled Chicken Diavolo

SERVES 4

WHY THIS RECIPE WORKS To make a fiery and smoky chicken diavolo, we took it to the grill. A mixture of herbs, spices, lemon, oil, sugar, and both black and red pepper performed double duty as a marinade and as a sauce. We built a two-level fire, starting the chicken on the cooler side of the grill to cook through and then searing it over the hotter side to char and crisp the skin. For extra smoky flavor, we added a foil-wrapped packet of soaked wood chips. We cooked the reserved marinade mixture to mellow the garlic, added a shot of lemon juice, and spooned our supercharged vinaigrette over the grilled chicken.

If you are buying a whole chicken and cutting it into pieces yourself, reserve the backbone and wings to make stock. To use wood chunks on a charcoal grill, substitute one medium wood chunk, soaked in water for 1 hour, for the wood chip packet.

- 3 pounds bone-in chicken pieces (split breasts cut in half, drumsticks, and/or thighs), trimmed
- ½ cup extra-virgin olive oil
- 4 garlic cloves, minced
- 1 tablespoon chopped fresh rosemary
- 2 teaspoons grated lemon zest plus 4 teaspoons juice
- 2 teaspoons red pepper flakes
- 1 teaspoon sugar
- Table salt and pepper
- ½ teaspoon paprika
- 1 cup wood chips

BBQ Chicken Thighs

3. Just before grilling, soak wood chips in water for 15 minutes, then drain. Using large piece of heavy-duty aluminum foil, wrap soaked chips in foil packet and cut several vent holes in top.

4a. For a Charcoal Grill Open bottom vent completely. Light large chimney starter mounded with charcoal briquettes (7 quarts). When top coals are partially covered with ash, pour into steeply banked pile against side of grill. Place wood chip packet on coals. Set cooking grate in place, cover, and open lid vent completely. Heat grill until hot and wood chips are smoking, about 5 minutes.

4b. For a Gas Grill Remove cooking grate and place wood chip packet directly on primary burner. Set grate in place, turn all burners to high, cover, and heat grill until hot and wood chips are smoking, about 15 minutes. Leave primary burner on high and turn off other burners. (Adjust primary burner as needed to maintain grill temperature of 350 to 375 degrees.)

The Complete Cook's Country TV Show Cookbook

Grilled Chicken Diavolo

2b. For a Gas Grill Place wood chip packet over primary burner. Turn all burners to high, cover, and heat grill until hot and wood chips are smoking, about 15 minutes. Turn primary burner to medium and turn other burner(s) to low. (Adjust primary burner as needed to maintain grill temperature of 400 to 425 degrees.)

3. Remove chicken from marinade and pat dry with paper towels. Discard used marinade. Clean and oil cooking grate. Place chicken on cooler side of grill, skin side up. Cover and cook until underside of chicken is lightly browned, 8 to 12 minutes. Flip chicken, cover, and cook until white meat registers 155 degrees and dark meat registers 170 degrees, 7 to 10 minutes.

4. Transfer chicken to hotter side of grill, skin side down, and cook (covered if using gas) until skin is well browned, about 3 minutes. Flip and continue to cook (covered if using gas) until white meat registers 160 degrees and dark meat registers 175 degrees, 1 to 3 minutes. Transfer chicken to platter, tent loosely with foil, and let rest for 5 to 10 minutes.

5. Meanwhile, heat reserved oil mixture in small saucepan over low heat until fragrant and garlic begins to brown, 3 to 5 minutes. Off heat, whisk in lemon juice and ¼ teaspoon salt. Spoon sauce over chicken. Serve.

Barbecued Pulled Chicken

MAKES ENOUGH FOR 8 SANDWICHES

WHY THIS RECIPE WORKS Barbecuing is the perfect method for cooking fatty cuts of pork or beef, but relatively lean chicken is another story. For barbecued pulled chicken with a smoky flavor and moist, tender meat, we'd have to come up with some tricks. Brining the birds kept the white meat moist and juicy, and arranging the chickens on the grill with the breast meat farther from the heat source than the dark meat evened out the cooking times. We tweaked our favorite barbecue sauce to better complement the chicken, increasing the vinegar to balance the sweetness and swapping the root beer for coffee to boost the smoky flavor.

We prefer to halve the chickens ourselves, but you may be able to buy halved chickens from your butcher.

1. Pat chicken dry with paper towels. Whisk oil, garlic, rosemary, lemon zest, pepper flakes, sugar, 1 teaspoon pepper, and paprika together in bowl until combined. Reserve ¼ cup oil mixture for sauce. (Oil mixture can be covered and refrigerated for up to 24 hours.) Whisk 2¼ teaspoons salt into oil mixture remaining in bowl and transfer to 1-gallon zipper-lock bag. Add chicken, turn to coat, and refrigerate for at least 1 hour or up to 24 hours. Just before grilling, soak wood chips in water for 15 minutes, then drain. Using large piece of heavy-duty aluminum foil, wrap soaked chips in foil packet and cut several vent holes in top.

2a. For a Charcoal Grill Open bottom vent halfway. Light large chimney starter filled with charcoal briquettes (6 quarts). When top coals are partially covered with ash, pour two-thirds evenly over half of grill, then pour remaining coals over other half of grill. Place wood chip packet on larger pile of coals. Set cooking grate in place, cover, and open lid vent halfway. Heat grill until hot and wood chips are smoking, about 5 minutes.

THE STATE OF GRILLING

Chicken

- 1 cup table salt
- 2 (4-pound) whole chickens, giblets discarded
  Pepper
- 2 cups wood chips, soaked in water for 15 minutes and drained

Sauce

- 2 teaspoons vegetable oil
- 1 onion, chopped fine
- 4 cups chicken broth
- 1¼ cups cider vinegar
- 1 cup brewed coffee
- ¾ cup molasses
- ½ cup tomato paste
- ½ cup ketchup
- 2 tablespoons brown mustard
- 1 tablespoon hot sauce
- ½ teaspoon garlic powder
- ¼ teaspoon liquid smoke

1. For the Chicken Dissolve salt in 4 quarts cold water in large container. Remove backbones from chickens and split chickens in half lengthwise through center of breastbone. Using metal skewer, poke 20 holes all over each chicken half. Submerge chicken halves in brine, cover, and refrigerate for 1 hour. Remove chicken halves from brine, pat dry with paper towels, and season with pepper. Using large piece of heavy-duty aluminum foil, wrap soaked wood chips in foil packet and cut several vent holes in top.

2. For the Sauce Meanwhile, heat oil in Dutch oven over medium-high heat until shimmering. Add onion and cook until softened, about 5 minutes. Whisk in broth, vinegar, coffee, molasses, tomato paste, ketchup, mustard, hot sauce, and garlic powder and bring to boil. Reduce heat to medium-low and simmer until mixture is thick and reduced to 4 cups, about 65 to 75 minutes. Stir in liquid smoke; reserve 1 cup sauce for serving. (Sauce can be refrigerated for up to 2 days.)

3a. For a Charcoal Grill Open bottom vent halfway. Light large chimney starter filled with charcoal briquettes (6 quarts). When top coals are partially covered with ash, pour into steeply banked pile against side of grill. Place wood chip packet on coals. Set cooking grate in place, cover, and open lid vent halfway. Heat grill until hot and wood chips are smoking, about 5 minutes.

3b. For a Gas Grill Place wood chip packet over primary burner. Turn all burners to high, cover, and heat grill until hot and wood chips are smoking, about 15 minutes. Leave primary burner on high and turn off other burner(s).

4. Clean and oil cooking grate. Place chicken halves skin side up on cool side of grill with legs closest to heat source. Cover and cook until breasts register 160 degrees and thighs register 175 degrees, 75 to 85 minutes. Transfer chicken to carving board, tent loosely with foil, and let rest until cool enough to handle, about 15 minutes. Remove and discard skin. Pull meat off bones, separating dark and light meat. Roughly chop dark meat into ½-inch pieces. Shred white meat into thin strands.

5. Add chicken to pot with sauce and cook over medium-low heat until chicken is warmed through, about 5 minutes. Serve on hamburger rolls, passing reserved sauce separately.

Tennessee Pulled Turkey Sandwiches

SERVES 8 TO 10

WHY THIS RECIPE WORKS We love a good pulled pork sandwich, so we were interested in an equally moist, smoky version using turkey. Salting the turkey a day ahead helped keep the lean meat juicy. Positioning the boneless breasts on the grill so that the thicker ends were closer to the heat source evened out the cooking time. We then transferred the breasts to a disposable pan partway through cooking and topped them with butter to add richness and help keep the meat moist. And for even more moisture, we mixed the shredded meat with the juices and butter leftover in the pan. The crowning touch was a tangy white barbecue sauce.

We prefer a natural (unbrined) turkey breast here, but both self-basting and kosher work well. Plan ahead: The salted meat needs to be refrigerated for at least 8 hours. Skip the salting step if you buy a kosher or self-basting breast. Some stores sell only boneless turkey breasts with the skin still attached; the skin can be removed easily with a paring knife. If you don't have ½ cup of juices from the rested turkey, supplement with chicken broth.

Turkey

- 2 (1¾- to 2-pound) boneless, skinless split turkey breasts, trimmed
- Kosher salt and pepper
- 2 cups wood chips
- ½ teaspoon cayenne pepper
- 1 (13 by 9-inch) disposable aluminum roasting pan
- 4 tablespoons unsalted butter, cut into 4 pieces

White Barbecue Sauce

- 1 cup mayonnaise
- ⅓ cup cider vinegar
- 1 tablespoon prepared horseradish, drained
- 1½ teaspoons kosher salt
- 1 teaspoon Worcestershire sauce
- 1 garlic clove, minced
- 1 teaspoon pepper
- ¼ teaspoon cayenne pepper

- 8 hamburger buns
- Shredded iceberg lettuce

1. For the Turkey Pat turkey dry with paper towels, place on large sheet of plastic wrap, and sprinkle with 1 tablespoon salt. Wrap in plastic and refrigerate for at least 8 hours or overnight.

2. Just before grilling, soak wood chips in water for 15 minutes, then drain. Using large piece of heavy-duty aluminum foil, wrap soaked chips in 8 by 4½-inch foil packet. (Make sure chips do not poke holes in sides or bottom of packet.) Cut 2 evenly spaced 2-inch slits in top of packet.

3a. For a Charcoal Grill Open bottom vent completely. Light large chimney starter three-quarters filled with charcoal briquettes (4½ quarts). When top coals are partially covered with ash, pour evenly over half of grill. Place wood chip packet on coals. Set cooking grate in place, cover, and open lid vent completely. Heat grill until hot and wood chips are smoking, about 5 minutes.

3b. For a Gas Grill Remove cooking grate and place wood chip packet directly on primary burner. Set grate in place, turn all burners to high, cover, and heat grill until hot and wood chips are smoking, about 15 minutes. Leave primary burner on medium-high and turn off other burner(s). (Adjust primary burner as needed to maintain grill temperature between 300 and 350 degrees.)

Barbecued Pulled Chicken

Tennessee Pulled Turkey Sandwiches

4. Clean and oil cooking grate. Unwrap turkey and sprinkle with 2 teaspoons pepper and cayenne. Place turkey on cooler side of grill, with thicker parts of breasts closest to fire. Cover grill (positioning lid vent directly over turkey if using charcoal) and cook until breasts register 120 degrees, 30 to 40 minutes.

5. Transfer turkey to disposable pan and top with butter. Cover pan tightly with foil and return to cooler side of grill. Cover grill and continue to cook until breasts register 160 degrees, 25 to 35 minutes longer. Remove pan from grill and let turkey rest in covered pan for 20 minutes.

6. For the White Barbecue Sauce Whisk all ingredients in bowl until smooth.

7. Transfer turkey to cutting board. Using two forks or your hands, shred turkey into bite-size pieces. Transfer to large bowl. Add ½ cup juices from pan to shredded turkey and toss to combine. Season with salt and pepper to taste.

8. Serve turkey on buns with white barbecue sauce and lettuce.

Barbecued Burnt Ends

SERVES 8 TO 10

WHY THIS RECIPE WORKS Burnt ends are the extra crispy and slightly meaty pieces left after cutting brisket. They are the brainchild of Arthur Bryant, a legendary African American barbecuer in Kansas City who gave them to his customers as they waited for their food instead of throwing them away. Real burnt ends are all about moist meat and flavorful, charred bark, but most pit masters use fatty point-cut brisket. To make leaner, more widely available flat-cut brisket work, we cut it into strips and brined it for maximum moisture and flavor. Three hours of smoke on the grill plus a few hours in a low oven ensured tender brisket with plenty of char.

Look for a brisket with a significant fat cap. This recipe takes about 8 hours to prepare. The meat can be brined ahead of time, transferred to a zipper-lock bag, and refrigerated for up to a day. If you don't have ½ cup of juices from the rested brisket, supplement with beef broth.

Brisket and Rub

- 2 cups plus 1 tablespoon kosher salt
- ½ cup granulated sugar
- 1 (5- to 6-pound) beef brisket, flat cut, untrimmed
- ¼ cup packed brown sugar
- 2 tablespoons pepper
- 4 cups wood chips
- 1 (13 by 9-inch) disposable aluminum roasting pan (if using charcoal) or 2 (8½ by 6-inch) disposable aluminum pans (if using gas)

Barbecue Sauce

- ¾ cup ketchup
- ¼ cup packed brown sugar
- 2 tablespoons cider vinegar
- 2 tablespoons Worcestershire sauce
- 2 teaspoons granulated garlic
- ¼ teaspoon cayenne pepper

1. For the Brisket and Rub Dissolve 2 cups salt and granulated sugar in 4 quarts cold water in large container. Slice brisket with grain into 1½-inch-thick strips. Add brisket strips to brine, cover, and refrigerate for 2 hours. Remove brisket from brine and pat dry with paper towels.

2. Combine brown sugar, pepper, and remaining 1 tablespoon salt in bowl. Season brisket all over with rub. Just before grilling, soak wood chips in water for 15 minutes, then drain. Using 2 large pieces of heavy-duty aluminum foil, wrap soaked chips in 2 foil packets and cut several vent holes in tops.

3a. For a Charcoal Grill Open bottom vent halfway and place disposable pan filled with 2 quarts water on one side of grill, with long side of pan facing center of grill. Arrange 3 quarts unlit charcoal briquettes on opposite side of grill and place 1 wood chip packet on coals. Light large chimney starter filled halfway with charcoal briquettes (3 quarts). When top coals are partially covered with ash, pour evenly over unlit coals and wood chip packet. Place remaining wood chip packet on lit coals. Set cooking grate in place, cover, and open lid vent halfway. Heat grill until hot and wood chips are smoking, about 5 minutes.

3b. For a Gas Grill Add ½ cup ice cubes to 1 wood chip packet. Remove cooking grate and place both wood chip packets directly on primary burner; place disposable pans each filled with 2 cups water directly on secondary burner(s). Set grate in place, turn all burners to high, cover, and heat grill until hot and wood chips are smoking, about 15 minutes. Leave primary burner on high and turn off other burner(s). (Adjust primary burner as needed to maintain grill temperature of 275 to 300 degrees.)

4. Clean and oil cooking grate. Arrange brisket on cooler side of grill as far from heat source as possible. Cover (positioning lid vent over brisket for charcoal) and cook without opening for 3 hours.

5. Adjust oven rack to middle position and heat oven to 275 degrees. Remove brisket from grill and transfer to rimmed baking sheet. Cover sheet tightly with foil. Roast until fork slips easily in and out of meat and meat registers 210 degrees, about 2 hours. Remove from oven, leave covered, and let rest for 1 hour. Remove foil, transfer brisket to carving board, and pour accumulated juices into fat separator.

6. For the Barbecue Sauce Combine ketchup, sugar, vinegar, Worcestershire, granulated garlic, cayenne, and ½ cup defatted brisket juices in medium saucepan. Bring to simmer over medium heat and cook until slightly thickened, about 5 minutes.

7. Cut brisket strips crosswise into 1- to 2-inch chunks. Combine brisket chunks and barbecue sauce in large bowl and toss to combine. Serve.

Barbecued Burnt Ends

Shashlik-Style Beef Kebabs

SERVES 4 TO 6

WHY THIS RECIPE WORKS Shashlik—a favorite street food in the Caucasus—is a grilled kebab with juicy, well-charred meat with a vibrant marinade. We chose sirloin steak tips because their loose grain enables them to soak up more marinade and they have big, beefy flavor. For our marinade we blended red wine vinegar, vegetable oil, chopped onion, and garlic with a blend of warm cumin, citrusy coriander, savory bay leaf, and aromatic cinnamon. Adding a little sugar and grilling the kebabs over a hot fire gave us excellent charring in spite of the wet marinade. A tangy sauce of caramelized onion and tart yogurt provided the perfect complement to the flame-kissed beef.

Sirloin steak tips are often sold as flap meat; we prefer to buy one large piece and cut it into pieces ourselves. We cook this beef past medium-rare in order to get more charring and to keep it from being too chewy. If you prefer it less cooked, remove it from the grill sooner (125 degrees for medium-rare).

Shashlik-Style Beef Kebabs

Marinade

- ½ cup coarsely chopped onion
- ¼ cup vegetable oil
- 2 tablespoons red wine vinegar
- 4 garlic cloves
- 1 tablespoon soy sauce
- 1 tablespoon kosher salt
- 1 tablespoon sugar
- 1 teaspoon ground cumin
- ½ teaspoon pepper
- ½ teaspoon ground coriander
- ¼ teaspoon ground cinnamon
- ¼ teaspoon cayenne pepper
- 1 bay leaf, crumbled

Beef and Sauce

- 2 pounds sirloin steak tips, trimmed and cut into 1-inch pieces
- 1 onion, chopped fine
- ⅓ cup water
- 1 tablespoon vegetable oil
- ½ cup plain whole-milk yogurt
- ⅓ cup chopped fresh cilantro
- 2 teaspoons lemon juice
- 6 (10-inch) wooden skewers, soaked in water for at least 30 minutes

1. For the Marinade Process all ingredients in blender until smooth, about 30 seconds. Measure out 2 tablespoons marinade and set aside.

2. For the Beef and Sauce Combine beef and remaining marinade in 1-gallon zipper-lock bag. Press out air, seal bag, and turn to coat beef in marinade. Refrigerate for 1 to 2 hours.

3. While beef marinates, combine onion, water, oil, and reserved marinade in 10-inch skillet. Cover and cook over medium-high heat until liquid has evaporated and onion is beginning to brown, 5 to 7 minutes, stirring occasionally. Uncover, reduce heat to medium, and continue to cook until onion is well browned, 8 to 10 minutes longer. Transfer onion to bowl and stir in yogurt, cilantro, and lemon juice. Season with salt and pepper to taste.

4. Thread beef tightly onto skewers, leaving ends of skewers slightly exposed.

5a. For a Charcoal Grill Open bottom vent completely. Light large chimney starter mounded with charcoal briquettes (7 quarts). When top coals are partially covered with ash, pour evenly over half of grill. Set cooking grate in place, cover, and open lid vent completely. Heat grill until hot, about 5 minutes.

5b. For a Gas Grill Turn all burners to high, cover, and heat grill until hot, about 15 minutes. Leave all burners on high.

6. Clean and oil cooking grate. Arrange kebabs on grill (over hotter side if using charcoal) and cook (covered if using gas), turning every 2 to 3 minutes, until beef is well browned, charred around edges, and registering between 135 and 145 degrees, 8 to 12 minutes. Transfer kebabs to platter, tent with aluminum foil, and let rest for 5 minutes. Serve with sauce.

Grilled Bourbon Steaks

SERVES 6 TO 8

WHY THIS RECIPE WORKS We tried the Whiskey Steak at Jesse's Restaurant in Magnolia Springs, Alabama, and it was something special. Why marinate rib eyes in bourbon? The bourbon not only enhances the beef's meatiness, it also increases the char. To maximize the steaks' flavor, we soaked four hefty rib eyes in a mixture of bourbon, Worcestershire, shallot, and garlic. After marinating the meat for four hours, we fired up the grill, brushed the steaks with oil and a liberal dose of salt and pepper, and cooked them to a juicy medium-rare. The boozy marinade really delivered, giving us sweet-savory flavors and perfect char.

Use a bourbon you'd be happy drinking. Plan ahead: These steaks need to marinate for at least 4 hours before grilling.

- 1 cup bourbon
- 1 cup Worcestershire sauce
- 1 shallot, minced
- 2 garlic cloves, minced
  Kosher salt and pepper
- 4 (1-pound) boneless rib-eye steaks, 1 to 1½ inches thick, trimmed
- 2 tablespoons vegetable oil

1. Whisk bourbon, Worcestershire, shallot, garlic, 2 teaspoons salt, and 2 teaspoons pepper together in bowl. Place 2 steaks in each of two 1-gallon zipper-lock bags and divide bourbon mixture between bags, about 1 cup each. Seal bags, turn to distribute marinade, and refrigerate for at least 4 hours or up to 24 hours, flipping occasionally.

2. Remove steaks from marinade and pat dry with paper towels; discard marinade. Brush steaks all over with oil and season liberally with salt and pepper.

3a. For a Charcoal Grill Open bottom vent completely. Light large chimney starter filled with charcoal briquettes (6 quarts). When top coals are partially covered with ash, pour evenly over grill. Set cooking grate in place, cover, and open lid vent completely. Heat grill until hot, about 5 minutes.

3b. For a Gas Grill Turn all burners to high, cover, and heat grill until hot, about 15 minutes. Turn all burners to medium-high. (Adjust burners as needed to maintain grill temperature between 350 and 400 degrees.)

4. Clean and oil cooking grate. Place steaks on grill and cook (covered if using gas) until well charred and meat registers 125 degrees (for medium-rare), 6 to 8 minutes per side.

5. Transfer steaks to wire rack set in rimmed baking sheet, tent with aluminum foil, and let rest for 10 minutes. Serve.

Grilled Bourbon Steaks

Grilled Thick-Cut Porterhouse Steaks

SERVES 6

Grilled Thick-Cut Porterhouse Steaks

WHY THIS RECIPE WORKS A giant, special-occasion steak can vex even experienced grillers. We wanted a simple route to perfect medium-rare. Setting up a half-grill fire with a cooler side and a hotter side allowed us to control the amount of crusty exterior and achieve a rosy interior for these steaks. To protect the leaner, quicker-cooking tenderloin portion of the porterhouse, we positioned the steaks with the tenderloins facing the cooler side of the grill. The T-shaped bone acted as a heat shield, further protecting the tenderloins from the heat. A final drizzle of melted butter added an even richer flavor before serving.

Flare-ups may occur when grilling over charcoal. If the flames become constant, slide the steaks to the cooler side of the grill until the flames die down.

- 2 (2½- to 3-pound) porterhouse steaks, 2 inches thick, fat trimmed to ¼ inch
  Kosher salt and pepper
- 4 teaspoons extra-virgin olive oil (if using gas)
- 3 tablespoons unsalted butter, melted

1. Pat steaks dry with paper towels and sprinkle each side of each steak with 1 teaspoon salt. Transfer steaks to large plate and refrigerate, uncovered, for at least 1 hour or up to 24 hours.

2a. For a Charcoal Grill Open bottom vent completely. Light large chimney starter filled with charcoal briquettes (6 quarts). When top coals are partially covered with ash, pour evenly over half of grill. Set cooking grate in place, cover, and open lid vent completely. Heat grill until hot, about 5 minutes.

2b. For a Gas Grill Turn all burners to high, cover, and heat grill until hot, about 15 minutes. Leave primary burner on high and turn off other burner(s). (Adjust primary burner [or, if using three-burner grill, primary burner and second burner] as needed to maintain grill temperature of 450 degrees.)

3. Pat steaks dry with paper towels. If using gas, brush each side of each steak with 1 teaspoon oil. Sprinkle each side of each steak with ½ teaspoon pepper.

4. Clean and oil cooking grate. Place steaks on hotter side of grill, with tenderloins facing cooler side. Cook (covered if using gas) until evenly charred on first side, 6 to 8 minutes. Flip steaks and position so tenderloins are still facing cooler side of grill. Continue to cook (covered if using gas) until evenly charred on second side, 6 to 8 minutes longer.

5. Flip steaks and transfer to cooler side of grill, with bone side facing fire. Cover and cook until thermometer inserted 3 inches from tip of strip side of steak registers 115 to 120 degrees (for medium-rare), 8 to 12 minutes, flipping halfway through cooking. Transfer steaks to wire rack set in rimmed baking sheet, tent with aluminum foil, and let rest for 10 minutes.

6. Stir ¼ teaspoon salt into melted butter. Transfer steaks to carving board. Carve strips and tenderloins from bones. Place bones on platter. Slice steaks thin against grain, then reassemble sliced steaks around bones. Drizzle with melted butter and season with salt and pepper to taste. Serve.

Grilled Steak Fajitas
SERVES 6

WHY THIS RECIPE WORKS Sizzling fajitas are always an exciting option at a Tex-Mex restaurant. For an at-home version, we marinated skirt steak in soy sauce to enhance its meaty flavor and pineapple juice for balanced sweetness and acidity. Leaving bell peppers whole and onions in thick rounds secured by toothpicks prevented any from slipping through the grates. We seared them before moving them to gently steam in a disposable pan while we cooked our steak on the hotter side of the grill, yielding tender meat with a caramelized exterior.

Serve the fajitas with Pico de Gallo (recipe follows), avocado pieces or guacamole, sour cream, and lime wedges. One (6-ounce) can of pineapple juice will yield ¾ cup. We cook the skirt steak to between medium and medium-well so that its texture is less chewy and the steak is therefore easier to eat.

- ¾ cup pineapple juice
- ½ cup plus 1 tablespoon vegetable oil
- ¼ cup soy sauce
- 3 garlic cloves, minced
- 2 pounds skirt steak, trimmed and cut crosswise into 6 equal pieces
- 3 yellow, red, orange, or green bell peppers
- 1 large red onion, sliced into ½-inch-thick rounds
- Table salt and pepper
- 12 (6-inch) flour tortillas
- 1 (13 by 9-inch) disposable aluminum pan
- 1 tablespoon chopped fresh cilantro

1. Whisk pineapple juice, ½ cup oil, soy sauce, and garlic together in bowl. Reserve ¼ cup marinade. Transfer remaining 1¼ cups marinade to 1-gallon zipper-lock bag. Add steak, press out air, seal bag, and turn to distribute marinade. Refrigerate for at least 2 hours or up to 24 hours.

2. Using paring knife, cut around stems of bell peppers and remove cores and seeds. Push toothpick horizontally through each onion round to keep rings intact while grilling. Brush bell peppers and onion evenly with remaining 1 tablespoon oil and season with salt and pepper. Remove steak from marinade and pat dry with paper towels; discard marinade. Sprinkle steak with ¾ teaspoon salt and ½ teaspoon pepper. Wrap tortillas in aluminum foil; set aside.

3a. For a Charcoal Grill Open bottom vent completely. Light large chimney starter filled with charcoal briquettes (6 quarts). When top coals are partially covered with ash, pour evenly over half of grill. Set cooking grate in place, cover, and open lid vent completely. Heat grill until hot, about 5 minutes.

3b. For a Gas Grill Turn all burners to high, cover, and heat grill until hot, about 15 minutes. Leave primary burner on high and turn other burner(s) to low.

4. Clean and oil cooking grate. Place bell peppers and onion on hotter side of grill and place tortilla packet on cooler side of grill. Cook (covered if using gas) until vegetables are char-streaked and tender, 8 to 13 minutes, flipping and moving as needed for even cooking, and until tortillas are warmed through, about 10 minutes, flipping halfway through cooking.

5. Remove tortillas from grill; keep wrapped and set aside. Transfer vegetables to disposable pan, cover pan tightly with foil, and place on cooler side of grill. (If using gas, cover grill and allow hotter side to reheat for 5 minutes.) Place steak on hotter side of grill and cook (covered if using gas) until charred and meat registers 135 to 140 degrees, 2 to 4 minutes per side. Transfer steak to cutting board and tent with foil. Remove disposable pan from grill.

6. Carefully remove foil from disposable pan (steam may escape). Slice bell peppers into thin strips. Remove toothpicks from onion rounds and separate rings. Return vegetables to disposable pan and toss with cilantro and reserved marinade. Season with salt and pepper to taste. Slice steak thin against grain. Transfer steak and vegetables to serving platter. Serve with tortillas.

Pico de Gallo
SERVES 4

To make it spicier, include the jalapeño seeds.

- 3 tomatoes, cored and chopped
  Table salt and pepper
- ¼ cup finely chopped red onion
- ¼ cup chopped fresh cilantro
- 1 jalapeño chile, stemmed, seeded, and minced
- 1 tablespoon lime juice
- 1 garlic clove, minced

Toss tomatoes with ¼ teaspoon salt in bowl. Transfer to colander and let drain for 30 minutes. Combine drained tomatoes, onion, cilantro, jalapeño, lime juice, and garlic in bowl. Season with salt and pepper to taste. Serve.

Grilled Steak Fajitas

Grilled Flank Steak with Basil Dressing
SERVES 6

WHY THIS RECIPE WORKS For a grilled flank steak with a char-kissed exterior and a perfectly cooked interior, we skipped the marinade. Instead, we seasoned our steak with salt and sugar—since they dissolve and penetrate deep into the meat—and pepper. To cook this wedge-shaped cut to a consistent internal temperature, we set up our grill with a cooler side and a hotter side. After briefly grilling the steak on the hotter side, we positioned the steak so the thinner end was over the cooler side of the grill to prevent overcooking. Finally, we converted our marinade into a sauce that we drizzled over our perfectly grilled steak.

We season this steak with sugar in addition to salt and pepper to help promote browning during the relatively short cooking time.

THE STATE OF GRILLING   483

Steak

- 1 (2-pound) flank steak, trimmed
- 2 teaspoons sugar
- ½ teaspoon table salt
- ½ teaspoon pepper

Basil Dressing

- ¼ cup extra-virgin olive oil
- ¼ cup chopped fresh basil
- 1 shallot, minced
- 2 tablespoons red wine vinegar
- 2 teaspoons lemon juice
- 1 teaspoon honey
- 1 garlic clove, minced
- ½ teaspoon red pepper flakes
- ½ teaspoon table salt
- ¼ teaspoon pepper

1. For the Steak Pat steak dry with paper towels and sprinkle with sugar, salt, and pepper. Transfer steak to plate, cover with plastic wrap, and refrigerate for at least 1 hour or up to 24 hours.

2. For the Basil Dressing Whisk all ingredients in bowl until sugar has dissolved; set aside.

3a. For a Charcoal Grill Open bottom vent completely. Light large chimney starter mounded with charcoal briquettes (7 quarts). When top coals are partially covered with ash, pour evenly over half of grill. Set cooking grate in place, cover, and open lid vent completely. Heat grill until hot, about 5 minutes.

3b. For a Gas Grill Turn all burners to high, cover, and heat grill until hot, about 15 minutes. Leave primary burner on high and turn off other burner(s).

4. Set wire rack in rimmed baking sheet. Clean and oil cooking grate. Place steak on hotter side of grill and cook (covered if using gas) until browned on both sides, about 2 minutes per side. Flip steak again and rotate so that thin end is over cooler side of grill and thick end remains over hotter side. Continue to cook (covered if using gas), flipping steak every 2 minutes, until thick end of steak registers 125 degrees (for medium-rare) or 130 degrees (for medium), 2 to 6 minutes longer.

5. Transfer steak to prepared rack, tent with aluminum foil, and let rest for 10 minutes. Transfer steak to carving board and cut in half lengthwise with grain to create 2 narrow steaks. Slice each steak thin on bias against grain. Transfer steak to shallow platter and pour dressing over top. Serve.

California Barbecued Tri-Tip

SERVES 4 TO 6

WHY THIS RECIPE WORKS California barbecued tri-tip recipes call for cooking the meat (bottom sirloin roast) over high heat and seasoning it only with salt, pepper, garlic, and the smoke of the grill. This consistently produces a charred exterior and very rare center—but we wanted the outside cooked less and the inside cooked more. To do this, we pushed all the coals l to one side, which created a hot zone for cooking and a cooler one for finishing the meat slowly. To prevent the meat from tasting too smoky, we held off on the wood chips until after we'd seared the meat.

If you can't find tri-tip, bottom round steak will also work. Two medium wood chunks, soaked in water for 1 hour, can be substituted for the wood chips on a charcoal grill. Serve with Santa Maria Salsa (recipe follows) and California Barbecued Beans (page 501). We prefer this roast cooked medium-rare.

Grilled Flank Steak with Basil Dressing

  6 garlic cloves, minced
  2 tablespoons extra-virgin olive oil
  ¾ teaspoon table salt
  1 (2-pound) tri-tip roast, trimmed
  1 teaspoon pepper
  ¾ teaspoon garlic salt
  2 cups wood chips, soaked in water for 15 minutes and drained

1. Combine garlic, oil, and salt in bowl. Pat meat dry with paper towels, poke it about 20 times on each side with fork, and rub it evenly with garlic mixture. Wrap meat in plastic wrap and let sit at room temperature for at least 1 hour or refrigerate for up to 24 hours. (If refrigerated, let sit at room temperature for 1 hour before grilling.) Before cooking, unwrap meat, wipe off garlic paste using paper towels, and rub it evenly with pepper and garlic salt. Using large piece of heavy-duty aluminum foil, wrap soaked chips in foil packet and cut several vent holes in top.

2a. For a Charcoal Grill Open bottom vent completely. Light large chimney starter filled with charcoal briquettes (6 quarts). When top coals are partially covered with ash, pour evenly over half of grill. Set cooking grate in place, cover, and open lid vent completely. Heat grill until hot, about 5 minutes.

2b. For a Gas Grill Turn all burners to high, cover, and heat grill until hot, about 15 minutes.

3. Clean and oil cooking grate. Grill meat on hot side of grill until well browned on both sides, about 10 minutes. Transfer meat to plate.

4. Place wood chip packet directly on coals or primary burner. If using gas, leave primary burner on high and turn other burner(s) off.

5. Place meat on cool side of grill. Cover (positioning lid vent over meat if using charcoal) and cook until meat registers 120 to 125 degrees (for medium-rare), about 20 minutes.

6. Transfer meat to carving board, tent loosely with aluminum foil, and let rest for 20 minutes. Slice meat thin against grain and serve.

Santa Maria Salsa
MAKES ABOUT 4 CUPS

The distinct texture of each ingredient is part of this salsa's identity and appeal, so we don't recommend using a food processor.

California Barbecued Tri-Tip

  2 pounds tomatoes, cored and chopped
  2 teaspoons table salt
  2 jalapeño chiles, stemmed, seeded, and chopped fine
  1 small red onion, chopped fine
  1 celery rib, chopped fine
  ¼ cup lime juice (2 limes)
  ¼ cup chopped fresh cilantro
  1 garlic clove, minced
  ⅛ teaspoon dried oregano
  ⅛ teaspoon Worcestershire sauce

1. Place tomatoes in strainer set over bowl and sprinkle with salt; drain for 30 minutes. Discard liquid. Meanwhile, combine jalapeños, onion, celery, lime juice, cilantro, garlic, oregano, and Worcestershire in large bowl.

2. Add drained tomatoes to jalapeño mixture and toss to combine. Cover with plastic wrap and let stand at room temperature for 1 hour before serving. (Salsa can be refrigerated for up to 2 days.)

Shredded Barbecued Beef

SERVES 8 TO 10

WHY THIS RECIPE WORKS We sped up the process for our shredded barbecued beef by cutting a chuck roast into quarters, which cook faster and absorb more smoke flavor. After cooking the meat in a roasting pan on the cooler side of the grill for a few hours, we flipped the pieces, wrapped the pan in foil, and placed it in the oven to finish cooking. For a richer barbecue sauce, we sautéed the onions in beef fat. Chili powder and pepper added bite, while ketchup, vinegar, coffee, Worcestershire sauce, brown sugar, and the beef juices rounded out the flavors.

If you prefer a smooth barbecue sauce, strain the sauce before tossing it with the beef in step 5. We like to serve this beef on white bread with plenty of pickle chips. Three medium wood chunks, soaked in water for 1 hour, can be substituted for the wood chips on a charcoal grill.

- 1 tablespoon table salt
- 1 tablespoon pepper
- 1 teaspoon cayenne pepper
- 1 (5- to 6-pound) boneless beef chuck-eye roast, trimmed and quartered
- 1 (13 by 9-inch) disposable aluminum roasting pan
- 3 cups wood chips, soaked in water for 15 minutes and drained
- 1 onion, chopped fine
- 4 garlic cloves, minced
- ½ teaspoon chili powder
- 1¼ cups ketchup
- ¾ cup brewed coffee
- ½ cup cider vinegar
- ½ cup packed brown sugar
- 3 tablespoons Worcestershire sauce
- ½ teaspoon pepper

1. Combine salt, pepper, and cayenne in small bowl. Pat meat dry with paper towels and rub evenly with spice mixture. Wrap meat in plastic wrap and let sit at room temperature for at least 1 hour or refrigerate up to 24 hours. (If refrigerated, let sit at room temperature for 1 hour before grilling.) Before cooking, unwrap meat and transfer to disposable pan. Using 2 large pieces of heavy-duty aluminum foil, wrap soaked chips in 2 foil packets and cut several vent holes in tops.

Texas Barbecue Brisket

2a. For a Charcoal Grill Open bottom vent completely. Light large chimney starter half filled with charcoal briquettes (3 quarts). When top coals are partially covered with ash, pour into steeply banked pile against 1 side of grill. Place wood chip packets on coals. Set cooking grate in place, cover, and open lid vent halfway. Heat grill until hot and wood chips are smoking, about 5 minutes.

2b. For a Gas Grill Place wood chip packets directly on primary burner. Turn all burners to high, cover, and heat grill until hot and wood chips are smoking, about 15 minutes. Leave primary burner on high and turn other burner(s) off. (Adjust primary burner as needed to maintain grill temperature between 250 and 300 degrees.)

3. Place pan of meat on cool side of the grill. Cover (positioning lid vent over meat if using charcoal) and cook until meat is deep red, about 2 hours. During final 20 minutes of grilling, adjust oven rack to lower-middle position and heat oven to 300 degrees.

4. Flip meat over in pan, cover pan tightly with foil, and roast beef in oven until fork slips easily in and out of beef, 2 to 3 hours.

5. Transfer meat to large bowl, tent loosely with foil, and let rest for 30 minutes. While meat rests, skim fat from accumulated juices in pan; reserve 2 tablespoons fat. Strain defatted juices; reserve ½ cup juice. Combine onion and reserved fat in medium saucepan and cook over medium heat until onion has softened, about 10 minutes. Add garlic and chili powder and cook until fragrant, about 30 seconds. Stir in ketchup, coffee, vinegar, sugar, Worcestershire, pepper, and any accumulated meat juices and simmer until thickened, about 15 minutes. Using 2 forks, pull meat into shreds, discarding any excess fat or gristle. Toss meat with ½ cup barbecue sauce. Serve, passing remaining sauce separately.

Texas Barbecue Brisket

SERVES 12 TO 15

WHY THIS RECIPE WORKS A proper Texas-style smoked brisket is sublime; tender juicy meat encased in a dark, peppery crust or "bark." But smoking a 10-pound brisket on a charcoal grill took some creative thinking. We used a charcoal snake, a C-shaped array of briquettes that slowly burns from one end to the other. Topped with wood chips, it provided hours of low, smoky heat, with just one refuel. Cooking the brisket fat side down protected it from the coals, and wrapping it in aluminum foil toward the end of its cooking time and letting it rest in an insulated cooler kept the meat ultramoist.

We developed this recipe using a 22-inch Weber Kettle charcoal grill. Plan ahead: The brisket must be seasoned at least 12 hours before cooking. We call for a whole beef brisket here, with both the flat and point cuts intact; you may need to special-order this cut. We recommend reading the entire recipe before starting.

- 1 (10- to 12-pound) whole beef brisket, untrimmed
- ¼ cup kosher salt
- ¼ cup pepper
- 5 (3-inch) wood chunks
- 1 (13 by 9-inch) disposable aluminum pan

1. With brisket positioned point side up, use sharp knife to trim fat cap to ½- to ¼-inch thickness. Remove excess fat from deep pocket where flat and point are attached. Trim and discard short edge of flat if less than 1 inch thick. Flip brisket and remove any large deposits of fat from underside.

2. Combine salt and pepper in bowl. Place brisket on rimmed baking sheet and sprinkle all over with salt mixture. Cover loosely with plastic wrap and refrigerate for 12 to 24 hours.

3. Open bottom vent of grill completely. Set up charcoal snake: Arrange 58 briquettes, 2 briquettes wide, around perimeter of grill, overlapping slightly so briquettes are touching, leaving 8-inch gap between ends of snake. Place second layer of 58 briquettes, also 2 briquettes wide, on top of first. (Completed snake should be 2 briquettes wide by 2 briquettes high.)

4. Starting 4 inches from 1 end of snake, evenly space wood chunks on top of snake. Place disposable pan in center of grill. Fill disposable pan with 6 cups water. Light chimney starter filled with 10 briquettes (pile briquettes on 1 side of chimney). When coals are partially covered with ash, pour over 1 end of snake. (Make sure lit coals touch only 1 end of snake.)

5. Set cooking grate in place. Clean and oil cooking grate. Place brisket, fat side down, directly over water pan, with point end facing gap in snake. Insert temperature probe into side of upper third of point. Cover grill, open lid vent completely, and position lid vent over gap in snake. Cook, undisturbed and without lifting lid, until meat registers 170 degrees, 4 to 5 hours.

6. Place 2 large sheets of aluminum foil on rimmed baking sheet. Remove temperature probe from brisket. Using oven mitts, lift brisket and transfer to center of foil, fat side down. Wrap brisket tightly with first layer of foil, minimizing air pockets between foil and brisket. Rotate brisket 90 degrees and wrap with second layer of foil. (Use additional foil, if necessary, to completely wrap brisket.) Make small mark on foil with marker to keep track of fat/point side. Foil wrap should be airtight.

7. Remove cooking grate. Starting at still-unlit end of snake, pour 3 quarts unlit briquettes about halfway around perimeter of grill over gap and spent coals. Replace cooking grate. Return foil-wrapped brisket to grill over water pan, fat side down, with point end facing where gap in snake used to be. Reinsert temperature probe into point. Cover grill and continue to cook until meat registers 205 degrees, 1 to 2 hours longer.

8. Remove temperature probe. Transfer foil-wrapped brisket to cooler, point side up. Close cooler and let rest for at least 2 hours or up to 3 hours. Transfer brisket to carving board, unwrap, and position fat side up. Slice flat against grain ¼ inch thick, stopping once you reach base of point. Rotate point 90 degrees and slice point against grain (perpendicular to first cut) ⅜ inch thick. Serve.

Jucy Lucy Burgers

Jucy Lucy Burgers

SERVES 4

WHY THIS RECIPE WORKS Minneapolis taverns are famous for the Jucy Lucy, a moist beef burger stuffed with American cheese. Our first attempts, cooked to well-done to melt the cheese inside, were dry and tough or the cheese melted through the meat, leaving an empty cavern behind. To keep the cheese in place, we wrapped it inside a small beef patty and then molded a second patty around it. Adding a panade of bread and milk to the ground beef kept the burgers moist and juicy.

Buy the American cheese from the deli counter, and ask them to slice it into a ½-inch slab from which you can cut four big cubes to fill the center of the burgers. One or two percent low-fat milk can be substituted for the whole milk. The cheesy center of these burgers is molten hot when first removed from the grill, so be sure to let the burgers rest for at least 5 minutes before serving.

- 2 slices hearty white sandwich bread, torn into 1-inch pieces
- ¼ cup whole milk
- 1 teaspoon garlic powder
- ¾ teaspoon table salt
- ½ teaspoon pepper
- 1½ pounds 85 percent lean ground beef
- 1 slice deli American cheese (½-inch-thick), quartered

1. In large bowl using potato masher, mash bread, milk, garlic powder, salt, and pepper into smooth paste. Add beef and lightly knead mixture until well combined.

2. Divide meat into 4 equal portions. Using half of each portion of meat, encase cheese to form mini burger patty. Mold remaining half-portion of meat around mini patty and seal edges to form ball. Flatten ball with palm of your hand, forming ¾-inch-thick patty. Cover and refrigerate patties for at least 30 minutes or up to 24 hours.

3a. For a Charcoal Grill Open bottom vent completely. Light large chimney starter half filled with charcoal briquettes (3 quarts). When top coals are partially covered with ash, pour evenly over grill. Set cooking grate in place, cover, and heat grill until hot, about 5 minutes.

3b. For a Gas Grill Turn all burners to high, cover, and heat grill until hot, about 15 minutes. Turn all burners to medium.

4. Clean and oil cooking grate. Lay burgers on grill and cook, without pressing on them, until well browned on both sides and cooked through, 12 to 16 minutes, flipping burgers halfway through grilling. Transfer burgers to platter, tent loosely with aluminum foil, and let rest for 5 minutes before serving.

How to Form a Jucy Lucy
To avoid a burger blowout, it's essential to completely seal in the cheese.

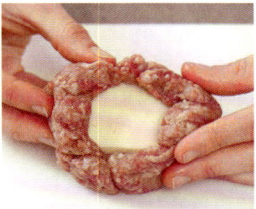
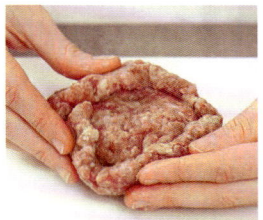

1. Using half of each portion of meat, encase cheese to form mini burger patty.

2. Mold remaining half-portion of meat around mini patty and seal edges to form a ball and flatten to form ¾-inch patty.

The Great Lucy Debate
A debate still rages as to where the Jucy Lucy was created. Two Minnesota taverns, Matt's Bar and the 5–8 Club, claim to have created the burger in the 1950s. As the story goes, a customer requested a burger with the cheese sealed in the middle. When he bit in, the hot cheese spurted out and he exclaimed, "That's one juicy Lucy!" As for the unusual spelling, that's still a mystery.

Grilled Bacon Burgers with Caramelized Onion

SERVES 4

WHY THIS RECIPE WORKS Bacon is a no-brainer burger topping, but we wanted bacony bliss in every bite, not just on top. Combining raw bacon with ground beef, however, led to overworked, dry patties, while adding crumbled cooked bacon left us with crunchy burgers. But we found that blitzing raw bacon in the food processor and then cooking it just until some of the fat was rendered before mixing it into our ground beef helped it incorporate easily, ensuring optimal flavor distribution. To take these burgers to even higher heights, we topped them with crumbled blue cheese (a classic pairing) and onion that we sautéed in some of the leftover bacon fat.

Martin's Sandwich Potato Rolls are our favorite hamburger buns, and Oscar Mayer Naturally Hardwood Smoked Bacon is our favorite thin-sliced bacon. Be gentle when shaping the patties, taking care not to overwork the meat, or the burgers will become dense. Serve the burgers with lettuce and tomato, if desired.

- 8 slices bacon
- 1 large onion, halved and sliced thin
  Table salt and pepper
- 1½ pounds 85 percent lean ground beef
- 4 ounces blue cheese, crumbled and chilled (1 cup) (optional)
- 4 hamburger buns, toasted

1. Process bacon in food processor to smooth paste, about 1 minute, scraping down sides of bowl as needed. Cook bacon in 12-inch nonstick skillet over medium heat until lightly browned in spots but still pink (do not cook until crispy), about 5 minutes, breaking up pieces with spoon. Drain bacon in fine-mesh strainer set over bowl. Transfer bacon to paper towel–lined plate and let cool completely. Reserve bacon fat.

2. Add 2 tablespoons reserved fat to now-empty skillet and heat over medium heat until shimmering. Add onion and ¼ teaspoon salt and cook until well browned, about 20 minutes. Transfer to bowl and set aside.

Grilled Bacon Burgers with Caramelized Onion

3. Spread beef in even layer in rimmed baking sheet. Sprinkle bacon, 1 teaspoon pepper, and ⅛ teaspoon salt over beef. Toss gently with 2 forks to combine. Divide beef mixture into 4 equal mounds. Gently shape each mound into ¾-inch-thick patty about 4½ inches in diameter. Using your fingertips, press center of each patty down until about ½ inch thick, creating slight indentation. (Patties can be covered and refrigerated for up to 24 hours.)

4a. For a Charcoal Grill Open bottom vent completely. Light large chimney starter filled with charcoal briquettes (6 quarts). When top coals are partially covered with ash, pour evenly over grill. Set cooking grate in place, cover, and open lid vent completely. Heat grill until hot, about 5 minutes.

4b. For a Gas Grill Turn all burners to high, cover, and heat grill until hot, about 15 minutes. Leave all burners on high.

5. Clean and oil cooking grate. Season patties with pepper. Cook patties indentation side down, uncovered, until browned, about 3 minutes. Flip patties and top each with ¼ cup blue cheese, if using. Cover and continue to cook until burgers register 125 degrees (for medium-rare) or 130 degrees (for medium), about 2 minutes longer. Transfer burgers to buns, top with onion, and serve.

Green Chile Cheeseburgers

SERVES 4

WHY THIS RECIPE WORKS For our version of New Mexico's green chile cheeseburgers—ground beef patties grilled to a crusty brown and topped with chopped fire-roasted chiles and a slice of cheese—we preferred the flavor and fat of 85 percent lean ground beef. For the topping, we used mild Anaheim chiles and spicy jalapeños for a complex chile flavor. We grilled the chiles with onions, then quickly chopped them with fresh garlic in the food processor. For even more chile flavor, we pureed some of the chile topping into a smooth paste and mixed it into the raw ground beef. This gave us burgers with satisfying heat through and through.

Green Chile Cheeseburgers

In step 3, you may need to add a teaspoon or two of water to the food processor to help process the chile mixture. Pressing a shallow indentation in the center of each patty keeps the burgers flat during grilling.

- 3 Anaheim chiles, stemmed, halved, and seeded
- 3 jalapeño chiles, stemmed, halved, and seeded
- 1 onion, sliced into 1/2-inch-thick rounds
- 1 garlic clove, minced
- Table salt and pepper
- 1½ pounds 85 percent lean ground beef
- 4 slices deli American cheese

1a. For a Charcoal Grill Open bottom vent completely. Light large chimney starter filled with charcoal briquettes (6 quarts). When top coals are partially covered with ash, pour evenly over grill. Set cooking grate in place, cover, and open lid vent completely. Heat grill until hot, about 5 minutes.

1b. For a Gas Grill Turn all burners to high, cover, and heat grill until hot, about 15 minutes.

2. Clean and oil cooking grate. Place Anaheims, jalapeños, and onion on grill, cover, and cook until vegetables are lightly charred and tender, 4 to 6 minutes, flipping halfway through cooking. Transfer vegetables to bowl, cover, and let cool 5 minutes. Remove skins from chiles and discard; separate onion rounds into rings.

3. Transfer chiles and onion to food processor, add garlic, and pulse until coarsely chopped, about 5 pulses. Transfer all but ¼ cup chopped chile mixture to empty bowl and season with salt and pepper; set aside. Process remaining mixture until finely chopped, about 45 seconds, scraping down bowl as needed.

4. Combine beef, finely chopped chile mixture, ½ teaspoon salt, and ¼ teaspoon pepper in large bowl and lightly knead until well combined. Shape into four ¾-inch-thick patties and press shallow depression in center of each.

5. Place burgers on grill, cover, and cook until well browned on first side, 3 to 5 minutes. Flip burgers, top with reserved coarsely chopped chile mixture and cheese, and continue to cook, covered, until cheese is melted and burgers are cooked to desired doneness, 3 to 5 minutes. Serve.

Chicago-Style Barbecued Ribs

Chicago-Style Barbecued Ribs

SERVES 4 TO 6

WHY THIS RECIPE WORKS Chicago-style barbecued ribs recipes typically call for smoking the ribs at about 200 degrees for at least 8 hours. This slow-and-low cooking method delivers the moist, tender meat that defines Chicago ribs. We wanted to replicate the same method at home. To shorten cooking time, we started our recipe on the grill—where the ribs picked up good color and smoke flavor—and finished them in the oven. Placing pans of water on the grill and in the oven steamed the ribs, making them extra moist and tender. For Chicago-style barbecue sauce, we used celery salt, allspice, and plenty of cayenne pepper.

THE STATE OF GRILLING 491

The dry spices are used to flavor both the rub and the barbecue sauce. One medium wood chunk, soaked in water for 1 hour, can be substituted for the wood chips on a charcoal grill. When removing the ribs from the oven, be careful to not spill the hot water in the bottom of the baking sheet.

Spice Rub and Ribs

- 1 tablespoon dry mustard
- 1 tablespoon paprika
- 1 tablespoon packed dark brown sugar
- 1½ teaspoons garlic powder
- 1½ teaspoons onion powder
- 1½ teaspoons celery salt
- 1 teaspoon cayenne pepper
- ½ teaspoon ground allspice
- 2 racks baby back ribs (about 1½ pounds each), trimmed
- 1 cup wood chips, soaked in water for 15 minutes and drained
- 1 (13 by 9-inch) disposable aluminum roasting pan

Sauce

- 1¼ cups ketchup
- ¼ cup molasses
- ¼ cup cider vinegar
- ¼ cup water
- ⅛ teaspoon liquid smoke

1. For the Spice Rub and Ribs Combine dry mustard, paprika, sugar, garlic powder, onion powder, celery salt, cayenne, and allspice in bowl. Measure out and reserve 2 tablespoons spice mixture for sauce. To remove chewy membrane from ribs, loosen it with tip of paring knife and, with aid of paper towel, pull it off slowly in 1 big piece. Pat ribs dry with paper towels and rub evenly with spice mixture. Wrap meat in plastic wrap and let sit at room temperature for at least 1 hour or refrigerate for up to 24 hours. (If refrigerated, let sit at room temperature for 1 hour before grilling.)

2. For the Sauce Whisk all ingredients with reserved 2 tablespoons spice rub in bowl. Using large piece of heavy-duty aluminum foil, wrap soaked chips in foil packet and cut several vent holes in top.

3a. For a Charcoal Grill Open bottom vent completely. Light large chimney starter filled with charcoal briquettes (6 quarts). Add 2 cups water to disposable pan and place it on 1 side of grill. When top coals are partially covered with ash, pour into steeply banked pile against other side of grill, opposite pan of water. Place wood chip packet on coals. Set cooking grate in place, cover, and open lid vent completely. Heat grill until hot and wood chips are smoking, about 5 minutes.

3b. For a Gas Grill Place wood chip packet directly on primary burner. Add 2 cups water to disposable pan and place it on secondary burner. Turn all burners to high, cover, and heat grill until hot and wood chips are smoking, about 15 minutes. Turn primary burner to medium and turn other burner(s) off. (Adjust primary burner as needed to maintain grill temperature around 325 degrees.)

4. Clean and oil cooking grate. Place ribs meat side down on grill over water-filled pan; ribs may overlap slightly. Cover (positioning lid vent over meat if using charcoal) and cook until ribs are deep red and smoky, about 1½ hours, flipping and rotating racks halfway through grilling. During final 20 minutes of grilling, adjust oven rack to middle position and heat oven to 250 degrees.

5. Set wire rack in rimmed baking sheet and add just enough water to cover pan bottom. Transfer ribs to rack and cover tightly with foil. Continue to cook ribs in oven until fork slips easily in and out of meat, 1½ to 2 hours.

6. Remove ribs from oven, tent with foil, and let rest for 30 minutes. Brush ribs evenly with half of sauce. Slice ribs between bones and serve with remaining sauce.

Texas Barbecued Beef Ribs

SERVES 4

WHY THIS RECIPE WORKS Traditional Texas barbecued beef ribs are placed in pits for up to 10 hours. The smoke slowly permeates the meat, melting away fat, building flavor, and creating an unforgettable crust. We wanted a streamlined recipe. To speed things up, we first turned to steaming the ribs in the oven on a tray of water covered with aluminum foil, which tenderized the ribs. We then moved the ribs to the grill, where we smoked them over indirect heat (banking all the coals to one side of the grill and placing the ribs on the empty side) using wood chips. The surface of the meat dried and formed a spicy, crusty bark.

Beef ribs are sold in slabs with up to seven bones, but slabs with three to four bones are easier to manage on the grill. If you cannot find ribs with a substantial amount of meat on the bones, don't bother making this recipe. One medium wood chunk, soaked in water for 1 hour, can be substituted for the wood chips on a charcoal grill.

Texas Barbecue Sauce

- 2 tablespoons unsalted butter
- ½ small onion, chopped fine
- 2 garlic cloves, minced
- 1½ teaspoons chili powder
- 1½ teaspoons pepper
- ½ teaspoon dry mustard
- 2 cups tomato juice
- 6 tablespoons distilled white vinegar
- 2 tablespoons Worcestershire sauce
- 2 tablespoons packed brown sugar
- 2 tablespoons molasses
- Table salt

Ribs

- 3 tablespoons packed brown sugar
- 4 teaspoons chili powder
- 1 tablespoon table salt
- 2 teaspoons pepper
- ½ teaspoon cayenne pepper
- 3–4 beef rib slabs (3 to 4 ribs per slab, about 5 pounds total), trimmed
- 1 cup wood chips, soaked in water for 15 minutes and drained

1. For the Texas Barbecue Sauce Melt butter in medium saucepan over medium heat. Add onion and cook until softened, about 5 minutes. Stir in garlic, chili powder, pepper, and dry mustard and cook until fragrant, about 30 seconds. Stir in tomato juice, vinegar, Worcestershire, sugar, and molasses and simmer until sauce is reduced to 2 cups, about 20 minutes. Season with salt to taste. (Sauce can be refrigerated for 1 week.)

2. For the Ribs Combine sugar, chili powder, salt, pepper, and cayenne in bowl. Pat ribs dry with paper towels and rub them evenly with spice mixture. Cover ribs with plastic wrap and let sit at room temperature for 1 hour.

3. Adjust oven rack to middle position and heat oven to 300 degrees. Set wire rack in rimmed baking sheet and add just enough water to cover pan bottom. Arrange ribs on rack and cover tightly with aluminum foil. Bake until fat has rendered and meat begins to pull away from bones, about 2 hours. Using large piece of heavy-duty foil, wrap soaked chips in foil packet and cut several vent holes in top.

Texas Barbecued Beef Ribs

4a. For a Charcoal Grill Open bottom vent halfway. Light large chimney starter filled with charcoal briquettes (6 quarts). When top coals are partially covered with ash, pour into steeply banked pile against 1 side of grill. Place wood chip packet on coals. Set cooking grate in place, cover, and open lid vent halfway. Heat grill until hot and wood chips are smoking, about 5 minutes.

4b. For a Gas Grill Place wood chip packet directly on primary burner. Turn all burners to high, cover, and heat grill until hot and wood chips are smoking, about 15 minutes. Leave primary burner on high and turn other burner(s) off. (Adjust primary burner as needed to maintain grill temperature between 250 and 300 degrees.)

5. Clean and oil cooking grate. Place ribs meat side down on cool side of grill; ribs may overlap slightly. Cover (positioning lid vent over meat if using charcoal) and cook until ribs are lightly charred and smoky, about 1½ hours, flipping and rotating racks halfway through grilling. Transfer to cutting board, tent with foil, and let rest for 10 minutes. Serve with barbecue sauce.

Texas-Style Smoked Beef Ribs

SERVES 6 TO 8

WHY THIS RECIPE WORKS To ensure a dark crust and a pink smoke ring surrounding extra-tender beef, we started at our butcher. We ordered two racks of beef plate ribs, each with 1 to 1½ inches of meat on top of the bone to ensure that they wouldn't shrivel down during cooking. To smoke them on our charcoal grill, we set up a charcoal snake, a C-shaped arrangement of smoldering briquettes that provided low, slow, indirect heat. Arranging five wood chunks on top of the briquettes provided a steady supply of smoke. Placing a pan of water inside the snake stabilized the grill temperature over the prolonged cook time, allowing the collagen to melt. Cooking the ribs to 210 degrees ensured ultratender, juicy beef.

We developed this recipe using a 22-inch Weber Kettle charcoal grill. We call for beef plate ribs here; you may need to special-order these. We recommend reading the entire recipe before starting.

- 3 tablespoons kosher salt
- 3 tablespoons pepper
- 2 (4- to 5-pound) racks beef plate ribs, 1 to 1½ inches of meat on top of bone, trimmed
- 5 (3-inch) wood chunks
- 1 (13 by 9-inch) disposable aluminum pan

1. Combine salt and pepper in bowl, then sprinkle ribs all over with salt-pepper mixture.

2. Open bottom vent completely. Set up charcoal snake: Arrange 60 briquettes, 2 briquettes wide, around perimeter of grill, overlapping slightly so briquettes are touching, leaving 8-inch gap between ends of snake. Place second layer of 60 briquettes, also 2 briquettes wide, on top of first. (Completed snake should be 2 briquettes wide by 2 briquettes high.)

3. Starting 4 inches from 1 end of snake, evenly space wood chunks on top of snake. Place disposable pan in center of grill so short end of pan faces gap in snake. Fill disposable pan with 4 cups water. Light chimney starter filled with 15 briquettes (pile briquettes on 1 side of chimney to make them easier to ignite). When coals are partially covered with ash, pour over 1 end of snake. (Make sure lit coals touch only 1 end of snake.)

4. Set cooking grate in place. Clean and oil cooking grate. Position ribs next to each other on cooking grate, bone side down, crosswise over disposable pan and gap in snake (they will be off-center; this is OK). Cover grill, position lid vent over gap in snake, and open lid vent completely. Cook undisturbed until rack of ribs overhanging gap in snake registers 210 degrees in meatiest portion, 5½ to 6¼ hours.

5. Transfer ribs to carving board, tent with aluminum foil, and let rest for 30 minutes. Cut ribs between bones and serve.

Texas-Style Smoked Beef Ribs

Buy the Right (Very Big!) Ribs
Individual beef short ribs (left) are too small to work here. This recipe is specifically engineered for racks of beef plate ribs (right), which you may need to special-order from a butcher.

Smoked Prime Rib

SERVES 8 TO 10

WHY THIS RECIPE WORKS Smoked prime rib is the specialty of Texas barbecue joints like Lockhart Smokehouse and Kreuz Market—and you don't need a professional-grade smoker to make it. Though it takes some patience (including a 24-hour minimum rest after seasoning the rib roast to ensure deep flavor and juicy meat), the final product will steal the show at your next barbecue. We mimicked the low, slow heat of a smoker with our charcoal snake method, which burned steady and long in a kettle grill without needing to refresh the briquettes. Some barbecue spots choose to smoke their prime rib until it's well-done, but we preferred smoking it to medium-rare for a delightful mix of textures. The finished roast had a deeply charred crust, a tender middle layer, and a juicy, rosy center. We sliced it thick and enjoyed with a stir-together spicy horseradish sauce.

We developed this recipe using a 22-inch Weber kettle charcoal grill. If you intend to make the Smoked Prime Rib Sandwiches with Green Chile Queso (recipe follows), reserve a 12-ounce chunk of meat after carving the roast in step 7. Be sure to also reserve 3 tablespoons of the horseradish sauce.

Prime Rib

- 1 (6- to 7-pound) first-cut beef standing rib roast (3 bones), fat cap trimmed to ¼ inch
- 2 tablespoons kosher salt
- 1 tablespoon pepper
- 3 (3-inch) wood chunks
- 1 (13 by 9-inch) disposable aluminum pan

Horseradish Sauce

- ½ cup mayonnaise
- ⅓ cup prepared horseradish
- 2 tablespoons lemon juice
- 1 garlic clove, minced
- 1 teaspoon Worcestershire sauce
- 1 teaspoon pepper
- ¾ teaspoon kosher salt
-   Pinch cayenne pepper

1. For the Prime Rib Using sharp knife, cut 1-inch crosshatch pattern in fat cap of roast, being careful not to cut into meat. Rub salt and pepper over entire roast and into crosshatch. Transfer to large plate and refrigerate, uncovered, for at least 24 hours or up to 4 days.

2. Open bottom vent of charcoal grill completely. Arrange 40 charcoal briquettes, 2 briquettes wide, around half of perimeter of grill, overlapping slightly so briquettes are touching, to form C shape. Place second layer of 40 briquettes, also 2 briquettes wide, on top of first. (Completed arrangement should be 2 briquettes wide by 2 briquettes high.)

3. Place 2 wood chunks on top of charcoal 2 inches from each end of C. Place remaining chunk in center of C. Place disposable pan in center of grill, running lengthwise into arc of C. Pour 6 cups water into disposable pan.

4. Light chimney starter filled with 10 briquettes (pile briquettes on 1 side of chimney so they catch). When coals are partially covered with ash, use tongs to place them at 1 end of C.

5. Set cooking grate in place, then clean and oil grate. Place roast over water pan, fat side up, with bones facing arc in C. Insert temperature probe into center of roast. Cover grill, open lid vent completely, and position lid vent over roast. Cook until meat registers 115 degrees (for medium-rare), 2½ to 3¼ hours.

6. For the Horseradish Sauce Meanwhile, combine all ingredients in bowl. Cover and refrigerate for at least 30 minutes to allow flavors to meld. (Sauce can be refrigerated for up to 2 days.)

7. Transfer roast to carving board, tent with aluminum foil, and let rest for 45 minutes. Carve meat from bones and slice ¾ inch thick. Serve with sauce. (Leftover meat can be refrigerated for up to 2 days.)

Smoked Prime Rib Sandwiches with Green Chile Queso

SERVES 2

WHY THIS RECIPE WORKS Lewis Barbecue in Charleston, South Carolina, sells a Beef N' Cheddar special on Fridays that nods to Arby's signature sandwich. We loved the combination of rich beef, chile-spiced queso, and sliced onions; here's our version. It's the best way to use up leftover Smoked Prime Rib and horseradish sauce. We sliced the chilled meat thin and then lightly crisped up the tender slices on the stovetop. The green chile queso came together quickly in the microwave using American cheese and milk for creamy, melty goodness and pepper Jack cheese and salsa verde for a spicy kick. We piled the beef and thin-sliced onions on a soft kaiser roll spread with homemade horseradish sauce and topped it off with queso.

This recipe, inspired by a recipe from Lewis Barbecue in Charleston, South Carolina, calls for leftover Smoked Prime Rib (page 495). We recommend chilling the leftover meat overnight to make it easier to slice thin.

- 3 tablespoons horseradish sauce from Smoked Prime Rib (page 495)
- 2 kaiser rolls, split and toasted
- ½ small white onion, sliced into thin rounds
- 1 tablespoon vegetable oil
- 12 ounces Smoked Prime Rib, sliced thin on bias
- 1 ounce American cheese, shredded (¼ cup)
- 1 ounce pepper Jack cheese, shredded (¼ cup)
- 2 tablespoons jarred salsa verde
- 2 tablespoons whole milk

1. Spread horseradish sauce on cut sides of bun tops (1½ tablespoons per bun top). Divide onion between bun bottoms.

2. Heat vegetable oil in 12-inch nonstick skillet over medium-high heat until just smoking. Add prime rib and cook until warmed through and fat is lightly crisped, about 3 minutes. Cover to keep warm.

Smoked Prime Rib Sandwiches with Green Chile Queso

3. Combine American cheese, pepper Jack, salsa verde, and milk in medium bowl. Microwave until cheeses begin to melt around edges of bowl, 30 to 60 seconds. Stir and continue to microwave until cheeses are completely melted and just beginning to bubble around edges of bowl, 1 to 2 minutes longer, whisking halfway through microwaving.

4. Divide prime rib between bun bottoms. Pour half of queso (or more, if desired) over prime rib. Cap with bun tops. Serve, passing any extra queso separately.

The Right Slice
Holding knife at angle, slice leftover prime rib thin on bias. (Note that meat is easier to slice when cold.)

Buy American
The mild, milky taste of American cheese is a great draw on its own, but we use it here because it melts beautifully and makes for a creamy, silky queso. We recommend buying a hunk from the deli counter and shredding it on a box grater at home.

496   *The Complete Cook's Country TV Show Cookbook*

Kalbi (Korean Grilled Flanken-Style Short Ribs)

SERVES 4

Kalbi (Korean Grilled Flanken-Style Short Ribs)

WHY THIS RECIPE WORKS Kalbi, which means "rib" in Korean, is an iconic Korean dish of tender, slightly sweet short ribs that char beautifully on the grill. A savory-sweet marinade was the key to achieving their characteristic flavor. The sweetness of a kalbi marinade comes from sugar and some kind of fruit, traditionally Asian pear. Since good Asian pears can be tough to find year-round, we found reliable alternatives. Canned pineapple added consistent sweetness, while fresh kiwi added a sweet-tart flavor (and contains enzymes that helped tenderize the meat). The thin shape of flanken-style ribs means that the fat rendered and the connective tissue broke down quickly, so the ribs got tender on the grill in a short amount of time.

We call for clear rice wine here; michiu, cheongju, or mirin can be used. This recipe can easily be doubled (you will need to marinate the ribs in two separate dishes, and you may need more charcoal if using a charcoal grill). We don't typically wash our proteins before cooking, but flanken-style short ribs tend to have a fair amount of bone fragments stuck to them because they are cut with a band saw. Rinsing is necessary to remove those fragments. An 8-ounce can of pineapple chunks will yield enough for this recipe. The flavor of green kiwi is preferred here over yellow kiwi. Garnish the kalbi with sliced scallions, if desired.

- ¾ cup packed dark brown sugar
- ⅔ cup soy sauce
- 1 cup coarsely chopped onion
- ½ cup canned pineapple chunks, plus 3 tablespoons juice
- ½ green kiwi, peeled
- 6 garlic cloves, smashed and peeled
- ¼ cup clear rice wine
- 2 tablespoons toasted sesame oil
- 3 pounds flanken-style beef short ribs, ¼ inch thick, trimmed

1. Combine sugar and soy sauce in small saucepan and cook over medium-high heat, stirring occasionally, until sugar is dissolved. Let cool completely off heat.

2. Combine onion, pineapple and juice, kiwi, and garlic in blender and puree until smooth, about 30 seconds. Transfer onion mixture to 13 by 9-inch baking dish; stir in wine, oil, and soy sauce mixture until combined.

3. Line rimmed baking sheet with triple layer of paper towels. Rinse ribs under cold running water to remove any bone fragments, then transfer to prepared sheet. Pat tops of ribs dry with additional paper towels.

4. Working with a few ribs at a time, transfer ribs to marinade, turn gently to coat, and submerge in marinade. Cover dish with plastic wrap and refrigerate for at least 24 hours or up to 2 days.

5a. For a Charcoal Grill Open bottom vent completely. Light large chimney starter three-quarters filled with charcoal briquettes (4½ quarts). When top coals are partially covered with ash, pour evenly over grill. Set cooking grate in place, cover, and open lid vent completely. Heat grill until hot, about 5 minutes.

5b. For a Gas Grill Turn all burners to high; cover; and heat grill until hot, about 15 minutes. Turn all burners to medium.

THE STATE OF GRILLING   497

6. Clean and oil cooking grate. Grill ribs, uncovered, until evenly browned on first side, about 6 minutes, moving ribs as needed for even cooking and to prevent flare-ups. Flip ribs and continue to grill until evenly browned on second side, about 6 minutes longer. Transfer ribs to platter, tent with aluminum foil, and let rest for 5 minutes. Serve.

> ### The Right Ribs
> Unlike English-style short ribs, flanken-style beef short ribs are cut thin across the bones. The thin shape means that the fat is rendered and the connective tissue breaks down faster, so the ribs get tender more quickly on the grill.

South Carolina Smoked Fresh Ham
SERVES 8 TO 10

WHY THIS RECIPE WORKS For a new take on pulled pork, we started with a shank-end fresh ham. We rubbed it with only salt to keep the flavor pure and let it rest overnight for deeply seasoned, juicy meat. To speed up the usually long cooking time, we smoked the ham on the grill to infuse it with flavor before covering it with foil and transferring it to the oven. For crisp and crackling skin, we removed the skin when the meat hit 200 degrees and roasted it separately. From there, we chopped the ham, stirring in the crisp bits of skin and the flavorful rendered juices, and served it on soft buns with a smear of tangy mustard sauce.

Plan ahead: The ham must be salted at least 18 hours before cooking. You'll have about 2½ cups of mustard sauce.

Ham
- 1 (6- to 8-pound) bone-in, skin-on shank-end fresh ham
  Kosher salt
- 2 cups wood chips

Mustard Sauce
- 1½ cups yellow mustard
- ½ cup cider vinegar
- 6 tablespoons packed brown sugar
- 2 tablespoons ketchup
- 2 teaspoons hot sauce
- 2 teaspoons Worcestershire sauce
- 1 teaspoon pepper

Hamburger buns

1. For the Ham Pat ham dry with paper towels. Place ham on large sheet of plastic wrap and rub all over with 2 tablespoons salt. Wrap tightly in plastic and refrigerate for 18 to 24 hours.

2. Just before grilling, soak wood chips in water for 15 minutes, then drain. Using large piece of heavy-duty aluminum foil, wrap soaked chips in 8 by 4½-inch foil packet. (Make sure chips do not poke holes in sides or bottom of packet.) Cut 2 evenly spaced 2-inch slits in top of packet.

3a. For a Charcoal Grill Open bottom vent completely. Light large chimney starter three-quarters filled with charcoal briquettes (4½ quarts). When top coals are partially covered with ash, pour evenly over half of grill. Place wood chip packet on coals. Set cooking grate in place, cover, and open lid vent completely. Heat grill until hot and wood chips are smoking, about 5 minutes.

3b. For a Gas Grill Remove cooking grate and place wood chip packet directly on primary burner. Set cooking grate in place, turn all burners to high, cover, and heat grill until hot and wood chips are smoking, about 15 minutes. Turn primary burner to medium-high and turn off other burner(s). (Adjust primary burner as needed to maintain grill temperature of 300 degrees.)

4. Clean and oil cooking grate. Unwrap ham and place flat side down on cooler side of grill. Cover grill (position lid vent directly over ham if using charcoal) and cook for 2 hours. Thirty minutes before ham comes off grill, adjust oven rack to middle position and heat oven to 300 degrees.

5. For the Mustard Sauce Meanwhile, whisk all ingredients together in bowl. (Sauce can be refrigerated for up to 1 week.)

6. Transfer ham to 13 by 9-inch baking pan, flat side down. Cover pan tightly with foil. Transfer to oven and roast until fork inserted in ham meets little resistance and meat registers 200 degrees, about 2½ hours.

7. Remove ham from oven and increase oven temperature to 400 degrees. Line rimmed baking sheet with foil. Using tongs, remove ham skin in 1 large piece. Place skin fatty side down on prepared sheet. Transfer to oven and roast until skin is dark and crispy and sounds hollow when tapped with fork, about 25 minutes, rotating sheet halfway through roasting. Tent ham with foil and let rest while skin roasts.

8. Transfer ham to carving board. Strain accumulated juices from pan through fine-mesh strainer set over bowl; discard solids. Trim and discard excess fat from ham. Remove bone and chop meat into bite-size pieces; transfer to large bowl.

9. When cool enough to handle, chop skin fine. Rewarm reserved ham juices in microwave for 1 minute. Add juices and chopped skin to ham and toss to combine. Season with salt to taste. Serve on buns, topped with mustard sauce.

North Carolina Barbecue Pork

SERVES 8 TO 10

WHY THIS RECIPE WORKS Head to North Carolina, and you'll encounter two schools of barbecue pork: eastern North Carolina style and Lexington style. We set out to make both possible for a backyard barbecue. This recipe requires some forethought so that the meat can be seasoned for at least 18 hours before firing up the grill. We used a charcoal snake method to create a long-burning, low, smoky heat source that needed to be refreshed only once. Over the course of a few hours, the pork absorbed plenty of smoky flavor and formed a well-browned crust. Pulling the meat off the heat and letting it finish cooking wrapped in foil kept the inside tender while preventing the exterior from darkening too much and turning bitter. Then, we could choose our own adventure: chopped finely with a tangy, spicy sauce for eastern North Carolina style; or coarse-chopped with a sweeter, thicker sauce for Lexington style. Either is delicious served topped with coleslaw on soft buns.

Plan ahead: The pork butt must be seasoned at least 18 hours before it is cooked. Pork butt roast is often labeled Boston butt in the supermarket. We developed this recipe using a 22-inch Weber kettle grill.

South Carolina Smoked Fresh Ham

North Carolina Barbecue Pork

3   tablespoons kosher salt
1½   tablespoons pepper
1   (6-pound) bone-in pork butt roast, with ¼-inch fat cap
1   (13 by 9-inch) disposable aluminum pan
4   (3-inch) wood chunks
1   recipe Lexington-Style Barbecue Sauce or Eastern North Carolina–Style Barbecue Sauce (recipe follows)

1. Combine salt and pepper in bowl. Place pork on large sheet of plastic wrap and sprinkle all over with salt mixture. Wrap tightly with plastic and refrigerate for 18 to 24 hours.

2. Open bottom grill vent completely. Set up charcoal snake: Arrange 60 briquettes, 2 briquettes wide, around perimeter of grill, overlapping slightly so briquettes are touching, leaving 6-inch gap between ends of snake. Place second layer of 60 briquettes, also 2 briquettes wide, on top of first. (Completed snake should be 2 briquettes wide by 2 briquettes high.)

3. Starting 4 inches from 1 end of snake, evenly space wood chunks on top of snake. Place disposable pan in center of grill so that short end of pan runs parallel to gap in snake. Fill pan with 4 cups water.

4. Light chimney starter filled with 15 briquettes. When coals are partially covered with ash, pour over 1 end of snake. Make sure lit coals touch only 1 end of snake. Use tongs if necessary to move any coals that touch other end of snake.

5. Set cooking grate in place. Clean and oil cooking grate. Unwrap pork and position fat side down over water pan. Insert temperature probe into thickest part of pork. Cover grill, positioning lid vent over gap in snake, and open lid vent completely. Cook, without opening grill, until pork registers 170 degrees, 4 to 5 hours.

6. Place 2 large sheets of aluminum foil on rimmed baking sheet. Remove probe from pork. Using oven mitts, lift pork and transfer to center of 1 sheet of foil, fat side down. Wrap tightly with first sheet of foil, minimizing air pockets between foil and pork. Wrap with second sheet of foil. (Use additional foil, if necessary, to completely wrap pork.) Foil wrap should be airtight. Make small mark on foil with marker to keep track of fat side.

7. Remove cooking grate. Starting at still-unlit end of snake, pour 2 quarts unlit briquettes about one-third of way around perimeter of grill over gap in snake and spent coals. Replace cooking grate. Return wrapped pork to grill over water pan, fat side down. Reinsert probe into thickest part of pork. Cover grill and continue to cook until pork registers 200 degrees, 1 to 1½ hours longer.

8. Remove probe. Transfer pork to carving board, fat side up, and let rest in foil for 1½ hours. Remove bone from pork. For eastern North Carolina style, chop pork into ¼-inch pieces. For Lexington style, chop pork with cleaver into 1-inch pieces. Toss with ⅔ cup sauce. Serve, passing remaining sauce separately.

Eastern North Carolina–Style Barbecue Sauce
MAKES ABOUT 2½ CUPS

This sauce is meant to be tangy and spicy to balance the rich smoked pork. One 12-ounce bottle of Texas Pete Original Hot Sauce will yield more than enough for this recipe.

1½   cups cider vinegar
1   cup Texas Pete Original Hot Sauce
¼   cup packed light brown sugar
2   teaspoons kosher salt
1   teaspoon pepper
1   teaspoon red pepper flakes

Whisk all ingredients together in bowl.

Lexington-Style Barbecue Sauce
MAKES ABOUT 2½ CUPS

This sauce is meant to be tangy and salty to balance the rich smoked pork.

2   cups cider vinegar
1   cup ketchup
2   teaspoons granulated garlic
2   teaspoons pepper
1½   teaspoons kosher salt
1   teaspoon red pepper flakes

Combine all ingredients in small saucepan and bring to boil over medium-high heat. Reduce heat to medium-low and simmer for 5 minutes. Transfer sauce to bowl and let cool completely.

Lexington-Style Pulled Pork

Lexington-Style Pulled Pork

SERVES 8

WHY THIS RECIPE WORKS Traditional vinegar-based Lexington-style pulled pork recipes take hours to prepare. We wanted to simplify this recipe without sacrificing flavor. To do so, we used a combination of grilling and oven roasting to reduce the cooking time from all day to just a few hours. To infuse our Lexington-Style Pulled Pork with ample smoke flavor despite the abbreviated cooking time, we doubled the amount of wood chips we used.

Boneless pork butt (also labeled Boston butt) is often wrapped in elastic netting; be sure to remove the netting before rubbing the meat with the spices in step 1. Four medium wood chunks, soaked in water for 1 hour, can be substituted for the wood chips on a charcoal grill.

Spice Rub and Pork
- 2 tablespoons paprika
- 2 tablespoons pepper
- 2 tablespoons packed brown sugar
- 1 tablespoon table salt
- 1 (4- to 5-pound) boneless pork butt roast, trimmed
- 4 cups wood chips, soaked in water for 15 minutes and drained

Lexington Barbecue Sauce
- 1 cup water
- 1 cup cider vinegar
- ½ cup ketchup
- 1 tablespoon granulated sugar
- ¾ teaspoon table salt
- ½ teaspoon pepper
- ½ teaspoon red pepper flakes

1. For the Spice Rub and Pork Combine paprika, pepper, sugar, and salt in bowl. Pat meat dry with paper towels and rub it evenly with spice mixture. Wrap meat in plastic wrap and let sit at room temperature for at least 1 hour or refrigerate for up to 24 hours. (If refrigerated, let sit at room temperature for 1 hour before grilling.) Using 2 large pieces of heavy-duty aluminum foil, wrap soaked chips in 2 foil packets and cut several vent holes in tops.

2a. For a Charcoal Grill Open bottom vent halfway. Light large chimney starter half filled with charcoal briquettes (3 quarts). When top coals are partially covered with ash, pour into steeply banked pile against 1 side of grill. Place wood chip packets on coals. Set cooking grate in place, cover, and open lid vent halfway. Heat grill until hot and wood chips are smoking, about 5 minutes.

2b. For a Gas Grill Place wood chip packets directly on primary burner. Turn all burners to high, cover, and heat grill until hot and wood chips are smoking, about 15 minutes. Turn primary burner to medium and turn other burner(s) off. (Adjust primary burner as needed to maintain grill temperature around 275 degrees.)

3. Clean and oil cooking grate. Place meat on cool side of grill. Cover (positioning lid vent over meat if using charcoal) and cook until pork has dark, rosy crust, about 2 hours. During final 20 minutes of grilling, adjust oven rack to lower-middle position and heat oven to 325 degrees.

4. Transfer pork to large roasting pan, cover pan tightly with foil, and roast pork in oven until fork slips easily into and out of meat, 2 to 3 hours. Remove pork from the oven and let rest, still covered with foil, for 30 minutes.

5. For the Lexington Barbecue Sauce Whisk together all ingredients until sugar and salt are dissolved. When cool enough to handle, unwrap pork and pull meat into thin shreds, discarding excess fat and gristle. Toss pork with ½ cup barbecue sauce, serving remaining sauce at table.

> ### North Carolina Barbecue Battle
> In the eastern part of North Carolina, it's just not barbecue unless it's a whole hog. Known as a pig pickin', this type of barbecue starts with a split hog and ends with succulent meat and crackling-crisp skin. The meat is then literally picked from the bones and lightly seasoned with a thin vinegar-and-pepper sauce. Western Carolinians eschew the whole hog and go straight for the pork shoulder—the most marbled and meatiest chunk of the animal. The pork shoulder is cooked just like the whole hog, but the sauce is enriched with just enough ketchup and sugar to take the edge off the acidity.

South Carolina Pulled Pork

South Carolina Pulled Pork

SERVES 8

WHY THIS RECIPE WORKS This regional recipe, nicknamed Carolina Gold, demands more than just a last-minute dose of bold flavors. A combination of grilling and oven roasting reduces the cooking time from all day to just four or five hours. We used a spice rub, which included dry mustard to jump-start the mustard flavor of the sauce. Most South Carolina barbecue sauce recipes use yellow mustard, which our tasters praised for its bright tang. Brushing the pork with the sauce before it went into the oven produced a second hit of mustard flavor; tossing the shredded pork with the remaining sauce gave the meat a final layer of mustard flavor.

Boneless pork butt (also labeled Boston butt) is often wrapped in elastic netting; be sure to remove the netting before rubbing the meat with the spices in step 1. The cooked meat can be shredded or chopped. Four medium wood chunks, soaked in water for 1 hour, can be substituted for the wood chip packet on a charcoal grill.

Spice Rub and Pork
- 3 tablespoons dry mustard
- 2 tablespoons table salt
- 1½ tablespoons packed light brown sugar
- 2 teaspoons pepper
- 2 teaspoons paprika
- ¼ teaspoon cayenne pepper
- 1 (4- to 5-pound) boneless pork butt roast, trimmed
- 4 cups wood chips, soaked in water for 15 minutes and drained

Mustard Barbecue Sauce
- ½ cup yellow mustard
- ½ cup packed light brown sugar
- ¼ cup distilled white vinegar
- 2 tablespoons Worcestershire sauce
- 1 tablespoon hot sauce
- 1 teaspoon table salt
- 1 teaspoon pepper

1. For the Spice Rub and Pork Combine dry mustard, salt, sugar, pepper, paprika, and cayenne in bowl. Pat meat dry with paper towels and rub it evenly with spice mixture. Wrap meat in plastic wrap and let sit at room temperature for at least 1 hour or refrigerate up to 24 hours. (If refrigerated, let sit at room temperature for 1 hour before grilling.) Using 2 large pieces of heavy-duty aluminum foil, wrap soaked chips in 2 foil packets and cut several vent holes in tops.

2a. For a Charcoal Grill Open bottom vent completely. Light large chimney starter half filled with charcoal briquettes (3 quarts). When top coals are partially covered with ash, pour into steeply banked pile against 1 side of grill. Place wood chip packets on coals. Set cooking grate in place, cover, and open lid vent halfway. Heat grill until hot and wood chips are smoking, about 5 minutes.

2b. For a Gas Grill Place wood chip packets directly on primary burner. Turn all burners to high, cover, and heat grill until hot and wood chips are smoking, about 15 minutes. Turn primary burner to medium-high and turn other burner(s) off. (Adjust primary burner as needed to maintain grill temperature around 325 degrees.)

3. Clean and oil cooking grate. Place meat on cool side of grill. Cover (positioning lid vent over meat if using charcoal) and cook until pork has dark, rosy crust, about 2 hours. During final 20 minutes of grilling, adjust oven rack to lower-middle position and heat oven to 325 degrees.

4. For the Mustard Barbecue Sauce Whisk yellow mustard, sugar, vinegar, Worcestershire, hot sauce, salt, and pepper in bowl until smooth. Measure out ½ cup sauce and set aside for cooking, reserving remaining sauce for serving.

5. Transfer pork to roasting pan and brush evenly with sauce for cooking. Cover pan tightly with foil and roast pork in oven until fork slips easily in and out of meat, 2 to 3 hours.

6. Remove pork from oven and let rest, still covered with foil, for 30 minutes. When cool enough to handle, unwrap pork and pull meat into thin shreds, discarding excess fat and gristle. Toss pork with reserved sauce and serve.

Tennessee Pulled Pork Sandwiches

Tennessee Pulled Pork Sandwiches

SERVES 8 WITH LEFTOVERS

WHY THIS RECIPE WORKS Inspired by a central Tennessee sandwich of pulled pork on cornmeal griddle cakes called hoecakes, we wanted pork shredded so finely that it resembled pâté. A combination of grill smoking and oven roasting brought our meat to a higher temperature for a softer pork butt roast. Instead of hand-shredding the meat, we used a stand mixer fitted with a paddle attachment to handily get a superfine shred. To keep the meat moist, we returned some of the pork juices to the shredded meat and served our sandwich with barbecue sauce just like they do at Papa KayJoe's (see "A 30-Year Journey to Pulled Pork Perfection," page 505).

In step 8, shred the pork while it's still hot. Leftover pork can be refrigerated for up to three days.

THE STATE OF GRILLING   503

Pork
- 1 (5- to 6-pound) bone-in pork butt roast, trimmed
- Kosher salt
- 2 cups wood chips
- 1 (13 by 9-inch) disposable aluminum roasting pan

Barbecue Sauce
- 1 cup ketchup
- ¼ cup cider vinegar
- ¼ cup water
- 2 tablespoons yellow mustard
- 1 tablespoon Worcestershire sauce
- 1 teaspoon granulated garlic
- 1 teaspoon pepper

- 1 recipe Hoecakes (recipe follows)
- Dill pickle chips
- Coleslaw

1. For the Pork Using sharp knife, cut 1-inch crosshatch pattern about ¼ inch deep in fat cap of roast, being careful not to cut into meat. Pat roast dry with paper towels. Place roast on large sheet of plastic wrap and rub 2 tablespoons salt over entire roast and into slits. Wrap tightly with plastic and refrigerate for 18 to 24 hours.

2. Just before grilling, soak wood chips in water for 15 minutes, then drain. Using large piece of heavy-duty aluminum foil, wrap soaked chips in foil packet and cut several vent holes in top.

3a. For a Charcoal Grill Open bottom vent completely. Light large chimney starter three-quarters filled with charcoal briquettes (4½ quarts). When top coals are partially covered with ash, pour evenly over half of grill. Place wood chip packet on coals. Set cooking grate in place, cover, and open lid vent completely. Heat grill until hot and wood chips are smoking, about 5 minutes.

3b. For a Gas Grill Remove cooking grate and place wood chip packet directly on primary burner. Set cooking grate in place, turn all burners to high, cover, and heat grill until hot and wood chips are smoking, about 15 minutes. Turn primary burner to medium-high and turn off other burner(s). (Adjust primary burner as needed to maintain grill temperature of 300 degrees.)

4. Unwrap pork and place fat side down in disposable pan. Place disposable pan on cooler side of grill. Cover grill (with lid vent directly over pork for charcoal) and cook until pork registers 120 degrees, about 2 hours. Thirty minutes before pork comes off grill, adjust oven rack to middle position and heat oven to 300 degrees.

5. Transfer disposable pan from grill to rimmed baking sheet. Cover pan tightly with foil and transfer to oven (still on sheet). Cook until fork inserted in pork meets little resistance and meat registers 210 degrees, about 3 hours.

6. For the Barbecue Sauce Meanwhile, combine all ingredients in medium saucepan and bring to boil over medium-high heat. Reduce heat to medium-low and simmer, whisking constantly, until slightly thickened, about 3 minutes. Transfer sauce to bowl and let cool completely.

7. Carefully remove foil from disposable pan (steam will escape). Remove blade bone from roast using tongs. Immediately transfer hot pork to bowl of stand mixer fitted with paddle attachment. Strain accumulated juices from pan through fine-mesh strainer set over separate bowl; discard solids.

8. Mix pork on low speed until meat is finely shredded, about 1½ minutes. Whisk pork juices to recombine, if separated, and add 1½ cups juices to shredded pork. Continue to mix pork on low speed until juices are incorporated, about 15 seconds longer. Season with salt to taste, adding more pork juices, if desired. Serve pork on hoecakes with barbecue sauce, pickles, and coleslaw.

Hoecakes

MAKES 16 HOECAKES

WHY THIS RECIPE WORKS To fully re-create our Papa KayJoe's experience in Centerville, Tennessee, we felt obligated to serve our Tennessee pulled pork on hoecakes. These cornmeal griddle cakes can be served on their own (with butter and syrup) or, in this case, as the perfect vehicle for a delicious barbecue sandwich. A loose batter with plenty of tangy buttermilk flavor gives the hoecakes a light texture, and the cornmeal makes them sturdy enough to hold up to a sandwich filling. Frying them in bacon fat adds a nice hit of smoky pork richness. Although our pulled pork is great on hamburger buns, we prefer to serve it on hoecakes.

Papa KayJoe's makes their hoecakes with bacon fat.

- 3 cups (15 ounces) white cornmeal
- 2 tablespoons sugar
- 2 teaspoons baking powder
- 1½ teaspoons table salt
- 2 cups buttermilk
- 2 large eggs
- 2 tablespoons bacon fat or vegetable oil

Hoecakes

1. Adjust oven rack to middle position and heat oven to 200 degrees. Set wire rack in rimmed baking sheet and place in oven. Whisk cornmeal, sugar, baking powder, and salt together in large bowl. Beat buttermilk and eggs together in separate bowl. Whisk buttermilk mixture into cornmeal mixture until combined.

2a. For a Skillet Heat 1 teaspoon fat in 12-inch nonstick skillet over medium heat until shimmering. Using level ¼-cup dry measuring cup, drop 3 evenly spaced scoops of batter into skillet, smoothing tops slightly if necessary.

2b. For a Griddle Heat 1 tablespoon fat on 400-degree nonstick griddle until shimmering. Using level ¼-cup dry measuring cup, drop 8 evenly spaced scoops of batter onto griddle, smoothing tops slightly if necessary.

3. Cook until small bubbles begin to appear on surface of cakes and edges are set, about 2 minutes. Flip and cook until second side is golden brown, about 2 minutes longer. Transfer hoecakes to prepared sheet in oven. Repeat with remaining fat and batter: 5 additional batches for skillet or 1 additional batch for griddle. Serve.

On The Road: A 30-Year Journey to Pulled Pork Perfection

Papa KayJoe's in Centerville, Tennessee, is a gray wooden building with a red tin roof at the end of a steep driveway. In the dining room, patrons tuck into Papa KayJoe's for their signature sandwiches—pulled pork on cornmeal griddle cakes—and share local news. Each morning owner Devin Pickard feeds armloads of hickory sticks into an outdoor furnace, where they slowly burn down to coals. Pickard then carries the hot embers to a nearby dirt-floored barbecue shack where a pair of cinder block pits sit waiting. At 11 a.m., Pickard lines up 24 heavily salted pork butts on the thick, black metal grate that sits over the pit and covers them with sheets of corrugated steel to trap the heat. The pork spends 6 to 8 hours on the grill, picking up the woodsy aroma of the smoldering hickory. After a day on the grill, the pork butts are packed into large aluminum roasting pans and transferred to a low oven where they'll spend the night. The next morning, Pickard slips on a pair of thick fireproof rubber gloves, picks out a pork butt, removes the blade bone and attacks the meat. In a clapping motion, he brings his fingertips together, pinching the pork; in less than a minute, the pork is in tiny shreds. He works in cupfuls of the juices that have accumulated in the roasting pan, moistening the pork with its own essence. Inside, Pickard's mother (Debbie) and daughter (Ruby) help pile the pork onto hot cornmeal griddle cakes (hoecakes) made to order with buttermilk and bacon fat. They'll produce dozens of these sandwiches today, and every day—including one for Pickard. "I would eat a barbecue sandwich every day of my life, that's how much I love it."

Grilled Pork Burgers

Grilled Sausages with Bell Peppers and Onions

Grilled Pork Burgers
SERVES 4

WHY THIS RECIPE WORKS Pork burgers can be notoriously dry and crumbly. To fix that problem, we looked toward meatballs for inspiration. They use a bread and milk mixture (called a panade) to stay moist, so we adopted that technique to keep our burgers juicy. Bumping up the seasoning with Worcestershire and soy sauces provided big flavor. After adding the pork to this flavorful mix, we formed patties and pressed divots into each to prevent the burgers from bulging on the grill. Cooking the patties over moderate heat kept them moist. We like these burgers topped with an easy horseradish sauce.

We developed this recipe with whole milk, but low-fat will work, too.

- 1 slice hearty white sandwich bread, torn into pieces
- 1 shallot, minced
- 2 tablespoons milk
- 4 teaspoons soy sauce
- 1 tablespoon Worcestershire sauce
- 1¼ teaspoons minced fresh thyme
- 1 teaspoon pepper
- ½ teaspoon table salt
- 1½ pounds 80 to 85 percent lean ground pork
- 4 hamburger buns, toasted and buttered
- 1 recipe Horseradish Burger Sauce (optional; recipe follows)

1. Combine bread, shallot, milk, soy sauce, Worcestershire, thyme, pepper, and salt in large bowl. Mash to paste with fork. Using your hands, add pork and mix until well combined.

2. Divide pork mixture into 4 equal balls. Flatten balls into even ¾-inch-thick patties, about 4 inches in diameter. Using your fingertips, press centers of patties down until about ½ inch thick, creating slight divot.

3a. For a Charcoal Grill Open bottom vent completely. Light large chimney starter filled with charcoal briquettes (6 quarts). When top coals are partially covered with ash, pour evenly over grill. Set cooking grate in place, cover, and open lid vent completely. Heat grill until hot, about 5 minutes.

3b. For a Gas Grill Turn all burners to high, cover, and heat grill until hot, about 15 minutes. Turn all burners to medium.

4. Clean and oil cooking grate. Grill patties (covered if using gas) until browned on first side, 5 to 7 minutes. Flip and continue to grill until burgers register 150 degrees, 5 to 7 minutes longer. Serve burgers on buns with sauce, if using.

Horseradish Burger Sauce
MAKES ½ CUP

Buy refrigerated prepared horseradish, not the shelf-stable kind, which contains preservatives and additives. Horseradish strength varies, so add it according to your taste.

- ¼ cup mayonnaise
- 2 tablespoons sour cream
- 1–2 tablespoons prepared horseradish
- 1 tablespoon whole-grain mustard
- 1 garlic clove, minced
-   Pinch sugar
-   Table salt and pepper
-   Hot sauce

Whisk mayonnaise, sour cream, horseradish, mustard, garlic, and sugar together in bowl. Season with salt, pepper, and hot sauce to taste.

Grilled Sausages with Bell Peppers and Onions

SERVES 6

WHY THIS RECIPE WORKS To get ballpark-worthy sausages with bell peppers and onions at home, we discovered that it's all about timing. We cooked the sausages gently on the cooler side of the grill until they were nearly done and then moved them to the hotter side to develop nice grill marks and a slight char. We used the microwave to parcook the vegetables and then transferred them to a disposable pan set on the hotter side of the grill, which mimicked a flat-top grill. The vegetables softened and browned just as the sausages finished cooking.

You can substitute hot Italian sausages for sweet, if desired. Minimal flare-ups are to be expected when grilling the sausages on the hotter side of the grill; they give the sausages color and flavor.

- 3 red bell peppers, stemmed, seeded, and cut into ¼-inch-wide strips
- 2 onions, halved and sliced ¼ inch thick
- 3 tablespoons distilled white vinegar
- 2 tablespoons sugar
- 1 tablespoon vegetable oil
- ½ teaspoon table salt
- ½ teaspoon pepper
- 1 (13 by 9-inch) disposable aluminum pan
- 2 pounds sweet Italian sausages
- 12 (6-inch) sub rolls (optional)

1. Toss bell peppers, onions, vinegar, sugar, oil, salt, and pepper together in bowl. Microwave, covered, until vegetables are just tender, about 6 minutes. Pour vegetable mixture and any accumulated juices into disposable pan.

2a. For a Charcoal Grill Open bottom vent completely. Light large chimney starter filled with charcoal briquettes (6 quarts). When top coals are partially covered with ash, pour evenly over half of grill. Set cooking grate in place, cover, and open lid vent completely. Heat grill until hot, about 5 minutes.

2b. For a Gas Grill Turn all burners to high, cover, and heat grill until hot, about 15 minutes. Leave primary burner on high and turn off other burner(s). (Adjust primary burner [or, if using three-burner grill, primary burner and second burner] as needed to maintain grill temperature between 375 and 400 degrees.)

3. Clean and oil cooking grate. Place disposable pan on hotter side of grill (over primary burner if using gas). Cover and cook for 20 minutes.

4. Place sausages on cooler side of grill and stir vegetable mixture; cover and cook for 8 minutes. Flip sausages and stir vegetable mixture again; cover and cook until sausages register 150 degrees and vegetables are softened and beginning to brown, about 8 minutes.

5. Transfer sausages to disposable pan with vegetables; slide disposable pan to cooler side of grill, then transfer sausages from disposable pan to hotter side of grill. Cook sausages, uncovered, turning often, until well browned and registering 160 degrees, 2 to 3 minutes (there may be flare-ups).

6. Return sausages to disposable pan with vegetables. Remove disposable pan from grill, tent with aluminum foil, and let rest for 5 minutes. Divide sausages and vegetables among rolls, if using. Serve.

Texas Thick-Cut Smoked Pork Chops

SERVES 8

WHY THIS RECIPE WORKS Big chops demand big flavor. Soaking thick pork chops in a salt and sugar brine promised juicy, seasoned meat that would brown beautifully on the grill. For true Hill Country flavor, we applied a rub of kosher salt, pepper, onion powder, and granulated garlic and smoked the chops over mesquite chips. Before firing up the grill, we readied a kicked-up barbecue sauce, rendering strips of bacon and stirring in grated onion and cider vinegar for a pop of acidity; liquid smoke added extra flavor and hot sauce introduced some heat. Brushing the chops with some sauce before serving doubled down on the pork's smoky goodness.

Each chop can easily serve two people. Grate the onion for the sauce on the large holes of a box grater. If you'd like to use wood chunks instead of wood chips when using a charcoal grill, substitute two medium chunks, soaked in water for 1 hour, for the wood chip packet.

Texas Thick-Cut Smoked Pork Chops

Pork
- Kosher salt and pepper
- 3 tablespoons sugar
- 4 (18- to 20-ounce) bone-in pork rib chops, 2 inches thick
- 2 teaspoons onion powder
- 2 teaspoons granulated garlic
- 2 cups mesquite wood chips

Barbecue Sauce
- 2 slices bacon
- ¼ cup grated onion
- Kosher salt and pepper
- ¾ cup cider vinegar
- 1¼ cups chicken broth
- 1 cup ketchup
- 2 tablespoons hot sauce
- ½ teaspoon liquid smoke

1. For the Pork Dissolve 6 tablespoons salt and sugar in 1½ quarts cold water in large container. Submerge chops in brine, cover, and refrigerate for 1 hour. Combine onion powder, granulated garlic, 1½ tablespoons salt, and 2 tablespoons pepper in bowl; set aside.

2. For the Barbecue Sauce Cook bacon in medium saucepan over medium heat until fat begins to render and bacon begins to brown, 4 to 6 minutes. Add onion and ¼ teaspoon salt and cook until softened, 2 to 4 minutes. Stir in vinegar, scraping up any browned bits, and cook until slightly thickened, about 2 minutes.

3. Stir in broth, ketchup, hot sauce, liquid smoke, and ¼ teaspoon pepper. Bring to simmer and cook until slightly thickened, about 15 minutes, stirring occasionally. Discard bacon and season with salt and pepper to taste. Remove from heat, cover, and keep warm.

4. Just before grilling, soak wood chips in water for 15 minutes, then drain. Using large piece of heavy-duty aluminum foil, wrap soaked chips in 8 by 4½-inch foil packet. (Make sure chips do not poke holes in sides or bottom of packet.) Cut 2 evenly spaced 2-inch slits in top of packet. Remove chops from brine and pat dry with paper towels. Season chops all over with reserved spice mixture.

5a. For a Charcoal Grill Open bottom vent completely. Light large chimney starter three-quarters filled with charcoal briquettes (4½ quarts). When top coals are partially covered with ash, pour evenly over half of grill.

Place wood chip packet on coals. Set cooking grate in place, cover, and open lid vent completely. Heat grill until hot and wood chips are smoking, about 5 minutes.

5b. For a Gas Grill Remove cooking grate and place wood chip packet directly on primary burner. Set grate in place, turn all burners to high, cover, and heat grill until hot and wood chips are smoking, about 15 minutes. Leave primary burner on medium-high and turn off other burner(s). (Adjust primary burner as needed to maintain grill temperature around 325 degrees.)

6. Clean and oil cooking grate. Arrange chops on cooler side of grill with bone ends toward fire. Cook, covered (positioning lid vent over chops if using charcoal), until chops register 140 degrees, 45 to 50 minutes, flipping halfway through cooking.

7. Transfer chops to platter, tent with foil, and let rest for 10 minutes. Brush chops generously with warm sauce and serve, passing remaining sauce separately.

Smoked Double-Thick Pork Chops

SERVES 6 TO 8

Smoked Double-Thick Pork Chops

WHY THIS RECIPE WORKS Most grilled double-thick pork chop recipes result in a charred exterior and raw meat, or gray meat that tastes steamed. We wanted our pork chops to have great taste and tenderness. Cooking our pork chops over indirect heat made for juicy and tender meat. We used wood chips on the grill to infuse the pork with a nice level of smoke flavor. Coating the double-thick pork chops with a rub of brown sugar and potent herbs and spices helped produce a flavorful crust, and quick grilling over hot coals at the end of cooking gave the crust a crisp texture and rich mahogany color.

We prefer blade chops, which have more fat to prevent drying out on the grill, but leaner loin chops will also work. Two medium wood chunks, soaked in water for 1 hour, can be substituted for the wood chips on a charcoal grill. These chops are huge. You may want to slice the meat off the bone before serving.

- 1/4 cup packed dark brown sugar
- 1 tablespoon ground fennel
- 1 tablespoon ground cumin
- 1 tablespoon ground coriander
- 1 tablespoon paprika
- 1 teaspoon table salt
- 1 teaspoon pepper
- 4 (1 1/4- to 1 1/2-pound) bone-in blade-cut pork chops, about 2 inches thick, trimmed
- 2 cups wood chips, soaked in water for 15 minutes and drained

1. Combine sugar, fennel, cumin, coriander, paprika, salt, and pepper in bowl. Pat pork chops dry with paper towels and rub them evenly with spice mixture. Wrap chops in plastic wrap and refrigerate for at least 1 hour or up to 24 hours. Using large piece of heavy-duty aluminum foil, wrap soaked chips in foil packet and cut several vent holes in top.

2a. For a Charcoal Grill Open bottom vent halfway. Light large chimney starter filled with charcoal briquettes (6 quarts). When top coals are partially covered with ash, pour into pile on 1 side of grill. Place wood chip packet on coals. Set cooking grate in place, cover, and open lid vent halfway. Heat grill until hot and wood chips are smoking, about 5 minutes.

THE STATE OF GRILLING   509

2b. For a Gas Grill Place wood chip packet directly on primary burner. Turn all burners to high, cover, and heat grill until hot and wood chips are smoking, about 15 minutes. Turn primary burner to medium and turn other burner(s) off. (Adjust primary burner as needed to maintain grill temperature around 275 degrees.)

3. Clean and oil cooking grate. Place pork chops on cool side of grill with bone sides facing hot side of grill. Cover (positioning lid vent over pork if using charcoal) and cook until meat registers 145 degrees, 50 minutes to 1 hour. Slide chops directly over fire (hot side on gas grill) and cook, uncovered, until well browned, about 4 minutes, flipping chops halfway through grilling. Transfer to platter and let rest for 20 minutes. Serve.

Grilled Thin-Cut Pork Chops

SERVES 4 TO 6

Grilled Thin-Cut Pork Chops

WHY THIS RECIPE WORKS To ensure that our thin-cut pork chops would brown quickly on the grill, we partially froze them to eliminate excess moisture from the exterior. Salting them first kept them from drying out and let us skip brining. A combination of butter and brown sugar spread over the chops resulted in a flavorful golden-brown crust when they came off the grill. A chive-mustard butter added even more flavor to the finished chops.

To prevent the chops from curling, cut two slits 2 inches apart through the fat around the outside of each raw chop.

- 6 bone-in rib or center-cut pork chops, about ½ inch thick, trimmed
- ¾ teaspoon table salt
- 4 tablespoons unsalted butter, softened, divided
- 1 teaspoon packed brown sugar
- ½ teaspoon pepper
- 1 teaspoon minced fresh chives
- ½ teaspoon Dijon mustard
- ½ teaspoon grated lemon zest

1. Set wire rack in rimmed baking sheet. Pat chops dry with paper towels. Cut 2 slits, about 2 inches apart, through outer layer of fat and silverskin on each chop. Rub chops with salt. Arrange on prepared rack and freeze until chops are firm, at least 30 minutes but no more than 1 hour. Combine 2 tablespoons butter, sugar, and pepper in small bowl; set aside. Mix remaining 2 tablespoons butter, chives, mustard, and zest in second small bowl and refrigerate until firm, about 15 minutes. (Butter-chive mixture can be refrigerated, covered, for 1 day.)

2a. For a Charcoal Grill Open bottom vent completely. Light large chimney starter filled with charcoal briquettes (6 quarts). When top coals are partially covered with ash, pour evenly over grill. Set cooking grate in place, cover, and open lid vent completely. Heat grill until hot, about 5 minutes.

2b. For a Gas Grill Turn all burners to high, cover, and heat grill until hot, about 15 minutes.

3. Pat chops dry with paper towels. Spread softened butter-sugar mixture evenly over both sides of each chop. Grill, covered, over hot fire until well browned and meat registers 145 degrees, 6 to 8 minutes, flipping chops halfway through grilling. Transfer chops to platter and top with chilled butter-chive mixture. Tent with aluminum foil and let rest for 5 minutes. Serve.

Spicy Grilled Thin-Cut Pork Chops with Cilantro and Lime

Substitute 1½ teaspoons chili-garlic sauce, 1 teaspoon minced fresh cilantro, and ½ teaspoon grated lime zest for chives, mustard, and lemon zest.

Grilled Thin-Cut Pork Chops with Thyme and Ginger

Substitute 1 teaspoon grated fresh ginger, ½ teaspoon minced fresh thyme, and ½ teaspoon grated orange zest for chives, mustard, and lemon zest.

Grilled Thin-Cut Pork Chops with Olive Tapenade

Substitute 1½ teaspoons black olive tapenade and ½ teaspoon minced fresh oregano for chives and mustard.

Monroe County–Style Pork Chops

SERVES 4

Monroe County–Style Pork Chops

WHY THIS RECIPE WORKS The paper-thin pork "steaks" flash-grilled over hickory coals in Monroe County, Kentucky, stay moist and flavorful thanks in part to a healthy dose of a fiery crimson-colored sauce (ordering it "dipped" means the meat is dunked in the lip-numbing sauce). For our version of this spicy, smoky, and intoxicating delicacy, we used bone-in blade pork chops (thin enough to not require at-home slicing) with just enough fat to keep the pork tender while grilling over a screaming-hot fire. For our "dip," we browned butter to bring out its nuttiness and dialed back the cayenne pepper, delivering a flavor-packed yet balanced heat.

Thin pork chops buckle during cooking. To prevent this, we snip the fat surrounding the loin portion of each chop. In Monroe County, these chops are considered finger food.

- 2 tablespoons kosher salt
- 2 tablespoons pepper
- 1 tablespoon paprika
- ¾ teaspoon cayenne pepper
- 1 tablespoon cornstarch
- 8 (6-ounce) bone-in blade-cut pork chops, ½ inch thick, trimmed
- 8 tablespoons unsalted butter
- ½ cup distilled white vinegar

1. Combine salt, pepper, paprika, and cayenne in bowl. Transfer 2 tablespoons spice mixture to separate bowl and stir in cornstarch. Using kitchen shears, snip interior portion of fat surrounding loin muscle of each chop in 2 places, about 2 inches apart. Season chops all over with cornstarch mixture. Reserve remaining spice mixture for sauce.

2. Heat butter in small saucepan over medium-low heat. Cook, swirling pan constantly, until butter turns dark golden brown and has nutty aroma, 4 to 5 minutes. Add reserved spice mixture and cook until fragrant, about 30 seconds. Carefully add vinegar (mixture will bubble up), bring to quick simmer, then remove from heat. Let cool completely, but do not let butter solidify.

3a. For a Charcoal Grill Open bottom vent completely. Light large chimney starter mounded with charcoal briquettes (7 quarts). When top coals are partially covered with ash, pour evenly over grill. Set cooking grate in place, cover, and open lid vent completely. Heat grill until hot, about 5 minutes.

3b. For a Gas Grill Turn all burners to high, cover, and heat grill until hot, about 15 minutes. Leave all burners on high.

4. Clean and oil cooking grate. Place chops on grill and cook without moving them (covered if using gas) until well charred on first side, 3 to 5 minutes. Flip chops and continue to cook on second side until well charred and meat registers 140 degrees, 3 to 5 minutes longer.

5. Transfer chops to rimmed baking sheet. Pour sauce over chops, flipping to evenly coat. Tent with aluminum foil and let rest for 5 minutes, flipping chops halfway through resting. Serve.

On the Road: All About That Dip

Barbecue in Monroe County, Kentucky, is known (or rather not known) for being a little different. Take the 'cue found at Collins Bar-B-Q in Gamaliel. There, you won't find the slow-smoked fall-apart-tender hunk of pork prevalent at most Southern barbecue joints. Instead, you'll find slices of bone-in pork shoulder, cut thin on the butcher's band saw and quickly grilled over hickory coals.

The sauce, which doubles as the basting liquid, is atypical, too. Known locally as "dip"—basting or saucing is thus "dipping"—it's more spicy than traditional barbecue sauce. Made with lard, butter, vinegar, and black and cayenne peppers, it's thin, oily, and potent. It comes together in a tall pot that's left to sit on the back of the stove where the oily portion naturally rises to the top and the vinegary spice-laden part sinks to the bottom. Since much of the capsaicin in the peppers is oil-soluble, that's where most of the heat resides. If you like your shoulder spicy, the pit master will dip from the top of the pot; less spicy and they'll dive the ladle to the bottom, where it collects more of the spent pepper and sharp vinegar. It's as much about the dip as it is the pork. The shoulder is mopped with dip on the grill, smothered with dip on your plate, and then served with more dip on the side for dunking. And while this is essentially a bone-in pork chop, this is 100 percent finger food. Tear off a piece, dip, eat, repeat.

St. Louis BBQ Pork Steaks

SERVES 4

WHY THIS RECIPE WORKS St. Louis BBQ pork steaks are little-known in other parts of America, but in St. Louis, they are so popular that pork steaks are on permanent sale in family packs at the supermarket. We found there was no substitute for pork steak, so the only option was to cut our own. We ordered a boneless Boston butt and cut it in half crosswise, then turned each piece on end to slice 1-inch-thick steaks. Inspired by a test kitchen recipe for brats and beer, we used a method of sear, simmer, sear again. This untraditional process gives the steaks a nice char, candy-like edges, and succulent, slightly chewy interiors.

Boneless pork butt is also labeled Boston butt. If pork steaks are available, use them and increase the cooking time in the sauce to 1 to 1½ hours. We use Budweiser in this recipe, since it's made in St. Louis, but any mild-tasting beer will do.

Spice Rub and Pork Steaks

- 1 tablespoon packed brown sugar
- 1 tablespoon paprika
- 2 teaspoons dry mustard
- 2 teaspoons pepper
- 1 teaspoon onion powder
- 1 teaspoon garlic powder
- 1 teaspoon ground cumin
- 1 teaspoon table salt
- ¼ teaspoon cayenne pepper
- 1 (5- to 6-pound) boneless pork butt roast, sliced crosswise, trimmed, and each half cut into three or four 1-inch-thick steaks

Barbecue Sauce

- 2 cups beer
- 1½ cups ketchup
- ¼ cup Heinz 57 Steak Sauce
- ¼ cup packed dark brown sugar
- 2 tablespoons cider vinegar
- 2 tablespoons Worcestershire sauce
- 1 teaspoon garlic powder
- 1 teaspoon hot sauce
- 1 teaspoon liquid smoke
- 1 (13 by 9-inch) disposable aluminum roasting pan

1. For the Spice Rub and Pork Steaks Combine sugar, paprika, dry mustard, pepper, onion powder, garlic powder, cumin, salt, and cayenne in bowl. Pat pork steaks dry with paper towels and rub them evenly with spice mixture. Wrap pork in plastic wrap and refrigerate for at least 1 hour or up to 24 hours.

2. For the Barbecue Sauce Whisk all ingredients together in bowl and transfer to disposable pan.

3a. For a Charcoal Grill Open bottom vent halfway. Light large chimney starter filled with charcoal briquettes (6 quarts). When top coals are partially covered with ash, pour evenly over grill. Set cooking grate in place, cover, and open lid vent halfway. Heat grill until hot, about 5 minutes.

3b. For a Gas Grill Turn all burners to high, cover, and heat grill until hot, about 15 minutes. Leave primary burner on high and turn other burner(s) off. (Adjust primary burner as needed to maintain grill temperature around 350 degrees.)

4. Clean and oil cooking grate. Place pork steaks on hot side of grill. Cook (covered if using gas) until well browned on both sides, about 10 minutes, flipping steaks halfway through grilling.

5. Transfer pork steaks to sauce in pan and coat thoroughly. Cover pan with aluminum foil and place on grill. Cover (positioning lid vent over pan if using charcoal) and cook steaks until fork-tender and they register 190 degrees, 45 minutes to 1 hour. Remove steaks from pan and grill until lightly charred around edges, 4 to 8 minutes, flipping steaks halfway through grilling.

6. Transfer steaks to serving platter, tent loosely with foil, and let rest for 10 minutes. Skim excess fat from sauce and serve with steaks.

St. Louis BBQ Pork Steaks

Making Pork Steaks

1. Slice pork crosswise in half and remove any large pieces of fat.

2. Rotate and stand each half of pork butt on its cut end and cut each half into three or four 1-inch-thick steaks.

THE STATE OF GRILLING   513

Chinese-Style Glazed Pork Tenderloin

SERVES 4 TO 6

WHY THIS RECIPE WORKS For an easy take on Chinese-style glazed and charred pork, we opted for pork tenderloin, which cooks quickly over a hot fire. Butterflying and pounding the meat gave us maximum surface area for our glaze. A combination of apricot preserves and ketchup flavored with hoisin, fresh ginger, sesame oil, sherry, garlic, and five-spice powder made a salty-sweet sauce that acted as both marinade and glaze. Continuously flipping and glazing the pork created a charred, caramelized exterior.

Leftover pork makes an excellent addition to fried rice or noodle soup.

- 2 (12- to 16-ounce) pork tenderloins, trimmed
- ½ cup soy sauce
- ½ cup apricot preserves
- ¼ cup hoisin sauce
- ¼ cup dry sherry
- 2 tablespoons grated fresh ginger
- 1 tablespoon toasted sesame oil
- 2 garlic cloves, minced
- 1 teaspoon five-spice powder
- 1 teaspoon pepper
- ¼ cup ketchup
- 1 tablespoon molasses
- 2 teaspoons vegetable oil

1. Lay tenderloins on cutting board with long side running parallel to counter edge. Cut horizontally down length of each tenderloin, stopping ½ inch from edge so tenderloin remains intact. Working with one at a time, open up tenderloins, place between 2 sheets of plastic wrap, and pound to ¾-inch thickness.

2. Combine soy sauce, preserves, hoisin, sherry, ginger, sesame oil, garlic, five-spice powder, and pepper in bowl. Reserve ¾ cup marinade. Place pork in large zipper-lock bag and pour remaining marinade into bag with pork. Seal bag, turn to coat, and refrigerate for at least 30 minutes or up to 4 hours.

3. Combine reserved marinade, ketchup, and molasses in small saucepan. Cook over medium heat until syrupy and reduced to ¾ cup, 3 to 5 minutes. Reserve ¼ cup glaze for glazing cooked pork.

4a. For a Charcoal Grill Open bottom vent completely. Light large chimney starter filled with charcoal briquettes (6 quarts). When top coals are partially covered with ash, pour evenly over grill. Set cooking grate in place, cover, and open lid vent completely. Heat grill until hot, about 5 minutes.

4b. For a Gas Grill Turn all burners to high, cover, and heat grill until hot, about 15 minutes. Turn all burners to medium-high.

5. Clean and oil cooking grate. Pat pork dry with paper towels, then rub with vegetable oil. Grill pork (covered if using gas) until lightly charred on first side, about 2 minutes. Flip and brush grilled side of pork evenly with 2 tablespoons glaze. Continue grilling until lightly charred on second side, about 2 minutes. Flip and brush evenly with 2 more tablespoons glaze. Repeat flipping and glazing twice more, until pork registers 140 degrees and is thickly glazed, about 4 minutes longer. Transfer pork to cutting board and brush with reserved glaze. Tent loosely with aluminum foil and let rest for 5 minutes. Slice and serve.

Chinese-Style Barbecued Spareribs

SERVES 6

WHY THIS RECIPE WORKS We began our Chinese-Style Barbecued Spareribs by removing the tough membrane on the underside of the ribs. Instead of cooking the ribs on the grill the entire time, we found that cooking them in the sauce in the oven and then finishing them on the grill allowed for deeply seasoned Chinese-style ribs and eliminated the need to marinate them. Since the smoke from wood chips was overpowering, we replaced the wood chips with orange spice or Earl Grey tea bags soaked in water, wrapped in foil, and placed on the hot coals for a mellow, smoky flavor that complemented the seasonings in the sauce.

Full-size spareribs are fatty; plus, they're too large to fit on the grill. If you can't find St. Louis–style spareribs (which have been trimmed of the brisket bone and surrounding meat), substitute baby back ribs and begin to check for doneness after 1 hour on the grill. Cover the edges of the ribs loosely with foil if they begin to burn while grilling.

- 2 (2½- to 3-pound) racks St. Louis–style spareribs, trimmed
- 8 black tea bags, preferably orange spice or Earl Grey
- 1½ cups ketchup
- 1 cup soy sauce
- 1 cup hoisin sauce
- 1 cup sugar
- ½ cup dry sherry
- 6 garlic cloves, minced
- 2 tablespoons grated fresh ginger
- 2 teaspoons toasted sesame oil
- 1½ teaspoons cayenne pepper
- 1 (13 by 9-inch) disposable aluminum roasting pan
- 1 cup red currant jelly

1. To remove chewy membrane from ribs, loosen it with tip of paring knife and, with aid of paper towel, pull it off slowly in 1 big piece. Cut rib racks in half. Cover tea bags with water in small bowl and soak for 5 minutes. Squeeze water from tea bags. Using large piece of heavy-duty aluminum foil, wrap tea bags in foil packet and cut several vent holes in top.

2. Adjust oven rack to middle position and heat oven to 300 degrees. Whisk 1 cup ketchup, soy sauce, hoisin sauce, sugar, sherry, garlic, ginger, sesame oil, and cayenne in large bowl; reserve ½ cup for glaze. Arrange ribs, meaty side down, in disposable pan and pour remaining ketchup mixture over ribs. Cover pan tightly with foil and cook until fat has rendered and meat begins to pull away from bones, 2 to 2½ hours. Transfer ribs to large plate. Pour pan juices into fat separator. Let liquid settle and reserve 1 cup defatted pan juices.

3. Simmer reserved pan juices in medium saucepan over medium-high heat until reduced to ½ cup, about 5 minutes. Stir in jelly, reserved ketchup mixture, and remaining ½ cup ketchup and simmer until reduced to 2 cups, 10 to 12 minutes. Reserve one-third of glaze for serving.

4a. For a Charcoal Grill Open bottom vent completely. Light large chimney starter filled with charcoal briquettes (6 quarts). When top coals are partially covered with ash, pour evenly over half of grill. Place tea packet on coals. Set cooking grate in place, cover, and open lid vent completely. Heat grill until hot and tea is smoking, about 5 minutes.

4b. For a Gas Grill Place tea packet directly on primary burner. Turn all burners to high, cover, and heat grill until hot and tea is smoking, about 15 minutes. Leave primary burner on high and turn other burner(s) off.

5. Clean and oil cooking grate. Arrange ribs, meaty side down, on cool side of grill and cook, covered, until ribs are smoky and edges begin to char, about 30 minutes.

Chinese-Style Glazed Pork Tenderloin

Chinese-Style Barbecued Spareribs

6. Brush ribs with glaze, flip, rotate, and brush again. Cover and cook, brushing with glaze every 30 minutes, until ribs are fully tender and glaze is browned and sticky, 1 to 1½ hours. Transfer ribs to cutting board, tent with foil, and let rest for 10 minutes. Serve with reserved glaze.

To Make Ahead Ribs and glaze can be prepared through step 3 up to 2 days in advance. Once ribs are cool, wrap tightly in foil and refrigerate. Transfer glaze to microwave-safe bowl, cover with plastic wrap, and refrigerate. Before proceeding with step 4, allow ribs to stand at room temperature for 1 hour. Before proceeding with step 6, microwave glaze until warm, about 1 minute.

Barbecued Country-Style Ribs

SERVES 4 TO 6

WHY THIS RECIPE WORKS Boneless country-style ribs present several cooking challenges. Each piece not only varies wildly from the next, but is also a mishmash of lean white meat and rich dark meat. Unfortunately, if the ribs are cooked to optimize the white meat, then the dark meat stays tough, and if they are cooked to optimize the dark meat, the white meat turns dry. To even out the cooking, we brined the ribs so that the white meat would stay juicy and pounded the ribs to an even ¾-inch thickness to "break down" the fattier dark meat. As for flavor, a double layer of barbecue spice and sauce and a quick smoke on the grill worked wonders.

For easier pounding, cut any ribs that are longer than 5 inches in half crosswise.

- 1 tablespoon table salt
- 2 pounds boneless country-style pork ribs, trimmed
- ¾ cup packed dark brown sugar
- 2 tablespoons chili powder
- 2 tablespoons paprika
- 1 tablespoon dry mustard
- 1 tablespoon onion powder
- ¾ teaspoon pepper
- ¼ teaspoon cayenne pepper
- 6 tablespoons ketchup
- 1 tablespoon cider vinegar
- ¼ cup wood chips, soaked in water for 15 minutes and drained

1. Dissolve salt in 2 cups cold water in large container. Place ribs, cut side down, between 2 sheets of plastic wrap and pound to ¾ inch thickness. Submerge pork in brine, cover, and refrigerate for 30 minutes to 1 hour.

2. Combine sugar, chili powder, paprika, dry mustard, onion powder, pepper, and cayenne in shallow dish. Transfer half of mixture to bowl and stir in ketchup and vinegar; set aside.

3. Remove pork from brine and pat dry with paper towels. Dredge pork in remaining spice mixture and transfer to plate. Using large piece of heavy-duty aluminum foil, wrap soaked chips in foil packet and cut several vent holes in top.

4a. For a Charcoal Grill Open bottom vent halfway. Light large chimney starter filled with charcoal briquettes (6 quarts). When top coals are partially covered with ash, pour evenly over half of grill. Place wood chip packet on coals. Set cooking grate in place, cover, and open lid vent halfway. Heat grill until hot and wood chips are smoking, about 5 minutes.

4b. For a Gas Grill Place wood chip packet directly on primary burner. Turn all burners to high, cover, and heat grill until hot and wood chips are smoking, about 15 minutes. Leave primary burner on high and turn other burner(s) off.

5. Clean and oil cooking grate. Place pork on cool side of grill, cover (positioning lid vent over meat if using charcoal), and cook until meat registers 125 degrees, 3 to 5 minutes. Brush pork with ketchup mixture and grill, brushed side down, over hot side of grill until lightly charred, 2 to 3 minutes. Brush second side of pork, flip, and grill until lightly charred and meat registers 145 degrees, 2 to 3 minutes. Transfer pork to platter, tent loosely with foil, and let rest for 5 to 10 minutes. Serve.

South Dakota Corncob-Smoked Ribs

SERVES 4 TO 6

WHY THIS RECIPE WORKS Corncob smoking is a South Dakota specialty and pit master Larry Mart is its undisputed king. It gives meat a subtle smokiness hardwoods can't match. For barbecued ribs with mild, nutty sweetness but without a barbecuing rig, we layered charcoal on our grill with fresh corncobs (with the kernels removed) and a foil packet of cornmeal. The cornmeal gave the ribs an initial blast of smoky flavor, and the fresh cobs offered long-lasting smoke and a nutty aroma. We basted the ribs with a simple ketchup-based barbecue sauce with plenty of garlic and some celery seeds for sticky, sweet ribs that we couldn't get enough of.

A gas grill can't do these corncob ribs justice, so please use charcoal. To use up some of the leftover corn, try our recipe for Sweet Corn Spoonbread (page 376).

Sauce
- 1 cup ketchup
- ¼ cup water
- 1 tablespoon pepper
- 1 tablespoon onion powder
- 1 tablespoon Worcestershire sauce
- 1 tablespoon light corn syrup
- 1 tablespoon granulated garlic
- 2 teaspoons celery seeds
- ½ teaspoon liquid smoke

Ribs
- 5 tablespoons packed light brown sugar
- 1 teaspoon table salt
- ½ teaspoon pepper
- 2 (2½- to 3-pound) racks baby back pork ribs, trimmed and membrane removed
- 1 cup cornmeal
- 6 corncobs, kernels removed and reserved for another use
- 1 (13 by 9-inch) disposable aluminum roasting pan

1. For the Sauce Whisk all ingredients together in medium bowl; set aside.

2. For the Ribs Combine sugar, salt, and pepper in bowl. Pat ribs dry with paper towels and rub with sugar mixture; set aside. Using large piece of heavy-duty aluminum foil, wrap cornmeal in foil packet and cut several vent holes in top.

3. Open bottom vents of charcoal grill halfway. Place disposable pan on 1 side of grill and fill pan with 2 quarts water. Arrange 3 quarts unlit charcoal briquettes on opposite side of grill. Place cobs on top of unlit briquettes. Light large chimney starter filled halfway with charcoal briquettes (3 quarts). When top coals are partially covered with ash, pour over cobs and unlit briquettes. Place cornmeal packet on coals. Set cooking grate in place, cover, and open lid vent halfway. Heat grill until hot and cornmeal is smoking, about 5 minutes.

Barbecued Country-Style Ribs

South Dakota Corncob-Smoked Ribs

4. Clean and oil cooking grate. Place ribs, meat side up, on cool part of grill opposite coals. Cover, positioning lid vent over ribs, and cook until ribs are deep red and tender, 3½ to 4 hours, rotating and switching ribs every hour. (Do not flip ribs.) During last 30 minutes of cooking, baste ribs every 10 minutes, rotating and switching ribs each time. Transfer ribs to carving board, tent loosely with foil, and let rest for 15 to 20 minutes. Cut ribs in between bones. Serve, passing remaining sauce separately.

Grilled Mustard-Glazed Pork Loin

SERVES 6 TO 8

WHY THIS RECIPE WORKS Two surefire ways to dress up a pork roast are to give it a flavorful, deeply caramelized crust on the grill and serve it with a savory-sweet mustard glaze. Our mustard-glazed pork loin has the best of both worlds. Leaving our roast untrimmed added moisture and flavor—and scoring the fat kept it from tasting too fatty. For the mustard glaze, apple jelly was a perfect complement to the spicy crunch of grainy mustard, and both married well with the other glaze ingredients. We applied the glaze before, during, and after grilling for the best flavor infusion.

Dijon and yellow mustards also work well in the glaze, but make certain to use apple jelly, not apple butter. Look for a pork roast with about ¼ inch of fat on top and tie the roast at 1-inch intervals to ensure an even shape.

- ½ cup whole-grain mustard
- 6 tablespoons apple jelly
- 2 tablespoons packed dark brown sugar
- 2 tablespoons extra-virgin olive oil
- 1 large garlic clove, minced
- 2 teaspoons minced fresh thyme
- ¾ teaspoon pepper
- ½ teaspoon table salt
- 1 boneless pork loin roast (2½ to 3 pounds), fat scored lightly, tied at 1-inch intervals

1. Whisk mustard, jelly, sugar, oil, garlic, thyme, pepper, and salt together in bowl. Measure out ⅔ cup sauce and set aside for cooking; reserve remaining sauce for serving. Before grilling, pat pork loin dry with paper towels and coat it evenly with ⅓ cup sauce for cooking.

2a. For a Charcoal Grill Open bottom vent halfway. Light large chimney starter filled with charcoal briquettes (6 quarts). When top coals are partially covered with ash, pour evenly over half of grill. Set cooking grate in place, cover, and open lid vent halfway. Heat grill until hot, about 5 minutes.

2b. For a Gas Grill Turn all the burners to high, cover, and heat grill until hot, about 15 minutes. Leave primary burner on high and turn other burner(s) off. (Adjust primary burner as needed to maintain grill temperature around 350 degrees.)

3. Clean and oil cooking grate. Place pork loin on hot side of grill. Cook (covered if using gas) until well browned on all sides, 12 to 15 minutes, turning as needed.

4. Flip pork loin fat side up and slide to cool side of grill. Brush pork with 2 tablespoons sauce for cooking. Cover (positioning lid vent over pork if using charcoal) and continue to cook until meat registers 140 degrees, 25 to 40 minutes longer, brushing every 10 minutes with remaining sauce for cooking.

5. Transfer pork loin to carving board, tent loosely with aluminum foil, and let rest for 15 minutes. Remove twine, cut meat into ¼-inch-thick slices, and transfer to serving platter. Whisk any accumulated juices into reserved sauce, spoon over meat, and serve.

Grilled Mustard-Glazed Pork Loin

Grilled Bone-In Leg of Lamb with Charred-Scallion Sauce

SERVES 10 TO 12

WHY THIS RECIPE WORKS The figure of this grand cut is iconic, but when grilled, its tapered shape can result in a wide range of doneness. To avoid this, we set up a half-grill fire—all the briquettes arranged on one side of the grill—to give us two heat zones. We started the lamb on the cooler side before searing it over the hotter side. This both minimized flare-ups and ensured a charred exterior and a lovely medium-rare interior. We smeared a powerful paste of fresh thyme, dried oregano, garlic, lemon zest, salt, and pepper onto the exterior and refrigerated the leg overnight to fully season the meat. For a beautiful sauce, we stirred charred scallions into a mixture of olive oil, red wine vinegar, parsley, and garlic.

The seasoned meat must be refrigerated for at least 12 hours before cooking. For an accurate temperature reading in step 5, insert your thermometer into the thickest part of the leg until you hit bone, then pull it about ½ inch away from the bone.

Lamb
- 12 garlic cloves, minced
- 2 tablespoons vegetable oil
- 2 tablespoons kosher salt
- 1½ tablespoons pepper
- 1 tablespoon fresh thyme leaves
- 1 tablespoon dried oregano
- 2 teaspoons finely grated lemon zest
- 1 teaspoon ground coriander
- 1 (8-pound) bone-in leg of lamb, trimmed

Scallion Sauce
- ¾ cup extra-virgin olive oil
- ¼ cup chopped fresh parsley
- 1 tablespoon red wine vinegar
- 2 garlic cloves, minced
- 1 teaspoon pepper
- ¾ teaspoon kosher salt
- ¼ teaspoon red pepper flakes
- 12 scallions, trimmed

1. For the Lamb Combine garlic, oil, salt, pepper, thyme, oregano, lemon zest, and coriander in bowl. Place lamb on rimmed baking sheet and rub all over with garlic paste. Cover with plastic wrap and refrigerate for at least 12 hours or up to 24 hours.

2. For the Scallion Sauce Combine oil, parsley, vinegar, garlic, pepper, salt, and pepper flakes in bowl; set aside.

3a. For a Charcoal Grill Open bottom vent completely. Light large chimney starter filled with charcoal briquettes (6 quarts). When top coals are partially covered with ash, pour evenly over half of grill. Set cooking grate in place, cover, and open lid vent completely. Heat grill until hot, about 5 minutes.

3b. For a Gas Grill Turn all burners to high, cover, and heat grill until hot, about 15 minutes. Leave primary burner on high and turn off other burner(s). (Adjust primary burner [or, if using 3-burner grill, primary burner and second burner] as needed to maintain grill temperature between 350 and 400 degrees.)

4. Clean and oil cooking grate. Place scallions on hotter side of grill. Cook (covered if using gas) until lightly charred on both sides, about 3 minutes per side. Transfer scallions to plate.

Grilled Bone-In Leg of Lamb with Charred-Scallion Sauce

5. Uncover lamb and place fat side up on cooler side of grill, parallel to fire. (If using gas, it may be necessary to angle thicker end of lamb toward hotter side of grill to fit.) Cover grill (position lid vent directly over lamb if using charcoal) and cook until thickest part of meat (½ inch from bone) registers 120 degrees, 1¼ hours to 1¾ hours.

6. Transfer lamb, fat side down, to hotter side of grill. Cook (covered if using gas) until fat side is well browned, 7 to 9 minutes. Transfer lamb to carving board, fat side up, and tent with aluminum foil. Let rest for 30 minutes.

7. Cut scallions into ½-inch pieces, then stir into reserved oil mixture. Season sauce with salt and pepper to taste. Slice lamb thin and serve with sauce.

Pomegranate-Glazed Grilled Lamb Chops

SERVES 4 TO 6

Pomegranate-Glazed Grilled Lamb Chops

WHY THIS RECIPE WORKS This recipe draws inspiration from the flavors of the Middle East. We achieved deeper flavor by seasoning individual lamb chops rather than a whole rack. The sugar in our seasoning mix, combined with the sweet and acidic pomegranate molasses, helped the chops pick up incredible char from the hot grill. When using charcoal, we loved how the concentrated heat from using only half the grill boosted the charring while yielding perfect, medium-rare chops. Though these chops were beautiful enough when brushed with a final coat of pomegranate molasses right off the grill, they are even better served with a mixture of fresh mint, parsley, garlic, and pomegranate seeds with enough olive oil to make the mixture spoonable over the chops.

We prefer domestic lamb here, which is typically grass-fed and finished on grain, for its less gamy flavor and better fat marbling. Some lamb racks come pretrimmed; if this is the case, look for a weight of about 1½ pounds. If you can find only precut chops, 16 of the largest single-bone rib chops will work just fine here.

- 2 (1¾- to 2-pound) racks of lamb, fat trimmed to ⅛ inch
- 1½ tablespoons plus ¼ teaspoon kosher salt, divided
- 1 tablespoon sugar
- 1 teaspoon ground allspice
- 1 teaspoon ground fennel
- 1 teaspoon granulated garlic
- 1 teaspoon pepper
- 5 tablespoons pomegranate molasses, divided
- ½ cup chopped fresh mint
- ½ cup pomegranate seeds
- 6 tablespoons extra-virgin olive oil
- ¼ cup chopped fresh parsley
- 1 garlic clove, minced

1. Cut lamb racks between ribs to separate chops. Combine 1½ tablespoons salt, sugar, allspice, fennel, granulated garlic, and pepper in bowl. Pat chops dry with paper towels and sprinkle all over with salt mixture.

2a. For a Charcoal Grill Open bottom vent completely. Light large chimney starter filled with charcoal briquettes (6 quarts). When top coals are partially covered with ash, pour evenly over half of grill. Set cooking grate in place, cover, and open lid vent completely. Heat grill until hot, about 5 minutes.

2b. For a Gas Grill Turn all burners to high; cover; and heat grill until hot, about 15 minutes. Leave all burners on high.

3. Clean and oil cooking grate. Brush chops all over with ¼ cup pomegranate molasses. Place chops on grill (over coals, if using charcoal) and cook (covered, if using gas) until chops are charred and register 135 to 140 degrees, about 2 minutes per side, rearranging chops as needed for even browning.

4. Transfer chops to serving platter, tent with aluminum foil, and let rest for 10 minutes. Stir mint, pomegranate seeds, oil, parsley, garlic, and remaining ¼ teaspoon salt together in small bowl. Brush tops of chops with remaining 1 tablespoon pomegranate molasses. Spoon mint mixture over chops. Serve.

Wood-Grilled Salmon

SERVES 4

WHY THIS RECIPE WORKS To create the flavor of cedar planks in our wood-grilled salmon (without having to mail-order them), we placed salmon fillets over wood chips in aluminum foil trays. To keep the salmon from sticking, we left the skin on, which easily separated from the cooked fish. Poking a few slits in the bottom of the foil let more heat reach the wood chips, releasing their woodsy flavor. A bit of olive oil and sugar produced a golden exterior.

Any variety of wood chips will work, but aromatic woods such as cedar and alder give the most traditional flavor.

- 1½ teaspoons sugar
- ½ teaspoon table salt
- ¼ teaspoon pepper
- 4 (6- to 8-ounce) skin-on salmon fillets, about 1¼ inches thick
- 1 tablespoon extra-virgin olive oil
- 2 cups wood chips, soaked in water for 15 minutes and drained

1. Combine sugar, salt, and pepper in bowl. Pat salmon fillets dry with paper towels, then brush flesh sides with oil and rub evenly with sugar mixture. Using 4 large sheets of heavy-duty aluminum foil, crimp edges of each sheet to make 4 trays, each measuring 7 by 5 inches. Perforate bottom of each tray with tip of paring knife. Divide wood chips among trays and lay 1 fillet skin side down on top of wood chips in each tray.

2a. For a Charcoal Grill Open bottom vent completely. Light large chimney starter filled with charcoal briquettes (6 quarts). When top coals are partially covered with ash, pour evenly over grill. Set cooking grate in place, cover, and open lid vent completely. Heat grill until hot, about 5 minutes.

2b. For a Gas Grill Turn all burners to high, cover, and heat grill until hot, about 15 minutes.

3. Clean and oil cooking grate. Place trays on grill. Cook (covered if using gas) until center is still translucent when checked with tip of paring knife and registers 125 degrees (for medium-rare), about 10 minutes.

4. Transfer trays to wire rack, tent loosely with foil, and let rest for 5 minutes. Slide metal spatula between skin and flesh of fish, transfer fish to platter, and serve.

Barbecued Wood-Grilled Salmon
Add ¾ teaspoon chili powder and ¼ teaspoon cayenne pepper to sugar mixture and substitute 1 tablespoon Dijon mustard mixed with 1 tablespoon maple syrup for oil in step 1.

Lemon-Thyme Wood-Grilled Salmon
Add 2 teaspoons minced fresh thyme and 1½ teaspoons grated fresh lemon zest to sugar mixture and substitute 2 tablespoons Dijon mustard for oil in step 1.

Wood-Grilled Salmon

Cedar-Planked Salmon with Cucumber-Yogurt Sauce

SERVES 4

Cedar-Planked Salmon with Cucumber Yogurt Sauce

WHY THIS RECIPE WORKS Our smoky, succulent salmon is surprisingly easy to make. While the cedar plank soaked in water, we seasoned the salmon with brown sugar, kosher salt, fresh dill, and pepper. We preheated the plank on the grill before adding the salmon to get the right amount of woodsy flavor. Opting for skinless fillets allowed just enough cedar flavor to permeate the salmon. A yogurt–cucumber sauce balanced the fish's richness.

Be sure to buy an untreated cedar plank specifically intended for cooking. To ensure uniform pieces of fish, we prefer to purchase a whole center-cut salmon fillet and cut it into four equal pieces. The seasoned fillets must be refrigerated for at least 1 hour before grilling. When preheating the cedar plank, you will know it's ready when it is just barely smoking. It should not ignite. Serve with lemon wedges and our Cucumber-Yogurt Sauce (recipe follows).

- 1 (2-pound) center-cut, skinless salmon fillet, about 1½ inches thick
- 2 tablespoons packed brown sugar
- 1½ tablespoons kosher salt
- 1 tablespoon chopped fresh dill
- 1 teaspoon pepper
- 1 (16 by 7-inch) cedar plank
- 1 teaspoon vegetable oil
-   Lemon wedges

1. Cut salmon crosswise into 4 equal fillets and pat dry with paper towels. Combine sugar, salt, dill, and pepper in bowl. Sprinkle salmon all over with sugar mixture, place on plate, and refrigerate, uncovered, for at least 1 hour or up to 24 hours. One hour before grilling, soak cedar plank in water for 1 hour (or according to manufacturer's directions).

2a. For a Charcoal Grill Open bottom vent completely. Light large chimney starter filled with charcoal briquettes (6 quarts). When top coals are partially covered with ash, pour evenly over grill. Set cooking grate in place. Place cedar plank in center of grill. Cover and open lid vent completely. Heat grill until plank is lightly smoking and crackling (it should not ignite), about 5 minutes.

2b. For a Gas Grill Place cedar plank in center of grill. Turn all burners to medium-low, cover, and heat grill until plank is smoking and crackling (it should not ignite), about 15 minutes. Leave all burners on medium-low. Adjust burners as needed to maintain grill temperature between 300 and 325 degrees.

3. Brush 1 side of salmon fillets with oil, then place oiled side down on plank. Cover grill and cook until center of salmon is translucent when checked with tip of paring knife and registers 125 degrees (for medium-rare), 12 to 15 minutes. Using tongs, transfer plank with salmon to baking sheet, tent with aluminum foil, and let rest for 5 minutes. Serve with lemon wedges.

Cucumber-Yogurt Sauce
MAKES ABOUT ¾ CUP

A spoon makes easy work of removing the cucumber seeds. Using Greek yogurt here is key; don't substitute regular plain yogurt, or the sauce will be very watery.

½ cucumber, peeled, halved lengthwise, and seeded
½ cup plain whole-milk Greek yogurt
1 tablespoon extra-virgin olive oil
1 tablespoon chopped fresh mint
1 tablespoon chopped fresh dill
1 small garlic clove, minced
¼ teaspoon pepper
⅛ teaspoon table salt

Shred cucumber on large holes of box grater. Combine yogurt, oil, mint, dill, garlic, pepper, salt, and shredded cucumber in bowl. Cover and refrigerate until chilled, about 20 minutes. Serve.

Grilled Salmon Steaks with Lemon-Caper Sauce

SERVES 4

WHY THIS RECIPE WORKS Salmon steaks are a common choice for grilling: Their bone and thickness make them a far sturdier cut than a fillet. But the steak's thickness can also work against it, making it difficult for the interior and exterior to finish cooking at the same time. We began by tucking the belly flaps in toward the center of the steak and tying them to create medallions that would cook evenly and be easily maneuvered. To make sure our steaks were packed with flavor, we finished cooking them in a pan of zesty sauce on the cooler part of the grill. When they were done, our salmon steaks were flavorful, juicy, and moist.

Before eating, lift out the small circular bone from the center of each steak.

4 (10-ounce) salmon steaks, 1 to 1½ inches thick
  Table salt and pepper
2 tablespoons extra-virgin olive oil
1 teaspoon grated lemon zest and 6 tablespoons juice (2 lemons)
1 shallot, minced
3 tablespoons unsalted butter, cut into 3 pieces
1 tablespoon capers, rinsed
2 tablespoons minced fresh parsley
1 (13 by 9-inch) disposable aluminum pan

1. Pat salmon steaks dry with paper towels. Working with 1 steak at a time, carefully trim 1½ inches of skin from 1 tail. Tightly wrap other tail around skinned portion and tie steaks with kitchen twine. Repeat with remaining salmon steaks. Season salmon steaks with salt and pepper and brush both sides with oil. Combine lemon zest, lemon juice, shallot, butter, capers, and ⅛ teaspoon salt in disposable pan.

2a. For a Charcoal Grill Open bottom vent completely. Light large chimney starter filled with charcoal briquettes (6 quarts). When top coals are partially covered with ash, pour evenly over half of grill. Set cooking grate in place, cover, and open lid vent completely. Heat grill until hot, about 5 minutes.

2b. For a Gas Grill Turn all burners to high, cover, and heat grill until hot, about 15 minutes. Leave primary burner on high and turn off other burner(s).

3. Clean and oil cooking grate. Place salmon medallions on hot part of grill. Cook until browned, 2 to 3 minutes per side. Meanwhile, set pan on cool part of grill and cook until butter has melted, about 2 minutes. Transfer medallions to pan and gently turn to coat. Cook (covered if using gas) until center is still translucent when checked with tip of paring knife and registers 125 degrees (for medium-rare), 6 to 14 minutes, flipping salmon and rotating pan halfway through grilling. Remove twine and transfer salmon to platter. Off heat, whisk parsley into sauce and drizzle sauce over salmon. Serve.

Prepping Salmon Medallions

1. For salmon steaks sturdy enough to grill easily, remove 1½ inches of skin from 1 tail of each steak.

2. Tuck skinned portion into center of steak, wrap other tail around it, and tie with kitchen twine.

THE STATE OF GRILLING

Smoked Fish Tacos

SERVES 4 TO 6

WHY THIS RECIPE WORKS The smoked salmon taco we ate at Ruddell's Smokehouse in Cayucos, California, won us over with its unbeatable combination of smoky fish, creamy mustard sauce, and a crunchy-sweet apple slaw. For our version, we seasoned the salmon in a salt-sugar cure to firm up the flesh and brushed on an apricot glaze. Then we built a two-level fire and added some wood chips. Cooked gently on the grill's cooler side, the salmon took on smoky flavor and a silky texture without drying out.

We prefer the flavor that applewood chips impart to the fish, but hickory wood chips are widely available and work fine in this recipe. To ensure even cooking, we prefer to purchase a whole center-cut salmon fillet and cut it into four equal pieces. Note that the seasoned fillets must be refrigerated for at least 4 hours before grilling. You can serve the salmon as whole fillets rather than as a flaked taco filling.

Salmon
- 1 cup packed brown sugar
- Kosher salt
- 1 tablespoon granulated garlic
- 1 (2-pound) center-cut, skin-on salmon fillet, about 1½ inches thick
- 1 cup wood chips
- 2 tablespoons apricot preserves
- 1 tablespoon water

Tacos
- ½ cup mayonnaise
- ¼ cup spicy brown mustard
- 2 teaspoons lemon juice
- ¼ teaspoon ground cumin
- 1 small Granny Smith apple, peeled and chopped fine
- 1 small celery rib, chopped fine
- 1 small carrot, peeled and shredded
- 12 (6-inch) flour tortillas, warmed
- 3 ounces (3 cups) mesclun

1. For the Salmon Combine sugar, ¼ cup salt, and granulated garlic in bowl. Cut salmon crosswise into 4 equal fillets. Transfer salmon and sugar mixture to 1-gallon zipper-lock bag. Press out air, seal bag, and turn to evenly coat salmon with sugar mixture. Refrigerate for at least 4 hours or up to 24 hours.

Smoked Fish Tacos

2. Just before grilling, soak wood chips in water for 15 minutes, then drain. Using large piece of heavy-duty aluminum foil, wrap soaked chips in 8 by 4½-inch foil packet. (Make sure chips do not poke holes in sides or bottom of packet.) Cut 2 evenly spaced 2-inch slits in top of packet.

3. Remove salmon from sugar mixture; discard sugar mixture. Rinse excess sugar mixture from salmon and pat salmon dry with paper towels. Whisk preserves and water together in small bowl; microwave until mixture is fluid, about 30 seconds.

4a. For a Charcoal Grill Open bottom vent completely. Light large chimney starter one-third filled with charcoal briquettes (2 quarts). When top coals are partially covered with ash, pour evenly over half of grill. Place wood chip packet on coals. Set cooking grate in place, cover, and open lid vent completely. Heat grill until hot and wood chips are smoking, about 5 minutes.

4b. For a Gas Grill Remove cooking grate and place wood chip packet directly on primary burner. Set cooking grate in place, turn all burners to high, cover, and heat grill until hot and wood chips are smoking, about

524   *The Complete Cook's Country TV Show Cookbook*

15 minutes. Turn primary burner to medium and turn off other burner(s). (Adjust primary burner as needed to maintain grill temperature between 250 and 275 degrees.)

5. Clean and oil cooking grate. Brush tops and sides of salmon fillets evenly with apricot mixture. Place fillets, skin side down, on cooler side of grill, with thicker ends facing fire. Cover grill (position lid vent over salmon if using charcoal) and cook until centers of fillets register 135 degrees (for medium-well), 28 to 35 minutes. Transfer salmon to plate, tent with foil, and let rest for 5 minutes. (If skin sticks to cooking grate, insert fish spatula between skin and fillet to separate and lift fillet from skin.)

6. For the Tacos Meanwhile, whisk mayonnaise, mustard, lemon juice, and cumin together in bowl. Combine apple, celery, and carrot in second bowl.

7. Remove and discard salmon skin. Flake salmon into bite-size pieces and season with salt to taste. Divide salmon evenly among tortillas, about ⅓ cup per tortilla. Serve, topping each taco with desired amounts of mesclun, mayonnaise mixture, and apple mixture.

Grilled Jalapeño and Lime Shrimp Skewers

SERVES 4

WHY THIS RECIPE WORKS We wanted tender, juicy, shrimp with a smoky, charred crust and chile flavor that was more than just superficial. To achieve this, we sprinkled one side of the shrimp with sugar to promote browning and cooked the shrimp sugar side down over the hot side of the grill for a few minutes. We then flipped the skewers to gently finish cooking on the cool side of the grill. Creating a flavorful marinade that doubled as a sauce gave our shrimp skewers a spicy, assertive kick. And butterflying the shrimp before marinating and grilling them opened up more shrimp flesh for the marinade and finishing sauce to flavor.

We prefer flat metal skewers that are at least 14 inches long for this recipe.

Marinade
- 1–2 jalapeño chiles, stemmed, seeded, and chopped
- 3 tablespoons extra-virgin olive oil
- 6 garlic cloves, minced
- 1 teaspoon grated lime zest plus 5 tablespoons juice (3 limes)
- ½ teaspoon ground cumin
- ¼ teaspoon cayenne pepper
- ½ teaspoon table salt

Shrimp
- 1½ pounds extra-large shrimp (21 to 25 per pound), peeled and deveined
- ½ teaspoon sugar
- 1 tablespoon minced fresh cilantro

1. For the Marinade Process all ingredients in food processor until smooth, about 15 seconds. Reserve 2 tablespoons marinade; transfer remaining marinade to medium bowl.

2. For the Shrimp Pat shrimp dry with paper towels. To butterfly shrimp, use paring knife to make shallow cut down outside curve of shrimp. Add shrimp to bowl with marinade and toss to coat. Cover and refrigerate for 30 minutes to 1 hour.

3a. For a Charcoal Grill Open bottom vent completely. Light large chimney starter filled with charcoal briquettes (6 quarts). When top coals are partially covered with ash, pour evenly over half of grill. Set cooking grate in place, cover, and open lid vent completely. Heat grill until hot, about 5 minutes.

Grilled Jalapeño and Lime Shrimp Skewers

3b. For a Gas Grill Turn all burners to high, cover, and heat grill until hot, about 15 minutes.

4. Clean and oil cooking grate. Thread marinated shrimp on skewers. (Alternate direction of each shrimp as you pack them tightly on skewer to allow about a dozen shrimp to fit snugly on each skewer.) Sprinkle 1 side of skewered shrimp with sugar. Grill shrimp, sugared side down, over hot side of grill (covered if using gas), until lightly charred, 3 to 4 minutes. Flip skewers and move to cool side of grill (if using charcoal) or turn all burners off (if using gas), and cook, covered, until other side of shrimp is no longer translucent, 1 to 2 minutes. Using tongs, slide shrimp into clean medium bowl and toss with reserved marinade. Sprinkle with cilantro and serve.

Grilled Red Chile and Ginger Shrimp Skewers

Replace marinade with 1 to 3 seeded and chopped small red chiles (or jalapeños), 1 minced scallion, 3 tablespoons rice vinegar, 2 tablespoons soy sauce, 1 tablespoon toasted sesame oil, 1 tablespoon grated fresh ginger, 2 teaspoons sugar, and 1 minced garlic clove. Prepare and grill shrimp as directed. Replace cilantro with 1 thinly sliced scallion and serve with lime wedges.

Grilled Habanero and Pineapple Shrimp Skewers

Replace marinade with 1 to 2 seeded and chopped habanero or serrano chiles, ¼ cup pineapple juice, 2 tablespoons extra-virgin olive oil, 1 tablespoon white wine vinegar, 3 minced garlic cloves, 1 teaspoon grated fresh ginger, 1 teaspoon packed brown sugar, 1 teaspoon dried thyme, ½ teaspoon salt, and ¼ teaspoon ground allspice. Prepare and grill shrimp as directed. Replace cilantro with 1 tablespoon minced fresh parsley.

Husk-Grilled Corn

SERVES 6

WHY THIS RECIPE WORKS Corn is the perfect vegetable to grill because its sweet flavor loves a smoky accent and it's large enough not to fall through the grate. Our goal was to prevent the corn from drying out while achieving a classic char. To keep the kernels moist, we found that initially cooking the ears of corn within their husks worked best. We then shucked the hot corn, rolled the ears in seasoned butter, and returned them to the grill to caramelize. This way, the kernels achieved a good char but weren't on the grill long enough to dry out. One last roll in the butter and our corn was ready.

The flavored butter can be made ahead and refrigerated for up to three days; bring it to room temperature before using. Set up a cutting board and knife next to your grill to avoid traveling back and forth between the kitchen and grill.

- 6 ears corn (unshucked)
- 6 tablespoons unsalted butter, softened
- ½ teaspoon table salt
- ½ teaspoon pepper

1. Cut and remove silk protruding from top of each ear of corn. Combine butter, salt, and pepper in bowl. Fold one 14 by 12-inch piece heavy-duty aluminum foil in half to create 7 by 12-inch rectangle; then crimp into boat shape long and wide enough to accommodate 1 ear of corn. Transfer butter mixture to prepared foil boat.

2a. For a Charcoal Grill Open bottom vent completely. Light large chimney starter mounded with charcoal briquettes (7 quarts). When top coals are partially covered with ash, pour evenly over half of grill. Set cooking grate in place, cover, and open lid vent completely. Heat grill until hot, about 5 minutes.

2b. For a Gas Grill Turn all burners to high, cover, and heat grill until hot, about 15 minutes.

3. Clean and oil grate. Place corn on grill (over coals, with stem ends facing cooler side of grill, for charcoal). Cover and cook, turning corn every 3 minutes, until husks have blackened all over, 12 to 15 minutes. (To check for doneness, carefully peel down small portion of husk. If corn is steaming and bright yellow, it is ready.) Transfer corn to cutting board. Using chef's knife, cut base from corn. Using dish towel to hold corn, peel away and discard husk and silk with tongs.

4. Roll each ear of corn in butter mixture to coat lightly and return to grill (over coals for charcoal). Cook, turning as needed to char corn lightly on each side, about 5 minutes total. Remove corn from grill and roll each ear again in butter mixture. Transfer corn to platter. Serve, passing any remaining butter mixture.

Husk-Grilled Corn with Mustard-Paprika Butter

Stir 2 tablespoons spicy brown mustard and 1 teaspoon smoked paprika into butter mixture in step 1.

Husk-Grilled Corn with Cilantro-Lime Butter

Stir ¼ cup minced fresh cilantro, 2 teaspoons grated lime zest plus 1 tablespoon juice, and 1 minced small garlic clove into butter mixture in step 1.

Husk-Grilled Corn with Rosemary-Pepper Butter

Increase pepper to 1 teaspoon. Stir 1 tablespoon minced fresh rosemary and 1 minced small garlic clove into butter mixture in step 1.

Husk-Grilled Corn with Brown Sugar–Cayenne Butter

Stir 2 tablespoons packed brown sugar and ¼ teaspoon cayenne pepper into butter mixture in step 1.

Grilled Corn on the Cob

SERVES 4 TO 6

WHY THIS RECIPE WORKS Grilling corn sounds like a simple proposition—but the right technique makes all the difference. For a recipe that produced corn with a distinctly grilled taste and lightly charred kernels, we grilled the corn unhusked. The grill imparted great flavor to our grilled corn, but also made the kernels tough and dry. To avoid this, we soaked the husked corn in salted water before grilling, which kept the kernels moist and seasoned them as well.

If your corn isn't as sweet as you'd like, stir ½ cup sugar into the water along with the salt. Avoid soaking the corn for more than 8 hours, or it will become overly salty.

- Table salt and pepper
- 8 ears corn, husks and silks removed
- 8 tablespoons unsalted butter, softened, or 1 recipe flavored butter (recipes follow)

1. In large pot, stir ½ cup salt into 4 quarts cold water until dissolved. Add corn and let soak for at least 30 minutes or up to 8 hours.

2a. For a Charcoal Grill Open bottom vent completely. Light large chimney starter filled with charcoal briquettes (6 quarts). When top coals are partially covered with ash, pour evenly over grill. Set cooking grate in place, cover, and open lid vent completely. Heat grill until hot, about 5 minutes.

Husk-Grilled Corn

Grilled Corn on the Cob

2b. For a Gas Grill Turn all burners to high, cover, and heat grill until hot, about 15 minutes.

3. Clean and oil cooking grate. Grill corn, turning every 2 to 3 minutes, until kernels are lightly charred all over, 10 to 14 minutes. Remove corn from grill, brush with softened butter, and season with salt and pepper. Serve.

Chesapeake Bay Butter
MAKES ABOUT ½ CUP

Using fork, beat 8 tablespoons softened, unsalted butter with 1 tablespoon hot sauce, 1 teaspoon Old Bay seasoning, and 1 minced garlic clove.

Cilantro-Chipotle Butter
MAKES ABOUT ½ CUP

Using fork, beat 8 tablespoons softened, unsalted butter with 1 teaspoon chili powder, ½ teaspoon ground cumin, ½ teaspoon grated lime zest, and 1 minced garlic clove. (Sprinkle cobs with ½ cup grated Parmesan, if desired.)

Basil Pesto Butter
MAKES ABOUT ½ CUP

Using fork, beat 8 tablespoons softened, unsalted butter with 1 tablespoon basil pesto and 1 teaspoon lemon juice.

Barbecue-Scallion Butter
MAKES ABOUT ½ CUP

Using fork, beat 8 tablespoons softened, unsalted butter with 2 tablespoons barbecue sauce and 1 minced scallion.

Backyard Barbecue Beans
SERVES 12 TO 16

WHY THIS RECIPE WORKS For a standout backyard barbecue side, we turned canned beans into a savory showstopper. Baked beans gave us an easy starting point, and mixing in pinto and cannellini beans built a multifaceted bean base. We boosted the flavor with a sauce made with cider vinegar, granulated garlic, cayenne, and liquid smoke. Browned bratwurst gave the sauce some meaty heft. We stirred the beans into this mixture, arranged bite-size pieces of bacon over the surface, and baked until the bacon crisped, infusing the dish with its smoky flavor.

Backyard Barbecue Beans

Be sure to use a 13 by 9-inch metal baking pan; the volume of the beans is too great for a 13 by 9-inch ceramic baking dish, and it will overflow. We found that Bush's Original Recipe Baked Beans are the most consistent product for this recipe.

- ½ cup barbecue sauce
- ½ cup ketchup
- ½ cup water
- 2 tablespoons spicy brown mustard
- 2 tablespoons cider vinegar
- 1 teaspoon liquid smoke
- 1 teaspoon granulated garlic
- ¼ teaspoon cayenne pepper
- 1¼ pounds bratwurst, casings removed
- 2 onions, chopped
- 2 (28-ounce) cans baked beans
- 2 (15-ounce) cans pinto beans, drained
- 2 (15-ounce) cans cannellini beans, drained
- 1 (10-ounce) can Ro-Tel Original Diced Tomatoes and Green Chilies, drained
- 6 slices thick-cut bacon, cut into 1-inch pieces

1. Adjust oven rack to middle position and heat oven to 350 degrees. Whisk barbecue sauce, ketchup, water, mustard, vinegar, liquid smoke, granulated garlic, and cayenne together in large bowl; set aside.

2. Cook bratwurst in 12-inch nonstick skillet over medium-high heat, breaking up into small pieces with spoon, until fat begins to render, about 5 minutes. Stir in onions and cook until sausage and onions are well browned, about 15 minutes.

3. Transfer bratwurst mixture to bowl with sauce. Stir in baked beans, pinto beans, cannellini beans, and tomatoes. Transfer bean mixture to 13 by 9-inch baking pan and place pan on rimmed baking sheet. Arrange bacon pieces in single layer over top of beans.

4. Bake until beans are bubbling and bacon is rendered, about 1½ hours. Let cool for 15 minutes. Serve.

To Make Ahead At end of step 3, beans can be wrapped in plastic and refrigerated for up to 24 hours. Proceed with recipe from step 4, increasing baking time to 1¾ hours.

California Barbecued Beans

SERVES 4 TO 6

California Barbecued Beans

WHY THIS RECIPE WORKS California barbecued beans recipes use a bean variety and chili sauce rarely found outside of California. We wanted to re-create this recipe with nationally available supermarket ingredients. Pink kidney beans proved to be a good stand-in for the traditional pinquito beans. Some recipes suggest using jarred taco sauce alone if the original recipe's requisite red chili sauce can't be found, but we found its taste and texture too thin. Instead, augmenting the sauce with a combination of fried bacon, ham, onion, and garlic with tomato puree, brown sugar, and dry mustard perfectly captured the chili sauce's bite.

If you can find them, pinquito beans (a variety grown in the Santa Maria Valley) are traditional in this dish. Bottled taco sauce is available in the Latin American aisle of most grocery stores. Don't add the tomato puree, taco sauce, brown sugar, and salt before the beans have simmered for an hour; they will hinder the proper softening of the beans.

- 4 slices bacon, chopped fine
- ½ pound deli ham, chopped fine
- 1 onion, chopped fine
- 4 garlic cloves, minced
- 1 pound pink kidney beans, soaked in 6 cups water overnight and drained
- 6 cups water
- 1 cup canned tomato puree
- ½ cup bottled taco sauce
- 5 tablespoons packed light brown sugar
- 1 tablespoon dry mustard
- Table salt
- ¼ cup chopped fresh cilantro
- 2 tablespoons cider vinegar

1. Cook bacon and ham in Dutch oven over medium heat until fat renders and bacon and ham are lightly browned, 5 to 7 minutes. Add onion and cook until softened, about 5 minutes. Stir in garlic and cook until fragrant, about 30 seconds. Add beans and water and bring to simmer. Reduce heat to medium-low, cover, and cook until beans are just soft, about 1 hour.

2. Stir in tomato puree, taco sauce, sugar, dry mustard, and 2 teaspoons salt. Continue to simmer, uncovered, until beans are completely tender and sauce is thickened, about 1 hour. (If mixture becomes too thick, add water.) Stir in cilantro and vinegar and season with salt. Serve. (Beans can be refrigerated for up to 4 days.)

> ### Quick-Soaking Beans
> If you don't want to soak the beans overnight, there is a faster way. Simply cover the beans with water in a Dutch oven, bring them to a boil over high heat, and let them boil for 5 minutes. Remove the beans from the heat and allow them to sit, covered, in the hot water for 1 hour. Drain the beans and proceed with the recipe as directed. The quick-soaked beans taste just as good as beans that are soaked overnight.

> ### Sorting Dried Beans
> It is important to rinse and pick over dried beans to remove any stones or debris before cooking. To make the task easier, sort dried beans on a large white plate or on a white, rimmed cutting board. The neutral background makes any unwanted matter a cinch to spot and discard.

Grilled Potato Packs

SERVES 4

WHY THIS RECIPE WORKS We wanted to rescue this campfire classic, which too often results in unevenly cooked spuds. After multiple tests, we found that Yukon Golds were preferred to starchy, mealy russets and "slippery" red potatoes. To ensure evenly grilled potatoes, we cut them into evenly sized wedges and microwaved them for a few minutes before grilling them. Tossing the potatoes with a little oil prevented them from sticking to the foil.

To keep the packs from tearing, use heavy-duty aluminum foil or two layers of regular foil. Also, scrape the cooking grate clean before grilling.

- 2 pounds Yukon Gold potatoes (about 3 large), scrubbed
- 1 tablespoon extra-virgin olive oil
- 2 garlic cloves, peeled and chopped
- 1 teaspoon minced fresh thyme
- 1 teaspoon table salt
- ½ teaspoon pepper

1. Cut each potato in half crosswise, then cut each half into 8 wedges. Place potatoes in large bowl and wrap tightly with plastic wrap. Microwave until edges of potatoes are translucent, 4 to 7 minutes, shaking bowl (without removing plastic) to redistribute potatoes halfway through cooking. Carefully remove plastic and drain well. Gently toss potatoes with oil, garlic, thyme, salt, and pepper.

2. Cut four 14 by 10-inch sheets of heavy-duty aluminum foil. Working with 1 at a time, spread one-quarter of potato mixture over half of foil, fold foil over potatoes, and crimp edges tightly to seal.

3a. For a Charcoal Grill Open bottom vent completely. Light large chimney starter filled with charcoal briquettes (6 quarts). When top coals are partially covered with ash, pour evenly over grill. Set cooking grate in place, cover, and open lid vent completely. Heat grill until hot, about 5 minutes.

3b. For a Gas Grill Turn all burners to medium-high, cover, and heat grill until hot, about 15 minutes.

4. Grill hobo packs over hot fire, covered, until potatoes are completely tender, about 10 minutes, flipping packs halfway through cooking. Cut open foil and serve.

Spanish-Style Grilled Potato Packs
Add 6 ounces thinly sliced cured chorizo sausage, 1 seeded and chopped red bell pepper, and 1 teaspoon paprika to cooked potatoes as they are tossed in step 1.

Vinegar and Onion Grilled Potato Packs
Microwave 1 halved and thinly sliced small onion with potatoes in step 1. Add 2 tablespoons white wine or red wine vinegar to cooked potatoes as they are tossed in step 1.

Spicy Home Fry Grilled Potato Packs
Omit chopped garlic. Add 1 teaspoon paprika, ½ teaspoon garlic powder, ½ teaspoon onion powder, and ¼ teaspoon cayenne pepper to cooked potatoes as they are tossed in step 1.

Grilled Sweet Potatoes with Maple Chile Crisp

SERVES 4 TO 6

WHY THIS RECIPE WORKS This recipe is inspired by the sweet potatoes with maple chile crisp served by chef, author, and educator Sean Sherman at Owamni in Minneapolis, Minnesota (see page 312). We started by roasting white sweet potatoes (which are firmer and starchier than orange varieties) until they were fully tender. Roasting the potatoes before grilling ensured that their interiors were exquisitely creamy while their exteriors became crisp, craggy, and caramelized. We love these potatoes drizzled with smoky-sweet maple chile crisp.

The potatoes can be made on an outdoor grill or an indoor grill pan. The chile crisp needs to sit for at least 4 hours before using; the potatoes should cool for at least 2 hours before grilling. The chile crisp yields about 1¾ cups. It's important to combine all the ingredients in step 2 in a metal bowl because the shock of adding hot oil to a Pyrex or glass bowl could cause it to shatter. This recipe makes a medium-spiced chile crisp. If you prefer your chile crisp slightly milder, reduce the arbol and chipotle chiles to two each. To serve a larger crowd, the potato portion of the recipe can be doubled.

Chile Crisp
- 3 dried chipotle chiles
- 3 arbol chiles
- 2 ancho chiles
- 2 guajillo chiles
- 2 dried New Mexico chiles
- 3 scallions, sliced thin
- 2 tablespoons maple sugar
- 3 garlic cloves, minced
- 1½ teaspoons fine sea salt
- 1½ cups sunflower oil

Potatoes
- 2 (12- to 16-ounce) white sweet potatoes, unpeeled, each lightly pricked with fork in 6 places
- 4 teaspoons sunflower oil, divided
- ½ teaspoon fine sea salt, divided
- ½ teaspoon flake sea salt
- 1 scallion, sliced thin on bias

Grilled Potato Packs

Grilled Sweet Potatoes with Maple Chile Crisp

1. For the Chile Crisp Adjust oven rack to middle position and heat oven to 400 degrees. Spread chipotle, arbol, ancho, guajillo, and New Mexico chiles on rimmed baking sheet. Roast until fragrant, 3 to 5 minutes. Let chiles cool completely on sheet, about 10 minutes.

2. Stem and seed chiles. Break chiles into 1- to 2-inch pieces. Working in batches, pulse chiles in spice grinder until pieces no larger than ¼ inch remain, about 6 pulses. Transfer ground chiles to medium metal bowl. Add scallions, sugar, garlic, and salt to chile mixture.

3. Heat oil in small saucepan over medium-high heat to 375 degrees. Carefully pour hot oil over chile mixture in bowl (mixture will bubble aggressively). Let sit, stirring occasionally, until cooled completely, about 30 minutes. Transfer chile crisp to jar and let sit for at least 4 hours before using. (Chile crisp will keep at room temperature for at least 1 month.)

4. For the Potatoes Meanwhile, adjust oven rack to middle position and heat oven to 400 degrees. Line rimmed baking sheet with parchment paper and place potatoes on sheet. Bake potatoes until paring knife inserted in center meets no resistance, 1¼ to 1½ hours. Let potatoes cool completely, at least 2 hours. (Potatoes can be baked and refrigerated up to 2 days in advance.)

5. Prepare medium-hot grill or grill pan (if using grill pan, preheat over medium-high heat for 10 minutes). Clean and oil cooking grate. Cut potatoes in half lengthwise. Brush cut sides of potatoes with 2 teaspoons sunflower oil and sprinkle with ¼ teaspoon fine sea salt. Place potatoes cut side down on grill and cook until potatoes are char-streaked and easily release from grill, 3 to 5 minutes.

6. Brush skin sides of potatoes with remaining 2 teaspoons sunflower oil and sprinkle with remaining ¼ teaspoon fine sea salt. Using firm metal spatula, flip potatoes and cook until lightly browned on skin side and heated through, 3 to 5 minutes.

7. Transfer potatoes to cutting board. Cut each potato in half lengthwise, then in half crosswise. Arrange potatoes on platter and spoon generous ½ cup chile crisp over top, plus extra to taste. Sprinkle with flake sea salt and scallion. Serve.

Grilled Broccoli with Lemon and Parmesan

SERVES 4

WHY THIS RECIPE WORKS Steaming or sautéing broccoli is fine, but if you want vivid green florets with flavorful char, there's no beating the grill. To avoid toughness, we peeled the stalks with a vegetable peeler and cut the head into spears small enough to cook quickly but large enough to grill easily. Since grilling alone would yield dry broccoli, we tossed the spears in olive oil and water and steamed them in sealed foil packets on the grill. As soon as the stems and florets were evenly cooked, we placed them directly on the grill to give them plenty of char. A squeeze of grilled lemon and a sprinkling of Parmesan sealed the deal.

To keep the packs from tearing, use heavy-duty aluminum foil. Use the large holes of a box grater to shred the Parmesan.

- ¼ cup extra-virgin olive oil, plus extra for drizzling
- 1 tablespoon water
-   Table salt and pepper
- 2 pounds broccoli
- 1 lemon, halved
- ¼ cup shredded Parmesan cheese

1. Cut two 26 by 12-inch sheets of heavy-duty aluminum foil. Whisk oil, water, ¾ teaspoon salt, and ½ teaspoon pepper together in large bowl.

2. Trim stalk ends so each entire head of broccoli measures 6 to 7 inches long. Using vegetable peeler, peel away tough outer layer of broccoli stalks (about ⅛ inch). Cut stalks in half lengthwise into spears (stems should be ½ to ¾ inch thick and florets 3 to 4 inches wide). Add broccoli spears to oil mixture and toss well to coat.

3. Divide broccoli between sheets of foil, cut side down and alternating direction of florets and stems. Bring short sides of foil together and crimp tightly. Crimp long ends to seal packs tightly.

4a. For a Charcoal Grill Open bottom vent completely. Light large chimney starter filled with charcoal briquettes (6 quarts). When top coals are partially covered with ash, pour evenly over half of grill. Set cooking grate in place, cover, and open lid completely. Heat grill until hot, about 5 minutes.

4b. For a Gas Grill Turn all burners to high, cover, and heat grill until hot, about 15 minutes. Turn all burners to medium-high. (Adjust burners as needed to maintain grill temperature around 400 degrees.)

5. Clean and oil cooking grate. Arrange packs evenly on grill (over coals if using charcoal), cover, and cook for 8 minutes, flipping packs halfway through cooking.

6. Transfer packs to rimmed baking sheet and, using scissors, carefully cut open, allowing steam to escape away from you. (Broccoli should be bright green and fork inserted into stems should meet some resistance.)

7. Discard foil and place broccoli and lemon halves cut side down on grill (over coals if using charcoal). Grill (covered if using gas), turning broccoli about every 2 minutes, until stems are fork-tender and well charred on all sides, 6 to 8 minutes total. Transfer broccoli to now-empty sheet as it finishes cooking. Grill lemon halves until well charred on cut side, 6 to 8 minutes.

8. Transfer broccoli to cutting board and cut into 2-inch pieces; transfer to platter. Season with salt and pepper to taste. Squeeze lemon over broccoli to taste, sprinkle with Parmesan, and drizzle with extra oil. Serve.

Grilled Broccoli with Anchovy-Garlic Butter

Omit lemon and Parmesan cheese. In step 1, whisk together 4 tablespoons melted unsalted butter, 3 rinsed and minced anchovy fillets, 1 minced garlic clove, 1 teaspoon lemon juice, ¼ teaspoon red pepper flakes, ½ teaspoon salt, and ⅛ teaspoon pepper. Set aside, then rewarm in step 8 and drizzle over broccoli before serving.

Grilled Caesar Salad

SERVES 6

WHY THIS RECIPE WORKS Grilled salad may seem like an oxymoron, but we were intrigued by the idea of the flavors of a classic Caesar salad enriched with the smoky char of the grill. We found that compact romaine hearts held their shape better than whole heads. We halved them lengthwise to increase their surface area, making sure to keep the core intact so the leaves didn't fall apart on the grill. To prevent sticking, we brushed the leaves with dressing. Just 1 to 2 minutes over a hot grill gave us a smoky and charred (not wilted) exterior. To keep things simple, we replaced the croutons with slices of crusty bread grilled alongside the lettuce.

Grilled Broccoli with Lemon and Parmesan

Grilled Caesar Salad

Our favorite Parmesan cheese is Boar's Head Parmigiano-Reggiano.

Dressing

- 1 tablespoon lemon juice
- 1 garlic clove, minced
- ½ cup mayonnaise
- ½ ounce Parmesan cheese, grated (¼ cup)
- 1 tablespoon white wine vinegar
- 1 tablespoon Worcestershire sauce
- 1 tablespoon Dijon mustard
- 2 anchovy fillets, rinsed
- ½ teaspoon table salt
- ½ teaspoon pepper
- ¼ cup extra-virgin olive oil

Salad

- 1 (12-inch) baguette, cut on bias into 5-inch-long, ½-inch-thick slices
- 3 tablespoons extra-virgin olive oil
- 1 garlic clove, peeled
- 3 romaine lettuce hearts (18 ounces), halved lengthwise through cores
- ½ ounce Parmesan cheese, grated (¼ cup)

1. For the Dressing Combine lemon juice and garlic in bowl and let stand for 10 minutes. Process mayonnaise, Parmesan, lemon-garlic mixture, vinegar, Worcestershire, mustard, anchovies, salt, and pepper in blender for about 30 seconds. With blender running, slowly add oil. Reserve 6 tablespoons dressing for brushing romaine.

2a. For a Charcoal Grill Open bottom vent completely. Light large chimney starter filled with charcoal briquettes (6 quarts). When top coals are partially covered with ash, pour evenly over half of grill. Set cooking grate in place, cover, and open lid vent completely. Heat grill until hot, about 5 minutes.

2b. For a Gas Grill Turn all burners to high, cover, and heat grill until hot, about 15 minutes. Leave all burners on high.

3. For the Salad Clean and oil cooking grate. Brush bread with oil and grill (over coals if using charcoal), uncovered, until browned, about 1 minute per side. Transfer to platter and rub with garlic clove. Brush cut sides of romaine with reserved dressing; place half of romaine, cut side down, on grill (over coals if using charcoal). Grill, uncovered, until lightly charred, 1 to 2 minutes. Move to platter with bread. Repeat. Drizzle romaine with remaining dressing. Sprinkle with Parmesan. Serve.

Tangy Apple Cabbage Slaw

Tangy Apple Cabbage Slaw

SERVES 6 TO 8

WHY THIS RECIPE WORKS We wanted to discover the secrets to tender cabbage, crunchy apples, and the sweet and spicy dressing that brings them together in this Southern barbecue side dish. Because cabbage is relatively watery, we salted the cut cabbage to draw out excess moisture before dressing it, which prevented moisture from diluting the dressing later and leaving us with a watery slaw. Granny Smith apples work best here—tasters loved their crunch and tart bite. Cider vinegar gave the dressing a fruity flavor, while red pepper flakes, chopped scallions, and mustard added some punch.

In step 1, the salted, rinsed, and dried cabbage can be refrigerated in a zipper-lock bag for up to 24 hours. To prep the apples, cut the cored apples into ¼-inch-thick planks, then stack the planks and cut them into thin matchsticks.

- 1 medium head green cabbage (2 pounds), cored and chopped fine (12 cups)
- 2 teaspoons table salt
- 2 Granny Smith apples, cored and cut into thin matchsticks
- 2 scallions, sliced thin
- 6 tablespoons vegetable oil
- ½ cup cider vinegar
- ½ cup sugar
- 1 tablespoon Dijon mustard
- ¼ teaspoon red pepper flakes

1. Toss cabbage and salt in colander set over medium bowl. Let stand until wilted, about 1 hour. Rinse cabbage under cold water, drain, dry well with paper towels, and transfer to large bowl. Add apples and scallions and toss to combine.

2. Bring oil, vinegar, sugar, mustard, and pepper flakes to boil in saucepan over medium heat. Pour over cabbage mixture and toss to coat. Cover with plastic wrap and refrigerate at least 1 hour or up to 24 hours. Serve.

Memphis Chopped Coleslaw

SERVES 8 TO 10

WHY THIS RECIPE WORKS The high water content of cabbage is typically to blame for watery slaws. We salted our cabbage to draw out the excess moisture. This style of slaw is usually studded with celery seeds and crunchy green peppers and tossed with a sugary mustard dressing that's balanced by a bracing hit of vinegar. To ensure our slaw boasted brash, balanced flavor, we quickly cooked the spicy dressing to meld the flavors and tossed the hot dressing with the cabbage. The salted cabbage absorbed the dressing and became seasoned inside and out.

In step 1, the salted, rinsed, and dried cabbage mixture can be refrigerated in a zipper-lock bag for up to 24 hours.

- 1 head green cabbage (2 pounds), cored and chopped fine (12 cups)
- 1 jalapeño chile, stemmed, seeded, and minced
- 1 carrot, peeled and shredded on box grater
- 1 small onion, peeled and shredded on box grater

Memphis Chopped Coleslaw

- 2 teaspoons table salt
- ¼ cup yellow mustard
- ¼ cup chili sauce
- ¼ cup mayonnaise
- ¼ cup sour cream
- ¼ cup cider vinegar
- 1 teaspoon celery seeds
- ⅔ cup packed light brown sugar

1. Toss cabbage, jalapeño, carrot, onion, and salt in colander set over medium bowl. Let stand until wilted, about 1 hour. Rinse cabbage mixture under cold water, drain, dry well with paper towels, and transfer to large bowl.

2. Bring mustard, chili sauce, mayonnaise, sour cream, vinegar, celery seeds, and sugar to boil in saucepan over medium heat. Pour over cabbage and toss to coat. Cover with plastic wrap and refrigerate 1 hour or up to 24 hours. Serve.

Shredded Carrot and Serrano Chile Salad

SERVES 4

WHY THIS RECIPE WORKS A classic carrot salad leans toward the sweet side by including raisins, but we wanted to take our flavors in a different direction. To make quick work of shredding the carrots, we set aside the hand-held box grater and opted for the shredding disk on a food processor; this gave us finer shreds (which in turn soaked up more dressing). For the dressing, we found that using potent fish sauce gave a salty, complex umami boost that amplified the flavor of the earthy, sweet carrot shreds. We cut serrano chiles into thin rings to add a bit of heat with good pepper flavor. Chopped cilantro, mint, and scallions provided a range of fresh notes and an extra touch of color. Toasted sesame oil brought a savory, deep element that anchored the bright flavors, and chopped peanuts added a nutty crunch with nibs of richness.

If you don't have a shredding disk for your food processor, shred the carrots on the large holes of a box grater. If you're spice averse, use only one chile and consider halving the chile and removing the ribs and seeds. We recommend wearing rubber gloves when handling the chiles. Brown sugar can be substituted for the granulated sugar.

- 1 pound carrots, peeled
- 1/2 cup dry-roasted peanuts, chopped
- 1/3 cup chopped fresh mint
- 1/3 cup chopped fresh cilantro
- 1/4 cup thinly sliced scallions
- 1–2 serrano chiles, stemmed and sliced into thin rings
- 1 tablespoon fish sauce
- 1 tablespoon sugar
- 1 tablespoon toasted sesame oil
- 2 teaspoons grated lime zest plus 3 tablespoons juice (2 limes)
- 1 garlic clove, minced
- 1 teaspoon table salt

1. Fit food processor with shredding disk and shred carrots.

2. Combine carrots, peanuts, mint, cilantro, scallions, serranos, fish sauce, sugar, oil, lime zest and juice, garlic, and salt in bowl and toss to thoroughly combine. Let sit for 30 minutes for flavors to meld. Serve. (Salad can be refrigerated for up to 24 hours.)

Shredded Carrot and Serrano Chile Salad

All-American Potato Salad

SERVES 4 TO 6

WHY THIS RECIPE WORKS For flavorful all-American potato salad, we decided to use firm-textured Yukon Gold potatoes because they hold their shape after cooking and won't turn mushy in the salad. Our recipe benefited from the sweetness of an unexpected ingredient: pickle juice. We drizzled the still-warm potatoes with a mixture of pickle juice and mustard. The hot potatoes easily absorbed the acidic liquid and tasted seasoned through to the middle. A combination of mayonnaise and sour cream formed the base of our creamy dressing, seasoned with classic additions like celery seeds, celery, and chopped hard-cooked eggs.

Make sure not to overcook the potatoes or the salad will be sloppy. Keep the water at a gentle simmer and use the tip of a paring knife to judge the doneness of the potatoes. If the knife inserts easily into the potato pieces, they are done.

- 2 large eggs
  Table salt
- 2 pounds Yukon Gold potatoes, peeled and cut into ¾-inch cubes
- 3 tablespoons dill pickle juice, divided, plus ¼ cup finely chopped dill pickles
- 1 tablespoon yellow mustard
- ¼ teaspoon pepper
- ½ teaspoon celery seeds
- ½ cup mayonnaise
- ¼ cup sour cream
- ½ small red onion, chopped fine
- 1 celery rib, chopped fine

1. Bring eggs, 1½ teaspoons salt, and 1 quart water to boil in small saucepan. Remove pan from heat, cover, and let sit for 10 minutes. Transfer eggs to bowl filled with ice water and let cool for 5 minutes, then peel and chop coarse.

2. Place potatoes in large saucepan with cold water to cover by 1 inch. Bring to boil over high heat, add 1 teaspoon salt, reduce heat to medium-low, and simmer until potatoes are tender, 10 to 15 minutes.

3. Drain potatoes thoroughly, then spread out on rimmed baking sheet. Mix 2 tablespoons pickle juice and mustard together in small bowl, drizzle pickle juice mixture over hot potatoes, and toss until evenly coated. Refrigerate until cooled, about 30 minutes.

4. Mix remaining tablespoon pickle juice, chopped pickles, ½ teaspoon salt, pepper, celery seeds, mayonnaise, sour cream, red onion, and celery in large bowl. Toss in cooled potatoes, cover, and refrigerate until well chilled, about 30 minutes. (Salad can be refrigerated for up to 2 days.) Gently stir in eggs, just before serving.

Smoky Potato Salad

SERVES 8

WHY THIS RECIPE WORKS For a grilled potato salad featuring smoky, tender potatoes with crispy outsides, we used unpeeled red potatoes: The skin helped them to stay intact, and their firm texture stood up to the heat. We coated them with bacon fat and grilled them with onions for extra smokiness. A spicy, smoky vinaigrette was a great pairing.

Use small red potatoes 1½ to 2 inches in diameter. If you don't have 2 tablespoons of fat in the skillet after frying the bacon, add olive oil to make up the difference.

All-American Potato Salad

Smoky Potato Salad

6 slices bacon
3 tablespoons red wine vinegar
2 tablespoons mayonnaise
2 teaspoons minced canned chipotle chile in adobo sauce
   Table salt and pepper
3 tablespoons extra-virgin olive oil, plus extra for brushing
3 pounds small red potatoes, unpeeled, halved
1 large onion, sliced into 1/2-inch-thick rounds
4 scallions, sliced thin

1. Cook bacon in 12-inch skillet over medium heat until crispy, 7 to 9 minutes; transfer to paper towel–lined plate. Set aside 2 tablespoons bacon fat. When cool enough to handle, crumble bacon and set aside. Whisk vinegar, mayonnaise, chile, 1/2 teaspoon salt, and 1/2 teaspoon pepper together in large bowl. Slowly whisk in 3 tablespoons oil until combined; set aside.

2a. For a Charcoal Grill Open bottom vent completely. Light large chimney starter three-quarters filled with charcoal briquettes (4 1/2 quarts). When top coals are partially covered with ash, pour evenly over grill. Set cooking grate in place, cover, and open lid vent completely. Heat grill until hot, about 5 minutes.

2b. For a Gas Grill Turn all burners to high, cover, and heat grill until hot, about 15 minutes. Turn all burners to medium.

3. Clean and oil cooking grate. Toss potatoes with reserved bacon fat and 1/2 teaspoon salt. Push a toothpick horizontally through each onion round to keep rings intact while grilling. Brush onion rounds lightly with extra oil and season with salt and pepper. Place potatoes, cut side down, and onion rounds on grill and cook, covered, until charred on first side, 10 to 14 minutes.

4. Flip potatoes and onion rounds and continue to cook, covered, until well browned all over and potatoes are easily pierced with tip of paring knife, 10 to 16 minutes longer. Transfer potatoes and onion rounds to rimmed baking sheet and let cool slightly.

5. When cool enough to handle, halve potatoes; remove toothpicks and coarsely chop onion rounds. Add potatoes, onion, scallions, and bacon to dressing and toss to combine. Season with salt and pepper to taste. Serve warm or at room temperature.

Amish Potato Salad

SERVES 8

WHY THIS RECIPE WORKS Amish potato salad is distinct for its creamy cooked dressing and sweet-and-sour flavor. The labor-intensive dressing is traditionally enriched with eggs and gently cooked over a double-boiler. To keep the rich taste with less work, we processed a hard-cooked egg yolk into the dressing base. We infused the hot potatoes with some of the dressing, then tossed the cooled potatoes with the rest, enriched with sour cream.

You can substitute an equal amount of celery salt for the celery seed, but if you do, eliminate the table salt from the dressing. Make sure to use sturdy Yukon Golds here; fluffy russets will fall apart in the salad.

3 pounds Yukon Gold potatoes, peeled and cut into 3/4-inch chunks
   Table salt and pepper
1/3 cup cider vinegar
1/4 cup sugar
2 tablespoons yellow mustard
1 recipe Foolproof Hard-Cooked Eggs (recipe follows)
1/2 teaspoon celery seeds
3/4 cup sour cream
1 celery rib, chopped fine

1. Bring potatoes, 1 tablespoon salt, and enough water to cover by 1 inch to boil in large pot over high heat. Reduce heat to medium and simmer until potatoes are just tender, about 10 minutes.

2. Meanwhile, microwave vinegar and sugar in small bowl until sugar dissolves, about 30 seconds. Process vinegar mixture, mustard, 1 hard-cooked egg yolk (reserve white), celery seeds, and 1/2 teaspoon salt in food processor until smooth, about 30 seconds. Transfer to medium bowl.

3. Drain potatoes thoroughly and transfer to large bowl. Drizzle 2 tablespoons dressing over hot potatoes and, using rubber spatula, toss gently until evenly coated. Refrigerate until cooled, at least 30 minutes, stirring gently once to redistribute dressing.

4. Whisk sour cream into remaining dressing. Add reserved egg white and 3 hard-cooked eggs to dressing and, using potato masher, mash until only small pieces remain. Add dressing and celery to cooled potatoes, tossing gently to combine. Cover and refrigerate until chilled, about 30 minutes. Season with salt and pepper to taste. Serve. (Salad can be refrigerated for up to 2 days.)

Foolproof Hard-Cooked Eggs
MAKES 4 EGGS

You can double or triple this recipe as long as you use a pot large enough to hold the eggs in a single layer, covered by an inch of water.

    4   large eggs

Bring eggs and enough water to cover by 1 inch to boil in medium saucepan over high heat. Remove pan from heat, cover, and let sit 10 minutes. Meanwhile, fill medium bowl with 4 cups water and 1 tray of ice cubes. Transfer eggs to ice water bath with slotted spoon; let sit for 5 minutes. Peel eggs.

Ranch Potato Salad
SERVES 6 TO 8

WHY THIS RECIPE WORKS Bottled ranch dressing sounds like a quick way to dress up potato salad, but many recipes are surprisingly dull and bland. We found that peeling the potatoes (we liked red spuds) allowed them to absorb more dressing. For the dressing, we doubled the amount of cilantro used in most recipes and added fresh garlic and scallions for a welcome bite. Dijon mustard and vinegar provided acidity and bite, while chopped roasted red peppers made a sweet counterpoint. To season the potatoes, we tossed the hot spuds first with just the Dijon and vinegar. A dash of dried dill lent more herb flavor.

We prefer white wine vinegar here, but white and cider vinegars are acceptable substitutes.

    3   pounds red potatoes, peeled and cut into 3/4-inch chunks
         Table salt
   3/4 cup mayonnaise
   1/2 cup buttermilk
   1/4 cup white wine vinegar, divided
   1/4 cup drained jarred roasted red peppers, chopped fine
    3   tablespoons finely chopped fresh cilantro
    3   scallions, chopped fine
    1   garlic clove, minced
   1/8 teaspoon dried dill
    2   teaspoons pepper
    2   tablespoons Dijon mustard

Amish Potato Salad

Ranch Potato Salad

1. Bring potatoes, 1 tablespoon salt, and enough water to cover potatoes by 1 inch to boil in large pot over high heat. Reduce heat to medium and simmer until potatoes are just tender, about 10 minutes. While potatoes simmer, whisk mayonnaise, buttermilk, 2 tablespoons vinegar, red peppers, cilantro, scallions, garlic, dill, 1 teaspoon salt, and pepper in large bowl.

2. Drain potatoes thoroughly, then spread out on rimmed baking sheet. Whisk mustard and remaining vinegar in small bowl. Drizzle mustard mixture over hot potatoes and toss until evenly coated. Refrigerate until cooled, about 30 minutes.

3. Transfer cooled potatoes to bowl with mayonnaise mixture and toss to combine. Cover and refrigerate until well chilled, about 30 minutes. Serve. (Salad can be refrigerated for up to 2 days.)

Dill Potato Salad
SERVES 8

WHY THIS RECIPE WORKS We wanted potato salad with vibrant dill flavor through and through. We seasoned our potato salad with three rounds of dill: first as an herb sachet while the potatoes simmered, next as a piquant dill vinegar, and finally as a fresh sprinkle. A dressing based on a combination of mayonnaise and sour cream, accented with Dijon mustard, let our dill flavor shine.

Use both dill stems and chopped leaves (sometimes called fronds) in the herb sachet. Trois Petits Cochons is our favorite brand of Dijon mustard.

- ¼ cup white wine vinegar
- 3 tablespoons minced fresh dill, divided, plus ½ cup leaves and stems, chopped coarse
- 3 pounds Yukon Gold potatoes, peeled and cut into ¾-inch pieces
  Table salt and pepper
- ½ cup mayonnaise
- ¼ cup sour cream
- 1 tablespoon Dijon mustard
- 3 scallions, green parts only, sliced thin

1. Combine vinegar and 1 tablespoon minced dill in bowl and microwave until steaming, 30 to 60 seconds. Set at room temperature until cool, 15 to 20 minutes.

2. Meanwhile, place chopped dill inside disposable coffee filter and tie closed with kitchen twine. Bring potatoes, dill sachet, 1 tablespoon salt, and enough water to cover potatoes by 1 inch to boil in large pot over high heat. Reduce heat to medium and simmer until potatoes are just tender, about 10 minutes.

3. Drain potatoes thoroughly, then transfer to large bowl; discard sachet. Drizzle 2 tablespoons dill vinegar over hot potatoes and toss gently until evenly coated. Refrigerate until cooled, about 30 minutes, stirring once.

4. Whisk mayonnaise, sour cream, remaining dill vinegar, mustard, ½ teaspoon salt, and ¼ teaspoon pepper together until smooth. Add dressing to cooled potatoes. Stir in scallions and remaining 2 tablespoons minced dill. Cover and refrigerate to let flavors meld, about 30 minutes. Season with salt and pepper to taste. Serve. (Salad can be refrigerated for up to 2 days.)

Texas Potato Salad
SERVES 8

WHY THIS RECIPE WORKS Texans take their potato salad up a notch with plenty of mustard and spicy chopped jalapeños. For our version, we started with classic potato salad, using firm Yukon Gold potatoes and a mayonnaise-based dressing seasoned with onion, celery seeds, and dill pickles. To this we added plenty of yellow mustard and spicy jalapeños. We tempered the jalapeños' bite by quick-pickling them, then used the leftover solution to flavor the hot potatoes. A pinch of cayenne added extra kick.

Heinz is our favorite brand of yellow mustard.

- ½ cup red wine vinegar
- 1½ tablespoons sugar
  Table salt and pepper
- 1 teaspoon yellow mustard seeds
- ½ small red onion, sliced thin
- 2 jalapeño chiles (1 sliced into thin rings; 1 stemmed, seeded, and minced)
- 3 pounds Yukon Gold potatoes, peeled and cut into ¾-inch pieces
- 6 tablespoons mayonnaise
- 6 tablespoons yellow mustard
- ¼ teaspoon cayenne pepper
- 2 large hard-cooked eggs, cut into ¼-inch pieces
- 1 celery rib, minced

1. Combine vinegar, sugar, 1½ teaspoons salt, and mustard seeds in bowl and microwave until steaming, about 2 minutes. Whisk until sugar and salt are dissolved. Add onion and jalapeños and set aside until cool, 15 to 20 minutes. Strain onion and jalapeños through fine-mesh strainer set over bowl. Reserve pickled vegetables and vinegar mixture separately.

2. Meanwhile, combine potatoes, 8 cups water, and 1 tablespoon salt in Dutch oven and bring to boil over high heat. Reduce heat to medium and simmer until potatoes are just tender, 10 to 15 minutes.

3. Drain potatoes thoroughly, then transfer to large bowl. Drizzle 2 tablespoons reserved vinegar mixture over hot potatoes and toss gently until evenly coated. (Reserve remaining vinegar mixture for another use.) Refrigerate until cool, about 30 minutes, stirring once halfway through chilling.

4. Whisk mayonnaise, mustard, ½ teaspoon pepper, and cayenne together in bowl until combined. Add mayonnaise mixture, reserved pickled vegetables, eggs, and celery to potatoes and stir gently to combine. Season with salt and pepper to taste. Cover and refrigerate to let flavors blend, about 30 minutes. Serve. (Salad can be refrigerated for up to 2 days.)

Dill Potato Salad

Smashed Potato Salad

SERVES 8 TO 10

WHY THIS RECIPE WORKS For our take on this Southern picnic staple, wanted both the creamy texture of mashed potatoes and the tender chunks of traditional potato salad. Yukon Gold potatoes worked best—their soft skins cooked up tender and saved us from peeling. For a mix of textures, we smashed a third of the boiled spuds with some vinegar before tossing the mashed portion with the cubes. Yellow mustard contributed some extra bite, which we balanced with chopped sweet pickles, and a touch of cayenne. Hard-cooked eggs, scallions, celery, and onion added even more textural variety to finish off our smooth-yet-chunky potato salad.

Use the tip of a paring knife to judge the doneness of the potatoes. If the tip inserts easily into the potato pieces, they are done. Hellmann's Real Mayonnaise is our favorite nationally available mayonnaise. Note that the salad needs to be refrigerated for about 2 hours before serving.

Texas Potato Salad

Smashed Potato Salad

3	pounds Yukon Gold potatoes, unpeeled, cut into 1-inch chunks
	Table salt and pepper
2	tablespoons distilled white vinegar, divided
1	cup mayonnaise
3	tablespoons yellow mustard
¼	teaspoon cayenne pepper
3	hard-cooked large eggs, chopped
3	scallions, sliced thin
½	cup chopped sweet pickles
½	cup finely chopped celery
¼	cup finely chopped onion

1. Combine potatoes, 8 cups water, and 1 tablespoon salt in Dutch oven and bring to boil over high heat. Reduce heat to medium and cook at vigorous simmer until potatoes are tender, 14 to 17 minutes.

2. Drain potatoes in colander. Transfer 3 cups potatoes to large bowl, add 1 tablespoon vinegar, and coarsely mash with potato masher. Transfer remaining potatoes to rimmed baking sheet, drizzle with remaining 1 tablespoon vinegar, and toss gently to combine. Let cool completely, about 15 minutes.

3. Whisk mayonnaise, ½ cup water, mustard, cayenne, 1 teaspoon salt, and 1 teaspoon pepper together in bowl. Stir mayonnaise mixture into mashed potatoes. Fold in eggs, scallions, pickles, celery, onion, and remaining potatoes until combined. (Mixture will be lumpy.)

4. Cover and refrigerate until fully chilled, about 2 hours. Season with salt and pepper to taste. Serve.

Lemon and Herb Red Potato Salad

SERVES 8

Lemon and Herb Red Potato Salad

WHY THIS RECIPE WORKS Too often potato salad is weighed down by a heavy mayonnaise-based dressing; we sought a lighter alternative. We used waxy red potatoes, as they are lower in starch than russets and more colorful than Yukon Golds. To prevent them from breaking down too much, we added vinegar to the cooking water, giving us tender but firm potatoes that held their shape. A mixture of capers, olive oil, and lemon juice and zest complemented the potatoes' earthiness, while tarragon, parsley, and chives provided freshness. Adding some of the herbed vinaigrette while the potatoes were still hot ensured that they best absorbed all of its flavor.

To rinse the onion, place it in a fine-mesh strainer and run it under cold water. This removes some of the onion's harshness. Drain, but do not rinse, the capers here.

- 3 pounds red potatoes, unpeeled, cut into 1-inch chunks
- 2 tablespoons distilled white vinegar
- Table salt and pepper
- 2 teaspoons grated lemon zest plus 3 tablespoons juice
- 1/3 cup extra-virgin olive oil
- 1/2 cup finely chopped onion, rinsed
- 3 tablespoons minced fresh tarragon
- 3 tablespoons minced fresh parsley
- 3 tablespoons minced fresh chives
- 2 tablespoons capers, minced

1. Combine potatoes, 8 cups water, vinegar, and 2 tablespoons salt in Dutch oven and bring to boil over high heat. Reduce heat to medium and cook at strong simmer until potatoes are just tender, 10 to 15 minutes.

2. Meanwhile, whisk lemon zest and juice, 1 teaspoon salt, and 1/2 teaspoon pepper together in large bowl. Slowly whisk in oil until emulsified; set aside.

3. Drain potatoes thoroughly, then transfer to rimmed baking sheet. Drizzle 2 tablespoons dressing over hot potatoes and toss gently until evenly coated. Let potatoes cool, about 30 minutes, stirring once halfway through cooling.

4. Whisk dressing to recombine and stir in onion, tarragon, parsley, chives, and capers. Add cooled potatoes to dressing and stir gently to combine. Season with salt and pepper to taste. Serve warm or at room temperature.

Potato, Green Bean, and Tomato Salad

SERVES 4

WHY THIS RECIPE WORKS We wanted a substantial salad that was simple to make and heavy on the vegetables. The secret to getting tender potatoes and vibrant green beans was to stagger the cooking. We boiled the potatoes until just tender and then added the beans so they finished cooking at the same time. Marinating the tomatoes in the dressing infused them with flavor. An easy vinaigrette plus lots of fresh parsley leaves and dill tied our hearty salad together.

Make sure to scrub the potatoes well. High-quality extra-virgin olive oil makes a big difference here. You can substitute cherry tomatoes for the grape tomatoes, if desired. For the best results, use a rubber spatula to combine the ingredients in steps 3 and 4.

- 1 1/2 pounds Yukon Gold potatoes, unpeeled, cut into 3/4-inch chunks
- 3/4 teaspoon table salt, plus salt for cooking vegetables
- 1 pound green beans, trimmed and cut into 1-inch pieces
- 1/2 cup extra-virgin olive oil
- 1/4 cup white wine vinegar
- 3/4 teaspoon pepper
- 6 ounces grape tomatoes, halved
- 1/4 cup capers
- 1 shallot, sliced thin
- 2 anchovy fillets, rinsed and minced (optional)
- 1/2 cup fresh parsley leaves
- 1/4 cup chopped fresh dill

1. Place potatoes and 2 teaspoons salt in large saucepan and cover with water by 1 inch. Bring to boil over high heat. Reduce heat to medium-low and simmer until potatoes are almost tender, about 7 minutes. Add green beans and continue to cook until both vegetables are tender, about 7 minutes longer.

2. Meanwhile, whisk oil, vinegar, pepper, and salt together in large bowl; measure out 1/4 cup dressing and set aside. Add tomatoes; capers; shallot; and anchovies, if using, to bowl with remaining dressing and toss to coat; set aside.

3. Drain potatoes and green beans thoroughly in colander, then spread out on rimmed baking sheet. Drizzle reserved dressing over potatoes and green beans and, using rubber spatula, toss gently to combine. Let cool slightly, about 15 minutes.

4. Add parsley, dill, and potato mixture to bowl with tomato mixture and toss to combine. Season with salt and pepper to taste. Serve.

rise-and-shine breakfast and breads

546	Fluffy Diner-Style Cheese Omelet	**569**	Beer-Batter Cheese Bread
547	"Impossible" Ham-and-Cheese Pie	**570**	Spicy Cheese Bread
548	Breakfast Pizza	**571**	Perfect Popovers
549	Adjaruli Khachapuri	**572**	Whole-Wheat Blueberry Muffins
550	Texas Breakfast Tacos	**573**	Morning Glory Muffins
551	Brunch Burgers	**573**	Browned Butter Chocolate Chunk Muffins
553	Homemade Breakfast Sausage	**575**	Muffin Tin Doughnuts
554	Short-Order Home Fries	**576**	Ultimate Cinnamon Buns
555	Better-Than-the-Box Pancake Mix	**577**	Quicker Cinnamon Buns
556	Fluffy Cornmeal Pancakes	**578**	Triple-Chocolate Sticky Buns
557	Dutch Baby	**579**	Morning Buns
557	Cheese Blintzes with Raspberry Sauce	**580**	New Jersey Crumb Buns
558	Beignets	**582**	Alabama Orange Rolls
560	Malasadas	**583**	Kolaches
561	Cornmeal Biscuits	**584**	Cream Cheese Kringle
561	Butter and Lard Biscuits	**586**	Chocolate Babka
563	Cat Head Biscuits	**587**	Monkey Bread
564	Blueberry Biscuits	**588**	Amish Cinnamon Bread
565	Mixed Berry Scones	**589**	English Muffin Bread
566	Jalapeño-Cheddar Scones	**590**	Brown Soda Bread
567	Blueberry Cornbread	**591**	Dakota Bread
568	Southern-Style Skillet Cornbread	**592**	Mana'eesh Za'atar (Za'atar Flatbreads)

Recipe Photos (from left to right): Jalapeño-Cheddar Scones, Alabama Orange Rolls

Fluffy Diner-Style Cheese Omelet

SERVES 2

WHY THIS RECIPE WORKS For a tall, fluffy diner-worthy omelet, we ditched the whisk for an electric mixer, which helped us incorporate air into the eggs. Cream added richness, but when we added it to the whipped eggs, the omelet lost its fluffiness. Combining the cream and eggs before whipping didn't work either—the fat in the cream made it impossible to whip air into the eggs. Instead, we whipped the dairy first, then folded it into the whipped eggs. After letting the bottom of the omelet set on the stovetop, we popped the skillet into a preheated oven, and just six minutes later had a puffy, fluffy omelet, cooked to perfection.

Although this recipe will work with a stand mixer, a handheld mixer makes quick work of whipping such a small amount of cream. To make two omelets, double this recipe and cook the omelets simultaneously in two skillets. If you have only one skillet, prepare a double batch of ingredients and set half aside for the second omelet. Be sure to wipe out the skillet in between omelets.

- 3 tablespoons heavy cream, chilled
- 5 large eggs, room temperature
- ¼ teaspoon table salt
- 2 tablespoons unsalted butter
- 2 ounces sharp cheddar cheese, shredded (½ cup), divided
- 1 recipe omelet filling, divided (optional) (recipes follow)

1. Adjust oven rack to middle position and heat oven to 400 degrees. Using stand mixer fitted with whisk, whip cream on medium-low speed until foamy, about 1 minute. Increase speed to high and whip until soft peaks form, 1 to 3 minutes. Set whipped cream aside. Using dry, clean bowl and whisk attachment, whip eggs and salt on high speed until frothy and eggs have tripled in size, about 2 minutes. Gently fold whipped cream into eggs.

2. Melt butter in ovensafe 10-inch nonstick skillet over medium-low heat, swirling pan to coat bottom and sides. Add egg mixture and cook until edges are nearly set, 2 to 3 minutes. Sprinkle with ¼ cup cheddar and half of omelet filling, if using, and transfer to oven. Bake until eggs are set and edges are beginning to brown, 6 to 8 minutes.

3. Carefully remove pan from oven (handle will be very hot), sprinkle eggs with remaining ¼ cup cheddar and remaining omelet filling, if using, and let sit, covered, until cheese begins to melt, about 1 minute. Tilt pan and, using rubber spatula, push half of omelet onto cutting board, then fold omelet over itself to form half-moon shape. Cut omelet in half and serve.

Sausage and Pepper Filling
MAKES ABOUT 1 CUP

- 4 ounces hot or sweet Italian sausage, casings removed
- 1 tablespoon unsalted butter
- 1 small onion, chopped
- ½ red bell pepper, chopped
- Table salt and pepper

Cook sausage in 10-inch nonstick skillet over medium heat, breaking up clumps with wooden spoon, until browned, about 6 minutes. Transfer to paper towel–lined plate. Add butter, onion, and bell pepper to now-empty skillet and cook until softened, about 10 minutes. Stir in sausage and season with salt and pepper to taste.

Loaded Baked Potato Filling
MAKES ABOUT 1 CUP

- 1 large Yukon Gold potato, peeled and cut into ½-inch pieces
- 4 slices bacon, chopped
- 2 scallions, sliced thin
- Table salt and pepper

Microwave potato, covered, in large bowl until just tender, 2 to 5 minutes. Cook bacon in 10-inch nonstick skillet over medium heat until crispy, about 8 minutes. Transfer bacon to paper towel–lined plate; pour off all but 1 tablespoon bacon fat. Add potato to skillet and cook until golden brown, about 6 minutes. Transfer potato to bowl, add cooked bacon, and stir in scallions. Season with salt and pepper to taste.

"Impossible" Ham-and-Cheese Pie

SERVES 8

WHY THIS RECIPE WORKS "Impossible" pie is a 1970s phenomenon that promises a pie "crust" without rolling out finicky dough. Traditionally, a simple Bisquick batter was whisked with eggs and poured over vegetables, meat, and cheese and baked. To give our "crust" a crispy, browned exterior, we buttered the pie dish and coated it with Parmesan cheese. We replaced the Bisquick with a simple batter of flour, baking powder, eggs, and creamy half-and-half. Doubling the number of eggs made for a richer, custardy pie. For the filling, we chose ingredients that required a minimum of prep work: scallions, diced deli ham, and Gruyère cheese.

Use a rasp-style grater or the smallest holes on a box grater for the Parmesan.

- 1 tablespoon unsalted butter, softened, plus 2 tablespoons melted
- 3 tablespoons finely grated Parmesan cheese
- 8 ounces Gruyère cheese, shredded (2 cups)
- 4 ounces thickly sliced deli ham, chopped
- 4 scallions, minced
- ½ cup (2½ ounces) all-purpose flour
- ¾ teaspoon baking powder
- ½ teaspoon pepper
- ¼ teaspoon table salt
- 1 cup half-and-half
- 4 large eggs, lightly beaten
- 2 teaspoons Dijon mustard
- ⅛ teaspoon ground nutmeg

1. Adjust oven rack to lowest position and heat oven to 350 degrees. Grease 9-inch pie plate with softened butter, then coat plate evenly with Parmesan.

2. Combine Gruyère, ham, and scallions in bowl. Sprinkle cheese-and-ham mixture evenly in bottom of prepared pie dish. Combine flour, baking powder, pepper, and salt in now-empty bowl. Whisk in half-and-half, eggs, melted butter, mustard, and nutmeg until smooth. Slowly pour batter over cheese-and-ham mixture in pie dish.

3. Bake until pie is light golden brown and filling is set, 30 to 35 minutes. Let cool on wire rack for 15 minutes. Slice into wedges. Serve warm.

Fluffy Diner-Style Cheese Omelet

"Impossible" Ham-and-Cheese Pie

Breakfast Pizza

Adjaruli Khachapuri

Breakfast Pizza

SERVES 6

WHY THIS RECIPE WORKS Eggs and bacon on a cheese pizza? Sounded like an excellent breakfast to us. Our challenge was to achieve a crisp, golden-brown crust without overcooking the eggs. We gave the crust a head start by parbaking it for 5 minutes. The remaining oven time cooked the eggs and other toppings to perfection. To keep the eggs in place while they cooked, we created wells in the cheese. Though we initially used ricotta, it became dry and grainy in the oven. Then we tried cottage cheese and were pleasantly surprised to find the curds melted in the oven, leaving a creamy, silky cheese layer that tied everything together.

Small-curd cottage cheese is sometimes labeled "country-style." Room-temperature dough is much easier to shape than cold, so pull the dough from the fridge about 1 hour before you start cooking.

- 3 tablespoons extra-virgin olive oil, divided, plus extra for drizzling
- 6 slices bacon
- 8 ounces mozzarella cheese, shredded (2 cups)
- 1 ounce Parmesan cheese, grated (½ cup)
- 4 ounces (½ cup) small-curd cottage cheese
- ¼ teaspoon dried oregano
  Table salt and pepper
  Pinch cayenne pepper
- 1 pound store-bought pizza dough, room temperature
- 6 large eggs
- 2 scallions, sliced thin
- 2 tablespoons minced fresh chives

1. Adjust oven rack to lowest position and heat oven to 500 degrees. Grease rimmed baking sheet with 1 tablespoon oil.

2. Cook bacon in 12-inch skillet over medium heat until crispy, 7 to 9 minutes. Transfer to paper towel–lined plate; when cool enough to handle, crumble bacon. Combine mozzarella and Parmesan in bowl; set aside. Combine cottage cheese, oregano, ¼ teaspoon pepper, cayenne, and 1 tablespoon oil in separate bowl; set aside.

3. Press and roll dough into 15 by 11-inch rectangle on lightly floured counter, pulling on corners to help make distinct rectangle. Transfer dough to prepared sheet and press to edges of sheet. Brush edges of dough with remaining 1 tablespoon oil. Bake dough until top appears dry and bottom is just beginning to brown, about 5 minutes.

4. Remove crust from oven and, using spatula, press down on any air bubbles. Spread cottage cheese mixture evenly over top, leaving 1-inch border around edges. Sprinkle bacon evenly over cottage cheese mixture.

5. Sprinkle mozzarella mixture evenly over pizza, leaving ½-inch border. Create 2 rows of 3 evenly spaced small wells in cheese, each about 3 inches in diameter (6 wells total). Crack 1 egg into each well, then season each with salt and pepper.

6. Return pizza to oven and bake until crust is light golden around edges and eggs are just set, 9 to 10 minutes for slightly runny yolks or 11 to 12 minutes for soft-cooked yolks, rotating sheet halfway through baking.

7. Transfer pizza to wire rack and let cool for 5 minutes. Transfer pizza to cutting board. Sprinkle with scallions and chives and drizzle with extra oil. Slice and serve.

Smoked Salmon Breakfast Pizza

In step 7, after cooling, omit scallions and top pizza with ¼ cup sliced red onion, 3 ounces sliced smoked salmon (cut into thin strips), and ¼ cup sour cream. Sprinkle with chives and 1 tablespoon chopped fresh dill and drizzle with extra oil.

Sausage and Red Bell Pepper Breakfast Pizza

Substitute 6 ounces bulk breakfast sausage for bacon and extra-sharp cheddar for mozzarella. Combine sausage; 1 stemmed, seeded, and chopped red bell pepper; 1 chopped onion; and ¼ teaspoon salt in 12-inch skillet. Cook over medium heat, breaking up sausage with spoon, until sausage begins to brown and bell pepper and onion are translucent, about 6 minutes. Transfer to paper towel–lined plate. Let mixture cool completely before proceeding.

Chorizo and Manchego Breakfast Pizza

Substitute 6 ounces chorizo sausage, halved lengthwise and cut into ½-inch slices, for bacon and 1 cup shredded Manchego cheese for Parmesan. Cook chorizo in 12-inch skillet over medium heat until lightly browned, 7 to 9 minutes. Let cool completely before proceeding.

Adjaruli Khachapuri

SERVES 6

WHY THIS RECIPE WORKS Adjaruli khachapuri is a bread stuffed with melty cheese hailing from the country of Georgia. When the bread is hot from the oven, the molten cheese is topped with an egg and butter and stirred together. We used a simple pizza dough since it was easy to shape, provided structure to contain the cheese, and had a chewy texture. We found that a mix of mozzarella and feta approximated the tang and stringy texture found in Georgian cheeses. Stirring in an egg yolk and a pat of butter right before serving kept the cheese filling smooth and stretchy. While khachapuri is perfect party food, it can also be enjoyed as a savory breakfast.

Using cold water in the dough keeps it from overheating in the food processor. Use block mozzarella, not fresh, here.

1¾ cups (8¾ ounces) all-purpose flour
1½ teaspoons sugar
 1   teaspoon instant or rapid-rise yeast
 ¾   teaspoon table salt
 ½   cup plus 2 tablespoons cold water
 1   tablespoon extra-virgin olive oil
 6   ounces whole-milk mozzarella cheese, shredded (1½ cups)
 6   ounces feta cheese, crumbled (1½ cups)
 1   large egg yolk
 1   tablespoon unsalted butter

1. Process flour, sugar, yeast, and salt in food processor until combined, about 3 seconds. With processor running, slowly add cold water and oil and process until dough forms sticky ball that clears sides of bowl, 30 to 60 seconds.

2. Transfer dough to counter and knead until smooth, about 1 minute. Shape dough into tight ball and place in greased bowl. Cover bowl with plastic wrap and let dough rise at room temperature until almost doubled in size, 2 to 2½ hours. (Alternatively, dough can rise in refrigerator until doubled in size, about 24 hours. Let come to room temperature, about 2 hours, before proceeding.)

3. Turn out dough onto lightly floured 16 by 12-inch sheet of parchment paper and coat lightly with flour. Flatten into 8-inch disk using your hands. Using rolling pin, roll dough into 12-inch circle, dusting dough lightly with flour as needed.

4. Roll bottom edge of dough 2½ inches in toward center. Rotate parchment 180 degrees and roll bottom edge of dough (directly opposite first rolled side) 2½ inches toward center. (Opposing edges of rolled sides should be 7 inches apart.)

5. Roll ends of rolled sides toward centerline and pinch firmly together to form football shape about 12 inches long and about 7 inches across at its widest point. Transfer parchment with dough to rimmed baking sheet. Cover loosely with plastic and let rise until puffy, 30 minutes to 1 hour. Adjust oven rack to middle position and heat oven to 450 degrees.

6. Combine mozzarella and feta in bowl. Fill dough with cheese mixture, lightly compacting and mounding in center (cheese will be piled higher than edge of dough). Bake until crust is well browned and cheese is bubbly and beginning to brown in spots, 15 to 17 minutes. Transfer sheet to wire rack. Add egg yolk and butter to cheese filling and stir with fork until fully incorporated and cheese is smooth and stretchy. Lift parchment off sheet and slide bread onto serving dish. Serve immediately.

Stages of Beauty and Bliss

1. Add egg yolk and butter to molten cheese filling and stir with fork.

2. Stir until fully incorporated and cheese is smooth and stretchy.

3. Serve immediately, dipping torn crust into the melted filling.

Texas Breakfast Tacos

SERVES 4 TO 6

WHY THIS RECIPE WORKS We love tacos for lunch and dinner, so why not for the most important meal of the day? For our take on southern Texas egg-stuffed tacos, we made flour tortillas from scratch, which was well worth the effort. After kneading and chilling the dough, we rolled out 6-inch rounds and cooked them in a skillet. For the hearty filling, we crisped bacon, leaving some of its fat in the skillet to help soften and flavor chopped onion and minced jalapeño. We added the eggs last, scrambling them with the vegetables and bacon, and topped the tacos with Monterey Jack cheese, our cooked red salsa, and a squeeze of lime.

If you're using an electric stovetop for the eggs, heat a second burner on low and move the skillet to it when it's time to adjust the heat. You can substitute 12 (6-inch) store-bought tortillas for the homemade.

- 1 pound plum tomatoes, cored and chopped
- 2 garlic cloves, chopped
- 2 jalapeño chiles, stemmed, seeded, and chopped, divided
- 2 tablespoons chopped fresh cilantro
- 1 tablespoon lime juice
  Table salt and pepper
- ¼ teaspoon red pepper flakes
- 12 large eggs
- 6 slices thick-cut bacon, cut into ½-inch pieces
- 1 small onion, chopped fine
- 1 recipe Homemade Taco-Size Flour Tortillas (recipe follows)
  Shredded Monterey Jack cheese
  Thinly sliced scallions
  Lime wedges

1. Microwave tomatoes and garlic in bowl until liquid begins to pool in bottom of bowl, about 4 minutes; transfer to fine-mesh strainer set over bowl and let drain for 5 minutes; discard liquid.

2. Process tomato mixture, half of jalapeños, cilantro, lime juice, 1 teaspoon salt, and pepper flakes in blender until smooth, about 45 seconds. Season with salt to taste; set aside for serving. (Salsa can be refrigerated for up to 3 days.)

3. Whisk eggs, ½ teaspoon salt, and ¼ teaspoon pepper in bowl until thoroughly combined and mixture is pure yellow, about 1 minute. Set aside.

The Complete Cook's Country TV Show Cookbook

4. Cook bacon in 12-inch nonstick skillet over medium heat until crispy, 8 to 10 minutes. Pour off all but 2 tablespoons fat from skillet (leaving bacon in skillet). Add onion and remaining jalapeños and cook until vegetables are softened and lightly browned, 4 to 6 minutes.

5. Add egg mixture and, using rubber spatula, constantly and firmly scrape along bottom and sides of skillet until eggs begin to clump and spatula leaves trail on bottom of skillet, 1½ to 2½ minutes.

6. Reduce heat to low. Gently but constantly fold egg mixture until it has clumped and is still slightly wet, 30 to 60 seconds. Season with salt and pepper to taste. Fill tortillas with egg mixture and serve immediately, passing salsa, Monterey Jack, scallions, and lime wedges separately.

Homemade Taco-Size Flour Tortillas
MAKES 12 (6-INCH) TORTILLAS

Lard can be substituted for the shortening, if desired.

- 2 cups (10 ounces) all-purpose flour
- 1¼ teaspoons table salt
- 5 tablespoons vegetable shortening, cut into ½-inch chunks
- ⅔ cup warm tap water
- 1 teaspoon vegetable oil

1. Combine flour and salt in large bowl. Using your fingers, rub shortening into flour mixture until mixture resembles coarse meal. Stir in warm water until combined.

2. Turn dough out onto counter and knead briefly to form smooth, cohesive ball. Divide dough into 12 equal portions; roll each into smooth 1-inch ball between your hands. Transfer to plate, cover with plastic wrap, and refrigerate until dough is firm, at least 30 minutes or up to 2 days.

3. Cut twelve 6-inch squares of parchment paper. Roll 1 dough ball into 6-inch circle on lightly floured counter. Transfer to parchment square; set aside. Repeat with remaining dough balls, stacking tortillas with parchment squares in between.

4. Heat oil in 12-inch nonstick skillet over medium heat until shimmering. Wipe out skillet with paper towels, leaving thin film of oil. Cook 1 tortilla until spotty brown and beginning to bubble, about 45 seconds per side, adjusting heat as needed. Transfer to plate and cover with clean dish towel. Repeat with remaining tortillas. (Cooled tortillas can be layered between parchment squares, covered, and refrigerated for up to 3 days. Before serving, discard plastic and parchment, wrap tortillas with clean dish towel, and microwave at 50 percent power until heated through, about 20 seconds.)

Texas Breakfast Tacos

Brunch Burgers
SERVES 4

WHY THIS RECIPE WORKS For a burger with the perfect balance of brunch flavors, adding a fried egg and bacon on top was just the beginning. Mixing breakfast sausage in with ground beef ensured savory porkiness and extra flavor in every bite. (For food safety, you'll have to cook the patty through to well-done, but don't worry: The extra fat from the sausage ensures that the patty stays moist and juicy.) Spiking mayonnaise with maple syrup provided a sugary hit that cut through the richness and added an unmistakable breakfast-y taste. A dollop of minced chipotle chile brought smoky heat to enliven the heavier components. Toasted brioche buns tied it all together, their eggy sweetness complementing the other ingredients perfectly.

Brunch Burgers

Homemade Breakfast Sausage

(And for even more breakfast flavor and a welcome crunch, try coating the buns with everything bagel seasoning!)

If you're spice averse, use less chipotle chile. We like the sweetness that maple syrup adds to the sauce, but you can omit it for a more savory flavor. You can use 80 percent lean ground beef here, but the burgers will exude more fat while they cook. If desired, serve these burgers on Everything Bagel–Seasoned Buns (recipe follows). We like to serve these burgers as is, but they're also good topped with your favorite burger fixings (such as lettuce, tomatoes, pickles, or sautéed onions) or thinly sliced apples.

½ cup mayonnaise
1–1½ tablespoons minced canned chipotle chile in adobo sauce
1 tablespoon Worcestershire sauce
1 tablespoon maple syrup (optional)
¾ teaspoon pepper, divided
1 pound 85 percent lean ground beef
8 ounces bulk breakfast sausage
4 slices thick-cut bacon, halved crosswise
¼ teaspoon plus pinch table salt, divided
4 slices cheddar cheese (4 ounces)
4 large eggs
4 brioche hamburger buns, toasted

1. Combine mayonnaise; chipotle; Worcestershire; maple syrup, if using; and ½ teaspoon pepper in bowl. Set aside.

2. Combine ground beef and sausage in large bowl and knead with your hands until roughly combined. Divide meat mixture into 4 equal portions, then shape each portion into 4½-inch-wide patty. Using your fingertips, press center of each patty to create slight divot. (Patties can be covered with plastic wrap and refrigerated for up to 24 hours.)

3. Cook bacon in 12-inch nonstick skillet over medium heat, flipping occasionally, until crispy, 8 to 10 minutes. Transfer bacon to paper towel–lined plate. Pour off and reserve all but 1 teaspoon fat from skillet.

4. Heat fat left in skillet over medium-high heat until just smoking. Sprinkle patties with ¼ teaspoon salt and remaining ¼ teaspoon pepper. Transfer patties to skillet and cook until well browned on first side, 4 to 6 minutes. Flip patties, top with cheddar, and reduce heat to medium-low. Continue to cook until browned on second side and meat registers 160 degrees, 5 to 7 minutes longer.

> **Making Brunch Burger Patties**
>
>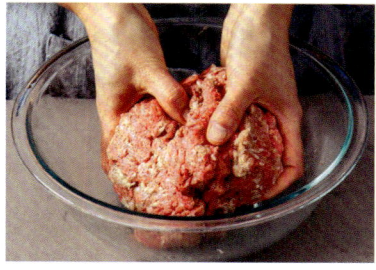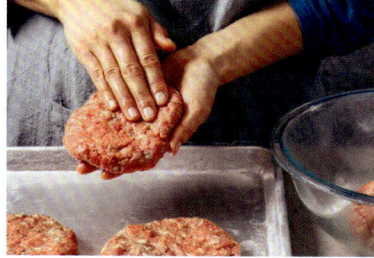
>
> **1.** Combine ground beef and sausage in large bowl and knead with your hands until roughly combined.
>
> **2.** Divide meat mixture into 4 equal portions, then shape each portion into 4½-inch-wide patty.
>
> **3.** Using your fingertips, press center of each patty, creating slight divot to keep patties flat during cooking.

5. Transfer burgers to paper towel–lined plate. Pour off fat from skillet. Wipe skillet clean with paper towels.

6. Crack eggs into 2 small bowls (2 eggs per bowl) and sprinkle with remaining pinch salt. Add 1 tablespoon reserved bacon fat to now-empty skillet and heat over medium-high heat until shimmering. Swirl to coat skillet with fat, then, working quickly, pour 1 bowl of eggs in 1 side of skillet and second bowl of eggs in other side. Cover and cook for 1 minute. Remove skillet from heat and let sit, covered, for 15 to 45 seconds for runny yolks (white around edge of yolk will be barely opaque), 45 to 60 seconds for soft but set yolks, or about 2 minutes for medium-set yolks.

7. Spread mayonnaise mixture on cut sides of buns. Place burgers on bun bottoms, then top with bacon, eggs, and bun tops. Serve.

Everything Bagel–Seasoned Buns
SERVES 4

Use a store-bought seasoning, or make your own by mixing ½ teaspoon each sesame seeds, poppy seeds, dried minced garlic, dried onion flakes, and kosher salt.

- 4 brioche hamburger buns
- 1 large egg, lightly beaten
- 2½ teaspoons everything bagel seasoning

Adjust oven rack to middle position and heat oven to 350 degrees. Arrange buns on rimmed baking sheet. Brush tops of buns with egg (you needn't use all of it) and sprinkle with everything bagel seasoning. Bake until egg is dry and set, about 5 minutes. Serve.

Homemade Breakfast Sausage
MAKES 16 PATTIES

WHY THIS RECIPE WORKS Commercially made breakfast sausage always disappoints when it comes to flavor, tasting either too sweet or salty, or too bland or highly seasoned, so we decided to make our own. We started with ground pork with some fat in it (lean meat was neither fatty nor flavorful enough) and amped up its mild flavor with classic breakfast sausage flavors: garlic, sage, thyme, and cayenne pepper. A spoonful of maple syrup sweetened the patties nicely. To combine the meat mixture, we kneaded it gently with our hands, but were careful not to overmix it, which would toughen the meat.

Avoid lean or extra-lean ground pork; it makes the sausage dry, crumbly, and less flavorful.

- 2 pounds ground pork
- 1 tablespoon maple syrup
- 1 garlic clove, minced
- 2 teaspoons dried sage
- 1½ teaspoons pepper
- 1 teaspoon table salt
- ½ teaspoon dried thyme
- ⅛ teaspoon cayenne pepper
- 2 tablespoons unsalted butter

RISE-AND-SHINE BREAKFAST AND BREADS

1. Combine pork, maple syrup, garlic, sage, pepper, salt, thyme, and cayenne in large bowl. Gently mix with hands until well combined. Using greased ¼-cup measure, divide mixture into 16 patties and place on rimmed baking sheet. Cover patties with plastic wrap, then gently flatten each one to ½-inch thickness.

2. Melt 1 tablespoon butter in 12-inch nonstick skillet over medium heat. Cook half of patties until well browned and cooked through, 6 to 10 minutes. Transfer to paper towel–lined plate and tent with aluminum foil. Wipe out skillet. Repeat with remaining butter and patties. Serve.

To Make Ahead Follow recipe through step 1. Refrigerate uncooked patties for up to 1 day or freeze for up to 1 month. To serve, proceed as directed in step 2, increasing cooking time to 14 to 18 minutes.

Short-Order Home Fries

SERVES 4

WHY THIS RECIPE WORKS Though a commercial-grade griddle helps our local diner serve up home fries with a perfectly crispy exterior, the real secret is precooking the potatoes. Roasting or boiling our spuds took too much time for a quick breakfast side, so we turned to the microwave to jump-start their cooking before frying them in a large skillet. We found that packing the potatoes down with a spatula and cooking them a few minutes before turning them and then repeating these steps ensured that they were evenly browned and extra-crunchy. Finally, we stirred in some sautéed onion and garlic salt to give our home fries a deep, savory flavor.

Although we prefer the sweetness of Yukon Gold potatoes, other medium-starch potatoes, such as red potatoes, can be substituted. If you want to spice things up, add a pinch of cayenne pepper.

- 1½ pounds Yukon Gold potatoes, cut into ¾-inch pieces
- 4 tablespoons unsalted butter, divided
- 1 onion, chopped fine
- ½ teaspoon garlic salt
- ½ teaspoon table salt
  Pepper

1. Place potatoes and 1 tablespoon butter in large bowl and microwave, covered, until edges of potatoes begin to soften, 5 to 7 minutes, stirring halfway through cooking.

2. Meanwhile, melt 1 tablespoon butter in 12-inch nonstick skillet over medium heat. Add onion and cook until softened and golden brown, 8 to 10 minutes. Transfer to small bowl.

3. Melt remaining 2 tablespoons butter in now-empty skillet over medium heat. Add potatoes and pack down with spatula. Cook, without moving, until bottoms of potatoes are brown, 5 to 7 minutes. Turn potatoes, pack down again, and continue to cook until well browned and crisp, 5 to 7 minutes. Reduce heat to medium-low and continue to cook until potatoes are crusty, 9 to 12 minutes, stirring occasionally. Stir in onion, garlic salt, and salt and season with pepper to taste. Serve.

Greek Diner–Style Home Fries
Omit garlic salt and add 1 tablespoon lemon juice, 2 minced garlic cloves, and ½ teaspoon dried oregano to potatoes along with onion in step 3.

Home Fries with Fresh Herbs
Add 1 teaspoon each chopped fresh basil, parsley, thyme, and tarragon to potatoes along with onion in step 3.

> **The Right Spuds for Home Fries**
>
> High-starch, low-moisture potatoes, such as russets, may be great for baking and mashing, but when it comes to home fries, they are not the best choice. The fluffy flesh of these potatoes breaks down in the skillet, leaving nothing but a greasy pool of stodgy spuds. For tender tubers that retain their texture, we prefer medium-starch varieties, such as Yukon Gold and red potatoes. They hold their shape in the skillet, develop a great crust, and fry up to a beautiful golden brown.
>
>
>
> **RUSSET POTATOES**
> A falling-apart mess
>
>
>
> **YUKON GOLD POTATOES**
> Intact, crisp, and browned

Better-Than-the-Box Pancake Mix

MAKES ABOUT 6 CUPS; ENOUGH FOR 24 PANCAKES

WHY THIS RECIPE WORKS For our take on pancake mix that delivers both store-bought ease and from-scratch taste, we combined all-purpose flour with cake flour; this duo yielded sturdy yet tender cakes. To give pancakes made from our mix complexity and depth, we added an unusual ingredient, malted milk powder, which imparted a sweet, nutty flavor. Though most mixes call for shortening, we opted for butter, which gave us moister, more flavorful pancakes. Using buttermilk instead of milk when mixing the batter gave us high-rising pancakes—the acid of the buttermilk reacts with the baking soda, causing the batter to bubble and rise.

Malted milk powder might seem odd here, but it gives the pancakes a deeper, more complex flavor.

- 2 cups (10 ounces) all-purpose flour
- 2 cups (8 ounces) cake flour
- 1 cup (3 ounces) nonfat dry milk powder
- ¾ cup (3⅓ ounces) malted milk powder
- ⅓ cup (2⅓ ounces) sugar
- 2 tablespoons baking powder
- 1 teaspoon baking soda
- 1 tablespoon table salt
- 12 tablespoons unsalted butter, cut into ½-inch pieces

Process all ingredients in food processor until no lumps remain and mixture resembles wet sand, about 2 minutes. (Pancake mix can be frozen for up to 2 months.)

Better-Than-the-Box Pancakes

To make 8 pancakes, whisk 2 cups Better-Than-the-Box Pancake Mix, 2 lightly beaten large eggs, and ½ cup buttermilk in large bowl until smooth. Using ¼-cup measure, portion batter into lightly oiled 12-inch nonstick skillet or griddle in 4 places and cook over medium-low heat until golden brown, about 2 minutes per side. Repeat with remaining batter. Serve. (If you don't have buttermilk, whisk 1½ teaspoons lemon juice or white vinegar into ½ cup whole or low-fat milk and let sit until slightly thickened, about 10 minutes.)

Short-Order Home Fries

Better-Than-the-Box Pancake Mix

Fluffy Cornmeal Pancakes

MAKES ABOUT 15 (4-INCH) PANCAKES

WHY THIS RECIPE WORKS Getting the height and lightness of traditional pancakes with the robust flavor and texture of cornmeal pancakes is tougher than it seems. Coarsely ground cornmeal can be sandy, and it lacks the gluten necessary to support a fluffy internal structure. We found that we could use more cornmeal by heating it with some of the buttermilk to soften it first. Soaking the cornmeal also thickened the batter, helping it ride higher in the pan instead of spreading out. Letting the batter sit for a few minutes before griddling the cakes allowed the buttermilk to react with the baking soda, which resulted in fluffier, airier pancakes.

Our favorite cornmeal is Anson Mills Fine Yellow Cornmeal.

- 1¾ cups buttermilk, divided
- 1¼ cups (6¼ ounces) cornmeal
- 2 tablespoons unsalted butter, cut into ¼-inch pieces
- ¾ cup (3¾ ounces) all-purpose flour
- 2 tablespoons sugar
- 1¾ teaspoons baking powder
- ½ teaspoon baking soda
- ½ teaspoon table salt
- 2 large eggs
- 2½ teaspoons vegetable oil

1. Adjust oven rack to middle position and heat oven to 200 degrees. Set wire rack inside rimmed baking sheet and place in oven. Whisk 1¼ cups buttermilk and cornmeal together in medium bowl. Stir in butter, cover, and microwave until slightly thickened around edges, about 90 seconds, stirring once halfway through cooking. Let sit, covered, for 5 minutes.

2. Whisk flour, sugar, baking powder, baking soda, and salt in large bowl. Beat eggs and remaining ½ cup buttermilk together in 1-cup liquid measuring cup. Whisk egg mixture into cornmeal mixture. Whisk cornmeal mixture into flour mixture. Let sit for 10 minutes.

3. Heat ½ teaspoon oil in 12-inch nonstick skillet over medium-low heat until shimmering. Using paper towels, carefully wipe out oil, leaving thin film on bottom of pan. Using level ¼-cup measure for each pancake, drop batter for 3 pancakes into pan. Cook until edges are set and bubbles begin to form on tops of pancakes, about 90 seconds. Flip, then cook until

Fluffy Cornmeal Pancakes

Dutch Baby

second side is golden brown, about 2 minutes longer. Transfer to prepared baking sheet in oven, cover loosely with aluminum foil, and repeat with remaining oil and batter. Serve.

> **The Virtues of Pancake Patience**
>
> For the fluffiest pancakes, let the finished batter sit for 10 minutes before griddling the cakes. The rest gives the baking soda extra time to react and form large air bubbles, lightening the batter, ergo the pancakes. With a hearty whole grain like cornmeal, you want all the lift you can get. This trick works with any pancake batter made with whole grains.

Dutch Baby

SERVES 4

WHY THIS RECIPE WORKS A big, puffy pancake, a Dutch baby puffs and rises as it bakes, then falls in the center a few minutes out of the oven, resulting in a bowl-shaped breakfast treat with crisp sides and a thin, custardy bottom. For our version, we started with a 12-inch skillet; its gently sloping walls promoted an even rise. Brushing the pan with oil and preheating it in the oven helped ensure that the sides had the texture we wanted and jump-started the pancake's rise. Since fats tend to make baked goods tender rather than crisp, we used skim milk in our batter. For even more crispness, we replaced some of the flour with cornstarch.

You can use whole or low-fat milk instead of skim, but the texture won't be as crisp. Serve with an assortment of berries and lightly sweetened whipped cream, if desired.

- 2 tablespoons vegetable oil
- 1 cup (5 ounces) all-purpose flour
- ¼ cup cornstarch
- 2 teaspoons grated lemon zest plus 2 tablespoons juice
- 1 teaspoon table salt
- 3 large eggs
- 1¼ cups skim milk
- 1 tablespoon unsalted butter, melted and cooled
- 1 teaspoon vanilla extract
- 3 tablespoons confectioners' sugar

1. Adjust oven rack to middle position and heat oven to 450 degrees. Brush bottom and sides of 12-inch skillet with oil. Heat skillet in oven until oil is shimmering, about 10 minutes.

2. Meanwhile, combine flour, cornstarch, lemon zest, and salt in large bowl. Whisk eggs in second bowl until frothy and light, about 1 minute. Whisk milk, butter, and vanilla into eggs until incorporated. Whisk one-third of milk mixture into flour mixture until no lumps remain, then slowly whisk in remaining milk mixture until smooth.

3. Carefully pour batter into skillet and bake until edges are deep golden brown and crisp, about 20 minutes. Transfer skillet to wire rack, sprinkle pancake with lemon juice and confectioners' sugar, and cut into wedges. Serve.

Cheese Blintzes with Raspberry Sauce

MAKES 12 BLINTZES, SERVES 4 TO 6

WHY THIS RECIPE WORKS We wanted to create a streamlined version of this eastern European specialty. For our filling, we replaced farmer's cheese with ricotta. Cream cheese added tanginess, while confectioners' sugar provided sweetness and body. We didn't need a crepe pan; a traditional skillet worked just fine, turning out larger crepes that were easier to fill and fold. A bright, quick-cooking raspberry sauce balanced the rich filling.

The batter makes about 15 crepes to account for any mistakes. When making the crepes, if the batter doesn't stick to the skillet when swirling, that means the skillet is too greased and/or not hot enough. Return the skillet to the heat and cook 10 seconds longer; then try again to swirl the batter. With the next try, use less butter to brush the skillet. If the filled and rolled blintzes split on the sides, be careful while searing them because the filling may sputter when it hits the skillet. You do not need to thaw the raspberries.

Filling

- 11 ounces (1¼ cups plus 2 tablespoons) whole-milk ricotta cheese
- ½ cup (2 ounces) confectioners' sugar
- 1 ounce cream cheese, softened
- ¼ teaspoon table salt

Sauce

- 10 ounces (2 cups) frozen raspberries
- ¼ cup (1¾ ounces) granulated sugar
- ¼ teaspoon table salt

Crepes

- 2 cups (10 ounces) all-purpose flour
- 2 teaspoons granulated sugar
- ½ teaspoon table salt
- 3 cups whole milk
- 4 large eggs
- 4 tablespoons unsalted butter, melted and cooled, divided, plus 4 tablespoons unsalted butter, divided

1. For the Filling Whisk all ingredients in bowl until no lumps of cream cheese remain. Refrigerate until ready to use. (Filling can be refrigerated for up to 2 days.)

2. For the Sauce Combine raspberries, sugar, and salt in small saucepan. Cook over medium heat, stirring occasionally, until slightly thickened, 8 to 10 minutes. (Sauce can be refrigerated for up to 2 days.)

3. For the Crepes Whisk flour, sugar, and salt together in medium bowl. Whisk milk and eggs together in separate bowl. Add half of milk mixture to flour mixture and whisk until smooth. Whisk in 3 tablespoons melted butter until incorporated. Whisk in remaining milk mixture until smooth. (Batter can be refrigerated for up to 2 days before cooking. It will separate; rewhisk it before using.)

4. Brush bottom of 12-inch nonstick skillet lightly with some of remaining 1 tablespoon melted butter and heat skillet over medium heat until hot, about 2 minutes. Add ⅓ cup batter to center of skillet and simultaneously lift and rotate skillet in circular motion to swirl batter, allowing batter to run and fully cover bottom of skillet. Cook crepe until edges look dry and start to curl and bottom of crepe is light golden, about 1 minute. Using rubber spatula, lift edge of crepe and slide it onto plate. Repeat with remaining batter, stacking crepes and brushing skillet with melted butter every other time. (Adjust burner between medium-low and medium heat as needed toward end of crepe-making process.)

5. Working with 1 crepe at a time, spoon 2 tablespoons filling onto crepe about 2 inches from bottom edge and spread into 4-inch line. Fold bottom edge of crepe over filling, then fold sides of crepe over filling. Gently roll crepe into tidy package about 4 inches long and 2 inches wide. Repeat with remaining crepes and filling. (Assembled blintzes can be transferred to plate, covered with plastic wrap, and refrigerated for up to 24 hours.)

6. Melt 2 tablespoons butter in now-empty skillet over medium heat. Add half of blintzes, seam sides down, and cook until golden brown, 2 to 4 minutes, gently moving blintzes in skillet as needed for even browning. Using spatula, gently flip blintzes and continue to cook until golden brown on second side, 2 to 4 minutes longer. Transfer blintzes to platter, seam sides down, and wipe skillet clean with paper towels. Repeat with remaining 2 tablespoons butter and remaining blintzes. Serve with raspberry sauce.

To Make Ahead At end of step 5, transfer blintzes to rimmed baking sheet and freeze. Transfer frozen blintzes to zipper-lock bag and freeze for up to 1 month. When ready to cook, do not thaw blintzes. Reduce heat in step 6 to medium-low and cook blintzes, covered, until golden brown, 6 to 9 minutes per side.

Beignets

MAKES 24 BEIGNETS

WHY THIS RECIPE WORKS To replicate the crisp, airy texture and tangy flavor of these classic New Orleans doughnuts, we began by using plenty of yeast, kick-starting it with warm water and sugar to develop its flavor. We added extra water for a super-hydrated dough, so that as soon as the wet dough hit the hot oil, it created lots of steam, giving our beignets an open, honeycombed structure. Since wet dough is tricky to roll out, we let it rise in the refrigerator to firm it up. A few minutes of frying and a shower of powdered sugar, and our beignets were ready to be enjoyed, Big Easy style.

This dough is very wet and sticky, so flour the counter and baking sheet generously. Use a Dutch oven that holds 6 quarts or more for this recipe.

- 1 cup water, heated to 110 degrees
- 3 tablespoons granulated sugar, divided
- 1 tablespoon instant or rapid-rise yeast
- 3 cups (15 ounces) all-purpose flour
- ¾ teaspoon table salt
- 2 large eggs
- 2 tablespoons plus 2 quarts vegetable oil for frying
  Confectioners' sugar

1. Combine water, 1 tablespoon granulated sugar, and yeast in large bowl and let sit until foamy, about 5 minutes. Combine flour, remaining 2 tablespoons granulated sugar, and salt in second bowl. Whisk eggs and 2 tablespoons oil into yeast mixture. Add flour mixture and stir vigorously with rubber spatula until dough comes together. Cover bowl with plastic wrap and refrigerate until nearly doubled in size, about 1 hour.

2. Set wire rack inside rimmed baking sheet. Line second sheet with parchment paper and dust generously with flour. Place half of dough on well-floured counter and pat into rough rectangle with floured hands, flipping to coat with flour. Roll dough into ¼-inch-thick rectangle (roughly 12 by 9 inches). Using pizza wheel, cut dough into twelve 3-inch squares and transfer to floured baking sheet. Repeat with remaining dough.

3. Add remaining oil to large Dutch oven until it measures about 1½ inches deep and heat over medium-high heat to 350 degrees. Fry 6 beignets, adjusting burner as necessary to maintain oil temperature between 325 and 350 degrees, until golden brown, about 3 minutes, flipping halfway through frying. Using slotted spoon or tongs, transfer beignets to prepared baking sheet. Return oil to 350 degrees and repeat with remaining beignets. Dust beignets with confectioners' sugar and serve immediately.

Cheese Blintzes with Raspberry Sauce

> ### Forming Beignets
> This dough is very wet, which allows a network of delicate holes to develop in the beignets. However, wet dough can be tricky to work with. Here's how to easily shape and cut the beignets:
>
>
>
> **1.** Dust counter and rolling pin generously with flour before you roll out chilled beignet dough.
>
> **2.** Cut 3-inch squares with pizza wheel.

Beignets

Malasadas

Cornmeal Biscuits

Malasadas

MAKES 12 MALASADAS

WHY THIS RECIPE WORKS These hole-less doughnuts, which originated in Portugal and found their way to Portuguese American enclaves all over the United States, boast a soft and slightly chewy interior with a crunchy exterior. Since malasada dough is traditionally very wet and difficult to work with, we played with the ratio of the wet and dry ingredients to yield a slightly more workable mixture. To keep our counter clean, we transferred the risen dough to a greased rimmed baking sheet and used a greased bench scraper to create 12 even pieces with minimal mess. For frying, we carefully slipped each disk into 2 quarts of hot oil; a quick, fairly shallow fry was all that was needed to get our malasadas to puff and turn deep golden brown.

This dough is very wet and sticky; be sure to grease your hands to make it easier to work with.

- 2¼ cups (12⅓ ounces) bread flour
- ¼ cup (1¾ ounces) sugar, plus 1 cup for coating
- 2¼ teaspoons instant or rapid-rise yeast
- ½ teaspoon table salt
- ¾ cup whole milk
- 2 large eggs
- 2 tablespoons unsalted butter, melted and cooled
- 1 tablespoon vegetable oil
- 2 quarts vegetable oil for frying

1. Whisk flour, ¼ cup sugar, yeast, and salt together in bowl of stand mixer. Whisk milk, eggs, and melted butter in separate bowl until combined. Add milk mixture to flour mixture. Fit mixer with dough hook and mix on low speed until dough comes together, about 2 minutes. Increase speed to medium and knead until dough is uniform, shiny, and sticky, about 8 minutes (dough will not clear bottom or sides of bowl).

2. Using greased rubber spatula, transfer dough to greased large bowl. Cover with plastic wrap and let rise at room temperature until doubled in size, 1½ to 2 hours.

3. Brush rimmed baking sheet with oil. Turn out dough onto sheet and gently press down to deflate. Divide dough into 12 equal pieces and evenly space pieces on sheet. Using your greased hands, pat each piece of dough into 3½-inch disk (about ⅜ inch thick). Cover sheet with plastic and let dough rise at room temperature until puffy, 30 to 45 minutes.

4. Set wire rack in second rimmed baking sheet. Add 2 quarts oil to large Dutch oven until it measures about 1½ inches deep and heat over medium-high heat to 350 degrees. Gently drop 4 dough disks into hot oil and fry until golden brown, about 3 minutes, flipping disks halfway through frying. Adjust burner, if necessary, to maintain oil temperature between 325 and 350 degrees.

5. Using slotted spoon or spider skimmer, transfer malasadas to prepared wire rack. Return oil to 350 degrees and repeat with remaining dough disks in 2 batches. Place remaining 1 cup sugar in large bowl. Lightly toss malasadas, one at a time, in sugar to coat. Transfer to platter. Serve immediately.

Cornmeal Biscuits

MAKES 12 BISCUITS

WHY THIS RECIPE WORKS A good cornmeal biscuit combines the tender, fluffy crumb of a traditional biscuit with the distinct cornmeal flavor of cornbread. To make the dough, we used a food processor to cut chilled butter quickly into our dry ingredients. So our biscuits would taste like cornmeal, but wouldn't have its dry, gritty texture, we soaked the cornmeal in buttermilk; just 10 minutes was enough to soften it. A bit of honey provided a subtle sweetness that drew out the corn flavor even more. Kneading the dough briefly prior to cutting out rounds ensured evenly textured biscuits that rose to an impressive height.

If you don't have buttermilk, you can substitute clabbered milk: Whisk 1 tablespoon lemon juice into 1¼ cups of milk and let the mixture sit until slightly thickened, about 10 minutes. Avoid coarsely ground cornmeal, which makes gritty biscuits.

- 1 cup (5 ounces) cornmeal
- 1¼ cups buttermilk
- 1 tablespoon honey
- 2 cups (10 ounces) all-purpose flour
- 1 tablespoon baking powder
- ½ teaspoon baking soda
- 1 teaspoon table salt
- 12 tablespoons unsalted butter, cut into ½-inch pieces and chilled

1. Adjust oven rack to middle position and heat oven to 450 degrees. Line rimmed baking sheet with parchment paper. Whisk cornmeal, buttermilk, and honey together in large bowl; let sit for 10 minutes.

2. Pulse flour, baking powder, baking soda, and salt in food processor until combined, about 3 pulses. Scatter butter evenly over top and continue to pulse until mixture resembles coarse meal, about 15 pulses. Add flour mixture to buttermilk mixture and stir until dough forms.

3. Turn dough out onto lightly floured counter and knead until smooth, 8 to 10 times. Pat dough into 9-inch circle, about ¾ inch thick. Using 2½-inch biscuit cutter dipped in flour, cut out rounds and transfer to prepared baking sheet, dipping cutter in flour after each cut. Pat remaining dough into ¾-inch-thick circle, cut rounds from dough, and transfer to baking sheet.

4. Bake until biscuits begin to rise, about 5 minutes, then reduce oven temperature to 400 degrees and bake until golden brown, 8 to 12 minutes longer, rotating baking sheet halfway through baking. Let biscuits cool on baking sheet for 5 minutes, then transfer to wire rack. Serve warm or let cool to room temperature. (Biscuits can be stored at room temperature for up to 2 days.)

Butter and Lard Biscuits

SERVES 9

WHY THIS RECIPE WORKS Butter and lard each play a role in producing these flaky, tender biscuits. After thoroughly combining the dry ingredients in a food processor, we added chilled pieces of lard and butter to the bowl and cut them small enough to distribute them evenly throughout. Buttermilk not only hydrated the mixture but also added a slight tang. As the biscuits baked, steam from the melting butter (which contains water) created flaky layers, while the melted lard (which doesn't contain water) added tenderness and flavor. Rolling the dough into a square and trimming ¼ inch off the edges ensured that the biscuits rose unimpeded in the oven. Cutting the dough into nine squares made even-size biscuits and avoided any wasted scraps (or tough rerolls).

Butter and Lard Biscuits

We developed this recipe using John Morrell Snow Cap Lard. If you have leftover buttermilk, it can be frozen in ice cube trays, transferred to zipper-lock bags, and frozen for up to a month. Upon thawing, the whey and the milk solids will separate; simply whisk the buttermilk back together before using it.

- 6 ounces lard
- 12 tablespoons unsalted butter
- 4½ cups (22½ ounces) all-purpose flour
- 1½ tablespoons sugar
- 1½ tablespoons baking powder
- ¾ teaspoon baking soda
- 1½ teaspoons table salt
- 1¼ cups buttermilk

1. Cut lard and butter into ½-inch pieces and freeze until firm, 20 to 30 minutes.

2. Line rimmed baking sheet with parchment paper. Process flour, sugar, baking powder, baking soda, and salt in food processor until combined, about 3 seconds. Scatter frozen lard and butter over top and pulse until mixture resembles coarse crumbs with visible pea-size pieces, about 14 pulses.

3. Transfer flour mixture to large bowl. Stir in buttermilk until very shaggy dough forms and some bits of dry flour remain. (Do not overmix.) Turn out dough onto lightly floured counter and knead briefly until dough comes together, 4 to 6 turns. Using your floured hands and bench scraper, shape dough into 8-inch square, about 1½ inches thick. (Dough may be sticky; reflour your hands as needed.)

4. Using sharp, floured chef's knife, trim ¼ inch of dough from each side of square and discard. Cut remaining dough into 9 squares (2 cuts by 2 cuts), flouring knife after each cut. Arrange biscuits at least 1 inch apart on prepared sheet. Cover sheet with plastic wrap and refrigerate for at least 30 minutes or up to 24 hours. Adjust oven rack to upper-middle position and heat oven to 450 degrees.

5. Bake until biscuits begin to rise, about 5 minutes. Rotate sheet and reduce oven temperature to 400 degrees. Bake until biscuits are golden brown, 12 to 14 minutes. Transfer sheet to wire rack and let biscuits cool for at least 5 minutes. Serve warm.

Why Two Fats?

While you can make biscuits with just butter or just lard, we call for both here for the richest, flakiest, most tender biscuits. Butter can contain almost 20 percent water, while lard is 100 percent fat. Because lard doesn't contain any water, it doesn't encourage gluten development. When the dough is worked, the lard coats the gluten strands to prevent them from bonding, in essence "shortening" the strands, thus creating more tender biscuits. Butter has a lower melting point than lard, which means that it melts faster. During baking, this allows the butter to form more air pockets in the dough as its water converts to steam, resulting in flakier, more leavened biscuits. Butter is also helpful for browning due to the sugar and protein in its milk solids, which undergo Maillard browning when heated. Some lards, such as U.S. Dreams Lard, can impart a porky flavor, a plus for many; John Morrell Snow Cap Lard is more neutral-tasting.

How to Make Butter and Lard Biscuits

1. Turn out dough onto lightly floured counter and knead briefly until dough comes together, 4 to 6 turns. Then press dough into 8-inch square, about 1½ inches thick.

2. Trim ¼ inch of dough from sides of square using sharp, floured chef's knife. Then cut dough into 9 squares, reflouring knife after each cut.

3. Arrange biscuits at least 1 inch apart on parchment paper–lined baking sheet.

Cat Head Biscuits

Cat Head Biscuits

MAKES 6 BISCUITS

WHY THIS RECIPE WORKS As big as a cat's head, these tender, moist biscuits that originated in Appalachia boast a golden-brown, craggy top and downy, soft sides. Many Southern bakers rely on White Lily flour to ensure a tender texture, but since this flour isn't readily available everywhere, we substituted an equal mix of cake flour and all-purpose flour. For a fluffy texture, we relied on softened butter and shortening, worked in with warm hands. Scooping the dough into a round pan, so that the mounds were touching, gave us baked biscuits with soft sides.

If you don't have buttermilk, you can substitute clabbered milk: Whisk 1 tablespoon lemon juice into 1¼ cups milk and let the mixture sit until slightly thickened, about 10 minutes. The recipe will also work with 3 cups White Lily flour in place of both the all-purpose and cake flours.

1½ cups (7½ ounces) all-purpose flour
1½ cups (6 ounces) cake flour
1 tablespoon baking powder
½ teaspoon baking soda
1 teaspoon table salt
8 tablespoons unsalted butter, cut into ½-inch pieces and softened
4 tablespoons vegetable shortening, cut into ½-inch pieces
1¼ cups buttermilk

1. Adjust oven rack to upper-middle position and heat oven to 425 degrees. Grease 9-inch round cake pan. Combine all-purpose flour, cake flour, baking powder, baking soda, and salt in large bowl. Using fingertips, rub butter and shortening into flour mixture until mixture resembles coarse meal. Stir in buttermilk until combined.

2. Using greased ½-cup measure or large spring-loaded ice cream scoop, transfer 6 heaping portions of dough into prepared pan, placing five around edge and one in center.

RISE-AND-SHINE BREAKFAST AND BREADS   563

3. Bake until puffed and golden brown, 20 to 25 minutes, rotating pan halfway through baking. Let biscuits cool in pan for 10 minutes, then transfer to wire rack. Serve. (Biscuits can be stored at room temperature for up to 2 days.)

Forming Cat Head Biscuits
Instead of kneading, rolling, and stamping, Cat Head Biscuits are scooped.

Scoop dough and nestle biscuits in cake pan using spring-loaded ice cream scoop.

Blueberry Biscuits
SERVES 9 (MAKES 9 BISCUITS)

WHY THIS RECIPE WORKS Inspired by the Bo-Berry Biscuits at Bojangles, the Southern fast-food chain, we set out to create our own recipe for blueberry biscuits using fresh blueberries. Smashing some chilled butter into the flour mixture with our fingertips gave the biscuits their signature flaky interior; the large pieces of butter melted in the oven and produced steam that helped create a light texture. To avoid dirtying the kitchen counter and rolling and stamping out biscuits, we pressed the biscuit dough into a square baking pan and cut it into squares. Lightly salted honey butter, brushed over the biscuits while they were still hot, provided luster and a salty-sweet finish.

We prefer the flavor of fresh blueberries here, but you can also use 7½ ounces (1½ cups) of frozen blueberries that have been thawed, drained, and then patted dry with paper towels. If you have leftover buttermilk, it can be frozen in ice cube trays, transferred to zipper-lock freezer bags, and frozen for up to a month. Upon thawing, the whey and the milk solids will separate; simply whisk the buttermilk back together before using it.

Blueberry Biscuits

Biscuits
- 1 tablespoon unsalted butter, melted, plus 10 tablespoons unsalted butter, cut into ½-inch pieces and chilled
- 3 cups (15 ounces) all-purpose flour
- ½ cup (3½ ounces) sugar
- 2 teaspoons baking powder
- ½ teaspoon baking soda
- 1¼ teaspoons table salt
- 7½ ounces (1½ cups) blueberries
- 1⅔ cups buttermilk, chilled

Honey Butter
- 2 tablespoons unsalted butter
- 1 tablespoon honey
- Pinch table salt

1. For the Biscuits Adjust oven rack to middle position and heat oven to 425 degrees. Brush bottom and sides of 8-inch square baking pan with melted butter.

The Complete Cook's Country TV Show Cookbook

2. Whisk flour, sugar, baking powder, baking soda, and salt together in large bowl. Add chilled butter to flour mixture and smash butter between your fingertips into flat, irregular pieces. Add blueberries and toss with flour mixture. Gently stir in buttermilk until no dry pockets of flour remain.

3. Using rubber spatula, transfer dough to prepared pan and spread into even layer and into corners of pan. Using bench scraper sprayed with vegetable oil spray, cut dough into 9 equal squares (2 cuts by 2 cuts), but do not separate. Bake until browned on top and paring knife inserted into center biscuit comes out clean, 40 to 45 minutes.

4. For the Honey Butter Meanwhile, combine butter, honey, and salt in small bowl and microwave until butter is melted, about 30 seconds. Stir to combine; set aside.

5. Remove pan from oven and let biscuits cool in pan for 5 minutes. Turn biscuits out onto baking sheet, then reinvert biscuits onto wire rack. Brush tops of biscuits with honey butter (use all of it). Let cool for 10 minutes. Using serrated knife, cut biscuits along scored marks and serve warm.

Mixed Berry Scones

MAKES 8 SCONES

Mixed Berry Scones

WHY THIS RECIPE WORKS A random stop at a rural Massachusetts antique store—which had a coffee shop attached—provided the inspiration for these berry-filled scones. To re-create them, we discovered that treating the butter in two different ways was key: We processed half the cold butter to fully incorporate it into the dough, then we pulsed in the remaining butter, processing it to pea-size pieces that created pockets of steam as the scones baked. Adding confectioners' sugar to the frozen berries counteracted their tartness and helped control them from "bleeding" into the dough. A simple glaze added a nice sheen and sweet finish.

Work the dough as little as possible, just until it comes together. Work quickly to keep the butter and berries as cold as possible for the best results. Note that the butter is divided in this recipe. An equal amount of frozen blueberries, raspberries, blackberries, or strawberries (halved) can be used in place of the mixed berries.

Scones

- 1¾ cups (8¾ ounces) frozen mixed berries
- 3 tablespoons confectioners' sugar
- 3 cups (15 ounces) all-purpose flour
- 12 tablespoons unsalted butter, cut into ½-inch pieces, chilled, divided
- ⅓ cup (2⅓ ounces) granulated sugar
- 1 tablespoon baking powder
- 1¼ teaspoons table salt
- ¾ cup plus 2 tablespoons whole milk
- 1 large egg plus 1 large yolk

Glaze

- 2 tablespoons unsalted butter, melted
- 1 tablespoon honey

1. For the Scones Adjust oven rack to upper-middle position and heat oven to 425 degrees. Line rimmed baking sheet with parchment paper. (If your berry mix contains strawberries, cut them in half.) Toss berries with confectioners' sugar in bowl; freeze until needed.

RISE-AND-SHINE BREAKFAST AND BREADS   565

2. Combine flour, 6 tablespoons butter, granulated sugar, baking powder, and salt in food processor and process until butter is fully incorporated, about 15 seconds. Add remaining 6 tablespoons butter and pulse until butter is reduced to pea-size pieces, 10 to 12 pulses. Transfer mixture to large bowl. Stir in berries.

3. Beat milk and egg and yolk together in separate bowl. Make well in center of flour mixture and pour in milk mixture. Using rubber spatula, gently stir mixture, scraping from edges of bowl and folding inward until very shaggy dough forms and some bits of flour remain. Do not overmix.

4. Turn out dough onto well-floured counter and, if necessary, knead briefly until dough just comes together, about 3 turns. Using your floured hands and bench scraper, shape dough into 12 by 4-inch rectangle, about 1½ inches tall. Using knife or bench scraper, cut dough crosswise into 4 equal rectangles. Cut each rectangle diagonally into 2 triangles (you should have 8 scones total). Transfer scones to prepared sheet. Bake until scones are lightly golden on top, 16 to 18 minutes, rotating pan halfway through baking.

5. For the Glaze While scones bake, combine melted butter and honey in small bowl.

6. Remove scones from oven and brush tops evenly with glaze mixture. Return scones to oven and continue to bake until golden brown on top, 5 to 8 minutes longer. Transfer scones to wire rack and let cool for at least 10 minutes before serving.

To Make Ahead Unbaked scones can be frozen for several weeks. After cutting scones into triangles in step 4, freeze them on baking sheet. Transfer frozen scones to zipper-lock freezer bag. When ready to bake, heat oven to 375 degrees and extend cooking time in step 4 to 23 to 26 minutes. Glaze time in step 6 will remain at 5 to 8 minutes.

Jalapeño-Cheddar Scones

MAKES 12 SCONES

WHY THIS RECIPE WORKS Scones don't have to be relegated to breakfast or tea time; with the right add-ins, they can be a savory accompaniment to any meal. We found that a hefty amount of extra-sharp cheddar brought plenty of cheesiness to the dough, which we studded with jarred jalapeños. A bit of sugar balanced the saltiness and encouraged browning in the oven. Once they were partially baked, we slathered the scones with honey butter and returned them to the oven until they were beautifully golden brown. The sweet-spicy mix of jalapeños, cheddar, and honey makes these scones great as a hearty snack or as an accompaniment to chilis or soups. They also make an outstanding breakfast sandwich with bacon, eggs, and extra cheese.

Work the dough as little as possible, just until it comes together.

Scones

- 3 cups (15 ounces) all-purpose flour
- 12 tablespoons unsalted butter, cut into ½-inch pieces and chilled, divided
- ¼ cup (1¾ ounces) sugar
- 1 tablespoon baking powder
- 1¼ teaspoons table salt
- 6 ounces extra-sharp cheddar cheese, cut into ½-inch pieces
- ½ cup jarred sliced jalapeños, drained and chopped
- 1 cup whole milk
- 1 large egg plus 1 large yolk

Honey Butter

- 3 tablespoons unsalted butter, melted
- 1½ tablespoons honey

1. For the Scones Line rimmed baking sheet with parchment paper. Combine flour, 6 tablespoons butter, sugar, baking powder, and salt in food processor and process until butter is fully incorporated, about 15 seconds. Add cheddar and remaining 6 tablespoons butter and pulse until cheddar and butter are reduced to pea-size pieces, 10 to 12 pulses. Transfer mixture to large bowl. Stir in jalapeños until coated with flour mixture.

2. Beat milk and egg and yolk together in separate bowl. Make well in center of flour mixture and pour in milk mixture. Gently stir mixture with rubber spatula, scraping from edges of bowl and folding inward, until very shaggy dough forms and some bits of dry flour remain. Do not overmix.

3. Turn out dough onto well-floured counter and knead briefly until dough just comes together, about 3 turns. Using your floured hands and bench scraper, shape dough into 15 by 3-inch rectangle with long side parallel to edge of counter, dusting with extra flour if it begins to stick.

4. Using knife or bench scraper, cut dough crosswise into 6 equal rectangles. Cut each rectangle diagonally into 2 triangles (you should have 12 scones total). Transfer scones to prepared sheet, spacing about 1 inch apart. Cover sheet with plastic wrap and refrigerate for at least 30 minutes or up to 24 hours. Adjust oven rack to middle position and heat oven to 425 degrees.

5. For the Honey Butter Meanwhile, combine melted butter and honey in small bowl.

6. Uncover scones and bake until lightly golden on top, 15 to 17 minutes, rotating sheet halfway through baking. Remove scones from oven and brush tops with honey butter. Return scones to oven and continue to bake until golden brown on top, 3 to 5 minutes longer. Transfer scones to wire rack and let cool for at least 10 minutes before serving.

> **The American Table:**
> **The History of Scones and Biscuits**
> Centuries ago, Scottish cooks griddled yeasted oatmeal or barley "cakes" and cut them into wedges. Wheat flour was a later addition throughout the United Kingdom, as were, eventually, chemical leaveners that made the yeast unnecessary. As scones traveled to the United States, they were further adapted. In the American South, scones evolved into biscuits made with lard, buttermilk, and soft wheat flour. The softer and fluffier versions of both scones and biscuits that we know today are a product of the leaveners as well as the introduction of butter.

Blueberry Cornbread

Blueberry Cornbread

SERVES 8

WHY THIS RECIPE WORKS A far cry from savory, dense cornbread, our rendition of blueberry cornbread is slightly sweet, moist, and studded with juicy berries. We opted for a higher ratio of flour to cornmeal, yielding a cornbread that was tender and cake-like, yet sturdy enough to keep a full two cups of blueberries from sinking. A dusting of cornmeal into the greased pan before pouring in the batter added a burst of corn flavor and crunch, and a sprinkling of sugar over the batter gave the top a golden crust. While the cornbread baked, we whipped up a honey butter that we slathered on the still-warm, blueberry-laden wedges.

We developed this recipe using commonly available Quaker Yellow Corn Meal. If you're using our favorite cornmeal, Anson Mills Fine Yellow Cornmeal, you will need to use 1¼ cups to yield 5 ounces for the batter. If you use a dark-colored cake pan, reduce the baking time in step 3 to 35 to 40 minutes. You can use frozen blueberries; if doing so, leave the berries in the freezer until the last possible moment and toss them with 2 tablespoons of all-purpose flour before stirring them into the batter. Then, increase the baking time to 45 to 50 minutes.

- 1½ tablespoons cornmeal, plus 1 cup (5 ounces)
- 1½ cups (7½ ounces) all-purpose flour
- ¾ cup (5¼ ounces) plus 1 tablespoon sugar, divided
- 2 teaspoons baking powder
- ¾ teaspoon table salt
- 1 cup whole milk
- 12 tablespoons unsalted butter, melted
- 2 large eggs
- 10 ounces (2 cups) blueberries

RISE-AND-SHINE BREAKFAST AND BREADS 567

1. Adjust oven rack to middle position and heat oven to 375 degrees. Grease bottom and sides of light-colored 9-inch round cake pan, then dust pan with 1½ tablespoons cornmeal.

2. Whisk flour, ¾ cup sugar, baking powder, salt, and remaining 1 cup cornmeal together in large bowl. Whisk milk, melted butter, and eggs together in second bowl (butter may form clumps; this is OK). Stir milk mixture into flour mixture until just combined. Stir in blueberries until just incorporated. Transfer batter to prepared pan and smooth top with rubber spatula. Sprinkle remaining 1 tablespoon sugar over top.

3. Bake until golden brown and paring knife inserted in center comes out clean, 40 to 45 minutes. Let cornbread cool in pan on wire rack for 20 minutes. Run paring knife between cornbread and side of pan. Remove cornbread from pan and let cool on rack for 20 minutes. Serve warm.

Honey Butter
MAKES ABOUT ⅓ CUP

This honey butter also tastes great on roasted root vegetables, boiled corn, pork chops, pancakes, muffins, biscuits, and dinner rolls.

- 4 tablespoons unsalted butter, softened
- 2 tablespoons honey
- ¼ teaspoon table salt
-   Pinch cayenne pepper

Using fork, mash all ingredients in bowl until combined. Serve.

Southern-Style Skillet Cornbread

SERVES 12

WHY THIS RECIPE WORKS Savory skillet-baked Southern-style cornbread should boast hearty corn flavor, a sturdy, moist crumb, and a dark brown crust. For the right texture, we used finely ground cornmeal. Toasting it in the oven for a few minutes intensified the corn flavor. Buttermilk added a sharp tang that worked well with the corn, and soaking the cornmeal in the buttermilk helped to soften it so our cornbread was moist and tender. When it came to the fat, a combination of butter (for flavor) and vegetable oil (which can withstand high heat without burning) worked best, and greasing the pan with both delivered the crisp crust we were after.

If you don't have buttermilk, you can substitute clabbered milk: Whisk 2 tablespoons lemon juice into 2 cups of milk and let the mixture sit until slightly thickened, about 10 minutes. We prefer a cast-iron skillet here, but any ovensafe 10-inch skillet will work fine. Avoid coarsely ground cornmeal, as it will make the cornbread gritty.

Southern-Style Skillet Cornbread

- 2¼ cups (11¼ ounces) cornmeal
- 2 cups buttermilk
- ¼ cup vegetable oil
- 4 tablespoons unsalted butter, cut into 4 pieces
- 2 large eggs
- 1 teaspoon baking powder
- 1 teaspoon baking soda
- ¾ teaspoon table salt

1. Adjust oven racks to lower-middle and middle positions and heat oven to 450 degrees. Heat 10-inch cast-iron skillet on middle rack for 10 minutes. Spread cornmeal over rimmed baking sheet and bake on lower-middle rack until fragrant and color begins to deepen, about 5 minutes. Transfer hot cornmeal to large bowl and whisk in buttermilk; set aside.

2. Carefully add oil to hot skillet and continue to bake until oil is just smoking, about 5 minutes. Remove skillet from oven and add butter, carefully swirling pan until butter is melted. Pour all but 1 tablespoon oil mixture into cornmeal mixture, leaving remaining oil mixture in pan. Whisk eggs, baking powder, baking soda, and salt into cornmeal mixture.

3. Pour cornmeal mixture into hot skillet and bake until top begins to crack and sides are golden brown, 12 to 16 minutes, rotating pan halfway through baking. Let cornbread cool in pan for 5 minutes, then turn out onto wire rack. Serve.

Beer-Batter Cheese Bread

SERVES 10 TO 12 (MAKES 1 LOAF)

WHY THIS RECIPE WORKS The beauty of a quick bread is that it can be on the table in less than an hour, but that convenience is worth it only if the final product tastes good. Recipes for beer-batter cheese bread often produce loaves that taste sour or have weak cheese flavor. We wanted a lighter loaf enhanced with the yeasty flavor of beer and a rich hit of cheese—and one that was still quick and easy. We put more than a cup of cheese into the batter and then sprinkled extra on top to create a lovely, craggy crust. Making the bread in a cast-iron skillet gave it a great bottom crust and helped it bake through quickly and evenly.

We prefer to use a mild American lager, such as Budweiser, here; strongly flavored beers will make this bread bitter.

- 2½ cups (12½ ounces) all-purpose flour
- ½ cup minced fresh chives
- 2 tablespoons sugar
- 4 teaspoons baking powder
- 1 teaspoon table salt
- ½ teaspoon pepper
- 8 ounces Gruyère cheese, shredded (2 cups), divided
- 1¼ cups mild lager, such as Budweiser
- 3 tablespoons unsalted butter, melted

Beer-Batter Cheese Bread

1. Adjust oven rack to middle position and heat oven to 450 degrees. Grease 10-inch cast-iron skillet.

2. Whisk flour, chives, sugar, baking powder, salt, and pepper together in large bowl. Stir in 1½ cups Gruyère, breaking up any clumps, until coated with flour. Stir beer and melted butter into flour mixture until just combined. Batter will be heavy and thick; do not overmix.

3. Scrape batter into prepared skillet and smooth top. Sprinkle with remaining ½ cup Gruyère. Transfer skillet to oven and bake until loaf is golden brown and toothpick inserted into center comes out clean, 20 to 25 minutes, rotating skillet halfway through baking.

4. Using potholders, transfer skillet to wire rack and let loaf cool for 10 minutes. Being careful of hot skillet handle, remove loaf from skillet, return to rack, and let cool for at least 20 minutes before serving.

Spicy Cheese Bread

MAKES 1 LOAF

WHY THIS RECIPE WORKS Stella's Bakery in Madison, Wisconsin, is known for its spicy cheese bread. When re-creating this irresistible bread, we found that the key was to let the cheese cubes come to room temperature before adding them to the dough so they wouldn't stunt the dough's rise. To help keep its shape, we baked the bread in a cake pan. An egg wash and a generous sprinkle of red pepper flakes finished off the loaf. A final brush of melted butter helped the crust stay supple and gave it a nice shine.

Take the cheese out of the refrigerator when you start the recipe to ensure that it comes to room temperature by the time you need it. Cold cheese will slow rising. The dough needs to rise for several hours before baking.

Bread
- 3¼ cups (16¼ ounces) all-purpose flour
- ¼ cup (1¾ ounces) sugar
- 1 tablespoon instant or rapid-rise yeast
- 1½ teaspoons red pepper flakes
- 1¼ teaspoons table salt
- ½ cup warm water (110 degrees)
- 2 large eggs plus 1 large yolk
- 4 tablespoons unsalted butter, melted
- 6 ounces Monterey Jack cheese, cut into ½-inch cubes (1½ cups), room temperature
- 6 ounces provolone cheese, cut into ½-inch cubes (1½ cups), room temperature

Topping
- 1 large egg, lightly beaten
- 1 teaspoon red pepper flakes
- 1 tablespoon unsalted butter, melted

1. For the Bread Whisk flour, sugar, yeast, pepper flakes, and salt together in bowl of stand mixer. Whisk warm water, eggs and yolk, and melted butter together in liquid measuring cup. Add egg mixture to flour mixture. Fit stand mixer with dough hook and knead on medium speed until dough clears bottom and sides of bowl, about 8 minutes.

2. Transfer dough to unfloured counter, shape into ball, and transfer to greased bowl. Cover with plastic wrap and let rise in warm place until doubled in size, 1½ to 2 hours.

3. Grease 9-inch round cake pan. Transfer dough to unfloured counter and press to deflate. Roll dough into 18 by 12-inch rectangle with long side parallel to counter's edge. Distribute Monterey Jack and provolone evenly over dough, leaving 1-inch border around edges. Starting with edge closest to you, roll dough into log. Pinch seam and ends to seal, then roll log so seam side is down. Roll log back and forth on counter, applying gentle, even pressure, until log reaches 30 inches in length. If any tears occur, pinch to seal.

4. Starting at one end, wind log into coil; tuck end underneath coil. Place loaf in prepared cake pan and cover loosely with clean dish towel. Let rise in warm place until doubled in size, 1 to 1½ hours. Adjust oven rack to lower-middle position and heat oven to 350 degrees.

5. For the Topping Brush top of loaf with egg, then sprinkle with pepper flakes. Place cake pan on rimmed baking sheet. Bake until loaf is golden brown, about 25 minutes. Rotate loaf, tent with aluminum foil, and continue to bake until loaf registers 190 degrees, 25 to 30 minutes longer.

6. Transfer pan to wire rack and brush bread with butter. Let cool for 10 minutes. Run knife around edge of pan to loosen bread. Slide bread onto wire rack, using spatula as needed for support. Let cool for 30 minutes before slicing. Serve warm.

Spicy Cheese Bread

Perfect Popovers

MAKES 6 POPOVERS

WHY THIS RECIPE WORKS For golden-brown popovers that really popped, we used bread flour instead of all-purpose flour—the bread flour's high protein content ensured the highest rise and crispiest crust. Resting the batter before baking kept the popovers from setting up too quickly. We baked our popovers at a high temperature to jump-start the initial rise, then turned the oven down so that they would cook through evenly. To prevent collapse, we let steam escape by poking a hole in each popover when they were nearly done baking and then again as they cooled.

Greasing the pan with shortening ensures the best release, but vegetable oil spray may be substituted; do not use butter. Bread flour makes for the highest and sturdiest popovers, but 2 cups (10 ounces) of all-purpose flour may be substituted.

- 3 large eggs
- 2 cups 1 percent or 2 percent low-fat milk, heated to 110 degrees
- 3 tablespoons unsalted butter, melted and cooled
- 2 cups (11 ounces) bread flour
- 1 teaspoon table salt
- 1 teaspoon sugar

1. Adjust oven rack to lower-middle position and heat oven to 450 degrees. Grease 6-cup popover pan with shortening, then flour pan lightly. Whisk eggs until light and foamy in medium bowl. Slowly whisk in milk and butter until incorporated.

2. Combine flour, salt, and sugar in large bowl. Whisk three-quarters of milk mixture into flour mixture until no lumps remain, then whisk in remaining milk mixture. Transfer batter to 4-cup liquid measuring cup, cover with plastic wrap, and let sit at room temperature for 1 hour. (Alternatively, batter can be refrigerated for up to 24 hours. Bring to room temperature before proceeding.)

3. Whisk batter to recombine, then pour into prepared pan (batter will not reach top of cups). Bake until just beginning to brown, about 20 minutes. Without opening oven door, decrease oven temperature to 300 degrees and continue to bake until popovers are golden brown, 35 to 40 minutes longer. Poke small hole in top of each popover with skewer and continue to bake until deep golden brown, about 10 minutes longer. Transfer pan to wire rack, poke popovers again with skewer, and let cool for 2 minutes. Remove from pan and serve.

To Make Ahead Cooled popovers can be stored at room temperature for up to 2 days. To serve, adjust oven rack to middle position and heat oven to 400 degrees. Heat popovers on rimmed baking sheet until crisp and heated through, 5 to 8 minutes.

Muffin Tin Popovers

If you don't have a popover pan, you can bake the popovers in a 12-cup muffin tin—with a sacrifice in stature. To ensure even cooking, use only the outer 10 cups of the tin.

Grease and flour outer 10 cups of muffin tin, then fill ¼ inch from the top (you may have some batter left over). Reduce initial baking time in step 3 to 15 minutes, and reduce secondary baking time to 20 to 25 minutes after oven temperature has been lowered. Poke popovers as directed and continue to bake for another 10 minutes.

Perfect Popovers

Whole-Wheat Blueberry Muffins

Morning Glory Muffins

Whole-Wheat Blueberry Muffins
MAKES 12 MUFFINS

WHY THIS RECIPE WORKS When it comes to baking with whole wheat, the benefits—added fiber, bran, and nutty sweetness—are often trumped by the drawbacks: dense texture and squat appearance. To use one hundred percent whole wheat, we added two leaveners and several high-moisture ingredients (buttermilk, eggs, blueberries, melted butter, and oil) to ensure light, tender muffins. We added a crumbly streusel topping to round out our delicate muffins.

Do not overmix the batter. You can substitute frozen (unthawed) blueberries for fresh in this recipe.

Streusel
- 3 tablespoons granulated sugar
- 3 tablespoons packed brown sugar
- 3 tablespoons whole-wheat flour
- Pinch table salt
- 2 tablespoons unsalted butter, melted

Muffins
- 3 cups (16 1/2 ounces) whole-wheat flour
- 2 1/2 teaspoons baking powder
- 1/2 teaspoon baking soda
- 1 teaspoon table salt
- 1 cup (7 ounces) granulated sugar
- 2 large eggs
- 4 tablespoons unsalted butter, melted
- 1/4 cup vegetable oil
- 1 1/4 cups buttermilk
- 1 1/2 teaspoons vanilla extract
- 7 1/2 ounces (1 1/2 cups) blueberries

1. For the Streusel Combine granulated sugar, brown sugar, flour, and salt in bowl. Add melted butter and toss with fork until evenly moistened and mixture forms large chunks with some pea-size pieces throughout; set aside.

2. For the Muffins Adjust oven rack to middle position and heat oven to 400 degrees. Spray 12-cup muffin tin, including top, generously with vegetable oil spray. Whisk flour, baking powder, baking soda, and salt together in large bowl. Whisk sugar, eggs, melted butter, and oil together in separate bowl until combined, about 30 seconds. Whisk buttermilk and vanilla into sugar mixture until combined.

3. Stir sugar mixture into flour mixture until just combined. Gently stir in blueberries until incorporated. Using a heaping ¼-cup dry measuring cup, divide batter evenly among prepared muffin cups (cups will be filled to rim); sprinkle evenly with streusel.

4. Bake until golden brown and toothpick inserted in center comes out with few crumbs attached, 18 to 20 minutes, rotating muffin tin halfway through baking. Let muffins cool in muffin tin on wire rack for 5 minutes. Remove muffins from muffin tin and let cool 5 minutes longer. Serve.

Morning Glory Muffins
MAKES 12 MUFFINS

WHY THIS RECIPE WORKS Created by Pam McKinstry at her café in Nantucket, morning glory muffins are chock-full of nuts, fruit, carrots, and spices. But all these tempting add-ins can make for heavy, dense muffins, so our first move was to strain the fruit and press out the extra juice to prevent our muffins from being soggy. To keep the bright, fruity flavor intact, we simply saved the released fruit juice, reduced it on the stovetop, and added the concentrated syrup back to the batter. To keep the nuts and coconut from becoming mealy or soggy in the finished muffins, we toasted and processed them. At last, our muffins were truly glorious.

Though we prefer golden raisins here, ordinary raisins will work too.

- ¾ cup (2¼ ounces) sweetened shredded coconut, toasted
- ½ cup walnuts, toasted
- 2¼ cups (11¼ ounces) all-purpose flour
- ¾ cup (5¼ ounces) sugar
- 1½ teaspoons baking soda
- ½ teaspoon baking powder
- 1 teaspoon ground cinnamon
- ¾ teaspoon table salt
- 1 (8-ounce) can crushed pineapple
- 1 Granny Smith apple, peeled, cored, and shredded
- 8 tablespoons unsalted butter, melted
- 3 large eggs
- 1 teaspoon vanilla extract
- 1½ cups shredded carrots (2 to 3 carrots)
- 1 cup golden raisins

1. Adjust oven rack to middle position and heat oven to 350 degrees. Spray 12-cup muffin tin with vegetable oil spray. Process coconut and walnuts in food processor until finely ground, 20 to 30 seconds. Add flour, sugar, baking soda, baking powder, cinnamon, and salt and pulse until combined. Transfer mixture to large bowl.

2. Place pineapple and shredded apple in fine-mesh strainer set over liquid measuring cup. Press fruit dry (you should have about 1 cup juice). Bring juice to boil in 12-inch skillet over medium-high heat and cook until reduced to ¼ cup, about 5 minutes. Let cool slightly. Whisk melted butter, cooled juice, eggs, and vanilla together until smooth. Stir wet mixture into dry mixture until combined. Stir in pineapple-apple mixture, carrots, and raisins.

3. Divide batter evenly among muffin cups. Bake until toothpick inserted in center comes out clean, 24 to 28 minutes, rotating pan halfway through baking. Let muffins cool in muffin tin on wire rack for 10 minutes. Remove muffins from tin and let cool for at least 10 minutes before serving. (Muffins can be stored at room temperature for up to 3 days.)

Browned Butter Chocolate Chunk Muffins
MAKES 12 MUFFINS

WHY THIS RECIPE WORKS These muffins look and taste like they're fresh from your favorite bakery, thanks to the complexity of browned butter and the use of homemade paper liners. In addition to creating a depth of nutty flavor, browning the butter reduced the water content of the batter, making these muffins rich and crumbly rather than dense and gummy. Chopped bar chocolate (which doesn't have the stabilizers used in chocolate chips) melted beautifully in every bite—no waxiness here. The parchment paper liners helped these muffins rise to new heights, and a bit of sugar sprinkled on top gave them a professional-looking crackly crust.

Using homemade parchment paper liners gives the muffins their tall, neat shape and ensures that the muffins will release easily. If you don't want to make your own, you can use tulip liners. Standard muffin liners will also work but won't result in the same tall shape. If you don't have a small drinking glass, a 6-ounce can of tomato paste works well to form the parchment liners in step 1.

- 2 cups (10 ounces) all-purpose flour
- 1 tablespoon baking powder
- 1 teaspoon table salt
- 8 ounces semisweet chocolate, chopped coarse
- 16 tablespoons unsalted butter
- 1¼ cups (8¾ ounces) sugar, plus ¼ cup sugar for sprinkling
- 2 large eggs
- 2 cups sour cream
- 4 teaspoons vanilla extract

1. Adjust oven rack to upper-middle position and heat oven to 400 degrees. Cut twelve 6-inch squares of parchment paper. Press each square around bottom of tapered drinking glass with 1¾- to 2-inch base, creasing paper to form cup shape. Place parchment liners in muffin cups, allowing excess parchment to protrude vertically from cups.

2. Whisk flour, baking powder, and salt together in medium bowl. Stir in chocolate and set aside. Melt butter in 10-inch skillet over medium-high heat. Cook, stirring constantly with heat-resistant rubber spatula, until butter is dark golden brown and has nutty aroma, 2 to 4 minutes. Transfer browned butter to second bowl and let cool slightly, about 10 minutes.

3. Whisk 1¼ cups sugar and eggs in large bowl until thick and creamy, about 1 minute. Whisk in sour cream, vanilla, and browned butter. Fold in flour mixture with rubber spatula until just moistened; do not overmix. (Batter will be thick and lumpy with spots of dry flour.)

4. Using greased ⅓-cup dry measuring cup, portion heaping ⅓ cup batter into each parchment-lined muffin cup; evenly distribute any remaining batter among cups (cups will be full). Sprinkle remaining ¼ cup sugar evenly over batter (about 1 teaspoon per muffin).

5. Bake until muffins are golden brown and toothpick inserted in center comes out with few crumbs attached, 20 to 25 minutes, rotating muffin tin halfway through baking. Let muffins cool in muffin tin on wire rack for 5 minutes. Transfer muffins to rack and let cool for at least 30 minutes. Serve warm or at room temperature.

Browned Butter Chocolate Chunk Muffins

Why Brown the Butter?

When butter makes muffins dense, it's because of the water that butter is contributing to the recipe, which gets absorbed by the starch and weighs it down. Browning the butter removes its water, effectively turning the butter into oil. Instead of making the muffin heavy, browned butter keeps it short, rich, and crumbly.

Unlike oil, browned butter is solid at room temperature, which keeps the muffins from tasting greasy. Since butter melts at body temperature, when you take a bite, the butter softens, giving the muffins a lush, moist mouthfeel.

MELTED

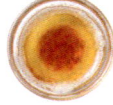
LIGHT BROWN

DARK BROWN

BURNT

> **Homemade versus Standard Liners**
>
> We found that making our own parchment paper liners was worth it to encourage the muffins to rise high and prevent them from sticking to the tin.
>
>
>
> **STANDARD LINERS**
> Muffin "mushrooms" out over the liner.
>
> **PARCHMENT PAPER LINERS**
> Muffin rises high and releases easily.

Muffin Tin Doughnuts

MAKES 12 DOUGHNUTS

WHY THIS RECIPE WORKS To capture the best of breakfast baking, we set out to create a muffin that tasted like a cake doughnut in disguise, with a tender crumb, a crisp exterior, and a buttery, spiced coating. Adding an extra yolk and cutting all-purpose flour with cornstarch gave the muffins a tender crumb that wouldn't break apart. To replicate a fried exterior, we turned up the oven temperature, which crisped the crust nicely. Lastly, we brushed the muffins with butter and rolled them in cinnamon sugar. From coating to crumb, these doughnut muffins combined the essence of a doughnut and the ease of a muffin (without a deep fryer in sight).

In step 3, brush the doughnuts generously, using up all the melted butter. Use your hand to press the cinnamon sugar onto the doughnuts to coat them completely.

Doughnuts
- 2¾ cups (13¾ ounces) all-purpose flour
- 1 cup (7 ounces) sugar
- ¼ cup cornstarch
- 1 tablespoon baking powder
- 1 teaspoon table salt
- ½ teaspoon ground nutmeg
- 1 cup buttermilk
- 8 tablespoons unsalted butter, melted
- 2 large eggs plus 1 large yolk

Muffin Tin Doughnuts

Coating
- 1 cup sugar
- 2 teaspoons ground cinnamon
- 8 tablespoons unsalted butter, melted

1. For the Doughnuts Adjust oven rack to middle position and heat oven to 400 degrees. Spray 12-cup muffin tin with vegetable oil spray. Whisk flour, sugar, cornstarch, baking powder, salt, and nutmeg together in bowl. Whisk buttermilk, melted butter, and eggs and yolk together in separate bowl. Add wet ingredients to dry ingredients and stir with rubber spatula until just combined.

2. Scoop batter into prepared tin. Bake until doughnuts are lightly browned and toothpick inserted in center comes out clean, 19 to 22 minutes. Let doughnuts cool in tin for 5 minutes.

3. For the Coating Whisk sugar and cinnamon together in bowl. Remove doughnuts from tin. Working with 1 doughnut at a time, brush all over with melted butter, then roll in cinnamon sugar, pressing lightly to adhere. Transfer to wire rack and let cool for 15 minutes. Serve.

RISE-AND-SHINE BREAKFAST AND BREADS   575

Ultimate Cinnamon Buns

MAKES 8 BUNS

WHY THIS RECIPE WORKS Gooey, softball-size cinnamon buns are the ultimate breakfast treat. For the base of ours, we turned to a buttery, tender brioche dough. Adding cornstarch to the all-purpose flour in the dough made the buns especially tender. For a filling with great flavor, we combined a good amount of cinnamon—no other spices necessary—with brown sugar. Softened butter helped keep the filling from spilling out as we rolled up the dough. Baked together, the butter and cinnamon sugar turned into a rich, gooey filling. A thick, tangy glaze of cream cheese, confectioners' sugar, and milk ensured that our buns really looked the part.

For smaller cinnamon buns, cut the dough into 12 pieces in step 3.

Dough

- ¾ cup whole milk, heated to 110 degrees
- 2¼ teaspoons instant or rapid-rise yeast
- 3 large eggs, room temperature
- 4¼ cups (21¼ ounces) all-purpose flour
- ½ cup cornstarch
- ½ cup (3½ ounces) granulated sugar
- 1½ teaspoons table salt
- 12 tablespoons unsalted butter, cut into 12 pieces and softened

Filling

- 1½ cups packed (10½ ounces) light brown sugar
- 1½ tablespoons ground cinnamon
- ¼ teaspoon table salt
- 4 tablespoons unsalted butter, softened

Glaze

- 1½ cups confectioners' sugar
- 4 ounces cream cheese, softened
- 1 tablespoon whole milk
- 1 teaspoon vanilla extract

1. For the Dough Make foil sling for 13 by 9-inch baking pan by folding 2 long sheets of aluminum foil; first sheet should be 13 inches wide and second sheet should be 9 inches wide. Lay sheets of foil in pan perpendicular to each other, with extra foil hanging over edges of pan. Push foil into corners and up sides of pan, smoothing foil flush to pan. Grease foil. Whisk milk and yeast together in liquid measuring cup until yeast dissolves, then whisk in eggs.

2. Adjust oven rack to middle position and place loaf or cake pan on bottom of oven. Using stand mixer fitted with dough hook, mix flour, cornstarch, sugar, and salt on low speed until combined. Add warm milk mixture in steady stream and mix until dough comes together, about 1 minute. Increase speed to medium and add butter, 1 piece at a time, until incorporated. Continue to mix until dough is smooth and comes away from sides of bowl, about 10 minutes (if dough is still wet and sticky, add up to ¼ cup flour, 1 tablespoon at a time, until it releases from bowl). Turn dough out onto counter and knead to form smooth, round ball. Transfer dough to medium greased bowl, cover with plastic wrap, and transfer to middle rack of oven. Pour 3 cups boiling water into loaf pan in oven, close oven door, and let dough rise until doubled in size, about 2 hours.

3. For the Filling Combine sugar, cinnamon, and salt in small bowl. Remove dough from oven and turn out onto lightly floured counter. Roll dough into 18-inch square and, leaving ½-inch border around edges, spread with butter, then sprinkle evenly with sugar mixture and lightly press sugar mixture into dough. Starting with edge closest to you, roll dough into tight cylinder, pinch lightly to seal seam, and cut into 8 pieces. Transfer pieces, cut side up, to prepared pan. Cover with plastic and let rise in oven until doubled in size, about 1 hour.

4. For the Glaze Remove buns and water pan from oven and heat oven to 350 degrees. Whisk all glaze ingredients together in medium bowl until smooth. Remove plastic and bake buns until deep golden brown and filling is melted, 35 to 40 minutes, rotating pan halfway through baking. Transfer to wire rack, top buns with ½ cup glaze, and let cool for 30 minutes. Using foil overhang, lift buns from pan and top with remaining glaze. Serve.

To Make Ahead Follow recipe through step 3, skipping step of letting buns rise. Place buns in pan, cover with plastic wrap, and refrigerate for up to 1 day. To bake, let sit at room temperature for 1 hour. Remove plastic and proceed with step 4.

Quicker Cinnamon Buns

MAKES 8 BUNS

WHY THIS RECIPE WORKS Rich, gooey, homemade cinnamon buns can take upwards of 3 hours to prepare. We wanted the same results in half the time. For a quicker rise, we supplemented the yeast (which we proofed in warm milk for extra speed) with baking powder. Two minutes of hand-kneading and a single 30-minute rise were enough to give us the flavor and texture we were looking for. We used a cooler-than-normal oven to give the yeast time to rise and develop flavor before the tops of the buns set. Brown sugar and butter in the filling and vanilla in our cream cheese glaze made these buns ultra-rich and indulgent.

Since the filling, dough, and glaze all require melted butter, it's easier to melt all 10 tablespoons in a liquid measuring cup and divvy it up as needed. Stir the melted butter before each use to redistribute the milk solids. We developed this recipe using a dark cake pan, which produces deeply caramelized buns. If your cake pan is light-colored, adjust the oven rack to the lowest position, heat the oven to 375 degrees, and increase the baking time to 29 to 32 minutes.

Filling
- ¾ cup packed (5¼ ounces) light brown sugar
- ¼ cup (1¾ ounces) granulated sugar
- 1 tablespoon ground cinnamon
- ⅛ teaspoon table salt
- 2 tablespoons unsalted butter, melted
- 1 teaspoon vanilla extract

Dough
- 1¼ cups whole milk, room temperature, divided
- 4 teaspoons instant or rapid-rise yeast
- 2 tablespoons granulated sugar, divided
- 2¾ cups (13¾ ounces) all-purpose flour
- 2½ teaspoons baking powder
- ¾ teaspoon table salt
- 6 tablespoons unsalted butter, melted, divided

Glaze
- 3 ounces cream cheese, softened
- 2 tablespoons unsalted butter, melted
- 2 tablespoons whole milk
- ½ teaspoon vanilla extract
- ⅛ teaspoon table salt
- 1 cup (4 ounces) confectioners' sugar, sifted

Ultimate Cinnamon Buns

Quicker Cinnamon Buns

1. For the Filling Combine brown sugar, granulated sugar, cinnamon, and salt in bowl. Stir in melted butter and vanilla until mixture resembles wet sand; set aside.

2. For the Dough Grease dark 9-inch round cake pan, line with parchment paper, and grease parchment. Pour ¼ cup milk in small bowl and microwave until 110 degrees, 15 to 20 seconds. Stir in yeast and 1 teaspoon sugar and let sit until mixture is bubbly, about 5 minutes.

3. Whisk flour, baking powder, salt, and remaining 5 teaspoons sugar together in large bowl. Stir in 2 tablespoons butter, yeast mixture, and remaining 1 cup milk until dough forms (dough will be sticky). Transfer dough to well-floured counter and knead until smooth ball forms, about 2 minutes.

4. Roll dough into 12 by 9-inch rectangle, with long side parallel to counter edge. Brush dough all over with 2 tablespoons butter, leaving ½-inch border on far edge. Sprinkle dough evenly with filling, then press filling firmly into dough. Using bench scraper or metal spatula, loosen dough from counter. Roll dough away from you into tight log and pinch seam to seal.

5. Roll log seam side down and cut into 8 equal pieces. Stand buns on end and gently re-form ends that were pinched during cutting. Place 1 bun in center of prepared pan and others around perimeter of pan, seam sides facing in. Brush tops of buns with remaining 2 tablespoons butter. Cover buns loosely with plastic wrap and let rise for 30 minutes. Adjust oven rack to middle position and heat oven to 350 degrees.

6. Discard plastic and bake buns until edges are well browned, 23 to 25 minutes. Loosen buns from sides of pan with paring knife and let cool for 5 minutes. Invert large plate over cake pan. Using potholders, flip plate and pan upside down; remove pan and parchment. Reinvert buns onto wire rack, set wire rack inside parchment-lined rimmed baking sheet, and let cool for 5 minutes.

7. For the Glaze Place cream cheese in large bowl and whisk in butter, milk, vanilla, and salt until smooth. Whisk in sugar until smooth. Pour glaze evenly over tops of buns, spreading with spatula to cover. Serve.

Triple-Chocolate Sticky Buns

SERVES 12

Triple-Chocolate Sticky Buns

WHY THIS RECIPE WORKS To take these sticky buns over the top, we incorporated three types of chocolate. We used the tangzhong technique—microwaving a portion of the flour and milk, turning it into a gel. The gel locked in moisture, so the dough was soft without becoming too sticky. For the filling, we made a ganache to spread over the rolled-out dough, then sprinkled it with milk chocolate chips. When baked, this delivered just the right amount of sweetness with pockets of creamy flavor. Cocoa powder added another dose of chocolate to the topping.

Be sure to use a metal baking pan. The tackiness of the dough aids in stretching it in step 7, so resist using a lot of dusting flour. Rolling the dough cylinder too tightly in step 8 will result in misshapen rolls.

Flour Paste and Dough

- ⅔ cup whole milk
- ¼ cup (1¼ ounces) all-purpose flour
- 1 large egg plus 1 large yolk
- 3¼ cups (16¼ ounces) all-purpose flour
- 2¼ teaspoons instant or rapid-rise yeast
- 3 tablespoons granulated sugar
- 1½ teaspoons table salt
- 6 tablespoons unsalted butter, cut into 6 pieces and softened

Topping and Filling
- ¾ cup packed (5¼ ounces) brown sugar
- 6 tablespoons unsalted butter, melted, plus 4 tablespoons unsalted butter
- ¼ cup dark corn syrup
- 2 tablespoons water
- 1 tablespoon unsweetened cocoa powder
- ¼ teaspoon table salt
- 4 ounces bittersweet chocolate, chopped fine
- 1 cup (6 ounces) milk chocolate chips

1. For the Flour Paste and Dough Whisk milk and flour in small bowl until no lumps remain. Microwave, whisking every 25 seconds, until mixture thickens to stiff paste, 50 to 75 seconds. Whisk until smooth.

2. In bowl of stand mixer, whisk flour paste and milk until smooth then whisk in egg and yolk. Add flour and yeast. Fit mixer with dough hook and mix on low speed until all flour is moistened, 1 to 2 minutes. Cover bowl and let stand for 15 minutes.

3. Add sugar and salt and mix on medium-low speed for 5 minutes. Add butter and mix until incorporated, scraping down dough hook and bowl as needed (dough will be sticky), about 5 minutes.

4. Transfer dough to lightly floured counter and knead briefly to form ball. Transfer, seam side down, to greased large bowl, cover tightly with plastic, and let rise until doubled in size, about 1 hour.

5. For the Topping and Filling Meanwhile, whisk brown sugar, melted butter, corn syrup, water, cocoa, and salt together until combined. Spray 13 by 9-inch metal baking pan with vegetable oil spray. Using rubber spatula, spread topping to edges of prepared pan; set aside.

6. About 30 minutes before dough is done rising, microwave bittersweet chocolate and remaining 4 tablespoons butter in bowl at 50 percent power, stirring occasionally, until melted, about 2 minutes. Refrigerate until matte and firm, 30 to 40 minutes.

7. Transfer dough to lightly floured counter and lightly flour top of dough. Roll and stretch dough to 18 by 15-inch rectangle with long side parallel to counter's edge. Stir bittersweet chocolate mixture with rubber spatula until smooth and spreadable (mixture should have similar texture to frosting); spread over dough, leaving 1-inch border along top edge. Sprinkle evenly with chocolate chips.

8. Beginning with long edge nearest you, loosely roll dough away from you into even log, pushing in ends to create even thickness. Pinch seam to seal. Roll log seam side down and slice into 12 equal portions. Place buns, cut side down, in prepared pan in 3 rows of four, lightly reshaping buns as needed. Cover tightly with plastic and let rise until buns are puffy and touching one another, about 1 hour.

9. Adjust oven racks to lowest and lower-middle positions and heat oven to 375 degrees. Place rimmed baking sheet on lower rack to catch any drips. Bake buns on upper rack until golden brown on top, about 20 minutes. Cover loosely with aluminum foil and continue to bake until center buns register at least 200 degrees, about 15 minutes longer.

10. Carefully remove foil from pan (steam may escape) and immediately run paring knife around edge of pan. Place large platter or second rimmed baking sheet over pan and carefully invert. Remove pan and let buns cool for 15 minutes. Serve.

To Make Ahead Follow recipe through step 8, then refrigerate buns for at least 8 hours or up to 24 hours. When ready to bake, let buns sit on counter for 30 minutes before proceeding with step 9. Increase uncovered baking time by 10 minutes.

Morning Buns
MAKES 12 BUNS

WHY THIS RECIPE WORKS Morning buns rely on a complicated croissant-like dough that requires substantial effort and time. For an easier path, we switched to a quick dough closer to puff pastry. We rolled the butter with the dry ingredients in a zipper-lock bag. To produce multiple layers in the pastry, we next rolled the dough into a rectangle, then a cylinder, then patted it flat. A blend of sugars and orange zest made a multifaceted filling.

If the dough becomes too soft to work with at any point, refrigerate it until it's firm enough to handle easily.

Dough
- 3 cups (15 ounces) all-purpose flour
- 1 tablespoon sugar
- 2¼ teaspoons instant or rapid-rise yeast
- ¾ teaspoon table salt
- 24 tablespoons (3 sticks) unsalted butter, cut into ¼-inch-thick slices and chilled
- 1 cup sour cream, chilled
- ¼ cup orange juice, chilled
- 3 tablespoons ice water
- 1 large egg yolk

New Jersey Crumb Buns

SERVES 12

WHY THIS RECIPE WORKS For buns piled high with big crumbs the way they do in Jersey, we had to pay special attention to the types of flour and sugar we used in each layer. For a chewy texture in our cake base, we used all-purpose flour. But instead of using this same flour for the topping, we reached for cake flour, which is finer and lower in protein than all-purpose flour and gave the topping its signature soft crumbs. We used just granulated sugar to sweeten the cake layer, but found that a combination of white and brown sugars was key for the optimal flavor and texture of the crumb topping.

Note that we call for both all-purpose and cake flours in this recipe. Do not substitute all-purpose flour for the cake flour (or vice versa), or the cake will be airy and fluffy and the topping will be tough and dry. We developed this recipe using Pillsbury Softasilk bleached cake flour; the topping will be slightly drier if you substitute unbleached cake flour. You can use either light or dark brown sugar in the topping.

Cake

- 2¼ cups (11¼ ounces) all-purpose flour
- ¾ cup milk
- ¼ cup (1¾ ounces) granulated sugar
- 1 large egg
- 2¼ teaspoons instant or rapid-rise yeast
- ¾ teaspoon table salt
- 6 tablespoons unsalted butter, cut into 6 pieces and softened

Topping

- 18 tablespoons (2¼ sticks) unsalted butter, melted
- ¾ cup (5¼ ounces) granulated sugar
- ¾ cup packed (5¼ ounces) brown sugar
- 1½ teaspoons ground cinnamon
- ½ teaspoon table salt
- 4 cups (16 ounces) cake flour
- Confectioners' sugar

1. For the Cake Adjust oven rack to middle position and heat oven to 350 degrees. Grease 13 by 9-inch baking dish. In bowl of stand mixer fitted with dough hook, combine flour, milk, sugar, egg, yeast, and salt. Knead on low speed until dough comes together, about 2 minutes.

2. With mixer running, add butter 1 piece at a time, waiting until each piece is incorporated before adding next. Increase speed to medium-high and continue to knead until dough forms stretchy, web-like strands on sides of bowl, about 6 minutes longer (dough will be soft and sticky).

3. Using greased rubber spatula, transfer dough to prepared dish. Using your floured hands, press dough into even layer to edges of dish. Cover dish tightly with plastic wrap and let dough rise at room temperature until slightly puffy, about 1 hour.

4. For the Topping Ten minutes before dough has finished rising, whisk melted butter, granulated sugar, brown sugar, cinnamon, and salt together in bowl. Add flour and stir with rubber spatula or wooden spoon until mixture forms thick, cohesive dough; let sit for 10 minutes to allow flour to hydrate.

5. If dough has pulled away from sides of dish after rising, gently pat it back into place using your floured fingers. Break topping mixture into rough ½-inch pieces using your fingers and scatter in even layer over dough in dish. (Be sure to scatter all crumbs even though it may seem like too much.)

6. Bake until crumbs are golden brown, wooden skewer inserted in center of cake comes out clean, and cake portion registers about 215 degrees in center, about 35 minutes. Transfer dish to wire rack and let cake cool completely. Using spatula, transfer cake to cutting board; cut cake into 12 squares. Dust squares with confectioners' sugar and serve.

To Make Ahead Once dough has been pressed into even layer in baking dish and dish has been wrapped tightly in plastic wrap, dough can be refrigerated for at least 4 hours (to ensure proper rising) or up to 24 hours. When ready to bake, let dough sit on counter for 10 minutes before proceeding with step 4. Increase baking time to 40 minutes.

> ### All Crumb Trails Lead to . . . Hackensack?
>
> Since 1948, B&W Bakery in Hackensack, New Jersey, has been at the center of the crumb bun universe. At the bakery, staffers use industrial-size baking sheets to bake the cakes before sprinkling them with a thick layer of streusel (they go through 2,000 pounds of crumbs a week) and cutting them into slabs or squares, depending on your order. Fans from across northern New Jersey make it a weekly stop.

Morning Buns

New Jersey Crumb Buns

Alabama Orange Rolls

MAKES 8 ROLLS

WHY THIS RECIPE WORKS At All Steak restaurant in Cullman, Alabama, crowds go crazy for the famous orange rolls that deliver an outsized punch of citrus flavor. To replicate these sweet spirals, we used oranges in every step of the process. Incorporating balanced amounts of orange juice into the yeasted dough and orange zest into the filling helped the rolls bake up with lots of bright citrus flavor without any bitterness. A mixture of orange juice, sugar, and cream boiled quickly into a vibrant and syrupy glaze that gave the fresh-baked rolls an additional punch of citrus and a lovely sheen.

Be sure to zest the oranges before juicing them. When zesting the orange, remove just the outer part of the peel—the inner white pith is very bitter. We bake these rolls in a dark-colored cake pan because they brown better. If you only have a light-colored pan, increase the baking time to 45 to 50 minutes.

Dough
- 3 cups (15 ounces) all-purpose flour
- ¼ cup (1¾ ounces) sugar
- 2¼ teaspoons instant or rapid-rise yeast
- 1 teaspoon table salt
- ½ cup orange juice, warm (110 degrees)
- ¼ cup heavy cream
- 6 tablespoons unsalted butter, cut into 6 pieces and softened
- 1 large egg plus 1 large yolk

Filling
- ½ cup (3½ ounces) sugar
- 2 teaspoons grated orange zest
- 2 tablespoons unsalted butter, softened

Glaze
- ¼ cup heavy cream
- ¼ cup (1¾ ounces) sugar
- 2 tablespoons orange juice
- 2 tablespoons unsalted butter
- ⅛ teaspoon table salt

1. For the Dough In bowl of stand mixer, whisk flour, sugar, yeast, and salt together. Add orange juice, cream, butter, and egg and yolk. Fit mixer with dough hook and knead on medium speed until dough comes together, about 2 minutes. Increase speed to medium-high and continue to knead dough until smooth and elastic, about 8 minutes longer. Dough will be soft.

2. Transfer dough to lightly floured counter and knead until smooth ball forms, about 30 seconds. Place dough in greased large bowl, cover tightly with plastic wrap, and let rise in warm place until doubled in size, 1½ to 2 hours.

Making Alabama Orange Rolls

1. Roll dough into 16 by 8-inch rectangle with long side parallel to counter's edge. Spread butter over surface of dough with small offset spatula, then sprinkle buttered surface evenly with sugar mixture.

2. Roll dough away from you into tight, even log. Pinch seam between forefinger and thumb along entire length of log to seal tightly.

3. Use serrated knife to cut log into eight 2-inch-thick slices.

4. Arrange slices in cake pan, one roll in center and remaining rolls around perimeter, with seam sides facing inward.

3. For the Filling Combine sugar and zest in small bowl. Transfer dough to lightly floured counter. Roll dough into 16 by 8-inch rectangle with long side parallel to counter's edge. Spread butter over surface of dough using small offset spatula, then sprinkle evenly with sugar mixture. Roll dough away from you into tight, even log and pinch seam to seal.

4. Grease dark-colored 9-inch cake pan, line bottom with parchment paper, then grease parchment. Roll log seam side down and cut into eight 2-inch-thick slices using serrated knife. Place 1 roll in center of prepared pan and others around perimeter of pan, seam sides facing center. Cover with plastic and let rise in warm place until doubled in size, 1 to 1½ hours. Adjust oven rack to middle position and heat oven to 325 degrees.

5. Discard plastic and bake rolls until golden brown on top and interior of center roll registers 195 degrees, 40 to 45 minutes. Let rolls cool in pan on wire rack for 30 minutes.

6. For the Glaze Once rolls have cooled for 30 minutes, combine all ingredients in small saucepan and bring to boil over medium heat. Cook, stirring frequently, until large, slow bubbles appear and mixture is syrupy, about 4 minutes.

7. Using spatula, loosen rolls from sides of pan and slide onto platter; discard parchment. Brush glaze over tops of rolls and serve warm.

Kolaches

MAKES 16 KOLACHES

WHY THIS RECIPE WORKS We learned the secrets to great kolaches from Denise Mazal at Little Gretel in Boerne, Texas. Brought to Texas by Czech immigrants, kolaches are palm-size rounds of sweetened bread with dollops of sweet cheese or fruit filling and a streusel topping. We discovered that long mixing with a dough hook developed plenty of stretchy gluten, making the finished pastries light and pleasantly chewy. For a Texas-style filling, a combination of tangy cream cheese and milkier, slightly salty ricotta created a perfect base, while a little sugar and lemon zest balanced the flavor. At the end of the day, our kolaches were subtly sweet, tender, buttery, and . . . gone.

Do not use nonfat ricotta cheese in this recipe. In step 1, if the dough hasn't cleared the sides of the bowl after 12 minutes, add more flour, 1 tablespoon at a time, up to 2 tablespoons. In step 6, to prevent sticking, reflour the bottom of the measuring cup (or drinking glass) after making each indentation.

Dough

- 1 cup whole milk
- 10 tablespoons unsalted butter, melted
- 1 large egg plus 2 large yolks
- 3½ cups (17½ ounces) all-purpose flour
- ⅓ cup (2⅓ ounces) sugar
- 2¼ teaspoons instant or rapid-rise yeast
- 1½ teaspoons table salt

Cheese Filling

- 6 ounces cream cheese, softened
- 3 tablespoons sugar
- 1 tablespoon all-purpose flour
- ½ teaspoon grated lemon zest
- 6 ounces (¾ cup) whole-milk or part-skim ricotta cheese

Streusel

- 2 tablespoons plus 2 teaspoons all-purpose flour
- 2 tablespoons plus 2 teaspoons sugar
- 1 tablespoon unsalted butter, cut into 8 pieces and chilled

- 1 large egg beaten with 1 tablespoon milk

1. For the Dough Grease large bowl. Whisk milk, melted butter, and egg and yolks together in 2-cup liquid measuring cup (butter will form clumps). Whisk flour, sugar, yeast, and salt together in bowl of stand mixer. Fit stand mixer with dough hook, add milk mixture to flour mixture, and knead on low speed until no dry flour remains, about 2 minutes. Increase speed to medium and knead until dough clears sides of bowl but still sticks to bottom, 8 to 12 minutes.

2. Transfer dough to greased bowl and cover with plastic wrap. Adjust oven racks to upper-middle and lower-middle positions. Place dough on lower-middle rack and place loaf pan on bottom of oven. Pour 3 cups boiling water into loaf pan, close oven door, and let dough rise until doubled, about 1 hour.

3. For the Cheese Filling Using stand mixer fitted with paddle, beat cream cheese, sugar, flour, and lemon zest on low speed until smooth, about 1 minute. Add ricotta and beat until just combined, about 30 seconds. Transfer to bowl, cover with plastic, and refrigerate until ready to use.

RISE-AND-SHINE BREAKFAST AND BREADS 583

Kolaches

4. For the Streusel Combine flour, sugar, and butter in bowl and rub between fingers until mixture resembles wet sand. Cover with plastic and refrigerate until ready to use.

5. Line 2 rimmed baking sheets with parchment paper. Punch down dough and place on lightly floured counter. Divide into quarters and cut each quarter into 4 equal pieces. Form each piece into rough ball by pulling dough edges underneath so top is smooth. On unfloured counter, cup each ball in your palm and roll into smooth, tight ball. Arrange 8 balls on each prepared sheet and cover loosely with plastic. Place sheets on oven racks. Replace water in loaf pan with 3 cups boiling water, close oven door, and let dough rise until doubled, about 90 minutes.

6. Remove sheets and loaf pan from oven. Heat oven to 350 degrees. Grease and flour bottom of ⅓-cup measuring cup (or 2¼-inch-diameter drinking glass). Make deep indentation in center of each dough ball by slowly pressing until cup touches sheet. (Perimeter of balls may deflate slightly.)

7. Gently brush kolaches all over with egg-milk mixture. Divide filling evenly among kolaches (about 1½ tablespoons per kolache) and smooth with back of spoon. Sprinkle streusel over kolaches, avoiding filling. Bake until golden brown, about 25 minutes, switching and rotating sheets halfway through baking. Let kolaches cool on pans for 20 minutes. Serve warm.

Cream Cheese Kringle

Cream Cheese Kringle

MAKES 2 KRINGLES, EACH SERVING 8

WHY THIS RECIPE WORKS In Racine, Wisconsin, kringle is king. This oval-shaped Danish combines the richness of sweet yeast dough with some of the flakiness of puff pastry. A traditional kringle takes three days of careful folding and chilling to achieve its tender layers, but we used a few tricks to achieve the same result in a fraction of the time. A generous amount of sour cream in the dough weakened the gluten structure, in effect mimicking the flaky texture of an authentic kringle. Lots of butter is key to a kringle's rich flavor and tenderness, but too much can cause greasiness. We replaced some with shortening, which is a tenderizer that helped balance the texture and flavor. A stir-together cream cheese filling and a quick glaze completed the kringle.

If the dough appears shaggy and dry after adding the sour cream in step 2, add up to 2 tablespoons ice water until the dough is smooth. If the capacity of your food processor is less than 11 cups, pulse the butter and shortening into the dry mixture in two batches at the beginning of step 2.

Filling

- 8 ounces softened cream cheese
- ¼ cup (1¾ ounces) granulated sugar
- ½ teaspoon lemon zest

Dough

- 4 cups (20 ounces) all-purpose flour
- 2 tablespoons confectioners' sugar
- 1 envelope (2¼ teaspoons) rapid-rise or instant yeast
- ¾ teaspoon salt
- 16 tablespoons (2 sticks) unsalted butter, cut into ½-inch pieces and chilled
- 4 tablespoons vegetable shortening, chilled, cut into ½-inch pieces
- 2 cups sour cream
- 1 large egg, lightly beaten

Glaze

- 1 cup (4 ounces) confectioners' sugar
- 2 tablespoons whole or low-fat milk
- ½ teaspoon vanilla extract

1. For the Filling Combine cream cheese, sugar, and lemon zest in bowl.

2. For the Dough Add flour, sugar, yeast, salt, butter, and shortening to empty food processor and pulse until mixture resembles coarse meal. Transfer to bowl and stir in sour cream until dough forms. Turn dough out onto lightly floured surface and divide in half. Pat each half into 7 by 3-inch rectangle and wrap in plastic. Refrigerate dough for 30 minutes, then freeze until firm, about 15 minutes.

3. Roll dough following photos 1 to 4 (right), roll one dough half into 28 by 5-inch rectangle, cover bottom half of strip with half of filling, fold dough over filling, and pinch seams closed. Shape into oval, tuck one end inside of other, and pinch to seal. Transfer to parchment-lined, rimmed baking sheet, cover with plastic wrap, and refrigerate at least 4 or up to 24 hours. Repeat with remaining dough and filling.

4. Adjust oven racks to upper-middle and lower-middle positions and heat oven to 350 degrees. Discard plastic, brush kringles with egg, and bake until golden brown, 40 to 50 minutes, switching and rotating sheets halfway through baking. Transfer kringles to wire rack and cool 30 minutes.

5. For the Glaze Whisk sugar, milk, and vanilla in bowl until smooth. Drizzle glaze over kringles. Let glaze set 10 minutes. Serve warm or at room temperature. (Kringle can be stored in airtight container at room temperature for 2 days.)

Kringle Construction

Working with one piece of chilled dough at a time, follow these steps to roll and shape the kringle.

1. Working on a lightly floured surface, roll the dough into a 28 by 5-inch strip with one long side closest to you. The dough will be about ¼ inch thick.

2. Leaving a ½-inch border around the bottom and side edges, spread half of the filling over the bottom half of the dough.

3. Brush the edge of the uncovered dough with water and fold the dough over the filling, pinching to close the long seam.

4. Fit one end of the folded dough inside the other to make an oval and press together to seal.

Pecan Filling

Prepare Cream Cheese Kringle, omitting cream cheese filling. In step 1, process ¾ cup packed light brown sugar, 1 cup toasted pecans, ¼ teaspoon ground cinnamon, and ⅛ teaspoon salt in food processor until pecans are coarsely ground. Add 4 tablespoons chilled unsalted butter, cut into ½-inch pieces, and pulse until mixture resembles coarse meal. Transfer to bowl. In step 3, spread half of pecan mixture over bottom of dough and continue with recipe as directed. Repeat with remaining dough and pecan mixture.

Double Berry Filling

Do not substitute raspberry jam for the preserves; it will leach out of the kringle.

Prepare Cream Cheese Kringle, omitting cream cheese filling. In step 1, combine ½ cup raspberry preserves and ¼ cup finely chopped dried cranberries in bowl. In step 3, spread half of preserves mixture over bottom half of dough and continue with recipe as directed. Repeat with remaining dough and preserves mixture.

Chocolate Babka

Chocolate Babka

SERVES 8

WHY THIS RECIPE WORKS This rich, chocolaty loaf features a yeasted dough flavored with orange zest and vanilla. We made a luscious chocolate filling by microwaving melted butter and chocolate together and stirring in confectioners' sugar, cocoa, and salt. To combine them, we rolled the dough out into a rectangle, spread the filling over it, and rolled it into a tight log. Splitting the log in half lengthwise and twisting the halves together ensured layers of chocolate throughout the loaf. A sugar syrup brushed over the warm babka provided an extra-special finish.

The test kitchen's preferred loaf pan, the USA Pan Loaf Pan, 1 lb Volume, measures 8½ by 4½ inches; if you use a 9 by 5-inch pan, start checking for doneness 15 minutes early. If the chocolate filling becomes too stiff to spread in step 6, use a rubber spatula to work it back to a softer texture. We developed this recipe using Ghirardelli 60% Cacao Bittersweet Chocolate Premium Baking Bar. Do not overflour the counter when rolling out the dough in step 5, or it may slide when rolling and shaping. It will feel like a lot of syrup when brushing the loaf in step 10, but use all of it. As hard as it is to do, let the babka cool for the full 3 hours before slicing it.

Dough

- 2¼ cups (12⅓ ounces) bread flour
- 1½ teaspoons instant or rapid-rise yeast
- ½ cup whole milk
- 2 large eggs
- 1 tablespoon grated orange zest (optional)
- 1 teaspoon vanilla extract
- ¼ cup (1¾ ounces) granulated sugar
- ½ teaspoon table salt
- 6 tablespoons unsalted butter, cut into 6 pieces and softened, plus 1 tablespoon for greasing pan

Filling

- 8 ounces bittersweet chocolate, chopped fine
- 8 tablespoons unsalted butter
- ½ cup (2 ounces) confectioners' sugar, sifted
- ½ cup (1½ ounces) unsweetened cocoa powder, sifted
- ½ teaspoon table salt

Syrup

- ½ cup (3½ ounces) granulated sugar
- ¼ cup water

1. For the Dough Whisk flour and yeast together in bowl of stand mixer. Add milk; eggs; orange zest, if using; and vanilla. Fit mixer with dough hook and mix on medium-low speed until cohesive dough comes together and no dry flour remains, about 2 minutes. Turn off mixer, cover bowl with dish towel or plastic wrap, and let dough stand for 15 minutes.

2. Add sugar and salt to dough and knead on medium speed until incorporated, about 30 seconds. Increase speed to medium-high and, with mixer running, add 6 tablespoons butter, 1 piece at a time, allowing each piece to incorporate before adding next, about 3 minutes total, scraping down bowl and dough hook as needed. Continue to knead on medium-high speed until dough begins to pull away from sides of bowl, 7 to 10 minutes longer.

3. Transfer dough to greased large bowl. Cover tightly with plastic and let rise at room temperature until slightly puffy, about 1 hour. Refrigerate until firm, at least 2 hours or up to 24 hours.

4. For the Filling Just before removing dough from refrigerator, place chocolate in medium bowl. Melt butter in small saucepan over medium heat. Immediately pour melted butter over chocolate and stir to combine. Microwave at 50 percent power, stirring often, until chocolate is fully melted and smooth, about 30 seconds. Stir in sugar, cocoa, and salt until combined; set aside.

5. Adjust oven rack to middle position and heat oven to 325 degrees. Grease 8½ by 4½-inch loaf pan with 1 tablespoon butter. Remove dough from refrigerator and turn out onto lightly floured counter. Using floured rolling pin, roll dough into 18 by 12-inch rectangle, with short side parallel to edge of counter.

6. Using offset spatula, spread chocolate mixture evenly over dough, leaving ½-inch border along top edge. Beginning with edge nearest you, tightly roll dough away from you into even 12-inch log, pushing in ends to create even thickness. Pinch seam to seal.

7. Using greased serrated knife and slicing in only 1 direction, gently cut log in half lengthwise and lay halves next to each other cut sides up. Forming tight twist, cross left log over right log. Continue twisting, 5 times total, keeping cut sides facing up as much as possible. Pinch ends together and carefully transfer to prepared loaf pan cut sides up. Tap loaf pan on counter to pack dough into pan.

8. Set wire rack in rimmed baking sheet and center loaf pan on wire rack. Bake for 30 minutes. Remove from oven and cover babka with aluminum foil. Return to oven and continue to bake until center registers 200 to 205 degrees, 50 minutes to 1 hour.

9. For the Syrup Meanwhile, combine sugar and water in small saucepan and heat over medium heat until sugar dissolves. Set aside off heat.

10. Remove babka from oven. Leaving babka in loaf pan, brush syrup evenly over entire surface of hot babka (use all of it). Let cool in loaf pan on wire rack for 1 hour. Carefully remove babka from pan and let cool completely on wire rack, about 2 hours. Slice 1 inch thick and serve.

Monkey Bread

SERVES 6 TO 8

WHY THIS RECIPE WORKS It might have a funny name, but monkey bread is a soft, sweet, sticky, ultra-cinnamony treat (its moniker probably refers to how it's pulled apart and stuffed into eager mouths). To expedite the rising and proofing of the dough and add yeasty flavor, we used a good amount of instant yeast. Butter and milk kept the dough rich and moist, and a little sugar added sweetness to the bread. A dip in butter and cinnamon sugar gave the monkey bread a caramel-like coating after its stint in the oven. A drizzle of glaze finished it off.

Make sure to use light brown sugar in the coating mix; dark brown sugar has a stronger molasses flavor that can be overwhelming. After baking, don't let the bread cool in the pan for more than 5 minutes or it will stick to the pan and come out in pieces. Monkey bread is best served warm.

Dough

- 2 tablespoons unsalted butter, softened, plus 2 tablespoons melted
- 1 cup milk, heated to 110 degrees
- ⅓ cup water, heated to 110 degrees
- ¼ cup (1¾ ounces) granulated sugar
- 2¼ teaspoons instant or rapid-rise yeast
- 3¼ cups (16¼ ounces) all-purpose flour
- 2 teaspoons table salt

Brown Sugar Coating

- 1 cup packed (7 ounces) light brown sugar
- 2 teaspoons ground cinnamon
- 8 tablespoons unsalted butter, melted

Glaze

- 1 cup (4 ounces) confectioners' sugar
- 2 tablespoons milk

1. **For the Dough** Grease 12-cup nonstick Bundt pan with softened butter; set aside. Combine milk, water, melted butter, sugar, and yeast in 2-cup liquid measuring cup.

2. Adjust oven rack to middle position and place loaf or cake pan on bottom of oven. Using stand mixer fitted with dough hook, mix flour and salt on low speed. Slowly add milk mixture and mix until dough comes together (if dough is too wet and doesn't come together, add up to 2 tablespoons more flour). Increase speed to medium and knead until dough is shiny and smooth, 6 to 7 minutes. Turn dough onto lightly floured counter and knead briefly to form smooth, round ball. Place dough in large greased bowl, coat surface with vegetable oil spray, and transfer to oven. Pour 3 cups boiling water into loaf pan in oven, close oven door, and let dough rise until doubled in size, 50 minutes to 1 hour.

3. **For the Brown Sugar Coating** While dough rises, combine sugar and cinnamon in small bowl. Place melted butter in second bowl. Set aside.

4. Gently remove dough from bowl and pat into rough 8-inch square. Using bench scraper or knife, cut square into quarters, then cut each quarter into 16 pieces. Roll each piece of dough into a ball. Working with one at a time, dip each ball in melted butter, allowing excess butter to drip off, then roll in sugar mixture. Layer dough balls in prepared pan, staggering seams where dough balls meet. Cover pan tightly with plastic wrap, transfer to oven, and let rest until dough balls are puffy and have risen 1 to 2 inches from top of pan, 50 minutes to 1 hour, 10 minutes.

5. Remove Bundt pan and water pan from oven; adjust oven rack to medium-low position and heat oven to 350 degrees. Remove plastic and bake until top of dough is deeply browned and caramel begins to bubble around edges, 30 to 35 minutes, rotating pan halfway through baking. Let monkey bread cool in pan for 5 minutes, then turn out on platter and let cool slightly, about 10 minutes.

6. **For the Glaze** Meanwhile, whisk sugar and milk together in small bowl until smooth. Using whisk, drizzle glaze over warm monkey bread, letting it run over top and sides of bread. Serve warm.

Forming Monkey Bread

After forming dough balls, dip each one in melted butter and sugar and then place in greased Bundt pan, staggering seams where dough balls meet.

Monkey Bread

Amish Cinnamon Bread

MAKES 2 LOAVES

WHY THIS RECIPE WORKS Recipes for this "friendship bread" traditionally include two unusual ingredients: a sourdough starter shared by friends and vanilla pudding mix. We set out to develop a recipe that would capture the flavor and spirit of the original without the need for a lengthy starter. Testing revealed that there was almost no difference between breads baked with and without a starter; the bread's sweetness rendered any tang from the starter undetectable. Rather than use packaged vanilla pudding mix, we increased the sugar and added extra vanilla extract. We designed our recipe to make two soft, delicious loaves—give one to a friend.

Amish Cinnamon Bread

We developed this recipe using an 8½ by 4½-inch metal loaf pan. If you use a glass loaf pan, increase the baking time in step 3 to 1¼ hours to 1 hour 20 minutes; if you use a 9 by 5-inch loaf pan, start checking for doneness 5 minutes early. If you own only one loaf pan, refrigerate half the batter and set aside half the coating so you can bake a second loaf after turning out the first onto a wire rack to cool in step 4. Be sure to clean the loaf pan and brush it with oil before baking the second loaf.

Cinnamon-Sugar Coating

- ½ cup (3½ ounces) sugar
- 1 teaspoon ground cinnamon
- 2 teaspoons vegetable oil

Bread

- 3¾ cups (18¾ ounces) all-purpose flour
- 3 cups (21 ounces) sugar
- 1 tablespoon ground cinnamon
- 1½ teaspoons baking powder
- ¾ teaspoon baking soda
- ¾ teaspoon table salt
- 1¾ cups milk
- 1⅓ cups vegetable oil
- 3 large eggs, lightly beaten
- 2 teaspoons vanilla extract

1. For the Cinnamon-Sugar Coating Combine sugar and cinnamon in bowl. Brush 2 loaf pans evenly with oil (1 teaspoon per pan). Add 2 tablespoons cinnamon-sugar coating to each prepared pan and shake and tilt pans until bottoms and sides are evenly coated. Set aside remaining ¼ cup cinnamon-sugar coating.

2. For the Bread Adjust oven rack to middle position and heat oven to 325 degrees. Whisk flour, sugar, cinnamon, baking powder, baking soda, and salt together in large bowl. Whisk milk, oil, eggs, and vanilla together in second bowl. Stir milk mixture into flour mixture until just combined (batter will be lumpy).

3. Divide batter evenly between prepared pans (about 3¾ cups or 2¼ pounds batter per pan). Sprinkle remaining cinnamon-sugar coating evenly over top of batter (2 tablespoons per pan). Bake until paring knife inserted in centers of loaves comes out clean, 1 hour 5 minutes to 1 hour 10 minutes.

4. Let bread cool in pans on wire rack for 1 hour. Run paring knife around edges of pans to thoroughly loosen loaves. Working with 1 loaf at a time, tilt pan and gently remove bread. Serve warm or at room temperature. (Cooled bread can be wrapped in aluminum foil and stored at room temperature for up to 3 days.)

English Muffin Bread

MAKES 2 LOAVES

WHY THIS RECIPE WORKS With their chewy interiors, crunchy crusts, and craggy texture, English muffins are a treat—but they're also a lot of work. For a no-fuss recipe without the kneading, rolling, cutting, or griddling, we made a simple loaf bread with the flavor and texture of English muffins. Protein-rich bread flour gave the loaf a chewy yet light consistency, and baking soda created the all-important honeycombed texture. Heating the milk before mixing the dough activated the yeast and shortened the rising time. We simply mixed the dough, let it rise, then baked it in loaf pans until the crust was well browned and the interior was perfectly craggy.

Serve this bread with butter and jam.

RISE-AND-SHINE BREAKFAST AND BREADS   589

Cornmeal
- 5 cups (27½ ounces) bread flour
- 4½ teaspoons instant or rapid-rise yeast
- 1 tablespoon sugar
- 2 teaspoons table salt
- 1 teaspoon baking soda
- 3 cups whole milk, heated to 120 degrees

1. Grease two 8½ by 4½-inch loaf pans and dust with cornmeal. Combine flour, yeast, sugar, salt, and baking soda in large bowl. Stir in hot milk until combined, about 1 minute. Cover dough with greased plastic wrap and let rise in warm place for 30 minutes, or until dough is bubbly and has doubled.

2. Stir dough and divide between prepared loaf pans, pushing into corners with greased rubber spatula. (Pans should be about two-thirds full.) Cover pans with greased plastic and let dough rise in warm place until it reaches edges of pans, about 30 minutes. Adjust oven rack to middle position and heat oven to 375 degrees.

3. Discard plastic and transfer pans to oven. Bake until loaves are well browned and register 200 degrees, about 30 minutes, rotating and switching pans halfway through baking. Turn loaves out onto wire rack and let cool completely, about 1 hour. Slice, toast, and serve.

English Muffin Bread

A Well-Dressed Table

By the end of the 19th century, the English were losing their taste for English-style muffins, but in the U.S. they had become such a popular breakfast bread that the properly set breakfast table required special dishes for serving them. Victorians, of course, were ardent believers that the correct home environment shaped correct behavior; proper dining and tableware, especially, equated with proper civilization. So wealthy families had specific dishware for everything, from glass or silver vases for celery to custom dishes to hold bananas to specialized vessels and utensils for serving sardines. And don't forget asparagus forks.

Brown Soda Bread

MAKES 1 LOAF

WHY THIS RECIPE WORKS For a brown soda bread with good wheaty flavor but without a gummy, dense texture, we started by finding the right ratio of whole-wheat to all-purpose flour. The addition of toasted wheat germ played up the sweet, nutty flavor of the whole wheat. To keep the texture light, we needed lots of leavening; baking soda alone gave the bread a soapy taste, so we used a combination of baking soda and baking powder. Just a bit of sugar and a few tablespoons of butter kept our bread wholesome but not bland, and brushing a portion of the melted butter on the loaf after baking gave it a rich crust.

Toasted wheat germ is sold in jars at well-stocked supermarkets.

- 2 cups (10 ounces) all-purpose flour
- 1½ cups (8¼ ounces) whole-wheat flour
- ½ cup toasted wheat germ
- 3 tablespoons sugar
- 1½ teaspoons table salt
- 1 teaspoon baking powder
- 1 teaspoon baking soda
- 1¾ cups buttermilk
- 3 tablespoons unsalted butter, melted, divided

1. Adjust oven rack to lower-middle position and heat oven to 400 degrees. Line rimmed baking sheet with parchment paper. Whisk all-purpose flour, whole-wheat

Brown Soda Bread

Fastest Bread Ever	
\multicolumn{2}{l}{No yeast, no rise time, and almost no kneading or shaping.}
Measure and whisk dry ingredients	5 minutes
Measure and combine wet ingredients	2 minutes
Stir wet into dry	1 minute
Knead briefly	1 minute
Shape simply	1 minute
Total work time	10 minutes

flour, wheat germ, sugar, salt, baking powder, and baking soda together in large bowl. Combine buttermilk and 2 tablespoons melted butter in 2-cup liquid measuring cup.

2. Add wet ingredients to dry ingredients and stir with rubber spatula until dough just comes together. Turn out dough onto lightly floured counter and knead until cohesive mass forms, about 8 turns. Pat dough into 7-inch round and transfer to prepared baking sheet. Using sharp serrated knife, make ¼-inch-deep cross about 5 inches long on top of loaf. Bake until skewer inserted in center comes out clean and loaf registers 195 degrees, 45 to 50 minutes, rotating baking sheet halfway through baking.

3. Remove bread from oven. Brush with remaining 1 tablespoon melted butter. Transfer loaf to wire rack and let cool for at least 1 hour. Serve.

Brown Soda Bread with Currants and Caraway
Add 1 cup dried currants and 1 tablespoon caraway seeds to dry ingredients in step 1.

Dakota Bread
MAKES ONE 10-INCH LOAF

WHY THIS RECIPE WORKS This hearty loaf from the breadbasket of America usually contains a daunting variety of flours and seeds. We shortened the ingredient list by using seven-grain cereal mix to give our loaf hearty texture and complex flavor. To round it out, we stirred some seeds into the batter and sprinkled more on top. Starting the bread in a hot oven created an initial "spring" for a lighter crumb. We then lowered the temperature to keep the seeds from burning. High-protein bread flour allowed our loaf to rise high, and a pan of water in the oven kept the crust from setting before the bread had fully risen.

In step 2, if the dough is still sticking to the sides of the mixing bowl after 2 minutes, add more flour 1 tablespoon at a time, up to 3 tablespoons. Be sure to use hot cereal mix, not boxed cold breakfast cereals, which may also be labeled "seven-grain." The latter will harm the texture of the loaf.

- 2 cups warm water (110 degrees)
- 1½ cups (7½ ounces) seven-grain hot cereal mix
- 2 tablespoons honey
- 2 tablespoons vegetable oil
- 3½ cups (19¼ ounces) bread flour
- 1¾ teaspoons table salt
- 1 teaspoon instant or rapid-rise yeast
- 3 tablespoons raw, unsalted pepitas, divided
- 3 tablespoons raw, unsalted sunflower seeds, divided
- 1 teaspoon sesame seeds
- 1 teaspoon poppy seeds
- 1 large egg, lightly beaten

RISE-AND-SHINE BREAKFAST AND BREADS

Dakota Bread

1. Grease large bowl. Line rimmed baking sheet with parchment paper. In bowl of stand mixer, combine water, cereal, honey, and oil and let sit for 10 minutes.

2. Add flour, salt, and yeast to cereal mixture. Fit stand mixer with dough hook and knead on low speed until dough is smooth and elastic, 4 to 6 minutes. Add 2 tablespoons pepitas and 2 tablespoons sunflower seeds to dough and knead for 1 minute longer. Turn out dough onto lightly floured counter and knead until seeds are evenly distributed, about 2 minutes.

3. Transfer dough to greased bowl and cover with plastic wrap. Let dough rise at room temperature until almost doubled in size and fingertip depression in dough springs back slowly, 60 to 90 minutes.

4. Gently press down on center of dough to deflate. Transfer dough to lightly floured counter and shape into tight round ball. Place dough on prepared sheet. Cover dough loosely with plastic and let rise at room temperature until almost doubled in size, 60 to 90 minutes.

5. Adjust oven racks to upper-middle and lowest positions and heat oven to 425 degrees. Combine remaining 1 tablespoon pepitas, remaining 1 tablespoon sunflower seeds, sesame seeds, and poppy seeds in small bowl. Using sharp knife, make ¼-inch-deep cross, 5 inches long, on top of loaf. Brush loaf with egg and sprinkle seed mixture evenly over top.

6. Place 8½ by 4½-inch loaf pan on lowest oven rack and fill with 1 cup boiling water. Place baking sheet with dough on upper-middle rack and reduce oven to 375 degrees. Bake until crust is dark brown and bread registers 200 degrees, 40 to 50 minutes. Transfer loaf to wire rack and let cool completely, about 2 hours. Serve.

Mana'eesh Za'atar (Za'atar Flatbreads)

SERVES 4 TO 6 (MAKES THREE 9-INCH FLATBREADS)

WHY THIS RECIPE WORKS In Lebanon, mana'eesh are both a street food and a specialty of dedicated bakeries. According to Maroun (Mario) Ellakis, owner of Mario's Lebanese Bakery in Fall River, Massachusetts, they are eaten at nearly every Lebanese meal. To make our za'atar flatbreads, we turned to the food processor. Its high-speed blades turned the flour, water, salt, yeast and olive oil into a dough quickly. Before baking the dough rounds, we pressed them with our fingers to prevent uneven puffing

Mana'eesh Za'atar (Za'atar Flatbreads)

and spread a mixture of za'atar, olive oil, and salt over each. Baking them on a preheated baking stone in a 500-degree oven gave them chewy yet tender interiors and a crispy crust.

You can purchase za'atar in the spice section of many grocery stores or online, or you can make own (recipe follows).

Dough
- 2½ cups (12½ ounces) all-purpose flour
- 1½ teaspoons instant or rapid-rise yeast
- 1 teaspoon table salt
- ¾ cup plus 2 tablespoons cold water
- 2 tablespoons extra-virgin olive oil

Topping
- 3 tablespoons za'atar (recipe follows)
- 3 tablespoons extra-virgin olive oil
- ½ teaspoon table salt

1. For the Dough Process flour, yeast, and salt in food processor until combined, about 3 seconds. Combine cold water and oil in liquid measuring cup. With processor running, slowly add water mixture and process until dough forms sticky ball that clears sides of bowl, 30 to 60 seconds.

2. Transfer dough to clean counter and knead into cohesive ball, about 1 minute. Place dough in greased bowl. Cover bowl with plastic wrap and let dough rise at room temperature until almost doubled in size, 2 to 2½ hours. One hour before baking, adjust oven rack to middle position, set baking stone on rack, and heat oven to 500 degrees.

3. For the Topping Meanwhile, combine za'atar, oil, and salt in bowl.

4. On clean counter, divide dough into 3 equal pieces, about 7 ounces each. Shape each piece of dough into ball; cover loosely with plastic and let rest for 15 minutes.

5. Working with 1 dough ball at a time on lightly floured counter, coat lightly with flour and flatten into 6- to 7-inch disk using your fingertips.

6. Using rolling pin, roll dough into 9- to 10-inch circle. Slide dough round onto floured baking peel. Spread one-third of za'atar mixture (about 1½ tablespoons) over surface of dough with back of dinner spoon, stopping ½ inch from edge.

7. Firmly tap dough all over with your fingertips, about 6 times. Slide dough onto baking stone and bake until lightly bubbled and brown on top, about 5 minutes. Using baking peel, transfer man'oushe to wire rack. Repeat with remaining dough and za'atar mixture. Slice or tear and serve.

Za'atar
MAKES ABOUT ⅓ CUP

The combination of dried herbs; toasted sesame seeds; and tart, citrusy sumac makes for an earthy yet brightly flavored seasoning.

- 2 tablespoons dried thyme
- 1 tablespoon dried oregano
- 1½ tablespoons sumac
- 1 tablespoon sesame seeds, toasted
- ¼ teaspoon table salt

Grind thyme and oregano using spice grinder or mortar and pestle until finely ground and powdery. Transfer to bowl and stir in sumac, sesame seeds, and salt. (Za'atar can be stored in airtight container at room temperature for up to 1 year.)

On the Road: Following the (Saintly) Signs

From a young age Maroun (Mario) Ellakis was drawn to the kitchen. "When I was 13 years old I started working in kitchens in Lebanon. I learned [cooking] little by little." Baking was a passion he developed over the years.

When Mario came to the United States from Lebanon in 2004, he knew he wanted to open his own business. In 2008, his dream became a reality. At Mario's Lebanese Bakery in Fall River, Massachusetts, he can be found five days a week in the early morning hours feeding mana'eesh za'atar dough onto the revolving steel plates of his custom-built brick oven. After 90 seconds in the 1,200-degree oven, his mana'eesh emerge char-flecked on top and crisp on the bottom. These flatbreads are based on a family recipe, which he explains he cooks from memory because he knows their "correct taste."

RISE-AND-SHINE BREAKFAST AND BREADS 593

great american cakes and cookies

596	Red Velvet Cake	**622**	Hot Fudge Pudding Cake
596	Chocolate Blackout Cake	**624**	Lemon Pudding Cake
598	Wellesley Fudge Cake	**624**	Lemon Icebox Cheesecake
599	Tunnel of Fudge Cake	**626**	Strawberry Cheesecake Bars
600	Lane Cake	**627**	Milk Chocolate Cheesecake
601	Clementine Cake	**629**	La Viña–Style Cheesecake
602	Orange Upside-Down Cake	**630**	Cowboy Cookies
603	Blueberry Jam Cake	**631**	Thin and Crispy Chocolate Chip Cookies
605	Strawberry Dream Cake	**632**	Chocolate Chip Skillet Cookie
606	Strawberry Poke Cake	**632**	M&M Cookies
607	Texas Sheet Cake	**634**	Gooey Butter Cake Bars
608	Chocolate Éclair Cake	**635**	Melting Moments
609	Magic Chocolate Flan Cake	**636**	Slice-and-Bake Cookies
611	Tres Leches Cake	**637**	New Mexico Biscochitos
612	Swiss Hazelnut Cake	**639**	Fairy Gingerbread
613	Blitz Torte	**640**	Joe Froggers
614	Angel Food Cake	**641**	Black and White Cookies
615	Chiffon Cake	**642**	Whoopie Pies
616	Italian Cream Cake	**643**	Oatmeal Creme Pies
618	Cream Cheese Pound Cake	**645**	Basic Chocolate Truffles
619	Cold-Oven Pound Cake	**646**	Buckeye Candies
620	Carrot Snack Cake	**647**	Chocolate Fudge
621	Chocolate Cream Cupcakes	**648**	Vanilla No-Churn Ice Cream

Recipe Photos (clockwise from top right): Fairy Gingerbread, Lane Cake

Red Velvet Cake

SERVES 12

WHY THIS RECIPE WORKS Although the exact origins of this cake are muddled, the appeal of a tender, shockingly bright red cake swathed in fluffy cream cheese frosting is undeniable. For a cake with an extra-tender crumb, we used two unexpected ingredients: buttermilk and vinegar. They reacted with our recipe's baking soda to create a fine, tender crumb. We also zeroed in on the perfect amount of cocoa that would add a dark hue to our cake as well as lending it a pleasant cocoa flavor.

This recipe must be prepared with natural cocoa powder. Dutch-processed cocoa will not yield the proper color or rise.

Cake
- 2¼ cups (11¼ ounces) all-purpose flour
- 1½ teaspoons baking soda
- Pinch table salt
- 1 cup buttermilk
- 2 large eggs
- 1 tablespoon distilled white vinegar
- 1 teaspoon vanilla extract
- 2 tablespoons cocoa powder
- 2 tablespoons (1 ounce) red food coloring
- 12 tablespoons unsalted butter, softened
- 1½ cups (10½ ounces) granulated sugar

Frosting
- 16 tablespoons unsalted butter, softened
- 4 cups (16 ounces) confectioners' sugar
- 16 ounces cream cheese, cut into 8 pieces, softened
- 1½ teaspoons vanilla extract
- Pinch table salt

1. For the Cake Adjust oven rack to middle position and heat oven to 350 degrees. Grease two 9-inch round cake pans, line with parchment paper, grease parchment, then flour pans. Whisk flour, baking soda, and salt in medium bowl. Whisk buttermilk, eggs, vinegar, and vanilla in 4-cup liquid measuring cup. Mix cocoa with food coloring in small bowl until smooth paste forms.

2. Using stand mixer fitted with paddle, beat butter and sugar together on medium-high speed until pale and fluffy, about 3 minutes. Reduce speed to medium-low and add flour mixture in 3 additions, alternating with buttermilk mixture in 2 additions, scraping down bowl as needed. Add cocoa mixture and beat on medium speed until completely incorporated, about 30 seconds. Give batter final stir by hand. Scrape batter into prepared pans and bake until toothpick inserted in center comes out clean, about 25 minutes. Let cakes cool in pans on wire rack for 10 minutes. Remove cakes from pans, discarding parchment, and let cool completely on rack, about 2 hours. (Cooled cakes can be wrapped tightly in plastic wrap and kept at room temperature for up to 1 day.)

3. For the Frosting Using stand mixer fitted with paddle, beat butter and sugar on medium-high speed until pale and fluffy, about 2 minutes. Add cream cheese, 1 piece at a time, and beat until incorporated, about 30 seconds. Beat in vanilla and salt. Refrigerate until ready to use.

4. When cakes are cooled, cover edges of cake platter with strips of parchment. Place 1 cake layer on platter. Spread 2 cups frosting evenly over top, right to edge of cake. Top with second cake layer, press lightly to adhere, then spread remaining frosting evenly over top and sides of cake. Carefully remove parchment strips before serving. (Cake can be refrigerated for up to 3 days.)

Lost and Found
Red velvet cake fell out of fashion in the 1970s amidst health scares relating to red dye #2 (a similar fate befell red M&Ms, even though the candies never contained the dye in question). Once consumers were convinced that other red dyes were safe, red candies made it back into the M&Ms assortment (in 1987) and red velvet cakes started a comeback in bakeries.

Chocolate Blackout Cake

SERVES 10 TO 12

WHY THIS RECIPE WORKS Chocolate blackout cake, a tender chocolate layer cake sandwiched together with a puddinglike filling and covered with cake crumbs, was created by the now-shuttered Ebinger's bakery in Brooklyn. We set out to create our own version. We started by adding cocoa powder to the butter we were already melting for the cake. Heating the cocoa in the butter produced a cake that was dark and rich. And to complement the chocolate flavor of the cake, we made a chocolaty, dairy-rich pudding with a combination of milk and half-and-half, which gave it a velvety, lush quality.

Be sure to give the pudding and the cake enough time to cool or you'll end up with runny pudding and gummy cake.

Pudding
- 1¼ cups (8¾ ounces) granulated sugar
- ¼ cup cornstarch
- ½ teaspoon table salt
- 2 cups half-and-half
- 1 cup whole milk
- 6 ounces unsweetened chocolate, chopped
- 2 teaspoons vanilla extract

Cake
- 1½ cups (7½ ounces) all-purpose flour
- 2 teaspoons baking powder
- ½ teaspoon baking soda
- ½ teaspoon table salt
- 8 tablespoons unsalted butter
- ¾ cup (2¼ ounces) Dutch-processed cocoa powder
- 1 cup brewed coffee
- 1 cup buttermilk
- 1 cup packed (7 ounces) light brown sugar
- 1 cup (7 ounces) granulated sugar
- 2 large eggs
- 1 teaspoon vanilla extract

1. For the Pudding Whisk sugar, cornstarch, salt, half-and-half, and milk in large saucepan. Set pan over medium heat. Add chocolate and whisk constantly until chocolate melts and mixture begins to bubble, 2 to 4 minutes. Stir in vanilla and transfer pudding to large bowl. Place plastic wrap directly on surface of pudding and refrigerate until cold, at least 4 hours or up to 24 hours.

2. For the Cake Adjust oven rack to middle position and heat oven to 325 degrees. Grease two 8-inch round cake pans, line with parchment paper, grease parchment, then flour pans. Whisk flour, baking powder, baking soda, and salt in bowl.

3. Melt butter in large saucepan over medium heat. Stir in cocoa and cook until fragrant, about 1 minute. Off heat, whisk in coffee, buttermilk, brown sugar, and granulated sugar until dissolved. Whisk in eggs and vanilla, then slowly whisk in flour mixture.

4. Divide batter evenly between prepared pans and bake until toothpick inserted in center comes out clean, 30 to 35 minutes. Let cakes cool in pans on wire rack for 15 minutes. Remove cakes from pans, discarding parchment, and let cool completely on wire rack, about 2 hours.

Red Velvet Cake

Chocolate Blackout Cake

5. Working with 1 cake layer at a time, cut cakes horizontally into 2 layers using long, serrated knife. Crumble 1 cake layer into medium crumbs and set aside. Cover edges of cake platter with strips of parchment. Place 1 cake layer on platter. Spread 1 cup pudding over top, right to edge of cake. Top with second layer; press lightly to adhere. Repeat with 1 cup pudding and last cake layer. Spread remaining pudding evenly over top and sides of cake. Sprinkle cake crumbs evenly over top and sides of cake, pressing lightly to adhere crumbs. Carefully remove parchment strips before serving. (Cake can be refrigerated for up to 2 days.)

Lost Icon

Ebinger's Baking Company opened in 1898 on Flatbush Avenue in Brooklyn and grew into a chain of more than 60 stores before going bankrupt in 1972. Started by Arthur Ebinger, a baker who emigrated from Germany with a vast collection of recipes, the business grew to include his wife and their three sons. During its heyday, Ebinger's was a point of bragging rights for Brooklynites, as celebrities and the well-to-do from Manhattan never went to Brooklyn without taking home a cake or one of Ebinger's other specialties, which included challah, rye bread, pumpkin pie, Othellos (filled mini sponge cakes covered in chocolate), and crumb buns.

Wellesley Fudge Cake

Wellesley Fudge Cake

SERVES 12

WHY THIS RECIPE WORKS Created a century ago at Wellesley College, this fudge cake consists of an extra-fudgy frosting atop a sturdy cake. We turned to all-purpose flour to provide more structure than the original pastry flour, plus cocoa powder bloomed in hot water for deep chocolate flavor. For its signature frosting, we created a base of evaporated milk, butter, and brown sugar. Stirring in more butter and evaporated milk off the heat cooled the base and prevented the chocolate from separating. Adding sifted confectioners' sugar and cooling the mixture helped to thicken the frosting to a spreadable consistency.

We prefer the deep color and balanced flavor of Dutch-processed cocoa powder, but natural cocoa can be used. Although not traditional, two 9-inch round cake pans will also work.

Cake

- 2½ cups (12½ ounces) all-purpose flour
- 2 teaspoons baking soda
- 1 teaspoon baking powder
- ½ teaspoon table salt
- ¾ cup hot water
- ½ cup Dutch-processed cocoa powder
- 16 tablespoons unsalted butter, cut into 16 pieces and softened
- 2 cups (14 ounces) granulated sugar
- 2 large eggs
- 1 cup buttermilk, room temperature
- 2 teaspoons vanilla extract

Frosting

8	tablespoons unsalted butter, cut in half, and softened, divided
1½	cups packed (10½ ounces) light brown sugar
½	teaspoon table salt
1	cup evaporated milk, divided
8	ounces bittersweet chocolate, chopped
1	teaspoon vanilla extract
3	cups (12 ounces) confectioners' sugar, sifted

1. For the Cake Adjust oven rack to middle position and heat oven to 350 degrees. Grease and flour two 8-inch-square cake pans. Combine flour, baking soda, baking powder, and salt in bowl; set aside. In a small bowl, whisk hot water with cocoa powder until smooth; set aside. With electric mixer on medium-high speed, beat butter and granulated sugar until light and fluffy, about 3 minutes. Add eggs, 1 at a time, and mix until incorporated. Add flour mixture in 3 additions, alternating with 2 additions of buttermilk, until combined. Reduce speed to low and slowly add cocoa mixture and vanilla until incorporated.

2. Scrape equal amounts of batter into prepared pans and bake until toothpick inserted in center comes out with a few crumbs attached, 25 to 30 minutes. Cool cakes in pans 15 minutes, then turn out onto wire rack. Cool completely, about 1 hour. (Cooled, wrapped cakes can be stored at room temperature for 2 days.)

3. For the Frosting Heat 4 tablespoons butter, brown sugar, salt, and ½ cup evaporated milk in large saucepan over medium heat until small bubbles appear around perimeter of pan, 4 to 8 minutes. Reduce heat to low and simmer, stirring occasionally, until mixture has thickened and turned deep golden brown, about 6 minutes. Transfer to large bowl. Slice remaining butter into 4 pieces and stir in with remaining evaporated milk until mixture is slightly cool. Add chocolate and vanilla and stir until smooth. Whisk in confectioners' sugar until incorporated. Cool to room temperature, stirring occasionally, about 1 hour.

4. Place 1 cake square on serving platter. Spread 1 cup frosting over cake, then top with second cake square. Generously spread remaining frosting evenly over top and sides of cake. Refrigerate cake until frosting is set, about 1 hour. Serve. (Cake can be refrigerated, covered, for 2 days. Bring to room temperature before serving.)

Tunnel of Fudge Cake

Tunnel of Fudge Cake

SERVES 12 TO 14

WHY THIS RECIPE WORKS We wanted to resurrect the classic tunnel of fudge cake without using prepackaged cake mix. Dutch-processed cocoa gave our cake deep chocolate flavor. Adding melted chocolate to the batter contributed more moisture and chocolate punch. Slightly underbaking the cake helped achieve the ideal consistency for the tunnel. Replacing some of the granulated sugar with brown sugar and cutting back on the flour and butter provided the perfect environment for the fudgy interior to form.

For an accurate measurement of boiling water, bring a full kettle of water to a boil, then measure out the desired amount. Do not use a cake tester, toothpick, or skewer to test the cake—the fudgy interior won't give an accurate reading. Instead, remove the cake from the oven when the sides just begin to pull away from the pan and the surface of the cake springs back when pressed gently.

Cake

- ¾ cup (2¼ ounces) Dutch-processed cocoa powder, plus extra for dusting pan
- ½ cup boiling water
- 2 ounces bittersweet chocolate, chopped
- 2 cups (10 ounces) all-purpose flour
- 2 cups pecans or walnuts, chopped fine
- 2 cups (8 ounces) confectioners' sugar
- 1 teaspoon table salt
- 5 large eggs, room temperature
- 1 tablespoon vanilla extract
- 20 tablespoons (2½ sticks) unsalted butter, softened
- 1 cup (7 ounces) granulated sugar
- ¾ cup packed (5¼ ounces) light brown sugar

Chocolate Glaze

- ¾ cup heavy cream
- ¼ cup light corn syrup
- 8 ounces bittersweet chocolate, chopped
- ½ teaspoon vanilla extract

1. For the Cake Adjust oven rack to lower-middle position and heat oven to 350 degrees. Grease 12-cup Bundt pan and dust with cocoa powder. Pour boiling water over chocolate in medium bowl and whisk until smooth. Let cool to room temperature. Whisk cocoa, flour, pecans, confectioners' sugar, and salt in large bowl. Whisk eggs and vanilla in 4-cup liquid measuring cup.

2. Using stand mixer fitted with paddle, beat butter, granulated sugar, and brown sugar on medium-high speed until light and fluffy, about 2 minutes. On low speed, add egg mixture until combined, about 30 seconds. Add chocolate mixture and beat until incorporated, about 30 seconds. Beat in flour mixture until just combined, about 30 seconds.

3. Scrape batter into prepared pan, smooth batter, and bake until edges are beginning to pull away from pan, about 45 minutes. Let cool in pan on wire rack for 1½ hours, then invert onto serving plate and let cool completely, at least 2 hours.

4. For the Chocolate Glaze Heat cream, corn syrup, and chocolate in small saucepan over medium heat, stirring constantly, until smooth. Stir in vanilla and set aside until slightly thickened, about 30 minutes. Drizzle glaze over cake and let set for at least 10 minutes. Serve. (Cake can be stored at room temperature for up to 2 days.)

Lane Cake

SERVES 10 TO 12

WHY THIS RECIPE WORKS Emma Rylander Lane of Clayton, Alabama, is credited with creating this county fair winner more than 100 years ago. Lane cake is a tall, fluffy, snow white cake filled with a rich, sweet mixture of egg whites, butter, raisins, and "a wineglass full of good whiskey." Our simplified recipe capped the number of layers at two, and using a food processor streamlined much of the tedious prep work. Replacing sugar with boiled corn syrup in our frosting quickly brought the whipped egg whites to a safe temperature without resorting to a candy thermometer or complicated (and unreliable) guesswork.

Cake

- 1 cup whole milk, room temperature
- 6 large egg whites, room temperature
- 2 teaspoons vanilla extract
- 2¼ cups (9 ounces) cake flour
- 1¾ cups (12¼ ounces) sugar
- 4 teaspoons baking powder
- 1 teaspoon table salt
- 12 tablespoons unsalted butter, cut into 12 pieces and softened

Filling

- 5 tablespoons bourbon
- 1 tablespoon heavy cream
- 1 teaspoon cornstarch
- Pinch table salt
- ⅓ cup sweetened shredded coconut
- ¾ cup pecans
- ¾ cup golden raisins
- 4 tablespoons unsalted butter
- ¾ cup sweetened condensed milk
- ½ teaspoon vanilla extract

Frosting

- 2 large egg whites, room temperature
- ¼ teaspoon cream of tartar
- ¼ cup (1¾ ounces) sugar
- ⅔ cup light corn syrup
- 1 teaspoon vanilla extract

The Complete Cook's Country TV Show Cookbook

Clementine Cake

SERVES 8

WHY THIS RECIPE WORKS Clementine cake is a bright, delicious, citrus-kissed dessert. For maximum clementine flavor, we put clementines both inside and on top of our cake. For the batter, we used a standard creaming process and added ground whole clementines that we softened in the microwave and processed until smooth. Baking the cake in a greased springform pan allowed it to soufflé slightly, which gave us the tall cake that we wanted. While it was baking, we quickly candied sliced clementines in a sugar solution. For a showstopping finish, we topped the cake with a white glaze that accentuated the vivid orange candied fruit slices.

Look for clementines that are about 2 inches in diameter (about 1¾ ounces each). We recommend using a mandoline to get consistent slices of clementine to arrange on top of the cake; you can also use a chef's knife. We found it easier to slice the clementines when they were cold. You will have a few more candied clementine slices than you will need; use the nicest-looking ones for the cake's top.

1. **For the Cake** Adjust oven rack to middle position and heat oven to 350 degrees. Grease two 9-inch round cake pans, line with parchment paper, grease parchment, then flour pans. Whisk milk, egg whites, and vanilla in 4-cup liquid measuring cup. Using stand mixer fitted with paddle, mix flour, sugar, baking powder, and salt on low speed until combined. Add butter, 1 piece at a time, and beat until only pea-size pieces remain. Add half of milk mixture, increase speed to medium-high, and beat until light and fluffy, about 1 minute. Reduce speed to medium-low, add remaining milk mixture, and beat until incorporated, about 30 seconds. Give batter final stir by hand.

2. Scrape batter into prepared pans and bake until toothpick inserted in center comes out clean, 20 to 25 minutes. Let cakes cool in pans on wire rack for 10 minutes. Remove cakes from pans, discarding parchment, and let cool completely on racks, about 2 hours. (Cooled cakes can be tightly wrapped in plastic wrap and stored at room temperature for up to 2 days.)

3. **For the Filling** Whisk bourbon, cream, cornstarch, and salt in bowl until smooth. Process coconut in food processor until finely ground, about 15 seconds. Add pecans and raisins and pulse until coarsely ground, about 10 pulses. Melt butter in large skillet over medium-low heat. Add processed coconut mixture and cook, stirring occasionally, until golden brown and fragrant, about 5 minutes. Stir in bourbon mixture and bring to boil. Remove from heat and add condensed milk and vanilla. Transfer to medium bowl and let cool to room temperature, about 30 minutes. (Filling can be refrigerated for 2 days. Bring filling to room temperature before using.)

4. **For the Frosting** Using stand mixer fitted with whisk, whip egg whites and cream of tartar on medium-high speed until frothy, about 30 seconds. With mixer running, slowly add sugar and whip until soft peaks form, about 2 minutes; set aside. Bring corn syrup to boil in small saucepan over medium-high heat and cook until large bubbles appear around perimeter of pan, about 1 minute. With mixer running, slowly pour hot syrup into whites (avoid pouring syrup onto beaters or it will splash). Add vanilla and beat until mixture has cooled and is very thick and glossy, 3 to 5 minutes.

5. Cover edges of cake platter with strips of parchment. Place 1 cake layer on platter. Spread filling over cake, then top with second cake layer, pressing lightly to adhere. Spread remaining frosting evenly over top and sides of cake. Carefully remove parchment strips before serving. (Cake can be refrigerated for up to 2 days.)

Clementine Cake

Cake

- 9 ounces clementines, unpeeled, stemmed (about 5 clementines)
- 2¼ cups (7½ ounces) sliced blanched almonds, toasted
- 1 cup (5 ounces) all-purpose flour
- 1¼ teaspoons baking powder
- ¼ teaspoon table salt
- 10 tablespoons unsalted butter, cut into 10 pieces and softened
- 1½ cups (10½ ounces) granulated sugar
- 5 large eggs

Candied Clementines

- 4 clementines, unpeeled, stemmed
- 1 cup water
- 1 cup (7 ounces) granulated sugar
- ⅛ teaspoon table salt

Glaze

- 2 cups (8 ounces) confectioners' sugar
- 2½ tablespoons water, plus extra as needed
- Pinch table salt

1. For the Cake Adjust oven rack to middle position and heat oven to 325 degrees. Spray 9-inch springform pan with vegetable oil spray, line bottom with parchment paper, and grease parchment. Microwave clementines in covered bowl until softened and some juice is released, about 3 minutes. Discard juice and let clementines cool for 10 minutes.

2. Process almonds, flour, baking powder, and salt in food processor until almonds are finely ground, about 30 seconds; transfer to second bowl. Add clementines to now-empty processor and process until smooth, about 1 minute, scraping down sides of bowl as needed.

3. Using stand mixer fitted with paddle, beat butter and sugar on medium-high speed until pale and fluffy, about 3 minutes. Add eggs, one at a time, and beat until combined, scraping down bowl as needed. Add clementine puree and beat until incorporated, about 30 seconds.

4. Reduce speed to low and add almond mixture in 3 additions until just combined, scraping down bowl as needed. Using rubber spatula, give batter final stir by hand. Transfer batter to prepared pan and smooth top. Bake until toothpick inserted in center comes out clean, 55 minutes to 1 hour. Let cake cool completely in pan on wire rack, about 2 hours.

5. For the Candied Clementines Meanwhile, line baking sheet with triple layer of paper towels. Slice clementines ¼ inch thick perpendicular to stem; discard rounded ends. Bring water, sugar, and salt to simmer in small saucepan over medium heat and cook until sugar has dissolved, about 1 minute. Add clementines and cook until softened, about 6 minutes. Using tongs, transfer clementines to prepared sheet and let cool for at least 30 minutes, flipping halfway through cooling to blot away excess moisture.

6. For the Glaze Whisk sugar, water, and salt in bowl until smooth. Adjust consistency with extra water as needed, ½ teaspoon at a time, until glaze has consistency of thick craft glue and leaves visible trail in bowl when drizzled from whisk.

7. Carefully run paring knife around cake and remove side of pan. Using thin metal spatula, lift cake from pan bottom; discard parchment and transfer cake to serving platter. Pour glaze over cake and smooth top with offset spatula, allowing some glaze to drip down sides. Let sit for 1 hour to set.

8. Just before serving, select 8 uniform candied clementine slices (you will have more than 8 slices; reserve extra slices for another use) and blot away excess moisture with additional paper towels. Arrange slices around top edge of cake, evenly spaced. Serve. (Cake can be wrapped in plastic wrap and stored at room temperature for up to 2 days.)

Orange Upside-Down Cake

SERVES 8

WHY THIS RECIPE WORKS This buttery cake is crowned with jewellike rounds of fresh citrus fruit swathed in a sticky glaze. Peeling the oranges by hand (instead of cutting away the peel and pith with a knife) ensured perfectly round slices. We used white sugar in the fruit layer (rather than brown sugar or a caramel) for a cleaner taste that didn't obstruct the subtle floral flavor of the oranges. Cornstarch helped trap the excess juices to prevent a soggy cake. A thin layer of orange marmalade brushed over the cooled cake made for an extra-shiny and extra-citrusy finish.

For the most striking visual, we like to use a combination of navel oranges, blood oranges, and Cara Cara oranges. Look for oranges no larger than a tennis ball; you'll be able to use more slices and cover a greater area. Peel the oranges by hand instead of with a knife: Leaving the exterior membrane intact helps maintain a circular shape. We recommend using a serrated knife to slice this cake to get clean slices. Serve the cake with whipped cream, if desired.

Orange Upside-Down Cake

- 1 pound small navel oranges, blood oranges, Cara Cara oranges, or a combination (2 to 3 oranges), divided
- 10 tablespoons unsalted butter, melted, divided
- 1½ cups (10½ ounces) sugar, divided
- 1 teaspoon cornstarch
- ⅛ teaspoon plus ½ teaspoon table salt, divided
- 1 cup (5 ounces) all-purpose flour
- 1 teaspoon baking powder
- ½ cup sour cream
- 2 large eggs
- 1 teaspoon vanilla extract
- 2 tablespoons orange marmalade

1. Adjust oven rack to middle position and heat oven to 350 degrees. Grease 9-inch round cake pan, line with parchment paper, then grease parchment. Grate 2 teaspoons zest from 1 orange; set aside. Using your hands, peel oranges. Using sharp chef's knife or serrated knife, trim ends and slice oranges crosswise ¼ inch thick, removing any seeds.

2. Pour 4 tablespoons melted butter over bottom of prepared pan and swirl to evenly coat. Whisk ½ cup sugar, cornstarch, and ⅛ teaspoon salt together in bowl, then sprinkle evenly over melted butter in pan. Arrange orange slices in single layer over sugar mixture, nestling slices snugly together and pressing them flat (you may have fruit left over).

3. Whisk flour, baking powder, and remaining ½ teaspoon salt together in large bowl. Whisk sour cream, eggs, vanilla, orange zest, and remaining 1 cup sugar in second large bowl until smooth, about 1 minute. Whisk remaining 6 tablespoons melted butter into sour cream mixture until combined. Add flour mixture and whisk until just combined.

4. Pour batter over oranges in pan and smooth top with rubber spatula. Bake until deep golden brown and toothpick inserted in center comes out clean, 50 to 55 minutes.

5. Let cake cool in pan on wire rack for 20 minutes. Run knife around edge of pan to loosen cake, then invert cake onto serving platter. Discard parchment. Let cake cool for at least 1 hour.

6. Microwave marmalade in bowl until fluid, about 20 seconds. Using pastry brush, brush marmalade over top of cake. Serve.

Blueberry Jam Cake

SERVES 10 TO 12

WHY THIS RECIPE WORKS Blueberry shines in this stunning—but not tricky—cake, which features three layers of downy white cake, a blueberry jam filling, and tangy cream cheese frosting. To emphasize the fruit's flavor, we made our own jam—blueberries, lemon juice, pectin, and some sugar—and used it both to fill the cake layers and to color (and flavor) the frosting. To create the beautiful ombre design, we strained different amounts of jam into three bowls of frosting (the pectin prevented the frosting from thinning) to create increasingly darker hues, which we spread on the cake from light to dark, before smoothing the shades together.

Having a cake stand with a turntable is a must for this cake. If your kitchen is warm, chilling the dark shades of frosting helps.

Blueberry Jam Cake

Strawberry Dream Cake

White Layer Cakes
- 1 cup whole milk, room temperature
- 6 large egg whites, room temperature
- 2 teaspoons vanilla extract
- 2¼ cups (9 ounces) bleached cake flour
- 1¾ cups (12¼ ounces) granulated sugar
- 1 tablespoon baking powder
- 1 teaspoon table salt
- 12 tablespoons unsalted butter, cut into 12 pieces and softened but still cool

Jam Filling and Frosting
- ½ cup (3½ ounces) granulated sugar
- 2 tablespoons low- or no-sugar-needed fruit pectin
- Pinch table salt
- 15 ounces (3 cups) fresh or thawed frozen blueberries
- 1 tablespoon lemon juice
- 8 tablespoons unsalted butter, softened
- 1½ cups (6 ounces) confectioners' sugar
- 8 ounces cream cheese, cut into 8 pieces and softened
- 2 teaspoons vanilla extract

1. For the White Layer Cakes Adjust oven rack to middle position and heat oven to 350 degrees. Grease three 8-inch round cake pans, line with parchment paper, grease parchment, and flour pans. Whisk milk, egg whites, and vanilla together in bowl.

2. Using stand mixer fitted with paddle, mix flour, sugar, baking powder, and salt on low speed until combined, about 5 seconds. Add butter, 1 piece at a time, until only pea-size pieces remain, about 1 minute. Add half of milk mixture, increase speed to medium-high, and beat until light and fluffy, about 30 seconds. Reduce speed to medium-low, add remaining milk mixture, and mix until incorporated, about 15 seconds (batter may look curdled). Give batter final stir by hand; do not overmix.

3. Divide batter evenly between prepared pans and smooth tops with rubber spatula. Gently tap pans on counter to settle batter. Bake until toothpick inserted in center comes out clean, 18 to 22 minutes, switching and rotating pans halfway through baking.

4. Let cakes cool in pans on wire rack for 10 minutes. Remove cakes from pans, discarding parchment, and let cool completely on rack, about 2 hours.

5. For the Jam Filling Process granulated sugar, pectin, and salt in food processor until combined, about 3 seconds. Add blueberries and pulse until chopped coarse, 6 to 8 pulses. Transfer blueberry mixture to medium saucepan and bring to simmer over medium heat, stirring occasionally, until mixture is bubbling and just starting to thicken, 6 to 8 minutes. Off heat, stir in lemon juice. Transfer 1⅓ cups jam to small bowl, cover, and refrigerate until firm, about 3 hours. Strain remaining jam through fine-mesh strainer set over bowl, cover, and set aside at room temperature. (You should have at least ¼ cup.)

6. For the Frosting Using stand mixer fitted with paddle, beat butter and confectioners' sugar on medium-high speed until light and fluffy, about 3 minutes. Add cream cheese, 1 piece at a time, and beat until no lumps remain. Add vanilla and 2 tablespoons strained jam and mix until incorporated. Transfer ⅓ cup frosting to each of 2 small bowls. Add 1 teaspoon strained jam to first bowl and 1 tablespoon strained jam to second bowl, stirring well to combine. (You should have 3 shades of frosting.)

7. Place 1 cake layer on cake turntable. Spread ⅔ cup chilled jam evenly over top. Repeat with 1 more cake layer, pressing lightly to adhere, and remaining chilled jam. Top with remaining cake layer, pressing lightly to adhere. Spread small amount of lightest-colored frosting in even layer over top and sides of cake. Using offset spatula, spread darkest-colored frosting over bottom third of sides of cake; medium-colored frosting over middle third; and remaining lightest-colored frosting over top third. While spinning cake turntable, run spatula from bottom to top of side of cake to blend frosting colors. While spinning cake turntable, run spatula over top of cake, working from outside in to create spiral. Serve.

Strawberry Dream Cake

SERVES 8 TO 10

WHY THIS RECIPE WORKS Strange as it may seem, the vast majority of existing strawberry cake recipes turn to strawberry Jell-O for flavor. Hoping to avoid this artificial solution, we performed test after test to figure out the best way to flavor our cake with actual strawberries. Any strawberry solids wreaked havoc on the tender cake, but strained and reduced strawberry juices kept our cake light and packed a strawberry punch. Not to be left behind, the reserved strawberry solids enriched the frosting with more berry flavor.

Be sure to allow the cream cheese to soften so that it blends into a smooth frosting.

Cake

- 10 ounces frozen whole strawberries (2 cups)
- ¾ cup whole milk, room temperature
- 6 large egg whites, room temperature
- 2 teaspoons vanilla extract
- 2¼ cups (9 ounces) cake flour
- 1¾ cups (12¼ ounces) granulated sugar
- 4 teaspoons baking powder
- 1 teaspoon table salt
- 12 tablespoons unsalted butter, cut into 12 pieces and softened

Frosting

- 10 tablespoons unsalted butter, softened
- 2¼ cups (9 ounces) confectioners' sugar
- 12 ounces cream cheese, cut into 12 pieces and softened
  Pinch table salt
- 8 ounces fresh strawberries, hulled and sliced thin (about 1½ cups), divided

1. For the Cake Adjust oven rack to middle position and heat oven to 350 degrees. Grease two 9-inch round cake pans, line with parchment paper, grease parchment, then flour pans.

2. Transfer strawberries to bowl, cover, and microwave until strawberries are soft and have released their juices, about 5 minutes. Place in fine-mesh strainer set over small saucepan. Firmly press fruit dry (juice should measure at least ¾ cup); reserve strawberry solids. Bring juice to boil over medium-high heat and cook, stirring occasionally, until syrupy and reduced to ¼ cup, 6 to 8 minutes. Whisk milk into juice until combined.

3. Whisk strawberry-milk mixture, egg whites, and vanilla in bowl. Using stand mixer fitted with paddle, mix flour, sugar, baking powder, and salt on low speed until combined. Add butter, 1 piece at a time, and mix until only pea-size pieces remain, about 1 minute. Add half of milk mixture, increase speed to medium-high, and beat until light and fluffy, about 1 minute. Reduce speed to medium-low, add remaining milk mixture, and beat until incorporated, about 30 seconds. Give batter final stir by hand.

4. Scrape batter into prepared pans and bake until toothpick inserted in center comes out clean, 20 to 25 minutes, rotating pans halfway through baking. Let cakes cool in pans on wire rack for 10 minutes. Remove cakes from pans, discarding parchment, and let cool completely on rack, about 2 hours. (Cooled cakes can be tightly wrapped with plastic wrap and stored at room temperature for up to 2 days.)

5. For the Frosting Using stand mixer fitted with paddle, mix butter and sugar on low speed until combined, about 30 seconds. Increase speed to medium-high and beat until pale and fluffy, about 2 minutes. Add cream cheese, 1 piece at a time, and beat until incorporated, about 1 minute. Add reserved strawberry solids and salt and mix until combined, about 30 seconds. Refrigerate until ready to use, up to 2 days.

6. Pat strawberries dry with paper towels. Cover edges of cake platter with strips of parchment. Place 1 cake layer on platter. Spread ¾ cup frosting evenly over top, right to edge of cake. Press 1 cup strawberries in even layer over frosting and cover with additional ¾ cup frosting. Top with second cake layer, press lightly to adhere, then spread remaining frosting evenly over top and sides of cake. Garnish with remaining strawberries. Carefully remove parchment strips before serving. (Cake can be refrigerated for up to 2 days.)

Strawberry Poke Cake

SERVES 12

Strawberry Poke Cake

WHY THIS RECIPE WORKS Strawberry poke cake was invented in 1969 as a way to increase Jell-O sales. It quickly became popular thanks to its festive look and easy assembly. But we encountered two problems: dull strawberry flavor and soggy box mix cake. For a sturdier cake that would hold up to hot gelatin, we opted to make our own white cake from scratch. And to improve the strawberry flavor of the Jell-O, we combined it with the juice from cooked strawberries. Making a homemade "jam" from the berry solids and spreading the mixture on top of the cake gave our cake an extra layer of flavor.

The top of the cake will look slightly overbaked—this keeps the crumb from becoming too soggy after the gelatin is poured on top.

Cake
- 2¼ cups (11¼ ounces) all-purpose flour
- 4 teaspoons baking powder
- 1 teaspoon table salt
- 1 cup whole milk
- 2 teaspoons vanilla extract
- 6 large egg whites
- 12 tablespoons unsalted butter, softened
- 1¾ cups (12¼ ounces) sugar

Syrup and Topping
- 4 cups frozen strawberries, divided
- ½ cup water
- 6 tablespoons (2⅔ ounces) sugar, divided
- 2 tablespoons orange juice
- 2 tablespoons strawberry-flavored gelatin
- 2 cups heavy cream, chilled

1. For the Cake Adjust oven rack to middle position and heat oven to 350 degrees. Grease 13 by 9-inch baking pan, line with parchment paper, grease parchment, then flour pan. Whisk flour, baking powder, and salt in bowl. Whisk milk, vanilla, and egg whites in 4-cup liquid measuring cup.

2. Using stand mixer fitted with paddle, beat butter and sugar on medium-high speed until pale and fluffy, about 2 minutes, scraping down bowl as needed. Reduce speed to low and add flour mixture in 3 additions, alternating with milk mixture in 2 additions, beating after each addition until combined, about 30 seconds each time, scraping down bowl as needed. Give batter final stir by hand. Scrape into prepared pan and bake until toothpick inserted in center comes out clean, about 35 minutes. Let cake cool completely in pan, at least 1 hour. (Once cool, cake can be wrapped in plastic wrap and kept at room temperature for up to 2 days.)

3. For the Syrup and Topping Heat 3 cups strawberries, water, 2 tablespoons sugar, and orange juice in medium saucepan over medium-low heat. Cover and cook until strawberries are softened, about 10 minutes. Strain liquid into bowl, reserving solids, then whisk gelatin into liquid. Let cool to room temperature, at least 20 minutes.

4. Meanwhile, poke 50 deep holes all over top of cake with skewer, taking care not to poke through to dish bottom and twisting skewer to enlarge holes. Pour cooled liquid over top of cake. Wrap with plastic wrap and refrigerate until gelatin is set, at least 3 hours or up to 2 days.

5. Pulse reserved strained strawberries, 2 tablespoons sugar, and remaining 1 cup strawberries in food processor until mixture resembles strawberry jam, about 15 pulses. Spread mixture evenly over cake. Using stand mixer fitted with whisk, whip cream with remaining 2 tablespoons sugar on medium-low speed until foamy, about 1 minute. Increase speed to high and whip until soft peaks form, 1 to 3 minutes. Spread cream over strawberries. Serve. (Cake can be refrigerated for up to 2 days.)

Perfecting the Poke

Finding the right poking device wasn't as simple as you might think. Toothpicks were too small, while straws, handles of wooden spoons, pencils, and fingers were too big. A wooden skewer finally did the trick. But just poking didn't create a large enough hole for the liquid to seep into. In order to create deep lines of red color against the white crumb, we had to poke and then twist the skewer to really separate the crumb.

1. Using skewer, poke about 50 deep holes over cake, being careful not to poke through to bottom. Twist skewer to enlarge holes.

2. Slowly pour cooled gelatin mixture evenly over surface of cake and it will slowly soak into cake.

Texas Sheet Cake

SERVES 24

WHY THIS RECIPE WORKS Texas sheet cake is a huge, pecan-topped chocolate-glazed cake. For the cake, we relied on a combination of butter and vegetable oil, which produced a dense, brownie-like texture. To increase the fudgy chocolate flavor, we used both cocoa powder and melted semisweet chocolate. Replacing milk with heavy cream gave the icing more body, while adding corn syrup produced a lustrous finish. The key to creating the signature fudgy layer between cake and icing was to let the warm icing soak into the hot cake. We poured the icing over the sheet cake straight out of the oven and smoothed it with a spatula.

Toast the pecans in a dry skillet over medium heat, shaking the pan occasionally, until golden and fragrant, about 5 minutes.

Cake

- 2 cups (10 ounces) all-purpose flour
- 2 cups (14 ounces) granulated sugar
- ½ teaspoon baking soda
- ½ teaspoon table salt
- 2 large eggs plus 2 large yolks
- ¼ cup sour cream
- 2 teaspoons vanilla extract
- 8 ounces semisweet chocolate, chopped
- ¾ cup vegetable oil
- ¾ cup water
- ½ cup (1½ ounces) Dutch-processed cocoa powder
- 4 tablespoons unsalted butter

Chocolate Icing

- 8 tablespoons unsalted butter
- ½ cup heavy cream
- ½ cup (1½ ounces) Dutch-processed cocoa powder
- 1 tablespoon light corn syrup
- 3 cups (12 ounces) confectioners' sugar
- 1 tablespoon vanilla extract
- 1 cup pecans, toasted and chopped

Texas Sheet Cake

1. For the Cake Adjust oven rack to middle position and heat oven to 350 degrees. Grease 18 by 13-inch rimmed baking sheet. Combine flour, sugar, baking soda, and salt in large bowl. Whisk eggs and yolks, sour cream, and vanilla in another bowl until smooth.

2. Heat chocolate, oil, water, cocoa, and butter in large saucepan over medium heat, stirring occasionally, until smooth, 3 to 5 minutes. Whisk chocolate mixture into flour mixture until incorporated. Whisk egg mixture into batter, then pour into prepared baking pan. Bake until toothpick inserted into center comes out clean, 18 to 20 minutes. Transfer to wire rack.

3. For the Chocolate Icing About 5 minutes before cake is done, heat butter, cream, cocoa, and corn syrup in large saucepan over medium heat, stirring occasionally, until smooth. Off heat, whisk in sugar and vanilla. Spread warm icing evenly over hot cake and sprinkle with pecans. Let cake cool to room temperature on wire rack, about 1 hour, then refrigerate until icing is set, about 1 hour longer. Cut into 3-inch squares. Serve. (Cake can be refrigerated for up to 2 days.)

Chocolate Éclair Cake
SERVES 15

WHY THIS RECIPE WORKS This no-bake dessert is typically made by layering a mixture of instant vanilla pudding and Cool Whip between graham crackers and topping it with chocolate frosting. We loved the convenience of these store-bought items, but our enthusiasm waned when confronted by their flavor. With a couple of easy techniques (a quick stovetop pudding, whipped cream, and a microwave-and-stir glaze) and very little active time, we produced a from-scratch version that easily surpassed its inspiration.

Six ounces of finely chopped semisweet chocolate can be used in place of the chips.

- 1¼ cups (8¾ ounces) sugar
- 6 tablespoons cornstarch
- 1 teaspoon table salt
- 5 cups whole milk
- 4 tablespoons unsalted butter, cut into 4 pieces
- 5 teaspoons vanilla extract
- 1¼ teaspoons unflavored gelatin
- 2 tablespoons water
- 2¾ cups heavy cream, chilled, divided
- 14 ounces graham crackers
- 1 cup semisweet chocolate chips
- 5 tablespoons light corn syrup

1. Combine sugar, cornstarch, and salt in large saucepan. Whisk milk into sugar mixture until smooth and bring to boil, scraping bottom of pan with heatproof rubber spatula, over medium-high heat. Immediately reduce heat to medium-low and cook, continuing to scrape bottom, until thickened and large bubbles appear on surface, 4 to 6 minutes. Off heat, whisk in butter and vanilla. Transfer pudding to large bowl and place plastic wrap directly on surface of pudding. Refrigerate until cool, about 2 hours.

2. Sprinkle gelatin over water in bowl and let sit until gelatin softens, about 5 minutes. Microwave until mixture is bubbling around edges and gelatin dissolves, 15 to 30 seconds. Using stand mixer fitted with whisk, whip 2 cups cream on medium-low speed until foamy, about 1 minute. Increase speed to high and whip until soft peaks form, 1 to 3 minutes. Add gelatin mixture and whip until stiff peaks form, about 1 minute.

Chocolate Éclair Cake

The American Table: Worst College Food Ever

The Reverend Sylvester Graham, the inventor of the graham cracker, wasn't quite as much fun as that crisp treat might have you believe. In fact, he was a food zealot, convinced that a diet of nothing but water and graham crackers—originally a "health food" made from whole-wheat flour and honey—would turn you into a better person. Some 170 years ago, the administrators at Oberlin College, a small liberal arts school in Ohio, grew enamored of Graham's ideas and decided to feed students according to his principles. (And you think your college food was bad?) Oberlin students were encouraged to abstain from consuming meat, tea, and coffee—except for "crust coffee" made from toast and boiled water. They were discouraged from eating butter and pastries and even from seasoning their food. (As legend has it, a professor actually lost his job for bringing a pepper shaker to the dining hall.) Oberlin students complained so vociferously that the college was forced to abandon its dining plan, and the Graham diet (if not his eponymous cracker) faded into culinary history.

3. Whisk one-third of whipped cream into chilled pudding, then gently fold in remaining whipped cream, 1 scoop at a time, until combined. Cover bottom of 13 by 9-inch baking dish with layer of graham crackers, breaking crackers as necessary to line bottom of pan. Top with half of pudding–whipped cream mixture (about 5½ cups) and another layer of graham crackers. Repeat with remaining pudding–whipped cream mixture and remaining graham crackers.

4. Microwave chocolate chips, remaining ¾ cup cream, and corn syrup in bowl, on 50 percent power, stirring occasionally, until smooth, 1 to 2 minutes. Let glaze cool to room temperature, about 10 minutes. Cover graham crackers with glaze and refrigerate cake for 6 to 24 hours. Serve. (Cake can be refrigerated for up to 2 days.)

Magic Chocolate Flan Cake

SERVES 16

WHY THIS RECIPE WORKS This unique dessert combines a layer of fudgy chocolate cake and a layer of rich, caramel-coated flan that "magically" switch places as they bake. We started with an easy dump-and-stir cake recipe. The cake's flavor was great, but it was soggy due to the moisture from the flan. Cutting some of the buttermilk and sugar from the cake batter did the trick. To help our flan firm up, we swapped some of the egg yolks for whole eggs and added cream cheese. The cream cheese also lent the flan a tanginess that offset its sweetness. Convenient store-bought caramel sauce topped it all off.

It's worth using good-quality caramel sauce, such as Fat Toad Farm Goat's Milk Caramel. If your blender doesn't hold 2 quarts, process the flan in two batches. The cake needs to chill for at least 8 hours before you can unmold it.

GREAT AMERICAN CAKES AND COOKIES   609

Cake

- ½ cup caramel sauce or topping
- ½ cup plus 2 tablespoons (3⅛ ounces) all-purpose flour
- ⅓ cup (1 ounce) cocoa powder
- ½ teaspoon baking soda
- ⅛ teaspoon table salt
- 4 ounces bittersweet chocolate, chopped
- 6 tablespoons unsalted butter
- ½ cup buttermilk
- ½ cup (3½ ounces) sugar
- 2 large eggs
- 1 teaspoon vanilla extract

Flan

- 2 (14-ounce) cans sweetened condensed milk
- 2½ cups whole milk
- 6 ounces cream cheese
- 6 large eggs plus 4 large yolks
- 1 teaspoon vanilla extract

1. For the Cake Adjust oven rack to middle position and heat oven to 350 degrees. Grease 12-cup nonstick Bundt pan. Microwave caramel until easily pourable, about 30 seconds. Pour into pan to coat bottom. Combine flour, cocoa, baking soda, and salt in bowl; set aside. Combine chocolate and butter in large bowl and microwave at 50 percent power, stirring occasionally, until melted, 2 to 4 minutes. Whisk buttermilk, sugar, eggs, and vanilla into chocolate mixture until incorporated. Stir in flour mixture until just combined. Pour batter over caramel in pan.

2. For the Flan Process all ingredients in blender until smooth, about 1 minute. Gently pour flan over cake batter and place Bundt pan in large roasting pan. Place roasting pan on oven rack and pour warm water into roasting pan until it reaches halfway up side of Bundt pan. Bake until toothpick inserted in cake comes out clean and flan registers 180 degrees, 75 to 90 minutes. Transfer Bundt pan to wire rack. Let cool to room temperature, about 2 hours, then refrigerate until set, at least 8 hours. (Remove roasting pan from oven once water has cooled.)

3. Place bottom third of Bundt pan in bowl of hot tap water for 1 minute. Invert completely flat cake platter, place platter over top of pan, and gently turn platter and pan upside down. Slowly remove pan, allowing caramel to drizzle over top of cake. Serve.

Magic Chocolate Flan Cake

Modulate the Heat

A water bath, or bain-marie, makes for a more even, temperate baking environment. Simply place your baking vessel in a larger vessel (we use a roasting pan) and partially fill the latter with water.

Tres Leches Cake

SERVES 12

WHY THIS RECIPE WORKS A great tres leches cake—a sponge cake soaked with a mixture of "three milks" (heavy cream, evaporated milk, and sweetened condensed milk)—should be moist but not mushy and sweet but not sickeningly so. For an ideal version, we needed to make our cake sturdy enough to handle the milk mixture, so we used whipped whole eggs instead of the usual egg whites. Although some tres leches recipes use equal amounts of evaporated milk, sweetened condensed milk, and cream, we found that cutting back on the cream produced a thicker mixture that didn't oversaturate the cake.

The cake is best frosted right before serving.

Milk Mixture
- 1 (14-ounce) can sweetened condensed milk
- 1 (12-ounce) can evaporated milk
- 1 cup heavy cream
- 1 teaspoon vanilla extract

Cake
- 2 cups (10 ounces) all-purpose flour
- 2 teaspoons baking powder
- 1 teaspoon table salt
- ½ teaspoon ground cinnamon
- 8 tablespoons unsalted butter
- 1 cup whole milk
- 4 large eggs, room temperature
- 2 cups (14 ounces) sugar
- 2 teaspoons vanilla extract

Topping
- 1 cup heavy cream
- 3 tablespoons corn syrup
- 1 teaspoon vanilla extract

1. For the Milk Mixture Pour condensed milk into large bowl. Microwave covered at 50 percent power, stirring every 3 to 5 minutes, until slightly darkened and thickened, 9 to 15 minutes. Remove from microwave and slowly whisk in evaporated milk, cream, and vanilla. Let cool to room temperature.

2. For the Cake Adjust oven rack to middle position and heat oven to 325 degrees. Grease and flour 13 by 9-inch baking dish. Whisk flour, baking powder, salt, and cinnamon in bowl. Heat butter and milk in small saucepan over low heat until butter is melted; remove from heat and set aside.

3. Using stand mixer fitted with whisk, whip eggs on medium speed until foamy, about 30 seconds. Slowly add sugar and continue to whip until fully incorporated, 5 to 10 seconds. Increase speed to medium-high and whip until mixture is thick and glossy, 5 to 7 minutes. Reduce speed to low, add milk-butter mixture and vanilla, and mix until combined, about 15 seconds. Add flour mixture in 3 additions, mixing on medium speed after each addition and scraping down bowl as needed, until flour is fully incorporated, about 30 seconds. Using rubber spatula, scrape batter into prepared dish. Bake until toothpick inserted in center comes out clean, 30 to 35 minutes. Transfer cake to wire rack and let cool for 10 minutes.

4. Using skewer, poke holes at ½-inch intervals in top of cake. Slowly pour milk mixture over cake until completely absorbed. Let sit at room temperature for 15 minutes, then refrigerate, uncovered, for 3 hours or up to 24 hours.

5. For the Topping Remove cake from refrigerator 30 minutes before serving. Using stand mixer fitted with whisk, whip cream, corn syrup, and vanilla on medium-low speed until foamy, about 1 minute. Increase speed to high and whip until soft peaks form, 1 to 3 minutes. Spread over cake and cut into 3-inch squares. Serve.

Tres Leches Cake

Swiss Hazelnut Cake

SERVES 12 TO 16

WHY THIS RECIPE WORKS We wanted to replicate the sweet, nutty cake famous at the Swiss Haus in Philadelphia. We knew that beaten egg whites would give the cake base a fluffy texture. For full hazelnut flavor, we substituted finely ground hazelnuts for a portion of the cake flour. We found an excellent shortcut to meringue buttercream by using marshmallow crème. To prevent the chocolate from melting, we froze it before and after shaving.

We toast and grind the hazelnuts with their skins for better color and flavor. When working with the marshmallow crème, grease the inside of your measuring cup and spatula with vegetable oil spray to prevent sticking. You may use a vegetable peeler or the large holes of a box grater to shave the chocolate.

Cake

- ½ cup (2 ounces) skin-on hazelnuts, toasted and cooled
- 1¼ cups (5 ounces) cake flour
- 1 cup (7 ounces) granulated sugar
- 1½ teaspoons baking powder
- ½ teaspoon table salt
- ½ cup vegetable oil
- ¼ cup water
- 3 large egg yolks, plus 5 large whites
- 2½ teaspoons vanilla extract
- ¼ teaspoon cream of tartar

Frosting

- 24 tablespoons (3 sticks) unsalted butter, softened
- ¼ teaspoon table salt
- 1¾ cups (7 ounces) confectioners' sugar
- 12 ounces (2⅔ cups) Fluff brand marshmallow crème
- 2 tablespoons hazelnut liqueur
- 6 ounces bittersweet chocolate

1. For the Cake Adjust oven rack to middle position and heat oven to 350 degrees. Line the bottoms of 2 light-colored 9-inch round cake pans with parchment paper; grease parchment but not pan sides.

2. Process hazelnuts in food processor until finely ground, about 30 seconds. Whisk flour, sugar, baking powder, salt, and ground hazelnuts together in large bowl. Whisk oil, water, egg yolks, and vanilla together in separate bowl. Whisk egg yolk mixture into flour mixture until smooth batter forms.

3. Using stand mixer fitted with whisk, whip egg whites and cream of tartar on medium-low speed until foamy, about 1 minute. Increase speed to medium-high and whip until soft peaks form, 2 to 3 minutes. Gently whisk one-third of whipped egg whites into batter. Using rubber spatula, gently fold remaining egg whites into batter until incorporated.

4. Divide batter evenly between prepared pans and gently tap pans on counter to release air bubbles. Bake until tops are light golden brown and cakes spring back when pressed lightly in center, 25 to 28 minutes, rotating pans halfway through baking.

5. Let cakes cool in pans for 15 minutes. Run knife around edges of pans; invert cakes onto wire rack. Discard parchment and let cakes cool completely, at least 1 hour. (To prepare to make chocolate shavings, place food processor shredding disk and chocolate in freezer.)

6. For the Frosting Using clean stand mixer fitted with whisk, whip butter and salt on medium speed until smooth, about 1 minute. Reduce speed to low and slowly add sugar. Increase speed to medium and whip until smooth, about 2 minutes, scraping down sides of bowl as needed. Add marshmallow crème, increase speed to medium-high, and whip until light and fluffy, 3 to 5 minutes. Reduce speed to low, add hazelnut liqueur, return speed to medium-high, and whip to incorporate, about 30 seconds.

7. Line rimmed baking sheet with parchment paper. Fit food processor with chilled shredding disk. Turn on processor and feed chocolate through hopper. Transfer shaved chocolate to prepared baking sheet and spread into even layer. Place in freezer to harden, about 10 minutes.

8. Place 1 cake layer on cake stand. Spread 2 cups frosting evenly over top, right to edge of cake. Top with second cake layer, pressing lightly to adhere. Spread remaining 2 cups frosting evenly over top and sides of cake.

9. Fold 16 by 12-inch sheet of parchment paper into 6 by 4-inch rectangle. Using parchment rectangle, scoop up half of chocolate shavings and sprinkle over top of cake. Once top of cake is coated, scoop up remaining chocolate shavings and press gently against sides of cake to adhere, scooping and reapplying as needed. Serve.

Blitz Torte

SERVES 8 TO 10

WHY THIS RECIPE WORKS The beauty of blitz torte is that you get five impressive layers for about the same amount of work as a two-layer cake. That's because each meringue layer is baked directly atop the yellow cake batter. The recipe is also pleasingly symmetrical: The egg yolks go into the cake, while the whites go into the meringue. We mimicked the rich egginess of custard filling by folding store-bought lemon curd into whipped cream, stabilizing it with gelatin, and layering it with raspberries.

If your pans are dark, reduce the baking time in step 6 to 30 to 35 minutes.

Filling
- 1 teaspoon unflavored gelatin
- 2 tablespoons water
- 1 cup heavy cream, chilled
- 1 teaspoon vanilla extract
- ½ cup lemon curd
- 10 ounces (2 cups) raspberries
- 2 tablespoons orange liqueur
- 1 tablespoon sugar

Cake
- ½ cup whole milk
- 4 large egg yolks
- 1½ teaspoons vanilla extract
- 1¼ cups (5 ounces) cake flour
- 1 cup (7 ounces) sugar
- 1½ teaspoons baking powder
- ½ teaspoon table salt
- 12 tablespoons unsalted butter, cut into 12 pieces and softened

Meringue
- 4 large egg whites
- ¼ teaspoon cream of tartar
- ¾ cup (5¼ ounces) sugar
- ½ teaspoon vanilla extract
- ½ cup sliced almonds

Swiss Hazelnut Cake

Blitz Torte

1. For the Filling Sprinkle gelatin over water in small bowl and let sit until gelatin softens, about 5 minutes. Microwave until mixture is bubbling around edges and gelatin dissolves, 15 to 30 seconds. Using stand mixer fitted with whisk, whip cream and vanilla on medium-low speed until foamy, about 1 minute. Increase speed to medium-high and whip until soft peaks form, about 2 minutes. Add gelatin mixture and whip until firm, stiff peaks form, about 1 minute.

2. Whisk lemon curd in large metal bowl to loosen. Fold whipped cream mixture into curd. Refrigerate cream filling for 1½ to 3 hours.

3. For the Cake Meanwhile, adjust oven rack to middle position and heat oven to 325 degrees. Grease 2 light-colored 9-inch round cake pans, line with parchment paper, grease parchment, and flour pans.

4. Beat milk, yolks, and vanilla together with fork. Using stand mixer fitted with paddle, mix flour, sugar, baking powder, and salt on low speed until combined, about 5 seconds. Add butter, 1 piece at a time, and mix until only pea-size pieces remain, about 1 minute. Add half of milk mixture, increase speed to medium-high, and beat until light and fluffy, about 1 minute. Reduce speed to medium-low, add remaining milk mixture, and beat until incorporated, about 30 seconds. Give batter final stir by hand. Divide batter evenly between prepared pans and spread into even layer using small offset spatula.

5. For the Meringue Using clean, dry stand mixer fitted with a whisk, whip egg whites and cream of tartar on medium-low speed until foamy, about 1 minute. Increase speed to medium-high and whip whites to soft, billowy mounds, 1 to 3 minutes. Gradually add sugar and whip until glossy, stiff peaks form, 3 to 5 minutes. Add vanilla and whip until incorporated.

6. Divide meringue evenly between cake pans and spread evenly over cake batter to edges of pan. Use back of spoon to create peaks in meringue. Sprinkle meringue with almonds. Bake cakes until meringue is golden and has pulled away from sides of pan, 50 to 55 minutes, switching and rotating pans halfway through baking. Let cakes cool completely in pans on wire rack. (Cakes can be baked up to 24 hours in advance and stored, uncovered, in pans at room temperature.)

7. To finish filling, 10 minutes before assembling cake, combine raspberries, liqueur, and sugar in bowl.

8. Gently remove cakes from pans, discarding parchment. Place 1 cake layer on platter, meringue side up. Spread half of cream filling evenly over top. Using slotted spoon, spoon raspberries evenly over filling. Gently spread remaining cream filling over raspberries, covering raspberries completely. Top with second cake layer, meringue side up. Serve cake within 2 hours of assembly.

Angel Food Cake

SERVES 10 TO 12

WHY THIS RECIPE WORKS The key to angel food cake is voluminous, stable egg whites. A mere speck of yolk prevents them from whipping to peaks. We had success with both cold and room-temperature egg whites; cold egg whites just took a few minutes longer to reach full volume. The acidity of cream of tartar helped stabilize the egg whites, and cake flour produced a tender crumb.

Do not use all-purpose flour in this recipe as it will give the cake a breadlike texture. You will need a 12-cup tube pan with a removable bottom for this recipe. If your pan has "feet" that rise above the top edge of the pan, let the cake cool upside down; otherwise, invert the tube pan over a large metal kitchen funnel or the neck of a sturdy bottle. Cake can be served plain or dusted with confectioners' sugar.

- 1 cup plus 2 tablespoons (4½ ounces) cake flour
- ¼ teaspoon table salt
- 1¾ cups (12¼ ounces) sugar, divided
- 12 large egg whites
- 1½ teaspoons cream of tartar
- 1 teaspoon vanilla extract

1. Adjust oven rack to lower-middle position and preheat oven to 325 degrees. Whisk flour and salt in bowl. Process sugar in food processor until fine, about 1 minute. Reserve half of sugar in small bowl. Add flour mixture to food processor with remaining sugar and process until aerated, about 1 minute.

2. Using stand mixer fitted with whisk, whip egg whites and cream of tartar on medium-low speed until foamy, about 1 minute. Increase speed to medium-high. Slowly add reserved sugar and whip until soft peaks form, about 6 minutes. Add vanilla and mix until incorporated.

3. Sift flour-sugar mixture over egg whites in 3 additions, folding gently with rubber spatula after each addition until incorporated. Scrape mixture into 12-cup ungreased tube pan.

4. Bake until skewer inserted into center comes out clean and cracks in cake appear dry, 40 to 45 minutes. Let cool, inverted, to room temperature, about 3 hours. To unmold, run knife along interior of pan. Turn out onto platter. Serve.

Chocolate-Almond Angel Food Cake
Replace ½ teaspoon vanilla extract with ½ teaspoon almond extract in step 2. Fold 2 ounces finely grated bittersweet chocolate into batter following flour in step 3.

Café au Lait Angel Food Cake
Add 1 tablespoon instant coffee or espresso powder to food processor along with flour in step 1. Replace ½ teaspoon vanilla with 1 tablespoon coffee liqueur in step 2.

> **Cool Upside Down**
> Invert cake until it is completely cool, about 3 hours. If you don't have pan with feet, invert it over neck of sturdy bottle.
>
>

Angel Food Cake

Chiffon Cake

Chiffon Cake
SERVES 10 TO 12

WHY THIS RECIPE WORKS Chiffon cake should have the airy height of angel food cake with the richness of pound cake. For our chiffon cake recipe, we eliminated the unnecessary step of sifting the dry ingredients. We also perfected the method for beating our egg whites—slowly adding sugar once the eggs had been beaten to soft peaks and then continuing to beat them until just stiff and glossy—to avoid little pockets of cooked egg whites.

Separate the eggs when they're cold; it's easier. You will need a 16-cup tube pan with a removable bottom for this recipe. If your pan has "feet" that rise above the top edge of the pan, let the cake cool upside down; otherwise, invert the tube pan over a large metal kitchen funnel or the neck of a sturdy bottle.

- 5 large eggs, separated
- 1 teaspoon cream of tartar
- 1½ cups (10½ ounces) sugar, divided
- 1⅓ cups (5⅓ ounces) cake flour
- 2 teaspoons baking powder
- ½ teaspoon table salt
- ¾ cup water
- ½ cup vegetable oil
- 1 tablespoon vanilla extract

1. Adjust oven rack to lower-middle position and heat oven to 325 degrees. Using stand mixer fitted with whisk, whip egg whites and cream of tartar on medium-high speed until soft peaks form, about 2 minutes. With mixer running, slowly add 2 tablespoons sugar and whip until just stiff and glossy, about 1 minute; set aside.

2. Combine flour, remaining sugar, baking powder, and salt in large bowl. Whisk water, oil, egg yolks, and vanilla in medium bowl until smooth. Whisk wet mixture into flour mixture until smooth. Whisk one-third whipped egg whites into batter, then gently fold in remaining whites, 1 scoop at a time, until well combined. Scrape mixture into 16-cup ungreased tube pan.

3. Bake until skewer inserted into center comes out clean and cracks in cake appear dry, 55 minutes to 1 hour, 5 minutes. Let cool, inverted, to room temperature, about 3 hours. To unmold, turn pan right side up and run flexible knife around tube and outer edge. Use tube to pull cake out of pan and set it on inverted baking pan. Cut bottom free. Invert cake onto serving plate and gently twist tube to remove. Serve.

Orange Chiffon Cake

Reduce total sugar to 1¼ cups. Replace water with ¾ cup orange juice and add 1 tablespoon grated orange zest along with vanilla in step 2. For glaze, whisk 3 tablespoons orange juice, 2 tablespoons softened cream cheese, and ½ teaspoon grated orange zest in medium bowl until smooth. Add 1½ cups confectioners' sugar and whisk until smooth. Pour glaze over cooled cake. Let glaze set for 15 minutes. Serve.

Italian Cream Cake
SERVES 8 TO 10

WHY THIS RECIPE WORKS Although there's nothing Italian about this cake, this Southern specialty of tender yellow cake with coconut, pecan, and cream cheese frosting is appealing. Cake flour made a tender crumb, and heat-activated baking powder ensured the cake would rise evenly in the oven. We used coconut twice—pulverized, toasted

Let Me Outta Here!
Like angel food cake, chiffon cake is baked in an ungreased pan. Why? The stiffly beaten egg whites need to cling to the pan to rise. If the pan were greased, they couldn't. Here's how to remove it from the pan.

1. When cake is cool, turn pan right side up and run flexible knife around tube and outer edge.

2. Use tube to pull cake out of pan and set it on inverted baking pan. Cut bottom free.

3. Invert cake onto serving plate and gently twist tube to remove.

coconut added flavor to the cake without drying it out, and cream of coconut amped up the frosting. Finally, we coated the sides in toasted pecans.

Toast the coconut and nuts in a 350-degree oven until golden brown, 10 to 12 minutes. Watch carefully and stir occasionally to prevent burning.

Cake

- 1½ cups sweetened shredded coconut, toasted
- 1 cup buttermilk, room temperature
- 2 teaspoons vanilla extract
- 2½ cups (10 ounces) cake flour
- 2 teaspoons baking powder
- ¾ teaspoon table salt
- ½ teaspoon baking soda
- 12 tablespoons unsalted butter, cut into 12 pieces and softened
- 4 tablespoons shortening, cut into 4 pieces
- 1¾ cups (12¼ ounces) sugar
- 5 large eggs, room temperature
- 2 cups (8 ounces) pecans, toasted and chopped, divided

Frosting

- 12 tablespoons unsalted butter, softened
- 2¼ cups (9 ounces) confectioners' sugar
- ½ cup cream of coconut
- ½ teaspoon vanilla extract
- Pinch table salt
- 16 ounces cream cheese, cut into 8 pieces and softened

1. For the Cake Adjust oven rack to middle position and heat oven to 350 degrees. Grease two 9-inch round cake pans, line with parchment paper, grease parchment, then flour pans. Process coconut in food processor until finely ground, about 1 minute. Combine coconut, buttermilk, and vanilla in 2-cup liquid measuring cup and let sit until coconut is slightly softened, about 10 minutes; reserve.

2. Combine flour, baking powder, salt, and baking soda in bowl. Using stand mixer fitted with paddle, beat butter, shortening, and sugar on medium-high speed until pale and fluffy, about 3 minutes. Add eggs, one at a time, and beat until combined. Reduce speed to low and add flour mixture in 3 additions, alternating with 2 additions of reserved coconut-buttermilk mixture, scraping down bowl as needed. Add ¾ cup pecans and give batter final stir by hand.

Italian Cream Cake

3. Scrape equal amounts of batter into prepared pans and bake until toothpick inserted in center comes out clean, 28 to 32 minutes. Cool cakes in pans on wire rack for 10 minutes. Remove cakes from pans, discarding parchment, and cool completely, about 2 hours. (Cooled cakes can be wrapped with plastic wrap and stored at room temperature for up to 2 days.)

4. For the Frosting Using stand mixer fitted with paddle, mix butter and sugar on low speed until combined, about 30 seconds. Increase speed to medium-high and beat until pale and fluffy, about 2 minutes. Add cream of coconut, vanilla, and salt and beat until smooth, about 30 seconds. Add cream cheese, one piece at a time, and beat until incorporated, about 1 minute. Refrigerate until ready to use.

5. When cakes are cooled, spread 1½ cups frosting over 1 cake round. Top with second cake round and spread remaining frosting evenly over top and sides of cake. Press remaining pecans onto sides of cake. Serve. (Cake can be refrigerated for up to 2 days. Bring to room temperature before serving.)

GREAT AMERICAN CAKES AND COOKIES

Cream Cheese Pound Cake

SERVES 12 TO 14

WHY THIS RECIPE WORKS In this delicious variation on classic pound cake, we added cream cheese for richness, tangy flavor, and an especially velvety texture. We let the pure flavors of eggs, butter, and the cream cheese take center stage, adding only a few teaspoons of vanilla and a moderate amount of sugar. To achieve a tight, fine crumb and a velvety texture, we left the leavener out altogether and used lower-protein cake flour. Extra egg yolks kept the cake moist and tender. Finally, a low oven took a little longer, but it produced a perfect golden-brown crust and a moist, tender interior.

If you do not have cake flour on hand, you can substitute 7/8 cup all-purpose flour and 2 tablespoons cornstarch for each cup of flour. Serve with Strawberry-Rhubarb Compote (recipe follows).

- 3 cups (12 ounces) cake flour
- 1 teaspoon table salt
- 4 large eggs plus 2 large yolks, room temperature
- 1/4 cup milk
- 2 teaspoons vanilla extract
- 3 cups (21 ounces) sugar, divided
- 24 tablespoons (3 sticks) unsalted butter, softened
- 6 ounces cream cheese, softened

1. Adjust oven rack to middle position and heat oven to 300 degrees. Grease and flour 12-cup nonstick Bundt pan. Combine flour and salt in bowl. Whisk eggs and yolks, milk, and vanilla together in 2-cup liquid measuring cup.

2. Using stand mixer fitted with paddle, beat sugar, butter, and cream cheese on medium-high speed until pale and fluffy, about 3 minutes. Reduce speed to low and very slowly add egg mixture, mixing until incorporated (batter may look slightly curdled). Add flour mixture in 3 additions, scraping down bowl as needed. Give batter final stir by hand.

3. Scrape batter into prepared pan and gently tap pan on counter to release air bubbles. Bake until toothpick inserted in center comes out clean, 80 to 90 minutes, rotating pan halfway through baking. Cool cake in pan on wire rack for 15 minutes. Remove cake from pan and cool completely, about 2 hours. Serve. (Cake can be stored, wrapped in plastic wrap, at room temperature for 3 days.)

Cream Cheese Pound Cake

Strawberry-Rhubarb Compote
MAKES 4 CUPS

The compote can be refrigerated for up to one week. It's delicious drizzled on Cream Cheese Pound Cake or ice cream or stirred into yogurt or oatmeal.

- 1 pound strawberries, hulled and chopped (3 cups)
- 1 cup (7 ounces) sugar
- 1 tablespoon lemon juice
- 1 pound rhubarb, sliced 1/4-inch thick
- Pinch table salt

1. Toss strawberries with 1/2 cup sugar and lemon juice in medium bowl. Transfer strawberry mixture to fine-mesh strainer set over medium saucepan and let stand, stirring occasionally, for 30 minutes. Do not wash bowl.

2. Return strawberries to bowl. Add rhubarb, remaining 1/2 cup sugar, and salt to strawberry juices in pan and bring to boil over medium-high heat. Reduce heat to medium-low and cook, stirring occasionally, until rhubarb is soft and liquid has thickened, 6 to 8 minutes.

3. Stir strawberries into pan and remove from heat. Transfer compote to bowl and let cool to room temperature, about 45 minutes. Serve.

Preparing a Bundt Pan
To ensure a clean release, apply paste of 1 tablespoon melted butter and 1 tablespoon flour to pan using pastry brush.

Cold-Oven Pound Cake
SERVES 12

Cold-Oven Pound Cake

WHY THIS RECIPE WORKS This thrifty pound cake, which was designed to save on gas by not requiring a preheated oven, is an especially tall cake and boasts a crisp crust. To create a light crumb, we used leaner whole milk instead of the heavy cream called for in most recipes. Swapping out all-purpose flour for cake flour yielded an even finer, more delicate crumb for our pound cake. We also used baking powder, which produced carbon dioxide bubbles that gave our cake its rise. Putting the pound cake into a cold oven, as is tradition, gave the carbon dioxide more time to produce greater rise.

You'll need a 16-cup tube pan for this recipe; if not using a nonstick pan, make sure to thoroughly grease a traditional pan. In step 2, don't worry if the batter looks slightly separated.

- 3 cups (12 ounces) cake flour
- ½ teaspoon baking powder
- 1 teaspoon table salt
- 1 cup whole milk
- 2 teaspoons vanilla extract
- 20 tablespoons (2½ sticks) unsalted butter, softened
- 2½ cups (17½ ounces) sugar
- 6 large eggs

1. Adjust oven rack to lower-middle position. Grease and flour 16-cup tube pan. Combine flour, baking powder, and salt in bowl. Whisk milk and vanilla in measuring cup.

2. Using stand mixer fitted with paddle, beat butter and sugar on medium-high speed until light and fluffy, about 2 minutes. Beat in eggs, one at a time, until combined. Reduce speed to low and add flour mixture in 3 additions, alternating with milk mixture in 2 additions, scraping down bowl as needed. Mix on low until smooth, about 30 seconds. Give batter final stir by hand.

3. Pour batter into prepared pan and smooth top. Place cake in cold oven. Adjust oven temperature to 325 degrees and bake, without opening oven door, until cake is golden brown and skewer inserted in center comes out clean, 1 hour 5 minutes to 1 hour 20 minutes.

4. Let cake cool in pan on wire rack for 15 minutes. Remove cake from pan and let cool completely on rack about 2 hours. Serve. (Cake can be stored at room temperature for up to 2 days.)

Why Pay for Preheating?

Gas ovens became widely available in the United States during the first decades of the 20th century. Because these ovens were more expensive than their wood- and coal-fired counterparts, gas companies had to get creative in marketing them. One popular tactic was to develop and promote recipes started in a cold oven, with the hook that consumers could save money in their gas ovens by not paying for "needless" preheating. Hence: cold-oven pound cake.

Carrot Snack Cake

SERVES 12 TO 16

WHY THIS RECIPE WORKS We wanted an incredibly tasty carrot cake that was easier, faster, and more moist than ever. To that end, we skipped the stacking of layers and fiddling with piping bags and opted to make an easy-to-prepare sheet cake in a 13 by 9-inch baking pan. Shredding the carrots and making the cream cheese frosting in a food processor made quick work of these otherwise tedious steps. A couple of easy but uncommon techniques ensured an ultramoist and superflavorful cake. First, we plumped and softened golden raisins in orange juice before stirring them into the batter. Then, we soaked the still-hot, just-baked cake in a stir-together buttermilk syrup, moistening the cake and balancing its sweetness while enhancing the tanginess of the cream cheese frosting.

Shred the carrots in a food processor fitted with the shredding disk or on the large holes of a box grater. One pound of carrots is about six medium carrots and will yield about 12 ounces of shredded carrots after peeling and trimming.

Cake

- 1 cup golden raisins
- ¼ cup orange juice
- 2½ cups (12½ ounces) all-purpose flour
- 1 tablespoon pumpkin pie spice
- 2 teaspoons baking powder
- 1 teaspoon baking soda
- ¾ teaspoon table salt
- 1½ cups packed (10½ ounces) light brown sugar
- 1¼ cups vegetable oil
- 4 large eggs
- 1 tablespoon vanilla extract
- 1 pound carrots, peeled and shredded (3 cups)
- 1 cup (4 ounces) confectioners' sugar
- ⅔ cup buttermilk

Frosting

- 12 ounces cream cheese, softened
- 2 cups (8 ounces) confectioners' sugar
- 8 tablespoons unsalted butter, softened
- 1 teaspoon vanilla extract
- ⅛ teaspoon table salt
- 1 cup pecans, toasted and chopped

1. For the Cake Adjust oven rack to middle position and heat oven to 350 degrees. Spray 13 by 9-inch baking pan with vegetable oil spray. Combine raisins and orange juice in small bowl. Microwave, covered, until hot, about 1 minute. Let stand, covered, until raisins are soft, about 5 minutes.

2. Whisk flour, pumpkin pie spice, baking powder, baking soda, and salt together in medium bowl; set aside. Whisk brown sugar, oil, eggs, and vanilla in large bowl until smooth; stir in carrots and raisin mixture. Stir in flour mixture with rubber spatula until just combined.

3. Transfer batter to prepared pan and smooth top with rubber spatula. Bake until toothpick inserted in center of cake comes out clean, 33 to 38 minutes, rotating pan halfway through baking. Transfer pan to wire rack.

4. Immediately whisk confectioners' sugar and buttermilk together until smooth. Brush buttermilk syrup evenly over entire surface of hot cake (use all of syrup). Let cake cool completely in pan on wire rack, about 3 hours.

5. For the Frosting Process cream cheese, sugar, butter, vanilla, and salt in food processor until smooth, about 30 seconds, scraping down sides of bowl with rubber spatula as needed.

6. Spread frosting evenly over surface of cake, leaving ½-inch border. Sprinkle frosting evenly with pecans. Serve.

To Make Ahead Frosted cake can be covered with plastic wrap and refrigerated for up to 2 days.

Carrot-Ginger Snack Cake with Cardamom

Substitute 1 teaspoon ground cinnamon and 1 teaspoon ground cardamom for pumpkin pie spice. Stir in 1½ tablespoons grated fresh ginger with carrots and raisin mixture in step 2. Sprinkle 2 tablespoons finely chopped crystallized ginger over top of frosted cake with pecans in step 6.

Chocolate Cream Cupcakes

MAKES 12 CUPCAKES

Carrot Snack Cake

WHY THIS RECIPE WORKS Packaged chocolate cream cupcakes are a childhood treat. But try one today and you're met with wan chocolate cake encasing salty whipped vegetable shortening. We knew we could do better. Blooming cocoa powder in boiling water and adding chocolate chips and espresso powder gave our cupcakes plenty of chocolate depth. Combining marshmallow crème and the right amount of gelatin gave us the perfect creamy filling. To fill our cupcakes without a pastry bag, we used a paring knife to cut inverted cones from the tops of the cupcakes, added the frosting, and plugged the holes.

To ensure an appropriately thick filling, be sure to use marshmallow crème (such as Fluff), not marshmallow sauce. For an accurate measurement of boiling water, bring a full kettle of water to a boil, then measure out the desired amount.

Cupcakes

- 1 cup (5 ounces) all-purpose flour
- ½ teaspoon baking soda
- ¼ teaspoon table salt
- ½ cup boiling water
- ⅓ cup (1 ounce) cocoa powder
- ⅓ cup (2 ounces) semisweet chocolate chips
- 1 tablespoon instant espresso powder
- ¾ cup (5¼ ounces) sugar
- ½ cup sour cream
- ½ cup vegetable oil
- 2 large eggs
- 1 teaspoon vanilla extract

Chocolate Cream Cupcakes

Filling
- ¾ teaspoon unflavored gelatin
- 3 tablespoons water
- 4 tablespoons (½ stick) unsalted butter, softened
- 1 teaspoon vanilla extract
- Pinch table salt
- 1¼ cups marshmallow crème

Glaze
- ½ cup semisweet chocolate chips
- 3 tablespoons unsalted butter

1. For the Cupcakes Adjust oven rack to middle position and heat oven to 325 degrees. Spray 12-cup muffin tin with vegetable oil spray and flour. Combine flour, baking soda, and salt in bowl. Whisk water, cocoa, chocolate chips, and espresso powder in large bowl until smooth. Add sugar, sour cream, oil, eggs, and vanilla and mix until combined. Whisk in flour mixture until incorporated. Divide batter evenly among muffin cups. Bake until toothpick inserted in center comes out with few dry crumbs attached, 18 to 22 minutes. Let cupcakes cool in tin on wire rack for 10 minutes, then turn out onto wire rack and let cool completely.

2. For the Filling Sprinkle gelatin over water in large bowl and let sit until gelatin softens, about 5 minutes. Microwave until mixture is bubbling around edges and gelatin dissolves, about 30 seconds. Stir in butter, vanilla, and salt until combined. Let mixture cool until just warm to touch, about 5 minutes, then whisk in marshmallow crème until smooth; refrigerate until set, about 30 minutes. Transfer ⅓ cup marshmallow mixture to pastry bag fitted with small plain tip; reserve remaining mixture for filling cupcakes.

3. For the Glaze Microwave chocolate and butter in small bowl, stirring occasionally, until smooth, about 30 seconds. Let glaze cool to room temperature, about 10 minutes.

4. Insert tip of paring knife at 45-degree angle and about ¼ inch from edge of cupcake, cut cone from top of each cupcake, and cut off all but top ¼ inch of cone, leaving circular disk of cake. Fill cupcakes with 1 tablespoon filling each. Replace tops, frost with 2 teaspoons cooled glaze, and let sit 10 minutes. Using pastry bag, pipe curlicues across glazed cupcakes. Serve. (Cupcakes can be stored at room temperature for up to 2 days.)

Filling the Cupcakes

1. Insert tip of paring knife at 45-degree angle about ¼ inch from edge of cupcake. Cut out and remove cake cone. Cut off all but top ¼ inch of cone, leaving circular disk of cake.

2. Using spoon, fill each cupcake with marshmallow mixture and then top with reserved cake "plug." The glaze and the curlicues will hide your handiwork.

Hot Fudge Pudding Cake
SERVES 6 TO 8

WHY THIS RECIPE WORKS Most hot fudge pudding cakes end up looking rich and fudgy but have very little chocolate flavor. For chocolate pudding cake that tasted as good as it looked, we folded semisweet chocolate chips into the batter, which added another layer of chocolate flavor and ensured plenty of gooey pockets in the baked cake. Vegetable oil, which most recipes call for, was flavorless, and we found substituting melted butter improved our pudding cake's flavor. Using Dutch-processed cocoa, which is less acidic than natural cocoa powder, produced a richer chocolate taste.

For an accurate measurement of boiling water, bring a kettle of water to a boil, then measure out the desired amount. Store leftovers, covered with plastic wrap, in the refrigerator. Reheat individual servings in a microwave on high power until hot (about 1 minute).

- 1 cup (7 ounces) sugar, divided
- ½ cup (1½ ounces) Dutch-processed cocoa powder, divided
- 1 cup (5 ounces) all-purpose flour
- 2 teaspoons baking powder
- ¼ teaspoon table salt
- ½ cup milk
- 4 tablespoons unsalted butter, melted
- 1 large egg yolk
- 2 teaspoons vanilla extract
- ½ cup semisweet chocolate chips
- 1 cup boiling water
- Vanilla ice cream or whipped cream

1. Adjust oven rack to middle position and heat oven to 350 degrees. Spray 8-inch square baking pan with vegetable oil spray. Whisk ½ cup sugar with ¼ cup cocoa in small bowl.

2. Whisk flour, remaining ½ cup sugar, remaining ¼ cup cocoa, baking powder, and salt in large bowl. Whisk milk, butter, egg yolk, and vanilla in medium bowl until smooth. Stir milk mixture into flour mixture until just combined. Fold in chocolate chips (batter will be stiff).

3. Using rubber spatula, scrape batter into prepared pan and spread into corners. Sprinkle reserved cocoa mixture evenly over top. Gently pour boiling water over cocoa. Do not stir.

4. Bake until top of cake looks cracked, sauce is bubbling, and toothpick inserted into cakey area comes out with moist crumbs attached, about 25 minutes. Let cool in pan on wire rack for at least 10 minutes. To serve, scoop warm cake into individual serving bowls and top with vanilla ice cream or whipped cream.

Baby Pudding Cakes
Put a fancy spin on this homey recipe by baking up individual pudding cakes.

Spray eight 6-ounce ovenproof ramekins or coffee cups with vegetable oil spray. Fill each with 2 tablespoons batter. Top each with 1½ tablespoons cocoa mixture, followed by 2 tablespoons boiling water. Arrange cups on rimmed baking sheet and bake until tops are just cracked, 20 to 25 minutes.

Is It Done Yet?
This highly unconventional cake breaks most of the usual rules, including how to judge when it's ready to come out of the oven.

 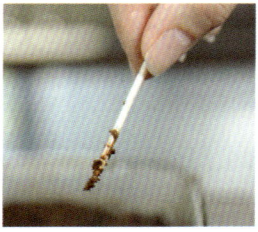

1. Start testing for doneness when top is crackled like a brownie and sauce is bubbling up from bottom. Insert toothpick close to the edge, where the cake is firmest. (Don't insert the toothpick in center, where cake should be gooey.)

2. Toothpick should have large, moist crumbs—but no gooey batter—attached. Check at least two spots to be certain that what's sticking to toothpick isn't just melted chocolate.

Hot Fudge Pudding Cake

Lemon Pudding Cake

SERVES 8

WHY THIS RECIPE WORKS For the brightest lemon flavor in our lemon pudding cake, we used a half cup of lemon juice. To coax even more flavor from the lemons, we creamed a bit of grated zest with the butter and sugar. A bit of cornstarch gently firmed the pudding layer without muddying the lemon flavor. To prevent the top layer of the cake from deflating, we beat sugar into the egg whites. This stabilized the whites and resulted in a high, golden, and fluffy cake. For the creamiest texture, it was important to bake the cake in a water bath. The hot water protected the pudding from cooking too quickly.

This dessert is best served warm or at room temperature the same day it is made.

- ¼ cup (1¼ ounces) all-purpose flour
- 2 teaspoons cornstarch
- 1¼ cups (8¾ ounces) sugar, divided
- 5 tablespoons unsalted butter, softened
- 2 tablespoons grated zest and ½ cup juice from 4 lemons
- 5 large eggs, separated
- 1¼ cups whole milk, room temperature
- 2 quarts boiling water

1. Adjust oven rack to lowest position and heat oven to 325 degrees. Grease 8-inch square baking dish. Whisk flour and cornstarch in bowl. Using stand mixer fitted with paddle, beat ½ cup sugar, butter, and lemon zest on medium-high speed until light and fluffy, about 2 minutes. Beat in egg yolks, 1 at a time, until incorporated. Reduce speed to medium-low. Add flour mixture and mix until incorporated. Slowly add milk and lemon juice, mixing until just combined.

2. Using clean bowl and whisk attachment, beat egg whites on medium-high speed until soft peaks form, about 2 minutes. With mixer running, slowly add remaining ¾ cup sugar until whites are firm and glossy, about 1 minute. Whisk one-third of whites into batter, then gently fold in remaining whites, 1 scoop at a time, until well combined.

3. Place clean dish towel in bottom of roasting pan and arrange prepared baking dish on towel. Spoon batter into prepared dish. Carefully place pan on oven rack and pour boiling water into pan until water comes halfway up sides of baking dish. Bake until surface is golden brown and edges are set (center should jiggle slightly when gently shaken), about 1 hour. Transfer dish to wire rack and let cool for at least 1 hour. To serve, scoop warm cake into individual serving bowls.

Using a Water Bath

The water lowers the temperature surrounding the baking dish for gentle, even cooking.

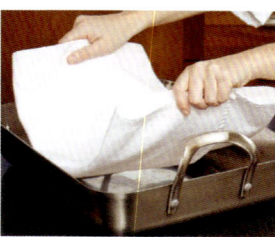

1. To prevent baking dish from sliding, line bottom of roasting pan with clean dish towel and place baking dish on top.

2. Set roasting pan on oven rack and carefully pour boiling water into pan, halfway up sides of baking dish.

3. After baking, promptly remove baking dish from water. Let water cool before moving water bath.

Lemon Icebox Cheesecake

SERVES 12 TO 16

WHY THIS RECIPE WORKS In a baked cheesecake, tart lemon juice is mellowed by the heat of the oven. For our icebox version of lemon cheesecake, we needed to dial back the lemon juice to compensate for the lack of baking. Lemon curd, a rich, tangy spread made from eggs, butter, cream, sugar, and lemon juice, added crisp lemon flavor without the undesirable chewiness of zest or the processed flavor of lemon extract. Using lemon cookies instead of graham crackers for the crust created an additional layer of lemon flavor.

Let the dissolved gelatin mixture cool down for a few minutes, or the gelatin will seize before combining with the filling. We tested our cheesecake with several store brands of lemon sandwich cookies; all worked well.

Crust
- 10 lemon sandwich cookies, broken into pieces (about 1¼ cups)
- 2 tablespoons unsalted butter, melted
- 1 teaspoon grated lemon zest

Curd
- ¼ cup (1¾ ounces) sugar
- 1 large egg plus 1 large yolk
- Pinch table salt
- 2 tablespoons lemon juice
- 1 tablespoon unsalted butter
- 1 tablespoon heavy cream

Filling
- 2¾ teaspoons unflavored gelatin
- ¼ cup lemon juice (2 lemons)
- 1½ pounds cream cheese, cut into 1-inch pieces and softened
- ¾ cup (5¼ ounces) sugar
- Pinch table salt
- 1¼ cups heavy cream, room temperature

1. For the Crust Adjust oven rack to middle position and heat oven to 350 degrees. Process cookies in food processor until finely ground, about 30 seconds. Add butter and zest and pulse until combined, about 10 pulses. Press mixture into bottom of 9-inch springform pan. Bake until lightly browned and set, about 10 minutes. Let cool completely on wire rack, at least 30 minutes.

2. For the Curd While crust is cooling, whisk sugar, egg and yolk, and salt together in small saucepan. Add lemon juice and cook over medium-low heat, stirring constantly, until thick and puddinglike, about 3 minutes. Remove from heat and stir in butter and cream. Press through fine-mesh strainer into small bowl and refrigerate lemon curd until needed.

3. For the Filling Sprinkle gelatin over lemon juice in small bowl and let stand until gelatin softens, about 5 minutes. Microwave until mixture is bubbling around edges and gelatin dissolves, about 30 seconds. Set aside.

Lemon Pudding Cake

Lemon Icebox Cheesecake

4. Using stand mixer fitted with paddle beat cream cheese, sugar, and salt on medium speed until smooth and creamy, scraping down sides of bowl as needed, about 2 minutes. Slowly add cream and beat until light and fluffy, about 2 minutes. Add gelatin mixture and ¼ cup curd, increase speed to medium-high, and beat until smooth and airy, about 3 minutes.

5. Pour filling into cooled crust and smooth top. Pour thin lines of remaining curd on top of cake and lightly drag paring knife or skewer perpendicularly through lines to create marbled appearance. Refrigerate until set, at least 6 hours. Remove sides of pan. Serve. (Cheesecake can be refrigerated for up to 3 days.)

Swirl Showstopper

Making a swirl with the lemon curd on top of the cheesecake is absurdly easy and awfully impressive.

1. Use measuring cup to pour curd in 4 thin lines on top of cheesecake.

2. Drag paring knife or skewer perpendicularly through lines to create marbled design.

Strawberry Cheesecake Bars

MAKES TWENTY-FOUR 2-INCH SQUARES

WHY THIS RECIPE WORKS Bright strawberries combined with tangy, rich cheesecake make for a perfect dessert. But trying to add fresh strawberries directly to the cheesecake filling compromised its creamy texture and prevented our bars from firming up. Instead, we pureed fresh berries and stirred them into a sour cream topping that we spread over the cheesecake layer. This gave strong strawberry flavor that didn't sacrifice the signature creaminess of cheesecake. A simple graham cracker crust is a test kitchen favorite for cheesecakes, and it was supereasy to put together. A single strawberry slice on top of each bar was the perfect finishing touch.

Be sure to let the crust cool completely before starting the filling.

Crust
- 9 whole graham crackers, broken into pieces
- ½ cup (3½ ounces) sugar
- ¾ cup (3¾ ounces) all-purpose flour
- ¼ teaspoon table salt
- 8 tablespoons unsalted butter, melted

Filling
- 1½ pounds cream cheese
- 1 cup (7 ounces) sugar
- 3 large eggs
- 2 teaspoons vanilla extract

Topping
- 6 ounces strawberries, hulled (1 heaping cup), plus 5 hulled strawberries
- ½ cup (3½ ounces) plus 1 teaspoon sugar, divided
- 2 cups sour cream

1. Adjust oven rack to middle position and heat oven to 300 degrees. Make foil sling for 13 by 9-inch baking pan by folding 2 long sheets of aluminum foil; first sheet should be 13 inches wide and second sheet should be 9 inches wide. Lay sheets of foil in pan perpendicular to each other, with extra foil hanging over edges of pan. Push foil into corners and up sides of pan, smoothing foil flush to pan. Spray with vegetable oil spray.

2. For the Crust Process cracker pieces and sugar in food processor until finely ground, about 30 seconds. Add flour and salt and pulse to combine, about 2 pulses. Add melted butter and pulse until crumbs are evenly moistened, about 10 pulses.

3. Using your hands, press crumb mixture evenly into bottom of prepared pan. Using bottom of dry measuring cup, firmly pack crust into pan. Bake until fragrant and beginning to brown around edges, about 20 minutes. Let cool completely.

4. For the Filling In clean, dry processor bowl, process cream cheese and sugar until smooth, about 3 minutes, scraping down sides of bowl as needed. With processor running, add eggs, one at a time, until just incorporated, about 30 seconds total. Scrape down sides of bowl. Add

Strawberry Cheesecake Bars

Milk Chocolate Cheesecake

SERVES 12

WHY THIS RECIPE WORKS Too often, chocolate's bitter side can clash with the tangy flavor of cream cheese, but we were determined to create a fluffy chocolate cheesecake without the bitterness. After making dozens of versions, we figured out that switching from dark to mild-mannered milk chocolate was the secret to a sweet, creamy cheesecake. Adding cocoa powder provided depth and rounded out the chocolate flavor. Unlike traditional cheesecake that is baked in a water bath, we simplified our recipe by baking it in a low 250-degree oven. For an easy and crunchy, chocolaty crust, we used Oreo cookies processed with butter and a bit of sugar.

Our favorite milk chocolate is Endangered Species Chocolate Smooth + Creamy Milk Chocolate. For the crust, use the entirety of the Oreo cookies, filling and all. The cheesecake needs to be refrigerated for at least 8 hours before serving.

- 16 Oreo sandwich cookies, broken into rough pieces
- 1 tablespoon sugar plus 1/2 cup (3 1/2 ounces), divided
- 2 tablespoons unsalted butter, melted
- 8 ounces milk chocolate, chopped, divided
- 1/3 cup heavy cream
- 2 tablespoons unsweetened cocoa powder
- 1/4 teaspoon table salt
- 1 1/2 pounds cream cheese, softened
- 4 large eggs, room temperature
- 2 teaspoons vanilla extract

1. Adjust oven rack to middle position and heat oven to 350 degrees. Grease bottom and sides of 9-inch nonstick springform pan.

2. Process cookies and 1 tablespoon sugar in food processor until finely ground, about 30 seconds. Add melted butter and pulse until combined, about 6 pulses. Transfer crumb mixture to prepared pan and press firmly with bottom of dry measuring cup into even layer in bottom of pan. Bake until fragrant and set, about 10 minutes. Let cool completely on wire rack.

vanilla and process to combine, about 10 seconds. Pour cream cheese mixture over cooled crust. Bake until center is almost set but still jiggles slightly when pan is shaken, about 45 minutes.

5. For the Topping Meanwhile, in clean, dry processor bowl, process 6 ounces strawberries and 1/2 cup sugar until pureed, about 30 seconds. Stir strawberry puree and sour cream in bowl until combined.

6. Remove cheesecake from oven. Pour strawberry mixture over cheesecake (cheesecake layer should be completely covered). Return pan to oven and bake until topping is just set, about 15 minutes.

7. Transfer pan to wire rack and let cheesecake cool completely, about 2 hours. Refrigerate until cold and set, at least 4 hours or up to 24 hours. Slice remaining 5 strawberries thin and toss gently with remaining 1 teaspoon sugar in bowl. Using foil overhang, lift cheesecake out of pan. Cut into 24 squares. Garnish each square with 1 strawberry slice and serve.

Milk Chocolate Cheesecake

La Viña–Style Cheesecake

3. Reduce oven temperature to 250 degrees. Combine 6 ounces chocolate and cream in medium bowl and microwave at 50 percent power, stirring occasionally, until melted and smooth, 60 to 90 seconds. Let cool for 10 minutes. In small bowl, whisk cocoa, salt, and remaining ½ cup sugar until no lumps remain.

4. Using stand mixer fitted with paddle, beat cream cheese and cocoa mixture on medium speed until creamy and smooth, about 3 minutes, scraping down bowl as needed. Reduce speed to medium-low, add chocolate mixture, and beat until combined. Gradually add eggs, one at a time, until incorporated, scraping down bowl as needed. Add vanilla and give batter final stir by hand until no streaks of chocolate remain.

5. Pour cheesecake mixture into cooled crust and smooth top with spatula. Tap cheesecake gently on counter to release air bubbles. Cover pan tightly with aluminum foil (taking care not to touch surface of cheesecake with foil) and place on rimmed baking sheet. Bake for 1 hour, then remove foil. Continue to bake until edges are set and center registers 150 degrees and jiggles slightly when shaken, 30 to 45 minutes. Let cool completely on wire rack, then cover with plastic wrap and refrigerate in pan until cold, about 8 hours. (Cake can be refrigerated for up to 4 days.)

6. To unmold cheesecake, remove sides of pan, slide thin metal spatula between crust and pan bottom to loosen, and slide cake onto serving platter. Microwave remaining 2 ounces chocolate in small bowl at 50 percent power, stirring occasionally, until melted, 60 to 90 seconds. Let cool for 5 minutes. Transfer to small zipper-lock bag, cut small hole in corner, and pipe chocolate in thin zigzag pattern across top of cheesecake. Let cheesecake stand at room temperature for 30 minutes. Using warm, dry knife, cut into wedges and serve.

Melt Milk Chocolate Carefully

Because milk chocolate contains milk solids, its protein content is generally higher than that of dark chocolate. The extra protein means that milk chocolate melts at a slightly lower temperature than dark; what's more, when you add heat to protein and sugar, new molecules may form, introducing unwelcome scorched or burned flavors. Microwaves are generally gentle, but notoriously inconsistent, so choose 50 percent power, keep a close eye on the chocolate, and give it a stir every 15 seconds.

La Viña–Style Cheesecake

SERVES 8 TO 12

WHY THIS RECIPE WORKS We adapted this recipe from a recipe developed by Santiago "Santi" Rivera at La Viña in Donostia-San Sebastián, Basque Country, Spain. Our version of this crustless cheesecake boasts a lightly caramelized exterior and an ultracreamy interior. For the smoothest texture, we used a food processor rather than a stand mixer, slightly adjusting the amount of cream to make it easier to process the ingredients in a single batch. Starting with room-temperature ingredients was also key to repeatedly producing perfect results. Lining a round pan with parchment paper can be awkward, so we lightly moistened the paper before crumpling and uncrumpling it, making it easier to work with.

If you don't have a 14-cup food processor, use a large, deep bowl and an immersion blender. Do not use cream cheese spread, whipped or low-fat cream cheese, or neufchatel. To ensure that the cheesecake cooks properly within the given time frame, be sure all ingredients are at room temperature (65 to 70 degrees). Use an oven thermometer to be sure that your oven is reading 425 degrees before baking. To avoid overcooking, we strongly recommend using a thermometer in step 3 to confirm when the center of the cheesecake reaches 155 degrees. Serve with Basque Cider Salted Caramel Sauce (recipe follows), if desired.

- 7 large eggs, room temperature
- 2 cups (14 ounces) sugar
- 2¼ pounds (36 ounces) cream cheese, room temperature
- 1 cup heavy cream, room temperature
- ¼ cup (1¼ ounces) all-purpose flour

1. Adjust oven rack to middle position and heat oven to 425 degrees. Spray or lightly sprinkle 2 approximately 16 by 12-inch pieces of parchment paper evenly with cold water. Crumple each piece of parchment into ball, then gently uncrumple. Overlap parchment pieces slightly to form approximately 16-inch square. Press parchment into bottom and sides of 9-inch springform pan. Fold overhanging parchment outward, over edge of pan. Using scissors or kitchen shears, trim overhanging parchment to about 1 inch past edge of pan.

2. Process eggs and sugar in large (14-cup) food processor until mixture is frothy and pale yellow, about 1 minute. Add cream cheese, heavy cream, and flour and pulse until cream cheese is broken into large, even pieces, 8 to 10 pulses. Process until mixture is completely smooth, about 2 minutes, scraping down sides of bowl and breaking up any large clumps of cream cheese as needed (processor bowl will be very full).

3. Transfer batter to prepared pan and place pan on rimmed baking sheet. Bake until top of cheesecake is deeply browned, edges are set, and center of cheesecake registers 155 degrees, 45 to 55 minutes (center will be very jiggly). Remove cheesecake from oven and transfer to wire rack. Let cheesecake cool in pan for at least 2 hours.

4. Remove side of pan. Gently peel parchment away from sides of cheesecake until parchment is flush with counter. To slice, dip sharp knife in very hot water and wipe dry after each cut. Serve slightly warm (after 2 hours cooling) or at room temperature. (Cheesecake can be refrigerated for up to 3 days; let sit at room temperature for 1 to 2 hours before serving.)

Basque Cider Salted Caramel Sauce
SERVES 8 TO 12 (MAKES ABOUT 1 CUP)

If you can't find Basque cider (also known as sagardoa), substitute another dry hard cider. You can reheat the sauce either in a microwave or in a small saucepan over low heat, whisking often, until the sauce is warm and smooth.

- 1 (750-ml) bottle Basque hard cider
- 1⅔ cups (11⅔ ounces) sugar
- ¾ cup heavy cream
- ¼ teaspoon table salt

1. Bring cider and sugar to boil in large heavy-bottomed saucepan over medium-high heat. Cook without stirring until mixture is syrupy and full of large bubbles and registers about 250 degrees, 25 to 35 minutes.

2. Reduce heat to medium-low and continue to cook, swirling saucepan occasionally, until mixture is deep amber–colored and registers 320 to 330 degrees, 10 to 15 minutes longer. (Watch caramel closely during final minutes of cooking since temperature can increase quickly.)

3. Off heat, carefully whisk in cream and salt (mixture will bubble and steam). Continue to whisk until sauce is smooth. Let sauce cool slightly before serving, about 15 minutes. (Sauce will thicken as it cools. Cooled sauce can be refrigerated for up to 2 weeks; reheat before serving.)

Cowboy Cookies

MAKES 16 COOKIES

WHY THIS RECIPE WORKS A product of 1950s nostalgia for the wild West, cowboy cookies—packed with rolled oats, chocolate chips, toasted nuts, and flakes of coconut—are perfect for tucking into your saddlebag to enjoy at high noon. When we set out to wrangle this recipe, we discovered that the mix-ins absorbed moisture in the dough, making for one tough cookie, so we melted our butter to keep the dough moist. Staggering ¼-cup portions of dough onto our baking sheets gave these oversize cookies enough room to spread, and deliberately underbaking them ensured that they had a perfectly crisp exterior and soft chew once cooled.

We prefer old-fashioned rolled oats in this recipe, but you can use quick or instant oats in a pinch. Do not use thick-cut oats here; the cookies will spread too much. These cookies are big and benefit from the extra space provided by a rimless cookie sheet when baking. Our favorite cookie sheet is the Wear-Ever Cookie Sheet (Natural Finish) by Vollrath.

1¼	cups (6¼ ounces) all-purpose flour
¾	teaspoon baking powder
½	teaspoon baking soda
½	teaspoon table salt
1½	cups packed (10½ ounces) light brown sugar
12	tablespoons unsalted butter, melted and cooled
1	large egg plus 1 large yolk
1	teaspoon vanilla extract
1¼	cups (3¾ ounces) old-fashioned rolled oats
1	cup pecans, toasted and chopped coarse
1	cup (3 ounces) sweetened shredded coconut
⅔	cup (4 ounces) semisweet chocolate chips

1. Adjust oven rack to middle position and heat oven to 350 degrees. Line 2 rimless cookie sheets with parchment paper. Whisk flour, baking powder, baking soda, and salt together in bowl.

2. Whisk sugar, melted butter, egg and yolk, and vanilla in large bowl until combined. Stir in flour mixture until no dry streaks remain. Stir in oats, pecans, coconut, and chocolate chips until fully combined (mixture will be sticky).

3. Lightly spray ¼-cup dry measuring cup with vegetable oil spray. Drop level ¼-cup portions of dough onto prepared sheets, staggering 8 portions per sheet and spacing them about 2½ inches apart. Divide any remaining dough among portions.

4. Bake cookies, 1 sheet at a time, until edges are browned and set and centers are puffed with pale, raw spots, 15 to 17 minutes, rotating sheet halfway through baking. Do not overbake.

5. Let cookies cool on sheet for 5 minutes, then transfer to wire rack and let cool completely before serving. (Cookies can be stored in airtight container for up to 3 days.)

To Make Ahead At end of step 3, wrap sheets tightly in plastic wrap and refrigerate for up to 2 days. When ready to bake, increase baking time to 16 to 18 minutes. To freeze, portion dough onto parchment-lined sheet and freeze until solid. Transfer frozen portions to zipper-lock bag and freeze for up to 2 months. Do not thaw before baking. Increase baking time to 17 to 19 minutes.

Cowboy Cookies

Don't Fence Them In

Cowboy Cookies need lots of room to expand and bake evenly. To ensure that they don't spread into each other while baking, we arrange no more than 8 portions of dough on each parchment-lined cookie sheet.

Thin and Crispy Chocolate Chip Cookies

Thin and Crispy Chocolate Chip Cookies

MAKES 16 COOKIES

WHY THIS RECIPE WORKS Thin and crunchy, butterscotchy chocolate chip cookies can't be beat. Melted butter helps the dough spread quickly so the cookies bake without burning. However, the batter needs more flour to keep them from spreading too much. Just ¼ cup more did the trick, but the extra flour made the cookies too chewy. Switching to a lighter cake flour, which contains less protein, made for more-tender cookies. But the cookies still weren't crisp enough. The solution was adding a bit of whole milk. The milk provided extra moisture, so the cookies didn't dry out with the additional baking time required to crisp up. Now that's the way these cookies crumble.

Note that this recipe calls for cake flour and mini (not full-size) chocolate chips.

1¼ cups (5 ounces) cake flour
¾ teaspoon table salt
¼ teaspoon baking soda
8 tablespoons unsalted butter, melted and cooled
⅓ cup (2⅓ ounces) granulated sugar
⅓ cup packed (2⅓ ounces) dark brown sugar
2 large egg yolks
1½ tablespoons whole milk
2 teaspoons vanilla extract
¾ cup (4½ ounces) mini semisweet chocolate chips

1. Adjust oven rack to middle position and heat oven to 350 degrees. Line 2 baking sheets with parchment paper. Whisk flour, salt, and baking soda together in bowl.

2. Using stand mixer fitted with paddle, mix melted butter, granulated sugar, and brown sugar on low speed until fully combined. Increase speed to medium-high and beat until mixture is lightened in color, about 1 minute. Reduce speed to low; add egg yolks, milk, and vanilla; and mix until combined. Slowly add flour mixture and mix until just combined, scraping down bowl as needed. Using rubber spatula, stir in chocolate chips.

GREAT AMERICAN CAKES AND COOKIES

3. Using greased 1-tablespoon measure, divide dough into 16 heaping-tablespoon portions on prepared sheets, 8 portions per sheet. Divide any remaining dough evenly among portions. Using your moistened fingers, press dough portions to ½-inch thickness. Bake cookies, 1 sheet at a time, until deep golden brown, 16 to 18 minutes, rotating sheet halfway through baking. Let cookies cool on sheet for 20 minutes. Serve. (Cookies can be stored at room temperature for up to 3 days.)

Keys to the Perfect Texture

Cake flour makes the batter light.

Mini chocolate chips keep a low profile.

Plenty of butter helps the cookies spread.

Chocolate Chip Skillet Cookie

SERVES 8

WHY THIS RECIPE WORKS A cookie in a skillet? Unlike baking a traditional batch of cookies, a skillet cookie can go straight from the oven to the table for a fun, hands-on dessert. This scaled-up cookie benefits from the hot bottom and tall sides of a well-seasoned cast-iron pan to create a great crisp crust. Reeling in the butter and chocolate chips from our usual cookie dough recipe allowed our oversized cookie to bake through in the middle while staying perfectly chewy. We increased the baking time to accommodate the giant size, but otherwise this recipe was simpler and faster than baking regular cookies.

Top with ice cream for an extra-decadent treat.

- 12 tablespoons unsalted butter, divided
- ¾ cup packed (5¼ ounces) dark brown sugar
- ½ cup (3½ ounces) granulated sugar
- 2 teaspoons vanilla extract
- 1 teaspoon table salt
- 1 large egg plus 1 large yolk
- 1¾ cups (8¾ ounces) all-purpose flour
- ½ teaspoon baking soda
- 1 cup (6 ounces) semisweet chocolate chips

1. Adjust oven rack to upper-middle position and heat oven to 375 degrees. Melt 9 tablespoons butter in 12-inch cast-iron skillet over medium heat. Continue to cook, stirring constantly, until butter is dark golden brown, has nutty aroma, and bubbling subsides, about 5 minutes; transfer to large bowl. Stir remaining 3 tablespoons butter into hot butter until completely melted.

2. Whisk brown sugar, granulated sugar, vanilla, and salt into melted butter until smooth. Whisk in egg and yolk until smooth, about 30 seconds. Let mixture sit for 3 minutes, then whisk for 30 seconds. Repeat process of resting and whisking 2 more times until mixture is thick, smooth, and shiny.

3. Whisk flour and baking soda together in separate bowl, then stir flour mixture into butter mixture until just combined, about 1 minute. Stir in chocolate chips, making sure no flour pockets remain.

4. Wipe skillet clean with paper towels. Transfer dough to now-empty skillet and press into even layer with spatula. Transfer skillet to oven and bake until cookie is golden brown and edges are set, about 20 minutes, rotating skillet halfway through baking. Using potholders, transfer skillet to wire rack and let cookie cool for 30 minutes. Slice cookie into wedges and serve.

M&M Cookies

MAKES 16 COOKIES

WHY THIS RECIPE WORKS For our version of this nostalgic recipe, we wanted cookies that were big and colorful, soft and chewy, sweet and buttery, and just salty enough to make us want to eat another one. To start, we skipped the creaming of the butter and sugar because that added extra air that produced taller, more tender cookies. Instead, we whisked together brown sugar, granulated sugar, and melted butter; the extra moisture in the brown sugar made for moist, chewy cookies. Following the advice of an M&M cookie expert we visited in Portland, Oregon, we increased the baking soda, upped the oven temperature to 425 degrees, and pulled the cookies out of the oven sooner (after only 8 minutes). Each of these strategies resulted in cookies that stayed soft and chewy longer.

Use standard, not mini, M&M'S in this recipe. The cookies will seem underdone when you pull them from the oven. This is OK; they will continue baking as they cool on the baking sheet for 5 minutes. This method ensures that the cookies remain chewy once they are cooled.

2¼ cups (11¼ ounces) all-purpose flour
1 teaspoon table salt
¾ teaspoon baking soda
12 tablespoons unsalted butter, melted
1 cup packed (7 ounces) light brown sugar
½ cup (3½ ounces) granulated sugar
1 large egg plus 1 large yolk
2 teaspoons vanilla extract
1¼ cups (9 ounces) M&M'S

1. Adjust oven rack to middle position and heat oven to 425 degrees. Line 2 baking sheets with parchment paper. Combine flour, salt, and baking soda in bowl.

2. Whisk melted butter, brown sugar, and granulated sugar in large bowl until thoroughly combined, about 30 seconds. Whisk in egg and yolk and vanilla until fully combined and mixture looks emulsified, about 30 seconds. Stir in half of flour mixture with rubber spatula or wooden spoon. Stir in candies and remaining flour mixture.

3. Divide dough into sixteen 2¼-ounce portions, about 2 heaping tablespoons each; divide any remaining dough evenly among dough portions. Roll dough portions between your hands to make smooth balls.

4. Evenly space dough balls on prepared sheets, 8 balls per sheet. Using your hand, flatten balls to ¾-inch thickness.

5. Bake cookies, 1 sheet at a time, until centers of cookies are puffed and still very blond, about 8 minutes; cookies will seem underdone. Let cookies cool on sheet for 5 minutes. Using spatula, transfer cookies to wire rack and let cool for 10 minutes before serving.

To Make Ahead At end of step 4, transfer flattened dough balls to parchment paper–lined plate and freeze until very firm, at least 1 hour. Transfer to 1-gallon zipper-lock bag and freeze for up to 1 month. Bake from frozen, increasing baking time to 12 minutes.

Chocolate Chip Skillet Cookie

M&M Cookies

Gooey Butter Cake Bars

SERVES 10 TO 12

Gooey Butter Cake Bars

WHY THIS RECIPE WORKS A riff on a favorite St. Louis cake, gooey butter cake bars feature three layers of goodness: an ultrabuttery crust; a custardy middle layer; and a chewy, meringue-like top. In our version, a sturdy shortbread base offers just enough salt to balance out the bar's sweetness. For our custard filling, we wanted to avoid using a double boiler and found that swapping some butter for cream cheese prevented the eggs from curdling and yielded a filling with the ideal pudding-like consistency. Poured on top of the cooled crust and baked on the upper oven rack, this filling transformed into a gooey middle layer and a perfectly crackled top.

A 2-pound bag of confectioners' sugar will yield enough for both the crust and filling with leftovers for dusting. Do not use a glass or ceramic baking dish here. Scrape down the sides and bottom of the mixer bowl with a rubber spatula as often as needed to make sure all the ingredients are fully combined.

Crust
- 2½ cups (12½ ounces) all-purpose flour
- ¾ cup (3 ounces) confectioners' sugar
- ¾ teaspoon table salt
- 12 tablespoons unsalted butter, melted

Filling
- 8 ounces cream cheese, softened
- 8 tablespoons unsalted butter, softened
- 4 cups (1 pound) confectioners' sugar, plus extra for dusting
- 2 large eggs plus 2 large yolks
- 2 tablespoons vanilla extract
- ¼ teaspoon table salt

1. Adjust oven rack to upper-middle position and heat oven to 350 degrees. Make foil sling for 13 by 9-inch baking pan by folding 2 long sheets of aluminum foil; first sheet should be 13 inches wide and second sheet should be 9 inches wide. Lay sheets of foil in pan perpendicular to each other, with extra foil hanging over edges of pan. Push foil into corners and up sides of pan, smoothing foil flush to pan. Spray foil with vegetable oil spray.

2. For the Crust Combine flour, sugar, and salt in bowl. Add melted butter and stir with rubber spatula until evenly moistened. Crumble dough over bottom of prepared pan. Using bottom of dry measuring cup, press dough into even layer. Using fork, poke dough all over, about 20 times. Bake until edges are light golden brown, about 20 minutes. Transfer pan to wire rack and let cool completely, about 30 minutes.

3. For the Filling Combine cream cheese and butter in bowl of stand mixer fitted with paddle. With mixer running on low speed, slowly add sugar and mix until fully combined, about 1 minute, scraping down sides and bottom of bowl as needed. Increase speed to medium-high and mix until light and fluffy, about 2 minutes.

4. Reduce speed to low; add eggs and yolks, one at a time, and mix until incorporated. Add vanilla and salt and mix until incorporated, about 20 seconds, scraping down sides and bottom of bowl as needed. Increase speed to medium-high and mix until light and fluffy, about 2 minutes (mixture should have consistency of frosting). Spread filling evenly over cooled crust. Tap pan gently on counter to release air bubbles.

5. Bake until top is golden brown, edges have cracked, and center jiggles slightly when pan is gently shaken, about 30 minutes. Transfer pan to wire rack and let cool completely, at least 3 hours.

6. Using foil overhang, lift bars out of pan. Cut into 12 pieces. Dust with extra sugar and serve. (Bars can be stored in airtight container at room temperature for up to 3 days.)

Melting Moments
MAKES ABOUT 70 COOKIES

WHY THIS RECIPE WORKS These delicate butter cookies literally melt in your mouth, thanks to the generous amount of cornstarch in the dough. Unfortunately, the cornstarch leaves behind a chalky residue with each bite. After settling on the maximum amount of cornstarch we could use without detection, we scoured supermarket shelves in search of other low-protein dry ingredients to replace the remainder. We replaced all-purpose flour with cake flour and chose confectioners' sugar over granulated, but we still needed more bulk. The solution? Rice Krispies! The ground cereal added the volume we were looking for without toughening the crumb.

If the dough gets too soft to slice, return it to the refrigerator to firm up.

- ½ cup Rice Krispies cereal
- 16 tablespoons unsalted butter, cut into 16 pieces and softened, divided
- 3 tablespoons heavy cream
- 1 teaspoon vanilla extract
- 1¼ cups (5 ounces) cake flour
- ¼ cup (1¼ ounces) cornstarch
- ⅛ teaspoon table salt
- ⅔ cup (2⅔ ounces) confectioners' sugar

1. Process Rice Krispies in blender until finely ground, about 30 seconds. Combine 4 tablespoons butter and cream in large bowl and microwave until butter is melted, about 30 seconds. Whisk in processed Rice Krispies and vanilla until combined. Let cool slightly, 5 to 7 minutes.

2. Combine flour, cornstarch, and salt in medium bowl; reserve. Whisk sugar into cooled butter mixture until incorporated. Add remaining 12 tablespoons butter, whisking until smooth. Stir in flour mixture until combined.

3. Working with half of dough at a time, dollop dough into 8-inch strip down center of 14 by 12-inch sheet of parchment paper. Fold 1 long side of parchment over dough. Using ruler, press dough into tight 1-inch-wide log. Repeat with remaining dough and another sheet of parchment. Refrigerate dough until firm, about 1 hour. (Dough can be wrapped in plastic wrap and aluminum foil and frozen for up to 1 month.)

4. Adjust oven racks to upper-middle and lower-middle positions and heat oven to 300 degrees. Line 2 baking sheets with parchment. Cut dough into ¼-inch slices and place 1 inch apart on prepared baking sheets. Bake until set but not brown, 18 to 22 minutes, switching and rotating baking sheets halfway through baking. Let cool completely on sheets, about 15 minutes. Repeat with remaining dough. Serve. (Cookies can be stored at room temperature for up to 2 days.)

Crescent Cookies
After step 2, transfer dough to pastry bag fitted with ½-inch star tip. Pipe 1½-inch-long crescents onto prepared baking sheets. Refrigerate dough until firm, about 30 minutes. Bake as directed.

Melting Moments

Jam Thumbprint Cookies

After step 2, transfer dough to pastry bag fitted with ½-inch plain tip. Pipe 1-inch-wide and ½-inch-high dough rounds onto prepared baking sheets. Using back of ¼-teaspoon measuring spoon dipped in water, make indentation in center of each round. Refrigerate dough until firm, about 30 minutes. Bake until set, 18 to 20 minutes, switching and rotating sheets halfway through baking. Fill each dimple with ½ teaspoon jam and bake for 5 minutes.

Round Spritz Cookies

After step 2, transfer dough to pastry bag fitted with ½-inch star tip. Pipe 1-inch-wide and ½-inch-high dough rounds onto prepared baking sheets. Refrigerate dough until firm, about 30 minutes. Bake as directed.

Handling Soft Dough

The high proportion of butter to flour makes the dough for these cookies very soft and challenging to handle. With this technique, you can easily roll it into a log.

1. Dollop half of dough in strip down center of sheet of parchment.

2. Pulling parchment taut, use ruler to press dough into tight log.

Slice-and-Bake Cookies

MAKES ABOUT 40 COOKIES

WHY THIS RECIPE WORKS We set out to create a slice-and-bake cookie recipe that would combine both crispness and rich butter and vanilla flavors—in effect, shortbread shaped into a convenient slice-and-bake log. Using both granulated sugar and light brown sugar gave the cookies a richness and complexity that tasters liked. We used the food processor to combine our recipe ingredients quickly without whipping in too much air—our cookies had the fine, shortbread-like texture we were after.

Be sure that the cookie dough is well chilled and firm so that it can be uniformly sliced.

- ⅓ cup (2⅓ ounces) granulated sugar
- 2 tablespoons packed light brown sugar
- ½ teaspoon table salt
- 12 tablespoons unsalted butter, cut into pieces and softened
- 2 teaspoons vanilla extract
- 1 large egg yolk
- 1½ cups (7½ ounces) all-purpose flour

1. Process granulated sugar, brown sugar, and salt in food processor until no lumps of brown sugar remain, about 30 seconds. Add butter, vanilla, and yolk and process until smooth and creamy, about 20 seconds. Scrape down sides of bowl, add flour, and pulse until dough forms, about 15 seconds.

2. Turn out dough onto lightly floured counter and roll into 10-inch log. Wrap tightly with plastic wrap and refrigerate until firm, at least 2 hours or up to 3 days. (Dough can be wrapped in foil and frozen for up to 1 month.)

3. Adjust oven racks to upper-middle and lower-middle positions and heat oven to 350 degrees. Line 2 baking sheets with parchment paper. Slice chilled dough into ¼-inch rounds and place 1 inch apart on prepared baking sheets. Bake until edges are just golden, about 15 minutes, switching and rotating baking sheets halfway through baking. Let cool 10 minutes on sheets, then transfer to wire rack and let cool completely. Repeat with remaining dough. (Cookies can be stored at room temperature for up to 1 week.)

Coconut-Lime Cookies

In step 1, add 2 cups sweetened shredded coconut and 2 teaspoons grated lime zest to food processor along with sugars and salt.

Walnut–Brown Sugar Cookies

In step 1, add 2 more tablespoons brown sugar and 1 cup chopped walnuts to food processor along with sugars and salt.

Orange–Poppy Seed Cookies

In step 1, add ¼ cup poppy seeds and 1 tablespoon grated orange zest to food processor along with sugars and salt.

Glaze Me

We love the simplicity of our Slice-and-Bake Cookies, but a confectioners' sugar glaze is an easy way to dress them up. If the glaze is too thick to spread, thin it with 1 tablespoon water. Each glaze makes enough for 1 recipe Slice-and-Bake Cookies.

Ginger-Lime Glaze Whisk 1 tablespoon softened cream cheese, 1 teaspoon ground ginger, and 2 tablespoons lime juice in medium bowl until combined. Whisk in 1½ cups confectioners' sugar until smooth.

Malted Milk Glaze Whisk 1 tablespoon softened cream cheese, 1 tablespoon malted milk powder, 1 teaspoon vanilla extract, and 2 tablespoons milk in medium bowl until combined. Whisk in 1½ cups confectioners' sugar until smooth.

Cappuccino Glaze Whisk 1 tablespoon softened cream cheese, 1 tablespoon instant espresso powder, and 2 tablespoons milk in medium bowl until combined. Whisk in 1½ cups confectioners' sugar until smooth.

Peanut Butter and Jelly Glaze Whisk 1 tablespoon creamy peanut butter, 2 tablespoons strawberry jelly, and 1 tablespoon water in medium bowl until combined. Whisk in 1½ cups confectioners' sugar until smooth.

Slice-and-Bake Cookies

New Mexico Biscochitos

MAKES ABOUT 48 COOKIES

WHY THIS RECIPE WORKS Biscochitos are cinnamon- and-anise-flavored shortbread cookies that have rightly earned the title of New Mexico's state cookie. While many home cooks prepare the cookies with butter and shortening, we preferred the delectable savory-sweet flavor of cookies made with lard (rendered pork fat). We shaped the dough into logs to chill so that we could slice and bake the cookies for clean, crisp edges. Tossing the baked cookies in cinnamon sugar gave them a sweet-spicy, crunchy exterior.

New Mexico Biscochitos

We developed this recipe using John Morrell Snow Cap Lard. We prefer the flavor and texture lard gives these cookies, but ⅔ cup of softened unsalted butter or vegetable shortening can be substituted, if desired.

1¾	cups (8¾ ounces) all-purpose flour
¼	teaspoon baking powder
¼	teaspoon plus pinch table salt, divided
1½	teaspoons anise seeds
⅔	cup (4⅔ ounces) lard
¾	cup (5¼ ounces) sugar, divided
1	large egg
½	teaspoon vanilla extract
¼	teaspoon ground cinnamon

1. Whisk flour, baking powder, and ¼ teaspoon salt together in bowl; set aside. Place anise seeds in zipper-lock bag, seal bag, and crush seeds coarse with rolling pin or meat pounder.

2. Using stand mixer fitted with paddle, beat lard, ½ cup sugar, and crushed anise seeds on medium-high speed until light and fluffy, about 3 minutes. Add egg and vanilla and beat until combined, scraping down bowl as needed. Reduce speed to low, slowly add flour mixture, and mix until just combined.

3. Turn out dough onto counter. Divide dough in half (about 9 ounces per half) and roll each half into 6-inch log. Wrap dough logs tightly in plastic wrap, roll against counter to form tight cylinder, and refrigerate until firm, at least 3 hours or up to 3 days.

4. Adjust oven rack to middle position and heat oven to 350 degrees. Line 2 baking sheets with parchment paper. Slice dough logs into ¼-inch-thick rounds, rolling logs as you cut to keep circular shape of dough. Evenly space cookies on prepared sheets (about 24 cookies per sheet). Bake cookies, 1 sheet at a time, until edges are lightly browned, 13 to 15 minutes, rotating sheet halfway through baking. Let cookies cool on sheets for at least 5 minutes.

5. Combine cinnamon, remaining pinch salt, and remaining ¼ cup sugar, in shallow dish. Gently toss cookies, a few at a time, in cinnamon sugar. Transfer to wire rack and let cookies cool completely, at least 30 minutes, before serving. (Cookies can be stored in airtight container for up to 3 days.)

On the Road: Baking Biscochitos with the Queen

Angie Delgado pulls a 1-pound block of lard from her shopping bag; it's the most important ingredient in her biscochitos. For her, butter just won't do if you're after the real thing. She's arrived with all her ingredients premeasured and portioned, along with a sturdy white cookie press that looks like a caulking gun, her preferred method for shaping biscochitos. The recipe was passed down to her from her great-grandmother, and she puts tremendous value on preserving that legacy. "Although," she whispers, "I don't follow all the directions."

Angie is the former First Lady of Santa Fe and a past Fiesta Queen of the Fiesta de Santa Fe. She's eaten these cookies all her life. They've shown up at every birthday, wedding, baptism, holiday, and family gathering for generations. When going through the ingredients, she nods at a small vial of whiskey, giggles, and says that while she prefers Jack Daniel's, wine is a suitable substitute. "But I'm happy when Jack's in the house," she says as her smile widens and her laugh fills the colorfully tiled kitchen. Time to make cookies.

Fairy Gingerbread

MAKES 60 COOKIES

WHY THIS RECIPE WORKS Original recipes for fairy gingerbread, a cookie popular in the 19th century, melted in our mouths but were also severely lacking in flavor. A bit of vanilla extract and salt helped boost the flavor. Doubling the ginger added a much-needed kick, but without any competing flavors it was overwhelming. We cut back a little and toasted the ground ginger to bring out its natural flavor. Grating fresh ginger straight into the batter added even more intense ginger flavor. Switching from bread flour to all-purpose flour made the batter slightly easier to spread. A little baking soda helped retain the cookies' airy crispness.

Use cookie or baking sheets that measure at least 15 by 12 inches. Don't be disconcerted by the scant amount of batter: You really are going to spread it very thin. Use the edges of the parchment paper as your guide, covering the entire surface thinly and evenly. For easier grating, freeze a 2-inch piece of peeled ginger for 30 minutes, then use a rasp-style grater.

1½ teaspoons ground ginger
¾ cup plus 2 tablespoons (4⅜ ounces) all-purpose flour
½ teaspoon baking soda
¼ teaspoon table salt
5 tablespoons unsalted butter, softened
9 tablespoons (4 ounces) packed light brown sugar
4 teaspoons grated fresh ginger
¾ teaspoon vanilla extract
¼ cup whole milk, room temperature

1. Adjust oven racks to upper-middle and lower-middle positions and heat oven to 325 degrees. Spray 2 rimless baking sheets (or inverted rimmed baking sheets) with vegetable oil spray and cover each with 15 by 12-inch sheet parchment paper. Heat ground ginger in small skillet over medium heat until fragrant, about 1 minute. Combine flour, toasted ginger, baking soda, and salt in medium bowl.

2. Using stand mixer fitted with paddle, beat butter and sugar on medium-high speed until light and fluffy, about 2 minutes. Add fresh ginger and vanilla and mix until incorporated. Reduce speed to low and add flour mixture in 3 additions, alternating with milk in 2 additions; scrape down bowl as needed.

Making Fairy Gingerbread

While making several dozen batches of Fairy Gingerbread, we had time to perfect our technique. The cookies are made with an unusual method we'd never encountered before. Here's how.

1. To form cookies of requisite thinness, use small offset spatula to spread batter to edges of 15 by 12-inch sheet of parchment paper.

2. Immediately after removing cookies from oven, use chef's knife or pizza wheel to score 3 by 2-inch rectangles. Work quickly to prevent breaking.

3. Once cookies are cool, trace over scored lines with paring knife and gently break cookies apart along lines.

GREAT AMERICAN CAKES AND COOKIES

3. Evenly spread ¾ cup batter to cover parchment on each prepared sheet (batter will be very thin). Bake until deep golden brown, 16 to 20 minutes, switching and rotating baking sheets halfway through baking. Immediately score cookies into 3 by 2-inch rectangles. Let cool completely, about 20 minutes. Using tip of paring knife, separate cookies along score marks. (Cookies can be stored at room temperature for 3 days.)

Joe Froggers
MAKES 24 COOKIES

WHY THIS RECIPE WORKS Joe froggers, from a recipe that dates back more than 200 years, are incredibly moist, spicy, slightly salty cookies, found in bakeries along the North Shore of Massachusetts. We wanted to develop our own recipe. Dissolving salt into our recipe's rum and water gave the cookie its distinctive salty flavor while ginger, allspice, nutmeg, and cloves contributed warm spice flavor. Many recipes we found in our research called for lard, but we found that using butter made for a more flavorful cookie.

Place only six cookies on each baking sheet—they will spread. If you don't own a 3½-inch cookie cutter, use a drinking glass. Use mild (not robust or blackstrap) molasses. Make sure to chill the dough for a full 8 hours or it will be too hard to roll out.

- ⅓ cup dark rum (such as Myers's)
- 1 tablespoon water
- 1½ teaspoons table salt
- 3 cups (15 ounces) all-purpose flour
- ¾ teaspoon ground ginger
- ½ teaspoon ground allspice
- ¼ teaspoon ground nutmeg
- ⅛ teaspoon ground cloves
- 1 cup molasses
- 1 teaspoon baking soda
- 8 tablespoons unsalted butter, softened but still cool
- 1 cup (7 ounces) sugar

1. Stir rum, water, and salt in small bowl until salt dissolves. Whisk flour, ginger, allspice, nutmeg, and cloves in medium bowl. Stir molasses and baking soda in liquid measuring cup (mixture will begin to bubble) and let sit until doubled in volume, about 15 minutes.

2. Using stand mixer fitted with paddle, beat butter and sugar on medium-high speed until fluffy, about 2 minutes. Reduce speed to medium-low and gradually beat in rum mixture. Add flour mixture in 3 additions, beating on medium-low until just incorporated, alternating with molasses mixture in 2 additions, scraping down sides of bowl as needed. Give dough final stir by hand (dough will be extremely sticky). Cover bowl with plastic wrap and refrigerate until stiff, at least 8 hours or up to 3 days.

3. Adjust oven racks to upper-middle and lower-middle positions and heat oven to 375 degrees. Line 2 baking sheets with parchment paper. Working with half of dough at a time on heavily floured counter, roll out to ¼-inch thickness. Using 3½-inch cookie cutter, cut out 12 cookies. Transfer 6 cookies to each baking sheet, spacing cookies about 1½ inches apart. Bake until cookies are set and just beginning to crack, about 8 minutes, switching and rotating baking sheets halfway through baking time. Let cookies cool on sheets on wire rack 10 minutes, then transfer cookies to rack to cool completely. Repeat with remaining dough. (Cookies may be stored for up to 1 week.)

Salty History

Joe froggers date back more than 200 years to Black Joe's Tavern, located in Marblehead, Massachusetts, a seaside town north of Boston. A formerly enslaved person and Revolutionary War veteran, Joseph Brown, and his wife, Lucretia, opened the tavern in a part of Marblehead called Gingerbread Hill. Besides serving drinks (mostly rum), Joe and Lucretia baked cookies: large, moist, molasses and rum cookies made salty by the addition of Marblehead seawater. These cookies were popular sustenance on long fishing voyages, as they had no dairy to spoil and the combination of rum, molasses, and seawater kept them chewy for weeks.

According to Samuel Roads Jr.'s *History and Traditions of Marblehead*, published in 1879, the funny name for these cookies referred to the lily pads (similar in size and shape to the cookies) and large croaking frogs that would fill the pond behind Joe's tavern. Thus the cookies became known as Joe froggers.

Black and White Cookies

MAKES 12 COOKIES

WHY THIS RECIPE WORKS These chocolate-vanilla, cakey cookies are a deli favorite in New York, but often they do not live up to the hype. To get the "cookie" just right, we made several small but high-impact adjustments. We dialed back the amount of baking soda and baking powder to get rid of unwanted air bubbles, added more vanilla extract to heighten the flavor, and used just enough sour cream to make the cookies tender but not sticky. Corn syrup made the glaze thick and shiny, while milk made it creamy and spreadable. Cocoa powder kept the chocolate glaze flavorful and simple.

Twelve cookies doesn't sound like much, but these cookie are huge. You'll get neater cookies if you spread on the vanilla glaze first. This recipe provides a little extra glaze, just in case.

Cookies
- 1¾ cups (8¾ ounces) all-purpose flour
- ½ teaspoon baking powder
- ¼ teaspoon baking soda
- ⅛ teaspoon table salt
- 10 tablespoons unsalted butter, softened
- 1 cup (7 ounces) granulated sugar
- 1 large egg
- 2 teaspoons vanilla extract
- ⅓ cup sour cream

Glaze
- 5 cups (20 ounces) confectioners' sugar, sifted
- 7 tablespoons whole milk, divided
- 2 tablespoons corn syrup
- 1 teaspoon vanilla extract
- ½ teaspoon table salt
- 3 tablespoons Dutch-processed cocoa powder, sifted

1. For the Cookies Adjust oven racks to upper-middle and lower-middle positions and heat oven to 350 degrees. Line 2 baking sheets with parchment paper. Combine flour, baking powder, baking soda, and salt in bowl.

2. Using stand mixer fitted with paddle, beat butter and sugar on medium-high speed until pale and fluffy, about 2 minutes. Add egg and vanilla and beat until combined. Reduce speed to low and add flour mixture in 3 additions, alternating with 2 additions of sour cream, scraping down bowl as needed. Give dough final stir by hand.

Joe Froggers

Black and White Cookies

3. Using greased ¼-cup measure, drop cookie dough 3 inches apart onto prepared baking sheets. Bake until edges are lightly browned, 15 to 18 minutes, switching and rotating sheets halfway through baking. Let cookies cool on sheets for 5 minutes, then transfer to wire rack to cool completely, about 1 hour.

4. **For the Glaze** Whisk sugar, 6 tablespoons milk, corn syrup, vanilla, and salt together in bowl until smooth. Transfer 1 cup glaze to small bowl; reserve. Whisk cocoa and remaining 1 tablespoon milk into remaining glaze until combined.

5. Working with 1 cookie at a time, spread 1 tablespoon vanilla glaze over half of underside of cookie. Refrigerate until glaze is set, about 15 minutes. Cover other half of cookies with 1 tablespoon chocolate glaze and let cookies sit at room temperature until glaze is firm, at least 1 hour. Serve. (Cookies can be stored at room temperature for up to 2 days.)

Glazing Black and White Cookies

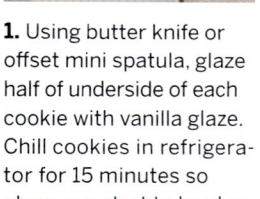

1. Using butter knife or offset mini spatula, glaze half of underside of each cookie with vanilla glaze. Chill cookies in refrigerator for 15 minutes so glaze can start to harden.

2. Glaze other half of each cookie with chocolate glaze, and let cookies sit until glaze sets, about 1 hour.

Whoopie Pies

MAKES 6 PIES

WHY THIS RECIPE WORKS We wanted a light, airy cake for our whoopie pies, so we used the creaming mixing method—blending the butter and sugar with a mixer until fluffy and nearly white in color. We also used lots of Dutch-processed cocoa powder and vanilla in our recipe for full flavor and a deep, dark-colored crumb. And for a cleaner, fuller flavor, we replaced the shortening (or lard) found in most recipes with butter.

Don't be tempted to bake all the cakes on one baking sheet; the batter needs room to spread in the oven.

Cakes

- 2   cups (10 ounces) all-purpose flour
- ½   cup (1½ ounces) Dutch-processed cocoa powder
- 1   teaspoon baking soda
- ½   teaspoon table salt
- 8   tablespoons unsalted butter, softened but still cool
- 1   cup packed (7 ounces) light brown sugar
- 1   large egg, room temperature
- 1   teaspoon vanilla extract
- 1   cup buttermilk

Filling

- 12 tablespoons unsalted butter, softened but still cool
- 1¼ cups (5 ounces) confectioners' sugar
- 1½ teaspoons vanilla extract
- ⅛   teaspoon table salt
- 2½ cups marshmallow crème

1. **For the Cakes** Adjust oven racks to upper-middle and lower-middle positions and heat oven to 350 degrees. Line 2 baking sheets with parchment paper. Whisk flour, cocoa, baking soda, and salt in medium bowl.

2. Using stand mixer fitted with paddle, beat butter and sugar on medium-high speed until fluffy, about 4 minutes. Beat in egg until incorporated, scraping down sides of bowl as necessary, then beat in vanilla. Reduce speed to low and beat in flour mixture in 3 additions, alternating with buttermilk in 2 additions. Give batter final stir by hand.

3. Using ⅓-cup measure, scoop 6 mounds of batter onto each baking sheet, spacing mounds about 3 inches apart. Bake until cakes spring back when pressed, 15 to 18 minutes, switching and rotating baking sheets halfway through baking. Let cool completely on baking sheets, at least 1 hour.

4. **For the Filling** Using stand mixer fitted with paddle, beat butter and sugar on medium speed until fluffy, about 2 minutes. Beat in vanilla and salt. Beat in marshmallow crème until incorporated, about 2 minutes. Refrigerate filling until slightly firm, about 30 minutes. (Bowl can be wrapped and refrigerated for up to 2 days.)

5. Dollop ⅓ cup filling on center of flat side of 6 cakes. Top with flat side of remaining 6 cakes and gently press until filling spreads to edges of cakes. Serve. (Whoopie pies can be refrigerated for up to 3 days.)

What's Up, Whoopie Pie?

Where did whoopie pies originate? Both Maine and Pennsylvania—the Pennsylvania Dutch of Lancaster County, to be specific—claim whoopie pies as their own. Maine's earliest claim dates back to 1925, when Labadie's Bakery in Lewiston first sold whoopie pies to the public. Some research showed that the Berwick Cake Company began manufacturing Whoopie! Pies (the exclamation point was part of the name) in 1927. These sources claim that whoopie pies were named after the musical Whoopie; Whoopie had its debut in Boston in 1927. In addition, Marshmallow Fluff, a key ingredient in many whoopie pie recipes, had been invented in nearby Lynn seven years earlier.

What about Pennsylvania's claim on whoopie pies? We found an article in a copy of the *Gettysburg Times* from 1982 that spoke of a chocolate cake sandwich with a fluffy cream center. These sandwiches were called gobs and were sold by the Dutch Maid Bakery of Geistown. While the name was different, the description (and a huge picture) showed that these were no doubt whoopie pies. The Dutch Maid Bakery purchased the rights to the gob in 1980 from the Harris and Boyer Baking Company, also of Pennsylvania, which had started manufacturing gobs in 1927. Maine might have a few years on Pennsylvania when it comes to whoopie pies, but who's to know for sure?

Whoopie Pie

Oatmeal Creme Pies
MAKES 12 SANDWICH COOKIES

WHY THIS RECIPE WORKS To develop a freshly baked version of Little Debbie's most iconic snack, we began with our recipe for oatmeal raisin cookies, tweaking both the ingredient list and method. Grinding oats and raisins into a paste gave our cookies the appropriate uniform texture and look while ensuring nutty flavor and bright sweetness. Mixing molasses into the cookie dough added complexity and color, and a bit of cinnamon brought in aromatic depth. Upping the amount of baking soda and baking the

Oatmeal Creme Pies

cookies at a high temperature caused them to spring up in the oven and then deflate as they cooled, re-creating the distinct dark cracks of the Little Debbie cookies. Finally, making the filling proved as easy as combining marshmallow crème, softened butter, and confectioners' sugar (plus vanilla extract and salt) in the food processor.

Regular old-fashioned rolled oats work best in this recipe. Do not use extra-thick rolled oats, as they will bake up tough in the cookies. For cookies with just the right amount of spread and chew, we strongly recommend that you weigh your ingredients. The cookies will seem underdone when you pull them from the oven. This is OK; they will continue to bake as they cool on the baking sheet. This method ensures that the cookies stay chewy once they have cooled.

Cookies

- 1 cup (5 ounces) all-purpose flour
- 1 teaspoon table salt
- ¾ teaspoon baking soda
- 3 cups (9 ounces) old-fashioned rolled oats
- ½ cup (3 ounces) raisins
- ¾ cup packed (5¼ ounces) dark brown sugar
- ½ cup (3½ ounces) granulated sugar
- ½ cup vegetable oil
- 4 tablespoons unsalted butter, melted
- 2 teaspoons molasses
- ¼ teaspoon ground cinnamon
- 1 large egg plus 1 large yolk
- 1 teaspoon vanilla extract

Filling

- 5 ounces (1¼ cups) Fluff brand marshmallow crème
- ¾ cup (3 ounces) confectioners' sugar
- 6 tablespoons unsalted butter, softened
- ½ teaspoon vanilla extract
- ¼ teaspoon table salt

1. For the Cookies Adjust oven rack to middle position and heat oven to 400 degrees. Line 2 rimmed baking sheets with parchment paper. Whisk flour, salt, and baking soda together in medium bowl; set aside. Process oats and raisins in food processor until very finely ground, about 1 minute.

2. Whisk brown sugar, granulated sugar, oil, melted butter, molasses, and cinnamon in large bowl until smooth. Whisk in egg and yolk and vanilla until smooth. Using wooden spoon or spatula, stir in flour mixture until evenly combined and no dry flour remains. Stir in oat-raisin mixture until evenly distributed. (Mixture will be stiff; once dough begins to stiffen, you can mix with your hands until dough is evenly combined.)

3. Divide dough into twenty-four 1⅓-ounce portions, about 1½ tablespoons each. Roll dough portions between your hands to form smooth balls. Evenly space dough balls on prepared sheets, 12 balls per sheet. Using your hand or bottom of dry measuring cup, flatten balls to ½-inch thickness.

4. Bake cookies, 1 sheet at a time, until tops are beginning to crack at edges, 5 to 7 minutes. Let cookies cool on sheet for 5 minutes. Using spatula, transfer cookies to wire rack and let cool completely, about 45 minutes.

The American Table: The American Dream of Cookies

O.D. McKee, who created the Oatmeal Creme Pie—the cookie upon which he and his wife, Ruth, built the Little Debbie snack empire—got his start in sales in Mississippi as a young teenager going door to door persuading people to buy books. Though dyslexia and a stutter meant that he struggled to read and often floundered in school, he possessed a preternatural knack for business.

After the family lost its savings in a bank failure in the 1930s Great Depression, O.D. found work as a traveling cookie salesman for a bakery in Chattanooga, Tennessee, parlaying his success in that role into becoming the owner of Jack's Cookie Company. Jack's had three cookies (oatmeal, vanilla, and raisin), each selling for $0.01 apiece. But O.D. was an innovator, adding a soft oatmeal sandwich cookie to the menu that the bakery could sell for $0.05. The Oatmeal Creme Pie immediately increased the bakery's profits and went on to become a huge success, driving the growth of the family business and becoming the first and most enduring snack under the Little Debbie brand (named after O.D. and Ruth's granddaughter).

5. For the Filling Process all ingredients in now-empty processor until smooth and fluffy, about 30 seconds, scraping down sides of bowl as needed. Transfer to bowl and stir to incorporate any dry sugar.

6. Spread scant 1 tablespoon creme filling on bottoms (flat sides) of each of 12 cookies. Top with remaining cookies to form sandwiches. Serve. (Assembled cookies can be stored in airtight container for up to 3 days.)

Basic Chocolate Truffles

MAKES 24 TRUFFLES

WHY THIS RECIPE WORKS Chocolate truffles are often reserved for special occasions because they can be laborious to make. We wanted a streamlined, failproof recipe, making the process as simple as possible. We utilized the microwave to melt the chocolate and cream ganache base, stirred the mixture with a rubber spatula (a whisk incorporates too much air), and chilled it. Rolling truffles can get messy, so we wore disposable gloves for easy cleanup. A dusting of cocoa powder and confectioners' sugar keeps the truffles from sticking together during chilling and storing.

Basic Chocolate Truffles

Wear latex gloves when forming the truffles to keep your hands clean.

- ¼ cup (¾ ounce) unsweetened cocoa powder
- 1 tablespoon confectioners' sugar
- 8 ounces bittersweet chocolate, chopped fine
- ½ cup heavy cream
- Pinch table salt

1. Sift cocoa and sugar through fine-mesh strainer into pie plate. Microwave chocolate, cream, and salt in bowl at 50 percent power, stirring occasionally with rubber spatula, until melted, about 1 minute. Stir truffle mixture until fully combined; transfer to 8-inch square baking dish and refrigerate until set, about 45 minutes.

2. Using heaping teaspoon measure, scoop truffle mixture into 24 portions, transfer to large plate, and refrigerate until firm, about 30 minutes. Roll each truffle between your hands to form uniform balls (balls needn't be perfect).

3. Transfer truffles to cocoa mixture and roll to evenly coat. (Coated truffles can be refrigerated along with excess cocoa mixture for up to 1 week.) Lightly shake truffles in your hand over pie plate to remove excess coating; transfer to platter. Refrigerate for 30 minutes. Let sit at room temperature for 10 minutes before serving.

Chocolate-Almond Truffles

Substitute 1 cup sliced almonds, toasted and chopped fine, for cocoa mixture coating. Add ½ teaspoon almond extract to chocolate mixture before microwaving in step 2.

Chocolate-Cinnamon Truffles

Sift ¼ teaspoon ground cinnamon with cocoa powder and sugar for coating. Add 1 teaspoon ground cinnamon and ⅛ teaspoon cayenne pepper to chocolate mixture before microwaving.

Chocolate-Ginger Truffles

Add 2 teaspoons ground ginger to chocolate mixture before microwaving.

Chocolate-Lemon Truffles

Add 1 teaspoon grated lemon zest to chocolate mixture before microwaving.

Buckeye Candies

Chocolate Fudge

Buckeye Candies
MAKES 32 CANDIES

WHY THIS RECIPE WORKS This sweetened peanut butter ball dipped in melted chocolate is named for the nut of Ohio's state tree. The ingredient list is simple: peanut butter, butter, chocolate, and confectioners' sugar. Since the mixture of butter and peanut butter is difficult to work with, most recipes call for adding confectioners' sugar to reduce the stickiness. For our version, we found that we could reduce the amount of sugar (and reduce the sweetness) by slightly softening the chilled butter. To quickly and easily temper the chocolate, we used the microwave. Refrigerating the dough made the candies easier to roll and also ensured that the coating set the to perfect snappy texture.

We developed this recipe with Ghirardelli 60% Cacao Bittersweet Chocolate Premium Baking Bars. You can substitute bittersweet chocolate chips for the bar chocolate, but be sure to finely chop the chips. Do not use natural peanut butter here. The butter should be about 67 degrees and give slightly when pressed; it should not be so warm that it loses its shape. The chocolate is divided here, so if you don't have a scale, note that each Ghirardelli bar weighs 4 ounces. You will need 32 toothpicks for this recipe.

- 1 cup creamy peanut butter
- 8 tablespoons unsalted butter, cut into 8 pieces, softened but still cold
- ¼ teaspoon table salt
- 2½ cups (10 ounces) confectioners' sugar
- 12 ounces bittersweet chocolate, chopped fine, divided

1. Using stand mixer fitted with paddle, mix peanut butter, butter, and salt on medium speed until mixture is nearly combined with some visible pieces of butter remaining, about 30 seconds. Reduce speed to low and slowly add sugar. Mix until just combined, scraping down bowl as needed. Refrigerate for 15 minutes.

2. Line 2 large plates with parchment paper. Divide dough into 32 pieces (about 1 tablespoon each). Using your hands, gently roll dough into balls and transfer to prepared plates. Insert 1 toothpick three-quarters of the way into each ball. Freeze balls until firm, about 1 hour.

3. Microwave 10 ounces chocolate in 4-cup liquid measuring cup at 50 percent power, stirring with rubber spatula every 30 seconds, until nearly melted, 2 to 3 minutes (chocolate should still be slightly lumpy). Remove measuring cup from microwave and stir in remaining 2 ounces chocolate until melted and smooth.

4. Tilt measuring cup slightly so chocolate pools on 1 side. Working with 1 plate of balls at a time (keeping second plate in freezer), grasp toothpicks and dip balls in chocolate until covered by two-thirds. Return balls to prepared plate. Refrigerate balls, uncovered, until chocolate is set and dough is no longer frozen, about 30 minutes.

5. Remove toothpicks and serve. (Buckeyes can be refrigerated for up to 1 week.)

Coating the Balls

1. Using your hands, gently roll dough into balls and transfer to prepared plates. Insert 1 toothpick three-quarters of the way into each ball. Freeze balls until firm, about 1 hour.

2. While tilting measuring cup slightly so melted chocolate pools on 1 side, grasp ends of toothpicks and dip balls into melted chocolate until covered by two-thirds. Return dipped balls to the prepared plate.

Chocolate Fudge
MAKES ABOUT 3 POUNDS

WHY THIS RECIPE WORKS This creamy, rich fudge doesn't take hours or an arm workout to put together. Cooking a brown sugar syrup to what candymakers call the "softball stage" ensured fudge that was firm yet pliable after cooling. The brown sugar offered a deep, caramelly flavor that enhanced the chocolate. We stirred marshmallows into the hot brown sugar syrup for a smooth, melt-in-your-mouth texture. Bittersweet, rather than milk or unsweetened, chocolate struck the perfect balance— still sweet enough to taste like candy but also deeply and satisfyingly chocolaty.

You will need a digital or candy thermometer for this recipe. We developed this recipe using Kraft Jet-Puffed Marshmallows. With this brand, 21 marshmallows yield 5 ounces. Be sure to use evaporated milk here, not sweetened condensed milk. We developed this recipe using Ghirardelli 60% Cacao Bittersweet Chocolate Premium Baking Bar. You can substitute semisweet chocolate bars or bars labeled "dark chocolate," but we do not recommend using chocolate that's 85 percent cacao or higher. If you're using an electric stove, the mixture will likely take longer than 5 minutes to reach 234 degrees in step 2.

- 3 cups packed (21 ounces) light brown sugar
- 12 tablespoons unsalted butter, cut into 12 pieces
- ⅔ cup evaporated milk
- ½ teaspoon table salt
- 12 ounces bittersweet chocolate, chopped
- 5 ounces large marshmallows (about 3 cups)
- 1½ cups walnuts, toasted and chopped coarse (optional)

1. Make foil sling for 8-inch square baking pan by folding 2 long sheets of aluminum foil so each is 8 inches wide. Lay sheets of foil in pan perpendicular to each other, with extra foil hanging over edges of pan. Push foil into corners and up sides of pan, smoothing foil flush to pan. Spray foil with vegetable oil spray.

2. Combine sugar, butter, evaporated milk, and salt in large saucepan. Bring to boil over medium-high heat, stirring frequently. Once boiling, reduce heat to medium-low and simmer, stirring frequently, until mixture registers 234 degrees, 3 to 5 minutes.

3. Off heat, add chocolate and marshmallows and whisk until smooth and all marshmallows are fully melted, about 2 minutes (fudge will thicken to consistency of frosting). Stir in walnuts, if using. Transfer mixture to prepared pan. Let cool completely, about 2 hours. Cover and refrigerate until set, about 2 hours.

4. Using foil overhang, lift fudge out of pan. Cut into 1-inch cubes. Let sit at room temperature for 15 minutes before serving. (Fudge can be stored in airtight container at room temperature for up to 2 weeks.)

Chocolate-Peppermint Fudge
Omit walnuts. Add 1 teaspoon peppermint extract with chocolate and marshmallows in step 3. After transferring fudge to prepared pan, sprinkle with ¼ cup crushed soft peppermint candies before letting fudge cool.

Chocolate-Toffee Fudge

Omit walnuts. Add 1½ tablespoons instant espresso powder with chocolate and marshmallows in step 3. Stir ¼ cup Heath Toffee Bits into fudge before transferring to prepared pan. After transferring fudge to prepared pan, sprinkle with additional ¼ cup toffee bits before letting fudge cool.

> ### Easy Removal
> In many of our baking recipes, we call for lining the pan with overlapping sheets of aluminum foil to create a "sling" that discourages sticking and aids in lifting.
>
>
>
> To create a sling, simply overlap two long sheets of aluminum foil in an 8-inch square pan.

Vanilla No-Churn Ice Cream

SERVES 8 TO 10 (MAKES ABOUT 1 QUART)

WHY THIS RECIPE WORKS We found an easy way to ditch the ice cream maker by whipping cream in a blender. The air in the whipped cream stood in for the air normally incorporated by churning. Using two liquid sweeteners—sweetened condensed milk and corn syrup—kept the ice cream soft and scoopable. A hefty tablespoon of vanilla extract and a bit of salt (to enhance the flavor) produced an intensely flavored vanilla ice cream.

The cream mixture freezes more quickly in a loaf pan than in a taller, narrower container. If you don't have a loaf pan, use an 8-inch square baking pan.

- 2 cups heavy cream, chilled
- 1 cup sweetened condensed milk
- ¼ cup whole milk
- ¼ cup light corn syrup
- 2 tablespoons sugar
- 1 tablespoon vanilla extract
- ¼ teaspoon table salt

1. Process cream in blender until soft peaks form, 20 to 30 seconds. Scrape down sides of blender jar and continue to process until stiff peaks form, about 10 seconds longer. Using rubber spatula, stir in condensed milk, whole milk, corn syrup, sugar, vanilla, and salt. Process until thoroughly combined, about 20 seconds, scraping down sides of blender jar as needed.

2. Pour cream mixture into 8½ by 4½-inch loaf pan. Press plastic wrap flush against surface of cream mixture. Freeze until firm, at least 6 hours. Serve.

Birthday Cake

Decrease vanilla to 2 teaspoons. Add ½ cup store-bought vanilla frosting and ⅛ teaspoon yellow food coloring with condensed milk. After transferring cream mixture to loaf pan, gently stir in 2 tablespoons rainbow sprinkles before freezing.

Banana-Walnut–Chocolate Chunk
Omit vanilla. Add 2 very ripe bananas with condensed milk. After transferring cream mixture to loaf pan, gently stir in ¼ cup chopped toasted walnuts and ¼ cup coarsely chopped bittersweet chocolate before freezing.

Milk Chocolate
Decrease vanilla to 1 teaspoon. Add 6 ounces melted milk chocolate with condensed milk.

Peach Cobbler
Omit sugar. Substitute bourbon for vanilla. Add ½ cup peach preserves and ¼ teaspoon ground cinnamon with condensed milk in step 1. After transferring cream mixture to loaf pan, gently stir in ½ cup coarsely chopped shortbread cookies before freezing.

Salted Caramel–Coconut
Decrease vanilla to 1 teaspoon. Increase salt to ½ teaspoon. Substitute caramel sauce for corn syrup. After transferring cream mixture to loaf pan, gently stir in ¼ cup toasted sweetened shredded coconut. Dollop additional ⅓ cup caramel sauce over top and swirl into cream mixture using tines of fork before freezing.

Mint-Cookie
Substitute ¾ teaspoon peppermint extract for vanilla. Add ⅛ teaspoon green food coloring with condensed milk. After transferring cream mixture to loaf pan, gently stir in ½ cup coarsely crushed Oreo cookies before freezing.

Key Lime
Omit vanilla. Substitute buttermilk for whole milk. Add ½ cup limeade concentrate with condensed milk. After transferring cream mixture to loaf pan, gently stir in ½ cup coarsely chopped graham crackers before freezing.

Dark Chocolate
Decrease vanilla to 1 teaspoon. Add 6 ounces melted bittersweet chocolate and ½ teaspoon instant espresso powder with condensed milk.

No-Churn Ice Cream

Strawberry-Buttermilk
Substitute ½ cup buttermilk for whole milk and 1 teaspoon lemon juice for vanilla. After transferring cream mixture to loaf pan, dollop ⅓ cup strawberry jam over top. Swirl jam into cream mixture using tines of fork before freezing.

Peanut Butter Cup
Omit vanilla. Add ½ cup creamy peanut butter with condensed milk. After transferring cream mixture to loaf pan, gently stir in ½ cup coarsely chopped peanut butter cups before freezing.

Malted Milk Chocolate
Decrease vanilla to 1 teaspoon. Add 6 ounces melted milk chocolate and 6 tablespoons malted milk powder with condensed milk.

old-fashioned fruit desserts and puddings

652 Baked Apple Dumplings
653 Apple Fritters
654 Apple Pandowdy
655 Tarte Tatin
656 Cranberry-Apple Crisp
657 Mixed Berry Buckle
659 Maine Blueberry Grunt

660 Easy Blueberry Cobbler
661 Skillet Peach Cobbler
661 Dakota Peach Kuchen
663 Banana Pudding
664 New Orleans Bourbon Bread Pudding
665 Summer Berry Pudding
666 Old-Fashioned Vanilla Frozen Custard

Recipe Photos (left to right): Tarte Tatin, Cranberry-Apple Crisp

Baked Apple Dumplings

MAKES 8 DUMPLINGS

WHY THIS RECIPE WORKS Apple dumplings are a homespun combination of warm pastry, concentrated apple flavor, raisins, butter, and cinnamon, but too often the apples turn too soft or are unevenly baked. The pastry can also turn gummy from the apples' juices. We found that biscuit dough was easier to work with than pie dough and did a great job of absorbing the liquid from the apples without getting mushy. Rather than baking the dumplings in syrup as some recipes instruct, we served our sauce on the side, which preserved the dumplings' texture.

Use a melon baller or a metal teaspoon measure to core the apples. Serve warm, with Cider Sauce (recipe follows).

Dough
- 2½ cups (12½ ounces) all-purpose flour
- 3 tablespoons sugar
- 2 teaspoons baking powder
- ¾ teaspoon table salt
- 10 tablespoons unsalted butter, cut into ½-inch pieces and chilled
- 5 tablespoons vegetable shortening, cut into ½-inch pieces and chilled
- ¾ cup cold buttermilk

Apple Dumplings
- 6 tablespoons (2⅔ ounces) sugar
- 1 teaspoon ground cinnamon
- 3 tablespoons unsalted butter, softened
- 3 tablespoons golden raisins, chopped
- 4 Golden Delicious apples
- 2 egg whites, lightly beaten

1. For the Dough Process flour, sugar, baking powder, and salt in food processor until combined, about 15 seconds. Scatter butter and shortening over flour mixture and pulse until mixture resembles wet sand, about 10 pulses; transfer to bowl. Stir in buttermilk until dough forms. Turn out onto lightly floured work surface and knead briefly until dough is cohesive. Press dough into 8 by 4-inch rectangle. Cut in half, wrap each half tightly in plastic wrap, and refrigerate until firm, about 1 hour.

2. For the Apple Dumplings Adjust oven rack to middle position and heat oven to 425 degrees. Combine sugar and cinnamon in small bowl. In second bowl, combine butter, raisins, and 3 tablespoons cinnamon sugar mixture. Peel apples and halve crosswise. Remove core and pack butter mixture into each apple half.

3. On lightly floured counter, roll each dough half into 12-inch square. Cut each 12-inch square into four 6-inch squares. Working with one at a time, lightly brush edges of dough square with egg white and place apple, cut side up, in center of each square. Gather dough, 1 corner at a time, on top of apple, crimping edges to seal. Using paring knife, cut vent hole in top of each dumpling.

4. Line rimmed baking sheet with parchment paper. Arrange dumplings on prepared baking sheet, brush tops with egg white, and sprinkle with remaining cinnamon sugar. Bake until dough is golden brown and juices are bubbling, 20 to 25 minutes. Let cool on baking sheet for 10 minutes. Serve.

Cider Sauce
MAKES ABOUT 1½ CUPS

- 1 cup apple cider
- 1 cup water
- 1 cup (7 ounces) sugar
- ½ teaspoon ground cinnamon
- 2 tablespoons unsalted butter
- 1 tablespoon lemon juice

Bring cider, water, sugar, and cinnamon to simmer in small saucepan and cook over medium-high heat until thickened and reduced to 1½ cups, about 15 minutes. Off heat, whisk in butter and lemon juice. Drizzle over dumplings to serve.

Wrapping Dumplings

1. Fold corners of dough up to enclose apple halves, overlapping and crimping to seal.

2. Arrange dumplings on baking sheet, brush with egg white, and sprinkle with cinnamon sugar.

Apple Fritters

MAKES 10 FRITTERS

WHY THIS RECIPE WORKS Apple fritters should be crisp on the outside, moist within, and sing out apple flavor. Too often, recipes for fritters produce leaden, soggy pastries with undercooked interiors. We found that the best solution was to dry the apples with paper towels and mix them with the dry ingredients. The dry ingredients absorbed the moisture that would otherwise have leached out during frying. As for the batter, we found that replacing the milk with apple cider reinforced the sweet apple flavor. And a quick glaze, spiked with more cider and warm spices and spooned over the warm fritters, added another layer of apple flavor.

We like Granny Smith apples in these fritters because they are tart and crisp. Apple juice doesn't have enough flavor—you really do need the cider.

Fritters

- 2 Granny Smith apples, peeled, cored, and cut into ¼-inch pieces
- 2 cups (10 ounces) all-purpose flour
- ⅓ cup (2⅓ ounces) granulated sugar
- 1 tablespoon baking powder
- 1 teaspoon table salt
- 1 teaspoon ground cinnamon
- ¼ teaspoon ground nutmeg
- ¾ cup apple cider
- 2 large eggs, lightly beaten
- 2 tablespoons unsalted butter, melted
- 3 cups peanut or vegetable oil for frying

Glaze

- 2 cups (8 ounces) confectioners' sugar
- ¼ cup apple cider
- ½ teaspoon ground cinnamon
- ¼ teaspoon ground nutmeg

1. For the Fritters Spread prepared apples in single layer on paper towel–lined baking sheet and pat thoroughly dry with paper towels. Combine flour, sugar, baking powder, salt, cinnamon, and nutmeg in large bowl. Whisk cider, eggs, and melted butter in medium bowl until combined. Stir apples into flour mixture. Stir in cider mixture until incorporated.

Baked Apple Dumplings

Apple Fritters

2. Set wire rack in rimmed baking sheet. Heat oil in Dutch oven over medium-high heat to 350 degrees. Use ⅓-cup measure to transfer 5 heaping portions of batter to oil. Press batter lightly with back of spoon to flatten. Fry, adjusting burner as necessary to maintain oil temperature between 325 and 350 degrees, until deep golden brown, 2 to 3 minutes per side. Transfer fritters to prepared wire rack. Bring oil back to 350 degrees and repeat with remaining batter. Let fritters cool for 5 minutes.

3. For the Glaze While fritters cool, whisk sugar, cider, cinnamon, and nutmeg in medium bowl until smooth. Top each fritter with 1 heaping tablespoon glaze. Let glaze set for 10 minutes. Serve.

Apple Pandowdy

SERVES 6

WHY THIS RECIPE WORKS Unlike traditional skillet pie, apple pandowdy's crust is gently pressed into the filling (or "dowdied") during baking so the juices flood the top and caramelize in the oven. We tossed wedges of buttery Golden Delicious apples in cinnamon and brown sugar for sweet-spiced flavor and partially cooked them before simmering in an apple cider–lemon juice slurry to thicken the filling. Topping the apples with squares of dough allowed steam to escape during baking, preventing the apples from overcooking. Dowdying the crust partway through created the dessert's sweet finish.

Disturbing the crust, or "dowdying," allows juices from the filling to rise over the crust and caramelize as the dessert continues to bake. Removing the skillet from the oven allows you to properly press down on the crust. Do not use store-bought pie crust in this recipe; it yields gummy results.

Pie Dough
- 3 tablespoons ice water
- 1 tablespoon sour cream
- ⅔ cup (3⅓ ounces) all-purpose flour
- 1 teaspoon granulated sugar
- ½ teaspoon table salt
- 6 tablespoons unsalted butter, cut into ¼-inch pieces and frozen for 15 minutes

Filling
- 2½ pounds Golden Delicious apples, peeled, cored, halved, and cut into ½-inch-thick wedges
- ¼ cup packed (1¾ ounces) light brown sugar
- ½ teaspoon ground cinnamon
- ¼ teaspoon table salt
- 3 tablespoons unsalted butter
- ¾ cup apple cider
- 1 tablespoon cornstarch
- 2 teaspoons lemon juice

Topping
- 1 tablespoon granulated sugar
- ¼ teaspoon ground cinnamon
- 1 large egg, lightly beaten

Vanilla ice cream

1. For the Pie Dough Combine ice water and sour cream in bowl. Process flour, sugar, and salt in food processor until combined, about 3 seconds. Add butter and pulse until size of large peas, 6 to 8 pulses. Add sour cream mixture and pulse until dough forms large clumps and no dry flour remains, 3 to 6 pulses, scraping down sides of bowl as needed.

2. Form dough into 4-inch disk, wrap tightly in plastic wrap, and refrigerate for 1 hour. (Wrapped dough can be refrigerated for up to 2 days or frozen for up to 1 month. If frozen, let dough thaw completely on counter before rolling.)

3. Adjust oven rack to middle position and heat oven to 400 degrees. Let chilled dough sit on counter to soften slightly, about 5 minutes, before rolling. Roll dough into 10-inch circle on lightly floured counter. Using pizza cutter, cut dough into four 2½-inch-wide strips, then make four 2½-inch-wide perpendicular cuts to form squares. (Pieces around edges of dough will be smaller.) Transfer dough pieces to parchment paper–lined baking sheet, cover with plastic, and refrigerate until firm, at least 30 minutes.

4. For the Filling Toss apples, sugar, cinnamon, and salt together in large bowl. Melt butter in 10-inch skillet over medium heat. Add apple mixture, cover, and cook until apples become slightly pliable and release their juices, about 10 minutes, stirring occasionally.

Apple Pandowdy

5. Whisk cider, cornstarch, and lemon juice in bowl until no lumps remain; add to skillet. Bring to simmer and cook, uncovered, stirring occasionally, until sauce is thickened, about 2 minutes. Off heat, press lightly on apples to form even layer.

6. **For the Topping** Combine sugar and cinnamon in small bowl. Working quickly, shingle dough pieces over filling until mostly covered, overlapping as needed. Brush dough pieces with egg and sprinkle with cinnamon sugar.

7. Bake until crust is slightly puffed and beginning to brown, about 15 minutes. Remove skillet from oven. Using back of large spoon, press down in center of crust until juices come up over top of crust. Repeat four more times around skillet. Make sure all apples are submerged and return skillet to oven. Continue to bake until crust is golden brown, about 15 minutes longer.

8. Transfer skillet to wire rack and let cool for at least 20 minutes. Serve with ice cream, drizzling extra sauce over top.

Tarte Tatin

SERVES 6 TO 8

WHY THIS RECIPE WORKS Tarte Tatin is a French upside-down caramelized apple tart. We were after a version that boasted big chunks of juicy apples glazed with a sticky, buttery caramel sitting atop a flaky crust. We started with an all-butter pie dough, which we rolled out immediately and then let rest in the refrigerator. We parcooked apples on the stovetop to drive off moisture and prevent the finished tart from being too liquid-y. Using a separate saucepan to cook the caramel (instead of making the caramel in the skillet with the apples) gave us greater control over the final color of the caramel and the texture of the apples. Letting the baked tart cool for a bit in the skillet ensured safe and easy flipping.

We like Gala or Golden Delicious apples here because they retain their shape and provide mild sweetness. If your apples are on the large side, you may have one or two pieces that won't fit. Serve with vanilla ice cream, if desired.

Dough
- 1 cup (5 ounces) all-purpose flour
- 2 teaspoons sugar
- ½ teaspoon table salt
- 8 tablespoons unsalted butter, cut into ½-inch pieces and chilled
- ¼ cup ice water

Filling
- 4 tablespoons unsalted butter, cut into 1-tablespoon pieces, divided
- 5 Gala or Golden Delicious apples (6 to 7 ounces each), peeled, quartered, and cored
- ¼ teaspoon table salt
- ¾ cup (5¼ ounces) sugar
- ¼ cup water
- 2 tablespoons light corn syrup

1. **For the Dough** Line large, flat plate with parchment paper. Process flour, sugar, and salt in food processor until combined, about 3 seconds. Scatter butter over top and pulse until irregular, large chunks of butter form with some small pieces throughout, about 5 pulses. Add ice water and process until little balls of dough form and almost no dry flour remains, about 10 seconds, scraping down sides of bowl after 5 seconds.

OLD-FASHIONED FRUIT DESSERTS AND PUDDINGS 655

2. Turn out dough onto clean counter and gather into ball. Sprinkle dough and counter generously with flour and shape dough into 5-inch disk, pressing any cracked edges back together. Roll dough into 9-inch circle, reflouring counter and dough as needed. Loosely roll dough around rolling pin and gently unroll it onto prepared plate. Cut three 2-inch slits in center of dough. Cover dough loosely with plastic wrap and refrigerate until dough is very firm, at least 2 hours or up to 2 days.

3. For the Filling After dough has chilled for at least 2 hours, adjust oven rack to middle position and heat oven to 350 degrees.

4. Melt 1 tablespoon butter in 10-inch ovensafe nonstick skillet over medium-low heat. Off heat, arrange apple quarters on their sides in melted butter in circular pattern around edge of skillet, nestling fruit snugly. Tuck remaining apples into center (it is not necessary to maintain circular pattern in center). Sprinkle salt over apples.

5. Cover and cook over medium-low heat until apples have released enough juice to cover bottom of skillet and juice just begins to reduce, 10 to 15 minutes. Uncover and continue to cook until liquid has mostly evaporated, 3 to 5 minutes longer (apples may brown on undersides). Remove skillet from heat and set aside.

6. Bring sugar, water, and corn syrup to boil in large heavy-bottomed saucepan over medium-high heat. Cook, without stirring, until mixture begins to turn straw-colored around edge of saucepan, 4 to 8 minutes. Reduce heat to medium-low and continue to cook, swirling saucepan occasionally, until mixture is light amber–colored and registers 355 to 360 degrees, 2 to 5 minutes longer. (To take temperature, remove saucepan from heat and tilt to 1 side; stir with thermometer to equalize hotter and cooler spots, avoiding bottom of saucepan.)

7. Off heat, carefully stir in remaining 3 tablespoons butter (mixture will bubble and steam). Working quickly, pour caramel over apples (caramel will not completely cover apples). Place dough over apples.

8. Bake tart until thick, syrupy bubbles form around edge and crust is golden brown, 50 minutes to 1 hour. Transfer skillet to wire rack and let sit until cool enough to handle, 20 to 30 minutes.

9. Run thin rubber spatula or plastic knife around edge of skillet to loosen tart. Invert large serving platter over skillet (make sure platter is larger than skillet and has sloped sides to catch any excess caramel). Swiftly and carefully invert tart onto platter (if apples shift or stick to skillet, rearrange with spoon). Cut into wedges and serve warm or at room temperature.

To Make Ahead Let baked tart cool completely in skillet. Cover and refrigerate for up to 24 hours. To serve, reheat tart in 300-degree oven until hot, about 25 minutes, then cool and invert.

A Slice of History

Tarte Tatin was created by sisters Stéphanie and Caroline Tatin at the hotel they ran in Lamotte-Beuvron, France, in the 1880s. It is fabled that Stéphanie created the tart by accident. Stories vary: Her apples got too dark, the tart was assembled upside down, she dropped it . . .

Patrons enjoyed the tart, but the Tatin sisters didn't put tarte Tatin on the menu nor publish the recipe. The dish as we know it was popularized in the 1930s at the Parisian restaurant Maxim's, where it is still served today.

Cranberry-Apple Crisp

SERVES 8 TO 10

WHY THIS RECIPE WORKS Although it's hard to imagine that apple crisp needs much improving upon, we liked the tartness and texture that cranberries added to one of our favorite standard dessert recipes. Raw cranberries proved too bitter, but we found that dried cranberries and cooked fresh berries made cranberry-apple crisp with the best taste and texture. And we used tapioca to thicken the fruit juices instead of cornstarch or flour.

656 *The Complete Cook's Country TV Show Cookbook*

If you can't find Braeburn apples, Golden Delicious will work. Serve with vanilla ice cream or whipped cream.

Topping
- ¾ cup (3¾ ounces) all-purpose flour
- ½ cup packed (3½ ounces) light brown sugar
- ½ cup (3½ ounces) granulated sugar
- 1 teaspoon ground cinnamon
- 12 tablespoons unsalted butter, cut into ½-inch pieces and chilled
- ¾ cup (2¼ ounces) old-fashioned rolled oats

Filling
- 1 pound (4 cups) fresh or frozen cranberries
- 1¼ cups (8¾ ounces) granulated sugar, divided
- ¼ cup water
- 2½ pounds Granny Smith apples, peeled, cored, halved, and cut into ½-inch pieces
- 2½ pounds Braeburn apples, peeled, cored, halved, and cut into ½-inch pieces
- 1 cup dried sweetened cranberries
- 3 tablespoons instant tapioca

1. For the Topping Adjust oven rack to middle position and heat oven to 400 degrees. Pulse flour, brown sugar, granulated sugar, cinnamon, and butter in food processor until mixture has texture of coarse crumbs (some pea-size pieces of butter will remain), about 12 pulses. Transfer to medium bowl, stir in oats, and use fingers to pinch topping into peanut-size clumps. Refrigerate while preparing filling.

2. For the Filling Bring fresh cranberries, ¾ cup sugar, and water to simmer in Dutch oven over medium-high heat and cook until cranberries are completely softened and mixture is jamlike, about 10 minutes. Scrape mixture into bowl. Add apples, remaining ½ cup sugar, and dried cranberries to now-empty Dutch oven and cook over medium-high heat until apples begin to release their juices, about 5 minutes.

3. Off heat, stir cranberry mixture and tapioca into apple mixture. Pour into 13 by 9-inch baking dish set in rimmed baking sheet and smooth surface evenly with spatula.

4. Mound topping over filling in center of dish, then use your fingers to rake topping out toward edges of dish. Bake until juices are bubbling and topping is deep golden brown, about 30 minutes. (If topping is browning too quickly, loosely cover with piece of aluminum foil.) Let cool on wire rack for 10 minutes. Serve.

Cranberry-Apple Crisp

To Make Ahead After pinching topping into small clumps in step 1, transfer mixture to zipper-lock bag and refrigerate for up to 5 days or freeze for up to 1 month. The cooked filling can be refrigerated for up to 2 days. To bake, sprinkle chilled topping evenly over chilled filling, loosely cover with foil, and bake for 20 minutes. Uncover and bake until juices are bubbling and topping is deep golden brown, 15 to 20 minutes longer.

Mixed Berry Buckle

SERVES 8

WHY THIS RECIPE WORKS A buckle, cousin to crumble and crisp, is a classic New England dessert that consists of a thick cake batter mixed with fruit and baked under a crunchy streusel topping. Using peak-season berries allowed us to make the most of their flavor. Tossing them with sugar helped bring out their natural sweetness while a

OLD-FASHIONED FRUIT DESSERTS AND PUDDINGS

bit of lemon zest added punch. We packed as many berries as we could into our batter and then sprinkled the rest on top. When baked, the dense, buttery cake suspended the berries, creating a luscious, summery dessert.

We prefer the flavor of fresh mixed berries, but you can also use a single variety of berries as long as the total amount equals 15 ounces (3 cups). If using all fresh blueberries, omit the 1/4 cup sugar for tossing the berries in step 4; blueberries are sweet on their own. You can also use 15 ounces (3 cups) of frozen mixed berries that have been thawed, drained for 30 minutes in a colander, and then patted dry.

Streusel
- 1 cup (5 ounces) all-purpose flour
- 1/2 cup packed (3 1/2 ounces) light brown sugar
- 6 tablespoons unsalted butter, melted
- 1/2 teaspoon table salt

Cake
- 1/2 cup whole milk
- 2 large eggs
- 4 tablespoons unsalted butter, melted
- 1 teaspoon vanilla extract
- 1 cup (5 ounces) all-purpose flour
- 1/2 cup (3 1/2 ounces) granulated sugar, divided
- 1 1/2 teaspoons baking powder
- 1 teaspoon grated lemon zest
- 1/2 teaspoon table salt
- 5 ounces (1 cup) blackberries, cut in half crosswise
- 5 ounces (1 cup) blueberries
- 5 ounces (1 cup) raspberries, cut in half crosswise

1. For the Streusel Stir all ingredients in bowl until no dry spots remain and mixture forms clumps. Refrigerate until streusel is firm, at least 10 minutes. Keep refrigerated until ready to use.

2. For the Cake Adjust oven rack to middle position and heat oven to 350 degrees. Grease light-colored 9-inch round cake pan, line with parchment paper, grease parchment, and flour pan.

3. Whisk milk, eggs, melted butter, and vanilla in bowl until well combined. Whisk flour, 1/4 cup sugar, baking powder, lemon zest, and salt together in large bowl. Stir milk mixture into flour mixture until just combined.

4. Toss blackberries, blueberries, and raspberries with remaining 1/4 cup sugar in separate bowl until coated. Using rubber spatula, gently fold half of berry mixture into batter until evenly distributed. Transfer batter to prepared pan and spread to edges of pan with spatula. Sprinkle remaining half of berry mixture evenly over top.

5. Break streusel into pea-size crumbs and distribute evenly over berries. Bake until top of buckle is golden brown and toothpick inserted in center comes out clean, about 50 minutes, rotating pan halfway through baking. Let buckle cool in pan on wire rack for 2 hours.

6. Run paring knife around edges of pan to release buckle from pan. Place inverted plate on top of pan (do not use plate or platter on which you intend to serve buckle). Invert buckle, remove pan, and discard parchment. Reinvert buckle onto serving platter. Cut into wedges and serve.

Berry Important Stuff
How you treat the berries can make or break your buckle.

1. Cut blackberries and raspberries in half crosswise. Toss with blueberries and sugar.

2. Fold half of sugared berries into batter.

3. Sprinkle remaining berries on top of batter before baking.

Maine Blueberry Grunt

SERVES 12

Mixed Berry Buckle

WHY THIS RECIPE WORKS This 19th-century fruit dessert boasts sweetened stewed berries topped with drop biscuit dough that is covered to let it steam and cook through. For our version of this simple stovetop fruit dessert, we cooked down half of the berries until jammy, and then stirred in the remaining berries. A bit of cornstarch further thickened the filling. For a fluffy biscuit topping, we placed a dish towel under the lid during cooking to absorb condensation. A sprinkle of cinnamon sugar over the finished dessert provided sweet crunch.

Do not use frozen blueberries here, as they will make the filling watery. You will need a clean dish towel for this recipe.

Filling
- 2½ pounds (8 cups) blueberries, divided
- ½ cup (3½ ounces) sugar
- ½ teaspoon ground cinnamon
- 2 tablespoons water
- 1 teaspoon grated lemon zest plus 1 tablespoon juice
- 1 teaspoon cornstarch

Topping
- ¾ cup buttermilk
- 6 tablespoons unsalted butter, melted and cooled slightly
- 1 teaspoon vanilla extract
- 2¼ cups (11¼ ounces) all-purpose flour
- 1½ teaspoons baking powder
- ½ teaspoon baking soda
- ½ teaspoon table salt
- ½ cup (3½ ounces) sugar, divided
- ½ teaspoon ground cinnamon

1. For the Filling Cook 4 cups blueberries, sugar, cinnamon, water, and lemon zest in Dutch oven over medium-high heat, stirring occasionally, until mixture is thick and jamlike, 10 to 12 minutes. Whisk lemon juice and cornstarch in small bowl, then stir into blueberry mixture. Add remaining 4 cups blueberries and cook until heated through, about 1 minute; remove pot from heat, cover, and keep warm.

Maine Blueberry Grunt

Easy Blueberry Cobbler

Skillet Peach Cobbler

2. For the Topping Combine buttermilk, butter, and vanilla in 2-cup liquid measuring cup. Whisk flour, baking powder, baking soda, salt, and 6 tablespoons sugar in large bowl. Slowly stir buttermilk mixture into flour mixture until dough forms.

3. Using small ice cream scoop or 2 large spoons, spoon golf ball–size dough pieces on top of warm berry mixture (you should have 14 pieces). Wrap lid of Dutch oven with clean dish towel (keeping towel away from heat source) and cover pot. Simmer gently until biscuits have doubled in size and toothpick inserted in center comes out clean, 16 to 22 minutes.

4. Combine remaining 2 tablespoons sugar and cinnamon in small bowl. Remove lid and sprinkle biscuit topping with cinnamon sugar. Serve immediately.

Easy Blueberry Cobbler

SERVES 8 TO 10

WHY THIS RECIPE WORKS Many cobbler recipes call for numerous ingredients, multiple components, and many steps. To streamline this version, we replaced four of the standard ingredients—flour, salt, baking soda, and some of the sugar—with self-rising flour and sweetened condensed milk. Self-rising flour is simply flour with leavener and salt added. Sweetened condensed milk, which contains added sugar, is cooked down to eliminate water, making it thick and resistant to curdling. This switch shortened the ingredient list and also the prep time. We just whisked together the batter ingredients, poured the batter into a prepared baking dish, and sprinkled the berries and sugar (to help with browning) over the batter.

Serve with vanilla ice cream.

- 1 (14-ounce) can sweetened condensed milk
- 1¼ cups (6 ounces) self-rising flour
- ½ cup whole milk
- 8 tablespoons unsalted butter, melted
- 10 ounces (2 cups) blueberries
- ¼ cup (1¾ ounces) sugar

1. Adjust oven rack to middle position and heat oven to 350 degrees. Grease 13 by 9-inch baking dish. Whisk condensed milk, flour, milk, and melted butter together in bowl. Pour batter into prepared baking dish. Sprinkle blueberries and sugar evenly over surface.

2. Bake until deep golden brown and toothpick inserted in center comes out clean, about 35 minutes. Transfer cobbler to wire rack; let cool for 10 minutes. Serve warm.

Skillet Peach Cobbler

SERVES 6 TO 8

WHY THIS RECIPE WORKS We wanted a peach cobbler that avoided a watery filling and soggy topping. To do this, we turned to a skillet and concentrated the peach flavor by first sautéing the peaches in butter and sugar to release their juices, then cooking them down until all the liquid had evaporated. To keep the filling from being too mushy, we withheld some of the peaches from sautéing, adding them just before baking. We also made the biscuits sturdy enough to stand up to the fruit by mixing melted butter rather than cold butter into the dry ingredients.

You can substitute 4 pounds of frozen sliced peaches for fresh; there is no need to defrost them. Start step 2 when the peaches are almost done.

Filling
- 4 tablespoons unsalted butter
- 5 pounds peaches, peeled, halved, pitted, and cut into ½-inch wedges, divided
- 6 tablespoons (2⅔ ounces) sugar
- ⅛ teaspoon table salt
- 1 tablespoon lemon juice
- 1½ teaspoons cornstarch

Topping
- 1½ cups (7½ ounces) all-purpose flour
- 6 tablespoons (2⅔ ounces) sugar, divided
- 1½ teaspoons baking powder
- ¼ teaspoon baking soda
- ¼ teaspoon table salt
- ¾ cup buttermilk
- 4 tablespoons unsalted butter, melted and cooled
- 1 teaspoon ground cinnamon

1. For the Filling Adjust oven rack to middle position and heat oven to 425 degrees. Melt butter in 12-inch ovensafe nonstick skillet over medium-high heat. Add two-thirds of peaches, sugar, and salt and cook, covered, until peaches release their juices, about 5 minutes. Remove lid and simmer until all liquid has evaporated and peaches begin to caramelize, 15 to 20 minutes. Add remaining peaches and cook until heated through, about 5 minutes. Whisk lemon juice and cornstarch in small bowl, then stir into peach mixture. Cover skillet and set aside off heat.

2. For the Topping Meanwhile, whisk flour, 5 tablespoons sugar, baking powder, baking soda, and salt in medium bowl. Stir in buttermilk and butter until dough forms. Turn dough out onto lightly floured work surface and knead briefly until smooth, about 30 seconds.

3. Combine remaining 1 tablespoon sugar and cinnamon. Break dough into rough 1-inch pieces and space them about ½ inch apart on top of hot peach mixture. Sprinkle with cinnamon sugar and bake until topping is golden brown and filling is thickened, 18 to 22 minutes. Let cool on wire rack for 10 minutes. Serve.

Dakota Peach Kuchen

MAKES TWO 9-INCH KUCHENS

WHY THIS RECIPE WORKS Kuchen, the official state dessert of South Dakota, features a tender yeasted dough, peaches full of flavor, and a layer of smooth, delicately sweet custard. We created a buttery crust by slowly adding softened butter to the dough, letting the dough rise and then rest in the fridge. An extra egg yolk made our custard thick and rich, without the eggy flavor found in egg whites. Finally, to ready the peaches, we sprinkled them with sugar and let them sit in a colander to pull out their excess juice and prevent the kuchen from becoming soggy. This dessert might come from South Dakota, but it felt right at home in our kitchen.

The dough will need 2 hours to rise plus 1 hour to chill in the refrigerator. We developed this recipe using dark cake pans; if your pans are light, increase the baking time in step 7 to 55 to 60 minutes.

Crust

- ½ cup whole milk
- 2 large eggs
- 2½ cups (12½ ounces) all-purpose flour
- 1 tablespoon sugar
- 2 teaspoons instant or rapid-rise yeast
- ½ teaspoon table salt
- 8 tablespoons unsalted butter, cut into 8 pieces and softened

Fruit and Custard

- 1 pound fresh peaches, peeled, halved, pitted, and cut into ½-inch wedges or 12 ounces frozen sliced peaches, thawed
- 2 tablespoons plus ¾ cup (5¼ ounces) sugar, divided
- 1 large egg plus 1 large yolk
- ¼ teaspoon table salt
- 1¼ cups heavy cream
- 4 tablespoons unsalted butter, cut into 4 pieces
- ½ teaspoon vanilla extract
- ¼ teaspoon ground cinnamon

1. For the Crust Grease large bowl. Whisk milk and eggs in 2-cup liquid measuring cup until combined. Using stand mixer fitted with dough hook, mix flour, sugar, yeast, and salt on medium-low speed until combined, about 5 seconds. With mixer running, slowly add milk mixture and knead until dough forms, about 1 minute.

2. With mixer still running, add butter 1 piece at a time until incorporated. Continue kneading until dough clears sides of bowl but still sticks to bottom, 8 to 12 minutes (dough should be soft and sticky).

3. Transfer dough to greased bowl, cover with plastic wrap, and let rise on counter until doubled in size, about 1 hour. Punch down dough and divide into 2 equal balls. Wrap each ball in plastic, transfer to refrigerator, and let rest for at least 1 hour or up to 24 hours.

4. Grease 2 dark-colored 9-inch round cake pans. Roll each chilled dough ball into a 9-inch disk on lightly floured counter. Transfer to prepared pans, pushing dough to edges of pans. Cover pans loosely with plastic and let rise on counter until puffy, about 1 hour. Adjust oven rack to middle position and heat oven to 350 degrees.

5. For the Fruit and Custard Meanwhile, toss peaches with 2 tablespoons sugar in bowl, then transfer to colander set in sink; let sit for 25 minutes. Whisk remaining ¾ cup sugar, egg and yolk, and salt in medium bowl until combined. Heat cream in medium saucepan over medium heat until just beginning to simmer.

6. Slowly whisk hot cream into egg mixture. Transfer cream mixture back to saucepan and cook over medium-low heat, stirring constantly, until mixture thickens and coats back of spoon, 3 to 5 minutes. Strain custard through fine-mesh strainer set over medium bowl. Whisk in butter and vanilla and transfer to refrigerator to cool until dough is ready. (Custard can be made up to 24 hours in advance but does not need to be fully chilled before going into crust.)

7. Leaving 1-inch border all around, press down centers of doughs with bottom of dry measuring cup to deflate and create wells for peaches and custard. Arrange peaches, evenly spaced, in circular pattern in depressed dough, avoiding border. Pour custard evenly over peaches in each pan, about 1 cup per pan (you may have a few tablespoons extra). Sprinkle with cinnamon. Bake until crusts are golden brown and centers jiggle slightly when shaken, 35 to 40 minutes, switching and rotating pans halfway through baking. Let cool completely. Remove kuchens from pans using flexible spatula. Slice and serve.

Peeling Peaches

1. With paring knife, score small X at base of each peach.

2. Lower peaches into boiling water and simmer until skins loosen, 30 to 60 seconds.

3. Transfer peaches immediately to ice water and let cool for about 1 minute.

4. Use paring knife to remove strips of loosened peel, starting at X on base of each peach.

Banana Pudding

SERVES 12

WHY THIS RECIPE WORKS We wanted our banana pudding to be rich and creamy, so we opted for half-and-half instead of milk in the pudding component. Roasting the bananas intensified their flavor and helped break them down so we could incorporate them into the pudding. A squeeze of lemon juice on the bananas kept them from browning in the fridge. To prevent soggy cookies, we waited for the pudding to cool before assembling the dessert.

If your food processor bowl holds less than 11 cups, puree half the pudding with the roasted bananas and lemon juice in step 3, transfer it to a large bowl, and whisk in the rest of the pudding.

Pudding

- 7 slightly underripe large bananas (2½ pounds), unpeeled, divided
- 1½ cups (10½ ounces) sugar, divided
- 8 large egg yolks
- 6 tablespoons cornstarch
- 6 cups half-and-half
- ½ teaspoon table salt
- 3 tablespoons unsalted butter
- 1 tablespoon vanilla extract
- 3 tablespoons lemon juice, divided
- 1 (12-ounce) box vanilla wafers

Whipped Topping

- 1 cup heavy cream, chilled
- 1 tablespoon sugar
- ½ teaspoon vanilla extract

1. For the Pudding Adjust oven rack to upper-middle position and heat oven to 325 degrees. Place 3 unpeeled bananas on baking sheet and bake until skins are completely black, about 20 minutes. Let cool for 5 minutes.

2. Meanwhile, whisk ½ cup sugar, egg yolks, and cornstarch in medium bowl until smooth. Bring half-and-half, remaining 1 cup sugar, and salt to simmer over medium heat in large saucepan. Whisk ½ cup simmering half-and-half mixture into egg yolk mixture to temper. Slowly whisk tempered yolk mixture into saucepan. Cook, whisking constantly, until mixture is thick and large bubbles appear at surface, about 2 minutes. Remove from heat and stir in butter and vanilla.

Dakota Peach Kuchen

Banana Pudding

3. Transfer pudding to food processor. Add warm peeled roasted bananas and 2 tablespoons lemon juice and process until smooth. Scrape into large bowl and place plastic wrap directly on surface of pudding. Refrigerate until slightly cool, about 45 minutes.

4. Peel and cut remaining bananas into ¼-inch slices and toss in bowl with remaining 1 tablespoon lemon juice. Spoon one-quarter of pudding into 3-quart trifle dish and top with layer of cookies, layer of sliced bananas, and another layer of cookies. Repeat twice, ending with pudding. Place plastic wrap directly on surface of pudding and refrigerate until wafers have softened, at least 8 hours or up to 2 days.

5. For the Whipped Topping Using stand mixer fitted with whisk, whip cream, sugar, and vanilla on medium-low speed until foamy, about 1 minute. Increase speed to high and whip until stiff peaks form, 1 to 3 minutes. (Whipped cream can be refrigerated for 4 hours.) Top banana pudding with whipped cream. Serve.

Toasted Coconut Banana Pudding

Replace 2 cups half-and-half with one 16-ounce can unsweetened coconut milk in step 2. Sprinkle ¼ cup toasted sweetened shredded coconut over whipped cream–topped pudding before serving.

Peanut-y Banana Pudding

In step 4, sandwich 2 vanilla wafers around 1 banana slice and ½ teaspoon creamy peanut butter (you'll need ½ cup total). Assemble by alternating layers of pudding and cookie-banana sandwiches, ending with pudding. Sprinkle ¼ cup chopped salted dry-roasted peanuts over whipped cream–topped pudding before serving.

New Orleans Bourbon Bread Pudding

SERVES 8 TO 10

WHY THIS RECIPE WORKS The best bourbon bread pudding is a rich, "scoopable" custard that envelops the bread with a balance of sweet spiciness and robust bourbon flavor. Tearing a crusty baguette into ragged pieces, then toasting them, gave the pudding a rustic look and kept the bread from turning soggy in the custard. We used a mixture of 3 parts cream to 1 part milk and replaced the whole eggs with yolks for a rich, creamy custard that didn't curdle. Once the custard set up in the oven, we sprinkled cinnamon, sugar, and butter on top and let it bake until the topping was caramelized.

This bread pudding is great on its own, but for a little more punch, drizzle Bourbon Sauce over individual servings (recipe follows). A bakery-quality French baguette makes this dish even better.

- 1 (18- to 20-inch) baguette, torn into 1-inch pieces (10 cups)
- 1 cup golden raisins, divided
- ¾ cup bourbon, divided
- 6 tablespoons unsalted butter, cut into 6 pieces and chilled, plus extra for baking dish
- 8 large egg yolks
- 1½ cups packed (10½ ounces) light brown sugar
- 3 cups heavy cream
- 1 cup whole milk
- 1 tablespoon vanilla extract
- 1½ teaspoons ground cinnamon, divided
- ¼ teaspoon nutmeg
- ¼ teaspoon table salt
- 3 tablespoons granulated sugar

1. Adjust oven rack to middle position and heat oven to 450 degrees. Arrange bread in single layer on baking sheet and bake until crisp and browned, about 12 minutes, turning pieces over and rotating sheet halfway through baking. Let bread cool. Reduce oven temperature to 300 degrees.

2. Meanwhile, heat raisins with ½ cup bourbon in small saucepan over medium-high heat until bourbon begins to simmer, 2 to 3 minutes. Strain mixture, reserving bourbon and raisins separately.

3. Butter 13 by 9-inch broiler-safe baking dish. Whisk egg yolks, brown sugar, cream, milk, vanilla, 1 teaspoon cinnamon, nutmeg, and salt together in large bowl. Whisk in reserved bourbon plus remaining ¼ cup bourbon. Add toasted bread and toss until evenly coated. Let mixture sit until bread begins to absorb custard, about 30 minutes, tossing occasionally. If majority of bread is still hard, continue to soak for 15 to 20 minutes.

4. Pour half of bread mixture into prepared baking dish and sprinkle with half of raisins. Pour remaining bread mixture into dish and sprinkle with remaining raisins. Cover with aluminum foil and bake for 45 minutes.

5. Meanwhile, mix granulated sugar and remaining ½ teaspoon cinnamon in small bowl. Using your fingers, cut 6 tablespoons butter into sugar mixture until size of small peas. Remove foil from pudding, sprinkle with butter mixture, and bake, uncovered, until custard is just set, 20 to 25 minutes. Remove pudding from oven and heat broiler.

6. Once broiler is heated, broil pudding until top forms golden crust, about 2 minutes. Transfer to wire rack and cool at least 30 minutes or up to 2 hours. Serve.

Bourbon Sauce
MAKES ABOUT 1 CUP

- 1½ teaspoons cornstarch
- ¼ cup bourbon, divided
- ¾ cup heavy cream
- 2 tablespoons sugar
- Pinch table salt
- 2 teaspoons unsalted butter, cut into small pieces

Whisk cornstarch and 2 tablespoons bourbon in small bowl until well combined. Heat cream and sugar in small saucepan over medium heat until sugar dissolves. Whisk in cornstarch mixture and bring to boil. Reduce heat to low and cook until sauce thickens, 3 to 5 minutes. Off heat, stir in salt, butter, and remaining 2 tablespoons bourbon. Drizzle warm sauce over individual servings. (Sauce can be refrigerated for up to 5 days.)

New Orleans Bourbon Bread Pudding

The American Table: The History of Bourbon

How did Kentucky bourbon (the name given to whiskey distilled from at least 51 percent corn) end up playing such an important role in New Orleans's signature dessert? Right after the Revolutionary War, settlers in what eventually became Kentucky planted significant amounts of corn. Because there weren't many passable roads on which to transport this much grain back over the mountains to populated areas along the East Coast, many farmers distilled their crop to make whiskey. Bottles were packed in crates (stamped with the words "Old Bourbon," after the region of Kentucky where this liquor was produced) and shipped down the Ohio and Mississippi rivers to New Orleans and, eventually, the rest of the world.

Summer Berry Pudding
SERVES 6

WHY THIS RECIPE WORKS Although our initial tests of this traditional British "pudding" were fairly disastrous, we knew that good bread and fresh summer berries could make a delicious dessert. The rectangular shape of a loaf pan proved a more stable mold than traditional round bowls. We staled challah bread (our top choice for its flavor and texture) in the oven for added support. Since the moisture content of fresh berries can vary, we strained the juice from the filling and dipped the bread in it ourselves. Cooking only half of the berries and mixing the rest in later brightened the filling, and apricot preserves and gelatin helped the pudding keep its shape.

Fill in any gaps in pudding crusts with toast trimmings.

OLD-FASHIONED FRUIT DESSERTS AND PUDDINGS 665

Summer Berry Pudding

- 8 (¼-inch-thick) slices challah, crusts removed, divided
- 12 ounces strawberries, hulled and chopped (2 cups), divided
- 8 ounces blackberries, halved (1½ cups)
- 8 ounces (1½ cups) blueberries
- 5 ounces (1 cup) raspberries
- ½ cup (3½ ounces) granulated sugar
- 1 teaspoon unflavored gelatin
- 2 tablespoons cold water
- ½ cup (5½ ounces) apricot preserves
- 1 cup heavy cream, chilled
- 1 tablespoon confectioners' sugar

1. Adjust oven rack to middle position and heat oven to 350 degrees. Line 8½ by 4½-inch loaf pan with plastic wrap, pushing plastic into corners and up sides of pan and allowing excess to overhang long sides. Make cardboard cutout just large enough to fit inside pan.

2. Place challah on wire rack set in rimmed baking sheet. Bake until dry, about 10 minutes, flipping challah and rotating sheet halfway through baking. Let challah cool completely.

3. Combine strawberries, blackberries, blueberries, and raspberries in bowl. Transfer half of mixture to medium saucepan, add granulated sugar, and bring to simmer over medium-low heat, stirring occasionally. Reduce heat to low and continue to cook until berries release their juices and raspberries begin to break down, about 5 minutes. Off heat, stir in remaining berries. After 2 minutes, strain berries through fine-mesh strainer set over medium bowl for 10 minutes, stirring berries once halfway through straining (do not press on berries). Reserve berry juice. (You should have ¾ to 1 cup.)

4. Sprinkle gelatin over water in bowl and let sit until gelatin softens, about 5 minutes. Microwave until mixture is bubbling around edges and gelatin dissolves, about 30 seconds. Whisk preserves and gelatin mixture together in large bowl. Fold in strained berries.

5. Trim 4 slices of challah to fit snugly side by side in bottom of loaf pan (you may have extra challah). Dip slices in reserved berry juice until saturated, about 30 seconds per side, then place in bottom of pan. Spoon berry mixture over challah. Trim remaining 4 slices of challah to fit snugly side by side on top of berries (you may have extra challah). Dip slices in reserved berry juice until saturated, about 30 seconds per side, then place on top of berries. Cover pan loosely with plastic and place in 13 by 9-inch baking dish. Place cardboard cutout on top of pudding. Top with 3 soup cans to weigh down pudding. Refrigerate pudding for at least 8 hours or up to 24 hours.

6. Using stand mixer fitted with whisk, whip cream and confectioners' sugar on medium-low speed until foamy, about 1 minute. Increase speed to high and whip until soft peaks form, 1 to 3 minutes. Transfer to serving bowl. Remove cans, cardboard, and plastic from top of pudding. Loosen pudding by pulling up on edges of plastic. Place inverted platter over top of loaf pan and flip platter and pan upside down to unmold pudding. Discard plastic. Slice pudding with serrated knife and serve with whipped cream.

Old-Fashioned Vanilla Frozen Custard

MAKES ABOUT 1 QUART

WHY THIS RECIPE WORKS There's nothing like a cone of creamy frozen custard on a hot summer day—or really any day. While stores use industrial condensers to produce the consistency we know and love, we set out to find a way to achieve supersmooth custard at home without a machine. After combining our heated cream and egg yolk mixtures, we strained the custard to remove any pieces of cooked egg. To achieve the smoothest possible custard, we cooled the mixture on ice, let it chill in the refrigerator, and then whipped it in a stand mixer to add air. This prevented ice crystals from building up and made the final texture silky and creamy.

One teaspoon of vanilla extract can be substituted for the vanilla bean; stir the extract into the strained custard in step 3. Use an instant-read thermometer for the best results.

- 6 large egg yolks
- ¼ cup (1¾ ounces) sugar
- 2 tablespoons nonfat dry milk powder
- 1 cup heavy cream
- ½ cup whole milk
- ⅓ cup light corn syrup
- ⅛ teaspoon table salt
- 1 vanilla bean

1. Whisk egg yolks, sugar, and milk powder in bowl until smooth, about 30 seconds; set aside. Combine cream, milk, corn syrup, and salt in medium saucepan. Cut vanilla bean in half lengthwise. Using tip of paring knife, scrape out vanilla seeds and add to cream mixture, along with vanilla bean. Heat cream mixture over medium-high heat, stirring occasionally, until it steams steadily and registers 175 degrees, about 5 minutes. Remove saucepan from heat.

2. Slowly whisk heated cream mixture into yolk mixture to temper. Return cream-yolk mixture to saucepan and cook over medium-low heat, stirring constantly, until mixture thickens and registers 180 degrees, 4 to 6 minutes.

3. Immediately pour custard through fine-mesh strainer set over large bowl; discard vanilla bean. Fill slightly larger bowl with ice and set custard bowl in bowl of ice. Transfer to refrigerator and let chill until custard registers 40 degrees, 1 to 2 hours, stirring occasionally.

4. Transfer chilled custard to stand mixer fitted with whisk and whip on medium-high speed for 3 minutes, or until mixture increases in volume to about 3¾ cups. Pour custard into airtight 1-quart container. Cover and freeze until firm, at least 6 hours, before serving. (Frozen custard is best eaten within 10 days.)

Old-Fashioned Chocolate Frozen Custard

Omit vanilla bean. Add ½ ounce finely chopped 60 percent cacao bittersweet chocolate and 1 tablespoon Dutch-processed cocoa powder to cream mixture in step 1 before cooking. Add ½ teaspoon vanilla extract to strained custard in step 3.

> **Frozen Custard vs. Ice Cream: Cracking Open the Difference**
>
> According to guidelines administered by the U.S. Food and Drug Administration, both ice cream and frozen custard must contain at least 10 percent milk fat (along with milk, cream, sweeteners, flavorings, and so forth). The main difference between them is eggs: While egg yolks are optional in ice cream bases (and occasionally do appear on ingredient lists), they are absolutely required in frozen custard. Frozen custards must contain at least 1.4 percent yolks by weight. The resulting frozen treat is eggier and richer than ice cream.

Old-Fashioned Frozen Custard

save room for pie

- **670** Double-Crust Pie Dough
- **670** Classic Single-Crust Pie Dough
- **671** No-Fear Single-Crust Pie Dough
- **672** Shaker Lemon Pie
- **673** North Carolina Lemon Pie
- **674** Mile-High Lemon Meringue Pie
- **674** Sour Orange Pie
- **676** Really Good Key Lime Pie
- **677** Icebox Key Lime Pie
- **678** Peaches and Cream Pie
- **679** Fried Peach Hand Pies
- **680** Oregon Blackberry Pie
- **682** Pennsylvania Dutch Apple Pie
- **683** Apple Pie with Cheddar Crust
- **684** Apple Slab Pie
- **685** Old-Fashioned Pecan Pie
- **687** Sweet Potato Pie
- **687** French Coconut Pie
- **689** Coconut Cream Pie
- **690** Banana Pudding Pie
- **691** Raspberry Chiffon Pie
- **692** Icebox Strawberry Pie
- **693** Blueberry Cream Pie
- **694** French Silk Chocolate Pie
- **696** Chocolate Angel Pie
- **697** Mississippi Mud Pie
- **698** S'Mores Pie

Recipe Photos (from left to right): S'Mores Pie, Blueberry Cream Pie

Double-Crust Pie Dough

MAKES ENOUGH FOR ONE 9-INCH PIE

- 2½ cups (12½ ounces) all-purpose flour
- 2 tablespoons sugar
- 1 teaspoon table salt
- 8 tablespoons vegetable shortening, cut into ¼-inch pieces and chilled
- 12 tablespoons unsalted butter, cut into ¼-inch pieces and chilled
- 6–8 tablespoons ice water

1. Process flour, sugar, and salt in food processor until combined, about 5 seconds. Scatter shortening over top and process until mixture resembles coarse cornmeal, about 10 seconds. Scatter butter over top and pulse until mixture resembles coarse crumbs, about 10 pulses. Transfer to bowl.

2. Sprinkle 6 tablespoons water over flour mixture. Using rubber spatula, stir and press dough until it sticks together. If dough does not come together, stir in remaining water, 1 tablespoon at a time, until it does.

3. Divide dough into 2 even pieces and flatten each into 4-inch disk. Wrap disks tightly in plastic wrap and refrigerate for 1 hour. Let chilled dough soften slightly on counter before rolling.

Classic Single-Crust Pie Dough

MAKES ENOUGH FOR ONE 9-INCH PIE

- 1¼ cups (6¼ ounces) all-purpose flour
- 1 tablespoon sugar
- ½ teaspoon table salt
- 4 tablespoons vegetable shortening, cut into ¼-inch pieces and chilled
- 6 tablespoons unsalted butter, cut into ¼-inch pieces and chilled
- 3–4 tablespoons ice water

1. Process flour, sugar, and salt in food processor until combined, about 5 seconds. Scatter shortening over top and process until mixture resembles coarse cornmeal, about 10 seconds. Scatter butter over top and pulse until mixture resembles coarse crumbs, about 10 pulses. Transfer to bowl.

2. Sprinkle 3 tablespoons water over flour mixture. Using rubber spatula, stir and press dough until it sticks together. If dough does not come together, add remaining 1 tablespoon water. Flatten dough into 4-inch disk, wrap tightly in plastic wrap, and refrigerate for 1 hour.

3. Let chilled dough soften slightly. Lightly flour counter, then roll dough into 12-inch circle and fit it into 9-inch pie plate. Trim, fold, and crimp edges of dough. Wrap dough-lined pie plate in plastic and place in freezer until dough is fully chilled and firm, about 30 minutes, before using.

Rolling and Fitting Pie Dough

1. Roll dough outward from its center into 12-inch circle. Between every few rolls, give dough quarter turn.

2. Toss additional flour underneath dough as needed to keep dough from sticking to counter.

3. Loosely roll dough around rolling pin, then gently unroll it over pie plate.

4. Lift dough and gently press it into pie plate, letting excess hang over plate.

No-Fear Single-Crust Pie Dough

MAKES ENOUGH FOR ONE 9-INCH PIE

Anyone can make this pat-in-the-pan pie dough—no rolling or transferring of dough to the dish required. Cream cheese helps make this dough easy to handle and helps ensure a tender crust. Make sure you press the dough evenly into a glass pie plate; if you hold the dough-lined plate up to the light, you will be able to clearly see any thick or thin spots.

1¼	cups (6¼ ounces) all-purpose flour
2	tablespoons sugar
¼	teaspoon table salt
8	tablespoons unsalted butter, softened but still cool
2	ounces cream cheese, softened but still cool

1. Lightly coat 9-inch Pyrex pie plate with vegetable oil spray. Whisk flour, sugar, and salt together in bowl.

2. Using stand mixer fitted with paddle, beat butter and cream cheese on medium-high speed until completely homogeneous, about 2 minutes, stopping once or twice to scrape down beater and sides of bowl. Add flour mixture and mix on medium-low speed until mixture resembles coarse cornmeal, about 20 seconds. Scrape down sides of bowl. Increase mixer speed to medium-high and beat until dough begins to form large clumps, about 30 seconds. Reserve 3 tablespoons of dough. Turn remaining dough onto lightly floured counter, gather into ball, and flatten into 6-inch disk. Transfer disk to greased pie plate.

3. Press dough evenly over bottom of pie plate toward sides, using heel of your hand. Hold plate up to light to ensure that dough is evenly distributed. With your fingertips, continue to work dough over bottom of plate and up sides until evenly distributed.

4. On floured counter, roll reserved dough into 12-inch rope. Divide into 3 pieces and roll each piece into 8-inch rope. Arrange ropes, evenly spaced, around top of pie plate, pressing and squeezing to join them with dough in plate and form uniform edge. Use your fingers to flute edge of dough. Wrap dough-lined pie plate in plastic wrap and place in freezer until dough is fully chilled and firm, about 30 minutes, before using.

No-Fear Pie Dough

1. Hold pie plate up to light to check thickness of dough; it should be translucent, not opaque. Pay attention to curved edges.

2. Roll reserved dough into three 8-inch ropes. Arrange ropes around perimeter of pie plate, leaving small (about 1-inch) gaps between them.

3. Squeeze ropes together.

4. Create a fluted edge, dipping your fingers in flour if dough is sticky.

Shaker Lemon Pie

North Carolina Lemon Pie

Shaker Lemon Pie
SERVES 8

WHY THIS RECIPE WORKS Most Shaker lemon pie recipes mix lemon slices—peel and all—with sugar and eggs to form a custardy filling. But unless we macerated the lemon slices for 24 hours, the pie turned out bitter. We wanted to speed things up. First, we squeezed the seeded lemon slices and reserved the juice for the filling. Then, we simmered the slices and added them to the filling with the uncooked juice for bright lemon flavor in a flash.

Have an extra lemon on hand in case the three sliced lemons do not yield enough juice. See page 670 for more information on rolling and fitting pie dough.

- 1 recipe Double-Crust Pie Dough (page 670)
- 3 large lemons, sliced thin and seeded
- 1¾ cups (12¼ ounces) sugar
- ⅛ teaspoon table salt
- 1 tablespoon cornstarch
- 4 large eggs
- 1 tablespoon heavy cream, divided

1. Roll 1 disk of dough into 12-inch circle on lightly floured counter, then fit it into 9-inch pie plate, letting excess dough hang over edge; cover with plastic wrap and refrigerate for 30 minutes. Roll other disk of dough into 12-inch circle on lightly floured counter, then transfer to parchment paper–lined baking sheet; cover with plastic and refrigerate for 30 minutes.

2. Adjust oven rack to lowest position and heat oven to 425 degrees. Squeeze lemon slices in fine-mesh strainer set over bowl; reserve juice (you should have 6 tablespoons). Bring drained slices and 2 cups water to boil in saucepan, then reduce heat to medium-low and simmer until slices are softened, about 5 minutes. Drain well and discard liquid. Combine softened lemon slices, sugar, salt, and ¼ cup reserved lemon juice in bowl; stir until sugar dissolves.

3. Whisk cornstarch and remaining 2 tablespoons lemon juice in large bowl. Whisk eggs into cornstarch mixture, then slowly stir in lemon slice mixture until combined. Pour into chilled pie shell. Brush edges of dough with 1 teaspoon cream. Loosely roll second piece of dough around rolling pin then gently unroll it over pie. Trim, fold, and crimp edges, and cut 4 vent holes in top. Brush top with remaining 2 teaspoons cream.

4. Bake until light golden, about 20 minutes, then decrease oven temperature to 375 degrees and continue to bake until golden brown, 20 to 25 minutes. Let pie cool on wire rack for at least 1 hour. Serve. (Pie can be refrigerated for 2 days.)

> ### The Slice Is Right
> While developing our recipe for Shaker Lemon Pie, we found that cutting the lemons into paper-thin slices was a difficult and time-consuming task. We had better results with a mandoline, which produced perfectly thin slices in no time at all. If you don't have a mandoline, another piece of kitchen equipment will make the process easier: the freezer. Freezing the lemons for about 30 minutes firms them up for better hand slicing, which is best accomplished with a serrated knife.

> ### Shaker Cooking
> The Shakers' food was never ornate and was always healthy and hearty enough to support their industrious, hard-working lifestyle. Shakers scrubbed—rather than peeled—their vegetables (and, in the case of Shaker Lemon Pie, their citrus fruit) to minimize waste. They were also pioneers in using exact measurements in cooking at a time when many recipes called for a "dash," "glob," or "handful" of something.

North Carolina Lemon Pie

MAKES ONE 9-INCH PIE

WHY THIS RECIPE WORKS This light, bright lemon pie has a perfect balance of sweet, salty, and sour. Plus, it's dead simple to make. Inspired by the North Carolina coast, its unique crust is made with saltine crackers. To keep the custard filling easy, we used both lemon zest and juice for plenty of citrus flavor, and heavy cream to soften the lemon's sharpness. Sweetened whipped cream was the perfect finishing touch.

You will need about 53 saltines, roughly one and a half sleeves, to equal 6 ounces.

Crust
- 6 ounces saltines
- 1/8 teaspoon table salt
- 10 tablespoons unsalted butter, melted
- 1/4 cup light corn syrup

Filling
- 1 (14-ounce) can sweetened condensed milk
- 4 large egg yolks
- 1/4 cup heavy cream
- 1 tablespoon grated lemon zest plus 1/2 cup juice (3 lemons)
- 1/8 teaspoon table salt

Topping
- 1/2 cup heavy cream, chilled
- 2 teaspoons sugar
- 1/2 teaspoon vanilla extract

1. For the Crust Adjust oven rack to middle position and heat oven to 350 degrees. Combine saltines and salt in food processor and pulse to coarse crumbs, about 15 pulses. Add melted butter and corn syrup and pulse until crumbs are broken down into oatmeal-size pieces, about 15 pulses.

2. Transfer saltine mixture to greased 9-inch pie plate. Using bottom of dry measuring cup, press crumbs into even layer on bottom and sides of plate, using your hand to keep crumbs from spilling over plate edge. Place plate on baking sheet and bake until light golden brown and fragrant, 17 to 19 minutes.

3. For the Filling Whisk condensed milk, egg yolks, cream, lemon zest, and salt in bowl until fully combined. Whisk in lemon juice until fully incorporated.

4. With pie plate still on sheet, pour filling into crust (crust needn't be cool). Bake pie until edges are beginning to set but center still jiggles when shaken, 15 to 17 minutes. Place pie on wire rack and let cool completely. Refrigerate pie until fully chilled, about 4 hours.

5. For the Topping Using stand mixer fitted with whisk, whip cream, sugar, and vanilla on medium-low speed until foamy, about 1 minute. Increase speed to high and whip until stiff peaks form, 1 to 3 minutes. Spread whipped cream over top of pie. Serve.

Mile-High Lemon Meringue Pie

SERVES 8 TO 10

WHY THIS RECIPE WORKS We wanted a lemon meringue pie with an impressively tall and fluffy topping, so we made the meringue with a hot sugar syrup and added a bit of cream of tartar to the egg whites as we beat them. This ensured that the meringue was cooked through and stable enough to be piled high on top of the filling. For our pie's bright citrus flavor, we flavored the filling with lemon zest and lemon juice and then, to ensure the filling was silky smooth, we strained out the zest.

You can use Classic Single-Crust Pie Dough (page 670) or No-Fear Single-Crust Pie Dough (page 671) for this pie. This pie is best served on the day it's made.

- 1 recipe single-crust pie dough, fitted into 9-inch pie plate and chilled

Lemon Filling
- 1¼ cups (8¾ ounces) sugar
- 1 cup lemon juice plus 2 tablespoons grated zest (5 lemons)
- ½ cup water
- 3 tablespoons cornstarch
- ¼ teaspoon table salt
- 8 large egg yolks
- 4 tablespoons unsalted butter, cut into 4 pieces and softened

Meringue
- 1 cup (7 ounces) sugar
- ½ cup water
- 4 large egg whites
- Pinch table salt
- ½ teaspoon cream of tartar
- ½ teaspoon vanilla extract

1. Adjust oven rack to middle position and heat oven to 375 degrees. Line chilled crust with double layer of aluminum foil and fill with pie weights. Bake until pie dough looks dry and is light in color, 25 to 30 minutes. Remove weights and foil and continue to bake crust until deep golden brown, 10 to 12 minutes longer. Let crust cool on wire rack to room temperature.

2. For the Lemon Filling Whisk sugar, lemon juice, water, cornstarch, and salt together in large saucepan until cornstarch is dissolved. Bring to simmer over medium heat, whisking occasionally until mixture becomes translucent and begins to thicken, about 5 minutes. Whisk in egg yolks until combined. Stir in lemon zest and butter. Bring to simmer and stir constantly until mixture is thick enough to coat back of spoon, about 2 minutes. Strain through fine-mesh strainer into cooled pie shell and scrape filling off underside of strainer. Place plastic wrap directly on surface of filling and refrigerate until set and well chilled, at least 2 hours or up to 1 day.

3. For the Meringue Adjust oven rack to middle position and heat oven to 400 degrees. Combine sugar and water in small saucepan. Bring to vigorous boil over medium-high heat. Once syrup comes to rolling boil, cook 4 minutes (mixture will become slightly thickened and syrupy). Remove from heat and set aside while beating whites.

4. Using stand mixer fitted with whisk, whip egg whites in large bowl at medium-low speed until frothy, about 1 minute. Add salt and cream of tartar and whip, gradually increasing speed to medium-high, until whites hold soft peaks, about 2 minutes. With mixer running, slowly pour hot syrup into whites (avoid pouring syrup onto whisk or it will splash). Add vanilla and whip until meringue has cooled and becomes very thick and shiny, 5 to 9 minutes.

5. Using rubber spatula, mound meringue over filling, making sure meringue touches edges of crust. Use spatula to create peaks all over meringue. Bake until peaks turn golden brown, about 6 minutes. Let pie cool on wire rack to room temperature. Serve.

Sour Orange Pie

MAKES ONE 9-INCH PIE

WHY THIS RECIPE WORKS Think of sour orange pie as northern Florida's answer to key lime: Its custard-like filling is made with the juice of wild sour oranges. Since fresh sour oranges are hard to source outside of Florida, we re-created their ultrasour taste with frozen orange juice concentrate, lemon juice, and orange and lemon zests. We mixed the juice with sweetened condensed milk for sweetness and egg yolks for structure. Slightly sweet animal crackers made a crunchy crust to contrast the tart filling. Chilled and topped with orange-flavored whipped cream, this sunny pie was bright and refreshing.

If available, you can use ¾ cup strained sour orange juice in place of the lemon juice and orange juice concentrate.

Crust
- 5 ounces animal crackers
- 3 tablespoons sugar
- Pinch table salt
- 4 tablespoons unsalted butter, melted

Filling
- 1 (14-ounce) can sweetened condensed milk
- 6 tablespoons thawed orange juice concentrate
- 4 large egg yolks
- 2 teaspoons grated lemon zest plus 6 tablespoons juice (2 lemons)
- 1 teaspoon grated orange zest
- Pinch table salt

Whipped Cream
- ¾ cup heavy cream, chilled
- 2 tablespoons sugar
- ½ teaspoon grated orange zest

1. For the Crust Adjust oven rack to middle position and heat oven to 325 degrees. Process crackers, sugar, and salt in food processor until finely ground, about 30 seconds. Add melted butter and pulse until combined, about 8 pulses. Transfer crumbs to 9-inch pie plate.

2. Using bottom of dry measuring cup, press crumbs firmly into bottom and up sides of pie plate. Bake until fragrant and beginning to brown, 12 to 14 minutes. Cool to room temperature, about 30 minutes.

3. For the Filling When crust is cool, whisk condensed milk, orange juice concentrate, egg yolks, lemon zest and juice, orange zest, and salt together in bowl until fully combined. Pour filling into cooled crust.

4. Bake until center of pie jiggles slightly when shaken, 15 to 17 minutes. Cool to room temperature, then refrigerate until fully chilled, at least 3 hours; or cover with greased plastic wrap and refrigerate for up to 24 hours.

5. For the Whipped Cream Whisk cream, sugar, and orange zest together in medium bowl until stiff peaks form, 2 to 4 minutes.

6. Slice chilled pie and serve with whipped cream.

Mile-High Lemon Meringue Pie

Sour Orange Pie

Really Good Key Lime Pie

SERVES 8

WHY THIS RECIPE WORKS We started with the recipe on the back of the bottle of Nellie & Joe's Famous Key West Lime Juice, increasing ingredient amounts and adding heavy cream for structure. Next, we baked three pies—one with bottled key lime juice, one with freshly squeezed key lime juice, and one with fresh Persian lime juice—and settled on using regular lime juice. The bottled-juice version was a bit bitter, and the version made with key limes, while floral and nuanced, was a little astringent. To embellish our graham cracker crust, we added pulverized pretzels. The pretzels provided a buttery saltiness that balanced the sweet-tart filling. A pillowy meringue topping added a contrasting texture and a stunning look.

Note that two of the egg whites from the filling are used to make the meringue topping—don't discard them when separating the eggs. Remember to zest the limes first before juicing them. Do not use a disposable aluminum pie plate; the volume of the filling will not fit. In place of the meringue, you can top the pie with our Failproof Whipped Cream (recipe follows). You'll need two 14-ounce cans of sweetened condensed milk to yield the 1½ cups called for. To substitute key lime juice for the regular lime juice, you'll need to squeeze about 18 key limes to get ¾ cup of juice.

Crust
- 6 ounces graham crackers, broken into 1-inch pieces (about 11 crackers)
- 2 ounces mini pretzel twists (about 35 twists)
- ¼ cup packed (1¾ ounces) light brown sugar
- ¼ teaspoon table salt
- 8 tablespoons unsalted butter, melted

Filling
- 1½ cups sweetened condensed milk
- ¾ cup lime juice (6 limes)
- 6 tablespoons heavy cream
- 4 large egg yolks
- ⅛ teaspoon table salt

Meringue
- 2 large egg whites
- ¼ teaspoon table salt
- ¼ teaspoon cream of tartar
- ½ cup (3½ ounces) granulated sugar
- ¼ cup water
- 1 tablespoon vanilla extract
- 2 teaspoons grated lime zest

1. For the Crust Adjust oven rack to middle position and heat oven to 350 degrees. Process cracker pieces, pretzels, sugar, and salt in food processor until finely ground, about 30 seconds. Add melted butter and pulse until combined, about 8 pulses.

2. Transfer cracker mixture to 9-inch pie plate. Using bottom of dry measuring cup, press crumbs firmly into bottom and up sides of plate. Place plate on baking sheet and bake until crust is fragrant and set, about 17 minutes. Transfer sheet to wire rack.

3. For the Filling Whisk all ingredients in bowl until fully combined. With pie plate still on sheet, carefully pour filling into crust (crust needn't be cool). Transfer sheet to oven and bake pie until edge of filling is set but center still jiggles slightly when shaken, about 30 minutes.

4. Place pie on wire rack and let cool completely, about 1 hour. Refrigerate until fully chilled, at least 4 hours, or cover with greased plastic wrap and refrigerate for up to 24 hours.

5. For the Meringue Combine egg whites, salt, and cream of tartar in bowl of stand mixer fitted with whisk attachment. Whip on medium-high speed until soft peaks form, 2 to 4 minutes.

6. Combine sugar and water in small saucepan. Bring to rolling boil over medium-high heat and cook until syrup registers 240 degrees, 1 to 3 minutes.

7. Working quickly, turn mixer to medium speed. With mixer running, slowly and carefully pour hot syrup into egg white mixture (avoid pouring syrup onto whisk, if possible). Add vanilla. Increase speed to medium-high and whip until shiny, stiff peaks form, about 2 minutes.

8. Spread meringue over pie filling, leaving 1-inch border around pie. Working gently, use spatula or spoon to create swirls and cowlicks over surface of meringue. Sprinkle meringue with lime zest. Slice pie into wedges with wet knife, wiping knife clean between slices. Serve.

Failproof Whipped Cream
SERVES 6 TO 8 (MAKES ABOUT 2 CUPS)

If your kitchen is warm, chill the mixer bowl and whisk attachment in the freezer for 20 minutes before whipping the cream. This recipe can be doubled or tripled, if desired.

1 cup heavy cream, chilled
¼ cup (1¾ ounces) sugar
½ teaspoon vanilla extract

Using stand mixer fitted with whisk attachment, whip cream, sugar, and vanilla on medium-low speed until foamy, about 1 minute. Increase speed to medium-high and whip until just shy of either soft or stiff peaks (depending on desired final texture), 1 to 2 minutes. Remove bowl and whisk attachment from mixer and whip by hand to desired texture.

Icebox Key Lime Pie

SERVES 8 TO 10

WHY THIS RECIPE WORKS Early key lime pie recipes used to be simple and uncooked—but they contained raw eggs, a no-no in modern times. We wanted to develop an eggless key lime pie recipe as bright and custardy as the original. In lieu of using egg yolks, we found the right ratio of instant vanilla pudding, gelatin, and cream cheese to thicken our Icebox Key Lime Pie's filling into a perfect, smooth consistency. A full cup of fresh lime juice produced a pie with bracing lime flavor. Lime zest added another layer of flavor, and processing the zest with a little sugar offset its sourness and eliminated the annoying chewy bits.

Use instant pudding, which requires no stovetop cooking, for this recipe. Do not use bottled lime juice, which lacks depth of flavor.

Crust
8 whole graham crackers, broken into small pieces
2 tablespoons sugar
5 tablespoons unsalted butter, melted

Filling
¼ cup (1¾ ounces) sugar
1 tablespoon grated lime zest plus 1 cup juice (8 limes)
8 ounces cream cheese, softened
1 (14-ounce) can sweetened condensed milk
⅓ cup instant vanilla pudding mix
1¼ teaspoons unflavored gelatin
1 teaspoon vanilla extract

Really Good Key Lime Pie

Icebox Key Lime Pie

1. For the Crust Adjust oven rack to middle position and heat oven to 350 degrees. Process crackers and sugar in food processor until finely ground, about 30 seconds. Add melted butter in steady stream while pulsing until crumbs resemble damp sand. Sprinkle mixture into 9-inch pie plate and use bottom of dry measuring cup to press crumbs firmly into bottom and sides. Bake until fragrant and browned around edges, 12 to 14 minutes. Let cool completely.

2. For the Filling Process sugar and zest in clean food processor until sugar turns bright green, about 30 seconds. Add cream cheese and process until combined, about 30 seconds. Add condensed milk and pudding mix and process until smooth, about 30 seconds. Scrape down sides of bowl. Sprinkle gelatin over 2 tablespoons lime juice in small bowl and let sit until gelatin softens, about 5 minutes. Heat in microwave for 15 seconds; stir until dissolved. With processor running, pour in gelatin mixture, remaining lime juice, and vanilla and mix until thoroughly combined, about 30 seconds.

3. Pour filling into cooled crust, cover with plastic wrap, and refrigerate for at least 3 hours or up to 2 days. To serve, let pie sit at room temperature for 10 minutes before slicing.

A Mystery of Pie History

Before Gail Borden invented sweetened condensed milk in 1856, drinking milk was a health risk, as there was no pasteurization or refrigeration for fresh milk. The shelf-stability and safety of sweetened condensed milk made it especially popular in areas like the Florida Keys, where the hot climate promoted rapid spoilage of anything perishable. Like many of our iconic foods, no one knows for sure when or by whom the first key lime pie was made, but with canned milk in every pantry by the 1870s and an abundance of tiny key limes throughout the area, it was only a matter of time. Most food historians trace the history of this pie back to the 1890s, but there are those—especially in the Keys—who claim the recipe is decades older.

Peaches and Cream Pie

SERVES 8

WHY THIS RECIPE WORKS Old-fashioned recipes for this pie call for simply arranging peaches in a pie crust, dousing them with fresh cream, and baking. But today's commercial cream gave us a milky, lumpy, and bland puddle rather than a rich filling. To thicken the cream, we whisked in a little flour and two egg yolks. But the juicy peaches wreaked watery havoc on our custardy pie filling. Roasting them in the oven evaporated their excess liquid, and a dusting of sugar encouraged caramelizing for even more flavor. Prebaking the crust kept it crisp and flaky after the roasted fruit and filling were added.

Keep an eye on the peaches at the end of their baking time to ensure that they don't scorch. You can use Classic Single-Crust Pie Dough (page 670) or No-Fear Single-Crust Pie Dough (page 671) for this pie.

- 1 recipe single-crust pie dough, fitted into 9-inch pie plate and chilled
- 2 pounds ripe but firm peaches, peeled, halved, and pitted
- 2 tablespoons plus ½ cup (4⅓ ounces) sugar
- 3 tablespoons all-purpose flour
- ¼ teaspoon table salt
- ⅓ cup heavy cream
- 2 large egg yolks
- ½ teaspoon vanilla extract

1. Adjust oven racks to upper-middle and lower-middle positions and heat oven to 375 degrees. Line chilled crust with double layer of aluminum foil and fill with pie weights.

2. Place peach halves cut side up on foil-lined rimmed baking sheet and sprinkle with 2 tablespoons sugar. Bake peaches on upper-middle rack until softened and juice is released, about 30 minutes, flipping halfway through baking.

3. After 30 minutes, place crust on lower-middle rack and, while peaches continue to roast, bake until edges are lightly browned, about 15 minutes. Remove crust from oven and carefully remove foil and weights. Continue to bake until bottom of crust is light golden brown and peaches are caramelized, about 5 minutes longer. Cool crust and peaches for 15 minutes.

4. Reduce oven temperature to 325 degrees. Cut peach halves lengthwise into quarters. Arrange peaches in single layer over crust. Combine remaining ½ cup sugar, flour, and salt in bowl. Whisk in cream, egg yolks, and vanilla until smooth. Pour cream mixture over peaches. Bake until filling is light golden brown and firm in center, 45 to 55 minutes. Cool pie on wire rack for at least 3 hours. Serve.

> ### Blind-Baking a Pie Crust
> The crusts for many pies and tarts are baked before filling (this is called blind baking) so that they stay golden brown, crisp, and flaky once filled.
>
>
>
> **1.** Line chilled pie crust with double layer of aluminum foil, fill crust with pie weights or pennies, and bake until lightly browned, about 15 minutes.
>
> **2.** Remove pie weights and foil and continue to bake until light golden brown, about 5 minutes longer.

Fried Peach Hand Pies

MAKES 8 HAND PIES

WHY THIS RECIPE WORKS These hand pies have it all: a crust that is delicate and tender but crumbly and a filling that's pure peach flavor. Starting with the filling, we cooked peeled, sliced peaches with sugar and a pinch of salt on the stovetop before gently mashing the fruit and letting it thicken. A bit of lemon juice added vibrancy. For the crust, we created a soft dough using melted butter and flour. Adding baking powder and milk created the dainty crumble we wanted. We divided, rolled out, and filled the dough, sealing in the filling before frying the pies in a Dutch oven, achieving peachy little pie perfection in minutes.

Peaches and Cream Pie

Fried Peach Hand Pies

If using frozen peaches, purchase a no-sugar-added product; we prefer Earthbound Farm or Cascadian Farm frozen peaches. There is no need to thaw the frozen peaches, but they will take longer to cook; times for both fresh and frozen are given in step 1. Use a Dutch oven that holds 6 quarts or more for frying. The assembled pies can be refrigerated for up to 24 hours before frying.

- 4 ripe peaches, peeled, halved, pitted, and cut into ½-inch wedges, or 20 ounces frozen peaches
- ½ cup (3½ ounces) sugar
- ¾ teaspoon plus ⅛ teaspoon table salt
- 2 teaspoons lemon juice
- 2 cups (10 ounces) all-purpose flour
- 2 teaspoons baking powder
- 6 tablespoons unsalted butter, melted and cooled
- ½ cup whole milk
- 2 quarts peanut or vegetable oil for frying

1. Combine peaches, sugar, and ⅛ teaspoon salt in medium saucepan. Cover and cook over medium heat, stirring occasionally and breaking up peaches with spoon, until tender, about 5 minutes for fresh peaches and 16 to 19 minutes for frozen peaches.

2. Uncover and continue to cook, stirring and mashing frequently with potato masher to coarse puree, until mixture is thickened and measures about 1⅔ cups, 7 to 13 minutes. Remove from heat, stir in lemon juice, and let cool completely. (Filling can be refrigerated for up to 3 days.)

3. Line rimmed baking sheet with parchment paper. Pulse flour, baking powder, and ¾ teaspoon salt in food processor until combined, about 3 pulses. Add melted butter and pulse until mixture resembles wet sand, about 8 pulses, scraping down sides of bowl as needed. Add milk and process until no floury bits remain and dough looks pebbly, about 8 seconds.

4. Turn dough onto lightly floured counter, gather into disk, and divide into 8 equal pieces. Roll each piece between your hands into ball, then press to flatten into round. Place rounds on prepared sheet, cover with plastic wrap, and refrigerate for 20 minutes.

5. Working with 1 piece of dough at a time, roll into 6- to 7-inch circle about ⅛ inch thick on lightly floured counter. Place 3 tablespoons filling in center of circle. Brush edges of dough with water and fold dough over filling to create half-moon shape, lightly pressing out air at seam. Trim any ragged edges and crimp edges with tines of fork to seal. Return pies to prepared sheet, cover with plastic, and refrigerate until ready to fry, up to 24 hours.

6. Line platter with triple layer of paper towels. Add oil to large Dutch oven until it measures about 1½ inches deep and heat over medium-high heat to 375 degrees. Gently place 4 pies in hot oil and fry until golden brown, about 1½ minutes per side, using slotted spatula or spider to flip. Adjust burner, if necessary, to maintain oil temperature between 350 and 375 degrees. Transfer to prepared platter. Return oil to 375 degrees and repeat with remaining 4 pies. Let cool for 10 minutes before serving.

On the Road: Peach Park

The massive, peach-shaped water tower looming over Clanton, Alabama, heralds Peach Park, a roadside retail attraction and restaurant that serves as the spiritual center of Alabama's peach-producing region. Out front, an open-air market sells fresh produce (peaches, mostly) and peach-based pantry products; inside, a long cafeteria case houses meat-and-three fare (preludes, perhaps, to peach ice cream and peach cobbler). Portraits of the reigning Miss Peach and her younger counterparts Junior Miss Peach, Young Miss Peach, and Little Miss Peach honor their regal stone-fruit court.

But the best reason to visit Peach Park is the fried peach hand pies. Rumor has it that these sweet, warm pies were created as a way to use up overripe peaches, too soft and ugly to sell as is but still full of peach flavor. At Peach Park, we left no leftovers.

Oregon Blackberry Pie

SERVES 8

WHY THIS RECIPE WORKS The hallmark of Oregon blackberry pie is its thick, fruity filling that retains its shape after slicing instead of oozing into a mess. Re-creating that perfect texture required trying a number of different thickeners. We ultimately landed on cornstarch, which provided the best texture and didn't impact the flavor. Tossing the blackberries in sugar, cornstarch, salt, and lemon juice kept the focus on the fruit. Adding a bit of sour cream to the pie dough inhibited gluten development, preventing the dough from becoming tough. An attractive faux lattice top allowed steam to escape, preventing a soggy crust.

Do not substitute frozen berries. Freezing the butter for the dough before processing it in step 1 is crucial to the flaky texture of this crust. Plan ahead: The pie dough needs to chill for at least an hour before rolling. When brushing the lattice strips with egg wash, be sure to leave the ends of each strip unbrushed so the wash doesn't impede the crimping process.

Pie Dough

- 1/3 cup ice water, plus extra as needed
- 3 tablespoons sour cream
- 2½ cups (12½ ounces) all-purpose flour
- 1 tablespoon sugar
- 1 teaspoon table salt
- 16 tablespoons unsalted butter, cut into ¼-inch pieces and frozen for 15 minutes

Filling

- ¾ cup (5¼ ounces) sugar, plus 1 teaspoon for topping
- 5 tablespoons (1¼ ounces) cornstarch
- ¼ teaspoon table salt
- 20 ounces (4 cups) blackberries, rinsed and dried
- 2 tablespoons lemon juice
- 2 tablespoons unsalted butter, cut into ½-inch pieces

- 1 large egg, lightly beaten

1. For the Pie Dough Mix ice water and sour cream in bowl. Process flour, sugar, and salt in food processor until combined, about 5 seconds. Scatter butter over top and pulse until butter is size of large peas, about 10 pulses.

2. Pour half of sour cream mixture into bowl with flour mixture and pulse until incorporated, about 3 pulses. Scrape down bowl and repeat with remaining sour cream mixture. Pinch dough with your fingers; if dough feels dry and does not hold together, sprinkle 1 to 2 tablespoons extra ice water over mixture and pulse until dough forms large clumps and no dry flour remains, 3 to 5 pulses.

3. Transfer dough to lightly floured counter. Divide dough in half and form each half into 4-inch disk. Wrap disks tightly in plastic wrap and refrigerate for 1 hour. (Wrapped dough can be refrigerated for up to 2 days or frozen for up to 1 month. If frozen, let dough thaw completely on counter before rolling.)

4. Adjust oven rack to lower-middle position and heat oven to 400 degrees. Let chilled dough sit on counter to soften slightly, about 10 minutes, before rolling. Roll 1 disk of dough into 12-inch circle on lightly floured counter. Loosely roll dough around rolling pin and gently unroll it onto 9-inch pie plate, letting excess dough hang over edge. Ease dough into plate by gently lifting edge of dough with your hand while pressing into plate bottom with your other hand.

5. Wrap dough-lined plate loosely in plastic and refrigerate until dough is firm, about 30 minutes. Roll other disk of dough into 12-inch circle on lightly floured counter, then transfer to parchment paper–lined baking sheet. Using pizza cutter, cut dough into twelve 1-inch strips. Discard 4 short end pieces, then cover remaining 8 long strips with plastic and refrigerate for 30 minutes.

6. For the Filling Whisk sugar, cornstarch, and salt together in large bowl. Add blackberries and toss gently to coat. Add lemon juice and toss until no dry sugar mixture remains. (Blackberries will start to exude some juice.)

7. Transfer blackberry mixture to dough-lined pie plate and dot with butter. Lay 4 dough strips parallel to each other across pie, about 1 inch apart. Brush strips with egg, leaving ½ inch at ends unbrushed. Lay remaining 4 strips perpendicular to first layer of strips, about 1 inch apart.

8. Pinch edges of lattice strips and bottom crust firmly together. Trim overhang to ½ inch beyond lip of plate. Tuck overhang under itself; folded edge should be flush with edge of plate. Crimp dough evenly around edge of plate using your fingers.

Oregon Blackberry Pie

9. Brush lattice top and crimped edge with egg and sprinkle with remaining 1 teaspoon sugar. Set pie on parchment-lined baking sheet. Bake until golden brown and juices bubble evenly along surface, 45 to 50 minutes, rotating sheet halfway through baking. Let cool on wire rack for at least 4 hours before serving.

Pennsylvania Dutch Apple Pie

SERVES 8 TO 10

WHY THIS RECIPE WORKS The hallmark of Dutch apple pie is its creamy apple and vanilla-flavored filling. We used melted vanilla ice cream in the apple filling for extra creaminess and rich flavor. We let sliced apples sit in the melted ice cream along with cinnamon, sugar, and lemon juice until they were soft and pliable. Before baking, we sprinkled a streusel mixture over the top of the pie for a buttery crumble topping. Letting the pie cool completely before slicing into it produced beautifully clean wedges.

We prefer Golden Delicious or Gala apples here, but Fuji, Braeburn, or Granny Smith varieties also work well. You may substitute ½ cup of heavy cream for the melted ice cream, if desired. This pie is best when baked a day ahead of time and allowed to rest overnight. Serve with vanilla ice cream.

Crust
- ¼ cup ice water
- 4 teaspoons sour cream
- 1¼ cups (6¼ ounces) all-purpose flour
- 1½ teaspoons granulated sugar
- ½ teaspoon table salt
- 8 tablespoons unsalted butter, cut into ¼-inch pieces and frozen for 15 minutes

Filling
- 2½ pounds apples, peeled, cored, halved, and sliced ¼ inch thick
- ½ cup melted vanilla ice cream
- ½ cup raisins (optional)
- ½ cup (3½ ounces) granulated sugar
- 1 tablespoon lemon juice
- 1 teaspoon vanilla extract
- 1 teaspoon ground cinnamon
- ½ teaspoon table salt

Topping
- 1 cup (5 ounces) all-purpose flour
- ½ cup packed (3½ ounces) light brown sugar
- 6 tablespoons unsalted butter, melted
- ½ teaspoon table salt

1. For the Crust Combine water and sour cream in bowl. Process flour, sugar, and salt in food processor until combined, about 5 seconds. Scatter butter over top and pulse until butter is size of large peas, about 10 pulses. Add sour cream mixture and pulse until dough forms clumps and no dry flour remains, about 12 pulses, scraping down sides of bowl as needed.

2. Turn dough onto sheet of plastic wrap and form into 4-inch disk. Wrap tightly in plastic and refrigerate for 1 hour. (Wrapped dough can be refrigerated for up to 2 days or frozen for up to 1 month. If frozen, let dough thaw completely on counter before rolling.)

3. For the Filling Toss all ingredients in large bowl until apples are evenly coated. Let sit at room temperature for at least 1 hour or up to 2 hours.

4. Adjust oven rack to lower-middle position and heat oven to 350 degrees. Let chilled dough sit on counter to soften slightly, about 10 minutes, before rolling. Roll dough into 12-inch circle on lightly floured counter. Loosely roll dough around rolling pin and gently unroll it onto 9-inch pie plate, letting excess dough hang over edge. Ease dough into plate by gently lifting edge of dough with your hand while pressing into plate bottom with your other hand.

5. Trim overhang to ½ inch beyond lip of plate. Tuck overhang under itself; folded edge should be flush with edge of plate. Crimp dough evenly around edge of plate using your fingers. Wrap dough-lined plate loosely in plastic and refrigerate until dough is firm, at least 30 minutes.

6. For the Topping Stir all ingredients in bowl until no dry spots remain and mixture forms clumps. Refrigerate until ready to use.

7. Place dough-lined plate on parchment paper–lined rimmed baking sheet. Working with 1 large handful at a time, distribute apple mixture in plate, pressing into even layer and filling in gaps before adding more. Take care not to mound apple mixture in center of plate. Pour any remaining liquid from bowl into pie. Break topping (it will harden in refrigerator) into pea-size crumbs and distribute evenly over apple mixture. Pat topping lightly to adhere.

8. Bake pie on sheet until top is golden brown and paring knife inserted in center meets no resistance, about 1 hour 10 minutes, rotating sheet halfway through baking. Let pie cool on wire rack for at least 4 hours or preferably overnight. Serve.

Apple Pie with Cheddar Crust

SERVES 8

WHY THIS RECIPE WORKS Apple pie and cheddar cheese share a history, and we wanted to incorporate this sweet-savory pairing into a single recipe. For a flaky crust infused with cheesy flavor, extra-sharp cheddar and a teaspoon of dry mustard amped up the crust's savory qualities. Traditional apple filling got a kick from some cayenne, and precooking the filling allowed us to cram in twice as many apples. Starting with a hotter oven browned the bottom crust, and then reducing the heat kept the top from burning. The result: a moist, sweet-tart filling that perfectly complemented our flaky, cheesy crust.

For the best flavor, be sure to use extra-sharp cheddar here. Freezing the butter for 15 minutes promotes flakiness in the crust—do not skip this step.

Crust
- 2½ cups (12½ ounces) all-purpose flour
- 1 tablespoon granulated sugar
- 1 teaspoon table salt
- 1 teaspoon dry mustard
- ⅛ teaspoon cayenne pepper
- 8 ounces extra-sharp cheddar cheese, shredded (2 cups)
- 8 tablespoons unsalted butter, cut into ¼-inch pieces and frozen for 15 minutes
- ⅓ cup ice water, plus extra as needed

Filling
- 2 pounds Granny Smith, Empire, or Cortland apples, peeled, cored, halved, and sliced ¼-inch thick
- 2 pounds Golden Delicious, Jonagold, or Braeburn apples, peeled, cored, halved, and sliced ¼-inch thick
- 6 tablespoons (2⅔ ounces) granulated sugar
- ¼ cup packed (1¾ ounces) light brown sugar
- ½ teaspoon grated lemon zest plus 1 tablespoon juice
- ¼ teaspoon table salt
- ⅛ teaspoon ground cinnamon

1. For the Crust Process flour, sugar, salt, mustard, and cayenne in food processor until combined, about 5 seconds. Scatter cheddar and butter over top and pulse until butter is size of large peas, about 10 pulses.

Pennsylvania Dutch Apple Pie

Apple Pie with Cheddar Crust

2. Pour half of ice water over flour mixture and pulse until incorporated, about 3 pulses. Repeat with remaining ice water. Pinch dough with your fingers; if dough feels dry and does not hold together, sprinkle 1 to 2 tablespoons extra ice water over mixture and pulse until dough forms large clumps and no dry flour remains, 3 to 5 pulses.

3. Divide dough in half and form each half into 4-inch disk. Wrap disks tightly in plastic wrap and refrigerate for 1 hour. Let chilled dough sit on counter to soften slightly, about 10 minutes, before rolling. (Wrapped dough can be refrigerated for up to 2 days or frozen for up to 1 month. If frozen, let dough thaw completely on counter before rolling.)

4. **For the Filling** Stir apples, granulated sugar, brown sugar, lemon zest, salt, and cinnamon together in Dutch oven. Cover and cook over medium heat, stirring frequently, until apples are just tender but still hold their shape, 10 to 15 minutes. Off heat, stir in lemon juice. Spread apple mixture on rimmed baking sheet and let cool completely, about 30 minutes. (Filling can be refrigerated for up to 24 hours.)

5. Roll 1 disk of dough into 12-inch circle between 2 sheets of parchment paper or plastic. Loosely roll dough around rolling pin and gently unroll it onto 9-inch pie plate, letting excess dough hang over edge. Ease dough into plate by gently lifting edge of dough with your hand while pressing into plate bottom with your other hand. Trim overhang to ½ inch beyond lip of pie plate. Wrap dough-lined pie plate loosely in plastic and refrigerate until dough is firm, about 15 minutes.

6. Adjust oven rack to lowest position and heat oven to 425 degrees. Fill pie shell with apple mixture. Roll other disk of dough into 12-inch circle between 2 sheets of parchment or plastic. Loosely roll dough around rolling pin and gently unroll it onto filling.

7. Trim overhang to ½ inch beyond lip of pie plate. Pinch edges of top and bottom crusts firmly together. Tuck overhang under itself; folded edge should be flush with edge of pie plate. Crimp dough around edge of pie plate using your fingers. Cut four 2-inch slits in top of dough.

8. Set pie on foil or parchment-lined baking sheet and bake for 20 minutes. Reduce oven temperature to 375 degrees and continue to bake until crust is deep golden brown and filling is bubbling, 35 to 45 minutes. Transfer pie to wire rack and let cool for at least 1½ hours. Serve.

Apple Slab Pie

Apple Slab Pie

SERVES 18 TO 20

WHY THIS RECIPE WORKS Unlike a traditional apple pie, a slab pie is prepared in a baking sheet and can feed up to 20 people. Its filling is thickened to ensure neat slicing, and its crust is topped with a sugary glaze. But rolling out the dough for this mammoth pie proved problematic, as did making the filling thick enough to hold up to slicing. Gluing two sturdy store-bought crusts together with water and then rolling the dough into a large rectangle allowed us to get the crust into the large pan without a tear. To give the crust a sweet, buttery flavor, we rolled it in crushed animal crackers. Tapioca thickened the filling well without making it starchy.

We prefer an 18 by 13-inch nonstick rimmed baking sheet for this pie. If using a conventional baking sheet, coat it lightly with vegetable oil spray.

Pie

- 3½ pounds Granny Smith apples, peeled, cored, halved, and sliced thin
- 3½ pounds Golden Delicious apples, peeled, cored, halved, and sliced thin
- 1½ cups (10½ ounces) granulated sugar, divided
- ½ teaspoon table salt
- 1½ cups (4 ounces) animal crackers
- 2 (16-ounce) boxes refrigerated pie dough
- 4 tablespoons unsalted butter, melted and cooled
- 6 tablespoons instant tapioca
- 2 teaspoons ground cinnamon
- 3 tablespoons lemon juice

Glaze

- 2 tablespoons lemon juice
- 1 tablespoon unsalted butter, softened
- 1¼ cups (5 ounces) confectioners' sugar

1. For the Pie Combine apples, 1 cup sugar, and salt in colander set over large bowl. Let sit, tossing occasionally, until apples release their juices, about 30 minutes. Press gently on apples to extract liquid and reserve ¾ cup juice. Adjust oven rack to lower-middle position and heat oven to 350 degrees.

2. Pulse crackers and remaining ½ cup sugar in food processor until finely ground, about 20 pulses. Dust counter with cracker mixture, brush half of 1 pie round with water, overlap with second pie round, and dust top with cracker mixture. Roll out dough to 19 by 14 inches and transfer to rimmed baking sheet. Brush dough with butter, cover loosely with plastic wrap and refrigerate.

3. Roll remaining 2 dough rounds together with remaining cracker mixture to a 19 by 14-inch rectangle.

4. Toss drained apples with tapioca, cinnamon, and lemon juice and arrange evenly over bottom crust, pressing lightly to flatten. Brush edges of bottom crust with water and arrange top crust on pie. Press crusts together. Use paring knife to trim any excess dough. Use fork to crimp and seal outside edge of pie and then pierce top of pie at 2-inch intervals. Bake until pie is golden brown and juices are bubbling, about 1 hour. Let pie cool on wire rack for 1 hour.

5. For the Glaze While pie is cooling, simmer reserved apple juice in saucepan over medium heat until syrupy and reduced to ¼ cup, about 6 minutes. Stir in lemon juice and butter and let cool to room temperature. Whisk in sugar and brush glaze evenly over warm pie. Let pie cool completely, at least 1 hour longer. Serve. (Pie can be refrigerated for up to 24 hours.)

How to Make Apple Slab Pie

1. Use water to "glue" together 2 store-bought pie crusts.

2. Add flavor to the bottom crust by rolling it out in mixture of crushed cookie crumbs and sugar.

3. After transferring bottom crust to baking sheet, brush with melted butter for extra richness.

4. Top filled pie with second "double" crust and use fork to tightly seal edges of crust.

Old-Fashioned Pecan Pie

SERVES 8 TO 10

WHY THIS RECIPE WORKS Could we re-create old-fashioned pecan pie without using modern-day processed corn syrup? Many traditional syrups (cane, sorghum) produced a great pie, but we had to mail away for those ingredients. In the end, combining maple syrup with brown sugar and molasses replicated the old-fashioned versions perfectly. We started the pie at a high oven temperature to ensure a crisp, golden-brown bottom crust and then dropped the temperature to finish baking.

Old-Fashioned Pecan Pie

Sweet Potato Pie

Serve with Bourbon Whipped Cream (recipe follows), if desired. You can use Classic Single-Crust Pie Dough (page 670) or No-Fear Single-Crust Pie Dough (page 671) for this pie.

- 1 cup maple syrup
- 1 cup packed (7 ounces) light brown sugar
- ½ cup heavy cream
- 1 tablespoon molasses
- 4 tablespoons unsalted butter, cut into ½-inch pieces
- ½ teaspoon table salt
- 6 large egg yolks, lightly beaten
- 1½ cups (6 ounces) pecans, toasted and chopped
- 1 recipe single-crust pie dough, fitted into 9-inch pie plate and chilled

1. Adjust oven rack to lowest position and heat oven to 450 degrees. Heat syrup, sugar, cream, and molasses in saucepan over medium heat, stirring occasionally, until sugar dissolves, about 3 minutes. Remove from heat and let cool for 5 minutes. Whisk butter and salt into syrup mixture until combined. Whisk in egg yolks until incorporated.

2. Scatter pecans in pie shell. Carefully pour filling over. Place pie in oven and immediately reduce oven temperature to 325 degrees. Bake until filling is set and center jiggles slightly when pie is gently shaken, 45 minutes to 1 hour. Let pie cool on rack for 1 hour, then refrigerate until set, about 3 hours or up to 24 hours. Bring to room temperature before serving.

Bourbon Whipped Cream
MAKES ABOUT 2 CUPS

Although any style of whiskey will work here, we like the smokiness of bourbon.

- 1 cup heavy cream
- 2 tablespoons bourbon
- 1½ tablespoons packed light brown sugar
- ½ teaspoon vanilla extract

Using stand mixer fitted with whisk, whip cream, bourbon, sugar, and vanilla on medium-low speed until foamy, about 1 minute. Increase speed to high and whip until stiff peaks form, about 2 minutes. (Whipped cream can be refrigerated for 4 hours.)

Sweet Potato Pie

SERVES 8

WHY THIS RECIPE WORKS Hoping to streamline this holiday dessert, we started by "baking" whole sweet potatoes in the microwave. A food processor made quick work of pureeing the flesh and lent a super-smooth texture. Sour cream added subtle tang while smoothing out the custard even more, and supplementing whole eggs with extra yolks added richness and helped with sliceability. We heated the spices in butter to intensify (or bloom) their flavor before adding them, along with some bourbon and vanilla, to the filling. We also sprinkled brown sugar onto the crust, which melted into a gooey faux caramel and took this pie to the next level.

The best pies use homemade crust. You can use Classic Single-Crust Pie Dough (page 670) or No-Fear Single-Crust Pie Dough (page 671) for this pie. If you're pressed for time, try our favorite store-bought crust, Pillsbury Refrigerated Pie Crusts. Choose sweet potatoes that are about the same size so that they'll cook evenly. Serve with Bourbon Whipped Cream (at left), if desired.

- 1 (9-inch) single-crust pie dough
- 1¼ cups packed (8¾ ounces) light brown sugar, divided
- 1¾ pounds sweet potatoes, unpeeled
- ½ teaspoon table salt
- 4 tablespoons unsalted butter
- ½ teaspoon ground cinnamon
- ¼ teaspoon ground nutmeg
- 1 cup sour cream
- 3 large eggs plus 2 large yolks
- 2 tablespoons bourbon (optional)
- 1 teaspoon vanilla extract

1. Adjust oven rack to middle position and heat oven to 375 degrees. Roll dough into 12-inch circle on lightly floured counter. Loosely roll dough around rolling pin and gently unroll it onto 9-inch pie plate, letting excess dough hang over edge. Ease dough into plate by gently lifting edge of dough with your hand while pressing into plate bottom with your other hand. Trim overhang to ½ inch beyond lip of pie plate. Tuck overhang under itself; folded edge should be flush with edge of pie plate. Crimp dough evenly around edge of pie using your fingers. Wrap dough-lined pie plate loosely in plastic and freeze until dough is firm, about 15 minutes.

2. Line chilled pie shell with two 12-inch squares of parchment paper, letting parchment lie over edges of dough, and fill with pie weights. Bake until lightly golden around edges, 18 to 25 minutes. Carefully remove parchment and weights, rotate crust, and continue to bake until center begins to look opaque and slightly drier, 3 to 6 minutes. Remove from oven. Let crust cool completely. Sprinkle ¼ cup sugar over bottom of crust; set aside. Reduce oven temperature to 350 degrees.

3. Meanwhile, prick potatoes all over with fork. Microwave on large plate until potatoes are very soft and surface is slightly wet, 15 to 20 minutes, flipping every 5 minutes. Immediately slice potatoes in half to release steam. When cool enough to handle, scoop flesh into bowl of food processor. Add salt and remaining 1 cup sugar and process until smooth, about 60 seconds, scraping down sides of bowl as needed. Melt butter with cinnamon and nutmeg in microwave, 15 to 30 seconds; stir to combine. Add spiced butter, sour cream, eggs and yolks, bourbon, if using, and vanilla to potatoes and process until incorporated, about 10 seconds, scraping down sides of bowl as needed.

4. Pour potato mixture into prepared pie shell. Bake until filling is set around edges but center registers 165 degrees and jiggles slightly when pie is shaken, 35 to 40 minutes. Let pie cool completely on wire rack, about 2 hours. Serve.

French Coconut Pie

SERVES 8 TO 10

WHY THIS RECIPE WORKS French coconut pie, a Southern favorite, is a coconut-custard pie that is often too eggy, too sweet, or lacking in coconut flavor. We set out to tackle all of these issues. First, we found that two whole eggs plus one extra yolk provided just the right amount of richness. To better control the sweetness, we tried unsweetened shredded coconut, which also intensified the coconut flavor. Since the dried coconut was not fully softening as the pie baked, we soaked it in buttermilk and vanilla before adding it to the filling. The finished pie was golden brown—from the pie crust to the lovely sugar crust that formed on top of the custard.

Look for shredded unsweetened coconut, about ¼ inch in length, in the natural foods section of the supermarket. It sometimes goes by the name "coconut flakes." Do not use large flaked coconut in this recipe. Our favorite shredded unsweetened coconut is Now Real Food Organic Unsweetened Coconut, Shredded.

- 1 (9-inch) store-bought pie dough round
- 1¼ cups (3¾ ounces) unsweetened shredded coconut
- ½ cup buttermilk
- 1 teaspoon vanilla extract
- 1 cup (7 ounces) sugar
- 8 tablespoons unsalted butter, melted and cooled
- 2 large eggs plus 1 large yolk
- 2 tablespoons all-purpose flour
- ¼ teaspoon table salt

1. Adjust oven rack to lower-middle position and heat oven to 325 degrees. Roll dough into 12-inch circle on lightly floured counter. Loosely roll dough around rolling pin and gently unroll it onto 9-inch pie plate, letting excess dough hang over edge. Ease dough into plate by gently lifting edge of dough with your hand while pressing into plate bottom with your other hand.

2. Trim overhang to ½ inch beyond lip of plate. Tuck overhang under itself; folded edge should be flush with edge of plate. Crimp dough evenly around edge of plate using your fingers. Wrap dough-lined plate loosely in plastic wrap and freeze until dough is firm, about 15 minutes.

3. Discard plastic wrap and line chilled pie shell with two 12-inch squares of parchment paper, letting parchment lie over edges of dough, and fill with pie weights. Bake until lightly golden around edges, 18 to 25 minutes. Transfer to wire rack and carefully remove parchment and weights. (Pie shell needn't cool completely before proceeding.)

4. Meanwhile, combine coconut, buttermilk, and vanilla in bowl. Cover with plastic and let sit for 15 minutes.

5. Whisk sugar, butter, eggs and yolk, flour, and salt together in large bowl. Stir in coconut mixture until fully incorporated. Pour filling into warm pie shell. Bake until custard is set and golden-brown crust forms on top of pie, 40 to 55 minutes.

6. Transfer pie to wire rack and let cool completely, about 4 hours. Serve at room temperature. (Cooled pie can be covered with plastic and refrigerated for up to 2 days. Let come to room temperature before serving.)

French Coconut Pie

Crimping a Single-Crust Pie Shell

Our easy crimping technique makes a decorative, sturdy edge.

1. Use scissors to trim overhanging dough to uniform ½ inch.

2. Tuck dough under to form thick, even edge on lip of pie plate.

3. Use both hands to pinch dough into ridges, working around perimeter.

Coconut Cream Pie

SERVES 8 TO 10

WHY THIS RECIPE WORKS To do justice to this retro classic—the star of the diner dessert case with its lofty profile and shaggy coconut garnish—we packed each component with coconutty goodness. We ground sweetened shredded coconut together with Nilla Wafers and melted butter for a snappy cookie crust (a hit with tasters) and prebaked it until it was golden brown and aromatic. More sweetened shredded coconut added tropical flavor to our custard filling, which we spooned into our cooled crust. After a three-hour rest in the refrigerator, we piled the pie high with whipped cream, and dressed it up with a sprinkling of toasted coconut.

Be sure to let the cookie crust cool completely before you begin making the filling—at least 30 minutes. Plan ahead: For the filling to set completely, this pie needs to be refrigerated for at least 3 hours or up to 24 hours before serving.

Crust
- 2 cups (4½ ounces) Nilla Wafer cookies (34 cookies)
- ½ cup (1½ ounces) sweetened shredded coconut
- 2 tablespoons sugar
- 1 tablespoon all-purpose flour
- ¼ teaspoon table salt
- 4 tablespoons unsalted butter, melted

Filling
- 3 cups whole milk, divided
- 5 large egg yolks
- 5 tablespoons cornstarch
- ¼ teaspoon table salt
- ½ cup (3½ ounces) sugar
- ½ cup (1½ ounces) sweetened shredded coconut
- ½ teaspoon vanilla extract

Topping
- 1½ cups heavy cream, chilled
- 3 tablespoons sugar
- 1 teaspoon vanilla extract
- ¼ cup (¾ ounce) sweetened shredded coconut, toasted

1. For the Crust Adjust oven rack to middle position and heat oven to 325 degrees. Process cookies, coconut, sugar, flour, and salt in food processor until finely ground, about 30 seconds. Add melted butter and pulse until combined, about 6 pulses. Transfer mixture to 9-inch pie plate. Using bottom of dry measuring cup, press crumbs firmly into bottom and up sides of plate. Bake until fragrant and set, 18 to 22 minutes. Transfer plate to wire rack and let crust cool completely.

2. For the Filling Whisk ¼ cup milk, egg yolks, cornstarch, and salt together in large bowl. Bring sugar and remaining 2¾ cups milk to simmer in large saucepan over medium heat. Slowly whisk half of hot milk mixture into yolk mixture to temper.

3. Return milk-yolk mixture to remaining milk mixture in saucepan. Whisking constantly, cook over medium heat until custard is thickened and registers 180 degrees, 30 to 90 seconds. Remove from heat and stir in coconut and vanilla. Pour filling into cooled crust and spread into even layer.

4. Spray piece of parchment paper with vegetable oil spray and press flush onto surface of custard to cover completely and prevent skin from forming. Refrigerate until cold and set, at least 3 hours or up to 24 hours.

5. For the Topping Using stand mixer fitted with whisk attachment, whip cream, sugar, and vanilla on medium-low speed until foamy, about 1 minute. Increase speed to high and whip until stiff peaks form, 1 to 3 minutes. Spread whipped cream evenly over pie. Sprinkle coconut over top. Serve.

Coconut Cream Pie

Banana Pudding Pie

SERVES 8

WHY THIS RECIPE WORKS Our take on the signature dessert at Buxton Hall Barbecue in Asheville, North Carolina, is a reimagining of the classic layered dessert of vanilla pudding, Nilla Wafers, and sliced bananas. Nilla Wafers formed the base of our crust, and flour and gelatin helped set the pudding layer. A pinch each of ground cinnamon and allspice rounded out the pudding's sweet flavor, which we complemented with sliced fresh bananas. We topped the pie with meringue, made with some brown sugar for caramel undertones. Browning the meringue added toasty notes.

For the best results, use either fully yellow or lightly spotted bananas here (avoid bananas that are green on top or all brown). Peel and slice the bananas just before using to help prevent browning. Plan ahead: The pie needs to be refrigerated for at least 4 hours or up to 24 hours before it's topped. Chilling the topped pie for longer than 4 hours may cause the top to deflate. Don't worry; it will still be delicious.

Crust
- 4 cups (8⅓ ounces) Nilla Wafer cookies
- 3 tablespoons packed light brown sugar
- 1 tablespoon all-purpose flour
- ¼ teaspoon table salt
- 6 tablespoons unsalted butter, melted

Filling
- 2 teaspoons unflavored gelatin
- 1¾ cups half-and-half, divided
- ¾ cup (5¼ ounces) granulated sugar
- 5 large egg yolks
- 2 tablespoons all-purpose flour
- ¼ teaspoon table salt
- Pinch ground cinnamon
- Pinch ground allspice
- 2 tablespoons unsalted butter, cut into 2 pieces and chilled
- 1 tablespoon vanilla extract
- 2 ripe bananas, peeled and sliced ¼ inch thick (1½ cups)

Meringue
- ⅓ cup (2⅓ ounces) granulated sugar
- ⅓ cup packed (2⅓ ounces) light brown sugar
- 4 large egg whites
- ¼ teaspoon cream of tartar
- ⅛ teaspoon table salt

1. For the Crust Adjust oven rack 8 inches from broiler element and heat oven to 325 degrees. Pulse cookies, sugar, flour, and salt in food processor until finely ground, about 10 pulses. Add melted butter and pulse until combined, about 8 pulses, scraping down sides of bowl as needed. Transfer mixture to 9-inch pie plate (it will seem like a lot of crumbs).

2. Using your hands, press crumbs firmly up sides of plate, building walls about ¼ inch thick and leveling top edge. Press remaining crumbs into even layer on bottom of plate, firmly pressing crumbs into corners of plate. Bake until fragrant and beginning to darken at edges, 18 to 20 minutes. Transfer plate to wire rack.

3. For the Filling Meanwhile, sprinkle gelatin over ½ cup half-and-half in small bowl and let mixture sit until gelatin softens, about 5 minutes. Whisk sugar, egg yolks, flour, salt, cinnamon, allspice, and remaining 1¼ cups half-and-half in large saucepan until fully combined. Cook over medium heat, whisking constantly and scraping corners of saucepan, until mixture thickens, bubbles burst across entire surface, and mixture registers 180 degrees in several places, 5 to 7 minutes. Off heat, whisk in butter, vanilla, and gelatin mixture until combined.

4. Stir bananas into hot filling. Pour filling into crust (crust needn't be completely cooled). Press parchment paper directly onto surface of filling and refrigerate until set, at least 4 hours or up to 24 hours.

5. For the Meringue Whisk all ingredients together in bowl of stand mixer. Place bowl over saucepan filled with 1 inch of barely simmering water, making sure water does not touch bottom of bowl. Whisking gently but constantly, cook until mixture registers 160 to 165 degrees, 5 to 8 minutes.

6. Fit mixer with whisk attachment and whip on high speed until meringue forms stiff peaks and is smooth and creamy, 2 to 3 minutes.

7. Gently peel off parchment from filling (if any filling sticks to parchment, scrape off and smooth back over surface of pie). Spread meringue over filling, making sure meringue touches edges of crust. Working gently, use spatula or spoon to create swirls over surface.

8a. For a Broiler Heat broiler. Broil until meringue is well browned, 1 to 2 minutes, rotating plate as needed for even browning.

8b. For a Torch Ignite torch; continuously sweep flame about 2 inches above meringue until well browned.

9. Slice pie into wedges with wet knife, wiping knife clean between slices. Serve immediately. (Topped pie can be refrigerated for up to 4 hours.)

Raspberry Chiffon Pie

SERVES 8 TO 10

WHY THIS RECIPE WORKS Raspberry chiffon pie can often be weak on berry flavor. We wanted to produce an intensely flavored pie, so we included a layer of sweetened, thickened fruit on the crust and beneath the chiffon. We also stiffened our recipe's chiffon filling by using extra gelatin and a little cream cheese, which enabled it to hold additional raspberry puree for even more flavor.

You can use Classic Single-Crust Pie Dough (page 670) or No-Fear Single-Crust Pie Dough (page 671) for this pie. The raspberry-flavored gelatin is important for the color and flavor of the chiffon layer; do not substitute unflavored gelatin. For an accurate measurement of boiling water, bring a full kettle of water to a boil, then measure out the desired amount.

- 1 recipe single-crust pie dough, fitted into 9-inch pie plate and chilled

Fruit
- 12 ounces (2½ cups) frozen raspberries
- 3 tablespoons pectin (Sure-Jell)
- 1½ cups (10½ ounces) sugar
- Pinch table salt
- 5 ounces (1 cup) fresh raspberries

Chiffon
- 3 tablespoons raspberry-flavored gelatin
- 3 tablespoons boiling water
- 3 ounces cream cheese, softened
- 1 cup heavy cream, chilled

Topping
- 1¼ cups heavy cream, chilled
- 2 tablespoons sugar

1. Adjust oven rack to middle position and heat oven to 375 degrees. Line chilled crust with double layer of aluminum foil and fill with pie weights. Bake until pie dough looks dry and is light in color, 25 to 30 minutes. Remove weights and foil and continue to bake crust until deep golden brown, 10 to 12 minutes longer. Let crust cool on wire rack to room temperature.

Banana Pudding Pie

Raspberry Chiffon Pie

2. For the Fruit Cook frozen berries in medium saucepan over medium-high heat, stirring occasionally, until berries begin to give up their juices, about 3 minutes. Stir in pectin and bring to full boil, stirring constantly. Stir in sugar and salt and return to full boil. Cook, stirring constantly, until slightly thickened, about 2 minutes. Pour through fine-mesh strainer into medium bowl, pressing on solids to extract as much puree as possible. Scrape puree off underside of strainer into bowl.

3. Transfer ⅓ cup raspberry puree to small bowl and let cool to room temperature. Gently fold fresh raspberries into remaining puree. Spread fruit mixture evenly over bottom of cooled pie shell and set aside.

4. For the Chiffon Dissolve gelatin in boiling water in bowl of stand mixer. Fit stand mixer with paddle, add cream cheese and reserved ⅓ cup raspberry puree, and beat on high speed, scraping down bowl once or twice, until smooth, about 2 minutes. Add cream and beat on medium-low speed until incorporated, about 30 seconds. Scrape down bowl. Increase speed to high and beat until cream holds stiff peaks, 1 to 2 minutes. Spread evenly over fruit in pie shell. Cover pie with plastic wrap. Refrigerate until set, at least 3 hours or up to 2 days.

5. For the Topping When ready to serve, fit stand mixer with whisk and whip cream and sugar on medium-low speed until foamy, about 1 minute. Increase speed to high and whip until stiff peaks form, 1 to 3 minutes. Spread or pipe over chilled filling. Serve.

Two Layers, Two Thickeners

For the Fruit Layer
For the bottom layer, we used Sure-Jell (pectin) to achieve a concentrated raspberry flavor and texture. There are two formulations of Sure-Jell. We found that the original formula made the smoothest, thickest bottom layer of fruit.

For the Chiffon Layer
A few tablespoons of raspberry gelatin made for great stability and color in the creamy chiffon layer and reinforced the berry flavor.

Icebox Strawberry Pie

SERVES 8

WHY THIS RECIPE WORKS Frozen strawberries, which are great for cooking, form the base of our strawberry pie. We cooked them down in a dry saucepan until they released their juice and the mixture was thick, concentrated, and flavorful. Because strawberries are low in pectin, the natural thickener found in citrus fruits and many other plants, we added some lemon juice, which perked up the flavor and tightened the texture of the filling a little. To thicken the filling further, we added a bit of unflavored gelatin. Then we mixed in fresh strawberries for a fresh finish with big berry flavor.

You can use Classic Single-Crust Pie Dough (page 670) or No-Fear Single-Crust Pie Dough (page 671) for this pie. In step 2, it is imperative that the cooked strawberry mixture measures 2 cups; any more and the filling will be loose. If your fresh berries aren't fully ripe, you may want to add extra sugar to taste in step 3.

- 1 recipe single-crust pie dough, fitted into 9-inch pie plate and chilled

Filling
- 2 pounds (7 cups) frozen strawberries
- 1 tablespoon unflavored gelatin
- 2 tablespoons lemon juice
- 2 tablespoons water
- 1 cup (7 ounces) sugar
- Pinch table salt
- 1 pound fresh strawberries, hulled and sliced thin

Topping
- 4 ounces cream cheese, softened
- 3 tablespoons sugar
- ½ teaspoon vanilla extract
- 1 cup heavy cream

1. Adjust oven rack to middle position and heat oven to 375 degrees. Line chilled crust with double layer of aluminum foil and fill with pie weights. Bake until pie dough looks dry and is light in color, 25 to 30 minutes. Remove weights and foil and continue to bake crust until deep golden brown, 10 to 12 minutes longer. Let crust cool to room temperature on wire rack.

Blueberry Cream Pie

SERVES 8 TO 10

WHY THIS RECIPE WORKS The flavor of fresh blueberries takes center stage in this fruit-packed pie with a decadent whipped cream cheese topping. Cooking down some of the blueberries into a puree while keeping others whole created a filling that had a balance of flavors and textures. The puree provided structure and deepened sweetness, while the fresh berries brought bright, juicy pops of tartness. We piled it all onto a buttery graham cracker crust, and topped it with beautiful rosettes of fluffy whipped cream cheese frosting. It was the perfect way to show off the best of the season's berries.

This pie highlights the flavor and texture of fresh blueberries, so use high-quality berries that you enjoy eating by themselves. Do not use frozen blueberries. We prefer Honey Maid Honey Graham Crackers for this crust. The finished pie will look best on the day it's made; it will still taste delicious the next day, but the topping might not look as fresh.

Crust
- 12 whole graham crackers, broken into pieces (6½ ounces)
- 2 tablespoons sugar
- Pinch table salt
- 6 tablespoons unsalted butter, melted

Filling
- ½ cup (3½ ounces) sugar
- 4 teaspoons cornstarch
- ¼ teaspoon table salt
- 1½ pounds (about 4¾ cups) blueberries, divided
- 1 tablespoon lemon juice

Topping
- 8 ounces cream cheese, softened
- ¼ cup (1¾ ounces) sugar
- 1 teaspoon vanilla extract
- 1 cup heavy cream, chilled

Icebox Strawberry Pie

2. For the Filling Cook frozen berries in large saucepan over medium-low heat until berries begin to release juice, about 3 minutes. Increase heat to medium-high and cook, stirring frequently, until thick and jamlike, about 25 minutes (mixture should measure 2 cups).

3. Sprinkle gelatin over lemon juice and water in small bowl. Let stand until gelatin is softened and mixture has thickened, about 5 minutes. Stir gelatin mixture, sugar, and salt into cooked berry mixture and return to simmer, about 2 minutes. Transfer to bowl and cool to room temperature, about 30 minutes.

4. Fold fresh berries into filling. Spread evenly in pie shell and refrigerate until set, about 4 hours. (Filled pie can be refrigerated for 24 hours.)

5. For the Topping Using stand mixer fitted with whisk, beat cream cheese, sugar, and vanilla on medium speed until smooth, about 30 seconds. With mixer running, add cream and whip until stiff peaks form, about 2 minutes. Dollop individual slices of pie with topping and serve.

1. For the Crust Adjust oven rack to middle position and heat oven to 325 degrees. Process cracker pieces in food processor until finely ground, about 30 seconds. Add sugar and salt and pulse to combine, about 3 pulses. Add melted butter and pulse until combined, about 8 pulses. Transfer crumbs to 9-inch pie plate. Using bottom of dry measuring cup, press crumbs into bottom and up sides of plate. Bake until crust is fragrant and beginning to brown, 16 to 18 minutes. Transfer plate to wire rack.

2. For the Filling Meanwhile, whisk sugar, cornstarch, and salt in medium saucepan until no lumps of cornstarch remain. Process 2 cups blueberries in clean, dry workbowl until smooth, about 2 minutes, scraping down sides of bowl as needed. Strain puree through fine-mesh strainer into sugar mixture in saucepan, pressing on solids to extract as much liquid as possible; discard solids. Whisk puree into sugar mixture until combined.

3. Bring puree mixture to simmer over medium heat, whisking frequently. Continue to cook, whisking constantly, until whisk leaves trail that slowly fills in, about 1 minute longer. Off heat, whisk in lemon juice. Reserve 2 tablespoons puree for piping. Stir remaining blueberries into remaining puree in saucepan. Spread filling evenly over bottom of pie crust (crust needn't be completely cool).

4. For the Topping Using stand mixer fitted with whisk attachment, whip cream cheese, sugar, and vanilla on medium-high speed until very smooth, about 2 minutes, scraping down bowl as needed. With mixer running, slowly pour in cream and whip until stiff peaks form, 1 to 3 minutes, scraping down bowl as needed.

5. Fit large pastry bag with large closed star tip. Using small spatula, apply 3 vertical stripes of reserved puree up sides of pastry bag. Fill pastry bag with topping. Pipe rosettes (spiraling from inside out) in concentric circles over surface of pie, covering filling. Pipe stars in any gaps between rosettes. Refrigerate pie for at least 4 hours or up to 24 hours. Serve.

No Pastry Bag? No Problem.

After step 4, spread cream cheese topping over filling. If reserved puree has thickened, microwave until loosened, 10 to 20 seconds. Drizzle reserved puree over topping. Using butter knife, swirl puree through topping, making marbled pattern.

Simple Steps to Pretty Piping

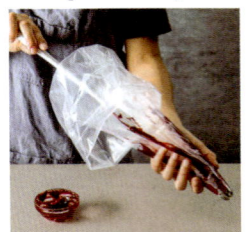

1. Fit large pastry bag with large closed star tip. Using small spatula, apply 3 vertical stripes of reserved blueberry puree up sides of pastry bag.

2. Fill pastry bag with cream cheese topping. Twist bag shut and apply pressure to push cream cheese topping to tip.

3. For rosettes (left): Holding bag upright, pipe center of rosette and then swirl around center in counterclockwise circle.
For stars: Holding bag upright, pipe straight down, then pull bag away.

French Silk Chocolate Pie

SERVES 8 TO 10

WHY THIS RECIPE WORKS This prize-winning icebox pie with a sophisticated name originally called for raw eggs. Testing showed that we could cook the eggs with sugar on the stovetop, almost like making a custard. Once the egg and sugar mixture was light and thick, we removed it from the heat and continued whipping it until it was fully cooled. Bittersweet chocolate folded into the cooled egg and sugar mixture made for a pie with more intense chocolate flavor. And to lighten the filling's texture, we incorporated whipped cream.

You can use Classic Single-Crust Pie Dough (page 670) or No-Fear Single-Crust Pie Dough (page 671) for this pie. Serve with lightly sweetened whipped cream.

French Silk Chocolate Pie

- 1 recipe single-crust pie dough, fitted into 9-inch pie plate and chilled
- 1 cup heavy cream, chilled
- 3 large eggs
- ¾ cup (5¼ ounces) sugar
- 2 tablespoons water
- 8 ounces bittersweet chocolate, melted and cooled
- 1 tablespoon vanilla extract
- 8 tablespoons unsalted butter, cut into ½-inch pieces and softened

1. Adjust oven rack to middle position and heat oven to 375 degrees. Line chilled crust with double layer of aluminum foil and fill with pie weights. Bake until pie dough looks dry and is light in color, 25 to 30 minutes. Remove weights and foil and continue to bake crust until deep golden brown, 10 to 12 minutes longer. Let crust cool on wire rack to room temperature.

2. Using stand mixer fitted with whisk, whip cream on medium-low speed until foamy, about 1 minute. Increase speed to high and whip until stiff peaks form, 1 to 3 minutes. Transfer whipped cream to small bowl and refrigerate.

3. Combine eggs, sugar, and water in large heatproof bowl set over medium saucepan filled with ½ inch barely simmering water (don't let bowl touch water). Using hand-held mixer set at medium speed, beat egg mixture until thickened and registers 160 degrees, 7 to 10 minutes. Remove bowl from heat and continue to beat egg mixture until fluffy and cooled to room temperature, about 8 minutes.

4. Add chocolate and vanilla to cooled egg mixture and beat until incorporated. Beat in butter, few pieces at a time, until well combined. Using spatula, fold in whipped cream until no streaks of white remain. Scrape filling into pie shell and refrigerate until set, at least 3 hours or up to 24 hours. Serve.

The Pillsbury Bake-Off

In 1949, General Mills launched the "Grand National Recipe and Baking Contest" (later known as the Pillsbury Bake-Off). It was held at the posh Waldorf-Astoria Hotel in New York. The grand-prize winner (for No-Knead Water Rising Twists) brought home $50,000; Eleanor Roosevelt was one of the luminaries on hand to present the awards. Since then, many prize-winning Pillsbury recipes have become part of our culinary heritage, among them French Silk Chocolate Pie (the name reflects the international curiosity of postwar America), Open Sesame Pie (which caused a run on sesame seeds nationwide), and Peanut Blossom Cookies (with a Hershey's Kiss in the middle).

Whisking Chocolate into Silk

1. Beat eggs and sugar together in double boiler to incorporate air for filling with light, ethereal texture. Remove from heat when egg mixture reaches 160 degrees.

2. Continue beating egg mixture until fluffy and cool. Add melted chocolate and beat in softened butter for rich flavor and silky-smooth texture.

SAVE ROOM FOR PIE 695

Chocolate Angel Pie

SERVES 8 TO 10

WHY THIS RECIPE WORKS Chocolate angel pie is a lavish version of chocolate cream pie with creamy chocolate mousse, fluffy whipped cream, and an airy meringue crust. For a light, crisp crust, 2½ hours in a low oven was necessary. To prevent the crust from sticking to the pan, we relied on cornstarch, both in the egg whites and dusted over the pie plate. We loaded nearly a pound of chocolate into the filling by making a cooked custard. Using two kinds of chocolate lent depth and complexity. To finish, we topped the pie with lightly sweetened whipped cream and a sprinkling of cocoa powder for a decadent, supremely chocolaty dessert.

Serve the assembled pie within 3 hours of chilling.

Filling
- 9 ounces milk chocolate, chopped fine
- 5 ounces bittersweet chocolate, chopped fine
- 3 large egg yolks
- 1½ tablespoons granulated sugar
- ½ teaspoon table salt
- ½ cup half-and-half
- 1¼ cups heavy cream, chilled

Meringue Crust
- 1 tablespoon cornstarch, plus extra for pie plate
- ½ cup (3½ ounces) granulated sugar
- 3 large egg whites
-   Pinch cream of tartar
- ½ teaspoon vanilla extract

Topping
- 1⅓ cups heavy cream, chilled
- 2 tablespoons confectioners' sugar
-   Unsweetened cocoa powder

1. For the Filling Microwave milk chocolate and bittersweet chocolate in large bowl at 50 percent power, stirring occasionally, until melted, 2 to 4 minutes. Whisk egg yolks, sugar, and salt together in medium bowl until combined, about 1 minute. Bring half-and-half to simmer in small saucepan over medium heat. Whisking constantly, slowly add hot half-and-half to egg yolk mixture in 2 additions until incorporated. Return half-and-half mixture to now-empty saucepan and cook over low heat, whisking constantly, until thickened slightly, 30 seconds to 1 minute. Stir half-and-half mixture into melted chocolate until combined. Let cool slightly, about 8 minutes.

2. Using stand mixer fitted with whisk, whip cream on medium-low speed until foamy, about 1 minute. Increase speed to high and whip until soft peaks form, 1 to 3 minutes. Gently whisk one-third of whipped cream into cooled chocolate mixture. Fold in remaining whipped cream until no white streaks remain. Cover and refrigerate for at least 3 hours, or until ready to assemble pie. (Filling can be made up to 24 hours in advance.)

3. For the Meringue Crust Adjust oven rack to lower-middle position and heat oven to 275 degrees. Grease 9-inch pie plate and dust well with extra cornstarch, using pastry brush to distribute evenly. Combine sugar and 1 tablespoon cornstarch in bowl. Using stand mixer fitted with whisk, whip egg whites and cream of tartar on medium-low speed until foamy, about 1 minute. Increase speed to medium-high and whip whites to soft, billowy mounds, 1 to 3 minutes. Gradually add sugar mixture and whip until glossy, stiff peaks form, 3 to 5 minutes. Add vanilla to meringue and whip until incorporated.

Chocolate Angel Pie

4. Spread meringue into prepared pie plate, following contours of plate to cover bottom, sides, and edges. Bake for 1½ hours. Rotate pie plate, reduce oven temperature to 200 degrees, and bake until completely dried out, about 1 hour longer. (Shell will rise above rim of pie plate; some cracking is OK.) Let cool completely, about 30 minutes.

5. For the Topping Spoon cooled chocolate filling into cavity of pie shell, distributing evenly. Using stand mixer fitted with whisk, whip cream and sugar on medium-low speed until foamy, about 1 minute. Increase speed to high and whip until stiff peaks form, 1 to 3 minutes. Spread whipped cream evenly over chocolate. Refrigerate until filling is set, about 1 hour. Dust with cocoa. Slice with sharp knife and serve.

Busted Crust

The egg white crust is part of what distinguishes angel pie. To avoid a sticky, broken meringue shell, we added cornstarch to the whites, and we greased the pie plate and dusted it with more cornstarch.

MERINGUE MESS
Don't let this happen to you.

Mississippi Mud Pie

SERVES 8 TO 12

WHY THIS RECIPE WORKS This pie is so named because its chocolate layers are reminiscent of the Mississippi River's silty bottom, but there's nothing muddy about its flavor. To simplify each layer of the pie, we started with a press-in chocolate wafer cookie crust. For a perfectly soft, chewy middle layer, we created a brownie-like batter and underbaked it slightly. Once this layer was fully chilled, we spread on a simple milk chocolate mousse and sprinkled on a crunchy chocolate cookie topping to finish.

This recipe takes at least 5 hours from start to finish. We used Nabisco Famous Chocolate Wafers in this recipe. Be sure to use milk chocolate in the mousse, as bittersweet chocolate will make the mousse too firm. Do not begin making the mousse until the brownie layer is fully chilled.

Crust
- 25 chocolate wafer cookies (5½ ounces), broken into coarse pieces
- 4 tablespoons unsalted butter, melted

Brownie Layer
- 4 ounces bittersweet chocolate, chopped fine
- 3 tablespoons unsalted butter
- 3 tablespoons vegetable oil
- 1½ tablespoons Dutch-processed cocoa powder
- ⅔ cup packed (4⅔ ounces) dark brown sugar
- 2 large eggs
- 2 teaspoons vanilla extract
- ¼ teaspoon table salt
- 3 tablespoons all-purpose flour

Topping
- 10 chocolate wafer cookies (2 ounces)
- 2 tablespoons confectioners' sugar
- 1 tablespoon Dutch-processed cocoa powder
- ⅛ teaspoon table salt
- 2 tablespoons unsalted butter, melted

Mousse
- 6 ounces milk chocolate, chopped fine
- 1 cup heavy cream, chilled, divided
- 2 tablespoons Dutch-processed cocoa powder
- 2 tablespoons confectioners' sugar
- ⅛ teaspoon table salt

1. For the Crust Adjust oven rack to middle position and heat oven to 325 degrees. Process cookie pieces in food processor until finely ground, about 30 seconds. Add melted butter and pulse until combined, about 6 pulses. Using bottom of dry measuring cup, press crumbs firmly into bottom and up sides of 9-inch pie plate. Bake until fragrant and set, about 15 minutes. Transfer to wire rack.

2. For the Brownie Layer Combine chocolate, butter, oil, and cocoa in bowl and microwave at 50 percent power, stirring often, until melted, about 1½ minutes. In separate bowl, whisk sugar, eggs, vanilla, and salt until smooth. Whisk in chocolate mixture until incorporated. Whisk in flour until just combined.

SAVE ROOM FOR PIE   697

6. Microwave 3 tablespoons cream in small bowl until it registers 105 to 110 degrees, about 15 seconds. Whisk in cocoa until homogeneous. Combine cocoa-cream mixture, sugar, salt, and remaining cream in bowl of stand mixer. Fit mixer with whisk and whip cream mixture on medium speed until beginning to thicken, about 30 seconds, scraping down bowl as needed. Increase speed to high and whip until soft peaks form, 30 to 60 seconds.

7. Using whisk, fold one-third of whipped cream mixture into melted chocolate to lighten. Using rubber spatula, fold in remaining whipped cream mixture until no dark streaks remain. Spoon mousse into chilled pie and spread evenly from edge to edge. Sprinkle with cooled topping and refrigerate for at least 3 hours or overnight. Serve.

S'Mores Pie

SERVES 10 TO 12

WHY THIS RECIPE WORKS We captured nostalgic campfire flavors in a show-stopping pie by breaking it down into layers. We started with a graham cracker crust that was both flavorful and sturdy enough to support the filling. For the chocolate, we combined a thick, gooey brownie layer with a layer of chocolate ganache. Adding extra heavy cream and a bit of corn syrup to the ganache replicated the melty texture of the chocolate on a s'more while keeping it stable enough to hold up when sliced. Then came the marshmallow topping: an easy meringue that we browned to toasty perfection with a blowtorch (though a broiler worked too). Just one slice had us wanting s'more.

We prefer Honey Maid Honey Graham Crackers for this crust. If your kitchen is particularly hot and the fudge layer is not fully set before spreading meringue layer over it in step 7, place the pie in the freezer, uncovered, for up to 30 minutes.

Crust

- 12 whole graham crackers, broken into pieces
- 2 tablespoons granulated sugar
- ⅛ teaspoon table salt
- 6 tablespoons unsalted butter, melted

Mississippi Mud Pie

3. Pour brownie batter into crust (crust needn't be cool at this point). Bake pie until edges begin to set and toothpick inserted in center comes out with thin coating of batter attached, about 15 minutes. Transfer to wire rack and let cool for 1 hour, then refrigerate until fully chilled, about 1 hour longer.

4. **For the Topping** Meanwhile, line rimmed baking sheet with parchment paper. Place cookies in zipper-lock bag, press out air, and seal bag. Using rolling pin, crush cookies into ½- to ¾-inch pieces. Combine sugar, cocoa, salt, and crushed cookies in bowl. Stir in melted butter until mixture is moistened and clumps begin to form. Spread crumbs in even layer on prepared sheet and bake until fragrant, about 10 minutes, shaking sheet to break up crumbs halfway through baking. Transfer sheet to wire rack and let cool completely.

5. **For the Mousse** Once brownie layer has fully chilled, microwave chocolate in large bowl at 50 percent power, stirring often, until melted, 1½ to 2 minutes. Let cool until just barely warm and registers between 90 and 100 degrees, about 10 minutes.

Brownie Layer

- 6 ounces bittersweet chocolate, chopped fine
- 5 tablespoons vegetable oil
- 4 tablespoons unsalted butter
- 2 tablespoons Dutch-processed cocoa powder
- 1 cup packed (7 ounces) light brown sugar
- 3 large eggs
- 1 tablespoon vanilla extract
- ½ teaspoon table salt
- ¼ cup (1¼ ounces) all-purpose flour

Fudge Layer

- 4 ounces milk chocolate, chopped fine
- ⅓ cup heavy cream
- 2 tablespoons light corn syrup

Meringue

- ¾ cup (5¼ ounces) granulated sugar
- 3 large egg whites
- ½ teaspoon vanilla extract
- ¼ teaspoon cream of tartar
- Pinch table salt

1. For the Crust Adjust oven rack 8 inches from broiler element and heat oven to 325 degrees. Process graham cracker pieces in food processor until finely ground, about 30 seconds. Add sugar and salt and pulse to combine. Add melted butter and pulse until combined, about 8 pulses. Transfer crumbs to 9-inch pie plate. Using bottom of dry measuring cup, press crumbs into bottom and up sides of plate. Bake until crust is fragrant and beginning to brown, 16 to 18 minutes. Transfer plate to wire rack.

2. For the Brownie Layer Combine chocolate, oil, butter, and cocoa in large bowl. Microwave at 50 percent power until chocolate is fully melted, about 2 minutes, stirring every 30 seconds. Let cool for 5 minutes. Whisk sugar, eggs, vanilla, and salt into chocolate mixture until fully combined. Whisk in flour until just incorporated. Pour brownie batter into crust (crust needn't be fully cooled).

3. Bake pie until edges of brownie begin to set and toothpick inserted in center comes out with few moist crumbs attached, about 40 minutes. Let pie cool for at least 10 minutes or up to 1 hour.

4. For the Fudge Layer Meanwhile, combine chocolate, cream, and corn syrup in medium bowl and microwave at 50 percent power until chocolate is fully melted, 1 to 2 minutes, stirring halfway through microwaving. Let cool completely, about 30 minutes.

5. Pour cooled fudge mixture over brownie layer and smooth into even layer. Let set completely at room temperature, at least 3 hours. (Fudge-topped pie can be loosely wrapped with greased plastic and stored at room temperature for up to 2 days.)

6. For the Meringue Whisk all ingredients together in bowl of stand mixer. Place bowl over saucepan filled with 1 inch simmering water, making sure water does not touch bottom of bowl. Whisking gently but constantly, heat until sugar is dissolved and mixture registers 160 to 165 degrees, 4 to 7 minutes.

7. Fit stand mixer with whisk attachment and whip on high speed until meringue forms stiff peaks and is smooth and creamy, about 3 minutes (bowl may still be slightly warm to touch). Spread meringue over filling, making sure meringue touches edges of crust. Use spatula or spoon to create swirls all over meringue.

8a. For a Torch Ignite torch and continually sweep flame about 2 inches above meringue until well browned, 1 to 2 minutes.

8b. For a Broiler Heat broiler. Broil until meringue is well browned, 1 to 2 minutes, rotating halfway through broiling.

9. Slice pie into wedges with wet knife, wiping knife clean between slices. Serve. (Topped pie can be held at room temperature for up to 4 hours before serving.)

Torch It

Torches are used to brown desserts like crème brûlée and pies with meringue toppings, such as this one. (If you don't have a torch, you can also brown the meringue under a broiler.) Using a cake stand makes it easier to brown the pie evenly.

While rotating cake stand, ignite torch and continually sweep flame about 2 inches above meringue until well browned.

Shopping For Equipment

With a well-stocked kitchen, you'll be able to take on any recipe. But there's so much equipment out there on the market, how do you figure out what's what? Price often correlates with design, not performance. Over the years, our test kitchen has evaluated thousands of products. We've gone through copious rounds of testing and have identified the most important attributes in every piece of equipment so that when you go shopping, you'll know what to look for. And because our test kitchen accepts no support from product manufacturers, you can trust our ratings. See AmericasTestKitchen.com for updates to these testings.

KNIVES AND MORE	ITEM	WHAT TO LOOK FOR	TEST KITCHEN FAVORITES
MUST-HAVE ITEMS	CHEF'S KNIFE	• High-carbon stainless steel knife • Thin, curved 8-inch blade • Lightweight • Comfortable grip and nonslip handle	**Victorinox Swiss Army Fibrox Pro 8" Chef's Knife**
	PARING KNIFE	• 3- to 3½-inch blade • Thin, flexible blade with pointed tip • Comfortable grip	**Victorinox Swiss Army Spear Point Paring Knife**
	SERRATED KNIFE	• 10-inch blade • Fewer broader, deeper, pointed serrations • Thinner blade angle • Comfortable, grippy handle • Medium weight	**Mercer Culinary Millenia 10" Bread Knife**
	SLICING/CARVING KNIFE	• Tapered 12-inch blade for slicing large cuts of meat • Oval scallops (called a granton edge) carved into blade • Fairly rigid blade with rounded tip	**Victorinox Swiss Army 12" Granton Slicing Knife**
	STEAK KNIVES	• Supersharp, straight-edged blade • Sturdy, not wobbly, blade	**Victorinox Swiss Army 6-Piece Rosewood Steak Set** Best Buy: **Chicago Cutlery Walnut 4-Piece Steak Knife Set**

KNIVES AND MORE	ITEM	WHAT TO LOOK FOR	TEST KITCHEN FAVORITES
	SANTOKU KNIFE	• Narrow, curved, and short blade • Comfortable grip	**Misono UX10 Santoku 7.0"**
	BIRD'S BEAK PARING KNIFE	• Narrow tip makes near-surgical incisions • Lightweight with a relatively grippy wood veneer handle • Comfortable to hold for long periods	**MAC Paring Knife, Bird's Beak, 2½"**
	BONING KNIFE	• 5.5-inch blade • Ultrasharp, moderately flexible blade • Slightly shorter length gives more control • Slim plastic handle easy to grip in different ways	**Zwilling Pro 5.5" Flexible Boning Knife** Best Buy: **Victorinox Swiss Army Fibrox Pro 6" Flexible Boning Knife**
	MEAT CLEAVER	• Well-made and durable with an ultra-keen blade • Grippy wood handle that's comfortable for hands of all sizes to hold	**Masui AUS8 Stainless Meat Cleaver 180mm**
	GYUTOU	• High-carbon stainless steel knife • Lightweight • Thin blade that tapers from spine to cutting edge and from handle to tip	**Masamoto VG-10 Gyutou, 8.2"** Co-Winner: **Hitohira FJ 210mm Gyuto VG10 Ho**
	ELECTRIC KNIFE	• Good slicing ability • Low noise level • Comfortable rounded handle with start button located conveniently underneath	**Black + Decker ComfortGrip 9" Electric Knife**
	MANDOLINE	• Razor-sharp blade(s) • No fixed thickness settings for customization with slicing • Simple plank shape can be used vertically or hooked over a bowl	Best Overall: **Super Benriner Mandoline Slicer**
		• Clearly marked, accurate dial allows thickness adjustments in both 1/16-inch and 1-millimeter increments • Rubber-coated kickstand • Spring-loaded food pusher helps protect hands	Easiest to Use: **OXO Good Grips Chef's Mandoline Slicer 2.0**

SHOPPING FOR EQUIPMENT 701

KNIVES AND MORE	ITEM	WHAT TO LOOK FOR	TEST KITCHEN FAVORITES
MUST-HAVE ITEMS	CARVING BOARD	• Trenches can contain ½ cup of liquid • Large and stable enough to hold large roasts • Midweight for easy carrying, carving, and cleaning	**J.K. Adams Maple Reversible Carving Board**
	CUTTING BOARD	• Roomy work surface at least 20 by 15 inches • Teak board for minimal maintenance • Durable edge-grain construction (wood grain runs parallel to surface of board)	**Teakhaus Edge Grain Cutting Board (XL)**
	KNIFE SHARPENER	• Diamond abrasives and a spring-loaded chamber to precisely guide blade • Quickly removes nicks in blades • Can convert a 20-degree edge to a sharper 15 degrees	Electric: **Chef'sChoice Trizor XV Knife Sharpener** Electric, Best Buy: **Chef'sChoice 315XV Knife Sharpener** Manual: **Chef'sChoice Pronto Diamond Hone Knife Sharpener**

POTS AND PANS	ITEM	WHAT TO LOOK FOR	TEST KITCHEN FAVORITES
MUST-HAVE ITEMS	TRADITIONAL SKILLET	• Stainless-steel interior and fully clad for even heat distribution • 12-inch diameter and flared sides • Comfortable, ovensafe handle • Tight-fitting lid included	**All-Clad D3 Stainless 12" Fry Pan with Lid**
	NONSTICK SKILLET	• Dark, nonstick surface • 12- or 12½-inch diameter, thick bottom • Cooking surface of at least 9 inches • Lightweight, easy to lift	12-inch: **OXO Good Grips Non-Stick Pro 12" Open Frypan** 10-inch: **OXO Good Grips Non-Stick Pro 10" Open Frypan** 8-inch: **OXO Good Grips Hard Anodized Pro Nonstick 8-Inch Fry Pan**

POTS AND PANS	ITEM	WHAT TO LOOK FOR	TEST KITCHEN FAVORITES
	CERAMIC NONSTICK SKILLET	• Durable nonstick coating • Broad cooking surface, gently sloped walls, and a comfortable handle • Runs a little hotter than traditional nonstick pans	**GreenPan Valencia Pro Hard Anodized Nonstick Frypan** Best Buy: **Kyocera Ceramic-Coated 12" Nonstick Frypan**
	CAST-IRON SKILLET	• Smooth, polished interior, virtually nonstick • Heavy weight for excellent heat retention • Roomy cooking surface • Sides at least 2 inches tall, deep enough for shallow frying	**Smithey Ironware No. 12 Cast Iron Skillet** Best Buy: **Lodge 12 Inch Cast Iron Skillet**
	BRAISER	• Comes in 5 quart, 3.5 quart, and 2.25 quart sizes • Light interior makes it easy to monitor browning and a moderately thick bottom ensures good heat retention • Large, comfortable looped handles and a stainless-steel lid knob provide secure grip	**Le Creuset Enameled Cast-Iron 3.5-Quart Braiser**
MUST-HAVE ITEMS	DUTCH OVEN	• Enameled cast iron or stainless steel • Capacity of at least 6 quarts • Diameter of at least 9 inches • Tight-fitting lid • Wide, sturdy handles	**Le Creuset 7¼ Quart Round Dutch Oven** Best Buy: **Cuisinart Chef's Enameled Cast Iron Casserole**
	SAUCEPAN	• Large saucepan with 3- to 4-quart capacity and small nonstick saucepan with 2- to 2½-quart capacity • Tight-fitting lids • Pans with rounded corners that a whisk can reach into • Long, comfortable handles that are angled for even weight distribution	Large: **All-Clad Stainless 4-Qt Sauce Pan** Best Buy: **Tramontina Gourmet Tri-Ply 4 Qt. Sauce Pan** Small Nonstick: **Calphalon Contemporary Nonstick 2½ Quart Saucepan**
	RIMMED BAKING SHEET	• Light-colored surface (heats and browns evenly) • Thick, sturdy pan • Dimensions of 18 by 13 inches • Good to have at least two	**Nordic Ware Baker's Half Sheet**

SHOPPING FOR EQUIPMENT

POTS AND PANS	ITEM	WHAT TO LOOK FOR	TEST KITCHEN FAVORITES
	SAUTÉ PAN	• Broad cooking surface • High walls that contain food • Moderate weight • Long offset yet straight handle with a small divot that acts as a thumb rest	**Made In Stainless Clad Saute Pan**
	STOCKPOT	• Lightweight • Stainless-steel interior • Lid that easily slides into place • Comfortable handles with rubber grips	**Cook N Home Stainless Steel Stockpot with Lid 12 Quart**
MUST-HAVE ITEM	ROASTING PAN WITH RACK	• At least 15 by 11 inches • Stainless-steel interior with aluminum core for even heat distribution • Upright handles for easy gripping • Light interior for better food monitoring	**Cuisinart MultiClad Pro 16" Roasting Pan with Rack**
	COOKWARE SET	• Fully clad stainless steel with aluminum core for even heat distribution • Moderately heavy, durable construction • Lids included • Ideal mix of pans includes 12-inch skillet, 10-inch skillet, 2-quart saucepan, 4-quart saucepan, 8-quart stockpot	**All-Clad D3 Tri-Ply Bonded Cookware Set, 10 Piece** Best Buy: **Goldilocks Cookware Set**

HANDY TOOLS	ITEM	WHAT TO LOOK FOR	TEST KITCHEN FAVORITES
MUST-HAVE ITEMS	KITCHEN SHEARS	• Take-apart scissors (for easy cleaning) • Supersharp blades • Sturdy construction • Work for both right- and left-handed users	**Shun Multi-Purpose Shears** Best Buy: **J.A. Henckels International Take-Apart Kitchen Shears**
	KITCHEN TONGS	• Scalloped edges • Slightly concave pincers • Length of 12 inches (to keep your hand far from the heat) • Open and close easily	**OXO Good Grips 12-Inch Tongs**
	SLOTTED SPOON	• Wide, shallow, thin bowl • Long, hollow, comfortable handle • Steep, ladle-like angle between handle and bowl	**Cuisinart Stainless Steel Slotted Spoon**
	ALL-AROUND SPATULA	• Head about 3 inches wide and 5½ inches long • 11 inches in length (tip to handle) • Long, vertical slots • Good to have a metal spatula to use with traditional cookware and plastic for nonstick cookware	Metal: **Wüsthof Gourmet 7" Slotted Fish Spatula** Nonstick-Safe: **Matfer Bourgeat Exoglass Pelton Spatula**
	SILICONE SPATULA	• Firm, wide blade ideal for efficient scraping and scooping • All-silicone design for easy cleanup	**Di Oro Living Seamless Silicone Spatula–Large**
	WOODEN SPOON	• "Spootle" (a combination spoon and spatula) has slim, long scraping edge and rounded bowl for scooping food • Cherry wood has a smooth texture and resists becoming overly dried out and rough • Available in right- or left-handed versions	Co-Winner: **Jonathan's Spoons Spootle**
		• Light, long, and maneuverable—keeps hands far from the heat • Rounded, tapered handle is comfortable and easy to grip in a variety of ways • Wood resists staining or drying out, retains its color, and resists becoming rough to touch	Co-Winner & Best Buy: **FAAY 13.5" Teak Cooking Spoon**

SHOPPING FOR EQUIPMENT

HANDY TOOLS	ITEM	WHAT TO LOOK FOR	TEST KITCHEN FAVORITES
MUST-HAVE ITEMS	OFFSET SPATULA	• Flexible blade offset to a roughly 30-degree angle • Enough usable surface area to frost the radius of a 9-inch cake • Comfortable handle	Large: **OXO Good Grips Bent Icing Knife** Mini: **Wilton 9-inch Angled Spatula**
	PIE SERVER	• Comfortable, balanced, and rubbery grip • Slides neatly under pie wedges for easy removal • Sharp serrated blade slices pie effortlessly	**OXO Steel Pie Server** Best Nonstick-Safe Option: **OXO Good Grips Nylon Flexible Pie Server**
	COMPACT SPATULA	• Generous handle • Flexible silicone head	**OXO Good Grips Silicone Cookie Spatula**
	ALL-PURPOSE WHISK	• At least 10 wires • Wires of moderate thickness • Comfortable rubber handle • Balanced, lightweight feel	**OXO Good Grips 11" Balloon Whisk**
	PEPPER MILL	• Easy-to-adjust, clearly marked grind settings • Efficient, comfortable grinding mechanism • Generous capacity	**Cole & Mason Derwent Pepper Mill** Best Buy: **OXO Good Grips Contoured Mess-Free Pepper Grinder**
	CONFECTIONERS' SUGAR SHAKER	• Mesh head that produces a fine, even dusting • Narrow cylinder that fits comfortably in your hand	**Ateco Stainless Steel Fine Mesh Shaker**
MUST-HAVE ITEM	LADLE	• Stainless steel • Hook handle • Pouring rim to prevent dripping • Handle 9 to 10 inches in length	**Rösle Hook Ladle with Pouring Rim** Best Buy: **Cuisinart Stainless Steel Ladle**

706   *The Complete Cook's Country TV Show Cookbook*

HANDY TOOLS	ITEM	WHAT TO LOOK FOR	TEST KITCHEN FAVORITES
MUST-HAVE ITEM	CAN OPENER	• Long driving handle makes it easy and comfortable to rotate • Thick, rubber-sheathed arms make it especially secure to operate	Best Traditional: **OXO Good Grips Soft Handled Can Opener** Best Safety: **Fissler Magic Can Opener**
	JAR OPENER	• Strong, sturdy clamp grip • Adjusts quickly to any size jar	**Amco Swing-A-Way Jar Opener**
MUST-HAVE ITEM	GARLIC PRESS	• Conical holes that press garlic through efficiently • Solid, stainless-steel construction • Comfortable handle • Easy to clean	**Kuhn Rikon Epicurean Garlic Press**
	GARLIC PEELER	• Thick, comfortable silicone sleeve • Removes skins without bruising • Easy to wash	**Zak! Designs Silicone Garlic Peeler**
	SERRATED FRUIT/ VEGETABLE PEELER	• Comfortable grip and nonslip handle • Sharp blade	**OXO Good Grips Serrated Peeler**
	VEGETABLE PEELER	• Sharp, carbon-steel blade • 1-inch space between blade and peeler to prevent jamming • Lightweight and comfortable	**Kuhn Rikon Original Swiss Peeler** Best Straight Peeler: **OXO Good Grips Swivel Peeler**
MUST-HAVE ITEMS	RASP-STYLE GRATER	• Sharp teeth (require little effort or pressure when grating) • Maneuverable over round shapes • Soft, grippy, secure handle	**Microplane Premium Classic Zester/Grater**
	GRATERS	• Large, long grating surface with stamped holes • Grippy plastic bumper around base for stability • Large, comfortable handle	Best Box-Style: **Cuisinart Box Grater** Best Paddle-Style: **Rösle Coarse Grater**
	ROTARY GRATER	• Drum and handle separate for easy interior cleaning • Comfortable handle • Crank can switch sides for left-or right-handed use	**Zyliss Classic Cheese Grater**

SHOPPING FOR EQUIPMENT

HANDY TOOLS	ITEM	WHAT TO LOOK FOR	TEST KITCHEN FAVORITES
	MANUAL JUICER	• Directs juice in a steady stream with no splattering or overflowing • Large, rounded handles that are easy to squeeze	**Chef'n FreshForce Citrus Juicer**
	ICE CREAM SCOOP	• Forms perfectly round orbs that release easily • Wide, comfortable handle contains heat-conductive fluid that warms up instantly when a hand grips the exterior and also warms the bowl, making scooping easy	**Zeroll Original Ice Cream Scoop**
	MEAT POUNDER	• At least 1½ pounds in weight • Vertical handle for better leverage and control	**Norpro GRIP EZ Meat Pounder**
	BENCH SCRAPER	• Sturdy blade • Thin, beveled edge for easy cutting and scraping • Comfortable plastic handle	**Dexter-Russell Sani-Safe 6" x 3" Dough Cutter/Scraper**
MUST-HAVE ITEMS	ROLLING PIN	• Moderate weight (1 to 1½ pounds) • 19-inch straight barrel • Slightly textured wooden surface to grip dough for easy rolling	Best Dowel: **JK Adams Plain Rolling Dowel Pin** Best Tapered Pin: **JK Adams French Rolling Pin**
	MIXING BOWLS	• Good to have both stainless steel and glass (for mixing, microwaving, and holding prepped ingredients) • Sets of 3 to 4 nesting bowls ranging in capacity from about 1 quart to 4 quarts (for glass) and 1½ quarts to 5 quarts (for stainless steel)	Stainless Steel: **Vollrath Economy Stainless Steel Mixing Bowls** Glass: **Pyrex Smart Essentials Mixing Bowl Set with Colored Lids**
	MINI PREP BOWLS	• Wide, shallow bowls • Easy to hold, fill, empty, and clean • Microwave-safe and ovensafe	**Anchor Hocking Custard Cups**

HANDY TOOLS	ITEM	WHAT TO LOOK FOR	TEST KITCHEN FAVORITES
MUST-HAVE ITEM	OVEN MITT	• Silicone is heavily textured for better grip • Flexed with hands, making it easy to pinch cookie sheets and small handles or knobs • Machine-washable	**OXO Silicone Oven Mitt**
	PASTRY BRUSH	• Bristles of moderate length and density • Grippy handle • Loses few bristles	**Winco Flat Pastry and Basting Brush, 1½ inch**
	CHINOIS SIEVE	• Conical shape • Depth of 7 to 8 inches • At least one hook on rim for stability	**Winco Reinforced Extra Fine Mesh Bouillon Strainer**
MUST-HAVE ITEMS	COLANDER	• 4- to 7-quart capacity • Metal ring attached to bottom for stability • Many holes for quick draining • Small holes so pasta doesn't slip through	**RSVP International Precision Pierced 5 Qt. Colander**
	FINE-MESH STRAINER	• Stiff, tightly woven mesh • Capacity of at least 5 cups with large, durable hooks for support over bowls and pots	**Rösle Fine Mesh Strainer, 7.9 inches**
	SPIDER SKIMMER	• Long handle is easy to maneuver and clean • Capable of handling fragile items like ravioli with care	**Rösle Wire Skimmer** Best Buy: **WMF Profi Plus Spider Strainer 14" (5" dia.)**

SHOPPING FOR EQUIPMENT

HANDY TOOLS	ITEM	WHAT TO LOOK FOR	TEST KITCHEN FAVORITES
	FOOD MILL	• Large capacity • Smooth turning mechanism	**Cuisipro Deluxe Food Mill**
	FAT SEPARATOR	• Easy-to-read measurement lines • Tightly sealed bottom release valve • Large strainer dotted with many small perforations	**OXO Good Grips Good Gravy Fat Separator–4 Cup**
	SPLATTER SCREEN	• 8-, 10-, and 12-inch sizes • Ring design • Dishwasher-safe silicone • Rolls up for storage	**Frywall Stovetop Splatter Guard**
MUST-HAVE ITEMS	POTATO MASHER	• Solid mashing disk with many small holes • Comfortable grip • Long handle	**Zyliss Stainless Steel Potato Masher**
	SALAD SPINNER	• Ergonomic and easy-to-operate hand pump • Wide base for stability • Flat lid for easy cleaning and storage	**OXO Good Grips Salad Spinner**
	STEAMER BASKET	• Collapsible stainless-steel basket with feet • Adjustable and removable center rod for easy removal from pot and easy storage	**OXO Good Grips Stainless Steel Steamer with Handle**
	MORTAR AND PESTLE AND MOLCAJETE	• Heavy, stable base keeps it firmly on counter while in use • Rough interior to help grip and grind ingredients • Comfortable, heavy pestle	Best Mortar and Pestle: **Cilio by Frieling Goliath Mortar & Pestle** Best Molcajete: **Masienda Molcajete**

The Complete Cook's Country TV Show Cookbook

MEASURING EQUIPMENT	ITEM	WHAT TO LOOK FOR	TEST KITCHEN FAVORITES
MUST-HAVE ITEMS	DRY MEASURING CUPS	• Accurate measurements • Easy-to-read measurement markings • Durable measurement markings • Strong and durable design • Handles perfectly flush with cups • Stacks and stores neatly	**OXO Good Grips Stainless Steel Measuring Cups**
	LIQUID MEASURING CUP (GLASS)	• Bold, easy-to-read measurement lines that clearly correspond to specific numbers • Heatproof and durable glass resists staining	**Pyrex 1 Cup Measuring Cup**
	LIQUID MEASURING CUP (PLASTIC)	• Lightweight cup has a secondary set of measurements located on a U-shaped strip set in the cup so it can be read from above • Dishwasher safe	**OXO Good Grips 1 Cup Angled Measuring Cup**
	ADJUSTABLE MEASURING CUP	• Plungerlike bottom (with a tight seal between plunger and tube) that you can set to correct measurement, then push up to cleanly extract sticky ingredients (such as shortening or peanut butter) • 1- or 2-cup capacity • Dishwasher-safe	**KitchenArt Pro 2 Cup Adjust-A-Cup Satin**
MUST-HAVE ITEMS	MEASURING SPOONS	• Metal construction is remarkably sturdy • Ingredients don't cling to the stainless steel • Simple design allows for a continuous, bump-free sweep, with a ball-chain connector that is easy to open and close	**Cuisipro Stainless Steel 5-Piece Measuring Spoons**
	KITCHEN RULER	• Stainless steel and easy to clean • 18 inches in length • Large, easy-to-read markings	**Empire 18-inch Stainless Steel Ruler**
	DIGITAL SCALE	• Easy-to-read display not blocked by weighing platform • At least 7-pound capacity • Accessible buttons • Gram-to-ounce conversion feature • Roomy platform	**OXO Good Grips 11-lb Food Scale with Pull Out Display** Best Buy: **Ozeri Pronto Digital Multifunction Kitchen and Food Scale**

SHOPPING FOR EQUIPMENT 711

THERMOMETERS AND TIMERS	ITEM	WHAT TO LOOK FOR	TEST KITCHEN FAVORITES
MUST-HAVE ITEMS	INSTANT-READ THERMOMETER	• Digital model with automatic shut-off • Quick-response readings in 1 second • Wide temperature range (-58 to 572 degrees) • Long stem that can reach interior of large cuts of meat • Water-resistant	**ThermoWorks Thermapen ONE** Best Inexpensive Option: **ThermoWorks ThermoPop** Best Midpriced: **Lavatools Javelin PRO Duo**
	OVEN THERMOMETER	• Wide, sturdy base • Clear temperature markings • Fairly easy to read	**CDN Pro Accurate Oven Thermometer**
	LEAVE-IN TEMPERATURE PROBE	• Large, easy-to-read display • High and low alarms, maximum and minimum temperatures, and timer • Magnetic back, stand, and pot clip	Best One-Probe Option: **ThermoWorks ChefAlarm** Best Two-Probe Option: **ThermoWorks Square DOT** Best Buy: **ThermoPro TP16**
	BARBECUE THERMOMETER	• Simultaneously checks food and grill temperature • Easy to read • Heatproof finger-grip	**Polder Dual Sensor Meat and Oven Thermometer**
	REFRIGERATOR/ FREEZER THERMOMETER	• Large, easy-to-read display • Accurate, and carefully monitors fluctuations in temperature	**ThermoWorks Fridge/ Freezer Alarm**

THERMOMETERS AND TIMERS	ITEM	WHAT TO LOOK FOR	TEST KITCHEN FAVORITES
	KITCHEN TIMER	• Displays three events at once • Screen clearly displays which event is being modified • Adjustable volume • Events have unique beep patterns	Multiple-Event: **OXO Good Grips Triple Timer** Single-Event: **ThermoWorks Extra Big & Loud Timer**
	WEARABLE TIMER	• Combines a clock, timer, and stopwatch • Vertical orientation fits comfortably in hand and pockets • 38-inch lanyard is comfortable and long enough to slip over head	**ThermoWorks TimeStick**

BAKEWARE	ITEM	WHAT TO LOOK FOR	TEST KITCHEN FAVORITES
MUST-HAVE ITEM	GLASS BAKING DISH	• Dimensions of 13 by 9 inches • Lightweight with large handles for easy grip and maneuvering	**Pyrex Easy Grab 3-Quart Oblong Baking Dish**
	13 BY 9-INCH BROILER-SAFE BAKING DISH	• Dish has looped handles that are easy to grab • Capacity of 14.25 cups • Easy cleanup whether by hand or in the dishwasher	**Mrs. Anderson's Baking Lasagna Pan with Handle (Rose)**
MUST-HAVE ITEMS	METAL BAKING PAN	• Dimensions of 13 by 9 inches • Straight sides • Nonstick surface for even browning and easy release of cakes and bar cookies	**Williams Sonoma Goldtouch Pro Nonstick Rectangular Cake Pan**
	8-INCH SQUARE BAKING PAN	• Nonstick coating for easy cleanup • Wide handles makes maneuvering easy • Durable	**All-Clad Pro-Release Nonstick Bakeware 8 inch Square Cake Pan** Best Buy: **Wilton Perfect Results Premium Non-Stick Bakeware Square Cake Pan**

SHOPPING FOR EQUIPMENT

BAKEWARE	ITEM	WHAT TO LOOK FOR	TEST KITCHEN FAVORITES
MUST-HAVE ITEMS	ROUND CAKE PAN	• Best for cake • Straight sides • Light finish for tall, even baking • Nonstick surface for easy release	**Williams Sonoma Goldtouch Pro Nonstick Round Cake Pan** Best Buy: **Nordic Ware Naturals Nonstick 9" Round Cake Pan**
	PIE PLATE	• Gold-hued metal produces crisp and flaky bottom crusts • Nonfluted lip allows for maximum crust-crimping flexibility • Good to have two • Ceramic nonstick coating	**Williams Sonoma Goldtouch Nonstick Pie Dish**
	LOAF PAN	• Folded loaf pan • Produces tall, picture-perfect pound cake • Corrugated pattern on the metal doesn't affect the appearance of baked goods	Best Results: **USA Pan Loaf Pan, 1 lb Volume** Best for Cleanup: **OXO Good Grips Non-Stick Pro 1 Lb Loaf Pan**
	SPRINGFORM PAN	• Tall sides make for an easy grip • Gold-hued pan produces evenly baked crusts • Wide, 9-inch raised base provides support	Co-Winner: **Williams Sonoma Goldtouch Leakproof Springform Pan** Co-Winner and Best Buy: **Nordic Ware 9" Leakproof Springform Pan**
	COOKIE SHEET	• Thick aluminum heats and browns evenly • Won't warp with repeated use • Raised edges for easy maneuvering • Nonstick, spacious surface	**Vollrath Wear-Ever Cookie Sheet (Natural Finish)**

The Complete Cook's Country TV Show Cookbook

BAKEWARE	ITEM	WHAT TO LOOK FOR	TEST KITCHEN FAVORITES
MUST-HAVE ITEMS	MUFFIN TIN	• Gold-hued nonstick surface ensures prefect browning and easy release • Wide, extended rims and raised lip for easy handling	**OXO Good Grips Non-Stick Pro 12-Cup Muffin Pan**
	WIRE RACK	• Reinforced with extra support bar • Fits inside a standard 18 by 13-inch rimmed baking sheet • Dishwasher-safe	**Checkered Chef Cooling Rack**
	BISCUIT CUTTERS	• Sharp edges • A set with a variety of sizes	**Ateco 5357 11-Piece Plain Round Cutter Set**
	BUNDT PAN	• Heavyweight cast aluminum • Thick, easy-to-grip handles • Clearly defined ridges for elegant cakes • 15-cup capacity	**Nordic Ware Anniversary Bundt Pan**
	TART PAN	• Nonstick mold released tarts more readily than traditional finish • Deep grooves for impressive edges • Dark surface for deeply, evenly browned edges	**Matfer Steel Non-Stick Tart Mold with Removable Bottom**
	TUBE PAN	• Heavy pan (at least 1 pound) • Heavy bottom for leak-free seal • Dark nonstick surface for even browning and easy release • 16-cup capacity • Feet on rim	**Chicago Metallic 2-Piece Angel Food Cake Pan with Feet**
	PULLMAN LOAF PAN	• Squared-off pan (4 by 4 inches) • Nonstick aluminized steel for easy cleanup • Light surface for even browning	**USA Pan 13 by 4-inch Pullman Loaf Pan & Cover**

SHOPPING FOR EQUIPMENT

BAKEWARE	ITEM	WHAT TO LOOK FOR	TEST KITCHEN FAVORITES
	BAKER'S EDGE PAN	• Dark nonstick surface for easy release	**Baker's Edge Brownie Pan**
	RAMEKIN	• Heavy, sturdy ceramic • Thick walls for gentle insulation • Straight sides • Stacks securely for easy storage	**Le Creuset Stackable Ramekin** Best Buy: **Mrs. Anderson's Baking Souffle (also sold as HIC)**
	BAKING STEEL	• Absolutely flat with no handholds or cutouts that waste space • Easy cleanup	**The Original Baking Steel**
		• Tough, unbreakable steel is a great choice for home pizza making or bread baking	Co-Winner: **Nerd Chef Steel Stone, Standard ¼"**

SMALL APPLIANCES	ITEM	WHAT TO LOOK FOR	TEST KITCHEN FAVORITES
MUST-HAVE ITEM	FOOD PROCESSOR	• 14-cup capacity • Sharp and sturdy blades • Wide feed tube • Should come with basic blades and discs: steel blade, dough blade, shredding/slicing disc	**Cuisinart Custom 14 Cup Food Processor** Small Food Processor: **Cuisinart Elite Collection 4-Cup Chopper/Grinder**
	STAND MIXER (HIGH-END)	• Powerful enough to mix dense doughs • Heavy, for better stability • Multiple distinct speeds • Simple, intuitive controls	**Ankasrum Original 6230 7 Liter Stand Mixer**

SMALL APPLIANCES	ITEM	WHAT TO LOOK FOR	TEST KITCHEN FAVORITES
MUST-HAVE ITEMS	STAND MIXER	• Fits all KitchenAid attachments, from meat grinder to ice cream maker (sold separately), so it could stand in for several other appliances • Highly efficient and powerful mixing action	Midpriced: **KitchenAid Classic Series 4.5 Quart Tilt-Head Stand Mixer** Best Buy: **Farberware 6 Speed 4.7 Quart Professional Stand Mixer**
	HAND MIXER	• Lightweight model • Slim wire beaters without central post • Range of speed settings	**Breville Handy Mix Scraper** Best Buy: **Cuisinart Power Advantage Plus 9 Speed Hand Mixer**
	BLENDER	• Mix of straight and serrated blades at different angles • Jar with curved base • At least 44-ounce capacity • Heavy base for stability	High-End: **Vitamix 5200** Midpriced: **Breville Fresh & Furious** Inexpensive: **NutriBullet Full Size Blender**
	IMMERSION BLENDER	• Easy to maneuver and lightweight with a slim, grippy body • Well-designed blade and cage • Detachable handle for easy cleanup	**Braun MultiQuick 5 Hand Blender**
	ELECTRIC GRIDDLE	• Large cooking area (about 20 by 12 inches) • Attached pull-out grease trap (won't tip over) • Nonstick surface for easy cleanup	**BroilKing Professional Griddle with Backsplash** Best Buy: **Presto 19-Inch Electric Tilt-n-Fold Griddle**

SMALL APPLIANCES	ITEM	WHAT TO LOOK FOR	TEST KITCHEN FAVORITES
	ELECTRIC JUICER	• Straightforward to assemble, with parts that fit together well • Fast • Easy to clean • Contained debris fairly well	Centrifugal Juicer: **Breville Juice Fountain Cold**
		• Easy to assemble • Helpful auger • Chewed through carrots, kale, and grapes with ease • Relatively easy to clean	Masticating Juicer: **Omega VSJ843QS Vertical Square Low Speed Juicer**
	ELECTRIC KETTLE	• Heats water rapidly • Secure base and wide, comfortable handle • Removable filter in spout	**OXO Brew Cordless Glass Electric Kettle** Best Buy: **Cosori Original Electric Glass Kettle**
	COFFEE MAKER (AUTOMATIC DRIP)	• Thermal carafe that keeps coffee hot for 2 hours • Powerful copper element that transfers heat rapidly and steadily • Water stays at ideal temperature for 91 percent of brewing cycle • Short 6-minute brewing time • Clear, intuitive controls	**Technivorm Moccamaster KBT** Best Buy: **Zojirushi ZUTTO Coffee Maker**
	COLD BREW COFFEE MAKER	• Coffee steeps 12–24 hours for full, smooth flavor • Spacious coffee grounds basket • Double filtration guarantees little to no sediment	**Toddy Cold Brew System**
	MEAT GRINDER	• Grinds pounds of meat easily, even on older KitchenAid stand mixers • Mostly dishwasher-safe	**KitchenAid Food Grinder Attachment**
	ICE CREAM MAKER	• Simple to use and very compact • Modestly priced • Made ice cream that rivaled the smooth texture of our favorite store-bought ice creams	**Cuisinart Frozen Yogurt, Ice Cream & Sorbet Maker**

SMALL APPLIANCES	ITEM	WHAT TO LOOK FOR	TEST KITCHEN FAVORITES
	STOVETOP PRESSURE COOKER	• Stainless steel rather than aluminum for more durable construction that doesn't react to acidic foods • Stovetop model with low sides and wide base for easy access and better browning and heat retention • Pressure indicator that is easy to see and interpret at a glance	**Fissler Vitaquick 8½-Quart Pressure Cooker** Best Buy: **Zavor Duo 8.4 Quart Pressure Cooker**
	SLOW COOKER	• At least 6-quart capacity (4-quart capacity for small slow cookers) • Insert has handles • Clear lid to see progress of food • Dishwasher-safe insert • Intuitive controls with programmable timer and warming mode	**KitchenAid 6-Quart Slow Cooker with Solid Glass Lid** Co-Winner: **Traditional Slow Cooker Hamilton Beach Temp T**
	ELECTRIC DEEP FRYER	• Large basket holds lots of food and is easy to lower and lift during use • High walls and lid contain messes • Built-in filter and handy oil storage container	**T-Fal Ultimate EZ-Clean Fryer**
	LONG-SLOT TOASTER	• Produced great toast with little fuss • Reliable, with no scorching even with darkest setting • Slim profile • Extra rack for warming buns and croissants	**Russell Hobbs Glass Accent Long Slot 2-Slice Toaster**
	TOASTER OVEN	• Quartz heating elements for steady, controlled heat • Roomy but compact interior • Simple to use	**Breville Smart Oven**
	WAFFLE IRON	• Indicator lights and audible alert • Timer gives two alerts: when the waffle is done and one minute before being done	**Presto Flipside Belgian Waffle Maker**
	PANINI PRESS	• Floating hinge with lid settings for thicker foods • Removable, reversible, dishwasher-safe plates • Simple controls	**Breville Sear & Press Grill** Best Buy: **Proctor Silex Panini Press Sandwich Maker and Electric Indoor Grill** Bargain Choice: **Dash Express Griddle**

SHOPPING FOR EQUIPMENT

GRILLING EQUIPMENT	ITEM	WHAT TO LOOK FOR	TEST KITCHEN FAVORITES
	TORTILLA PRESS	• Hefty construction • Design that applies steady, even pressure	**Doña Rosa x Masienda Tortilla Press**
		• Wide plates that prevent dough from squeezing out the sides • Compact size for easy storage	Best Buy: **Victoria 8" Tortilla Press**
	GAS GRILL	• Large main grate • Built-in thermometer • Two burners for varying heat levels (three is even better) • Made of thick, heat-retaining materials such as cast aluminum and enameled steel	**Weber Spirit II E-310 Gas Grill**
	CHARCOAL GRILL	• Sturdy construction, with well-designed cooking grate, handles, lids, and wheels • Generous cooking surface and charcoal capacity • Well-positioned vents control air flow • Gas ignition instantly and easily lights coals • Ash catcher for easy cleanup	**Weber Original Kettle Premium Charcoal Grill, 22-Inch** Upgrade Pick: **Weber Performer Deluxe Charcoal Grill**
	PORTABLE CHARCOAL GRILL	• Ample cooking surface with raised lip • Cover that can be secured for travel • Lightweight but durable	**Weber Smokey Joe Premium**
	SMOKER	• Large cooking area • Water pan • Multiple vents for precise temperature control • Generously sized charcoal basket	Best Overall: **Weber Smokey Mountain Cooker Smoker 18"** Best No Frills Model: **18.5" Classic Pit Barrel Cooker**

GRILLING EQUIPMENT	ITEM	WHAT TO LOOK FOR	TEST KITCHEN FAVORITES
	FIRE PIT FOR COOKING	• Keeps air clearer • Holds up to rigorous use • Makes adjusting food easy	Best Overall: **Breeo X19 Smokeless Fire Pit Grilling Bundle** Best Portable Fire Pit: **Barebones Cowboy Fire Pit Grill–23"**
	CHIMNEY STARTER	• 6-quart capacity • Holes in canister so air can circulate around coals • Sturdy construction • Heat-resistant handle • Dual handle for easy control	**Weber Rapidfire Chimney Starter**
	GRILL TONGS	• 16 inches in length • Scalloped, not sharp and serrated, edges • Opens and closes easily • Lightweight • Moderate amount of springy tension	**OXO Good Grips Grilling Tongs**
	GRILL BRUSH	• Short metal bristles and triangular head shape easily clean grill grates by sweeping the top or by wedging it between the bars • Shorter handle gives good leverage	**Weber 12" Three-Sided Grill Brush**
	GRILL SPATULA	• Front edge is 3 inches across • Head flares out toward the handle to support wider items • Rounded handle with silicone grip	**Char-Broil Comfort-Grip Grill Spatula**
	BARBECUE BASTING BRUSH	• Silicone bristles • Handle between 8 and 13 inches • Heat-resistant	**OXO Good Grips Grilling Basting Brush**
	GRILL GLOVES	• Effective insulation • Forearm protection • Flexible suede • Available in multiple sizes	Best Overall: **WZQH Leather Forge Welding Gloves** Best For Easy Cleanup: **Kitchen Perfection Silicone Smoker Oven Gloves**

SHOPPING FOR EQUIPMENT

GRILLING EQUIPMENT	ITEM	WHAT TO LOOK FOR	TEST KITCHEN FAVORITES
	SKEWERS	• Flat and metal • 3/16 inch thick	**Norpro 12-Inch Stainless Steel Skewers**
	GRILL LIGHTER	• Flexible neck • Refillable chamber with large, easy-to-read fuel window • Comfortable grip	**Zippo Flexible Neck Utility Lighter**
	OUTDOOR GRILL PAN	• Narrow slits and raised sides so food can't fall through or off • Sturdy construction with handles	**Weber Professional-Grade Grill Pan**
	SMOKER BOX	• Cast iron for slow heating and steady smoke • Easy to fill, empty, and clean	**GrillPro Cast Iron Smoker Box made by Onward Manufacturing Company**
	VERTICAL ROASTER	• Helps poultry cook evenly • 8-inch shaft keeps chicken above fat and drippings in pan • Attached basin catches drippings for pan sauce • Sturdy construction	**Vertical Roaster with Infuser by Norpro** Best Buy: **Elizabeth Karmel's Grill Friends Porcelain Chicken Sitter**
	GRILL LIGHT	• Durable and waterproof • Sturdy, simple clamp • Can be configured to stand freely on a side table for grills without handles	**Blackfire Clamplight Waterproof**
SPECIALTY PIECES	**ITEM**	**WHAT TO LOOK FOR**	**TEST KITCHEN FAVORITES**
	APPLE CORER	• Comfortable grip with offset handle • Sharp teeth • Wide blade diameter	Best Push-Style: **Norpro Grip EZ Fruit Wedger, 16 Slices with Base** Best Crank-Style: **VKP Brands Johnny Apple Peeler, Suction Base, Stainless Steel Blades, Red**

SPECIALTY PIECES	ITEM	WHAT TO LOOK FOR	TEST KITCHEN FAVORITES
	CORN STRIPPER	• Two sets of plastic prongs helped center the corn for more efficient cutting • Contains mess well	**RSVP International Deluxe Corn Stripper**
	TOMATO CORER	• Sharp teeth make easy, clean cuts • Lightweight, rounded-off plastic handle • Comfortable head-handle combination	**Norpro Tomato Core It**
	NUT CHOPPER	• Sharp, sturdy stainless steel chopping tines • Dishwasher-safe	**Prepworks from Progressive Nut Chopper with Non-Skid Base**
	GRILL PAN	• Well-seasoned surface releases food and cleans up easily • Tall, well-defined ridges produce excellent grill marks	Co-Winner: **Lodge Chef Collection Cast Iron Grill Pan**
		• Smooth finished and preseasoned patina • Tall ridges and low, flared sides • Doubles as a lid for the company's 12-inch skillet	Co-Winner: **Borough Furnace Grill Pan/ Braising Lid**
	STOVETOP GRIDDLE	• Heats quickly and evenly • Tall sides to contain grease • Upright, sturdy, easy-to-grab handles • Compatible with gas, electric, and induction stoves	**Cuisinart Chef's Classic Nonstick Double Burner Griddle**
	OYSTER KNIFE	• Upturned tip and unsharpened blade • Grippy, comfortable handle • Can handle oysters of all sizes	**R. Murphy Knives New Haven Shucker** Best for Experienced Users: **F. Dick Oyster Opener** Best Buy: **OXO Good Grips Oyster Knife**

SHOPPING FOR EQUIPMENT

SPECIALTY PIECES	ITEM	WHAT TO LOOK FOR	TEST KITCHEN FAVORITES
	SEAFOOD SCISSORS	• Curved blade neatly snips off shells • Tidy removal of shrimp vein	**RSVP International Endurance Seafood Scissors**
	SILICONE MICROWAVE LID	• Thin, silicone round to cover splatter-prone food during microwave heating • Easy to clean • Doubles as jar opener	**Piggy Steamer**
	PIPING SET	• Contains all of the essentials: twelve 16-inch pastry bags; four plastic couplers; and the following Wilton tips: #4 round, #12 round, #70 leaf, #103 petal, #2D large closed star, #1M open star • All parts available at most crafts stores	**Test Kitchen Self-Assembled à la Carte Decorating Set**
	PIZZA CUTTER	• Ultrasharp blade makes clean cuts on the first try • Grippy, textured handle	**Mercer Culinary Millennia Pizza Cutter 4"**
	POTATO RICER	• Large hopper that can hold 1¼ cups sliced potatoes • Interchangeable fine and coarse disks • Sturdy, ergonomic handles	**RSVP International Potato Ricer**
	TORTILLA WARMER	• Triple-layered sides with two layers of fabric around sheet of insulating plastic • 12-inch diameter to fit large wraps	**IMUSA 12" Cloth Tortilla Warmer**
	INSULATED FOOD CARRIER	• Keeps food piping hot for over 3 hours • Fits two 13 by 9-inch baking dishes • Handy zippered pocket holds serving utensils	**Rachael Ray Expandable Lasagna Lugger**
	CUPCAKE AND CAKE CARRIER	• Fits both round and square cakes and cupcakes • Snap locks • Nonskid base • Collapses for easy storage	**Progressive Collapsible Cupcake and Cake Carrier**

The Complete Cook's Country TV Show Cookbook

SPECIALTY PIECES	ITEM	WHAT TO LOOK FOR	TEST KITCHEN FAVORITES
	CAKE LIFTER	• Sturdy but small and slightly flexible • Rounded corners for visibility • Comfortable offset handle	**Fat Daddio's Cake Lifter**
	CAKE STAND	• Elevated rotating stand so you can hold the spatula steady for easy frosting • Solid, light construction	**Winco Revolving Cake Decorating Stand**
	CREAM WHIPPER	• Responsive lever for better control and easy piping • Grips on handle and neck for easy refilling and cleanup	**iSi Gourmet Whip**
	BLADE GRINDER	• Electric, not manual, grinders • Deep bowl to hold ample amount of coffee beans • Good to have two, one each for coffee grinding and spice grinding	**Krups Coffee and Spice Grinder**
	INNOVATIVE TEAPOT	• Contained, ultrafine-mesh strainer keeps tea leaf dregs separate • One-piece design for easy cleaning	**IngenuiTEA by Adagio Teas**
	TRAVEL MUG	• Simple, leakproof lid design • Good heat retention • Easy to clean and dishwasher-safe	**Zojirushi Stainless Steel Mug (SM-SE)**
	WATER BOTTLE	• Large capacity yet lightweight • Superdurable • Easy-to-use screw-on spout	Plastic: **YETI Yonder 1L/34 oz Water Bottle** Stainless-Steel: **YETI Rambler 26 oz Water Bottle** Glass: **Lifefactory 22 oz Glass Bottle with Classic Cap**

SPECIALTY PIECES	ITEM	WHAT TO LOOK FOR	TEST KITCHEN FAVORITES
	WINE OPENER	• Durable design • Teflon-coated worm	**Pulltap's Classic Evolution Corkscrew by Pulltex** Best Buy: **Trudeau Double Lever Corkscrew**
	ELECTRIC WINE OPENER	• Sleek, streamlined, and easy to use • Transparent window to see corkscrew in action	**Secura Electric Wine Opener**
	WINE AERATOR	• Long, tubelike design that exposes wine to air as it is being poured • Neat, hands-free aerating	**Nuance Wine Finer**
	COCKTAIL SHAKER	• Holds at least 18 ounces to make one or two cocktails at once • Comfortable carafe-like shape • Wide mouth for easy filling, muddling, and cleaning	Cobbler Style: **Tovolo Stainless Steel 4-in-1 Cocktail Shaker** Boston Shaker: **Houdini by Rabbit 24oz Stainless Steel & Glass Boston Cocktail Shaker**
	BEER SAVERS	• Fits both glass and plastic bottles • Preserves carbonation for up to 2 days	**SaveBrands Beer Savers**
	COOLER	• Ice lasted 7 days, and soda stayed at 50 degrees for five days • Durable construction	**Yeti Tundra 45** Best Buy: **Coleman 50 QT Xtreme Wheeled Cooler**
	SOFT COOLER	• Thick, closed-cell foam insulation • Smooth zippers • Box shape • Side handles	**Engel HD20 22qt Heavy-Duty Soft Sided Cooler Tote Bag**
	ICE PACK	• Convenient handle for easy transporting • No bulges formed upon freezing • Remained cold for almost 14 hours when sitting at room temperature	**Arctic Ice Alaskan Series, X-Large**

SPECIALTY PIECES	ITEM	WHAT TO LOOK FOR	TEST KITCHEN FAVORITES
	PICNIC BASKET	• Portable to carry • Padded straps • Equipped with silverware, plates, wine glasses • Collapses with all items inside	Most Comfortable: **Sunflora Picnic Backpack for 4** Easiest to Store: **Picnic at Ascot Collapsible Picnic Basket for 4**
	SPORK AND TRAVEL UTENSIL SET	• Lightweight set • Held together by magnets • Variety of utensils	**Full Windsor Magware Magnetic Camping Utensils Set** Best Buy: **UCO Switch Spork Utensil** Best Spork: **Light My Fire Spork Titanium**
	PORTABLE BURNER	• Powerful cooking • Easy to use and clean • Dual fuel option of butane or propane	Overall Winner/Best Gas Burner: **Grill Boss 90057 Dual Fuel Camp Stove** Best Buy/Best Electric Burner: **IMUSA USA GAU-80305 Electric Single Burner 1100-Watts**
	SELTZER MAKER	• Can customize carbonation from mildly fizzy to very bubbly • Water bottles are a convenient size and dishwasher-safe • Uses SodaStream "quick-connect" CO^2 canisters	**SodaStream Terra**
	COUNTERTOP VACUUM SEALER	• Digital screen tracks the machine's progress • Intuitive control panel • Gentle setting for vacuum sealing fragile foods • Built-in storage for plastic roll	**Nesco Deluxe Vacuum Sealer**
	COMPOST BIN	• Lightweight yet spacious • Body and lid are dishwasher-safe • Easy-to-open lid • Handle is fastened securely in place	**OXO Good Grips Easy-Clean Compost Bin—1.75 Gal** For Larger Households: **Exaco Eco 2000 Kitchen Compost Pail**
MUST-HAVE ITEM	FIRE EXTINGUISHER	• Fast and effective • Intuitive to use and easy to figure out • Powerful spray worked well on grease fire and burning fabric	**Kidde ABC Multipurpose Home Fire Extinguisher**

SHOPPING FOR EQUIPMENT

KITCHEN SUPPLIES	ITEM	WHAT TO LOOK FOR	TEST KITCHEN FAVORITES
MUST-HAVE ITEMS	PARCHMENT PAPER	• Sturdy paper for heavy doughs • Easy release of baked goods • 12 by 16 inches fits in standard rimmed baking sheets	**King Arthur Flour Parchment Paper 100 Half-Sheets**
	PLASTIC WRAP	• Clings to vessels of different materials • Dispenses easily • Resilient and strong over long periods of time	**Freeze-Tite Clear High Cling Freezer Wrap**
	HERB KEEPER	• Adjustable height makes it easy to add or remove herbs • Vented lid prevents condensation from building up • Internal dividers keep things nice and tidy	**Cole & Mason Fresh Herb Keeper**
	PLASTIC FOOD STORAGE CONTAINER	• Clear, lightweight material stays as stain-free as glass • Snug seal doesn't leak • Flat top makes for secure, compact stacking	**Rubbermaid Brilliance Food Storage Container, Large, 9.6 Cup**
	DISH TOWEL	• Thin cotton for absorbency and flexibility • Dries glassware without streaks • Washes clean without shrinking	**Williams Sonoma Striped Towels, Set of 4**
	DISPOSABLE PLATES	• Roomy eating surface with steep lip • Thick bagasse (dried sugarcane pulp) holds up to 2 pounds of food	**Hefty ECOSAVE Compostable 10 1/8 inch Plates**
	DISPOSABLE UTENSIL SETS	• Sturdy and rigid • Pointy, sharp fork tines • Thin knife blades with sharp serrations • Moderately deep spoon bowl • Flat, smooth, and comfortable handles	**Ecovita 100% Compostable Cutlery Combo 380 Set** Best Set Under 100 Pieces: **The Diamond Entertaining 96 Combo**
	SWEDISH DISHCLOTHS	• Standard dishcloth size • Durable, absorbent cloth • Multiple colors help with organization and sanitation • Great for scrubbing • Easy to clean	Co-winner: **SWEDEdishcloths** Co-winner: **Skoy Cloth**

728   *The Complete Cook's Country TV Show Cookbook*

KITCHEN SUPPLIES	ITEM	WHAT TO LOOK FOR	TEST KITCHEN FAVORITES
	PAPER TOWELS	• Thick, soft, sturdy sheets • Single sheet holds nearly ½ cup of water • Easily tear off half or full-size sheets	**Bounty Select-A-Size Paper Towels**
	APRON	• Adjustable neck strap and long strings • Full coverage; chest area reinforced with extra layer of fabric • Stains wash out completely	**Bragard Travail Bib Apron**
	LIQUID DISH SOAP	• High concentration of surfactants to wash away oil • Clean scent	**Mrs. Meyer's Clean Day Liquid Dish Soap, Lavender**
	SPRAY MOP	• Large, absorbent, machine-washable microfiber pad • Lightweight yet sturdy • Long handle • Comfortable grip with large spray trigger • Powerful spraying mechanism	**O-Cedar ProMist MAX Microfiber Spray Mop**
	DISH DRYING RACK	• Two roomy utensil holders • Seven-slot knife block • Ledge that can hang four wineglasses upside down for spot-free drying • Raised feet to hold it up off the counter	Innovative, Large: **simplehuman Steel Frame Dishrack**
		• Readily fits smaller items • Folds flat for easy storage • Best choice for small spaces or light loads	Innovative, Small: **Progressive Prepworks Collapsible Over-The-Sink Dish Drainer**
		• Fits dishes for a family of four • Angled mat tidily drains off water	Traditional/Best Buy: **Rubbermaid Antimicrobial Sink Drainer, Large and Antimicrobial Drain Board, Large**

SHOPPING FOR EQUIPMENT

Stocking Your Pantry

Using the best ingredients is one way to guarantee success in the kitchen. But how do you know what to buy? Shelves are filled with a dizzying array of choices—and price does not equal quality. Over the years, the test kitchen's blind-tasting panels have evaluated thousands of ingredients, brand by brand, side by side, plain and in prepared applications, to determine which brands you can trust and which brands to avoid. In the chart that follows, we share the results, revealing our top-rated choices and the attributes that made them stand out among the competition. And because our test kitchen accepts no support from product manufacturers, you can trust our ratings. See AmericasTestKitchen.com for updates to these tastings.

TEST KITCHEN FAVORITE	WHY WE LIKE IT	RUNNERS-UP
ANCHOVIES **Merro Flat Fillets of Anchovies in Pure Olive Oil**	• Firm, meaty texture • Savory without being fishy • Moderate saltiness	Ortiz Anchovies in Olive Oil
APPLESAUCE **Musselman's Lite**	• An unusual ingredient, sucralose, sweetens this applesauce without overpowering its fresh, bright apple flavor • Pinch of salt boosts flavor above weak, bland, and too-sweet competitors • Coarse, almost chunky texture, not slimy like applesauces sweetened with corn syrup	Musselman's Home Style, Santa Cruz Organic
BACON, SUPERMARKET **Oscar Mayer Naturally Hardwood Smoked**	• Good balance of chew and crispness • Not too smoky, with a mildly meaty flavor	Smithfield Hometown Original, Hormel Black Label Original
BACON, ARTISANAL **Vande Rose Applewood Smoked Artisan Dry Cured**	• Perfectly balanced salt, sugar, and smoke levels • Substantial, thick and chewy texture	Burger's Smokehouse Original Country
BAKING POWDER **Argo Double Acting**	• Easy-to-use plastic tub • Makes chewy cookies, fluffy biscuits, and moist but airy cakes	Bob's Red Mill, Calumet, Clabber Girl

	TEST KITCHEN FAVORITE	WHY WE LIKE IT	RUNNERS-UP
	BEANS, CANNED BAKED **B&M Vegetarian**	• Firm and pleasant texture with some bite • Sweetened with molasses for complexity and depth	Bush's Best Original, Van Camp's Original
	BEANS, CANNED BLACK **Bush's Best**	• Clean, mild, and slightly earthy flavor • Firm, almost al dente texture, not mushy or pasty • Good amount of salt	Goya, Progresso
	BEANS, CANNED CHICKPEAS **Goya**	• Nutty flavor • Plump, buttery • Nicely seasoned with just enough salt	Pastene, Bush's
	BEANS, CANNED WHITE **Goya**	• Clean, earthy flavor • Smooth, creamy interior with tender skins and a nice, firm bite • Not full of broken beans like some competitors	Bush's Best
	BREAD, MULTIGRAIN **Nature's Own Specialty 12 Grain**	• Substantial, chewy slices • Nutty, hearty seeds throughout and topped with rolled oats • Uses no white flour	Arnold 12 Grain, Pepperidge Farm 15 Grain
	BREAD, WHITE SANDWICH **Arnold Country White**	• Subtle sweetness, not tasteless or sour • Perfect structure, not too dry or too soft	Pepperidge Farm Farmhouse Hearty White
	BREAD, WHOLE-WHEAT SANDWICH **Arnold Whole Grains 100% Whole Wheat**	• Mild nuttiness with clean wheat flavor and a touch of sweetness • Tender and chewy with crunchy flecks of bulgur on the crust	Pepperidge Farm Farmhouse 100% Whole Wheat
	BREAD CRUMBS, PLAIN **Progresso Bread Crumbs Plain**	• Finely ground, uniform pieces • Neutral, pleasant flavor	4C
	BREAD CRUMBS, PANKO **Kikkoman Panko Japanese Style**	• Consistently sized pieces • Slightly sweet flavor	JFC, 4C, Progresso

STOCKING YOUR PANTRY

TEST KITCHEN FAVORITE	WHY WE LIKE IT	RUNNERS-UP
BROTH, BEEF **Better Than Bouillon Roasted Beef Base**	• Contains good amount of salt and multiple powerful flavor enhancers • Paste is economical, stores easily, and dissolves quickly in hot water	
BROTH, CHICKEN **Swanson Chicken Stock**	• Rich and meaty flavor • Hearty and pleasant aroma • Not sour, rancid, or salty like some competitors • Flavor-boosting ingredients include carrots, celery, and onions	Better Than Bouillon Premium Roasted Chicken Base
BROTH, VEGETARIAN **Orrington Farms Vegan Chicken Flavored Broth Base & Seasoning**	• Savory depth without off-tasting vegetable undertones • Easy to store • Yeast extract adds depth and richness	Swanson Certified Organic Vegetable Broth; Better Than Bouillon Vegetable Base, Reduced Sodium
BROWNIE MIX Mail-Order: **King Arthur All-American Brownie Mix**	• Fudgy, chewy consistency • Intense chocolate flavor • Easy to make	
Supermarket: **Ghirardelli Chocolate Supreme**	• Chewy and moist • Crackly top and fudgy middle • Strong, chocolate-forward flavor	Trader Joe's, Pillsbury, Stonewall Kitchen, Duncan Hines
BUNS, HAMBURGER **Martin's Sandwich Potato Rolls**	• Potato starch provides soft, moist crumb • Tender, fluffy texture • Rich sweetness complements saltiness of burgers • Primarily available in East Coast grocery stores or online	Pepperidge Farm, Arnold's
BUTTER, UNSALTED **Challenge**	• Clean, strong dairy flavor • Sticks are wrapped in aluminum foil, which may protect them from picking up off-flavors during shipping and storage	Kate's Creamery, Land O'Lakes
BUTTER, SALTED **Lurpak Slightly Salted**	• Made with cultured cream • Rich, creamy texture	Kate's Homemade, Plugrá European-Style, Land O'Lakes
CHEESE, AMERICAN, **Boar's Head**	• Strong cheesy flavor, unlike some competitors • Higher content of cheese culture contributes to better flavor	Kraft Deli Deluxe, Land O'Lakes

732   *The Complete Cook's Country TV Show Cookbook*

TEST KITCHEN FAVORITE	WHY WE LIKE IT	RUNNERS-UP
CHEESE, BLUE, CRUMBLED **Roth Buttermilk Blue Crumbles**	• Assertive, clean, well-balanced flavor • Lush, creamy crumbles cooked and uncooked	Boar's Head, Athenos
CHEESE, CHEDDAR, SHARP **Cabot Vermont Sharp Cheddar**	• Buttery, creamy texture • Nutty, complex sharpness	Tillamook, Cracker Barrel
CHEESE, CHEDDAR, EXTRA-SHARP **Cracker Barrel Extra Sharp White**	• Perfect balance of tang • Moderate amounts of fat and moisture ensure toothsome, crumbly texture when eaten plain and melty, creamy texture when cooked	Cabot Vermont Extra-Sharp, Kerrygold Reserve
CHEESE, CHEDDAR, LOW-FAT **Cracker Barrel Reduced Fat Sharp**	• Ample creaminess • Strong cheesy flavor • Good for cooking	Cabot 50% Light Sharp
CHEESE, COTTAGE **Daisy 4%**	• Large, uniform curds • Thick, creamy consistency • Clean, tart flavor	Good Culture, Breakstone's 4%
CHEESE, CREAM **Philadelphia Brick Original**	• Rich, tangy, and milky flavor • Thick, creamy texture, not pasty, waxy, or chalky	Philadelphia Cream Cheese Spreads Original, Organic Valley
CHEESE, FETA Block: **Real Greek**	• Silky, luxurious texture • Savory, complex flavor	Dodoni, Boar's Head
Crumbled: **Athenos Crumbled**	• High fat and relatively moderate sodium levels • Nice, big chunks that keep their shape	Boar's Head Creamy Feta Cheese Crumbles
CHEESE, FONTINA Real deal: **Mitica Fontina Val d'Aosta**	• Impressively complex: savory and earthy, with a nutty sweetness • Aged in caves for at least 80 days • Melts well	Zerto Fontal, Carr Valley, Fontina
Supermarket winner: **Boar's Head Fontina Cheese**	• Soft, creamy texture and a buttery, tangy flavor • Blends well with other ingredients	
CHEESE, GOAT **Laura Chenel Original Fresh Goat Cheese Log**	• Rich-tasting, grassy, tangy flavor • Smooth and creamy both unheated and baked • High salt content	Vermont Creamery, Chevrion

	TEST KITCHEN FAVORITE	WHY WE LIKE IT	RUNNERS-UP
	CHEESE, GRUYÈRE **1655 Le Gruyère AOP**	• Aged between 12 and 14 months • Crystalline structure with dense, fudgy texture • Deeply aged, caramelized, grassy flavors shine through even when cooked	Mifroma Le Gruyère Cavern AOP, Emmi Roth Grand Cru Surchoix
	CHEESE, MOZZARELLA Block: **Polly-O Whole Milk**	• Creamy, rich flavor with a hint of salt reminiscent of fresh mozzarella • Elastic but not gooey when melted	Galbani Whole Milk, Boar's Head Whole Milk Low Moisture
	Shredded: **Sargento Off the Block Shredded Low Moisture Part-Skim**	• Short strands easily spreadable over pizza dough • Classic creamy milkiness and slight tang	Kraft Low-Moisture Part-Skim
	CHEESE, PARMESAN, SUPERMARKET **Boar's Head Parmigiano-Reggiano**	• Rich and complex flavor balances tanginess and nuttiness • Dry, crumbly texture yet creamy with a crystalline crunch, not rubbery or dense • Aged for 24 months for better flavor and texture	Il Villagio Parmigiano-Reggiano 18 Month, SarVecchio
	CHEESE, PARMESAN, SHREDDED **Sargento Artisan Blends**	• Mix of small and large shreds • Blend of 10- and 18-month-aged Parmesan • Rich, nutty flavor	Kraft Natural Cheese
	CHEESE, PEPPER JACK **Boar's Head Monterey Jack with Jalapeño**	• Buttery, tangy cheese • Clean, balanced flavor with assertive spice	Tillamook
	CHEESE, AMERICAN PROVOLONE **Organic Valley Cheese Slices**	• Pleasantly tangy with subtle sharpness • High salt content intensifies flavor	Kraft Sliced Provolone Cheese, Applegate Naturals
	CHEESE, RICOTTA **Belgioioso Ricotta con Latte Whole Milk**	• Rich, dense consistency • Slight sweetness thanks to sweet whey and small amount of milk	Galbani Whole Milk, Calabro Whole Milk

TEST KITCHEN FAVORITE	WHY WE LIKE IT	RUNNERS-UP
CHEESE, SWISS For eating out of hand: **Edelweiss Creamery Emmentaler Switzerland**	• Produced using traditional Swiss methods, including copper vats for flavor development • Grassy, nutty notes	Emmi Kaltbach Cave-Aged Emmentaler Switzerland AOC
For cooking: **Boar's Head Gold Label Switzerland**	• Mildly nutty flavor • Smooth texture when melted	
For eating out of hand or cooking: **Emmi Emmentaler Cheese AOC**	• Pleasantly pungent • Creamy texture preferable for grilled cheese sandwiches	
CHICKEN, WHOLE **Mary's Free Range Air Chilled (also sold as Pitman's)**	• Great, savory chicken flavor • Very tender • Air-chilled for minimum water retention and cleaner flavor	Bell & Evans Air Chilled Premium Fresh
CHICKEN, BREASTS, BONELESS, SKINLESS **Bell & Evans Air Chilled**	• Juicy and tender with clean chicken flavor • Not salted or brined • Air-chilled • Aged on bone for at least six hours for significantly more tender meat	
CHILI POWDER **Morton & Bassett**	• Bold, full-flavored heat • Multidimensional flavor • Spices that complement but don't overwhelm the chiles	Penzeys Spices Medium Hot
CHOCOLATE, DARK **Ghirardelli 60% Cacao Bittersweet Chocolate Premium Baking Bar**	• Creamy texture • Complex flavor with notes of cherry and wine with slight smokiness	Callebaut Intense Dark L-60-40NV
CHOCOLATE, MILK **Endangered Species Chocolate Smooth + Creamy Milk Chocolate**	• Rich and intense with a balanced sweetness thanks to its high cacao percentage • Smooth and snappy texture	Scharffen Berger Extra Rich Milk Chocolate

STOCKING YOUR PANTRY

TEST KITCHEN FAVORITE	WHY WE LIKE IT	RUNNERS-UP
CHOCOLATE, DARK CHIPS **Ghirardelli 60% Premium Baking Chips**	• Rich chocolate flavor • Higher cacao and fat percentages	Guittard Extra Dark Chocolate Chips 63%
CHOCOLATE, MILK CHIPS **Hershey's Kitchens**	• Bold chocolate flavor outshines too-sweet, weak chocolate flavor of other chips • Deep cocoa flavor and creamy texture	Guittard, Ghirardelli
CHOCOLATE, UNSWEETENED **Baker's Baking Chocolate Bar 100% Cacao**	• Familiar, classic flavor • Makes a rich and caramel-y hot fudge sauce, and brownies with a deep cocoa flavor	Hershey's Kitchens Baking Bar
CHOCOLATE, WHITE CHIPS **Ghirardelli Classic White Baking Chips**	• Milky flavor with hints of vanilla, caramel, and butterscotch • Pleasantly creamy when eaten plain	Ghirardelli White Melting Wafers
CIDER, HARD APPLE **Angry Orchard Crisp**	• Crisp and refreshing • Strong apple flavor	Strongbow Gold Apple, Woodchuck Amber
CINNAMON **Morton & Bassett**	• The perfect balance of sweet and spicy • Mellow in baked applications	Penzeys Vietnamese, McCormick
COCOA POWDER **Droste Cacao**	• Earthy and woodsy deep chocolate flavor • High fat content and less starch yields perfectly chewy, rich, and moist baked goods	Guittard Cocoa Rouge, Valrhona
COCONUT MILK **Aroy-D**	• Velvety, luxurious, and not overly thick texture • Balanced, clean coconut flavor	Roland, Goya

The Complete Cook's Country TV Show Cookbook

	TEST KITCHEN FAVORITE	WHY WE LIKE IT	RUNNERS-UP
	COCONUT, UNSWEETENED SHREDDED **Now Real Food Organic**	• Nutty, tropical flavor • Fluffy, crisp texture	Woodstock Foods Organic
	COFFEE, SUPERMARKET MEDIUM-ROAST **Peet's Coffee Café Domingo**	• Extremely smooth, but bold-tasting with a strong finish • Rich chocolate and toast flavors • Few defective beans, low acidity, and optimal moisture	Millstone Breakfast Blend
	COFFEE, DECAFFEINATED **Maxwell House Decaf Original Roast**	• Smooth, mellow flavor without being acidic or harsh • Complex, with a slightly nutty aftertaste • Made with only flavorful Arabica beans	Peet's Decaf House Blend Ground, Starbucks Coffee Decaf House Blend
	COOKING SPRAY **Pam Original Cooking Spray**	• Sprays evenly • Food releases quickly and easily • Neutral flavor	Crisco Original No-Stick, Pam Olive Oil, LouAna Coconut Oil
	COOKING SPRAY, PROPELLANTLESS **Chosen Foods Avocado Oil Spray**	- 100% avocado oil - High smoke point	
	CORNMEAL **Anson Mills Fine Yellow**	• Slightly muted flavor, less corn forward and more buttery • Cornbread made with this cornmeal was soft and tender, with a smooth, cakey texture	Goya Fine Yellow Corn Meal, Pearl Milling Company Yellow Cornmeal, Quaker Yellow Cornmeal
	CREOLE SEASONING **Tony Chachere's Original Creole Seasoning**	• Strong garlic and red pepper notes • Vibrant and zesty with a punch of heat	McCormick Perfect Pinch Cajun Seasoning

STOCKING YOUR PANTRY 737

	TEST KITCHEN FAVORITE	WHY WE LIKE IT	RUNNERS-UP
	CUMIN **Simply Organic**	• Ground, flavorful, and robust with earthiness and warmth • Bright, with a touch of sweetness	Spice Islands Ground Cumin Seed
	CURRY POWDER **Penzeys Sweet**	• Balanced, neither too sweet nor too hot • Complex and vivid earthy flavor; not thin, bland, or one-dimensional NOTE: Available at penzeys.com, or on Amazon	Durkee
	DINNER ROLLS, FROZEN **Pepperidge Farm Stone Baked Artisan French**	• Tender on the inside with crispy crust • Has only seven ingredients • Tastes homemade, with a hint of salt	Rhodes Warm-N-Serv French Crusty Rolls
	EGG SUBSTITUTE **Judee's Vegan Egg Replacer Mix**	• Makes moist, airy cakes and pleasantly chewy cookies • No savory flavorings	Namaste Foods Vegan Egg Replacer, Bob's Red Mill Gluten Free Vegan Egg Replacer
	Best for scrambled eggs: **JUST Egg Plant Based Liquid Egg**	• Texture closely mimics bounce and chew of traditional scrambled eggs	
	EGG WHITES, PROCESSED **Eggology 100% Egg Whites**	• Work well in egg white omelets • Pasteurized; safe for use in uncooked applications • Make satisfactory baked goods	
	ESPRESSO POWDER **Civilized Coffee Espresso Powder**	• Coffee as the main ingredient • Fresh-brewed, complex flavor	
	FIVE-SPICE POWDER **Frontier Natural Products Co-op**	• Nice depth, not one-dimensional • Balanced heat and sweetness	Dynasty Chinese, McCormick Gourmet Collection Chinese
	FLOUR, WHOLE-WHEAT **King Arthur Premium**	• Finely ground for hearty but not overly coarse texture in bread and pancakes • Sweet, nutty flavor	Bob's Red Mill Organic

TEST KITCHEN FAVORITE	WHY WE LIKE IT	RUNNERS-UP
FREEZE-DRIED BACKPACKING MEAL **Peak Refuel Beef Stroganoff**	• Easy to make • Very flavorful • Filling	Packit Gourmet Skillet Biscuits & Sausage Gravy, Patagonia Provisions Organic Black Bean Soup
FRENCH FRIES, FROZEN **Alexia Organic Yukon Select**	• Crispy exteriors with fluffy, creamy interiors • Earthy, potato-y flavor	Ore-Ida Golden
GARLIC SUBSTITUTES **Spice World Fresh Peeled Organic Garlic**	• Tastes practically identical to freshly peeled cloves • Great shortcut to avoid fussing with papery skins	Dorot Gardens Crushed Garlic
GIARDINIERA **Pastene**	• Sharp, vinegary tang • Crunchy mix of vegetables • Mellow heat that's potent but not overpowering	Scala Hot
GRITS **Anson Mills Pencil Cob**	• Full, ripe, fresh corn flavor • Nice chew while still thick and creamy	Arrowhead Mills Organic Yellow, Bob's Red Mill
HAM, BLACK FOREST DELI **Dietz & Watson Smoked with Natural Juices**	• Good texture • Nice ham flavor	
HAM, COUNTRY **Burgers' Smokehouse Ready to Cook**	• Balanced, nuanced, and rich and fatty ham flavor • Slices are silky, tender, and slightly dry	Tripp Country Hams Whole, Edwards Virginia Traditions Uncooked Virginia
HAM, SPIRAL-SLICED, BONE-IN **Burgers' Smokehouse Spiral-Sliced City**	• Very smoky flavor that is assertive but not over the top • Texture is moist and tender	Applewood Farms

STOCKING YOUR PANTRY

TEST KITCHEN FAVORITE	WHY WE LIKE IT	RUNNERS-UP
HOISIN SAUCE **Kikkoman**	• Balances sweet, salty, pungent, and spicy flavors • Initial burn mellows into harmonious and aromatic blend without bitterness	Koon Chun
HORSERADISH **Woeber's Pure**	• Pleasant, slow burn is strong but not overwhelming • Distinct shreds of grated horseradish mixed together with a little vinegar	Silver Springs Prepared, Kelchner's
Inglehoffer Cream Style (also sold as Beaver Brand Grandma Rose's Hot Cream Horseradish)	• Lots of heat up front and a mustardy burn that lingers	
HOT DOGS **Nathan's Famous Skinless Beef Franks**	• Meaty, robust, and hearty flavor; not sweet, sour, or too salty • Juicy but not greasy • Firm, craggy texture; not rubbery, mushy, or chewy	Kayem Skinless Beef
HOT FUDGE SAUCE **Hershey's**	• True fudge flavor; not weak or overly sweet • Thick, smooth, and buttery texture	
ICE CREAM BARS **Dove Bar Vanilla Ice Cream with Milk Chocolate**	• Rich, prominent chocolate flavor • Thick, crunchy chocolate coating • Dense, creamy ice cream with pure vanilla flavor • Milk chocolate, not coconut oil, listed first in coating ingredients	Häagen-Dazs Vanilla Milk Chocolate All Natural, Blue Bunny Big Alaska
ICE CREAM CONES **Joy Waffle**	• Lightly sweet, with vanilla, toasty, and nutty flavors • Crunchy and crisp but not overly hard • Individual paper jackets keep things neat	Joy Sugar, Keebler Waffle
ICE CREAM, CHOCOLATE **Turkey Hill Premium Dutch**	• Ultra-creamy, smooth texture • Milk chocolate taste	Breyers, Edy's (known as Dreyer's in the Western United States and Texas)
ICE CREAM, VANILLA **Turkey Hill Original Premium**	• Silky and creamy with a rich vanilla flavor • Spoonable and airy, but still velvety from the use of viscous corn syrup	Ben & Jerry's

The Complete Cook's Country TV Show Cookbook

	TEST KITCHEN FAVORITE	WHY WE LIKE IT	RUNNERS-UP
	ICED TEA, LOOSE LEAF **Tazo**	• Distinctive flavor with floral notes • Balanced level of strength and astringency	Luzianne, Tetley Premium Blend
	ICED TEA, BOTTLED, WITH LEMON **Lipton PureLeaf Black Tea with Lemon**	• Bright, balanced, and natural tea and lemon flavors • Uses concentrated tea leaves to extract flavor	Gold Peak
	JUICE, GRAPEFRUIT **Natalie's 100% Florida**	• Balanced and bright flavor, not too sweet • Clean and refreshing crispness	Florida's Natural Ruby Red
	JUICE, ORANGE **Natalie's 100% Florida Orange Juice, Gourmet Pasteurized**	• Fresh, sweet, and fruity flavor without overly acidic, sour, or from-concentrate taste • Gentler pasteurization helps retain fresh-squeezed flavor • Pleasant amount of light pulp	Simply Orange Not from Concentrate 100% Pure Squeezed Pasteurized, Medium Pulp
	JUICE, FROZEN ORANGE CONCENTRATE **Minute Maid Original**	• Full-bodied orange flavor • Good texture, includes some pulp	Tropicana 100% Juice
	KETCHUP **Heinz Organic**	• Smooth, viscous consistency • Bold, harmonious punch of saltiness, sweetness, tang, and tomato flavor • Classic, familiar flavor	Heinz Tomato Ketchup
	KING CAKE **Joe Gambino's Bakery**	• Moist, with a light and fluffy texture • Buttery, vanilla flavor with mellow cinnamon notes • DIY frosting keeps the cake from getting messy in transit	Poupart Bakery Incorporated – Cinnamon, Haydel's Bakery "Piece of Cake" Package – Traditional
	LARD Artisanal: **U.S. Dreams** Supermarket: **John Morrell Snow Cap**	• Preservative-free, nonhydrogenated lard • Clean and rich flavor while remaining light • Partial hydrogenation helps ensure firmness • Neutral flavor leaves food very tasty	
	LEMONADE Sweet: **Tropicana Lively Lemonade** Tart: **Natalie's Natural**	• 10 percent fruit juice sweetened with sugar • Bright, refreshing lemon flavor • 20 percent fruit juice sweetened with sugar • Perfectly balances sweetness with tartness	Simply, Newman's Own, Minute Maid, Florida's Natural

STOCKING YOUR PANTRY 741

	TEST KITCHEN FAVORITE	WHY WE LIKE IT	RUNNERS-UP
	MACARONI & CHEESE **Kraft Velveeta Original Shells & Cheese**	• Strong and rich cheese flavor • Thick liquid sauce made from real cheese and milk • Dry shell pasta, instead of frozen, gives substantial texture	
	MAYONNAISE **Blue Plate**	• Great balance of taste and texture • Tastes close to homemade NOTE: While it's one of the top-selling brands in the country, you'll have to mail-order it unless you live in the South or Southeast	Hellmann's Real, Hellmann's Light, Spectrum Organic, Duke's
	MAYONNAISE, LIGHT **Hellmann's Light**	• Bright, balanced flavor close to full-fat counterpart; not overly sweet • Not as creamy as full-fat but passable texture NOTE: Hellmann's is known as Best Foods west of the Rocky Mountains	
	MOLASSES **Brer Rabbit All Natural Unsulphured Mild Flavor**	• Acidic yet balanced • Strong and straightforward raisin-y taste • Pleasantly bitter bite	Plantation Barbados Unsulphured, Grandma's Unsulphured Original
	MUSTARD, BROWN **Gulden's Spicy**	• Complex flavor with both heat and gentle tang • Smooth, creamy texture that goes perfectly with hot dogs	French's, Beaver Deli
	MUSTARD, COARSE-GRAIN **Grey Poupon Harvest Coarse Ground** and **Grey Poupon Country Dijon**	• Spicy, tangy burst of mustard flavor • High salt content amplifies flavor • Contains no superfluous ingredients that mask mustard flavor • Big, round seeds add pleasant crunch • Just enough vinegar, not too sour or thin	Woeber's Reserve Whole Grain
	MUSTARD, DIJON **Trois Petits Cochons Moutarde de Dijon**	• Potent, bold, and very hot; not weak or mild • Good balance of sweetness, tanginess, and sharpness • Not overly acidic, sweet, or one-dimensional like competitors	Maille Dijon Originale, Roland Extra Strong

	TEST KITCHEN FAVORITE	WHY WE LIKE IT	RUNNERS-UP
	MUSTARD, YELLOW **Heinz**	• Moderate acidity • Mild sweetness • Smooth texture	French's Classic, Koops' Original
	OATS, ROLLED **Bob's Red Mill Old Fashioned**	• Toasty flavor, even in cookies • Tender texture with just the right amount of chew • Hearty, tender texture and nutty flavor in oatmeal	Bob's Red Mill Extra Thick, Quaker Old Fashioned
	OATS, STEEL-CUT **Bob's Red Mill Organic**	• Rich and complex oat flavor with buttery, earthy, nutty, and whole-grain notes • Creamy yet toothsome texture • Moist but not sticky NOTE: Not recommended for baking	Arrowhead Mills Organic Hot Cereal, Country Choice Organic
	OLIVE OIL, EXTRA-VIRGIN **Carapelli Original Extra Virgin**	• Buttery, sweet, and herbaceous • Fresh flavor with a peppery finish	Bertolli; Botticelli; Star; Colavita Premium Selection; Pompeian Extra Virgin, Smooth; California Olive Ranch, 100% California
	OLIVE OIL, EXTRA-VIRGIN, PREMIUM Mild: **Castelines Classic AOP Vallée des Baux de Provence;**	• Starts out mild and buttery and builds to be bright and fruity • Green and herbal notes	Nicolas Alziari Cuvée Prestige, Acushla Green, Entelia
	Medium-intensity: **Castillo de Canena Reserva Familiar Picual;**	• Herbaceous, peppery, and aromatic • Smooth, rounded texture	Cobram Estate 100% Australian Select, Familia Zuccardi Arauco, Frantoio Grove Organic, Goutis Estate Bitter Grey, Merula
	Robust: **McEvoy Ranch Certified Organic**	• Sharp, intense, and rich • Notes of citrus, vanilla, and cinnamon	Frescobaldi Laudemio, Les Moulins Mahjoub Organic

STOCKING YOUR PANTRY 743

TEST KITCHEN FAVORITE	WHY WE LIKE IT	RUNNERS-UP
PANCAKE MIX **Hungry Jack Buttermilk Pancake and Waffle**	• Flavorful balance of sweetness and tang well-seasoned with sugar and salt • Light, extra-fluffy texture • Requires vegetable oil (along with milk and egg) to reconstitute the batter	Pearl Milling Company Original Pancake and Waffle
PAPRIKA, SWEET **The Spice House Hungarian Sweet**	• Complex flavor with earthy, fruity notes • Bright and bold, not bland and boring • Rich, toasty aroma NOTE: Available only through mail order, 312-274-0378 or thespicehouse.com	Penzeys Hungarian Sweet Kulonleges NOTE: Available at penzeys.com, or on Amazon
PASTA, CHEESE TORTELLINI **Barilla Three Cheese**	• Robustly flavored filling from combination of ricotta, Emmentaler, and Grana Padano cheeses • Tender pasta that's sturdy enough to withstand boiling but not so thick that it becomes doughy	Seviroli, Buitoni Three Cheese
PASTA, EGG NOODLES **Pennsylvania Dutch Wide (also sold as Mueller's)**	• Balanced, buttery flavor with no off-flavors • Light and fluffy texture, not gummy or starchy	Manischewitz Wide, Manischewitz Yolk Free Wide
PASTA, ELBOW MACARONI **Creamette**	• Buttery flavor • Firm but slightly tender texture • Longer noodles, close to 1 inch in length	De Cecco
PASTA, FETTUCCINE **Garofalo**	• Wide, thick noodles that cook up plump and springy with mild, clean flavor • Retained perfect chew when tossed with sauce	De Cecco, Barilla Classic Blue Box
PASTA, LASAGNA NOODLES No-boil: **Barilla**	• Taste and texture of fresh pasta • Delicate, flat noodles	Ronzoni Oven Ready, Pasta DeFino
Whole-wheat: **Bionaturae Organic 100% Whole Wheat**	• Complex nutty, rich wheat flavor • Substantial chewy texture without any grittiness	DeLallo 100% Organic Whole Wheat, Ronzoni Healthy Harvest
PASTA, PENNE **Mueller's Penne Rigate**	• Hearty texture, not insubstantial or gummy • Wheaty, slightly sweet flavor; not bland	Benedetto Cavalieri Penne Rigate, De Cecco

TEST KITCHEN FAVORITE	WHY WE LIKE IT	RUNNERS-UP
PASTA, SPAGHETTI **De Cecco Spaghetti No. 12**	• Rich, nutty, wheaty flavor • Firm, ropy strands with good chew, not mushy, gummy, or mealy	Rustichella d'Abruzzo Pasta Abruzzese di Semola di Grano Duro, Garofalo
PASTA, SPAGHETTI, GLUTEN-FREE **Jovial Organic Gluten-Free Brown Rice**	• High in fiber and protein • No gumminess or off-flavors as experienced with other brands • Delicate and thin strands	Barilla Gluten Free Spaghetti
PASTA, SPAGHETTI, WHOLE-WHEAT **Bionaturae Organic 100% Whole Wheat**	• Chewy and firm, not mushy or rubbery • Full and nutty wheat flavor	Barilla PLUS Multigrain
PASTA SAUCE, JARRED **Rao's Homemade Marinara**	• Vibrant, bright, aromatic sauce • Adds buttery, creamy richness to dishes • Uses imported whole tomatoes	Victoria Fine Foods Premium Marinara
PEANUT BUTTER, CREAMY **Skippy**	• Smooth, creamy, and spreadable • Good balance of sweet and salty flavors	Jif, Peter Pan Natural
PEPPERCORNS, BLACK **Tone's Whole Black Peppercorns**	• Whole peppercorns (not preground) • Moderate, balanced heat with subtle floral and smoky notes • No overpowering or off-flavors	Penzeys Whole Telicherry Indian Peppercorns
PEPPERONI, SLICED **Margherita Italian Style**	• Nice balance of meatiness and spice • Tangy, fresh flavor with hints of fruity licorice and peppery fennel • Thin slices with the right amount of chew	Boar's Head
PEPPERS, ROASTED RED **Dunbars Sweet**	• Balance of smokiness and sweetness • Mild, sweet, and earthy red pepper flavor • Firm texture, not slimy or mushy • Packed in simple yet strong brine of salt and water without distraction of other strongly flavored ingredients	Cento

STOCKING YOUR PANTRY

TEST KITCHEN FAVORITE	WHY WE LIKE IT	RUNNERS-UP
PICKLES, BREAD-AND-BUTTER **Bubbies Chips**	• Subtle, briny tang • All-natural solution that uses real sugar, not high-fructose corn syrup	
PICKLES, WHOLE KOSHER DILL **Boar's Head**	• Pleasantly crisp with a great snap • Slightly spicy and very garlicky; has a homemade pickle flavor	Mt. Olive Kosher Dills
PIE CRUST, READY-MADE **Pillsbury Refrigerated**	• Flaky, buttery texture • Fits in standard pie plate • Enough overhang to crimp edges nicely	
PIZZA, PEPPERONI, FROZEN **Pizzeria! by DiGiorno Primo Pepperoni**	• Thick, crisp, and airy crust with a browned and charred bottom • Herby, zesty sauce • Very meaty pepperoni	Freschetta Brick Oven Crust Pepperoni and Italian Style Cheese, Red Baron Fire Baked
POPCORN, BAGGED **Smartfood Smart50 Sea Salt**	• Subtle saltiness and nice, toasty flavor • Round, fluffy kernels that are crunchy on the outside with a tender interior	Kettle Sea Salt, Popcorn Indiana Sea Salt
PORK, PREMIUM **Snake River Farms American Kurobuta (Berkshire)**	• Deep pink tint, which indicates higher pH level and more flavorful meat • Tender texture and juicy, intensely pork-y flavor	D'Artagnan Berkshire Chops (Milanese-Style Cut)
POTATO CHIPS Kettle Style: **Utz's Kettle Classics, Original**	• Perfectly salted, flavorful chips • Slightly thick chips that are crunchy • Not too greasy	
 Regular: **Herr's Crisp 'N Tasty**	• Thin and crispy without being flimsy	

746 *The Complete Cook's Country TV Show Cookbook*

TEST KITCHEN FAVORITE	WHY WE LIKE IT	RUNNERS-UP
PRESERVES, PEACH **American Spoon Red Haven**	• Bold, ripe peach taste and balanced sweetness • Loose and spreadable texture, similar to homemade preserves	Bonne Maman, Smucker's
PRESERVES, RASPBERRY **Smucker's**	• Clean, strong raspberry flavor; not too tart or sweet • Not overly seedy • Ideal, spreadable texture; not too thick, artificial, or overprocessed	Trappist Jam
RICE, ARBORIO **RiceSelect**	• Creamier than competitors • Smooth grains • Characteristic good bite of Arborio rice in risotto where al dente is ideal	Riso Baricella Superfino, Rienzi Premium Gourmet
RICE, BASMATI **Daawat**	• Pleasantly chewy, long, intact, fluffy grains • Fragrant, aromatic flavor • Aged 18 to 24 months • Imported from India	Goya, Royal
RICE, BROWN **Lundberg Organic Long Grain**	• Firm yet tender grains • Bold, toasty, nutty flavor • Works with a range of cooking methods • Includes the best instructions	Riceland Extra Long Grain Natural, Carolina Whole Grain (also sold as Mahatma)
RICE, LONG-GRAIN WHITE **Lundberg Organic Long Grain**	• Nutty, buttery, and toasty flavor • Distinct, smooth grains that offer some chew without being overly chewy	Carolina Enriched Extra-Long-Grain
RICE, READY **Minute Ready to Serve**	• Parboiled long-grain white rice that is ready in less than 2 minutes • Toasted, buttery flavor • Firm grains with al dente bite	
SALSA, JARRED GREEN **Frontera Tomatillo**	• Sweet and nuanced flavor with a roasted, smoky taste from charred tomatillo skins • A good amount of heat • Has no preservatives or stabilizers	

	TEST KITCHEN FAVORITE	WHY WE LIKE IT	RUNNERS-UP
	SALSA, JARRED HOT **Pace Hot Chunky**	• Good balance of bright tomato, chile, and vegetal flavors • Chunky, almost crunchy texture; not mushy or thin • Spicy and fiery but not overpowering	Frontera Hot Habanero with Roasted Tomatoes and Cilantro, Newman's Own All Natural Chunky
	SALSA, JARRED, MILD **Chi-Chi's Mild Thick & Chunky**	• Hint of heat with good balance and sweet, satisfying tomato flavor • Thick, smooth base fortified with concentrated crushed tomatoes and chunks of vegetables	
	SALT, KOSHER **Diamond Crystal**	• Flakes have a soft, delicate texture that is easy to crush between your fingers • Contains no anticaking agents • Dissolves rapidly	Morton Kosher Salt
	SAUERKRAUT **Eden Organic**	• Slight sweetness and subtle zing, bright tanginess • Small, soft shreds with just enough chew	Libby's
	SAUSAGE, BREAKFAST **Jimmy Dean Fully Cooked Original Pork Links**	• Meaty chew and a crisp, golden crust • Balance of sweet and spicy for a rich pork taste	Odom's Tennessee Pride Fully Cooked Original Sausage Links, Bob Evans Fully Cooked Original Pork Sausage Links
	SOUP, CANNED CHICKEN NOODLE **Muir Glen Organic**	• Organic chicken and vegetables and plenty of seasonings give it a fresh taste and spicy kick • Firm, not mushy, vegetables and noodles • No off-flavors	Progresso Traditional
	SOUP, TOMATO **Progresso Vegetable Classics Hearty**	• Includes fresh, unprocessed tomatoes, not just tomato puree like some competitors • Tangy, slightly herbaceous flavor • Balanced seasoning and natural sweetness • Medium body and slightly chunky texture	Imagine Organic Vine Ripened
	SPREAD, STRAWBERRY **Smucker's Preserves**	• Robust, natural strawberry flavor without any added flavoring • Pleasing consistency, neither too runny nor too thick	Welch's Natural Strawberry Spread, Crofter's Organic Strawberry Just Fruit Spread

748   *The Complete Cook's Country TV Show Cookbook*

TEST KITCHEN FAVORITE	WHY WE LIKE IT	RUNNERS-UP
STEAK SAUCE **Heinz 57 Sauce**	• Mellow, restrained flavor that doesn't overpower the meat • Fruity, sweet, and tangy flavor with hints of heat and smoke • Smooth texture with enough body to cling to steak without being gluey	Lea & Perrins Traditional
SWEETENED CONDENSED MILK **Borden Eagle Brand** and **Nestlé Carnation**	• Made with whole milk • Thick, smooth, velvety	
TARTAR SAUCE **McCormick Original**	• Rich and eggy sauce with good acidity • Abundance of sweet pickle bits	
TEA, BLACK For plain tea: **Twinings English Breakfast**	• Bright, bold, and flavorful yet not too strong • Fruity, floral, and fragrant • Smooth, slightly astringent profile preferred for tea without milk	Lipton Black Tea, Bigelow English Teatime
With milk and sugar: **Tetley British Blend**	• Boasts caramel notes and full, deep, smoky flavors • Bold, fruity flavor	Celestial Seasonings English Breakfast Estate Tea
TERIYAKI SAUCE **Soy Vay Veri Veri Teriyaki Marinade & Sauce**	• Contains sesame seeds and small chunks of onion • Strong garlic flavor	
TOMATOES, CANNED CRUSHED **San Merican Crushed Tomatoes**	• Bright, clear tomato flavor • Crushed tomatoes in liquid contribute thick, hearty texture	RedPack Crushed Tomatoes in Puree (also sold as Red Gold), Pastene Kitchen Ready Chunky Style Ground Peeled Tomatoes
TOMATOES, CANNED DICED **San Merican Diced Tomatoes**	• Fresh and bright tomato flavor • Perfectly sized pieces	Tutturosso Diced Tomatoes, Muir Glen Organic Diced Tomatoes, Cento Petite Diced Tomatoes

STOCKING YOUR PANTRY

	TEST KITCHEN FAVORITE	WHY WE LIKE IT	RUNNERS-UP
	TOMATOES, CANNED WHOLE **Cento San Marzano Certified Peeled Tomatoes**	• Bright, fresh, sweet tomato flavor • Velvety smooth texture • Produces great cooked results	Red Gold Whole Peeled Tomatoes
	TOMATO PASTE, CANNED **Cento Tomato Paste**	• Savory, with good fruity flavors • Bright and acidic but not bitter or harsh	Contadina Tomato Paste
	TOMATO PASTE, TUBED **Cento Double Concentrated Tomato Paste**	• Intense, robust tomato flavors • Balance of sweet and tart flavors	Mutti Double Concentrated Tomato Paste
	TORTILLA CHIPS **Tostitos Original Restaurant Style Tortilla Chips**	• Delicate yet substantial chip that holds up well when dipping • Delightfully salty • Relatively large size	Tortiyahs!, Mission, Santitas, Calidad, On the Border, Juanita's
	TORTILLAS, CORN/WHEAT BLEND **Maria and Ricardo's Handmade Style Soft Corn Tortillas, Yellow**	• Subtle corn flavor and slight nuttiness • Pleasantly chewy	
	TORTILLAS, ALL-CORN **Guerrero White Corn Tortillas**	• Soft and pliable, thin but not frail • Tender with some chew	
	TORTILLAS, FLOUR **Old El Paso Flour Tortillas for Soft Tacos & Fajitas**	• Thin, flaky, tender tortilla • Made with plenty of fat and salt	Guerrero Tortillas de Harina Caseras

	TEST KITCHEN FAVORITE	WHY WE LIKE IT	RUNNERS-UP
	TOSTADAS, CORN **Mission Tostadas Estilo Casero**	• Crisp, crunchy texture • Good corn flavor • Flavor and texture that are substantial enough to stand up to hearty toppings	Charras
	TUNA PACKED IN OIL **Tonnino Tuna Fillets in Olive Oil**	• Meaty yellowfin tuna that has a clean and bright taste • Large, lovely flakes	
	Ortiz Bonito del Norte Albacore White Tuna in Olive Oil	• Firm but with delicate layers • Very well seasoned	
	TUNA PACKED IN WATER **American Tuna Pole Caught Wild Albacore**	• Seasoned well with lots of flavor • Moist but not mushy • Creamy texture	
	TURKEY, WHOLE **Mary's Free-Range Non-GMO Verified**	• Turkey flavor that is rich and robust • Tender and juicy meat • Untreated vegetarian-fed turkeys have clean turkey flavor	Plainville Farms Young, Diestel Turkey Ranch Non-GMO Verified
	TURKEY, WHOLE HERITAGE **Mary's Free-Range Heritage Turkey**	• Richly flavored • Great texture and moisture • Exquisitely crisp skin	Elmwood Stock Farm Organic, Good Shepherd Poultry Ranch, Heritage Turkey Farm

TEST KITCHEN FAVORITE	WHY WE LIKE IT	RUNNERS-UP
VANILLA BEANS **McCormick Madagascar**	• Moist, seed-filled pods • Complex, robust flavor with caramel notes	Spice Islands Bourbon, Nielsen-Massey Madagascar Bourbon Gourmet
VANILLA PURE EXTRACT **Simply Organic** Imitation: **McCormick Premium Vanilla Flavoring**	• Good vanilla presence • Complex flavor	
VEGETABLE OIL, ALL-PURPOSE **Crisco Blends**	• Unobtrusive, mild flavor for stir-frying and sautéing and for use in baked goods and in uncooked applications such as mayonnaise and vinaigrette • Neutral taste and absence of fishy or metallic flavors when used for frying	Mazola Canola Oil, Crisco Pure (Soybean)
VINEGAR, APPLE CIDER **Heinz Filtered**	• Right amount of acidity • Distinct apple flavor with a floral aroma and assertive, tangy qualities • Sharp and punchy	White House, Bragg Organic
VINEGAR, BALSAMIC **Bertolli of Modena**	• Tastes of dried fruit such as figs, raisins, and prunes • Tastes pleasantly sweet once reduced or whisked into vinaigrette	Monari Federzoni of Modena, Colavita of Modena
VINEGAR, RED WINE **Laurent du Clos**	• Crisp red wine flavor balanced by stronger than average acidity and subtle sweetness • Complex yet pleasing taste from multiple varieties of grapes	Pompeian Gourmet

The Complete Cook's Country TV Show Cookbook

	TEST KITCHEN FAVORITE	WHY WE LIKE IT	RUNNERS-UP
	VINEGAR, WHITE WINE **Napa Valley Naturals Organic**	• Balanced sweetness and acidity • Fruity and vibrant in vinaigrettes • Floral and aromatic notes with robust acidity in pickled vegetables	Star, Colavita Aged
	**WHIPPED TOPPING** **Cool Whip Extra Creamy**	• Thick, silky, and luscious • Excellent, fresh cream flavor and just enough sweetness	Land O'Lakes Whipped Heavy Cream
	WORCESTERSHIRE SAUCE **Lea & Perrins Original**	• Balanced notes of vinegar, pepper, and tamarind • Distinctly punchy, bright tanginess in marinades	French's, Annie's Organic Vegan
	YOGURT, WHOLE-MILK **Brown Cow Cream Top Plain**	• Rich, well-rounded flavor; not sour or bland • Especially creamy, smooth texture; not thin or watery • Higher fat content contributes to flavor and texture	Stonyfield Farm Organic Plain

STOCKING YOUR PANTRY 753

episode directory

2008
season one

EPISODE 101
Forgotten Cakes
Strawberry Poke Cake 606
Chocolate Blackout Cake 596

EPISODE 102
Sunday Dinner
Sunday-Best Garlic Roast Beef 329
Mashed Potato Casserole 370

EPISODE 103
Feeding a Crowd, Italian-Style
Slow-Cooker Italian Sunday Gravy 420
Meatballs and Marinara 432

EPISODE 104
Southern Regional Recipes
Lexington-Style Pulled Pork 501
Memphis Chopped Coleslaw 535

EPISODE 105
Autumn Supper
Old-Fashioned Roast Pork 347
Cranberry-Apple Crisp 656

EPISODE 106
All-American Picnic
Extra-Crunchy Fried Chicken 166
All-American Potato Salad 536

EPISODE 107
Easy as Pie
Raspberry Chiffon Pie 691
No-Fear Single-Crust Pie Dough 671

EPISODE 108
Steakhouse Favorites
Broiled Steaks 277
Super-Stuffed Baked Potatoes 301

EPISODE 109
Barbecued Chicken
Classic Barbecued Chicken 461
Best Potluck Macaroni and Cheese 124

EPISODE 110
Regional Chops
Tennessee Whiskey Pork Chops 227
Smoked Double-Thick Pork Chops 509

EPISODE 111
Midwestern Favorites
Chicago-Style Barbecued Ribs 491
Cincinnati Chili 241

EPISODE 112
California Grilling
California Barbecued Tri-Tip 484
Santa Maria Salsa 485
California Barbecued Beans 529

EPISODE 113
Diner Favorites
Fluffy Diner-Style Cheese Omelet 546
Short-Order Home Fries 554

2009
season two

EPISODE 201
Old-Fashioned Roast Beef Dinner
Classic Roast Beef and Gravy 331
Perfect Popovers 571

EPISODE 202
Pucker-Up Pies
Mile-High Lemon Meringue Pie 674
Icebox Key Lime Pie 677

EPISODE 203
Rise and Shine
Ultimate Cinnamon Buns 576
Better-Than-the-Box Pancake Mix 555

EPISODE 204
Surefire Seafood
Wood-Grilled Salmon 521
Baked Stuffed Shrimp 288
Grilled Jalapeño and Lime Shrimp Skewers 525

EPISODE 205
Fudgy Cakes
Tunnel of Fudge Cake 599
Hot Fudge Pudding Cake 622

EPISODE 206
Texas Chili
Easy Chili con Carne 409
Southern-Style Skillet Cornbread 568

EPISODE 207
Southern BBQ
Alabama Barbecued Chicken 460
Tangy Apple Cabbage Slaw 534

754   *The Complete Cook's Country TV Show Cookbook*

EPISODE 208
Fail-Safe Thanksgiving
Old-Fashioned Roast Turkey
 with Gravy 310
Garlic Mashed Potatoes 290

EPISODE 209
Fried Chicken Dinner
Creole Fried Chicken 165
Grilled Corn on the Cob 537

EPISODE 210
Ranch-Style Barbecue
Shredded Barbecued Beef 486
Ranch Potato Salad 539

EPISODE 211
Stovetop Desserts
Skillet Peach Cobbler 661
Maine Blueberry Grunt 659

EPISODE 212
Perfect Pork
Grilled Mustard-Glazed
 Pork Loin 518
Cider-Braised Pork Chops 158

EPISODE 213
Historical Cakes
Red Velvet Cake 596
Cold-Oven Pound Cake 619

2010
season three

EPISODE 301
Two Perfect Pies
Shaker Lemon Pie 672
Icebox Strawberry Pie 692

EPISODE 302
Family Dinner Favorites
Glazed Meatloaf 143
Crunchy Potato Wedges 259

EPISODE 303
Old-Fashioned Pork
Pan-Fried Pork Chops 156
Slow-Cooker Pork Pot Roast 346
Creamy Mashed Sweet Potatoes 371

EPISODE 304
Southern Comfort Food
Batter-Fried Chicken 164
Sweet Corn Spoonbread 376

EPISODE 305
Beef Meets Grill
Texas Barbecued Beef Ribs 492
Char-Grilled Steaks 279

EPISODE 306
Everybody Loves Chocolate
Chocolate Cream Cupcakes 621
Texas Sheet Cake 607

EPISODE 307
Hearty Italian Meals
Italian Pot Roast 448
Baked Manicotti with
 Meat Sauce 441

EPISODE 308
Northern Cookout
Cornell Barbecued Chicken 459
Syracuse Salt Potatoes 370
Jucy Lucy Burgers 488

EPISODE 309
The Chemistry of Cakes
Lemon Pudding Cake 624
Angel Food Cake 614

EPISODE 310
Southwestern Suppers
Beef Enchiladas 406
Easy Chicken Tacos 391

EPISODE 311
Breakfast Showstoppers
Monkey Bread 587
Dutch Baby 557

EPISODE 312
Chicken Two Ways
Roast Lemon Chicken 316
Skillet Chicken Parmesan 446

EPISODE 313
Ultimate Ham Dinner
Cider-Baked Ham 353
Delmonico Potato Casserole 293
Cornmeal Biscuits 561

2011
season four

EPISODE 401
Roast Beef Dinner
Herbed Roast Beef 331
Whipped Potatoes 368

EPISODE 402
Icebox Desserts
Lemon Icebox Cheesecake 624
French Silk Chocolate Pie 694

EPISODE 403
Fancy Chicken
Failproof Chicken Cordon Bleu 289
Apple Cider Chicken 317

EPISODE DIRECTORY 755

EPISODE 404
Chicken and Spareribs
Huli Huli Chicken 458
Chinese-Style Barbecued
  Spareribs 514

EPISODE 405
Southern Classics
Gumbo 192
Lane Cake 600

EPISODE 406
Retro Desserts
Banana Pudding 663
Chiffon Cake 615

EPISODE 407
Family Favorites
Swiss Steak with Tomato Gravy 150
Crispy Baked Potato Fans 300

EPISODE 408
Not Just for Kids
Chicken Nuggets 178
Macaroni and Cheese
  with Tomatoes 126

EPISODE 409
Fried Chicken and Biscuits
Nashville Hot Fried Chicken 168
Cat Head Biscuits 563

EPISODE 410
Road Food at Home
Slow-Cooker BBQ Beef Brisket 226
Beer-Battered Onion Rings 265

EPISODE 411
Autumn Desserts
Baked Apple Dumplings 652
Old-Fashioned Pecan Pie 685

EPISODE 412
Grilling
Grilled Thin-Cut Pork Chops 510
Grilled Potato Packs 530
Grilled Butterflied
  Lemon Chicken 467

EPISODE 413
St. Louis Cooking
St. Louis–Style Pizza 249
St. Louis BBQ Pork Steaks 512

2012
season five

EPISODE 501
Hearty Autumn Dinner
Smothered Pork Chops 157
Apple Fritters 653

EPISODE 502
Breakfast Breads
Morning Glory Muffins 573
Morning Buns 579

EPISODE 503
Chicken Pie and Stew
Chicken and Slicks 324
Moravian Chicken Pie 325

EPISODE 504
Italian Favorites Revisited
Slow-Cooker Meatballs
  and Marinara 433
Spinach and Tomato Lasagna 439

EPISODE 505
Simple Summer Supper
Grilled Steakhouse Steak Tips 276
Dill Potato Salad 540

EPISODE 506
Fun Modern Cakes
Strawberry Dream Cake 605
Chocolate Éclair Cake 608

EPISODE 507
Upscale Meat and Potatoes
Herb-Crusted Beef Tenderloin 332
Duchess Potatoes 369

EPISODE 508
Thrill of the Grill
Grilled Chicken Wings 468
South Carolina Pulled Pork 502

EPISODE 509
Forgotten Cookies
Melting Moments 635
Fairy Gingerbread 639

EPISODE 510
Super-Easy Comfort Food
Slow-Cooker French Onion Soup 275
Chuck Roast in Foil 342

EPISODE 511
Roast Chicken and Chimichangas
One-Pan Roast Chicken with
  Root Vegetables 318
Easier Chicken Chimichangas 400
Smoky Salsa Verde 401

EPISODE 512
Great American Cookout
Baltimore Pit Beef 235
Barbecued Country-Style Ribs 516

EPISODE 513
Dinner at the Diner
Patty Melts 220
Crispy Potato Tots 260

2013
season six

EPISODE 601
Picnic in the Country
Honey Fried Chicken 170
Amish Potato Salad 538

EPISODE 602
Company's Coming
Crown Roast of Pork 344
Parmesan-Crusted Asparagus 361

EPISODE 603
Old-Fashioned Sweet Endings
Peaches and Cream Pie 678
Cream Cheese Pound Cake 618

EPISODE 604
Great American Meat and Potatoes
Atlanta Brisket 225
Roasted Salt-and-Vinegar
  Potatoes 297

EPISODE 605
Italian Made Easy
Grandma Pizza 444
Slow-Cooker Minestrone 419

EPISODE 606
Backyard Barbecue
Barbecued Pulled Chicken 475
South Dakota Corncob-Smoked Ribs 516

EPISODE 607
Homespun Breakfast Treats
Fluffy Cornmeal Pancakes 556
English Muffin Bread 589

EPISODE 608
Irish Country Cooking
Guinness Beef Stew 328
Brown Soda Bread 590

EPISODE 609
Sweet on Texas
Tres Leches Cake 611
Magic Chocolate Flan Cake 609

EPISODE 610
Get Your Chile Fix
Green Chile Cheeseburgers 490
Five-Alarm Chili 410

EPISODE 611
Dessert on Bourbon Street
New Orleans Bourbon Bread Pudding 664
Beignets 558

EPISODE 612
Glazed Pork and Chicken Salad
Chinese-Style Glazed Pork Tenderloin 514
Chinese Chicken Salad 206

EPISODE 613
Comfort Food Classics
Meatloaf with Mushroom Gravy 145
Herb Roast Chicken 315

2014
season seven

EPISODE 701
Short-Order Breakfast Classics
Quicker Cinnamon Buns 577
"Impossible" Ham-and-Cheese Pie 547

EPISODE 702
Dressing Up Meat and Potatoes
Holiday Strip Roast 335
Olive Oil Potato Gratin 295

EPISODE 703
Black and White Desserts
Chocolate Angel Pie 696
Black and White Cookies 641

EPISODE 704
Pork Pernil and Fish Tacos
Pork Pernil 348
California-Style Fish Tacos 387

EPISODE 705
Old-Fashioned Sunday Suppers
Skillet-Roasted Chicken with Stuffing 322
Pork Chops with Vinegar Peppers 450

EPISODE 706
Steakhouse Specials Off the Grill
Grilled Cowboy-Cut Rib Eyes 282
Grilled Caesar Salad 533

EPISODE 707
Dinner from the Prairie
Milk-Can Supper 155
Dakota Bread 591

EPISODE 708
Memphis Ribs and Pretzel Salad
Memphis-Style Wet Ribs for a Crowd 228
Strawberry Pretzel Salad 129

EPISODE 709
Sweet Endings from the Icebox
Italian Cream Cake 616
Summer Berry Pudding 665

EPISODE 710
New Orleans Shrimp and Creamy Grits
New Orleans Barbecue Shrimp 196
Creamy Cheese Grits 128

EPISODE 711
Great Grilled Chicken and Texas Potato Salad
Grilled Chicken Leg Quarters 472
Texas Potato Salad 540

EPISODE 712
Oklahoma Onion Burgers and Louisiana Meat Pies
Oklahoma Fried Onion Burgers 223
Natchitoches Meat Pies 244

EPISODE 713
Colorado Chili and Slow-Cooker Baked Ziti
Colorado Green Chili 242
Slow-Cooker Baked Ziti 434

2015
season eight

EPISODE 801
American Classics with a Twist
Frosted Meatloaf 145
Apple Pie with Cheddar Crust 683

EPISODE 802
Muffins and Doughnuts Get a Makeover
Muffin Tin Doughnuts 575
Whole-Wheat Blueberry Muffins 572

EPISODE 803
Pasta for Every Plate
Pork Ragu 421
Pasta with Roasted Garlic Sauce, Arugula, and Walnuts 425

EPISODE 804
Grilled and Smoked
Barbecued Burnt Ends 478
Smoky Potato Salad 537

EPISODE 805
Enchiladas and Huevos Rancheros
Tex-Mex Cheese Enchiladas 403
Huevos Rancheros 383

EPISODE 806
Southern Comfort
Delta Hot Tamales 245
Charleston Shrimp Perloo 194

EPISODE 807
A Hearty Fall Dinner
Skillet-Roasted Chicken
 and Potatoes 321
Brussels Sprout Salad 363

EPISODE 808
Simplified Showstoppers
One-Pan Prime Rib and
 Roasted Vegetables 340
Blitz Torte 613

EPISODE 809
Chow Mein and Barbecued Pork
Slow-Cooker Chinese
 Barbecued Pork 214
Chicken Chow Mein 207

EPISODE 810
All-American Sweet Dough Desserts
Dakota Peach Kuchen 661
Kolaches 583

EPISODE 811
Fried Chicken and Grilled Peppers
Garlic-Lime Fried Chicken 386
Grill-Roasted Peppers 304

EPISODE 812
Break Out the Bourbon
Smoked Bourbon Chicken 466
Sweet Potato Pie 687

EPISODE 813
Grilled Salmon and Stuffed Tomatoes
Grilled Salmon Steaks with
 Lemon-Caper Sauce 523
Stuffed Tomatoes 307

2016
season nine

EPISODE 901
Badger State Favorites
Spicy Cheese Bread 570
Old-Fashioned Vanilla
 Frozen Custard 666

EPISODE 902
Picnic Gamechangers
Ranch Fried Chicken 175
Husk-Grilled Corn 583
Classic Tuna Salad 132

EPISODE 903
Sweet Indulgences
Milk Chocolate Cheesecake 627
Swiss Hazelnut Cake 612
Basic Chocolate Truffles 645

EPISODE 904
Surf and Turf Goes Regional
Cedar-Planked Salmon with
 Cucumber-Yogurt Sauce 522
Grilled Sugar Steak 276
Lemon and Herb Red
 Potato Salad 542

EPISODE 905
Big Family Breakfast
Mixed Berry Scones 565
Breakfast Pizza 548

EPISODE 906
A Taste of Tennessee
Tennessee Pulled Pork
 Sandwiches 503
Hoecakes 504
French Coconut Pie 687

EPISODE 907
The Devil Made Me Do It
Deviled Beef Short Ribs 338
Grilled Chicken Diavolo 474

EPISODE 908
Tacos and Chilaquiles
Puffy Tacos 393
Chicken Chilaquiles 408

758   *The Complete Cook's Country TV Show Cookbook*

EPISODE 909
All Wrapped Up
Bacon-Wrapped Meatloaf 146
Chicken Baked in Foil with Sweet
    Potato and Radish 323

EPISODE 910
Southern Stews
Brunswick Stew 326
Shrimp and Grits 195

EPISODE 911
Biting into the Big Easy
Pork Grillades 287
New Orleans Muffulettas 216

EPISODE 912
Prime Rib with All the Fixings
Prime Rib with Potatoes and
    Red Wine–Orange Sauce 341
Roasted Green Beans with
    Goat Cheese and Hazelnuts 130
Green Goddess Dressing 132

EPISODE 913
Big Flavors from Little Italy
Zeppoles 454
Pasta with Mushroom Sauce 426
Slow-Cooker Chicken Stock 120

2017
season ten

EPISODE 1001
Pork and Pierogi
Cider-Braised Pork Roast 349
Potato-Cheddar Pierogi 257

EPISODE 1002
Arroz con Pollo and Sour Orange Pie
Arroz con Pollo 384
Sour Orange Pie 674

EPISODE 1003
Smoky Barbecue Favorites
Texas Thick-Cut Smoked
    Pork Chops 508
Backyard Barbecue Beans 528

EPISODE 1004
Smothered and Dowdied
Southern-Style Smothered
    Chicken 136
Apple Pandowdy 654

EPISODE 1005
BBQ Thighs and Fried Peach Pies
BBQ Chicken Thighs 473
Fried Peach Hand Pies 679

EPISODE 1006
Ribs and Mashed Potatoes Revisited
Slow-Cooker Memphis-Style
    Wet Ribs 229
Mashed Potato Cakes 291

EPISODE 1007
Bourbon and Broccoli Hit the Grill
Grilled Bourbon Steaks 480
Grilled Broccoli with Lemon
    and Parmesan 532

EPISODE 1008
Pork Tacos and Churros
Citrus-Braised Pork Tacos 398
So-Cal Churros 414

EPISODE 1009
Southern Discoveries
South Carolina Smoked
    Fresh Ham 498
Smashed Potato Salad 541

EPISODE 1010
Cast-Iron Comforts
Cast Iron Skillet Pizza 445
Chocolate Chip Skillet Cookie 632

EPISODE 1011
Plenty of Garlic and Parm
Garlic Fried Chicken 171
Crispy Parmesan Potatoes 299

EPISODE 1012
When Only Chocolate Will Do
Mississippi Mud Pie 697
Whoopie Pies 642

EPISODE 1013
The Italian-American Kitchen
Pasta with Sausage Ragu 422
Fluffy Baked Polenta with
    Red Sauce 430

EPISODE DIRECTORY   759

2018
season eleven

EPISODE 1101
Ultimate Comfort Foods
Wellesley Fudge Cake 598
Chicken and Pastry 122

EPISODE 1102
Ballpark Classics
Grilled Sausages with Bell Peppers and Onions 507
Ballpark Pretzels 269

EPISODE 1103
A Trip to Tarheel Country
North Carolina Dipped Fried Chicken 172
North Carolina Lemon Pie 673

EPISODE 1104
New Recipes for the Grill
Grill-Fried Chicken Wings 469
Grilled Pork Burgers 506

EPISODE 1105
Spaghetti House Classics
Hearty Beef Lasagna 437
Chicken Scarpariello 448

EPISODE 1106
Tex-Mex Favorites
Flank Steak in Adobo 406
Texas Breakfast Tacos 550

EPISODE 1107
Pacific Northwest Supper
Oregon Blackberry Pie 680
One-Pan Roasted Salmon with Broccoli and Red Potatoes 357

EPISODE 1108
Summer Steak and Salad
Grilled Thick-Cut Porterhouse Steaks 481
Caesar Green Bean Salad 305

EPISODE 1109
Reimagining Italian American Classics
Detroit-Style Pizza 253
Fettuccine with Butter and Cheese 422

EPISODE 1110
Southern Specialties
Tennessee Pulled Turkey Sandwiches 476
Eastern North Carolina Fish Stew 187

EPISODE 1111
Tri-State Treats
New Jersey Crumb Buns 580
Cheese Blintzes with Raspberry Sauce 557

EPISODE 1112
Holiday Roast and Potatoes
Boneless Rib Roast with Yorkshire Pudding and Jus 339
Lighthouse Inn Potatoes 294

EPISODE 1113
Pub-Style Seafood
Fish and Chips 184
South Carolina Shrimp Burgers 199

2019
season twelve

EPISODE 1201
Texas Barbecue Brisket
Texas Barbecue Brisket 487

EPISODE 1202
Italian Comfort Food Classics
Chicago Thin-Crust Pizza 250
Pasta e Fagioli 418

EPISODE 1203
Fish Tacos and Steak Fajitas
Smoked Fish Tacos 524
Grilled Steak Fajitas 482

EPISODE 1204
Beef, Dressed Up
Spice-Crusted Steaks 280
Grilled Bacon Burgers with Caramelized Onion 489

EPISODE 1205
Regional Italian American Favorites
Prosciutto Bread 453
Drop Meatballs 431

EPISODE 1206
Aloha State Favorites
Hawaiian-Style Fried Chicken 175
Hawaiian Macaroni Salad 268

EPISODE 1207
Chicken and Cornbread
Cast Iron Baked Chicken 134
Blueberry Cornbread 567

EPISODE 1208
The Perfect Cake
Blueberry Jam Cake 603

EPISODE 1209
Roast Beef and Potatoes
Classic Roast Beef Tenderloin 334
Lyonnaise Potatoes 292

EPISODE 1210
Pork and Pie
Monroe County–Style Pork Chops 511
Coconut Cream Pie 689

EPISODE 1211
Holiday Feast
Crumb-Crusted Rack of Lamb 354
Brussels Sprout Gratin 362

EPISODE 1212
A Trip to the Big Easy
Shrimp Po' Boys 198
Chicken Sauce Piquant 180

EPISODE 1213
Comfort Food Done Right
Double-Crust Chicken Pot Pie 142
Cowboy Cookies 630

2020
season thirteen

EPISODE 1301
Regional Seafood Specialties
Monterey Bay Cioppino 188
Shrimp Mozambique 194

EPISODE 1302
Taste of Summer
Grilled Flank Steak with
   Basil Dressing 483
Fresh Tomato Galette 374

EPISODE 1303
Beef Kebabs and Cheese Bread
Shashlik-Style Beef Kebabs 479
Adjaruli Khachapuri 549

EPISODE 1304
Grilled Chicken, Two Ways
Grilled Jerk Chicken 462
Smoked Chicken Wings 471

EPISODE 1305
Let's Taco 'bout It
Pork Carnitas 399
Shrimp Tacos 390

EPISODE 1306
**Bread, Cheese, and Meat
Can't Be Beat**
Sliders 222
Croque Monsieur 217

EPISODE 1307
Herbaceous Chicken and Potatoes
Greek Chicken 180
Crushed Red Potatoes with Garlic
   and Herbs 296

EPISODE 1308
Italian Comfort Food
Cheesy Stuffed Shells 442
Eggplant Pecorino 440

EPISODE 1309
Chicken and Biscuits
One-Batch Fried Chicken 135
North Carolina Cheese Biscuits 258

EPISODE 1310
Pennsylvania Dutch Country
Pennsylvania Dutch Apple Pie 682
Amish Cinnamon Bread 588

EPISODE 1311
Motor City Favorites
Bottom Round Roast Beef with
   Zip-Style Sauce 336
Almond Boneless Chicken 209

EPISODE 1312
Never Enough Chocolate
Triple-Chocolate Sticky Buns 578
Thin and Crispy Chocolate
   Chip Cookies 631

EPISODE 1313
Spring Feast
Slow-Roasted Fresh Ham 352
Gooey Butter Cake Bars 634

2021
season fourteen

EPISODE 1401
Fried Bites
Popcorn Chicken 179
Gobi Manchurian 262
Crispy Vegetable Fritters 263

EPISODE 1402
Roast Chicken and Salad
Green Goddess Roast Chicken 133
Potato, Green Bean, and
   Tomato Salad 543

EPISODE 1403
Summer Berry Desserts
Mixed Berry Buckle 657
Strawberry Cheesecake Bars 626

EPISODE 1404
Carne Guisada and Enchiladas
Carne Guisada 392
Easy Green Chili Chicken
   Enchiladas 405

EPISODE 1405
One-Pot Meals
One-Pot Chicken Jardinière 141
Baked Shrimp with Fennel, Potatoes,
   and Olives 358

EPISODE 1406
Italian Comforts
Italian Meatloaf 435
Chicken Scampi 447

EPISODE 1407
Regional Sandwich Roundup
Iowa Skinny 234
Boogaloo Wonderland
   Sandwiches 218
St. Paul Sandwich 215

EPISODE 1408
Thanksgiving Simplified
One-Pan Turkey Breast
   and Stuffing 312
Roasted Butternut Squash
   and Apple 372

EPISODE 1409
Paprikash and Stroganoff
Chicken Paprikash and
   Buttered Spaetzle 137
Ground Beef Stroganoff 148

EPISODE 1410
Pork, Peaches, and Potatoes
Bacon-Wrapped Pork Roast with
   Peach Sauce 350
Texas Potato Pancakes 263

EPISODE 1411
French Fare
Easy Steak Frites 281
French Onion Soup 274

EPISODE 1412
Chicken Soup and Cheesy Bread
Old-Fashioned Chicken
   Noodle Soup 120
Beer-Batter Cheese Bread 569

EPISODE 1413
Elegant and Orange
Slow-Roasted Salmon with
   Chives and Lemon 356
Clementine Cake 601

2022
season fifteen

EPISODE 1501
Cast Iron Everything
Japanese Steakhouse Steak and Vegetables 284
Charred Cherry Tomatoes with Roasted Red Bell Peppers and Fresh Mozzarella 268

EPISODE 1502
New England for Everyone
Woodman's-Style Clam Chowder 189
Hot Buttered Lobster Rolls 201

EPISODE 1503
Low Country Party
Okra and Shrimp Stew 191
Pickled Shrimp 197

EPISODE 1504
Midwestern Favorites
Tater Tot Hotdish 149
Wisconsin Butter Burgers 224

EPISODE 1505
Fried Chicken and Biscuits
Lard Fried Chicken 167
Blueberry Biscuits 564

EPISODE 1506
Thai Comforts
Khao Man Gai (Thai-Style Chicken and Rice) 210
Pad Gra Prow (Holy Basil Stir-Fry) 213

EPISODE 1507
Seafood Two Ways
Seafood Fra Diavolo 427
Salmon Piccata 451

EPISODE 1508
Two Tastes from the Bay Area
Sinigang (Filipino Pork and Vegetable Stew) 231
Neorm Sach Moan 205

EPISODE 1509
Never Enough Chocolate
Chocolate Babka 586
Chocolate Fudge 647

EPISODE 1510
Pennsylvanian Melting Pot
Transylvanian Goulash 327
Beans and Greens 451

EPISODE 1511
Cajun Country
Cajun Rice Dressing 247
Cajun Stuffed Turkey Wings 183

EPISODE 1512
Endless Dessert
Banana Pudding Pie 690
No-Churn Ice Cream 648

EPISODE 1513
Old New Mexico
Gorditas 396
New Mexico Biscochitos 637

EPISODE 1514
Chuck Roast and Potatoes
Roasted Beef Chuck Roast with Horseradish-Parsley Sauce 337
Torn and Fried Potatoes 298

EPISODE 1515
Saucy Italian-Inspired Dinners
Spaghetti Carbonara 425
Instant Mashed Potato Gnocchi 428

EPISODE 1516
Pork Roast and Orange Cake
Roast Pork Loin with 40 Cloves of Garlic 343
Orange Upside-Down Cake 602

EPISODE 1517
Bar Snacks
New England Bar Pizza 252
Lemon Pepper Chicken Wings 182

EPISODE 1518
The Cuban Sandwich Show
Cuban Sandwiches 237

762   *The Complete Cook's Country TV Show Cookbook*

2023
season sixteen

EPISODE 1601
Texas Cookout
Texas-Style Smoked Beef Ribs 494
Easy Blueberry Cobbler 298

EPISODE 1602
Fish Tacos and Fried Shrimp
San Diego Fish Tacos 388
Crispy Fried Shrimp 159

EPISODE 1603
Never Enough Citrus
Smoked Citrus Chicken 465
Really Good Key Lime Pie 676

EPISODE 1604
Sisig and Wings
Sisig 232
Garlic Fried Rice 233
Soy Sauce Chicken Wings 210

EPISODE 1605
Hawaiian Melting Pot
Tuna Poke 202
Salmon Teriyaki Poke 203
Malasadas 560

EPISODE 1606
Grilled Lamb and Cheesecake
Grilled Bone-In Leg of Lamb with Charred-Scallion Sauce 519
La Viña–Style Cheesecake 629

EPISODE 1607
Puerto Rican Classics
Guanimes con Bacalao (Cornmeal Dumplings with Salt Cod) 203
Piña Coladas 271

EPISODE 1608
A Love Letter to the South
Pan-Fried Pork Chops with Milk Gravy 157
Pimento Mac and Cheese 124

EPISODE 1609
Biscuits and Chicken
Butter and Lard Biscuits 561
Mimosa Fried Chicken 173

EPISODE 1610
Jamaican Feast
Jamaican Oxtail 151
Jamaican Rice and Peas 152

EPISODE 1611
New Mexican Bounty
New Mexican Bean-and-Cheese Turnovers with Green Chile 402
Southwestern Tomato and Corn Salad 413

EPISODE 1612
Mediterranean Meze
Mana'eesh Za'atar (Za'atar Flatbread) 592
Baba Ghanoush 270
Roasted Beets with Lemon-Tahini Dressing 373

EPISODE 1613
The Best Diner Food
Diner-Style Patty Melts 221
Ultimate Extra-Crunchy Onion Rings 264

EPISODE 1614
French-Inspired Dinner
Trout Amandine 355
Lentilles du Puy with Spinach and Crème Fraîche 375

EPISODE 1615
Sausages and Salad
Olympia Provisions–Style Choucroute Garnie 153
Endive Salad with Oranges and Blue Cheese 366

2024
season seventeen

EPISODE 1701
North Carolina Barbecue
North Carolina Barbecue Pork 499
Lemonade with Honey 161

EPISODE 1702
Inspired by Japanese Immigrants
Chicken Teriyaki 464
Miso Black Cod 186

EPISODE 1703
Unexpected Beef and Potatoes
Smoked Prime Rib & Smoked Prime Rib Sandwiches with Green Chile Queso 495
Torn Potato Salad with Toasted Garlic and Herb Dressing 367

EPISODE 1704
Mexican American Comfort Food
Quesabirria Tacos 394
Sopa Seca 384

EPISODE 1705
Southwestern Vegetarian Fare
Vegetarian Chili 411
Jalepeño-Cheddar Scones 566

EPISODE 1706
Spiced Chicken Dinners
Kombdi, Jira Ghalun (Cumin-Scented Chicken) 212
Hot-Honey Chicken 138

EPISODE 1707
A Bold Brunch
Brunch Burgers 551
Browned Butter Chocolate Chunk Muffins 573

EPISODE 1708
From the Indigenous Pantry
Cider-Braised Turkey 311
Grilled Sweet Potatoes with Maple Chile Crisp 531

EPISODE 1709
Just Some Darn Good Desserts
S'Mores Pie 698
M&M Cookies 632

EPISODE 1710
Short Ribs and Baked Potatoes
Slow-Roasted Medium-Rare Beef Short Ribs 283
Twice-Baked Potatoes with Bacon and Cheddar Cheese 302

EPISODE 1711
Seafood in a Skillet
Clams with Chorizo 360
Gambas Al Ajillo (Spanish-Style Sizzling Garlic Shrimp) 359

EPISODE 1712
Duck and Dessert
Duck Breasts with Port Wine–Fig Sauce 315
Tarte Tatin 655

EPISODE 1713
From the Dairyland
Cream Cheese Kringle 584
Fried Cheese Curds with Ranch Dressing 266

EPISODE 1714
Southern Staples
Fried Catfish with Comeback Sauce 185
Extra-Cheesy Grits 129

EPISODE 1715
Pantry Shortcuts
Okinawan Taco Rice 230
Pepperoni French Bread Pizza 256

EPISODE 1716
Snack Cake and Sandwich Cookies
Carrot Snack Cake 620
Oatmeal Creme Pies 643

EPISODE 1717
Italian Food from Philly
Philadelphia Pork Sandwiches 236
Philly Tomato Pie 255

EPISODE 1718
The Power of Southern Cooking
Hoppin' John 248
Alabama Orange Rolls 582

EPISODE 1719
Pork Any Way You Like
Pork Chops with Bourbon-Cherry Sauce and Sweet Potatoes 351
South Carolina Barbecue Hash 240

EPISODE 1720
Crescent City Comforts
Beef Yakamein (New Orleans Spicy Beef Noodle Soup) 243
Bourbon Chicken 208

EPISODE 1721
Dinner in a Skillet
Cast Iron Chicken and Vegetables 319
Cheeseburger Mac 127

EPISODE 1722
Hearty and Light Pastas
Sausage Lasagna 438
Aglio e Olio (Spaghetti with Garlic and Olive Oil) 424

EPISODE 1723
Fresh Mexican-Inspired Dinners
Ahi-Chile Tostadas 389
Skillet Corn with Mexican Chorizo 414

EPISODE 1724
All-American Cookout
Blueberry Cream Pie 693
Sweet Tea–Brined Fried Chicken Thighs 177

EPISODE 1725
Korean from the Grill
Kalbi (Korean Grilled Flanken-Style Short Ribs) 497
Shredded Carrot and Serrano Chile Salad 536

EPISODE 1726
Celebrating Springtime
Pomegranate-Glazed Grilled Lamb Chops 520
Asparagus Salad with Radishes, Pecorino Romano, and Croutons 364

2025
season eighteen

EPISODE 1801
Georgia Food On My Mind
Coastal Georgia Paella 50
Peach Ripple Ice Cream 114

EPISODE 1802
Portuguese Baking
Pastéis De Nata 98
Bolos Lêvados (Portuguese Muffins) 95

EPISODE 1803
Italian-American Feast
Porchetta Abruzzese 34
Quick-Braised Broccoli Rabe with Garlic and Anchovies 80

EPISODE 1804
Bar Snacks, Perfected
Indoor Barbecued Ribs 36
Air-Fryer Jalapeño Poppers 86

EPISODE 1805
Chips on the Menu
Frito Pie 16
Chocolate-Dipped Potato Chip Cookies 104

EPISODE 1806
Southern Sandwiches
Pickle-Brined Fried Chicken Sandwiches 6
Chocolate-Marshmallow Sandwich Cookies 106

EPISODE 1807
Chocolate Baked Delights
Double Chocolate Banana Bread 92
Chocolate Brownie Cookies 108

EPISODE 1808
New England Sandwiches
Jitto's-Style Steak Bombs 19
Cutty's-Inspired Eggplant Spuckie 72

EPISODE 1809
Elevated Friendsgiving Mains
Slow Roasted Ducks with Blackberry Sauce 12
Bean Bourguignon 70

EPISODE 1810
Jewish Donuts and Potatoes
Sufganiyot (Hanukkah Jelly Donuts) 100
Cast Iron Potato Kugel 88

EPISODE 1811
Feast of the Seven Fishes
Clams Casino 58
Seafood Risotto 52

EPISODE 1812
Greens for Dinner
Pesto Lasagna 64
Ultimate Caesar Salad 76

EPISODE 1813
Upper Midwest Classics
Chicken Cordon Bleu 10
Cornish Pasties 22

EPISODE 1814
Inspiring Shrimp Suppers
Shrimp with Garlic and Jalapeño Butter 56
Zephyr Wright-Inspired Shrimp Curry 54

EPISODE 1815
Glazed Pork and Potatoes
Honey-Glazed Pork Shoulder 38
Creamy Potatoes and Leeks 82

EPISODE 1816
Chinese Noodles and Egg Rolls
Shanghai Scallion Oil Noodles 68
American-Style Egg Rolls 44

EPISODE 1817
When Southern Women Cook
Aunt Jule's Pie 112
Gullah Lowcountry Red Rice 90

EPISODE 1818
Cajun Cooking
Rillons 42
Cajun Meatball Fricassee 20

EPISODE 1819
Sweet and Savory Brunch
Conchas 102
Skillet Eggs Sardou 40

EPISODE 1820
Mediterranean Burgers and Fritters
Grilled Lamb Burgers 46
Sweet Potato Fritters with Feta, Dill, and Cilantro 84

EPISODE 1821
Tuscon Tacos and Tomatillos
Mesquite-Grilled Tacos Rasurados 26
Tomatillo and Bibb Lettuce Salad with Tomatillo Ranch Dressing 74

EPISODE 1822
From Texas, With Love
Barbecued Chuck Roast 15
Green Spaghetti 62

EPISODE 1823
Spring Dinner and Dessert
Grilled Brined Pork Chops with Garlic-Herb Oil 32
Rhubarb Shortcakes with Buttermilk Whipped Cream 110

EPISODE 1824
Flavorful Chicken and Fonduta
Grilled Hilltribe Chicken with Kua Txob 3
Tomatoes with Fontina Sauce and Cornichon Dressing 78

EPISODE 1825
Puerto Rican Flavors
Alcapurrias 28
Coquito 116

EPISODE 1826
Seafood in a Snap
Grilled Mussels 60
One-Pot Shrimp Piccata Pasta 66

conversions and equivalents

Some say cooking is a science and an art. We would say that geography has a hand in it too. Flour milled in the United Kingdom and elsewhere will feel and taste different from flour milled in the United States. So we cannot promise that the loaf of bread you bake in Canada or England will taste the same as a loaf baked in the States, but we can offer guidelines for converting weights and measures. We also recommend that you rely on your instincts when making our recipes. Refer to the visual cues provided. If the bread dough hasn't "come together in a ball," as described, you may need to add more flour—even if the recipe doesn't tell you to. You be the judge.

The recipes in this book were developed using standard U.S. measures following U.S. government guidelines. The charts below offer equivalents for U.S., metric, and imperial (U.K.) measures. All conversions are approximate and have been rounded up or down to the nearest whole number.

EXAMPLE:
1 teaspoon = 4.9292 milliliters, rounded up to 5 milliliters
1 ounce = 28.3495 grams, rounded down to 28 grams

VOLUME CONVERSIONS

U.S.	METRIC
1 teaspoon	5 milliliters
2 teaspoons	10 milliliters
1 tablespoon	15 milliliters
2 tablespoons	30 milliliters
¼ cup	59 milliliters
⅓ cup	79 milliliters
½ cup	118 milliliters
¾ cup	177 milliliters
1 cup	237 milliliters
1¼ cups	296 milliliters
1½ cups	355 milliliters
2 cups (1 pint)	473 milliliters
2½ cups	591 milliliters
3 cups	710 milliliters
4 cups (1 quart)	0.946 liter
1.06 quarts	1 liter
4 quarts (1 gallon)	3.8 liters

WEIGHT CONVERSIONS

OUNCES	GRAMS
½	14
¾	21
1	28
1½	43
2	57
2½	71
3	85
3½	99
4	113
4½	128
5	142
6	170
7	198
8	227
9	255
10	283
12	340
16 (1 pound)	454

CONVERSIONS FOR INGREDIENTS COMMONLY USED IN BAKING

Baking is an exacting science. Because measuring by weight is far more accurate than measuring by volume, and thus more likely to achieve reliable results, in our recipes we provide ounce measures in addition to cup measures for many ingredients. Refer to the chart below to convert these measures into grams.

INGREDIENT	OUNCES	GRAMS
1 cup all-purpose flour*	5	142
1 cup whole-wheat flour	5½	156
1 cup granulated (white) sugar	7	198
1 cup packed brown sugar (light or dark)	7	198
1 cup confectioners' sugar	4	113
1 cup cocoa powder	3	85
4 tablespoons butter[†] (½ stick or ¼ cup)	2	57
8 tablespoons butter[†] (1 stick or ½ cup)	4	113
16 tablespoons butter[†] (2 sticks or 1 cup)	8	227

[*] U.S. all-purpose flour, the most frequently used flour in this book, does not contain leaveners, as some European flours do. These leavened flours are called self-rising or self-raising. If you are using self-rising flour, take this into consideration before adding leavening to a recipe.

[†] In the United States, butter is sold both salted and unsalted. We generally recommend unsalted butter. If you are using salted butter, take this into consideration before adding salt to a recipe.

OVEN TEMPERATURES

FAHRENHEIT	CELSIUS	GAS MARK
225	105	¼
250	120	½
275	135	1
300	150	2
325	165	3
350	180	4
375	190	5
400	200	6
425	220	7
450	230	8
475	245	9

CONVERTING TEMPERATURES FROM AN INSTANT-READ THERMOMETER

We include doneness temperatures in many of the recipes in this book. We recommend an instant-read thermometer for the job. Refer to the above table to convert Fahrenheit degrees to Celsius. Or, for temperatures not represented in the chart, use this simple formula:

Subtract 32 degrees from the Fahrenheit reading, then divide the result by 1.8 to find the Celsius reading.

EXAMPLE:
"Roast chicken until thighs register 175 degrees."
To convert:

175°F − 32 = 143°
143° ÷ 1.8 = 79.44°C, rounded down to 79°C

index

Note: Page references in *italics* indicate photographs.

A

Adjaruli Khachapuri, *548,* 549–50
Aglio e Olio (Spaghetti with Garlic and Olive Oil), *424, 424*
Ahi-Chile Tostadas, *389,* 389–90
Aioli, Lemon, 453
Air-Fryer Jalapeño Poppers, 86, *87*
Alabama Barbecued Chicken, *460,* 460–61
Alabama Orange Rolls, *544,* 582–83
Alcapurrias, 28–29, *30*–31
Almond(s)
　Boneless Chicken, *209,* 209–10
　-Chocolate Truffles, 645
　Grapes, and Goat Cheese, Asparagus Salad with, 364–65
　and Mint, Roasted Green Beans with, 131
　Trout Amandine, 355–56, *356*
American cheese
　Best Potluck Macaroni and Cheese, 124, *125*
　Boogaloo Wonderland Sandwiches, 218–19, *219*
　Diner-Style Patty Melts, *220,* 221–22
　Jitto's-Style Steak Bombs, 19, *19*
　Jucy Lucy Burgers, *488,* 488–89
　Sliders, 222–23, *223*
　Smoked Prime Rib Sandwiches with Green Chile Queso, 495–96, *496*
　St. Louis–Style Pizza, *248,* 249–50
　Wisconsin Butter Burgers, *224, 224*
American-Style Egg Rolls, 44–45, *45*
Amish Cinnamon Bread, 588–89, *589*
Amish Potato Salad, *538,* 539
Anchovy(ies)
　and Garlic, Quick-Braised Broccoli Rabe with, 80, *81*
　-Garlic Butter, Grilled Broccoli with, 533
　Green Goddess Dressing, 132–33, *133*
　Green Goddess Roast Chicken, *133,* 133–34

Anchovy(ies) *(cont.)*
　Grilled Caesar Salad, *533,* 533–34
　Salsa Verde, 336
　Ultimate Caesar Salad, 76, *77*
Angel Food Cake, 614–15, *615*
　Café au Lait, 615
　Chocolate-Almond, 615
Appetizers
　Air-Fryer Jalapeño Poppers, 86, *87*
　Charred Cherry Tomatoes with Roasted Bell Peppers and Fresh Mozzarella, 268, *269*
　Clams Casino, 58, *59*
　Fried Cheese Curds with Ranch Dressing, 266–67, *267*
　Grilled Mussels, 60, *61*
　"Impossible" Ham-and-Cheese Pie, 547, *547*
　Pickled Shrimp, 197–98, *198*
　Tomatoes with Fontina Sauce and Cornichon Dressing, 78, *79*
　Ultimate Spicy Beef Nachos, 380, *381*
　see also Dips; Salsa
Apple cider. *See* **Cider**
Apple(s)
　Cabbage Slaw, Tangy, *534,* 534–35
　Cheddar, and Hazelnuts, Brussels Sprout Salad with, 363
　Cider-Braised Pork Roast, *349,* 349–50
　Cider Chicken, 317–18, *318*
　-Cranberry Crisp, 656–57, *657*
　Dumplings, Baked, 652, *653*
　Fritters, *653,* 653–54
　Morning Glory Muffins, *572,* 573
　Pandowdy, 654–55, *655*
　Pie, Pennsylvania Dutch, 682, *683*
　Pie with Cheddar Crust, *683,* 683–84
　Roasted Butternut Squash and, *372,* 372–73
　Slab Pie, *684,* 684–85
　Tarte Tatin, *650,* 655–56
　Walnuts, and Tarragon, Tuna Salad with, 132

INDEX　769

Appliances, small, ratings of, 716–19
Artichoke(s)
    Fried, *452,* 452–53
    Skillet Eggs Sardou, 40–41, *41*
    -Spinach Dip, 376–77, *377*
Arugula, Roasted Garlic Sauce, and Walnuts, Pasta with, *425,* 425–26
Asparagus
    Parmesan-Crusted, *361,* 361–62
    Salad with Grapes, Goat Cheese, and Almonds, 364–65
    Salad with Oranges, Feta, and Hazelnuts, 365
    Salad with Radishes, Pecorino Romano, and Croutons, 364, *364*
Atlanta Brisket, 225, *225*
Aunt Jule's Pie, 112, *113*
Avocados
    Ahi-Chile Tostadas, *389,* 389–90
    Chicken Chilaquiles, 408–9, *409*
    Chunky Guacamole, *382, 382*
    Huevos Rancheros, 383, *383*
    Mesquite-Grilled Tacos Rasurados, 26–27, *27*
    Salmon Teriyaki Poke, *202,* 203
    San Diego Fish Tacos, 388–89, *389*
    Ultimate Seven-Layer Dip, *381,* 381–82
    Ultimate Smoky Seven-Layer Dip, 382

B

Baba Ghanoush, 270, *271*
Babka, Chocolate, *586,* 586–87
Bacon
    Air-Fryer Jalapeño Poppers, 86, *87*
    Backyard Barbecued Beans, *528,* 528–29
    BLT Salad, *306,* 306–7
    and Blue Cheese Baked Potato Fans, 300
    and Blue Cheese Mashed Potato Cakes, 292
    Breakfast Pizza, *548,* 548–49
    Brunch Burgers, 551–53, *552*
    Burgers, Grilled, with Caramelized Onion, 489–90, *490*
    and Cheddar Cheese, Twice-Baked Potatoes with, *272,* 302
    Clams Casino, 58, *59*
    and Cornbread Stuffing, 314
    Loaded Baked Potato Omelet Filling, 546
    -Ranch Potato Tots, 262
    Smoked Salmon Breakfast Pizza, 549
    Smokehouse Mashed Sweet Potatoes, 372

Bacon *(cont.)*
    Smoky Potato Salad, *537,* 537–38
    Texas Breakfast Tacos, 550–51, *551*
    Twice-Baked Potatoes with Pancetta and Mozzarella, 302
    Ultimate Smoky Seven-Layer Dip, 382
    -Wrapped Meatloaf, 146–47, *147*
    -Wrapped Pork Roast with Peach Sauce, 350–51, *351*
Bakeware, ratings of, 713–16
Baltimore Pit Beef, *234,* 235
Banana(s)
    Bread, Double-Chocolate, 92, *93*
    Pudding, *663,* 663–64
    Pudding, Peanut-y, 664
    Pudding, Toasted-Coconut, 664
    Pudding Pie, 690, *691*
    ripening, 92
    -Walnut–Chocolate Chunk No-Churn Ice Cream, 649
Barbecue Sauce
    Creamy BBQ, 260
    Eastern North Carolina–Style, 500
    Lexington-Style, 500
Barbecue-Scallion Butter, 528
Barley
    Vegetarian Chili, *411,* 411–12
Bars
    Gooey Butter Cake, *634,* 634–35
    Strawberry Cheesecake, *626,* 626–27
Basil
    Dressing, Grilled Flank Steak with, 483–84, *484*
    Holy, Stir-Fry (Pad Gra Prow), *213,* 213–14
    Pesto Butter, 528
    Pesto Lasagna, 64–65, *65*
    Prosciutto, and Blue Cheese, Shredded Swiss Chard Salad with, *365,* 365–66
    -Tomato Sauce, 429
Basque Cider Salted Caramel Sauce, *628,* 629
Bean(s)
    -and-Cheese Turnovers, New Mexican, with Green Chile, *402,* 402–3
    Backyard Barbecued, *528,* 528–29
    Bourguignon, 70, *71*
    Brunswick Stew, 326–27, *327*
    California Barbecued, *529,* 529–30
    dried, quick-soaking, 530
    dried, sorting, 530
    Easier Chicken Chimichangas, 400–401, *401*
    Five-Alarm Chili, *410,* 410–11
    and Greens, 451–52, *452*
    Jamaican Oxtail, *151,* 151–52
    Jamaican Rice and Peas, 152–53, *153*

Bean(s) *(cont.)*
    Pasta e Fagioli, 418, *418*
    Pinto, Texas-Style, 412, *413*
    Slow-Cooker Minestrone, 419, *419*
    Ultimate Seven-Layer Dip, *381*, 381–82
    Ultimate Smoky Seven-Layer Dip, 382
    Ultimate Spicy Beef Nachos, 380, *381*
    Vegetarian Chili, *411*, 411–12
    see also Green Bean(s)

Beef
    Alcapurrias, 28–29, *30–31*
    Atlanta Brisket, 225, *225*
    Bacon-Wrapped Meatloaf, 146–47, *147*
    Baked Manicotti with Meat Sauce, *441*, 441–42
    Baltimore Pit, *234*, 235
    Barbecued Burnt Ends, 478–79, *479*
    Barbecued Chuck Roast, 15, *15*
    Birria Ramen, 395–96, *396*
    Boneless Rib Roast with Yorkshire Pudding and Jus, *338*, 339–40
    Boogaloo Wonderland Sandwiches, 218–19, *219*
    Bottom Round Roast with Zip-Style Sauce, 336, *337*
    Brisket, Slow-Cooker BBQ, *226*, 226–27
    Broiled Steaks, 277–78, *278*
    Brunch Burgers, 551–53, *552*
    Burgers
        Diner-Style Patty Melts, *220*, 221–22
        Green Chile Cheeseburgers, *490*, 490–91
        Grilled Bacon, with Caramelized Onion, 489–90, *490*
        Grilled Steak, 286–87, *287*
        Jucy Lucy, *488*, 488–89
        Oklahoma Fried Onion, *223*, 223–24
        Patty Melts, *220*, 220–21
        Sliders, 222–23, *223*
        Wisconsin Butter, 224, *224*
    Cajun Meatball Fricassee, 20, *21*
    California Barbecued Tri-Tip, 484–85, *485*
    Carne Guisada, 392–93, *393*
    Char-Grilled Steaks, 279, *279*
    Cheeseburger Mac, 127, *127*
    Chuck, Roasted, with Horseradish-Parsley Sauce, *337*, 337–38
    chuck eye, tying, 338
    chuck roast, preparing for stew, 329
    Chuck Roast in Foil, 342–43, *343*
    Cincinnati Chili, *241*, 241–42
    Classic Roast, and Gravy, *330*, 331
    Cornish Pasties, 22–23, *23*
    Delta Hot Tamales, 245–46, *246*

Beef *(cont.)*
    Diner-Style Patty Melts, *220*, 221–22
    Drop Meatballs, *431*, 431–32
    Easy Chili con Carne, *409*, 409–10
    Easy Steak Frites, *281*, 281–82
    Enchiladas, 406, *407*
    Five-Alarm Chili, *410*, 410–11
    Flank Steak in Adobo, 406–8, *407*
    Frito Pie, 16, *17*
    Frosted Meatloaf, 144, *145*
    Garlic Roast, Sunday-Best, 329–31, *330*
    Glazed Meatloaf, 143–44, *144*
    Gorditas, 396–97, *397*
    Grilled Bourbon Steaks, 480–81, *481*
    Grilled Cowboy-Cut Rib Eyes, *282*, 283
    Grilled Flank Steak with Basil Dressing, 483–84, *484*
    Grilled Steak Fajitas, 482–83, *483*
    Grilled Steakhouse Steak Tips, 276, *276*
    Grilled Sugar Steak, 276–77, *277*
    Grilled Thick-Cut Porterhouse Steaks, *481*, 481–82
    Ground, Stroganoff, 148, *149*
    Herbed Roast, 331–32, *333*
    Holiday Strip Roast, *335*, 335–36
    Italian Meatloaf, *416*, 435–36
    Italian Pot Roast, 448–49, *449*
    Jamaican Oxtail, *151*, 151–52
    Japanese Steakhouse Steak and Vegetables, 284–85, *285*
    Jitto's-Style Steak Bombs, 19, *19*
    Kalbi (Korean Grilled Flanken-Style Short Ribs), *497*, 497–98
    Kebabs, Shashlik-Style, *479*, 479–80
    Lasagna, Hearty, *437*, 437–38
    Meatballs and Marinara, 432–33, *433*
    Meatloaf with Mushroom Gravy, 145–46, *147*
    Mesquite-Grilled Tacos Rasurados, 26–27, *27*
    Nachos, Ultimate Spicy, 380, *381*
    Natchitoches Meat Pies, 244, *244–45*
    Okinawan Taco Rice, 230–31, *231*
    One-Pan Prime Rib and Roasted Vegetables, 340–41, *341*
    Prime Rib with Potatoes and Red Wine–Orange Sauce, 341–42, *343*
    Puffy Tacos, 393–94, *394*
    Quesabirria Tacos, 394–95, *395*
    ribs, flanken-style, about, 498
    Ribs, Texas Barbecued, 492–93, *493*
    Ribs, Texas-Style Smoked, 494, *494*
    Salisbury Steak, 148–49, *149*
    Short Ribs, Deviled, *338*, 338–39
    Short Ribs, Slow-Roasted Medium-Rare, *283*, 283–84

Beef *(cont.)*
    Short Ribs, Spice-Crusted Slow-Roasted Medium-Rare, 284
    Shredded Barbecued, *486,* 486–87
    Skillet Lasagna, *436, 436*
    Slow-Cooker Italian Sunday Gravy, *420,* 420–21
    Slow-Cooker Meatballs and Marinara, 433–34, *434*
    Smoked Prime Rib, *446,* 495
    Smoked Prime Rib Sandwiches with Green Chile Queso, 495–96, *496*
    Spice-Crusted Steaks, *280,* 280–81
    steaks, broiling times for, 278
    Stew, Guinness, 328–29, *329*
    Swiss Steak with Tomato Gravy, 150–51, *151*
    Tater Tot Hotdish, 149–50, *150*
    Tenderloin, Classic Roast, 334, *335*
    Tenderloin, Herb-Crusted, 332–34, *333*
    Texas Barbecue Brisket, *486,* 487–88
    Yakamein (New Orleans Spicy Beef Noodle Soup), 243–44, *244*

Beer
    -Batter Cheese Bread, *569, 569*
    -Battered Onion Rings, 265–66, *266*
    Guinness Beef Stew, 328–29, *329*
    Milk-Can Supper, *154,* 155

Beets, Roasted, with Lemon-Tahini Dressing, *372,* 373–74
Beignets, 558–59, *559*
Belgian endive
    Endive Salad with Oranges and Blue Cheese, *366,* 366–67
    preparing, 367

Berry(ies)
    Blitz Torte, *613,* 613–14
    Cranberry-Apple Crisp, 656–57, *657*
    Double, Cream Cheese Kringle Filling, 586
    Mixed, Buckle, 657–58, *659*
    Mixed, Scones, *565,* 565–66
    Oregon Blackberry Pie, 680–81, *681*
    Slow Roasted Ducks with Blackberry Sauce, 12–13, *13*
    Summer, Pudding, 665–66, *666*
    see also Blueberry(ies); Raspberry(ies); Strawberry(ies)

Birria Ramen, 395–96, *396*
Birthday Cake No-Churn Ice Cream, 648
Biscochitos, New Mexico, *637,* 637–38
Biscuits
    Blueberry, *564,* 564–65
    Butter and Lard, 561–63, *562*
    Cat Head, *563,* 563–64
    Cornmeal, *560,* 561
    North Carolina Cheese, *258,* 258–59

Black and White Cookies, *641,* 641–42
Blackberry(ies)
    Mixed Berry Buckle, 657–58, *659*
    Pie, Oregon, 680–81, *681*
    Sauce, Slow Roasted Ducks with, 12–13, *13*
    Summer Berry Pudding, 665–66, *666*

Black Cod, Miso, 186–87, *187*
Blintzes, Cheese, with Raspberry Sauce, 557–58, *559*
Blitz Torte, *613,* 613–14
BLT Salad, *306,* 306–7
Blueberry(ies)
    Biscuits, *564,* 564–65
    Cobbler, Easy, *660,* 660–61
    Cornbread, *567,* 567–68
    Cream Pie, *668,* 693–94
    Grunt, Maine, *659,* 659–60
    Jam Cake, 603–5, *604*
    Mixed Berry Buckle, 657–58, *659*
    Muffins, Whole-Wheat, *572,* 572–73
    Summer Berry Pudding, 665–66, *666*

Blue Cheese
    and Bacon Baked Potato Fans, 300
    and Bacon Mashed Potato Cakes, 292
    and Oranges, Endive Salad with, *366,* 366–67
    Prosciutto, and Basil, Shredded Swiss Chard Salad with, *365,* 365–66
    Sauce, Buffalo, 260

Bolos Lêvedos (Portuguese Muffins), *95,* 95–96, *97*
Bolos Lêvedos (Portuguese Muffins) with Lemon and Cinnamon, 96
Boogaloo Wonderland Sandwiches, 218–19, *219*
Bourbon
    Bread Pudding, New Orleans, 664–65, *665*
    -Cherry Sauce and Sweet Potatoes, Pork Chops with, *308,* 351–52
    Chicken, 208, *208*
    Chicken, Smoked, *466,* 466–67
    Lane Cake, *594,* 600–601
    Sauce, 665
    Steaks, Grilled, 480–81, *481*
    Whipped Cream, 686

Bread croutons
    BLT Salad, *306,* 306–7
    Caesar Green Bean Salad, 305–6, *306*
    French Onion Soup, *274,* 274–75
    Grilled Caesar Salad, *533,* 533–34
    Slow-Cooker French Onion Soup, *272,* 275
    Ultimate Caesar Salad, 76, *77*

Bread Pudding
  New Orleans Bourbon, 664–65, *665*
  Summer Berry Pudding, 665–66, *666*
Breads
  Adjaruli Khachapuri, *548,* 549–50
  Alabama Orange Rolls, *544,* 582–83
  Amish Cinnamon, 588–89, *589*
  Ballpark Pretzels, *162,* 269–70
  Banana, Double-Chocolate, 92, *93*
  Beignets, 558–59, *559*
  Blueberry Cornbread, *567,* 567–68
  Brown Soda, 590–91, *591*
  Brown Soda, with Currants and Caraway, 591
  Cheese, Beer-Batter, *569, 569*
  Cheese, Spicy, 570, *570*
  Chocolate Babka, *586,* 586–87
  Chocolate Conchas, 103, *103*
  Conchas, 102–3, *103*
  Cream Cheese Kringle, *584,* 584–86
  Cuban, *239,* 239–40
  Dakota, 591–92, *592*
  English Muffin, 589–90, *590*
  Jalapeño-Cheddar Scones, *544,* 566–67
  Kolaches, 583–84, *584*
  Malasadas, *560,* 560–61
  Mana'eesh Za'atar (Za'atar Flatbreads), *592,* 592–93
  Mixed Berry Scones, *565,* 565–66
  Monkey, 587–88, *588*
  Muffin Tin Doughnuts, *575, 575*
  Muffin Tin Popovers, 571
  Perfect Popovers, 571, *571*
  Prosciutto, 453–54, *455*
  Roasted Garlic–Parmesan, 303, *303*
  Southern-Style Skillet Cornbread, *568,* 568–69
  see also Biscuits; Buns; Muffins; Tortilla(s)
Bread stuffing. See Stuffing
Broccoli
  Chicken Divan, 139–40, *140*
  Grilled, with Anchovy-Garlic Butter, 533
  Grilled, with Lemon and Parmesan, 532–33, *533*
  and Red Potatoes, One-Pan Roasted Salmon with, 357–58, *359*
Broccolini
  Philadelphia Pork Sandwiches, *236,* 236–37
Broccoli Rabe, Quick-Braised, with Garlic and Anchovies, 80, *81*
Broiler pans, cooking with, 278
Brown Soda Bread, 590–91, *591*
Brown Soda Bread with Currants and Caraway, 591

Brown Sugar–Cayenne Butter, Husk-Grilled Corn with, 527
Brunswick Stew, 326–27, *327*
Brussels Sprout(s)
  Gratin, 362, *363*
  One-Pan Prime Rib and Roasted Vegetables, 340–41, *341*
  One-Pan Roast Chicken with Root Vegetables, 318–19, *319*
  Salad, 363, *363*
  Salad with Cheddar, Hazelnuts, and Apple, 363
  Salad with Smoked Gouda, Pecans, and Dried Cherries, 363
Buckeye Candies, *646,* 646–47
Buckle, Mixed Berry, 657–58, *659*
Buffalo Blue Cheese Sauce, 260
Buffalo-Style Grill-Fried Chicken Wings, 470
Buns
  Everything Bagel-Seasoned, *552,* 553
  Morning, 579–80, *581*
  New Jersey Crumb, 580–81, *581*
  Quicker Cinnamon, *577,* 577–78
  Triple-Chocolate Sticky, *578,* 578–79
  Ultimate Cinnamon, 576, *577*
Burgers
  Brunch, 551–53, *552*
  Diner-Style Patty Melts, *220,* 221–22
  Fried Onion, Oklahoma, *223,* 223–24
  Green Chile Cheeseburgers, *490,* 490–91
  Grilled Bacon, with Caramelized Onion, 489–90, *490*
  Grilled Lamb, 46, *47*
  Grilled Pork, *506,* 506–7
  Grilled Steak, 286–87, *287*
  Jucy Lucy, *488,* 488–89
  Patty Melts, *220,* 220–21
  Shrimp, South Carolina, 199–200, *200*
  Sliders, 222–23, *223*
  Wisconsin Butter, 224, *224*
Burger Sauce, Horseradish, 507
Butter
  Barbecue-Scallion, 528
  Basil Pesto, 528
  Browned, –Caper Sauce, 430
  Browned, Chocolate Chunk Muffins, 573–74, *574*
  Chesapeake Bay, 528
  Cilantro-Chipotle, 528
  Honey, *567,* 568
Buttermilk
  -Strawberry No-Churn Ice Cream, 649
  Whipped Cream, Rhubarb Shortcakes with, 110–11, *111*

INDEX 773

C

Cabbage
    American-Style Egg Rolls, 44–45, *45*
    Apple Slaw, Tangy, *534*, 534–35
    California-Style Fish Tacos, *387*, 387–88
    Chinese Chicken Salad, 206, *206*
    Memphis Chopped Coleslaw, 535, *535*
    Milk-Can Supper, *154*, 155
    Neorm Sach Moan (Cambodian Chicken Salad), *204*, 205
    San Diego Fish Tacos, 388–89, *389*
    see also Sauerkraut
Caesar Green Bean Salad, 305–6, *306*
Caesar Salad, Grilled, *533*, 533–34
Caesar Salad, Ultimate, 76, *77*
Café au Lait Angel Food Cake, 615
Cajun Meatball Fricassee, 20, *21*
Cajun Stuffed Turkey Wings, *183*, 183–84
Cakes
    Angel Food, 614–15, *615*
        Café au Lait, 615
        Chocolate-Almond, 615
    Baby Pudding, 623, *623*
    Blitz Torte, *613*, 613–14
    Blueberry Jam, 603–5, *604*
    Carrot-Ginger Snack, with Cardamom, 621
    Carrot Snack, 620–21, *621*
    Chiffon, *615*, 615–16
    Chiffon, Orange, 616
    Chocolate Blackout, 596–98, *597*
    Chocolate Cream Cupcakes, *621*, 621–22
    Chocolate Éclair, 608–9, *609*
    Clementine, *601*, 601–2
    Hot Fudge Pudding, 622–23
    Italian Cream, 616–17, *617*
    Lane, *594*, 600–601
    La Viña–Style Cheesecake, *628*, 629
    Lemon Icebox Cheesecake, 624–26, *625*
    Lemon Pudding, 624, *625*
    Magic Chocolate Flan, 609–10, *610*
    Milk Chocolate Cheesecake, 627–28, *628*
    Mixed Berry Buckle, 657–58, *659*
    Orange Upside-Down, 602–3, *603*
    Pound, Cold-Oven, *619*, 619–20
    Pound, Cream Cheese, 618, *618*
    Red Velvet, 596, *597*
    Strawberry Dream, *604*, 605–6
    Strawberry Poke, *606*, 606–7
    Swiss Hazelnut, 612, *613*

Cakes (*cont.*)
    Texas Sheet, 607–8, *608*
    Tres Leches, 611, *611*
    Tunnel of Fudge, *599*, 599–600
    Wellesley Fudge, *598*, 598–99
    Whoopie Pies, 642–43, *643*
California Barbecued Beans, *529*, 529–30
California Barbecued Tri-Tip, 484–85, *485*
Cambodian Chicken Salad (Neorm Sach Moan), *204*, 205
Candies
    Buckeye, *646*, 646–47
    see also Fudge; Truffles
Caper(s)
    –Browned Butter Sauce, 430
    Hard-Cooked Eggs, and Radishes, Tuna Salad with, 132
    -Lemon Sauce, Grilled Salmon Steaks with, *446*, 523
    One-Pot Shrimp Piccata Pasta, 66, *67*
    and Oregano, Crushed Red Potatoes with, 297
    Salmon Piccata, *450*, 451
Cappuccino Glaze, 637
Caramel, Salted
    –Coconut No-Churn Ice Cream, 649
    Sauce, Basque Cider, *628*, 629
Cardamom, Carrot-Ginger Snack Cake with, 621
Carrot(s)
    Cast Iron Chicken and Vegetables, 319–20, *321*
    Chuck Roast in Foil, 342–43, *343*
    Cutty's-Inspired Eggplant Spuckie, 72, *73*
    -Ginger Snack Cake with Cardamom, 621
    Guinness Beef Stew, 328–29, *329*
    Milk-Can Supper, *154*, 155
    Morning Glory Muffins, *572*, 573
    One-Pan Prime Rib and Roasted Vegetables, 340–41, *341*
    One-Pan Roast Chicken with Root Vegetables, 318–19, *319*
    One-Pot Chicken Jardinière, *141*, 141–42
    and Potatoes, Chicken Baked in Foil with, 323
    Shredded, and Serrano Chile Salad, 536, *536*
    Slow-Cooker Pork Pot Roast, 346, *347*
    Snack Cake, 620–21, *621*
Catfish, Fried, *185*, 185–86
Cat Head Biscuits, *563*, 563–64
Cauliflower
    Gobi Manchurian, *262*, 262–63
Charleston Shrimp Perloo, *162*, 194–95
Cheddar
    Air-Fryer Jalapeño Poppers, 86, *87*
    Beef Enchiladas, 406, *407*
    Best Potluck Macaroni and Cheese, 124, *125*
    Brunch Burgers, 551–53, *552*
    Cheese and Bacon, Twice-Baked Potatoes with, *272*, 302

Cheddar *(cont.)*
    Cheeseburger Mac, 127, *127*
    and Chipotle, Sweet Potato Fritters with, 84
    Creamy Cheese Grits, 128, *128*
    Crust, Apple Pie with, *683*, 683–84
    Easier Chicken Chimichangas, 400–401, *401*
    Easy Green Chile Chicken Enchiladas, *405*, 405–6
    Extra-Cheesy Grits, *128*, 129
    Fluffy Diner-Style Cheese Omelet, 546, *547*
    Fried Cheese Curds with Ranch Dressing, 266–67, *267*
    Frito Pie, 16, *17*
    Hazelnuts, and Apple, Brussels Sprout Salad with, 363
    -Jalapeño Scones, *544*, 566–67
    Macaroni and Cheese with Tomatoes, *126*, 126–27
    New England Bar Pizza, 252–53, *253*
    New Mexican Bean-and-Cheese Turnovers with Green Chile, *402*, 402–3
    North Carolina Cheese Biscuits, *258*, 258–59
    Pimento Mac and Cheese, 124–25, *125*
    -Potato Pierogi, *257*, 257–58
    Sausage and Red Bell Pepper Breakfast Pizza, 549
    and Scallion Mashed Potato Cakes, 292
    Tex-Mex Cheese Enchiladas, 403–4, *404*

Cheese
    Adjaruli Khachapuri, *548*, 549–50
    aged, melting, 125
    -and-Ham Pie, "Impossible," *547*, 547
    Asparagus Salad with Oranges, Feta, and Hazelnuts, 365
    Asparagus Salad with Radishes, Pecorino Romano, and Croutons, 364, *364*
    Baked Manicotti with Meat Sauce, *441*, 441–42
    Beef Enchiladas, 406, *407*
    Blintzes with Raspberry Sauce, 557–58, *559*
    Blue, and Bacon Baked Potato Fans, 300
    Blue, and Bacon Mashed Potato Cakes, 292
    Blue, and Oranges, Endive Salad with, *366*, 366–67
    Blue, Prosciutto, and Basil, Shredded Swiss Chard Salad with, *365*, 365–66
    Blue, Sauce, Buffalo, 260
    Boogaloo Wonderland Sandwiches, 218–19, *219*
    Bread, Beer-Batter, 569, *569*
    Bread, Spicy, 570, *570*
    Brussels Sprout Salad, 363, *363*
    Brussels Sprout Salad with Smoked Gouda, Pecans, and Dried Cherries, 363
    Brussels Sprouts Gratin, 362, *363*
    Cheeseburger Mac, 127, *127*
    Cheesy Stuffed Shells, 442–43, *443*
    Chicken Cordon Bleu, 10–11, *11*

Cheese *(cont.)*
    Chorizo and Manchego Breakfast Pizza, 549
    Creamy Potatoes and Leeks, 82–83, *83*
    Crispy Baked Potato Fans, 300, *301*
    Croque Madame, 218
    Croque Monsieur, 217–18, *218*
    Cuban Sandwiches, 237–38, *238*
    Detroit-Style Pizza, 253–55, *254*
    Diner-Style Patty Melts, *220*, 221–22
    Eggplant Pecorino, *440*, 440–41
    Enchiladas, Tex-Mex, 403–4, *404*
    Failproof Chicken Cordon Bleu, *289*, 289–90
    Fluffy Baked Polenta with Red Sauce, 430–31, *431*
    Fontina, Sauce, 429–30
    French Onion Soup, *274*, 274–75
    Fresh Tomato Galette, 374, *375*
    Goat, and Hazelnuts, Roasted Green Beans with, 130–31, *131*
    Goat, Grapes, and Almonds, Asparagus Salad with, 364–65
    Gorditas, 396–97, *397*
    Green Chile Cheeseburgers, *490*, 490–91
    Grits, Creamy, 128, *128*
    Hearty Beef Lasagna, *437*, 437–38
    Huevos Rancheros, 383, *383*
    Italian Meatloaf, *416*, 435–36
    Jitto's-Style Steak Bombs, 19, *19*
    Jucy Lucy Burgers, *488*, 488–89
    Kolaches, 583–84, *584*
    Mac and, Pimento, 124–25, *125*
    Macaroni and, Best Potluck, 124, *125*
    Macaroni and, with Tomatoes, *126*, 126–27
    New Orleans Muffulettas, *216*, 216–17
    Okinawan Taco Rice, 230–31, *231*
    Olive Oil Potato Gratin, *295*, 295–96
    Pasta with Mushroom Sauce, *426*, 426–27
    Patty Melts, *220*, 220–21
    Philadelphia Pork Sandwiches, *236*, 236–37
    Roasted Green Beans with Pecorino and Pine Nuts, 131
    Sausage Lasagna, *416*, 438–39
    Shrimp Tacos, 390–91, *391*
    Skillet Chicken Parmesan, 446, *447*
    Skillet Lasagna, 436, *436*
    Skillet Lasagna with Sausage and Peppers, 436
    Sliders, 222–23, *223*
    Slow-Cooker Baked Ziti, *434*, 434–35
    Slow-Cooker French Onion Soup, *272*, 275
    Smoked Prime Rib Sandwiches with Green Chile Queso, 495–96, *496*

INDEX   775

Cheese *(cont.)*
    Smokehouse Mashed Sweet Potatoes, 372
    Southwestern Potato Tots, 262
    Southwestern Tomato and Corn Salad, 413, *413*
    Spaghetti Carbonara, *424*, 425
    Spinach and Tomato Lasagna, *439*, 439–40
    Spinach-Artichoke Dip, 376–77, *377*
    St. Louis–Style Pizza, *248*, 249–50
    Stuffed Tomatoes, *272*, 307
    Super-Stuffed Baked Potatoes, *301*, 301–2
    Sweet Potato Fritters with Feta, Dill, and Cilantro, 84, *85*
    Tomatoes with Fontina Sauce and Cornichon Dressing, 78, *79*
    Twice-Baked Potatoes with Chorizo and Chipotle, 302
    Ultimate Seven-Layer Dip, *381*, 381–82
    Ultimate Smoky Seven-Layer Dip, 382
    Ultimate Spicy Beef Nachos, *380*, *381*
    Wisconsin Butter Burgers, *224*, 224
    see also Cheddar; Cream Cheese; Mozzarella; Parmesan

Cheesecake
    Bars, Strawberry, *626*, 626–27
    La Viña–Style, *628*, 629
    Lemon Icebox, 624–26, *625*
    Milk Chocolate, 627–28, *628*

Cherry(ies)
    -Bourbon Sauce and Sweet Potatoes, Pork Chops with, *308*, 351–52
    Dried, Smoked Gouda, and Pecans, Brussels Sprout Salad with, 363

Chesapeake Bay Butter, 528
Chicago-Style Barbecued Ribs, *491*, 491–92
Chicago Thin-Crust Pizza, 250–51, *251*

Chicken
    Almond Boneless, *209*, 209–10
    Apple Cider, 317–18, *318*
    Arroz con Pollo, 384–85, *385*
    Baked in Foil
        with Fennel and Sun-Dried Tomatoes, 323
        with Potatoes and Carrots, 323
        with Sweet Potato and Radish, *322*, 323
    Barbecued
        Alabama, *460*, 460–61
        Classic, 461–62, *463*
        Cornell, 459–60, *460*
        Pulled, 475–76, *477*
    Bourbon, 208, *208*
    breasts, preparing cutlets from, 446
    breasts, splitting and trimming, 136
    Brunswick Stew, 326–27, *327*

Chicken *(cont.)*
    Cast Iron Baked, 134, *134*
    Chilaquiles, 408–9, *409*
    Chimichangas, Easier, 400–401, *401*
    Chow Mein, 207, *207*
    Cordon Bleu, 10–11, *11*
    Cordon Bleu, Failproof, *289*, 289–90
    Cumin-Scented (Kombdi, Jira Ghalun), 212, *213*
    Diavolo, Grilled, 474–75, *475*
    Divan, 139–40, *140*
    Enchiladas, Easy Green Chile, *405*, 405–6
    Florentine, *140*, 140–41
    Fried
        Batter-, 164, *165*
        Creole, *165*, 165–66
        Extra-Crunchy, *166*, 166–67
        Extra-Spicy, Extra-Crunchy, 167
        Garlic, *171*, 171–72
        Garlic-Lime, *386*, 386–87
        Hawaiian-Style, *174*, 175
        Honey, *170*, 170–71
        Lard-, 167–68, *168*
        Mimosa, 173–74, *174*
        Nashville Extra-Hot, 169
        Nashville Hot, 168–69, *169*
        North Carolina Dipped, 172–73, *173*
        One-Batch, *135*, 135–36
        Pickle-Brined, Sandwiches, 6, *7*
        Ranch, 175–77, *176*
        Thighs, Sweet Tea–Brined, *176*, 177
    Greek, 180, *181*
    Grilled Hilltribe, with Kua Txob, 3–4, *5*
    Gumbo, 192–93, *193*
    Hot-Honey, 138–39, *139*
    Huli Huli, *458*, 458–59
    Jardinière, One-Pot, *141*, 141–42
    Jerk, Grilled, 462–63, *463*
    Leg Quarters, Grilled, 472, *473*
    Lemon, Grilled Butterflied, 467–68, *468*
    Noodle Soup, Old-Fashioned, 120, *121*
    Nuggets, 178, *178*
    Paprikash and Buttered Spaetzle, 137–38, *138*
    Parmesan, Skillet, 446, *447*
    and Pastry, *122*, 122–23
    Pie, Moravian, *325*, 325–26
    Popcorn, *179*, 179–80
    and Potatoes, Skillet-Roasted, 321, *321*
    Pot Pie, Double-Crust, 142–43, *143*

Chicken *(cont.)*
    and Rice, Thai-Style (Kaho Man Gai), 210–12, *211*
    Roast
        with Fennel and Parsnips, One-Pan, 319
        Green Goddess, *133*, 133–34
        Herb, 315–16, *317*
        Lemon, 316–17, *317*
        with Root Vegetables, One-Pan, 318–19, *319*
    Salad, Cambodian (Neorm Sach Moan), *204*, 205
    Salad, Chinese, 206, *206*
    Sauce Piquant, 180–81, *181*
    Scampi, *447*, 447–48
    Scarpariello, 448, *449*
    shredding, 392
    Skillet-Roasted, with Stuffing, *322*, 322–23
    and Slicks, *324*, 324–25
    Smoked Bourbon, *466*, 466–67
    Smoked Citrus, *465*, 465–66
    Smothered, Southern-Style, 136–37, *137*
    Stock, Slow-Cooker, 120–21, *121*
    Tacos, Easy, 391–92, *392*
    Teriyaki, *456*, 464
    Thighs, BBQ, 473–74, *474*
    and Vegetables, Cast Iron, 319–20, *321*
    whole, breaking down, 167
    whole, butterflying, 4, 320, 468
    whole, cutting in half, 467
    Wings
        Grilled, 468–69, *469*
        Grilled, BBQ, 469
        Grilled, Creole, 469
        Grilled, Tandoori, 469
        Grill-Fried, 469–70, *470*
        Grill-Fried Buffalo-Style, 470
        Lemon Pepper, *182*, 182–83
        Smoked, *471*, 471–72
        Soy Sauce, 210, *211*

Chicken livers
    Cajun Rice Dressing, *247*, 247–48
    South Carolina Barbecue Hash, 240–41, *241*

Chiffon Cake, *615*, 615–16
Chiffon Cake, Orange, 616
Chilaquiles, Chicken, 408–9, *409*
Chile(s)
    Air-Fryer Jalapeño Poppers, 86, *87*
    ancho, about, 412
    canned chipotle in adobo, about, 412
    Chicken Chilaquiles, 408–9, *409*
    Cilantro-Chipotle Butter, 528
    Colorado Green Chili, 242–43, *243*

Chile(s) *(cont.)*
    Crisp, Maple, Grilled Sweet Potatoes with, *531*, 531–32
    Easy Chicken Tacos, 391–92, *392*
    Easy Chili con Carne, *409*, 409–10
    Five-Alarm Chili, *410*, 410–11
    Flank Steak in Adobo, 406–8, *407*
    Green, Cheeseburgers, *490*, 490–91
    Green, Chicken Enchiladas, Easy, *405*, 405–6
    Green, New Mexican Bean-and-Cheese Turnovers with, *402*, 402–3
    Green Spaghetti, 62, *63*
    Grilled Habanero and Pineapple Shrimp Skewers, 526
    Grilled Jalapeño and Lime Shrimp Skewers, *525*, 525–26
    Grilled Jerk Chicken, 462–63, *463*
    Grilled Red Chile and Ginger Shrimp Skewers, 526
    guajillo, about, 412
    Guanimes con Bacalao (Cornmeal Dumplings with Salt Cod), 203–5, *204*
    Huevos Rancheros, 383, *383*
    Jalapeño-Cheddar Scones, *544*, 566–67
    jalapeños, seeding, 382
    Mesquite-Grilled Tacos Rasurados, 26–27, *27*
    One-Minute Salsa, 380, *381*
    Pique, 29
    poblano, about, 412
    Quesabirria Tacos, 394–95, *395*
    Santa Maria Salsa, 485
    Serrano, and Shredded Carrot Salad, 536, *536*
    Shrimp with Garlic and Jalapeño Butter, 56, *57*
    Smoky Salsa Verde, 401–2, *402*
    Sofrito, 29
    Sweet Potato Fritters with Cheddar and Chipotle, 84
    Texas Potato Salad, 540–41, *541*
    Tex-Mex Cheese Enchiladas, 403–4, *404*
    Ultimate Seven-Layer Dip, *381*, 381–82
    Ultimate Smoky Seven-Layer Dip, 382
    Ultimate Spicy Beef Nachos, 380, *381*
    Vegetarian Chili, *411*, 411–12

Chili
    Cincinnati, *241*, 241–42
    Colorado Green, 242–43, *243*
    con Carne, Easy, *409*, 409–10
    Five-Alarm, *410*, 410–11
    Vegetarian, *411*, 411–12

Chili powder
    Homemade Taco Seasoning, 231

Chimichangas, Easier Chicken, 400–401, *401*
Chinese Chicken Salad, 206, *206*
Chinese-Style Barbecued Spareribs, 514–16, *515*
Chinese-Style Glazed Pork Tenderloin, 514, *515*

Chive(s)
- Green Goddess Dressing, 132–33, *133*
- Green Goddess Roast Chicken, *133*, 133–34
- and Lemon, Slow-Roasted Salmon with, 356–57, *357*
- Sour Cream, *298*, 299

Chocolate
- -Almond Angel Food Cake, 615
- Babka, *586*, 586–87
- Baby Pudding Cakes, 623, *623*
- Black and White Cookies, *641*, 641–42
- Blackout Cake, 596–98, *597*
- Brownie Cookies, 108, *109*
- Buckeye Candies, *646*, 646–47
- Chip Cookies, Thin and Crispy, *631*, 631–32
- Chip Skillet Cookie, 632, *633*
- Chunk–Banana-Walnut No-Churn Ice Cream, 649
- Chunk Browned Butter Muffins, 573–74, *574*
- Conchas, 103, *103*
- Cowboy Cookies, *630*, 630–31
- Cream Cupcakes, *621*, 621–22
- Dark, No-Churn Ice Cream, 649
- -Dipped Potato Chip Cookies, 104–5, *105*
- Double-, Banana Bread, 92, *93*
- Éclair Cake, 608–9, *609*
- Flan Cake, Magic, 609–10, *610*
- Frozen Custard, Old-Fashioned, *667*, 667
- Fudge, *646*, 647
- Hot Fudge Pudding Cake, 622–23
- Malted Milk, No-Churn Ice Cream, 649
- -Marshmallow Sandwich Cookies, 106–7, *107*
- Milk, Cheesecake, 627–28, *628*
- milk, melting, note about, 628
- Milk, No-Churn Ice Cream, 649
- Mississippi Mud Pie, 697–98, *698*
- -Peppermint Fudge, *646*, 647
- Pie, Angel, *696*, 696–97
- Pie, French Silk, 694–95, *695*
- S'mores Pie, *668*, 698–99
- So-Cal Churros, 414–15, *415*
- Texas Sheet Cake, 607–8, *608*
- -Toffee Fudge, *646*, 648
- Triple-, Sticky Buns, *578*, 578–79
- Truffles, Basic, 645, *645*
  - -Almond, 645
  - -Cinnamon, 645
  - -Ginger, 645
  - -Lemon, 645
- Tunnel of Fudge Cake, *599*, 599–600
- Wellesley Fudge Cake, *598*, 598–99
- Whoopie Pies, 642–43, *643*

Chorizo and Manchego Breakfast Pizza, 549
Choucroute Garnie, Olympia Provisions–Style, 153–54, *154*
Chowder, Clam, Woodman's-Style, 189–90, *190*
Chow Mein, Chicken, 207, *207*
Churros, So-Cal, 414–15, *415*
Chutney, Five-Spice Tomato, 47, *47*

Cider
- Apple, Chicken, 317–18, *318*
- -Baked Ham, *353*, 353–54
- Basque, Salted Caramel Sauce, *628*, 629
- -Braised Pork Chops, 158–59, *159*
- -Braised Pork Roast, *349*, 349–50
- -Braised Turkey, *310*, 311–12
- Sauce, 652

Cilantro
- -Chipotle Butter, 528
- Easy Chicken Tacos, 391–92, *392*
- Feta, and Dill, Sweet Potato Fritters with, 84, *85*
- Green Spaghetti, 62, *63*
- Kua Txob, 4
- and Lime, Grilled Thin-Cut Pork Chops with, 511
- -Lime Butter, Husk-Grilled Corn with, 527
- One-Minute Salsa, 380, *381*
- Pork Pernil, *348*, 348–49
- and Scallions, Eggplant Dip with, 271
- Smoky Salsa Verde, 401–2, *402*
- Sofrito, 29

Cincinnati Chili, 241, 241–42

Cinnamon
- Bread, Amish, 588–89, *589*
- Buns, Quicker, *577*, 577–78
- Buns, Ultimate, 576, *577*
- -Chocolate Truffles, 645
- and Lemon, Bolos Lêvedos (Portuguese Muffins) with, 96
- and Lemon, Pastéis de Nata with, 99
- Monkey Bread, 587–88, *588*
- Morning Buns, 579–80, *581*
- Muffin Tin Doughnuts, 575, *575*
- New Mexico Biscochitos, *637*, 637–38

Cioppino, Monterey Bay, 188–89, *189*
Citrus-Braised Pork Tacos, 398, *399*

Clam(s)
- Casino, 58, *59*
- with Chorizo, *308*, 360–61
- Chowder, Woodman's-Style, 189–90, *190*
- Coastal Georgia Paella, 50, *51*

Clementine Cake, *601*, 601–2
Cobbler, Easy Blueberry, *660*, 660–61

Cocktails
    Coquito, 116, *117*
    Piña Coladas, 271, *271*

Coconut
    Coquito, 116, *117*
    Cowboy Cookies, *630,* 630–31
    cream of, about, 116
    Cream Pie, 689, *689*
    Italian Cream Cake, 616–17, *617*
    Lane Cake, *594,* 600–601
    -Lime Cookies, 636
    Morning Glory Muffins, *572,* 573
    Pie, French, 687–88, *688*
    Piña Coladas, 271, *271*
    –Salted Caramel No-Churn Ice Cream, 649
    Toasted-, Banana Pudding, 664

Cod
    Salt, Cornmeal Dumplings with (Guanimes con Bacalao), 203–5, *204*
    San Diego Fish Tacos, 388–89, *389*

Coffee
    Café au Lait Angel Food Cake, 615
    Cappuccino Glaze, 637

Colorado Green Chili, 242–43, *243*
Comeback Sauce, *185,* 186
Conchas, 102–3, *103*
Conchas, Chocolate, 103, *103*

Cookies
    Black and White, *641,* 641–42
    Chocolate Brownie, 108, *109*
    Chocolate Chip, Thin and Crispy, *631,* 631–32
    Chocolate Chip Skillet, *632, 633*
    Chocolate-Marshmallow Sandwich, 106–7, *107*
    Coconut-Lime, 636
    Cowboy, *630,* 630–31
    Crescent, 635
    Fairy Gingerbread, *594,* 639–40
    Jam Thumbprint, *635,* 636
    Joe Froggers, 640, *641*
    Melting Moments, *635, 635*
    M&M, 632–33, *633*
    New Mexico Biscochitos, *637,* 637–38
    Oatmeal Creme Pies, *643,* 643–45
    Orange–Poppy Seed, 636
    Round Spritz, *635,* 636
    Slice-and-Bake, 636–37, *637*
    Walnut–Brown Sugar, 636
    Whoopie Pies, 642–43, *643*

Coquito, 116, *117*

Corn
    Brunswick Stew, 326–27, *327*
    on the Cob, Grilled, *527,* 527–28
    Cornbread and Bacon Stuffing, 314
    Creamy Cheese Grits, 128, *128*
    Husk-Grilled, 526, *527*
        with Brown Sugar–Cayenne Butter, 527
        with Cilantro-Lime Butter, 527
        with Mustard-Paprika Butter, 526
        with Rosemary-Pepper Butter, 527
    Milk-Can Supper, *154,* 155
    Skillet, with Mexican Chorizo, *378,* 414
    Sweet, Spoonbread, *376,* 377
    Sweet, Spoonbreads, Individual, 376
    and Tomato Salad, Southwestern, 413, *413*

Cornbread
    and Bacon Stuffing, 314
    Blueberry, *567,* 567–68
    and Sausage Stuffing, 313–14, *314*
    Southern-Style Skillet, *568,* 568–69

Corncob-Smoked Ribs, South Dakota, 516–18, *517*
Cornell Barbecued Chicken, 459–60, *460*

Corn husks
    cooking with, 245
    Delta Hot Tamales, 245–46, *246*

Cornichon(s)
    Dressing and Fontina Sauce, Tomatoes with, 78, *79*
    and Whole-Grain Mustard, Tuna Salad with, 132

Cornish Pasties, 22–23, *23*

Cornmeal
    about, 129
    Biscuits, *560,* 561
    Blueberry Cornbread, *567,* 567–68
    Delta Hot Tamales, 245–46, *246*
    Dumplings with Salt Cod (Guanimes con Bacalao), 203–5, *204*
    Fluffy Baked Polenta with Red Sauce, 430–31, *431*
    Hoecakes, 504–5, *505*
    Individual Sweet Corn Spoonbreads, 376
    Pancakes, Fluffy, *556,* 556–57
    Southern-Style Skillet Cornbread, *568,* 568–69
    Sweet Corn Spoonbread, *376,* 377

Cottage cheese
    Breakfast Pizza, *548,* 548–49
    Chorizo and Manchego Breakfast Pizza, 549
    Hearty Beef Lasagna, *437,* 437–38
    Sausage and Red Bell Pepper Breakfast Pizza, 549
    Sausage Lasagna, *416,* 438–39
    Smoked Salmon Breakfast Pizza, 549

Couscous
    Stuffed Tomatoes, *272,* 307
Cowboy Cookies, *630,* 630–31
Cranberry(ies)
    -Apple Crisp, 656–57, *657*
    Double Berry Cream Cheese Kringle Filling, 586
Cream Cheese
    Air-Fryer Jalapeño Poppers, 86, *87*
    Blueberry Cream Pie, *668,* 693–94
    Blueberry Jam Cake, 603–5, *604*
    Carrot Snack Cake, 620–21, *621*
    Gooey Butter Cake Bars, *634,* 634–35
    Green Spaghetti, 62, *63*
    Icebox Key Lime Pie, *677,* 677–78
    Italian Cream Cake, 616–17, *617*
    Kolaches, 583–84, *584*
    Kringle, *584,* 584–86
    La Viña–Style Cheesecake, *628,* 629
    Lemon Icebox Cheesecake, 624–26, *625*
    Magic Chocolate Flan Cake, 609–10, *610*
    Milk Chocolate Cheesecake, 627–28, *628*
    Pound Cake, *618,* 618
    Red Velvet Cake, 596, *597*
    Spinach-Artichoke Dip, 376–77, *377*
    Strawberry Cheesecake Bars, *626,* 626–27
    Strawberry Dream Cake, *604,* 605–6
    Strawberry Pretzel Salad, 129–30, *131*
Crema, Mexican, about, 414
Crème Fraîche and Spinach, Lentilles du Puy with, 375, *375*
Creole Baked Stuffed Shrimp with Sausage, 289
Creole Fried Chicken, *165,* 165–66
Creole Grilled Chicken Wings, 469
Crescent Cookies, 635
Croque Madame, 218
Croque Monsieur, 217–18, *218*
Cuban Bread, *239,* 239–40
Cuban Pork Roast with Mojo, 238–39, *239*
Cuban Sandwiches, 237–38, *238*
Cucumber(s)
    Salmon Teriyaki Poke, *202,* 203
    -Yogurt Sauce, 522–23
Cumin
    Homemade Taco Seasoning, 231
    Onion Raita, *213,* 213
    -Scented Chicken (Kombdi, Jira Ghalun), *212,* 213
Cupcakes, Chocolate Cream, *621,* 621–22
Currants and Caraway, Brown Soda Bread with, 591
Curried Chutney Sauce, 260
Curry, Shrimp, Zephyr Wright–Inspired, 54, *55*

Curry and Grapes, Tuna Salad with, 132
Custard, Old-Fashioned Frozen
    Chocolate, 667, *667*
    Vanilla, 666–67, *667*
Cutty's-Inspired Eggplant Spuckie, 72, *73*

D

Dakota Bread, 591–92, *592*
Dakota Peach Kuchen, 661–62, *663*
Dates
    Aunt Jule's Pie, 112, *113*
Delmonico Potato Casserole, *293,* 293–94
Delta Hot Tamales, 245–46, *246*
Desserts
    Apple Fritters, *653,* 653–54
    Apple Pandowdy, 654–55, *655*
    Baked Apple Dumplings, 652, *653*
    Banana Pudding, *663,* 663–64
    Chocolate Conchas, 103, *103*
    Conchas, 102–3, *103*
    Cranberry-Apple Crisp, 656–57, *657*
    Dakota Peach Kuchen, 661–62, *663*
    Easy Blueberry Cobbler, *660,* 660–61
    Gooey Butter Cake Bars, *634,* 634–35
    Maine Blueberry Grunt, *659,* 659–60
    Mixed Berry Buckle, 657–58, *659*
    New Orleans Bourbon Bread Pudding, 664–65, *665*
    Pastéis de Nata (Portuguese Egg Tarts), 98–99, *99*
    Pastéis de Nata with Lemon and Cinnamon, 99
    Peanut-y Banana Pudding, 664
    Rhubarb Shortcakes with Buttermilk Whipped Cream, 110–11, *111*
    Skillet Peach Cobbler, *660,* 661
    So-Cal Churros, 414–15, *415*
    Strawberry Cheesecake Bars, *626,* 626–27
    Strawberry-Elderflower Rhubarb Shortcakes with Buttermilk Whipped Cream, 111
    Sufganiyot (Hanukkah Jelly Doughnuts), 100–101, *101*
    Summer Berry Pudding, 665–66, *666*
    Tarte Tatin, *650,* 655–56
    Toasted-Coconut Banana Pudding, 664
    Zeppoles, 454–55, *455*
    see also Cakes; Candies; Cookies; Fudge; Ice Cream; Pies (sweet); Truffles
Detroit-Style Pizza, 253–55, *254*

Dill
    Feta, and Cilantro, Sweet Potato Fritters with, 84, *85*
    and Garlic, Slow-Roasted Salmon with, 357
    Potato Salad, 540, *541*

Dips
    Baba Ghanoush, 270, *271*
    Buffalo Blue Cheese Sauce, 260
    Chive Sour Cream, *298, 299*
    Chunky Guacamole, *382, 382*
    Creamy BBQ Sauce, 260
    Curried Chutney Sauce, 260
    Eggplant, with Scallions and Cilantro, 271
    Honey-Mustard Sauce, 178
    One-Minute Salsa, 380, *381*
    Santa Maria Salsa, 485
    Seven-Layer, Ultimate, *381*, 381–82
    Seven-Layer, Ultimate Smoky, 382
    Smoky Salsa Verde, 401–2, *402*
    Spinach-Artichoke, 376–77, *377*
    Sweet and Sour Sauce, 179
    see also Salsa

Doughnuts
    Beignets, 558–59, *559*
    Hanukkah Jelly (Sufganiyot), 100–101, *101*
    Malasadas, *560*, 560–61
    Muffin Tin, 575, *575*

Dressing, Cajun Rice, *247*, 247–48
Dressing, Green Goddess, 132–33, *133*
Drinks
    Coquito, 116, *117*
    Ginger Lemonade, 161
    Lemonade with Honey, 161, *161*
    Mint Lemonade, 161
    Piña Coladas, 271, *271*

Duchess Potatoes, 369, *369*
Duck(s)
    Breasts with Port Wine–Fig Sauce, *314*, 315
    Slow Roasted, with Blackberry Sauce, 12–13, *13*

Dumplings
    Baked Apple, 652, *653*
    Cornmeal, with Salt Cod (Guanimes con Bacalao), 203–5, *204*
    Instant Mashed Potato Gnocchi, *428*, 428–29
    Potato-Cheddar Pierogi, *257*, 257–58

Dutch Baby, *556*, 557

Eastern North Carolina Fish Stew, 187–88, *189*
Eastern North Carolina–Style Barbecue Sauce, 500
Eggplant
    Baba Ghanoush, 270, *271*
    Dip with Scallions and Cilantro, 271
    Pecorino, *440*, 440–41
    Spuckie, Cutty's-Inspired, 72, *73*

Egg Rolls, American-Style, 44–45, *45*
Egg(s)
    Adjaruli Khachapuri, *548*, 549–50
    Beef Yakamein (New Orleans Spicy Beef Noodle Soup), 243–44, *244*
    Breakfast Pizza, *548*, 548–49
    Brunch Burgers, 551–53, *552*
    Chorizo and Manchego Breakfast Pizza, 549
    Croque Madame, 218
    Eastern North Carolina Fish Stew, 187–88, *189*
    Fluffy Diner-Style Cheese Omelet, 546, *547*
    Foolproof Hard-Cooked, 539
    Hard-Cooked, Radishes, and Capers, Tuna Salad with, 132
    Huevos Rancheros, 383, *383*
    Pastéis de Nata with Lemon and Cinnamon, 99
    Sardou, Skillet, 40–41, *41*
    Sausage and Red Bell Pepper Breakfast Pizza, 549
    Simple Hibachi-Style Fried Rice, *285*, 285–86
    Sisig, 232–33, *233*
    Smoked Salmon Breakfast Pizza, 549
    Spaghetti Carbonara, *424*, 425
    St. Paul Sandwich, 215–16, *216*
    Tarts, Portuguese (Pastéis de Nata), 98–99, *99*
    Texas Breakfast Tacos, 550–51, *551*
    Thai-Style Fried (Kai Dao), 213, *214*
    whites, whipping, 376

Elderflower-Strawberry Rhubarb Shortcakes with Buttermilk Whipped Cream, 111
Enchiladas
    Beef, 406, *407*
    Cheese, Tex-Mex, 403–4, *404*
    Green Chile Chicken, Easy, *405*, 405–6

English Muffin Bread, 589–90, *590*

INDEX   781

Equipment, ratings of
    bakeware, 713–16
    grilling equipment, 720–22
    handy tools, 705–10
    kitchen supplies, 728–29
    knives and more, 700–702
    measuring equipment, 711
    pots and pans, 702–4
    small appliances, 716–19
    specialty pieces, 722–27
    thermometers and timers, 712–13

Escarole
    Beans and Greens, 451–52, *452*

Everything Bagel-Seasoned Buns, *552,* 553

Fairy Gingerbread, *594,* 639–40
Fajitas, Grilled Steak, 482–83, *483*
Fennel
    Cast Iron Chicken and Vegetables, 319–20, *321*
    and Parsnips, One-Pan Roast Chicken with, 319
    Pasta with Sausage Ragu, 422, *423*
    Potatoes, and Olives, Baked Shrimp with, 358–59, *359*
    Sausage Lasagna, *416,* 438–39
    and Sun-Dried Tomatoes, Chicken Baked in Foil with, 323

Feta
    Adjaruli Khachapuri, *548,* 549–50
    Dill, and Cilantro, Sweet Potato Fritters with, 84, *85*
    Oranges, and Hazelnuts, Asparagus Salad with, 365

Fettuccine with Butter and Cheese, 422–23, *423*
Fig–Port Wine Sauce, Duck Breasts with, *314,* 315
Filipino Stew with Meat and Vegetables (Sinigang), *231,* 231–32

Fish
    Ahi-Chile Tostadas, *389,* 389–90
    buying, for poke, 203
    and Chips, 184–85, *185*
    Fried Catfish, *185,* 185–86
    Guanimes con Bacalao (Cornmeal Dumplings with Salt Cod), 203–5, *204*
    Miso Black Cod, 186–87, *187*

Fish *(cont.)*
    Monterey Bay Cioppino, 188–89, *189*
    Smoked, Tacos, *524,* 524–25
    Stew, Eastern North Carolina, 187–88, *189*
    Sticks, Crispy, with Tartar Sauce, 160, *161*
    Tacos, California-Style, *387,* 387–88
    Tacos, San Diego, 388–89, *389*
    Trout Amandine, 355–56, *356*
    Tuna Poke, 202, *202*
    Tuna Salad
        with Apple, Walnuts, and Tarragon, 132
        Classic, *118,* 132
        with Cornichons and Whole-Grain Mustard, 132
        with Curry and Grapes, 132
        with Hard-Cooked Eggs, Radishes, and Capers, 132
    see also Anchovy(ies); Salmon

Five-Alarm Chili, *410,* 410–11
Five-Spice Tomato Chutney, *47, 47*
Fontina
    Cheese Sauce, 429–30
    Cheesy Stuffed Shells, 442–43, *443*
    Eggplant Pecorino, *440,* 440–41
    Italian Meatloaf, *416,* 435–36
    Sauce and Cornichon Dressing, Tomatoes with, 78, *79*

French Coconut Pie, 687–88, *688*
French Onion Soup, *274,* 274–75
French Onion Soup, Slow-Cooker, *272,* 275
French Silk Chocolate Pie, 694–95, *695*
Frito Pie, 16, *17*
Fritters
    Apple, *653,* 653–54
    Crispy Vegetable, 263–64, *265*
    Sweet Potato, with Cheddar and Chipotle, 84
    Sweet Potato, with Feta, Dill, and Cilantro, 84, *85*
    Zeppoles, 454–55, *455*

Frozen Custard, Old-Fashioned
    Chocolate, *667, 667*
    Vanilla, 666–67, *667*

Fudge
    Chocolate, *646,* 647
    Chocolate-Peppermint, *646,* 647
    Chocolate-Toffee, *646,* 648

Furikake
    Salmon Teriyaki Poke, *202,* 203
    Tuna Poke, 202, *202*

G

Galette, Fresh Tomato, 374, *375*
Gambas al Ajillo (Spanish-Style Sizzling Garlic Shrimp), 359–60, *360*
Garlic
    and Anchovies, Quick-Braised Broccoli Rabe with, 80, *81*
    -Anchovy Butter, Grilled Broccoli with, 533
    Chicken Scampi, *447*, 447–48
    40 Cloves of, Roast Pork Loin with, 343–44, *344*
    Fried Chicken, *171*, 171–72
    Fried Rice, 233
    -Herb Oil, Grilled Brined Pork Chops with, 32, *33*
    and Herbs, Crushed Red Potatoes with, *296*, 296
    and Jalapeño Butter, Shrimp with, 56, *57*
    -Lime Fried Chicken, *386*, 386–87
    Mashed Potatoes, 290–91, *291*
    and Olive Oil, Spaghetti with (Aglio e Olio), *424*, 424
    One-Pot Shrimp Piccata Pasta, 66, *67*
    -Parsley Steak Sauce, 280
    Pique, 29
    Roast Beef, Sunday-Best, 329–31, *330*
    Roasted, 303
    Roasted, –Parmesan Bread, 303, *303*
    Roasted, Sauce. Arugula, and Walnuts, Pasta with, *425*, 425–26
    Shrimp, Spanish-Style Sizzling (Gambas al Ajillo), 359–60, *360*
    and Smoked Paprika, Crushed Red Potatoes with, 296
    Sofrito, 29
    Toasted, and Herb Dressing, Torn Potato Salad with, *367*, 367–68
Ginger
    -Carrot Snack Cake with Cardamom, 621
    -Chocolate Truffles, 645
    Fairy Gingerbread, *594*, 639–40
    Joe Froggers, 640, *641*
    Lemonade, 161
    -Lime Glaze, 637
    Sauce, Sweet, 286
    and Thyme, Grilled Thin-Cut Pork Chops with, 511
Glazes
    Cappuccino, 637
    Ginger-Lime, 637
    Malted Milk, 637
    Peanut Butter and Jelly, 637
Gnocchi, Instant Mashed Potato, *428*, 428–29
Goat Cheese
    Grapes, and Almonds, Asparagus Salad with, 364–65
    and Hazelnuts, Roasted Green Beans with, 130–31, *131*
Gobi Manchurian, *262*, 262–63
Gooey Butter Cake Bars, *634*, 634–35
Gorditas, 396–97, *397*
Gouda cheese
    Smokehouse Mashed Sweet Potatoes, 372
    Southwestern Potato Tots, 262
    Spinach-Artichoke Dip, 376–77, *377*
Graham crackers
    Blueberry Cream Pie, *668*, 693–94
    Chocolate Éclair Cake, 608–9, *609*
    Icebox Key Lime Pie, *677*, 677–78
    Really Good Key Lime Pie, *676*, 677
    S'mores Pie, *668*, 698–99
    Strawberry Cheesecake Bars, *626*, 626–27
Grains
    Dakota Bread, 591–92, *592*
    polenta, about, 129
    Vegetarian Chili, *411*, 411–12
    see also Cornmeal; Grits; Rice
Grandma Pizza, *444*, 444–45
Grapes
    and Curry, Tuna Salad with, 132
    Goat Cheese, and Almonds, Asparagus Salad with, 364–65
Gravy
    Classic Roast Beef and, *330*, 331
    Milk, Pan-Fried Pork Chops with, *156*, 157
    Mushroom, Meatloaf with, 145–46, *147*
    Old-Fashioned Roast Turkey with, *310*, 310–11
Greek Chicken, 180, *181*
Greek Diner-Style Home Fries, 554
Green Bean(s)
    Potato, and Tomato Salad, *446*, 543
    Roasted, with Almonds and Mint, 131
    Roasted, with Goat Cheese and Hazelnuts, 130–31, *131*
    Roasted, with Pecorino and Pine Nuts, 131
    Salad, Caesar, 305–6, *306*
Green Goddess Dressing, 132–33, *133*
Green Goddess Roast Chicken, *133*, 133–34
Greens
    and Beans, 451–52, *452*
    Belgian endive, preparing, 367
    Endive Salad with Oranges and Blue Cheese, *366*, 366–67
    mizuna, about, 205
    Pasta with Roasted Garlic Sauce, Arugula, and Walnuts, *425*, 425–26

Greens *(cont.)*
    Shredded Swiss Chard Salad with Prosciutto, Basil, and Blue Cheese, *365,* 365–66
    Slow-Cooker Minestrone, 419, *419*
    Swiss chard, stemming, 366
    see also Cabbage; Lettuce; Spinach

Grilled dishes
    Alabama Barbecued Chicken, *460,* 460–61
    Baltimore Pit Beef, *234,* 235
    Barbecued Burnt Ends, 478–79, *479*
    Barbecued Chuck Roast, 15, *15*
    Barbecued Country-Style Ribs, 516, *517*
    Barbecued Pulled Chicken, 475–76, *477*
    Barbecued Wood-Grilled Salmon, 521
    BBQ Chicken Thighs, 473–74, *474*
    Buffalo-Style Grill-Fried Chicken Wings, 470
    California Barbecued Tri-Tip, 484–85, *485*
    Cedar-Planked Salmon with Cucumber-Yogurt Sauce, 522, *522*
    Char-Grilled Steaks, 279, *279*
    Chicago-Style Barbecued Ribs, *491,* 491–92
    Chicken Teriyaki, *446,* 464
    Chinese-Style Barbecued Spareribs, 514–16, *515*
    Chinese-Style Glazed Pork Tenderloin, 514, *515*
    Classic Barbecued Chicken, 461–62, *463*
    Cornell Barbecued Chicken, 459–60, *460*
    Green Chile Cheeseburgers, *490,* 490–91
    Grilled Bacon Burgers with Caramelized Onion, 489–90, *490*
    Grilled Bone-In Leg of Lamb with Charred-Scallion Sauce, *519,* 519–20
    Grilled Bourbon Steaks, 480–81, *481*
    Grilled Brined Pork Chops with Garlic-Herb Oil, 32, *33*
    Grilled Broccoli with Anchovy-Garlic Butter, 533
    Grilled Broccoli with Lemon and Parmesan, 532–33, *533*
    Grilled Butterflied Lemon Chicken, 467–68, *468*
    Grilled Caesar Salad, *533,* 533–34
    Grilled Chicken Diavolo, 474–75, *475*
    Grilled Chicken Leg Quarters, 472, *473*
    Grilled Chicken Wings, 468–69, *469*
        BBQ, 469
        Creole, 469
        Tandoori, 469
    Grilled Corn on the Cob, *527,* 527–28
    Grilled Cowboy-Cut Rib Eyes, 282, *283*
    Grilled Flank Steak with Basil Dressing, 483–84, *484*
    Grilled Habanero and Pineapple Shrimp Skewers, 526
    Grilled Hilltribe Chicken with Kua Txob, 3–4, *5*
    Grilled Jalapeño and Lime Shrimp Skewers, *525,* 525–26

Grilled dishes *(cont.)*
    Grilled Jerk Chicken, 462–63, *463*
    Grilled Lamb Burgers, 46, *47*
    Grilled Mussels, 60, *61*
    Grilled Mustard-Glazed Pork Loin, 518, *518*
    Grilled Pork Burgers, 506, *506*–7
    Grilled Potato Packs, 530, *531*
        Spanish-Style, 530
        Spicy Home Fry, 530
        Vinegar and Onion, 530
    Grilled Red Chile and Ginger Shrimp Skewers, 526
    Grilled Salmon Steaks with Lemon-Caper Sauce, *446,* 523
    Grilled Sausages with Bell Peppers and Onions, *506,* 507
    Grilled Steak Burgers, 286–87, *287*
    Grilled Steak Fajitas, 482–83, *483*
    Grilled Steakhouse Steak Tips, 276, *276*
    Grilled Sugar Steak, 276–77, *277*
    Grilled Sweet Potatoes with Maple Chile Crisp, *531,* 531–32
    Grilled Thick-Cut Porterhouse Steaks, *481,* 481–82
    Grilled Thin-Cut Pork Chops, 510, *510*
        with Olive Tapenade, 511
        Spicy, with Cilantro and Lime, 511
        with Thyme and Ginger, 511
    Grill-Fried Chicken Wings, 469–70, *470*
    Grill-Roasted Peppers, 304–5, *305*
    Huli Huli Chicken, *458,* 458–59
    Husk-Grilled Corn, 526, *527*
        with Brown Sugar–Cayenne Butter, 527
        with Cilantro-Lime Butter, 527
        with Mustard-Paprika Butter, 526
        with Rosemary-Pepper Butter, 527
    Jucy Lucy Burgers, *488,* 488–89
    Lemon-Thyme Wood-Grilled Salmon, 521
    Lexington-Style Pulled Pork, *501,* 501–2
    Memphis-Style Wet Ribs for a Crowd, 228–29, *229*
    Mesquite-Grilled Tacos Rasurados, 26–27, *27*
    Monroe County–Style Pork Chops, *511,* 511–12
    North Carolina Barbecue Pork, *499,* 499–500
    Pomegranate-Glazed Grilled Lamb Chops, *520,* 520–21
    Shashlik-Style Beef Kebabs, *479,* 479–80
    Shredded Barbecued Beef, *486,* 486–87
    Smoked Bourbon Chicken, *466,* 466–67
    Smoked Chicken Wings, *471,* 471–72
    Smoked Citrus Chicken, *465,* 465–66
    Smoked Double-Thick Pork Chops, *509,* 509–10
    Smoked Fish Tacos, *524,* 524–25
    Smoked Prime Rib, *446,* 495
    Smoked Prime Rib Sandwiches with Green Chile Queso, 495–96, *496*

Grilled dishes *(cont.)*
    Smoky Potato Salad, *537,* 537–38
    South Carolina Pulled Pork, *502,* 502–3
    South Carolina Smoked Fresh Ham, 498–99, *499*
    South Dakota Corncob-Smoked Ribs, 516–18, *517*
    St. Louis BBQ Pork Steaks, 512–13, *513*
    Tennessee Pulled Pork Sandwiches, *503,* 503–4
    Tennessee Pulled Turkey Sandwiches, 476–78, *477*
    Texas Barbecue Brisket, *486,* 487–88
    Texas Barbecued Beef Ribs, 492–93, *493*
    Texas-Style Smoked Beef Ribs, *494,* 494
    Texas Thick-Cut Smoked Pork Chops, *508,* 508–9
    Wood-Grilled Salmon, 521, *521*
Grilling equipment, ratings of, 720–22
Grits
    about, 129
    Cheese, Creamy, *128, 128*
    Extra-Cheesy, *128,* 129
    Shrimp and, *195,* 195–96
Gruyère cheese
    Beer-Batter Cheese Bread, *569, 569*
    Brussels Sprouts Gratin, *362, 363*
    Chicken Cordon Bleu, 10–11, *11*
    Creamy Potatoes and Leeks, 82–83, *83*
    Croque Madame, 218
    Croque Monsieur, 217–18, *218*
    French Onion Soup, *274,* 274–75
    Fresh Tomato Galette, 374, *375*
    "Impossible" Ham-and-Cheese Pie, *547, 547*
    Slow-Cooker French Onion Soup, *272,* 275
    Stuffed Tomatoes, *272,* 307
Guacamole
    Chunky, 382, *382*
    Ultimate Seven-Layer Dip, *381,* 381–82
    Ultimate Smoky Seven-Layer Dip, 382
Guanciale
    Spaghetti Carbonara, *424,* 425
Guanimes con Bacalao (Cornmeal Dumplings with Salt Cod), 203–5, *204*
Guinness Beef Stew, 328–29, *329*
Gullah Lowcountry Red Rice, 90, *91*
Gumbo, 192–93, *193*

Ham
    -and-Cheese Pie, "Impossible," *547, 547*
    California Barbecued Beans, *529,* 529–30
    Chicken Cordon Bleu, 10–11, *11*
    Cider-Baked, *353,* 353–54
    Croque Madame, 218
    Croque Monsieur, 217–18, *218*
    Cuban Sandwiches, 237–38, *238*
    Failproof Chicken Cordon Bleu, *289,* 289–90
    Fresh, Slow-Roasted, *352,* 352–53
    Fresh, South Carolina Smoked, 498–99, *499*
    Hoppin' John, *248,* 248–49
    Okra and Shrimp Stew, *190,* 191–92
    Olympia Provisions–Style Choucroute Garnie, 153–54, *154*
    Prosciutto Bread, 453–54, *455*
    Shredded Swiss Chard, with Prosciutto, Basil, and Blue Cheese, *365,* 365–66
    Skillet Eggs Sardou, 40–41, *41*
    St. Paul Sandwich, 215–16, *216*
    Texas-Style Pinto Beans, 412, *413*
Handy tools, ratings of, 705–10
Hanukkah Jelly Doughnuts (Sufganiyot), 100–101, *101*
Hash, South Carolina Barbecue, 240–41, *241*
Hawaiian Macaroni Salad, 268–69, *269*
Hawaiian-Style Fried Chicken, *174,* 175
Hazelnut(s)
    Cake, Swiss, 612, *613*
    Cheddar, and Apple, Brussels Sprout Salad with, 363
    and Goat Cheese, Roasted Green Beans with, 130–31, *131*
    Oranges, and Feta, Asparagus Salad with, 365
Herb(ed)
    -Crusted Beef Tenderloin, 332–34, *333*
    and Lemon Red Potato Salad, *542,* 542–43
    Mashed Sweet Potatoes with Caramelized Onion, 372
    Pan-Fried Pork Chops, 157
    Ranch Fried Chicken, 175–77, *176*
    Roast Beef, 331–32, *333*
    Roast Chicken, 315–16, *317*
    and Toasted Garlic Dressing, Torn Potato Salad with, *367,* 367–68
    see also specific herbs
Hoecakes, 504–5, *505*
Holy Basil Stir-Fry (Pad Gra Prow), *213,* 213–14
Home Fries with Fresh Herbs, 554
Hominy grits, about, 129

Honey
    Butter, *567*, 568
    Fried Chicken, *170*, 170–71
    -Glazed Pork Shoulder, 38, *39*
    Hot-, Chicken, 138–39, *139*
    Lemonade with, 161, *161*
    -Mustard Sauce, 178

Hoppin' John, *248*, 248–49

Horseradish
    Boneless Rib Roast with Yorkshire Pudding and Jus, *338*, 339–40
    Burger Sauce, 507
    Cream Sauce, 334
    -Parsley Sauce, Roasted Beef Chuck with, *337*, 337–38
    Smoked Prime Rib, *446*, 495

Hot Fudge Pudding Cake, 622–23

Hot sauce
    Eastern North Carolina–Style Barbecue Sauce, 500
    Hot-Honey Chicken, 138–39, *139*
    Nashville Extra-Hot Fried Chicken, 169
    Nashville Hot Fried Chicken, 168–69, *169*
    Texas Pete, about, 173

Huevos Rancheros, 383, *383*

Huli Huli Chicken, *458*, 458–59

Husk-Grilled Corn, 526, *527*
    with Brown Sugar–Cayenne Butter, 527
    with Cilantro-Lime Butter, 527
    with Mustard-Paprika Butter, 526
    with Rosemary-Pepper Butter, 527

I

Icebox Key Lime Pie, *677*, 677–78

Icebox Strawberry Pie, 692–93, *693*

Ice Cream
    Old-Fashioned Chocolate Frozen Custard, 667, *667*
    Old-Fashioned Vanilla Frozen Custard, 666–67, *667*
    Peach Ripple, 114–15, *115*

Ice Cream, No-Churn
    Banana-Walnut–Chocolate Chunk, 649
    Birthday Cake, 648
    Dark Chocolate, 649
    Key Lime, 649
    Malted Milk Chocolate, 649
    Milk Chocolate, 649
    Mint-Cookie, 649

Ice Cream, No-Churn *(cont.)*
    Peach Cobbler, 649
    Peanut Butter Cup, 649
    Salted Caramel–Coconut, 649
    Strawberry-Buttermilk, 649
    Vanilla, 648–49, *649*

"Impossible" Ham-and-Cheese Pie, 547, *547*

Ingredients, tastings of, 730–53
    anchovies, 730
    applesauce, 730
    bacon, 730
    baking powder, 730
    beans, canned, 731
    bread crumbs, 731
    breads, 731
    broths, 732
    brownie mix, 732
    buns, hamburger, 732
    butter, 732
    cheeses, 732–35
    chicken, 735
    chili powder, 735
    chocolate and chocolate chips, 735–36
    cider, hard, 736
    cinnamon, 736
    cocoa powder, 736
    coconut, shredded, 737
    coconut milk, 736
    coffee, 737
    cooking spray, 737
    cornmeal, 737
    Creole seasoning, 737
    cumin, 738
    curry powder, 738
    dinner rolls, frozen, 738
    egg substitute, 738
    egg whites, processed, 738
    espresso powder, 738
    five-spice powder, 738
    flour, whole-wheat, 738
    freeze-dried backpacking meal, 739
    French fries, frozen, 739
    garlic substitutes, 739
    giardiniera, 739
    grits, 739
    ham, 739
    hoisin sauce, 740
    horseradish, 740
    hot dogs, 740

Ingredients, tastings of *(cont.)*
    hot fudge sauce, 740
    ice cream, 741
    ice cream bars, 740
    ice cream cones, 740
    iced tea, 741
    juice, grapefruit, 741
    juice, orange, 741
    ketchup, 741
    king cake, 741
    lard, 741
    lemonade, 741
    macaroni and cheese, 742
    mayonnaise, 742
    molasses, 742
    mustard, 742–43
    oats, 743
    olive oils, 743
    pancake mix, 744
    paprika, 744
    pastas, 744–45
    pasta sauces, 745
    peanut butter, 745
    peppercorns, 745
    pepperoni, 745
    peppers, roasted red, 745
    pickles, 746
    pie crust, ready-made, 746
    pizza, frozen, 746
    popcorn, 746
    pork, premium, 746
    potato chips, 746
    preserves, 747
    rice, 747
    salsa, 747–48
    salt, 748
    sauerkraut, 748
    sausages, 748
    soups, canned, 748
    spread, strawberry, 748
    steak sauce, 749
    sweetened condensed milk, 749
    tartar sauce, 749
    tea, 749
    teriyaki sauce, 749
    tomatoes, canned, 749–50
    tomato paste, 750
    tortilla chips, 750
    tortillas, 750

Ingredients, tastings of *(cont.)*
    tostadas, 751
    tuna, canned, 751
    turkey, 751
    vanilla beans and extract, 752
    vegetable oil, 752
    vinegars, 752–53
    whipped topping, 753
    Worcestershire sauce, 753
    yogurt, 753
Iowa Skinny, 234, *234*
Italian Cream Cake, 616–17, *617*
Italian Meatloaf, *416,* **435–36**
Italian Pot Roast, 448–49, *449*

J

Jamaican Oxtail, *151,* **151–52**
Jamaican Rice and Peas, 152–53, *153*
Jam Thumbprint Cookies, *635,* **636**
Japanese Steakhouse Steak and Vegetables, 284–85, *285*
Jelly Doughnuts, Hanukkah (Sufganiyot), 100–101, *101*
Jerk Chicken, Grilled, 462–63, *463*
Jitto's-Style Steak Bombs, 19, *19*
Joe Froggers, 640, *641*
Jucy Lucy Burgers, *488,* **488–89**

K

Kai Dao (Thai-Style Fried Eggs), *213,* **214**
Kalbi (Korean Grilled Flanken-Style Short Ribs), *497,* **497–98**
Khao Man Gai (Thai-Style Chicken and Rice), 210–12, *211*
Kitchen supplies, ratings of, 728–29
Knives and more, ratings of, 700–702
Kolaches, 583–84, *584*
Kombdi, Jira Ghalun (Cumin-Scented Chicken), 212, *213*
Korean Grilled Flanken-Style Short Ribs (Kalbi), *497,* **497–98**
Kringle, Cream Cheese, *584,* **584–86**
Kua Txob, 4
Kugel, Cast Iron Potato, 88, *89*

INDEX   787

L

Lamb
    Bone-In Leg of, Grilled, with Charred-Scallion Sauce, *519*, 519–20
    Burgers, Grilled, 46, *47*
    Chops, Pomegranate-Glazed Grilled, *520*, 520–21
    Crumb-Crusted Rack of, *354*, 354–55

Lane Cake, *594*, 600–601

Lard
    cooking with, 399
    -Fried Chicken, 167–68, *168*
    Pork Carnitas, *399*, 399–400

Lasagna
    Beef, Hearty, *437*, 437–38
    Pesto, 64–65, *65*
    Sausage, *416*, 438–39
    Skillet, *436*, *436*
    Skillet, with Sausage and Peppers, 436
    Spinach and Tomato, *439*, 439–40

La Viña–Style Cheesecake, *628*, 629

Leeks
    and Potatoes, Creamy, 82–83, *83*
    prepping, 82

Lemonade
    Ginger, 161
    with Honey, 161, *161*
    Mint, 161

Lemon(s)
    Aioli, 453
    -Caper Sauce, Grilled Salmon Steaks with, *446*, 523
    Chicken, Grilled Butterflied, 467–68, *468*
    Chicken, Roast, 316–17, *317*
    and Chives, Slow-Roasted Salmon with, 356–57, *357*
    -Chocolate Truffles, 645
    and Cinnamon, Bolos Lêvedos (Portuguese Muffins) with, 96
    and Cinnamon, Pastéis de Nata with, 99
    Ginger Lemonade, 161
    Greek Chicken, 180, *181*
    and Herb Red Potato Salad, *542*, 542–43
    Icebox Cheesecake, 624–26, *625*
    Lemonade with Honey, 161, *161*
    Meringue Pie, Mile-High, 674, *675*
    Mint Lemonade, 161
    One-Pot Shrimp Piccata Pasta, 66, *67*
    Pepper Chicken Wings, *182*, 182–83
    Pepper Seasoning, 182
    Pie, North Carolina, *672*, 673

Lemon(s) *(cont.)*
    Pie, Shaker, *672*, 672–73
    Pudding Cake, 624, *625*
    Salsa Verde, 336
    -Tahini Dressing, Roasted Beets with, *372*, 373–74
    -Thyme Wood-Grilled Salmon, 521

Lentilles du Puy with Spinach and Crème Fraîche, *375*, 375

Lettuce
    Almond Boneless Chicken, *209*, 209–10
    Bibb, and Tomatillo Salad with Tomatillo Ranch, 74, *75*
    BLT Salad, *306*, 306–7
    Chinese Chicken Salad, 206, *206*
    Grilled Caesar Salad, *533*, 533–34
    Ultimate Caesar Salad, 76, *77*

Lexington-Style Barbecue Sauce, 500

Lexington-Style Pulled Pork, *501*, 501–2

Lighthouse Inn Potatoes, *294*, 294

Lime
    -Cilantro Butter, Husk-Grilled Corn with, 527
    -Coconut Cookies, 636
    -Garlic Fried Chicken, *386*, 386–87
    -Ginger Glaze, 637
    Key, No-Churn Ice Cream, 649
    Key, Pie, Icebox, *677*, 677–78
    Key, Pie, Really Good, 676, *677*

Liquid smoke, about, 37

Liver
    Cajun Rice Dressing, *247*, 247–48
    South Carolina Barbecue Hash, 240–41, *241*

Lobster
    removing meat from, 201
    Rolls, Hot Buttered, 201, *201*

Louisiana Seasoning, 181

Lyonnaise Potatoes, *292*, 292

M

Macadamia nuts
    Tuna Poke, 202, *202*

Macaroni
    and Cheese, Best Potluck, 124, *125*
    and Cheese, Pimento, 124–25, *125*
    Cheeseburger Mac, 127, *127*
    and Cheese with Tomatoes, *126*, 126–27
    Salad, Hawaiian, 268–69, *269*

Magic Chocolate Flan Cake, 609–10, *610*

Maine Blueberry Grunt, *659*, 659–60

Malasadas, *560,* 560–61
Malted Milk Chocolate No-Churn Ice Cream, 649
Malted Milk Glaze, 637
Mana'eesh Za'atar (Za'atar Flatbreads), *592,* 592–93
Manchego and Chorizo Breakfast Pizza, 549
Manicotti, Baked, with Meat Sauce, *441,* 441–42
Maple Chile Crisp, Grilled Sweet Potatoes with, *531,* 531–32
Marinara Sauce, 452–53
Marshmallow crème
    Chocolate Cream Cupcakes, *621,* 621–22
    Oatmeal Creme Pies, *643,* 643–45
    Swiss Hazelnut Cake, 612, *613*
    Whoopie Pies, 642–43, *643*
Marshmallows
    Chocolate Fudge, *646,* 647
    Chocolate-Peppermint Fudge, *646,* 647
    Chocolate-Toffee Fudge, *646,* 648
Masa harina
    Gorditas, 396–97, *397*
    Puffy Tacos, 393–94, *394*
Mashed Potato Cakes, *291,* 291–92
Mashed Potato Casserole, 370, *370*
Mayonnaise, Spicy (Yum-Yum Sauce), 286
Mayonnaise-based sauces
    Buffalo Blue Cheese Sauce, 260
    Comeback Sauce, *185,* 186
    Creamy BBQ Sauce, 260
    Curried Chutney Sauce, 260
    Green Goddess Dressing, 132–33, *133*
    Horseradish Burger Sauce, 507
    Tartar Sauce, 185, *185*
Measuring equipment, ratings of, 711
Meat. *See* **Beef; Lamb; Pork; Veal**
Meatball(s)
    Drop, *431,* 431–32
    Fricassee, Cajun, 20, *21*
    and Marinara, 432–33, *433*
    and Marinara, Slow-Cooker, 433–34, *434*
Meatloaf
    Bacon-Wrapped, 146–47, *147*
    Frosted, *144,* 145
    Glazed, *143,* 143–44
    Italian, *416,* 435–36
    with Mushroom Gravy, 145–46, *147*
Melting Moments, 635, *635*
Memphis Chopped Coleslaw, 535, *535*
Memphis-Style Wet Ribs for a Crowd, 228–29, *229*
Mesquite-Grilled Tacos Rasurados, 26–27, *27*
Mexican crema, about, 414

Milk-Can Supper, *154,* 155
Milk Gravy, Pan-Fried Pork Chops with, *156,* 157
Mimosa Fried Chicken, 173–74, *174*
Minestrone, Slow-Cooker, *419,* 419
Mint
    and Almonds, Roasted Green Beans with, 131
    Asparagus Salad with Grapes, Goat Cheese, and Almonds, 364–65
    Asparagus Salad with Oranges, Feta, and Hazelnuts, 365
    Asparagus Salad with Radishes, Pecorino Romano, and Croutons, 364, *364*
    Chocolate-Peppermint Fudge, *646,* 647
    -Cookie No-Churn Ice Cream, 649
    Lemonade, 161
    Pomegranate-Glazed Grilled Lamb Chops, *520,* 520–21
    Salsa Verde, 35, *35*
    Sauce, Fresh, *354,* 355
Miso Black Cod, 186–87, *187*
Mississippi Mud Pie, 697–98, *698*
Mizuna, about, 205
M&M Cookies, 632–33, *633*
Monkey Bread, 587–88, *588*
Monroe County–Style Pork Chops, *511,* 511–12
Monterey Bay Cioppino, 188–89, *189*
Monterey Jack
    Beef Enchiladas, 406, *407*
    Best Potluck Macaroni and Cheese, 124, *125*
    Creamy Cheese Grits, *128,* 128
    Crispy Baked Potato Fans, 300, *301*
    Detroit-Style Pizza, 253–55, *254*
    Okinawan Taco Rice, 230–31, *231*
    Shrimp Tacos, 390–91, *391*
    Spicy Cheese Bread, 570, *570*
    St. Louis–Style Pizza, *248,* 249–50
    Tex-Mex Cheese Enchiladas, 403–4, *404*
    Twice-Baked Potatoes with Chorizo and Chipotle, 302
Moravian Chicken Pie, *325,* 325–26
Morning Buns, 579–80, *581*
Morning Glory Muffins, *572,* 573
Mozzarella
    Adjaruli Khachapuri, *548,* 549–50
    Baked Manicotti with Meat Sauce, *441,* 441–42
    Breakfast Pizza, *548,* 548–49
    Cast-Iron Skillet Pizza, *444,* 445
    Chicago Thin-Crust Pizza, 250–51, *251*
    Chorizo and Manchego Breakfast Pizza, 549
    Cutty's-Inspired Eggplant Spuckie, 72, *73*
    Fresh, and Roasted Bell Peppers, Charred Cherry Tomatoes with, 268, *269*

INDEX   789

Mozzarella *(cont.)*
    Grandma Pizza, *444,* 444–45
    Hearty Beef Lasagna, *437,* 437–38
    New England Bar Pizza, 252–53, *253*
    and Pancetta, Twice-Baked Potatoes with, 302
    Pepperoni French Bread Pizza, 256, *257*
    Pineapple and Bacon French Bread Pizza, 256, *257*
    Quesabirria Tacos, 394–95, *395*
    Sausage Lasagna, *416,* 438–39
    Skillet Chicken Parmesan, *446, 447*
    Slow-Cooker Baked Ziti, *434,* 434–35
    Smoked Salmon Breakfast Pizza, 549
    Spinach and Tomato Lasagna, *439,* 439–40
    Supreme French Bread Pizza, 256, *257*
Muffins
    Browned Butter Chocolate Chunk, 573–74, *574*
    homemade liners, 575
    Morning Glory, *572,* 573
    parchment paper liners, 575
    Portuguese (Bolos Lêvedos), *95,* 95–96, *97*
    Portuguese (Bolos Lêvedos) with Lemon and Cinnamon, *96*
    Whole-Wheat Blueberry, *572,* 572–73
Muffin Tin Doughnuts, *575, 575*
Muffin Tin Popovers, 571
Mushroom(s)
    Bean Bourguignon, 70, *71*
    Classic Roast Beef and Gravy, *330,* 331
    Gravy, Meatloaf with, 145–46, *147*
    Ground Beef Stroganoff, 148, *149*
    Italian Pot Roast, 448–49, *449*
    Japanese Steakhouse Steak and Vegetables, 284–85, *285*
    Jitto's-Style Steak Bombs, *19, 19*
    One-Pot Chicken Jardinière, *141,* 141–42
    Salisbury Steak, 148–49, *149*
    Sauce, Pasta with, *426,* 426–27
    Tater Tot Hotdish, 149–50, *150*
Mussels
    Grilled, 60, *61*
    Monterey Bay Cioppino, 188–89, *189*
    Seafood Fra Diavolo, *427,* 427–28
    Seafood Risotto, 52, *53*
Mustard
    Deviled Beef Short Ribs, *338,* 338–39
    -Glazed Pork Loin, Grilled, 518, *518*
    -Honey Sauce, 178
    -Paprika Butter, Husk-Grilled Corn with, 526
    Sauce, White, 286
    Whole-Grain, and Cornichons, Tuna Salad with, 132

N

Nachos, Ultimate Spicy Beef, 380, *381*
Nashville Extra-Hot Fried Chicken, 169
Nashville Hot Fried Chicken, 168–69, *169*
Natchitoches Meat Pies, *244,* **244–45**
Neorm Sach Moan (Cambodian Chicken Salad), *204,* **205**
New England Bar Pizza, 252–53, *253*
New Jersey Crumb Buns, 580–81, *581*
New Mexican Bean-and-Cheese Turnovers with Green Chile, *402,* **402–3**
New Mexico Biscochitos, *637,* **637–38**
New Orleans Barbecue Shrimp, 196–97, *197*
New Orleans Bourbon Bread Pudding, 664–65, *665*
New Orleans Muffulettas, *216,* **216–17**
New Orleans Spicy Beef Noodle Soup (Beef Yakamein), 243–44, *244*
Nilla wafers
    Banana Pudding, 690, *691*
    Coconut Cream Pie, 689, *689*
Noodle(s)
    American-Style Egg Rolls, 44–45, *45*
    Birria Ramen, 395–96, *396*
    Chicken and Slicks, *324,* 324–25
    Chicken Chow Mein, 207, *207*
    Chicken Soup, Old-Fashioned, 120, *121*
    Ground Beef Stroganoff, 148, *149*
    Shanghai Scallion Oil, 68, *69*
North Carolina Barbecue Pork, *499,* **499–500**
North Carolina Cheese Biscuits, *258,* **258–59**
North Carolina Dipped Fried Chicken, 172–73, *173*
North Carolina Lemon Pie, *672,* **673**
Nuts. *See specific nuts*

O

Oats
    Oatmeal Creme Pies, *643,* 643–45
Okinawan Taco Rice, 230–31, *231*
Oklahoma Fried Onion Burgers, *223,* **223–24**
Okra
    Gumbo, 192–93, *193*
    and Shrimp Stew, *190,* 191–92
Olive Oil Potato Gratin, *295,* **295–96**

790   *The Complete Cook's Country TV Show Cookbook*

Olive(s)
    Alcapurrias, 28–29, *30–31*
    Cutty's-Inspired Eggplant Spuckie, 72, *73*
    Fennel, and Potatoes, Baked Shrimp with, 358–59, *359*
    New Orleans Muffulettas, *216*, 216–17
    Supreme French Bread Pizza, 256, *257*
    Tapenade, Grilled Thin-Cut Pork Chops with, 511

Olympia Provisions–Style Choucroute Garnie, 153–54, *154*

Onion(s)
    and Bell Peppers, Grilled Sausages with, *506*, 507
    Caramelized, Grilled Bacon Burgers with, 489–90, *490*
    Caramelized, Herbed Mashed Sweet Potatoes with, 372
    Diner-Style Patty Melts, *220*, 221–22
    Fried, Burgers, Oklahoma, *223*, 223–24
    Patty Melts, *220*, 220–21
    Raita, 213, *213*
    Red, Pickled, 389
    Rings, Beer-Battered, 265–66, *266*
    Rings, Ultimate Extra-Crunchy, 264–65, *265*
    Smothered Pork Chops, 157–58, *158*
    Sofrito, 29
    Soup, French, *274*, 274–75
    Soup, French, Slow-Cooker, *272*, 275
    spring, about, 27

On the Road
    Angie Delgado (Santa Fe, NM), 638
    Ansots (Boise, ID), 361
    Bastien's Restaurant (Denver, CO), 277
    Buddy's (Detroit, MI), 255
    Central Bakery (Tiverton, RI), 94–95
    Chef Greg's Soul "N" the Wall (Detroit, MI), 219
    Cochon de Lait Festival (Mansura, LA), 247
    Collins Bar-B-Q (Gamaliel, KY), 512
    Cuban Sandwich Festival (Tampa, FL), 238
    Dairyland Old-Fashioned Frozen Custard & Hamburgers (Milwaukee, WI), 267
    Gilliard Farms (Brunswick, GA), 48–49
    The Harvey House (Madison, WI), 9
    Ishnala Supper Club (Lake Delton, WI), 8–9
    Jitto's Super Steak (Portsmouth, NH), 18
    John's Roast Pork (Philadelphia, PA), 237
    Józsa Corner (Hazelwood, PA), 328
    Kreuz Market (Lockhkart, TX), 14–15
    La Segunda Bakery (Ybor City, FL), 239
    Laura's II (Lafayette, LA), 184
    Mario's Lebanese Bakery (Fall River, MA), 593
    Mariscos German Beyer (San Diego, CA), 390
    Ms. Emily (Edisto Island, SC), 249

On the Road *(cont.)*
    Olympia Provisions (Portland, OR), 155
    Original Gullah Festival (Beaufort, SC), 192
    Owamni by The Sioux Chef (Minneapolis, MN), 312
    Papa Kay Joe's (Centerville, TN), 505
    Park Chop Suey (St. Paul, MN), 216
    Peach Park (Clanton, AL), 680
    Pyrenees Cafe (Bakersfield, CA), 171
    Tacos Apson (Tucson, AZ), 24–25
    Today's Cajun Seafood (New Orleans, LA), 208
    Tommy DiNic's (Philadelphia, PA), 237
    Toshi's Teriyaki Grill (Centerville, TN), 464
    Union Hmong Kitchen (Minneapolis, MN), 2–3
    Woodman's (Essex, MA), 191

Orange(s)
    and Blue Cheese, Endive Salad with, *366*, 366–67
    Chiffon Cake, 616
    Chinese Chicken Salad, 206, *206*
    Feta, and Hazelnuts, Asparagus Salad with, 365
    how to supreme, 367
    Mimosa Fried Chicken, 173–74, *174*
    –Poppy Seed Cookies, 636
    Porchetta Abruzzese, 34–35, *35*
    –Red Wine Sauce, 342
    Rolls, Alabama, *544*, 582–83
    Smoked Citrus Chicken, *465*, 465–66
    Sour, Pie, 674–75, *675*
    Upside-Down Cake, 602–3, *603*

Oregano
    and Capers, Crushed Red Potatoes with, 297
    Grilled Brined Pork Chops with Garlic-Herb Oil, 32, *33*
    Za'atar, 593

Oregon Blackberry Pie, 680–81, *681*
Oxtail, Jamaican, *151*, 151–52

P

Pad Gra Prow (Holy Basil Stir-Fry), *213*, 213–14
Paella, Coastal Georgia, 50, *51*
Pancake(s)
    Better-Than-the-Box, 555, *555*
    Dutch Baby, *556*, 557
    Fluffy Cornmeal, *556*, 556–57
    Hoecakes, 504–5, *505*
    Mix, Better-Than-the-Box, 555
    Texas Potato, *162*, 263

Pancetta and Mozzarella, Twice-Baked Potatoes with, 302
Pandowdy, Apple, 654–55, *655*
Paprika
    Chicken Paprikash and Buttered Spaetzle, 137–38, *138*
    Louisiana Seasoning, 181
    Smoked, and Garlic, Crushed Red Potatoes with, 296
Parmesan
    Blue Cheese and Bacon Baked Potato Fans, 300
    Brussels Sprouts Gratin, 362, *363*
    Caesar Green Bean Salad, 305–6, *306*
    Cajun Meatball Fricassee, 20, *21*
    Chicken Divan, 139–40, *140*
    Creamed Spinach, 304, *305*
    Crispy Baked Potato Fans, 300, *301*
    -Crusted Asparagus, *361*, 361–62
    Delmonico Potato Casserole, *293*, 293–94
    Extra-Cheesy Grits, *128*, 129
    Fettuccine with Butter and Cheese, 422–23, *423*
    Grilled Caesar Salad, *533*, 533–34
    Herb-Crusted Beef Tenderloin, 332–34, *333*
    Italian Meatloaf, *416*, 435–36
    and Lemon, Grilled Broccoli with, 532–33, *533*
    Lighthouse Inn Potatoes, *294*, 294
    Mashed Potato Cakes, *291*, 291–92
    Pesto Lasagna, 64–65, *65*
    Potatoes, Crispy, *298*, 299
    –Roasted Garlic Bread, 303, *303*
    -Rosemary Potato Tots, 262
    Skillet Chicken, 446, *447*
    Skillet Eggs Sardou, 40–41, *41*
    Skillet Lasagna, 436, *436*
    Skillet Lasagna with Sausage and Peppers, 436
    Spinach and Tomato Lasagna, *439*, 439–40
    Spinach-Artichoke Dip, 376–77, *377*
    Tater Tot Hotdish, 149–50, *150*
    Tomatoes with Fontina Sauce and Cornichon Dressing, 78, *79*
    Ultimate Caesar Salad, 76, *77*
Parsley
    and Cayenne, Slow-Roasted Salmon with, 357
    -Garlic Steak Sauce, 280
    Green Goddess Dressing, 132–33, *133*
    Green Goddess Roast Chicken, *133*, 133–34
    -Horseradish Sauce, Roasted Beef Chuck with, *337*, 337–38
    Mint Salsa Verde, 35, *35*
    -Pomegranate Sauce, One-Pan Turkey Breast and Stuffing with, 312–13, *313*
    Salsa Verde, 336

Parsnips
    and Fennel, One-Pan Roast Chicken with, 319
    One-Pan Prime Rib and Roasted Vegetables, 340–41, *341*
    Slow-Cooker Pork Pot Roast, 346, *347*
Pasta
    Baked Manicotti with Meat Sauce, *441*, 441–42
    Beef Yakamein (New Orleans Spicy Beef Noodle Soup), 243–44, *244*
    Best Potluck Macaroni and Cheese, 124, *125*
    Cheeseburger Mac, 127, *127*
    Cheesy Stuffed Shells, 442–43, *443*
    Chicken and Slicks, *324*, 324–25
    Cincinnati Chili, *241*, 241–42
    e Fagioli, *418*, 418
    Fettuccine with Butter and Cheese, 422–23, *423*
    Green Spaghetti, 62, *63*
    Hawaiian Macaroni Salad, 268–69, *269*
    Hearty Beef Lasagna, *437*, 437–38
    Instant Mashed Potato Gnocchi, *428*, 428–29
    Macaroni and Cheese with Tomatoes, *126*, 126–27
    with Mushroom Sauce, *426*, 426–27
    One-Pot Shrimp Piccata, 66, *67*
    Pesto Lasagna, 64–65, *65*
    Pimento Mac and Cheese, 124–25, *125*
    Pork Ragu, *420*, 421
    with Roasted Garlic Sauce, Arugula, and Walnuts, *425*, 425–26
    Sausage Lasagna, *416*, 438–39
    with Sausage Ragu, *422*, 423
    Seafood Fra Diavolo, *427*, 427–28
    Shrimp Piccata, One-Pot, 66, *67*
    Skillet Lasagna, 436, *436*
    Skillet Lasagna with Sausage and Peppers, 436
    Slow-Cooker Baked Ziti, *434*, 434–35
    Slow-Cooker Minestrone, *419*, 419
    Sopa Seca, *378*, 384
    Spaghetti Carbonara, *424*, 425
    Spaghetti with Garlic and Olive Oil (Aglio e Olio), 424, *424*
    Spinach and Tomato Lasagna, *439*, 439–40
    Stuffed Tomatoes, *272*, 307
    see also Noodle(s)
Pastéis de Nata (Portuguese Egg Tarts), 98–99, *99*
Pastéis de Nata with Lemon and Cinnamon, 99
Pastry, Chicken and, *122*, 122–23
Patty Melts, *220*, 220–21
Patty Melts, Diner-Style, *220*, 221–22
Peach(es)
    Cobbler, Skillet, *660*, 661
    Cobbler No-Churn Ice Cream, 649

Peach(es) *(cont.)*
    and Cream Pie, 678–79, *679*
    Hand Pies, Fried, *679,* 679–80
    Kuchen, Dakota, 661–62, *663*
    peeling, 662
    Ripple Ice Cream, 114–15, *115*
    Sauce, Bacon-Wrapped Pork Roast with, 350–51, *351*

Peanut Butter
    Buckeye Candies, *646,* 646–47
    and Jelly Glaze, 637
    Peanut Butter Cup No-Churn Ice Cream, 649
    Peanut-y Banana Pudding, 664

Pear and Pancetta, Roasted Butternut Squash with, 373

Peas
    Hoppin' John, *248,* 248–49

Pecan(s)
    Aunt Jule's Pie, 112, *113*
    Carrot Snack Cake, 620–21, *621*
    Chocolate-Dipped Potato Chip Cookies, 104–5, *105*
    Cowboy Cookies, *630,* 630–31
    Cream Cheese Kringle Filling, 586
    Italian Cream Cake, 616–17, *617*
    Lane Cake, *594,* 600–601
    Pie, Old-Fashioned, 685–86, *686*
    Smoked Gouda, and Dried Cherries, Brussels Sprout Salad with, 363
    Texas Sheet Cake, 607–8, *608*
    Tunnel of Fudge Cake, *599,* 599–600

Pecorino Romano
    Cheesy Stuffed Shells, 442–43, *443*
    Eggplant Pecorino, *440,* 440–41
    Fluffy Baked Polenta with Red Sauce, 430–31, *431*
    Hearty Beef Lasagna, *437,* 437–38
    Pasta with Mushroom Sauce, *426,* 426–27
    Radishes, and Croutons, Asparagus Salad with, 364, *364*
    Roasted Green Beans with Pecorino and Pine Nuts, 131
    Sausage Lasagna, *416,* 438–39
    Spaghetti Carbonara, *424,* 425

Pennsylvania Dutch Apple Pie, 682, *683*

Pepper Jack cheese
    Huevos Rancheros, 383, *383*
    Smoked Prime Rib Sandwiches with Green Chile Queso, 495–96, *496*
    Ultimate Seven-Layer Dip, *381,* 381–82
    Ultimate Smoky Seven-Layer Dip, 382
    Ultimate Spicy Beef Nachos, 380, *381*

Peppermint
    -Chocolate Fudge, *646,* 647
    Mint-Cookie No-Churn Ice Cream, 649

Pepperoni
    French Bread Pizza, 256, *257*
    Supreme French Bread Pizza, 256, *257*

Pepper(s)
    Bell, and Onions, Grilled Sausages with, *506,* 507
    Chicken Paprikash and Buttered Spaetzle, 137–38, *138*
    Chicken Scampi, *447,* 447–48
    Chicken Scarpariello, 448, *449*
    Crispy Vegetable Fritters, 263–64, *265*
    Grilled Steak Fajitas, 482–83, *483*
    Grill-Roasted, 304–5, *305*
    Jitto's-Style Steak Bombs, 19, *19*
    Milk-Can Supper, *154,* 155
    pimento, about, 128
    Pimento Mac and Cheese, 128, *129*
    Red, Steak Sauce, Spicy, 280
    Red Bell, and Sausage Breakfast Pizza, 549
    Roasted Bell, and Fresh Mozzarella, Charred Cherry Tomatoes with, 268, *269*
    and Sausage Omelet Filling, 546
    and Sausages, Skillet Lasagna with, 436
    Sofrito, 29
    Supreme French Bread Pizza, 256, *257*
    Vinegar, Pork Chops with, *450,* 450–51
    see also Chile(s)

Perloo, Charleston Shrimp, *162,* 194–95

Pesto
    Basil, Butter, 528
    Lasagna, 64–65, *65*

Philadelphia Pork Sandwiches, *236,* 236–37
Philly Tomato Pie, *254,* 255–56
Pickle-Brined Fried Chicken Sandwiches, 6, *7*
Pickled Red Onion, 389
Pickled Shrimp, 197–98, *198*
Pico de Gallo, 483, *483*

Pie Dough
    blind baking, 679
    Double-Crust, 670
    rolling and fitting, 670
    Single-Crust, Classic, 670
    single-crust, crimping edge, 688
    Single-Crust, No-Fear, 671

Pierogi, Potato-Cheddar, *257,* 257–58

Pies (savory)
    Double-Crust Chicken Pot Pie, 142–43, *143*
    Frito, 16, *17*
    "Impossible" Ham-and-Cheese, 547, *547*
    Moravian Chicken, *325,* 325–26
    Natchitoches Meat, *244,* 244–45
    Tomato, Philly, *254,* 255–56

Pies (sweet)
- Apple, Pennsylvania Dutch, 682, *683*
- Apple, with Cheddar Crust, *683,* 683–84
- Apple Slab, *684,* 684–85
- Aunt Jule's Pie, 112, *113*
- Banana Pudding, 690, *691*
- Blackberry, Oregon, 680–81, *681*
- Blueberry Cream, *668,* 693–94
- Chocolate, French Silk, 694–95, *695*
- Chocolate Angel, *696,* 696–97
- Coconut, French, 687–88, *688*
- Coconut Cream, 689, *689*
- Fried Peach Hand, *679,* 679–80
- Key Lime, Icebox, *677,* 677–78
- Key Lime, Really Good, 676, *677*
- Lemon, North Carolina, *672,* 673
- Lemon, Shaker, *672,* 672–73
- Lemon Meringue, Mile-High, 674, *675*
- Mississippi Mud, 697–98, *698*
- Peaches and Cream, 678–79, *679*
- Pecan, Old-Fashioned, 685–86, *686*
- Raspberry Chiffon, *691,* 691–92
- S'mores, *668,* 698–99
- Sour Orange, 674–75, *675*
- Strawberry, Icebox, 692–93, *693*
- Sweet Potato, *686,* 687

Pimento(s)
- about, 128
- Mac and Cheese, 128, *129*

Piña Coladas, 271, ***271***

Pineapple
- Ahi-Chile Tostadas, *389,* 389–90
- and Bacon French Bread Pizza, 256, *257*
- and Habanero Shrimp Skewers, Grilled, 526
- Huli Huli Chicken, *458,* 458–59
- Kalbi (Korean Grilled Flanken-Style Short Ribs), *497,* 497–98
- Morning Glory Muffins, *572,* 573
- Piña Coladas, 271, *271*

Pine Nuts
- Brussels Sprout Salad, 363, *363*
- and Pecorino, Roasted Green Beans with, 131
- Pesto Lasagna, 64–65, *65*

Pique, 29

Pizza
- Breakfast, *548,* 548–49
- Cast-Iron Skillet, *444,* 445
- Chicago Thin-Crust, 250–51, *251*
- Chorizo and Manchego Breakfast, 549
- Detroit-Style, 253–55, *254*

Pizza *(cont.)*
- Dough, Classic, 445–46
- Grandma, *444,* 444–45
- New England Bar, 252–53, *253*
- Pepperoni French Bread, 256, *257*
- Philly Tomato Pie, *254,* 255–56
- Pineapple and Bacon French Bread, 256, *257*
- Sauce, No-Cook, 446
- Sausage and Red Bell Pepper Breakfast, 549
- Smoked Salmon Breakfast, 549
- St. Louis–Style, *248,* 249–50
- Supreme French Bread, 256, *257*

Plantains
- Alcapurrias, 28–29 30–31

Plum Sauce, 45, ***45***

Poke
- buying fish for, 203
- Salmon Teriyaki, *202,* 203
- Tuna, 202, *202*

Polenta
- about, 129
- Fluffy Baked, with Red Sauce, 430–31, *431*

Pomegranate
- -Glazed Grilled Lamb Chops, *520,* 520–21
- -Parsley Sauce, One-Pan Turkey Breast and Stuffing with, 312–13, *313*

Popcorn Chicken, *179,* **179–80**

Popovers
- Muffin Tin, 571
- Perfect, 571, *571*

Poppers, Air-Fryer Jalapeño, 86, ***87***

Porchetta Abruzzese, 34–35, ***35***

Pork
- American-Style Egg Rolls, 44–45, *45*
- Barbecued Country-Style Ribs, 516, *517*
- Burgers, Grilled, *506,* 506–7
- butt roast, removing bone from, 350
- Cajun Rice Dressing, *247,* 247–48
- Carnitas, *399,* 399–400
- Chicago-Style Barbecued Ribs, *491,* 491–92
- Chinese Barbecued, Slow-Cooker, 214–15, *215*
- Chinese-Style Barbecued Spareribs, 514–16, *515*
- Chops
  - BBQ Pan-Fried, 157
  - with Bourbon-Cherry Sauce and Sweet Potatoes, *308,* 351–52
  - Cider-Braised, 158–59, *159*
  - Grilled Brined, with Garlic-Herb Oil, 32, *33*
  - Grilled Thin-Cut, 510, *510*
  - Grilled Thin-Cut, Spicy, with Cilantro and Lime, 511

Pork, Chops *(cont.)*
    Grilled Thin-Cut, with Olive Tapenade, 511
    Grilled Thin-Cut, with Thyme and Ginger, 511
    Herbed Pan-Fried, 157
    Monroe County–Style, *511,* 511–12
    Pan-Fried, *156,* 156–57
    Pan-Fried, with Milk Gravy, *156,* 157
    Smoked Double-Thick, *509,* 509–10
    Smothered, 157–58, *158*
    Tennessee Whiskey, *227,* 227–28
    Texas Thick-Cut Smoked, *508,* 508–9
    with Vinegar Peppers, *450,* 450–51
Citrus-Braised, Tacos, 398, *399*
Colorado Green Chili, 242–43, *243*
Crown Roast of, 344–45, *345*
Cuban Sandwiches, 237–38, *238*
Drop Meatballs, *431,* 431–32
Frosted Meatloaf, *144,* 145
Glazed Meatloaf, *143,* 143–44
Grillades, *287,* 287–88
Indoor Barbecued Ribs, 36, *37*
Iowa Skinny, 234, *234*
Loin, Grilled Mustard-Glazed, *518,* 518
Loin, Roast, with 40 Cloves of Garlic, 343–44, *344*
Memphis-Style Wet Ribs for a Crowd, 228–29, *229*
Natchitoches Meat Pies, *244,* 244–45
North Carolina Barbecue, *499,* 499–500
Olympia Provisions–Style Choucroute Garnie, 153–54, *154*
Pad Gra Prow (Holy Basil Stir-Fry), *213,* 213–14
Pepperoni French Bread Pizza, 256, *257*
Pernil, *348,* 348–49
Porchetta Abruzzese, 34–35, *35*
Pot Roast, Slow-Cooker, 346, *347*
Pulled
    Lexington-Style, *501,* 501–2
    South Carolina, *502,* 502–3
    Tennessee, Sandwiches, *503,* 503–4
Ragu, *420,* 421
Rillons, 42, *43*
Roast
    Bacon-Wrapped, with Peach Sauce, 350–51, *351*
    Cider-Braised, *349,* 349–50
    Cuban, with Mojo, 238–39, *239*
    Old-Fashioned, *347,* 347–48
Sandwiches, Philadelphia, *236,* 236–37
Shoulder, Honey-Glazed, 38, *39*
shoulder, slicing thin, 237
Sinigang (Filipino Stew with Meat and Vegetables), *231,* 231–32
Sisig, 232–33, *233*

Pork *(cont.)*
Skillet Lasagna, 436, *436*
Slow-Cooker Italian Sunday Gravy, *420,* 420–21
Slow-Cooker Memphis-Style Wet Ribs, *229,* 229–30
South Carolina Barbecue Hash, 240–41, *241*
South Dakota Corncob-Smoked Ribs, 516–18, *517*
Spaghetti Carbonara, *424,* 425
steaks, cutting your own, 513
Steaks, St. Louis BBQ, 512–13, *513*
Supreme French Bread Pizza, 256, *257*
Tenderloin, Chinese-Style Glazed, 514, *515*
Transylvania Goulash, *327,* 327–28
see also Bacon; Ham; Sausage(s)
Portuguese Egg Tarts (Pastéis de Nata), 98–99, *99*
Portuguese Muffins (Bolos Lêvedos), *95,* **95–96,** *97*
Portuguese Muffins (Bolos Lêvedos) with Lemon and Cinnamon, 96
Port Wine–Fig Sauce, Duck Breasts with, *314,* **315**
Potato Chip Cookies, Chocolate-Dipped, 104–5, *105*
Potato(es)
Baked
    Fans, Blue Cheese and Bacon, 300
    Fans, Crispy, 300, *301*
    Super-Stuffed, *301,* 301–2
Brunswick Stew, 326–27, *327*
Carne Guisada, 392–93, *393*
and Carrots, Chicken Baked in Foil with, 323
Casserole, Delmonico, *293,* 293–94
Cast Iron Chicken and Vegetables, 319–20, *321*
-Cheddar Pierogi, *257,* 257–58
and Chicken, Skillet-Roasted, 321, *321*
Chuck Roast in Foil, 342–43, *343*
Cornish Pasties, 22–23, *23*
Crispy Parmesan, *298,* 299
Crown Roast of Pork, 344–45, *345*
Duchess, 369, *369*
Eastern North Carolina Fish Stew, 187–88, *189*
Easy Steak Frites, *281,* 281–82
Fennel, and Olives, Baked Shrimp with, 358–59, *359*
Fish and Chips, 184–85, *185*
Frosted Meatloaf, *144,* 145
Gorditas, 396–97, *397*
Gratin, Olive Oil, *295,* 295–96
Greek Diner-Style Home Fries, 554
Green Bean, and Tomato Salad, *446,* 543
Guinness Beef Stew, 328–29, *329*
Home Fries with Fresh Herbs, 554
Instant Mashed, Gnocchi, *428,* 428–29
Kugel, Cast Iron, 88, *89*
and Leeks, Creamy, 82–83, *83*

INDEX   795

Potato(es) *(cont.)*
- Lighthouse Inn, 294, *294*
- Loaded Baked, Omelet Filling, 546
- Lyonnaise, 292, *292*
- Mashed
    - Cakes, *291*, 291–92
    - Cakes, Blue Cheese and Bacon, 292
    - Cakes, Cheddar and Scallion, 292
    - Casserole, 370, *370*
    - Garlic, 290–91, *291*
- Milk-Can Supper, *154*, 155
- One-Pan Roast Chicken with Fennel and Parsnips, 319
- One-Pan Roast Chicken with Root Vegetables, 318–19, *319*
- One-Pot Chicken Jardinière, *141*, 141–42
- Packs, Grilled, 530, *531*
    - Spanish-Style, 530
    - Spicy Home Fry, 530
    - Vinegar and Onion, 530
- Pancakes, Texas, *162*, 263
- Red
    - and Broccoli, One-Pan Roasted Salmon with, 357–58, *359*
    - Crushed, with Garlic and Herbs, 296, *296*
    - Crushed, with Garlic and Smoked Paprika, 296
    - Crushed, with Oregano and Capers, 297
- and Red Wine–Orange Sauce, Prime Rib with, 341–42, *343*
- Roasted Salt-and-Vinegar, 297, *297*
- Salad
    - All-American, *536*, 536–37
    - Amish, *538*, 539
    - Dill, 540, *541*
    - Ranch, *539*, 539–40
    - Red, Lemon and Herb, *542*, 542–43
    - Smashed, 541–42, *542*
    - Smoky, *537*, 537–38
    - Texas, 540–41, *541*
    - Torn, with Toasted Garlic and Herb Dressing, *367*, 367–68
- Short-Order Home Fries, 554, *555*
- Syracuse Salt, 370–71, *371*
- Tater Tot Hotdish, 149–50, *150*
- Torn and Fried, 298, *298*
- Tots
    - Bacon-Ranch, 262
    - Crispy, *260*, 260–61
    - Crispy, for a Crowd, 261
    - Parmesan-Rosemary, 262
    - Southwestern, 262

Potato(es) *(cont.)*
- Twice-Baked
    - with Bacon and Cheddar Cheese, *272*, 302
    - with Chorizo and Chipotle, 302
    - with Pancetta and Mozzarella, 302
- Wedges, Crunchy, 259–60, *261*
- Whipped, *368*, 368–69
- *see also* Sweet Potato(es)

Potato starch, about, 56
Pot Pie, Double-Crust Chicken, 142–43, *143*
Pots and pans, ratings of, 702–4
Poultry. *See* Chicken; Duck(s); Turkey
Pretzel(s)
- Ballpark, *162*, 269–70
- Really Good Key Lime Pie, 676, *677*
- Strawberry Salad, 129–30, *131*

Prosciutto
- Basil, and Blue Cheese, Shredded Swiss Chard Salad with, *365*, 365–66
- Bread, 453–54, *455*
- Chicken Cordon Bleu, 10–11, *11*

Provolone
- Baked Manicotti with Meat Sauce, *441*, 441–42
- New Orleans Muffulettas, *216*, 216–17
- Philadelphia Pork Sandwiches, *236*, 236–37
- Sausage Lasagna, *416*, 438–39
- Skillet Chicken Parmesan, 446, *447*
- Spicy Cheese Bread, 570, *570*

Pudding
- Banana, *663*, 663–64
- Banana, Peanut-y, 664
- Banana, Toasted-Coconut, 664
- Bread, New Orleans Bourbon, 664–65, *665*
- Summer Berry, 665–66, *666*

Q

Quesabirria Tacos, 394–95, *395*

R

Radish(es)
    Hard-Cooked Eggs, and Capers, Tuna Salad with, 132
    Pecorino Romano, and Croutons, Asparagus Salad with, 364, *364*
    and Sweet Potato, Chicken Baked in Foil with, *322*, 323

Raisins
    Aunt Jule's Pie, 112, *113*
    Carrot Snack Cake, 620–21, *621*
    Classic Steak Sauce, 279
    Lane Cake, *594*, 600–601
    Morning Glory Muffins, *572*, 573
    New Orleans Bourbon Bread Pudding, 664–65, *665*
    Oatmeal Creme Pies, *643*, 643–45
    Steak Sauce, 286–87, *287*

Raita, Onion, 213, *213*
Ramen, Birria, 395–96, *396*
Ranch Fried Chicken, 175–77, *176*
Ranch Potato Salad, *539*, **539–40**

Raspberry(ies)
    Blitz Torte, *613*, 613–14
    Chiffon Pie, *691*, 691–92
    Double Berry Cream Cheese Kringle Filling, 586
    Mixed Berry Buckle, 657–58, *659*
    Sauce, Cheese Blintzes with, 557–58, *559*
    Summer Berry Pudding, 665–66, *666*

Recipe and culinary history
    America's first restaurant, 282
    beef Stroganoff, 148
    Benihana, 285
    Big Bob Gibson's restaurant, 461
    B&W Bakery crumb buns, 581
    Campbell's Noodle with Chicken Soup, 120
    chuck roast in foil, 343
    cold-oven recipes, 620
    Colonel Sanders, 135
    cooking with lard, 399
    Cornell chicken, 460
    Cornish pasties, 23
    Delmonico potatoes, 293
    Delmonico's restaurant, 293
    Ebinger's Baking Company, 598
    Edna Lewis and Southern cooking, 123
    fra diavolo, 428
    Fritos corn chips, 16
    gelatin-based salads, 130
    grandma pizza, 445
    history of bourbon, 665

Recipe and culinary history *(cont.)*
    Horn and Hardart's automats, 126
    "huli"-ed chicken, 459
    innovative sandwiches, 221
    Joe froggers, 640
    Jucy Lucy burgers, 489
    ketchup, 210
    the Lighthouse Inn, 295
    macaroni and cheese, 126
    New Orleans Vietnamese community, 193
    North Carolina barbecue, 502
    North Carolina fish stews, 187
    Oatmeal Creme Pie, 644
    Oberlin College dining plan, 609
    patty melts, 222
    Pillsbury Bake-Off, 695
    po' boy sandwiches, 199
    potato chips, 105
    Prince's Hot Chicken Shack, 169
    proper dining and tableware, 590
    red velvet cake, 596
    scones and biscuits, 567
    Shaker Lemon Pie, 673
    shrimp and grits, 196
    Shrimp Shack, 200
    soy sauce, 210
    sufganiyot jelly doughnuts, 101
    sweetened condensed milk, 678
    tarte Tatin, 656
    Texas Pete hot sauce, 173
    Villa de Roma restaurant, 432
    whoopie pies, 643
    Zephyr Wright, 54

Red Velvet Cake, 596, *597*

Red Wine
    –Orange Sauce, 342
    Sauce, 334–35

Rhubarb
    Shortcakes, Strawberry-Elderflower, with Buttermilk Whipped Cream, 111
    Shortcakes with Buttermilk Whipped Cream, 110–11, *111*
    -Strawberry Compote, 618–19

Rice
    Arroz con Pollo, 384–85, *385*
    Charleston Shrimp Perloo, *162*, 194–95
    and Chicken, Thai-Style (Kaho Man Gai), 210–12, *211*
    Coastal Georgia Paella, 50, *51*
    Dressing, Cajun, *247*, 247–48
    Easier Chicken Chimichangas, 400–401, *401*
    Garlic Fried, 233

Rice *(cont.)*
    Hibachi-Style Fried, Simple, *285*, 285–86
    Hoppin' John, *248*, 248–49
    Okinawan Taco, 230–31, *231*
    and Peas, Jamaican, 152–53, *153*
    Red, Gullah Lowcountry, 90, *91*
    Seafood Risotto, 52, *53*

Ricotta cheese
    Baked Manicotti with Meat Sauce, *441*, 441–42
    Blintzes with Raspberry Sauce, 557–58, *559*
    Cheesy Stuffed Shells, 442–43, *443*
    Kolaches, 583–84, *584*
    Skillet Lasagna, 436, *436*
    Skillet Lasagna with Sausage and Peppers, 436
    Slow-Cooker Baked Ziti, *434*, 434–35
    Spinach and Tomato Lasagna, *439*, 439–40

Rillons, 42, *43*
Risotto, Seafood, 52, *53*
Rolls, Alabama Orange, *544*, **582–83**
Rosemary
    Grilled Brined Pork Chops with Garlic-Herb Oil, 32, *33*
    -Parmesan Potato Tots, 262
    -Pepper Butter, Husk-Grilled Corn with, 527

Roux, shades of, 21
Rum
    Coquito, 116, *117*
    Piña Coladas, 271, *271*

Rutabaga
    Cornish Pasties, 22–23, *23*

S

Salads
    Asparagus
        with Grapes, Goat Cheese, and Almonds, 364–65
        with Oranges, Feta, and Hazelnuts, 365
        with Radishes, Pecorino Romano, and Croutons, 364, *364*
    BLT, *306*, 306–7
    Brussels Sprout, 363, *363*
        with Cheddar, Hazelnuts, and Apple, 363
        with Smoked Gouda, Pecans, and Dried Cherries, 363
    Caesar, Ultimate, 76, *77*
    Caesar Green Bean, 305–6, *306*
    Chicken, Cambodian (Neorm Sach Moan), *204*, 205
    Chicken, Chinese, 206, *206*
    Endive, with Oranges and Blue Cheese, *366*, 366–67

Salads *(cont.)*
    Grilled Caesar, *533*, 533–34
    Macaroni, Hawaiian, 268–69, *269*
    Memphis Chopped Coleslaw, 535, *535*
    Potato
        All-American, *536*, 536–37
        Amish, *538*, 539
        Dill, 540, *541*
        Green Bean, and Tomato, *446*, 543
        Ranch, *539*, 539–40
        Red, Lemon and Herb, *542*, 542–43
        Smashed, 541–42, *542*
        Smoky, *537*, 537–38
        Texas, 540–41, *541*
        Torn, with Toasted Garlic and Herb Dressing, *367*, 367–68
    Shredded Carrot and Serrano Chile, 536, *536*
    Shredded Swiss Chard, with Prosciutto, Basil, and Blue Cheese, *365*, 365–66
    Strawberry Pretzel, 129–30, *131*
    Tangy Apple Cabbage Slaw, *534*, 534–35
    Tomatillo and Bibb Lettuce, with Tomatillo Ranch, 74, *75*
    Tomato and Corn, Southwestern, 413, *413*
    Tuna
        with Apple, Walnuts, and Tarragon, 132
        Classic, *118*, 132
        with Cornichons and Whole-Grain Mustard, 132
        with Curry and Grapes, 132
        with Hard-Cooked Eggs, Radishes, and Capers, 132

Salami
    Jitto's-Style Steak Bombs, 19, *19*

Salisbury Steak, 148–49, *149*
Salmon
    Barbecued Wood-Grilled, 521
    Cedar-Planked, with Cucumber-Yogurt Sauce, 522, *522*
    Lemon-Thyme Wood-Grilled, 521
    One-Pan Roasted, with Broccoli and Red Potatoes, 357–58, *359*
    Piccata, *450*, 451
    pin bones, removing, 357
    Slow-Roasted
        with Chives and Lemon, 356–57, *357*
        with Dill and Garlic, 357
        with Parsley and Cayenne, 357
    Smoked, Breakfast Pizza, 549
    Smoked Fish Tacos, *524*, 524–25
    Steaks, Grilled, with Lemon-Caper Sauce, *446*, 523
    Teriyaki Poke, *202*, 203
    Wood-Grilled, 521, *521*

Salsa
    One-Minute, 380, *381*
    Pico de Gallo, 483, *483*
    Santa Maria, 485
    Tomatillo, Quick, 400
    Verde, 336
    Verde, Mint, 35, *35*
    Verde, Smoky, 401–2, *402*

Salt Cod, Cornmeal Dumplings with (Guanimes con Bacalao), 203–5, *204*
Salted Caramel–Coconut No-Churn Ice Cream, 649
Salt Potatoes, Syracuse, 370–71, *371*
San Diego Fish Tacos, 388–89, *389*
Sandwiches
    Baltimore Pit Beef, *234*, 235
    Barbecued Pulled Chicken, 475–76, *477*
    Boogaloo Wonderland, 218–19, *219*
    Croque Madame, 218
    Croque Monsieur, 217–18, *218*
    Cuban, 237–38, *238*
    Cutty's-Inspired Eggplant Spuckie, 72, *73*
    Diner-Style Patty Melts, *220*, 221–22
    Iowa Skinny, 234, *234*
    Jitto's-Style Steak Bombs, 19, *19*
    New Orleans Muffulettas, *216*, 216–17
    Patty Melts, *220*, 220–21
    Pickle-Brined Fried Chicken, 6, *7*
    Pork, Philadelphia, *236*, 236–37
    Shrimp Po' Boys, *198*, 198–99
    Smoked Prime Rib, with Green Chile Queso, 495–96, *496*
    St. Paul, 215–16, *216*
    Tennessee Pulled Pork, *503*, 503–4
    Tennessee Pulled Turkey, 476–78, *477*
    Tuna Salad
        with Apple, Walnuts, and Tarragon, 132
        Classic, *118*, 132
        with Cornichons and Whole-Grain Mustard, 132
        with Curry and Grapes, 132
        with Hard-Cooked Eggs, Radishes, and Capers, 132
    see also Burgers

Santa Maria Salsa, 485
Sauces
    Barbecue, Eastern North Carolina–Style, 500
    Barbecue, Lexington-Style, 500
    Basque Cider Salted Caramel, *628*, 629
    BBQ, Creamy, 260
    Bourbon, 665
    Browned Butter–Caper, 430
    Buffalo Blue Cheese, 260
    Cider, 652

Sauces *(cont.)*
    Comeback, *185*, 186
    Cucumber-Yogurt, 522–23
    Curried Chutney, 260
    Fontina Cheese, 429–30
    Fresh Mint, *354*, 355
    Ginger, Sweet, 286
    Honey-Mustard, 178
    Horseradish Burger, 507
    Horseradish Cream, 334
    Kua Txob, 4
    Lemon Aioli, 453
    Marinara, 452–53
    Meatballs and Marinara, 432–33, *433*
    Mustard, White, 286
    One-Minute Salsa, 380, *381*
    Onion Raita, 213, *213*
    Pique, 29
    Pizza, No-Cook, 446
    Plum, 45, *45*
    Pork Ragu, *420*, 421
    Red Wine, 334–35
    Red Wine–Orange, 342
    Salsa Verde, 336
    Santa Maria Salsa, 485
    Slow-Cooker Italian Sunday Gravy, *420*, 420–21
    Slow-Cooker Meatballs and Marinara, 433–34, *434*
    Smoky Salsa Verde, 401–2, *402*
    Steak
        Classic, 279
        Garlic-Parsley, 280
        Spicy Red Pepper, 280
    Sweet and Sour, 179
    Tartar, 185, *185*
    Tomato-Basil, 429
    Yum-Yum (Spicy Mayonnaise), 286

Sauerkraut
    Olympia Provisions–Style Choucroute Garnie, 153–54, *154*
    Transylvania Goulash, *327*, 327–28

Sausage(s)
    Backyard Barbecued Beans, *528*, 528–29
    Baked Manicotti with Meat Sauce, *441*, 441–42
    Breakfast, Homemade, *552*, 553–54
    Brunch Burgers, 551–53, *552*
    Brunswick Stew, 326–27, *327*
    Chicago Thin-Crust Pizza, 250–51, *251*
    Chicken Scarpariello, 448, *449*
    Chorizo and Manchego Breakfast Pizza, 549
    Clams with Chorizo, *308*, 360–61
    and Cornbread Stuffing, 313–14, *314*

Sausage(s) *(cont.)*
    Creole Baked Stuffed Shrimp with, 289
    Grilled, with Bell Peppers and Onions, *506, 507*
    Gullah Lowcountry Red Rice, 90, *91*
    Gumbo, 192–93, *193*
    Italian Meatloaf, *416,* 435–36
    Jitto's-Style Steak Bombs, 19, *19*
    Lasagna, *416,* 438–39
    Meatballs and Marinara, 432–33, *433*
    Milk-Can Supper, *154,* 155
    New Orleans Muffulettas, *216,* 216–17
    Okra and Shrimp Stew, *190,* 191–92
    Olympia Provisions–Style Choucroute Garnie, 153–54, *154*
    One-Pan Turkey Breast and Stuffing with Pomegranate-Parsley Sauce, 312–13, *313*
    and Pepper Omelet Filling, 546
    and Peppers, Skillet Lasagna with, 436
    Prosciutto Bread, 453–54, *455*
    Ragu, Pasta with, *422, 423*
    and Red Bell Pepper Breakfast Pizza, 549
    Skillet Corn with Mexican Chorizo, *378,* 414
    Slow-Cooker Baked Ziti, *434,* 434–35
    Slow-Cooker Italian Sunday Gravy, *420,* 420–21
    Slow-Cooker Meatballs and Marinara, 433–34, *434*
    Spanish-Style Grilled Potato Packs, 530
    Supreme French Bread Pizza, 256, *257*
    Sweet Italian, Easy, *251,* 251–52
    Twice-Baked Potatoes with Chorizo and Chipotle, 302

Sazón, Homemade, 385
Scallion(s)
    Charred-, Sauce, Grilled Bone-In Leg of Lamb with, *519,* 519–20
    and Cilantro, Eggplant Dip with, 271
    Oil Noodles, Shanghai, 68, *69*

Scallops
    Monterey Bay Cioppino, 188–89, *189*
    Seafood Fra Diavolo, *427,* 427–28

Scones
    Jalapeño-Cheddar, *544,* 566–67
    Mixed Berry, *565,* 565–66

Seafood. *See* **Fish; Shellfish**
Seasonings
    Homemade Sazón, 385
    Lemon Pepper, 182
    Louisiana, 181
    Taco, Homemade, 231
    Za'atar, 593

Sesame seeds
    Za'atar, 593

Shaker Lemon Pie, *672,* 672–73

Shanghai Scallion Oil Noodles, 68, *69*
Shashlik-Style Beef Kebabs, *479,* 479–80
Shellfish
    Clams Casino, 58, *59*
    Clams with Chorizo, *308,* 360–61
    Coastal Georgia Paella, 50, *51*
    Grilled Mussels, 60, *61*
    Hot Buttered Lobster Rolls, 201, *201*
    Monterey Bay Cioppino, 188–89, *189*
    removing meat from lobster, 201
    Seafood Fra Diavolo, *427,* 427–28
    Seafood Risotto, 52, *53*
    Woodman's-Style Clam Chowder, 189–90, *190*
    see also Shrimp

Shortcakes
    Rhubarb, with Buttermilk Whipped Cream, 110–11, *111*
    Strawberry-Elderflower Rhubarb, with Buttermilk Whipped Cream, 111

Shrimp
    American-Style Egg Rolls, 44–45, *45*
    Baked, with Fennel, Potatoes, and Olives, 358–59, *359*
    Baked Stuffed, 288–89, *289*
    Baked Stuffed, Creole, with Sausage, 289
    Burgers, South Carolina, 199–200, *200*
    Coastal Georgia Paella, 50, *51*
    Crispy Fried, *118,* 159–60
    Curry, Zephyr Wright–Inspired, 54, *55*
    with Garlic and Jalapeño Butter, 56, *57*
    and Grits, *195,* 195–96
    Gumbo, 192–93, *193*
    Monterey Bay Cioppino, 188–89, *189*
    Mozambique, 194, *195*
    New Orleans Barbecue, 196–97, *197*
    and Okra Stew, *190,* 191–92
    Perloo, Charleston, *162,* 194–95
    Piccata Pasta, One-Pot, 66, *67*
    Pickled, 197–98, *198*
    Po' Boys, *198,* 198–99
    Seafood Fra Diavolo, *427,* 427–28
    Seafood Risotto, 52, *53*
    Skewers, Grilled
        Habanero and Pineapple, 526
        Jalapeño and Lime, *525,* 525–26
        Red Chile and Ginger, 526
    Spanish-Style Sizzling Garlic (Gambas al Ajillo), 359–60, *360*
    Tacos, 390–91, *391*

Simple Syrup, 271
Sinigang (Filipino Stew with Meat and Vegetables), *231,* 231–32

Sisig, 232–33, *233*
Slab Pie, Apple, *684,* 684–85
Slaws
    Memphis Chopped Coleslaw, 535, *535*
    Tangy Apple Cabbage, *534,* 534–35
Slice-and-Bake Cookies, 636–37, *637*
Sliders, 222–23, *223*
Slow-Cooker Baked Ziti, *434,* 434–35
Slow-Cooker BBQ Beef Brisket, *226,* 226–27
Slow-Cooker Chicken Stock, 120–21, *121*
Slow-Cooker Chinese Barbecued Pork, 214–15, *215*
Slow-Cooker French Onion Soup, *272,* 275
Slow-Cooker Italian Sunday Gravy, *420,* 420–21
Slow-Cooker Meatballs and Marinara, 433–34, *434*
Slow-Cooker Memphis-Style Wet Ribs, *229,* 229–30
Slow-Cooker Minestrone, 419, *419*
Slow-Cooker Pork Pot Roast, 346, *347*
Smoked Gouda, Pecans, and Dried Cherries, Brussels Sprout Salad with, 363
Smoked Paprika and Garlic, Crushed Red Potatoes with, 296
Smoked Salmon Breakfast Pizza, 549
Smokehouse Mashed Sweet Potatoes, 372
S'mores Pie, *668,* 698–99
So-Cal Churros, 414–15, *415*
Sofrito, 29
Sopa Seca, *378,* 384
Soups
    Beef Noodle, New Orleans Spicy (Beef Yakamein), 243–44, *244*
    Birria Ramen, 395–96, *396*
    Chicken and Pastry, *122,* 122–23
    Chicken Noodle, Old-Fashioned, 120, *121*
    French Onion, *274,* 274–75
    French Onion, Slow-Cooker, *272,* 275
    Minestrone, Slow-Cooker, 419, *419*
    Pasta e Fagioli, 418, *418*
    Tomato, Classic, *122,* 123–24
    Woodman's-Style Clam Chowder, 189–90, *190*
    see also Stews
Sour Cream, Chive, *298,* 299
Sour Orange Pie, 674–75, *675*
South Carolina Barbecue Hash, 240–41, *241*
South Carolina Pulled Pork, *502,* 502–3
South Carolina Shrimp Burgers, 199–200, *200*
South Carolina Smoked Fresh Ham, 498–99, *499*
South Dakota Corncob-Smoked Ribs, 516–18, *517*
Southern-Style Skillet Cornbread, *568,* 568–69
Southern-Style Smothered Chicken, 136–37, *137*
Southwestern Potato Tots, 262

Southwestern Tomato and Corn Salad, 413, *413*
Soy Sauce Chicken Wings, 210, *211*
Spaetzle, Buttered, 137–38, *138*
Spanish-Style Grilled Potato Packs, 530
Spanish-Style Sizzling Garlic Shrimp (Gambas al Ajillo), 359–60, *360*
Specialty pieces, ratings of, 722–27
Spice-Crusted Slow-Roasted Medium-Rare Beef Short Ribs, 284
Spice-Crusted Steaks, *280,* 280–81
Spinach
    -Artichoke Dip, 376–77, *377*
    Chicken Florentine, *140,* 140–41
    Creamed, 304, *305*
    and Crème Fraîche, Lentilles du Puy with, 375, *375*
    draining, 140
    Skillet Eggs Sardou, 40–41, *41*
    Stuffed Tomatoes, *272,* 307
    and Tomato Lasagna, *439,* 439–40
Spoonbread, Sweet Corn, 376, *377*
Spoonbreads, Individual Sweet Corn, 376
Squash
    Crispy Vegetable Fritters, 263–64, *265*
    Japanese Steakhouse Steak and Vegetables, 284–85, *285*
    Roasted Butternut, and Apple, *372,* 372–73
    Roasted Butternut, with Pear and Pancetta, 373
    Slow-Cooker Minestrone, 419, *419*
Squid
    Seafood Risotto, 52, *53*
Steak Sauce
    Classic, 279
    Garlic-Parsley, 280
    Spicy Red Pepper, 280
Stews
    Bean Bourguignon, 70, *71*
    Brunswick, 326–27, *327*
    Carne Guisada, 392–93, *393*
    Chicken Paprikash and Buttered Spaetzle, 137–38, *138*
    Filipino, with Meat and Vegetables (Sinigang), *231,* 231–32
    Fish, Eastern North Carolina, 187–88, *189*
    Guanimes con Bacalao (Cornmeal Dumplings with Salt Cod), 203–5, *204*
    Guinness Beef, 328–29, *329*
    Gumbo, 192–93, *193*
    Monterey Bay Cioppino, 188–89, *189*
    Okra and Shrimp, *190,* 191–92
    One-Pot Chicken Jardinière, *141,* 141–42
    Transylvania Goulash, *327,* 327–28
    see also Chili
Sticky Buns, Triple-Chocolate, *578,* 578–79

INDEX   801

St. Louis BBQ Pork Steaks, 512–13, *513*
St. Louis–Style Pizza, *248,* 249–50
Stocks
    Chicken, Slow-Cooker, 120–21, *121*
    storing, 121
St. Paul Sandwich, 215–16, *216*
Strawberry(ies)
    -Buttermilk No-Churn Ice Cream, 649
    Cheesecake Bars, *626,* 626–27
    Dream Cake, *604,* 605–6
    -Elderflower Rhubarb Shortcakes with Buttermilk Whipped Cream, 111
    Pie, Icebox, 692–93, *693*
    Poke Cake, *606,* 606–7
    Pretzel Salad, 129–30, *131*
    -Rhubarb Compote, 618–19
    Summer Berry Pudding, 665–66, *666*
Stuffing
    Cornbread and Bacon, 314
    Cornbread and Sausage, 313–14, *314*
    Skillet-Roasted Chicken with, *322,* 322–23
    and Turkey Breast, One-Pan, with Pomegranate-Parsley Sauce, 312–13, *313*
Sufganiyot (Hanukkah Jelly Doughnuts), 100–101, *101*
Sumac
    Za'atar, 593
Sweet and Sour Sauce, 179
Sweet Potato(es)
    and Bourbon-Cherry Sauce, Pork Chops with, *308,* 351–52
    Fritters with Cheddar and Chipotle, 84
    Fritters with Feta, Dill, and Cilantro, 84, *85*
    Grilled, with Maple Chile Crisp, *531,* 531–32
    Herbed Mashed, with Caramelized Onion, 372
    Mashed, Creamy, *371,* 371–72
    Pie, *686,* 687
    and Radish, Chicken Baked in Foil with, *322,* 323
    Smokehouse Mashed, 372
Swiss Chard
    Shredded, Salad with Prosciutto, Basil, and Blue Cheese, *365,* 365–66
    stemming, 366
Swiss cheese
    Cuban Sandwiches, 237–38, *238*
    Diner-Style Patty Melts, *220,* 221–22
    Failproof Chicken Cordon Bleu, *289,* 289–90
    Patty Melts, *220,* 220–21
Swiss Hazelnut Cake, 612, *613*
Swiss Steak with Tomato Gravy, 150–51, *151*
Syracuse Salt Potatoes, 370–71, *371*
Syrup, Simple, 271

T

Tacos
    Breakfast, Texas, 550–51, *551*
    Chicken, Easy, 391–92, *392*
    Citrus-Braised Pork, 398, *399*
    Fish, California-Style, *387,* 387–88
    Fish, San Diego, 388–89, *389*
    Puffy, 393–94, *394*
    Quesabirria, 394–95, *395*
    Rasurados, Mesquite-Grilled, 26–27, *27*
    Shrimp, 390–91, *391*
    Smoked Fish, *524,* 524–25
Taco Seasoning, Homemade, 231
Tahini
    Baba Ghanoush, 270, *271*
    Eggplant Dip with Scallions and Cilantro, 271
    -Lemon Dressing, Roasted Beets with, *372,* 373–74
Tamales, Delta Hot, 245–46, *246*
Tandoori Grilled Chicken Wings, 469
Tarragon, Apple, and Walnuts, Tuna Salad with, 132
Tartar Sauce, 185, *185*
Tarte Tatin, *650,* 655–56
Tarts
    Egg, Portuguese (Pastéis de Nata), 98–99, *99*
    Pastéis de Nata with Lemon and Cinnamon, 99
Tater Tot Hotdish, 149–50, *150*
Tea, Sweet, –Brined Fried Chicken Thighs, *176,* 177
Tennessee Pulled Pork Sandwiches, *503,* 503–4
Tennessee Pulled Turkey Sandwiches, 476–78, *477*
Tennessee Whiskey Pork Chops, *227,* 227–28
Teriyaki, Chicken, *446,* 464
Texas Barbecue Brisket, *486,* 487–88
Texas Barbecued Beef Ribs, 492–93, *493*
Texas Breakfast Tacos, 550–51, *551*
Texas Potato Pancakes, *162,* 263
Texas Potato Salad, 540–41, *541*
Texas Sheet Cake, 607–8, *608*
Texas-Style Pinto Beans, 412, *413*
Texas-Style Smoked Beef Ribs, *494,* 494
Texas Thick-Cut Smoked Pork Chops, *508,* 508–9
Tex-Mex Cheese Enchiladas, 403–4, *404*
Thai-Style Chicken and Rice (Kaho Man Gai), 210–12, *211*
Thai-Style Fried Eggs (Kai Dao), *213,* 214
Thermometers and timers, ratings of, 712–13
Thyme
    Za'atar, 593
Toffee-Chocolate Fudge, *646,* 648

Tomatillo(s)
    and Bibb Lettuce Salad with Tomatillo Ranch, 74, *75*
    Easy Green Chile Chicken Enchiladas, *405,* 405–6
    removing husk from, 74
    Salsa, Quick, 400
    Smoky Salsa Verde, 401–2, *402*

Tomato(es)
    Baked Manicotti with Meat Sauce, *441,* 441–42
    -Basil Sauce, 429
    BLT Salad, *306,* 306–7
    Cheesy Stuffed Shells, 442–43, *443*
    Cherry, Charred, with Roasted Bell Peppers and Fresh Mozzarella, 268, *269*
    Chicago Thin-Crust Pizza, 250–51, *251*
    Chicken Chilaquiles, 408–9, *409*
    Chicken Paprikash and Buttered Spaetzle, 137–38, *138*
    Chicken Sauce Piquant, 180–81, *181*
    Chutney, Five-Spice, 47, *47*
    and Corn Salad, Southwestern, 413, *413*
    Detroit-Style Pizza, 253–55, *254*
    Drop Meatballs, *431,* 431–32
    Eggplant Pecorino, *440,* 440–41
    Fluffy Baked Polenta with Red Sauce, 430–31, *431*
    with Fontina Sauce and Cornichon Dressing, 78, *79*
    Frito Pie, 16, *17*
    Galette, Fresh, 374, *375*
    Grandma Pizza, *444,* 444–45
    Gravy, Swiss Steak with, 150–51, *151*
    Gullah Lowcountry Red Rice, 90, *91*
    Hearty Beef Lasagna, *437,* 437–38
    Huevos Rancheros, 383, *383*
    Italian Meatloaf, *416,* 435–36
    Macaroni and Cheese with, *126,* 126–27
    Marinara Sauce, 452–53
    Meatballs and Marinara, 432–33, *433*
    New England Bar Pizza, 252–53, *253*
    No-Cook Pizza Sauce, 446
    One-Minute Salsa, 380, *381*
    Pasta with Sausage Ragu, 422, *423*
    Pico de Gallo, 483, *483*
    Pie, Philly, *254,* 255–56
    Pork Grillades, *287,* 287–88
    Pork Ragu, *420,* 421
    Potato, and Green Bean Salad, *446,* 543
    Santa Maria Salsa, 485
    Sausage Lasagna, *416,* 438–39
    Skillet Chicken Parmesan, 446, *447*
    Skillet Lasagna, *436, 436*
    Skillet Lasagna with Sausage and Peppers, 436
    Slow-Cooker Baked Ziti, *434,* 434–35

Tomato(es) *(cont.)*
    Slow-Cooker Italian Sunday Gravy, *420,* 420–21
    Slow-Cooker Meatballs and Marinara, 433–34, *434*
    Sopa Seca, *378,* 384
    Soup, Classic, *122,* 123–24
    and Spinach Lasagna, *439,* 439–40
    Stuffed, *272,* 307
    Sun-Dried, and Fennel, Chicken Baked in Foil with, 323
    Texas Breakfast Tacos, 550–51, *551*
    Ultimate Seven-Layer Dip, *381,* 381–82
    Ultimate Smoky Seven-Layer Dip, 382

Tools, handy, ratings of, 705–10

Tortilla(s)
    Ahi-Chile Tostadas, *389,* 389–90
    Chicken Chilaquiles, 408–9, *409*
    Easier Chicken Chimichangas, 400–401, *401*
    Flour, Homemade Taco-Size, 551, *551*
    Grilled Steak Fajitas, 482–83, *483*
    Huevos Rancheros, 383, *383*
    Pork Carnitas, *399,* 399–400
    Ultimate Spicy Beef Nachos, 380, *381*
    see also Enchiladas; Tacos

Tostadas, Ahi-Chile, *389,* 389–90

Transylvania Goulash, *327,* 327–28

Tres Leches Cake, 611, *611*

Trout Amandine, 355–56, *356*

Truffles, Chocolate
    -Almond, 645
    Basic, 645, *645*
    -Cinnamon, 645
    -Ginger, 645
    -Lemon, 645

Tuna
    Ahi-Chile Tostadas, *389,* 389–90
    Poke, 202, *202*

Tuna Salad
    with Apple, Walnuts, and Tarragon, 132
    Classic, *118,* 132
    with Cornichons and Whole-Grain Mustard, 132
    with Curry and Grapes, 132
    with Hard-Cooked Eggs, Radishes, and Capers, 132

Tunnel of Fudge Cake, *599,* 599–600

Turkey
    Breast and Stuffing, One-Pan, with Pomegranate-Parsley Sauce, 312–13, *313*
    Cider-Braised, *310,* 311–12
    Old-Fashioned Roast, with Gravy, *310,* 310–11
    Tennessee Pulled, Sandwiches, 476–78, *477*
    Wings, Cajun Stuffed, *183,* 183–84

Turnovers
  Cornish Pasties, 22–23, *23*
  New Mexican Bean-and-Cheese, with Green Chile, *402*, 402–3

Vanilla
  Frozen Custard, Old-Fashioned, 666–67, *667*
  No-Churn Ice Cream, 648–49, *649*
Veal
  Skillet Lasagna, 436, *436*
Vegetable(s)
  and Chicken, Cast Iron, 319–20, *321*
  Fritters, Crispy, 263–64, *265*
  and Meat, Filipino Stew with (Sinigang), *231*, 231–32
  Roasted, and Prime Rib, One-Pan, 340–41, *341*
  Root, One-Pan Roast Chicken with, 318–19, *319*
  Slow-Cooker Minestrone, 419, *419*
  see also specific vegetables
Vegetarian Chili, *411*, 411–12

Walnut(s)
  Apple, and Tarragon, Tuna Salad with, 132
  –Banana–Chocolate Chunk No-Churn Ice Cream, 649
  –Brown Sugar Cookies, 636
  Chocolate Fudge, *646*, 647
  Endive Salad with Oranges and Blue Cheese, *366*, 366–67
  Morning Glory Muffins, *572*, 573
  Roasted Garlic Sauce, and Arugula, Pasta with, *425*, 425–26
  Shredded Swiss Chard Salad with Prosciutto, Basil, and Blue Cheese, *365*, 365–66
  Tunnel of Fudge Cake, *599*, 599–600
Water baths, preparing, 624
Wellesley Fudge Cake, *598*, 598–99
Whipped Cream
  Bourbon, 686
  Buttermilk, Rhubarb Shortcakes with, 110–11, *111*
  Failproof, 676–77

Whiskey
  Tennessee, Pork Chops, *227*, 227–28
  see also Bourbon
White Mustard Sauce, 286
Whole-Wheat Blueberry Muffins, *572*, 572–75
Whoopie Pies, 642–43, *643*
Wine
  Port, –Fig Sauce, Duck Breasts with, *314*, 315
  Red, –Orange Sauce, 342
  Red, Sauce, 334–35
Wisconsin Butter Burgers, *224*, *224*
Wood-Grilled Salmon, 521, *521*
  Barbecued, 521
  Lemon-Thyme, 521
Woodman's-Style Clam Chowder, 189–90, *190*

Yakamein, Beef (New Orleans Spicy Beef Noodle Soup), 243–44, *244*
Yogurt
  -Cucumber Sauce, 522–23
  Onion Raita, 213, *213*
Yorkshire Pudding and Jus, Boneless Rib Roast with, *338*, 339–40
Yum-Yum Sauce (Spicy Mayonnaise), 286

Za'atar
  homemade, 593
  Mana'eesh (Za'atar Flatbreads), *592*, 592–93
Zephyr Wright–Inspired Shrimp Curry, 54, *55*
Zeppoles, 454–55, *455*
Zip-Style Sauce, Bottom Round Roast with, 336, *337*
Zucchini
  Crispy Vegetable Fritters, 263–64, *265*
  Japanese Steakhouse Steak and Vegetables, 284–85, *285*
  Slow-Cooker Minestrone, 419, *419*